Praise for *The Psychology of Personality*

"Bernie Carducci's *The Psychology of Personality* is a rare treat for both instructors and students. It is comprehensive and scholarly, but is written in an engaging and conversational style – one that makes the subject come alive."

Ronald E. Riggio, Director, Kravis Leadership Institute, Claremont McKenna College

"Lucid, engaging, and pedagogically sound – *The Psychology of Personality* by Bernie Carducci has all the essential elements of a first-class textbook. The whole of personality is covered, with theories, assessment, research, and application each receiving its due. The applications of personality psychology theory and research to a variety of everyday experiences help students to see the relevance of what they are studying and connect the textbook material more directly to their daily lives. Extra pluses include subheadings that point the student to the core issues of subsequent material; ancillaries written by the author with the same high standards as the text; thorough, well-written test questions that even cover tables and figures; and inventive and usable classroom enhancement ideas that make teaching easier and more fun."

Lisa Gray-Shellberg, California State University, Dominguez Hills

"My students have always found Carducci's textbook informative, engaging, and interesting, and I know this revision will be as enthusiastically received as the first. This revision keeps the approachable, readable style of writing, the blend of theory and current research, and the sections on anxiety, self, and gender differences that my students found particularly interesting and pertinent from the first edition and adds important current research and teaching aids, like mini-lectures. I can't wait to start using it in my class!"

Patricia Lee Llewellyn, Ph.D., Professor, Director of the Ainsworth Clinic, University of Virginia

"Bernardo J. Carducci's *The Psychology of Personality* clearly describes many of the key concepts in the field of personality psychology. The author's enthusiasm is evident throughout the book. The organization of the book allows the reader to easily follow the various theoretical viewpoints in a straightforward manner. I give this book my highest recommendation."

Karen Boyd White, Psy.D.

"Carducci offers a comprehensive and up-to-date review of theory and research in the field of personality, but importantly goes beyond traditional texts by emphasizing the applications of personality theory and research in contemporary life. The text also expands upon traditional approaches to include contributions of research in neuroscience and behavioral genetics to the study of personality. Carducci's use of biographical sketches of leading theorists pulls back the curtains on the lives of important figures in the field, helping students to see how their life experiences shaped their work. The 'Cutting Edge' feature puts a contemporary face on the face of personality psychology, such as by examining how Karen Horney's personality constructs shed light on our understanding of the tragic events at Columbine and by examining the relationship between Freudian theory and the therapeutic impact of expressive writing ('power of the pen'). All in all, this is a highly readable, student accessible, and thorough treatment of personality theory and research that contemporarizes the field in a way that makes the material interesting, relevant, and timely."

Jeffrey Nevid, Ph.D., Professor of Psychology and Clinical Director, St. John's University

About the Cover

"The Kiss" was painted by Gustav Klimt (1862–1918), a turn-of-the-century Viennese painter noted for his use of vibrant colors and striking and sensual images. I personally selected this painting for the cover of the book because it is my favorite work of art. In this painting, you get a sense of Klimt's passionate personality for art, for love, and for life. I have tried to emulate some of Klimt's passion in the writing of this book.

B.J.C.

The Psychology of Personality

Viewpoints, Research, and Applications

Second Edition

Bernardo J. Carducci

INDIANA UNIVERSITY SOUTHEAST

WILEY-BLACKWELL

A John Wiley & Sons, Ltd., Publication

This second edition first published 2009
© 2009 Bernardo J. Carducci

Edition history: Brooks/Cole Publishing Company (1e, 1998).

Blackwell Publishing was acquired by John Wiley & Sons in February 2007. Blackwell's publishing program has been merged with Wiley's global Scientific, Technical, and Medical business to form Wiley-Blackwell.

Registered Office
John Wiley & Sons Ltd, The Atrium, Southern Gate, Chichester, West Sussex, PO19 8SQ, United Kingdom

Editorial Offices
350 Main Street, Malden, MA 02148-5020, USA
9600 Garsington Road, Oxford, OX4 2DQ, UK
The Atrium, Southern Gate, Chichester, West Sussex, PO19 8SQ, UK

For details of our global editorial offices, for customer services, and for information about how to apply for permission to reuse the copyright material in this book please see our website at www.wiley.com/wiley-blackwell.

The right of Bernardo J. Carducci to be identified as the author of this work has been asserted in accordance with the Copyright, Designs and Patents Act 1988.

Wiley also publishes its books in a variety of electronic formats. Some content that appears in print may not be available in electronic books.

Designations used by companies to distinguish their products are often claimed as trademarks. All brand names and product names used in this book are trade names, service marks, trademarks or registered trademarks of their respective owners. The publisher is not associated with any product or vendor mentioned in this book. This publication is designed to provide accurate and authoritative information in regard to the subject matter covered. It is sold on the understanding that the publisher is not engaged in rendering professional services. If professional advice or other expert assistance is required, the services of a competent professional should be sought.

Library of Congress Cataloging-in-Publication Data

Carducci, Bernardo J.
  The psychology of personality : viewpoints, research, and applications / Bernardo J. Carducci. – 2nd ed.
    p. cm.
  Includes bibliographical references and index.
  ISBN 978-1-4051-3635-8 (hardcover : alk. paper)   1. Personality.   I. Title.
  BF698.C177 2009
  155.2–dc22

                                                                    2008044448

A catalogue record for this book is available from the British Library.

Set in 10/12pt Minion by Graphicraft Limited, Hong Kong
Printed in the USA

1   2009

In loving memory of Mary and Edward Carducci, my parents,

whose passion for each other and their children served as an

inspiration for the passion I now have for the study of personality

and the teaching of personality psychology to all of my

"adopted academic children" – my students.

About the Author

Bernardo J. Carducci (PhD, Kansas State University, 1981) is professor of psychology at Indiana University Southeast, where he has taught classes on personality psychology and introductory psychology for the past 28 years, and the director of the Indiana University Southeast Shyness Research Institute (www.ius.edu/ shyness). He is a fellow of Division 1: General Psychology and Division 2: Teaching of Psychology of the American Psychological Association, past national president of the Council of Teachers of Undergraduate Psychology, current member of the *Journal of Social Psychology* editorial board, and founding editorial board member of the *Journal of Business and Psychology*. In addition to his research interest in the study of shyness, Bernie's professional writings related to such topics as teaching activities to enhance classroom instruction, student development, and career opportunities for psychology majors have appeared in *Teaching of Psychology*, *Teaching Psychology: A Handbook*, and many American Psychological Association-sponsored publications on teaching. He is also the author of five popular-press books related to shyness, including *Shyness: A Bold New Approach* and *The Shyness Workbook: 30 Days to Dealing Effectively with Shyness*.

As well as sharing his interest in the study of personality and shyness with his colleagues and students, Bernie is also passionate about sharing this information with those outside of academia whenever and wherever asked to do so. Specifically, in addition to his multiple appearances on ABC's *Good Morning America* and other national and international media services, including the BBC, Bernie's writings and advice have been featured in such diverse sources as *Psychology Today*, *U.S.*

News and World Report, *USA Weekend Magazine*, *Vogue*, *Allure*, *YM*, *TWA Ambassador Magazine*, *Glamour*, *JET*, *Parenting Magazine*, *Walking Magazine*, *Good Housekeeping*, *Essence*, *Child Magazine*, *Reader's Digest*, *Patents*, *Redbook*, *First for Women Magazine*, *Cosmopolitan*, *The Futurist*, *Entrepreneur*, *Fitness Magazine*, *TIME.com*, *USA Today*, *WebMD*, *The Chicago Tribune*, *The Wall Street Journal*, the London *Times*, *The Los Angeles Times*, and *The New York Times*, to name just a few.

In addition to his academic activities, he is also involved in his community. For over 10 years, 8 of those as treasurer, Bernie served on the board of directors of the Southern Indiana Transitional Shelter, which provided independent-living housing to abused women and their children. As a reflection of the pride he has in his Italian heritage, Bernie is a longtime board member and president for the past 10 years of the Italian-American Association in Louisville, KY (www.LouisvilleItalians. com), and principal organizer of the city's Festa Italiana.

As a lover of all types of music, Bernie finally decided to try his hand at becoming a musician and, against the advice of family and friends, started taking accordion lessons a few years ago. On starting to play the accordion at his age, Bernie said, "Trying to learn something totally different, like playing the accordion, has given me a greater appreciation for students who are taking a course in personality psychology for the first time. It has helped me to become a more sensitive teacher and writer, but has done nothing to improve the quality of my playing of the accordion."

Finally, as his crowning life achievement, he is the loving father of his only child, Rozana Carducci.

Brief Contents

Contents

Part II The Viewpoints of Personality: Different Perspectives of the Person   75

3 The Psychodynamic Viewpoint: Forging Personality out of Conflict Resolution   77

Features

A Closer Look

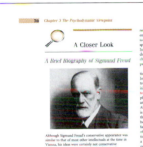

Applications in Personality Psychology

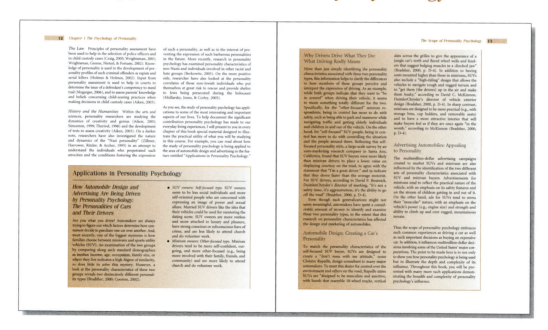

You Can Do It

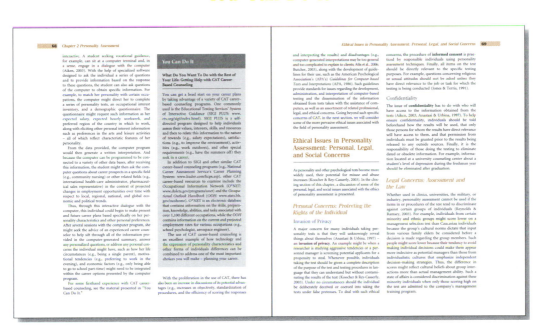

At the Cutting Edge of Personality Psychology

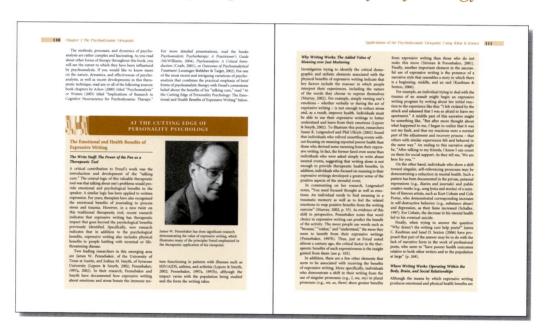

The Cultural Context of Personality Psychology

Summing It Up Tables

The "Personality" of this Personality Textbook: Special Features of this Book

Personality psychology is the study of people – what makes us unique – by people – personality psychologists. And personality textbooks, like people, can have a collection of unique characteristic features that help to distinguish them from each other. Before you start your formal reading of this textbook, I briefly want to tell you a little about why I decided to write it, and provide you with a summary description of some of the unique characteristic features that will help to define the "personality" of this personality psychology textbook.

Why I Wrote this Book: On Doing It "My Way"

When I initially began to consider writing a personality text, one of the first things I had to do was to think about the type of textbook I wanted to write. I began working on this book by looking at the personality textbooks I had used in my classes in the past and other books already available. When examining these books, I discovered that personality textbooks, like the personalities of various people, are very different from one another. Again, like people, it was as if each textbook had its own "personality," or characteristic way in which the material was presented. While each of these books did a good job in its own way, they did not provide the balance of personality theory, research, and the application of personality psychology in a manner consistent with what I wanted to present to the students in my classes. Because I could not find a book with the right "personality," I decided to write this book, and I decided that I would, as Frank Sanatra famously sang, do it "my way." In part, doing it "my way" involves combining two of my passions in life – the study of personality psychology and the teaching of personality psychology.

After deciding to write this book, I then had to think about the personality of this text. Thus, I not only had to think about what I wanted to say in the book but how I was going to say it. Following much consideration, I decided that I wanted to write a book that would have a style, or personality, that would be different from the other personality textbooks. Specifically, I wanted to write

a textbook that would provide a balanced coverage of personality theory, research, and applications in a manner that would be interesting to read and easy to learn from. In addition, I wanted to write a book that conveyed the enthusiasm and passion I have for the field of personality psychology. In a sense, I wanted to write a book that reflected my own personality both as an individual and as a teacher – a "people-person" orientation.

The "People-Person" Orientation: A Personality Textbook About People for People

Most of the people who know me well would probably describe me as a "people person." Whether it is in my day-to-day personal life in the community or my day-to-day professional life as a teacher of personality psychology, I am very interested in getting to know others, and using this knowledge to help us foster personal and professional success. As a result, I have tried to write a book that reflects a "people-person" orientation – "a book about people for people." Specifically, I wanted to write a book that would help people – students – learn more about themselves and others, which is the focus of the study of personality psychology, and, at the same time, to be able to use this knowledge to be more successful both in the classroom – learn more and get better grades – and outside of the classroom – see the value of personality in their everyday life. As a reflection of the "people-person" orientation, I have included in this textbook a number of special learning aids that are designed to help students foster a sense of academic and personal success. A brief description of these learning aids is presented next.

Special Learning Aids: To Ease Your Efforts and Maximize Your Success

While personality psychology involves the scientific study of helping people understand the uniqueness of each other, *pedagogy* is the science of teaching and understanding how to help people learn more effectively. In my attempt to combine the scientific study of understanding people with the scientific principles of how people learn, I have included in the writing of this textbook a number of pedagogical features in the form of special learning aids specifically designed to ease your efforts while reading and studying the material in this book and maximize your success when applying this information during the taking of tests in this class and while trying to understand yourself and those around you outside of class. In a sense, similar to the special characteristics that define an individual's personality, the special learning aids included in this textbook are the characteristics that help to define this book's personality. These special learning aids can be classified into two distinctive categories: special features *within each chapter* and special features *across all of the chapters*. A brief description of these features, along with an explanation of the rationale for including them, is presented in the following paragraphs.

Special Features Within Each Chapter: Plenty of Pedagogy to Go Around

Contained within each chapter are a number of pedagogical features specifically designed to enhance your ability to learn from, as well your instructor's ability to teach from, this textbook. These distinguishing pedagogical features include the following.

Chapter Outline: Serving an Integrative Pedagogical Function

At the beginning of each chapter there is a chapter outline of the principal headings and subheadings of the material contained in the chapter. In addition to helping you to see the overall organization of the chapter and guide your reading, the chapter outlines will also serve as the basis of the learning objectives (LOs) that are included in the *Student Study Guide* (SSG), *Test Bank* (TB), and *Instructor's Manual* (IM) that accompany this textbook. The study questions and items in the practice quizzes in the SSG and the essay questions and multiple-choice questions in the TB are written to be consistent with the LOs. The suggested classroom activities and supplemental lecture materials and supporting readings included in the IM are also designed to be consistent with the LOs. Thus, the chapter outline serves a vital pedagogical function designed to help guide your reading and studying of the textbook material and assist your instructor to

provide a seamless integration of the textbook and classroom material.

Chapter Overview: A Preview of Coming Attractions

The text of each chapter starts with a chapter overview, which is designed to provide a quick synopsis of the material to be discussed in the chapter and introduce some of the major topics and issues that will be featured in this discussion. Providing this overview will help you to place the information in a more specific mental framework that will allow you to integrate more easily the connecting themes and ideas throughout the chapter, which will serve to maximize your understanding and enjoyment of the material as you are reading it and organize the material more effectively while studying it.

Highlighting of Important Terms: Making Bold Statements

Throughout the book, the important terms are in **bold print**, like this. An explanation of each bold term is provided with its initial presentation, along with a more formal definition in a glossary at the end of each chapter. These terms will also be featured in the SSG as a reminder of their importance when you are studying the material from the chapter and preparing for your tests over this material.

Chapter Section Summaries: Hitting the Highlights

Each chapter contains a set of chapter section summary tables titled "Summing It Up" (SIU). These tables summarize the highlights of specific sections within the chapter. The tables include an explanation and supporting examples of the principal points discussed in that section of the chapter. In preparation for your exams, you can also use the SIU tables as study aids to review your understanding and mastery of the material contained within that section of the chapter. Examples of SIU tables can be seen in Chapter 3 on p. 81 and Chapter 9 on p. 383. A complete listing of the SIU tables is presented on pp. xxvi–xxviii above.

Five Types of Box Inserts: "Boxing Your Ears Off"

Throughout the chapter, you will encounter five different types of box inserts. These box inserts are designed to enhance your reading of the material, expand on material that is presented without disrupting the overall depth of coverage of the material in the body of the running text, and highlight unique and interesting illustrations of topics in the study of personality psychology. While these box inserts collectively are designed to have many different purposes, each of the five types has its own specific pedagogical purpose. Presented below is a description of each type of box insert.

- *A Closer Look: The More You Know, the Better You Will Know It.* The "A Closer Look" boxes are designed to examine in more detail the coverage of certain topics, such as presenting biographical information about a particular personality theorist or highlighting a significant program of research, without disturbing the overall depth of coverage of other topics in the chapter. In addition to helping you better understand the topic being presented, the depth of the material presented in these boxes will also serve to stimulate your thinking about how and why research is done in the study of personality psychology. For examples of this type of box, see Chapter 2, p. 57, Chapter 4, p. 134, and Chapter 7, p. 274. A complete listing of these boxes is presented on pp. xxi–xxii above.

- *Applications in Personality Psychology: Showing What Personality Psychology Can Do for You.* The "Applications in Personality Psychology" boxes present extended examples of how personality psychology has been applied to a variety of interesting and important areas in our everyday living experiences. Since all of the material appearing in the "Applications" boxes has a theoretical basis and a solid foundation in research, it will also serve to demonstrate and remind you of the relevance and implications of theory and research in the study of personality psychology and the important role they play when developing and implementing these applications of personality psychology to our lives. For examples of this type of box, see Chapter 1, p. 12 Chapter 3, p. 109, and Chapter 10, p. 444. A complete listing of these boxes is presented on pp. xxii–xxiii above.

- *You Can Do It: Behaving Like a Personality Psychologist.* Created to provide firsthand experience with doing some of your own "research" in the study of personality, the "You Can Do It" boxes will give you the opportunity to complete a variety of exercises and projects designed to illustrate specific concepts being discussed in the textbook. All of the exercises and projects are class-tested and can be performed without any elaborate equipment. Although they are designed to be performed indi-

vidually by you while reading or studying the textbook outside of class, your instructor might use some of them as in-class activities to supplement the classroom lecture and stimulate some in-class discussion. For examples of this type of box, see Chapter 5, p. 192, and Chapter 8, p. 341. A complete listing of these boxes is presented on pp. xxiii–xxiv above.

- *At the Cutting Edge of Personality Psychology: The Next Big Thing.* The "At the Cutting Edge of Personality Psychology" boxes illustrate a unique look at some of the more recent developments in the study of personality, ranging from highlighting a new research technique to up-to-date, innovative applications of personality psychology. For examples of this type of box, see Chapter 6, p. 220, Chapter 11, p. 461, and Chapter 13, p. 566. A complete listing of these boxes is presented on pp. xxiv–xxv above.

- *The Cultural Context of Personality Psychology: A World View of the Study of Personality.* "The Cultural Context of Personality Psychology" boxes are designed to illustrate to you how personality psychology is studied in different cultures, including making cross-cultural comparisons of various dimensions of personality and testing the dynamics of personality processes within an ethnic or cultural group. For examples of this type of box, see Chapter 9, p. 379, and Chapter 12, p. 524. A complete listing of these boxes is presented on pp. xxv–xxvi above.

Suggested Readings: Putting Them Where They Will Be Seen

Instead of the suggested readings being listed at the end of the chapter, where students oftentimes simply skip over them, the suggested readings in this textbook appear in the running text at those points in the chapter where they are most relevant, such as at the end of the discussion of a specific section within the chapter or within one of the many box inserts. In addition to being placed in a more strategic location, each suggested reading will also include a brief annotation in the running text to help you become familiar with the reference before seeking it out. Examples of the strategic placement of the suggested readings can be found in Chapter 7, p. 315, and Chapter 12, p. 506.

End-of-Chapter Summary: Reexamining the Highlights

The main points of the material presented in the chapter will be summarized in a bullet-point outline format at the end of the chapter. The format of the end-of-chapter summary will reflect the principal section headings of the chapter. Such a format will also serve as a study aid to you, since the bullet-point outline corresponds to the major points of the chapter. You can examine an end-of-chapter summary by going to the end of any of the chapters of this book (e.g., Chapter 1, p. 35).

End-of-Chapter Glossary: Words to the Wise

Each chapter contains a glossary of those important terms appearing in bold print throughout the chapter. In this glossary, the bold-print terms are listed in alphabetical order and defined at the end of the chapter, instead of being listed in an all-encompassing, end-of-book glossary. Providing you with these definitions at the end of the chapter will make it possible for you to get the meaning of important terms without having to interrupt your reading to turn to a glossary that is placed at the end of the book. These terms, along with their definitions, also appear in the corresponding chapter of the SSG as a list of "Important Terms to Remember" to reinforce their pedagogical significance. You can examine a chapter glossary by going to the end of any of the chapters of this book (e.g., Chapter 5, p. 203).

In summary, the material presented in this section describes some of principal pedagogical features that appear within each chapter of this textbook. The inclusion of these pedagogical features in each chapter is designed to create a standard level of consistency in the learning and teaching experiences for both you and your instructor, respectively, for each chapter.

Special Features Across All Chapters: Creating the Overall Look and Tone of the Textbook

While there are specific characteristic features that will appear within each chapter, there are also other more universal characteristic features that will help to define the overall tone, feel, and look of the textbook. Again, the principal rationale guiding the inclusion of these universal characteristic features is to help facilitate the ability of your instructor to provide you with an exciting and meaningful learning experience while teaching you from this book, and to stimulate your interest in the field of personality psychology while you read and study from this book. Presented below is a summary of these major characteristic features.

The Use of Examples: Variety is the Spice of Life

While reading this book, you will notice a few things about my writing style. One of the first things you will notice is that I have tried to supplement the material with a number of examples. Some of the examples will occur in parentheses within the sentence you are reading while others will be much more elaborate. Providing you with these examples will help make the material more concrete and, therefore, more meaningful and easier to learn. I have tried to select examples that not only illustrate the point being made or the concept being presented but also have some relevance to the type of "everyday living experiences" most of us have probably encountered. As you will see, these examples involve family, friends, and lovers; work, school, and leisure activities; and psychology, sociology, biology, criminology, medicine, the military, business, marketing, nursing, education, and personnel management, to name just a few. Through the extensive use of examples, I wanted to show you how this book is not only a textbook about personality psychology but about life in general.

The Use of Tables and Figures: A Picture is Worth a Thousand Words

You will also notice that I have included a number of pictorial and other visual aids in the form of photographs, tables, and figures. All of the photographs in this book have been selected by me to help illustrate in a more dramatic way a particular point being made in the book when words alone would not do (e.g., see the photograph in Chapter 7, p. 306). Some of the tables and figures will contain material summarizing the important points of particular sections of each chapter (e.g., see Figure 3.4 in Chapter 3, p. 102). When reading this book, it is possible for you to make sure you have mastered all the major points in a specific section by reviewing the material presented in these specially designed and strategically located figures and tables before going on to the next section. Some of the figures you will see will be used to illustrate certain concepts that are better understood when presented visually than simply reading about them (e.g., see Figure 1.1 in Chapter 1, p. 8). Other tables, figures, and graphs will be used to summarize the statistical results of research being discussed (see Figure 9.1 in Chapter 9, p. 380).

Emphasis on Applications: The Everyday Use of Personality Psychology

The study of personality psychology has its basis in systematic research guided by formal theories, just like any other discipline whose principal purpose it is to understand what people do and why they do it. In this textbook, I have made a serious attempt to include the latest findings and most up-to-date theories in the study of personality psychology. However, another characteristic feature of this textbook is the emphasis on the use of what we know about personality psychology to address many important personal concerns (e.g., enhancing one's self esteem – see Chapter 6, p. 238; overcoming test anxiety – see Chapter 13, p. 560) and social issues (e.g., the prevention of HIV – see Chapter 10, p. 402; sex discrimination in the workplace – see Chapter 12, p. 528). Throughout the textbook, you will see that I am committed to demonstrating that the material you will be reading about in this textbook is directly relevant to your everyday living experiences (e.g., consumer behavior – see Chapter 6, p. 246; overcoming shyness – see Chapter 13, p. 575). For example, each chapter will include a separate section subtitled "Using What Is Known." These distinctive sections will discuss in some detail and focus on the application of findings in the study of personality psychology to clinical psychology and personality assessment, and on many other interesting applications of the material presented in the chapter (e.g., subliminal advertising – see Chapter 3, p. 120; marital counseling – see Chapter 7, p. 278). Thus, I have made a variety of systematic and direct attempts to help you see the immediate utility of what you are reading and studying by the textbook's emphasis on the applications of personality psychology.

In summary, the material presented in this section describes some of universal pedagogical features that appear across this entire textbook. The inclusion of these overriding characteristics will give this textbook an engaging tone and sense of relevance to your everyday living experiences while you are reading and studying from it.

When we describe the unique personality of each individual, we focus on both the particular characteristics of the individual that help us to distinguish that person from others (e.g., "She likes to read 1970s Japanese crime-thriller novellas") and the person's general style across a variety of situations (e.g., "He is outgoing and conscientious"). As we noted previously, the same can be said for the pedagogical features described in this section. Specifically, all of the special features contained within each chapter and the universal characteristics appearing across the entire book are designed to give it its own personality. These features are also designed to make this book interesting and informative to read and easy to learn from. Finally, these features are designed to make this book fun and to convey the enjoyment I have when I teach, write, and talk about personality psychology. Just like the specific

characteristics of my own personality, all of these special features serve to define the unique personality of this personality textbook – "a people-person personality."

Beyond the Psychology of Personality: Getting Your Money's Worth from this Book

One of the most frequent comments I hear students make about their textbooks is the high price they must pay when purchasing them. Such comments are not only common but also very familiar; I can remember making those same comments when I was a student. While the pricing of this textbook is beyond my control, I have decided that I would deal with the price of textbooks by writing a book that would allow you to maximize your return on your initial investment. Specifically, I have tried to write a book that is not only about personality psychology but about many other aspects of life as well. As such, I have tried to present you with information that will be of benefit to you not only for this course in personality psychology but for other courses you will take throughout your college career. I believe you will find this book to be a valuable source of ideas as well as a reference book to help you write speeches and term papers in your other classes both inside and outside of psychology. I hope you will get your money's worth out of this book by using it again and again. I also hope that you will talk to friends, co-workers, family members, and acquaintances about what you are reading and learning from this book. Sharing what you are learning from this book will not only help you to learn the material better, but it will also help you to get more value for what you paid for it. The more people who benefit from what is written in this book, the greater the return will be on your initial investment. Specifically, you can share this book and the knowledge you have gained from studying it with others to help them see how personality psychology can be applied to their college career and beyond. In my view, keeping this book to use in your other classes and sharing it with others is the highest compliment you could pay to an author of a textbook. I hope my efforts are worthy of such a compliment from you.

The Pervasiveness of Personality Psychology: On Knowing How and Where to Look

I hope to make it possible for you, by reading this book, to realize that personality psychology is all around you.

All you have to do is know how and where to look for it. With the help of this book and your instructor, you should be able to start viewing the world through the eyes of a personality psychologist. Is such a view better than others? All I can say is that my life is much more interesting and exciting since I have become involved in the study of personality psychology. I hope my sense of excitement and enthusiasm is contagious.

From Me to You: "My Way" Is Really about "Your Way"

While I realize that personality textbooks, unlike people, really do not have personalities, after spending so much time and energy, after all of the good times and bad times, after all of the pleasant and unpleasant memories I have associated with writing this book, I have almost come to view it as a unique person with a unique personality for whom I care a great deal and want other people to like, as well. With this in mind, let me say that I have made every attempt to write a textbook that will give you a thorough coverage of the field of personality psychology in a manner that you will find interesting and with special fea-

tures that will make it possible for you to get the most out of this book in the time you spend reading it. So, in a sense, doing this book "my way" is really about doing it "your way." I hope that this book meets with your approval.

A Request for Help: Let's Keep in Touch

I would like to hear from you. Do you have examples, ideas for topics, or constructive criticism? If you care to contact me, here is how I can be reached:

Bernardo J. Carducci
Department of Psychology
Indiana University Southeast
New Albany, IN 47150
E-mail: bcarducc@IUS.edu

I look forward to hearing from you soon. And, I wish you continued success. Let's keep in touch.

Best regards,
Bernardo J. Carducci

Acknowledgments
Some Words of Thanks

While the many hours I spent alone at my computer might suggest that writing this book was an individual effort, nothing could be further from the truth. I would like to acknowledge those individuals who had a hand in making this book possible, whether they were aware of their contribution or not.

Madora Manson was a high school art teacher who always saw artistic greatness and a creative personality in the efforts of all of her students, even those without any artistic talent, like me. Chris Cozby was the person who sparked my initial interest in the study of psychology when I was an aimless undergraduate seeking a college major after my dismal three-week attempt to play community college-level football led me to reject physical education as a major. Stanley Woll taught an undergraduate course in personality psychology that excited my interest in the study of personality and served to solidify my career choice – to be a personality psychologist. Bill Griffitt, who left the field of personality psychology much too soon due to his premature death, taught me how to be a personality psychologist during those many informal discussions in his office.

I would like to acknowledge the support of Indiana University Southeast for creating the type of environment that makes writing a book possible. Within the university, there are several people whose efforts I must acknowledge. I want to thank Cliff Staten, my "boss," who always had words of encouragement that seemed to appear just when I needed to hear them. Thomas P. Wolf is a colleague who continues to serve as a source of inspiration by showing me that one's active involvement in scholarly activities does not stop with the onset of retirement. Brigette Colligan and Lesley Deal provided clerical and editorial assistance that kept many versions of the manuscript flowing. As members of the "Lunch Bunch," Kathleen Norvell and Lesley Deal helped to reduce the daily stress of working on this book by making going out to lunch so much fun. A special debt of gratitude goes to Melanie E. Hughes, Gabrielle Carr, Jacqueline Johnson, Marty Rosen, Benita Mason, Maria Accardi, and especially Nancy Totten, who are all reference librarians that, I am convinced, searched from here to the moon to obtain many of the reference sources I needed to write this book. To them, I owe a tremendous debt of gratitude.

Away from the university, there are also some folks to whom I would like to express my gratitude for their unique support while I worked on this book. Kathleen Norvell provided the type of special friendship that was so important whenever I had writer's block and needed someone to talk to and make me laugh. Joy and Lou Bailey always made me feel "just like family" on those special occasions when my real family was many miles away. At Kremer's Smoke Shoppe, Gayle Salle, "the other cigar guy," Robert Caudall, "a true cigar buddy," and all of the other members of the Derby City Cigar Club provided me with a place to relax and enjoy my favorite cigars, engage in great conversation, and obtain a sense of community, all which I discovered were very important after spending so much time alone working on this book.

At the publishing house of Wiley-Blackwell, there are several individuals that I wish to acknowledge. First and foremost, I want to express my gratitude to Christine M. Cardone, my editor. Even before she became my editor, Chris, during our initial 10-minute conversation about my research on shyness, impressed me as the type of person who was passionate about the ideas of others and knew intuitively how to make those ideas even better. A few years later, after becoming my editor, she has exceeded all of my expectations of what I hoped an editor would be. From the very beginning, she has supported me unconditionally in terms of what I wanted to do as the author of this book, even when others did not. And, most importantly, Chris, being the type of Italian that my full-blooded Italian parents would have loved, understood that writing a book, like preparing a great homemade pot of spaghetti sauce (or "gravy," as our folks called it), takes time. I am so grateful that Chris gave me the time to write the type of book that I truly wanted to write. My only regret about working with her as an editor is that my parents passed away before they had the opportunity to meet her. As I said, my parents would have loved her for the kindness and support she has given to "their boy." On their behalf, and in their cherished memory, I say to Chris, "*Grazie mille!*"

As my developmental editor, Susan Moss provided the type of feedback that was both critical and constructive. As the editorial assistants, Sarah Coleman and Constance Adler made sure all of the important tasks that need to get organized, coordinated, and done were completed in a timely manner, even in the face of my tendency to procrastinate. Kitty Bocking did a wonderful job of selecting the photographs that appear throughout the book. Hannah Rolls was masterful as she coordinated all of the production details associated with taking the electronic files of the manuscript I submitted and creating the highly reader-friendly book you are now holding in your hands.

I would also like to acknowledge those individuals who served as manuscript reviewers and provided me with a variety of insightful comments that helped to make my words into a book. These individuals are: Gordon Atlas, Alfred University; Patricia Lee Llewellyn, University of Virginia; Alan E. Martin, The University of Buckingham; Christie Napa Scollon, Singapore Management University; Isis H. Settles, Michigan State University; Lisa Gray-Shellberg, California University – Dominguez Hills; Steven C. Funk, Northern Arizona University; and one anonymous reviewer.

Finally, many very special acknowledgments are expressed to Rozana Carducci, my daughter, who continued to make me feel like a dad, not just a father, as she blossomed from "my little girl" to a fellow academic. The conversations we have had over the years about our individual lives and professional work have served to create a father–daughter bond that is so much thicker than blood and has transcended the time and miles we spent apart during those early years.

Like I said, this book is the product of many individuals. The personality of each of these individuals has found its way into this book about personality psychology, and this book is much better as a result of their efforts. To all, once again, I say, "Thanks."

Bernardo J. Carducci

The Scope and Methods of Personality Psychology
An Introduction to the Psychology of Personality

Part I

Welcome to the study of the psychology of personality. Part I serves as a general introduction to the study of personality. As part of this introduction, you will be exposed to information that will help you understand the scope of personality psychology by illustrating how personality is defined and what constitutes the study of personality psychology. You will also be exposed to the methods of personality psychology by considering the research strategies and assessment techniques personality psychologists use to gather information while studying the underlying nature, operation, and development of personality, as well as how this information can be used in applications to our everyday living experiences. The information you gain in Part I will lay the foundation for all of the viewpoints, research, and applications of personality psychology you will meet in the remainder of this book.

The Psychology of Personality
An Overview

1

Chapter Overview:
A Preview of Coming Attractions

People use the word *personality* every day. They say, "He has such a dynamic personality" or "She gets her personality from her mother's side of the family." But most people do not really understand what the study of **personality** is all about. Chapter 1 sets the stage for our study of personality. In this chapter, you will learn what **personality psychologists** mean by personality, as well as the types of questions they ask, the research methods they use, and the ethical parameters within which they operate.

Defining Personality

Welcome to the psychology of personality! Among all the research areas in the science of psychology, personality psychology is notable in the way it effortlessly meshes with the fabric of our lives – our everyday situations, problems, and relationships. You will see this demonstrated through the numerous applications of personality research woven throughout every chapter of this text.

This text has been carefully written to help you succeed in the class you are taking. As you read the chapters, you'll notice a number of special elements designed to help you monitor comprehension. The chapter outlines show the progression of topics and subtopics; key terms are printed in boldface; photos, figures, and tables dramatize and organize material; and chapter summaries provide a concise overview of the main points. Each chapter in this book also contains a number of special feature boxes that will challenge you to zero in on certain aspects of classic personality theory, research, assessment, and processes – and to expand your knowledge of contemporary findings, cross-cultural aspects, and applications of personality psychology.

Part I of this text will help you understand the general principles and scope of personality psychology. Part III comprises a survey of basic assumptions, principal processes, assessment techniques, and practical applications associated with each major theoretical viewpoint. In Part III, you will see a shift in emphasis from viewpoints to a consideration of selected topics addressing important personal and social issues with a rich tradition in personality psychology. I hope that you enjoy learning about the complexity of personality and the personal insights that come to you as you navigate this text.

How Personality Psychologists Define Personality

What does the word *personality* mean to you? The way personality psychologists define it has changed over the years (McAdams, 1997; Pervin, 1990; Winter & Barenbaum, 1999), reflecting theoretical and empirical advancements made in the study of personality, which you will be exposed to throughout this book. Think for a moment about the word and how it is used. Now compare your definition with those of some prominent personality psychologists:

- "That which permits a prediction of what a person will do in a given situation" – Raymond B. Cattell (1950, p. 2).
- "The most adequate conceptualization of a person's behavior in all its detail" – David McClelland (1951, p. 69).
- "A person's unique pattern of traits" – J. P. Guilford (1959, p. 5).
- "The dynamic organization within the individual of those psychophysical systems that determine his characteristic behavior and thought" – Gordon W. Allport (1961, p. 28).
- "The distinctive patterns of behavior (including thoughts as well as 'affects,' that is, feelings, and emotions and actions) that characterize each individual enduringly" – Walter Mischel (1999, p. 4).
- "Personality represents those characteristics of the person that account for consistent patterns of feeling, thinking, and behaving" – Lawrence A. Pervin and Oliver P. John (2001, p. 4).
- "Personality refers to an individual's characteristic patterns of thought, emotions, and behavior, together with the psychological mechanisms – hidden or not – behind those patterns" – David C. Funder (2001, p. 2).
- Traits of personality "are classified by the adaptive problems they were designed to solve and . . . traits evolve as a function of the adaptive problems faced by the organism over evolutionary time" – Figueredo et al. (2005, p. 871).

After reading these quotations from the experts, you might conclude that there are almost as many definitions of personality as there are authors (Pervin, 1990) – and you would be right. But note that each definition expresses a common concern for using personality to help predict and explain people's behavior. Keep in mind that like other complex concepts (e.g., the origin of the universe) and interesting phenomena (e.g., why people fall in love) the human personality is not easily defined. Thus, just as you are willing to accept a diversity of explanations for other complex and interesting phenomena in your own life, so should you be willing to accept a diversity of explanations for one of life's most interesting phenomena – the understanding of your personality and those around you. Ideally, as you make your way through this text you will develop a healthy tolerance for diversity and an appreciation that most of the important things in life do not come packaged in simple, concise categories.

Common Features of Definitions of Personality

Developing a definition of personality that is accepted by everyone studying personality does seem difficult. But it is useful to identify certain features common to most of these definitions.

Uniqueness of the Individual

Most definitions of personality include some statement about the uniqueness of an individual's personality. This uniqueness can be explained from various theoretical viewpoints held by different personality psychologists. A *biological* viewpoint, with its emphasis on genetics and physiological processes, might consider differences in bodily processes (e.g., hormonal levels and brain functioning). A *dispositional trait* viewpoint might assert that certain human qualities are stable even as they are displayed across diverse settings (e.g., being conscientious at work and while hiking in the mountains). A *learning* viewpoint, with its emphasis on the effect of experience on behavior, might consider distinctive reinforcement patterns (e.g., extraversion being rewarded). A *cognitive viewpoint* would emphasize individual differences in the interpretation of environmental cues and the behavioral expectations and consequences associated with these cues (e.g., being cooperative at work but aggressive when playing tennis). A *phenomenological* viewpoint might emphasize subjective experience and self-determination (e.g., your career as an expression of your passion for protecting the environment). An *evolutionary viewpoint* would emphasize the adaptive significance of certain personality characteristics (e.g., aggressive behavior serves as protection of territory and food sources). A *cross-cultural* viewpoint might highlight the impact of societal norms and local customs on the expression of individual differences. And a *Freudian* viewpoint, with its focus on internal forces, might emphasize early childhood experiences (e.g.,

parent–child interactions). But regardless of the theoretical viewpoint or perspective, any definition of explanation of personality should take into account that each person is unique.

Consistency of Behavior

Personality psychologists generally assume some degree of continuity in an individual's personality. As a result, another feature common to most definitions of personality is a concern for the consistency of behavior across time and situations. For example, by assuming consistency across time, personality psychologists can link high-risk behavior in high school (e.g., riding a motorcycle) with a decision in adulthood to enter a high-risk occupation (e.g., becoming a police officer). By assuming consistency across situations, researchers can link the competitive nature of a tennis player with the desire to be the top sales representative in his or her company. If behavioral consistency did not exist, studying personality would make little sense.

Emphasizing behavioral consistency does not mean an individual's personality never changes. Concerns with the consistency of behavior are at the heart of some of the most controversial debates in personality psychology. The degree of behavioral consistency is influenced by the extent to which situational factors, as well as one's personality, determine thoughts, feelings, and behavior.

Content and Process of Personality

In the words of highly regarded personality psychologist Gordon W. Allport, "Personality is something that *does* something" (1937, p. 48). By *is* something, Allport refers to the *content* of personality. Each major personality theory discussed in this book offers a somewhat different explanation of the basic content of the human personality. By *does* something, Allport refers to the *process* of personality, the dynamic nature by which the contents of the personality influence the individual's thoughts, feelings, and behavior.

The content and process features of personality are interrelated. Across time and situations, the basic makeup of the human personality directly influences how the personality operates. For example, some personality psychologists assume that various traits make up the basic content of the human personality and also influence behavior. They would explain the aggressive

Summing It Up *Common Features of Definitions of Personality*

Common Features	Examples	Research Issues
Uniqueness of the Individual: Each person is different.	While Joe responded to receiving a "D" on his history test by reviewing the quality of his class notes, Sam dealt with his "D" by going to a local pub to "drown" his misery.	What is the nature of this uniqueness (e.g., unique combinations of traits or genes or different learning histories)?
Uniformity of Behavior: Behavior of the individual is consistent over time and across situations.	Rosemary is very friendly toward her fellow employees at work and her guests at the parties she gives.	To what extent do situational and personality factors interact to determine our behavior?
Content and Processes: Personality consists of something that influences behavior.	Because Mary has failed her French test, she also expects to fail her psychology test and, therefore, does not study for it that night.	How do our expectations in one situation influence our behavior in others?

style of the office tyrant across a variety of situations as resulting from a personality that contains a combination of the traits of aggressiveness and hostility. They would attribute variations in the uniqueness and behavioral consistency of other office workers to other numerous combinations of personality traits.

Combining common features to formulate a definition of personality is significant, because it determines how a personality psychologist views the development, measurement, and modification of the human personality. Thus, a definition of personality is far more than simply a series of words. A summary of the major points discussed in this section is presented in "Summing It Up: Common Features of Definitions of Personality" above.

The Scope of Personality Psychology

The scope of personality psychology goes far beyond simply defining terms. What do personality psychologists do? Some general areas of study presented in this section include the formulation and testing of personality theories, the developmental aspects of personality, the assessment of personality, and the application of personality psychology to many aspects of our daily lives.

Theory Development: Viewpoints of Personality

Theory development is one of the most important areas of study within personality psychology. A **theory** is a systematic collection of explanations that are used to account for a set of observations and predict future observations. A theory serves many important purposes in the study of personality. A particular theoretical viewpoint determines the research questions that are asked about personality, the methodology used to answer these questions, what is done to influence personality development, and the treatment used to modify an individual's personality, if a change is necessary.

Many different theoretical viewpoints of the human personality exist, each explaining personality from a different perspective (Millon & Grossman, 2006; Sommers-Flanagan & Sommers-Flanagan, 2004; Wiggins, 1999). Figure 1.1 illustrates how the same behavior is interpreted differently from various theoretical viewpoints. *None of the different perspectives is right or wrong; they simply vary in how useful they are in helping personality psychologists to understand behavior.*

As an example of this important point, consider the two contrasting perspectives of personality provided by the biological and cultural viewpoints. The biological viewpoint of personality focuses on biological processes operating within the individual – such as genetic makeup, hormonal factors, physiological arousal, and brain chemistry – to explain the operation and expression of an individual's personality. The material presented in "At the Cutting Edge of Personality: Searching for Genetic Explanations of Personality" exemplifies such a biological explanation.

AT THE CUTTING EDGE OF PERSONALITY PSYCHOLOGY

Searching for Genetic Explanations of Personality

The Gene–Brain–Personality Chain: Creating Some Important Links

One of the most exciting areas of research in the study of personality psychology has to do with the identification of genes linked with personality traits (Azar, 2002; Canli, 2006; DiLalla, 2004). Although the term *personality* is often used to describe the characteristic manner in which an individual responds to environmental conditions (e.g., a "hot-headed individual" honks her horn when experiencing delays in traffic and expresses anger at the cashier while being held up at the checkout line at the supermarket), geneticists studying personality are searching for the underlying biological bases of these reactions. The goal of this research is to identify genes that affect brain function and then, in turn, to examine how the brain affects the way individuals interact with and adjust to their environments (Benjamin, Ebstein, & Belmaker, 2002; Nelson, 2006).

Although the possibility that many different genes may influence the expression of specific personality traits certainly complicates our understanding of the genetic influence on personality, some possible links are being identified in the gene–brain–personality relationship (Benjamin et al., 2002). For example, the personality trait of sensation seeking (e.g., a high level of brain arousal and the seeking of new and different experiences), more commonly know as "thrill seeking," has been linked with a protein-producing gene that is responsible for producing a dopamine receptor in the brain called DRD4 (Zuckerman, 2006). Dopamine, a chemical substance produced in the brain, stimulates arousal in the brain and triggers behavioral responses. Investigation of the DRD4 gene suggests that it is linked with certain thrill- or sensation-seeking tendencies, such as drug abuse and attention-deficit hyperactivity disorder (ADHD; Benjamin et al., 2002; Plomin & Crabbe, 2002). It is possible that an increased presence of this gene creates an elevated level of arousal in the brain that some individuals choose to satisfy with the novelty, excitement, and risk associated with drug abuse. In a similar manner, the inability of individuals with ADHD to concentrate, focus their attention, and control their impulses, all of which can lead to learning disabilities, may be due in part to an elevated arousal level created by increased presence of this gene.

Researchers do not yet understand how the presence of the DRD4 gene, along with its interaction with other genes, influences the way individuals react to their environments. However, this aspect of the study of the gene–brain–personality chain has some important implications. For example, the identification of the DRD4 gene may make it possible to initiate early intervention and precautionary measures for at-risk individuals living in stressful environments. A similar case could be made in school environments for children with an elevated risk of ADHD.

Without a doubt, the possible link between an individual's genetic makeup and personality is one of the most exciting and controversial current research topics in the study of personality psychology (Canli, 2006; DiLalla, 2004; Plomin, 2002; Plomin & Crabbe, 2002). You will read much more about this emerging area of research that is at the "cutting edge of personality psychology" in Chapter 8, in which the biological aspects of personality are discussed in greater depth.

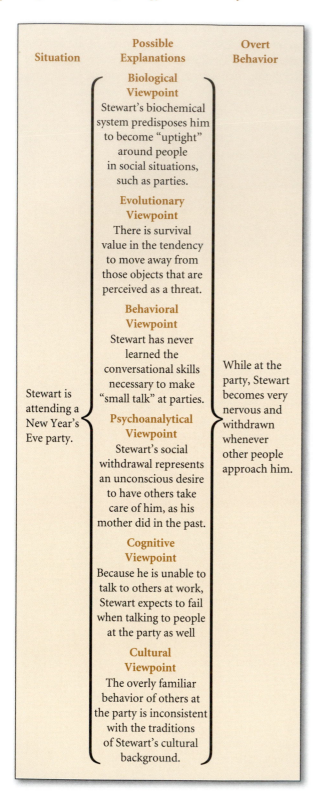

	Situation	Possible Explanations	Overt Behavior

Biological Viewpoint
Stewart's biochemical system predisposes him to become "uptight" around people in social situations, such as parties.

Evolutionary Viewpoint
There is survival value in the tendency to move away from those objects that are perceived as a threat.

Behavioral Viewpoint
Stewart has never learned the conversational skills necessary to make "small talk" at parties.

Psychoanalytical Viewpoint
Stewart's social withdrawal represents an unconscious desire to have others take care of him, as his mother did in the past.

Cognitive Viewpoint
Because he is unable to talk to others at work, Stewart expects to fail when talking to people at the party as well

Cultural Viewpoint
The overly familiar behavior of others at the party is inconsistent with the traditions of Stewart's cultural background.

Stewart is attending a New Year's Eve party.

While at the party, Stewart becomes very nervous and withdrawn whenever other people approach him.

Figure 1.1 Explaining the same overt behavior from six theoretical viewpoints

By contrast, the cross-cultural viewpoint of personality focuses on influences operating outside of the individual – such as societal norms, family expectations, and ethnic identification – to explain the operation and expression of an individual's personality. The material presented in "The Cultural Context of Personality Psychology" exemplifies a cultural explanation.

The Cultural Context of Personality Psychology

Cultural Conceptualizations and Considerations of Personality: Putting Personality in a Worldwide Perspective

Although it is easy to think of individuals as having different personalities, thinking of cultures as having different personalities may be harder. Yet they do. Specifically, North American and Western European countries are characterized by a view of personality that emphasizes the uniqueness of the individual's personality (Brislin & Lo, 2006; Cross & Markus, 1999). Such a viewpoint is seen in the definitions of personality presented on p. 4. These definitions tend to emphasize the principal role of personality as capturing the uniqueness of the individual, predicting what he or she will do, and explaining his or her thoughts, feelings, and behavior.

By contrast, Eastern countries such as Japan, India, and China, along with other Asian cultures, are characterized by a view of personality that places less emphasis on the unique personality of the individual and greater focus on the person's identification with a group, such as family, occupation, or caste, and the expectations, duties, and roles associated with being a member of that group as the principal source for understanding the individual (Brislin & Lo, 2006; Cross & Markus, 1999).

Looking for Love: Personality and Personal Ads

A dramatic example of the variability in cultural expression of personality can be seen in the nature of the information placed in "personal ads" (Cross & Markus, 1999, p. 378). The first two ads shown below originally appeared in the *San Francisco Chronicle*, a typical daily metropolitan newspaper:

> 28 SWM, 6′1″, 160 lbs. Handsome, artistic, ambitious, seeks attractive WF, 24-29, for friendship, romance, and permanent partnership.

> Very attractive, independent SWF, 29, 5′6″, 110 lbs., loves fine dining, the theater, gardening and quiet evenings at home. In search of handsome SWM 28-34 with similar interests.

Now compare these ads with the following two, which were placed on the same day in the *India Tribune*, a California newspaper with a readership of primarily immigrant families from India:

> Gujarati Vaishnav parents invite correspondence from never married Gujarati well settled, preferably green card holder from respectable family for green card holder daughter 29 years, 5′4″, good looking, doing CPA.

> Gujarati Brahmin family invites correspondence from a well cultured, beautiful Gujarati girl for 29 years, 5′8″, 145 lbs. handsome looking, well settled boy.

The first two ads reflect the typical Western viewpoint of personality by focusing on the uniqueness of the individual and emphasizing individual personality characteristics (e.g., "independent," "ambitious") and personal interests (e.g., "loves . . . theater, gardening"). The first two ads were placed by the seekers themselves. The second two, on the other hand, were placed by the *families* of the seekers. Note how they reflect the Eastern viewpoint of personality by focusing on information emphasizing group membership, such as indicating the family's region of origin in India (e.g., the state of Gujarat) and the caste of the family (e.g., Vaishnav, Brahmin).

As these ads illustrate, the contrasting expressions of personality in the lives of individuals, from establishing their uniqueness to helping them to attract potential mates, reflects the viewpoint of personality associated with different cultures. Being aware of and sensitive to these cultural characteristics of personality is critical to the efforts of personality psychologists who through their study seek to promote international understanding. Throughout this text you will be exposed to information that will expand your awareness of "the cultural context of personality psychology."

Personality psychologists use certain criteria to assess how much better one theory is than another (Hall, Lindzey, & Campbell, 1998; Levy, 1970). The criterion of *internal consistency* requires that assumptions, principles, and dynamics of a particular theory of personality fit with one another. The more logically the various pieces of the theory fit together, the more favorably it is evaluated. The criterion of *comprehensiveness* focuses on how many aspects of personality (e.g., morality, aggression, and anxiety) are covered by the theory. The more comprehensive a theory, the more favorably it is evaluated. The criterion of **parsimony** suggests, all other things being equal, that the simpler a theory is (e.g., fewer assumptions and principles), the more adequate it is. The criterion of *utility* has to do with how useful the theory is in stimulating additional research, predicting various outcomes, or being applied to different problems (e.g., personnel selection, reducing shyness, and treating depression). Thus, a good theory is internally consistent, comprehensive, simple, and useful.

Personality Research: The Testing of Theory

In addition to developing theories, personality psychologists must test those theories through systematic research involving hypothesis testing. A **hypothesis** is a statement made about the relationship between at least two variables in a manner consistent with a particular theory. For example, a learning theory of aggression might propose the following hypothesis: Viewers who see others rewarded for aggressive behavior will act more aggressively than those who observe others being punished for aggressive behavior. To test the hypothesized effect of observed outcome for aggressiveness on viewer aggressive behavior, a psychologist might have one group of children watch a videotape showing an adult being rewarded for behaving aggressively. At the same time, an equal number of other children would watch a videotape showing the adult being scolded for the aggressive behavior. After watching the videotapes, the children would be allowed to engage in a free-play period while the psychologist monitored the amount of aggressive play through a one-way mirror. Documenting more aggressive behavior in the children who observed the adult rewarded rather than scolded for aggressiveness would confirm the hypothesis and support this learning theory of personality.

Confirming the hypothesis would not mean the research was complete. Subsequent research would need to be done to determine whether such variables as the sex or age of the aggressive adult model or the nature of the reward (e.g., candy vs. verbal praise) made a difference in the children's tendency to imitate the aggressive behavior. Converging evidence from such additional research would more completely test the theory and allow for better understanding of the relationship between observed rewards and imitative aggressive behavior.

Based on additional research, a particular theory of personality is modified and refined to account for the observed results. If the theory cannot be modified to be consistent with the research results, it is usually abandoned and another one is proposed and tested in its place.

Personality Development: The Emergence of Personality

Researchers studying **personality development** examine those factors contributing to the emergence of an individual's personality (Caspi & Roberts, 1999; Costa & McCrae, 1997; Eder & Mangelsdorf, 1997; Halverson & Wampler, 1997; Hayslip, Neumann, Louden, & Chapman, 2006; Lewis, 1999; Pervin, 2002). Examining factors from the past can offer insight into the current state of an individual's personality (Block, 1971, 1993; Caspi, 2000; Caspi & Roberts, 1999, 2001; Roberts & Caspi, 2003). For example, examining such childhood factors as birth order, family size, parenting practices, and early trauma might provide insight into experiences of shyness in adulthood.

Personality development is an interactive process involving other aspects of human development. For example, research indicates that the rate of physical development (e.g., being big or small for one's age) influences personality development during adolescence (Kaplan, 2000; Papalia, Olds, & Feldman, 2001; Shaffer & Kipp, 2007), and these influences on personality development can remain into adulthood (Gross & Duke, 1980). The gradual effect of various physical changes (e.g., slowing down of motor responses) and social changes (e.g., retirement or death of a spouse) on the process of personality adjustment in the later years is also studied by psychologists in the area of personality development (Papalia et al., 2001).

As researchers in the field of personality psychology acquire more knowledge about the factors contributing to the development of certain aspects of personality, they can help individuals make decisions about changing and/or developing certain aspects of their own personality or the personality of others. For example, if certain parenting styles are known to foster high self-esteem (Coopersmith, 1967; Kaplan 2000) or a heightened sense of independence and achievement (Baumrind, 1971; Kaplan, 2000) in children, then deliberately adopting those styles will maximize the likelihood of children developing these personality characteristics.

Personality Assessment: The Measurement of Personality

Personality assessment refers to the development and use of techniques to accurately and consistently measure different aspects of personality (Aiken & Groth-Marnat, 2006; Cohen & Swerdlik, 2002; Lanyon & Goodstein, 1997). Personality assessment is a vital link to the other major aspects of personality psychology. Following are some ways researchers use personality assessment techniques:

- Testing various personality theories (e.g., test anxiety; extraversion vs. introversion).
- Measuring developmental changes in personality (e.g., moral reasoning) from childhood to adulthood.
- Evaluating the effectiveness of various psychotherapies (e.g., a stress-reduction workshop).

Personality psychologists and other professionals also use personality assessment in a variety of important applications to everyday situations, ranging from screening potential job applicants to assisting in the diagnosis of medical problems (Handler & Clemence, 2003).

Applications in Personality Psychology: Putting Personality Psychology to Use

The application of personality psychology involves utilizing what is known about personality theories, research, development, and assessment to help individuals lead happier, healthier, more productive lives. Effective applications of personality psychology have a solid theoretical framework and are based on systematic research. A long-standing application of personality psychology is to the area of **psychotherapy** – the process of treating maladaptive tendencies using principles of psychology (Trull & Phares, 2001). **Psychotherapists** – those individuals who perform psychotherapy – rely on theories of personality to help guide their thinking about what factors may have caused a client's emotional and behavioral difficulties and what should be done to modify the client's problem behavior. In fact, many major theories of personality and techniques of personality assessment were developed and refined in the context of the personality theorist's clinical experience and research (Sommers-Flanagan & Sommers-Flanagan, 2004). For example, to test her theory that a person's self-esteem will improve as he or she learns to deal successfully with minor failures, a psychotherapist might pose a series of difficult social situations (e.g., starting a conversation with others, asking for a raise at work) to her client and then help guide the individual through the successful resolution of these conflicts, after which the client's self-esteem would be measured and an increase from the beginning of the treatment noted. The results of the research would provide support for the psychotherapist's theory about the relationship between self-esteem and response to failure, as well as increase the likelihood of her using this form of psychotherapy in the future when dealing with other clients who might have similar issues with their self-esteem.

Outside of psychotherapy, the applications of personality research to our daily lives are numerous and diverse.

Medicine, Health, and Epidemiology   Personality researchers have examined which personality characteristics are linked with sickness (Contrada & Guyll, 2001) and how certain personality processes might be related to mortality (Danner, Snowdon, & Friesen, 2001), as well as the role personality factors play in the experience and treatment of individuals with chronic pain (Arbisi & Seime, 2006; Gatchel & Weisberg, 2000). In the area of health, researchers have examined the role of personality factors in the progression of HIV (Cole, Kemeny, & Taylor, 1997; DeAngelis, 2002), in the identification and treatment of the "addiction-prone personality" (Barnes, Murray, Patton, Bentler, & Anderson, 2000), and in the expression of high-risk sexual behaviors (e.g., unprotected sex, sex with strangers; Hoyle, Fejfar, & Miller, 2000). In the study of *epidemiology*, the branch of medicine dealing with the frequency of disease in large populations, researchers are investigating the role of personality as a consequential factor in a variety of social problems, including mental disorders, violence, and health-risk behaviors (Krueger, Caspi, & Moffitt, 2000).

Business   Research from personality psychology has been used in the process of personnel selection (Butcher, Ones, & Cullen, 2006; Ones & Viswesvaran, 2001; Schmidt & Hunter, 1998). Researchers study employees' effectiveness in diverse occupational settings ranging from sales, telemarketing, and public bus driving (Alge, Gresham, Heneman, Fox, & McMasters, 2002; Furnham, 2001; Von Emster & Harrison, 1998) to such high-risk, hazardous-duty occupational settings as emergency services (e.g., police officers, firefighters, ambulance personnel), nuclear power plants, military units, medical surgical departments, and the airline industry (Flin, 2001). The characteristics of effective and ineffective business leaders and executives have been investigated (Emler & Cook, 2001; Timmerman, 1997). The personality characteristics of those with good organizational citizenship (e.g., customer service orientation and conscientiousness) and those with antisocial organizational citizenship (e.g., substance abuse or violence on the job; theft of money, property, or time from an employer), along with evaluating the tests used to assess them (Avis, Kudisch, & Fortunato, 2002; Graham, McDaniel, Douglas, & Snell, 2002; Nicol & Paunonen, 2002; Sommers, Schell, & Vodanovich, 2002), have also been appraised and identified by researchers utilizing principles of personality psychology (Neuman & Kickul, 1999; Ones & Viswesvaran, 2001).

Technology and Economics   Researchers have investigated how individuals judge the personality of others based on information obtained from Internet home pages (Goldstein, 1998) and how they infer personality characteristics from computer-generated synthetic voices (Nass & Lee, 2001), as well as how computer-mediated communication can serve to influence the behavior of shy individuals during online interactions (Stritzke, Nguyen, & Durkin, 2004). In the study of economics, the relationship between personality and entrepreneurship, time spent working, saving patterns, and everyday financial decision making have been examined (Brandstätter, 1997; Carducci & Wong, 1998; Webley, Burgoyne, Lea, & Young, 2001; Wong & Carducci, 1991).

The Law   Principles of personality assessment have been used to help in the selection of police officers and in child custody cases (Craig, 2005; Wrightsman, 2001; Wrightsman, Greene, Nietzel, & Fortune, 2002). Knowledge of personality is used in the development of personality profiles of such criminal offenders as rapists and serial killers (Holmes & Holmes, 2002). Input from personality assessment is used to help in courts to determine the issue of a defendant's competency to stand trail (Megargee, 2006), and to assess parents' knowledge and beliefs concerning child-rearing practices when making decisions in child custody cases (Aiken, 2003).

History and the Humanities   Within the arts and sciences, personality researchers are studying the dynamics of creativity and genius (Aiken, 2003; Simonton, 1999; Therivel, 1998) and the development of tests to assess creativity (Aiken, 2003). On a darker note, researchers have also investigated the nature and dynamics of the "Nazi personality" (Zillmer, Harrower, Ritzler, & Archer, 1995) in an attempt to understand the individuals who perpetrated such atrocities and the conditions fostering the expression of such a personality, as well as in the interest of preventing the expression of such barbarous personalities in the future. More recently, research in personality psychology has examined personality characteristics of neo-Nazis and individuals involved in other racist and hate groups (Berkowitz, 2005). On the more positive side, researcher have also looked at the personality correlates of those non-Jewish individuals who put themselves at great risk to rescue and provide shelter to Jews being persecuted during the holocaust (Midlarsky, Jones, & Corley, 2005).

As you see, the study of personality psychology has applications to some of the most interesting and important aspects of our lives. To help document the significant contribution personality psychology has made to our everyday living experiences, I will present to you in every chapter of this book special material designed to illustrate the practical utility of what you will be studying in this course. For example, you can read about how the study of personality psychology is being applied to the area of automobile design and advertising in the feature entitled "Applications in Personality Psychology."

Applications in Personality Psychology

How Automobile Design and Advertising Are Being Driven by Personality Psychology: The Personalities of Cars and Their Drivers

Are you what you drive? Automakers are always trying to figure out which factors determine how consumers decide to purchase one car over another. And, most recently, one of the biggest mysteries is how families choose between minivans and sports utility vehicles (SUV). An examination of the two groups by comparing along such standard demographics as median income, age, occupation, family size, or where they live indicates a high degree of similarity, so does little to solve this mystery. However, a look at the personality characteristics of these two groups reveals two distinctively different personality types (Bradsher, 2000; Coomes, 2002).

- *SUV owners: Self-focused type.* SUV owners seem to be less social individuals and more self-oriented people who are concerned with expressing an image of power and sexual allure. Married SUV drivers like the idea that their vehicles could be used for reentering the dating scene. SUV owners are more restless and more attached to luxury and pleasure, have strong conscious or subconscious fears of crime, and are less likely to attend church and do volunteer work.
- *Minivan owners: Other-focused type.* Minivan drivers tend to be more self-confident, outgoing, and more other-focused (e.g., being more involved with their family, friends, and community) and are more likely to attend church and do volunteer work.

Why Drivers Drive What They Do: What Driving Really Means

More than just simply identifying the personality characteristics associated with these two personality types, this information helps to clarify the differences in how members of these groups perceive and interpret the experience of driving. As an example, while both groups indicate that they want to "be in control" when driving their vehicle, it seems to mean something totally different for the two. Specifically, for the "other-focused" minivan respondents, being in control has more to do with safety, such as being able to park and maneuver while navigating traffic and getting elderly individuals and children in and out of the vehicle. On the other hand, for "self-focused" SUV people, being in control has more to do with controlling the situation and the people around them. Reflecting this self-focused personality style, a large-scale survey by an auto-marketing research company in Santa Ana, California, found that SUV buyers were more likely than minivan drivers to place a lower value on displaying courtesy on the road, to agree with the statement that "I'm a great driver," and to indicate that they drove faster than the average motorist. For SUV drivers, according to David P. Bostwick, DaimlerChrysler's director of marketing, "It's not a safety issue, it's aggressiveness, it's the ability to go off the road" (Bradsher, 2000, p. D-4).

Even though such generalizations might not seem meaningful, automakers have spent a considerable amount of money to identify and examine these two personality types, to the extent that this research on personality characteristics has affected the design and marketing of automobiles.

Automobile Design: Creating a Car's Personality

To match the personality characteristics of the self-focused SUV buyer, SUVs are designed to create a "don't mess with me attitude," notes Clotaire Rapaille, design consultant to many major automakers. To meet this desire for control over the environment and others on the road, Rapaille states SUVs are "designed to be masculine and assertive, with hoods that resemble 18-wheel trucks, vertical slats across the grilles to give the appearance of a jungle cat's teeth and flared wheel wells and fenders that suggest bulging muscles in a clinched jaw" (Bradsher, 2000, p. D-4). In addition to having seats mounted higher than those in minivans, SUVs also include a "high-riding" design that allows the vehicles to navigate rough and rugged terrain and to "get them [the drivers] up in the air and make them husky," according to David C. McKinnon, DaimlerChrysler's director of vehicle exterior design (Bradsher, 2000, p. D-4). In sharp contrast, minivans are designed to be more practical (e.g., with storage bins, cup holders, and removable seats) and to have a more attractive interior that will make buyers feel as if they are once again "in the womb," according to McKinnon (Bradsher, 2000, p. D-4).

Advertising Automobiles: Appealing to Personality

The multimillion-dollar advertising campaigns created to market SUVs and minivans are also influenced by the identification of the two different sets of personality characteristics associated with SUV and minivan buyers. Advertisements for minivans tend to reflect the practical nature of the vehicle, with an emphasis on its safety features and on the stream of children getting in and out of it. On the other hand, ads for SUVs tend to stress their "muscular" nature, with an emphasis on the vehicle's power (e.g., engine size) and strength and ability to climb up and over rugged, mountainous terrain.

Thus the scope of personality psychology embraces such common experiences as driving a car as well as such important decisions as buying an expensive car. In addition, it influences multimillion-dollar decisions involving some of the United States' major corporations. The point to be made here is to not only to show you how personality psychology is being used but to illustrate the depth and complexity of its influence. Throughout this book, you will be presented with many more such applications demonstrating the breadth and complexity of personality psychology's influence.

Summing It Up *The Scope of the Study of Personality Psychology*

Area of Study	Brief Description	Related Research Examples
Theory Development	The formulation of theories to help explain and predict various aspects of personality	Is the motivating force behind human behavior striving for superiority or the resolution of unconscious conflict?
Personality Research	The testing of hypotheses based on a particular theory through a program of systematic research	Will individuals with a high score on a measure of test anxiety score lower on a math exam than individuals with a low test-anxiety score?
Personality Development	The investigation of those factors contributing to the nature of personality development across the life span	What personality factors contribute to successful adjustment to aging?
Personality Assessment	The development and utilization of assessment techniques designed to measure different aspects of the human personality	How can you measure a person's level of aggression or self-esteem?
Application of Personality Psychology	The utilization of personality psychology to help individuals and organizations function more effectively	How can physicians use personality tests to diagnose coronary heart disease?

A summary of the major ideas discussed in this section is presented in "Summing It Up: The Scope of the Study of Personality Psychology" above. In the next section, we will examine some of the research methods personality psychologists use to study topics falling with the scope of personality psychology.

Research Methods in Personality Psychology

Personality psychologists use various research methods in studying personality. The three major approaches are clinical, correlational, and experimental (Pervin, 2002). As you will discover in this section, each approach contributes a unique perspective to our knowledge about personality.

The Clinical Approach: Probing the Depths of the Individual

The characteristic feature of the clinical approach is the attention given to the in-depth study of the individual or a small group of individuals. Three methods illustrating the clinical approach are the case study, the individual interview, and the analysis of personal documents.

The Case Study

The **case study method** involves a detailed investigation and description of an individual's history and current status. A comprehensive case history includes information about the individual's past and present family history, educational background, previous history of emotional or adjustment problems, employment record, and medical history. Researchers elicit this valuable information by talking directly to the individual, by interviewing family members, friends, or co-workers, or by gaining access to certain records (e.g., college or employment records). See "A Closer Look" on p. 15 for an example of the kind of information gathered as part of a case study.

A Closer Look

Piecing Together the Picture of a Mass Murderer

What kind of person would do such a thing? Information about past and present circumstances of James Huberty's life, as obtained from acquaintances and assorted records, indicated that:

The killer, said neighbors, was "a sour man" who regularly exploded in towering rages against his wife Etna and their two daughters, 14 and 10. Even the bumper sticker on his car was testy: "I'M NOT DEAF, I'M IGNORING YOU." (*Time*, July 30, 1984, p. 91)

Acquaintances in Ohio were not altogether surprised.

One said, "I knew there was something wrong with him."

Another recalled that when Huberty lost his job at the Babcock & Wilcox plant in nearby Canton, "He said that if this was the end of his making a living for his family, he was going to take everyone with him. He was always talking about shooting somebody."

A portrait of Huberty, drawn from law enforcement officials and those who knew him, reveals an uncertain man who shifted directions several times in his life. One personality trait was consistent, however. Huberty struck others as a loner who did not much like people.

In Canton, Ohio, Brother Dave Lombardl, minister of the Trinity Gospel Temple, said he believed Huberty's problems went back to childhood, when the boy's mother deserted the family to become a religious missionary to an Indian reservation. Huberty grew up in Ohio, raised mainly by his father, Lombardl said.

"He had real inner conflicts," said Lombardl, who performed the marriage ceremony for Huberty and his wife in 1965. "He was pent-up; he was a loner, and he had kind of an explosive personality. When you talked to him, you knew he had nervous anxiety and was wound up inside."

In 1964 and 1965, while attending Malone College in Canton part-time, Huberty became an apprentice mortician at Don Williams Funeral Home.

"He was a very clean-cut chap and he was more or less of a loner type," Williams recalled yesterday. "He would rather just be off by himself."

Williams said Huberty was better at embalming bodies than dealing with clients. "I told him that I thought he was pursuing the wrong profession. He didn't seem to have the personality for it," Williams said.

Huberty married the former Etna Markland during this period, Williams said, and the couple had two children.

In the 1970s, Huberty appeared to achieve some success. He graduated from Malone with a bachelor's degree in sociology after on-again, off-again study there. He went to work as a welder for Babcock & Wilcox, reportedly making $25,000 to $30,000 a year.

He moved to Massillon eight years ago and bought a home and a six-unit apartment building next door, according to James Aslanes, a coworker at Babcock & Wilcox.

Aslanes got to know Huberty there but, before very long, he became wary of him.

"We first became friendly when he found out I was studying kung fu," Aslanes recalled. "He was inquiring about how to 'put his daughter into the program' for some kind of self-defense."

The two men visited each other's homes. Aslanes, a gun owner himself, noticed that Huberty's house was filled with guns: shotguns, rifles, handguns and an Israeli-made Uzi machine gun. While Aslanes said their mutual interest reinforced their friendship, one incident caused him concern.

"We went shooting one time with the Uzi," he said, "and he began shooting at a rock. It was dangerous. The bullets might come back to us. It shocked me that anybody that knowledgeable about guns would do that."

When Huberty was laid off in October 1982 after 10 years' employment, Aslanes said he became concerned about making his house payments.

"He became despondent," Aslanes said. "He worried. He blamed the whole country for his misfortune. He said that Ronald Reagan and the government were conniving against him. The working class were going to have to pay for this inflation. . . . He became so discouraged that he wrote the Mexican government and applied for residence. . . .

"He bought a lot of food, survival foods. He had tons and tons of ammunition, and when he left Massillon, I was under the impression that he was going to Mexico, a couple of miles south of Tijuana."

Huberty was well-known to Massillon police, although he was never charged with a violent crime. Sgt. Don Adams recalled that Huberty's two German shepherds repeatedly harassed motorcycle police.

When calls came in on minor matters, Adams recalled, officers often joked that it was "the Hubertys again" because of the numerous complaints that Huberty filed against others and the complaints filed against him. Adams said Huberty once was accused of shooting a dog with an airgun.

In October, 1980, Massillon police charged Huberty with disorderly conduct after a neighborhood quarrel.

In September 1981, neighbors accused Mrs. Huberty of threatening them with a 9mm pistol; she later pleaded guilty to a disorderly conduct charge, Massillon police said.

Huberty took his family to Southern California seven months ago. San Diego neighbors described Huberty as an angry, unsmiling man.

Although he had recently lost his job, Huberty did not fit the profile of the classically unemployed, according to neighbors. They described the family as well-clothed and Huberty as a clean-cut dresser, "like an executive."

Police officials said Huberty showed up at the restaurant wearing camouflage trousers. According to those who spoke of him yesterday, he had never been seen in such garb before.

Although Huberty's wife was quoted as saying he liked children, some neighbors said he hated them and people of Mexican descent. The massacre at the restaurant, a neighborhood gathering spot, took a heavy toll of both groups. (*The Courier-Journal*, July 20, 1984, p. A-12)

From Huberty's father and widow, we get some additional information:

SAN DIEGO – Adding depth to the portrait of mass murderer James Oliver Huberty, his father and widow have described him as a troubled, hot-tempered man who was often abusive to his family and once tried to kill himself.

Earl V. Huberty said Friday that a combination of medical problems and an unsuccessful career left his son "angry at the whole world." A clinical psychologist who sat in on an interview Thursday with Huberty's widow described the slayer's actions on his final day as a "grandiose last stand."

In an interview with the San Diego Union published Friday, Mrs. Huberty, 41, recalled that last year, when the family still lived in Ohio, her husband tried to kill himself.

She wrested the gun away and hid it, she said, adding, "When I came back, he was sitting on the sofa crying."

She told the newspaper that a couple of months ago, Huberty said, "You should have let me kill myself." (*The Courier-Journal*, July 22, 1984, p. A-10)

Mrs. Huberty said in the interview that her husband "would never have done this . . . if he had been in his right mind."

"If he . . . hadn't been hearing voices . . . I know definitely he would never have killed a child," she said. "He was very fond of children, extremely fond of children, and he always talked very vehemently about what should happen to people that hurt children." (*The Courier-Journal*, July 20, 1984, p. A-1)

While obtaining information from these various sources does give some understanding of what past and present social and emotional factors may have contributed to this incident, they make possible only "educated guesses":

Lt. Paul Ybarrondo, commander of the San Diego Police Department's homicide squad, said investigators had not determined a motive for the killings.

"I don't expect that we will," Ybarrondo said. "You're talking about getting into a deceased person's thought process. We might be able to come up with something in his background. . . . But as far as why he went over the brink at this very moment, I can't answer that, and I don't think we'll ever be able to." (*The Courier-Journal*, July 20, 1984, p. A-1)

Under such conditions, educated guesses seem to be better than nothing. But for more concrete answers, additional systematic research involving in-depth analyses of the case studies of other mass murderers is required. For example, personality researchers can begin to compare case studies of other mass murderers in an attempt to identify common personality characteristics (e.g., violent tendencies), underlying dynamics (e.g., pent-up rage), and life circumstances (e.g., feelings of alienation). Based on the identification of these common features, a theory could be developed and tested on other violent individuals (e.g., highly violent prisoners). In this case, a researcher might test a theory linking an excessive hormonal imbalance and feelings of alienation with the behavior of violent inmates. If such a link were found, an application of this research might be the development and implementation of a treatment program that combines the use of medication to deal with the hormonal imbalance, and teaching of communication skills to reduce feelings of alienation. Finally, an evaluation of the treatment program would also serve as an additional test of the proposed theory.

Documenting rare phenomena and helping to test theory are other important functions of the case study. Presenting a detailed case study of the successful treatment of a person with a rare form of dissociative identity disorder (previously referred to as multiple-personality disorder or simply multiple personality), in which the individual displays two or more complete and

separate personalities (e.g., a timid 7-year-old girl and an abusive 60-year-old man) without being aware of it, can help to document the existence of the disorder. Beyond just demonstrating the disorder's existence, a thorough case study can also provide support for testing the theory upon which the treatment is based, such as using hypnosis to help the individual to become aware of and integrate the different personalities. Such results would then encourage additional research, with a larger number of other individuals suffering from dissociative identity disorder being treated at different hospitals to test this theory.

The Individual Interview

The **individual interview** is a one-on-one verbal exchange for the purpose of obtaining important information about the interviewee. The general format is for one individual to ask a series of specific questions of another designed to elicit responses that will provide information for the purpose of addressing a particular issue. For example, after giving a client a series of personality tests, the career counselor begins to ask the client questions about the conditions under which she would like to work (e.g., "Do you like predictability or unpredictability in your workday?") in an attempt to match the results of her personality tests (e.g., high conscientiousness and moderate impulsiveness) with specific occupations (e.g., pharmaceutical sales representative – highly predictable workday – vs. emergency medical technician – very unpredictable workday). However, there is more to an individual interview than just asking and answering questions. Conducting a successful interview involves establishing rapport and considering both verbal and nonverbal communication.

- *Establishing rapport.* **Rapport** refers to the positive, warm relationship established between the interview participants. Establishing rapport makes the expression of intimate and oftentimes very painful information much easier. Refraining from expressing disapproval or from appearing judgmental of the individual's responses and offering confidentiality are effective ways to establish rapport.
- *Nonverbal behavior.* In addition to the verbal message and variety of verbal cues, a skillful interviewer is also sensitive to the individual's nonverbal messages (e.g., posture, gestures, and facial expressions). Subtle changes in the individual's nonverbal messages can help provide more information about the true meaning of the verbal message.

To help illustrate these points, "A Closer Look," below, examines the dynamics involved in an individual interview.

A Closer Look

Interview with a College Student: Sometimes Talking About It Can Help

The following excerpt illustrates many basic features of the individual interview, such as establishing rapport and the progressive "opening up" of the individual to the interviewer. This typifies an initial interview at a university psychological clinic with a student who is burdened by parental pressures, deciding on a major, test anxiety, and alcohol consumption. The comments presented opposite the dialogue are included to clarify the interviewer's objectives and to identify the significant topic being explored.

As you have seen, a considerable amount of personal information about the nature of the individual's problems at school was obtained by asking the right question at the right time. If performed appropriately, the individual interview is a very useful tool. As a side note, if you are having any personal concerns that are troubling you, consider seeking assistance from your school's counseling center because, as the subtitle of this box indicates, "sometimes talking about it can help."

Interview Dialogue	**Comments**
INTERVIEWER (I): Could you tell me why you decided to come to our clinic today?	Interviewer highlights significance of client's choice to come to the clinic at this particular time.
CLIENT (C): Well, I'm having real difficulties in school.	
I: OK I'd like to briefly explain what I hope we can accomplish in the next hour, to give you a clear idea of what to expect and how this interview can help you.	Interviewer provides basic goals and guidelines to reduce the client's uncertainty and to promote positive expectations.
Maybe we could start by talking about how you decided to come to come to the clinic at this particular point in your life.	Open-ended question, but with a focus of "why now?"
C: I can't have my way. My parents won't let me.	
I: Your parents have a powerful and hurtful impact on you. I hear you very clearly. I'm just wondering what you'd do if you could magically have control of your own future?	Acknowledges client's belief, but challenges the hopelessness. Facilitates exploration of alternatives.
C: Well, I guess I'd change my major to theatre, that's where my interests and talents are.	
I: I'd like to explore that, but first, let's get a picture of what it's like to be in your family. Could you describe your family, and how you fit it?	Holds off on specific issues, to get a general background.

(after some discussion about 20 minutes into the session)

I: Tell me about your relationships with friends, including both casual and close friends of both sexes.	Exploring social relationships.
C: Well, I'm afraid I'll flunk out of the university if I don't get over feeling anxious about tests (begins to clasp hands nervously and blushes while looking at the ground, some light laughter also).	Nonverbal cues reflecting anxiety.
I: I notice that you seem to be worried. Troubles at school can really be painful.	Gentle acknowledgment of client's nonverbal cues and distress.
C: Especially when your parents are pressuring you to get into law school.	An important tie-in: the family plays a role as well as school problems.

(after some discussion about 15 minutes later)

I: Well, you've given an excellent sketch of several important areas in your life. Have we missed some important sides of you or your situation?	Relying on client to fill in gaps.
C: I don't know if it's relevant, but I'm concerned about how much I've been drinking lately.	Another important life concern.
I: Why don't you tell me more about it.	

(after some discussion about 15 minutes later)

I: We may not have covered everything, but I'd like to use our remaining time to summarize my understanding of you and your situation, and then to have us both discuss what you might do next.	Acknowledges that more information may still be needed, but makes sure to provide a summary and a discussion of the client's alternatives.

(Adapted from Kendall & Norton-Ford, 1982, pp. 209–211)

Analysis of Personal Documents

A third research method characteristic of the clinical approach is the analysis of personal documents. According to Allport (1961), a **personal document** is "any freely written or spoken record that intentionally or unintentionally yields information regarding the structure and dynamics of the author's life" (p. 401). Personal documents include diaries, letters, autobiographies, and verbatim recordings. For a closer look at some excerpts taken from personal documents, read the feature "A Closer Look" below.

A Closer Look

Words from the Heart: Excerpts from the Personal Documents of President Nixon's Public and Private Farewell Speeches

In what is considered to be the lowest point in the history of the presidency of the United States, on August 9, 1974, the 37th president, Richard Nixon, became the only person in U.S. history to resign the nation's highest office. He did so because of his personal knowledge of the burglary of the Democratic headquarters in the Watergate Hotel, his efforts to cover it up, and his attempts to obstruct a subsequent investigation into the incident by the FBI. At the time of his resignation, Nixon was probably one of the most reviled figures in the United States.

What would make a man do such things? What was his personality like? How might the study of personality psychology help us answer these questions? A possible answer might come from conducting a **psychobiography** – that is, a detailed psychological case study of an individual (Elms, 1976, 1994). In his book *Personality and Politics*, Alan Elms (1976) illustrates how psychobiographies have been used to study the personality of famous politicians. In a discussion of the psychobiographies of President Nixon, Elms notes that:

> Nixon's formal statement of resignation from the Presidency was a calm and controlled performance.... It could almost have been the retirement speech by a respected President turning over the reins to his elected successor, or perhaps a State of the Union oration designed to comfort more than inform. It certainly

In sharp contrast to his public appearance, Nixon's private appearance when alone was very somber and projected a sense of weakness and defeat.

informed the audience very little about Nixon's internal state. (p. 103)

In contrast, in his farewell speech to his staff, "with sweat and tears streaming down his face" (Elms, 1976, p. 103), Nixon seems to have been speaking words from the heart. During a more emotional part of his speech, Nixon remembers his mother:

> Nobody will ever write a book about my mother. Well, I guess all of you would say this about your mother: my mother was a saint. And I think of her two boys dying of tuberculosis, nursing four others in order that she could take care of my older brother for three years in Arizona and seeing each of them die. And when they died it was like one of her own. Yes, she will have no books written about her. But she was a saint. (p. 103)

In his closing remarks, Nixon becomes philosophical:

> Because the greatness comes not only when things go always good for you, but the greatness comes when you're really tested, when you take some knocks and some disappointments, when sadness comes. . . . Always give your best. Never get discouraged. Never be petty. Always remember, others may hate you, but those who hate you don't win unless you hate them. And then you destroy yourself. (p. 104)

Bruce Mazlish (1973), in his rather detailed psychobiography of Nixon, emphasized many of the themes noted in his speeches as a means of identifying some of the major influences on the characteristics of Nixon's personality. For example, according to Mazlish, Nixon's "Protestant ethics" traits – emphasizing planning, hard work, and persistence – were influenced by his mother and maternal grandmother. On the other hand, an analysis of the personal recording made in his office revealed that his good qualities – intelligence, determination, a desire for world peace – were overtaken by more base elements of his personality – doing whatever needed to be done, no matter how dishonest, to achieve his goals and to humiliate and destroy his opponents and perceived enemies (Commire, 1994).

Information from such personal documents made possible some insights into Nixon's private personality not seen in public. Such personal insights reflect the real heartache and disappointment Nixon felt, as well as demonstrating his sense of vulnerability and sentimentality, which the most powerful leader in the free world had to hold in check when projecting a brave, bold front while appearing on the world stage. When he could let his guard down, Nixon's personality was less a reflection of extreme public power than one of defeat and, both literally and metaphorically, resignation.

Finally, as you will see throughout this book, psychobiographies have helped us understand how life events served to shape the personalities not only of politicians and other historical figures but also of many famous personality psychologists, as well as other influential psychologists, and the viewpoints of personality they expressed in their work (Runyan, 2006). For a good general introduction to the use of psychobiographies to gain insights into the work of many famous psychologists, see Runyan's (2006) article, "Psychobiography and the Psychology of Science: Understanding Relations between the Life and Work of Individual Psychologists."

Achieving an in-depth understanding of an individual's feelings and behavior involves much more than simply reading personal documents. As Allport (1961) notes, "Anyone, of course, can read these documents and form interpretations in a common-sense way" (p. 406). To go beyond common sense, researchers in personality psychology might conduct a content analysis of the document. A **content analysis** is a systematic assessment of the themes, ideas, and expressions presented in a document. In one form of content analysis, a researcher can identify the major overlapping themes by asking different raters to read the document and indicate what themes they observe. The "Applications in Personality Psychology" feature on p. 21 illustrates how the content analysis of personal documents is used to help increase our understanding of one of the most tragic examples of human suffering – suicide.

Applications in Personality Psychology

Closing Statements: Content Analysis of Suicide Notes

Psychologists and other mental health professionals cannot currently explain why people commit suicide. But researchers continue to analyze the contents of suicide notes in an attempt to better understand the motives and feelings of those who kill themselves (Leenaars, 1989: Lester & Linn, 1998; Stirman & Pennebaker, 2001). For example, Stirman and Pennebaker (2001) compared approximately 300 poems by 9 suicidal and nonsuicidal poets and found that the writings of the suicidal poets used more first-person singular references (e.g., *I*, *me*, *my*), supporting the notion that suicidal individuals are more socially detached from others and preoccupied with the self. In a very early and important study, Tuckman, Kleiner, and Lavell (1959) attempted to investigate more directly the writings of suicidal individuals by examining the suicide notes left by some. More specifically, of the 724 suicides examined, they found that approximately 24 percent left notes. Analyzing their content revealed four general emotional categories: positive, negative, neutral, and mixed affect.

- *Positive emotional content.* Fifty-one percent of the notes express what might be defined as positive affect, such as expressing affection, gratitude, and concern for others:

  > Please forgive me and please forget me. I'll always love you. All I have was yours. No one ever did more for me than you, oh please pray for me please. (p. 60)

- *Negative (hostile) emotional content.* Only 6 precent of the notes were classified as expressing primarily hostile or negative affect:

  > I hate all of you and all of your family and I hope you never have peace of mind. I hope I haunt this house as long as you live here and I wish you all the bad luck in the world. (p. 60)

- *Neutral emotional content.* Twenty-five percent of the notes contained a generally neutral affective tone. As you read the following note, notice it conveys neither a sense of anger nor a sense of relief, just a sense of order:

  > To Whom It May Concern,
  >
  > I, Mary Smith, being of sound mind, do this day, make my last will as follows – I bequeath my rings, Diamond and Black Opal to my daughter-in-law, Doris Jones and any other personal belongings she might wish. What money I have in my savings account and my checking account goes to my dear father, as he won't have me to help him. To my husband, Ed Smith, I leave my furniture and car.
  >
  > I would like to be buried as close to the grave of John Jones as possible. (Darbonne, 1969, p. 50)

- *Mixed emotional content.* Eighteen percent of the notes were classified as having a mixed emotional content, containing a combination of both positive and negative affect:

  > I am sorry I have to take this way out. But you can see there's no other way. She would just give me and the kids a hard time for the rest of our lives, also the club deal is away out of my hands. Contact. S——— about the Girls and the M———s about B———. All the money I have in the world is here. May God Bless you and your family and may he look after mine.
  >
  > May she rot in hell after me. (Tuckman et al., 1959, p. 60)

Information gained from such content analysis is used to test theories of suicide, assess others' reactions to it, and help individuals working with suicidal persons in such places as mental hospitals, counseling centers, and suicide intervention telephone centers (Comer, 2001).

Evaluating the Clinical Approach: Strengths and Limitations

Being aware of the characteristic strengths and limitations of the clinical approach will make evaluating its use easier.

Following are some strengths of the clinical approach:

- *In-depth understanding of the individual.* A major strength of the clinical approach is that it offers several ways of studying a particular individual or small group of individuals in considerable detail. An example is studying the personality development of female state governors in the 20th century.
- *Studying development and adjustment processes over time.* Taking an in-depth look at an individual over time makes it possible to observe developmental changes and their presumed effects (Funder, Parke, Tomlinson-Keasey, & Widaman, 1993). An example is a therapist examining changes in a client's self-esteem and job satisfaction over a two-year period.
- *Investigating extreme and rare events.* Studying extreme and rare events is made possible with the clinical approach. As an example, investigating the coping skills of survivors of a murderous prisoner-of-war camp makes studying the extremes of personality adaptability possible. Because they are so rare, such events must be studied when they can be found, and in as much depth as possible.

The following are some limitations of the clinical approach:

- *Limited generalizability.* The issue of **generalizability** involves extending the findings about one group of individuals to another group. Findings based on the clinical approach typically use a small number of individuals, which limits their extension to other groups. For example, it is unclear how information about the coping skills of a handful of prisoner-of-war camp survivors may be generalized to the development of a survival training program taught to thousands of other soldiers.
- *Personal biases.* The personal nature of the clinical approach introduces subject and researcher biases.

Subject biases are systematic alterations in the recall of an individual when reporting information to a researcher. Subjects may withhold information out of embarrassment or "fill in the gaps" of distant events.

Researcher biases are tendencies to gather and interpret information in a manner consistent with the researcher's point of view. For example, a researcher testing a theory of sibling rivalry may overemphasize the role of siblings when studying the personality development of U.S. presidents.

Thus, the clinical approach provides a variety of methods for in-depth study of individuals or a small group of individuals. A summary of the main points discussed in this section is presented in "Summing It Up: Characteristic Methods of the Clinical Approach" and "Summing It Up: Characteristic Strengths and Limitations of the Clinical Approach" opposite. In the next section, you will examine the correlation approach in the study of personality psychology.

The Correlational Approach: Knowledge by Association

As we have seen, the clinical approach provides insights into the personality of an individual or a very small number of individuals by identifying important personality variables. By contrast, the major purpose of **correlational research** is to investigate the extent to which any two variables are associated with one another. For example, a researcher might be interested in studying the relationship between shyness and loneliness or the need for achievement and worker productivity.

The Scatter Plot: Illustrating Relationships

A **scatter plot** is a graph summarizing the scores obtained by many individuals on two different variables. Figure 1.2a is a scatter plot showing the relationship between scores on a measure of shyness and a measure of loneliness. Each point on the scatter plot represents an individual's score for the two different variables. For example, the point on the scatter plot corresponding to Mike's scores indicates a score of 12 on the measure of loneliness and 20 on the measure of shyness. Interpreting correlational relationships involves identifying the direction and strength of the relationship between the two variables.

Summing It Up *Characteristic Methods of the Clinical Approach*

Method	Function	Application
Case Study	Provides a comprehensive investigation of past and present factors contributing to the behavior of an individual or small group of individuals	By talking with other members of the Native American tribe, the cultural anthropologists began to develop a profile of the social skills and personality qualities used in the selection of the tribe's chief.
Individual Interview	Obtains personal and vital information about an individual through systematically asking questions within an environment designed to elicit trust and cooperation in the individual answering the questions	During an interview, the potential military recruit expresses views about wanting to join the military to deal with her feelings of inadequacy and to rebel against what she considered as too much control over her personal and social life by her parents.
Analysis of Personal Documents	Yields information about the personality of a particular individual through the systematic analysis of information found in such personal documents as letters, speeches, stored files, and records	Looking at the records of the chat-room discussions stored on the computer of the high school shooter indicated a desire to please others, feelings of rejection, loneliness, and hate, and a history of interests in guns and playing violent video games.

Summing It Up *Characteristic Strengths and Limitations of the Clinical Approach*

Factor or Process	Strength or Limitation	Description
Understanding of the individual can be in depth	Strength	Various techniques are available to facilitate detailed study of research participants.
Developmental processes can be studied over time	Strength	Developmental changes in participants' thoughts and behaviors can be monitored and predicted.
Extreme and rare events can be investigated	Strength	Unusual phenomena can be illustrated and documented.
Limited generalizability	Limitation	Typically small sample sizes limit researchers' ability to generalize findings to larger or more diverse groups.
Personal bias	Limitation	Individuals may distort findings via selective reporting of information; researchers may distort findings via their own interpretations.

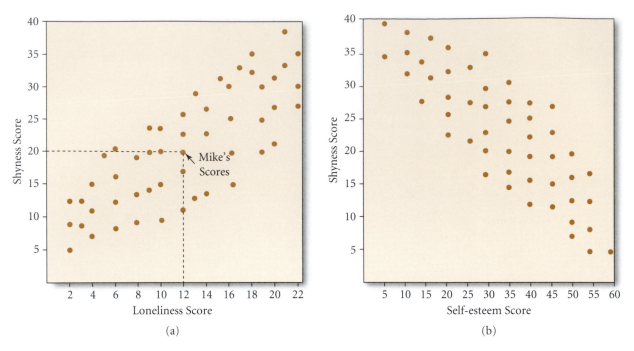

Figure 1.2   Scatter plots illustrating a positive and negative correlational relationship

Correlational Relationships: Identifying Associations

The direction of a correlational relationship reveals how the two variables are related. The two basic patterns indicating direction are the positive and negative correlational relationships. The general pattern of association of a **positive correlational relationship** reveals that as the scores on one variable increase, the corresponding scores on the other variable also tend to increase. Figure 1.2a shows that as the loneliness scores increase, the corresponding shyness scores also tend to increase. The general pattern of association of a **negative correlational relationship** reveals that as the scores on one variable increase, the corresponding scores on the other variable tend to decrease. Figure 1.2b shows that as the shyness scores increase, the corresponding self-esteem scores tend to decrease.

The Correlational Coefficient: Assessing the Strength of the Correlational Relationship

After determining the direction, the next step is to assess the strength of the correlational relationship by determining the extent to which scores on the two

variables are related. The index used to indicate the strength of association between two variables is called the **correlation coefficient** and is symbolized by the letter r. The strength of the association between two variables is reflected in a value ranging from $r = +1.00$ to 0.00 to -1.00 and is determined by a specific statistical formula. The closer to $+1.00$ or -1.00 the value for r, the stronger the association between the two variables. In a similar manner, the closer to zero the value of r, the weaker the association between the two variables.

The strongest relationship possible between two variables is $r = +1.00$ or -1.00. Figure 1.3a indicates that there is a perfect positive correlational relationship ($r = +1.00$) between the scores on measures of aggressiveness and hostility. Figure 1.3e indicates that there is a perfect negative correlational relationship ($r = -1.00$) between a measure of shyness and a popularity rating. In a perfect positive correlation, the value for one variable is associated with one and only one value of the second variable, creating a straight line on the graph. As will be discussed in more detail below, the correlation between two variables does not mean that one variable *caused* the changes in the values of the other variable, only that the changes in values are related.

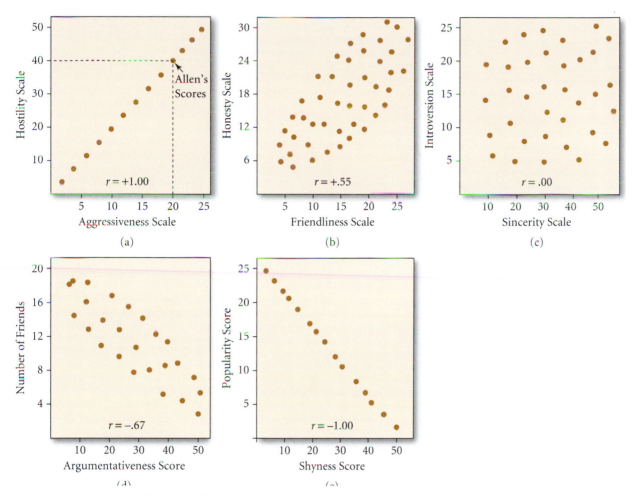

Figure 1.3 Scatter plots illustrating the strength of the correlation for five proposed relationships

Perfect correlational relationships in personality research are extremely rare. A less-than-perfect correlational relationship indicates that a particular score on one variable is not necessarily associated with one and only one value on the second variable, creating some spread in the scores in the scatter plot. Figure 1.3b is an example of a moderately strong positive correlational relationship ($r = +.55$) between friendliness and honesty. Figure 1.3d is an example of a moderately strong negative correlational relationship ($r = -.67$) between argumentativeness and number of friends.

The scatter plot in Figure 1.3c illustrates an uncorrelated relationship ($r = .00$) between scores on measures of sincerity and introversion. In uncorrelated relationships, the association between the two variables is extremely weak or nonexistent. In assessing the strength of a correlational relationship through visual inspection, a general rule of thumb is the less spread in the scores on the scatter plot, the stronger the relationship.

The Third-Variable Problem: Looking Beyond the Observed Relationship

Interpreting correlational relationships is made difficult by the potential presence of third variables. The **third-variable problem** exists when the observed relationship between two variables is actually produced by their relationship with another unobserved, or third, variable. Figure 1.4a illustrates a relationship between shyness and test anxiety. Figure 1.4b illustrates how this relationship is explained by considering the relationship of these two variables to a third variable – self-consciousness.

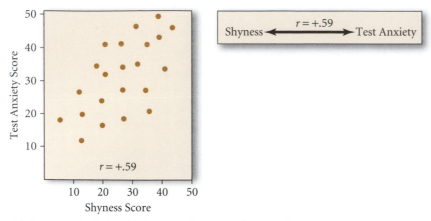

(a) A proposed relationship between shyness and test anxiety

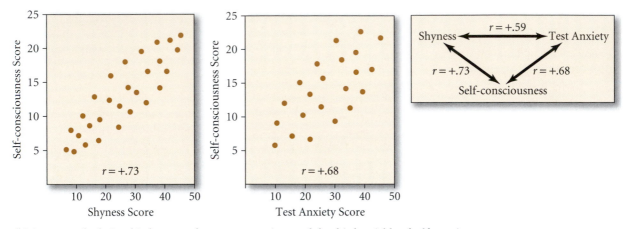

(b) A proposed relationship between shyness, test anxiety, and the third variable of self-conciousness

Figure 1.4 An illustration of the third-variable problem, (a) A proposed relationship between shyness and text anxiety, (b) A proposed relationship between shyness, test, anxiety, and the third variable of self-consciousness

Interpreting correlational relationships involves considering the direction and strength of the relationship and the third-variable problem.

Evaluating the Correlational Approach: Strengths and Limitations

An understanding of the correlational approach also involves considering its strengths and limitations. The following are some characteristic strengths of this approach:

- *Exploring and identifying relationships.* An important use of the correlational approach is in searching for relationships among variables

during early stages of research. A personality psychologist might first explore the relationship of shyness with such variables as self-esteem, social anxiety, self-consciousness, and loneliness to determine the strongest correlations and the best research potential.

- *Ethical considerations.* Using the correlational approach, researchers can investigate some important problems that they could not ordinarily study because of ethical restrictions. For example, it is not ethically permissible for a researcher to separate children from their parents in order to study personality development in single-parent families. But it is possible to correlate information about personality variables

by studying children who are already in single-parent families.

Here are some characteristic limitations of the correlational approach:

- *The third-variable problem*. The possibility of third variables going unidentified by the researcher decreases a thorough understanding of the relationship between two variables. But being aware of potential third variables and taking them into consideration can minimize their negative impact.
- *Undetermined causal relationships*. While the correlational approach can identify the nature and strength of the relationship between two variables, this does not mean that one variable causes the change in the other to occur. For example, in the relationship between shyness and self-esteem (see Figure 1.2b), it is not known whether shyness causes people to have low self-esteem or having low self-esteem causes people to be shy. Unfortunately, the results from such a correlational study do not tell researchers which explanation, if either, is correct. This is a serious limitation, since the goal of most personality research is to explain why the human personality operates as it does.

Thus, the correlational approach makes it possible to study the nature and the magnitude of the relationship between two variables of interest to personality psychologists. A summary of the main points discussed in this section is presented in "Summing It Up: Characteristic Features of the Correlational Approach" opposite, and "Summing It Up: Characteristic Strengths and Limitations of the Correlational Approach" on p. 29. In the next section, you will examine the experimental approach to the study of personality psychology.

The Experimental Approach: Knowledge by Systematic Intervention

The correlational approach can determine the degree to which two variables are associated, but not the causal nature of the relationship. Personality psychologists searching for causal relationships pursue knowledge by systematic intervention using the experimental approach.

Basic Principles of the Experimental Approach: Intervention, Observation, and Control

The **experimental research** approach requires three elements: intervention, observation, and control. The logic of the approach involves investigating how the systematic intervention of one variable creates changes that can be observed in a second variable. At the same time, researchers attempt to control for outside factors that might also produce changes in the second variable.

Systematic Intervention   Establishing a causal relationship involves determining that varying the level of one variable produces corresponding changes in a second variable. The **independent variable** is the factor that you believe causes the change in the second variable. For example, psychotherapists might wish to investigate how receiving positive comments causes changes in the self-esteem of clients. They divide 30 clients into three groups of 10 with the first group receiving five positive comments per 1-hour session, the second receiving 20 positive comments, and the third receiving no positive comments. The independent variable is the number of positive comments.

Observation   The behavior affected by the independent variable and being observed is called the **dependent variable**. The dependent variable in this example is the change in the clients' self-esteem. Figure 1.5 summarizes the changes in the clients' self-esteem by plotting the **group mean** (i.e., arithmetic average) of the self-esteem scores for each of the three feedback groups.

Experimental Control   **Experimental control** refers to the extent to which researchers control for the possibility that other explanations may account for the results observed. There are many ways to increase experimental control; following are three of the most common:

- *Randomly assigning subjects*. Decreases in experimental control occur whenever there is the possibility of bias in the way researchers assign individuals to different conditions of the experiment. **Random assignment** is a procedure designed to help control for biases in selection. According to the principle of random

Summing It Up *Characteristic Features of the Correlational Approach*

Characteristic Feature	Description	Example
Types of Correlational Relationships	A scatter plot provides a visual representation of the nature of the relationship between two variables.	A researcher looks at the relationship between test anxiety and test performance.
Positive Relationship	As the value of one variable gets larger, the corresponding value of the second variable shows an increase.	As scores on the measure of test anxiety get higher, heart-rate scores of the students also get higher.
Negative Relationship	As the value of one variable gets larger, the corresponding value of the second variable shows a decrease.	The higher the score on the measure of test anxiety, the lower the grade the students believe they will obtain on the math test.
Uncorrelated Relationship	As the value of one variable changes, there is no systematic pattern in the change of the second variable.	There is no identifiable pattern of change between the scores of test anxiety and friendliness.
The Correlation Coefficient	A numerical value indicates the strength of association between two variables.	The correlation coefficient of the relationship between self-esteem and loneliness is rather low.
The Index of the Correlation Coefficient	The index of the correlation coefficient is symbolized by the letter r and a value ranging from $r = +1.00$ to $r = 0.00$ to $r = -1.00$.	The correlation of self-esteem and test anxiety is $r = -.48$ while the correlation of self-esteem and creativity is $r = +.35$.
The Strength of the Association	The closer the value to $r = +1.00$ or $r = -1.00$, the stronger the association between the two variables. The closer the value to $r = 0.00$, the weaker the relationship.	The relationship between self-esteem and depression is stronger than that between self-esteem and creativity.
The Third-Variable Problem	The researcher fails to consider the possible presence of an outside variable correlated with the two variables being considered.	The correlation between self-esteem and depression may be due to the style of parenting experienced by the individual.

assignment, all research participants have an equal chance of being exposed to the different levels of the independent variable. For example, because individuals who have morning appointments may be somewhat different in age or employment status, assigning all clients with morning appointments to the no-feedback condition creates a bias. To avoid this bias, the group to which a client is assigned could be based on the order in which their names are drawn out of a box. This procedure increases the likelihood that the outcome of the study is due to the treatment itself rather than to the composition of the groups.

● *Standardizing procedures.* **Standardization of procedures** involves treating all of the subjects in a similar manner. In this way, the only difference among individuals in each group is the treatment produced by variations in the independent variable. Standardization of procedures might

Summing It Up *Characteristic Strengths and Limitations of the Correlational Approach*

Characteristic Feature	Strength or Limitation	Description
Exploring and Identifying Relationships	Strength	The correlational method provides an efficient means of exploring and identifying relationships between variables of interest in the early stages of theory development.
Ethical and Procedural Considerations	Strength	The correlational method makes it possible to investigate questions that could not normally be addressed due to serious ethical (e.g., harming people) or procedural (e.g., being at the site of a natural disaster to study stress reactions) limitations.
The Third-Variable Problem	Limitation	The problem of interpreting correlational relationships results when the researcher fails to consider the presence of outside variables.
Undetermined Causal Relationships	Limitation	The nature of correlational research does not make it possible to determine the causal relationship between two variables. Such causal statements are necessary if researchers desire to explain the operation of the human personality.

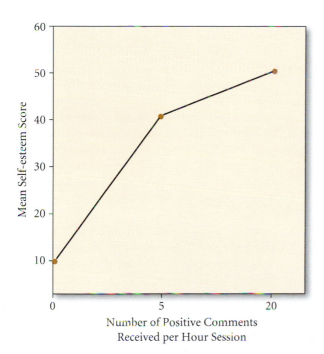

Figure 1.5   The hypothetical results in a study of the effects of positive feedback on self-esteem

include such things as testing subjects in rooms with similar lighting and temperature and at around the same time of day, or presenting the instructions on a tape recorder. As an example, to control for the possibility of acting friendlier when giving feedback than when not giving feedback, researchers must maintain a neutral facial expression and speak in a similar manner and tone of voice to all individuals.

- *Using a control group.* The **control group** contains individuals who are otherwise treated the same as other groups but are not exposed to the treatment conditions of the independent variable. The control group serves as a basis of comparison for the treatment groups. In the self-esteem example (Figure 1.5), the group receiving no positive feedback is the control group.

Experimental control is not an either–or situation; it varies in degree. Experimental control is increased through careful planning of the research. Careful planning helps to control for or eliminate other factors that can serve as erroneous explanations of the results.

Meta-Analysis: A tool for the Comparison of Experimental Research

Meta-analysis is a statistical technique used in determining the consistency and magnitude of the findings from different experimental studies that address a similar issue by combining and averaging their results. Meta-analysis is an important technique because it makes possible the identification of general trends across the many different studies on a particular topic, and aids in the interpretation of these trends. Although the actual statistical computations for performing a meta-analysis are complex and well beyond the scope of this discussion, the underlying logic of this technique is very simple.

Meta-analysis has been used to address the critical issue of gender differences in aggressive behavior (Archer, 2004; Eagly & Steffen, 1986; Hyde, 1984, 1986). An excellent example of how meta-analysis is used to identify general trends in these differences in aggressive behavior is the work of John Archer of the University of Central Lancashire in the United Kingdom. In a recent meta-analysis, Archer (2004) examined the results of 200 different studies that looked at sex differences in different forms of aggression (e.g., hitting, verbal, and nonphysical forms of aggression) from different perspectives (e.g., self-report ratings and ratings from teachers and peers) in various real-world settings (e.g., school, military base, prison) across 13 different countries. Some of the general trends that were observed in this meta-analysis indicated that males displayed a greater amount of physical (e.g., hitting) and dangerous (e.g., use of weapons) aggression than females, who were more likely to use indirect or relational forms of aggression (e.g., deliberate social exclusion and ostracism). Another more general but important finding was that the magnitude of the differences varied depending on the methods of aggression observed (e.g., direct observation of behavior vs. peer ratings vs. self-report vs. teacher ratings), suggesting a certain amount of ambiguity in the expression, measurement, and interpretation of gender differences in aggression (Archer, 2004; Hyde, 2005).

Because it would not be possible to examine so many different factors in a single study, the ability to make comparisons across a number of different studies contributes significantly to our understanding of sex differences in aggression. Another rather extensive meta-analysis of 133 studies drawn from 17 countries assessed the extent to which conformity was related to certain general cultural characteristics (Bond & Smith, 1996). You can explore additional examples and more information about meta-analysis in *Meta-analysis: New Developments and Applications in Medical and Social Sciences* (Schulze, Holling, & Böhning, 2003) and *Systematic Reviews and Meta-analysis* (Torgerson, 2003).

Evaluating the Experimental Approach: Strengths and Limitations

The experimental approach is one of the most powerful research tools personality psychologists have at their disposal. But it also has its characteristic strengths and limitations.

Following are some of the strengths of the experimental approach:

- *Controlled observations.* Much of the research employing the experimental approach is **laboratory research**, conducted in a very structured and controlled setting. The major advantage of laboratory research is that it gives the researcher control over how and when the independent variable is introduced, what the surrounding conditions are like, and how the dependent variable is assessed. Such experimental control greatly increases the ability to eliminate alternative explanations of the results.
- *Causal explanations.* Conclusions about the independent variable causing observable changes in the dependent variable increase when the experimental approach is used correctly. The ability to make causal statements creates a level of understanding that allows a researcher to know "why" something happens. Knowing why personality operates the way it does is a principal objective of the systematic study of personality psychology.

Following are some characteristic limitations of the experimental approach:

- *Group means vs. the individual.* Statements made about causal relationships are based on reporting group means, which indicate how the average person in that group behaved. Studying groups of people and reporting group means indicate the "average" response but may or may not accurately describe how each person responds (Block, 1995; Lamiell, 1997; McAdams, 1992). This heavy emphasis on the experimental study of personality and reporting of group means has led some personality psychologists to ask "whatever happened to the person in personality psychology?" (Carlson, 1971, 1984).

- *Generalizability of results from the laboratory to the real world.* A concern with research conducted under well-controlled laboratory conditions is how fully the results can be generalized to the real world. For example, how much can studying frustration and aggression in college students for 45 minutes in a laboratory help researchers in understanding the reactions of workers being laid off after many years on a job? A partial solution to this issue is to conduct field research whenever possible. **Field research** includes investigations done outside the controlled conditions of the laboratory in such places as counseling centers, personnel offices, nursing homes, and shopping malls. Although it is somewhat more difficult when doing field research, the researcher still attempts to achieve experimental control over as many external factors as possible.

- *Experimenter bias.* **Experimenter bias** refers to any intentional or unintentional influences the experimenter exerts on the participants of the experiment to behave in a manner consistent with his or her hypothesis (Rosenthal, 1966, 1969). In the example investigating the effects of positive feedback on self-esteem (Figure 1.5), the experimenter might intentionally have been very friendly and nice to those individuals while giving them positive feedback and quite unfriendly to those not receiving any feedback, in an attempt to find support for the hypothesis. Such behavior is dishonest, inexcusable, and rare. Much more likely are unintentional influences involving the researcher unwittingly communicating to the participants (e.g., smiling, nodding one's head) when they behave in a way that supports the hypothesis. Employing research assistants who are not aware of the hypothesis to carry out the experimental procedures helps to control for such unintentional but damaging communication; it is difficult to communicate unintentionally what participants are expected to do if the assistant is unaware of the hypothesis.

Thus, the experimental approach makes it possible for personality psychology to investigate cause-and-effect relationships in the study of personality psychology. A summary of the major points discussed in this section is presented in "Summing It Up: Basic Principles of the Experimental Approach" on p. 32, and "Summing It Up: Characteristic Strengths and Limitations of the Experimental Approach" on p. 33. In the next section, you will examine some of the ethical issues associated with the study of personality psychology.

Research Ethics: Protecting the Individual's Rights

The participants in personality research have contributed greatly to our knowledge of personality. To maintain a favorable relationship with them, personality researchers must follow certain ethical standards of behavior. This section presents a discussion of the ethical issues associated with conducting personality research and considers some potential solutions.

Some Ethical Concerns: Hurting, Lying, and Justifying

Some of the ethical concerns associated with conducting research in personality psychology include inducing stress, using deception, and justifying research procedures.

Inducing Stress

Minimizing any emotional harm experienced by participating in personality research is an important ethical concern. But in certain cases, inducing some harm is a byproduct of the type of research. Such is the case when the researcher studying the effects of failure on self-esteem or need for achievement gives participants false feedback by telling some of them they did very poorly on a task and others they did very well.

Deception

Sometimes participants in research attempt to guess what the researcher is trying to find out and modify their behavior accordingly. Such modifications can alter the research results. To help minimize this threat to experimental control, researchers may disguise the true

Summing It Up *Basic Principles of the Experimental Approach*

Basic Principle	Description	Example
Independent Variable	This variable is varied systematically throughout the experiment to observe what changes it creates in that aspect of personality being investigated.	A researcher exposes participants to either a high-, medium-, or no-noise condition to assess their sensitivity to stress.
Dependent Variable	This variable is the specific aspect of personality being investigated for changes created in it by the independent variable.	The measure of stress sensitivity involves assessing changes in muscle tension in response to the different levels of noise.
Experimental Control	Precautions are taken by the researcher to rule out the possibility of other explanations besides the presence of the independent variable being proposed to account for the changes in the dependent variable.	To control for other environmental factors, the researcher tests each participant separately in the same room with the same temperature at the same time of day.
Random Assignment	This technique is used to control for the possibility of individuals being assigned to groups in a systematic manner by guaranteeing each individual has an equal chance of being assigned to any treatment group.	The participants are assigned to one of the three noise conditions by the researcher drawing the number 1 (high), 2 (medium), or 3 (no noise) out of a box.
Standardization of Procedures	Procedures are standardized to make sure individuals in the different treatment groups are treated identically with the exception of the level of the independent variable.	With the exception of the noise level, all of the participants receive the same instructions and forms to complete under similar room conditions.
The Control Group	This group contains subjects who do not receive any level of the independent variable and serve as a basis of comparison for those groups of subjects who do.	The no-noise condition serves as the control group for comparison to the high- and medium-noise conditions.
Meta-Analysis	This statistical technique is designed to compare the outcomes of different studies examining a specific issue to determine the similarity and strength of the outcomes across the studies.	The researcher combines the results of 35 other similar studies examining the effect of different noise levels on various types of stress measures to determine the general effect of noise on stress reactions.

purpose of the study by employing a certain amount of deception. **Deception** involves the researcher withholding the true purpose of the research from the individual or deliberately misleading him or her as to the true nature of the experiment (Bröder, 1998; Ortmann & Hertwig, 1998). The degree of deception can range from modifying the title of the survey to providing the participants with false feedback to staging fake injuries, arguments, and property destruction. As an example, a researcher may have an assistant fake an

Summing It Up *Characteristic Strengths and Limitations of the Experimental Approach*

Characteristic Feature	Strength or Limitation	Description
Controlled Observations	Strength	The researcher can exercise control over such things as environmental conditions and the administration of the independent variable.
Causal Explanations	Strength	Controlling for alternative explanations strengthens the assumption that the independent variable caused the changes in the dependent variable.
Group Means vs. the Individual	Limitation	Because group means, or the "average response," are analyzed, the behavior of any one particular individual is lost.
Ethical Constraints	Limitation	The administration of certain procedures is ethically not possible.
Experimental Biases	Limitation	The researcher might communicate a variety of intentional or unintentional cues to the individual about what is being investigated and how the persons "ought to" respond.

epileptic seizure in a busy mall to study the effect of certain personality factors on helping behavior in stressful situations.

Justifying Research Procedure

Deception is not the rule in personality research; it is justified only as a last resort, when the researcher believes that results from such research will contribute to a greater understanding of the human personality. For example, faking injuries may be justified if the results of the study increase our understanding of how to make people more responsive to the needs of others. Allowing researchers to make decisions justifying their own research introduces the potential of biased judgments. Problems may occur when personal biases about the importance of one's research begin to overshadow concerns for the protection of research participants.

Some Solutions to Ethical Issues: Trying to Make Things Right

The ethical issues just described illustrate some of the special considerations personality psychologists must address when planning the procedures of their research. Some solutions for dealing with these and other ethical considerations include informed consent, debriefing, establishing ethical guidelines, and ethics review boards.

Informed Consent

Informed consent involves giving individuals the chance to decide whether they wish to participate before the actual start of the research. The decision to participate should be based on a reasonable description of the procedures being given to the individuals. Informed consent also involves informing individuals of their right to terminate their participation in the research project at any time they wish for *any* reason. Finally, assuring individuals that their responses will be kept confidential is another important element of informed consent.

Debriefing

Debriefing participants after their participation is designed to help deal with the issue of deception. During a **debriefing session**, the researcher explains to the individual what the purpose of the project was, why it was necessary to use the deception, and how participants contributed to the project. The purpose of the debriefing session is to minimize any harm or ill feelings the individual might have experienced during his or her participation in the research project. In the debriefing session, explaining what is being studied and why can help to make the individual's participation a more educational and rewarding experience. In the example of the research investigating helping behavior, the researcher would explain that the assistant's injury was fake, say that no one outside the study would know how individual participants

behaved, and describe how their participation contributed to our understanding of why people help others.

Are such debriefing sessions effective? Research on the effectiveness of debriefing seems to indicate that while some negative reactions to deception are reported based on receiving negative feedback (Epley & Huff, 1998), most participants perceive such temporary uses of deception as acceptable (Rogers, 1980) and express more positive feelings about psychological research when such deception is followed by a thorough debriefing session (Smith & Richardson, 1983).

Summing It Up *Some Ethical Concerns and Possible Solutions in Conducting Personality Research*

Ethical Concern	Description	Possible Solution	Example
Inducing Stress and Psychological Harm	Research participants may experience psychological discomfort owing to the nature of the procedures used by the researcher.	*Informed consent:* Giving participants the opportunity to decide, based on a reasonable description of the procedures, if they wish to participate in the research project.	In a study supposedly examining "interpersonal dynamics," the participants are told that there is the possibility of some individuals receiving harsh feedback after the group discussion but they can withdraw from the session any time they desire.
Deception	Investigators may withhold a certain amount of information or deliberately mislead research participants regarding the actual purpose of the research.	*Debriefing:* After completing their participation, the individuals are given a complete explanation of the research, the rationale for the deception, and how their participation contributed to the research.	At the end of the research session, the individuals are told that the real purpose of the study was to examine the effect of feedback on self-esteem and that all of the feedback ratings were made up and randomly assigned.
Justification of Research Procedures	Investigators may exaggerate the importance of the research as a means of justifying stress-producing procedures.	*Ethical guidelines:* There are codes of conduct that researchers must follow when conducting research in personality. *Ethical review boards:* Individuals not associated with the research project evaluate it to make sure it meets standard ethical guidelines.	Before being able to conduct the research on feedback and self-esteem, the project is reviewed by a panel of judges on the university's research review committee.

Ethical Guidelines

In addition to informed consent and debriefing, many other ethical considerations are involved when designing and implementing a research project (Blanck, Bellack, Rosnow, Rotheram-Borus, & Schooler, 1992; Koocher & Keith-Spiegel, 1998). To help researchers identify and resolve potential ethical issues, the **American Psychological Association** (APA) has formulated a set of ethical principles to be used as guidelines when planning and conducting research (APA, 1981a, 1982, 1992a, 1992b, 2002). Psychologists who conduct research involving humans are obligated to conform to this set of ethical guidelines. The APA has also developed a set of guidelines for research conducted with animal subjects (APA, 1981a; APA's Committee on Animal Research and Ethics, 2002) and for many of the other activities engaged in by professional psychologists, such as testing, teaching, and counseling (APA, 1977, 1981b, 1990, 2002; Turner, DeMers, Fox, & Reed, 2001) and providing services over the phone and Internet (APA's Ethics Committee, 1997/2002). Finally, any student of psychology who assumes the role of a researcher is also expected to adhere to the ethical standards of professional psychologists (APA, 1977, 1981a, 1982, 2002). For example, any student assisting with the research of a professor must behave in a manner consistent with these ethical principles.

Ethics Review Boards

Preventing researchers from exaggerating the importance of their research as a means of justifying deception or the presence of stress is the major function of an **ethics review board**. The review board evaluates research proposals with respect to their adherence to certain ethical standards (Bullock, 2002). Board members include psychologists and nonpsychologists. Because the board members are not connected directly with the proposals being considered, they can take a much more objective stand on evaluating the ethical nature of the procedures.

Thus, being aware of the ethical issues associated with the study of personality psychology makes it possible to increase our knowledge of personality psychology through systematic research while protecting the rights and safety of those individuals who provide a valuable service by serving as participants in this research. For more information about the ethical issues discussed in this section, read *Ethics in Research with Human Participants* (Sales & Folkman, 2000) or visit the APA's Ethics Office home page (http://www.apa.org/ethics/homepage.html). A summary of the major ideas examined in this section is presented in "Summing It Up: Some Ethical Concerns and Possible Solutions in Conducting Personality Research" opposite.

This concludes our discussion of the scope of and the methods used in the study of personality psychology. In the next chapter we will examine personality assessment by considering the nature of and the techniques used in the measurement of personality.

Chapter Summary: Reexamining the Highlights

- *Defining Personality*. Although personality psychologists define personality in many different ways, the definitions have three common features: uniqueness of the individual, consistency of behavior, and explanations of the content and process of personality.

- *The Scope of Personality Psychology*. The study of personality psychology covers such areas as theory development, personality research, personality development, personality assessment, and applications in personality psychology.

- *Research Methods in Personality Psychology*

  – The clinical approach involves in-depth study of the individual or a small group of individuals through such techniques as case study, individual interview, and analysis of personal documents. Strengths of this approach are its usefulness in gaining a deeper understanding of the individual, studying development and adjustment processes over time, and investigating extreme and rare cases. Limitations include decreased generalizability of results and the potential for personal biases.

– The correlational approach identifies the relationship between two variables. The relationships can be positive or negative and vary in the strength of association between the two variables. Strengths of this approach include the ability to explore and identify relationships between variables and overcome certain ethical considerations. Limitations include the potential presence of the third-variable problem and undetermined causal relationships.

– The experimental approach helps to establish causal relationships among variables. This approach involves systematic intervention of the independent variable to observe any changes it produces in the dependent variable while maintaining experimental control over outside influences. Three techniques for increasing experimental control are random assignment of subjects, standardization of procedures, and use of a control group. Meta-analysis compares the results across different experimental studies. Strengths of this approach include making controlled observations and providing causal explanations. Limitations include an emphasis on the group mean over the individual, limited generalizability of results from the controlled laboratory to the real world, and the potential for experimenter biases.

● *Research Ethics.* Some ethical issues and concerns associated with doing research in personality psychology involve inducing stress, using deception, and justifying research procedures. Possible solutions for dealing with these ethical issues include using informed consent, debriefing, following APA ethics guidelines, and consulting ethics review boards.

Glossary

American Psychological Association The largest national professional organization of psychologists in the United States.

case study method A research method involving an extensive investigation of an individual.

content analysis The identification of recurring themes and ideas through the systematic analysis of a specific set of documents.

control group The comparison group in experimental research that does not receive any level of the independent variable.

correlation coefficient A numerical value indicating the strength of the association between two variables.

correlational research An approach to research designed to identify the relationship between two variables.

debriefing session A period at the end of the experimental session when a complete explanation of the research is given to the participants.

deception The partial withholding of information about the experiment from the participants.

dependent variable That variable in experimental research for which observed changes are attributed to the independent variable.

ethics review board A panel of judges made up of individuals from different disciplines who independently evaluate the ethical standards of proposed research procedures.

experimenter bias Any attempt by the researcher to influence the behavior of the subjects in order to achieve support for the hypothesis.

experimental control The elimination of outside influences on the changes observed in the dependent variable.

experimental research A method of research designed to identify causal relationships.

field research Research conducted in locations other than the controlled conditions of the laboratory.

generalizability The extent to which the information obtained from one situation can be extended to new and different situations.

group mean The arithmetic average of a set of scores from a particular group.

hypothesis A statement expressing the predicted outcome of the relationships between variables.

independent variable That variable in experimental research believed to be the causal factor.

individual interview A one-to-one verbal exchange designed to yield critical information about the interviewee.

informed consent Individuals making their decision to participate on the basis of information about the procedures of the research received before their actual participation.

laboratory research Research done in the controlled conditions of a laboratory.

meta-analysis   A statistical technique used to compare the results from different studies addressing a similar issue.

negative correlational relationship   A correlational relationship between two variables characterized by a downward trend in the points in the scatter plot.

parsimony   A condition of being simple or economical.

personal document   Any document a person uses to reveal personal thoughts, feelings, or ideas.

personality   The characteristics of the individual that create a unique expression of thoughts, feelings, and behavior.

personality assessment   An area of study emphasizing the development of techniques designed to measure different aspects and dimensions of personality.

personality development   The study of the factors and processes associated with the development of personality across the life span and in conjunction with other aspects of individual development.

personality psychologist   A psychologist whose professional training and research interests are in studying the different aspects and dimensions of personality.

positive correlational relationship   A correlational relationship between two variables characterized by an upward trend in the points in the scatter plot.

psychobiography   A case study of an individual for the purpose of formulating statements about the individual's psychological characteristics.

psychotherapy   The systematic application of principles of psychology in modifying the thoughts, feelings, and behavior of individuals experiencing difficulty coping with life.

psychotherapist   A psychologist specially trained to provide psychotherapy.

random assignment   A procedure guaranteeing that all individuals have an equal chance of being assigned to any of the treatment groups.

rapport   The sense of warmth and trust the interviewer creates with the interviewee.

researcher biases   The systematic distortion of information by researchers in support of their position.

scatter plot   A graph illustrating the relationship between two variables.

standardization of procedures   Treating all subjects in all treatment groups in a similar manner.

subject biases   The systematic distortion of information by individuals when they report it to the researcher.

third-variable problem   The mediating influence of an outside variable on the observed correlation between two other variables.

theory   A systematic collection of ideas and explanations designed to account for a set of observations and predict future observations.

Personality Assessment
An Introduction to the Measurement of Personality

2

Chapter Overview:
A Preview of Coming Attractions

Personality assessment involves the development, evaluation, and utilization of personality tests in diverse settings (Aiken, 2003; Cohen & Swerdlik, 2002; Handler & Clemence, 2003; Murphy & Davidshofer, 2005; Plante, 2005). In this chapter you will learn about the basic nature of personality assessment. The material that follows describes the procedures for evaluating measures of personality, gives examples of classic personality assessment devices, illustrates the diverse settings in which personality tests are utilized, and discusses some of the associated ethical and legal issues.

Personality Assessment: What, Why, and Where

This section gives an overview of personality assessment in the study of personality psychology, discussing what personality assessment is, why it is done, and where it is done.

What Is Personality Assessment?

Personality assessment is the systematic measurement of the many aspects of personality. A few examples of these include motivation (e.g., achievement striving), personality pathology (e.g., depression), various personality traits (e.g., aggression, self-esteem, and introversion), personality dynamics (e.g., reactions to anxiety), and personality development (e.g., styles of aging). Personality tests are characterized by a variety of different techniques, including paper-and-pencil or computerized inventories, direct observation of behavior, physiological recordings (e.g., heart rate monitoring), and verbal responses (e.g., comments about ink blots).

Why Assess Personality?

Personality assessment has three major functions:

- To help obtain information about people in a meaningful and precise manner.
- To help communicate this information in a useful way to personality psychologists and other professionals (e.g., psychiatrists and personnel managers) utilizing personality tests.
- To help in the prediction of future behavior based on information obtained from the results of the test (e.g., predict the ability of military recruits to handle stress under combat conditions).

Promoting Purpose and Precision in Assessment

Personality assessment utilizes many specialized techniques designed to perform a particular function. For example, some personality tests are used by mental health workers in assigning clients to specific treatment programs, by business managers or executives to select sales representatives, and by the FBI to screen potential agents.

Before a personality test is put into use, it is evaluated through systematic research to make sure that it measures what it says it will measure in a precise manner. For example, research in the development of a personality test designed to select sales representatives might involve administering the test to existing sales representatives and correlating their test scores with their total dollars-in-sales performance records for each of the previous four years. Only if the test scores were highly related to sales performance in a consistent manner over time would the test be used in the actual hiring of future sales representatives.

Promoting Effective Communication

The ability to communicate precise descriptions of personality is vital when important decisions rest on them. For example, the decision to admit an individual to a police academy may depend on a description of the applicant's personality provided by a personality psychologist to the members of the selection committee. Since personality factors and job stress have been linked to indices of poorer mental health in police personnel (Girodo, 1991), effective communication of this information has serious consequences for the future safety and protection of many citizens.

To provide a more effective means of communicating information about personality, personality psychologists typically compare an individual's test scores with some type of **group norm**. A group norm is a summary of the scores on a measure obtained from a specific group of individuals who have taken the test previously. For example, a prospective police officer applicant's score on a test measuring adjustment to stress is compared to that of the group norm of successful police officers. If the applicant's score is above the norm, the application qualifies to go forward. If the score is below it, the application process ends. Because group norms for many personality tests are readily available to qualified individuals who are responsible for interpreting test results, a precise description of a person's score-based personality can easily be communicated to others in different locations.

Promoting the Prediction of Future Behavior

For personality assessment to be of some value, it must demonstrate the ability to predict future behavior from the results of the test being used. For example, to help determine the most effective course of psychiatric treatment, a therapist working in a psychiatric hospital might use the results of a series of personality tests to help diagnosis an individual's psychological disorder. From the diagnosis, the therapist could then select and implement the treatment program with the greatest likelihood of success. Because the issue of predictability is such a critical concern in the development and use of personality tests, you will be exposed to some of the different methods used to assess their ability to predict future behavior.

Where Is Personality Assessment Done?

Personality assessment is utilized in many different settings (Aiken, 2003; Cohen & Swerdlik, 2002; Handler & Clemence, 2003). The assessment of psychological attributes, including personality, is utilized by a variety of individuals, such as clinical psychologists, psychiatrists, personnel managers, social workers, guidance counselors, law enforcement officials, and consumer marketers. The assessment of personality is also utilized, although to a lesser extent, by anthropologists, criminologists, and sociologists. Six major areas in which personality is assessed are clinical, counseling, legal, educational and vocational guidance, human resources, and research settings.

Clinical Settings

Clinical settings include psychiatric hospitals, community mental health centers, and the private offices of **psychometricians** (i.e., individuals licensed to purchase, administer, and interpret psychological tests) and of some psychotherapists. The principal purpose of psychological assessment in clinical settings is to help diagnose and classify individuals' emotional or behavioral problems (Nevid, Rathus, & Greene, 2000). This type of information is very useful in determining the most effective treatment plan (Kring, Davison, Neale, & Johnson, 2007; Plante, 2005; Trull & Phares, 2001).

Counseling Settings

Counseling settings include colleges, rehabilitation centers, and a variety of industrial settings (Gladding, 2003; Trull & Phares, 2001). In counseling settings **counseling psychologists** work to help individuals cope with and adjust more effectively to problems in their daily life (e.g., job dissatisfaction or loneliness). For example, a counseling psychologist implementing a two-month stress-management treatment program for the employees of an auto manufacturing plant might use a personality test measuring stress reactions to assess the program's effectiveness.

Legal Settings

Personality tests are also used in such legal settings as the courtroom, prisons, and law enforcement agencies (Craig, 2005; Goodman-Delahunty, Forsterlee, & Forsterlee, 2005; Handler & Clemence, 2003; Wrightsman, Greene, Nietzel, & Fortune, 2002). Information from personality tests is used as evidence in judicial proceedings to help determine whether a person is sane and can be held responsible for criminal actions (Stafford & Ben-Porath, 2002) or whether an inmate is ready for probation (Walters, Revella, & Baltrusaitis, 1990). For example, on the basis of psychiatric interviews and various personality tests, John W. Hinckley, Jr., was found not guilty by reason of insanity in the shooting of President Reagan and three other individuals. Personality tests given to prospective jurors are also used by lawyers to help in the selection of jury members (Wrightsman et al., 2002). For example, personal information gathered from pretrial surveys of potential jurors proved to be critical in O. J. Simpson's defense and his subsequent not-guilty verdict in 1995 for the murder of his ex-wife and her friend in what was called the "trial of the century" (C. B. Murray, Kaiser, & Taylor, 1997). Personality assessment is also used to evaluate individuals involved in cases involving child custody, personal injury, sexual harassment, and sexual offenses (e.g., rape, incest, indecent exposure, and pedophilia; Craig, 2005).

Law enforcement agencies, from local police departments to U.S. marshals and Secret Service agents, use personality assessment to help solve and prevent crimes (Coggins, Pynchon, & Dvoskin, 1998). In such cases, a **personality profile** (i.e., a pattern of similar behavioral responses and/or results for a set of tests taken by a particular group of individuals) is created based on clinical interviews with and personality tests taken by incarcerated criminals who have committed a certain type of crime (e.g., serial killings). Information in the profile about the motives and behavior patterns of this type of criminal is used to help identify potential suspects or potential victims. The Secret Service uses similar information to help prevent physical attacks by identifying and monitoring individuals who have demonstrated the potential for violence against an individual being protected by the Service, such as the U.S. president. In addition, law enforcement agencies use personality assessment to help in the screening and selection of applicants for employment as police officers, as well as to develop personality profiles of successful and unsuccessful officers (Craig, 2005).

Educational and Vocational Guidance Settings

High schools, colleges, and vocational guidance centers use personality assessment to help individuals make educational and vocational decisions (Aiken, 2003; Gladding, 2003). For example, should group norms indicate that most successful forest rangers are independent-minded and enjoy physical exercise, then an individual whose test scores do not reflect these basic characteristics probably should not plan a career as a forest ranger. Personality assessment techniques have also been used to investigate the pre- and post-examination study strategies of college students (Drumheller, Eicke, & Scherer, 1991).

Corporate Settings

Personality assessment in the corporate setting involves the use of personality tests to address a variety of issues to help businesses operate more effectively. In the area of human resources, management uses information obtained from personality tests to help in the selection and placement of personnel, with the larger goal of promoting employee satisfaction and organizational productivity (Handler & Clemence, 2003; Hough & Furnham, 2003). To minimize corporate loss, assessments of personality and other related factors are used to eliminate prospective job applicants most likely to engage in counterproductive behavior, such as theft, property damage and waste, violence, and the use of drugs or alcohol on the job (Cascio, 2003; Sackett & Wanek, 1996; Schmitt, Cortina, Ingerick, & Wiechmann, 2003; Slora, Joy, & Terris, 1991; Terris & Jones, 1985).

In personnel placement, personality assessment techniques are used to help determine what job within a group of jobs seems to be most appropriate for an individual (Hough & Furnham, 2003; Riggio, 2002). For example, in a construction company, systematic placement might involve giving all new employees a test of "accident proneness" (Hansen, 1991; Jones & Wuebker, 1984; Schmitt et al., 2003). New employees

with high accident proneness scores might be placed in low-risk jobs. In addition, personality tests are used to assess the coping styles of individuals in the commercial fishing industry in response to the stress and dangers associated with being at sea for long periods of time (Riordan, Johnson, & Thomas, 1991). These measures can also predict the effectiveness of different personality styles on management performance (Gable & Topol, 1991). Thus, the use of personality assessment for both personnel selection and placement in an organization helps to maximize the probability of placing the right person in the right job.

Research Settings

Almost anyplace where personality assessment is utilized has the potential to be a research setting. Such settings include university research laboratories, counseling centers, psychiatric hospitals, community mental health centers, the military, and industry.

Personality assessment is used in research settings to evaluate treatment outcome, develop new assessment techniques, and test theories (Burger, 2004). For example, personality researchers in a psychiatric hospital might use a test of anxiety to assess changes in patients before and after receiving a new type of group therapy. Researchers in military and industrial settings might develop new personality tests to aid in the selection and placement of individuals in new technology jobs. A psychologist in a university setting developing a theory of body image might utilize personality assessment techniques to test hypotheses linking body image with various personality dimensions, such as loneliness and depression (Cash & Pruzinsky, 1990).

For a review of the major points discussed in this section, see "Summing It Up: The What, Why, and Where of Personality Assessment" opposite. In the next section, we will consider the basic indices for evaluating personality assessment techniques.

Evaluating Personality Assessment Techniques: Assessing Personality Assessment

Regardless of why or where they are utilized, all personality assessment techniques are subject to scrutiny.

Summing It Up *The What, Why, and Where of Personality Assessment*

Question	Answer	Example
What is it?	Any systematic attempt to measure personality characteristics using any one of a variety of measurement techniques	Measuring an individual's level of self-esteem using a paper-and-pencil test and their degree of dependency with an ink blot test
Why do it?	To develop measurement techniques designed to identify important differences in personality among people in a more precise manner	Executing research designed to develop a more effective means of identifying at-risk individuals best suited for a new treatment of depression
Where is it is done?	In a variety of settings for many different purposes	Utilizing assessment in business, the military, psychiatric hospitals, and high schools to help assess, select, and place individuals in a variety of programs to best meet their needs

Specifically, they are subject to the evaluation of certain standards of quality (Anastasi & Urbina, 1997; Cohen & Swerdlik, 2002; Riggio, 2002; Trull & Phares, 2001). Two of the most important of these standards are *reliability* and *validity*. Although the different issues of reliability and validity are discussed separately here, personality psychologists consider all aspects of both issues together when developing and evaluating assessment techniques.

Standards of Reliability: Looking for Consistency

Reliability is the extent to which a test is consistent in its assessment of what it says it is measuring. For example, a human resources manager might use a test of achievement striving (i.e., desire to succeed) when selecting potential employees for a management-training program. For the selection process to be effective, the manager has to assume that if a prospective employee took the test of achievement striving today or three weeks from today, the scores on the test would be similar. If the test does not produce reliable scores, the wrong individuals may be selected for the training program.

Although there are several types of reliability, the index used to evaluate the consistency of a particular technique of personality assessment is referred to as the **reliability coefficient** (Aiken, 2003; Anastasi & Urbina,

1997; Cohen & Swedlik, 2002; Lanyon & Goodstein, 1997). The logic and evaluation of the reliability coefficient is very similar to those of the correlation coefficient discussed in Chapter 1 (see pp. 24–25). The major difference is that the pairs of scores used to calculate the reliability coefficient are based on the *same* measure instead of two different measures. As an example, to measure the reliability of a new test of extraversion, a researcher has a group of 60 students take the test and then take it again three weeks later. If the test is a reliable measure of extraversion, the correlation between the two scores should be high. As a general rule, a desirable value for a reliability coefficient is $r = .80$ or greater, suggesting that there is a relatively high degree of consistency in the measurement provided by the particular test (Aiken, 2003; Anastasi & Urbina, 1997).

Types of Reliability: Different Standards of Consistency

There are several different types of reliability, depending on the way consistency is measured. Two of the most important are *test-retest* and *examiner* reliability.

Test-Retest Reliability: Consistency Across Time

Test-retest reliability examines the consistency of assessment over time. A common method to assess the degree of test-retest reliability is to give the same group a personality test on two different occasions and calculate the reliability coefficient (r) between the two sets of scores. For example, researchers developing a measure of self-consciousness might give their test to a group on one day and then give them the same test 30 days later.

The test-retest reliability can be affected by the length of time between administrations of the tests (Aiken, 2003). If the interval is too short (i.e., two days), the similarity in the scores may simply be explained by individuals' ability to recall their recent responses. If the interval is too long (e.g., 10 months), the dissimilarity in the scores may be due to actual changes that have occurred in the individuals over time (e.g., development of acne resulting in an increase in one's self-consciousness). Although there is not a hard-and-fast rule, experts recommend that the interval between the two occasions of personality testing be at least one week but no more than two or three months (Kleinmuntz, 1982).

Examiner Reliability: Consistency Across Raters

Examiner reliability, by contrast, examines consistency across raters. The principal rationale of examiner reliability is to establish the extent to which different individuals administering and scoring a particular test will come to similar conclusions about the results. For example, a personality test assessing depression for the purpose of developing a plan of therapy is of little value if the test is scored differently by different clinical psychologists. A related issue is the extent to which an individual administering and scoring the test does so consistently over time. For example, it is extremely unfair if the answers to a standard set of questions given by applicants during a job interview are evaluated not on the basis of their content but on the mood of the personnel manager during the interview. Concerns regarding examiner reliability increase as the degree of subjective input by the rater increases, such as when the raters must interpret the meaning of verbal expressions used in response to a set of inkblots or the intent behind a behavior performed by an individual being tested (e.g., being helpful vs. trying to create a good impression during an interview).

Several precautions can be taken to increase the examiner reliability of a test. One involves providing detailed training and clear instructions on how to interpret the test results. For this reason, distributors of personality tests go to great lengths to develop and produce scoring manuals to accompany their tests. These manuals include detailed explanations and examples of how to interpret the results obtained from the tests. Another precaution is to standardize the procedures for scoring the tests so as to eliminate personal bias in the interpretations. The logic underlying standardization is to make the scoring procedures so consistent and straightforward that all who score the test will do so in the same manner. To accomplish this, distributors might provide a standard set of scoring keys or require that the test be scored by a computer (Cohen & Swerdlik, 2002; Riggio, 2002; Trull & Phares, 2001). Both of these precautions are designed to minimize the chance that human error will affect the scoring and interpretation of the test results.

For a review of the major points discussed in this section, see "Summing It Up: Indices of Reliability." In the next section, we will consider the topic of validity in personality assessment.

Summing It Up *Indices of Reliability*

Kind	Purpose	Example
Test-Retest Reliability	To establish the degree of stability of test scores over time	Give the same test of creativity to the same group of art majors on two different occasions.
Examiner Reliability	To establish the level of agreement between different raters of the same test	Have two different personnel managers score a potential applicant's personality test.

Note. For each kind of reliability, an acceptable reliability coefficient should have a positive r value equal to or greater than .80.

Standards of Validity: Measuring What You Say You're Measuring

Measures of personality must be valid as well as reliable. **Validity** of assessment is the extent to which a test measures what it says it is measuring. For example, to establish the validity of a measure of aggression, those school children with high scores on the aggression scale would be expected to demonstrate more aggressive play (e.g., tease, yell at, and hit others) in the schoolyard than those with low scores. The validity of the scores on the aggression scale demonstrate its ability to do what it says it is supposed to do – predict aggressive behavior. Validity of assessment is considered the most critical issue in the development of tests (Groth-Marnat, 2003; Messick, 1995). In this section, a discussion of some of the various types of validity will be presented, along with illustrative examples.

Types of Validity: Establishing the Meaning of Your Test

Types of validity include face validity, content validity, criterion validity, construct validity, and discriminate validity. Each considers a different aspect of the measure of personality.

Face Validity: Judging a Book by Its Cover

Face validity refers to the extent to which a test looks appropriate for what it is supposed to measure. One of the most important reasons for having a high degree of face validity is to help maintain the interest and involvement of individuals taking the test. For example, a test for selecting potential executives should include some questions about making financial and human resource decisions, as well as questions about personal goals. However, merely having face validity does not provide any valuable information concerning whether a test is really measuring what it says it is measuring. This type of information is provided by the other four types of validity.

Content Validity: It's What's Inside that Counts

Content validity refers to the extent to which the items (i.e., content) making up the test are a representative sample of that personality dimension supposedly being measured by the test. For example, the development of a test to measure shyness should contain items reflecting the personal (e.g., "Is your shyness a major source of personal unhappiness?"), social (e.g., "Do you find it difficult to talk in small groups of people?"), cognitive (e.g., "Do you believe that people are always evaluating you?"), and physiological (e.g., "Do you experience sweaty palms when talking to members of the opposite sex?") aspects of shyness. Because shyness involves all of these components (Carducci, 2000; Zimbardo, 1977), a valid test of shyness must measure all of them. To enhance content validity of a test, care must be taken to make sure all aspects of the dimension supposedly being measured are included.

A related issue is the extent to which the dimension of personality being measured by the test is clearly defined. For example, when developing a test to measure anxiety, there are many types of anxiety to consider, such as social anxiety, trait anxiety, state anxiety, moral anxiety, neurotic anxiety, and test anxiety, to name just a few. Defining a specific dimension of anxiety determines the type of items contained in the test. Since personality psychologists from different theoretical viewpoints do not necessarily agree on how a certain dimension of personality might be specified or defined, establishing content validity relies heavily on the definition of the concept used by the individuals developing the test.

Criterion Validity: Making Predictions

Criterion validity addresses the extent to which the scores of a test can predict the behavior of an individual in specific situations. The behavior predicted from the test score is called the **criterion measure**. The extent to which the criterion measure is predicted from the test score, indicated by the **validity coefficient,** involves correlating the test scores with an agreed-upon criterion measure. Two types of criterion validity are predictive validity and concurrent validity.

Predictive validity involves assessing the extent to which scores from the test are able to predict some specific criterion behavior in the future. For example, in the area of industrial security, scores on personality tests are used to help predict employee theft in a chain of home improvement centers (Jones & Terris, 1983, 1991) and in convenience stores (Terris & Jones, 1985). In these studies, the criterion measure was the amount of unexplained missing merchandise. In the large commercial rail industry, test scores were able to predict who would and would not have a work-related injury within a 12-month period (Sherry, 1991). In a more tragic example, researchers have utilized measures of hopelessness to predict suicide (Beck, Brown, Berchick, Stewart, & Steer, 1990)

Concurrent validity refers to the extent to which test scores are related to other currently existing criterion measures. For example, in a psychiatric hospital, a clinical psychologist trying to establish the concurrent validity of a personality test measuring paranoia might correlate patients' test scores with the ratings of paranoid tendencies made by other clinical psychologists who interviewed these same individuals. A high degree of correlation between the scores on the paranoia test and the paranoia ratings made by the clinicians would be evidence to support the concurrent validity of this test of paranoia.

Establishing predictive validity has its difficulties. One involves getting individuals to agree on an appropriate criterion measure. For example, when developing a test designed to measure happiness, a significant problem is arriving at a consensus about what is meant by *happiness* (Diener, 2000; Myers, 1992, 2000). Another problem concerns the issue of criterion contamination. **Criterion contamination** refers to a situation in which a researcher's knowledge about a person's score on one test influences the score the individual obtains on the second test. In the previous example involving the test of paranoid tendencies, a potential problem is created when the person scoring the test also has knowledge of the interview scores. Fortunately, this situation can be easily rectified by making sure that the same person is not making both ratings.

Construct Validity: Measuring What Cannot be Seen

In their classic article on construct validity, Cronbach and Meehl (1955) state, "A construct is some postulated attribute of people, assumed to be reflected in test performance" (p. 283). The term *postulated attribute* simply means a measurable human characteristic – such as cheerfulness, aggressiveness, or being in love – that can be used to help describe, explain, and/or predict behavior in a variety of situations. For example, although they have no physical embodiment, the concepts of intelligence and friendliness are constructs used to explain a variety of behaviors. Thus, *constructs* are invisible internal attributes, measurable by personality tests, whose existence can be used to help explain and predict behavior.

Construct validity represents the degree to which evidence is provided documenting the presence of the construct as defined by the researcher. The establishment of construct validity is a continuing process involving three basic steps:

1. Define the construct, making sure to include as many behavior references as possible.
2. Develop a test designed to measure the construct, making sure items in the test reflect the definition of the construct (i.e., content validity).
3. Conduct research designed to provide evidence that scores on the test can predict behaviors in a manner consistent with the definition of the construct.

For example, researchers have defined shyness as a tendency to avoid social interactions and fail to participate appropriately in social situations, and have developed a measure of "Personal Shyness" (Zimbardo, 1974) for research attempting to validate the construct of shyness. In support of this definition, researchers found that individuals scoring high on this measure tended to stand farther away from others (i.e., avoid social interactions) and speak less in groups (i.e., fail to participate appropriately) than individuals who scored low (Carducci & Webber, 1979; Pilkonis, 1977). Thus, because the shy individuals, as determined by their score on the shyness measure, responded in a manner consistent with the proposed definition of shyness, this research provides evidence supporting the existence and operation of the construct of shyness.

Discriminate Validity: Making a Clear Distinction

Discriminate validity is the extent to which your measure *does not relate* to other measures in an expected manner. An example of this would be to establish the distinction between a measure of shyness and one of introversion, two concepts that are frequently confused (Carducci, 2000). More specifically, while introverts prefer to participate in more sedate, solitary activities, shy individuals actually prefer to be around others socially but for a variety of reasons have difficulty approaching and interacting with them (Carducci, 2005). To establish the discriminate validity of a measure of shyness from a measure of introversion, a personality psychologist could present a list of 100 social activities that vary in the degree to which they involve interacting with others (e.g., spending an evening at home reading a novel, going to a small poetry reading, going to a popular mall, or attending a party) to a group of individuals that scored high on a measure of shyness and those who scored high on a measure of introversion. Evidence supporting the discriminate validity of the shyness measure would be provided if those individuals with the high shyness scores indicated a greater preference for attending highly social activities (e.g., going to a popular mall or party) than those individuals scoring high on the measure of introversion, who would be expected to prefer more sedate, solitary activities (e.g., spending an evening at home reading a novel or going to a small poetry reading) than the shy individuals. Being able to predict the difference between what shy individuals do and what introverted individuals do helps to establish a clear distinction between the measures of shyness and of introversion.

Generalizability: Providing Continued Support

Establishing validity is an ongoing process that requires supporting evidence from more than only one or two studies. In support of establishing validity, **generalizability** refers to the extent to which the results of one particular study can be replicated using other types of individuals or in other types of situations. With respect to establishing the generalizability of the shyness construct and the measure used to assess it, for example, researchers must continually determine its appropriateness by testing its ability to predict the behavior of shy individuals in different settings (e.g., at a party vs. business meeting), in different ages groups (e.g., teenagers vs. adults), and from different cultures (e.g., Eastern vs. Western; Carducci, 2000). The more consistent the evidence across these different groups of individuals and situations, the greater the degree of genalizability there is for the shyness construct and the measure used to assess it. Thus, the more supporting evidence the research provides, the more confidence there is in the validity of the existence, operation, and measurement of the construct.

For a review of the major points discussed in this section, see "Summing It Up: Forms of Validity" on p. 48. In the next section, we will consider some of the different methods to assess personality.

Methods of Personality Assessment: A Survey of Personality Assessment Techniques

How do we get information about an individual's personality? There are a number of different methods of measuring personality. Four categories of personality assessment techniques are objective self-report, projective, behavioral, and psychophysiological. In this section the characteristic features and examples of these techniques are discussed, along with their strengths and weaknesses. A discussion of the ever-increasing role played by computers in personality assessment is also presented.

Objective Self-Report Techniques: Treating Everybody the Same

With **objective self-report techniques**, individuals provide information about their thoughts, feelings, and behaviors in response to standardized items contained in personality tests. Both the response alternatives available for the items in these tests and the procedures for scoring the responses are standardized in that they are the same for anyone completing the test. The logic is that by treating all participants the same way, potential biases in interpretation of results, which might affect the person's test score, are controlled. The standardization of test items and procedures for scoring the responses add to the speed and ease of administration and to the increased level of reliability that is characteristic of objective self-report techniques. These characteristics make these techniques very attractive to many personality psychologists and other individuals who administer them.

Types of Objective Self-Report Techniques: Single- vs. Multiple-Dimension Personality Tests

Single-dimension personality tests attempt to measure only one dimension of personality (e.g., shyness, creativity, or aggressiveness) at a time. A classic example of a single-dimension objective self-report personality test is the **California F Scale** (Adorno, Frenkel-Brunswick, Levinson, & Sanford, 1950). The F Scale is

Summing It Up *Forms of Validity*

Kind	Purpose	Example
Face Validity	To make sure a test looks like what it is supposed to be measuring	Give the test a title that will have meaning to those taking it.
Content Validity	To make sure the items in the test represent all the dimensions of that aspect of personality being measured	A test for creativity should include items assessing concrete and abstract forms of thinking.
Criterion Validity (concurrent and predictive)	To make sure the test scores can predict a particular behavior in current and future situations	A child's score on a measure of aggression should correlate with aggressiveness ratings by teachers and the number of fights the child has had over a six-month period.
Construct Validity	To make sure that the construct being measured relates to other measures and behaviors in a manner consistent with the conceptualization of the construct	If it is assumed that anxiety is related to stress, then individuals under stress should score higher on a test of anxiety than individuals under less stress.
Discriminate Validity	To make sure that your measure is not too related to other measures, in a manner that is consistent with its theoretical formulation	To establish that assertiveness is not just verbal aggression, two researchers find that their measure of assertiveness does not correlate with a measure of verbal aggression.
Generalizability	To extend an established set of results to other groups of individuals in different settings	The increased tendency for teenagers to be more impulsive than adults in Western cultures is also found repeatedly in Eastern cultures.

designed to measure the personality dimension called authoritarianism. **Authoritarianism** is characterized by conventional attitudes and beliefs, submissiveness to authority, and intolerance of others perceived as different (e.g., members of racial minorities; Zillmer, Harrower, Ritzler, & Archer, 1995). The F Scale consists of 29 items having a standardized 6-point agreement-disagreement response option. A sample F-Scale item follows:

Obedience and respect for authority are the most important virtues children should learn.

___Strong Support, Agreement
___Moderate Support, Agreement
___Slight Support, Agreement
___Slight Opposition, Disagreement
___Moderate Opposition, Disagreement
___Strong Opposition, Disagreement

Another excellent example of a frequently used single-dimension test is the **Self-Monitoring Scale** (Synder, 1974). **Self-monitoring** refers to the extent to which individuals monitor or regulate the nature of their public appearance during their interactions with others, such as act surprised when they are not or appear sad when others around them are sad. The Self-Monitoring scale consists of 25 true–false items. To get some firsthand experience with assessing your own level of self-monitoring, try "You Can Do It" on p. 49.

You Can Do It

Identifying Interpersonal Actors: Assessment of Self-Monitoring

For each of the following six items, answer "true" or "false" to indicate whether or not the item describes you.

1. I find it hard to imitate the behavior of other people.
2. I guess I put on a show to impress or entertain people.
3. In a group of people, I am rarely the center of attention.
4. I have considered being an entertainer.
5. I am not particularly good at making other people like me.
6. I sometimes appear to others to be experiencing deeper emotions than I actually am.

Scoring

If you answered "false" to items 1, 3, and 5, give yourself one point. If you answered "true" to items 2, 4, and 6, give yourself one point. Now add the total number of points you have received. The higher your score, the more you express opinions characteristic of high self-monitoring.

Interpretation

High self-monitors perceive themselves as being able to convincingly produce whatever self-presentation image seems appropriate for the present situation. They also perceive themselves to be good actors in social situations. On the other hand, low self-monitors see themselves as not being skillful enough actors to present themselves in any other way than "being themselves" (Snyder, 1987). Be aware that most people are not exclusively high or low self-monitors, but typically fall somewhere in the middle when responding to the complete set of items on the Self-Monitoring Scale. Also be aware that there is some disagreement regarding what is being measured by the Scale (Briggs & Cheek, 1988; Briggs, Cheek, & Buss, 1980; Osborne, 1996).

Multiple-dimension personality tests attempt to measure more than one dimension of personality at a time and tend to contain a much larger number of items than single-dimension tests. The **California Psychological Inventory** (**CPI**; Gough, 1957, 1987) is a multiple-dimension personality test that contains 462 true–false questions and measures 20 different personality dimensions such as dominance, self-control, flexibility, socialization, self-acceptance, and a sense of well-being, to name just a few. Another well-established objective self-report personality test is the **Edwards Personal Preference Schedule** (**EPPS**; Edwards, 1954, 1959). The EPPS contains 210 forced-choice pairs of items assessing 15 separate personality dimensions expressed as need preferences in such domains as achievement, autonomy, affiliation, dominance, endurance, heterosexuality, and aggression, to name a few. However, a unique feature of the EPPS is that items associated with each specific need preference are paired with items from the remaining 14 need preferences. An example of an item similar to those in the EPPS follows:

a. I find it very satisfying to achieve success on my own.
b. The most enjoyable times I have involve being with other people.

By demonstrating a tendency to select options like (a), an achievement-type statement, over options like (b), an affiliation-type statement, an individual is assessed as possessing a high need for achievement and a low need for affiliation. The EPPS assesses the extent to which certain needs are more characteristic of the individual's personality than are other needs. Similarly, intelligence tests, like the Wechsler Adult Intelligence Scale-Revised, are objective tests assessing many different aspects of intelligence (Aiken, 2003; Cohen & Swerdlik, 2002; Murphy & Davidshofer, 2005).

In addition to these multiple-dimension personality tests, other such tests will be featured throughout the book, including the 240-item, five-dimension NEO Personality Inventory (Costa & McCrae, 1992), discussed in Chapter 7, and the Minnesota Multiphasic Personality Inventory, discussed next.

The Minnesota Multiphasic Personality Inventory

This is the most widely used and extensively researched clinical personality inventory (Groth-Marnat, 2003; Lanyon & Goodstein, 1997; Murphy & Davidshofer, 2005). The **Minnesota Multiphasic Personality Inventory-2** (**MMPI-2**; Butcher, Dahlstrom, Graham, Tellegen, &

Table 2.1   Illustrative Items and Interpretations of the Clinical and Supplementary Scales of the MMPI-2

Scale Name (Symbol)	Illustrative Items*	Interpretation**
The clinical scales:		
Hypochondriasis (*Hs*)	I am frequently bothered by chest pains and other body aches.	Tendency to have excessive bodily concerns and complain of chronic weakness, lack of energy, and sleep disturbances
Depression (*D*)	I have a negative outlook regarding my future.	Tendency to feel unhappy and depressed and be pessimistic about the future
Hysteria (*Hy*)	My heart begins to beat rapidly as soon as I feel stressed.	Tendency to react to stress by development of physical symptoms that appear and disappear suddenly
Psychopathic deviate (*Pd*)	I generally do not get along with individuals in positions of authority.	Tendency to be rebellious, impulsive, and lacking in warm attachments with others
Masculinity–Femininity (*Mf*)	Others would describe me as a warm and empathic person.	Tendency to distinguish male and female sex-role behavior.
Paranoia (*Pa*)	I generally do not get along with people because I feel they have it in for me.	Tendency to feel mistreated and picked on and to have delusions of persecution or grandeur
Psychasthenia (*Pt*)	I am frightened easily and worry a lot.	Tendency to be worried, fearful, apprehensive, high-strung, and jumpy
Schizophrenia (*Sc*)	My thoughts tend to be disorganized and very different from those around me.	Tendency to report unusual thoughts or attitudes or hallucinations; may be confused, disorganized, and disoriented
Hypomania (*Ma*)	I tend to go overboard in all the things I do but also lose interest in things quickly.	Tendency to be energetic and talkative and prefer action to thought
Social introversion (*Si*)	People would say it is hard to get to know me because I do not say much.	Tendency to be shy, reserved, timid, and retiring
The supplementary scales:		
Anxiety (*A*)	I tend to lack confidence in my abilities in social situations.	Tendency to be anxious, uncomfortable, shy, and retiring
Repression (*R*)	I tend to think about something a lot before I actually do it.	Tendency to be careful and cautious
Ego strength (*Es*)	I am not afaid to try new things.	Tendency to be stable, reliable, and self-confident
MacAndrew Alcoholism Revised Scale (MAC-R)	I tend to drink alcohol to feel more confident, comfortable, and outgoing in social situations.	Tendency to abuse alcohol and other substances, to be socially extroverted and exhibitionistic, and possibly to experience blackouts
Overcontrolled-Hostility Scale (*O-H*)	It takes a lot to make me get angry.	Tendency not to respond to provocation and to report few angry feelings, but may experience occasional exaggerated aggressive responses

Notes. *Since printing actual items from the MMPI is not possible in order to protect the integrity of the test, the statements presented are not actual test items but illustrative statements adapted from Graham's (1990) detailed descriptions of the clinical subscales (pp. 52–85) and the supplementary scales (pp. 141–168). ** Adapted from Graham (1990) and Butcher et al. (1989).

Kaemmer, 1989), like the original MMPI (Hathaway & McKinley, 1940, 1943), is a multiple-dimension personality test that was originally developed to help classify individuals with psychiatric disorders. The MMPI-2 contains 567 true–false questions. As shown in the upper portion of Table 2.1, 10 dimensions of personality are measured by the principal clinical scales appearing in the original MMPI and the revised MMPI-2. Table 2.1 also contains a sample item from each of the clinical scales and a brief interpretation of the characteristic features of someone scoring high on the scale. The nature of the labels of these scales reflects the principal function for which the MMPI was designed; that is, to help in the diagnosis and class-ification of individuals experiencing various psycho-pathological conditions. However, the MMPI is also utilized as a screening and diagnostic device in indus-trial, military, and educational settings (Butcher, 2006).

In addition to the 10 principal clinical scales appearing in the original MMPI and the MMPI-2, the MMPI-2 also contains 12 supplementary scales (Butcher et al., 1989). These supplementary scales were developed utilizing items from the existing MMPI and MMPI-2 item pool and recombining them using various statis-tical item-grouping techniques. Each supplementary scale was then validated against various clinical and nonclinical populations (Butcher et al., 1989; Graham, 2006). The lower portion of Table 2.1 contains a list-ing of five of the supplementary scales, a sample item, and a brief interpretation of the characteristic features of someone scoring high on the scale. The other sup-plementary scales and a brief interpretation of some-one scoring high on them include:

- *Dominance Scale (DO)* – tendency to feel con-fident and cope with life's stresses.
- *Social Responsibility Scale* (RE) – tendency to incorporate societal and cultural values and behave accordingly.
- *College Maladjustment Scale (MT)* – tendency to show general maladjustment, procrastinate, and be ineffectual.
- *Masculine Gender Role Scale (GM)* – tendency to be self-confident and free from fears and worries.
- *Feminine Gender Role Scale (GF)* – tendency toward religiosity and to abuse alcohol and non-prescription drugs.
- *Post-Traumatic Stress Disorder Scale (PK)* – tendency among veterans to report intense emotional distress and guilt.

- *Subtle–Obvious Subscales* – tendency to endorse items on the clinical scales that indicate obvious emotional disturbances (e.g., trying to appear emotionally disturbed).

The labeling used in these supplementary scales reflects their tendency to assess other aspects of per-sonality that might be helpful in the diagnostic process. However, note that the supplementary scales are not designed to replace the clinical scales but to be used in conjunction with them (Graham, 2006).

The MMPI-2 validity scales As one of its most important features, both MMPI and the MMPI-2 contain a set of **validity scales** designed to assess the validity of the responses given by individuals taking the test. The validity scales contained in the original MMPI include:

- *The Cannot Say Scale (?)* counts the number of items the individual leaves blank and is believed to reflect a desire to be evasive.
- *The Lie Scale (L)* contains 15 items (e.g., "I get angry sometimes. [False]") and assesses the extent to which individuals taking the test are trying to present themselves in a favorable or extremely positive manner by not answering the questions frankly and honestly. Individuals with a high *L* score are likely to lie in their responses to other items on the test, too, so their results have to be viewed with a high degree of caution.
- *The Infrequency Scale (F)* contains 64 items (e.g., "I have nightmares every few nights. [True]") and assesses a pattern of responses to this subset of questions that is not likely (i.e., infrequently) to be seen for individuals in the general, nonpsy-chiatric population. A high score might suggest that the person taking the test is trying to appear more psychologically disturbed than they actually are (e.g., a criminal trying to appear insane to avoid prosecution).
- *The Correction Scale (K)* contains 30 items (e.g., "I have very few fears compared to my friends. [False]") assessing the extent to which the person is responding in a defensive manner by demonstrating a tendency to guard against admitting to psychopathology, such as an indi-vidual whose actions demonstrate psychiatric problems trying to appear emotionally healthy.

In addition to these validity scales, the MMPI-2 also includes the Back-Page F Scale [*F(B)*], Variable Response Inconsistency Scale (*VRIN*), and True Response Inconsistency Scale (*TRIN*). The *F(B)* scale is designed to assess a pattern of randomness or carelessness to items appearing at the end of the test, which might suggest the individual is getting tired or simply trying to rush through the questions to "get the test over with." The *VRIN* scale assesses inconsistent patterns of responses to a set of differently worded questions throughout the test that have the same meaning. The *TRIN* scale assesses the tendency for individuals to answer the questions within this subscale in an inconsistent pattern by responding in the same direction, such as predominantly "true" or "false" to all of the subscale items. These new validity scales are designed to detect how careful and consistent individuals are when taking the test .

Taken together, these validity scales increase the likelihood of detecting individuals whose responses to the items indicate a lack of trustworthiness. They also help boost the test administrator's confidence in the results and in their interpretation. However, as seen in the next "Cultural Context of Personality Psychology," even the validity of the validity scales has come into question.

The Cultural Context of Personality Psychology

Cultural Diversity and the MMPI Validity Scale: Validity, Ethnicity, and Sensivity

As mainstream society becomes more culturally diverse, concerns about the appropriateness of the standard interpretations of the MMPI have been expressed (Gray-Little, 2002). In an attempt to address

The research of Bernadette Gray-Little and Danielle A. Kaplan highlights the importance of cross-cultural considerations when interpreting the results of the MMPI.

this issue, researchers are assessing the nature of the responses to the MMPI by individuals from diverse cultural backgrounds (Butcher, Mosch, Tsai, & Nezami, 2006; Okazaki, Kallivayalil, & Sue, 2002; Velásquez, Maness, & Anderson, 2002). An excellent example of this research is the work of Bernadette Gray-Little and Danielle A. Kaplan (1998), both of the University of North Carolina at Chapel Hill. In their review of this research, they note that there are certain areas of interpretation that deserve special attention when reviewing the MMPI results of individuals from certain cultural backgrounds. For example, in comparison to samples of white respondents, individuals of Hispanic descent tended to demonstrate an elevated score on the Lie (*L*) validity scale, African-Americans tended to display an elevated score on the Frequency (*F*) validity scale, and Asian-Americans tended to have elevated scores on the *L* and *F* validity scales. No clear pattern of results was obtained for samples of Native Americans. This inconsistency may be due, in part, to the fact that Native Americans represent many different linguistic and cultural traditions, making comparisons across different groups difficult. The point to be made here is that because individuals coming from different cultural backgrounds may bring certain characteristic patterns of responding to test items, personality psychologists interpreting the test results need to be sensitive to such patterns, since, as we have noted previously, the nature of these interpretations can have serious clinical, forensic, and occupational implications.

The MMPI-2 Personality Profile   Another distinctive feature of the MMPI-2 is that the subscales can be used to construct a personality profile. A **profile analysis** involves plotting the scores of each subscale on an MMPI-2 profile chart and then connecting these points to reveal a particular response pattern. Through extensive and systematic analysis of many MMPI and MMPI-2 profiles, researchers discovered that certain profiles are associated with particular psychiatric disorders and personality characteristics (Dahlstrom, Welsh, & Dahlstrom, 1972, 1975; Graham, 2006; Groth-Marnat, 2003; Hathaway & Meehl, 1951; Pope, Butcher, & Seelen, 2000).

For example, the profile pattern in Figure 2.1 has been identified as the "paranoid valley" (Dahlstrom & Welsh, 1960; Groth-Marnat, 2003) because patients suffering from paranoid schizophrenia tend to have this profile pattern. The "valley" is created by high scores on the Paranoia (*Pa*) and Schizophrenia (*Sc*) scales (numbers 6 and 8 on the profile chart) and relatively low scores on the Psychasthenia (*Pt*) and Hypomania (*Ma*) scales (numbers 7 and 9 on the profile chart). Because patients with certain psychiatric disorders produce certain profiles, the MMPI-2 is an extremely valuable tool for many mental health professionals in diagnosing psychiatric disorders and establishing treatment plans (Butcher, 1990; Graham, 2006; Trull & Phares, 2001).

The Problem of Response Sets: Subjective Influences on Objective Tests

Although the objective nature of these self-report tests helps to minimize any subjective influences when scoring and interpreting them, certain tendencies can influence the nature of the results obtained. A **response set** refers to a tendency to answer test items in a particular way regardless of how the person taking the test really feels about the content of the item (Cohen & Swerdlik, 2002; Lanyon & Goodstein, 1997; Murphy & Davidshofer, 2005).

The **acquiescence response set** refers to the tendency for the person to respond with agreement to test items for which there is some uncertainty. For example, a person may obtain a very high need-for-achievement score only because of a tendency to answer "true" to the many items on the test for whose meaning there was some uncertainty.

The **social desirability response set** is characterized by a tendency to select those responses appearing the most socially acceptable. For example, the individual might agree consistently with such statements as "I am very loyal to all of my friends" and disagree consistently with such statements as "I tell lies to cover my mistakes."

Although such response sets can be problematic, they can be minimized by developing and including

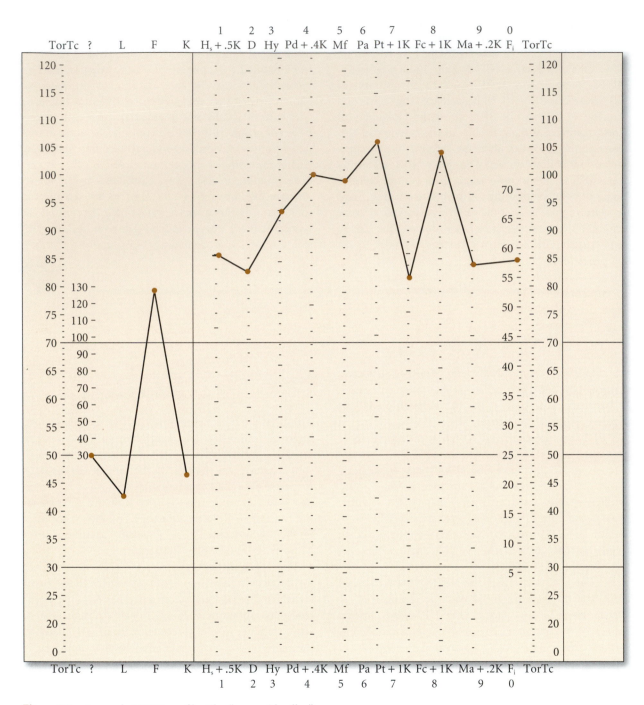

Figure 2.1 A sample MMPI profile: The "paranoid valley"
Source: Kleinmuntz (1982, p. 228); Groth-Marnat (1990, p. 226)

validity scales in the tests (e.g., MMPI-2 and EPPS) to identify and correct the test scores. The sets can also be minimized by carefully considering the wording of the test items and the scoring procedures. For example, wording the test items so half of the alternatives appearing most socially acceptable are scored as "true" and half as "false" can help to control for both the acquiescence and social desirability response sets.

Evaluating Objective Self-Report Techniques: Strengths and Limitations

A summary of the characteristic strengths and limitations of the objective self-report techniques is presented below.

Characteristic Strengths   The major strength of objective self-report personality tests is their objective and rather standardized nature. The objective nature makes it possible for them to be administered quite easily in both individual and group settings. Their standardized procedures make it possible for every person taking the test to be treated the same. In addition to contributing to the ease with which the test is scored, standard scoring procedures have the major advantage of minimizing any bias on the part of the test scorer, which helps to contribute to increased reliability of these tests. With the multiple-dimension tests, a major advantage is that it is possible to assess many different aspects of the individual's personality at the same time.

Characteristic Limitations   One of the major limitations of objective self-report tests is that they rely heavily on the person taking the test to provide honest and unbiased answers. Research on response sets makes it clear that test takers may not always provide answers that accurately describe themselves. Such response sets make interpretation difficult and decrease the validity of the test. Another limitation is that the standardized and limited response options available in objective self-report tests do not allow the persons taking the test to elaborate or clarify their answers. Still another limitation is the somewhat restricted ability of the test score, based on a specific set of items, to predict more general and complex behavioral patterns, as might be the case in personnel selection, educational placement, and the classification of psychiatric patients for psychotherapy.

For a review of the major points discussed in this section, see "Summing It Up: Objective Self-Report Techniques." Next we will consider projective techniques of personality assessment.

Projective Techniques: Assessing Personality Indirectly

Projective techniques of personality assessment involve asking individuals to respond to ambiguous test stimuli with no apparent meaning (Viglione & Rivera, 2003). The underlying assumption of projective techniques is that the meaning the person projects onto the ambiguous stimuli indicates the individual's unconscious feelings, needs, desires, attitudes, motives, and other core personality aspects (Frank, 1939). Thus, information about the individual's personality is revealed without the person realizing it (Murphy & Davidshofer, 2005). From this perspective, the major advantage of projective

Summing It Up *Objective Self-Report Techniques*

Basic Logic	To measure personality via completion of a test with standardized procedures for taking the test as well as for scoring and interpreting it.
Basic Types	Single-dimension personality tests measure one aspect of personality at a time. Example: California F Scale measures authoritarianism.
	Multiple-dimension personality tests measure several aspects of personality at a time. Example: Minnesota Multiphasic Personality Inventory (MMPI) measures 10 dimensions and has 4 validity scales.
Response Sets	Systematic responses to tests that do not reflect the content of the items but, rather, a pattern of acquiescence or social desirability.
Strengths	The standardized nature of these tests makes it possible to treat everyone the same and minimize the subjective decisions on the part of those scoring the tests.
Limitations	A heavy emphasis on self-report information and the standardization of procedures restrict freedom of response.

techniques is that the abstract nature of the stimuli minimizes the likelihood of an individual guessing what the test is all about and trying to respond in a socially desirable manner.

Although there is a variety of projective techniques, they share the following characteristic features (Rotter, 1954; Trull & Phares, 2001; Viglione & Rivera, 2003):

- *Ambiguous test stimuli*. In projective techniques, the testing stimuli are relatively ambiguous. For example, they might include responding to a series of inkblots or completing a series of sentences (e.g., "If I were president, . . .").
- *Indirect method*. Instead of responding directly to items on objective self-report techniques (e.g., "Are you anxious in public places?"), projective techniques take a much more indirect approach to personality assessment by requiring the individual to respond to ambiguous test stimuli. This makes individuals less certain as to the actual purpose of the test and makes it more difficult for them to modify their responses accordingly.
- *Freedom of response*. Projective techniques allow for more freedom in responses to the test stimuli. Because the stimuli are ambiguous, there are no "right" or "wrong" responses. As an example, the inkblot presented in Figure 3.7 on p. 115 could be perceived as almost anything.
- *Subjective nature of scoring procedures*. Although attempts have been made to standardize their scoring, a considerable amount of subjective interpretation of the responses by those scoring the tests is a common characteristic of projective techniques. For example, depending on the theoretical viewpoint of the individual scoring the test, a response of "If I were president, I would get rid of all the rules for paying taxes" could be interpreted as an expression of an individual's sense of freedom or an indication of a lack of responsibility.

Types of Projective Techniques: Many Methods of Indirect Assessment

An individual's personality is assessed and interpreted through the use of projective techniques by analyzing the themes and patterns of responses generated in reaction to the ambiguous stimuli contained in the test. One of the most interesting aspects of these techniques is the diversity of the stimuli employed. According to

Figure 2.2   A TAT card used in projective assessment
Reprinted by permission of the publishers from Henry A. Murray, THEMATIC APPERCEPTION TEST, Card 12 F, Cambridge, Mass.: Harvard University Press, Copyright © 1943 by the President and Fellows of Harvard College, © 1971 by Henry A. Murray

Lindzey (1961), projective techniques can be classified into the following five general categories:

- With **association techniques**, the individual is presented with a test stimulus and then asked to respond with the first word, thought, or feeling that comes to mind. The most famous example of this type of technique is the Rorschach Inkblot Test (Rorschach, 1942), discussed in more detail in Chapter 3.
- **Completion techniques** require individuals to complete a test stimulus that is presented to them unfinished. An example is the Rotter Incomplete Sentences Test (Rotter, Lah, & Rafferty, 1992; Rotter & Rafferty, 1950), where the individual is asked to complete a series of sentences such as: "Men seem to be anxious . . ." and "My secret desire is . . ."

- **Choice or ordering projective techniques** require the individual to select from or arrange in some preferred order a set of test stimuli. For example, the Szondi Test (Szondi, 1944) requires the respondents to select from a set of pictures those liked the most and those liked the least.
- **Expressive projective techniques** require individual expression through such activities as taking the role of another individual or drawing a picture. For example, in the Kinetic House-Tree-Person Test (Burns, 1987), the individual is asked to draw a picture of a person "doing something."
- **Constructive projective techniques** require the individual to create something, such as a story based on the test stimuli.

For a closer look at a famous constructive projective technique written about in over 1,800 articles (Groth-Marnat, 2003), consider the material presented in "A Closer Look" below.

A Closer Look

The Thematic Apperception Test: Of Pictures and Personality

The **Thematic Apperception Test** (**TAT**; Morgan & Murray, 1935; H. A. Murray, 1938, 1943) was developed by the famous American personality psychologist Henry Murray and colleagues at the Harvard Psychological Clinic and is based on Murray's (1938) theory of needs.

Administering the TAT

The TAT consists of 19 cards containing black-and-white pictures of an individual or individuals in rather ambiguous situations, plus one blank card. For example, the TAT card in Figure 2.2 depicts a scene where a much older woman is standing near, but behind, and looking past the shoulder of a much younger woman, who is looking off to the side. During the test, the individual is presented with each picture separately and is asked by the examiner to make up a story about what is

going on in the picture by telling what has led up to this moment in the story, what is happening now, what will happen next, and what the individuals in the pictures may be feeling, thinking, or saying to each other. The logic underlying the TAT is that important aspects of the individual's personality will be revealed by the nature of the stories created from these ambiguous pictures.

Scoring and Interpreting the TAT

Although alternative scoring procedures (Thompson, 1986; Westen, Barends, Leigh, Mendel, & Silbert, 1988) exist, according to Murray's procedures (Cohen & Swerdlik, 2002; Groth-Marnat, 2003; H. A. Murray, 1943), scoring the TAT involves evaluating the following five different aspects of the stories:

- *The hero.* Scoring for the **hero** involves identifying who is the central character(s) in the story. In reading the response to the TAT card depicting the images of the older and younger woman, it is clear that the younger woman is the hero, since all of the action seems to revolve around her.
- *Needs of the hero.* For Murray, it was also critical to identify the **needs**, motives, and desires of the hero. In the card containing the images of the older and younger woman, the hero seems to be expressing an intensive need for regaining control of her life and a desire to be independent.
- *Identifying the presses.* A **press** refers to any important environmental factor that may influence or interfere with the needs of the hero. For our female hero, a very important press is the older woman. Other presses might involve particular authority figures (e.g., parents or a boss), external obstacles (e.g., the lock on the door is broken), or physical disabilities (e.g., being sick or injured).
- *Scoring for themes.* Scoring for *themes* in TAT stories involves noting the nature of the interplay and conflict between the needs and presses, the types of emotions elicited by this conflict, and the way the conflict is resolved. A clear theme found in the response to the depiction of the older and younger woman is the struggle between the need of the younger woman to be free and the press created by the manipulative tendencies of the older woman.
- *Scoring for outcome.* Scoring for the *outcome* of the story involves analyzing how the stories end by noting a happy versus unhappy ending and

assessing the extent to which the ending is controlled by the strengths of the hero or forces (i.e., presses) in the environment. The outcome of the story represented in this particular card involves an unhappy ending with determining environmental forces.

Interpreting the TAT involves the overall assessment of the individual's personality from the general pattern of responses to the TAT cards in terms of what needs, motives, and modes of interacting with other people are expressed. The female hero's responses to the scenario depicted in this card and the other TAT cards stress the person's need to have control over her life and her feelings of being manipulated in her interactions with others.

Evaluating Projective Techniques: Strengths and Limitations

Following is a summary of the characteristic strengths and limitations of the projective techniques.

Characteristic Strengths The major strength of projective techniques is the freedom of response they allow. Their indirect method and the ambiguous nature of the stimuli make it possible to minimize any attempts by individuals to modify their responses in accordance with what they think the test is measuring and what the examiner supposedly wants to hear. Finally, because projective techniques attempt to measure many deep-seated core aspects of personality at the same time, the assumption is that a more global and meaningful assessment of the individual's personality emerges.

Characteristic Limitations Because of the tremendous freedom of response made available, the scoring procedures of projective techniques are oftentimes extremely complex. This complexity introduces many subjective decisions on the part of the examiner, which contribute to the characteristically low reliability coefficients of these techniques. The global nature of projective techniques also creates problems of validity in terms of what is actually being measured by these tests. If they supposedly measure different core aspects and dimensions of personality, which ones are they and what criterion measures should be used to assess their

Summing It Up *Projective Techniques*

Basic Logic	To assess personality by analyzing patterns of projected meaning onto ambiguous stimuli
Characteristic Features	Ambiguous test stimuli
	Considerable response freedom permitted by indirect assessment
	High degree of subjective interpretation
Response Pattern Types Analyzed	Idea association elicited by test stimuli
	Completion of unfinished test stimuli
	Choices among and ordering of test stimuli
	Expressive behavior in response to test stimuli
	Story construction based on test stimuli (example: TAT)
Strengths	The highly ambiguous nature of the test stimuli allows for a high degree of response flexibility while guarding against the presenting of socially desirable response patterns.
Limitations	The highly ambiguous nature of the test stimuli introduces subjective interpretation. The nature of the personality dimensions being assessed is not clear.

validity? Finally, there is a fundamental question of the validity of the process of projection as an indirect means of assessing personality. Specifically, to what extent can the ability of examiners be trusted to interpret accurately what the individual "really means" when responding to ambiguous stimuli?

For a review of the major points discussed in this section, see "Summing It Up: Projective Techniques" opposite. Next we will consider behavioral techniques of personality assessment.

Behavioral Techniques: Assessing Personality Directly

In sharp contrast to assessing constructs (e.g., traits or needs) that characterize the objective self-report and projective techniques, **behavioral techniques** of assessment emphasize the systematic observation of behavior as the basis for assessing the personality of individuals. Because behavior can be determined by many factors, personality psychologists using these techniques to study personality attributes (e.g., shyness) also focus on what cues in the environment elicit the behavior (e.g., being approached by a stranger), what thoughts and feelings influence the behavior (e.g., anxiety about being evaluated by that person), and what the consequences are for engaging in such behavior (e.g., reducing the anxiety by being a "wallflower"). Thus, behavioral techniques attempt to assess directly the more observable (e.g., actions) and less observable (e.g., thoughts and feelings) dimensions influenced by personality.

Types of Behavioral Assessment Techniques: Looking at What People are Doing

Although there is a variety of behavioral techniques (O'Brien, McGrath, & Haynes, 2003), they all share a characteristic emphasis on assessing behavior and the factors influencing it. Four categories of behavioral techniques are direct observations, self-monitoring, behavior inventories, and cognitive assessment.

Direct Observation Techniques   As the name implies, **direct observation techniques** involve obtaining actual samples of the individual's behavior (Cohen & Swerdlik, 2002). Such observations can be obtained in a variety of formats. **Naturalistic observations** involve viewing the individual's behavior in real-life settings (e.g., psychiatric hospitals, work settings, and classrooms). **Controlled observations** involve evaluating behavior in more structured situations (i.e., a laboratory room). For example, to study gender differences in aggression in children, a personality psychologist might observe the aggressive play of boys and girls in the playground or through a one-way mirror while they play with toys in a laboratory room. **Role playing**, which combines the naturalistic and controlled observational methods, involves a person playing an assigned role (e.g., having to terminate someone's employment) for the purpose of assessing the individual's behavior in various situations (e.g., assessing compassion in office managers).

Self-Monitoring Techniques   Whereas direct observation techniques typically involve others (e.g., therapists, researchers, teachers, or nursing staff) recording the observations, **self-monitoring techniques** require individuals to maintain observational records of their own behavior (e.g., noting when and where feelings of anxiety appear). An advantage of self-monitoring techniques is that they can be applied to a variety of different types of behavior (e.g., eating, sleeping, arguing, feeling anxious, talking on the phone). Another advantage is that they are very convenient and flexible in that they can be done almost anywhere and at almost any time. This is in contrast to direct observation techniques that require the presence of an outside observer.

Threats to the validity of self-monitoring techniques are created when observing one's own behavior results in a modification of that behavior (Aiken & Groth-Marnat, 2006; Pine, 2005). However, an interesting side-benefit of self-monitoring is that simply monitoring a behavior can be therapeutic by providing a concrete record of, for example, what, when, and how much an individual eats, as well as serving an incentive to modify the behavior in a constructive manner (Cohen & Swerdlik, 2002; Comer, 2007; Otten, 2004; Plante, 2005). For example, dieters are often encouraged to keep a daily journal of all food consumed (e.g., noting what is eaten and when it is eaten). This self-report technique can result in a reduction of food consumed by the individual. To illustrate this side-benefit of self-monitoring, try the exercise outlined in the feature "You Can Do It" on p. 60.

You Can Do It

Looking Over Your Own Shoulder: An Exercise in Self-Monitoring

If you are interested in gaining some information about your personality and why you do some of the things you do, try your hand at this simple self-monitoring exercise. Select some behavior that is important to you. Eating, drinking, smoking, studying, watching TV, surfing the Internet, or interacting with friends are all options that will work just fine. For the next several days, note very carefully when you engage in each of these behaviors and what were the surrounding conditions (e.g., what was happening at that time or just before you started doing the target behavior). Also note what happened when you engaged in this behavior. For example, did you stop studying, feel better, avoid some unpleasant task, and/or have fun? Record all of this information in a notebook, PDA, or other computer. After about a week of self-monitoring, go back over your records to gain some possible insight into why you do some of the things you do. What you find may surprise you!

A Closer Look

What Are You Afraid Of? A Look at a Fear Survey Schedule

On a scale of 1 (not at all afraid) to 5 (very afraid), indicate the level of fear you feel towards the 20 objects and situations listed here.

_____ 1. Sharp objects
_____ 2. Dead bodies
_____ 3. Being self-conscious
_____ 4. Mental illness
_____ 5. Being in an airplane
_____ 6. Worms
_____ 7. Rats and mice
_____ 8. Being alone
_____ 9. Giving a speech
_____ 10. Roller coasters
_____ 11. Being with drunks
_____ 12. Heights
_____ 13. Failing a test
_____ 14. Death
_____ 15. Meeting strangers
_____ 16. Snakes
_____ 17. Dark places
_____ 18. Thunderstorms
_____ 19. Blood
_____ 20. Crowded places

Adapted from Geer (1965).

Self-Report Behavioral Inventories   Self-report behavioral inventories typically require individuals to indicate the extent to which they have engaged in a series of specific behaviors in different situations. The "You can do it" activity above is a simple example of such a behavioral inventory. Another good example is what is called a *fear survey schedule* (Geer, 1965; Wolpe & Lang, 1964). In general, **fear survey schedules** include a list of common situations or objects to which individuals are asked to indicate their level of fear for each item. See "A Closer Look" for an example of a fear survey schedule.

Self-report behavioral inventories assess a wide variety of behaviors such as depression, assertiveness, and ability to resolve conflicts, to name just a few (Groth-Marnat, 2003). Possible threats to the reliability and validity of self-report behavior inventories exist because they tend to rely heavily on a respondent's memory and willingness to admit to such behaviors.

Cognitive Behavioral Assessment   **Cognitive events** are activities occurring in the person's brain that influence behavior. Techniques of **cognitive behavioral**

assessment attempt to measure a person's thoughts or feelings while in a particular situation. The technique of **thought sampling** requires the individual to monitor the thoughts (e.g., "All those people are evaluating me") experienced while in certain situations (e.g., giving a speech) that can be used to explain the observed behavior (e.g., fumbling over words). **Self-statement inventories** require respondents to read a series of statements describing the types of thoughts people may have and then to indicate the extent to which they endorse these statements for themselves. Two sample items from the Automatic Thoughts Questionnaire (Hollon & Kendall, 1980) are:

1. I feel like I'm up against the world.
2. I wish I were a better person.

Being able to assess the extent to which a person endorses such statements might help explain why a behavior pattern characteristic of depression is exhibited.

Evaluating Behavioral Assessment Techniques: Strengths and Limitations

A summary of the characteristic strengths and limitations of the behavior assessment techniques is presented next.

Characteristic Strengths A principal advantage of the techniques of behavioral assessment is that the emphasis on both overt (e.g., actions) and covert (e.g., thoughts) forms of behaviors clarifies the importance of environmental and cognitive variables in the study of personality. The behavioral techniques also represent a diverse collection of methods having the flexibility to be used almost anywhere (e.g., home, work, school) and by individuals with minimal formal training in personality assessment (e.g., truck drivers, office managers, high school students).

Characteristic Limitations One limitation associated with a variety of behavioral assessment techniques is the lack of standards or guidelines to indicate which behaviors are worthy of observation. For example, in studying depression or conflict resolution, what environmental, situational, and cognitive variables are of critical importance and should be viewed by the therapist or monitored by the client? Another limitation is the variety of potential biases associated with direct observations of behaviors made by an observer or with self-observations made by the individual. For example, the mere fact that one is being observed tends to alter the nature of one's actions. In addition, different observers may view the same behavior (e.g., avoiding eye contact) differently (e.g., shyness vs. boredom). Finally, potential biases in the ability of individuals to assess their own thoughts and behavior in a reliable and valid manner are also a limitation of certain techniques of behavioral assessment. For example, individuals may be too embarrassed to indicate all of the situations that actually make them fearful or the rather illogical nature of many of their thoughts.

For a review of the major points presented in this section, see "Summing It Up: Behavioral Assessment Techniques." Next, we will consider psychophysiological techniques of personality assessment.

Summing It Up *Behavioral Assessment Techniques*

Basic Logic	The assessment of observable behaviors and the environmental cues, cognitive processes, and behavioral consequences affecting them
Basic Types	Behavioral assessment techniques differ in the nature of the behaviors observed. Included in these techniques are: • The direct observation of behavior in naturalistic, controlled, and role-playing settings. • The self-monitoring of personal behavior and the factors affecting them. • The self-reporting of behavioral reactions retrospectively. • The assessment of cognitive processes affecting behavior.
Strengths	They represent a rather diverse collection of techniques emphasizing the direct and systematic assessment of many different forms of behavior.
Limitations	There is a lack of specific guidelines for what behaviors should be observed. There is a tendency to alter one's behavior when being systematically observed.

Psychophysiological Techniques: The Measurement of Bodily Processes

The essential logic of the psychophysiological techniques of personality assessment is that certain aspects of the individual's personality (e.g., aggression, anxiety, or risk-taking) are related to various bodily processes (e.g., blood chemistry, hormonal levels, heart rate). **Psychophysiological techniques** of assessment are characterized by their ability to measure a variety of physiological changes occurring "underneath the skin" and linking them with various interpersonal (Lieberman & Eisenberger, 2006; Taylor et al., 2002), cognitive (Cacioppo, Berntson, & Crites, 1996; Ito, Larsen, Smith, & Cacioppo, 2002; Mitchell, Mason, Macrae, & Banaji, 2006), and emotional (Ambady, Chiao, Chiu, & Deldin, 2006; Davidson & Irwin, 2002; Gross, 1999; LeDoux, 2002) aspects of behavior and personality differences (Cacioppo et al., 2002; Cacioppo, Visser, & Pickett, 2006; Eysenck, 1990; Nyborg, 1997; Zuckerman, 2005).

Types of Psychophysiological Assessment Techniques: Looking from the Inside Out

Although we will discuss the use of psychophysiological techniques of assessment again in more detail in Chapter 8, in this section we will round out our discussion of the different categories of personality assessment by presenting a survey of some of the more frequently used psychophysiological techniques in the study of personality (Geen, 1997; Gross, 1999; Nyborg, 1997; Stern, Ray, & Quigley, 2001; Zuckerman, 2005).

Electrophysiological Measures: Assessment that "Gets Under Your Skin" Although there is a variety of electrophysiological assessment techniques, they all measure some aspects of an underlying bodily process. Following are three common electrophysiological assessment techniques used in the study of personality:

- The **electrocardiogram (ECG)** is an instrument that assesses changes in electrical activity of the heart and, thus, makes it possible to assess heart rate (Kring et al., 2007). Changes in heart rate are associated with different levels of arousal and excitement, as well as indicating cardiac disorders. Personality researchers have used ECG measures

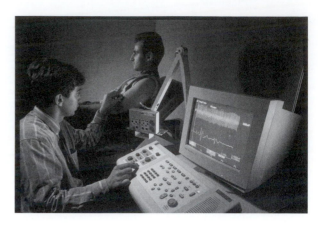

Personality psychologists employ a number of electrophysiological assessment techniques, including EMG, ECG, and EDA, to "get under the skin" of individuals to investigate how physiological processes are related to personality processes.

extensively to study the relationship between coronary heart disease and personality factors (Brannon & Feist, 2000).

- The **electromyograph (EMG)** is a technique that measures muscular activity associated with muscle tension and relaxation. The EMG is used extensively as a therapeutic technique to help individuals suffering from excessive stress and anxiety learn to relax by receiving muscle relaxation training (Brannon & Feist, 2000; Comer, 2007).
- Techniques assessing **electrodermal activity (EDA)** note changes occurring on the skin's surface in response to different emotional states (Stern et al., 2001). A frequently assessed EDA is **galvanic skin response (GSR)**. GSR is a measure of the skin's level of moisture (i.e., "sweat") in response to various physical and emotional states and is assessed using a **galvanometer**. A somewhat controversial topic is the accuracy of the GSR when used in the context of a polygraph ("lie detector") test (Cohen & Swerdlik, 2002; Jones & Terris, 1991). At the base of this controversy is the notion that the polygraph does not really detect lies but detects those bodily changes (e.g., perspiration or increased respiration rate) associated with the arousal assumed to be associated with telling a lie (Granhag & Vrij, 2005).

Biochemical Assessment: The Measurement of the Biological Bases of Personality In addition to electrophysiological measures, psychophysiological assessment of personality involves measuring an assortment of biochemical processes (Zuckerman, 1995, 1998, 2005). These biochemical measures include:

- Examining blood samples. This allows for assessing the levels of neurotransmitters such as monamine oxidase (MAO), serotonin, and dopamine (Canli, 2006; Zuckerman, 1994, 1998, 2005). Neurotransmitters affect the operation and communication of the neurological system in the brain. For example, MAO is a contributing factor in the desire for seeking excessive exciting stimulation associated with the "thrill-seeking personality" (Zuckerman, 2005).
- Measuring hormones such as testosterone and cortisol (Canli, 2006; Zuckerman, 1998, 2005). Biochemical assessment of neurotransmitters and hormones can be obtained by analyzing cerebrospinal fluid (CSF), blood, saliva, or urine. Testosterone has been linked to dominance, aggressiveness, and various forms of antisocial behavior (Dabbs, 2000) while cortisol is associated with coping and resistance to stress (Sinha, 2006).
- Analyzing the individual's genetic makeup. Genetic assessment is an important tool in determining the inherited dimensions of personality (Benjamin, Ebstein, & Belmaker, 2002; Plomin & Caspi, 1999; Plomin, DeFriies, McClearn, & McGuffin, 2001; Rowe, 1997; Tooby & Cosmides, 2005).

Cortical Measures: Assessment of Brain Activity
Cortical measures assess the neurological activity associated with different regions of the brain in response to various forms of stimulation (e.g., visual images, written scenarios). Three of the more common forms of cortical measures used in the study of personality follow:

- The **electroencephalograph (EEG)** is an instrument for assessing the electrical activity of the brain occurring in the form of various "brain waves" (wavelengths displayed on a visual monitor). A computer is used to convert the electrical activity to this visual display. While different wavelength patterns are not used as a direct measure of specific traits, researchers have associated them with personality characteristics such as extraversion and impulsivity (Geen, 1997; Matthews, Deary, & Whiteman, 2003; Zuckerman, 1991, 1997, 2005), with different states of arousal such as, sleep and excitement, and with certain

psychiatric disorders such as antisocial personality disorder (individuals with this were previously referred to as "psychopaths") and schizophrenia (Nevid et al., 2000).

- The **positron emission tomography (PET)** technique uses an X-ray-like scanning device to assess the rate at which brain cells use energy-providing substances (e.g. sugar, oxygen) when responding to stimulation – the faster the rate, the more activity associated with the cells in that area of the brain (Kring et al., 2007). A computer is used to create a visual image of the brain on a monitor that highlights in different colors the rate of energy used in different regions. Researchers have used PET scans to examine what areas of the brain are associated with modeling behavior to help understand how individuals process the actions of others (Puce & Perrett, 2004).
- The **functional magnetic resonance imaging (fMRI)** technique is similar to that of the PET scan but assesses the magnetic properties of blood before and after the oxygen is used as energy, in reference to an external magnet contained in a scanning device that takes rapid images of the brain while it is "at work" (i.e., as the brain is using energy). The greater the difference in the magnetic properties, the more activity in those brain

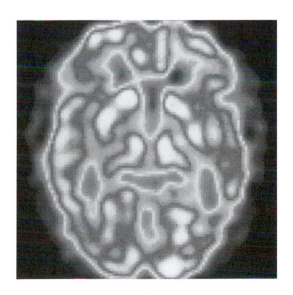

Personality psychologists employ a number of different measures of cortical activity, such as this image of the brain based on the PET technique, to "get into the head" of individuals to study the link between brain activity and personality processes.

cells responding to the external stimulation. Again, a computer is used to create a visual image of the brain on a monitor that highlights those areas of the brain with the greatest energy use. Researchers have used the fMRI technique to assess brain activity of individuals with problematic personalities (e.g., drug dependency, antisocial personality disorder; Raine, Lencz, Bihrle, & LaCasse, 2000) and healthy-functioning personalities (Herrington et al., 2005) in response to stressful stimuli, and to assess the cortical location associated with romantic love (Aron et al., 2005).

Evaluating Psychophysiological Assessment Techniques: Strengths and Limitations

Characteristic Strengths   A major strength of psychophysiological techniques is that they provide different

methods to assess bodily reactions, many of which can be measured at the same time, while avoiding the shortcomings associated with relying on self-report techniques. For example, researchers investigating aggressive adolescents simultaneously assess EEG and GSR recordings (Gilbert, Gilbert, Johnson, & McColloch, 1991). In addition, these techniques can be used in conjunction with other types of assessment techniques. For example, a researcher can monitor the heart rate of an individual in response to the stories being constructed from TAT pictures to assess the level of stress produced. These techniques have made it possible for personality psychologists to examine systematically possible biological bases of personality (see Chapter 8).

Characteristic Limitations   A frequent criticism of psychophysiological techniques of assessment is that any given bodily reaction can have several different meanings. For example, increased heart rate is

Summing It Up *Psychophysiological Techniques*

Basic Logic	The assessment of bodily reactions that can be linked to personality processes
Basic Types	Psychophysiological assessment techniques differ in the nature of the bodily process observed. Included in these techniques are: ● Electrophysiological measures assess underlying bodily processes: – Electrical activity of the heart (i.e., ECG). – Muscular activity and tension (i.e., EMG). – Changes in the skin's surface (i.e., EDA), such as assessing the level of skin moisture (i.e., GSR). ● Biochemical measures assess various forms of biochemical elements through the body: – Neurotransmitters, by examining blood samples. – Hormones, by examining saliva or urine. – The genetic properties of individuals. ● Cortical measures assess neurological activity in various regions of the brain in response to stimulation: – Electrical activity of the brain (i.e., EEG). – Consumption rate of energy-providing substances (i.e., PET). – Magnetic properties associated with the use of oxygen in the blood (i.e., fMRI).
Strengths	They provide a variety of techniques that make it possible to begin to link personality with biological processes.
Limitations	The rather ambiguous nature of the meaning of various bodily processes, the relative ease by which these processes can be altered, and individual variation in these processes are characteristic limitations.

characteristic of feelings of fear, love, happiness, and pain. Another limitation is that it is relatively easy to modify bodily processes and invalidate the readings obtained from many of these psychophysiological techniques. For example, being nervous about taking a polygraph test can increase the muscle tension of a person telling the truth. Another problem is that many different areas of the brain perform more than one function. For example, the frontal region is associated with abstract reasoning and interpretation of emotional stimuli. Finally, variation in the way individuals respond physiologically to the same stimuli can contaminate the results of research. For example, because some individuals might respond primarily by sweating when anxious while others may respond with increased muscle tension, a researcher using only a GSR measure when studying anxiety might mistakenly assume that an individual is very calm even though the person may have a great deal of muscle tension.

This concludes our discussion of the psychophysiological techniques. A review of the major points discussed in this section is presented in "Summing It Up: Psychophysiological Techniques" opposite.

Which Type of Technique to Use? Some General Guidelines and Closing Remarks

After such a survey of the various techniques of assessment, there is a tendency to wonder which one is the "best." In fact, there is no such thing as the "best technique." Each technique has its characteristic strengths and limitations. The determining factors for which assessment technique to use are the nature of the question being asked and the dimension of personality being assessed. For example, to study the effectiveness of a treatment program designed to increase an individual's assertive behavior, one of the behavioral techniques should be used. To study the interrelationship between various traits, a multiple-dimension objective self-report technique might be most useful. An even better possibility is to make an attempt to combine assessment approaches. For an example of some research that employed a number of different types of measures to investigate a rather interesting question, consider the material presented in "At the Cutting Edge of Personality Psychology: A Multi-Method Approach to the Assessment of Romantic Passion."

AT THE CUTTING EDGE OF PERSONALITY PSYCHOLOGY

A Multi-Method Approach to the Assessment of Romantic Passion

Searching for Feelings of the Heart in the Head: A Multi-Method Perspective

Whether of not you have been lucky enough to have experienced the feelings of intense pleasure associated with the early stages of being in love, a question that has been on the minds of many across the ages is from where these interesting feelings come. In response to such an age-old concern, recently individuals from a number of different fields have come together using a variety of assessment techniques in an attempt to answer this fascinating question. An excellent example of research that involves the use of different types of assessment techniques to investigate the areas of the brain associated with the heightened pleasure and euphoria characteristic of early-stage intense romantic love is the work of psychologist Arthur Aron, of the State University of New York at Stony Brook, anthropologist Helen Fisher, of Rutgers University, and their colleagues from radiology, neurology, and psychology (Aron et al., 2005).

The participants in this study were 10 women and 7 men, ranging in age between 18 and 26 years (average age = 20.6 years), who were recruited from within and around the New York City area by word of mouth and with flyers seeking individuals who were currently intensely in love. As a condition of their participation, the participants were asked to provide a photograph of the individual for whom he or she had the intense romantic feelings (positive stimulus object) and a similar photograph of another individual of the same age and sex for which the participant had emotionally neutral feelings (neutral stimulus object). All of the photographs were digitized and standardized to show the head only. Finally, as part of their participation, the participants were not to be taking antidepressants, were given an informed consent statement, and received $50.00 for their participation.

Three different types of measures were used to assess the intensity of the individual's feelings of early romantic love: oral interview, objective self-report, and fMRI. More specifically, the initial assessment technique used in this research was the oral interview, in which one of the researchers interviewed the participants individually to establish the duration, intensity, and range of his or her feelings of romantic love. Next, the individuals were asked to complete two objective self-report inventories: the Passionate Love Scale (PLS; Hatfield & Sprecher, 1986) and the Affect Intensity Measure (AIM; Larsen, Diener, & Cropanzano, 1987). The PLS assesses the degree of self-reported feelings of passion an individual has for his or her lover and includes such items as: "I want [name of lover] physically, emotionally, and mentally" and "Sometimes I cannot control my thoughts; they are obsessively on [name of lover]." The AIM is designed to assess the varying degree to which individuals experience emotions intensely and includes such items as: "I get overly enthusiastic" and "Sad movies deeply touch me." To assess cortical activity associated with feelings of early-stage romantic love, an fMRI was used. During the fMRI assessment, each participant was shown the image of the beloved and the neutral acquaintance for 30 seconds. The order in which the images of the beloved and neutral acquaintance were shown varied across the participants. After viewing each image, the participants were asked to count backwards from a different 4-digit number by 7 (e.g., 8472, 8465, 8458, . . .) for 40 seconds for the positive stimulus and 20 seconds for the neutral stimulus. The counting task was designed to eliminate any residual cortical arousal between the viewing of the two different stimuli, and it was determined from previous research that it would take a little longer to eliminate the residual arousal for the positive stimuli than the neutral stimuli.

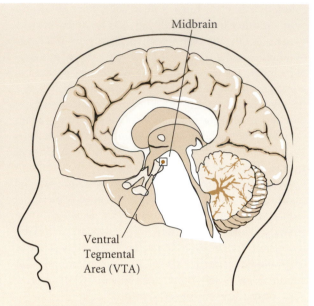

Figure 2.3   The location in the midbrain of the ventral tegmental area (VTA)
Source: Aron et al. (2005)

As can be seen in Figure 2.3, a summary of the fMRI recordings across all of the participants indicated that the ventral tegmental area (VTA) area of the midbrain, an area associated with feelings of pleasure and reward, was activated to a greater degree when the participants were viewing the positive stimuli (i.e., image of the beloved) than the neutral (i.e., emotionally neutral acquaintance). To make sure that this increased cortical activity in the VTA was linked to feelings of passionate love, and not some other emotion (e.g., excitement), the researchers checked that the increased neurological activity in this area was positively correlated with the scores on the PLS. The results also indicated that while the participants did show more arousal to the positive stimuli in this region, the magnitude of the response was positively correlated with the individual's AIM score. Such a pattern of results suggests a strong trait difference in how individuals experience a universal emotion such as love and supports the romantic idea that although the location of feelings of romantic love may be in the same cortical area for many individuals, each individual experiences such feelings in their own unique way. Finally, a lack of correlation among the AIM scores, PLS scores, sex of the participant, and duration of the relationship revealed in the interview suggests that it is the intensity of the feelings, not just the duration of being in love, that characterizes such early-stage intense romantic love.

While interesting in their own right, the results of this research are also highly illustrative of the principal point made earlier of using different assessment techniques within the same research project. This is critical because it serves to strengthen the validity of the results by providing convergent evidence obtained through very different sources. In addition, by using the fMRI, a technique frequently used to assess cortical arousal to a variety of other stimuli, the results of the present study seem to suggest that there is converging evidence that the VTA is not only associated with feelings of intense romantic love but linked to a pleasure center of the brain associated with the experience of a variety of highly pleasurable stimuli. For example, thoughts of money (Elliot, Newman, Longe, & Deakin, 2003) and the consumption of chocolate (Small, Zatorre, Dagher, Evans, & Jones-Gotman, 2001) serve to increase neurological activity in the VTA. And the injection of cocaine has also been shown to stimulate the VTA in fMRI studies with humans (Breiter et al., 1997),

which has led some researchers to conclude that the intense feelings and behavior of romantic love are similar to those activated by the reward qualities of cocaine, such as exhilaration, excessive energy, sleeplessness, and loss of appetite (Fisher, 1998), which serves to give new meaning to the phrase "addicted to love."

Thus, this collective body of research serves to link the study of personality and individual differences to many other diverse areas of study. Such "cutting edge" research is at the core of building a more comprehensive understanding of personality and individual differences in an attempt to work with researchers from different areas and using different techniques to answer some of life's most interesting questions. And while this cutting edge research may serve to demystify the metaphoric feelings of romance of the heart by noting that such feelings are actually located in a very specific area of the brain, I hope that it does not serve to dilute your sense of romanticism, because, after all, as anyone who has ever been fortunate enough to have such wonderful feelings will tell you, when you are experiencing a sense of intense romantic love, the location of their origin really does not matter all that much.

Computer Adaptive Testing (CAT): Computer Technology and Personality Assessment

Going beyond serving to help create visual images of cortical activity, the use of computers in the area of personality assessment is changing almost daily. Computers are used to help in the development of personality tests (e.g., the creation of test-item banks) and their administration (e.g., responding to items from a personality test presented on a computer screen). However, a significant use of **computer adaptive testing** (CAT) is in the interpretation of test results, which can be done at several different levels (Atlis, Hahn, & Butcher, 2006). At the most basic level, computers can be programmed to calculate the scores of tests. An example might be to compute separate scores on the various subscales of the

MMPI. At a more complex level, computers can be programmed to provide a printout containing written comments that are linked to certain test scores. As an example, a clinical psychologist working in a hospital might receive a computer-generated written summary, based on the MMPI responses of a patient who is to receive a gastric bypass operation, that describes the individual's personality tendencies and emotional condition as part of a presurgical psychological evaluation (Butcher, 2003). Based on the individual's pattern of scores and MMPI profile, the computer-generated written summary would then be used by the physician and therapist to assess the individual's potential psychological adjustment to the surgery and make recommendations for psychological counseling, rehabilitation programs, or other medical and emotional considerations.

At an even more complex level, computers can be programmed so that even the interpretation is interactive. A student seeking vocational guidance, for example, can sit at a computer terminal and, in a sense, engage in a dialogue with the computer (Aiken, 2003). With the help of specialized software designed to ask the individual a series of questions and to provide information based on the response to these questions, the student can also ask questions of the computer to obtain specific information. For example, to match her personality with certain occupations, the computer might direct her to complete a series of personality tests, an occupational interest inventory, and a demographic questionnaire. The questionnaire might request such information as her expected salary, expected hourly workweek, and preferred region of the country in which to work, along with eliciting other personal interest information such as preferences in the arts and leisure activities – all of which reflect characteristic features of her personality.

From the data provided, the computer program would then generate a written interpretation. And because the computer can be programmed to be connected to a variety of other data bases, after receiving this information, the student might then ask the computer questions about career prospects in a specific field (e.g., community nursing) or other related fields (e.g., international health-care administrator, pharmaceutical sales representative) in the context of projected changes in employment opportunities over time with respect to local, regional, national, and global economic and political trends.

Thus, through this interactive dialogue with the computer, this individual could begin to make present and future career plans based specifically on her personality characteristics and other personal preferences. After several sessions with the computer program, she might seek the advice of an experienced career counselor to help sift through all of the information provided in the computer-generated summary, answer any personalized questions, or address any personal concerns the individual might have, such as how her life circumstances (e.g., being a single parent), motivational tendencies (e.g., preferring to work in the evening), and economic factors (e.g., only being able to go to school part-time) might need to be integrated within the career options presented by the computer program.

For some firsthand experience with CAT career-based counseling, see the material presented in "You Can Do It."

You Can Do It

What Do You Want To Do with the Rest of Your Life: Getting Help with CAT Career-Based Counseling

You can get a head start on your career plans by taking advantage of a variety of CAT career-based counseling programs. One commonly used is the Educational Testing Services' System of Interactive Guidance (SIGI PLUS: www.ets.org/sigi/index.html). SIGI PLUS is a self-directed program designed to help individuals assess their values, interests, skills, and resources and then to relate this information to the nature of rewards (e.g., salary expectations), satisfactions (e.g., to improve the environment), activities (e.g., work outdoors), and other special requirements (e.g., have the summers off) they seek in a career.

In addition to SIGI and other similar CAT career-based counseling programs (e.g., National Career Assessment Service's Career Planning System: www.kuder.com/kcps.asp), other CAT career-based resources to examine include the Occupational Information Network (O*NET: www.doleta.gov/programs/onet) and the *Occupational Outlook Handbook* (*OOH*: www.stats.bls.gov/ocohome). O*NET is an electronic database that contains information on the skills, preparation, knowledge, abilities, and tasks associated with over 1,100 different occupations, while the *OOH* contains information on the current and projected employment rates for various occupations (e.g., school psychologist, aerospace engineer).

The use of CAT career-based counseling is an excellent example of how technology and the expression of personality characteristics and other forms of individuals differences can be combined to address one of the most important choices you will make – planning your career.

With the proliferation in the use of CAT, there has also been an increase in discussions of its potential advantages (e.g., increases in objectivity, standardization of procedures, and the efficiency of scoring the responses and interpreting the results) and disadvantages (e.g., computer-generated interpretations may be too general and too complicated to explain to clients; Atlis et al., 2006; Butcher, 2003), along with the development of guidelines for their use, such as the American Psychological Association's (APA's) *Guidelines for Computer-based Tests and Interpretations* (APA, 1986). Such guidelines provide standards for issues regarding the development, administration, and interpretation of computer-based testing and the dissemination of the information obtained from tests taken with the assistance of computers, as well as an assortment of related professional, legal, and ethical concerns. Going beyond such specific concerns of CAT, in the next section, we will consider some of the more pervasive ethical issues associated with the field of personality assessment.

Ethical Issues in Personality Assessment: Personal, Legal, and Social Concerns

As personality and other psychological tests become more widely used, their potential for misuse and abuse increases (Koocher & Rey-Casserly, 2003). In the closing section of this chapter, a discussion of some of the personal, legal, and social issues associated with the ethics of personality assessment is presented.

Personal Concerns: Protecting the Rights of the Individual

Invasion of Privacy

A major concern for many individuals taking personality tests is that they will unknowingly reveal things about themselves (Anastasi & Urbina, 1997) – an **invasion of privacy**. An example might be when a researcher is studying aggressive tendencies or a personnel manager is screening potential applicants for a propensity to steal. Whenever possible, individuals taking the test should be given a complete description of the purpose of the test and testing procedures in language that they can understand but without contaminating the results of the test (Koocher & Rey-Casserly, 2003). Under no circumstances should the individual be deliberately deceived or coerced into taking the tests under false pretenses. To deal with such ethical

concerns, the procedure of **informed consent** is practiced by responsible individuals using personality assessment techniques. Finally, all items on the test should be directly relevant to the specific testing purposes. For example, questions concerning religious or sexual attitudes should not be asked unless they have direct relevance to the job or task for which the testing is being conducted (Jones & Terris, 1991).

Confidentiality

The issue of **confidentiality** has to do with who will have access to the information obtained from the tests (Aiken, 2003; Anastasi & Urbina, 1997). To help ensure confidentiality, individuals should be told beforehand how the results will be used, that only those persons for whom the results have direct relevance will have access to them, and that permission from individuals must be granted prior to the results being released to any outside sources. Finally, it is the responsibility of those doing the testing to eliminate dated or obsolete information. For example, information located at a university counseling center about a student's level of depression during the freshman year should be eliminated after graduation.

Legal Concerns: Assessment and the Law

Whether used in clinics, universities, the military, or industry, personality assessment cannot be used if the items in or procedures of the test tend to discriminate against certain groups of individuals (Reynolds & Ramsey, 2003). For example, individuals from certain minority and ethnic groups might score lower on a management selection test than Caucasian individuals because the group's cultural norms dictate that input from various family elders be considered before a decision is made regarding the group members. Such people might score lower because their tendency to avoid making individual decisions could make them appear more indecisive as potential managers than those from individualistic cultures that emphasize independent decision-making strategies. Thus, the difference in scores might reflect cultural beliefs about group interactions more than actual management ability. Such a state of affairs is considered discrimination against these minority individuals when only those scoring high on the test are admitted to the company's management training program.

Equal Rights Legislation

The Equal Employment Opportunity Act of 1972, as well as guidelines published by the **Equal Employment Opportunity Commission** (**EEOC**) and other court decisions, have done much to reduce discrimination. With respect to testing, these laws state that institutions and organizations must be able to prove the validity of the tests; that is, that they do predict success and failure on the specific tasks for which they are being used. In addition, they must provide proof the tests do not unfairly discriminate against any minority or ethnic subgroups. In short, examiners must establish or have information to prove that the tests they use are valid and fair (Murphy & Davidshofer, 2005; Riggio, 2002).

A controversy addressed by the EEOC is whether screening potential employees with personality tests that use separate gender norms violates civil rights law (Adler, 1993). At the heart of this issue is the tendency of women to be more willing than men to reveal negative aspects of themselves when taking personality tests. For example, if women endorse an average of 10 items on an anxiety scale whereas men endorse an average of only 6, a female applicant who endorses 8 items might be considered highly anxious and perceived as a less desirable job candidate. A potential solution to this problem is to eliminate separate gender norms and have norms that combine the responses of both men and women. As reasonable as this solution seems, it still may discriminate against women because of their tendency to be more likely to report negative aspects of themselves in tests.

Impact of Equal Rights Legislation on Testing

Probably the biggest impact of such legislation is that it requires human resource managers who depend on personality tests in the process of selection and placement to examine the tests more closely (Riggio, 2002). It also requires those involved in the business of developing and marketing such tests to spend more time and money on research to establish their validity. Finally, it requires that more attention be paid to the nature of the individuals and groups included in research; and greater care be taken to ensure that test items are culturally fair.

As a result of this legislation, administrators of tests must ensure they are using the tests only for the particular purposes for which they are specifically designed. Greater knowledge of reliability and validity issues and more advanced training in test selection and administration are now required of those (e.g., admissions counselors and human resource managers) involved in testing others for selection and placement. As a result, increasingly sophisticated and legally sound decisions are made possible about the selection and use of tests, and the fair and equal treatment of the individuals taking the tests is ensured.

Social Concerns: Assessment and Society

One of the biggest social concerns about the large-scale use of assessment techniques is labeling. This issue has to do with what can happen when a negative label is attached to an individual on the basis of the results of these techniques (Cohen & Swerdlik, 2002). For example, consider what can happen to an individual who has been labeled as emotionally disturbed on the basis of a set of personality tests. First of all, other people may react to this person differently because of the label (e.g., they may treat him or her in an impersonal manner). Because people are now treating this person differently, the individual may eventually come to internalize the label of being emotionally disturbed and start exhibiting negative behaviors (e.g., hostility and social withdrawal). Such bizarre behavior will then serve to reinforce the label and the differential treatment the person now receives. In short, the label becomes the beginning of a **self-fulfilling prophecy**. Keep in mind that such problems are not created by the tests and labels themselves but by the way people react to and believe in the labels.

Ethical Guidelines: Rules for Assessment

The ethical issues associated with the assessment of personality are numerous and complex, and have serious legal and social implications. To help address and resolve these issues, the American Psychological Association (1981, 1990, 1992, 2000, 2002) has developed a set of ethical principles to be followed by its members when developing and administering psychological assessment techniques, interpreting and explaining test results, maintaining test security, and dealing with obsolete tests and outdated test results (see www.apa.org/ethics/code2002.html). In addition, to help provide a more universal set of ethical standards

Summing It Up *Ethical Issues in Personality Assessment*

Personal Concerns	Individuals unwittingly revealing information about themselves is an invasion of privacy. Regulations must be developed to increase confidentiality by restricting access to and the distribution of test results.
Legal Concerns	Discrimination is the unfair impact of testing procedures and results on a specific group of individuals. Equal rights legislation is designed to document the extent to which tests do what they say they will do without discriminating. Equal rights legislation will require more attention to the development and validation of tests and more specialized knowledge and training for those using them.
Social Concerns	Interpersonal consequences for individuals: • The unfair labeling of individuals on the basis of test results. • Treating individuals unfairly because of the label. • The self-fulfilling prophecy in the behavior of individuals being labeled.

for testing, professional organizations are working together to establish guidelines for the use of tests. For example, the American Educational Research Association (AERA), American Psychological Association (APA), and National Council on Measurement in Education (NCME) have developed jointly *The Standards for Educational and Psychological Testing* (1999; http://www.apa.org/science/standards.html), and the Association of Test Publishers has published the *Model Guidelines for Preemployment Integrity Testing Programs* (1996). These guidelines are published to: "ensure that both test publishers and test users adhere to effective ethical and legal integrity testing practices in the following areas: (1) test development and selec-

tion, (2) test administration, (3) scoring, (4) test fairness and confidentiality, and (5) public statements and test marketing practices" (Jones & Terris, 1991, p. 857). Such ethical guidelines are primarily concerned with protecting the rights of those taking the tests.

This concludes our discussion of the ethical concerns associated with the assessment of personality. A review of the major points discussed in this section is presented in "Summing It Up: Ethical Issues in Personality Assessment" above. In the next chapter, we will begin our examination of the various viewpoints of personality by considering perhaps the most famous individual associated with the study of personality, Sigmund Freud, and his psychodynamic viewpoint.

Chapter Summary: Reexamining the Highlights

- *Personality Assessment.* Personality assessment is the systematic measurement of various aspects of personality designed to increase precision and effectiveness in communication about the personality of individuals. The techniques are utilized in industrial, clinical, legal, military, and educational settings, to name just a few.

- *Evaluating Assessment Techniques.* Standards of reliability include test-retest reliability and examiner reliability. Indices of validity include face validity, content validity, criterion validity including predictive and concurrent validity, the process of construct validity, and discriminate validity, along with generalizability.

- *Methods of Personality Assessment.* Objective self-report techniques assess personality through single-dimension and multiple-dimension tests containing a standardized set of responses and scoring procedures. Acquiescence and social desirability response sets may influence the results of these techniques. A principal strength is their standardization, while a principal limitation is the lack of freedom of response they allow.

  – Projective techniques of assessment interpret personality from responses to ambiguous stimuli. Characteristic features of these techniques include ambiguous stimuli, indirect method of assessment, freedom of response, and increased possibility of subjective scoring procedures. The different types of projective techniques include association, completion, choice or ordering, expressive, and constructive. A major strength is the freedom of response allowed to the individual taking the tests. while principal limitations are the subjective nature of the scoring procedures and the uncertainty of what dimensions of personality they assess.

  – Behavioral techniques of assessment focus on observable behavior, environmental cues, and cognitive processes. The different types of behavioral assessment include direct observation, self-monitoring, self-report behavioral interviews, and cognitive assessment techniques. A principal strength is the emphasis on various types of behavior, while principal limitations include the uncertainty of what should be observed and biases in the recording and recalling of information.

  – Psychophysiological assessment techniques measure bodily responses associated with personality processes. Electrophysiological measurements include the electrocardiogram (ECG), the electromyograph (EMG), and techniques assessing electrodermal activity (EDA). Biochemical measurements include assessing various neurotransmitters, hormones, and genetic composition. Cortical measures of neurological activity include the electroencephalograph (EEG), positron emission tomography (PET), and functional magnetic resonance imaging (fMRI). A principal strength is the linking of bodily and personality processes, while principal limitations include the unclear meaning of measures of bodily processes and the extent to which they can be modified.

  – The nature of the question being asked about personality will determine the type of assessment technique to be used.

- *Computer Adaptive Testing (CAT).* Computers have been used in a variety of different aspects of personality testing, including test construction and validation, administration and scoring, interpretation of results, and interactive programs connected to a variety of different databases that can be tailored to the individual's personality characteristics, needs, and preferences.

- *Ethical Issues in Personality Assessment.* Preventing invasions of privacy and ensuring confidentiality are personal concerns associated with the ethics of personality assessment. Preventing discrimination, regulating who has access to the results of tests, and focusing more attention on the use of assessment techniques are associated legal concerns. The process of labeling and its consequences are associated social concerns.

Glossary

acquiescence response set   A tendency to respond with agreement to the items on a test for which the person is uncertain.

association technique   A projective technique that assesses personality on the basis of the individual's associations with test stimuli.

authoritarianism   A personality dimension characterized by conservative attitudes and submission to authority.

behavioral technique   A type of assessment that emphasizes observable behaviors and the environmental factors, cognitive processes, and consequences that affect them.

California F Scale   A single-dimension objective self-report technique assessing authoritarianism.

California Psychology Inventory (CPI)   A multiple-dimension test assessing 20 different aspects of personality.

choice or ordering projective technique A projective technique that assesses personality on the basis of individual's expressed preferences in choosing or ranking test stimuli.

cognitive behavior assessment The measure of cognitive events that serve to influence behavior.

cognitive events Any number of mental activities (e.g., reasoning and expectations).

completion technique A projective technique that assesses personality on the basis of the individual's completed responses to incomplete test stimuli.

computer adaptive testing The use of computers to help develop, administer, score, and interpret test results.

concurrent validity The ability of a test score to predict a currently existing criterion measure.

confidentiality A condition of testing in which access to the results of the test is restricted to ensure the privacy rights of those taking the test.

construct validity Establishing the relationship between a test score and a set of behaviors consistent with a particular theory.

constructive projective technique A projective technique that assesses personality on the basis of stories created in response to test stimuli.

content validity The extent to which a test contains items reflecting the dimension of personality being measured.

controlled observation The recording of behavior in environments with highly regulated environmental conditions.

counseling psychologists Psychologists who are trained professionally to help individuals cope more effectively with problems of everyday adjustments.

criterion contamination Biases introduced in the assessment of reliability and validity when the same person makes all the observations.

criterion measure A specific behavior to be predicted by the score on the test.

criterion validity The ability of a test to predict a behavior in a particular situation.

direct observation technique A behavioral assessment technique that emphasizes the recording of overt behaviors occurring in different situations.

discriminate validity The degree to which your measure does not relate to others in a predictable manner.

Edwards Personal Preference Schedule (EPPS) A multiple-dimension objective self-report technique assessing 15 aspects of personality as expressed by need preferences.

electrocardiogram (ECG) An electrical device for assessing the muscular activity of the heart.

electrodermal activity (EDA) The activity associated with changes in the skin's surface in response to various environmental and emotional stimuli.

electroencephalograph (EEG) A tool for assessing electrical activity in the brain in the form of electrical wavelengths.

electromyograph (EMG) An electrical recording device for assessing muscular activity.

Equal Employment Opportunity Commission (EEOC) A legislative body designed to protect individuals from discrimination in employment practices.

examiner reliability The extent to which different examiners scoring a test arrive at the same score.

expressive projective technique A projective technique that assesses personality on the basis of an individual's creative actions, such as drawing and role playing.

face validity The degree to which a test looks like what it says it is supposedly measuring.

fear survey schedule A self-report technique in which individuals indicate from many different options those objects or situations eliciting fear in them.

functional magnetic resonance imaging (fMRI) A computer image of brain activity as indicated by the rate of change in the magnetic properties of blood as a result of oxygen use by brain cells.

galvanic skin response (GSR) An activity of the skin's surface associated with changes in moisture level (e.g., perspiration).

galvanometer An electrical device for assessing galvanic skin response (GSR).

generalizability The extent to which the results obtained with one sample of individuals or in a particular situation can be established with a variety of other individuals or situations.

group norm A numerical index of how a specific group of individuals scored on a particular measure of personality.

hero The central figure in a story generated in response to a picture from the Thematic Apperception Test.

informed consent Individuals making their decision to participate on the basis of information about the procedures of the research received before their actual participation.

invasion of privacy The potential for individuals to unknowingly reveal personal information about themselves when taking a test.

Minnesota Multiphasic Personality Inventory-2 (MMPI-2) A multiple-dimension objective self-report technique assessing 10 different aspects of personality and containing four separate validity scales.

multiple-dimension personality tests Any personality test that attempts to measure more than one dimension of personality at a time.

naturalistic observations The recording of behavior in real-life settings.

need A state of deprivation that creates a desire or motivation for a particular object or state of affairs.

objective self-report techniques Techniques of personality assessment characterized by standardized administration and scoring procedures.

personality assessment The systematic measurement of different aspects of personality.

personality profile A summarized interpretation of a collection of personality characteristics in written and graphic form.

positron emission tomography (PET) A computer image of brain activity as indicated by the rate of usage of energy-producing substances by brain cells.

predictive validity The ability of a test score to predict a criterion measure in the future.

press An environmental factor that affects needs as measured by the Thematic Apperception Test.

profile analysis The identification of a specific personality pattern on the basis of scores of several dimensions of personality.

projective techniques Techniques of personality assessment based on an interpretation of the subject's responses to ambiguous stimuli.

psychometricians Individuals who have specialized professional training in administering, scoring, and interpreting the results of personality tests and other techniques of psychological assessment.

psychophysiological techniques Procedures for measuring bodily processes.

reliability The assessment consistency of a personality test.

reliability coefficient A numerical index of the consistency of a test score.

response set Answering test questions in a biased manner.

role playing The acting out of an assigned role for the purpose of assessing behavioral and emotional reactions.

self-fulfilling prophecy A tendency of individuals to begin to behave in a manner consistent with a diagnostic label attributed to them, thus providing after-the-fact support for the label.

self-monitoring A personality dimension expressing the tendency for an individual's behavior to reflect situational demands vs. personal beliefs.

Self-Monitoring Scale A personality test assessing individual differences in self-monitoring.

self-monitoring technique A form of behavioral assessment in which the recording of behavior is done by the individual.

self-statement inventory A self-report technique in which individuals choose from many alternatives in the thoughts that occur to them in certain situations.

single-dimension personality test A test of personality that measures one dimension of personality at a time.

social desirability response set A tendency to endorse items on a test in a pattern that creates a favorable impression.

test-retest reliability The consistency of a test score obtained on two separate occasions.

Thematic Apperception Test (TAT) A constructive projective technique that assesses personality by identifying the needs expressed in the stories generated by individuals in response to pictures with ambiguous themes.

thought sampling The assessment of the various thoughts occurring to an individual in certain situations.

validity The extent to which a test measures what it says it measures.

validity coefficient A numerical index of the ability of a test score to predict a criterion measure.

validity scale A set of items within a test designed specifically to detect certain biases in response patterns that can negatively affect the test results.

The Viewpoints of Personality
Different Perspectives of the Person

Part II

In Part I, the general principles for studying the psychology of personality were presented. Part II applies those principles to an examination of several viewpoints of the person as proposed by different personality theorists. Each chapter explores the basic assumptions, principal processes, assessment techniques, and practical applications associated with the viewpoints. As you read those chapters, do not feel compelled to find the "right" or "best" viewpoint; there is none. Instead, try to understand each one, evaluate it by the standards discussed in Part I, and select those aspects that are most applicable to your own view of personality.

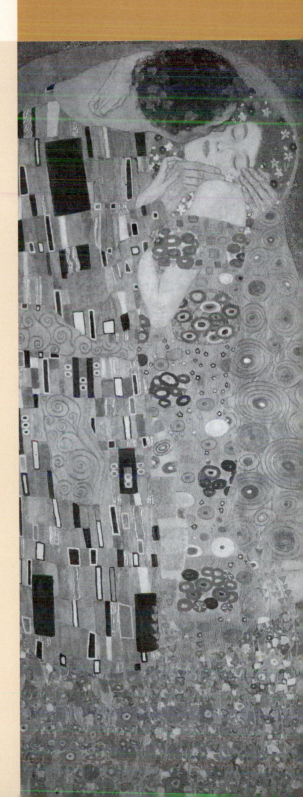

The Psychodynamic Viewpoint
Forging Personality out of Conflict Resolution

3

Chapter Overview:
A Preview of Coming Attractions

If you ask anyone from a personality psychologist to a person in the street, you will find that Sigmund Freud is by a wide margin the most famous personality theorist. It was Freud who postulated, in a staggering 23 volumes, the first comprehensive modern view of personality. This chapter gives you an overview of Freud's work and contributions to the study of personality psychology. We begin with a presentation of the basic assumptions, concepts, and processes associated with the psychodynamic viewpoint. Next are a discussion of personality development and an exploration of applications of the psychodynamic viewpoint to psychotherapy, personality assessment, and contemporary advertising. In addition, to illustrate Freud's enduring influence, throughout the chapter you will also be exposed to recent research in the study of personality psychology based on Freudian ideas (Cramer, 2000, 2006; Hassin, Uleman, & Bargh, 2005). The chapter ends with an evaluation of the characteristic strengths and limitations of the psychodynamic viewpoint. To learn more about the personal life of the man who forever changed the study of personality, consider the material in "A Closer Look" on p. 78.

A Closer Look

A Brief Biography of Sigmund Freud

Although Sigmund Freud's conservative appearance was similar to that of most other intellectuals at the time in Vienna, his ideas were certainly not conservative and helped change forever the study of personality.

Sigmund Freud was born on May 6, 1856, in the small town of Freidberg, Moravia (now called Pribor, Czech Republic). He was the oldest of seven children. In 1860, his father moved the family to Vienna, where Freud would live for almost 80 years. An extremely good student, he began reading Shakespeare at the age of 8 and excelled in science. He exhibited an unusual talent for writing and languages, mastering Latin, Greek, French, English, Italian, and Spanish; and he graduated at the head of his class.

Freud dreamed of becoming a great military general or minister of state, but in 1873 – at the age of 17 – he began studying medicine at the University of Vienna. He aspired to become a medical researcher and earned a minor reputation in the scientific community for exceptional research on the nervous system and other work. But limited employment opportunities and financial concerns got the better of him, resulting in episodes of anxiety and depression for which he began using cocaine. Although he used and researched the analgesic possibilities of cocaine, there is no evidence to suggest that he was ever addicted to the drug.

Freud's aspirations were derailed because of the limited opportunities for Jews in such areas as medical research, and because he fell in love with and became engaged to Martha Bernays. In 1881, in preparing to support a family, he established a private practice specializing in the treatment of the nervous system. In 1886 he and Martha married. They had six children – three girls and three boys. The youngest child, Anna, would eventually become a world-famous psychoanalyst.

Freud's career was enhanced greatly by his collaboration with the highly successful Viennese neurologist Joseph Breuer. In his practice, Breuer had successfully treated many patients suffering from physical disabilities (e.g., muscle twitching or paralysis) that seemed to be related to emotional problems by having them simply talk about their thoughts and feelings. In 1895, Breuer and Freud (1895/1955) published *Studies in Hysteria*. Although the book sold only 626 copies in 13 years, it is now considered a classic marking the beginning of the psychoanalytic movement. But shortly after the book was published, Freud and Breuer had a major falling out due to Freud's emphasis on the importance of sexual conflicts as a cause of **hysteria**, which, at the time, referred to a disorder characterized by the loss of a physical function (e.g., blindness or paralysis) without any neurological explanation but believed to be psychologically based. The disagreement completely ended their personal and professional relationship and resulted in Freud's dismissal from the Vienna Medical Society in 1896.

After the death of his father that same year, Freud began to experience intense feelings of depression and anxiety, including an unnatural fear of traveling by train. To help overcome these emotional difficulties, he began his historic self-analysis, from which he eventually formed many of the founding principles of the psychodynamic viewpoint (e.g., emphasizing the unconscious and dreams). One of the most significant outcomes of this analysis was a book called *The Interpretation of Dreams*, published in 1900 (1900/1935a). It is considered Freud's greatest work, although during its first six years only 351 copies were sold (Tolson, 1999).

As the twentieth century began, the fame of Freud increased in Europe, with the publication of *Psychopathology of Everyday Life* in 1901 (1901/1960a) and the founding in 1902 of the Vienna Psychoanalytical Society. The society boasted members from all over Europe, including Alfred Adler and Carl Jung – both of whom would eventually disagree with Freud and go on to develop their own schools of thought and theories of personality (see Chapter 4). In 1909, G. Stanley

Hall, a famous American psychologist, asked Freud to give a series of lectures at Clark University in Worcester, Massachusetts. Hall's invitation established Freud as an international figure, but it was to be his first and only visit to America. To help increase the visibility of Freud's ideas in America, Hall persuaded him to recreate his lectures in writing, which were translated from German to English and published in the *American Journal of Psychology* under the title "The Origin and Development of Psychoanalysis" (Freud, 1910). When commenting on this article almost 100 years after it was published, Fancher (2000) notes "This vivid and lucid account remains today among the best of Freud's popular introductions to the field he created" (p. 1026).

The publication of this article did much to increase interest in Freud's other works, which were then translated into English. The appearance and nature of his writings "helped to make Freud's name a veritable household word in the United States" (Fancher, 2000, p. 1026), culminating in the first of his three appearances on the cover of *Time* magazine in October 1924. In the Europe and United States of the 1920s, his fame rose to new heights through the establishment of the International Psychoanalytic Association and a supporting journal that helped spread the information throughout the world. Freud was offered lucrative contracts to write popular articles for *Cosmopolitan* magazine and to work for a movie studio as a consultant in making films of famous love stories. Although he was not a wealthy man, Freud turned down these offers, fearing they would compromise his scientific credibility. In 1923, he was diagnosed with cancer of the jaw. The cancer was linked to his lifelong habit of smoking 20 cigars a day, but he refused to give them up. Over the next 16 years, he would endure some 33 operations on his mouth and jaw, continuing to write and develop his ideas despite great physical pain.

As a Jew living in Europe in the 1930s, Freud found that his increased fame incited harassment by the Nazis, who burned his books, attacked his character, and raided his house. Although he was in great danger, he refused to leave his beloved city of Vienna, even after the Nazis invaded and occupied Austria in 1938. But shortly afterward, when his daughter Anna was arrested, detained, and subsequently released by the Gestapo, he consented to leave Austria for England. There he was accepted with all the warmth and honor deserved by a man of his stature. In London, on September 23, 1939, Freud died of cancer.

Much has been written about the relationship between Freud's personal biography and the development of his ideas (Runyan, 2006). You can learn more from *The Life and Work of Sigmund Freud* by Ernest Jones (1953, 1955, 1957), who was Freud's biographer, fellow psychoanalyst, and lifelong friend. For a much shorter account, read a book chapter titled "Sigmund Freud (1856–1939)" (Bragg & Gardiner, 1999) or the cover story in *Time* magazine titled "Sigmund Freud" (Gay, 1999). Finally, two other rather unusual sources for information on Freud's personal and professional life can be found in Irving Stone's (1971) *The Passions of the Mind*, which is a biographical novel of Freud's life, and *Berggasse 19: Sigmund Freud's Home and Offices, Vienna 1938* (Engelman, 1976), which is a collection of photographs, with accompanying commentary as well as a brief biography in the introduction, of various locations and personal artifacts in Freud's personal and professional residence, from where he developed many of his most significant ideas. Finally, on April 27, 2006, *Newsweek* had as its cover story an article titled "Freud in our Midst" (Adler, Underwood, & Bain, 2006) discussing his contribution and contemporary relevance in recognition of his 150th birthday. The wide array of biographical information about Freud is a testament to the degree of interest individuals still have in his life and work.

Foundations of the Psychodynamic Viewpoint

In this section, the core elements of Freud's comprehensive viewpoint of personality are presented. He used these elements as the foundation from which to account for the nature and operation of personality. The core elements to be discussed in this section include his underlying assumptions about, the basic concepts and processes associated with, and the developmental aspects of personality.

Basic Assumptions

The following four basic theoretical assumptions serve to link together the various components of Freud's comprehensive view of personality, such as the nature and dynamics of personality, personality development and psychopathology, and psychotherapy and personality change.

Psychic Determinism: Leaving Nothing to Chance

Psychic determinism refers to Freud's belief that behavior does not just happen by chance, but is governed by some purpose or meaning. As Brenner (1973) notes, "in the mind, as in physical nature . . . nothing happens by chance, or in a random way. Each psychic event is determined by the ones that preceded it" (p. 2). From this assumption, Freud theorized that such everyday occurrences as slips of the tongue, jokes, and dreams are expressions of psychic determinism (Freud, 1900/1953a, 1901/1960a, 1905/1960b). For example, according to Freud, the content of dreams is determined by an individual's unconscious wishes and desires.

Even seemingly innocent or meaningless behaviors are influenced by psychic determinism. For example, if you miss a turn while driving, you may be expressing the unconscious desire to avoid something or someone. Thus, according to the assumption of psychic determinism, nothing about behavior is left to chance (Sommers-Flanagan & Sommers-Flanagan, 2004).

The Influence of the Unconscious Mind: Powers of the Unknown

Freud also assumed that behavior is governed by powerful forces in the unconscious region of the mind (Freud, 1900/1953a; Kihlstrom, 1990, 1999; Westen & Gabbard, 1999). Freud said these forces are unconscious because they contain thoughts, ideas, desires, and impulses that individuals find threatening, shameful, or unacceptable; but these forces are still part of the personality and have to find ways to be expressed. For example, the telling of dirty jokes is a relatively safe expression of an individual's sexual desires and impulses. One possible explanation of the power of the unconscious suggests the automatic processing of mental activity that can influence our thoughts, feelings, and behaviors without our conscious awareness (E. R. Smith & DeCoster, 2000; Strack & Deutsch, 2004). Such automatic processing of information is typically very quick, requires little effort, and is unintentional. In an excellent examples of some recent research on such processing as it affects our perceptions of and actions towards others based on racial stereotypes (Greenwald, Nosek, & Banaji, 2003), black and white participants were placed in front of a video screen and were instructed to press a button that said "shoot" or "don't shoot" when images of either black or white males were rapidly flashed on the screen holding either a gun or a harmless object, such as a flashlight. The results indicated that both the black and white participants were more likely to mistakenly shoot the images of black males. While all of these participants would probably not report unacceptable racial attitudes and would say that they are not prejudiced, it is possible that the unintentional shooting of the black-male images was an acceptable unconscious expression of certain stereotypical beliefs. This, along with other research (Judd, Blair, & Chapleau, 2004; Payne, 2001), suggests that unconscious processes serve to influence our thoughts, feelings, and behaviors in some very powerful ways.

The Dynamic Nature of Personality

A claim for the dynamic nature of personality assumes that several different elements work together in a homeostatic fashion; that is, one in which balance and stability are maintained among different aspects of an individual's personality. You can experience **homeostasis** by taking a break after studying for a couple of hours, walking to a local coffee shop to chat with friends, and then resuming your studies. In balancing the studious and social aspects of your personality, you achieve homeostasis. Thus, the dynamic process of homeostasis is the creation of a state of arousal (e.g., being stressed out by studying too long) that motivates an individual to take action (e.g., take a break to socialize with friends) to stabilize and restore balance among the different motivational aspects (e.g., social vs. studious) within the individual (Geen, 1995).

Personality as a Closed System

Freud also viewed personality as a **closed system** that operates on a fixed amount of psychic energy, or **libido**. In such a system, the limited amount of energy is shifted continuously from one part to another in a dynamic and interactive manner in an attempt to maintain a sense of internal balance. In the preceding example, you shifted some of the energy away from studying to the activity of talking to friends, and later shifted back to studying. By taking a break, you can

Summing It Up *Basic Assumptions of the Psychodynamic Viewpoint*

Basic Assumption	Explanation	Example
Psychic Determinism	There is a psychic reason for all of our thoughts, feelings, and actions; nothing just happens.	Without being aware of it, certain individuals tend to be attracted to others who have a particular emotional problem, such as alcoholism.
Influence of the Unconscious Mind	Our behavior is determined by factors outside of conscious awareness.	A shopper's decision to select a red coat rather than a blue one reflects an unconscious desire to be perceived as daring.
The Dynamic Nature of Personality	The nature of our personality includes a number of elements interacting with each other.	As an effective manager, your personality style must include being firm, compassionate, and fair when dealing with subordinates.
Personality as a Closed System	The fixed amount of psychic energy used to operate personality is shifted from one part to another.	When playing volleyball, you shift your emotions from being rational when developing a setup to a team member to aggression when spiking the ball on an opposing player to friendly when shaking hands with the opposing players after the game.

actually save psychic energy by relaxing a bit and not wasting lots of energy trying to concentrate while tired.

Although these are not the only theoretical assumptions of the psychodynamic approach to personality (Sommers-Flanagan & Sommers-Flanagan, 2004; Westen, 1990; Westen & Gabbard, 1999), they helped to guide many of Freud's most important ideas about the nature and operation of personality. A basic understanding of these assumptions should help you understand more clearly how and why Freud viewed personality the way he did. A summary of the major ideas discussed in this section is presented in "Summing It Up: Basic Assumptions of the Psychodynamic Viewpoint" above. In the next section, we will examine some of the basic concepts and processes that serve as fundamental building blocks of the psychodynamic viewpoint.

Basic Concepts and Processes

This section examines some of the concepts that serve as fundamental building blocks of the psychodynamic viewpoint.

The Regions of the Mind

Very early in his career, in about 1900, Freud (1900/1953a) began to describe his view of how the mind was organized (Quintar, Lane, & Goeltz, 1998; Westen & Gabbard, 1999). As Figure 3.1 shows, Freud's map of the mind had three regions: the conscious, the preconscious, and the unconscious. He believed that each had unique features and special functions.

The Conscious Mind   As the "tip of the iceberg," the **conscious mind** is characterized by sensory awareness and is limited to what people are capable of hearing, seeing, smelling, touching, tasting, or thinking at any particular time. For example, while reading a book, you might find it difficult to hear the words of a favorite song on the radio. With its limited capacity, Freud believed the conscious mind had very little to do with determining behavior.

The Preconscious Mind   As shown in Figure 3.1, the **preconscious mind** is just below the level of conscious awareness. It contains pieces of information that can be brought into conscious awareness when needed (e.g., a word rhyming with *red*). Because he viewed it

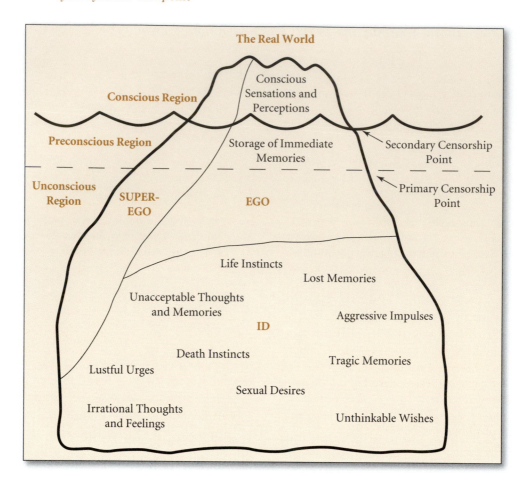

The Real World

Conscious
Sensations and
Perceptions

Conscious Region

Preconscious Region

Storage of Immediate
Memories

Secondary Censorship
Point

**Unconscious
Region**

**SUPER-
EGO**

EGO

Primary Censorship
Point

Life Instincts

Lost Memories

Unacceptable Thoughts
and Memories

Aggressive Impulses

ID

Death Instincts

Tragic Memories

Lustful Urges

Sexual Desires

Irrational Thoughts
and Feelings

Unthinkable Wishes

Figure 3.1   The three regions of the mind, with their corresponding features and psychic structures

as simply a storage bin for information, Freud did not believe the preconscious mind had much influence on behavior. But it was the location of the **secondary censorship** point for keeping threatening information out of our conscious awareness. Forgetting an appointment with the dentist until the day after is an example of the censorship function of the preconscious mind preventing the recall of threatening information until it is no longer a source of unpleasantness.

The Unconscious Mind   The largest and most influential region of the mind postulated by Freud is the **unconscious mind**. This holds unacceptable memories, urges, desires, and impulses that could seriously threaten a person's sense of self if they were expressed directly at the conscious level of awareness. A characteristic feature of the unconscious mind is its unlim-

ited capacity for storing information for an unlimited amount of time.

Freud proposed that unconscious information can also be expressed at the conscious level in ways that are not directly understood by the individual. For example, stored in the unconscious mind of an executive may be the tragic memory of being locked accidentally in a dark room as an infant. This experience is manifested consciously in adulthood by the individual's little-understood extreme fear of flying (i.e., in the confined space of airplanes). This threatening information is kept out of the preconscious mind and prevented from eventually being expressed at the conscious level of the mind by the **primary censorship** point, which Freud said is located between the unconscious and preconscious regions (Freud, 1900/1953a). Although research into the operation of the unconscious is still a topic of much discussion today (Anooshian & Seibert, 1996), nobody has yet managed to clearly explain how the censorship mechanism operates (Silverman, 1982). However, evidence supporting its operation continues to mount (Dixon, 1981; Greenwald, McGhee, & Schwartz, 1998; Kihlstrom, 1990; Silverman, 1976, 1980; Silverman, Ross, Adler, & Lustig, 1978; Westen, 1990; Westen & Gabbard, 1999), as well as evidence in support of other operational aspects of the unconscious consistent with the psychodynamic perspective (Bornstein & Masling, 1998). For example, a recent area of research investigating the operation of the unconscious is that involving compensatory automaticity (Glaser & Kihlstrom, 2005; Moskowitz, 2001). **Compensatory automaticity** is the unconscious strategic compensation for unintended thoughts, feelings, or behaviors. For example, in an interesting study demonstrating compensatory automaticity (Moskowitz, Gollwitzer, Wasel, & Schaal, 1999), individuals who scored high or low on a measure of egalitarianism (i.e., equal treatment of individuals) were exposed to photographs of either males or females that were paired with words that had female-relevant stereotypical attributes (e.g., *sexy*, *loving*, *sensitive*, *irrational*, *deceptive* or *cunning*, and *weak* or *dependent*) or non-female-relevant stereotypical attributes (e.g., *flexible*, *fair*, *easygoing*, *colorful*, *reliable*, and *creepy*) on a screen every 200 milliseconds, a rate that made it impossible to indicate at a conscious level (e.g., say what they saw) the nature of the stimuli. Shortly afterwards, when exposed to the words again at a rate that they could see and asked to pronounce them, the participants with high egalitarian scores (i.e., less prejudice) responded more slowly to the female-relevant stereotypical words than did those with the low egalitarian scores. The results suggest that the high-egalitarian individuals responded more slowly because they were trying to correct or compensate for any stereotypical responses that may have been activated at an unconscious level by being exposed to the stereotypical words previously, reflecting a form of unconscious censorship.

Instincts and Psychic Energy

Freud believed that the operation of personality was powered by a force of psychic energy fueled by **instincts** (Alford, 1998; Quintar et al., 1998; Westen, 1990; Westen & Gabbard, 1999). As defined by Freud, "an instinct is a mental representation of a physical or bodily need" (Freud, 1915/1957c, p. 122).

Physical or bodily needs include those for food, water, sleep, and mental and sexual stimulation. Mental representations of bodily needs manifest themselves in the form of a wish or desire. The mental representation of your state of hunger might involve wishing for pizza. However, because simply wishing for something does not make it so, a major function of instincts is to motivate you to do something to satisfy your desire, reduce tension, and maintain homeostasis.

Characteristics of Instincts Freud (1915/1957c) postulated that instincts have four basic characteristics: aim, pressure, object, and source. The **aim** of the instinct is to reduce an internal state of tension (e.g., reduce boredom). The **pressure** of an instinct is the amount of motivating influence it has on the individual (e.g., degree of boredom). To achieve the aim of tension reduction, the individual must seek out some instinctual **object** (e.g., the company of others or a movie). The **source** of the instinct refers to the area of the body from which the state of tension originates (e.g., the brain for boredom). Psychic instincts are variable and are expressed in each person in a unique combination of these four characteristics.

The Nature of Instincts Freud subdivided psychic instincts into two categories, defined as life instincts and death instincts (Freud, 1914/1957a). **Life instincts** use psychic energy for preserving the organism and achieving pleasure through such activities as reducing a state of hunger or thirst, taking action to avoid danger, reducing sexual arousal, resting when sleepy, and seeking company when bored or lonely. Satisfying all of these instinctual desires with an appropriate object reduces tension and contributes to a satisfying life.

In sharp contrast to the life instincts, Freud also postulated death instincts. According to him (1920/1955), **death instincts** represent the individual's desire to complete the life cycle by returning to an earlier inactive and tension-free state. Freud spoke of death not literally, but symbolically, by postulating a set of instincts that could be used to explain the destructive, aggressive, and dark side of human nature (e.g., war). But because the life instincts exert so much pressure and generally make it difficult for people to express their death instincts inwardly against themselves, we have a tendency to express them outwardly toward other people (e.g., arguing, fighting, and murder; Alford, 1998). In this manner, we can express the death instincts while still preserving the aim of the life instincts. In support of this reasoning, recent research indicates, "highly accessible unconscious thoughts of death are defended against with distal defenses, which, on the surface, bear no rational or logical relationship to the problem of death but defend against death by enabling the individual to construe himself or herself as a valuable participant in a meaningful universe" (Pyszczynski, Greenberg, & Solomon, 1999, p. 835). In other words, people can protect themselves against the thoughts associated with the possibility of their own death by believing that they are important in the lives of other people (e.g., family and friends) and that they make a significant contribution to life (e.g., volunteer at the homeless shelter).

Fostering a personal sense of communal worth is a strategy for creating distance (i.e., distal defenses) between expressions of the death and life instinct so individuals do not spend all their time worrying about death. At a more conscious level, think about what your life would be like if you were preoccupied with thoughts about dying, as might be the case for individuals on the brink of starvation or in war-torn nations or communities dominated by gang violence. Fortunately, you can avoid thinking about such threats because you have other thoughts to occupy you mind, such as your school work, career, social activities, and other activities that give meaning to you and the life you live.

The Id, Ego, and Superego: The Structural Elements of Personality

In a later theoretical modification, Freud (1923/1961) introduced his concept of three structures operating within the three regions of the mind (see Figure 3.1): the id, the ego, and the superego. Categorized by function (Jahoda, 1977; Westen & Gabbard, 1999), they were characterized as having their own special set of features and functions.

The Id: The Core of Personality   The **id** is seen as the core of personality because it is believed to be present and fully functional at birth. Located completely in the unconscious region of the mind and therefore having no actual contact with the external world, it operates within its own sense of reality. Because of its location, the id also reflects those characteristics associated with the unacceptable urges, desires, memories, and impulses found in the unconscious region. It expresses the contents of the unconscious in the form of

instincts that serve as the source of an individual's psychic energy.

The expression of these impulses and desires is based on the pleasure principle. The **pleasure principle** is the tendency for the id to seek immediate gratification of any unfulfilled impulse or desire when a state of tension in the individual is created (e.g., sexual arousal) without any regard for what is going on in the real world (e.g., sitting in a business meeting).

The **primary process action** is the mechanism by which this state of immediate gratification is achieved (Brown & Richards, 1998). It involves a set of behaviors and mental activities the id can use that immediately reduces tension, such as reflexive behaviors (e.g., an infant's automatic sucking) and fantasy (e.g., dreaming). Other primary process actions might be daydreaming of a loved one to immediately reduce the tension of being lonely, or thinking about food when you are hungry. A major limitation of these actions is that whereas they provide immediate gratification, the need or wish is not really satisfied; it eventually returns with even greater force (Quintar et al., 1998). For example, thinking about food when you are hungry helps for the moment, but you typically become even hungrier afterward.

The Ego: The Master of Reality   To deal more effectively with the demands created by impulses and desires, the id then channels some psychic energy into forming and developing the **ego**, whose major function is to help meet the needs and wishes of the id by serving as a buffer between it and the real world. The ego spans all three regions of the mind (see Figure 3.1); as a result, it has contact with the id at the unconscious level and with the external world at the conscious level. This characteristic enables the ego to be aware of the unconscious needs and wishes of the id and the external conditions under which it must operate to meet them.

The ego meets the needs and desires of the id by operating on the reality principle. The **reality principle** dictates that while trying to meet the unconscious and often irrational needs and wishes of the id, the ego must follow the rules of reality, one of which is delaying gratification. In its simplest sense, the **delay of gratification** involves postponing the satisfaction of the id's needs and wishes until a realistic object or method can be achieved. There is considerable evidence that by the end of the first year of life, infants develop a number of different strategies to help control their emotional expression (Shaffer & Kipp, 2007). For example, infants may rock themselves back and forth or chew on objects as a means of controlling unpleasant feelings.

The reality principle and delay of gratification operate through secondary process actions. **Secondary process actions** are behaviors and mental activities that the ego can utilize to meet realistically the needs of the id. Included in these actions are such phenomena as learning and memory strategies, planning alternatives, and modifying behavior in response to feedback (Quintar et al., 1998). For example, rather than coping with loneliness by fantasizing about being with others, enrolling in a course titled "How to Meet People" at the local community center is a much more realistic solution. By forgoing the immediate gratification based on fantasy and delaying the gratification by having the ego develop a more realistic solution to satisfying the id's needs, a greater degree of tension reduction and much more pleasure are achieved in the long run.

The Superego: The Moral Authority of Personality
The **superego** is conceptualized as an individual's center of moral standards (Westen & Gabbard, 1999). Like any moral authority, the superego's task is to make sure that thoughts, feelings, and behaviors stay within society's moral standards when the ego is dealing with the demands of the id. By dealing with the demands of the superego while trying to meet the needs of the id, the ego must consider not only what is realistic and unrealistic but also what is right and wrong. For example, although approaching others to chat is a realistic and immediate solution to reducing boredom and loneliness, bothering or harassing these individuals is morally wrong.

Characteristics of the superego include the ego ideal and the conscience. The **ego ideal** is the part of the superego that rewards all behavior that is considered right, appropriate, and morally acceptable. On the other hand, the **conscience** is the part that punishes all behavior that is considered wrong, inappropriate, and morally unacceptable. These two parts of the superego are used to help maintain a morally acceptable level of behavior. Whenever you behave in a way that is considered socially acceptable (e.g., returning lost money to its owner), your ego is rewarded by the superego in the form of pride or an increase in self-esteem. On the other hand, when the ego produces a set of actions the conscience considers unacceptable (e.g., failing to

return the money), the superego punishes the ego in the form of guilt feelings, embarrassment, shame, or loss of self-respect. Because the superego cuts across all three regions of the mind (see Figure 3.1), much of the control the superego exerts over the ego to behave in an acceptable manner occurs outside of a person's awareness. Returning to our example, this helps to explain why even when you need the money, you do not think twice about keeping it; the conflict concerning stealing between the ego and superego has already been resolved at an unconscious level. However, you should also realize that a superego expressing moral reasoning that is too excessive can be problematic. Individuals who are highly committed to their moral beliefs might be willing to jeopardize their own safety or that of others to promote their cause. For example, to promote their cause, extreme social activists might be willing to go on a hunger strike, while terrorists might be willing to become suicide bombers and kill themselves and many innocent people. Thus, the superego's expression of moral standards can range from logical to illogical and moderate to extreme, depending on who is judging the standards.

The Dynamic Interaction of the Id, Ego, and Superego: Maintaining a Balance of Psychic Power
Figure 3.2 graphically represents the dynamic relationships among the id, ego, and superego. With the ego placed in the middle, and if all demands are met, the system maintains its balance of psychic power and the outcome is an adjusted personality. If there is imbalance, the outcome is a maladaptive personality. For example, with a dominant id, the outcome could be an impulsive and uncontrollable individual (e.g., a criminal). With an overactive superego, the outcome might be an extremely moralistic individual (e.g., a television evangelist). An overpowering ego could create an individual who is caught up in reality (e.g., extremely rigid and unable to stray from rules or structure), is unable to be spontaneous (e.g., express id impulses), or lacks a personal sense of what is right and wrong (e.g., somebody who always goes by the book). Even with temporary states of imbalance (e.g., screaming and yelling when the id is out of control), most people are able to maintain psychic balance and exhibit a healthy personality.

The operation of structural relationship and the operational nature of the id, ego, and superego represent a major theoretical component of Freud's psychodynamic viewpoint. A summary of the main points

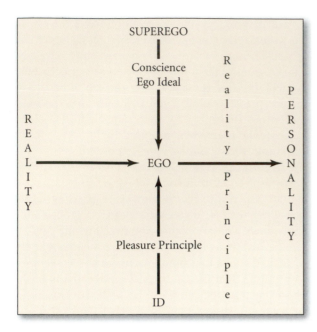

Figure 3.2 The nature of each personality is the outcome of the dynamic relationship involving the interaction of the id, ego, and superego.

outlining the characteristic features of the id, ego, and superego noted in this discussion is presented in "Summing It Up: The Structural Nature of Personality."

The Nature and Role of Anxiety: That "Alarming" Feeling

Although serving as a mediator between the id and superego, the ego does not have to work alone. Assistance comes in the form of anxiety. According to Freud (1926/1959), **anxiety** serves as a psychic warning sign to the ego that it is near danger. The ego is then in a much better position to protect itself by developing an appropriate strategy. Because the ego can experience many kinds of dangers, Freud postulated three types of anxiety: reality, neurotic, and moral (Quintar et al., 1998).

Reality Anxiety: A Signal for Danger in the Real World   **Reality anxiety** is the signal the ego receives when a source of danger exists in the real world. You might experience reality anxiety if you are caught in a smoke-filled room, see a mean-looking dog approaching quickly, or feel uneasy when walking down a dark street in a high-crime area. When this sense of real danger is signaled by feelings of reality anxiety, the ego

Summing It Up *The Structural Nature of Personality*

Characteristic Features	Personality Structures		
	Id	**Ego**	**Superego**
Level of Location within the Mind	Unconscious	Conscious Preconscious Unconscious	Conscious Preconscious Unconscious
Purpose	The source of psychic energy associated with basic instincts and desires	To meet the needs of the id within the context of reality and morality	To maintain an acceptable standard of moral behavior when the ego is meeting the id's needs
Basic Processes	Pleasure principle and primary process actions	Reality principle and secondary process actions	Ego ideal and conscience
Outcome of Excessive Influence on Personality	An overly impulsive individual seeking immediate gratification (e.g., a thief or rapist)	An individual overly concerned with reality (e.g., lacking the ability to fantasize)	An overly moralistic and righteous person (e.g., a fundamentalist preacher or political zealot)

is in a much better position to plan a coping strategy to minimize the anxiety.

Neurotic Anxiety: The Feeling of Losing Control
Neurotic anxiety is a feeling signaling the possible conscious expression of id impulses that have reached conscious awareness. Although no actual physical danger exists, neurotic anxiety is triggered by the superego when it believes the ego is losing control over the ability to inhibit these impulses. For example, even though they are safe, many people experience anxiety – even panic – when looking over the edge of a tall building because of the unconscious impulse (e.g., an expression of the death instinct) they feel to jump off. Their anxiety may be a result of the possibility of losing control over the impulse and jumping. As a result, the ego makes the individual step back. As a more extreme unconscious form of self-protection against the impulse to jump, the individual might begin to suffer from **acrophobia**, an irrational fear of heights.

Moral Anxiety: The Security Officer within Us
Moral anxiety is a signal by the superego given when the ego is contemplating doing something that violates the superego's moral standards. This signal often appears in the form of guilt feelings or shame, which are designed to prevent the ego from carrying out these unacceptable thoughts or behaviors. As an example, while on a date, two people might become sexually aroused, caught up in the moment, and desire to have unprotected sexual intercourse. However, because such casual, unprotected sex is considered socially unacceptable and physically dangerous, the superego of one or both people generates feelings of guilt that force their egos to engage in more restrictive and socially acceptable sexual behavior, such as intense kissing and fondling or delaying the immediate gratification by going to get some condoms before engaging in sexual intercourse. Thus, moral anxiety is a signal of internal conflict between the ego and the superego.

The ego generally tries to respond to the different types of anxiety by proposing and executing a course of action designed to minimize unpleasant feelings. In some situations, it becomes overwhelmed by the anxiety and takes actions that are more irrational and less effective as long-term solutions. These actions are referred to as ego defense mechanisms.

Ego Defense Mechanisms: A Psychic System of Defense Against Anxiety

Ego defense mechanisms are a series of unconscious actions taken by the ego as a form of self-defense that are designed to immediately reduce anxiety (e.g., forgetting a dentist appointment) and to help maintain psychic balance (Freud 1926/1959). By using these mechanisms, the ego can gain a sense of relief that allows it to divert its attention to other more pleasant activities (e.g., concentrate on a television program). However, while such a defensive action may offer the immediate benefit of tension relief, the cost to the individual is that she has to operate within a distorted reality (e.g., acting as if the appointment does not exist), which can create even more distressing circumstances. For example, forgetting about this routine, preventative checkup may result in the development of or increase in existing dental problems that will require even more dental work, appointments, and financial cost, producing an even greater level of anxiety, than if the initial appointment had been kept. Thus, defense mechanisms are characterized by their unconscious operation to remove an unpleasant emotional state while having no effect on external reality and creating the potential for distortions in the perception of reality (Cramer, 2006). Some common ego defense mechanisms are discussed below.

Repression: Out of Sight, Out of Mind According to Freud (1914/1957b), the most basic defense mechanism is repression. **Repression** occurs when the ego unconsciously removes threatening impulses, desires, and memories from conscious awareness. The logic is that things people are not aware of cannot cause problems. In addition, because the process of repression occurs at an unconscious level, the individual is not even aware that it is happening. But a problem develops: Because the repressed material is not resolved, it reappears more intensely when psychic defenses are lowered (e.g., when sleeping, when under hypnosis, or while intoxicated). For example, a rape victim might have a difficult time telling police the details of the assault, because thinking about it triggers a feeling of reliving the entire unpleasant experience. At the same time, she may have trouble sleeping because she cannot stop dreaming about the assault.

A recent controversy associated with the concept of repression has been that of **repressed memory**

syndrome (RMS) – the tendency for traumatic early childhood experiences (e.g., sexual abuse or physical trauma) to be blocked out until they are brought to conscious awareness. Concerns associated with RMS relate to their authenticity and the circumstances under which they are recalled (Loftus, 2003; McNally, 2003; McNally, Clancy, Barrett, & Parker, 2005). More specifically, such repressed memories are typically recalled within the context of psychotherapy through the use of certain therapeutic techniques, including hypnosis, dream interpretation, journal writing, and explanations of symptoms, under the guidance of a therapist that requires the individual to focus and elaborate on the imagination of the early traumatic experiences. The problem, it seems, is that by encouraging the individual to focus and elaborate on the traumatic memory, particularly if the therapist provides supporting evidence through clinical interpretation, the individual may eventually come to believe that such events actually happened even when they did not. For example, if a therapist suggests that the individual's inability to enjoy sexual activities may be related to an early sexual trauma and then begins to encourage the individual to reflect and elaborate on any early sexual experiences through the use of hypnosis and dream interpretation, the individual may come to believe that the traumatic experience happened even though it did not. In support of such reasoning, systematic research has documented the ability of researchers to create such false memories (Thomas, Bulevich, & Loftus, 2003). For example, in one study (Braum, Ellis, & Loftus, 2002), participants were encouraged to actively imagine that they shook hands with Bugs Bunny. Such elaborative imaging increased the false confidence that they actually *did* shake hands with Bugs Bunny. While such research calls into question the validity of such repressed memory, it should be clear that it in no way discounts the problem of childhood sexual abuse and the problems it can create during childhood and into adulthood (Chu, 2000; Knapp & VandeCreek, 2000).

Denial: That Can't Be True   The defense mechanism of **denial** occurs when the ego distorts reality to make dealing with threatening impulses and information easier. When reminded of the possibility of an early death, individuals tend to respond with a "not-me, not-now" reaction by denying that they may be vulnerable to those risk factors associated with an early death (Chaplin, 2000). For example, people engaging in unsafe sexual practices cope with the unpleasant possibility of getting AIDS by employing denial, claiming, "It won't happen to me." On the positive side, there is some evidence to suggest that the denial of a chronic illness (e.g., heart disease) can help individuals deal with the initial fear and distress of the illness by giving them some time to reflect on the diagnosis and the changes to their lifestyle it may produce (Taylor, 2006).

Reaction Formation: Expressing the Opposite Reaction
The defense mechanism of **reaction formation** involves dealing with unacceptable impulses by expressing just the opposite feeling. For example, people who are emotionally conflicted and unable to accept their own strong sexual desires may devote much of their time and considerable psychic energy waging strong protests against pornography and birth control clinics. There is considerable contemporary evidence to support the notion that people react against personal uncertainty and emotional conflict with an extreme defensive reaction consistent with reaction formation (McGregor, 2003, 2004). In one laboratory study designed to test for the expression of reaction formation (McGregor & Grippen, 2003, as cited in McGregor, 2004), students were asked by a researcher, but also given the option to refuse, to write an essay endorsing the position that students should take mandatory comprehensive exams at the university – an opinion that most students vehemently opposed. Other students were simply instructed to write the essay but not given any choice. The results indicated that those students given the choice wrote essays that were much more favorable toward the mandatory exams than those students who did not have any choice. It was suggested that freely expressing an opinion that was in direct opposition to their personal beliefs created emotional tension and conflict because it produced a sense of personal uncertainty by implying that they might actually have favorable attitudes toward the comprehensive exams, and that the individuals resolved this emotional conflict by taking a more extreme public stand – writing highly favorable essays – that was consistent with their free choice, and thus their actual beliefs, than those individual who did not have any choice, and therefore did not experience any emotional conflict. Thus, threats to personal beliefs can result in internal conflict that is resolved by expressing just the opposite belief in a manner consist with the defense mechanism of reaction formation.

Projection: Pointing the Finger at Others   With the defense mechanism of **projection**, an individual attributes his or her own negative characteristics to others. For example, to help justify his or her own angry feelings, a person arguing with a spouse might say, "Why is it that you are so angry with me?" In support of the expression of projection, individuals who hold negative attitudes about another racial group believe that lots of other individuals hold negative stereotypes, too (Krueger, 1996), and that those who sneak showers during shower bans, which are used as a water-conversation measurer, believe that others are doing the same thing to a greater degree than nonbathers (Monin & Norton, 2003).

Displacement: Finding a Safe and Easy Target
Displacement is a defense mechanism used by the ego to shift the expression of an impulse from an unacceptable or threatening target (e.g., person or object) to a more acceptable or less threatening one. The classic example of displacement is the woman who, after being "chewed out" by her boss, comes home and begins to express the anger toward the boss by yelling at her husband, who yells at their child, who then kicks the dog. Thus, each person selects a safe target at which to express their anger and frustration. In support of the expression of displacement, it has been noted that there is a tendency for individuals, when emotionally aroused by daily annoyances or irritations, to think in an irrational manner that may include expressing their anger against others who may not be the cause of the negative feelings (J. D. Lieberman & Greenberg, 1999; Pederson, Gonzelez, & Miller, 2000). More extreme examples of displaced aggression throughout history include the tendency for individuals to engage in some highly violent behaviors when taking their anger and frustration out on less fortunate or powerful groups. For example, "Following their defeat in World War I and their country's subsequent economic chaos, many Germans saw the Jews as villains" (Myers, 2005, p. 350) and took their frustration and anger out them. In the USA, there was an increase in the lynching of African-Americans between 1882 and 1930, which may have been an expression of the frustration felt by poor whites during a time when the price of cotton was low and economic difficulties were high (Hepworth & West, 1988; Hovland & Sears, 1940). As another example, during times of increased unemployment, hate crimes also tend to increase (Frank, 1999).

Rationalization: Seeing Our Faults in Others   With the defense mechanism of **rationalization**, an individual makes up what are supposed to be rational or logical explanations to justify unacceptable behavior. For example, a man might justify "cheating" on his income taxes by saying, "Well, everybody else is doing it, and besides, I don't want my money to buy bombs." Such explanations are seen by the individual as being rational. For example, individuals who lie to another begin to increase their belief that others are dishonest (Sagarin, Rhoads, & Cialdini, 1998).

Regression: Acting Like a Baby   **Regression** is a defense mechanism by which the individual attempts to cope with a threatening situation by retreating to earlier, less mature behavior patterns. For example, the screaming and yelling of a surgeon at the surgical staff each time she begins to have difficulties during an operation may represent regression to an early childhood tendency to get her way by throwing a tantrum. In a study of a more extreme form of acting out – taking one's own life – regression was associated with suicidal patients to a greater degree than with nonsuicidal patients hospitalized for a variety of other psychiatric reasons (Apter et al., 1989).

Undoing: Atoning for Your Sins   **Undoing** as a defense mechanism involves an individual engaging in some sort of behavior (e.g., saying "I'm sorry") designed to compensate or make amends for unacceptable feelings or actions expressed. For example, after having lustful feelings about a co-worker, an office supervisor may go home with a gift for his spouse to atone for these feelings. It has been suggested that an apology can serve as a means of reality negotiation (Snyder, Higgins, & Stucky, 1983) by which the offending individual can attempt to alter the victim's feelings or perception of the offense (M. E. McCullough & vanOyen Witvliet, 2002), such as make the victim feel less angry about the transgression.

Sublimation: Turning Bad Feelings into Good Actions   The defense mechanism of **sublimation** involves converting unacceptable impulses into actions serving a more socially acceptable purpose. For example, becoming a sex therapist and teaching courses in human sexuality might be an acceptable way of expressing unconscious sexual desires while helping others with their sexual problems. The major advantage of sublimation is that it makes possible the best of both worlds; both the individual and society benefit from the expression of unconscious impulses through the process. For this reason, Freud considered sublimation the only completely successful defense mechanism. In support of such reasoning, there is considerable evidence to suggest the feelings of guilt linked to acts of transgression are associated with increases feelings of empathy (Tangney & Mashek, 2004). For example, after parking in a handicap space, an individual might deal with the unacceptable negative feelings of being inconsiderate of the needs of the handicapped by giving a few dollars the following week in support of the Special Olympics Games, thus helping to improve the quality of life of handicapped people through his socially appropriate actions.

Evaluating Ego Defense Mechanisms: A Good-News/Bad-News Scenario   When used appropriately, ego defense mechanisms can provide an immediate sense of relief. But in the long term, they are not effective for coping with the actual source of anxiety: yelling at your spouse might make you feel better after being chewed out by your boss, but you still have not resolved the long-term problem of why your boss yelled at you in the first place. And now, you have the added problem of having hurt your spouse's feelings. Defense mechanisms can create more problems than they solve.

Another problem is that since defense mechanisms do not actually solve the problem, it typically returns in a more intense form. The bigger the problem gets, the more psychic energy is required to cope with it, which results in less energy being available for coping with other aspects of a person's life. For example, denying that she has a drinking problem helps Marie to cope with the problem in the short run. But as it gets worse, she spends more energy trying to cover it up and has less energy for coping with other more important tasks in life, such as doing her job and caring for loved ones. In support of this logic, "Recent research on thought suppression indicates that attempts to avoid unwanted thoughts can backfire, making intrusion more pervasive and troublesome than they otherwise would have been" (Wenzlaff & Bates, 2000, p. 1200).

Healthy vs. Unhealthy Use of Defense Mechanisms: A Word of Caution and Clarification   Considerable empirical evidence exists to suggest people use defensive processes to alter their conscious thoughts and feelings in an attempt to maximize positive feelings and minimize negative ones (Plutchik, 1998; Westen, 1998;

Westen & Gabbard, 1999). Although everybody uses defense mechanisms in one form or another, they can be used in an unhealthy manner. Most people who use them are generally aware of what they are doing (e.g., seeking temporary relief), but those who engage in maladaptive use of defense mechanisms are not aware of the defensive nature of their actions. In contrast to using many defense mechanisms to a modest degree, maladaptive use involves exclusively one or two of them to an extreme degree. For example, it is the emotionally unhealthy individual who deals with all problems by always denying reality and seems unaware of this denial.

In support of Freud's view on the use of defense mechanisms, research over the years has documented a relationship between their use, levels of anxiety (Hedegard, 1969), and personality maladjustment (Perry & Cooper, 1986, 1989; Vaillant, 1977, 1986; Vaillant & Drake, 1985; Westen & Gabbard, 1999). And, like individuals exhibiting more severe personality maladjustment, relatively healthy individuals during times of severe stress (e.g., the loss of a loved one, being assaulted) employ a style of defensive processing that is more rigid (e.g., extensive use of a single or selected few defense mechanisms) and characterized by a greater distortion of reality (e.g., the more pervasive use of the defensive process to a greater degree; A. Freud, 1936; Vaillant, 1992; Westen & Shedler, 1999). As well as in clinical and personality psychology, the operation of defense mechanisms has helped explain psychological functioning in developmental (Cramer, 2000, 2006) and social (Baumeister, Dale, & Sommer, 1998) psychology and as an adverse contributing factor to physical health (Contrada & Guyll, 2001; Shedler, Mayman, & Manis, 1993; T. W. Smith & Gallo, 2001; Weinberger, 1995), although their actual nature and level of operation at the conscious and unconscious level are still a source of controversy and debate (Cramer, 2001, 2006; Erdelyi, 2001; Newman, 2001). For more information about defense mechanisms, see Phebe Cramer's (2006) outstanding book titled *Protecting the Self: Defense Mechanisms in Action*.

At this point, you have gained a basic understanding of how Freud conceptualized the nature and operation of personality. A summary of the major points of discussion is presented in "Summing It Up: Basic Concepts and Processes of the Psychodynamic Viewpoint" opposite. The focus of this chapter shifts next to how Freud believed personality developed.

Summing It Up *Basic Concepts and Processes of the Psychodynamic Viewpoint*

Basic Concepts	Basic Processes	Supporting Concepts and Processes
Regions of the Mind	The mind is divided into three regions: conscious, preconscious, and unconscious.	These regions of the mind differ in their level of consciousness, storage capacity, contents, and influence on behavior.
Instincts and Psychic Energy	The operation of the personality is powered by a fixed amount of psychic energy; the source of this energy is instincts.	Instincts are characterized by their pressure, aim, object, and source; they are also subdivided into life and death instincts.
Structural Elements of Personality	The id, ego, and superego comprise the elements of personality.	Specialized features, such as the pleasure principle (id), reality principle and delay of gratification (ego), and ego ideal and conscience (superego) supplement the structural elements of personality.
Dynamic Interaction of Personality Structures	The ego must meet the demands of the id within the limits set by the superego and external reality; the outcome of this interaction reflects one's personality.	The three types of anxiety (reality, neurotic, and moral) and a variety of defense mechanisms (e.g., repression and sublimation) are used by the ego in its interaction with the id and superego.

Psychodynamic Personality Development

In addition to conceptualizing the structure and operation of personality, Freud also described the process by which personality develops (Freud, 1905/1953b). This section presents a discussion of the psychodynamic viewpoint of personality development (Arlow, 2000; Quintar et al., 1998).

Characteristic Features and Processes

For Freud, the basic purpose of personality development was to help prepare the individual to cope with the psychic conflicts and crises of life (Westen, 1990; Westen & Gabbard, 1999). This was done by the individual resolving a series of conflicts during early childhood. The skills developed then would serve as the basis for resolving conflicts that would occur later in life.

Psychosexual Stages: The Milestones of Personality Development

At the center of Freud's theory of personality development was the idea that individuals resolve a series of conflicts associated with a sequence of five **psychosexual stages:** the oral, anal, phallic, latent, and genital stages. In Freud's construct, these are viewed as milestones in personality development. We will explore them in detail in the section beginning on p. 93. **Psychosexual conflicts** involve the release of psychic energy (e.g., tension reduction) concentrated in various regions of the body, and external constraints against doing so (e.g., parents, social customs). **Erogenous zones** are those regions of the body containing this concentrated source of psychic energy. According to Freud, at each psychosexual stage, a different erogenous zone is the center of the psychosexual conflict.

The Importance of Early Experience: Getting It Right the First Time

The heavy emphasis on early childhood experiences in his theory was based on Freud's view that the way individuals learn to resolve the conflicts associated with each of the psychosexual stages in childhood determines, to some extent, the way they will cope with conflicts as adults. Failing to pass through these stages successfully means an individual might have trouble expressing and satisfying instinctual needs and desires as an adult. Thus, Freud viewed childhood as the time for individuals to acquire and practice those coping skills that would be valuable later in life (Westen, 1990; Westen & Gabbard, 1999).

Fixation and Regression: Barriers to Successful Personality Development

According to Freud, failure to resolve satisfactorily the conflicts at any of the psychosexual stages will result in the barriers to successful personality development known as fixation and regression. With **fixation**, an individual invests a considerable amount of psychic energy trying to resolve a particular psychosexual conflict. Because Freud viewed personality as a closed system, the more energy invested in a given psychosexual conflict, the less energy would remain for successfully solving later conflicts. Balanced and imbalanced distributions of psychic energy as part of personality development are illustrated in Figure 3.3.

Fixation is believed to occur on account of two reasons: overgratification and undergratification of instinctual desires. When these desires are overgratified, an individual might find the pleasure associated with one erogenous zone so powerful that she or he remains at that stage of development by investing an excess amount of psychic energy trying to continuously achieve that source of pleasure. When they are undergratified, the individual may invest an excessive amount of energy trying to satisfy an unfulfilled or denied source of pleasure associated with a particular erogenous zone. An example of fixation is an individual who was so happy during the 1960s that he continues to dress in clothes fashionable at the time (e.g., tie-dyed shirts), listens only to sixties guitar rock music, and decorates his house with posters popular at the time, as well as deals with life's daily crises by drinking and taking drugs, as he did back then.

Regardless of the reason, fixation at any psychosexual stage increases the likelihood of regression, or the tendency to return to an earlier, more immature behavior pattern associated with a specific psychosexual stage to cope with a psychic conflict. For example, eating, drinking, and smoking cigarettes are all associ-

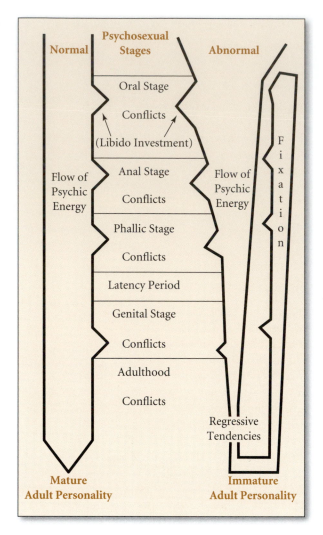

Figure 3.3 The fixation–regression relationship as illustrated by the normal and abnormal flow of psychic energy
Source: Adapted from Rychlak (1981)

ated with the oral region, which is the erogenous zone in the first psychosexual stage of personality development. The relationship between fixation and regression is such that the more a person has fixated at a particular psychosexual stage, the more likely he or she is to regress to a form of behavior associated with that stage later in life (see right side of Figure 3.3). Since returning to immature forms of coping prevents the learning of more mature and effective coping methods, both fixation and regression are major barriers to successful personality development.

The Psychosexual Stages: The Road to Personality Development

Probably one of the most controversial aspects of Freud's theory was his notion of the psychosexual stages occurring during childhood (Westen & Gabbard, 1999). Although the term *sexual* is used to describe the stages, it is an extreme oversimplification of Freud's view to assume that he used this term literally. Instead, he was referring primarily to the expression of libido and the pleasure associated with reducing bodily tension. The basic characteristics and dynamics of the psychosexual stages are discussed in this section.

The Oral Stage: Learning to Cope with Significant Losses

Infants tend to put everything in their mouths, mainly because most of the pleasure they receive in life comes from eating and reducing the tension associated with hunger. During the **oral stage** occurring during the first 18 to 24 months of an infant's life, Freud believed an excessive amount of libido was concentrated around the oral region. Thus, sucking, biting, chewing, licking, and swallowing were associated with eating and the seeking of pleasure in activities involving the mouth.

During the oral stage, nursing on the mother's breast is a primary source of pleasure (e.g., reduction of hunger tension) for the infant. But about half way through this stage, the infant is confronted with his or her first major psychosexual conflict. When the child is between 6 and 20 months old, the mother begins to wean it from breast feeding. Since the breast becomes an object of tension reduction and pleasure for the child, Freud believed that the manner in which the weaning process was resolved had important implications for subsequent personality development and the resolution of future psychosexual conflicts. For example, weaning that is too abrupt creates the undergratification of needs and frustration, while weaning that is prolonged creates overgratification of needs and dependency. In both cases, fixating at the early part of the oral stage might result in the individual developing an **oral incorporative personality**, characterized by the tendency to cope with the conflicts of adult life in an oral manner (e.g., eating or drinking). Toward the end of the oral stage, the infant also begins to develop teeth that can be used to express anger or frustration during the weaning process by biting the mother. Fixating at this later part of the oral stage produces what is known as an **oral aggressive** or **oral sadistic personality**, which in adults is characterized by the tendency to cope with conflicts by behaving in an orally aggressive manner (e.g., yelling or swearing).

If the conflict associated with the weaning process goes well, the infant develops the basic skills necessary to cope effectively with certain conflicts that may arise later in life. This person is better equipped to handle situations involving the loss of a significant source of pleasure, such as giving up a security blanket at age 5 or losing a love interest to a romantic rival at age 26. In addition, by learning to distinguish between objects of significance in the external environment (e.g., mother's breast) and an internal sense of his or her own needs and desires, the infant begins to show the first signs of an emerging ego – an independent sense of the self.

The Anal Stage: Learning When and Where

At age two, the primary erogenous zone begins to shift from the oral region to the anal region. For this reason, Freud referred to the second psychosexual stage as the **anal stage**. The principal source of pleasure associated with the anal stage is the reduction of tension that accompanies reducing bodily tension by urinating and defecating. The conflict arises when parents begin to make demands on the infant to regulate this source of pleasure during the process of toilet training. The basic task of toilet training is teaching the child to delay this source of gratification until proper toilet facilities are available.

Freud believed that difficulties in the course of toilet training also had implications for future personality development. Some infants may cope with the rather strict and harsh demands of neatness and cleanliness during toilet training by resisting or holding back and not defecating. Overextending psychic energy during the process of toilet training by holding back can result in fixating at the anal stage, creating an anal retentive personality as an adult. The **anal retentive personality** is characterized by the tendency to cope with conflicts later in life by demonstrating an extreme sense of cleanliness and orderliness, such as dusting furniture or waxing the car when troubled. The child may also respond to the challenge of toilet training with anger and aggression and fixate at the anal stage by developing an anal sadistic personality. The **anal sadistic personality** is characterized by the tendency to deal with stress in an explosive and unexpected manner, such as getting very angry over the slightest disturbance.

So the basic lessons the child is being taught through toilet training involve the need to consider external constraints and the process of delaying gratification – the expression of pleasures must be done at the proper time and place. This concern for what is acceptable and proper is the beginning of a sense of social conscience (i.e., superego).

The Phallic Stage: Laying the Foundation for Morality and Sex-Role Behavior

Around the fourth or fifth year of life, the individual enters what Freud called the **phallic stage**. The erogenous zone for the phallic stage is the genital region. With an increased sense of bodily awareness and the exploration of various body parts, the child discovers the sense of pleasure that can be achieved by touching the genitals. Because of the central role the mother has played in the previous stages in helping the child to achieve pleasure (e.g., breast feeding and teaching the child how to use the toilet), she is seen as the person most likely to maximize the child's pleasure during this stage as well. Although boys and girls both show similar interests in their genitals as a source of pleasure, Freud believed the course of personality development taken by each during the phallic stage was quite different.

For little boys, the principal conflict involves the father as a source of competition for the gratification provided by the mother (see Figure 3.4). Specifically, the boy supposedly realizes that because his father's penis is much bigger than his own, the father has a greater need for the mother's attention. With this realization, Freud believed boys begin to experience feelings of castration anxiety. **Castration anxiety** involves a boy's belief that his father will cut off the boy's penis so that he will not be in competition for the mother's attention. The psychosexual conflict this creates is between the little boy's desires to maximize his sense of pleasure via the mother versus the possibility of losing the entire source of pleasure if he tries to compete against the father. Freud called this "love triangle" involving the little boy and his parents the **Oedipus complex**, after the mythical Greek character King Oedipus, who unknowingly killed his father and married his mother.

Successful resolution of the Oedipus complex and the Electra complex during the phallic stage produces culturally appropriate sex-role identification. Children demonstrate this process of identification during play by engaging in activities that are consistent with their respective genders, such as the little girl wearing a dress and necklace and the little boy wearing a shirt and tie.

Freud proposed that in successfully resolving this conflict, the boy engages in the process of **identification with the aggressor**; that is, the boy acts like his father by adopting his values, attitudes, and characteristic behaviors. Thus, the boy becomes "mama's little man" and can experience a vicarious sense of genital pleasure by observing the pleasure his father receives from his mother. Resolving the Oedipus complex in this way serves two important functions of socialization. First, because the father's values and attitudes generally reflect the moral standards of society, the internalization of those values through the process of identification fosters the development of

THE FAMILY CIRCUS.   **By Bil Keane**

11-23
Copyright 1979
The Register and Tribune
Syndicate, Inc.

"Know what, Daddy? I love your wife."

Figure 3.4 During the phallic stage, the child expresses intense emotional affection for the opposite-sex parent while viewing the same-sex parent as a source of competition.

the superego (i.e., a conscience). Second, internalizing his father's behavior also helps the boy to learn how men are supposed to act in society (e.g., sex-typed behavior). At the end of a successfully resolved phallic stage, the boy has formed the basis of his superego and sex-role behavior patterns. On the other hand, unsuccessful resolution of the Oedipus complex can result in the formation of a weak superego that can be expressed in impulsive, criminal behavior or the development of more feminine sex-role behavior.

For a young girl, the phallic stage begins when she notices that little boys have a penis and little girls do not. This realization results in what Freud referred to as **penis envy**. The little girl feels that she is being denied the extra genital pleasure that a penis would allow her. As in the past, the girl turns to her mother as a means of achieving this additional pleasure. But her mother also lacks a penis, so the girl turns her affection toward her father. Knowing that the mother has no penis, the girl begins to feel that the mother also desires the father's penis. The psychosexual conflict this creates is between the little girl's desires to maximize her sense of pleasure via the father versus the

possibility of losing other sources of considerable pleasure by having the mother as a rival. The girl's mixed feelings for her parents form the basis of what Freud referred to as the **Electra complex**, so named after the mythical Greek character Electra, who persuaded her brother to kill their father.

The resolution of the Electra complex involves the little girl identifying with her mother and incorporating all of her characteristic behaviors, attitudes, and values. By acting like her mother, the little girl is then able to experience a vicarious sense of pleasure by observing the pleasure her mother receives from the father. As with the little boy, the process of identification results in the appearance of a superego that reflects society's moral standards and feminine sex-role behavior patterns. Freud proposed that to completely resolve the issue of penis envy, the woman will marry and have a baby boy of her own. Her son's penis then serves as a symbol of the penis she never had. Failure to completely resolve the Electra complex can result in an ever-active sense of penis envy and the development of a phallic personality as an adult. The **phallic personality** is characterized by a woman who deals with her penis envy by behaving in a very dominating or aggressive manner toward men (e.g., publicly or privately humiliating them), symbolically castrating them and decreasing their masculinity. Another manifestation of the phallic personality might involve the female having sexual relations with many men as a means of symbolically obtaining a penis. Such views of female personality development are not shared by all personality theorists, but seem to reflect the beliefs Freud developed while working in the primarily male-dominated Viennese society in the early 1900s.

The Latency Period: A Time of Peace for Practicing Sex Roles

Freud believed that after dealing with the extremely traumatic experiences of the phallic stage, children enter into the latency period, from around 5 to 7 years of age until about 13. The **latency period** is characterized by a reduction in the overall activity level of psychic energy. During this time, boys and girls begin to form closely knit same-sex peer groups. Boys typically form clubs "for boys only," playing games and other group activities considered socially appropriate for them. Little girls spend much of their time playing with dolls or other socially approved activities like soccer practice or ballet class. This exclusive same-sex interaction allows

During the genital stage of psychosexual development, there is an awakening of interest in the opposite sex as a source of emotional pleasure. Such emotional attachments during adolescence lay the foundation for the more mature and intimate relationships to be experienced in adulthood.

children to begin experimenting with the new roles and modes of behaviors that society says should be reflected in their superego as young adults. Because of the newness of these behaviors, it just seems easier for children to begin practicing them in the company of others sharing similar experiences. However, the down side of this is that spending too much time in the company of same-sex peers can create more opportunities and stronger pressures to conform to gender-related behaviors, making it more difficult for boys and girls to interact over time (Martin & Fabes, 2001).

The Genital Stage: Learning to Love

The onset of puberty, beginning at around age 12 to 14, initiates the **genital stage**, the final psychosexual stage. During adolescence, hormonal shifts produce bodily changes that are manifested in the development of **secondary sex characteristics**: the development of breasts in females, further development of the genitals for both sexes, appearance of pubic hair, and onset of nocturnal emissions ("wet dreams") for boys and menstruation for girls. All of these events reintroduce the genital region as a source of interest, tension, and pleasure, as was the case during the phallic stage. But instead of turning to the opposite-sex parent as an

agent of gratification and tension reduction, adolescents turn to their opposite-sex peers. During this time, adolescents begin to experience their first strong emotional feelings for someone other than their parents (e.g., a "crush" or puppy love). In coping with these new feelings, adolescents begin to use those sex-role behaviors first acquired and rehearsed during the phallic and latency stages. These early romantic relationships help to prepare individuals for the more significant emotional relationships that they will develop as adults.

During these relationships, adolescents first become aware not only of experiencing pleasure, but also of the rewards of giving pleasure to others. They display this consideration by giving things (romantic notes, such as text and messages and e-mails, or cards, class rings, and other gifts) to their love interest; and, ideally, these expressions of affection are reciprocated. The lesson learned is that by giving pleasure to others, it is possible to receive pleasure. Freud believed that such selflessness formed the basis for what is needed in the mature emotional relationships of adulthood. Thus Freud believed the genital stage continued from adolescence well into adulthood.

In adulthood, the major psychosexual conflict to be resolved involves expressing and releasing psychic energy in a socially acceptable manner. For Freud, successful resolution of this conflict involved the development of **genital sexuality** in romantic relationships, in which both partners gain pleasure by helping to reduce their partner's sexual tension while also meeting their own emotional needs. Freud believed that the most acceptable means of sexual release for adults is through the institution of marriage. Although starting out as very lustful in nature, partners in successful marriages develop a sense of affection and emotional commitment that involves considering the needs, desires, and pleasures of one's spouse. The nature of genital sexuality comes very close to what we might define as love. To take this process one step further, marriages based on genital sexuality also serve as models for children to incorporate during the development of the superego in the phallic stage. Thus, children learn that one of the things adults do is to treat others in a manner involving respect, commitment, and consideration.

Individuals who fail to establish a sense of genital sexuality run the risk of becoming involved with others selfishly – to satisfy their own sexual needs and desires while being unable to commit themselves to others in any emotional sense other than lust.

Psychosexual Stages: Some Closing Remarks

The conflicts encountered at each psychosexual stage are symbolic rather than literal (Westen, 1990: Westen & Gabbard, 1999), representing a "dress rehearsal" for events that are to come as adults. Thus, successful navigation through the psychosexual stages is the foundation for developing a healthy personality. Although Freud developed his theories around 1900, without the benefit of much of what we now know about personality development, recent research supports his views concerning the relationship between early childhood experiences – particularly with primary caregivers – and subsequent adjustment and interpersonal relationships (Ainsworth, 1979; Ainsworth, Blehar, Waters, & Wall, 1978; Bowlby, 1982; Bretherton, 1985; Fisher & Greenberg, 1996; Howes, Hamilton, & Philipsen, 1998; Mikulincer, 1998a, 1998b; Ricks, 1985; Sroufe & Fleeson, 1986; Westen, 1998; Zeanah & Zeanah, 1989). However, you should be aware that there are those who have questioned the ability of these psychosexual conflicts to predict future personality (Bem, 1989; Crews, 1996). Still, Freud's ideas continue to influence thinking on personality development. To read about the work of contemporary psychoanalytical thinkers who used as a basis Freud's views on the importance of early childhood in personality development, see "A Closer Look" below.

A Closer Look

Object Relations Theory: Recent Developments in Psychoanalytic Thinking on Development

One of the most recent and significant developments in psychodynamic thinking is object relations theory (Scharf & Scharf, 1998; St. Clair, 2004; Westen, 1990, 1991; 1998; Westen & Gabbard, 1999). According to **object relations theory** (St. Clair, 2004), the fundamental motivating force is the desire for interpersonal relationships and human connection that are first expressed in childhood as mental representations of the self (e.g., need for the help of others) and early caregiver figures (e.g., parents). These early internalized mental representations of these individuals and the nature of their relationships are carried into adulthood. Thus, like Freud, most object relations theorists greatly emphasize the importance of early childhood experience as a critical element in the formation of the adult personality. But in contrast to Freud's emphasis on intrapsychic conflict and tension reduction, object relations theorists place more emphasis on the interpersonal nature of relationships with significant objects (i.e., parents) and the development of a personal identity (i.e., mental representations of the self) during early childhood.

Early Thinking in Object Relations Theory

One of the earliest object relations theorists was the English psychoanalyst Melanie Klein, a contemporary of Freud. In her work, Klein (1937, 1948) focused on how infants developed a sense of self based on their perceptions of significant objects (e.g., parents or primary caregivers) in their lives (Bronstein, 2001; Sayers, 2000; St. Clair, 2004; Strean, 1994). Klein proposed that during the first year of life, infants classify significant pieces of the object into "good" and "bad" categories from their experiences with each piece of the object (Cashdan, 1988). For example, an infant perceives the mother's breast as "good" because it is a source of pleasure and her hand as "bad" because it is the object that takes the breast away from the baby's mouth. However, toward the end of the first year of life, the child begins to combine the good and bad pieces to formulate an image of the object as a whole unit.

The child's ability to form a sense of attachment to the object and use its image as a source of comfort is indicated by the extent to which the object is perceived as good, can be related to by the child to deal with discomfort, and is incorporated into the child's establishment of an independent sense of identity. Bad objects contribute to the infant's sense of discomfort and make identity formation difficult. Problems of adjustment in later life are related to the individual's relationship with these significant objects in infancy and those that are developed later (e.g., teachers, coaches, and bosses).

In a similar manner, Otto Kernberg (1975, 1976, 1984) proposed that these early object relationships set

Object relations theorists, such as Margaret Mahler, above, and Otto Kernberg, below, sought to expand Freud's ideas by taking an interpersonal viewpoint that emphasized the individual's relationships with significant others.

the stage for the way subsequent relations are internalized (Quintar et al., 1998; Westen & Gabbard, 1999). For example, a young man's feelings about seeking psychotherapy are related in part to the extent to which he was able to find comfort from significant others in his early childhood.

In a close approximation to Freud's psychosexual stages, Margaret Mahler (1968; Mahler, Pine, & Bergman, 1975) also proposed a theory of object relations. Mahler believes that the infant passes through a series of stages during the first three years of life. During this time, the infant attempts to establish

supportive object relationships that enable it to explore and take risks in order to establish its own sense of self. Like Klein and Kernberg, Mahler believes that the object relations developed very early in life are critical to establishing healthy and meaningful object relationships in adulthood (Stepansky, 1988).

Contemporary Thinking and Research in Object Relations

A more recent object relations theorist is Heinz Kohut (1971, 1977, 1984; Mollon, 2001). Like Freud, Kohut (1913–1981) received his medical training at the University of Vienna; but he was trained in psychoanalysis at the University of Chicago. Also like Freud, Kohut developed his theory from the observations of individuals he saw in his clinical practice.

Freud's observations were based primarily on clients whose experiences of anxiety produced symptoms of hysteria. Kohut, by contrast, noticed that the principal complaints of many of his clients were feelings of depression, a sense of emptiness, and a general dissatisfaction with life. These symptoms were viewed as characteristic of **narcissistic personality disorder**, which is characterized by a very shallow sense of self for which individuals require constant reassurance from others (Morf & Rhodewalt, 1993). Persons with this disorder are likely to spend a considerable amount of time in self-absorbed, attention-seeking activities trying to figure out who they are as a means of avoiding the feelings of depression and emptiness that accompany not having a sense of self or personal identity.

At the core of Kohut's view of personality is the bipolar self. The **bipolar self** is characterized by a desire for power and success on one hand and individual goals and personal values on the other hand. These two aspects of the self are linked by the individual's talents and skills. According to Kohut, personality development is the process through which the individual establishes a sense of self by using his or her talents and skills to achieve success and reach personal goals. For example, you are most likely using your intellectual skills and ability to pursue a college education because they will maximize the likelihood of reaching your intended career goal. Achieving career goals is important because what we do for a living is a significant aspect of our sense of self. Individuals who fail to establish a sense of self are likely to develop a sense of narcissism.

According to Kohut (1977), narcissism can be traced back to early childhood, when children are searching for objects in their lives that they can use to help define their sense of self. In this regard, parents are considered self-objects. **Self-objects** are primary objects with which children are most likely to identify in trying to establish their sense of identity. They are also objects that are so important to the children's lives that they are likely to view these as being part of their own sense of self. However, for some children, such identification with their parents does not occur, usually because the parents fail to give the child a sense of empathic mirroring. **Empathic mirroring** is the process by which parents provide attention and praise when the child tries to establish a sense of self by taking a risk or expressing an interest in a particular activity. For example, a parent who stays home to watch baseball on the television instead of going to his child's softball games is demonstrating a low level of empathic mirroring. By contrast, a parent who serves as a coach on the child's team or works at the ball park's concession stand is showing a high level. A lack of empathic mirroring can also exist when parents display behaviors that are not consistent with those their children aspire to model or incorporate as part of their own identity. For example, a parent who spends a lot of time watching television is not likely to be a good model for a child who wants to attend medical school, since the workload associated with going to medical does not permit a lot of time for watching television. A more effective role model would be a parent who spends a lot of time reading, since reading is an important activity associated with succeeding in medical school.

The development of a healthy personality is most likely to occur, according to Kohut, when individuals unite their talents, goals, and desire for success with the support of significant self-objects who provide empathic mirroring. For example, an adolescent who wants to be a rock star starts a band. His efforts are encouraged by his parents, who show their approval and support by taking him to music lessons and helping to pay for his equipment.

For Kohut, the healthy personality is defined as an autonomous self. The **autonomous self** is characterized by high self-esteem and self-assuredness. It includes an appreciation for the importance of social support provided by significant others in reaching one's goals, as well as the necessity of such support in the establishment of meaningful relationships. Individuals whose self-objects provide too little empathic mirroring are likely to seek attention by engaging in self-indulgent and adventurous lifestyles, such as drug abuse, promiscuous sexual behavior, or gang activities. Individuals whose self-objects provide too much attention are likely to develop an unrealistic sense of their abilities, which creates a greater likelihood of failure.

Presented here is only a brief summary of Heinz Kohut's ideas. To learn more about Kohut's perspective on the self, read *Releasing the Self: The Healing Legacy of Heinz Kohut* (Mollon, 2001).

A significant recent development in object relations theory is based on the work of Drew Westen of Emory University. Westen and his colleagues have expanded the thinking of object relations by combining it with research in the area of social cognition (Calabrese, 1998; Calabrese, Farber, & Westen, 2005; Westen, 1991; Westen & Gabbard, 1999; Westen & Heim, 2003). **Social cognition** is the process by which individuals perceive, attend to, remember, think about, interpret, and analyze information about themselves and others in an attempt to make sense of their social world (Moskowitz, 2005). According to Westen, one expression of social cognition is that of working representations (Westen & Gabbard, 1999). **Working**

Contemporary research by Drew Westen has done much to provide empirical support to for many of Freud's ideas on personality development.

representations are mental conceptualizations that individuals have about themselves, others, and their relationships with these others. These working representations form the basis of the object relations with significant others that serve to influence the thoughts and feelings individuals have about these relationships and determine the nature of the relationships and their interactions with these significant others. For example, an individual can have a working representation of herself as being analytical and industrious. She might also have a working representation of her boss as an overbearing person who wants to control her every move. Finally, the individual can have a working representation of her relationship with her boss that is characterized by a lack of trust and sense of insecurity. These working relationships might be triggered while she is surfing the Internet and comes across a classified ad for a job similar to hers, which would serve to influence her belief that she is qualified for that particular position and prompt her to e-mail her résumé.

In their research on personality development, Westen and others have gathered considerable evidence documenting how the nature of working representations of the self and significant others that are a result of different styles of caregiving (e.g., positive, secure vs. negative, insecure) during childhood can produce variations in the sense of attachment children experience with significant others. The nature of this sense of attachment, in turn, serves to influence the expression of their personality and the quality of their social interactions during later periods of development in a manner consistent with the psychodynamic viewpoint of development (Westen, 1998; Westen & Gabbard, 1999). Examples of this research include the influence of the quality of childhood attachment and the nature of working representations on mental processing in childhood, adolescent social development, adult interpersonal relationships, and adult health.

Working Representations and Attachment in Childhood

Consistent with Westen's emphasis on social cognition in the context of object relations, there is evidence to suggest that children who experience sensitive, responsive caregiving develop positive working mental representations of themselves (e.g., "I am loveable") and others (e.g., "People are dependable). These influence them to process information differently from children who experience insensitive or neglectful caregiving

and develop negative working mental representations of themselves (e.g., "I am unworthy") and others (e.g., "People cannot be trusted."). For example, when 3-year-old children were treated to a puppet show that included a series of positive (e.g., getting a birthday present) and negative (e.g., spilling juice) events, it was reported that even though the children did not differ in their attention to the events, those with the positive working representations recalled more positive events while those with the negative working representations recalled more of the negative ones (Belsky, Spritz, & Crnic, 1996).

In addition to affecting the way children process information, such positive and negative working representations also seem to have a significant impact on later development. For example, other research indicated that children with positive working representations of the self and caregivers tended to display self-confidence and earn higher grades during adolescence, develop better social skills and more positive representations of peers, and enjoy closer and more supportive friendships than children with less positive representations (Cassidy, Kirsh, Scolton, & Parke, 1996; Jacobsen & Hofmann, 1997; Verschueren & Marcoen, 1999). Such a pattern of results suggests that the nature of working representations formed in childhood has critical implications for later personal and social development (Waters & Cummings, 2000).

Working Representations and Attachment in Adulthood

Working representations have also been found to be important predictors of adult attachment. A study of such representations of one's self, significant others, and interpersonal relationships found they were better predictors of adult attachment than many standard, more objectives measures of self-representation (e.g., self-esteem) and interpersonal relationships (e.g., fear of intimacy scale; Calabrese et al., 2005). Individuals who expressed working representations of others as offering a more secure basis for emotional connection (i.e., the capacity to invest in emotional relationships) tended to have well-developed and complex representations of the self and others. These representations assume that people can be associated with a variety of personality characteristics (e.g., empathic, analytical, aggressive) and can operate on a variety of different levels (e.g., impulsively, methodically, irrationally). This reflects a more realistic and accepting view of how people really are and how they behave in the real world – people are, in fact, complex and multifaceted. In addition, such well-developed working representations were significant predictors of the individual's current involvement in a significant relationship and of their parents' marital status (i.e., whether the marriage was still intact), as compared to more standardized, self-report objective measures of self (e.g., self-esteem scale) and interpersonal (e.g., fear of intimacy scale) representations, which tended to predict only the scores on other self-reported measures. Such a pattern of results suggests that individuals with working representations of themselves and others that appear to be more emotionally secure (e.g., feel a sense of caring and emotional connection) and well-developed (e.g., others are multi-dimensional) tend to experience more healthy expressions of intimate attachment in adulthood.

Working Representations and Health in Adulthood

There is also evidence to suggest that the nature of one's working representations has health implications (Westen, 1998). For example, it has been demonstrated that the qualitative nature of the working representations of the relationships individuals have with others was a better predictor of self-reported health and visits to the doctor over a 12-month period than other more standard quantitative measures of social support (e.g., the number of individuals a person has in their social network; Costanzo, 1996). Finally, in a dramatic piece of research, the impact the long-term implications of the working representations that are formed in childhood can have on health issues in adulthood was investigated (Russek & Schwartz, 1997). In this research, individuals in college were asked to provide ratings based on their working representations of parental caring provided during their childhood. Thirty-five years later, the health status of these individuals was compared with their ratings of parental caring. The results indicated that those with mental representations of their parents as less caring were more likely during midlife to suffer from a variety of illnesses, including coronary artery disease, hypertension, ulcers, and alcoholism, even when such factors as family history of illness and adult-risk factors such as smoking were held constant.

Taken together, early conceptual developments and more contemporary research on object relations theories have extended and provided support for Freud's ideas about the importance of early childhood and the process of identifying with significant others. These are seen as critical dynamics in establishing a sense of identity and forming interpersonal relationships with important implications for various aspects of psychological, social, and physical development that continue well into adulthood. You will also see that many of the ideas proposed by object relations theorists are reflected in the neo-Freudian (see Chapter 5), humanistic (Chapter 6), and social-cognitive (Chapter 10) viewpoints of personality. For more information on object relations theory, read *Object Relations and Self Psychology: An Introduction* (St. Clair, 2004) or *Object Relations and Integrative Psychotherapy: Tradition and Innovation in Theory and Practice* (Nolen & Nolen, 2002).

Because there is so much information associated with Freud's view of personality development, the basic processes and dynamics of the psychosexual stages are summarized in Figure 3.5.

Maladaptive Personality Development: When Things Do Not Go According to the Plan

Failing to successfully resolve the psychosexual stages can result in the development of personality patterns that reflect serious emotional and behavioral problems that are carried over into adulthood (Arlow, 1995, 2000; Stuart & Noyes, 1999). For example, alcoholism is assumed to be a result of fixation at the oral stage. **Obsessive-compulsive disorders** – a condition involving uncontrollable intrusive thoughts (e.g., sensing germs all over the house) or reoccurring behavior patterns (e.g., washing the same dish 25 times to kill all the germs) – are believed to be linked to strict and excessive toilet training during the anal stage. **Dissociative identity disorder** (previously referred to as multiple-personality disorder) – a condition characterized by the individual developing at least two separate and independent identities – is believed to be associated with repressed, unresolved sexual urges and experiences during the phallic stage. To help people recover from such emotional disturbances, Freud developed a method of treatment known as psychoanalysis, which we will discuss in the next section.

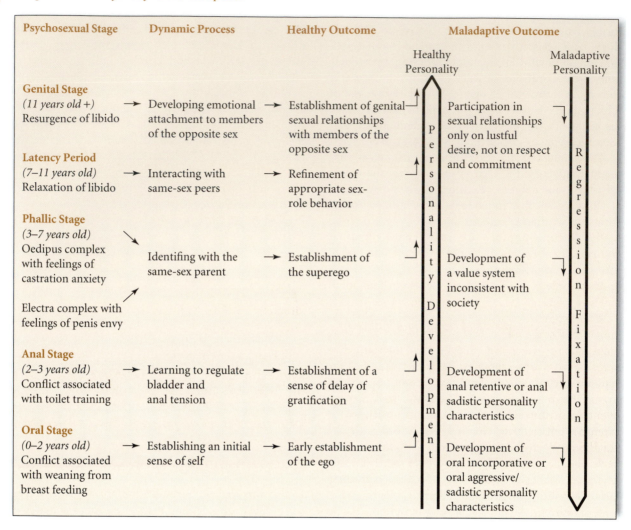

Figure 3.5   The psychosexual stages of development: A summary

Applications of the Psychodynamic Viewpoint: Using What Is Known

Few people have had a greater impact on Western civilization than Freud. His work has influenced such areas as psychiatry, literature, education, psychology, cultural anthropology, sociology, advertising, and philosophy, to name just a few. This section discusses the specific applications of psychodynamic principles to psychotherapy, personality assessment, and advertising.

The Application of Psychodynamic Principles to Psychotherapy: The Talking Cure of Psychoanalysis

The principal application of the psychodynamic approach has been in the clinical setting, as a form of psychotherapy referred to as *psychoanalysis*. This section examines its basic objectives, methods, and dynamics.

Basic Objectives of Psychoanalysis: To Provide Insight and Conflict Resolution

From Freud's belief that personality pathology is a result of unresolved unconscious conflict, he developed a form of psychotherapy known as **psychoanalysis**, a therapeutic technique permitting access to the operation of an individual's unconscious mind. The primary objectives of psychoanalysis are to provide insight – to help an individual to become aware of the unconscious motives and conflicts that negatively affect his or her behavior – and to resolve these conflicts (Sommers-Flanagan & Sommers-Flanagan, 2004).

The view into the operation of an individual's unconscious mind gained during psychoanalysis is referred to as **insight** (Trull & Phares, 2001). Insight is achieved when an individual relates information to the psychoanalyst, who then interprets the information to the client as it relates to his or her unconscious conflicts. So important to the client is insight through interpretation that Bibring (1954) referred to it as the "supreme agent in the hierarchy of therapeutic principles" (p. 763).

After insight is achieved, psychoanalysis helps the individual resolve the conflicts creating his or her existing emotional problems (Arlow, 2000). For example, during a session, a psychoanalyst explains to an office supervisor that his tendency to direct excessive criticism toward his co-workers is actually a manifestation of his own unconscious sense of uncertainty, fostered by the extensive criticism he received from parents during childhood. With this insight, the individual can then begin to resolve his childhood conflicts with his parents, which will then create less of a need for him to take his hostility out on his co-workers.

By dealing with the underlying unconscious conflict, instead of only the surface problem (i.e., giving negative feedback to co-workers), the psychoanalyst helps the client to minimize the problem of symptom substitution. **Symptom substitution** occurs when the symptoms of a problem occur in a different manner than they appeared originally (Kazdin, 1982). Continuing our example, if the office supervisor is simply taught to provide more constructive feedback to co-workers, the psychic tension reflecting the still-unresolved conflict might manifest itself again, in the form of chest pains and tension headaches. Although the assumption of symptom substitution is a critical element in the process of psychoanalysis, this construct is not universally accepted. Specifically, "not every patient's complaint can be labeled as a symptom of some underlying psychic illness – an illness that will surely return in the form of another symptom if the present one is removed without attending to the underlying pathology" (Trull & Phares, 2001, p. 398).

Psychoanalytic Methods: How It is Done

Although psychoanalysis involves many different methods, they all involve the process of catharsis. The logic behind **catharsis** is that when an individual expresses the feelings associated with an impulse or emotion, the pressure exerted by them is reduced (Arlow, 2000). By discussing the extensive parental criticism received during childhood, the individual repressing these feelings can release the tension they create. In addition to verbal expressions of catharsis (e.g., crying or yelling), there are also physical (e.g., hitting a pillow or writing in a diary) and mental (e.g., dreaming or fantasizing) forms of cathartic expression.

The Psychoanalytic Situation: The Therapeutic Setting
The process of psychoanalysis is conducted in a therapeutic environment referred to as the **psychoanalytic situation** (Arlow, 2000). The stereotypical view of a psychoanalytic situation is that of a client reclining on a couch while the psychoanalyst sits in the background with a notebook (see Figure 3.6). The creation of this situation was no accident. Freud believed that having the client in a comfortable position, with the psychoanalyst out of view, would help the individual feel less threatened and more willing to discuss emotionally

Figure 3.6 This somewhat amusing situation illustrates the "classic" psychoanalytic environment, with the client in a relaxed position and the psychoanalyst out of view.

significant topics. During the session, the psychoanalyst makes notes but does not express emotion or pass judgment on what the client says. This method was also designed by Freud to help the individual feel less self-conscious.

Free Association   With **free association**, the client simply tells the psychoanalyst whatever comes to mind, no matter how foolish or unimportant it sounds. Based on psychic determinism (see p. 80), the logic of free association is that everything said has value because uncensored pieces of information can offer insights into the client's unconscious mind and, by extension, the root causes of his or her emotional problems. To explore this psychoanalytic technique, try the exercise described in "You Can Do It."

You Can Do It

An Exercise in Free Association

To get a feel for the way free association works, simply sit back in a comfortable chair, close your eyes, and start to think about anything that comes into your mind. Do not filter out or censor your thoughts. If possible, try to do this for about 20 minutes. For the first few minutes, you might find yourself thinking about how ridiculous this is making you feel. But after a few more minutes, you will notice your thoughts are becoming a bit clearer. If you find yourself trying to suppress certain thoughts, try to recall their nature or meaning. If you continue the exercise for the entire 20 minutes, you may begin to notice certain recurring themes or topics.

According to Freud, the key to analyzing the information obtained from free association is a considerable amount of training in psychoanalysis and extensive information about the individual's patterns of associations. So do not despair if you do not completely understand the nature of your own patterns. After all, the purpose of this exercise is not for you to psychoanalyze yourself – something Freud said could not be done anyway – but to demonstrate what can surface from your unconscious mind when you just let your thoughts run free.

Dream Analysis: On Things that Go Bump in the Night
One of Freud's most famous statements is that "The interpretation of dreams is the royal road to a knowledge of the unconscious activities of the mind" (1900/1953s, p. 608). What he meant by this was that during sleep, the ego's censorship mechanisms weaken and unconscious wishes, desires, and impulses are allowed to surface to a conscious level in the individual's dreams. In **dream analysis**, the analyst listens to the client's reported dreams and interprets their unconscious meaning and psychic relationship to the individual's past and present experiences and conflicts. The **manifest content** of the dream is what the dreamer is able to recall about the dream, such as who was in it, where it took place, and the nature of the action. The **latent content**, or the true meaning of the dream, is believed to reflect the dreamer's unconscious motives and desires. Since dreams are such personal experiences, it is only by carefully analyzing the manifest content that the analyst is able to get some insight into the client's unconscious wishes, desires, and motives (Pesant & Zadra, 2004). As an interesting side note, Freud's views on the nature and operation of dreams were, in part, based on his own self-analysis (Arlow, 2000). For an example of Freud's dream analysis under unique circumstances, consider the material in "A Closer Look" below.

A Closer Look

Freud's Mail-Order Dream Analysis: Answering A Call for Help

On the morning of October 18, 1927, 20-year-old Mary Fields* awoke early from a dream that had been troubling her for weeks. To seek some relief from this dream, she decided to get a professional's opinion. So, on November 11, she described in a typed three-page letter the details of this dream and mailed it from her family's country home in the midwestern United States to Sigmund Freud in Vienna.

November 11th, 1927.

Professor Sigmund Freud,
Bertggasse 19,
Vienna, Austria.

Dear Professor Freud:

I am writing you because I have read a great many of your books and admire you immensely and also because I hope you can help me. In the event that you find yourself too busy to do so I hope that you can tell me who I can go to that will be able to overcome the difficulty.

My desired information is concerning dreams, or rather a dream. First I should like to know the meaning of the dream and secondly whether it will have any direct meaning or reference on my future. I must sound as if I wanted you to be a fortune teller or the like but this is not so because I realize that a man of your fame certainly would be anything but. You see among your books I have read your views on dreams and because of my great respect for you and because of my interest in your work I thought you might be able to help me. Now to go on with the dream and the series of events connected with it. I mention the events previously connected with the dream because if I remember your text on Dream Psychology rightly, you spoke many times of previous occurrences often times having a great deal of influence on dreams. Now for the basis of this letter.

But a short two months ago I met a young man who since has held a great fascination for me. Not being of age as yet of course my parents tyranize over me in many respects and one of them happens to be the choosing of my friends. Possibly you may think me an ungrateful child but still it is only a few short months until I reach the age of independence. Perhaps also I ought to mention the fact that I am the only child in our family. In the case of this young gentleman there have been some very hard words spoken. The reason for this is that the young man in question is an Italian and of course is Catholic. My parents are thoroughbred Americans and also are of a Protestant Religion and although they are not snobbish they feel that in going around with an Italian I am going around with some one who is not my equal. Of course the religious part of it comes in pretty strong as neither father or mother have a very strong love for the Catholic Religion. As for my self it does not bother me at all for I feel that because a person happened to be born into a family of the Catholic or Jewish Religion is nothing against them. In fact if I want to marry either a Jewish or Catholic fellow you may rest assured that I shall do so. But how well I shall accept that religion is another question.

The fascination which this young man has for me has twice transported us into a forbidden paradise, it is also a fool's paradise, leaving us forgetful of every day morals and conventions. Before I met the young man in question he had been going steady with a girl of his own station in life and was going steadily enough with her so that she was wearing his ring, but since he has practically given her up entirely and devoted his time to me. Those are the circumstances leading up to the dream. Now for the dream.

I saw myself sitting in a place that was unfamiliar to me still I seemed to be very much at home. It seemed to be a place poorly furnished so it could not have been home for our place is very beautifully furnished. My uncle, rather my mother's brother, and my father were sitting on the front porch talking and as it was a very hot day I was seated inside by an open window fanning my self, and while I was dreaming as I sat there the door bell rang. Upon answering the ring I found the brother of my young Italian friend. He was dressed very peculiarly wearing the modern civilian clothes of the average American but with a large gaudy colored Mexican Sombrero on his head. We passed the time of day and for several minutes conversed politely on daily news topics of interest, the both of us standing up he on the porch and [me] in the house. He did not disclose the object of his visit until he was ready to depart when he handed me a letter saying that it was from his brother. As a parting remark he told me that he was coming into the city to see me next week and probably there would be four or five other fellows along with him. To which I replied that I would be glad to see them. Upon that he left. In the meantime my father and uncle seemed to have disappeared when they went I have no recollection of but when I answered the doorbell they were not upon the porch. The young man who called upon me lives in a small town not far from my summer home and that is why he told me he was coming in to see me.

Well I opened the letter and I can still see the expression of horror, dismay, and despair which was shown on my face. The letter told me that this young Italian boy had been married on the afternoon of October 17th to a Miss Mildred Dowl. I cannot account for the girl's name because it is not the name of the girl to whom he was formerly engaged or even her initials. The name I cannot account for as I have never known any one by the whole name given above or even the last name.

Well in my despair I happened to look down on a small table standing near me and saw a large brass paper knife with a sharp edge. Grabbing the thing up I struck myself a hard blow around the region of the heart (I must sound quite dramatic, but I assure that I was and am far from feeling that way). I remember the sensation distinctly of the knife passing into my body. The first was the somewhat like the eternal thrill and it passed into something more powerful, lasting and serious, which cannot possibly be explained. I distinctly remember dropping to the floor without the slightest cry or shudder. I saw myself laying on the floor on my right side with my legs drawn up and my left hand outstretched and my right hand still clutching the paper knife. At this time I awoke and I was somewhat startled to find myself lying in the same position in bed as I was when I last saw myself lying on the floor presumably dead. Upon awakening I found the tears coursing down my face and it took me some little time before I could control myself. The next day I found myself thrown into the worst case of blues or dejection or whatever you want to call it and it was an impossibility to pull myself out of it. This comes back to me after I have been thinking about the dream and trying to find a solution of it myself.

This dream occurred during the early morning of the 18th of October. I hope that you will not think me bold for telling you the things I have and also for writing you and asking the favor that I have. If I have annoyed you with my troubles please dear Professor Freud forgive me I really did not intend to. Please believe me when I say that. And also please won't you help me for there seems to have been nothing on my mind but this confounded dream and as I am a stenographer it does not pay to have your mind occupied with anything other than business during business hours. I feel perhaps that just writing you and waiting a reply will relieve the sense of something formidable hanging over me which was caused by the dream.

Awaiting your reply, I am thanking you now for whatever help you can be to me, and begging you to pardon me for bothering you with my troubles.

Sincerely Yours,
Mary Fields

At the time he received this letter, Freud was 71 years old and at the height of this career, but he was also in failing health. Despite his poor health and an enormous work schedule, Freud took the time to answer Mary Field's letter in a one-and-a-half-page typed letter on his personal stationery. As you can see, Freud's response was polite and gracious but guarded in the amount of analysis he was able to do with such limited contact with Mary.

PROF. DR. FREUD
WIEN IX. BERGGASSE 19

Dec. 2nd 1927.

Dear Miss Fields,

I found your letter charming and I am willing to give you as much help as I can. Unhappily it does not reach very far. Dream interpretation is a difficult affair. As long as you cannot explain the name Mildred Dowl in your dream, find out what the source of these two names is, where you got it, a trustworthy explanation of the dream is not possible. You must have heard or read this name somewhere, a dream never creates, it only repeats or puts together. If you were here in Vienna and could talk to me in my study, we could detect where these names come from.

But you are not here and the fact is, you have forgotten it and not yet remembered.

Now for the little I can grasp of the hidden meaning of your dream. I see your emotions towards the young Italian are not undivided, not free from conflict. Besides the love you feel for him there is a trend of perhaps distrust, perhaps remorse. This antagonistic feeling is covered up during your waking life by the love-attraction you undergo and by another motive, your resistance against your parents. Perhaps if your parents did not dislike the boy, it would be much easier for you to become aware of the splitting in your feelings. So you are in a conflict about him and the dream is a way out of the maze. To be sure, you will not leave him and fulfill your parents' request. But if he drops you this is a solution. I guess that is the meaning of the dream and your emotional reaction is produced by the intensity of your love while the content of the dream is the result of the repressed antagonism which yet is active in your soul.

Please write me another letter if after receipt of mine you are able to explain the origin of the two names.

With best wishes

Yours sincerely
Freud

Mary Fields never married and was employed as a secretary her entire life. A carbon copy of her letter to Freud and a copy of his reply to her were found among her papers following her death in 1984. It is unclear if Freud's words helped her to lessen the pain of her dream. Perhaps it was relief enough to know that such a world-famous individual would take the time to reply to her request for help (Benjamin & Dixon, 1996).

*Mary Fields is a pseudonym, used at the request of the writer's surviving family. The writer's letter is reprinted with permission from her estate. Freud's letter is reprinted with permission from Mark Peterson & Associates.

Although Freud laid the foundation for how we think regarding the psychological nature and functions of dreams by emphasizing their operation and influence on thoughts, feelings, and behavior at the unconscious level (Zillmer & Spiers, 2001), more recent theorists place less emphasis on the unconscious aspects of dreams and more on the brain's neurological processes during sleep (Hobson, 1997, 2002) and the relationship between the emotions and thoughts expressed during dreams and recent waking experiences (Domhoff, 1999; Wegner, Wenzlaff, & Kozak, 2004). More specifically, there is evidence to suggest that thinking about something, or trying not to think about something, before you go to sleep can sometimes increase the likelihood of dreaming about it (O'Connor, 2004; Wegner et al., 2004). For, example, if you experience a crisis, such as having a heated argument with a co-worker, and you keep thinking about it for the rest of the day and evening, you are likely to dream about the argument that night. Thus, although recent research supports the notion that dream content is a product of daily concerns in the lives of individuals (Nikles, Brecht, Klinger, & Bursell, 1998), evidence suggests that the meaning of these dreams is closer to the surface, or conscious level of awareness, than deep-seated, unconscious symbolic representations (Crenson, 1999). If you would like to read more about recent perspectives on dreams and dreaming, which my experiences tells me that most students do, examine *The Scientific Study of Dreams* (Domhoff, 2003).

Additional Remarks about Psychoanalytic Methods
Although it may seem that the processes by which free associations are interpreted and dreams are analyzed are pretty straightforward, they are, in fact, extremely complex. According to Freud and other psychoanalysts, such interpretation and analysis can only be done when the analyst has a thorough knowledge of the individual's past and the way these past events relate to current unconscious forces. It takes a considerable amount of training, time, and effort on the analyst's part to progress through all the notes and other pieces of information obtained during the many years of psychoanalyzing an individual to achieve this level of knowledge.

The Dynamics of Psychoanalysis: What Happens in Analysis?

During psychoanalysis, a number of processes occur. The dynamics of insight facilitate the therapeutic process while the processes of resistance, transference, and countertransference hinder its.

The Dynamics of Insight: Meeting and Resolving Unconscious Conflict In addition to making the client aware of the unsuccessful resolution of uncon-

scious conflicts, the dynamics of insight (see p. 103) involve giving the client another chance to resolve them in a more satisfactory manner under the guidance of the psychoanalyst. For example, it is not enough for a client to discover that feelings of resentment toward authority figures are a result of his or her failure to identify completely with the same-sex parent during the phallic stage. In such a case, the client must reexperience, confront, and resolve these intense feelings to deal effectively with other authority figures in life, such as supervisors or police officers. Thus, the basic processes and dynamics of psychoanalysis involve the client having the opportunity to "work though" previously unresolved conflicts with the guidance, supervision, and assistance of the psychoanalyst in a structured and supportive environment (Luborsky, O'Reilly-Landry, & Arlow, 2008; Trull & Phares, 2001).

Resistance: Dragging One's Psychic Heels **Resistance** is a barrier to the psychoanalytic process that occurs when the client avoids facing difficult information during analysis, making it very hard to progress. Resistance can take many forms. In the therapeutic context, clients may begin to "forget" or show up late for their appointments, engage the analyst in conversation about current events to delay the start of the session, or abruptly stop a train of thought during free association. Outside of this context, the client might engage in self-defeating behaviors designed to deal with the increased level of anxiety being confronted during analysis, such as risky sexual behavior or drinking or taking drugs (Trull & Phares, 2001). The underlying dynamics of resistance involve the ego trying to protect the individual against unpleasant information.

Transference: The Therapist as a Symbol of a Significant Other **Transference** occurs when the client begins to express feelings and actions toward the analyst as if he or she were a significant other (e.g., spouse, parents, supervisor) in the client's life (Plante, 2005; Kivlighan, 2002). The thoughts, feelings, and actions revealed through the process of transference can be extremely helpful in analysis because they give clients another opportunity to face their unresolved unconscious conflicts (Arlow, 2000).

For example, a woman arguing with her analyst may be symbolically expressing the anger she feels toward the restrictive actions of her parents during childhood. In this case, the hostile feelings toward the parent would then be analyzed and a more acceptable resolution to the conflict achieved. During the past half century, over 3,000 professional publications have been devoted to the phenomenon of transference (Kivlighan, 2002). A considerable amount of research supports this proposed psychodynamic process (Glassman & Andersen, 1999; Luborsky & Crits-Christoph, 1998; Westen & Gabbard, 1999). However, although transference has been found to be a useful tool during psychoanalysis (Henry, Strupp, Schacht, & Gaston, 1994; Trull & Phares, 2001), other research on the process indicates that it can result in clients feeling criticized (Piper, Azim, Joyce, & McCallum, 1991) and responding defensively (L. McCullough et al., 1991; Porter, 1987).

Countertransference: The Client as a Significant Other   **Countertransference** is when the psychoanalyst begins to express feelings and actions toward the client as if the latter were a child or significant person from the past. The analyst might express affection or make sexual advances toward the client as a reflection of an unresolved Oedipal complex. In such a situation, the analyst runs the risk of undermining the process of analysis by introducing his or her own personal problems (Arlow, 2000). Thus, this phenomenon is a hindrance to successful psychoanalysis. As part of their training, analysts themselves are required to undergo psychoanalysis with a certified analyst to make sure they have no unresolved conflicts that might interfere with their ability to analyze others. Should an analyst become aware of any feelings of countertransference during the process of therapy, she or he might try to resolve the issue through self-analysis, seek the help of another analyst, or discuss the issue openly and honestly with the client and make arrangements to have the client transferred to another therapist (Arlow, 2000).

The Effectiveness of Psychoanalysis: How Good is It?

One of the biggest problems in assessing the effectiveness of psychoanalysis is determining what is meant by treatment effectiveness and for whom treatment is effective (Leuzinger-Bohleber & Target, 2002). As a subjective measure of effectiveness, many people who have gone through analysis report having benefited from the experience (Strupp, Fox, & Lessler, 1969). A more objective measure is found in research comparing clients in psychoanalysis both with those receiving

other types of therapy and with those not yet receiving treatment. This research suggests that the effectiveness of psychoanalytical or "insight-oriented therapy" is similar to that of other forms of therapy and more effective than no treatment at all (Crits-Christoph, 1992; Cross, Sheehan, & Khan, 1982; Slone, Staples, Cristol, Yorkston, & Whipple, 1975; M. L. Smith & Glass, 1977; M. L. Smith, Glass, & Miller, 1980; Svartberg & Stiles, 1991). But such research is not without critics (Eysenck, 1978; Gallo, 1978; Strahan, 1978), who question it on various methodological (e.g., the use of adequate control conditions) and theoretical (e.g., the operation of unconscious forces) grounds.

Certain client characteristics are associated with the effectiveness of psychoanalysis (Arlow, 1995, Luborsky & Spence, 1978; Svartberg & Stiles, 1991). Given its highly verbal nature, bright, articulate individuals are very good candidates for psychoanalysis, whereas severely mentally disturbed individuals with cognitive and communication deficits, such as individuals suffering from **schizophrenia** – a condition in which the individual loses touch with reality (e.g., the belief of being chased by FBI agents constantly) – would not generally benefit significantly from traditional psychoanalysis (D. Klein, 1980; Mosher & Keith, 1979). However, there is some evidence that practitioners implementing certain variations of traditional psychoanalysis based on object relations theory (see pp. 97–101; St. Clair, 2004) have had some success in treating more serious forms of psychopathology, including schizophrenia and severe depression (Teixeria, 1992).

Duration of treatment also seems to play a role. The effectiveness of psychoanalytic therapies seems to improve when there are more than 12 sessions (Grauwe, 1987), which seems reasonable, given the complexities of the associated processes. Recently, however, various forms of "short-term dynamic therapy" (Davanloo, 1999; Levenson, 2003; Luborsky, 1997; Strupp & Binder, 1984; Trull & Phares, 2001), such as "psychoanalytically oriented psychotherapy" and "time-limited dynamic psychotherapy" (Hoyt, 1995; Messer & Kaplan, 2004), have been developed. Driven by the recent emphasis on cost containment in health care systems (Cummings, 1986; Lambert, Bergin, & Garfield, 2004; Moran, 2000), these brief forms of psychodynamic therapy focus less on changing the defensive nature and character of personality and more on the development of strategies designed to deal more effectively with day-to-day problems (e.g., marital problems, stress of unemployment). This short-term, strategic work retains many significant aspects of traditional psychoanalytic therapy, such as the transference relationship (Connolly, Crits-Cristoph, & Barber, 2000; Goldfried, Greenberg, & Marmar, 1990; Luborsky & Crits-Cristoph, 1998). Evidence suggests these brief treatments are more effective than more traditional forms of psychoanalysis (Koss, Butcher, & Strupp, 1986) across a variety of clinical conditions (Koss & Shiang, 1994). In addition, research has shown the effectiveness of brief psychodynamic therapy to be similar to that of various forms of alternative psychological treatments (Crits-Christoph, 1992).

In summary, while the practice of classic psychoanalysis still exists today, its presence is not as pervasive as it was several decades ago (Gabbard, 2000, Horgan, 1996). However, such variations and developments in the psychodynamic approach have served to help it retain its influence and relevance among mental health professionals in a variety of therapeutic settings (Ball & Peake, 2006; Westen & Gabbard, 1999).

In this section we have explored the degree to which psychoanalysis is effective and some of the factors that determine its effectiveness. To learn about some serious and world-changing consequences of its effectiveness, consider the material in "Applications in Personality Psychology" below.

Applications in Personality Psychology

Military Applications of Psychoanalysis: Freud's Contribution to World War I

Because of his emphasis on sexual matters, Freud and his ideas were initially ignored, for the most part, by his German and Austrian colleagues. They viewed his "excessive concern" with such matters as both distasteful and depraved. It is very likely that Freud and his ideas might have remained of interest to a relatively small group of individuals, had it not been for World War I.

In reaction to horrendous experiences in the trenches during the war, many soldiers developed a variety of hysterical symptoms – including blindness, deafness, tremors, and paralysis – for which no medical basis could be determined. These unexplained symptoms rendered the soldiers unfit for combat duty (M. Stone, 1985). Because no medical basis for the symptoms could be determined, these soldiers were viewed as "fakers," treated as disciplinary problems, and punished for dishonorable behavior. But the punishment did not work; the symptoms continued. The incidence of these hysterical symptoms became so great that combat effectiveness was threatened. It was during the war that therapeutic interventions based on the principles of psychoanalysis were first developed and introduced as strategies for treating such combat-related stress reactions (Kennedy & McNeil, 2006).

In response to this crisis, British psychoanalysts offered their assistance. They first pointed out that these soldiers were not fakers or cowards; they were suffering from a mental condition called "shellshock." Defined as a nervous condition resulting from the cumulative emotional, physical, and psychological strains of prolonged warfare, shellshock could be treated by psychoanalysis. Because they had a label and an explanation for this condition, as well as a method for treating it, psychoanalysts were soon in great demand in Great Britain and, subsequently, the United States.

Following the war, psychoanalysis became influential in both countries. Freud's name and ideas began to spread, and although he had been shunned initially, his fame continued to increase. He was awarded honorary degrees, and his works was studied more extensively (Schwartz, 2000). It is interesting to speculate what might have happened if psychoanalysis had not "come to the rescue" with an effective treatment for shellshock and the serious consequences it was creating during World War I, which was supposed to be "the war to end all wars."

The methods, processes, and dynamics of psychoanalysis are rather complex and fascinating. As you read about other forms of therapy throughout this book, you will see the extent to which they have been influenced by psychoanalysis. If you would like to know more on the nature, dynamics, and effectiveness of psychoanalysis, as well as recent developments in this therapeutic technique, read any or all of the following sources: book chapters by Arlow (2000) titled "Psychoanalysis" or Westen (2005) titled "Implications of Research in Cognitive Neuroscience for Psychodynamic Therapy."

For more detailed presentations, read the books *Psychoanalytic Psychotherapy: A Practitioner's Guide* (McWilliams, 2004), *Psychoanalysis: A Critical Introduction* (Craib, 2001), or *Outcomes of Psychoanalytical Treatment* (Leuzinger-Bohleber & Target, 2002). For one of the most recent and intriguing variations of psychoanalysis that combines the practical emphasis of brief forms of psychoanalytic therapy with Freud's cornerstone belief about the benefits of his "talking cure," read "At the Cutting Edge of Personality Psychology: The Emotional and Health Benefits of Expressive Writing" below.

AT THE CUTTING EDGE OF PERSONALITY PSYCHOLOGY

The Emotional and Health Benefits of Expressive Writing

The Write Stuff: The Power of the Pen as a Therapeutic Tool

A critical contribution to Freud's work was the introduction and development of the "talking cure." The central logic of this valuable therapeutic tool was that talking about one's problems would provide emotional and psychological benefits to the speaker. A similar logic has been applied to written expression. For years, therapists have also recognized the emotional benefits of journaling to process stress and trauma. However, in a new twist on this traditional therapeutic tool, recent research indicates that expressive writing has therapeutic impact that goes beyond the psychological benefits previously identified. Specifically, new research indicates that in addition to the psychological benefits, expressive writing also includes physical benefits to people battling with terminal or life-threatening disease.

Two leading researchers in this emerging area are James W. Pennebaker, of the University of Texas at Austin, and Joshua M. Smyth, of Syracuse University (Lepore & Smyth, 2002; Pennebaker, 1997a, 2002). In their research, Pennebaker and Smyth have documented how expressive writing about emotions and stress boosts the immune sys-

James W. Pennebaker has done significant research demonstrating the value of expressive writing, which illustrates many of the principles Freud emphasized in the therapeutic application of his viewpoint.

tem functioning in patients with illnesses such as HIV/AIDS, asthma, and arthritis (Lepore & Smyth, 2002; Pennebaker, 1997a, 1997b), although the impact varies with the population being studied and the form the writing takes.

Why Writing Works: The Added Value of Meaning over Just Muttering

Investigators trying to identify the critical demographic and stylistic elements associated with the physical benefits of expressive writing indicate that key factors include the manner in which people interpret their experiences, including the nature of the words they choose to express themselves (Murray, 2002). For example, simply venting one's emotions – whether verbally or during the act of expressive writing – is not enough to reduce stress and, as a result, improve health. Individuals must be able to use their expressive writings to better understand and learn from their emotions (Lepore & Smyth, 2002). To illustrate this point, researchers Susan K. Lutgendorf and Phil Ullrich (2002) found that individuals who relived unsettling events without focusing on meaning reported poorer health than those who derived some meaning from their expressive writing. In fact, the former fared even worse than individuals who were asked simply to write about neutral events, suggesting that writing alone is not enough to provide therapeutic health benefits. In addition, individuals who focused on meaning in their expressive writings developed a greater sense of the positive aspects of the stressful event.

In commenting on her research, Lutgendorf notes, "You need focused thought as well as emotions. An individual needs to find meaning in a traumatic memory as well as to feel the related emotions to reap positive benefits from the writing exercise" (Murray, 2002, p. 55). As evidence of this shift in perspective, Pennebaker notes that word choice in expressive writing can predict the benefit of the activity. The more people use words such as "because," "realize," and "understand," the more they seem to benefit from their expressive writings (Pennebaker, 1997b). Thus, just as Freud noted almost a century ago, the critical factor in the therapeutic benefits of such expressiveness is the insight gained from them (see p. 103).

In addition, there are a few other elements that seem to be associated with receiving the benefits of expressive writing. More specifically, individuals who demonstrate a shift in their writing from the use of singular pronouns (e.g., *I*, *me*, *my*) to plural pronouns (e.g., *we*, *us*, *them*) show greater benefits from expressive writing than those who do not make this move (Stirman & Pennebaker, 2001). Finally, another important element in the successful use of expressive writing is the presence of a narrative style that resembles a story in which there is a beginning, middle, and an end (Kaufman & Sexton, 2006).

For example, an individual trying to deal with the trauma of an assault might begin an expressive writing program by writing about her initial reaction to the experience like this: "I felt violated by the attack and ashamed that I was so afraid to leave my apartment." A middle part of this narrative might be something like, "But after more thought about what happened to me, I began to realize that it was not my fault, and that my reactions were a normal part of the adjustment and recovery process – that others with similar experiences felt and behaved in the same way." An ending to this narrative might be, "After talking to my friends, I know I can count on them for social support. As they tell me, 'We are here for you.'"

On the other hand, individuals who show a shift toward singular, self-referencing pronouns may be demonstrating a reduction in mental health. Such a pattern has been documented in the private, personal expressions (e.g., diaries and journals) and public creative works (e.g., song lyrics and stories) of a number of famous artists, such as Kurt Cobain and Cole Porter, who demonstrated corresponding increases in self-destructive behavior (e.g., substance abuse) and depression, as their fame increased (Schaller, 1997). For Cobain, the decrease in his mental health led to his eventual suicide.

Finally, when trying to answer the question "Why doesn't the writing cure help poets?" James C. Kaufman and Janel D. Sexton (2006) have proposed that part of the answer may be to do with the lack of narrative form in the work of professional poets, who seem to "have poorer health outcomes relative to both other writers and to the population at large" (p. 268).

Where Writing Works: Operating Within the Body, Brain, and Social Relationships

Although the means by which expressive writing produces emotional and physical health benefits are

Kurt Cobain was a famous musical artist who demonstrated a pattern of expressive writing in his public and private works that has been found to be associated with decreases in mental health. He suffered from substance abuse and eventually committed suicide.

unclear, recent research indicates some possible explanations that include mechanisms within the body, brain, and social relationships.

Facilitating the Functioning of the Immune System

One possible explanation for the benefits of expressive writings is that it facilitates the functioning of the immune system. The **immune system** is the body's natural defense system. It fights against and removes toxic substances and destructive foreign cells entering the body, and it assists in the reproduction of healthy cells in response to illness and disease. In support of this reasoning, in a study of HIV/AIDS patients, individuals participating in a program of expressive writing measured higher on CD4$^+$ lymphocyte counts – an index of immune

system functioning – than did those who were simply asked to write about their daily schedules (Petrie, Fontanilla, Thomas, Booth, & Pennebaker, 2004).

The benefits of expressive writing appear to come from a number of specific changes in the thinking of and emotional expression by these individuals regarding their illness. These included the expression of more positive emotion words, while minimizing the expression of negative emotion words, and more causal (e.g., "because") and insight (e.g., "understand" and "realize") words. More specifically, the cognitive changes in the way they were now thinking about their illness were a result of the increased meaning and greater sense of understanding the individuals gleaned from the traumatic experience by engaging in expressive writing, which decreased the amount of self-reported HIV-related stress and anxiety that they felt, which then made it easier on their immune system because it had less stress to deal with. Stated more simply, the less energy your body has to divert to the immune system dealing with the stress of anxiety, the more energy it can devote to the immune system fighting off the deadly cells while producing healthy cells. In support of this reasoning, other research indicates that individuals who suppressed negative, traumatic thoughts exhibited a reduction in their immune system functioning while those who engaged in expressive writing visited the doctor less (Petrie, Booth, & Pennebaker, 1998) and displayed a stronger immune system response to the Hepatitis B vaccine (Petrie, Booth, Pennebaker, Davison, & Thomas, 1995). Again, such evidence is consistent with Freud's observations about 100 years ago regarding the dangers of suppressing anxiety-provoking thoughts and feelings and the benefits of expressing them in a meaningful way.

Controlling Pain in the Brain In addition to having a positive effect on the immune system, another possibility is that putting our feelings of emotional distress into words serves to trigger certain parts of the brain associated with the experience and reduction of negative feelings brought on by either physical (e.g., being hit) or social (e.g., being rejected or teased) sources of pain (Eisenberger &

Lieberman, 2005; M. D. Lieberman & Eisenberger, 2006). More specifically, using fMRI to record neuronal activity in the brain (see pp. 63–64 for a review), individuals were exposed to a series of images of faces depicting various emotions (e.g., being angry, scared, and happy) and then asked to match those faces either with images of others displaying the same emotion or with words that labeled the emotion (M. D. Lieberman et al., in press). The results indicated that those who used verbal expression to match the emotion showed less neurological activity in the amygdala – an area of the brain that responds to emotional distress – than those who responded with the visual expression. In addition, those using the verbal expression displayed more activity in that part of the brain associated with the verbalization of thoughts and the production of language than those employing the visual expression. Such a pattern of results suggests that verbalizing one's feelings may serve to trigger that part of the brain associated with the creation of verbal responses, which then controls that area of the brain responsible for creating emotional pain (Winerman, 2006).

Improving Intimate Relationships   There is considerable evidence documenting the role of social support in helping individuals to deal with their psychological distress (Rath, 2006; Taylor, 2006; Taylor, Dickerson, & Klein, 2002). In this regard, another mechanism by which the written expression of emotions can serve to help individuals deal with emotional distress is by fostering social support (Niederhoffer & Pennebaker, 2002). For example, dating couples who were asked to write about their deepest thoughts and feelings about the relationships for three consecutive days were more likely to still be dating three months later than couples who were asked simply to write about their daily activities (Slatcher & Pennebaker, 2006). An analysis of the content of the instant messages sent to each other after the three days revealed a greater use of more positive and negative emotions by those in the first group than in the second. In addition, in compar-

ison to individuals who were simply asked to write about how they managed their time during the day, individuals who were asked to write about traumatic experiences during a two-week writing program showed a greater tendency to talk to their friends more, laugh more, and use more positive emotions in their daily conversations, as well as a decrease in their blood pressure (Niederhoffer & Pennebaker, 2002). Thus, it seems that writing about your feelings can facilitate and strengthen your social support network, particularly when you express your emotions to those individuals with whom you already have some special commitment (e.g., significant others).

No matter what the specific mechanism for the benefits of expressive writing may be, the primary dynamic seems to be that "Putting upsetting experiences into words allows people to stop inhibiting their thoughts and feeling, to begin to organize their thoughts and perhaps find meaning in their traumas, and to reintegrate into their social networks" (Niederhoffer & Pennebaker, 2002, p. 581). Such an elegant summary of this research on the physical and psychological benefits of expressing your troubled feelings is very consistent with Freud's logic over 100 years ago, when he encouraged his clients to stop defending against (i.e., inhibiting) their unconscious emotions and talk about them during their therapeutic sessions. If you would like more information on the benefits of expressive writing, I would recommend you start by reading a book chapter by Niederhoffer & Pennebaker (2002) titled "Sharing one's story: On the benefits of writing or talking about emotional experience." I would also recommend reading Pennebaker's (1997a) *Opening Up: The Healing Power of Expressing Emotions*, which is a short, reader-friendly, and engaging account of this fascinating area of study, or Stephen J. Lepore and Joshua M. Smyth's (2002) *The Writing Cure: How Expressive Writing Promotes Health and Emotional Well-being*, which is a more scholarly presentation of this topic.

Summing It Up *The Purpose and Processes of Psychoanalysis*

Basic Element	Description	Example
Basic Objective	The development of insight brings awareness of unresolved unconscious conflicts and the opportunity to resolve them in a more appropriate and successful manner.	During therapy, an individual learns how problems related to strict care giving during his childhood may relate to his intimate relationships in adulthood.
Basic Methods	Tension is expressed and reduced through catharsis in a nonthreatening therapeutic environment.	The technique of *free association* makes possible the expression of the contents of the unconscious mind by unrestrained thinking. *Dream analysis* uncovers expressions from the unconscious mind via the latent content of dreams (i.e., the real meaning) by analyzing their manifest content (i.e., details that are recalled).
Basic Dynamics	Barriers to the therapeutic process include the misattribution of feelings of the client toward the therapist with transference and of the therapist toward the client with countertransference, and resistance by the client.	An individual begins to develop feelings of fear toward the therapist while the therapist begins to develop feelings of hostility toward the client. The client demonstrates resistance by canceling sessions at the last minute.
Basic Effectiveness	While subjective reports from clients support the benefits of psychoanalysis, there are conflicting reports of effectiveness, based on systematic research.	An individual reports feeling better about her relationships with her co-workers after her sessions of psychoanalysis, but interviews with co-workers indicate that some critical interpersonal problems still remain.

Psychoanalysis was developed to help Freud test his viewpoint of personality and help his clients deal with their psychological problems. A summary of the major points of discussion is presented in "Summing It Up: The Purpose and Processes of Psychoanalysis" above. Next we will consider some additional applications of the psychodynamic viewpoint.

The Application of Psychodynamic Principles to Personality Assessment: Another Look at Projective Techniques

Because the principal information related to personality is believed to be located in the unconscious mind, personality assessment based on psychodynamic prin-

ciples relies primarily on the use of projective techniques. As you will recall from the discussion in Chapter 2 (see pp. 56–59), projective techniques are characterized by the ambiguous nature of the testing stimuli and the freedom of response options available to the individuals being tested. For example, the testing stimuli can vary from pictures of clouds to an incomplete sentence, while the response options can vary from "Tell me what you see in these clouds" to "Complete the following sentence: If I were the president . . ." The logic underlying psychodynamic assessment is that the meaning given to the ambiguous test stimuli contained in projective techniques represents unconscious processes and hidden or repressed aspects of personality, such as unconscious needs, motives, desires, unacceptable thoughts and impulses, fantasies, and conflicts (Frank, 1939; Cohen & Swerdlik, 2005; K. R. Murphy &

Davidshofer, 2005; Viglione & Rivera, 2003). Because of their emphasis on their emphasis on unconscious dynamics, projective techniques are most often associated with the psychodynamic viewpoint.

While there is a variety of projective techniques, one in particular is based on a central feature of Freud's psychodynamic viewpoint – the psychosexual stages of development. The **Blacky Pictures Test** (Blum, 1949, 1950, 1968) is a projective technique consisting of 12 cartoon-like drawings featuring a dog named Blacky. The pictures are designed to elicit stories directly relevant to a specific psychosexual stage. For example, one drawing depicts Blacky nursing intensely on Mama. This picture is designed to trigger themes of oral eroticism, which – as would be predicted from psychodynamic theory – has been more closely linked to heavy smokers than to nonsmokers (Kimeldorf & Geiwitz, 1966). Although not used much today, the Blacky Pictures Test is an excellent example of how the psychodynamic theory was integrated into a specific test (Cohen & Swerdlik, 2005).

The Thematic Apperception Test (TAT) is another projective technique used in assessing the manifestation of unconscious needs (see pp. 57–58). With this test, individuals are asked to make up (i.e., project) stories in response to a series of pictures. But probably the best-known and most widely used projective technique for assessing unconscious processes is the Rorschach Inkblot Test (Erdberg & Exner, 1984; Gray-Little, 1995; Weiner, 1998), which "has been administered to hundreds of thousands of people, generated thousands of research studies, and become widely familiar to professional persons and the general public around the world" (Weiner, 1998, p. 3). It has been described as "associated in the public eye with psychology itself" (Cohen & Swerdlik, 1999, p. 437). To learn more about this famous test, see "A Closer Look" below.

fraternity nickname of "Klex" means "inkblot" in German (Mestel, 2003a; "Time capsule," 2000). Although constructed by the 27-year-old Rorschach in 1911, the test was not published until 1921 (Rorschach, 1921/1942), in a book titled *Psychodiagnostics: A Diagnostic Test Based on Perception*. In a tragic series of events, Rorschach was hospitalized on April 1, 1922, after complaining of abdominal pains for several days, which were determined to be caused by a ruptured appendix. After exploratory surgery, he died on April 2. In a related piece of irony, the entire first edition of the book went essentially unsold, and the publisher went bankrupt. In 1927, the book was purchased by Hans Huber Publishers, who still maintain the publishing rights to this day. Thus, due to his early and unexpected demise, Herman Rorschach, tragically, reaped essentially no financial reward from this most original contribution to psychology.

The Rorschach Inkblot Test (Rorschach, 1921/1942) consists of 10 inkblots on a white background. Five of the cards are black (with shades of gray) and five are colored. A sample inkblot card is presented in Figure 3.7. During administration of the test, the individual is shown each card separately and asked to indicate what the card looks like (e.g., two people dancing) and what factors influence the response (e.g., the middle part looks as though their hands are touching).

A Closer Look

The Rorschach Inkblot Test: The Most Famous Projective Technique

The **Rorschach Inkblot Test** was created by the Swiss psychiatrist Herman Rorschach (1884–1922), whose

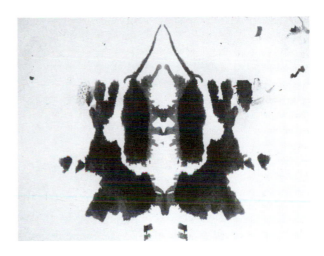

Figure 3.7   A sample inkblot card

Scoring and Interpreting the Rorschach

Although several different systems have been developed for scoring the almost unlimited number of responses to the Rorschach cards (Klopfer & Davidson, 1962; Lerner, 1996a, 1996b), Exner's Comprehensive System of scoring (Exner, 1991, 1993, 2002) is the most widely used (Cohen & Swerdlik, 2005; Trull & Phares, 2001; Weiner, 1998). In scoring and interpreting the results, the individual's responses to the cards are examined along a number of different dimensions to determine characteristic features of his or her personality. When scoring the test, the examiner might look at the number of responses the individual generates to the cards, the popularity of the responses (i.e., the extent to which the individual's responses are similar to others), and the individual's use of the whole or just part of the card (e.g., the tips at the top of the figure) to create their response, to name just a few determinants.

When interpreting the test, the examiner might note that a greater number of responses (e.g., "It looks like a donkey with wings flying, or an X-ray photo of the brain, or some road kill" vs. "It looks like a donkey with wings flying") suggests a higher degree of intelligence. A high degree of popular responses (e.g., "It looks like a bat") might indicate a tendency to conform to and think like other people. Individuals who use the whole cards (e.g., "The figures at the top look like radar antennae, and the stuff at the bottom reminds me of flames coming out of exhaust pipes. So it looks like a Martian spaceship hovering in space") demonstrate a high degree of abstract thinking and creativity. This brief presentation may make it seem that the scoring and interpretation of the Rorschach is simple and straightforward. However, you should realize that it takes many hours of training and supervision.

Validity and Reliability of the Rorschach

As was noted in Chapter 2, a characteristic limitation of the projective techniques of personality assessment is the rather low reliability and validity associated with them. Recent attempts to create more objective and consistent scoring systems, such as Exner's (Exner, 1991, 1993, 2002), have done much to improve reliability in the scoring of the Rorschach (McDowell & Acklin, 1996). However, critics note that even so, the sheer number of possible responses and the many subjective judgments made by the examiners bring into question the reliability and validity of the interpretations (Dawes, 1994; Hunsley & Bailey, 1999; Hunsley,

Lee, & Wood, 2003; Lilienfeld, Wood, & Garb, 2000; Wood, Nezworski, Lilienfeld, & Garb, 2003). For example, they can be influenced by the test administrator's assumptions and beliefs about those for whom the test is being interpreted (Ben-Shakhar, Bar-Hillel, Bilu, & Shefler, 1998). In addition, as with other types of projective techniques discussed previously (see pp. 56–59), the Rorschach's validity is questioned – including its ability to predict behavior and assess specific dimensions of personality (Mestel, 2003b; Wood et al., 2003). As a result of such concerns regarding the validity of the Rorschach and other projection techniques, they are not used very often in basic personality research, but they remain popular among clinical psychologists, particular those with a psychodynamic orientation, who use them in assessment of psychological disorders (Lilienfeld et al., 2000).

Despite its limitations, the Rorschach is still used widely by clinicians as a diagnostic tool (Camara, Nathan, & Puente, 1998; K. R. Murphy & Davidshofer, 2005). In addition to being the most frequently taught projective technique in many counseling programs (Watkins, Campbell, & Manus, 1990) and used in many training sites (Craig, 1990), the Rorschach has been used extensively in forensic work (Piotrowski, 1996a, 1996b) and widely accepted by courts of law (Meloy, Hansen, & Weiner, 1997; Weiner, Exner, & Sciara, 1996). In the face of conflicting views, what conclusion can we draw regarding this provocative test? According to University of South Florida Professor Irving B. Weiner, one of the world's leading experts on the Rorschach, "Widely used and highly valued by clinicians and researchers in many countries of the world, it appears despite its fame not yet to have received the academic respect it deserves and, it can be hoped, will someday enjoy" (Weiner, 1997, p. 17). Thus, because of the different ways it is used, a more specific evaluation of the quality of the Rorschach would be difficult.

If you would like more information on the Rorschach, see Exner's (2002) *The Rorschach: A Comprehensive System: Vol. 1*, Weiner's (1998) *Principles of Rorschach Interpretation*, or *Psychoanalytic Perspectives on the Rorschach* (Lerner, 1998). For a more critical look at the Rorschach, read *What's Wrong with the Rorschach? Science Confronts the Controversial Inkblot Test* (Wood et al., 2003).

An important asset of the Rorschach is the ambiguous nature of the stimuli, which makes it ideal for use with individuals from different cultures (Butcher, Nezami, & Exner, 1998). Specifically, since the socialization process influences the variety of personal experiences available to an individual and helps to shape the meaning given to these experiences, differences in socialization should be reflected in the nature of the projections. Similarly, cultural factors can influence Rorschach responses. To learn about the use of the Rorschach to study the influence of cultural factors on the projection process, see "The Cultural Context of Personality Psychology."

The Cultural Context of Personality Psychology

The Universal Utilization of the Rorschach

Take a moment to examine the card presented in Figure 3.7 on p. 115. What do you see in the inkblot? Next, take a moment to reflect on what made you see the things you did in response to the card. If you have the time, repeat this exercise with a few friends. Did you see any commonalties between your responses and those of your friends?

Now consider the responses presented below, which were provided by "Dawnlight," a middle-aged female Apache Indian shaman, to the card in Figure 3.7 (Boyer, De Vos, & Boyer, 1989). In various cultures around the world, **shamans** are believed to have supernatural powers used to heal the sick and trigger visions that provide insight into significant cultural, spiritual, medicinal, and agricultural events. Dawnlight's responses were obtained on two separate occasions, about two years apart, as part of an anthropological case study examining the intrapsychic dynamics associated with her personal and social adjustment to becoming a shaman. The first set of her responses was obtained just two days after she became a shaman. The second set was obtained two years later to assess the potential stress and strain associated with the heightened cultural expectations of her performing the duties of a shaman, a high-status social role typically held by a male of her tribe.

Card V: First Administration

1st Response: *Grasshopper, flying*
2nd Response: *Bat with webbed wings*
(60 second pause)
3rd Response: *Something else flies. A black owl.*

Interpretation

Dawnlight responds to Card V with the highly popular response of "bat," along with two other responses. The first response is that of a flying grasshopper while the third, after an extended pause, is that of a black owl. It is important to note that the Apache have a concern for grasshoppers, since at various times they have been literally plagued by them. In fact, at the time of this administration, there was a grasshopper invasion of the area. Finally, it should also be noted that for the Apache, the owl is symbolic of impending death. Thus, Dawnlight's responses appear to be symbolic of threat and anxiety. (based on Boyer et al., 1989, p. 396)

Card V: Second Administration

1st Response: *Bat*
2nd Response: *Grasshopper, no spine*

Interpretation

On Dawnlight's first response to Card V two years ago, her responses were interpreted by the testers to indicate anxiety. Here first response to the card then was that of a grasshopper, then a bat, and lastly an owl, which is a rather unusual response to this card, but one that reflected an adequate form level (i.e., tied the various components of the card together). As noted previously, at the time of the first administration of the test, there was a plague of grasshoppers, and Dawnlight was intensely worried about her garden. In this second set of responses, she initially gives the popular response of the bat but then responds with the spineless grasshopper again. Such a pattern of response seems to reflect her continued feelings of anxiety, but this time stemming from feelings of inadequacy and a lack of strength to deal with the crisis. As can be seen in her responses, she continues to deal with the lingering concern for the grasshoppers, but does so by displacing it from its source (i.e., shifting it to the bat). As can be seen in her responses to other cards during this second administration, such a defensive posture (i.e., displacement) against the anxiety did not work very well. (based on Boyer et al., 1989, p. 415)

The information presented in this feature illustrates clearly the significance of the cultural context of personality psychology. The corollary is that to truly understand the nature of an individual's responses to the inkblots, it is important to have some knowledge of his or her cultural background. In this case, knowing something about the impact of grasshoppers and the symbolic meaning of owls within the context of the Apache culture gives much deeper significance to Dawnlight's responses.

Although knowing the cultural background helps in understanding responses, it is the unstructured nature of the inkblot cards that gives them their universal appeal and utility. Evidence in support of the global utilization of the Rorschach includes the vigor of the International Rorschach Society, which typically draws participants from more than 30 countries to its international meeting every three years and sponsors the publication of *Rorschachiana*, a yearbook that concludes theoretical, research, and clinical contributions translated into English from many different languages (Weiner, 1998). In addition, as seen in the information presented here, the utility of the Rorschach extends to both developed cultures and primitive societies (Weiner, 1998). Thus, in a conclusion reached over 60 years ago (Vernon, 1935), "the Rorschach is an ideal instrument for exploring cross-cultural differences because, unlike verbal and more structured tests, it involves cultural-free stimuli" (Weiner, 1998, p. 46). If you would like more information about the cross-cultural aspects of the Rorschach, I recommend highly *Symbolic Analysis Cross-culturally: The Rorschach* (De Vos & Boyer, 1989).

This concludes our discussion of personality assessment from the psychodynamic viewpoint. In the next section, we will explore applications of the psychodynamic viewpoint to areas related to consumer decision making and marketing.

The Application of Psychodynamic Principles to Marketing and Buying Behaviors: Freud Meets Madison Avenue

Whether we realize it or not, our decision to purchase a particular product is influenced by many psycho-dynamic factors (e.g., fantasies and psychic needs, sexual desires) as well as the more common features of the product itself (e.g., price or ease of operation). From a marketing perspective, those in product development try to create new items that attempt to fulfill the needs of the id, ego, or superego while those in advertising use Freudian concepts (e.g., anxiety reduction) to create and develop advertising campaigns (Arnould, Price, & Zinkhan, 2002). In this section, we will discuss two phenomena in which Freudian concepts are applied to consumer behavior: motivation research/lifestyle analysis and subliminal advertising.

Motivation Research and Lifestyle Analysis: Classic and Contemporary Freudian Contributions to Marketing

One of the earliest and most influential applications of psychodynamic principles to consumer behavior was in the area of motivation research, a major force in marketing from the late 1940s to the early 1960s. At its peak of popularity, **motivation research** attempted to uncover the deep-seated reasons for purchasing particular products and unconscious influences on decision making. To overcome the ego's defenses, motivation researchers used many projective techniques (e.g., word association and picture-completion tests) and in-depth, psychoanalytically based interviews to get at these unconscious determinants of buying behavior (Dichter, 1949, 1964).

Motivation researchers also relied heavily on psychodynamic concepts and processes in explaining and interpreting their findings. Study results included these ideas: wearing suspenders reflects unresolved castration complexes, making cakes symbolizes giving birth, and people do not like to buy prunes because their wrinkled shape brings back memories of parental authority figures (Dichter, 1960). The use of motivation research principles became so popular that in 1957, Vance Packard published *The Hidden Persuaders* as a means of trying to cast "a penetrating light into the murky world of the motivational researchers. It tells how these shock troops of the advertising world are subtly charting your inner thoughts, fears, and dreams so that they can influence your daily living" (p. i).

Although its influence as the driving force in marketing has long since waned, motivation research remains significant in its focus on the underlying reasons why people buy. It has also demonstrated the usefulness of psychological theories and assessment techniques in identifying and interpreting consumer behavior patterns (Arnould et al., 2002; Foxall & Goldsmith, 1988; Hawkins, Best, & Coney, 2001). A clear illustration of the lingering impact of motivation research is the influence of Freudian dream analysis on contemporary marketing research through the use of manifest and latent motives to understand the decisions of consumers (Hawkins et al., 2001). **Manifest motives** are the reasons known to the consumer and admitted to the consumer researcher. For example, when explaining the decision to purchase a luxury car, an individual might tell co-workers such things as, "A large car is more comfortable and safe. Plus, this luxury car is really well built and will hold its value." **Latent motives** are reasons and beliefs affecting purchasing decisions that the consumer is unaware of or very reluctant to admit to others. For example, the latent motives for purchasing the luxury car, which the individual may not want to admit or tell others, might include, "This is a powerful and sexy car, which will make me look powerful and sexy, as well show off how successful I am, to others."

As in dream analysis, manifest motives are easily assessed with direct questions (Berstell & Nitterhouse, 1997), such as "Why did you by this car?" On the other hand, just as the psychodynamic viewpoint emphasizes the use of projective techniques to reveal the latent content of the unconscious mind, marketing researchers are returning to projective approaches to better understand consumer decisions and develop marketing campaigns (Hawkins et al., 2001), many of which are similar to those on p. 120. These include sentence completion techniques (e.g., "Complete the sentence: 'People buy a Cadillac _____'"), word association techniques (e.g., "Tell me the first word that comes to mind when I say 'Oreo'"), and picture response construction techniques (e.g., "Here is a picture of an individual buying an outfit. Tell me a story about this picture"). As an indication of the value of such projective techniques, investigators have noted that "these techniques are gaining use again as a way to enhance and enrich the insights that can be gained from more empirical sources" (Hawkins et al., 2001, p. 369). The basic logic of such an approach thus is to identify not only the surface meaning of why people buy certain products (e.g., because of quality workmanship or price) but, more importantly, the deeper psychological motives and consequences (e.g., higher self-esteem, being more popular, feeling secure) of such decisions (Peter & Olson, 2002). This logic is at the very core

of Freud's views on investigating and understanding personality.

The emphasis on personality dynamics (e.g., needs and desires) continues to be a major force in contemporary marketing research (Arnould et al., 2002; Berkowitz, Kerin, Hartley, & Rudelius, 2000). **Psychographics**, also known as **lifestyle analysis**, is a technique in which people's attitudes, interests, and behavior patterns are used to help market and advertise products in a manner that fits with the social (e.g., leisure activities) and psychological (e.g., status-seeking) profile of a particular segment of the buying public (e.g., young adults) at which the products are being targeted (Hawkins et al., 2001; Peter & Olson, 2002). To boost ticket sales at a local amusement park, marketing researchers might promote it as a quick and simple way to meet certain needs of busy working parents (e.g., to assuage their guilt about not spending enough time with their children).

One of the most widely used measures of psychographics is the **Values and Lifestyle (VALS™ 2) Program** (1989) developed by SRI Consulting and Business Intelligence (SRIC-BI, formally Stanford Research Institute [SRI] International). This program seeks to explain how and why consumers make decisions by asking individuals to indicate their degree of agreement with a series of 42 questions such as "I am often interested in theories," "I often crave excitement," and "I like being in charge of a group." From their responses to these items, individuals are grouped into three self-orientation categories:

- *Principle-oriented.* Individuals in this group use personal beliefs and principles to make consumer decisions rather than feelings, events, and the desire to seek approval from others. For example, such an individual might decide against purchasing a popular brand of sneakers because of a sense of guilt that these shoes are made by exploited workers in underdeveloped countries laboring in horrendous conditions.
- *Status-oriented.* Individuals in this group base their purchasing decisions on the actions and opinions of others (e.g., what others are wearing) and the desire to the seek approval of and the anxiety over being rejected by others. For example, an individual might decide to buy a type of sneaker only because "they are all the rage with celebrities and everyone at the hottest clubs in town is wearing them."

- *Action-oriented.* Individuals in this group base their purchasing decisions on social or physical activities, the pursuit of a variety of experiences, impulsiveness, risk taking, and the excitement and tensions such activities produce. For example, on the spur of the moment an individual might decide to buy distinctive sneakers to elicit attention and create excitement at work, where everyone else wears conservative shoes.

As you can see, many of the underlying dynamics discussed by Freud in terms of the operation of personality, such as guilt, anxiety, and the building of tension, are reflected in these three self-orientation categories. In addition to the self-orientation dimension, the VALS 2 program also utilizes a resources dimension, which reflects an individual's ability to pursue and express the desired self-orientation. This dimension includes both monetary resources and psychological (e.g., self-esteem, confidence) and social (e.g., peer support) ones. The VALS 2 program uses these to segment consumers into eight general psychographic categories: strugglers, believers, strivers, makers, fulfilled, achievers, experiencers, and actualizers. If you would like to know your VALS 2 profile, consider the material presented in the following "You Can Do It."

You Can Do It

Are You What You Buy? Examining Your VALS Profile

To what extent are your purchasing decisions a reflection of your underlying personality dynamics as assessed by the technique of psychographics? To examine your VALS profile, simply respond to the questions provided on the VALS 2 questionnaire at http://future.sri.com. You will also be able to examine the characteristic features of your profile and others in more detail. As you examine your profile, to what extent do you feel it is a reflection of the way your personality is expressed through the products you buy? Are you what you buy?

In an indirect manner, traditional Freudian concepts like tension reduction and defense mechanisms are major considerations in consumer decisions (Arnould et al., 2002; Hawkins et al., 2001). For example, to overcome feelings of loneliness, a person rationalizes the extra cost and responds to an advertisement suggesting an increase in popularity for those who use the advertised toothpaste. As another reflection of Freud's viewpoint, a common technique in advertising is the use of dream themes, for example by such major companies as Toyota, the Gap, Avon, Citibank, and British Airways (Garchik, 1996). The logic seems to be to promote dream themes as a form of wish fulfillment for the consumer (e.g., "I can be sexier with a new car" or "I can be slimmer with this exercise machine"). Such reasoning is consistent with primary process thought and the pleasure principle (i.e., the creation of mental images for the purpose of immediate gratification), but only at a more conscious level. As the real world becomes a harsher place, with massive employee downsizing and increases in violent crime, advertisers using dream themes hope to incorporate the less critical and more fluid thinking characteristic of the dream state. Of course, even though the individual fantasizes that having the car will make him sexier, the reality of the situation is that the car comes with a large monthly car payment. Such reality-based details are typically not part of the dream themes used in the advertisement. Thus, the Freudian influence is still very much alive on Madison Avenue.

Subliminal Advertising: Where the Message Supposedly Meets the Unconscious Mind

Beginning in the middle 1950s, in an interesting application of the psychodynamic contention that our unconscious mind influences our behavior, some marketing researchers began exploring the possibility of using subliminal advertising to influence consumer behavior. **Subliminal advertising** is an advertising technique by which product messages and images are presented to consumers without their conscious awareness. Although its use and effectiveness are controversial, subliminal advertising exemplifies the importance of the unconscious mind's influence on overt behavior (e.g., the purchase of products). Do you remember the cartoon character Joe Camel? Noticing the pairing of sexual overtones with the logic of subliminal cigarette advertising, "many observers declared that the cartoon character Joe Camel looked like a phallus, and Freudian theory provides an interesting framework for thinking about these unconscious urges" (Arnould et al., 2002, p. 382).

Essential to the logic of subliminal advertising is the concept of subliminal perception. **Subliminal perception** refers to a person's ability to perceive and respond to stimuli that are below the **limen**, or threshold of consciousness. In a very strict sense, a stimulus that is below the limen (i.e., subliminal) is presented so weakly that you would be conscious of it much less than 50 percent of the time yet it would still be strong enough, on *some occasions*, to reach your conscious level of awareness. But before discussing subliminal advertising, it is necessary to determine if subliminal perception is even possible.

Is Subliminal Perception Possible? Perceiving When You are Not Aware   There is considerable evidence that perception without awareness is possible (Dijksterhuis, Aart, & Smith, 2005). Research conducted by Robert Zajonc, of Stanford University, and Anthony Greenwald, of the University of Washington, as well as others, supports the contention that some stimuli that are not recognized can influence the affective reactions of individuals (Abrams & Greenwald, 2000; Greenwald & Draine, 1997; Greenwald, Draine, & Abrams, 1996; Kunst-Wilson & Zajonc, 1980; Monahan, Murphy, & Zajonc, 2000; S. T. Murphy & Zajonc, 1993; Zajonc, 1980). In a good example of this type of research, individuals were asked to watch a video of their performance on a number of trials during a computer game or a competitor's performance on that game (Tamir, Robinson, Clore, Martin, & Whitaker, 2004). While watching the video, images of smiling or frowning faces were flashed onto the screen at a rate that was too fast (i.e., every 32 milliseconds) for them to see consciously. The results indicated that the individuals rated their present and expected future performances as being better when they were exposed to smiling faces and their opponent's performances were paired with frowning ones, creating the belief that they were doing well and their opponent was doing poorly, than when the pairing was reversed, creating the belief that their opponent was doing well and they were doing poorly. Thus, there does seem to be sufficient evidence that people can be influenced by subliminal perception.

Does Subliminal Advertising Work? Purchasing Without Awareness   In 1956, James M. Vicary, a public

relations executive, used a special projector to flash the messages "Drink Coca-Cola" or "Eat Popcorn" on the screen every 5 seconds, for less than 1/1,000th of a second, while an audience was watching a movie. This subtle manipulation resulted in an increase in the sale of popcorn by 57.7 percent and Coca-Cola by 18.8 percent over the sales for the previous six weeks (Wilhelm, 1956). Vicary's results triggered a tremendous amount of interest and controversy surrounding the possible effects and use of subliminal advertising and messaging that is still very much alive today. For example, the families of two teen boys who committed suicide blamed it on the British rock band Judas Priest. In their suit, the families claimed that the band's music contained subliminal lyrics ("Do it") that promoted satanism and encouraged suicide (Rock group not liable for deaths, 1990).

A more recent illustration of the subliminal advertising controversy occurred during the 2000 U.S. presidential election (Democrats Smell a Rat, 2000). As part of their election efforts, the Bush campaign ran an attack ad on TV criticizing opponent Al Gore's health-care proposal. This ad contained the simple message "The Gore Prescription Plan: Bureaucrats Decide." However, for just a fraction of a second, the word "RATS" in large letters was also flashed across the screen, supposedly trying to link Gore with rats. When they became aware of the ad, the Gore campaign team accused the Bush team of trying to influence votes with subliminal messages. In response, George W. Bush denied having any knowledge of the use of the technique of subliminal messaging. In their defense, the producers of the "RATS" ad stated that it was not their intention to directly or indirectly insult Gore, but

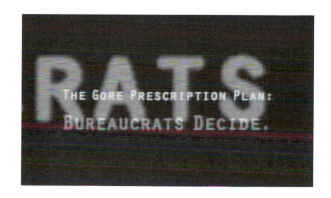

The "RATS" ad caused considerable controversy with its supposedly subliminal message during the 2000 U.S. presidential election.

simply to provide a visual cue to reminder viewers of the word "bureaucrats" (i.e., "rats" being the last four letters of the word). In response to all of the negative attention the ad drew, the Bush campaign team quickly pulled it from the campaign. Was all of this concern justified? Did the "RAT" ad, the lyrics of Judas Priest, or Vicary's "Drink Coca-Cola" and "Eat Popcorn" messages serve to influence the behavior of individuals without them being aware of it? In short, is there any evidence to support the use of subliminal messages?

Are these anecdotes impressive? They also might make you concerned about the potential for advertisers to control your mind without your knowledge. In fact, when discussing the general public's pervasive belief in subliminal advertising, it was reported that 75 percent of Americans had heard of it, and 75 percent of these believed that it worked (Dijksterhuis et al., 2005, p. 92). However, before you put too much confidence in the impact of subliminal advertising, you should know that Vicary later admitted that he made up the claims as a hoax and publicity stunt to boost sales of subliminal projectors (Moore, 1982; Pratkanis, 1992; Weir, 1984). In fact, the firm that supposedly helped to conduct the original subliminal advertising study in 1956 also happened to be in the business of selling subliminal projectors (Runyon, 1980). This alone should make you question the validity of those results. In addition, the families of the suicidal teens lost their case (Rock group not liable for death, 1990), and, although it did receive some attention, the "RATS" ad is not believed to have changed voting behavior (Aronson, Wilson, & Akert, 2002). A more systemic reason for not putting much faith in the power of subliminal advertising is that subliminal stimuli are less likely to influence behavior when individuals engage in considerable mental deliberation on the issue (e.g., an individual is listening to the stated position on taxes of a political candidate during a campaign message) or object (e.g., the individual notices the color or style of a pair of jeans in a commercial) being targeted for change (Olson & Fazio, 2001). Stated more concisely, instead of simply viewing advertisements passively, most individuals are actually paying some attention to and thinking about what they are viewing at a conscious level, thus minimizing any unconscious effects of the subliminal message in the advertisement.

However, the biggest reason you need not worry is that to date, the general consensus is that evidence collected over the years supporting the persuasive power of subliminal advertising is extremely weak (Berkowitz et al., 2000; Dixon, 1971; Greenwald, Spangenberg, Pratkanis, & Eskenazi, 1991; Hawkins et al., 2001; Heart & McDaniel, 1982; Kotler & Armstrong, 1994; McConnell, Cutler, & McNeil, 1958; Moore, 1982; Peter & Olson, 2002; Schoell & Guiltinan, 1995; K. H. Smith & Rogers, 1994; Vivian, 1993). It is inconclusive for the following reasons:

- *Individual differences.* There is a considerable amount of variation in what exactly is subliminal from person to person. As a result, it would be impossible to establish a "standard subliminal stimulus" that would be effective for a large enough group of people to make it cost-effective (Moore, 1982). In addition, individual consumers respond to advertisements by actively constructing and attaching personal meaning to the message based on a variety of personal (e.g., emotional states) and environmental (e.g., cost, ease of accessibility) factors, rather than simply to the general nature of the message itself (e.g., "Eat Popcorn"; Peter & Olson, 2002).

- *Poor generalizability of laboratory results.* Studies finding subliminal message effects have been done in controlled laboratory settings, where the participants were given strict instructions to concentrate on the screen (Greenwald & Draine, 1997; Moore, 1982, 1995). Specifically, "To get subliminal effects, researchers have to make sure that illumination of the room is just right, that people are seated just the right distance from a viewing screen, and that nothing else is occurring to distract them as the subliminal stimuli are flashed" (Aronson et al., 2002, p. 246). In more realistic settings, such as movie theaters with many distractions going on, it is very likely that people might not even attend to the message or possibly misinterpret it (Runyon, 1980). In addition, even in controlled laboratory settings, there is no evidence that subliminal messages can make people act against their wishes or beliefs (Neuberg, 1988). Research on subliminal advertising conducted in "real-life settings," such as on television, has failed to demonstrate its effectiveness (DeFleur & Petranoff, 1959).

- *Misleading claims.* A recent variation of subliminal advertising is the promotion of audiotapes with subliminal messages on them. The tapes supposedly help individuals with an assortment of problems, including losing weight, increasing motivation, raising self-esteem, improving memory, quitting smoking, and learning a foreign language. In 1990, the market for the sale of such self-help subliminal tapes was estimated to be $50 million dollars (Krajick, 1990). Are the sales figures for such tapes a testimony to their effectiveness? The answer to this question is a resounding "No." As with subliminal advertising, there is considerable evidence that subliminal self-help audiotapes are not effective (Brannon & Brock, 1994; Druckman & Bjork, 1991; Moore, 1982, 1992, 1995; Pratkanis, 1992; Pratkanis, Eskenazi, & Greenwald, 1994; Theus, 1994; Trappey, 1996), including those specifically designed for weight loss (Merikle & Skanes, 1992).

As a powerful and interesting illustration of the latter point, Greenwald and associates (Greenwald et al., 1991) provided study participants with a subliminal self-help tape labeled as either "Improving Memory" or "Improving Self-Esteem" and had them listen to the tapes for five weeks. For half of the individuals in each group, the message in the tape either matched the label or contained the message of the other tape. For the other half of the individuals in each group, the label did not match the message on the tape. When assessed five weeks later, scores on the measures of memory and self-esteem were no higher than those obtained before the tapes were distributed. What's more, regardless of whether or not the message on the tape matched the label, when asked about the tapes' effectiveness, individuals who listened to the one labeled "Improving Memory" believe their memory had improved; whereas those who listened to the one labeled "Improving Self-Esteem" believed their self-esteem had improved. Thus, even though there was no actual improvement, the perceived improvement was based on what was on the label, rather than on the actual content of the tape. A simple and eloquent summary of the effects of such subliminal self-help tapes is, "What you expect is what you believe, but not necessarily what you get" (Pratkanis et al., 1994, p. 251). So, do not be misled by the label on these subliminal self-help tapes or the claims made on their packaging and advertisements – buyer beware!

In conclusion, people do have the ability to be emotionally or physiologically influenced slightly by stimuli they may not be able to recognize or explain. But their recall of and preference for certain product

Summing It Up *Applications of the Psychodynamic Viewpoint*

Application	Description	Example
Personality Assessment	Personality assessment involves various projective techniques designed to measure aspects of personality operating in the unconscious mind.	The Blacky Pictures and the Rorschach Inkblot Test require individuals to make up a story and give meaning to ambiguous inkblots, respectively, as projections of their unconscious mind.
Consumer Behavior	Psychodynamic principles applied to consumer behavior involve determining how unconscious desires influence purchasing decisions.	Motivation research examines the role of unconscious motives in consumer decision making, while lifestyle analysis and psychographics match products to and develop advertisements for consumers with certain personality characteristics.
Subliminal Advertising	The rationale of subliminal advertising is to present consumer messages at a level that is below conscious awareness so as to trigger unconscious desires.	Although hidden messages presented in motion picture scenes, music lyrics, motivational audiotapes, and magazine ads are targeted at the unconscious mind, the effectiveness of subliminal advertising is highly questionable.

brands – or the modification of their behavior – seem to be unaffected by subliminal messages. Although the public is concerned about them, subliminal messages "do not present a threat to the general public," and there is no "evidence marketers are using subliminal messages" (Hawkins et al., 2001, p. 296). Thus, although Freud stated that we are controlled by our unconscious mind, you can rest assured that you are probably safe from any subliminal messages targeted at your unconscious mind by advertisers and marketing researchers who might be foolish enough to try to do so. If you would like to read more on the fascinating topic of subliminal perception, see a book chapter titled "The Power of the Subliminal: On Subliminal Persuasion and Other Potential Applications" (Dijksterhuis et al., 2005).

A summary of the main points of discussion is presented in "Summing It Up: Applications of the Psychodynamic Viewpoint" on p. 123. Next we will consider the characteristic strengths and limitations of the psychodynamic viewpoint.

Evaluating the Psychodynamic Viewpoint: Strengths and Limitations

Sigmund Freud is one of the most famous people of the twentieth century and beyond because of the impact his work has had on so many aspects of our lives. We conclude this discussion of the psychodynamic viewpoint that grew out of Freud's work by evaluating its strengths and limitations.

Characteristic Strengths

Following are some strengths of the psychodynamic viewpoint:

- *Comprehensiveness of Freud's theory: Freud said it all.* One of the most significant strengths of the psychodynamic viewpoint developed by Freud was its comprehensiveness in the behaviors it sought to explain. His viewpoint attempted to explain the overall nature and dynamics of personality, personality development, and personality pathology and its treatment (psychoanalysis).

- *Internal consistency of the psychodynamic viewpoint: Fitting the pieces together.* Freud went to great lengths to establish a high degree of internal consistency within his viewpoint by trying to explain how all the different aspects of personality (e.g., structure of the mind; id, ego, superego; and personality development) fit together theoretically. Given the comprehensiveness and complexity of his theory, this was not an easy task.

- *Attention to complex behavior: Creating a new point of view.* The development of the psychodynamic viewpoint brought to the world's attention a new appreciation for the complexity of personality (e.g., unconscious dynamics, psychosexual stages). The psychodynamic approach also produced innovative techniques (e.g., dream analysis) for studying the complex nature of personality.

- *Functional utility: Getting the ball rolling.* The theoretical utility of Freud's psychodynamic viewpoint is unparalleled. Because his was the first real modern psychological theory of personality, almost everything presented in this book is a direct extension of or reaction to his work. The impact it had on disciplines outside of personality (e.g., literature, marketing) is also extensive and impressive.

- *The birth of psychoanalysis: Offering a helping hand to the helping profession.* Many of the therapeutic techniques that Freud developed to treat his patients and test his theoretical ideas that formed the basis of psychoanalysis are still very much a part of the therapeutic environment today. For example, although many contemporary therapists may not adhere to the traditional tenets of Freudian psychoanalysis, clients may still be asked by such therapists to discuss their dreams, engage in free association, respond to an inkblot test, or deal with issues of resistance and transference, all within the Freud-inspired legendary 50-minute therapy session.

- *Freud as an observer: Making sense out of the senseless.* Probably the greatest strength of the approach is that it had Freud as its founder and principal investigator. He was an extremely skilled observer who used his abilities to extract from the seemingly meaningless statements, fantasies, and dreams of his clients the concepts that formed the foundation of the psychodynamic viewpoint.

Characteristic Limitations

Following are limitations of the psychodynamic viewpoint:

- *The psychodynamic view of the individual: People aren't all that bad.* A major criticism of the psychodynamic viewpoint is that it generally portrays human nature in negative terms. It assumes that for the most part, people are pleasure seekers who are simply at the mercy of an assortment of unconscious demands. In addition, too little attention is given to situational or social factors residing outside the individual as determinants of behavior.

- *Ambiguous terms and explanations: Definitional difficulties.* The ambiguity of the psychodynamic viewpoint is reflected in the unscientific manner in which terms used to explain concepts and processes are defined. For example, how do you objectively measure penis envy or the superego? Although the evidence supports many of Freud's concepts and processes (Blum, 1968; Bornstein, 1996; Bornstein & Masling, 1998a; Cramer, 2006; Erdelyi, 1985; Hassin et al., 2005; Holmes, 1974; Silverman, 1976; Westen, 1990; 1991; Westen & Gabbard, 1999), ambiguity makes testing them and communicating the results difficult.

- *Observational biases: Can you really believe what you are hearing?* Serious criticism has also focused on the observational way in which Freud collected information from his clients and the information they provided him. Critics question the extent to which he might have attended in a biased manner and recalled only those details from his clients that were consistent with his theory. Although Freud tried very hard to make his clients feel less self-conscious, the validity of what they told him and their ability to perceive and recall it in an unbiased manner is also worthy of consideration (see Figure 3.8).

- *Methodological problems: Shortcomings in the tools used to build the theory.* Critics of the psychodynamic viewpoint argue that many of the methods implemented by those developing it have serious limitations. Placing a heavy emphasis on using case studies, relying significantly on self-report information from clients, and using dream analysis and projective techniques

Figure 3.8 A criticism of information provided by clients is its accuracy.

as ways of tapping into the unconscious all have methodological problems.

- *Was Freud a sexist?* The psychodynamic viewpoint has been criticized because of the unflattering picture it paints of women (Kofman, 1985). This less-than-equal view of men and women is best exemplified by some of the ideas proposed during the phallic stage. The idea of penis envy seems to suggest that what all women really want is to be just like men. Without question, Freud's views about men and women were shaped by the culture and times in which he lived. But why is it that a man who – with his astute insights and powers of observation – almost single-handedly challenged many of the prevailing ideas about sexuality was not able to extend this wonderful insight into a construct concerning women? Long before the rise of contemporary feminism, Karen Horney, another famous psychoanalyst practicing in the 1930s and 1940s (see Chapter 5), was already busy questioning the assumptions underlying the notion of penis envy. For some contrasting views examining Freud and feminism, see *Feminism and Psychoanalytic Theory* (Chodorow, 1989) and "Freud, Feminism, and Postmodernism" (Elliott, 1999a).

Summing It Up *Characteristic Strengths and Limitations of the Psychodynamic Viewpoint*

Characteristic Strengths:

- *Comprehensive Nature.* The psychodynamic viewpoint was extremely comprehensive in attempting to account for many aspects of human behavior.
- *Internal Consistency.* By consistently modifying the viewpoint to account for new evidence, a high degree of theoretical internal consistency was maintained.
- *Examination of Complex Behavior.* The viewpoint focused attention on the complexities of personality processes (e.g., the unconsciousness, interplay of psychic structures, defense mechanisms) and developed techniques to study them.
- *Developments of Innovative Techniques.* To study complex behaviors, a variety of new techniques (e.g., free association and dream analysis) was developed.
- *Extended Functional Utility.* The tremendous functional utility of the viewpoint is illustrated by the impact it has had on the field of personality and many disciplines outside of personality psychology.
- *Observational Astuteness of Freud.* Freud used his considerable observational skills to forge his comprehensive theory of personality out of the clinical sessions he had with his clients.

Characteristic Limitations:

- *Negative View of Human Nature.* The psychodynamic viewpoint generally portrays human nature in a somewhat negative manner (e.g., governed by unconsciousness).
- *Ambiguous Terms and Explanations.* The rather loose nature of the language and explanations makes communicating about the viewpoint difficult.
- *Observational Biases.* Two sources of bias in the nature of the information used to develop the viewpoint were in the accuracy of Freud's recollections at the end of his therapy sessions and self-reports provided by his clients.
- *Methodological Limitations.* The validity of some of the principal methods used to develop the viewpoint, including projective techniques, case studies, and psychoanalysis, have been questioned.
- *View of Feminism.* The viewpoint has been criticized because of the inferior psychic position it has given to women, particularly during the phallic psychosexual stage.

This presentation completes the coverage of Freud's psychodynamic viewpoint. A summary of the main points of discussion is presented in "Summing It Up: Characteristic Strengths and Limitations of the Psychodynamic Viewpoint" above.

Without question, Freud is considered one of the most influential thinkers of our times, one whose ideas continued to attract interest throughout the twentieth century and beyond. As evidence of the enduring interest in his ideas, in addition to his first appearance on the cover of *Time* magazine in 1924, Freud appeared there twice more: in 1939, just before his death, labeled an "Intellectual Provocateur" and the subject of one of the longest articles in that magazine to be published up to that date (Gerow, 1988), and again on March 29, 1999, just months before the 100th anniversary of the publication of *The Interpretation of Dreams*, with an illustration of Freud analyzing Albert Einstein under a banner that read "The Century's Greatest Minds."

If you want to read more about Freud and his ideas, *A Primer of Freudian Psychology* (Hall, 1954) and *An Elementary Textbook on Psychoanalysis* (Brenner, 1955) are two excellent places to start. Information on the relationship between Freud's personal history and some of his theoretical developments can be found in an insightful book chapter titled "Freud and Leonardo: Why the First Psychobiography Went Wrong" (Elms, 2005). Vance Packard's (1957) *The Hidden Persuaders* is a very short paperback containing several interesting and amusing illustrations of how psychodynamic ideas were applied to marketing and advertising. Additional information on empirical research investigating many psychodynamic principles and processes is summarized in a well-written book chapter by Drew Westen and Glen O. Gabbard (1999) titled "Psychoanalytic Approaches to Personality," an article titled "Science and Psychodynamics: From Arguments about Freud to Data" (Weinberger & Westen, 2001), and Robert F. Bornstein and Joseph M. Masling's (1998a) book *Empirical*

Perspectives on the Psychoanalytic Unconscious, while *The New Unconscious* (Hassin et al., 2005) discusses many interesting developments in recent research focusing on the dynamics and influence of unconsciousness processing. Information on research on psychodynamic approaches to therapy can be found in Bornstein and Masling's (1998b) *Empirical Studies of the Therapeutic Hour*. A more philosophical presentation on Freud's ideas can be found in Abraham Drassinower's (2003) *Freud's Theory of Culture.* Finally, Anthony Elliott's (1999b) book *Freud 2000* "aims to provide a critical examination of the relevance and importance of Freud to contemporary culture" (p. 1). In the next chapter, you will learn about some of the reactions to Freud's ideas.

Chapter Summary: Reexamining the Highlights

- *Foundations of the Psychodynamic Viewpoint.* The basic assumptions of the psychodynamic viewpoint include the role of psychic determinism, the significant influence of the unconscious mind, and the dynamic nature of personality operating within a closed system.

  - *Basic Concepts and Processes.* The structural subdivision of the regions of the mind includes the conscious mind, the preconscious mind, and the unconscious mind, along with the primary and secondary censorship points.

    The energy source of personality comes in the form of instincts. Instincts are characterized by an aim to reduce tension, the amount of pressure exerted, their object of gratification, and their source of origin in the body. Life instincts involve the preservation of the organism and achievement of pleasure; death instincts involve the reduction of tension.

    The structural nature of the personality consists of the id, ego, and superego. The id, the core of personality, operates on the pleasure principle and primary process action. The ego, the mediator of personality, operates on the reality principle, delay of gratification, and secondary process actions. The superego, the moral center of personality, operates on rewards offered by the ego ideal and on punishment triggered by the conscience. Balance is maintained in the personality by the ego meeting the demands of the id within the constraints of reality and morality.

    The role of anxiety is to signal the presence of potential danger to the ego; it comes in the form of reality, neurotic, and moral anxiety. A series of ego defense mechanisms can be employed by the ego to achieve temporary relief from anxiety.

  - *Psychodynamic Personality Development.* Personality development is the process by which the individual passes through a series of psychosexual stages associated with resolving a set of conflicts designed to help develop coping skills for the future. The source of the conflicts is the external constraints placed on the expression of pleasure versus tension reduction. Unsatisfactory resolution of these conflicts can result in fixation and regressions.

    Each psychosexual stage corresponds to resolving a conflict involving the tension of a specific erogenous zone. Successful resolution of the conflict at the oral stage results in learning to cope with the loss of sources of pleasure and the emergence of the ego. Successful resolution of conflict at the anal stage results in learning to restrict expressions of pleasure to their proper time and place. Successful resolution of the phallic stage results in the emergence of the superego and the onset of sex-role behavior. The latency period is used to practice in same-sex groups the newly acquired sex-role behaviors. Successful resolution of the genital stage results in learning to consider first the needs of others. Failure to pass through the psychosexual stages successfully can result in maladaptive forms of personality development.

- *Applications of the Psychodynamic Viewpoint*

  - *Psychodynamic Principles in Psychoanalysis.* Psychoanalysis is a form of psychotherapy designed to help bring into awareness unresolved unconscious conflicts. Its structure involves creating a nonthreatening environment and employing free association and dream analysis to facilitate insight. Transference, countertransference, and resistance are dynamic processes that can serve as barriers to successful treatment.

– *Psychodynamic Principles in Personality Assessment.* Projective techniques have been utilized to assess unconscious processes and form the basis of personality assessment from the psychodynamic perspective. The Rorschach Inkblot Test assesses personality by interpreting the meaning individuals project onto ambiguous test stimuli, presented in the form of inkblots.

– *Psychodynamic Principles in Marketing and Buying Behaviors.* Motivation research, a marketing approach made popular in the 1940s through 1960s, applied psychodynamic principles to the process of determining and explaining purchasing decisions. More recent variations on the logic of motivation research include psychographics and lifestyle analysis.

Subliminal advertising attempts to influence consumer decisions by presenting messages to the unconscious mind. Perception without awareness has been demonstrated in the controlled conditions of the laboratory, but its effectiveness has not been demonstrated in real-life settings.

● *Evaluation of Psychodynamic Viewpoint*

– *Characteristic Strengths.* These include the viewpoint's comprehensive nature, its internal theoretical consistency, the attention it gives to studying complex personality processes, its functional utility in helping to develop the field of personality psychology, and the observational skills of Freud.

– *Characteristic Limitations.* These include the viewpoint's rather unfavorable view of human nature, the ambiguous nature of some of its principal elements, the potential for observational biases on the part of Freud and his clients, the methodological problems associated with some of the techniques used in its development and validation, and its unequal treatment of the personality development of women.

Glossary

acrophobia   An emotionally unrealistic fear of being in high places.

aim   The tension-reduction purpose of an instinct.

anal retentive personality   A maladaptive personality style characterized by withholding information and objects from others.

anal sadistic personality   A maladaptive personality style characterized by explosive tendencies during times of crisis.

anal stage   The second psychosexual stage, during which the erogenous zone is the anal region.

anxiety   A sense of unpleasantness produced to signal a possible threat to the ego.

autonomous self   According to Kohut, the expression of a healthy personality characterized by an independent sense of self and an appreciation for the social support of others.

bipolar self   Kohut's core of personality, consisting of opposing dimensions of ambition and personal goals, which are linked by the individual's abilities and expressed in personality development.

Blacky Pictures Test   A projective technique designed specifically to assess information relevant to psychosexual stages.

castration anxiety   The symbolic loss of a boy's penis, expressed as the fear a boy has of his father as a rival for the affection of his mother.

catharsis   Removing the symptoms of a disorder by discussing the thoughts and feelings underlying it.

closed system   A limited amount of energy operating within a system.

compensatory automaticity   The compensation of unintentional thoughts, feelings, and behaviors at an unconscious level.

conscience   The source of guilt when performing actions inconsistent with the standards of the superego.

conscious mind   The region of the mind in direct contact with sensory awareness.

countertransference   The therapist's expression of emotions toward the client in a manner reflecting feelings toward significant others.

death instinct   The driving force motivating the organism into achieving a tension-free state.

delay of gratification   The ego postponing the satisfaction of the needs of the id until a realistic solution is achieved.

denial   A defense mechanism by which information is altered to make it less threatening.

displacement A defense mechanism by which feelings of hostility are expressed toward a safe target instead of the original, more threatening source.

dissociative identity disorder A psychological disorder characterized by the formation of two or more complete identities as a means of coping with threatening situations.

dream analysis The interpretation of information obtained from dreams recalled, designed to reveal significant information from the unconscious.

ego A mediating psychic structure serving to meet the needs of the id.

ego defense mechanisms A set of actions designed to immediately reduce feelings of anxiety.

ego ideal The source of esteem for performing actions consistent with the standards of the superego.

Electra complex The expressed affection a girl has for her father while perceiving her mother as a rival for the father; named after the mythical Greek character Electra.

empathic mirroring The attention provided by parents and significant others to children as they engage in activities designed to help establish a personal identity.

crogenous zones Regions of the body associated with a high concentration of psychic energy within each psychosexual stage.

fixation The excessive attachment to a psychosexual stage as a result of the inability to resolve it successfully.

free association Unrestrained thinking and verbal expressions designed to reveal significant information from the unconscious.

genital sexuality The expression of affection through which pleasure is received by satisfying the needs of others first.

genital stage The fifth psychosexual stage, during which the genital region is once again the erogenous zone.

homeostasis The tendency of a system or organism to maintain a certain level of stability based on an internal system of feedback.

hysteria A psychiatric disorder characterized by a loss of physical abilities or paralysis with no corresponding physiological or neurological damage.

id The core and energy source of personality operating completely in the unconscious mind.

identification with the aggressor The process by which a boy internalizes the characteristics of his father as a means of successfully resolving the Oedipus complex.

immune system The body's defense system that acts against harmful substances and cells that enter the body and helps to reproduce healthy cells to restore normal bodily functioning.

insight The gaining of knowledge about unresolved unconscious conflicts, achieved through psychoanalysis.

instincts Psychic forces that motivate the individual.

latency period The fourth psychosexual stage, in which adolescents form same-sex groups for the purpose of practicing sex-role behaviors.

latent content The unconscious meaning of dreams determined through dream analysis.

latent motives The underlying reasons, which consumers are unable or reluctant to admit, for making their purchases.

libido A form of psychic energy responsible for helping to promote the preservation of the organism.

life instinct The driving force behind the preservation of the organism.

lifestyle analysis The use of psychographics to direct marketing strategies at social and psychological needs of consumers.

limen The point of awareness between conscious and unconscious perception.

manifest content The information about dreams recalled at the conscious level of awareness.

manifest motives The reasons consumers are willing to admit for making their purchases.

moral anxiety A signal to indicate that actions are being considered or performed that violate the superego's standards.

motivation research An approach to marketing using psychodynamic processes, techniques, and explanations to understand purchasing decisions and behaviors.

narcissistic personality disorder A form of psychopathology characterized by patterns of grandiosity, a chronic need for admiration, and a lack of empathy.

neurotic anxiety A signal for the existence of danger, created by the possible expression of unconscious impulses.

object Any item serving to satisfy the aim of an instinct.

object relations theory A variation of psychoanalytical thought emphasizing the infant's emotional attachment to individuals and the symbolic representation of these attachments in developing subsequent interpersonal relationships.

obsessive-compulsive disorder A psychological disorder characterized by recurring intrusive thoughts and behaviors.

Oedipus complex The expressed affection a boy feels for his mother while perceiving his father as a rival for the mother; named after Oedipus, the mythical Greek character.

oral aggressive or oral sadistic personality A maladaptive personality style characterized by expressions of verbal hostility to cope with stress.

oral incorporative personality   A maladaptive personality style characterized by taking in substances by the mouth to cope with crises.

oral stage   The first psychosexual stage, in which the erogenous zone is the mouth.

penis envy   The symbolic desire for a penis, expressed by little girls as the genital region becomes the focus of attention during the phallic stage.

phallic personality   A maladaptive personality style of females, characterized by expressions of hostility toward men or of sexual promiscuity as a means of symbolically resolving penis envy.

phallic stage   The third psychosexual stage in which the erogenous zone is the genital region.

pleasure principle   The seeking of immediate gratification by the id.

preconscious mind   The region of the mind that serves as a storage center for access of retrievable information by the conscious mind.

pressure   The degree of force exerted by an instinct.

primary censorship   A process that helps to keep threatening information in the unconscious mind from entering the preconscious mind.

primary process actions   A set of responses designed to produce immediate gratification.

projection   A defense mechanism by which one's unacceptable impulses are seen as existing in others.

psychic determinism   The assumption that all forms of behavior have some reason for occurring.

psychoanalysis   A form of psychotherapy designed to uncover unconscious emotional conflicts.

psychoanalyst   A mental health professional trained to perform psychoanalysis.

psychoanalytic situation   The specific physical arrangement of the client and the analyst, and the nonjudgmental demeanor of the analyst during psychoanalysis, designed to facilitate insight.

psychographics   The assessment of attitudes, interests, and behavior patterns to determine and develop marketing plans.

psychosexual conflicts   A set of dilemmas involving the expression of psychic impulses at different psychosexual stages.

psychosexual stages   A sequence of psychological milestones individuals pass through in the process of personality development.

rationalization   A defense mechanism by which unacceptable actions are given explanations to make them seem reasonable.

reaction formation   A defense mechanism by which just the opposite reaction to a threatening impulse is expressed.

reality anxiety   A signal for the existence of an objective source of danger.

reality principle   The process by which the ego seeks to satisfy the needs of the id within the constraints of reality.

regression   As a defense mechanism, the use of less mature forms of behavior to deal with threatening situations; as a process in psychosexual development, the increased tendency to return in times of crisis to a course of action characteristic of a fixated psychosexual stage.

repressed memory syndrome   The questionable recalling of traumatic early childhood memories under specific therapeutic conditions.

repression   A defense mechanism by which threatening information is removed from conscious awareness.

resistance   Responses made by a client to avoid confrontation with threatening information during psychoanalysis.

Rorschach Inkblot Test   A projective technique designed to assess information from the unconscious by analyzing the meaning given to a set of ambiguous inkblots.

schizophrenia   A serious psychological disturbance characterized by a separation from reality through the expression of inappropriate affect, bizarre behavior, and incoherent speech.

secondary censorship   A process that helps to keep threatening information in the preconscious mind from entering the conscious mind.

secondary process actions   A set of behaviors and mental processes designed to produce a realistic solution to meeting the needs of the id.

secondary sex characteristics   Physical features appearing during puberty that distinguish the masculine and feminine physiques.

self-objects   Individuals with whom infants form a deep emotional attachment and whom they incorporate as part of their own sense of personal identity.

shaman   A spiritual leader among tribal people who serves as an intermediary between the natural and supernatural worlds and uses magic for curing illnesses, controlling spiritual forces, and foretelling the future.

social cognition   The mental processing of information about our self and others in an attempt to understand our social world.

source   The location of origin of an instinct within the body.

sublimation   A defense mechanism by which unacceptable impulses are channeled into socially acceptable actions.

subliminal advertising An advertising technique by which the consumer message is presentedto the unconscious mind.

subliminal perception The perception of stimuli below the conscious level of awareness.

superego The psychic structure serving as the moral center of personality.

symptom substitution The resurfacing of an emotional disorder in a different form from the original symptoms.

transference The client's expression of emotions toward the therapist in a manner reflecting feelings toward significant others.

unconscious mind A region of the mind not in contact with conscious awareness, having an unlimited storage capacity, and containing unacceptable and threatening information.

undoing A defense mechanism that involves engaging in one form of action to compensate for another, less acceptable form.

Values and Lifestyle (VALS 2) Program A psychographic assessment technique designed to identify the motives underlying consumer decisions.

working representations The perceptions individuals have about themselves, others, and their relationship with others that serve to influence actions within these relationships.

The Viewpoints of Jung and Adler

Early Reactions to Freud

4

Chapter Overview:
A Preview of Coming Attractions

Asignificant aspect of Freud's work was the role he played in stimulating the thinking of other personality theorists. Carl Jung and Alfred Adler were two of the earliest of those whose thinking was influenced by their professional and personal associations with Freud. Initially, Jung and Adler were strong supporters of Freud's ideas. Over time, however, they both developed considerable theoretical differences with Freud. Each theorist formulated his own viewpoint of personality, and each view was very different from Freud's and from the other's. More specifically, Jung reacted to Freud by probing deeper into the individual's unconscious and the seeking of balance within the structure and dynamics of personality, instead of the focus on conflict that guided Freud's thinking. Adler, on the other hand, did just the opposite by giving more attention to the study of conscious motives and social factors as the principal determinants of personality, instead of the emphasis Freud provided on the intrapersonal factors operating within the individual. And like Freud, Jung and Adler developed ideas that served to influence the thinking and research in many areas of contemporary personality psychology. This chapter presents the perspectives of personality proposed by Jung and Adler.

Jung's Analytical Psychology: Probing Deeper into the Unconscious Mind

Jung's viewpoint was termed **analytical psychology**. In reaction to Freud, Jung probed deeper into the unconscious mind and expanded the role it played in maintaining balance among the different aspects of personality. For a glimpse into the life of one of personality psychology's most original thinkers, read "A Closer Look", below.

A Closer Look

The Life of Carl G. Jung

Carl Gustav Jung was born in the small Swiss country village of Kesswyl on July 26, 1875. His mother was described by Jung as having emotional problems. His father, a poor but extremely well-read country pastor, introduced his son to the study of Latin at age six. Jung describes his childhood as rather lonely and isolated.

Jung originally wanted to be an archaeologist. Because of limited financial resources, the only university he could attend was the University of Basel, which did not offer courses in that area. He decided to study medicine because of its greater career possibilities. Intending to be a surgeon, he switched to psychiatry to pursue his interests in dreams, fantasies, the occult, theology, and archaeology. Upon graduation, he received an appointment to the Burgholzli Mental Hospital in Zurich, where, from 1900 to 1909, he studied the nature of schizophrenia, established an extensive clinical practice, and developed into a world authority on abnormal behavior.

Jung was an early supporter of Freud because of their shared interest in the unconscious. In 1907, Jung traveled to Vienna for his first meeting with Freud, at which the two talked for 13 consecutive hours! In 1909, Jung traveled with Freud to America, where they were to give a series of lectures at Clark University. During this trip, a fissure in their relationship first developed when the two experts were analyzing each other's dreams. During one of their interactions, Freud reacted to Jung in a very condescending manner, as though he (Freud) was the greater authority. This stunned Jung, as he had come to Freud with a world-class reputation, rather than as an intellectual neophyte.

When the International Psychoanalytic Association was formed in 1910, Jung became its first president at the request of Freud. Jung was being groomed to be Freud's heir to the psychoanalytic movement. However, growing theoretical differences, especially over the importance of sexual energy, resulted in Jung's resignation from the group only four years later. The split was bitter and complete. The two men never met or spoke to each other again.

From 1913 to 1917, while experiencing some serious emotional difficulties in his own life and even contemplating suicide, Jung engaged in a monumental effort of self-analysis. The outcome produced some of Jung's most original theoretical concepts. After this self-analysis and the recovery from his emotional disturbances, Jung continued his work for over 60 years, establishing himself as one of the most noted psychological thinkers of the twentieth century. For example, he studied schizophrenic patients in Switzerland, Navajo Indians in America, native tribes in Africa, and African American patients in Washington, DC. He participated in archaeological and anthropological expeditions in such diverse cultures as Egypt, the Sudan, and India. He was extremely well read in theology, anthropology, archaeology, psychology,

Carl Jung reacted to his disagreements with Freud by developing a viewpoint of personality that expanded the nature and role of the unconscious mind.

ancient texts, the occult, and mythology, as well as psychiatry. He incorporated this diverse knowledge into his theory of personality.

Jung died on June 6, 1961, in Zurich at the age of 85. He was an active and productive researcher and writer his entire life, with a collection of works (20 volumes) second only in size to Freud's.

Basic Assumptions of Jung's Analytical Psychology

Most of the basic assumptions of Jung's analytical psychology reflect his major theoretical differences with Freud. The following subsections examine those differences in detail.

The Nature and Purpose of Libido

A major point of theoretical disagreement was the central focus Freud gave to sexual energy, or libido. For Jung (1948/1960b), libido was a much more generalized life energy source serving to motivate the individual in a number of different ways, including spiritually, intellectually, and creatively. It was also the individual's motivational source for seeking pleasure and reducing conflict. Thus, in reaction to Freud, Jung attempted to expand the nature of libido.

The Nature of the Unconscious

Jung also felt that Freud's views on the unconscious (i.e., as a storehouse for unacceptable desires) were rather limited. Jung viewed the unconscious as being a **phylogenetic** structure that has developed over the generations and contains certain elements shared by all individuals from all times that have been passed along from one generation to the next. For example, a common belief in some sort of supreme being is a concept that has been passed from one generation to another. A more recent expression of such ideas can be seen in the emerging field of positive psychology (C. R. Snyder & Lopez, 2002). **Positive psychology** seeks to understand and promote human virtues that emphasize personal strength and fulfillment. Recent cross-cultural perspectives on positive psychology (Lopez et al., 2002) discuss how most individuals express a sense of spirituality, "regardless of our historical roots or heritage" (Sweeney, 1995, p. vii). Such a shared sense

of spirituality helps individuals from diverse cultures, races, and ethnic groups to coexist by helping clarify guidelines about how life should be lived (e.g., finding a purpose in life).

The Retrospective and Teleological Nature of Behavioral Causality

While Freud took a rather **retrospective** view of personality (i.e., emphasis on early childhood experiences), Jung combined this retrospective view with a **teleological** perspective as a means of explaining the causes of behavior. For Jung, personality is pushed from the past, but is also pulled along by hope, goals, and future aims and aspirations. For example, both grade school experiences and career goals can act as important sources of motivation for college success. Again, such ideas involving looking to the future are clearly reflected in recent discussions in positive psychology of the purpose and value of having goals for life and their contribution to happiness (Locke, 2002). Thus, by considering both past and present influences on behavior, Jung felt that we could achieve a better understanding of how and why the personality operates.

Seeking Balance as the Motivational Nature of Personality

While Freud viewed the various aspects of personality (e.g., id, ego, and superego) as operating in opposition to each other, Jung assumed more of a balanced relationship. For Jung, the primary mode of interaction among the various elements of personality was a tendency to achieve a state of balance. This involves each element being fully developed and then integrated with the others into a well-developed sense of the self. Recent discussions in positive psychology suggest seeking balance in our acquisition wisdom as a guide for living a good life (Baltes, Glück, & Kunzmann, 2002). For example, at college it is important to develop equally the intellectual and social aspects of the self by going both to the library and to social events.

Although Jung developed many of his ideas at the beginning of the twentieth century, they have maintained their utility into the twenty-first. He and Freud began with very similar assumptions about the nature of personality, but their differences became clear. A comparison of these is presented in "Summing It Up: A Comparison of the Basic Assumptions of Jung and Freud" on p. 136.

Summing It Up *A Comparison of the Basic Assumptions of Jung and Freud*

Basic Assumption	Jung	Freud
Nature and Purpose of Libido	A generalized source of psychic energy serving to motivate different aspects of the individual's personality	A source of psychic energy specific to seeking sexual gratification
Nature of the Unconscious	A storehouse of repressed memories specific to the individual and of information passed from previous generations	A storehouse of repressed memories specific to the individual
Nature of Behavioral Causality	Past experiences as well as future expectations and aspirations	Past experiences, particularly those from childhood
Motivational Nature of Personality	To seek balance in the individual's personality by the separate development and eventual integration of its different elements	To reduce instinctual pressure and resolve conflict between the id, ego, and superego

The Structure of Personality: Redefining the Unconscious Mind

In comparison to Freud, Jung's view of the structural nature of personality clearly reflected a redefined, expanded view of the unconscious mind (Jung, 1934/1960a). Figure 4.1 gives a graphic representation of Jung's structural view of personality. The following subsections examine this viewpoint in greater detail.

The Conscious Ego as the Center of Conscious Awareness

The **conscious ego** is the center of conscious awareness of the self (Kaufmann, 1989). The major functions of the conscious ego are to make the individual aware of his or her internal processes (e.g., thoughts or feelings of pain) and the external world (e.g., surrounding noises) through sensations and perceptions at a level of awareness necessary for day-to-day functioning. For example, being aware consciously of the traffic problems ahead, a motorist recalls another route for driving into town.

The Personal Unconscious

Directly next to the conscious ego and completely below conscious awareness, Jung proposed the **personal unconscious** region of the mind. Its contents included all those thoughts, memories, and experiences that were momentarily not being thought about or were being repressed because they were too emotionally threatening.

Probably the most important elements in the personal unconscious are what Jung described as complexes (Jung, 1934/1960a, 1954/1959d). A **complex** is a collection of thoughts, feelings, attitudes, and memories that center on a particular concept. The more elements attached to the complex, the greater its influence on the individual. For example, the many elements associated with a rather strong power complex might include a desire to dominate the discussion in a study group, decide what's for dinner at home, and order around one's co-workers. If the complex becomes too strong, it can also become pathological, as was the case with the power complex often attributed to Hitler.

Jung also expanded the influence of the personal unconscious beyond simply being a storehouse of unconscious memories to include both a prospective and a compensatory function. Its **prospective function** served to help the individual look into the future (Jung, 1916/1969). For example, dreaming about what might happen in a job interview two days from now helps an individual to prepare for it. The **compensatory function** (Jung, 1916/1969) helps individuals balance out at an unconscious level the conscious aspects of personality being ignored. For example, a rather shy person may dream of being the life of the party.

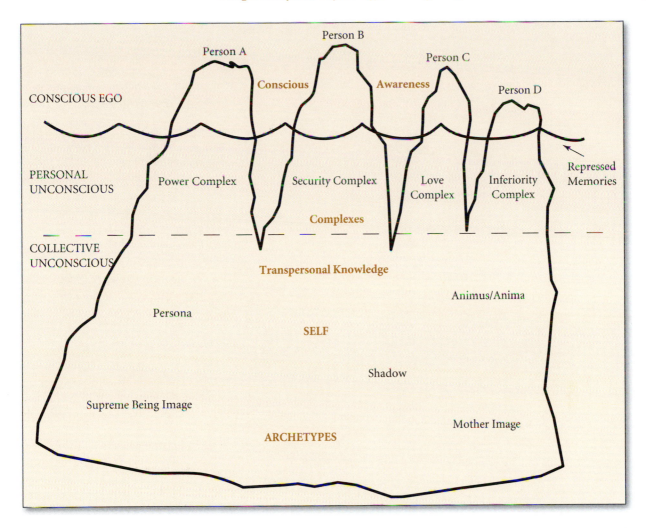

Figure 4.1   No one is an island. According to Jung's structural view of the mind, each person's separate conscious ego and personal unconscious are connected to a shared collective unconscious.

The Collective Unconscious

While the personal unconscious is unique to each individual, the **collective unconscious** is conceptualized as being **transpersonal** in nature (Jung, 1917/1966, 1936/1959b, 1943/1953a, 1945/1953b). The transpersonal nature of the collective unconscious reflected Jung's view that there is a region of the unconscious mind containing a collection of general wisdom that is shared by all people, has developed over time, and is passed along from generation to generation across the ages.

The principal function of this wisdom is to *predispose* individuals to respond to certain external situations in a given manner. This maximizes the development of the individual. For example, any time a group of individuals gets together, there is a natural tendency or predisposition for them to establish some sort of social order (e.g., a democracy, a division of labor by skill performed or by sheer size and strength). Such organizations seem to help in maximizing the possibility of survival of the individuals. Thus, because these predispositions, or hereditary wisdom, are passed along from generation to generation, individuals do not need to start all over again with each new generation, making the task of survival that much easier.

Archetypes

The most significant of these predispositions or images in the collective unconscious are referred to as archetypes. **Archetypes** (Jung, 1936/1959a, 1943/1953a) are universal thoughts, symbols, or images having a large

Table 4.1 Some Archetypes and Their Meanings, Images, and Manifestations

Archetype	Transpersonal Meaning	Symbolic Image	Contemporary Manifestation
Anima	The female side of males; males expressing feminine characteristics	Woman	The warmth and tenderness expressed by actor and comedian Bill Cosby
Animus	The male side of females; females expressing masculine characteristics	Man	Sigourney Weaver appearing as the alien-fighting Ripley in the *Alien* films
Child	The potentiality of adults; the future; goodness to come	The Christ child	The New Year's Eve baby wrapped in the banner of the coming year; E.T. in the movie *E.T.: The Extraterrestrial*
Hero	*Positive*: An individual or object that fights evil and suffers punishment for others	Christ on the cross; any martyr	The character Harry Potter from the *Harry Potter* books and films
	Negative: An individual or object that opposes goodness	The devil	Lord Voldemort in the *Harry Potter* books and films
Mother	*Positive*: A compassionate caregiver	Virgin Mary	The Statue of Liberty
	Negative: A wicked individual or object causing harm	A witch	The Wicked Witch in *The Wizard of Oz*
Persona	The public side of our personality; a positive image we create for the purpose of pleasing others	The actor and actress	The stereotypical smiling and friendliness of sales representatives
Self	The desire for unity, harmony, and balance within the individual	The circle; the principle of yin and yang in Chinese philosophy	The tremendous growth in psychotherapies designed to help people "get in touch with themselves"
Shadow	The dark side of personality; our base and instinctive tendencies	Various demons, such as snakes dragons, and monsters	Norman Bates in the classic film *Psycho*
Supreme being	A power beyond that on earth that can be used to explain phenomena outside of our control	God; the sun	"The Force" in the *Star Wars* films
Trickster or magician	A mythical figure fond of playing jokes and pranks	The clown; the court jester	Trapper John and Hawkeye Pierce of *M*A*S*H*; cartoon characters such as Bart Simpson, Bugs Bunny, and the Roadrunner
Wise old man	Learning from the past; receiving help from those older and stronger; valuing the past	A religious prophet; a witch doctor or medicine man	The Wizard in *The Wizard of Oz*; Obi Wan Kenobi in *Star Wars*

amount of emotion attached to them. Their special status comes from the importance they have gained across the many generations and the significant role they play in day-to-day living. For example, the archetype of "mother" is an image of a nurturing and compassionate individual that can take many forms (e.g., mother nature, mother earth, a mother's love). Table 4.1 provides some additional examples of archetypes, and four that play a significant role in the establishment of a balanced personality are discussed below: the persona, animus and anima, shadow, and self.

The Persona   The **persona** is an archetype that develops over time as a result of the tendency of people to adopt the social roles and norms that go along with living with other people. From the Latin word meaning "mask," the persona reflects what might be defined as our public personality (Jung, 1917/1966, 1945/1953b). For example, when interacting with potential business clients, a sales representative might behave in a very friendly and outgoing manner through the use of compliments, praise, and amusing remarks. However, attaching too much emotion and importance to the persona can result in the individual losing contact with his or her true feelings and identity, which then can become dictated by others (e.g., an individual with a very shallow and conforming personality; Kaufmann, 1989).

The Animus and Anima   Jung believed that individuals were psychologically bisexual in nature in that each individual possesses characteristic features and tendencies of the opposite sex (Kaufmann, 1989). Along these lines, Jung (1917/1966, 1945/1953b, 1954/1959e) formulated the archetypes of the animus and anima. The **animus** is the masculine aspect of females, such as being aggressive. The **anima** is the feminine aspect of males, such as being nurturant. The well-developed personality contains both masculine and feminine characteristics. Failing to recognize and integrate the alternate sexual aspects of one's personality can result in an individual who is sexist and chauvinistic with regard to members of the opposite sex.

The Shadow   The **shadow** represents the dark and more primitive side of personality (Jung, 1948/1959c). Like the id, the shadow represents all of the instinctive and impulsive aspects of personality typically kept out of the public personality and repressed in the unconscious regions of the mind. However, to deny the shadow would be like trying to assume that everyone is

perfect, without any sense of base desires (e.g., sexual needs) and impulses (e.g., wanting to hit your boss for yelling at you).

Jung proposed that well-adjusted individuals learn to incorporate these private aspects of their personality into the persona and to express them consciously in a socially acceptable form. For example, an employee can file a complaint instead of hitting the supervisor when feelings of hostility arise out of a sense of perceived injustice.

The Self   The most important archetype is that of the self. The **self** is that element of the personality predisposing the individual to unite all of the other aspects (Kaufmann, 1989). The development of the self as an archetype reflects the desire by people across the generations to seek unity and harmony (Wilhelm & Jung, 1931). Within the individual, the self is the motivating force seeking to achieve unity and harmony between all the private and public, masculine and feminine, and conscious and unconscious aspects. Failure on the part of the self to achieve this sense of unity and balance can result in the overdevelopment of one aspect of the personality at the expense of all others. An example would be a workaholic who becomes depressed after becoming alienated from family and friends. As illustrated in Figure 4.2, a major function of the self

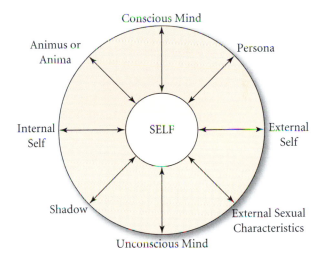

Figure 4.2 At the center of the personality is the self. The bidirectional nature of the arrows represents the self's attempt to seek unity and harmony among the various aspects of the personality. The circle represents a balanced expression of all aspects of the personality.

is to sit at the center and attempt to balance all of the different aspects of personality.

While there is a variety of archetypes, Jung noted the similarity in their expression across different cultures, suggesting a form of universality in their purpose and expression (Hopcke, 1989; Jung, 1964). An illustration of the cross-cultural expression of archetypes is presented in "The Cultural Context of Personality Psychology."

The Cultural Context of Personality Psychology

Similarities in the Hero Archetype Across Cultures

The basic assumption of Jung's concept of archetypes is that they were transpersonal in nature: figures or symbols appearing in many different forms and in different cultures throughout history but serving a similar purpose. One example is the archetype of the hero. Throughout history, the hero has appeared in many forms but always seems to share certain characteristics. These include a miraculous but humble birth, early proof of superhuman strength, and a rapid rise to prominence or power with the specific purpose of doing battle with the forces of evil. Examples of the hero as appearing throughout history and across cultures include Hercules of ancient Greek mythology, the sixth-century British mythical figure King Arthur, the American comic-strip hero Superman of the 1940s–1980s, and, most recently, Luke Skywalker of the *Star Wars* film series.

In addition to the above examples of the archetypes of heroes familiar to most individuals in Western cultures, presented below are some examples from cultures around the world.

- *Babylonian-Sumerian (Middle Eastern)*. Gilgamesh was an ancient semi-divine king (c.2650 BCE) and the hero of an epic collection of mythical tales. Legend says that he built great walls around his city in Iraq to keep his people safe. He is the hero of the oldest work of literature in the world, the *Epic of Gilgamesh*.

Luke Skywalker, as a young boy, demonstrating his special ability early on to use "the Force"

Luke Skywalker, as an adult, using "the Force" in battle with the forces of evil represents a contemporary manifestation of the classic example of the hero archetype.

- *Indian.* Shiva is the most important Hindu god and, according to Hindu folklore, does everything. All other Hindu gods and goddess are lesser than Shiva. Even though he represents destruction, Shiva is viewed as a positive force (e.g., the destroyer of evil), since creation follows destruction. Shiva is not merely a destroyer but performs five functions: creator, preserver, destroyer, hiding sins, and most importantly, blessing.

- *Chinese.* Guan-Yu, also known as Kuan-Kung, was legendary for his bravery. Although a Chinese god of war and martial arts, Guan-Yu tried to use his skills to avoid confrontations if at all possible.

- *Norse (Scandinavian).* Hengest and Horsa were two brothers whose legendary bravery in battle helped lead to the settlement of England by the Anglo-Saxons.

- *Polynesian (South Pacific).* Maui is the most famous folktale character of the Polynesian culture. He is the trickster hero who steals fire for man, fishes up the islands of the South Pacific, traps the sun to lengthen the day, and helps raise the sky. Pele, also known as "She-Who-Shapes-The-Sacred-Land," was a passionate fire goddess who commanded fear and respect and was considered both a destructive and creative force.

Thus, no matter in what culture or time period, the archetype of hero shares principal characteristics, which reflects Jung's view that people across time and cultures shared certain common ideas and beliefs that were passed along through the collective unconscious.

The Dynamics of Personality: The Ebb and Flow of Psychic Energy

Jung (1948/1960b) viewed psychic energy as a generalized motivational source designed to help the self achieve a sense of balance. The self does this within the personality by the ebb and flow of psychic energy among the various aspects of the self. The principles of opposites, equivalence, and entropy are three processes by which energy is shifted and balance is achieved.

- *The principle of opposites.* According to the **principle of opposites**, for each conscious or unconscious reaction within the personality, there is an opposite reaction to it somewhere else within the system. For example, a conscious desire to develop the more analytical side of the personality while at work is offset in the same person when seeking more creative pursuits by visiting art museums while on vacation.

- *The principles of equivalence and entropy.* The flow of psychic energy is based on the principle of opposites and is regulated by those of equivalence and entropy (Jung, 1948/1960b). According to the **principle of equivalence**, any psychic energy taken from one psychic structure is found somewhere else in the system. On the other hand, the **principle of entropy** states that when one aspect of the personality has a greater amount of psychic energy, the energy will flow back to the weaker aspect to create a sense of balance. Figure 4.3 presents a graphic summary of these two principles.

The Nature and Processes of Personality Development: A Lifetime Attempt to Achieve Balance

Jung conceptualized the development of personality as an ongoing process continuing throughout life (Jung, 1931a/1960). The principal objective of personality development is the balanced development of each separate aspect of personality and their harmonious integration as a single entity.

Developmental Processes: The Basics of Personality Development

To explain the development of personality, Jung proposed the following processes: individuation, the transcendent function, and self-realization.

Individuation In the process of **individuation**, the individual becomes aware of the different aspects of personality at both the conscious and unconscious level and expends psychic energy to develop them (Jung, 1921/1971, 1939/1959). An environmentally conscious young executive might try to invest psychic energy in career efforts that will demonstrate the greatest potential for developing both the conscious persona (e.g., potential for promotion to vice-president) and the unconscious persona (e.g., opportunities for creative

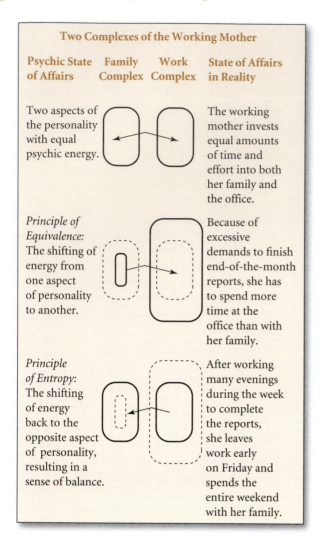

Two Complexes of the Working Mother

Psychic State of Affairs	Family Complex	Work Complex	State of Affairs in Reality
Two aspects of the personality with equal psychic energy.			The working mother invests equal amounts of time and effort into both her family and the office.
Principle of Equivalence: The shifting of energy from one aspect of personality to another.			Because of excessive demands to finish end-of-the-month reports, she has to spend more time at the office than with her family.
Principle of Entropy: The shifting of energy back to the opposite aspect of personality, resulting in a sense of balance.			After working many evenings during the week to complete the reports, she leaves work early on Friday and spends the entire weekend with her family.

Figure 4.3 As psychic energy is shifted away from one aspect of the personality, it flows back to the opposite aspect.

expression) when seeking employment with an environmental engineering company. Thus, by exploring both public and private forms of personal growth, the young executive can make career decisions that promote the development of all aspects of personality.

The Transcendent Function   Once the components of personality have developed separately through the processes of individuation, the transcendent function can occur. The **transcendent function** is an operation of the self that blends all aspects of the personality into a unified system with a meaningful purpose in life (Jung, 1916/1960, 1936/1959a). Extending the preceding example, the young executive might start to invest psychic energy in efforts to be a vice-president in the visual arts division of the company's marketing department. Thus, the self must rise above (i.e., transcend) the task (i.e., function) of simply supervising the separate expression and development of the various aspects of personality and work to blend them into a unifying purpose (i.e., preserving the environment).

Self-realization   The unifying purpose of the self takes the form of each person trying to establish or determine the true meaning of life through the process of self-realization. **Self-realization** refers to the tendency of the self to continue to explore and expand all the elements of personality in a never-ending attempt to gain a better understanding of the total personality and its purpose. For example, even while not at work, the environmentally conscious young executive continues to think about ways to help recycle products, or organizes letter-writing campaigns for local recycling legislation.

Figure 4.4 is a graphic summary of the processes associated with healthy personality development.

Maladaptive Personality Development: The Unbalanced Personality

Since the objective of healthy personality development is the balanced evolution and subsequent integration of the various elements of personality, maladaptive development is defined by the extent to which this process is not achieved. Investing too much psychic energy in the persona might result in an individual becoming extremely self-conscious and conforming. The anxiety and depression associated with retirement for some people reflect the loss of a significant and overly developed aspect of the self – what they did for a living. More serious forms of mental disorders occur when the pressure to express the severely neglected aspects of the unconscious become so great that something analogous to the breaking of a dam of psychic energy occurs. In this situation, the explosion produces an overwhelming rush of psychic energy from the unconscious into the individual's conscious awareness. For example, a person may become extremely depressed and immobile as a means of blocking out and completely avoiding the extreme shift of psychic energy.

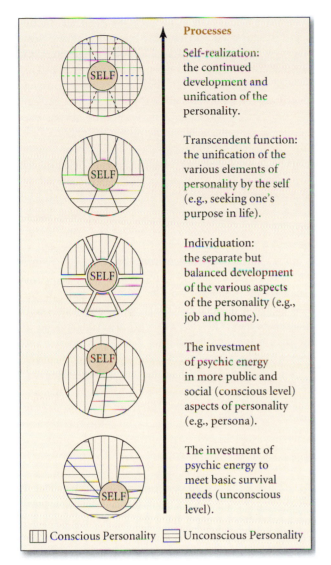

Processes

Self-realization: the continued development and unification of the personality.

Transcendent function: the unification of the various elements of personality by the self (e.g., seeking one's purpose in life).

Individuation: the separate but balanced development of the various aspects of the personality (e.g., job and home).

The investment of psychic energy in more public and social (conscious level) aspects of personality (e.g., persona).

The investment of psychic energy to meet basic survival needs (unconscious level).

⊞ Conscious Personality　⊞ Unconscious Personality

Figure 4.4　A summary of Jung's developmental processes. For Jung, the major objective of personality development is the continuous integration of all aspects of personality at both the conscious and unconscious levels.

Applications of Jung's Analytical Psychology: Using What is Known

In these sections, we will examine the applications of Jung's analytical psychology to the development of a form of psychotherapy to help treat individuals experiencing psychological problems of adjustment, the measurement of personality types, and the making of personnel and career decisions.

Analytical Psychotherapy: Confronting the Unconsciousness

From Jung's viewpoint, failure to achieve a satisfactory balance within the personality can have some serious consequences. To help cope with such psychic imbalances, Jung developed what he referred to as **analytical psychotherapy** (Kaufmann, 1989; Sommers-Flanagan & Sommers-Flanagan, 2004).

The Aim of Analytical Psychotherapy　Jung believed that much of personality pathology was a result of an imbalance between the development of the conscious and unconscious aspects of personality. As a result, he proposed that the principal aim of psychotherapy was to weaken the hold the conscious had on the imbalanced development of the self and help individuals utilize their unconscious as a guiding force in reestablishing a sense of psychic balance.

The Four Stages of Analytical Psychotherapy: A Step-By-Step Progression into the Unconscious

In his systematic attempt to help the client more effectively utilize unconscious psychic energy, Jung divided the process of analytical psychotherapy into four separate stages.

1. *The confession stage.* The **confession stage** includes those early therapy sessions characterized by uncertainty within the client. During this stage, clients talk about their problems and the feelings associated with them with a certain degree of confusion (e.g., unexplained feelings of anxiety).
2. *The elucidation stage.* After expressing their feelings, clients begin to enter into the **elucidation stage**. Clients now desire to seek answers and explanations for their problems by exploring how past events may have caused the current problem. As this stage progresses, a deeper exploration into the personal and collective unconscious begins with the aid of the therapist. This stage often includes dream analysis.
3. *The education stage.* Further exploration into the unconscious characterizes the **education stage**. In this stage, the therapist and the client begin to explore the variety of alternatives available to achieve a greater sense of balance. Jung was not specific about formulating a standard approach

to what clients should do to achieve psychic balance (Kaufmann, 1989). Instead, he approached each individual as a unique case, exploring various psychological, spiritual, and behavioral alternatives in the treatment process.

4. *The transformation stage.* The final step in the therapeutic process is the **transformation stage**, which requires the client to go beyond a state of psychic balance to achieve self-realization by establishing a sense of meaning in life. Establishing this sense of meaning is a task Jung typically found in many of his middle-aged clients, and involves a much deeper and more intense search of the unconscious. Such a search might involve switching careers to one that is more meaningful to the client (e.g., opening a restaurant or teaching the disadvantaged in a foreign country). One of Jung's most significant contributions was the attention and importance he gave to such midlife crises.

The Methods of Analytical Psychotherapy: How is It Done?

The Therapeutic Environment   For Jung, the therapeutic environment consisted of the client and analyst engaging in a free and reciprocal discussion. For example, Jung might share one of his dreams with a client. By making the nature of the communication mutual and egalitarian, the client would get the impression that the journey into the unconscious was a joint venture with the analyst. Two of the more common techniques developed by Jung to explore the unconscious were the word association test and the method of amplification.

The Word Association Test   In a **word association test**, the individual is given a word and asked to report the first word that comes to mind. Jung (1905/1973a, 1909/1973b, 1907; Peterson & Jung, 1907; Rickscher & Jung, 1908) was the first to employ word association tests systematically in the clinical setting (Bennet, 1983). His principal purpose was to use it to help identify the client's problematic complexes. More specifically, by examining what words produced various types of nervous behavior (e.g., stammering or changes in respiration rate) in the client, as well as the associations themselves, Jung was able to assess the degree of emotionality of the word associations and uncover their attachment to problematic complexes. For

example, a client with a problematic family complex might respond to the words "house," "father," and "vacations" with an increasing heart rate, by leaning back in the chair, and by stumbling verbally over the associations produced. With the problematic complex identified, the client and analyst would start to explore the root causes of the problem by probing deeper into the specific complexes and archetypes in the unconscious.

Method of Amplification   Going beyond the identification of problematic complexes, Jung used the analysis of dreams to explore clients' archetypes. For Jung, the dream was to be studied in great detail by elaborating, expanding, and reanalyzing the images in it (Kaufmann, 1989). To do this, he developed the method of amplification. In the **method of amplification**, the client not only reports what is going on in the dream but expands on the details as if actually a part of the dream. For example, an overly self-conscious client is asked to take the role of a sports car appearing in the dream by describing how it feels to be free and powerful. This active participation of the client in the dream reflected Jung's view that each archetype (e.g., the self as a car) could take many different forms.

To facilitate this process, Jung also used the **dream series method**. This technique involves amplifying and analyzing a series of dreams for the repeated occurrence of particular archetype symbols (e.g., the self appearing as the sun or a tall building). In addition, Jung used the **method of active imagination**, in which the client is asked to imagine having an interaction with the significant archetypes identified during treatment (e.g., talking to a "mechanic/therapist" about making the "car/self" perform more effectively). In many cases, Jung felt that these methods could be used to help clients prepare for solving problems in the future (e.g., preparing for questions to be asked by the therapist).

In summary, Jung used the word association test and the method of amplification to look in more detail at the contents of the unconscious as a means of enhancing the client's ability to achieve a sense of psychic balance.

Personality Assessment from a Jungian Perspective: The Identification of Personality Types

In this section, we will examine personality assessment from Jung's perspective, with a particular emphasis on the identification of personality types.

Jung's Personality Types: Personality Attitudes and Functions

Personality assessment in Jung's viewpoint focuses on identifying particular types of personality. According to Jung (1921/1971), there are two general types of personality attitudes by which individuals orient themselves toward their environment: extraversion and introversion.

The Extraverted and Introverted Attitudes The **extraverted attitude** is an outward orientation in which psychic energy is invested in events and objects in the external environment (e.g., prefers group activities). The **introverted attitude** reflects an inward orientation in which psychic energy is invested in internal and more personal experiences (e.g., prefers to spend time alone). While Jung believed that both types of attitudes are present within each personality, he also thought that in each person one attitude is expressed more at the conscious level than the other (Bennet, 1983; Ellenberger, 1970).

The Functions of Personality Besides the two basic attitudes of personality, Jung (1921/1971; Bennet, 1983; Ellenberger, 1970) also proposed the existence of four functions of personality. Each **function** is characterized by a specific orientation to understanding the events and experiences in the environment.

- The **sensation function** involves relating to the world through the senses (e.g., "To know something, you must be able to hear, smell, see, or feel it").
- The **thinking function** refers to the tendency to relate to the world through ideas and intellect (e.g., "If something is out there, what is its relation to other things?").
- The **feeling function** concerns reacting to the world on the basis of the affective quality of one's experiences with it (e.g., "Is that something good, valuable, acceptable, harmful, or unpleasant?").
- The **intuition function** goes beyond all of the other conscious functions and relies on a deeper, more internal sense of understanding (e.g., "Although knowing what something is and how it feels, it still does not seem quite right for some strange reason").

As with the two attitude types, Jung assumed that each personality possesses all four functions, but one is often expressed at a more conscious level and predominates over the others (Ellenberger, 1970). Thus, while a feeling-type person will have to "see it to believe it," an intuitive-type person will know by just having a "gut feeling about it."

A rather interesting application of Jung's four personality functions is studying how they are manifested in varying styles of literary criticism (Helson, 1978, 1982). According to Helson, sensation-dominant critics tend to stress the meaning of the material while intuition-dominant critics tend to go beyond the surface meaning and try to identify symbolism and hidden meaning by reading between the lines. Thinking-dominant critics tend to take a more analytical and logical approach to their reviews while feeling-dominant critics try to establish a sense of intimacy with the reader. The significance of this research is that it demonstrates a systematic link between differences in personality and specific styles of cognitive functioning.

Table 4.2 presents a summary of the eight personality types created when combining the two attitudes with the four functions.

The Myers-Briggs Type Indicator® Assessment Tool: The Assessment of Jungian Types

An instrument designed to assess the two attitude types and four functions is the Myers-Briggs Type Indicator® assessment tool (Brislin & Lo, 2006; Myers, 1962, 1980; Myers & McCaulley, 1985; Myers, McCaulley, Quenk, & Hammer, 1998). The **Myers-Briggs Type Indicator®** (MBTI®) assessment tool is based on Jung's (1921/1971) type theory concerning differences in the way individuals use perception and judgment as general orientations to their experiences. More specifically, the MBTI® instrument illustrates some of the "basic differences in the ways human beings take in information and make decisions" (McCaulley, 2000, p. 117).

Testing with the MBTI® Instrument The MBTI® instrument is an objective self-report inventory designed to measure four dimensions of Jung's typology: Extraversion–Introversion (E-I), Sensation–Intuition (S-N), Thinking–Feeling (T-F), and Judgment–Perception (J-P). Since the descriptions of the E-I, S-N, and T-F dimensions correspond to those given to these terms previously, only the J-P dimension

Table 4.2   Jungian Types and Their Characteristic Features: A Summary Table

Type	Characteristic	Example
Extrovert/Sensation	A constant search for novel sensory experiences; may develop sensory skills by becoming an art critic, wine-tasting expert, masseuse, or marksman	Indiana Jones in *Raiders of the Lost Ark*
Extrovert/Thinking	Places a lot of emphasis on external objects and ideas; ruled by logic and intellect – objective and rigid	Court Television celebrity Judge Judy
Extrovert/Feeling	Public expression of feelings and emotions; makes friends easily but highly influenced by the mood of the situation – intense and sociable	The stereotype of the "used car salesperson"
Extrovert/Intuition	Sudden changes in interests; when interested, the level reflects enthusiasm; a leader of causes when interested in them	The politician who jumps from one bandwagon to another
Introvert/Sensation	Dominated by internal feelings to external events in rather dichotomous ways (e.g., good or evil); may become disassociated from the external world in response to their feelings	Political or religious extremists who you are either for or against
Introvert/Thinking	Overly concerned with ideas for their own sake; tends to dwell on abstractions and ignore practical considerations – very theoretical	The stereotypical scientist working alone in the laboratory
Introvert/Feeling	Tendency to keep their feelings to themselves; makes them appear cold, aloof, and indifferent	Dr Spock of *Star Trek* or the character Dirty Harry
Introvert/Intuition	Generally unconcerned with the external world and its events; more concerned with finding meaning in reality satisfying to them – a dreamer	The "starving artist"

Note. From Ellenberger (1970) and Monte (1987).

needs to be defined. **Judging types** tend to be orderly, systematic, and try to regulate and control their life. On the other hand, **perceiving types** tend to be curious, open-minded, spontaneous, and try to understand life and adapt to it.

The MBTI® instrument contains 126 pairs of items, each containing two statements reflecting opposing orientations on the four separate dimensions. Scoring and interpreting the MBTI® instrument involves assessing the extent to which the individual's choices for the items are more characteristic of one or the other orientation on the four separate dimensions. Based on the choices made, scores on each of the four dimensions are calculated for the individual. These four scores are then used to classify the individuals into one of 16 possible types (e.g., ISTJ, ISTP, ENFJ, ENTJ, etc.).

To determine your own Jungian typology, try completing the exercise outlined in "You Can Do It" on p. 147.

Research with the MBTI® Instrument   An excellent example of a systematic program of research on the MBTI® instrument is the work of Rae Carlson and her colleagues, which links Jungian personality types with various cognitive and interpersonal processes. For example, that introvert/thinking types were better able to memorize information of an objective nature (e.g., numbers) than were extravert/feeling types, while just the opposite was true for information of a social nature (e.g., faces; Carlson & Levy, 1973). In addition, when asked to search their memories for their most vivid experience, extravert types reported more memories of a social nature than did introvert types, while feeling

You Can Do It

What Type are You? A Personal Examination of Jungian Types

For each of the 12 items below, indicate "true" (T) if the statement reflects a belief you have about yourself and "false" (F) if the opposite of the statement reflects a belief you have about your self.

1. While attending a party, I prefer interacting with a lot of different people than with just a few individuals.
   T or F
2. I prefer movies with a clear-cut story line over movies with a lot of flashbacks.
   T or F
3. I would consider myself to be more rational than emotional.
   T or F
4. I prefer to follow a set schedule than to cope with things as they occur.
   T or F
5. I would rather play games with people, like Pictionary, than read a book.
   T or F
6. I would describe my thoughts as being more conventional than novel.
   T or F
7. To me, my thoughts are more important than my feelings.
   T or F
8. I am considered by those who know me to be more orderly than easygoing.
   T or F
9. I am someone who is generally able to express my feelings.
   T or F
10. I would rather take college classes that emphasize facts than theoretical information.
    T or F
11. I would rather people think of me as a reasonable person than a compassionate person.
    T or F
12. I would rather be decisive than impulsive.
    T or F

Scoring

Items 1, 5, and 9: If you selected "T" more often than "F," then you indicated what might be described as an extraverted type; if you selected "F" more often for these items, then you might be described as an introverted type.

Items 2, 6, and 10: If you selected "T" more often than "F," then you indicated what might be considered a sensing type. More "F" responses to these items might be described as an intuitive type.

Items 3, 7, and 11: If you selected "T" more often than "F," then you indicated what might be called a thinking type; if you had more "Fs" than "Ts," your response pattern reflected what might be called a feeling type.

Items 4, 8, and 12: More "Ts" reflect what might be called a judging type, while more "Fs" reflect what might be considered a perceptive type.

What Type Are You?

Based on the scoring procedures described above, check those type categories that seem to reflect your response patterns.

Extravert Type (E) ____ or Introvert Type (I) ____
Sensing Type (S) ____ or Intuitive Type (N) ____
Thinking Type (T) ____ or Feeling Type (F) ____
Judging Type (J) ____ or Perceptive Type (P) ____

Note: These items are not from the MBTI® assessment and results derived from this exercise will not yield an "MBTI type". You can only obtain an MBTI type by taking the authentic MBTI instrument. For more information or to take the authentic MBTI assessment, visit www.mbticomplete.com.

types reported more memories of an affective tone (e.g., joy, fear) than did thinking types (Carlson, 1980). These differences in cognitive ability seem to be due to the tendency of introvert/thinking types to pay more attention to internal personal events and that of extravert/feeling types to pay more attention to external social events (Carlson & Levy, 1973; Carlson, 1980).

The tendency for the extrovert/intuitive types to be oriented toward others was demonstrated by identifying a greater percentage of them in a group of volunteers at a half-way house for disturbed children than in a comparison group of nonvolunteers (Carlson & Levy, 1973). In contrast, other research has identified the introvert/sensing combination to be characteristic of tax preparers, an occupation that involves working primarily with vast numbers of detailed facts and figures (Descouzis, 1989).

Although considerable research supports these Jungian concepts (Cann & Donderi, 1986; Maddi, 1996), Carlson's work is particularly important because it attempts to validate the unique Jungian contribution of combining different personality dimensions and linking them systematically with other cognitive and social indices of behavior (Maddi, 1996). While the work of Carlson and others (Capraro & Capraro, 2002; Dawes, 2004) serves to provide support for the reliability and validity of the MBTI® instrument, you should realize that others have expressed concerns regarding its psychometric properties (Arnau et al., 2003; Pittenger, 1993; Vacha-Haase & Thompson, 2002). Regardless of such criticism, the MBTI® instrument continues to be a widely used personality test involving a variety of interesting applications, as you will see in the next section.

The Application of Jungian Typologies in the World of Work: The Identification of Personality Types for Personnel Purposes

The MBTI® instrument is a popular method of personality assessment with a variety of applications, especially for those professionals involved in counseling and organizational consulting (Cohen & Swerdlik, 2005). In this section, we will consider the use of the MBTI® instrument with regard to helping individuals make career-related decisions (Kennedy & Kennedy, 2004).

Career Choices: Vocational Correlates of Jungian Types

One of the most frequent applications of the MBTI® instrument involves helping individuals to make career decisions. For employers, such decisions might involve using the MBTI® instrument to find the "best fit" between the personality characteristics of a potential employee and the nature of the job to be performed (Piotrowski & Armstrong, 2002). For example, the investigation of personality types has been used to help develop personality profiles for various occupations, such as software engineers (Capretz, 2003), managers vs. nonmanagers (Carr, 2006), and leadership positions (Levesque, 2001). For those individuals attempting to make personal career decisions, seeking the "best fit" might involve trying to identify those careers that seem to match their personality characteristics and vocational interests. As an example of such career-decision making, presented below are brief descriptions of some personal characteristics and possible vocational preferences of the eight different types based on the MBTI® instrument (Carlyn, 1977; Hammer, 1996; Stricker & Ross, 1964).

- *Extraverted types* desire novel situations and tend to be talkative and impulsive. Their vocational interests tend to be in such careers as sales, public administration, and personnel director.
- *Introverted types* tend to be reflective, self-sufficient, and like privacy. Their vocational interests tend to draw them to technical-scientific professions where they can work alone, such as being an engineer, mathematician, dentist, farmer, writer, or carpenter.
- *Sensing types* emphasize reality and authority and tend to be cooperative and pragmatic. They tend to be attracted to practical vocations, including banking, medicine, office management, business administration, and police work.
- *Intuitive types* evidence a high tolerance for complexity, enjoy mental activities (e.g., reading and reasoning), and desire independence. They tend to prefer professional vocations involving autonomy, such as being a psychologist, minister, musician, chemist, or architect.
- *Thinking types* are objective, are analytical, desire order, and demonstrate endurance. Their vocational preferences tend to include scientific,

technical, and business professions that require logical thinking.

- *Feeling types* are interested in human values and interpersonal relationships and tend to be nurturing. Their vocational interests tend to be in the helping professions, such as social work, counseling, nursing, customer relations, and preaching.
- *Judging types* tend to be responsible, industrious, and steady workers and like to have things decided and settled. Their vocational interests are directed at business-oriented professions emphasizing administrative skills.
- *Perceptive types* tend to be spontaneous, flexible, and open-minded. Their vocational choices tend to include writing, art, music, advertising, psychology, and architecture.

On a more personal note, although it is not possible to assess actual Jungian types from the limited number of items presented in the "You Can Do It" activity on p. 147, to what extent do those results and these summaries seem to fit your own career aspirations? For a more thorough examination of the use of the MBTI® instrument to help you make some personal career decisions, go to the Career Services and Placement Center (CSPC) on your campus. Most CSPCs offer the opportunity for interested students to take the MBTI® instrument as part of a career-decision-making program. For more information using the MBTI® instrument to help you make some career decisions, read *Do what you are: Discover the perfect career for you through the secrets of personality type* (Tieger & Barron-Tieger, 2001).

While we have focused on the application of the MBTI® instrument to career-decision making, there are many other applications. In business, these include using personality types to improve group communication and enhance team performance (Hirsh & Kise, 2006; Varvel, Adams, Pridie, & Ruiz Ulloa, 2004), to promote creative thinking in the design of information technology services (Vowler, 2004), to investigate the possibility that decreasing enrollment trends in accounting majors are associated with the negative perceptions of students of accounting as influenced by their personality type (McDanel, 2005), and to facilitate communication in the healthcare industry (Allen & Brock, 2002).

Evaluating Jung's Analytical Viewpoint: Strengths and Limitations

We will conclude our discussion of Jung's perspective by consider the characteristic strengths and limitations of his analytical psychology.

Characteristic Strengths

This section focuses on strengths of the analytical viewpoint.

- *Richness of ideas.* Jung's viewpoint produced many rich and novel ideas. Such concepts as the collective unconscious and archetypes demonstrate the novelty of his viewpoint while his emphasis on lifelong personality development through self-realization illustrates its richness.
- *An expanding view of personality.* Jung did much to expand the way personality is viewed. He made it clear that future expectations, as well as past events, are critical when trying to understand personality. His increased emphasis on the self as a major component of personality did much to expand the role of the self in defining the uniqueness of the person. Such a view is reflected in recent theoretical formulations of the self (Pervin, 1992). Interest in Jungian psychotherapy has expanded considerably in the United States since the early 1960s (Kaufmann, 1989). Jung's theoretical influence has also attracted the attention of individuals working in diverse areas, from sociology, religion, economics, and political science (Ellenberger, 1970) to interior design and apparel merchandising (Bonner, 1989). Additional evidence of the expanded interest in Jung's ideas is the number of books based on psychological types appearing in the "self-help" section of local bookstores.
- *Methodological impact on the study of personality.* Jung's most significant contribution to the way personality is studied is the word association test (Ellenberger, 1970). From a methodological perspective, the real significance of this test is the importance Jung placed on using it as an objective measure (e.g., obtaining physiological reactions to the words) of subjective psychological constructs (e.g., complexes). His introduction

Summing It Up *Characteristic Strengths and Limitations of Jung's Analytical Psychology*

Characteristic Strengths:

- *Richness of Ideas.* Jung's views on the nature and development of personality are extremely novel.
- *Expansion of the Nature of Personality.* Jung expanded our view of personality through his conceptualization of the collective unconscious, teleological perspective on the causes of behavior, and emphasis on personality development in adulthood.
- *Methodological Impact.* This can be seen in the popularity of the word association test, number of measurement techniques for assessing the extraversion–introversion dimension, and extensive use of the MBTI instrument.
- *Optimistic View of Human Nature.* Jung's concept of self-realization illustrates the belief he had in the individual's desire for self-awareness and personal growth.

Characteristic Limitations:

- *Difficulty of Testing Concepts.* While many of Jung's theoretical concepts are novel, they are also rather abstract and difficult to test empirically.
- *Limited Acceptance.* Acceptance of Jung's ideas has been rather limited, in part, because his writing style was difficult for most people to understand and he made reference to many ideas from the occult sciences.

of the psychological types, including those of introversion and extraversion, has also stimulated the work of many other researchers (Eysenck, 1990; Morris, 1979; Winter & Baren-baum, 1999).

- *A more optimistic view of human nature.* Unlike Freud, Jung proposed a view of human nature that was somewhat optimistic. The essence of this optimism is expressed in his concept of self-realization and the emphasis it placed on the individual striving for a greater self-awareness.

Characteristic Limitations

The analytical viewpoint put forth by Jung has the following limitations:

- *Difficulty of testing concepts.* As a major limitation, the novelty of many of Jung's principal concepts (e.g., archetypes, the collective unconscious) made them very difficult to test empirically. However, in all fairness, a very limited number of Jungian concepts, such as the psychological types, have received much supportive evidence (Cann & Donderi, 1986; Maddi, 1996).
- *Limited acceptance.* A major problem Jung has had in achieving a wider level of acceptance is that many of his original writings are very hard to

understand. He was an extremely well-read individual and used many obscure references to archaeology, theology, and mythology in his writings that were not known to most people. In addition, because he also studied and made many references to the occult sciences, Jung has not been well received by the scientific community.

A highlight of major points discussed in this section appears in "Summing It Up: Characteristic Strengths and Limitations of Jung's Analytical Psychology" above.

Adler's Individual Psychology: The Promotion of Social Interest

While Jung's reaction to Freud was to look inward and probe deeper into the unconscious mind, Alfred Adler's reaction was to look outward and examine interpersonal relationships. Adler's viewpoint of personality emphasized the individual's interpersonal actions with others at a very conscious level of awareness as critical factors in the operation and development of personality. For a glimpse into the life of Alfred Adler, read "A Closer Look" on p. 151.

A Closer Look

The Life of Alfred Adler

Alfred Adler reacted to his disagreement with Freud by developing a viewpoint of personality that focused on interpersonal relationships that promoted the welfare of others.

Alfred Adler was born in a suburb of Vienna on February 17, 1870. While his family was secure financially, Adler describes his childhood in less than pleasant terms. He perceived himself as being rather ugly and too small. Being the second of six children, he was constantly trying to compete with his older brother, who was a very good athlete. Adler's problems as a child were further complicated by the fact that he suffered from rickets, a disease that affects the bones. This made it difficult for him to walk or move about.

Adler recalls his mother pampering him as a small child – until the birth of his younger brother. At this time, he sensed that his mother was shifting her attention more and more fully to the new baby. Feeling dethroned, Adler turned his affection toward his father, who seems to have had high expectations for him.

During his childhood, Adler was run over twice in the streets. At the age of three, he saw his younger brother die in the bed next to him, and he almost died from pneumonia at age four. It was these brushes with death that Adler recalls as having triggered his interest in becoming a doctor.

Through all of these traumatic experiences, Adler remained a friendly and socially active child. In school, he was not a very good student, leading one of his teachers to recommend to his parents that he should be taken out of school and trained as a shoemaker, since he was not going to be able to do much else. However, with a tremendous display of sustained hard work, Adler was able to become an excellent student. He attended the University of Vienna and received a medical degree in 1895. He began by studying ophthalmology but then settled into psychiatry.

Adler's association with Freud started when he wrote a paper publicly defending Freud's position. As a result of this, Adler was asked by Freud in 1902 to attend weekly meetings where psychoanalysis was being discussed. This discussion group would later become the Vienna Psychoanalytic Society, with Adler serving as its first president. However, at these meetings, and in Freud's presence, Adler began expressing ideas and attitudes about such significant topics as sexuality, childhood experiences, repression, and the unconscious mind that were increasingly at odds with the views of Freud. In 1911, after a nine-year association as one of Freud's earliest colleagues, Adler resigned from the society and took about one third of the society's members with him. After this separation, Freud and Adler, although living in the same city, never met again. Adler and his followers subsequently formed the Society of Free Psychoanalytic Research, an obvious bit of sarcasm aimed at Freud's domineering tendencies.

After serving as a physician in the Austrian army during World War I, Adler was asked by the government to help open a number of child guidance clinics in Vienna. Through his work with the clinics, he spent a great deal of time lecturing to, writing for, and interacting with parents, teachers, and other members of the general public. Such efforts made him extremely popular in Vienna. This display of public concern, especially for children, was to be expressed in many different aspects of his theory.

In 1926, Adler made the first of many frequent and extensive trips to the United States and was well received by U.S. educators. As a result of the Nazi takeover in Europe, he settled permanently in the United States in 1935. Adler died on May 28, 1937, in Aberdeen, Scotland, while on a lecture tour.

More information about the life of Alfred Adler can be found in *Alfred Adler: A Biographical Essay* by Carl Furtmuller (1964), who has been described as having been probably the deepest and most lifelong friend of Adler (Bottome, 1957), and chapters titled "Alfred Adler and Individual Psychology" by Henri F. Ellenberger (in Ellenberger 1970) and "Alfred Adler and Adlerian Psychology: An Overview" by Harold H. Mosak and Michael P. Maniacci (in Mosak & Maniacci, 1999).

Basic Assumptions of Adler's Individual Psychology

Adler was a prolific writer (producing over 100 books and articles in his lifetime) and lecturer. Much of his lecturing was done to – and in a style geared directly for – the general public. Almost as a reflection of his own personality, he developed a viewpoint of personality that was rather straightforward, was easily understood by nonprofessionals, and emphasized a social concern for others (Ellenberger, 1970). He referred to this approach as individual psychology. The basis of **individual psychology** was his view of people as each being *unique* in the manner in which he or she elected to help promote the social well-being of others and the betterment of society. Adler's individual psychology focused on the whole individual – emphasizing how individuals attempted to unify their thoughts, feelings, actions, attitudes, and values to achieve their goals (Rule, 2006b; Sommers-Flanagan & Sommers-Flanagan, 2004).

The Social Nature of Motivation

For Freud, the primary motivational source of personality was the reduction of individual tension, especially psychosexual urges. In sharp contrast, Adler assumed that the principal motivating force in personality was for the individual to behave in ways that serve the interests of the group over those of the individual (Sommers-Flanagan & Sommers-Flanagan, 2004). Such thinking is reflected in contemporary research documenting the health benefits (e.g., reduced likelihood of illness and a faster recovery, lower mortality rates) for those individuals whose involvement with others results in developing a high quantity and quality of social relations (Taylor, Dickerson, & Klein, 2002).

Conscious Control of Personality and an Awareness of Helping Others

To a greater extent than Freud and Jung, Adler emphasized the operation of personality at the conscious level (Mosak, 1995; Mosak & Maniacci, 1999). More specifically, he believed behavior was governed by conscious processes related to the individual's desire to work with and for others.

A Teleological Perspective of Personality

Like Jung, Adler placed a great emphasis on teleological explanations of behavior. He assumed that behavior is governed by the future goals individuals set for themselves (e.g., a student's selection of a major while in college reflects future career goals; Sommers-Flanagan & Sommers-Flanagan, 2004). However, Adler did look into the past during psychotherapy to help identify the early childhood experiences that might have shaped the goal in its present form (e.g., more parental attention given to other siblings during childhood creating a desire to be a success).

Intrapersonal vs. Interpersonal Nature of Personality

While Freud stressed **intrapersonal** forces as the primary cause of behavior, Adler tended to stress **interpersonal** forces operating within the external social environment as the primary cause of behavior. For example, the nature of an individual's relationships with siblings and how teachers reacted to this person at school were two social environments Adler considered important in determining present and future goals and behavior.

The Role of the Self

More than just a mediator of intrapsychic conflict (e.g., the ego), Adler viewed the self as that component of personality serving to give each person a sense of uniqueness. The self helped to determine an individual's view of the world, the goals set on the basis of this view, and the strategy developed to achieve these goals.

As you can see, there were some distinctive differences in the beliefs about personality proposed by Adler and Freud. These differences are highlighted in "Summing It Up: A Comparison of the Basic Assumptions of Adler and Freud" on p. 153.

Summing It Up *A Comparison of the Basic Assumptions of Adler and Freud*

Basic Assumption	Adler	Freud
Nature of Motivation	Social motivation designed to maximize the benefit of the group over selfish personal interests	Satisfaction of the individual's psychosexual urges
Conscious Control of Personality	An emphasis on the conscious awareness and control of our thoughts and actions	An emphasis on the influence of the unconscious mind on personality while minimizing the influence of the conscious mind
Teleological Perspective on Personality	An emphasis on future aspirations found in goals as major explanations of behavior	An emphasis on past experiences as primary explanations of behavior
Intrapersonal vs. Interpersonal Nature of Personality	Personality is determined by both intrapersonal forces and interpersonal relationships with other individuals.	Personality is determined largely by intrapersonal forces operating within the individual.
The Role of the Self	The self plays a major role in creating a unique personality for each individual.	The ego (the concept in Freud's thought that is closest to the self) is primarily a mediating concept involved in reducing psychic conflict.

Basic Concepts of Adler's Individual Psychology

The concepts comprising Adler's viewpoint of personality had at their basis helping the individual to develop a sense of social concern for others.

Inferiority Feelings and Compensation

While operating a clinic near a famous amusement park early in his career and treating many of the circus performers, Adler noted that these individuals developed great skills as a reaction to their physical weaknesses or handicaps. For example, an individual with a deformed leg might display considerable skill as a trapeze performer and develop tremendous strength in the upper body and arms.

On the basis of such observations, Adler proposed the concept of organ inferiority (Adler, 1907/1956a). The basic idea of **organ inferiority** is that each person is born with some type of physical limitation, such as weak eyes, weak stomach, or being a slow runner. In response to this limitation, the person is motivated to either overcome it or develop another aspect of the self (Ellenberger, 1970; Mosak & Maniacci, 1999). For example, a weak and frail young person might develop the ability to be an effective speaker and become captain of the debate team.

However, Adler (1910/1956b) soon realized that just as important as actual physical inferiorities were perceived inferiorities. Adler used the more general phrase "inferiority feelings" to reflect this belief. **Inferiority feelings** involve the response to the real or imagined inferiorities individuals perceive themselves as possessing. For example, downplaying the potential quality of his or her contribution to a discussion in class, a shy student may be reluctant to make any comments.

Adler assumed that individuals would be motivated to overcome their inferiority feelings through some form of compensation (Ellenberger, 1970; Rule, 2006b). **Compensation** consists of the individual taking positive steps to deal with and overcome inferiority feelings. For example, to help overcome a sense of shyness, this shy student might start by trying to speak with classmates before class. Next, the individual might try asking just one question in class.

It is, however, possible to overcompensate for inferiority feelings. **Overcompensation** was viewed by Adler as an excessive reaction to these feelings. For example, in an effort to lose weight, an individual might become so involved with an exercise and diet routine that friends and family are ignored and the symptoms of anorexia nervosa begin to appear (e.g., self-induced vomiting after eating). To avoid such over-compensation, Adler (1931) recommended altering one's goals or seeking alternative methods of compensation. For example, the individual might try setting as a goal losing just 20 pounds in six months instead of 60. The individual might also decide to incorporate a moderate exercise program along with the diet. Thus, individuals develop their strengths by being motivated to overcome feelings of inferiority.

Striving for Superiority

Striving for superiority was the concept Adler developed to explain the desire to go beyond simple compensation in an attempt to achieve a superior level of competence (Adler, 1930). He used the term "superiority" to express his view that individuals should strive to be perfect by developing all aspects of their personality to their fullest potential (Sommers-Flanagan & Sommers-Flanagan, 2004). For example, dieting and exercise will help the individual improve the physical aspect of the self. However, helping others to lose weight by offering advice and moral support makes it possible for the individual to also strengthen the development of the social aspect of the self. From Adler's perspective, being in great physical shape is of little value if the person is self-centered and lonely.

While Adler assumed that striving for superiority was a fundamental part of human nature, he knew that it did not happen in isolation. It must be fostered by others (e.g., parents, friends, teachers, and employers) in supportive social environments (e.g., at home, school, work, and in the community). As an illustration of the role a supportive environment plays in helping others who are striving for superiority, read "Applications in Personality Psychology" below.

On the positive side, striving for superiority can motivate people to achieve their fullest potential. On the negative side, Adler also noted the possibility of its taking a turn for the worse and manifesting itself in the form of a superiority complex. An individual suffering from a **superiority complex** is someone who seeks to abuse, exploit, and dominate others in an attempt to achieve superiority over them. Examples of the superiority complex would be the playground bully or adults who practice a dog-eat-dog philosophy so they can advance their career.

Applications in Personality Psychology

Helping Others Strive for Superiority

In addition to teaching courses in personality psychology at Hawaii Community College in Hilo, Hawaii, Professor Trina Hahm-Mijo is an accomplished ballet dancer and professional choreographer. She has combined her interests in ballet and personality psychology when teaching ballet to and choreographing ballets for wheelchair-bound individuals.

Professor Hahm-Mijo talked about how this work relates to many of Adler's notions:

My wheelchair ballets have been inspired by the wheelchair performers themselves. They are a striking example of Adler's concept of how organ inferiority can lead to a striving for superiority or perfection. In these individuals, I discovered a wealth of personal victories as I learned how each dealt with their particular reality of physical limitations. The creativity and courage exhibited by these individuals willing to face their physical disabilities as a challenge rather than a burden underscores Adler's belief in the creative power of the self – the notion that an individual's attitude towards his or her circumstances has greater power than childhood events in shaping one's adult personality. In essence, these wheelchair ballets have taught me that the human universal handicap is not physical limitations but limited vision or perspective. They serve as a clear example of Adler's premise that all individual progress, growth, and development result from one's attempt to compensate for one's inferiorities.

Social Interest

The ultimate expression of striving for superiority occurs with the development of social interest (Adler, 1939). **Social interest** is the tendency for the individual to put the needs of others over one's personal needs when striving for superiority (Mosak & Maniacci, 1999). It reflects the feeling and commitment individuals have to others and the society in which they live. When expressing social interest, the primary goal of self-improvement is, in reality, the betterment of society. By making themselves better through striving for superiority, individuals are sometimes able to make society better, which in turn makes it possible for others to better themselves. This can improve society and start the cycle again. For example, an individual may compensate for poor athletic ability by becoming an outstanding teacher and helping others to strive for superiority.

Style of Life

Adler's (1929a, 1931) concept of a **style of life** refers to the unique way that each person seeks to express the universal desire to strive for superiority through social interest. For example, one individual may seek superiority by becoming a political activist while another might decide to write children's books designed to reduce prejudice.

The unique style of life an individual develops reflects both personal and environmental factors (Rule, 2006b; Sommers-Flanagan & Sommers-Flanagan, 2004). Personal factors include inferiority feelings based on objective (e.g., not being very tall) and subjective (e.g., seeing one's self as being dumb) perceptions and a desire to strive for superiority in order to overcome these shortcomings. Environmental factors include the structural and emotional nature of the family. Structural factors include the family size, presence of both parents, or an individual's birth-order position. Emotional factors within the family involve the nature of the emotional relationships among family members (e.g., the basic sense of mistrust in abusive families). Environmental factors might also include relationships outside the family (e.g., a compassionate teacher). Adler felt that one's style of life was determined by the age of five years.

Adler proposed that the major function of a style of life was to serve as a unifying force for all aspects of the individual's personality. So important was one's style of life, he believed that it determined literally everything a person does. For example, an individual with an artistic style of life might elect to enroll in art courses as electives instead of science or writing courses in high school, decide to major in art while in college, donate money to community art organizations, and desire to marry someone with a similar commitment to the arts. Thus, the style of life a person develops can have some important consequences.

The Creative Self

While a variety of factors can serve to influence the style of life, Adler believed that in the end, the individual must take personal responsibility for the style selected and its outcomes. The central concept Adler (1935) used to assume all of this responsibility was the creative self. The **creative self** is responsible for perceiving, analyzing, interpreting, and giving meaning to life's experiences. As such, the interpretation of and subjective meaning given to a situation determine a person's reaction to it. For example, one person from an abusive family might elect to major in social work in order to help other abuse victims, while another might express anger and abuse others. The creative self would produce a style of life high in social interest for the first individual, while it produced one low in social interest for the second. Because it has such a profound influence on the unique and characteristic way individuals respond to the world around them, Adler considered the creative self the crown jewel of his viewpoint of personality. Such an emphasis on personalized reactions to fostering one's style of life is consistent with contemporary research documenting the value associated with an individual's positive problem-solving ability to cope successfully with the challenges of everyday living (Heppner & Lee, 2002).

As a final point, while the basic concepts comprising Adler's viewpoint were discussed separately, Adler viewed them as operating in an interrelated manner. Figure 4.5 summarizes the relationships among the major concepts discussed in this section.

The Nature of Personality Development

The process of personality development was to prepare the individual to meet the challenges in what Adler (1931, 1933/1956c) believed to be life's three major tasks: social, occupational, and sexual. Successful personality development required the individual to resolve problems in each of these three areas in the direction of fostering greater social interest. While he assumed that

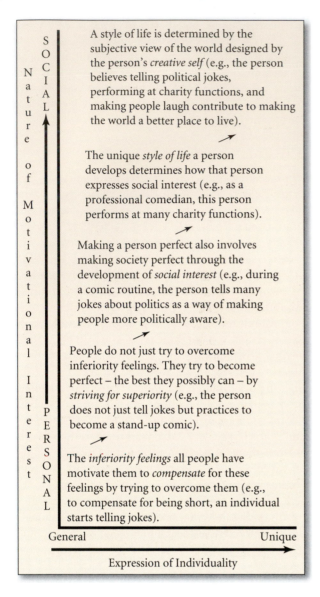

Figure 4.5   The basic concepts of Adler's individual viewpoint

During this period of life, the first life task is a social one that involves learning to cooperate and consider the needs of others. Two of the most significant social relationships to occur during this period are those with parents and siblings.

Parent–Child Interactions as the First Social Relationship   The nature of the child's early interactions with the parents can have a significant impact on the child's personality development and degree of social interest. Adler described two personality types that were a result of specific parent–child relationships: the pampered child and the rejected child.

The personality of the **pampered child** develops out of a parent–child relationship characterized by overprotection, overindulgence, or domination over the child. As adults, pampered children tend to rely on others, be rather unsure, and display a low level of social interest by placing their needs above those of others. On the other hand, children who are not pampered, are allowed to take small risks, and are taught to take responsibility feel more confident and display a healthy need for cooperation and social interest. These characteristics tend to be carried over into adulthood.

The personality of the **rejected child** develops out of parent–child relationships characterized by rejection and neglect that might be due to the presence of too many other children. Such children may develop a style of life that reflects a lack of trust and withdrawal from social participation. As adults, rejected children may become rather independent of others but feel socially isolated, display a low level of social interest, and possibly become criminals. Children who are not rejected grow up in an environment of warmth, acceptance, and trust. As adults they are not afraid to get involved with others, both socially (e.g., join clubs) and emotionally (e.g., fall in love). Such individuals tend to display a high degree of social interest.

personality development is a lifelong process, Adler believed experiences in early childhood played an important role in preparing the individual to confront life's challenges.

Childhood and Adolescence: Developing the Initial Sense of Cooperation with Others in Social Relationships

During childhood and adolescence, each person starts to develop an initial sense of social relationships.

Sibling Relationships and Birth Order as Determinants of Personality   Part of what constitutes the family environment is the **birth-order** relationship with one's brothers and sisters (Adler, 1931; Hoffman, 1991; Sulloway, 1996; Toman, 1993). Adler believed that one's birth order exposed the child to particular types of family environments that had systematic effects on personality development. Although there is a variety of possible birth-order combinations, Adler (1931) emphasized four: firstborn (oldest), secondborn, the youngest child, and the only child.

- *The first-born child.* The first-born child is, for a time, given special attention as being the only child. However, with the arrival of the second child, the oldest child is dethroned from this favored position. As adults, Adler believed firstborns tended to be more independent of others and try to solve their problems on their own, supposedly as a result of being abandoned by their parents. However, such feelings of dethronement in the first-born child can be minimized by parents encouraging the oldest child to serve as a "helper" with the newborn. Caring for younger siblings fosters the development of an initial sense of social interest in helping others who are less able.

- *The second-born child.* Because the second-born child lives in the shadow of the older sibling, feelings of inferiority are intensified and expressed by a heightened level of motivation to achieve and get ahead of the older sibling. In a healthy sense, this high degree of achievement motivation is channeled into the direction of helping others (e.g., becoming a superior community activist). It is interesting to note that Adler was a second-born child. In a negative sense, this high need for achievement can be expressed in a desire to dominate others (e.g., a cut-throat politician).

- *The youngest child.* Being the baby of the family can create a rather perplexing situation in that there are older siblings to contribute to feelings of inferiority. However, there are also more people around to care for and pamper the youngest child. In a healthy sense, the youngest child has many models from which to learn how to strive for superiority. In a negative sense, the youngest child can become discouraged by all of this competition and develop excessive feelings of inferiority and a lack of social interest. Next to the oldest child, Adler believed the youngest child had the greatest potential to be a problem child and develop neurotic tendencies as an adult.

- *The only child.* The only child is the most likely to be pampered by the parents and to spend a considerable amount of time around adults. In a healthy sense, spending a lot of time around adults as a child without siblings can contribute to a higher level of intellectual ability and academic success in school (Zajonc, 1976). In a negative sense, when no longer the center of attention, the only child as an adult may become timid, passive,

and withdrawn and still feel the need to be pampered by others.

Although Adler first introduced the notion of birth order as a determinant of personality development over 50 years ago, the idea is still receiving considerable research attention today. See "A Closer Look" below for more about the topic.

A Closer Look

Birth Order and Personality: Knowing One's Place in the Family

Does knowing a person's place in the family birth order reveal something about their personality? There is some evidence to support the relationship between birth order and various personality and interpersonal characteristics, such as achievement striving, intelligence, affiliation, and popularity (Sulloway, 1996).

Achievement Striving

There is extensive research to suggest that firstborns have a higher need for achievement than do later-born individuals (Howarth, 1980). For example, first-born children tend to score higher on personality tests measuring the need for achievement (Glass, Neulinger, & Brim, 1974) and tests measuring English, mathematical, and verbal achievement (Breland, 1974; Eysenck & Cookson, 1969; Glass et al., 1974) than do later-born children.

Going beyond simple test scores, a larger representation of firstborns than later-borns has been found among the ranks of eminent people and college students (Schachter, 1963; Warren, 1966). Firstborns have also been found to be overrepresented among those listed in *Who's Who* (Altus, 1966), individuals involved in American politics (Zweigenhaft, 1975), those who were U.S. astronauts (I. D. Harris, 1964), and women who were business executives (Hoyenga & Hoyenga, 1984).

One explanation for the high achievement of firstborns seems to be that parents tend to give the first-born child more attention and stimulation, and have higher expectations for them than they do for their

Table 4.3   More Illustrations of the Relationship Between Birth Order and Personality Characteristics and Social Behavior

Nature of the Relationship	Reference
Cigarette consumption: Youngest children of both sexes have the highest percentage of smokers.	Ernst & Angst, 1983
Alcohol consumption: Youngest male children with three or more siblings have the highest rate of alcohol consumption; no relationship found for females.	Ernst & Angst, 1983
Self-esteem: Firstborns tend to have a lower sense of self-esteem than later-born children.	Forer, 1976
Mate selection: Firstborns and later-borns tend to select as their mates others with a similar birth-order rank.	Ward, Castro, & Wilcox, 1974
Self-disclosure: Later-borns tended to reveal more about themselves than firstborns.	Dimond & Munz, 1968
Cheating at school: Among college students, more cheating was found in firstborns than later-born children.	Hetherington & Feldman, 1964
Alcoholism: No relationship between birth order and alcoholism has been established.	Ernst & Angst, 1983
Shyness: With four or more siblings, laterborns tend to be more shy than firstborns.	Sulloway, 1996
Criminal behavior: No relationship between birth order and criminal behavior has been established.	Ernst & Angst, 1983
Creativity: Firstborns have been found to be more creative than later-born individuals.	Corneau, 1980
Aggressiveness: No relationship between birth order and aggressiveness has been established.	Owyang, 1971
Risk-taking behavior: Laterborns seem to take more risks than first-born individuals.	Nisbett, 1968
Handedness: No relationship between birth order and being left- or right-handed.	Searleman, Porac, & Coren, 1989
Acceptance of new ideas: Later-born scientists and religious and political leaders tend to be more accepting and supportive of new ideas than firstborns.	Sulloway, 1990
Vocational choice: Firstborns tend to be overrepresented among eminent scientists, lawyers, members of congress, army officers, and medical and dental students; second-borns seem to be overrepresented among beauticians.	Rule & Comer, 2006
Parental affection: In multiple-child families, the youngest children receive the most from parents and the oldest one the least.	J. R. Harris, 2006
Clinical judgments: Only children are perceived by mental health professionals as having more personal problems and career-related concerns.	Stewart, 2004

later-born children (Belsky, Gilstrap, & Rovine, 1984; Boroson, 1973; Rothbart, 1971). It is possible that such early expectations of achievement for firstborns result in their becoming higher achievers than later-born children as adults.

Intelligence

Firstborns, as well as only children (Falbo & Polit, 1986), were found to have IQ scores that, on the average, were higher than those of later-born children (Belmont & Marolla, 1973; Falbo & Polit, 1986; Zajonc, 1975; Zajonc & Markus, 1975). To explain this relationship,

Zajonc (1975; Zajonc & Markus, 1975) proposed that, while they are alone, the first-born child is given a large amount of attention and verbal stimulation. As other children are added to the family, the amount of attention and stimulation the parents can give each child decreases, resulting in subsequently lower IQ scores. This relationship could also be due to socioeconomic status. More specifically, there is a tendency for families of high socioeconomic status to be small; consequently, there will be fewer later-born children (Blake, 1989). However, these birth-order differences in IQ among siblings are not that great, averaging only about 10 points, and may disappear by the age of 17 (McCall, 1984).

Affiliation

Under conditions of stress, firstborns display a greater desire to be with others than do later-born children (Darley & Aronson, 1966; Schachter, 1959; Zimbardo & Formica, 1963). This seems to be due to the increased anxiety created in and excessive comforting given to the child by inexperienced parents (Hilton, 1967; Ring, Lipinski, & Braginsky, 1965; Schachter, 1959). As a result, first-born children may become more anxious and, as both children and adults, dependent on others to reduce this anxiety and provide some emotional comfort.

Popularity

Later-born children, youngest children in particular, have been found to be more extraverted (Thompson, 1974) and popular among their peers than their first-born siblings or only children (Miller & Maruyama, 1976). This increased popularity of later-born children may be a consequence of their having developed social skills (e.g., negotiation, cooperation) to compensate for their lack of physical size when resolving power struggles with older siblings (Miller & Maruyama, 1976; Ickes & Turner, 1983).

Table 4.3 provides a brief sample of some additional relationships between birth order and other personality characteristics and social behaviors. More information on the subject of birth order and personality can be found in *Birth Order: Its Influence on Personality* (Ernst & Angst, 1983) and *Born to Rebel: Birth Order, Family Dynamics, and Creative Lives* (Sulloway, 1996), as well as a book chapter titled "Birth Order and Other Environmental Differences within the Family" (in J. R. Harris, 2006) for a more detailed discussion of various explanations of differences among siblings.

Young Adulthood: Developing a Sense of Society through Work

The major developmental task during young adulthood is to select an occupation that will make it possible to express one's style of life in a manner reflecting social interest. Adler (1933/1956c) believed that by striving for occupational superiority, the person would develop a purpose in life and make a positive contribution to the development of society. Adler also believed the fear of failure was a reason why some young adults avoid making career choices. Because he placed so much importance on the selection of an occupation as a means of overcoming feelings of inferiority and expressing social interest, Adler firmly believed that schools must provide young adults with career counseling.

Adulthood and Old Age: Demonstrating Social Interest through Love

In Adler's view, the major developmental task in adulthood involves expressing social interest in the form of love within an intimate relationship characterized by each individual being more concerned about the needs and happiness of the other person than his or her own. The expression of love in adulthood also involves raising children in a family environment which supports their efforts to strive for superiority and promotes a sense of social interest. Thus, teaching children to respect and care about the needs of others starts when the adults in the family demonstrate concern and respect for each other's needs.

In old age, the elderly can express their love by stepping aside and letting young people have their opportunity to exhibit social interest and strive for superiority. Continued involvement in society by the elderly (e.g., serving on advisory boards) demonstrates hope for the future and the life hereafter. Without such hope, the only thing elderly individuals will have to look forward to is death.

In summary, Adler's perspective on personality development emphasizes a sense of social interest that focuses on cooperation and helping to satisfy the needs of others. An outline of the major points discussed in this section appears in "Summing It Up: The Development of Social Interest Across the Life Span" on p. 160.

Applications of Adler's Individual Psychology: Using What Is Known

Our discussion of the applications of Adler's viewpoint will focus on psychotherapy and personality assessment.

Adlerian Psychotherapy

The major goal of Adlerian psychotherapy is to help individuals correct their maladaptive style of life. In its place, the therapist proposes a healthy style of life that

Summing It Up *The Development of Social Interest Across the Lifespan*

Period of Development	Description of the Developmental Task
Childhood and Adolescence	The early development of social skills requiring the child to learn to cooperate with and consider the needs of others – such development usually occurs through interaction with parents and siblings in the home.
Young Adulthood	The selection of and preparation for a career that will allow the individual to express social interest – such development usually occurs while going to high school, college, or a technical training institute.
Adulthood	The expression of love that manifests itself in teaching children to respect and care for others so that the concept of social interest is passed from one generation to the next – such development usually occurs within a marriage emphasizing the needs of one's spouse over one's own.
Old Age	The expression of love that manifests itself in a form of social interest that will go on forever – such development is usually achieved in the elderly by giving younger individuals the opportunity to participate actively in the betterment of society.

includes more constructive means of compensating for inferiority and a greater emphasis on social interest (Mosak & Maniacci, 1999; Sommers-Flanagan & Sommers-Flanagan, 2004). For example, providing vocational counseling and training to youth gang members might be one approach taken by a therapist to help them achieve a sense of superiority through a career instead of through antisocial behavior.

The Progression of Adlerian Psychotherapy: The Systematic Reconstruction of a Style of Life High in Social Interest

Adler divided his individual psychotherapy into three steps, described in the following subsections.

Step One: Establishing a Therapeutic Relationship Based on Confidence and Trust   The first step in Adlerian therapy involves the therapist gaining the client's confidence and trust (Adler, 1929b). The therapist begins by outlining clearly and optimistically the nature of the therapeutic procedures and processes. This approach presumably serves as a source of inspiration for the client and increases the client's confidence in the therapist's ability to provide help. To help gain the

client's trust, Adler (1927) felt the therapist must establish a level of mutual respect, demonstrating a willingness to take the perspective of the client by offering explanations that reflect the client's point of view (e.g., social norms of gang members) and are in language easily understood by the client (e.g., avoiding overly complicated psychological terminology). Such actions demonstrate a direct attempt by the therapist to create a therapeutic relationship with the client based on mutual respect and involvement.

Step Two: Tracing the Development of a Mistaken Style of Life   The second step in the therapeutic process involves modifying the self-defeating strategies being employed by the client to achieve superiority. This step requires making clear to the client the dangers of leading such a mistaken style of life (e.g., compensating for feelings of inferiority and alienation through gang violence will lead to a criminal lifestyle). In addition, the therapist must try to make the client understand how this maladaptive style of life developed initially and what functions it currently serves (e.g., gang violence brings social status).

Step Three: Developing Social Interest   Rather than simply replacing the mistaken style of life with one that is less self-defeating, the final step in the therapeutic process is an attempt to foster social interest in the newly developed style of life of the client. For example, in addition to a gang member dropping out of the gang and being successful in school, the individual could also help others succeed by serving as a volunteer at a day-care center helping young kids learn to read.

In summary, the major objective of Adlerian therapy is to foster a style of life that is high in social interest and so consistent with the needs of both the individual and society.

Some Techniques of Adlerian Psychotherapy: Trying to Understand from Where You Came

Because each person's style of life develops during childhood, Adler employed a number of therapeutic techniques in an attempt to trace the development of the mistaken style of life back to its source in the client's youth.

Identifying Early Recollections With the technique of **early recollections**, the client is asked to report the earliest memories he or she can recall (Rule, 2006a). Adler believed that since our style of life was formed in childhood, such early memories could provide us with hints as to its origin and development (Adler, 1931). For example, an early childhood recollection of the youth gang member might include images of the older boys in gangs receiving considerable attention and respect from the other neighborhood kids.

Investigating Early Childhood Experiences An investigation into childhood involves getting information from the client about the nature of early family experiences. By becoming aware of such things as how the client was treated by the parents or the nature of sibling relationships, a more effective treatment plan to offset the negative consequences of these experiences can be developed. For example, the client might have turned to gang activity to compensate for an emotionally distant relationship with parents during childhood. In the course of treatment, this client might be told that such emotional support can also be obtained by doing volunteer work at the local community center. Thus, these childhood experiences can provide the therapist with insights into the motivation for current behavior patterns.

Dream Analysis Adler viewed dreams as a means of providing information in the *present* about those feelings and aspirations the client wants to have in the *future* (Mosak, 1995; Mosak & Maniacci, 1999; Sommers-Flanagan & Sommers-Flanagan, 2004). By investigating dreams, the therapist can begin to see how the client "would like the world to be." For example, in his dream, the youth gang member dreams of being a powerful leader and commanding the respect of many people. The therapist might point out that instead of gang activity, such desires could manifest themselves more constructively through gaining some valuable experience by serving as an aide to a local politician.

Family Therapy Because Adler placed so much emphasis on the early childhood family environment, he was one of the first to practice family therapy. **Family therapy** is a form of psychotherapy that focuses on the interpersonal relationships among members of a family (Goldenberg & Goldenberg, 1995). Its logic is that some disturbances are caused or maintained by faulty family relationships. Its goal is to help create a more psychologically healthy environment by pointing out self-defeating relationships and providing instruction for rectifying the situation (e.g., parenting skills, group communication skills).

By employing these therapeutic techniques, the therapist is in a much better position to begin understanding the origins of the client's mistaken style of life and the underlying motivational forces that serve to maintain it into adulthood. More information on the therapeutic use of Adler's individual psychology can be found by reading *Adlerian Lifestyle Counseling: Practice and Research* (Rule & Bishop, 2006).

Personality Assessment from Adler's Viewpoint

In the tradition of the Adlerian viewpoint, Dr. James E. Crandall (1975) has developed the **Social Interest Scale** (SIS). The SIS is a 15-item scale containing a series of personal characteristics or traits arranged in pairs (e.g., respectful vs. original). A person's score on the SIS, ranging from 0 to 15, reflects the extent to which he or she would like to possess personal characteristics indicative of social interest. To examine your own level of social interest, complete the SIS in "You Can Do It" on p. 162.

You Can Do It

The Social Interest Scale: Measuring the Desire to Care for Others

For each of the item pairs listed below, select which one you would rather possess as one of your own personal characteristics. Indicate your choice by writing a "1" or "2" on the line next to each pair. The scoring directions are listed at the end of this feature.

_____ 1. respectful
        2. original
_____ 1. generous
        2. individualistic
_____ 1. trustworthy
        2. wise
_____ 1. forgiving
        2. gentle
_____ 1. considerate
        2. wise

_____ 1. neat
        2. sympathetic
_____ 1. alert
        2. cooperative
_____ 1. imaginative
        2. helpful
_____ 1. realistic
        2. moral
_____ 1. ambitious
        2. patient

Scoring

For the five items on the left, count the number of times you selected the first trait in the pair. Add that number to the number of times you selected the second trait in the pair for those five items listed on the right. The higher the score, the greater the degree of expressed social interest. Since only 10 items were selected, you should not consider this to be an absolute measure of your social interest.

Adapted from Crandall (1975).

Table 4.4 Mean Scores for Different Groups on the Social Interest Scale

Group	Mean Score
Ursuline sisters (6)	13.33
Adult church members (147)	11.21
Charity volunteers (9)	10.78
High social interest high school students (23)*	10.22
High social interest college students (21)*	9.48
University employees (165)	9.24
University students (1784)	8.17
Mental hospital patients (25)	7.56
Low social interest college students (35)*	7.40
Female professional models (54)	7.06
Low social interest high school students (22)*	6.86
Adult atheists (30)	6.70
Convicted felons (30)	6.37

Note. From Crandall (1980).
Group size is given in parenthesis. *Based on peer ratings.

Behavioral Correlates of Social Interest

In support of its validity, scores on the SIS have been found to be related to a variety of other personal attributes and social behaviors in a manner consistent with Adler's conceptualization of social interest. Table 4.4 illustrates that, consistent with Adler's views on social interest and personality adjustment, criminals and mental patients displayed a lower level of social interest than other groups such as church members and charity volunteers (Crandall, 1980). In addition, scores on the SIS were found to be positively correlated with measures of cooperation, helping, empathy, liking of others, being liked by others, and responsibility. On the other hand, SIS scores have been found to be negatively correlated with hostility and self-centeredness (Crandall, 1980, 1981).

Attitudinal Correlates of Social Interest

Do individuals with varying degrees of social interest view the world differently? There is some evidence to support this contention. For example, SIS scores have been found to be positively correlated with a personal value system emphasizing the importance of peace, equality, and family security (Crandall, 1975) and a positive view of others as being altruistic and trustworthy (Crandall, 1980). In a more global sense, SIS scores have also been found to be positively correlated with how interesting individuals perceive their day-to-day life to be and how much beauty and attractiveness they find in the world (Crandall & Putman, 1980).

It is possible that such an optimistic view of the world may lie at the foundation of social interest. In a simple sense, it could be that when people are in a good

AT THE CUTTING EDGE OF PERSONALITY PSYCHOLOGY

Volunteerism as an Expression of Social Interest

Motivational Factors that Promote Volunteerism: Doing Good for Self and Society

Volunteerism benefits the recipients of service and the broader community as well; as such, volunteer service is one way that people can help other people and, at the same time, help alleviate some of society's problems (Omoto & Snyder, 2002; M. Snyder & Omoto, 2004). But volunteer service also rewards volunteers by promoting community spirit, offering evidence of people's kindness and commitment to others, increasing feelings of helpfulness and self-worth, providing opportunities to develop and exercise one's skills, and actually improving physical health (Andrews, 1990; Omoto & Malsch, 2005; M. Snyder, Omoto, & Lindsay, 2004). To put it simply, volunteer service provides, at one and the same time, opportunities to do good for other people, for society, and for one's self (M. Snyder & Omoto, 2000, p. 128).

Such a statement illustrates beautifully the sentiments expressed by Adler through his emphasis on social interest. A significant application of the concept is the research on volunteerism by Allen M. Omoto, of Claremont Graduate University, and Mark Snyder, of the University of Minnesota. In their research, Omoto and Snyder Omoto, 1998; M. Snyder & Omoto, 2000) and their colleagues (Clary et al., 1998; M. Snyder, Omoto, & Crain, 1999) are "examining personal and social motivations that dispose people to volunteer and that sustain their involvement in such ongoing helping relationships" (M. Snyder & Omoto, 2000, p. 127). For example, as part of their research, Omoto, Snyder, and Steve C. Martino (2000) examined the motivational factors of adult hospice volunteers of varying ages over a six-month period. Their results indicate that younger volunteers (ages 19 to 39 years) expressed a greater degree of relationship motivation than did middle-aged (ages 40 to 54 years) and elderly volunteers (55 to 76 years), with the latter two groups not differing from each other. On the other hand, older volunteers reported a greater degree of service motivation than did the younger ones. Volunteers of all ages expressed the belief that their work would permit them to give something back to society. After volunteering for six months, younger volunteers reported experiencing closer relationships with their clients than did either the middle or older volunteers, who did not differ from each other on this measure. In contrast, older volunteers tended to report a greater sense of service and feelings of obligation to society than did younger ones. Increases in self-esteem as a result of volunteer actions were linked to their impact on their clients for younger volunteers and to the ability to alter feelings of obligation to society for older ones.

The significance of this research is that Omoto and Snyder have identified two differing motivational tendencies for volunteering appearing at different stages of life: the potential to fulfill social relationships for young volunteers and the potential to fulfill a sense of service and social obligation for older ones. By identifying such differing motives throughout the life course, volunteer agencies will increase the likelihood of attracting and sustaining individuals' efforts by matching appeals for volunteers with individuals' motives (Clary et al., 1994, 1998). Modifying the appeals to match individuals' changing motives as they enter different life stages also increases the ability to sustain volunteers' efforts throughout their lives, thus creating the potential for providing a lifetime of service to others. Such a sense of service to others while contributing to a positive sense of self (e.g., increases in self-esteem) truly is in the spirit of Adler's views on social interest – the outcome of service to others is "doing good for self and society."

mood, they are more likely to help others (Baron & Byrne, 2000). Another benefit of maintaining a high level of social interest is that individuals with high SIS scores report fewer stressful life experiences and fewer symptoms of stress than do those with low SIS scores (Crandall, 1984). It seems that having a more positive outlook and taking a more active role in one's own life and in the lives of others can serve to help reduce everyday stress. Such ideals are expressed in the contemporary research on volunteerism presented in "At the Cutting Edge of Personality Psychology: Volunteerism as an Expression of Social Interest" on p. 163.

Evaluating Adler's Viewpoint: Strengths and Limitations

We will conclude our discussion of Adler by considering some of the characteristics strengths and limitations of his viewpoint.

Characteristic Strengths

Adler's viewpoint has the following strengths:

- *Impact on contemporary psychology.* Although not as visible as Freud's, Adler's influence on contemporary psychology is reflected in a number of ways (Mosak & Maniacci, 1999). For example, his emphasis on striving for superiority is consistent with the humanistic viewpoint of personality discussed in Chapter 6. His concept of the creative self as an interpreter of information is consistent with some of the more cognitive and social learning viewpoints of personality discussed in Chapter 10. The research on birth order is clearly rooted in the Adlerian tradition.
- *Adler the optimist.* Adler offered a view of human nature that stressed compassion for others as the major motivating force of personality. Nothing illustrates this better than the tremendous significance he gave to social interest throughout his theory, and the theory's many applications based on social interest. For Adler, people are not only striving for self-perfection but for perfection of the society and the world in which they live.
- *Adler the pragmatist.* In trying to help individuals strive for superiority, Adler turned to those places most likely to have the greatest impact – the school and family (Mosak, 1995). Practicing what he preached, he lectured widely to groups of parents and teachers and helped to develop

family therapy and community intervention programs (Ellenberger, 1970; Mosak, 1995).

Characteristic Limitations

Adler's viewpoint has the following limitations:

- *Less systematic theorizing.* Adler developed a theory of personality consisting of relatively few concepts that were loosely related to each other. For example, his approach to therapy was not very well defined or linked systematically with his views on personality development.
- *Limited empirical investigations.* To some extent, Adler spent more effort on the clinical and social applications of his theory than on its empirical validation. Part of the problem may be that the looseness of his theory made formulating specific hypotheses difficult. But Crandall's work does provide supporting evidence for one of Adler's most important concepts – assessing social interest.

Summing It Up *Characteristic Strengths and Limitations of Adler's Individual Psychology*

Characteristic Strengths:

- *The Impact of Adler.* While not often acknowledged, Adler's influence can be found in a number of different viewpoints of personality proposed by other theorists.
- *Optimistic View of People.* Adler believed that people are motivated by the desire to help others.
- *Practicality.* Adler stressed looking to the family and school as being the basic foundation of successful personality development, adjustment, and therapeutic modification.

Characteristic Limitations:

- *Theoretical Simplicity.* Because Adler utilized a relatively small number of theoretical concepts, his viewpoint of personality might be described as rather simplistic.
- *Limited Empirical Research.* Because Adler was more concerned with the applications of his theory than with the systematic validation of it, he did not spend much time on empirical research.

Additional information on Adler's views of personality can be obtained from reading *Social Interest* (Adler, 1939) and *A Primer of Adlerian Psychology* (Mosak & Maniacci, 1999). The highlights of the major points in this section are presented in "Summing It Up: Characteristic Strengths and Limitations of Adler's Individual Psychology" on p. 164.

A final comment on the Freud–Jung–Adler relationship is in order at this point. Jung and Adler were among the first to propose alternatives to Freud's psychology of personality. Jung reacted to Freud by going deeper into the individual's unconscious (e.g., collective unconscious). Adler did just the opposite, focusing his attention on conscious motives (e.g., striving for superiority) and social factors (e.g., family and school) as the principal determinants of personality. The next chapter presents still other reactions to Freud's viewpoint.

Chapter Summary: Reexamining the Highlights

- *Jung's Analytical Psychology*

  - *Basic Assumptions of Analytical Psychology.* The basic assumptions of Jung's viewpoint include an expanded role for libido, extending the structure and nature of the unconscious, noting both the past and future as being critical determinants of behavior, and the seeking of psychic balance as being a principal motivator of personality.

  - *The Structure of Personality.* Jung viewed the structure of personality as consisting of the conscious ego, personal unconscious, and the collective unconscious, and as containing complexes in the personal unconscious and archetypes in the collective unconscious. Significant archetypes include the persona, animus and anima, the shadow, and the self.

  - *The Dynamics of Personality.* The dynamics of personality consist of the flow of psychic energy based on the principles of opposites, equivalence, and entropy.

  - *The Nature and Process of Personality Development.* Personality development is a lifelong process involving individuation, the transcendent function, and self-realization. Maladaptive personality development is characterized by a lack of balance among the various aspects of personality.

  - *Applications of Jungian Analytical Psychology.* The aim of Jungian analytical psychotherapy is to reestablish a balance among the various aspects of personality. The process of analytical psychotherapy includes stages of confession, elucidation, education, and transformation. Analytical psychotherapy includes creating a primarily egalitarian relationship between the client and analyst, the use of the word association test to identify significant complexes, and the method of amplification to analyze dreams and explore archetypes. Personality assessment from the Jungian perspective involves the identification of personality types. The extraverted and introverted attitudes are two personality types identified by Jung. The four functions of personality are sensation, thinking, feeling, and intuition. The Myers-Briggs Type Indicator® assessment tool is an objective self-report technique designed to assess these personality types and functions. The application of Jungian types to career-decision making involves using the Myers-Briggs Type Indicator® assessment tool to match individuals with occupations that reflect their personality characteristics.

  - *Evaluating Jung's Analytical Viewpoint.* Characteristic strengths associated with Jung's viewpoint include its rich and novel ideas, an expanded view of the nature of personality, the methodological developments it produced and stimulated, and an optimistic view of human nature. Its limitations include proposing concepts that were difficult to test and a limited acceptance due to Jung's sometimes rather esoteric writing style.

- *Adler's Individual Psychology*

  - *Basic Assumptions of Adler's Individual Psychology.* The basic assumptions of Adler's viewpoint include an emphasis on helping others as a primary motivational force, the conscious control of personality, an emphasis on the future and the importance of interpersonal relationships as principal determinants of behavior, and an expanded role for the self.

- *Basic Concepts of Individual Psychology.* The basic concepts of Adler's viewpoint include organ inferiority, inferiority feelings, and compensation and overcompensation for inferiority feelings through the striving for superiority and the expression of social interest. The creative self helps to produce a style of life high in social interest.

- *The Nature of Personality Development.* The basic goal of personality development is to learn to solve life's tasks with a high degree of social interest. During childhood and adolescence, learning to get along with parents and siblings establishes an initial sense of cooperation. Such factors as parent–child relationships and birth order can influence this aspect of development. In young adulthood, the developmental task is to learn to express social interest and striving for superiority through work and community involvement. In adulthood and old age, the developmental task involves providing love and support for those who are younger. The degree of personality adjustment is reflected in the amount of social interest demonstrated by the individual.

- *Adlerian Psychotherapy.* The goal of Adlerian psychotherapy is to establish a style of life high in social interest. The process requires that the client establish confidence and trust in the therapist, identify the origins of the maladaptive style of life, and develop an alternative style of life high in social interest. Therapeutic methods include the technique of early recollections, examining childhood experiences, the analysis of dreams for goals and aspirations, and family therapy.

- *Personality Assessment.* The Social Interest Scale (SIS) measures the tendency of an individual to desire characteristics indicative of social interest. SIS scores are associated with helping others and a more positive world view.

- *Evaluating Adler's Viewpoint.* Characteristic strengths associated with Adler's viewpoint include the somewhat pervasive but subtle impact he has had on contemporary personality psychology, his optimistic view of human nature, and his pragmatic approach to promoting changes in social interest. Characteristic limitations include the somewhat unsystematic nature of his theory and his limited attempts to gather empirical evidence in support of his viewpoint.

Glossary

analytical psychology The name given to Jung's viewpoint of personality.

analytical psychotherapy The process of treating emotional disorders, as practiced from the Jungian viewpoint.

anima The archetype for expressing the feminine characteristics within males.

animus The archetype for expressing the masculine characteristics within females.

archetypes Generalized or universal ideas and concepts.

birth order The order in which persons are born into a family.

collective unconscious The region of the unconscious mind Jung believed was shared by all individuals.

compensation Attempts made by individuals to overcome actual or perceived limitations and weaknesses.

compensatory function An activity of the personal unconscious that could be used to help the individual achieve psychic balance.

complex A collection of emotions or information around a particular concept.

confession stage The initial stage of Jungian psychotherapy, in which the client begins to express troubled feelings and ideas.

conscious ego The structure used by Jung to account for conscious awareness.

creative self That aspect of personality responsible for processing information in a manner that promotes the development of an individual's potential to the fullest.

dream series method The analysis of several dreams for consistency of contents and symbolism.

early recollections A technique in Adlerian psychotherapy in which individuals are asked to identify the earliest memories they can recall.

education stage The third stage of Jungian psychotherapy, in which more adaptive forms of behavior are explored.

elucidation stage The second stage of Jungian psychotherapy, in which explanations for problematic feelings are discussed.

extraverted attitude A personality style geared toward objects and events in the external or social environment.

family therapy A systematic attempt to modify the maladaptive behavioral patterns operating within families.

feeling function Using affective reactions as the dominant means of experiencing the environment.

function A systematic approach to experiencing the environment.

individual psychology The name given to Adler's viewpoint of personality.

individuation The systematic development of separate aspects of personality.

inferiority feelings Subjective limitations and weaknesses individuals perceive they possess.

interpersonal Dynamics operating between individuals.

intrapersonal Dynamics operating within the individual.

introverted attitude A personality style geared toward objects and events in the internal or personal environment.

intuition function Using an internal sense of judgment as the dominant means of experiencing the environment.

judging types Individuals who are orderly and systematic.

method of active imagination A technique of Jungian psychotherapy in which the client is asked to interact with the objects and symbols appearing in dreams.

method of amplification A technique in Jungian psychotherapy used to elaborate and explore the contents of dreams.

Myers-Briggs Type Indicator® assessment tool A personality test designed to assess Jungian personality types and functions.

organ inferiority Objective physical limitations and weakness possessed by individuals.

overcompensation Excessive attempts made by individuals to overcome actual or perceived limitations and weaknesses.

pampered child A style of personality characterized by overindulgence and self-centeredness.

perceiving types Individuals who are rather open-minded.

persona The archetype predisposing individuals to conform to social norms.

personal unconscious The region of the mind described by Jung as the storehouse of information not in awareness or that is too emotionally threatening.

phylogenetic A process of systematic development or evolution.

positive psychology A recent movement in psychology that emphasizes the study and understanding of human virtues and strengths and the promotion of positive personal experiences.

principle of entropy The compensatory flow of psychic energy from a high-concentration to a low-concentration area.

principle of equivalence The displacement of psychic energy from one aspect of personality to another.

principle of opposites The corresponding flow of psychic energy in an opposing direction within two aspects of personality.

prospective function An activity of the personal unconscious that could be used to help the individual think about future events.

rejected child A style of personality characterized by emotional isolation and social withdrawal.

retrospective The influence of the past on current behavior.

self The archetype that seeks balance and harmony.

self-realization The continuous development and integration of the separate aspects of personality to express their full potential.

sensation function Using the senses as the dominant means of experiencing the environment.

shadow The archetype representing the impulsive and instinctive characteristics of personality.

social interest Considering the needs of others while attempting to develop one's own potential to the fullest.

Social Interest Scale A personality test designed to assess an individual's tendency to express concern for the needs of and desire to help others.

striving for superiority Attempts made by individuals to develop themselves to their fullest potential.

style of life The general approach taken when developing one's potential to the fullest.

superiority complex Excessive attempts to develop one's own potential at the expense of others.

teleological The influence of the future on current behavior.

thinking function Using intellect and reasoning as the dominant means of experiencing the environment.

transcendent function The systematic reintegration of the developed aspects of the self.

transformation stage The final stage of Jungian psychotherapy, in which a sense of meaning in life is explored and developed.

transpersonal Sharing or passing along information across people, cultures, and generations.

word association test A projective test designed to assess unconscious content and problematic complexes.

The Viewpoints of Horney, Erikson, and Fromm

The Neo-Freudians

5

Chapter Overview:
A Preview of Coming Attractions

The reactions to Freud's viewpoint by Carl Jung and Alfred Adler were among the earliest and most significant of that time. However, they were followed by other **neo-Freudians** who proposed viewpoints of personality as an alternative to and extension of many of Freud's ideas. Most notably, these theorists shifted away from Freud's intrapsychic emphasis (i.e., conflict within the individual) to a more inter-personal emphasis (i.e., relationships between people). They also tended to place more emphasis on the conscious-level operation of personality and the role and significance of social relationships in the development and expression of personality. Three of the most prominent of the neo-Freudians are Karen Horney, Erik Erikson, and Erich Fromm. This chapter introduces you to the viewpoints of these three personality theorist, and demonstrates how their pioneering ideas served to influence contemporary research documenting the importance of social relationships for such issues as happiness, health, stress management, and longevity (Taylor, 2006).

Horney's Social Psychological Viewpoint: The Search for Social Security

Although Karen Horney was not a contemporary of Freud in the sense that Jung and Adler were, much of her theoretical development was in response to what she perceived as major limitations in the traditional Freudian thinking dominant at the time. Her theoretical focus was to place more importance on interpersonal relationships as a determinant of personality development and to reformulate the dynamics of the female personality. For a glimpse into the life of Karen Horney, read "A Closer Look" below.

Karen Horney pioneered the role of women in the psychology of personality with her astute observations on the role of cultural circumstances in the study of personality and a reformulation of the dynamics of the female personality.

A Closer Look

The Life of Karen Horney

Karen Danielson Horney was born on September 16, 1885, near Hamburg, Germany, into an upper-middle-class family. Although the economic climate of her childhood was secure, its emotional nature was less than tranquil. Her father, Berndt Wackels Danielson, was a sea captain. He was described as being rather stern and morose, and he was an extreme religious fundamentalist. In sharp contrast to his gruff and authoritarian personality was that of his second wife, Karen's mother. Eighteen years younger than her husband, Clothilde Danielson was a youthful, attractive, sophisticated, dynamic, spirited, and free-thinking woman.

The emotional climate of Horney's childhood could probably best be described as conflicted. Her father was critical of his daughter's appearance, interests, and intellectual desires, and he discouraged her from the idea of pursuing a career as a physician. Her mother, on the other hand, encouraged her to pursue her intellectual interests. Even so, Horney always felt that her mother loved her brother more than her, which made her feel unwanted. Horney dealt with these feelings of insecurity by immersing herself in her studies, reasoning that "If I couldn't be beautiful, I decided I would be smart" (Rubins, 1978, p. 14).

The result of this mixed emotional climate was that Horney developed a very warm and close relationship with her mother. But for a while during her thirties, Karen took to wearing a captain's-style cap, implying some positive identification with her father. In 1904 – when Karen was 19 – Clothilde, not being able to take any more of her husband's authoritarian ways, took her two children and separated from him. Growing up in an environment of such emotional turmoil created in Horney feelings of anxiety and insecurity she knew she would have to overcome if she was to be successful in life.

In 1906, Horney began to pursue her medical career in Freiburg, Germany, where she enrolled in one of the few medical schools accepting women at that time. In 1909, she married Oskar Horney, a Berlin lawyer. In 1913, she received her masters degree from the University of Berlin. From 1914 to 1918, she received psychoanalytic training at the Berlin Psychoanalytic Institute, where she was psychoanalyzed by Karl Abraham and Hanns Sachs, two of the most noted training analysts in Europe at that time. From 1918 to 1932, she taught at the Berlin Psychoanalytic Institute, maintained a private clinical practice, and wrote many professional articles, some expressing her disagreement with the dominant Freudian views of the time.

In 1923, the investment firm for which Oskar was working collapsed, making his salary worth almost nothing. As a result, he began to borrow heavily. Partly because of Oskar's personal and financial problems and partly because of her own demanding schedule, Horney's marriage began to deteriorate. In addition, shortly after, her brother, Berndt, died at the age of 40. Because of all of this emotional turmoil, Horney began to experience severe feelings of depression and contemplated suicide. In 1926, she and her three children separated from Oskar by moving into their own small apartment. The termination of the Horneys' marriage became final only in 1939, because she waited more than 10 years before actually filing for the divorce.

In 1932, Horney was invited to come to the United States and assume the associate directorship of the Chicago Institute for Psychoanalysis. Two years later, she left Chicago for a position at the New York Psychoanalytic Institute. But she was becoming more and more dissatisfied with traditional psychoanalysis and expressed her views openly. As a result, the more traditional supporters of Freud's ideas at the New York Psychoanalytic Institute voted in April 1941 to demote Horney from her roles of teacher and clinical supervisor to the position of "instructor" (Quinn, 1988).

In quick response, Horney and some of her followers left the institute and within three weeks had formed a new organization called the Association for the Advancement of Psychoanalysis. Shortly afterward, they published the first issue of the association's journal, the *American Journal of Psychoanalysis*. Before 1941 ended, they also established the American Institute of Psychoanalysis. The purpose of the new association, journal, and institute was to promote the study of psychoanalysis in a more democratic and open manner than was practiced by the more traditional Freudian approach dominant at the time. Horney remained as dean of the institute until her death on December 4, 1952.

Karen Horney's life was filled with the pressures of being a professional woman and single parent in a male-dominated profession. Her experience is not unlike those many professional women have today. In addition, she expressed ideas that seem to be well ahead of her time, such as the cultural context of psychopathology and thoughts on the psychology of women (Runyan, 2006). More on the life of this remarkable woman can be found in a major biography titled *Karen Horney: A Psychoanalyst's Search for Self-Understanding* (Paris, 1994).

Basic Assumptions of Horney's Social Psychological Viewpoint

The principal theoretical differences Horney had with the dominant Freudian thinking of the time are best expressed in the basic assumptions of her viewpoint on the motivational, social, and cultural nature of personality (Paris, 1994).

Motivational Nature of Personality

While Freud viewed personality as being motivated by a tendency to reduce psychic tension, Horney emphasized the individual's search for a sense of security in the world as the primary motivational force in personality. In attempting to establish a sense of security, Horney said, each person develops a particular personality style for coping with the world. For example, an insecure adult might develop a domineering personality as a means of establishing security and predictability at work and home.

Social Nature of Early Childhood

Horney agreed with Freud that many of the emotional problems people experience as adults can be traced back to early childhood. But she did not assume that these problems resulted from the unsuccessful resolution of a particular developmental stage, or by psychological regression. Like Freud and Adler, she assumed that the nature of the early social relationship between parent and child was extremely important in determining personality maladjustment in adulthood (Nevid, Rathus, & Greene, 2000). For example, if a boy is raised in a household with little expression of love, as an adult he may develop a personality style that involves agreeing with everybody in the hopes of gaining their approval and affection.

Cultural Nature of Personality

Horney was in considerable disagreement with Freud's view that the development of the female personality has

Summing It Up *Comparison of the Basic Assumptions of Horney and Freud*

Basic Assumption	Horney	Freud
Nature of Motivation	To seek security in one's own world	To reduce bodily tension
Nature of Childhood	Established the foundation of later social relationships	Emphasized the resolution of psychosexual stages
Cultural Determinants of Personality	Stressed cultural influences on the nature of personality development	Stressed intrapersonal influences on the nature of personality development

as its basis the desire of women to be like men (i.e., penis envy). Taking a more cultural perspective, she proposed that both men and women are motivated by the same desire to seek security. And since the culture in which Freud was working gave men a much more active role in determining their security, Horney stated that it only made sense to assume that women wanted to be like men. Had the cultural circumstances been reversed, it is doubtful that women would still have wanted to be like men. Thus, she emphasized specific cultural differences to account for personality development, not unconscious desires (Arlow, 1995; Nevid et al., 2000).

With such striking differences, it is clear why Horney's ideas were not well received by those in the prevailing pro-Freudian community at the time. A comparison of the theoretical differences is presented in "Summing It Up: A Comparison of the Basic Assumptions of Horney and Freud" above.

Basic Concepts of Horney's Social Psychological Viewpoint: The Causes and Consequences of Seeking Security

Like Adler, Horney emphasized the influence of social interactions on the nature of personality adjustment (Westen & Gabbard, 1999). But her emphasis was on the causes and consequences of feeling insecure in the social environment.

Basic Hostility

Horney (1937) noted that the two most powerful needs that children demonstrate are for safety and satisfaction. Being completely dependent on others for these needs creates feelings of insecurity in children. If the parents respond with genuine love and affection, the child perceives the environment as safe, anticipates that all needs will be met, and develops a sense of security. If the parents respond with a lack of affection or emotional concern, the child perceives the environment as threatening and unfriendly, acquires a sense of increased insecurity, and develops feelings of basic hostility toward the parents. **Basic hostility** is the sense of anger and betrayal the child feels toward parents who are not helping to create a secure environment. Since no parents can be entirely consistent and satisfying, basic hostility is an inevitable experience for the child.

In dealing with such feelings of insecurity and basic hostility, children may repress them and express overtly false feelings of affection toward the parents so they will not make the situation worse. An example of this is the child who says "I love you" at bedtime to a physically abusive parent. In a sense, the child is really saying, "I will act like I love you because I am afraid that if I don't, you will make my world even worse." When the child turns these feelings of hostility inward, the feelings of insecurity, helplessness, and basic hostility only increase (Horney, 1937).

Basic Anxiety

Basic anxiety refers to feelings of insecurity, insignificance, powerlessness, inferiority, and hopelessness in a social environment that an individual feels is full of hostility, betrayal, and unfaithfulness (Horney, 1945). Thus, basic anxiety involves an expanded sense of basic hostility being generalized from the parents to other people in the individual's personal and social environment. As a result, the individual behaves in a manner

Table 5.1 Neurotic Trends Defined by Horney

Neurotic Trends	Illustrations of the Trends
1. The neurotic need for affection and approval	The adolescent who will do or say anything to gain the acceptance of his or her peers
2. The neurotic need for a "partner" who will take over one's life	The "clinging vine" lover whose partner is expected to meet all of his or her emotional needs
3. The neurotic need to restrict one's life within narrow borders	The rather meek person who does not want to be a bother to anyone and settles for very little in life
4. The neurotic need for power	The military dictator who uses unscrupulous tactics to gain control over the people in that country
5. The neurotic need to exploit others	The thief or rapist who commits such acts for the sake of taking advantage of others
6. The neurotic need for prestige	The middle-aged person who defines his or her sense of self-worth by the size of the house owned or status of the car driven
7. The neurotic need for personal admiration	The politician who wishes to be seen on the basis of his or her own exaggerated sense of importance, not of what has actually been accomplished
8. The neurotic ambition for personal achievement	The student who spends so much time studying as a means of gaining recognition that it begins to affect his or her health
9. The neurotic need for self-sufficiency and independence	To avoid any more ridicule from his or her peers, the adolescent who becomes a "social loner," proclaiming no need of anyone
10. The neurotic need for perfection and unassailability	The compulsive student with low self-esteem who, because he or she spends so much time worrying about every little detail, never completes an assignment

Note. Based on Horney (1942).

reflecting this view of the world. For example, believing that people cannot be trusted, a person may become reluctant to fall in love or may become abusive as a means of maintaining emotional distance.

Neurotic Trends

Neurotic trends are irrational needs and desires developed by the individual in trying to achieve a sense of security. They are created by intense feelings of basic anxiety (Horney, 1942). The logic is that if the specific need is fulfilled, then the individual will feel safe and secure. The trends are described as neurotic because they represent unrealistic or irrational solutions to the problem of achieving psychological security. Table 5.1 presents the 10 neurotic trends noted by Horney. As you can see, a common feature of many of these trends is a sense of excessive expectations – perfectionism. In support of this common feature, there is a distinction between normal perfectionism (e.g., striving for success) and neurotic perfectionism (e.g., setting standards that are impossibly high; Kring, Davision, Neale, & Johnson, 2007). It is easy to see how individuals who are never able to experience a sense of success or personal satisfaction would be anxious and uncertain with themselves.

A more recent conceptualization of individuals who might express the characteristic features of these neurotic trends is that of neuroticism. **Neuroticism** characterizes individuals who tend to be highly anxious, irritable, pessimistic, uncertain, and generally negative in their thoughts (e.g., worry) and feelings (e.g., distress). Such individuals, for a variety of reasons, seem to be more vulnerable to experiencing anxiety, and this vulnerability tends to lead them to view situations as threatening (Rachman, 2004). Because of such an unfavorable view of the world, neuroticism is strongly associated with both anxiety and depression (Kring et al., 2007; Zuckerman, 2000). The sense of pessimism associated with neuroticism can result in such individuals adopting a coping style that is characterized by avoidance of a problem rather than dealing directly with it (Carver & Scheier, 2002). For example, when distressed by having to study for a big test, the pessimistic feature of neuroticism would result in an individual being likely to try to find some sort of distraction (e.g., calling a friend, playing a video game) to avoid studying and the negative feelings associated with the test. Another form of avoidance that has been linked to pessimism is alcohol consumption (Carver & Schier, 2002). For example, to avoid the unpleasantness of studying for the test, the individual may go to the local bar for a few drinks "to take her mind off" the troubling thoughts of the test. Obviously, such strategies of avoidance provide only a short-term solution and can contribute to other long-term problems, such as not being prepared for the test or the development of a drinking problem.

A critical example of such neurotic trends is that of morbid dependency. **Morbid dependency** is the neurotic tendency to seek and maintain affection through involvement in exploitative or manipulative relationships. Such a tendency can have its origin in dysfunctional families where children must sacrifice their own needs, desires, and expectations to obtain esteem and affection from parents (Horney, 1942). Morbid dependency is reflected in the dynamics associated with the contemporary phenomenon of codependency (Lyon & Greenberg, 1991).

Codependency describes the tendency of adults who were the children or spouses of alcoholics to find themselves in other dysfunctional relationships, which they make personal sacrifices in order to maintain (Cocores, 1987; Irvine, 1999; Schaef, 1986). Consistent with Horney's viewpoint, the roots of codependency seem to be traced back to childhood involving a history of chronic family stress, such as growing up with an alcoholic, mentally ill, or physically ill parent

(Fuller & Warner, 2000). Having learned to establish a sense of self-worth by conforming to the desires and expectations of dependent and exploitative alcoholic parents or spouses, codependent adults demonstrate a specific tendency to be interested in and want to help others who possess these same characteristics of being dependent and exploitative (Lyon & Greenberg, 1991), express feelings of depression (Martsolf, Sedlak, & Doheny, 2000), and demonstrate characteristic features of codependency in their significant relationships (Cretser & Lombardo, 1999).

Another social problem linked to pathological patterns of interpersonal dependency is that of domestic violence. Consistent with Horney's conceptualization of morbid dependency, recent research suggests that "high levels of emotional dependency in an abused partner may reduce the likelihood that the victimized person will terminate the relationship" (Bornstein, 2006, p. 595).

Strategies for Achieving Social Security: Moving Toward, Against, and Away from People

In fulfilling the neurotic trends noted in Table 5.1, people use various interpersonal coping strategies in an attempt to achieve a sense of security and minimize feelings of basic anxiety. In a general sense, these strategies are characterized by their inflexibility and limited effectiveness. Horney (1945) identified three broad interpersonal coping strategies for seeking social security: moving toward people, moving against people, and moving away from people.

Moving Toward People

As an interpersonal coping strategy, **moving toward people** involves believing that if you go along with people and give them what they want, they will give you love and a sense of affection, approval, and admiration (see Table 5.1, neurotic needs 1 and 2). For example, by going along with and catering to the needs of her abusive husband, the wife hopes he will not abuse her in the future and will continue to take care of her and the children. Thus, the salient belief here is "if I love you, you won't hurt me." In a more normal sense, each of us to some extent might be willing to be the butt of many jokes from our friends or "go along" with what the group decides to do because we really do like them and want their approval.

Moving Against People

Moving against people involves a style of interaction characterized by aggressiveness, hostility, and exploitation. This coping strategy is founded on the belief that the world is full of people who are only looking out for themselves and, as a result, will attempt to exploit others if given the chance. By taking advantage of others first, an individual is able to achieve the exaggerated need for power, exploitation of others, social recognition and prestige, personal admiration, and personal achievement reflected in neurotic needs 4 through 8 of Table 5.1. Examples of people using this strategy are the ruthless criminal, the corrupt government official, and the unscrupulous business owner who continue to take from others for their personal gain. The salient belief here is "if I have power, people can't hurt me." This extremely pessimistic view of others allows such individuals to justify their self-centered and exploitative behavioral pattern. In a more normal sense, most students would be more than willing to borrow someone's class notes if they really needed to do so. On the other hand, most students would probably be less willing to lend their notes to someone else, because that person might boost the grading curve in the class.

Moving Away from People

Moving away from people is a coping strategy characterized by withdrawing or detaching oneself from others. By retreating into his or her own world, the individual achieves a sense of self-sufficiency, independence, and perfection while gaining protection against attacks from others (see neurotic needs 3, 9, and 10 of Table 5.1). As an example, some adults can gain a sense of emotional self-sufficiency and safety by terminating a relationship each time they feel they are falling in love, but the price they may pay for their emotional independence and protection is loneliness. Thus, the salient belief here is that "if I withdraw, I can't be hurt." In a more normal sense, a person might elect to stand in the corner at a party rather than ask someone to dance and run the risk of being rejected.

Healthy vs. Maladaptive Strategies

Horney believed that some feelings of basic anxiety exist within all of us. As a result, she assumed that everyone would need to use interpersonal coping strategies at some time or another. She also made the distinction between healthy and maladaptive uses of the coping strategies and neurotic tendencies.

In general, the major differences have to do with the degree, flexibility, and emotionality of their use. The healthy person uses all three coping strategies to some extent, depending on the nature of the relationship (e.g., child, boss, spouse), type of situation (e.g., physically dangerous, emotionally threatening), and type of interaction (e.g., business, social, family). As an example of the healthy use of all three strategies, a person may go along (i.e., move toward) with the boss, take a firm stand (i.e., move against) when dealing with a teenager's demand for a later curfew, and withdraw (i.e., move away) from a potentially physical argument.

Maladaptive use of the three coping strategies involves the exclusive use of one strategy regardless of the nature and type of the relationship and an excessive emotional reaction when its use does not succeed. For example, a middle-aged man trying to please his spouse might become even more accommodating in an attempt to "save the marriage" when he discovers that his spouse is having an affair. When trying to be even more accommodating does not work, the man becomes extremely depressed. In this case, a more appropriate strategy might involve moving against and moving away from the unfaithful spouse with the aid of a good attorney and supportive psychotherapist. Thus, neurotic tendencies are classified as such because they are irrational, unrealistic solutions for overcoming basic anxiety and have little regard for their consequence (e.g., the development of codependency).

For two rather different perspectives on the utilization of Horney's three interpersonal coping strategies, "At the Cutting Edge of Personality Psychology" (on p. 176) presents an dramatic illustration of their rather unhealthy utilization by two high school students who went on a killing spree in Littleton, Colorado, while the "Applications in Personality Psychology" (on p. 178) examines their utilization in an interesting application designed to help understand the coping strategies used by some diabetics to adjust to the challenges of diabetes.

While the information presented above can be used to help us understand the extreme and violent reactions of these two emotionally troubled adolescents, the information in "Applications in Personality Psychology" provides a more positive consideration of Horney's perspective as it has been used to help diabetics deal more effectively with their diabetes.

An Analysis of the Columbine High School Tragedy

In Search of Social Security: Extreme Reactions to Alienation, Rejection, and Frustration

By now, almost everybody associates Columbine High School and Littleton, Colorado, with the shooting and killing spree of Columbine students Dylan Klebold and Eric Harris. Although there have been a number of possible explanations of why Klebold and Harris did what they did (Bai, Bagley, Johnson, & Levy, 1999; S. Schwartz, 2000), additional insight can be obtained by considering their actions in the context of Horney's social psychological viewpoint of personality.

Dylan Klebold and Eric Harris seemed to have a relatively normal family life in Littleton, Colorado. Both boys were considered shy and they shared a great enthusiasm for computers and computer games, which they would play together for hours. In high school, the boys were somewhat isolated from the other students and felt left out. Their sense of separation from the other students may have been due to their shyness, excessive interests in computers, disinterest in sports, or appearance.

Moving Toward People: In Response to Alienation

In response to their sense of alienation from the other students at the school, Klebold and Harris began associating with a group of students known as the "Trenchcoat Mafia." The students in this group wore long black trenchcoats and black-toned clothes to distinguish themselves from the style-conscious "prep" cliques and engaged in nonathletic activities, such as football (table soccer), to distinguish themselves from the sports-centered "jocks." However, while Harris and Klebold began wearing the group's signature item of clothing – the long trenchcoats – the other members of the group did not fully accept the two boys and, as a result, they were never really members of this clique.

Moving Away from People: In Response to Rejection

When trying to become part of the Trenchcoat Mafia to deal with their sense of social isolation did not seem to work, Klebold and Harris began to engage in a pattern of behavior characterized by moving away from others. More specifically, in their junior year, Klebold changed his clean-cut appearance and began wearing long hair and an unkempt beard. Both Harris and Klebold starting adorning their cloths with Nazi insignia and started speaking to each other in German on a regular basis. As you can imagine, such a pattern of behavior attracted a lot of attention, including being bullied, teased, and tormented by members of the school's football team.

Moving Against People: In Response to Frustration

It was also during their junior year that Harris and Klebold began to demonstrate a distinctive behavioral shift in their interactions with others. The shift featured a pattern of behavior that involved moving away from people to one that involved moving against people. The pattern of moving against people was characterized by an escalating tendency to threaten and do harm to others, as well as by brushes with the law. More specifically, both boys were convicted of burglarizing a van and stealing electronic equipment. A few months after the burglary, a police complaint was filed by the father of a fellow student against Harris. The complaint noted that Harris had threatened the student and smashed the windshield of the student's car. The police failed to follow up on the complaint or notify the officials of the criminal diversion program that Harris and Klebold were assigned to after their van burglary and theft charges.

Other evidence that suggested an increasing tendency to move against people by these two individuals was that a year before the shooting, Harris's diary contained a detailed map of the school, including notes on when large numbers of students would be in the cafeteria, and a number of references to Adolf Hitler. (In the aftermath of the hour-long shooting spree, a police search of the cafeteria and school grounds revealed dozens of homemade explosive devices, including a 20-pound propane bomb discovered in the school's kitchen that would have been capable of destroying the entire building.) In addition, Harris and Klebold made a video, submitted as a senior-year class project, of student actors in long coats going down school corridors and gunning down athletes. (In their actual killing spree later that year, Klebold and Harris went down the hall from room to room, with Harris supposedly saying, "All jocks stand up! We're going to kill every one of you.") Harris also began to create a website filled with references to death and destruction.

On the anniversary of Adolf Hitler's birthday, Tuesday, April 20, Harris and Klebold did not go to school in the morning but showed up at lunchtime heavily armed, with an assortment of handguns, an assault rife, sawn-off shotguns, and homemade hand grenades, prepared to engage in the ultimate expression of moving against people – killing them in cold blood. Starting in the parking lot and moving into the school, the two began shooting and killing their classmates. In total, over 30 people were wounded, some permanently paralyzed, and 15 killed, including 14 students, 1 teacher, and, as would be discovered several hours later, both Klebold and Harris of self-inflicted gunshot wounds.

A Final Comment: A Lesson Learned

Although there are other possible explanations for the actions of Dylan Klebold and Eric Harris, at the core were many of Horney's basic concepts, including:

- *Basic anxiety* – their feelings of insignificance and insecurity in a social environment, namely their high school, that they felt was full of hostility (e.g., being bullied by the "jocks") and unfaithfulness (e.g., being rejected by the other students).
- *Basic hostility* – their escalating feelings of anger and hatred for their fellow students in response to being rejected and mistreated by them.
- *Neurotic tendencies* – their extreme actions as an attempt to fulfill their irrational need for power, recognition, personal achievement, affection, and approval.
- *Maladaptive interpersonal coping strategies* – their escalating tendency toward self-isolation (i.e., moving away from people) and aggression and violence (i.e., moving against people) when their initial attempts to establish a social support network at school (i.e., moving toward people) failed.

In summary, one of the many lessons to be learned from this tragedy is the power of the need for social security and the extent to which people will go to achieve it. In response to such a lesson, the question we can all ask is: What can each one of us do to help others achieve a sense of social security?

The Nature of Personality Adjustment: The Overlapping of the Real and Ideal Self

Horney (1950) made a distinction between the real and the idealized self. The **real self** is what a person believes is true and unique about himself or herself. Information contained in the real self might involve personal likes and dislikes, strengths and weaknesses, and needs and desires. This self is also involved in motivating the individual toward healthy personal growth and achievement.

The **idealized self** is the individual's perception of how he or she would like to be. Information contained in the idealized self might include wanting to be more independent, powerful, outgoing, honest, emotionally involved with someone, or responsible. The idealized self is a yardstick by which people assess the extent of their personal growth and the realization of their true potential. This self is also used to develop strategies for overcoming basic anxiety and achieving a greater sense of security. For example, in an attempt to "move toward others," a lonely person might reason: "If I were 15 pounds lighter and more talkative and self-confident, I would have plenty of friends."

Applications in Personality Psychology

The Coping Strategies of Diabetics from a Horneyan Perspective

An estimated 20.8 million Americans, roughly 7 percent of the population, suffer from diabetes (http://www.diabetes.org/diabetes-statistics.jsp), which is the country's leading cause of death and of kidney failure, adult blindness, and amputations (Taylor, 2006). A recent estimate of the yearly economic costs of diabetes is approximately $132 billion. Unfortunately, diabetics' compliance with their treatment regimen is quite poor (Harris & Lustman, 1998). Failure to follow treatment programs for diabetes can lead to a variety of negative consequences from hypoglycemia (low blood sugar), which can result in heightened levels of depression and anxiety and decreases in cognitive functioning (Strachan, Deary, Ewing, & Frier, 2000), to less work satisfaction and more overall mood disturbance (U.K. Prospective Diabetes Study Group, 1999). The sexual functioning of both men and women can be affected by diabetes, and women diabetics who become pregnant often have difficult pregnancies (Brannon & Feist, 2000).

In an attempt to help diabetics become more effective in coping with their diabetes, a number of psychological approaches have been examined (Brannon & Feist, 2000), including the social psychological viewpoint of Karen Horney. More specifically, in their work with diabetics, physicians Michael Bergam, Saim Akin, and Philip Felig (1990) noted that although many patients do well in adjusting to the physical and psychological challenges of diabetes, others find these adjustments more difficult. The physicians suspected that these difficulties had something to do with the nature of the interpersonal relationships between the diabetic and significant others in the diabetic's life (e.g., medical personnel and family members).

In examining the interpersonal dynamics of diabetes management among patients who are poorly adjusted to the challenges of the disease, the doctors noted three distinct patterns corresponding closely to the three interpersonal coping styles described by Horney (1945). These coping styles were labeled self-effacement, need for mastery, and resignation.

Self-Effacement: Moving Toward People by Becoming Dependent

Bergam et al. characterized patients in the self-effacement group by their dependency on the care of others for the control of their diabetes. These patients may actually sabotage their control over diabetes when they feel ignored or despondent. They do so both unknowingly (e.g., accidentally forget to take the insulin) and sometimes knowingly (e.g., deliberately eat sweets). This sabotage typically results in additional hospital visits and more attention from medical personnel.

By gaining increased medical attention, those in the self-effacement group can remind family members of their inability to take care of themselves and of their "need" to have others care for them. Those family members, who are then expected to take more responsibility for controlling the individual's diabetes, often begin to feel anger and hostility toward the diabetic. But patients in this group are often successful in using the family's expressed anger and hostility to create a sense of guilt (e.g., "Don't you feel awful yelling at someone who is as sick as me?"). The patient then uses guilt feelings created in the family members to gain even more help from them, which in turn fosters even more dependency on others. Thus, becoming dependent on others to control their diabetes illustrates how patients in this group move toward people. In treating patients in this group, medical personnel need to help them realize how their actions are creating emotional difficulties for themselves and others around them. They also need to discuss how the patient can become more independent in controlling diabetes and in handling interpersonal relationships.

Need for Mastery: Moving Against People by Ignoring Their Assistance

Patients in the need for mastery group are characterized by the need to take control of their diabetes. They typically try to be masters of their own fate by moving against the medical personnel attempting to work with them. These patients often express a higher level of medical insight, knowledge, experience, and awareness of their condition than they actually possess. They also have rather high and unrealistic expectations concerning their own ability to cope effectively with diabetes.

With such an attitude, these patients typically ignore the true limitations of their life situation (e.g., what they can eat and how often they need to take insulin). No matter what is recommended, such patients tend to impose or substitute their own perceived solutions and remedies to their medical condition. They become angry and frustrated with their inability to meet the high expectations they have set for themselves and express this frustration through hostility toward and criticism of people who are trying to help them. Thus, attempting to take direct control of their own treatment program illustrates how individuals in this group move against people trying to help them. In helping these patients, medical personnel should focus on encouraging greater compliance with recommended procedures and on establishing more realistic expectations about the support these patients need from others.

Resignation: Moving Away from People by Withdrawing into the Treatment Program

Patients in the resignation group are characterized by a tendency to use their diabetes to isolate themselves from others. These patients, who often perceive themselves as being victimized by their condition, demonstrate a sense of martyrdom in trying to deal with and overcome diabetes. They tend to cope with their diabetes by becoming extremely regimented in their treatment program, to the point of removing themselves from more meaningful contacts with the healthcare system. Developing a sense of "perfectionism" is their way of avoiding dependency on the healthcare system and creating a sense of independence, which reinforces the tendency to move away from medical personnel.

The tendency of patients in the resignation group to be overly regimented in their treatment program also restricts their opportunities for social interactions (e.g., dating) and for establishing meaningful relationships with others. This form of social isolation is another manifestation of trying to move away from others by withdrawing. Praising these patients for their excessive efforts to cope with the diabetes only increases their sense of victimization and martyrdom and strengthens their efforts to withdraw from others. To help patients in the resignation group, healthcare personnel must try to make them realize the dangers of such overly regimented treatment efforts (e.g., administering too much insulin and producing hypoglycemia), especially when they have already established a tendency to withdraw from medical support.

Using Horney's three interpersonal coping styles to classify diabetics who have some difficulty in controlling the disease is helpful in several ways:

- It helps to illustrate the diversity of the interpersonal needs of diabetics and the strategies they use to meet these needs.
- It provides a framework for understanding the underlying psychological dynamics of these patients' interpersonal difficulties.
- It establishes specific objectives of psychological counseling in an effort to help these patients more successfully meet their interpersonal needs.
- It demonstrates how knowledge of personality psychology can be applied to important issues of medicine and health maintenance.

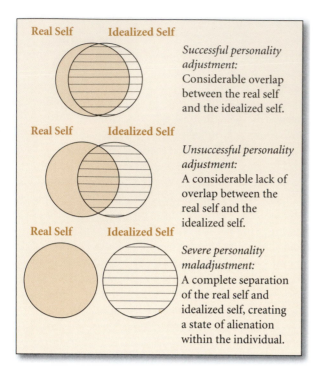

Real Self   Idealized Self

Successful personality adjustment: Considerable overlap between the real self and the idealized self.

Real Self   Idealized Self

Unsuccessful personality adjustment: A considerable lack of overlap between the real self and the idealized self.

Real Self   Idealized Self

Severe personality maladjustment: A complete separation of the real self and idealized self, creating a state of alienation within the individual.

Figure 5.1 Horney's conceptualization of personality adjustment as indicated by the degree of overlap between the real self and the idealized self

For Horney, the nature and extent of personality adjustment are determined by looking at the degree of overlap between the real self (e.g., a person's degree of emotional independence) and the idealized self (e.g., the desire to be more emotionally independent). The greater the degree of overlap, the greater the degree of personality adjustment. Figure 5.1 illustrates this relationship between the real and idealized self, and the degree of personality adjustment.

Successful Personality Adjustment

As shown in the top portion of Figure 5.1, successful personality development involves a considerable degree of overlap between the real and idealized self. This overlap creates a sense of satisfaction and security in the individual, who knows that he or she is capable of coping with and mastering events in the real world. For example, feeling that you have the necessary study skills (i.e., real self) to complete your education and attain your career goals (i.e., idealized self) should give you a pretty secure feeling about your present and future life situation.

Unsuccessful Personality Adjustment

The middle and bottom portions of Figure 5.1 indicate that moderate and more severe forms of personality maladjustment are characterized by the greater separation of the real from the ideal self. These conditions are often brought on by what Horney called the **tyranny of the should** – an excessive emphasis by the individual on what "should" be in life. It is an overemphasis on the idealized self to the point of ignoring the real self. For example, neurotic feelings and personality maladjustment are likely to be experienced by a man who expects never to show professional jealousy toward coworkers, express public disagreements with close friends, or experience amorous thoughts for anyone but his spouse. The point is that creating such a "state of shoulds" clearly ignores what are real human characteristics.

Horney believed that the neurotic individual employs the excessive tyranny of the should to escape reality. To extend the earlier example, rather than trying to resolve his feelings of professional jealousy toward coworkers, the man tries to deny them by assuming that such feelings should never happen. But the more separated he becomes from reality, the more insecure the man is going to feel. This is due to a perceived lack of competence to cope effectively with the life events occurring in the real world. When alienation from the real self becomes too excessive, Horney believed, the only hope for the individual is psychotherapy.

To conclude our discussion, the principal ideas examined in this section are presented in "Summing It Up: The Basic Concepts of Horney's Social Psychological Viewpoint" on p. 181. Next, we will explore the applications of Horney's viewpoint.

Applications of Horney's Social Psychological Viewpoint: Using What Is Known

Our discussion of the applications of Horney's viewpoint will focus on psychotherapy and personality assessment.

Horneyan Psychotherapy

For Horney, the basic goal of psychotherapy was to increase the client's sense of security and minimize the

Summing It Up *The Basic Concepts of Horney's Social Psychological Viewpoint*

Basic Concept	Definition	Illustration
Basic Hostility	Feelings of hostility toward parents experienced by children when sensing a home environment lacking security	The feelings of anger children have when their parents tell them they are getting a divorce
Basic Anxiety	Feelings of anxiety the individual experiences about being vulnerable in one's environment	A woman who stays married because she feels she can't make it on her own
Neurotic Trends	Unrealistic beliefs an individual develops in the desire to achieve security	Breaking the law in order to achieve status in a street gang
Strategies for Achieving Social Security	Three interpersonal strategies for achieving social security: (1) moving toward people, (2) moving against people, and (3) moving away from people.	(1) Always agreeing with one's lover for fear of losing this person; (2) constantly lying to cover one's mistakes; (3) not falling in love out of fear of rejection

maladaptive use of interpersonal coping styles. Achieving a sense of security helps the individual to gain a more accurate perception of the real self and makes possible more realistic interactions with others. To help people with maladjusted personalities achieve this sense of realism in their lives, Horney (1942; Paris, 1994) proposed her own form of psychotherapy, referred to as self-analysis.

Self-analysis is a process by which the person can gain (either alone or with the aid of a psychotherapist) a greater understanding and acceptance of the real self, while reducing the influence of the tyranny of the *should* that prevents them from gaining a sense of security. The process of self-analysis involves three basic stages: (1) achieving freedom of expression, (2) learning from this freedom of expression, and (3) using this freedom of expression to improve interpersonal relationships.

Achieving Freedom of Expression Self-analysis employs the technique of free association to help clients think more openly about problematic interpersonal relationships. Because there are no actual consequences of the thoughts and feelings experienced during free association, clients can be more open to a wider range of possible alternatives. More specifically, free association allows clients to consider more real-istic and personally rewarding responses to interpersonal problems instead of how they *should* have felt, thought, or acted. An example would be using free association to help an unhappy student realize that the decision to go to college has as its basis a desire to conform to her parents' expectations rather than any desire of her own.

Learning from Freedom of Expression The next step in the process of self-analysis involves learning from these free associations. Horney recommended that clients review the associations repeatedly, in great detail. A review might include starting to examine what neurotic needs are being met by engaging in a particular type of self-defeating coping strategy and the consequences of such actions. For the student in the example, a review might include realizing that being depressed and getting poor grades are two consequences of her neurotic tendency to stay in school to obtain parental respect.

Using Freedom of Expression to Improve Interpersonal Relationships As the final step in the process of self-analysis, clients use their new-found knowledge to develop more realistic perceptions of the self and relationships with other people. With a more realistic view of their strengths and limitations, clients are in a much better position to develop goals that will bring personal satisfaction. This satisfaction brings the real and the ideal self closer together. In the example, the unhappy student can work with the therapist to develop the sense of security necessary to tell her parents what would be more personally satisfying academic and career goals.

In summary, the process of self-analysis creates the opportunity to become more free in thinking. With this freedom, clients can more closely examine the true nature of their beliefs and relationships and formulate more realistic and beneficial alternatives for interacting with others. Horney's work has served to influence such contemporary forms of psychotherapy as cognitive therapy (Beck, 1999; Beck & Weishaar, 1995; Sommers-Flanagan & Sommers-Flanagan, 2004), interpersonal psychotherapy (Nevid et al., 2000; Trull & Phares, 2001), and feminist therapy (Sommers-Flanagan & Sommers-Flanagan, 2004).

Personality Assessment from Horney's Viewpoint

The CAD (Cohen, 1967) is a self-report inventory designed to measure the three interpersonal coping styles described by Horney (1945). It contains 35 items measuring three separate subscales: compliant, aggressive, and detached. The compliant subscale (C) measures the interpersonal style of moving toward others; the aggressive subscale (A) measures moving against people; and the detached subscale (D) measures moving away from people. Each item is measured on a six-point scale, from "extremely undesirable" to "extremely desirable." The compliant and detached subscales contain 10 items each, while the aggressive subscale contains 15

items. A separate score is calculated for each subscale. Here are some examples of items from the CAD:

> *Complaint Scale Items*
> To have something good to say about everybody seems:
> Putting myself out to be considerate of others' feelings is:
>
> *Aggressive Scale Items*
> To be able to spot and exploit weakness in others is:
> Having to compete with others for various rewards is:
>
> *Detached Scale Items*
> Being free of emotional ties with others is:
> If I could live all alone in a cabin in the woods or mountains it would be:

To support the validity of the CAD, the subscale scores for students with educational and career preferences in helping professions (e.g., social welfare, nursing), competitive professions (e.g., business), and scientific professions (e.g., geology) were compared (Cohen, 1967; Rendon, 1987). The results indicated that students in the helping professions group scored higher on the compliant subscale than did students in the competitive and scientific groups. Students in the competitive professions group scored higher on the aggressive subscale than did students in the helping and scientific groups. Finally, students in the scientific professions group scored higher on the detached subscale than did students in the helping and competitive groups.

In addition to establishing the validity of the CAD, the results of this research have implications for using it in academic and career advising. Another interesting attempt to validate the CAD while applying Horney's theory to marketing and consumer behavior is presented below in "Applications in Personality Psychology."

Applications in Personality Psychology

Personality and Preferences for Personal Grooming Products: Applying Horney's Theory to Buyer Behavior

A unique application of Horney's theory of personality is in the area of marketing and consumer

behavior. Joel Cohen (1967), professor of marketing at the University of Florida, used Horney's three interpersonal styles to help explain the purchasing behavior of consumers. In this research, 157 males were asked to complete the CAD and a questionnaire assessing their product and brand usage. The men were classified into high- or low-scoring groups on the basis of their scores for each of the three CAD subscales. After classifying the men, Cohen compared the purchasing preferences of the high- and low-scoring groups within each of the three subscales.

Compliant Group Preferred Fresh Breath and No Body Odor

The men who scored high on the compliant subscale of the CAD indicated a greater usage of personal grooming products, such as mouthwash and brand-name bath soap, than those who scored low on this subscale.

Cohen suggests that highly compliant people exhibit consumer preferences that will reassure them that they are capable of being liked by others. Since bad breath and offensive body odors are two very clear barriers to social relationships, it is understandable that compliant people, who seek reassurance by moving toward others, would be more likely to purchase products designed to combat these two personal hygiene problems. They might also be more willing than less compliant people to pay extra for brand-name products that are advertised as being highly effective.

Aggressive Group Preferred Smelling Good and Feeling Manly

The men who scored high on the aggressive subscale of the CAD expressed a greater preference for brand-name deodorant products with an advertised "masculine image." They used cologne and aftershave more often, and more of them reported using a manual razor (vs. an electric shaver) for shaving than did the men who scored low on this subscale.

Cohen suggests that men who scored high on the aggressive subscale exhibit consumer preferences designed to establish a distinct image that attracts attention and projects a sense of masculinity. Because cologne and aftershave are designed to help a person be noticed by others, it makes sense that aggressive men seeking to attract attention would be more likely to purchase these products than would men concerned with blending into the crowd (e.g., compliant group) or men not overly concerned with interpersonal relationships (e.g., detached group). Also, because projecting a macho image characterized by strength would aid aggressive men in their attempts to move against others, it seems natural that these men would be willing to engage in behavior designed to reinforce this type of self-image, such as shaving with a manual razor and paying more for brand-name deodorants advertised as being manly.

Detached Group Had No Real Preferences for Personal Hygiene Products

Cohen's results indicated that men who scored high on the detached subscale demonstrated no clear preferences for personal hygiene products that are designed to achieve certain interpersonal motives or whose advertisements stress interpersonal appeals (e.g., not offending others with bad breath or feeling manly). This makes sense since men in the detached group, with their desire to move away from others, would be the least likely of the three groups studied to be concerned with the success of their interpersonal relationships.

Finally, comparisons within the three groups indicated no differences in preferences for those personal hygiene products not designed to meet interpersonal needs, such as toothpaste (e.g., advertisements stressing dental health benefits) and hair dressings (e.g., advertisements stressing the benefits of healthy hair), healthcare products (e.g., headache remedies), and products to meet everyday needs (e.g., gasoline brands). Thus, Cohen observed specific consumer preferences only for those personal hygiene products that seem to meet each group's specific interpersonal needs. Such results suggest the importance of considering the specific psychological needs of the consumer (Engel, Blackwell, & Miniard, 1993; Murry, Latovicka, & Austin, 1997) and the social consequences of production selection (Peter & Olson, 1999) when conducting consumer research and when developing effective advertisements (Berkowitz, Kerin, Hartley, & Rudelius, 2000; Hawkins, Best, & Coney, 2001; Pride & Ferrell, 1993).

Although the research by Cohen and others (Kassarjian, 1971; Kernan, 1971; Wells & Beard, 1973) supports the validity and utility of the CAD, it is not without its critics. Other researchers have suggested that the CAD is more a measure of just two dimensions (compliant and aggressive) than of three (Munson & Spivey, 1982; Noerager, 1979), and that the CAD subscales do not consistently correlate with other related measures of personality traits (Munson & Spivey, 1982).

In addition to the work with the CAD, applications of Horney's theoretical principles have been incorporated into other areas, including behavioral correlates of coronary disease (Hamon, 1987), attitudes toward the physically disabled (Jabin, 1987), and the psychobiography of President Lyndon B. Johnson (Hyffamn, 1989).

Horney's Feminine Psychology

Horney (1939, 1967) is also known for her pioneering efforts in and contribution to feminine psychology (Paris, 1994) and feminist psychoanalytic theories (Bell, 2004). She published a total of 19 essays on feminine psychology between 1923 and 1935 (Paris, 1994). She reinterpreted Freud's conceptualization of the female personality, with particular reference to the phallic stage and the concept of penis envy (Sommers-Flanagan & Sommers-Flanagan, 2004). Horney (1939) proposed that it is the child's feelings of basic anxiety, hostility, and anger directed at the opposite-sex parent that make the child view this parent as not only a source of competition for the affection of the same-sex parent, but a direct threat to the child's sense of safety and security. Thus, in response to the phallic stage dilemma, Horney proposed a resolution based more on interpersonal dynamics (e.g., differences in social power) than on the more sexual dynamics proposed by Freud (e.g., reduction of tension in the erogenous zone).

In a similar manner, Horney (1967) approached the concept of penis envy by proposing a more cultural interpretation (Nevid et al., 2000; Paris, 1994). She pointed out that because of the greater social freedom and opportunities available to men during the time Freud was formulating his viewpoint, it was only natural for women to be envious of and desire the same quality of life as men. Thus, what Freud mistakenly believed to be women's envy of the male penis was nothing more than women wanting to express those natural needs for success and security characteristic of both sexes. Horney also pointed out that Freud's views of women were biased in that they were, for the most part, based on his interactions with the neurotic women he had as patients.

In taking her discussion and reinterpretation of penis envy one step further, Horney (1967) proposed the notion of **womb envy**: the feeling of admiration and respect men supposedly feel for the female's ability to give birth. She also proposed that since men could not give birth but still had the natural desire to be creative and productive, they expressed their womb envy indirectly through their achievements and successes in other areas. On a more negative side, womb envy could also lead men to express their jealousy by belittling the achievements of women. Men might also engage in various discriminatory practices that make it difficult for women to achieve success and obtain additional status (e.g., systematically overlooking women for promotions).

Going beyond certain evolutionary (i.e., instinctive) explanations for gender differences in nurturing behavior (Buss, 1999; Mealey, 2000), Westkott (1986a, 1986b, 1989), consistent with Horney's position, has also noted that the normative expectations for women to be more nurturing, empathic, and responsible for the maintenance and preservation of interpersonal relationships than men can also serve as cultural constraints on personal growth and fulfillment for women by reinforcing a particular "idealized" notion of femininity. An example of this situation would be the working mother who is perceived as neglecting the emotional well-being of her children by placing them in a day-care center while she pursues her career aspirations. Such evaluative statements are less likely to be made about men and their career aspirations.

It is no accident that Horney should be one of Freud's critics at a time when his views were enjoying considerable fame. After all, as a career woman and mother, Horney demonstrated that it was possible to be successful in what was at that time clearly a male-dominated profession (Sommers-Flanagan & Sommers-Flanagan, 2004). It was through her desire to see men and women as psychological equals in their attempts to meet basic security needs, as well as to point out the significance of cultural factors in this process, that Horney probably made her most important contribution to personality psychology.

Evaluating Horney's Social Psychological Viewpoint: Strengths and Limitations

Characteristic Strengths

Here are some strengths of Horney's viewpoint:

- *Reinterpretation of the female personality.* Horney's reinterpretation of the feminine personality is based on a set of needs designed to achieve security in a manner similar to those of males. Such thinking significantly contributed to equalizing the psychology of the sexes.
- *Emphasis on the contribution of culture.* Horney's continuous emphasis on the importance of cultural factors in determining the nature of personality was a reminder that in addition to psychological processes operating within the individual, social forces operating outside of the individual must be considered in order to achieve complete understanding of the person.

Characteristic Limitations

The main limitation of Horney's social psychological viewpoint is its lack of empirical evidence. In comparison to the other theorists discussed, Horney's work has generated very little empirical research among personality psychologists. Although her theoretical ideas were presented in a relatively straightforward manner, they have not stimulated much interest in others to investigate their validity. This may in part be due to the rejection of her ideas by the more traditional and influential Freudian tradition operating at the time. But thinking about such ideas as feminine psychology and the importance of social and cultural factors in personality has become more salient. Such changes in thinking have resulted in an increase in awareness of and research attempting to validate basic concepts of Horney's viewpoint (Cohen, 1967; Munson & Spivey, 1982) and to extend her ideas to areas within (Roemer, 1986, 1987) and outside (Bergman et al., 1990; Paris, 1989, 1994) of personality psychology. Perhaps this renewed interest in Horney's unique viewpoint will result in her contribution to personality psychology being fully realized.

For more information on Horney's social psychological viewpoint, an excellent source is Bernard J. Paris's (1994) *Karen Horney: A Psychoanalyst's Search for Self-Understanding*, which presents the development of her ideas in the context of her personal and professional life in a clear and engaging manner, and Janet Sayer's (1991) *Mothers of Psychoanalysis: Helene Deutsch, Karen Horney, Anna Freud, Melanie Klein*, which presents an interesting discussion of Horney's contribution to the development of psychoanalysis.

Erikson's Psychosocial Viewpoint: The Development of the Ego throughout the Life Span

Erik Erikson's fundamental reaction to Freud was to extend the stages of personality development throughout the life span, to define the stages as more social in nature, and to expand significantly the role of the ego as a component of personality. In addition, Erikson's early focus on the problems of adolescents as being very different from those being faced by adults is an idea that is shared today by most contemporary developmental psychologists (Shaffer & Kipp, 2007). For a glimpse into the life of Erik Erikson, read "A Closer Look" below.

A Closer Look

The Life of Erik Erikson

Erik H. Erikson was born on June 15, 1902, near Frankfurt, Germany. His birth was the result of an extramarital affair by his mother. His parents, both Danish, separated shortly before his birth. Wishing to be near her close friends, Erik's mother moved to Karlsruhe, Germany. When Erik was 3 years old, his mother married a local pediatrician, Theodore Homburger, who successfully treated Erik for a childhood disease. Dr Homburger adopted Erik and gave him his last name. But in what Erik would later call an act of "loving deceit," his parents concealed his adoption for several years. Erik used Homburger as his surname until shortly before he

Erik Erikson gave meaning to the term "identity crisis" and extended the notion of a stage theory of personality development to include young adulthood, middle age, and late adulthood.

emigrated to the United States in 1933. He then adopted the surname of Erikson, which means "son of Erik."

Although his stepfather was Jewish, Erik was not easily accepted by his Jewish peers because of his tall, blond, Aryan appearance. At the same time, he was rejected by his German peers because they knew he was Jewish. Having to confront being adopted and then being rejected by his peers may have affected Erikson's later concerns with what he was to call the identity crisis.

Unlike many of the personality theorists discussed so far, Erikson was not a particularly good student. He did show some promise in history and art. After graduating from high school and rejecting his stepfather's suggestions to go to medical school, Erik traveled around central Europe for a year. He then returned to Karlsruhe to attend art school. But he quickly became restless again and, until the age of about 25, spent time wandering through Italy and Germany.

In 1927, an old classmate invited Erikson to join him as a Montessori instructor at a private school run by Anna Freud for children whose parents were receiving psychoanalysis from her father. After Erikson had worked at the school for a short time, Anna asked him to consider beginning analysis with her and becoming a child analyst himself. During his training with Anna, which lasted from 1927 to 1933, he became a close friend of the Freud family.

Over the next few years, Erikson distinguished himself as a key figure in psychoanalysis through some of his early publications demonstrating how children could become more aware of themselves through artistic expression. Thus, with just a high school education and a diploma as a Montessori teacher, he combined his early talents in art and history to make a unique contribution to psychoanalysis by trying to understand emotional development during childhood.

On April 1, 1930, Erikson married Joan Serson. In 1933, he moved his wife and two sons to Boston, where he became a practicing children's analyst and accepted a position at the Harvard Medical School. At the same time, he began working on a PhD in the psychology program at Harvard. But realizing that he was not suited for formal education, he withdrew a short time later – after failing his first course. In 1936, he accepted a position at the Yale Institute of Human Relations. In 1938, he spent some time studying childrearing practices among the Sioux Indians in South Dakota.

In 1939, Erikson moved to San Francisco and continued his practice as a children's analyst. In 1942, he became a professor of psychology at the University of California at Berkeley; but he was released in 1950, along with other faculty members, for refusing to sign a loyalty oath. From 1951 to 1960, Erikson lived in Stockbridge, Massachusetts, where he served as a senior staff member at the Austin Riggs Center, a private hospital for disturbed adolescents, and simultaneously held several other part-time faculty appointments at neighboring institutions.

In 1960, he returned to an academic appointment as a lecturer and professor of human development at Harvard. Although he never actually received a college or university degree, Erikson was considered a strong intellectual by his colleagues and a popular teacher by his students. His book *Gandhi's Truth* (Erikson, 1969) won him a Pulitzer Prize and the National Book Award in philosophy and religion. Although he retired in 1970, he continued to be a productive researcher and writer. His last book addressed personality growth during the later years of life (Erikson, Erikson, & Kivnick, 1986). Erikson died on May 12, 1994, in Harwich, Massachusetts.

For more information about Erikson's life, read his article titled "Autobiographic Notes on the Identity Crisis" (Erikson, 1970) and his obituary (Hopkins, 1995).

Basic Assumptions of Erikson's Psychosocial Viewpoint

Although he was trained in traditional Freudian psychoanalysis, Erikson formulated certain basic assumptions of personality that were quite different from Freud's. Still, Erikson's reaction to Freud extends several aspects of the Freudian viewpoint (Westen & Gabbard, 1999).

The Nature and Function of the Ego

A major departure from traditional Freudian analysis was Erikson's conception of the ego. Erikson's view was more in line with that of ego psychology. **Ego psychology** views the ego as being more than just growing out of the id and serving as a mediator for the id and superego (Hartmann, 1958, 1964; Westen & Gabbard, 1999). Erikson made the ego a central feature in his theory of personality. He believed that it operates as an autonomous structure, giving a sense of meaning and coherence to personal experiences and creating consistency in behavior. The ego serves as the core of the healthy personality and is responsible for creative thinking, artistic expression, logical reasoning, and joyful expression of emotions. Thus, for Erikson, the ego did much more than simply resolve conflict.

The Psychosocial Nature of Ego Development

Erikson proposed that the ego operates in a manner characterized by psychosocial development. **Psychosocial development** refers to Erikson's belief that the ego develops as it successfully resolves crises that are distinctively social in nature. These involve establishing a sense of trust in others, developing a sense of identity in society, and helping the next generation prepare for the future.

A Life-span Perspective of Ego Development

Erikson assumed that ego development through psychosocial crises is a process that continues well into the later years of life. He proposed that preparing for death was the final stage of personality development. This is in sharp contrast to the Freudian view that most of personality development occurs during the first several years of life.

Summing It Up *Basic Assumptions of Erikson's Psychosocial Viewpoint*

Basic Assumptions	Example
The Nature and Function of the Ego: The ego serves as the unifying core of one's experiences.	Your ego integrates the sights, sounds, and emotions that allow you to experience the pleasure of your favorite movie again and again.
The Psychosocial Nature of Ego Development: The ego develops by resolving a series of crises that have as their goal the person functioning more effectively in society.	By successfully resolving these psychosocial crises, children learn how to initiate activities with others, adolescents learn the fundamental skills deemed important by society (e.g., reading), and young adults learn about love and intimacy.
A Life-Span Perspective of Ego Development: The ego continues to grow and develop throughout life, even in the face of death.	In infancy, the ego develops a sense of basic trust in others, while in late adulthood, it acquires a sense of acceptance and fulfillment that makes facing death less threatening.
Extending, Not Departing from, Freudian Thought: Erikson's viewpoint extended Freudian ideas by making them more social (vs. sexual) and conscious (vs. unconscious) in nature.	A mother makes a conscious decision to leave the office early two nights a week to serve as a mentor to a group of college students to help them make career choices, as she remembers her favorite high school teacher doing for her.

Extending, Not Departing from, Freudian Thought

Although his basic assumptions do differ considerably from Freud's, Erikson's views are not a departure from Freudian thought but an extension of it. Erikson extends Freudian thought by focusing on the adaptive and creative characteristics of the ego and expanding the notion of the stages of personality development to include the entire life span.

This concludes our presentation of the basic assumptions of Erikson's viewpoint. A summary of the principal points discussed in this section is presented in "Summing It Up: Basic Assumptions of Erikson's Psychosocial Viewpoint" on p. 187.

Basic Concepts of Erikson's Psychosocial Viewpoint: The Stages of Ego Development

A significant contribution made by Erikson to the study of personality was his investigation into the development of personality throughout the life span. In this next section, we will consider his views on the nature of ego development.

Characteristic Features of Psychosocial Stages

Erikson is probably best known for his work on the developmental stages of the ego throughout the life span (Erikson, 1950, 1963). The following paragraphs examine these characteristics of Erikson's developmental stages:

- They operate on an epigenetic principle.
- They involve the resolution of psychosocial crises.
- They result in the acquisition of basic virtues.

The Epigenetic Nature of Ego Development   Erikson's stages of development are said to operate on an epigenetic principle. This **epigenetic principle** assumes that the stages of development occur in a specific sequence and build upon each previous stage. In this manner, the development at one stage is related to development at other stages (Whitbourne, Zuschlag, Elliot, & Waterman, 1992). The sequence is based on certain expectations of the individual by society at certain periods in life. As an example of this sequencing of events, a person must establish a personal identity before being able to establish a meaningful, intimate relationship with another person.

Psychosocial Crises During Ego Development   Like Freud, Erikson assumed that a crisis occurs at each stage of development. For Erikson these crises are of a psychosocial nature, because they involve psychological needs of the individual (i.e., *psycho-*) conflicting with the expectations of society (i.e., *-social*; Erikson, 1963; Whitbourne et al., 1992). Successful resolution of each **psychosocial crisis** requires striking a balance between the needs of the individual and the expectations of society. For example, very early in life, people must learn not only to trust others enough to be able to fall in love as an adult but also to mistrust others enough to avoid becoming highly gullible.

The Acquisition of Basic Virtues   With the successful resolution of each of the psychosocial crises comes the acquisition of basic virtues. **Basic virtues** are characteristic strengths that the ego can use to help in resolving subsequent crises. For example, as a child develops a healthy sense of trust, the basic virtue of hope for the future is acquired and incorporated into the child's ego. The greater the amount of these basic virtues the ego is able to acquire during its course of development, the more strength it will have for coping with some of the more difficult crises occurring later in life, such as facing one's death.

The Eight Stages of Psychosocial Development

Because Erikson's psychosocial stages of ego development represent his most significant contribution to the study of personality, an appreciation of his viewpoint can be best achieved by examining these eight stages (see Table 5.2). The following subsections describe the processes and consequences associated with both successful and unsuccessful resolution of each psychosocial stage.

Stage One. Trust vs. Mistrust: Acquiring Hope   The first psychosocial crisis occurs during the first year or so of life, as did the oral stage of Freud's psychosexual crises. The crisis is one of **trust vs. mistrust**. During the first year of life, the infant is uncertain about the world in which he or she lives. To resolve these feelings of uncertainty, the infant looks to the primary caregiver

Table 5.2   Erikson's Eight Stages of Psychosocial Development

Stage	Psychosocial Crisis	Basic Virtue	Age
1	Trust vs. mistrust	Hope	Infancy (0 to $1^1/_2$)
2	Autonomy vs. shame and doubt	Will	Early childhood ($1^1/_2$ to 3)
3	Initiative vs. guilt	Purpose	Play age (3 to 5)
4	Industry vs. inferiority	Competency	School age (5 to 12)
5	Ego identity vs. role confusion	Fidelity	Adolescence (12 to 18)
6	Intimacy vs. isolation	Love	Young adult (18 to 40)
7	Generativity vs. stagnation	Care	Adulthood (40 to 65)
8	Ego integrity vs. despair	Wisdom	Maturity (65+)

Note. The ages listed are not to be taken as discrete points of development, but are estimates of when each psychosocial crisis is most likely to occur the first time.

for stability, consistency, familiarity, and continuity in the nature of these experiences.

By consistently meeting the child's basic needs over time, parents and other primary caregivers can provide this sense of stability and establish in their children a sense of certainty that their basic needs will be met. In addition, the more a child can generalize these feelings to others (e.g., older siblings, grandparents, and friends), the greater the sense of trust he or she will feel. On the other hand, an infant who experiences inconsistency in the meeting of its basic needs will develop a sense of mistrust.

If the child is able to resolve this crisis in the direction of trust, then comes the belief that the external world is protective and supportive. With this belief, the ego acquires the basic virtue of hope. By developing a sense of trust, the infant can have hope that as new needs and crises arise, there is a real possibility that other people will be there as a source of support. Failing to acquire this sense of hope will result in the development of a sense of fear. This fear involves having to live in an uncertain and unpredictable environment. For example, an individual who has failed to establish a sense of trust as a child may have difficulty establishing friendships as an adult for fear of being rejected. Consistent with Erikson's views on the importance of trust, more recent research has documented the implications of the quality of early experiences of attachment for the development of more successful interpersonal relationships later in life (Waters & Cummings, 2000).

Stage Two. Autonomy vs. Shame and Doubt: Acquiring Will The second psychosocial crisis appears some time around the end of the first year of life and

continues through the third year, thus corresponding to the anal stage of Freud's psychosexual crisis. This crisis involves **autonomy vs. shame and doubt**. During these early childhood years, the child is discovering that he or she has many skills and abilities, such as putting on clothes and shoes, playing with a variety of toys, and manipulating a variety of household objects, from lights to water faucets. All of these activities illustrate the child's growing independence and sense of autonomy.

It is critical for parents and others to let children begin to explore the limits of their abilities in an environment that is supportive, encouraging, and tolerant of failure. Rather than putting on the child's shirt, a supportive parent has the patience to allow the child to continue to try until he or she gets it on or asks for some assistance. As children get the opportunity to demonstrate the extent of their abilities, they begin to develop a sense of mastery over their environment and acquire feelings of being autonomous. On the other hand, if the parents do not allow the child to demonstrate his or her abilities or have expectations well above a child's abilities (i.e., create situations of failure), the child may experience a sense of shame and doubt over failing. This may result in the child becoming very dependent on or demanding of others. In support of Erikson's reasoning, both classic (McClelland, Atkinson, Clark, & Lowell, 1953) and contemporary (Kelly, Brownell, & Campbell, 2000) research has demonstrated that parents who stress their children doing things on their own, while providing indirect assistance (e.g., helping the child but not taking over the task), have children who display a sense of personal achievement, while parents who tend to criticize and punish failure foster children who shy away from challenges (Kelly et al., 2000).

If the child is able to resolve this second crisis in the direction of autonomy, the ego acquires the basic virtue of will. By developing a sense of will, the child does not have to fear being controlled and manipulated by surrounding events; he or she has a sense of being able to change them. Failing to acquire this sense of willpower will result in the child's developing a sense of self-doubt. For example, an adult who has failed to establish a sense of autonomy may lack the self-confidence necessary to enroll in college or pursue a particular career.

Stage Three. Initiative vs. Guilt: Acquiring Purpose
The third psychosocial crisis occurs during the fourth and fifth years of life, corresponding to the phallic stage of Freud's psychosexual crisis. The basic crisis at this time involves **initiative vs. guilt**. During this period, the principle activities involve the child's going to school and, for the first time, regularly interacting with a large number of people (e.g., classmates).

Erikson believed that central to this period is the activity of children playing together. Playing allows children to explore their interpersonal abilities through such behaviors as initiating activities (deciding what to play) and making plans related to the activity selected (deciding on the rules). By taking the initiative and making plans, children learn that they can make decisions, propose a course of action, and carry out the plan. With this, they are learning the basic skills of problem solving in the context of working with other people and developing a sense of curiosity. Such basic skills are the cornerstones of coping successfully in society. The way others react to these self-initiated actions is also extremely important. For example, if parents respond with excessive verbal or physical punishment when the child tries to take some initiative, the child may begin to feel guilty about taking such actions. As a result, the child may develop feelings of excessive self-consciousness.

Consist with the significance Erikson attributed to the importance of play during this psychosocial stage, recent research shows that in addition to helping to foster social (e.g., get along with others), personal (e.g., express one's feelings), and cognitive skills (e.g., promote creative thinking), play also serves to help teach cultural values (Goencue, Mistry, & Mosier, 2000). For example, the play of American children tends to involve demonstrating their abilities and exploits and

bossing others around – a more self-focused form of play. On the other hand, the play of Korean children tends to be more sedate and involves cooperating, seeking harmony, and focusing on the concerns of their playmates – a more other-focused form (Farver, Kim, & Lee-Shin, 2000). Consistent with the way these children play, as we will see in more detail in Chapter 11, a characteristic feature of the personality of individuals from Western cultures is the expression of the concerns of the self, while a characteristic features of the personality of individuals from Eastern cultures is the expression of the concerns of others.

Resolving this crisis in the direction of initiative makes it possible for the child to develop a sense of goal-directed behavior. By feeling comfortable with setting and pursuing goals, the ego acquires the basic virtue of purpose. With purpose, people of all ages begin to develop a sense of meaning in their life. An individual who fails to acquire this sense of purpose may develop a sense of unworthiness. For example, a college student without any sense of purpose will probably just wander from one major to another without doing well or being happy going to school.

Stage Four. Industry vs. Inferiority: Acquiring Competency   Erikson's fourth psychosocial crisis, involving **industry vs. inferiority** occurs in children from the ages 5 through 12. This stage corresponds to the latency period in Freud's psychosexual stages. But while Freud viewed these years as a time of reduced psychic activity, Erikson viewed them as one of significant development. During these years, the child is in school learning to acquire and develop the basic technical skills needed to be a productive individual in society. In our society these skills include learning to read, write, perform mathematical operations, and engage in deductive reasoning. In another society they may involve learning to set a bear trap or skin a wild animal.

As they begin to master these skills, children develop a sense of industry and start to use the skills in more unique and personal ways, such as writing love notes to each other or reading books of personal interest. While acquiring these skills together with their peers, some children may realize their level of skills may be lower than that of others, or they may discover that they do not have the skills deemed valuable in their social context (e.g., being humorous or athletic). Such realizations can lead the child to experience a sense of inferiority, and may cause him or her to lose interest in school activities. This in turn can limit employment and career opportunities in adulthood. According to one recent theory (Dweck, 2001), the basis of such feelings of failure and inferiority is that these individuals tend to give up and stop trying because they feel that they lack the ability and skills needed, and that there is nothing they can do about it. On the other hand, those students who persist in the face of failure tend to believe that they can improve their ability and acquire the needed skills through practice and increased effort, which reflects a sense of industry, or a "can-do" attitude.

Resolving this crisis in the direction of industry creates in the individual the belief that he or she has the basic skills to work and compete as a productive member of society. With this belief, the ego develops a sense of competency. This sense of competency helps the person in taking future risks. For example, an individual with a sense of competency has expectations for success during the process of selecting or changing a career. Failing to establish this sense of competency will result in the ego's developing a sense of incompetence. With such a belief, the individual may not be willing to try new experiences (e.g., make a career change) for fear of failing.

Stage Five. Ego Identity vs. Role Confusion: Acquiring Fidelity **Ego identity vs. role confusion**, the fifth psychosocial crisis, lasts from around 12 years of age to about 18 or 20. It is during this stage that the individual begins to make the transition from childhood to adulthood. Part of this transition involves an initial attempt to establish a sense of ego identity within the society. Ego identity involves establishing a sense of belonging to a society by determining the extent to which an individual feels he or she "fits into" it. In our society, such fitting in typically involves making some career decisions (e.g., wanting to be a clinical psychologist) and career planning (e.g., majoring in psychology).

Failing to establish a sense of identity within society can lead to what Erikson refers to as role confusion. Role confusion involves the individual's not being sure of his or her place in society. The feelings of uncertainty that such a state creates are referred to as an **identity crisis**. In response to this role confusion and identity crisis, young adults may begin to experiment with different lifestyles. Such experimentation might involve a person switching college majors or working at different jobs in an attempt to get some ideas about what he or she enjoys doing. In support of Erikson's reasoning, there is considerable research by James Marcia and

his associates (1966, 1980; Marcia & Friedman, 1970; Marcia, Waterman, Matteson, Archer, & Orlofsky, 1993) that young individuals actively involved in various identity-seeking activities through work, political involvement, and educational experiences tend to feel much better about themselves and their futures and make stronger commitments to occupational goals and ideological positions than do individuals who are less involved in identity-seeking activities. Thus, as Erikson proposed, such identity-seekers tend to come through this identity crisis with a clear and stronger sense of self. Given the significance of this task, what are you doing to help identify your identity? For some help, see the information in "You Can Do It" on p. 192.

Forcing an individual to accept an identity inconsistent with his or her own self-perceptions can result in a lot of unhappiness. Consider Sophie, a student who really does not want to be going to college but is there because of family pressures. She is not likely to be very happy, nor will she do very well in college. Pressuring someone into an identity can result in a rebellion in the form of establishing a negative identity. A **negative identity** is one that is in opposition to what others expect. For example, because of being pressured into going to college, Sophie may simply drop out and take a job as an unskilled laborer to demonstrate her independence and free will. It has been suggested that many adolescents stuck in a state of identity uncertainty are highly apathetic and express a sense of hopelessness about the future, leading some to become suicidal (Chandler, Lalonde, Sokol, & Hallett, 2003) or drift into delinquency to establish a sense of self-worth (Loeber & Stouthamer-Loeber, 1998). To avoid such rebellion, Erikson recommended that parents and significant others simply offer guidance and be supportive of the decisions their children make about what they want to do, instead of trying to make the decisions for them.

Resolving this crisis in the direction of ego identity allows the individual to develop a sense of being accepted by society for the person he or she is, rather than solely on the basis of what others want. With this sense of acceptance, the ego acquires the virtue of fidelity. **Fidelity** involves being able to commit one's self to others on the basis of accepting the individual even when there may be some ideological differences. For example, even when Peter decides not to go into the family sporting goods business as all had hoped, the family still encourages him in his decision to enroll in a culinary arts college to prepare for a career as a chef.

You Can Do It

Identity-Seeking Activities to Help You Identify Your Identity

Identity-seeking activities are all about providing you with a variety of opportunities to determine what you like and do not like, what you can and cannot do, what you want to believe, and what position you will take on various issues, to name just a few. Here are some identity-seeking activities that might help you explore various interests and abilities you might have:

At school:

- Enroll in courses from different disciplines.
- Attend the meetings of some different clubs and organizations on campus.
- Attend several different types of lectures, art performances, sporting events, or rallies sponsored by the college.
- Eat at and talk with other students at different locations on campus.

In your community:

- Volunteer at various agencies around town.
- Attend public meetings.
- Visit job fairs sponsored by area businesses.
- Become familiar with local political issues.

With your family and friends:

- Take family vacations that involve going to different places and doing different types of activities, instead of doing the same things year after year.
- Have discussions of books, movies, or current events with your friends to help you articulate your views and hear the views of others.
- Become involved with family and friends in various civic activities.
- Make an effort to make friends with different types of people.

As you participate in these various identity-seeking activities, here are some questions to ask yourself:

- Did you like or dislike the activity? Why?
- Did you learn anything new from this activity? If so, what?
- Would you consider doing this activity again? Why, or why not?
- To what extent were you able to incorporate the experience associated with this activity into your existing sense of self?
- To what extent did this activity make you want to alter your sense of self?

Having the support of significant others makes committing to personal decisions and goals in life and establishing a personal identity easier.

Stage Six. Intimacy vs. Isolation: Acquiring Love
Intimacy vs. isolation is the sixth psychosocial crisis. This crisis spans the ages of about 18 to 40, or the period of young adulthood. After establishing a sense of social identity, the individual is now ready to begin the task of establishing a meaningful emotional relationship with another person. People need a solid sense of their own personal identity before they are able to make the commitment and sacrifices expected in an intimate emotional relationship (Bellew-Smith & Korn, 1986).

An individual who has not established a firm personal identity will have trouble fusing his or her identity with another person and will feel isolated and lonely.

If the individual is able to resolve this crisis in the direction of intimacy, then comes the capacity to fuse his or her identity with that of another person without having to worry about losing it in the process. With this belief, the ego acquires the basic virtue of love. Beyond the traditional romantic sense, the virtue of love involves being able to commit one's self to someone else, even though this may mean compromising some of one's own needs. Expressions of the virtue of love also include showing respect, providing caring, and helping to take responsibility for significant others. Indeed, contemporary research on intimate relationships suggests that successful relationships are characterized by compassionate love (Mikulincer & Shaver, 2005; Miller, Perlman, & Brehm, 2007). **Compassionate love** goes beyond the intense emotional feelings typically associated with being in love to include a sensing of caring for and being concerned for the well-being of one's partner. In true Eriksonian form, those individuals feeling compassionate report extreme feelings of empathy for their partner (e.g., being able to feel the pain and joy their partner feels) and a willingness to suffer rather than have their partner suffer (Sprecher & Fehr, 2005), as well as demonstrating a true sense of caring, understanding, trust, and support for their partner (Fehr & Sprecher, 2004),

The major advantage of developing the virtue of love is that by fusing their egos in an intimate relationship, two people are able to have twice as much ego strength between them. Failing to acquire this sense of love will result in a lack of emotional commitment. People who fear commitment will avoid getting too close emotionally to others, or may have a series of meaningless love affairs as a way of obtaining a sense of acceptance without commitment.

Stage Seven. Generativity vs. Stagnation: Acquiring Care   The seventh psychosocial crisis, spanning the ages of about 40 to 65, corresponds to the period of middle adulthood. The principal crisis here involves **generativity vs. stagnation**. During this period of middle adulthood, the individual must realize that it is not only his or her own ego development that is important but also the ego development of the next generation of young people.

With this belief comes the individual's desire to make things better for the next generation by sharing the wisdom and strengths acquired during the years of ego development. Examples of this sense of commitment include caring for one's own children and political involvement (Peterson, Smirles, & Wentworth. 1997), along with doing volunteer work in the community and mentoring younger individuals (Lachman, 2004). The secondary gain to be achieved by such commitment to the next generation is that the person's ego will continue to develop through them: the lessons parents teach their children are then passed on to their children's children. This sense of commitment to the future is what Erikson called generativity, and there is contemporary research supporting his notion that generativity is a primary task of many adults during

midlife rather than when they were younger (Sheldon & Kasser, 2001; Zucker, Ostrove, & Stewart, 2002).

Not establishing a sense of commitment to the future can result in feelings of stagnation. Stagnation produces adults who live to satisfy only their own needs. An example of this might be the adult who simply packs up and leaves family members as part of what has become known as a midlife crisis. Less extreme examples might be having an extramarital affair to prove that one is still capable of attracting the sexual attention of others, particularly younger individuals, or buying a motorcycle to prove one is still adventurous and daring.

If this crisis is resolved in the direction of generativity, the individual develops the belief that the ego development of others matters. With this belief, the ego acquires the virtue of care. Care produces a sense of involvement and activity that results in the individual's putting back into society some of what he or she has taken out. An example of care might be a retired executive sharing her knowledge with local high school students as an advisor for an after-school junior entrepreneur program. Failing to establish the virtue of care results in feelings of apathy and self-centeredness.

While Erikson focused on the notion of generativity as being primarily a midlife issue, examinations of personality characteristics across the life span suggest that expressions of conscientiousness appear in young adulthood and continue well into old age (Roberts, Walton, & Viechtbauer, 2006). For details of a recent attempt to study the concept of generativity, read "A Closer Look" on pp. 194–196.

Stage Eight. Ego Integrity vs. Despair: Acquiring Wisdom   The last psychosocial crisis appears from about 65 years until death, occurring during what might be called late adulthood. This crisis is one of **ego integrity vs. despair**. During this part of life, the major task is for the individual to take a look at how his or her ego has developed and reflect on the choices that have been made. **Ego integrity** occurs when the individual can look back on the events of the past seven stages with pleasure about what has taken place and the people one has helped to develop. and a sense of having lived a complete life. Despair occurs when the elderly individual looks back on his or her life with a sense of incompleteness about what has not been done or will never be done and realizes that his or her time on earth is running out. Such despair leads to feelings of bitterness and anger.

Resolving this crisis in the direction of ego integrity results in the ego acquiring the virtue of wisdom. Wisdom makes it possible for people to look back on life with a sense of closure and completeness. The wisdom that we have gained throughout life also makes it possible for us to accept death without fear. An older person showing courage in the face of death can help the younger generation to fear death less and appreciate living more. Without this sense of wisdom, the mature individual experiences a sense of incompleteness and despair over what might have been or the opportunities missed.

In conclusion, Erikson made it clear that personality development is a lifelong process. He also helped to point out the significance of personality development during the twilight years of life – a time that was previously associated with little psychic activity and emotional growth. Additional praise for this aspect of Erikson's work emphasizes his appreciation of the multitude of factors that influences personality development: "from a comparative-culture perspective, Erikson's work is important because he consistently emphasized the dynamic, synthetic nature of developmental transformation. He insisted on viewing personality, biology, and culture as mutually integrating parts of the same system" (Valsiner & Lawrence, 1997, p. 74). Although support for Erikson's stages of personality development exists (McAdams, 1999), critics of his viewpoint and other developmental stage theories of personality provide evidence suggesting a lack of discrete stages of adult personality development (Costa & McCrae, 1997). However, part of the contradictory nature of the results may be linked to the use of different methodologies (analysis of personal stories vs. objective self-report tests).

A Closer Look

Measuring Generativity by Actions and Words

In their efforts to study Erikson's notion of generativity, Dan McAdams, of Northwestern University, and Ed de St. Aubin, of Marquette University, have developed

Dan McAdams and Ed de St. Aubin have made significant contributions to the measurement and validation of Erikson's concept of generativity, as well as serving to stimulate the work of others in this area.

the Loyola Generativity Scale (McAdams & de St. Aubin, 1992). The Loyola Generativity Scale (LGS) is a 20-item, objective self-report personality inventory. Its items are answered on a four-point fixed-format response scale, ranging from 0 (the statement never applies to you) to 3 (the statement applies to you very often). Here is a sample of items from the LGS:

1. I think I would like the work of a teacher.
2. I have a responsibility to improve the neighborhood in which I live.
3. I think I will be remembered for a long time after I die.
4. Other people say that I am a very productive person.
5. I have made many commitments to many different kinds of people, groups, and activities in my life.

The items contained in the LGS "cover many of the most salient ideas in the theoretical literature on generativity" (McAdams & de St. Aubin, 1992, p. 1007), including

- Passing knowledge and skills to others, especially the next generation (see item 1).
- Making significant contributions to improve the quality of one's community and neighborhood (see item 2).
- Engaging in activities that will have a lasting impact or create a legacy (see item 3).
- Being creative and productive (see item 4).
- Caring and taking responsibility for other people (see item 5).

Validating the LGS by What People Do

As part of their attempts to validate the LGS, McAdams and de St. Aubin had study participants complete a behavioral checklist containing 49 activities related to generativity (e.g., taught somebody a skill, performed a community service) and 16 activities not related to generativity (e.g., read a nonfiction book, began a diet to lose weight). People ranging in age from 25 to 74 years were asked to indicate the extent to which they had engaged in a given act during the previous 2 months. In support of the validity of the LGS, it was found that LGS scores were positively correlated with the number of generative behaviors and uncorrelated to the number of behaviors irrelevant to generativity.

Validating the LGS by What People Say

These participants were also asked to describe in writing five important autobiographical episodes involving a recent peak experience, a recent nadir (low point) experience, one related to commitment, one involving a goal, and an imagined future experience. The autobiographic episodes were analyzed on the basis of five generativity themes:

- Creativity (e.g., wrote a poem, built a patio).
- Maintaining (e.g., kept up a family tradition, followed up on a project).
- Offering (e.g., giving one's time or money to others).
- Next generation (e.g., purposeful and positive interactions with those of a younger generation).
- Symbolic immortality (e.g., doing something that will outlive one's existence).

In support of the validity of the LGS, it was found that the total number of generativity themes expressed across the five autobiographic episodes was positively correlated with the total LGS score and the number of generative behaviors performed within a 2-month period.

The results of this research support the validity of the LGS as a systematic measure of generativity by establishing its relationship with what people do and say with respect to their generative behavior. In addition, subsequent research with the LGS indicated that expressions of generativity were positively associated with life satisfaction (McAdams, de St. Aubin, & Logan, 1993), adult value socialization investment (Pratt, Norris, Arnold, & Filyer, 1999), parenting styles emphasizing high standards and discipline along with parental guidance and support that promote antonymous expression in children (Pratt, Danso, Arnold, Norris, & Filyer (2001), and involvement in religious, political, and community activities (Dillon & Wink, 2004; Hart, 1998; Hart, McAdams, Hirsch, & Bauer, 2001), all of which is consistent with Erikson's views. Finally, scores on the LGS were also positively correlated with scores on the Pet Attachment Survey, suggesting that folks who are concerned about caring for others also care about animals (Marks & Koepke, 1994). The research by McAdams and de St. Aubin (1992) and others (Rossi, 2001) indicates that a sense of generativity and generative forms of behavior appear in life much earlier than previously indicated by Erikson. This kind of research helps to clarify the nature and operation of Erikson's psychosocial stages in general and the stage of generativity in particular.

Additional information on the investigation of the concept of generativity from such diverse disciplines as psychology, history, philosophy, and the arts can be found in *Generativity and Adult Development: How and Why We Care for the Next Generation* (McAdams & de St. Aubin, 1998) and "What is Generativity?" (McAdams & Logan, 2004).

Applications of Erikson's Psychosocial Viewpoint: Using What Is Known

Our discussion of the applications of Erikson's viewpoint will focus on psychotherapy, the use of psychobiographies, and personality assessment.

Eriksonian Psychotherapy: Playing through the Conflict

Although Erikson had some theoretical differences with Freud, he regarded himself as a traditional psychoanalyst. He employed many standard techniques of psychoanalysis (e.g., free association), but with some modifications.

One of Erikson's unique therapeutic techniques was play therapy. In **play therapy**, children may be given drawing materials and draw pictures or take ordinary toy objects (e.g., dolls, puppets, and blocks) and arrange them any way they want during a period of free play as a means of expressing their conscious and unconscious concerns (Booth & Lindaman, 2000; Gladding, 2003; Nevid et al., 2000). Erikson regarded free play as a special form of free association, during which children could express with toys what they could not or dared not say (Erikson, 1963). As a means of expressing Oedipal feelings, a child might create a scene in which the mother doll is on one side of a block wall while the father doll and baby doll are on the other side. Play therapy enables children to express emotional conflict from a safe distance.

Psychobiography: The Ego Strength of Greatness

Another unique application of Erikson's viewpoint has been his work on the psychobiographies of famous people (Erikson, 1974, 1975; Runyan, 1997, 2006). **Psychobiography** is the study of an individual's life combining the methodology of differing theoretical viewpoints of personality psychology and historical

analysis (Runyan, 1988a, 1988b, 1997, 2006), such as the lives of Adolf Hitler (Waite, 1977), Sigmund Freud (Elms, 2005; Gay, 1988), Frank Lloyd Wright (de St. Aubin, 1998), Abraham Lincoln (Strozier & Offer, 1985), Elvis Presley, and Truman Capote (Schultz, 2005). In his psychobiographies, Erikson (1958, 1969) investigated how the ego strength of famous people contributed to their greatness. He tried to understand how these people took the conflicts from their own lives and resolved them in later life – in ways that in many cases altered the course of history. An example of Erikson's use of psychobiography is illustrated below in "The Cultural Context of Personality Psychology."

The Cultural Context of Personality Psychology

The Greatness of Gandhi

At the time of the Ahmedabad strike, Gandhi was forty-eight years old: middle-aged Mahatma, indeed. That the very next year he emerged as the father of his country only lends greater importance to the fact that the middle span of life is under the dominance of the universal human need and strength which I have come to subsume under the term *generativity*. I have said that in this stage a man and woman must have defined for themselves what and whom they have come to care for, what they care to do well, and how they plan to take care of what they have started and created. But it is clear that the great leader creates for himself and for many others new choices and new cares. These he derives from a mighty drivenness, an intense and yet flexible energy, a shocking originality, and a capacity to impose on his time what most concerns him – which he does so convincingly that his time believes this concern to have emanated "naturally" from ripe necessities. (Erikson, 1969, p. 395)

This quotation, from *Gandhi's Truth* (Erikson, 1969), is an excellent example of how Erikson combined his interest in personality psychology, psychobiography, and the cultural context of personality to understand how the ego strength of a great individual can inspire the collective ego development of an entire country. In this award-winning book, Erikson tried to explain how Gandhi's use of a personal hunger strike and other forms of nonviolent protest resulted in transforming the weak and negative identity of many Indians into a collective positive identity that enabled them to break away from British rule. In this case, by showing that he was not afraid to die for something in which he believed, Gandhi inspired ego development in millions of individuals.

Such an act is at the heart of three of Erikson's psychosocial crises: ego identity (e.g., Gandhi established clearly his purpose in life and a commitment to it), generativity (i.e., Gandhi's concern for the future), and ego integrity (i.e., Gandhi's acceptance of possible death during his hunger strike inspired others to live). Thus, Erikson was not concerned with tracing the pathological roots of famous people as a means of explaining maladaptive behavior. Instead, he was more concerned with looking to the future (e.g., Gandhi's impact on the future of India) than the past (e.g., what in Gandhi's childhood caused his behavior). And, as this example illustrates, his work was even more valuable because he demonstrated how his psychosocial principles, considered within the cultural context of personality psychology, served to help change the face of an entire culture and alter the course of history.

Personality Assessment from Erikson's Viewpoint

Several assessment techniques have been designed to measure personality development based on Erikson's viewpoint (Constantinople, 1969; McAdams & de St. Aubin, 1992; Walaskay, Whitbourne, & Nehrke, 1983–1984; Whitbourne et al., 1992). One of the most comprehensive is an objective self-report questionnaire developed by Rhona Ochse and Cornelis Plug (1986) from the University of South Africa. The scale consists of 76 statements related specifically to Erikson's first seven psychosocial stages and 17 validity items designed to assess social-desirability response tendencies. The individual is asked to indicate on a four-point scale the degree to which the statement applies to him or her. A score for each of the seven stages is then calculated. For a sample of items similar to those found in this questionnaire, see "You Can Do It."

You Can Do It

Assessing Identity vs. Role Confusion: Finding a Place in Society

As was noted earlier, for Erikson, a principal part of finding your place in society and establishing a sense of identity was making attempts to find a connection with other individuals around you on the basis of your interests and beliefs. In an attempt to help you reflect on your progress regarding this aspect of the issue of identity formation, consider the sample of items presented below.

Instructions

Respond to each of the 10 items below according to how frequently each statement applies to you: 0 = never applies; 1 = applies occasionally; 2 = applies fairly often; 3 = applies very often.

1. Others recognize my worth.
2. The opinion others have of me does not seem to change.
3. I feel sure about how others feel about me.
4. What I am doing in life, I feel, is worthwhile.
5. Wondering about the type of person I am is something I do not do.
6. The type of person I am seems to be agreed upon by most people.
7. Approving of me is something people seem to do.
8. Fitting well into the community in which I live is a feeling I have.
9. My way of life feels like it suits me.
10. Knowing what I should do with my life is something about which I feel certain.

Scoring

Add together the numerical values of your responses. The higher your score, the greater the degree to which you seem to have resolved this psychosocial crisis in the direction of identity.

Adapted from Ochse and Plug (1986).

Results obtained with the psychosocial questionnaire provide supporting evidence for Erikson's viewpoint (Ochse & Plug, 1986). For example, scores on a measure of well-being were significantly correlated with scores on the intimacy scale for young adults and the generativity scale for middle-aged adults. This pattern of results suggests that well-being is strongest within groups of people when it is achieved during the critical stage for one's age as outlined by Erikson.

In a similar manner, scores on the identity scale were related more closely to the intimacy scores for young adults and generativity scores for middle-aged adults than the identity and intimacy scores for adolescents. This pattern of results supports Erikson's contention that establishing an identity is critical for successfully resolving subsequent psychosocial crises. Additional research suggests that scores on subscales for earlier stages of psychosocial development are positively correlated with scores on subscales for later stages (Whitbourne et al., 1992). This pattern of results supports the epigenetic principle of Erikson's viewpoint that successful resolution of early psychosocial crises is related to successful resolution of later crises.

Evaluating Erikson's Psychosocial Viewpoint: Strengths and Limitations

Characteristic Strengths

The psychosocial viewpoint has the following strengths:

- *A comprehensive viewpoint.* A major strength of Erikson's viewpoint is that it combines psychological, social, and historical factors (Valsiner & Lawrence, 1997). His viewpoint has general appeal; he has influenced not only personality psychologists but also historians, anthropologists, educators, sociologists, and gerontologists. The everyday use of the term *identity crisis* is evidence of just how far Erikson's viewpoint is ingrained in contemporary thinking.
- *Extending the periods of personality development.* By extending the notion of personality development across the life span, Erikson portrays a more realistic view of how people develop their personality (McAdams, 1997, 1999). This approach has also done much to change the way the later years of life are viewed. Middle and late

adulthood are no longer seen as simply the passing of time; because of Erikson, they are now considered active and significant times of personal growth. Empirical evidence supporting the importance of the sequencing of personality based on Erikson's viewpoint includes documenting the impact of roles occupied early in life (Vandewater, Ostrove, & Stewart, 1997) and of regret over life choices in early adulthood on well-being later in life (Stewart & Vandewater, 1999). In addition, recent theoretical developments have also started to redefine the nature of the developmental period between adolescence and adulthood in an attempt to achieve a better understanding of the psychosocial development in the earlier stages of the life span (Arnett, 2000).

Characteristic Limitations

Here are some limitations of the psychosocial viewpoint:

- *A rehash of Freud.* Erikson has been criticized as attempting to water down Freudian theory. His views on expanding the role of the ego and extending the psychosocial stages are all seen as simply taking ideas already proposed by Freud and giving them labels that the general population would find easier to accept (e.g., *social crises* rather than *sexual conflicts*). Such a criticism makes sense only from the traditional Freudian viewpoint.
- *Using society as a measure of identity.* Erikson's critics say his viewpoint encourages the development of conformity rather than individuality, particularly within a historical and cultural context (Baumeister, 1997). More specifically, he has been criticized for maintaining that while the individual needs to establish an identity, that identity must be developed within the context of what is acceptable to society, particularly with respect to certain gender roles (Helson, Pals, & Solomon, 1997). Anything outside of this range is considered a negative identity. But as an individual who studied such nonconformists as Gandhi, Erikson can hardly be accused of emphasizing the status quo.

For more information about Erikson's unusual and creative approach to the study of personality, read his *Childhood and Society* (1963), *Identity, Youth, and Crisis* (1968), and *Gandhi's Truth* (1969).

Fromm's Sociological Viewpoint: Balancing Personal Independence and Social Interdependence

Another neo-Freudian who emphasized the role of social factors as critical determinants of personality was Erich Fromm. For a glimpse into the life of Fromm, read "A Closer Look."

A Closer Look

The Life of Erich Fromm

Erich Fromm was born in Frankfurt, Germany, in 1900. His childhood was not a happy one. He described his family environment as tense. His father was moody and his mother suffered from frequent episodes of intense depression. As an adolescent, Fromm was troubled by the suicide of a 25-year-old female friend of the family and the changes in the personalities of relatives, friends, and teachers as they began to express the hatred being promoted by the German government through propaganda during World War I. In college, he sought to find answers to the problems of personality adjustment experienced by his family members and friends. He received a PhD in political sociology in 1922 from the University of Heidelberg and obtained additional psychoanalytic training from the Berlin Psychoanalytic Institute in 1923, where he first met Karen Horney and, according to Jack Rubins (1978, p. 12), they "felt a mutual attraction," although he was married at the time. The attraction resulted in an affair between Horney and Fromm from approximately 1934 to 1939 (Runyan, 2006).

Fromm immigrated to the United States in 1933 and taught at the Chicago Psychoanalytic Institute, where he and Horney began to influence each other intellectually as well as develop their romantic relationship. In addition, at Horney's suggestion, in the summer of 1937, Fromm began to serve as the training analyst of her daughter Marianne, a psychiatric resident at the Payne-Whitney Clinic (Paris, 1994). After teaching at other universities, including Yale and Columbia, and establishing a private clinical practice in New York, he moved to Mexico City in 1949. There he joined the faculty of the National University of Mexico, where he established the department of psychiatric training at the medical school. He also became the director of the Mexico Psychoanalytic Institute. In the 1960s and 1970s, Fromm became very active in the peace movement and helped to establish SANE, the Organization for a Sane Nuclear Policy. In 1976, he moved to Switzerland, where he lived until his death in 1980.

Throughout his career, Fromm combined his interests in political sociology, philosophy, and psychoanalytic thinking to try to understand why people would be willing to give up their freedom to accept and support totalitarian leaders (e.g., the German people's support of Hitler). He wrote a number of books outlining his views. As a result of his ability to convey his ideas to the general public, some of his books have become bestsellers.

Basic Assumptions of Fromm's Sociological Viewpoint: The Desire for Independence vs. Interdependence

Like Horney and Erickson, Fromm stressed the social, political, and cultural factors in the development of the individual (Arlow, 1995). From a sociological perspective, he proposed that the fundamental dilemma of human nature is the struggle between wanting to be free and the desire to belong (Fromm, 1941). Consistent with his reasoning, more recent analysis of the role of social uncertainty has proposed that personal uncertainty (e.g., searching for meaning) increases the tendency of individuals to overidentify (i.e., become more extreme in their beliefs) with the norms, values, and ideals of specific groups (e.g., political parities or religious organizations) or social movements (e.g., skinheads or environmental activists) in an attempt to help themselves find a sense of personal identity and establish a purpose and direction in their life (McGregor, 2004). To help understand the reactions to an act of terrorism that created a tremendous sense of personal and social uncertainty – the attacks on 9/11 – consider the material presented in "Applications in Personality Psychology" on p. 200.

Applications in Personality Psychology

Terror Management Theory: Coping in the Aftermath of 9/11

Without a doubt, the events of 9/11, as well as other acts of terrorism around the world (e.g., subway and train bombings), changed the U.S. way of life (e.g., how we travel through airports) and our view of the world (e.g., our sense of national security and global stability). How do we account for the reactions of individuals following such extreme changes to their day-to-day experiences? One possible explanation is a significant recent development based on some of Fromm's ideas and referred to as terror management theory (Pyszczynski, Solomon, & Greenberg, 2003). **Terror management theory** (TMT) attempts to explain how and why individuals respond to psychological (e.g., feelings of uncertainty and vulnerability) and physical (e.g., injury and death) threats the way they do. According to TMT, individuals have an innate sense of anxiety about death and the unique human awareness of the certainty of death for all of us. Such a combination of intense apprehension about and the inevitability of our own deaths contributes to ongoing concerns regarding the possibility of acts of terrorism. To cope with such feelings of anxiety, TMT suggests that individuals respond by identifying with the values and ideals of specific group(s) and attempting to live up to their standards, thus creating a sense of order and security in their world. For example, in response to the attacks of 9/11, many individuals increased their religious and spiritual involvement and civic identification in order to find a sense of meaning (e.g., "God has a higher reason for the attacks") and security (e.g., "The government will take action to protect us"). In addition, TMT predicts that individuals will strengthen their identification with the values of the group(s) by striking out at those whom they perceive as being different, or blaming them as the cause of the real or imagined threat.

In support of TMT, after the attacks of 9/11, the media coverage was filled with anecdotal evidence in news reports documenting the increased number of individuals attending religious services and heightened expressions of patriotism (e.g., displaying the American flags on cars), as well as acts of aggression against symbols of Islam (e.g., attacks on individuals who looked Middle Eastern or on local mosques). According to TMT, such a pattern of behavior might be interpreted as the way individuals sought comfort from others in church and their community to deal with the threat to their everyday sense of security brought on by these attacks. The attacks on symbols of Islam could be interpreted as collective action designed to express a sense of frustration and anger against those who were perceived as being different and the cause of such attacks and the source of triggering these feelings of uncertainty and vulnerability. In addition, more systematic research indicates that group identification serves to strengthen the sense of self during times of threat and uncertainty to the sense of self (Mussweiller, Gabriel, & Bodenhausen, 2000), and that American evaluations of Islam post-9/11 were most negative in laboratory research for individuals who had an increased sense of personal uncertainty and experienced a threat to their sense of self (e.g., were asked to recall a recent vocational failure; McGregor, Zanna, Holmes, & Spencer, 2001).

As an extension of Fromm's viewpoint, TMT provides a fascinating account of how people deal with the threats to their sense of personal and social security, as well as serving to stimulate a considerable amount of systematic research over the last 20 years (Solomon, Greenberg, & Pyszczynski, 2004). For a more detailed discussion of the application of TMT to the attacks of 9/11, read *In the Wake of 9/11: The Psychology of Terror* (Pyszczynski, Solomon, & Greenberg, 2003).

Basic Needs: Freedom to Be vs. the Desire to Belong

Fromm emphasized the choices people make and the consequences of those choices (Mosak, 1995). Freedom of choice brings with it personal responsibility for the consequences of those choices. It can also increase the sense of separation people begin to feel from each other and can threaten their sense of belonging. Threats to this sense of belonging create feelings of isolation and loneliness and the belief that one is alone or insignificant (Fromm, 1941). The theme of alienation has emerged out of the twentieth century into a critical theme for our times in terms of the variety of the social roles we must play and the choices we must make when interacting with others (Harter, 2002).

Such feelings of alienation produce anxiety. As an example of this dilemma consider Jacob, who moves away from home to a much larger city in order to accept a promotion within the company. In this case, although the new promotion involves more money and the greater freedom of choice associated with it, Jacob has much more responsibility than before and less of the hometown social support of his family and longtime friends. Such a situation can create feelings of anxiety and loneliness. As a reflection on such thoughts based on Fromm's viewpoint, several recent popular books by academic researchers written for the general public, such as *Bowling Alone: The Collapse and Revival of American Community* (Putnam, 2000), *The American Paradox: Spiritual Hunger in an Age of Plenty* (Myers, 2000), and *The Paradox of Choice: Why More is Less* (B. Schwartz, 2004), have focused on the issues of increasing alienation and mental health problems (e.g., anxiety and depression) in a time of considerable mobility (e.g., it's easier for us to get around), heightened prosperity (e.g., we have more purchasing power than ever before), and an overabundance of choices (e.g., having to choose between a multitude of health insurance policies) in the United States, well as offering solutions to rectify such social and personal problems.

Character Types: Strategies for Coping with Anxiety and Isolation

In an attempt to deal with the anxiety produced by feelings of isolation, Fromm (1947) proposed that people develop certain dominant strategies (i.e., personality styles) that he classified as character types.

The **receptive character type** requires constant support from others, such as family members, friends, or the government, but does not reciprocate that support. Such an individual is rather passive and dependent on others and is willing to give up freedom (e.g., stay in abusive relationships) for the sake of security (e.g., the abuser pays the bills).

The **exploitative character type** also takes from others but does so in a more exploitative and manipulative manner. Such an individual will lie and cheat (e.g., falsely profess love) or seek out people who are vulnerable (e.g., those with low self-esteem) to fulfill the need for belonging.

The **hoarding character type** deals with insecurity by keeping all they produce and possess to themselves. These people tend to be selfish, aloof, and suspicious of others. They might establish a sense of security by collecting large numbers of possessions (e.g., a big house, many clothes) and forming emotional bonds with them (e.g., establishing an identity by the type of car they drive) instead of with other people.

The **marketing character type** perceives interpersonal relationships on the basis of their exchange value (e.g., marrying for money) and modifies their personality accordingly (e.g., being overly friendly to those who can be of some help to them). These individuals are characterized by a personality that is shallow, empty, and anxious.

The **productive character type** deals with feelings of anxiety and loneliness by engaging in productive work (e.g., creative self-expression) and fostering loving and compassionate relationships (e.g., being a supportive friend, parent, spouse, employer, co-worker, or teacher). The personality of this type of individual is characterized by caring, creativity, and being responsible. Of all the various character types, only the productive one is considered to have a healthy strategy for dealing with the issue of freedom vs. alienation.

Like those of the other neo-Freudians, Fromm's viewpoint of personality emphasizes the critical role social relationships play in determining the development and operation of personality.

Evaluating Fromm's Sociological Viewpoint: Strengths and Limitations

A characteristic strength of Fromm's viewpoint is the elaborated sense of importance he gave to interpersonal relationships as a critical factor in the development and operation of personality. In addition, he provided considerable insights into the nature and dynamics of the strategies people would develop for fostering these important interpersonal relationships His ideas on the importance of social relationships has served to stimulate more recent thinking on the role and value of our relationships with others, especially in times of personal and social uncertainty (i.e., terror management theory).

The characteristic limitation of Fromm's viewpoint is that he, personally, did not do much to provide empirical support for his viewpoint. As was just noted, however, he did stimulate the research of others.

A Final Comment on the Freud/Neo-Freudian Relationship

As a final comment on the Freud/neo-Freudian relationship, one of the major contributions of Freud's work was the impact it had on the thinking of others. His impact was not limited to his contemporaries, such as Jung and Adler; rather it extended to a new generation – the neo-Freudians. More specifically, Freud's influence appears in Horney's elaboration of feminine psychology, Erikson's extension of the stages of personality development, and Fromm's attention to broader societal concerns.

Chapter Summary: Reexamining the Highlights

- *Horney's Social Psychological Viewpoint*

  - *Basic Assumptions of the Social Psychological Viewpoint.* The basic assumptions of Horney's viewpoint include the individual's personality being motivated by a tendency to seek a sense of security, the importance of early parent–child interactions in determining personality adjustment in adulthood, and the significance of culture in shaping personality.

  - *Basic Concepts of Horney's Social Psychological Viewpoint.* The basic concepts of personality proposed by Horney include feelings of basic hostility and basic anxiety, and coping with these feelings through the use of neurotic tendencies, including moving toward people, moving against people, and moving away from people in the form of healthy or maladaptive strategies.

  - *The Nature of Personality Adjustment.* The degree of personality adjustment is reflected in the amount of overlap between the real self and the ideal self.

  - *Applications of Horney's Social Psychological Viewpoint.* In Horneyan psychotherapy, self-analysis is the therapeutic process by which the individual gains insights into the perceptions of

    the real and ideal self and the strategies used to seek a sense of security. Personality assessment based on Horney's viewpoint focuses on the CAD, assessing the three interpersonal coping styles proposed by Horney.

  - *Horney's Feminine Psychology.* Horney's perspective on the female personality emphasizes the importance of social roles as critical determinants of personality development.

  - *Evaluating Horney's Social Psychological Viewpoint.* Characteristic strengths of Horney's viewpoint include her reinterpretation of the female personality and recognition of the importance of social factors. Characteristic limitations include a lack of empirical research being generated to test it. Recent applications of Horney's viewpoint have served to offset this criticism.

- *Erikson's Psychosocial Viewpoint*

  - *Basic Assumptions of the Psychosocial Viewpoint.* The basic assumptions of Erikson's viewpoint include increasing the role played by the ego, developing the ego in a psychosocial context, and expanding the nature of personality development throughout the life span, all of which serve to extend basic principles of Freudian thought.

– *Basic Concepts of Erikson's Psychosocial Viewpoint.* The eight psychosocial stages are characterized by their epigenetic nature of development, the resolution of crises involving the needs of the person and the expectations of society, and the acquisition of basic virtues when these crises are successfully resolved.

– *Eriksonian Psychotherapy.* Play therapy is designed to help children express their emotional concerns through symbolic free-play activities. In an additional application of this viewpoint, psychobiographies involve analyzing retrospectively the lives of historical figures through the use of techniques of psychoanalysis and history.

– *Personality Assessment.* Recent research has attempted to develop assessment techniques designed to measure and validate Erikson's psychosocial stages of development.

– *Evaluating Erikson's Psychosocial Viewpoint.* Characteristic strengths of Erikson's viewpoint are that his thinking combines the importance of psychological, social, and historical factors and the extension of the psychosocial stages of development to the later years. Characteristic

limitations include the perception of his viewpoint as just a reinterpretation of basic Freudian thought and an overemphasis on personality development reflecting conformity to the expectations of society.

● *Fromm's Sociological Viewpoint*

– *Basic Assumptions of Fromm's Sociological Viewpoint.* The principal social task for individuals is the struggle between wanting to be free and the desire to belong.

– *Basic Needs.* Fromm characterized basic human needs as the desire to be free and independent and the fear of responsibility and loneliness such freedom brings.

– *Character Types.* The different strategies people develop to cope with these basic needs include the receptive, exploitative, hoarding, marketing, and productive character types.

– *Evaluating Fromm's Sociological Viewpoint.* Characteristic strengths of Fromm's viewpoint include his emphasis on interpersonal relationships and the strategies developed to foster these relationships. A characteristic limitation is that Fromm himself did not generate much empirical research in support of his viewpoint, although his ideas did serve to stimulate systematic research done by others.

Glossary

autonomy vs. shame and doubt   The second psychosocial crisis, involving the extent to which the child acquires an initial sense of independence.

basic anxiety   Feelings of insecurity in response to a threatening social environment.

basic hostility   Feelings experienced by children in reaction to parents when they do not create a secure environment for them.

basic virtues   The personal attributes a person gains after the successful resolution of each psychosocial crisis.

codependency   A tendency to become involved in dysfunctional interpersonal relationships in which personal sacrifices by one person give emotional support to the other person.

compassionate love   A type of love that is characterized by a desire to care and look out for the well-being of one's partner.

ego identity vs. role confusion   The fifth psychosocial crisis, involving the extent to which an adolescent develops an initial sense of belonging to the community.

ego integrity   The sense of satisfaction and little regret over the way life has been lived by the elderly, which reduces a fear of death in one's self and increases the zest for living in others.

ego integrity vs. despair   The eighth psychosocial crisis, involving the extent to which the elderly can look back on life with satisfaction and a lack of regrets.

ego psychology   A viewpoint of personality that emphasizes the importance and independent functioning of the ego.

epigenetic principle   The sequential and progressive development of personality through a specific set of stages.

exploitative character type   Persons who base their interactions on taking advantage of others in a manipulative manner.

fidelity   The basic virtue of being able to commit to the ideals and values of others to establish a sense of belonging.

generativity vs. stagnation   The seventh psychosocial crisis, involving the extent to which knowledge gained through life is shared with younger people as a means of commitment to future generations.

hoarding character type   Persons who maintain a sense of security from others through selfishness.

idealized self   An assessment of the ideal type of person one would like to be.

identity crisis   The sense of uncertainty experienced by an individual who lacks a sense of place or belonging in the community or society.

industry vs. inferiority   The fourth psychosocial crisis, involving the extent to which the child acquires a sense of mastery over basic technical skills such as reading, math, and reasoning.

initiative vs. guilt   The third psychosocial crisis, involving the extent to which the child acquires the basic skills of planning and problem solving.

intimacy vs. isolation   The sixth psychosocial crisis, involving the degree to which the identity of one person is combined with that of another within an intimate relationship.

marketing character type   Persons who base their interactions on what can be exchanged in the relationship.

morbid dependency   The seeking of security through excessive dependency on others within exploitative relationships.

moving against people   A behavioral tendency to deal with feelings of insecurity by responding with aggression and hostility for the purpose of obtaining an emotional advantage over others.

moving away from people   A behavioral tendency to deal with feelings of insecurity by withdrawing emotionally and physically from others.

moving toward people   A behavioral tendency to deal with feelings of insecurity by agreeing with people for the purpose of obtaining their affection.

negative identity   Establishing an identity that is the direct opposite of what others expect as a form of expressing independence.

neo-Freudians   A group of personality theorists emphasizing the importance of interpersonal processes as determinants of personality.

neurotic trends   A set of irrational needs and desires developed in an attempt to establish a sense of security.

neuroticism   A collection of personality characteristics featuring anxiety, uncertainty, and negativity in mood and thought.

play therapy   A form of psychotherapy in which children express their thoughts and emotions through free-play activities.

productive character type   Persons who base their interactions on concern for and care of others.

psychobiography   An investigation into the lives of historical figures through the use of viewpoints of personality psychology and historical analysis.

psychosocial crisis   A developmental task that involves balancing the needs of the individual and the expectations of society.

psychosocial development   A process of personality development that places increased emphasis on interpersonal and social factors.

real self   An assessment of the type of person one perceives himself or herself as being.

receptive character type   Persons who base their interactions on demanding support from others.

self-analysis   Horney's form of psychotherapy designed to increase the accuracy of self-perceptions and the effectiveness of interpersonal strategies for gaining a sense of security.

terror management theory   An explanation for the affective, cognitive, and behavior reactions of individuals to extreme events that threaten their sense of security and stability in their everyday lives.

trust vs. mistrust   The first psychosocial crisis, involving the extent to which the infant learns to develop a sense of trust and hope that security will be provided by significant others.

tyranny of the should   A set of excessive expectations a person has about the type of person he or she should be.

womb envy   The sense of envy males feel for the ability of women to give birth.

The Viewpoints of Rogers and Maslow

The Humanists

6

Chapter Overview:
A Preview of Coming Attractions

The **humanistic viewpoint** is characterized by a belief that people are good, active, creative individuals who live in the present and base their actions on the subjective perception of experience (Moss, 2001; Trull & Phares, 2001; Wong, 2006). This viewpoint stresses the positive, healthy aspects of personality and the uniqueness of the individual. People are seen as active agents in the perception and modification of their own reality and are assumed to be motivated to move toward personal growth and self-fulfillment (Maslow, 1962). This chapter will focus on two individuals who best represent the humanistic tradition in the study of personality: Carl R. Rogers and Abraham H. Maslow. In our discussion of the viewpoints of Rogers and Maslow, we will examine the basic assumptions, the basic concepts, and some applications of their ideas. In addition, our discussion will focus on how their ideas have served as a contemporary influence on such topics as the principles of and practices in psychotherapy, self-esteem, leadership, and human motivation (Moss, 2001; Tudor & Worrall, 2006).

The Phenomenological Viewpoint of Carl R. Rogers: Putting the Person at the Center of Personality

"The organism reacts to the field as it is experienced and perceived. This perceptual field is, for the individual, 'reality'" (Rogers, 1951, p. 484). This quotation illustrates Carl R. Rogers's phenomenological viewpoint of personality. The **phenomenological perspective** stresses that a person's feelings and behavior are determined by how she or he perceives and interprets events. The significance of this assumption is that it makes the person the "undisputed expert" on his or her feelings and behavior. Placing the person's perceptions at the center of the study of personality was in sharp contrast to the dominant Freudian viewpoint at the time, which discounted much of the individual's conscious perception and interpretation of events. For a glimpse into the life of Carl Rogers, who, beginning in the early 1940s and for almost the next 50 years, proposed a revolutionary perspective on the study of personality, read "A Closer Look."

A Closer Look

The Life of Carl R. Rogers

Carl Ransom Rogers was born on January 8, 1902, in the Chicago suburb of Oak Park, Illinois. He was the fourth of six children in what he described as a close-knit family. His childhood environment was financially secure and characterized by an almost fundamentalist atmosphere stressing hard work and conservative values. His parents discouraged the children from developing friendships outside of the family, because "outsiders" engaged in activities that they did not approve, including playing cards, smoking, and going to movies. Such solitude resulted in Rogers becoming an avid reader and a socially independent individual.

When Rogers was 12 years old, his parents moved the family to a farm. Because of his father's emphasis on running the farm scientifically, Rogers became very

Carl Rogers's lasting contribution to the study of personality psychology was his effort to verify and integrate his viewpoint of personality with social concerns of the individual and society.

interested in science and agriculture, reading about many agricultural experiments and studying insects on his own. With his tendency toward solitude and his love for reading, he had only two dates in high school, but he was almost a straight-A student. His chief interests as a student were in English and science.

Following in the family tradition of his parents, two brothers, and a sister, Rogers enrolled at the University of Wisconsin in 1919 to study agriculture. While at college, he became active in church work, then switched his academic emphasis and began to prepare for the ministry. In 1922, he was selected as one of 10 students to attend the World Student Christian Federation Conference in Peking, China. As he met others from a wide variety of cultural backgrounds at college and during the conference, Rogers found himself slipping away from the fundamentalist beliefs of his parents and becoming more liberal in his philosophy. In 1924, he received his BA degree in history.

Shortly after graduation, Rogers married Helen Elliott, a childhood sweetheart. The two of them drove in a secondhand Model-T coupe to New York, where he was to begin studying for the ministry at Union Theological Seminary in 1924. Becoming doubtful that his seminary training was preparing him to help people, he transferred to Columbia University Teachers College to study clinical and educational psychology. He earned his MA in 1928 and a PhD in 1931. His doctoral dissertation was concerned with measuring personality adjustment in children.

Rogers's first professional appointment was at the Rochester Guidance Center in the Child Study Department of the Society for the Prevention of Cruelty to Children. He started as a student intern and eventually became the center's director. The center's highly Freudian approach, stressing unconscious forces, was in sharp contrast to the very scientific and statistical training Rogers received at Columbia. It was during this time that he began to question the effectiveness of psychodynamic approaches to emotional problems. His interactions with the rather diverse staff at the center led him to begin trying to assess and document the critical factors in the therapeutic environment. The outcome of this effort was his first book, *The Clinical Treatment of the Problem Child* (1939).

In 1940, Rogers left the clinical setting for an academic appointment at Ohio State University, where he began to develop and test his view of personality. He left there and accepted a position as professor of psychology and director of the counseling center at the University of Chicago in 1945. While at the counseling center, Rogers, with the aid of many fine research-oriented clinical psychology graduate students, expanded the systematic investigation and verification of his viewpoint. The outcome of this work was a textbook titled *Client-Centered Therapy: Its Current Practice, Implications, and Theory* (1951), which is considered his most important textbook. In it, he took a very scientific view of studying the processes, dynamics, and effectiveness of his approach to psychotherapy.

In 1957, Rogers left the University of Chicago to return to the University of Wisconsin, where he was professor of both psychology and psychiatry. However, he become disenchanted with the departmental politics of the university environment and resigned his professorships to accept a position with the Western Behavioral Sciences Institute in La Jolla, California, in 1963. In 1968, he and several others from the institute left to form the Center for the Studies of the Person, also located in La Jolla. At the center, he continued to devote his life to investigating how to make psychotherapy more effective and to understanding human nature more completely.

After devoting more than 50 years of his life to the study of the person, Rogers died on February 4, 1987. In recognition of his contribution to psychology, he received numerous awards, including the Distinguished Scientific Contribution Award and Distinguished Professional Contribution Award of the American Psychological Association (APA), and being elected president of the APA. In addition, he was rated the single most influential psychotherapist in a survey of therapists (Smith, 1982). He not only provided "the central framework for the humanistic therapies. As a person, he provided leadership for three generations of humanistic clinicians" (Moss, 2001, p. 15).

More about the life of Carl Rogers can be found in an autobiography (Rogers, 1967) appearing in Boring and Lindzey's *A History of Psychology in Autobiography,* and an autobiographical paper titled "In Retrospect: Forty-six Years" (Rogers, 1974).

Basic Assumptions of the Rogerian Viewpoint: The Person = Personality

The assumptions of his theory illustrate clearly the emphasis Rogers placed on the person as being the center of attention in the study of personality (Raskin & Rogers, 1989, 1995; Raskin, Rogers, & Witty, 2008; Rogers, 1951, 1959; Tudor & Worrall, 2006). We begin our exploration of Rogers's viewpoint with a discussion of these basic assumptions.

The Reality of Subjective Experience

Subjective experience refers to the unique way each person views the world and his or her experiences in it. As a result of one's own unique perception, one's responses to these subjective experiences will also be unique: One person might respond to the loss of a job with anxiety and depression about the great loss of security, whereas another might respond with optimism at the challenges a new job might bring. Thus, from the phenomenological perspective, it becomes more important to know how the person views the event than it is to know the nature of the event itself (Watson & Greenberg, 1998). Or, in Rogers's own words, "The best vantage point for understanding behavior is from the internal frame of reference of the individual himself" (1951, p. 494).

Emphasis on the Here and Now

Related to Rogers's emphasis on the subjective experience was his emphasis on the *here and now* of each person's experiences. He stressed the importance of events as they are perceived and experienced by the person now, not as they were perceived in the past (Greening, 2001). He did not ignore the past; he simply felt that more could be gained by investigating the individual's perception and reactions to events in the present. For example, although the parents of a college student put pressure on her to succeed when she was in grade school, her anxiety over a test next week has more to do with her views of the current state of affairs of her life at college, such as perceiving a lack of time to squeeze in going to work, participating in a volunteer program with friends, and studying for the test.

The Actualizing Tendency

"The organism has one basic tendency and striving – to actualize, maintain, and enhance the experiencing organism" (Rogers, 1951, p. 487). The motivation underlying the desire for self-improvement is the actualizing tendency (Raskin et al., 2008; Tudor & Worrall, 2006). The **actualizing tendency** motivates a person to develop personal attributes (e.g., social, spiritual, and intellectual) and capabilities (e.g., physical and mental) in a direction of increasing autonomy through self-awareness. For example, by learning a new job skill (i.e., an occupational aspect of the person) and gaining more confidence in making her own decisions (i.e., a mental capability), a woman who is being physically abused by her husband can start taking more control over her life. Such changes will make it possible for her to live her life with a greater possibility of exploring and expanding her potential for personal growth than in the past.

The Organismic Valuing Process

To help guide the actualizing tendency, Rogers assumed the operation of a mechanism called the organismic valuing process. The purpose of the **organismic valuing process** is to evaluate subjective experiences as to their short-term and long-term potential for helping the individual toward self-enhancement (Kasser & Sheldon, 2004; Raskin et al., 2008; Rogers, 1959; Tudor & Worrall, 2006). Experiences judged as consistent with the objective of self-enhancement are evaluated positively, while those judged as inconsistent with this objective are evaluated negatively. For example, a person's decision to stop drinking at a party, even when there is peer pressure to continue drinking, is based on an assessment of the organismic valuing process that the short-term gain of peer acceptance is outweighed

by the long-term risks to the self associated with getting drunk (e.g., being arrested for drunk driving). Rogers was a firm believer that given the choice between what is good and bad for the individual, the emotionally healthy and highly self-aware individual would *always freely choose* those alternatives evaluated as promoting the actualizing tendency.

A summary of the principal ideas examined in this section is presented in "Summing It Up: Basic Assumptions of Rogers's Viewpoint" on p. 209.

Basic Concepts of the Rogerian Viewpoint: Defining Your Sense of Self

Like his basic assumptions, the concepts upon which Rogers developed his viewpoint of personality also emphasized the perceptions of the individual as being central to any attempt to understand personality (Raskin & Rogers, 1995).

The Phenomenal Field

Linked to subjective experience is what Rogers referred to as the phenomenal field (Rogers, 1951, 1959). The **phenomenal field** represents all of the possible sensory experiences that a person is aware of at any given moment (Trull & Phares, 2001) and the reactions a person might generate from these experiences (Tudor & Worrall, 2006). They can be occurring both inside (e.g., test anxiety) and outside (e.g., the announcement of a test) the individual. An important feature of the phenomenal field is that it is constantly changing. These changes can significantly affect the thoughts, feelings, and behavior of the individual. For example, the depression experienced by a firefighter can be lessened during group therapy when feedback from others helps her come to the realization that, even with the best of efforts, not everyone can be saved every time. By changing the phenomenal field in the direction of bravery instead of failure, the therapist is able to remove the depression and raise the person's self-esteem.

Subception

Rogers also assumed that the perceptual processes of the phenomenal field could operate at a level outside of conscious awareness, in the form of subception. Rogers (1951) defined **subception** as "a discriminating

Summing It Up *Basic Assumptions of Rogers's Viewpoint*

Basic Assumption	Description	Compared to Other Theorists
Reality of Subjective Experience	What is important about an event is how the individual perceives it from his or her point of view.	Similar to the influence of the creative self proposed by Adler; dissimilar to the lack of validity Freud attributed to the manifest content of verbal reports
Emphasis on the Here and Now	What is most important is how the individual is experiencing events in his or her life at the present time.	Dissimilar to Freud's retrospective viewpoint and the combined retrospective/teleological viewpoints of Jung and Adler
Actualizing Tendency	Each individual is motivated in his or her own unique way toward maximizing personal growth and self-enhancement.	Similar to Jung's concept of self-realization, Adler's striving for superiority, and Horney's ideal self; dissimilar to Freud's homeostatic view of personality
Organismic Valuing Process	This helps the individual to determine which experiences facilitate the actualizing tendency and which do not.	Similar to Freud's reality principle of the ego, Jung's archetype of the self, Adler's creative self, and the healthy use of Horney's three interpersonal coping strategies

evaluative physiological organismic response to experience, which may precede the conscious perception of such experience" (p. 507). This means that the individual may respond to something before it is actually consciously perceived. For example, sensing anxiety, a college student represses information about an assignment due early next week and agrees to participate in social events. Thus, to avoid the conscious-level feelings of anxiety, the student becomes preoccupied with other activities. The point is that decisions and actions are influenced by emotional and mental factors of which the person may not be completely aware.

The Self-Concept

"A portion of the total perceptual field gradually becomes differentiated as the self" (Rogers, 1951, p. 497). For Rogers, the unique sense of self is something that does not just happen; it is part of a continuous process forged through the experiences with the phenomenal field. Thus, a sense of self is achieved through the individual's encounters with and interpretations of life's events. The establishment of a sense of self involves the dynamic interaction of two somewhat different components of the self-concept: the organism and the self (Tudor & Worrall, 2006).

Closely related to the organismic valuing process is that aspect of the self-concept referred to as the organism. The **organism** is that part of the self-concept concerned with helping the individual to evaluate and categorize various experiences. The information gained from these experiences is used in helping the individual to define a sense of self. For example, suppose that in one semester, an individual takes courses in history, geology, and psychology but finds that only the psychology course is really enjoyable. In the next semester, the individual takes courses in math, psychology, and political science, and again enjoys only the psychology. After a few more favorable encounters with psychology, being a "psych major" becomes part of the individual's self-image. Thus, when experiences are incorporated into the individual's self-image by the organism, they become part of what Rogers called the "self."

The **self** is the sense of personal identity represented within the phenomenal field. The pronouns *I*, *me*, and *my* are all used to distinguish between each person's sense of self and all other objects in the phenomenal field (Trull & Phares, 2001). The unique perception of the individual's sense of self is a result of the ongoing organismic evaluative process and the interpretation of the information it provides (Tudor & Worrall, 2006;

Watson & Greenberg, 1998). For example, through a variety of experiences and affective reactions to them, an individual's self could be represented by such labels as "philosophy major," "animal-rights activist," "movie buff," "lover of art," "reader of mystery novels," "hospital volunteer," and "environmentalist." These various aspects of the self all help to produce personal opinions (e.g., views on fines for environmental polluters) and patterns of behavior (e.g., visiting certain types of museums while on vacation) that make each person unique (Trull & Phares, 2001).

Congruence and Incongruence

The different components of the self-concept are also related to the extent to which the individual is motivated to maintain a degree of consistency between the evaluative nature of the experiences by the organism and their incorporation into the individual's sense of self. When there is a close match between how a person feels about something and how these feelings are related to the sense of self, Rogers (1959) described this as a state of **congruence** within the individual. For example, having feelings of outrage over discrimination practices in the workplace is congruent with an individual's self-perception of not being a sexist or racist.

On the other hand, Rogers believed that a state of **incongruence** exists when there is some degree of discrepancy between a person's feelings about something and the sense of self. For example, a happily married individual might find feelings of sexual arousal for a co-worker incongruent with the self-perception of being a faithful spouse and moral individual. Incongruence leads to feelings of anxiety that the individual is motivated to reduce in order to bring the sense of self together (Rogers, 1959). The self-concept seeks to reduce this incongruence through the process of self-actualization.

This concludes the discussion of the basic concepts of Rogers's viewpoint. A summary of the principal ideas noted in this section is presented in "Summing It Up: Definitions and Examples of the Basic Concepts of Rogers's Viewpoint."

Summing It Up *Definitions and Examples of the Basic Concepts of Rogers's Viewpoint*

Definitions	Examples
Phenomenal Field: All of the potential experiences occurring in and around you at any single moment	While driving, you are aware of the storefront billboards, as well as the tension in your neck caused by a car that just cut in front of you.
Subception: Developing an emotional response to an event before it actually appears in your conscious awareness	An individual begins to feel really tired, so she goes to bed early and oversleeps the next morning and misses having to give a difficult presentation in her speech class.
Self-Concept: How you feel about your experiences and the sense of who you are	You feel excited when watching your favorite baseball team play, and have a sense of identification with that team (e.g., wearing a Reds' cap and t-shirt while shopping).
Organism: The part of the self-concept responsible for evaluating and categorizing your experiences	After enjoying your personality course, you decide to take more psychology courses.
The Self: The part of the self-concept that makes it possible for you to distinguish yourself from all other individuals	After taking several psychology courses, you decide to be a "psych major," giving you a sense of academic identity.
Congruence–Incongruence: The degree of consistency between your feelings about your experiences and your sense of self	You feel guilt about cheating on your income tax return, which is inconsistent with your self-perception as an honest and fair individual.

Self-Actualization: The Motivational Component of Personality

The actualizing tendency reflects Rogers's belief that people are motivated in the direction of self-understanding and self-enhancement (Raskin & Rogers, 1995). **Self-actualization** refers to the motivational process by which this actualizing tendency is expressed (Trull & Phares, 2001; Tudor & Worrall, 2006; Winter & Barenbaum, 1999). The principal objective of self-actualization is to help the individual meet this fundamental need of self-enhancement by maintaining continuous progress toward personal growth and improvement (Polkinghorne, 2001; Watson & Greenberg, 1998).

The process of self-actualization is facilitated by openness to emotional experiences and characterized by being ongoing in nature, expressed in a unique way by each person, and holistic in its response. These four features of the self-actualization process are as follows:

- *The necessity of experiential freedom and openness.* Rogers believed that the process of self-actualization is most likely to occur when the individual is willing to be completely free and open to his or her emotions and other experiences in the phenomenal field. For example, without having to distort and deny the reasons for selecting a particular major (e.g., to please family members), a college student is in a much better position to select a course of study that will allow personal interests and talents to flourish. Thus, experiential freedom reflects an honest and unbiased approach to the events in one's life.
- *The ongoing process of self-actualization.* Self-actualization is an ongoing process because the individual is innately motivated to move continuously in the direction of self-enhancement and personal growth. In this regard, as the individual experiences self-enhancement and personal growth, there is the tendency to want to become better. For example, no matter how good they are, outstanding teachers always search for ways to improve their teaching effectiveness.
- *The unique expression of self-actualization.* The uniqueness feature of the self-actualization process reflects Rogers's belief that each of us seeks self-enhancement in our unique way. For example,

when trying to get better grades in school, one student might enroll in a memory improvement course, another might seek out the professor after class for some special study tips, and a third might endeavor to spend more time studying by working fewer hours at an off-campus job.
- *The holistic nature of self-actualization.* The holistic nature of self-actualization refers to people's tendency to use all of their capabilities in a coordinated effort when moving toward self-enhancement. For example, to succeed in college, a student must coordinate cognitive abilities (e.g., studying for exams) with psychological abilities (e.g., the motivation to find time to study) and physical self-care (e.g., eating right and getting enough rest to stay healthy). If any aspect of this coordinated effort breaks down (e.g., losing the motivation to study), the student's progress toward personal growth is affected.

The self-actualization process is a fundamental part of each person's expression of uniqueness and desire for personal growth. A summary of the major points in the discussion of self-actualization is presented in "Summing It Up: Key Features of the Self-Actualization Process" on p. 212. The process of self-actualization is facilitated through successful personality development. In the next section, we begin our exploration of Rogers's views on personality development.

Personality Development: Developing Experiential Freedom

In a very general sense, the principal theme in Rogers's views on personality development concerns the reciprocal interaction between those needs reflecting the individual's desire for the regard of others and those needs reflecting a desire for personal regard (Mruk, 2006; Rogers, 1961). Central to this process are the concepts of need for positive regard, unconditional and conditional positive regard, need for self-regard, and conditions of worth.

The Regard of Others: External Considerations in the Development of the Self

For Rogers, an important part of personality development is the relationship we have with others and the nature of the feelings they have for us.

Summing It Up *Key Features of the Self-Actualization Process*

Key Feature	Example
Basic Objective: The process by which the individual is motivated in the direction of personal growth and self-enhancement	Although you get a "B" on your personality psychology exam, you spend more time studying for the next one, hoping to get a "B+" or an "A."
Characteristic Features: The process of self-actualization is facilitated by the following conditions:	A sense of self-enhancement and personal growth during college is more likely to be achieved when certain considerations are addressed.
Experiential Freedom and Openness: The individual must be open to and experience freely events and feelings in his or her phenomenal field.	Your decision to go to college must reflect your true feelings, not those of your parents or peers.
Ongoing: The basic desire for self-enhancement is continuous and never-ending.	You will constantly be making decisions directed at self-enhancement, while in college (e.g., what courses to take?), during your career (e.g., what job offer to accept?), and in your retirement (e.g., where will you be the happiest?).
Unique Expression: Each person expresses this process in his or her unique way.	While you decided to go to college for self-enhancement after high school, some of your friends decided to go into the military or get a full-time job as a means of personal growth.
Holistic Nature: All aspects of the individual are utilized in harmony during this process.	You must consider your psychological, educational, and occupational needs, as well as your emotional needs, when trying to decide if you should get married.

Need for Positive Regard The **need for positive regard** is the basic desire each person has for receiving the warmth, acceptance, sympathy, regard, and respect of others (Rogers, 1959). To put it simply, as an individual begins to develop and accept a sense of self, he or she wants others to accept it as well. For example, children engage in behaviors (e.g., clear their plates) that will elicit a smile or praise from their parents. As adults, we might express this need by buying some attractive new clothes with the hope that our friends will say how much they like them too. The experience of positive regard can take one of two forms: unconditional or conditional positive regard.

- *Unconditional Positive Regard* **Unconditional positive regard** is when a person receives the positive regard of others without any limitations set to it (Sommers-Flanagan & Sommers-Flanagan, 2004; Trull & Phares, 2001). It is the acceptance of people for who they are, not for what others would like them to be. For example, in successful relationships, good friends realize that they will not agree on all issues. With children, unconditional positive regard occurs when they realize that even though they may be afraid of the dark or dislike eating broccoli, they will be given acceptance with no strings attached. When such a situation exists, people are free to experience openly and freely the true nature of their feelings.

- *Conditional Positive Regard* **Conditional positive regard** involves placing limitations on the regard people give to others. For example, when a parent says, "I won't love you if you keep making that noise," the child can interpret this to mean that conditions of acceptance are being imposed. In a more complex example, when someone says, "If you really loved me, you'd have sex with me," this person is putting a price tag on the affection and acceptance to be granted. Such examples come close to what might be called emotional blackmail. As people become more and more responsive to conditional positive regard, they run the risk of having their sense of self defined by others and being the type of person others want them to be, not the type they really want to be. Such a situation is a serious barrier to the process of self-actualization.

The Regard of Self: Internal Considerations in the Development of the Self

So that personality development is not based totally on our relationships with others, Rogers also stipulated the need for positive regard.

The Need for Positive Self-Regard   The **need for positive self-regard** is the desire we have as individuals to accept our own experiences on an internal valuing

process. In this sense, everyone begins to judge for themselves what they like and dislike and what they will – and will not – incorporate into the sense of self. From the need for positive self-regard, each person develops self-acceptance and a unique identity. This process is most likely to occur when the individual experiences unconditional positive regard from others. An example would be supporting a spouse's decision to quit work for two years to pursue a lifelong dream of a career in acting.

Conditions of Worth   People can facilitate the process of self-actualization in others; they can also hinder it. More specifically, **conditions of worth** develop when significant others (e.g., parents, a lover, or a spouse) give a person labels that become incorporated into that person's self-concept. This occurs because the person begins to equate conditional positive regard and positive self-regard (Comer, 2007; Tudor & Worrall, 2006; Watson & Greenberg, 1999). That is, a person experiences a sense of self-acceptance only when meeting the expectations others have set as a condition of acceptance. An example of this process would be a young man who feels a sense of manhood only when he goes along with peer pressure to engage in various petty crimes. Because conditions of worth can undermine the true

Summing It Up *The Basic Concepts of Personality Development from Rogers's Viewpoint*

Basic Concept	Example
Need for Positive Regard: The need we all have for others to accept us	You wear certain types of clothes so that you will "fit in" at the office.
Unconditional Positive Regard: Granting others freedom of experience without passing judgment	While you don't like a friend's taste in clothes, your friend may not like your taste in movies. However, part of what keeps you friends is the respect you have for each other's freedom of expression.
Conditional Positive Regard: Giving esteem to others only when they meet certain expectations	The parents of an overweight child offer praise only after the child has taken and consumed a second helping of each dish on the table.
Need for Positive Self-Regard: Our basic desire to accept our sense of self	A peace-loving minister admits watching professional football for the sense of pleasure and excitement it offers.
Conditions of Worth: Accepting your sense of self only when it meets the expectations of others	A college student feels successful self only when getting all "A"s, which meets parental expectations.

organismic valuing process, Rogers (1959) felt that conditions of worth can threaten efforts toward self-actualization. From his perspective, personality development is a continuous process in which the person strives to promote self-actualization by acquiring a degree of experiential freedom (i.e., openness to experience) for the organismic valuing process.

A summary of the major points of discussion in this section is presented in "Summing It Up: The Basic Concepts of Personality Development from Rogers's Viewpoint" on p. 213. In the next section, we will discover some benefits of successful personality development by considering the nature of personality adjustment.

The Nature of Personality Adjustment: A Consequence of Experiential Freedom

For Rogers, the degree of successful personality adjustment was directly related to the amount of experiential freedom available during the process of personality development. He defined quite clearly the characteristic features and consequences associated with successful and unsuccessful personality development.

Personality Adjustment and the Fully Functioning Person: Living the Good Life

Being free and open to experience maximizes the possibility that the individual will maintain congruence within the self-concept. Rogers (1959, 1961, 1964) referred to the **fully functioning person** as an individual constantly experiencing a high degree of congruence. The fully functioning person, according to him, has a high degree of mental health and personality adjustment (Raskin & Rogers, 2000; Tudor & Worrall, 2006; Watson & Greenberg, 1998). More specifically, Rogers (1959, 1961, 1964) describes the fully functioning person as someone who can incorporate diverse information about his or her sense of self (e.g., David knows he is a good father but tends to be late for most appointments), tends to be open to new experiences (e.g., although not a fan of experimental theater, Sue agrees to see a new play at a local art house), and trusts his or her own judgment (e.g., Pete resists peer pressure to participate in a binge-drinking game while at a party).

A consequence of being a fully functioning person is living what Rogers (1961) called "the good life."

From this point of view, the good life involves more than having a big house and a fancy car. It involves how the fully functioning person lives his or her life and interacts with others. More specifically, for Rogers, the good life is characterized by a greater degree of independence (e.g., Debbie tends to express her opinions, regardless of how popular they are), creativity (e.g., being open to new experiences has helped Toni write better poems), trust by others (e.g., because Jan speaks her mind, her friends know where she stands), and richness of experience (e.g., Stu's willingness to participate in a variety of student activities enhanced the quality of his college experience). But as Rogers (1961) warns,

> This process of the good life is not, I am convinced, a life for the faint-hearted. It involves the stretching and growing of becoming more and more of one's potentialities. It involves the courage to be. It means launching oneself fully into the stream of life. Yet the deeply exciting thing about human beings is that when the individual is inwardly free, he chooses as the good life this process of becoming. (p. 196)

Thus, living the good life and developing a high degree of personality adjustment are the consequences of being a fully functioning person. For those who are unwilling or unable to do so, the consequences are a life characterized by a certain degree of personality maladjustment.

Personality Maladjustment: Living the Incongruent Life

If successful personality adjustment is linked with living the good life, personality maladjustment is linked with living the incongruent life. Basing too much on the conditional positive regard of others develops a sense of self that has attached to it conditions of worth. A person who relies too much on external influences for determining the nature of his or her experiences minimizes experiential freedom and maximizes the possibility of incongruence within the self-concept. This state of incongruence is at the core of psychological maladjustment (Rogers, 1959). It is likely to occur when conditional positive regard and conditions of worth are pitted against the need for positive self-regard.

When the self-actualization process is hindered, the individual begins to experience anxiety and tries to cope with it by engaging in defensive behavior (Tudor

& Warroll, 2006; Watson & Greenberg, 1998). Such behavior is characterized by distortions of awareness (e.g., Jane deals with her test anxiety by telling herself that doing poorly on her mid-term exam is "no big deal"), denial (e.g., to avoid having to think about and address his marital problems, Robert spends lots of additional time working), and rigid patterns of behavior (e.g., Alice stays at a very boring and unfulfilling job because of the risks associated with making a job or career change). Thus, while such defensive behavior helps the individual gain a certain degree of perceived congruence by distorting the situation, the actual level of incongruence produces feelings of anxiety and unpleasantness. When this level of anxiety gets to be too great, the individual may become disorganized. In a state of disorganization, feelings of anxiety resulting from incongruence come into conscious awareness (Rogers, 1959). When disorganization becomes too severe, the individual is motivated to seek psychotherapy in an attempt to regain congruence and positive self-regard. Rogers's views on psychotherapy are discussed in the next section.

A summary of the interrelated dynamics of Rogers's views on personality development and personality adjustment is presented in Figure 6.1.

Applications of the Rogerian Viewpoint: Using What Is Known

Like any other comprehensive and influential theory of personality, Rogers's viewpoint has found its way into many different applications. You will learn about two areas of application in this section: psychotherapy and personality assessment.

Person-Centered Therapy: Reestablishing Congruence

Rogers is best known for the application of his viewpoint to the type of psychotherapy he developed, called client-centered therapy (Rogers, 1951), which he later renamed **person-centered therapy** (Raskin et al., 2008; Rogers, 1977; Trull & Phares, 2001). As with everything else related to Rogers's viewpoint, the individual is the essential element in the therapeutic process. There is also a considerable amount of emphasis on the working relationship between the client and therapist (Greenberg, Elliott, & Lietaer, 1994; Lambert, Bergin, & Garfield, 2004; Raskin & Rogers, 1989, 1995, 2000; Sommers-Flanagan & Sommers-Flanagan,

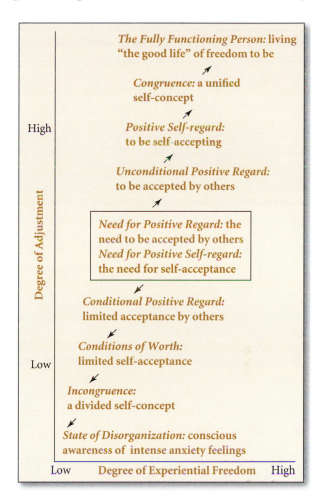

Figure 6.1 From Rogers's viewpoint, experiential freedom is positively related to personality adjustment.

2004). Finally, a basic premise is the belief that people are motivated to seek therapy by their desire to continue the process of self-actualization (Trull & Phares, 2001).

The Reintegration of the Self-Concept as the Basic Object of Person-Centered Therapy Since personality maladjustment is characterized by the conscious awareness of intense anxiety, which signals a state of incongruence, the goal of therapy should be to minimize this state of affairs. In person-centered therapy, the major objective is to reintegrate the self-concept by helping the individual to freely experience events in the phenomenal field. Once the individual can make judgments based on a true organismic valuing process, the barriers to the self-actualization process are removed. To achieve this objective, Rogers specified the conditions necessary to analyze the therapeutic process.

The Necessary Conditions of the Therapeutic Environment   As a means of helping the individual to begin establishing a state of congruence, Rogers (1957, 1959; Raskin & Rogers, 1989, 1995, 2000) and others (Greenberg et al., 1994; Moss, 2001; Nevid, Rathus, & Greene, 2000; Thorne & Lambers, 1998) noted that the therapeutic environment must include the following six conditions:

- *Client and therapist establish contact.* Having **contact** implies a purposeful relationship between the client and therapist. For the client, contact involves being able to share intimate experiences with the therapist. For the therapist, contact requires attempting to understand these experiences from the client's point of view. Their shared contact stresses trying to communicate in a manner that will bring about experiential freedom for the client.
- *The client is in a state of incongruence.* The client has to be experiencing a certain amount of emotional pain (i.e., incongruence) prior to therapy. It is the state of vulnerability and anxiety that motivates the individual to want to become more congruent and seek therapy. For example, as long as an unhappy spouse continues to distort the situation at home by simply hoping things will get better, it is unlikely that he or she will seek counseling.
- *The therapist is congruent in this relationship.* To accurately understand what the client says, and to react in a true and unbiased manner, the therapist should be operating with a unified self-concept when interacting with the client (Trull & Phares, 2001). That is, the therapist's own conditions of worth should not interfere with the therapeutic process. For example, although the therapist may be going through a very emotional divorce at the time, personal feelings should not bias his or her therapeutic responses to what a client may be saying about a spouse. The therapist is free, however, to express personal feelings that might help strengthen the relationship with the client (e.g., the therapist reveals having similar feelings of anxiety as a result of the divorce; Rogers & Sanford, 1985). In such situations, the therapist is responding to the client with genuine feelings and "avoiding the temptation to hide behind a mask of professionalism" (Rogers & Sanford, 1985, p. 1379).

- *The therapist expresses unconditional positive regard for the client.* The therapist should promote unconditional positive regard by not passing judgment on what the client says or by conveying conditions of worth (Trull & Phares, 2001). This point is crucial because unconditional positive regard is an important preliminary step in developing experiential freedom and critical for forward movement in the therapeutic process (Rogers, 1986a). If the client senses that the therapist is conveying conditions of worth, even through nonverbal behavior (e.g., looking away when infidelity is discussed), the client might begin to modify statements about his or her true feelings. This situation only hinders the therapeutic process. Even if the therapist does not approve of the client's behavior, it is important that unconditional positive regard be expressed. As an example, the therapist might disapprove of the emotional abuse of a spouse by the client. But the therapist still can express acceptance of the client as a person for seeking therapy to change this destructive behavior.
- *The therapist demonstrates empathic understanding.* The therapist should express empathic understanding by trying to experience what is said from the client's perspective (Bohart & Greenberg, 1997; Duan, Rose, & Kraatz, 2002; Greenberg et al., 1994; Trull & Phares, 2001). The therapist must realize that what is important is how the client perceives the events. For example, although the therapist can see that the client has many personal strengths, it is the client's perceived sense of helplessness that is creating much of the anxiety about the unhappy marriage.
- *The client is able to perceive the therapist's sense of unconditional positive regard and emphatic understanding.* It is not enough for the therapist to attempt to be accepting and understanding. The client must be able to see that this is the case. For example, sitting face to face with the client, the therapist might rephrase what the client has just said so that the client can see that what is being disclosed and discussed is being understood in a manner that is not judgmental.

While Rogers (1959) admits that other elements are usually present, he maintains that "These seem to be the necessary conditions of therapy" (p. 213). He believed that these six basic conditions are at the core of any form of successful therapy, not just person-centered therapy. As can be seen in "The Cultural Context of Personality Psychology," his ideals also seem to find support in culturally diverse treatment environments.

The Cultural Context of Personality Psychology

The Cultural Responsiveness Hypothesis: A Cross-Cultural Extension of Rogers's Ideals

Rogers spent a considerable amount of time trying to identify the critical factors and underlying dynamics of successful psychotherapeutic experiences. However, the clients that he and most other psychotherapists were dealing with in the 1940s, 1950s, and 1960s in the United States were probably in what Schofield (1964) describes as the YAVIS syndrome (young, attractive, verbally fluent, intelligent, and successful). As the diversity of our culture increases, mental health professions are providing services to a wider range of individuals, including those from lower socioeconomic classes and non-English-speakers (Trull & Phares, 2001). As a result of such shifts in client characteristics, concerns have been raised regarding the extent to which the ethnic match of client and therapist is a critical factor in treatment effectiveness.

At the core of the issue of client–therapist matching is the cultural responsiveness hypothesis. The **cultural responsiveness hypothesis** suggests that treatment effectiveness increases when the language and ethnic background of the therapist and the client are similar. (Nevid et al., 2000). While evidence from research on this hypothesis is mixed regarding whether or not ethnic matching increases therapeutic effectiveness, it does suggest that individuals who express a strong sense of ethnic identity with their own culture prefer ethnically similar counselors (H. L. K. Coleman, Wampold, & Casali, 1995) and that ethnic matching

has been associated with increases in treatment participation (e.g., less likelihood of terminating treatment after only one session, greater length of treatment) for a variety of ethnic groups (Sue, Fujino, Hu, Takeuchi, & Zane, 1991; Zane, Hall, Sue, Young, & Nunez, 2004).

Thus, although there may be some benefits of ethnic matching, "it is important to recognize that ethnicity alone is not a sole determinant of treatment effectiveness" (Nevid et al., 2000, p. 109). It is more likely that the sensitivity of the therapists and their ability to establish rapport are likely to be significant determinants of treatment effectiveness, whether working with clients of the same or different ethnicity (Sue, 1988; Zane et al., 2004). Such a conclusion provides a cross-cultural perspective in support of Rogers's own views on the determinants of treatment effectiveness.

In addition to identifying some of the necessary conditions associated with treatment effectiveness, Rogers developed a number of techniques for creating a therapeutic atmosphere of empathy and unconditional positive regard for the client (Rogers, 1952), as well as methods for assessing the outcome of treatment (Orlinsky, Rønnestad, & Willutzki, 2004). In the next section, we will consider Roger's efforts to measure treatment outcome.

Measuring the Outcome of Treatment: Assessing the Effects and Effectiveness of Person-Centered Therapy

Given his long association with some of the nation's most prestigious U.S. research universities, Carl Rogers was well aware of the valuable information that could be gained from rigorous research. It is through his research investigating the outcome of treatment that he made many significant contributions to the field of psychotherapy (Sommers-Flanagan & Sommers-Flanagan, 2004).

Rogers (1942a, 1942b) was one of the first major figures to systematically assess the effects and effectiveness of psychotherapy (Orlinsky et al., 2004). In his research on psychotherapy, he was concerned with assessing changes that occurred in the individual as a result of a successful therapeutic experience and identifying the factors associated with successful psychotherapy. He employed a number of methods to assess the effectiveness of person-centered therapy. For example, he and his colleagues would record the verbal dialogue of treatment sessions and perform content analysis on the type (e.g., belittling vs. self-affirming) and nature (e.g., blaming the self vs. blaming others) of statements clients made as therapy progressed. To assess changes in the clients, Rogers and his colleagues used various rating scales for measuring self-perceptions (e.g., ratings of the real and ideal self) and the nature of feelings expressed (e.g., degree of anxiety vs. happiness) at various points in the treatment process.

Assessing the Effects of Person-Centered Therapy Rogers (1958, 1959, 1961; Meador & Rogers, 1973; Raskin & Rogers, 1995) and others (Greenberg et al., 1994) noted several changes in the person, both during and after a successful therapeutic experience.

In the course of psychotherapy, one of the first changes clients begin to show is a greater tendency to express their feelings in words (e.g., an angry tone of voice) and behavior (e.g., pounding on the arm of the chair). Clients also begin to make more references to the self (e.g., "my feelings of anger") than to others (e.g., "my spouse's disappointment") as therapy progresses. Clients show a greater awareness of the incongruence within the self-concept and begin to express freely feelings that were directly related to it (e.g., anger with one's self for being so conforming). Clients also display a reduction in the distortion and denial of experiences related to feelings of incongruence (e.g., less likely to express anger for their own disappointments directed at a spouse or the children).

One of the most important breakthroughs that occurs during therapy is when the client becomes able to experience, without threat of removal, the therapist's unconditional positive regard. For example, sensing unconditional positive regard from the therapist, a client trying to make a career change might reveal deep feelings of disappointment related to the lack of support given by family members. Such changes within the person are at the basis of an increased level of congruence that Rogers believed would last after the successful therapeutic experience.

The Effectiveness of Person-Centered Therapy To maximize the possibility of achieving these positive outcomes, Rogers and others have concerned themselves with identifying the factors contributing to treatment

effectiveness. In two rather extensive reviews of the research investigating the interpersonal skills of certain therapists (Greenberg et al., 1994; Truax & Mitchell, 1971), it was noted that therapists or counselors who are accurately empathic (e.g., sensitive), nonpossessively warm in attitude (e.g., not dominating), and genuine (e.g., open-minded and not defensive) contribute to treatment effectiveness regardless of the type of treatment context (e.g., individual or group therapy), therapist's theoretical orientation (e.g., person-centered or psychoanalytical), and type of client (e.g., college underachievers, juvenile delinquents, or hospitalized schizophrenics). To consider two somewhat different sources of evidence in support of the relationship between treatment effectiveness from the Rogerian viewpoint, see "A Closer Look."

A Closer Look

The Impact of Therapist Warmth and Empathic Understanding: Learning to Touch Snakes and Love Yourself

The Impact of Therapeutic Warmth

The importance of "therapist warmth" was demonstrated in an interesting study done by Morris and Suckerman (1974), who looked at the effect of this variable on the treatment of snake phobias using a form of behavior therapy known as graduated practice. **Graduated practice** involves helping clients to overcome their fear of a specific object (e.g., dogs) or situation (e.g., public speaking) by gradually bringing them into closer proximity with it.

In their study, Morris and Suckerman initially assessed how close 23 snake-phobic female college students would be willing to get to a live, harmless, 3-foot king snake (e.g., be in the same room, touch the glass cage, or touch the snake) as a pretest measure of snake avoidance. Over the next couple of weeks, approximately two-thirds of the 23 women were then given six 20-minute sessions involving a standard treatment for snake phobia based on graduated practice. One group of these women received the treatment session from a therapist who behaved in a warm and compassionate manner. Another group received the *same* treatment from the *same* therapist who, for these women only, behaved in a cold and matter-of-fact manner. After completing all of the six sessions with either the "warm" or "cold" therapist, the extent to which the women were willing to approach the snake was assessed once again as a posttest measure. A third group of the women did not receive any type of treatment. The posttest measure of willingness to approach the snake for these women was obtained concurrently with that for the women in the warm and cold therapist conditions. For all of the women in the study, a second posttest measure was taken approximately $2^1/2$ months after the first measure.

The study results indicated that the women treated by the warm therapist exhibited a greater tendency to approach the snake during the posttest measures than did those treated by the cold therapist or those receiving no treatment at all. In addition, no difference was found between the approach behavior of the women treated by the cold therapist and those receiving no treatment at all. Such results demonstrate the significance of therapist warmth in affecting positive behavioral changes with treatment procedures other than the person-centered therapy approach.

The Impact of Empathic Understanding

One of the many sources of evidence Rogers used to evaluate the effectiveness of person-centered therapy was to look at the changes it brought about in clients. The following passage indicates that one important impact of empathic understanding is the greater level of self-acceptance and personal responsibility it can create in clients.

> ROGERS: A vivid example of this comes from a young man who has been the recipient of much sensitive understanding and who is now in the later stages of his therapy:
>
> CLIENT: I could not even conceive of it as a possibility that I could have a kind of tender concern for me. Still, how could I be tender, be concerned for *myself*, when they're one and the same thing? But yet I can feel it so clearly – you know, like taking care of a child. You want to give it this and give it that. I can kind of clearly see the purposes for somebody else, but I can never see them for myself, that I could do this for me, you know.

Is it possible that I can really want to take care of myself, and make that a major purpose of my life? That means I'd have to deal with the whole world as if I were guardian of the most cherished and most wanted possession, that this *I* was between this precious *me* that I wanted to take care of and the whole world. It's almost as if I *loved* myself; you know, that's strange – but it's true.

> ROGERS: It is, I believe, the therapist's caring understanding – exhibited in this excerpt – which has permitted this client to experience a high regard, even a love, for himself. (Rogers, 1980, p. 153)

Although these two sources of evidence are quite different, they have in common their support of the treatment effectiveness of a person-centered approach to therapy.

Although the effectiveness of person-centered therapy is well documented (Greenberg, Watson, & Lietaer, 1998), this therapeutic approach is not without its critics (K. M. Mitchell, Bozarth, & Krauft, 1977; Patterson, 2000; Stubbs & Bozarth, 1994). However, the extensive systematic research Rogers conducted and helped to inspire – investigating the effects of and factors responsible for effective person-centered therapy – can be used to support the validity of the Rogerian viewpoint of personality and psychotherapy. A survey of the research on these and other changes within the individual following successful therapy can be found in Rogers and Dymond's (1954) classic textbook *Psychotherapy and Personality Change* and a book chapter titled "Research on Experiential Psychotherapies" (Greenberg et al., 1994).

The principal ideas discussed in this section are outlined in "Summing It Up: The Essentials of Person-Centered Therapy" on p. 220.

It is safe to say that not since Freud has any single person influenced the field of psychotherapy as much as Carl Rogers (Smith, 1982). His development of person-centered therapy and his emphasis on investigating the therapeutic process and its outcomes are unparalleled contributions to psychotherapy. An example of his legacy in promoting the understanding of the therapeutic process can be seen in "At the Cutting Edge of Personality Psychology: Therapy and Technology" on p. 220.

Summing It Up *The Essentials of Person-Centered Therapy*

The Necessary Therapeutic Conditions:

- *The presence of contact*. The therapist and client interact in a meaningful manner.
- *The client is incongruent*. The client must be experiencing a sufficient degree of anxiety to be motivated to seek therapy.
- *The therapist is congruent*. The therapist is completely honest when interacting with the client.
- *The therapist expresses unconditional positive regard*. The therapist's interactions with the client are totally accepting and without judgment.
- *The therapist demonstrates empathic understanding*. During the process of therapy, the therapist tries to experience it from the client's point of view.
- *The client perceives the therapist's unconditional positive regard and empathic understanding*. Through the words and actions of the therapist, the client is able to sense the presence of the unconditional positive regard and empathic understanding.

Measuring the Outcome of Treatment:

- *The effects*. Changes occurring both during and after therapy indicate clients relate to themselves and others differently.
- *The effectiveness*. While being more effective than no treatment or other forms of psychotherapy, the effectiveness of person-centered therapy depends on characteristics of the therapist and client.

AT THE CUTTING EDGE OF PERSONALITY PSYCHOLOGY

Therapy and Technology

During much of his professional life, Rogers spent a considerable amount of time trying to identify and assess the underlying dynamics and critical factors

While e-therapy makes it possible for a therapist to conduct a therapy session with a client who might be hundreds of miles away, there are many unanswered questions regarding the effectiveness of such techniques.

of psychotherapy. Such pioneering efforts did much to lift the veil of mystery associated with psychotherapy for the general public. Some 50 years later, the Internet is a force adding new mysteries to the process of psychotherapy. With the increased presence of the Internet in our daily lives, it should come as no surprise that recent innovations in therapeutic processes involve a number of online services for helping individuals to deal with a variety of personal concerns (Rochlen, Zack, & Speyer, 2004; Rosen, 2005). **E-therapy** involves the delivery of therapeutic information and services to individuals over the Internet. For example, virtual support groups are online chat groups devoted to particular topics, such as depression, anxiety, sexual orientation issues, substance abuse, and shyness, that allow individuals to talk about their problems and concerns with others having similar problems and concerns. Another online therapeutic development is the appearance of computer software programs that offer help for specific disorders. For example,

MoodGYM is an interactive program that offers help to those experiencing depression (H. Christensen, Griffiths, Groves, & Korten, 2006; H. Christensen, Griffiths, & Jorm, 2004).

In the spirit of Rogers's efforts to assess the effectiveness of treatment outcome and the characteristic features associated with successful treatment, there is systematic research to indicate that some of these online services are indeed helpful (Lange, van de Ven, Schrieken, & Smith, 2004; Rochlen et al., 2004). In addition to making therapeutic services available on a 24-hour basis at a reasonable cost to a wide variety of individuals, the benefits noted by users of such online therapeutic services include offering individuals the opportunity to present their thoughts and feelings in a nonevaluative environmental context and receiving empathy from others (Griffiths & Christensen, 2006; Jacobs et al., 2001; Landau, 2001; Mortley, Wade, & Enderby, 2004).

However, along with these benefits, there are also some concerns that should be noted with the use of these online services, such as issues of confidentiality (e.g., online users revealing your personal information to others without your knowledge), the quality of the training of individuals who might be offering therapeutic advice to others, and the education of the general population with respect to the benefits and limitations of such services, to name just a few. In response to such concerns, the APA, the largest U.S. association of professional psychologists, is actively addressing the issues associated with the delivery of therapeutic services electronically (Rabasca, 2000; Zur, 2007).

These are only some of the concerns and issues that will need to be addressed in an attempt to lift the veil of mystery associated with online therapeutic services available to the general public, as well as for practitioners. However, as Rogers pointed out over 50 years ago, what still seems to be important for those seeking assistance for their emotional concerns, be it during an in-person interaction with a therapist or online in a virtual chat room, is a nonjudgmental setting (e.g., unconditional positive regard) and experiencing a sense of empathy from others. This seems to support the old saying of "The more things change, the more they remain the same." Thus, it is probably a safe bet that no matter what therapies look like 50 years from now, unconditional positive regard and empathy will certainly be critical factors in the therapeutic process, as Rogers noted initially.

Personality Assessment from the Rogerian Viewpoint: Measuring the Personal World

The focus of personality assessment from the Rogerian viewpoint is an attempt to measure the individual's personal world. Measuring this personal world involves trying to understand how the individual views his or her sense of self. The Q-Sort technique is a method most often associated with personality assessment from this viewpoint (R. J. Cohen & Swerdlik, 2005; Gregory, 2007).

The Q-Sort Technique The **Q-Sort technique** (Stephenson, 1953) is designed to systematically assess the way people perceive themselves through the use of a set of self-descriptive statements (R. J. Cohen & Swerdlik, 2005). When performing a Q-Sort, the individual is given a large number (e.g., 100) of self-descriptive statements printed on separate cards and asked to sort them into a limited number of piles (e.g., nine) ranging from "least like me" (i.e., "1") to "most like me" (e.g., "9").

Although there are a number of different instructional sets for sorting the statements, one of the most common is the self–ideal sort (R. J. Cohen & Swerdlik, 2005; Gregory, 2007). With the **self–ideal sort**, the individual is asked first to perform a self-sort. In a **self-sort**, the individual sorts the statements according to how he or she perceives himself or herself now. After it has been noted in which pile each statement is placed, the individual is then asked to perform an ideal sort. In an **ideal sort**, the individual sorts the statements into piles on the basis of ideal person he or she would like to be. Again, it is noted in which pile each statement is placed. Because each statement is assigned a number according to the pile in which it was placed after each sort, it is possible to calculate the correlation coefficient between the ratings of the statements for the different sorts. The higher this correlation, the greater the degree of similarity between the way the individual sees himself or herself and the way he or she would like to be.

A high degree of similarity in self-perceptions was seen by Rogers as a measure of personality adjustment (R. J. Cohen & Swerdlik, 2005; Gregory, 2007). Thus, from the Rogerian viewpoint, the significance of the Q-Sort technique is that it makes it possible to quantify objectively the subjective perception of the self-concept. As a means of obtaining some firsthand experience with a Q-Sort type of activity, try for yourself the exercise outlined in "You Can Do It."

You Can Do It

Using a Q-Sort Exercise: What "Sort" of Person Are You?

Instructions

Using the nine-point scale listed below, perform the following self-sort.

Self-sort:

For each of the 20 items listed below, rate the extent to which you feel each statement is characteristic of how you perceive yourself now.

After you have completed the self-sort, cover your responses with a piece of paper and complete the following ideal sort using the same nine-point scale.

Ideal sort:

For each of the 20 items below, rate the extent to which you feel each statement is characteristic of how you perceive your ideal self.

Rating Scale

Not at all characteristic	Moderately characteristic	Extremely characteristic
1 2 3	4 5 6	7 8 9

	Self-sort rating	Ideal sort rating
1. Relate well with opposite-sex others	____	____
2. Demonstrate a sense of humor	____	____
3. Accept others' faults	____	____
4. Tend to procrastinate	____	____
5. Am sensitive to the feelings of others	____	____
6. Handle criticism well	____	____

7. Exhibit sudden mood fluctuations	____	____
8. Am optimistic about most things	____	____
9. Am talkative in social situations	____	____
10. See myself as physically attractive	____	____
11. Express opinions openly	____	____
12. Relate well with same-sex others	____	____
13. Like to engage in daydreaming	____	____
14. Am basically anxious	____	____
15. Attract the confidence of others	____	____
16. Tend to self-indulgence	____	____
17. Prefer to be alone than with others	____	____
18. Feel self-confident	____	____
19. Trust the motives of others	____	____
20. Possess a sense of direction in life	____	____

Interpretation

Note that it is not the size of the numbers that is important (e.g., having all 8s or 9s), but the degree of similarity between the numbers in the self and ideal columns. The greater the similarity between the two sets of numbers, the closer you are to the type of person you would like to be. If you are like most other college students, your responses for the two sorts are probably close on some statements but far apart on others. It should be noted that this is not a true Q-Sort technique, since only a rather limited number of self-descriptive statements are used and the items are rated rather than sorted.

The Q-Sort technique has been used extensively to measure the effectiveness of psychotherapy by assessing changes in the degree of congruence that have occurred within individuals as a result of receiving therapy. The logic has been that if the therapy is effective, a higher correlation between the self- and ideal-sorts should be observed after therapy than before it.

One of the most frequently cited studies using the Q-Sort technique for this purpose is by Butler and Haigh (1954). They reported a self–ideal average correlation of $r = -.01$ for a group of clients before ther-

apy. When the self–ideal sorts were examined after therapy, the average correlations were $r = .34$ for the post-counseling sort and $r = .31$ for a follow-up sort obtained a period of time after therapy. As a basis of comparison, self–ideal sorts were also obtained for a control group of individuals not requiring therapy at approximately the same time. The correlations between the self–ideal sorts were $r = .58$ for the pre-therapy sort and $r = .59$ for the follow-up sort. A more extensive example of the application of the Q-Sort technique to assess the effectiveness of psychotherapy is presented in "Applications in Personality Psychology."

Applications in Personality Psychology

The Q-Sort Technique in Psychotherapy: "Sorting" Out the Outcome of the Therapeutic Experience

In an elaborate application of the Q-Sort technique to assess the effectiveness of psychotherapy, a study was done that included four different therapy groups and two separate control groups (Butler, 1968). Three of the therapy groups received traditional person-centered therapy. The fourth received treatment based on Adlerian therapy. The two control groups included a "normal" group and a "client" group. The normal control group consisted of people who did not appear to need therapy. The client control group consisted of people who had sought psychotherapy but were placed on a 10-week waiting list. This client control group was tested at the onset of the 10-week period and then again 10 weeks later. The inclusion of this group is important because it provides a more valid test of the effectiveness of therapy by directly comparing those who needed therapy and received it (i.e., the four therapy groups) with those who did not (i.e., the client control group).

The results of this study are summarized in Figure 6.2. The nature of the correlations for the pre- and posttest sorts for those receiving therapy increased in a positive direction. This pattern of results indicates a greater degree of congruence within the individual after therapy than before it. The correlations for those clients requiring but not receiving

therapy remained relatively low and unchanged. In addition to validating the Q-Sort technique, these results make it clear that it was the therapy, not just the passage of time, that produced the positive changes within the clients. Without the client control group, this conclusion would not have been possible.

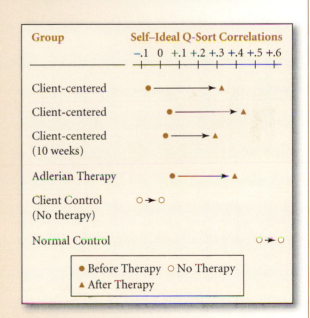

Group	Self–Ideal Q-Sort Correlations
	−.1 0 +.1 +.2 +.3 +.4 +.5 +.6
Client-centered	
Client-centered	
Client-centered (10 weeks)	
Adlerian Therapy	
Client Control (No therapy)	
Normal Control	

● Before Therapy ○ No Therapy
▲ After Therapy

Figure 6.2   A comparison of the mean correlations for self–ideal Q-Sorts before and after therapy for the treatment and control groups.
*The higher and more positive the correlation, the greater the degree of congruence within the self-concept.
Source: Based on Butler (1968)

Although the Q-Sort technique is used to study the effectiveness of psychotherapy (R. J. Cohen & Swerdlik, 2005; Gregory, 2007; Lambert & Hill, 1994; Rogers, 1959; Rogers & Dymond, 1954), it is not limited to this single application. Research involving theory testing used the technique to investigate the basic structure of personality and the stability of personality over time (Bem & Funder, 1978; Block, 1971; Caspi & Roberts, 1999; Funder & Block, 1989; Funder, Block, & Block, 1983; Funder, Parke, Tomlinson-Keasey, & Widaman, 1993; McCrae, Costa, & Busch, 1986; Ozer & Gjerde, 1989).

The Q-Sort technique has also been used to help distinguish career from noncareer naval officers, assess the importance of various aspects of nurses' work, obtain students' evaluations of teachers, study the views about children and family life held by the mothers of schizophrenic patients, and examine the services provided by a counseling agency over a four-year period (Wittenborn, 1961). Other areas of application of Q-Sort techniques include assessment in educational settings (Stephenson, 1980), of attachment security in preschoolers (DeMulder, Denham, Schmidt, & Mitchell, 2000), of leadership values in military personnel (Cassel, 1958), of perceived occupational desirability during vocational and occupational counseling (Tyler, 1961; Williams, 1978), and of variables associated with suicidal behavior (Yufit, 1988). In short, a major strength of the technique is its versatility. For more information about the various applications of the Q-Sort technique, Brown lists some 277 references from which to choose among the over 580 references in his "Bibliography on Q Technique and Its Methodology" (S. R. Brown, 1968).

Although the Q-Sort technique has been used extensively in a number of areas, a major criticism of it is based on the extent to which people can provide reliable and valid self-report information that is not biased by the desire to make themselves look good (Jackson & Messick, 1958; Lanyon & Goodstein, 1997). However, others have found self-report information to be extremely useful in the study of the structure of personality, classification of personality disorders, assessment of treatment effectiveness, and other related areas (Bem & Allen, 1974; Bem & Funder, 1978; Merluzzi, Glass, & Genest, 1981; Mischel, 1972, 1981; Westen & Gabbard, 1999; Westen & Shedler, 1999).

Additional Applications of Rogers's Viewpoint

Only three major applications of the Rogerian viewpoint have been discussed in this section, but Rogers made serious attempts to extend the application of his views to a wide variety of other areas (Raskin & Rogers, 1995). These include social issues (Rogers, 1977), classroom teaching and learning (Rogers, 1969, 1983), marriage and family life (Rogers, 1972), play therapy for children (Axline, 1947; Ellinwood & Raskin, 1993), group therapy (Rogers, 1970), medical education (Rogers, 1980), the reduction of interracial and intercultural tension (McGaw, Rice, & Rogers, 1973; Rogers, 1986b), nuclear proliferation (Rogers & Ryback, 1984), and world peace (Rogers, 1982, 1987).

Evaluating the Rogerian Viewpoint: Strengths and Limitations

Characteristic Strengths

Here are some strengths of the Rogerian viewpoint:

- *Emphasis on research.* Probably the most significant strength of Rogers's viewpoint is the emphasis he placed on systematic research as a means of verifying all aspects of his theory and applications (Comer, 2007; Lakin, 1998; Trull & Phares, 2001). Rogers wanted to understand and investigate systematically the underlying processes and dynamics that contributed to a successful therapeutic experience (Sommers-Flanagan & Sommers-Flanagan, 2004; Trull & Phares, 2001). In his research, he employed a number of innovative techniques (e.g., content analysis of recorded therapy sessions, Q-Sort methodology). His use of the therapy session as a "research laboratory" did much to take some of the mystery out of psychotherapy for the general public. It is probably safe to say that his emphasis on research, and the impact of that emphasis on the field of psychotherapy, are second only to the influence of Freud.

- *An emphasis on the person.* Rogers promoted the view of people as having free will and responsibility over their actions (Trull & Phares, 2001; Tudor & Worrall, 2006). He also emphasized the conscious and subjective experiences of the individual as critical factors in determining behavior. While such views seem rather straightforward today, they were extremely different from the Freudian and behavioristic viewpoints of the 1940s and 1950s that were so dominant at the time Rogers was formulating his theory of personality and psychotherapy.

- *The impact of the Rogerian viewpoint.* The impact of the Rogerian viewpoint is significant inside as well as outside the field of personality psychology (Sommers-Flanagan & Sommers-Flanagan, 2004). In personality psychology, the perspective offered a totally different way of viewing the individual and expressed this view most clearly in person-centered therapy. Not since psychoanalysis has a specific form of therapy so significantly influenced the way psychotherapy is conducted (Comer, 2007; Trull & Phares, 2001). The overall impact of the viewpoint was facilitated by Rogers's dedication to systematic research and the respect this brought him – and his ideas – in the academic and psychotherapeutic communities.

  In addition to having its substantial impact on psychotherapy, the Rogerian viewpoint can be found outside of personality psychology in such areas as education, child-rearing practices, management training, and employee relations. In short, the viewpoint has made quite a name for itself through its extensive application in a wide variety of areas.

Characteristic Limitations

The Rogerian viewpoint has the following limitations:

- *Emphasis on the subjective experience and self-report.* A major limitation of the Rogerian viewpoint is its emphasis on the subjective experiences and self-reports of individuals (Trull & Phares, 2001). The basis of this limitation is the extent to which we can rely on what people say about themselves. For example, how much should the therapist rely on the subjective experiences and self-perceptions of clients to identify the source of their problems? How much should a therapist rely on clients to tell the truth as opposed to what they think the therapist wants to hear? In defense of Rogers's position, it should be known that he was aware of such possibilities. He felt, however, that if a warm and nonjudgmental therapeutic environment were created, a skillful therapist would be able to help clients see the true nature of their problems and elicit honest responses. But the validity of what others say about themselves is still in question.

- *Theoretical simplicity.* The Rogerian viewpoint is said to be theoretically rather simplistic and naive. It has been labeled simplistic because of its reliance on a relatively small number of theoretical constructs. Much of what Rogers says about the nature and dynamics of personality can be summarized with two concepts: congruence and self-actualization.

  This theoretical simplicity is also reflected in the rather limited explanation of the nature of personality development. Although Rogers specifies which factors are important (e.g., unconditional positive regard and positive self-regard), he does not discuss or examine in much detail the specifics of the processes and dynamics involved. Instead, he assumes that the same processes and dynamics that foster the development of an adjusted personality in adults during therapy will operate in a similar manner for children. The naiveté of Rogers's viewpoint is also said to be reflected in his emphasis on the conscious mind and the validity he attributes to self-report information while almost completely ignoring the unconscious mind. Thus, his view of human nature has been characterized as somewhat superficial.

- *Criticisms of person-centered therapy.* Person-centered therapy has come under attack as being a technique more than a therapy (Trull & Phares, 2001). Critics say that anyone who can learn how to make reassuring and reflective responses is in a position to perform person-centered therapy. As more fuel for this argument, training in this approach is popular in educational programs for social workers, counselors, and seminarians. These programs tend to be relatively brief (e.g., two years), are conducted outside of psychology programs (e.g., schools of sociology, education, and religious studies), and require only a minimal amount of education in psychology. Sometimes the training is viewed as nothing more than hand-holding that treats all clients alike regardless of their disorder.

  In his defense, Rogers spent more than 20 years in association with the Center for the Studies of the Person in La Jolla, California, a training and research institute for person-centered therapy. He was deeply committed to training qualified therapists and examining the dynamics of psychotherapy. He would certainly not have accepted the argument that simply being able to reflect what was said back to the client would constitute "doing therapy."

A final criticism of person-centered therapy is that its effectiveness seems to be limited to helping people suffering from mild to moderate emotional problems of adjustment related to everyday living (e.g., loneliness, family- or job-related stress, and problems of self-esteem; Trull & Phares, 2001). However, like any other form of treatment, person-centered therapy was never meant to be a therapeutic cure-all.

A summary of the principal ideas discussed in this section is presented in "Summing It Up: Characteristic Strengths and Limitations of the Rogerian Viewpoint."

Summing It Up *Characteristic Strengths and Limitations of the Rogerian Viewpoint*

Characteristic Strengths:

- *Emphasis on Research.* Rogers was deeply committed to empirical investigation in a systematic attempt to validate his theoretical and therapeutic contributions.
- *Emphasis on the Person.* Rogers promoted a humanistic view of the individual that stressed conscious awareness and free will.
- *The Impact of the Rogerian Viewpoint.* In addition to having a major impact on the nature of psychotherapy, the Rogerian viewpoint has been applied to a wide variety of areas outside of the field of personality psychology.

Characteristic Limitations:

- *Emphasis on the Subjective Experience.* The Rogerian viewpoint has been criticized for the emphasis and validity it gives to the individual's perception of reality and its impact on behavior.
- *Theoretical Simplicity.* The Rogerian viewpoint has been criticized because of the relatively few constructs making up the theory and its naive assumptions about behavior, including a lack of emphasis on unconscious influences.
- *Person-Centered Therapy as a Technique.* Person-centered therapy has been viewed as an easily taught technique consisting of relatively few types of verbal responses automatically applied to all forms of psychological disorders.

Some Closing Remarks on Rogers's Viewpoint

Rogers's ideas were unique in that he, like Freud, proposed a viewpoint of personality that sharply contrasted with the dominant thinking at the time. Rogers's attention and devotion to systematic research made contributions to the study of personality that will remain for many years. More information about the Rogerian viewpoint can be found in *Person-Centered Therapy: A Clinical Philosophy* (Tudor & Worral, 2006), a comprehensive historical and contemporary discussion of the basic principles and processes. A more personal account of Rogers's viewpoint can be found in his book *A Way of Being* (1980), a very readable account of his general theory, his thoughts on many important social issues, and recent developments in his philosophy. Of particular interest are his thoughts concerning "the person of tomorrow" (pp. 348–356).

With our discussion of Rogers's viewpoint complete, we will now turn our attention to another individual who help to establish the humanistic tradition in the study of personality psychology – Abraham H. Maslow.

Maslow's Motivational Perspective: Meeting the Needs of the Person

Like Carl Rogers, Abraham Maslow formulated his viewpoint of personality in reaction to the pessimistic psychodynamic explanation of the unconsciously controlled individual and to **behaviorism**, a dominant school of thought in psychology during the first three-quarters of the twentieth century, and its emphasis on the role of environmental factors as principal determinants of behavior (Maslow, 1970b). Maslow felt that individuals are motivated by the desire for self-enhancement and self-actualization in a manner that goes well beyond satisfying base unconscious needs and simply reacting to external stimuli (Rathus & Nevid, 2002). He emphasized the creative, spontaneous, and optimistic side of human nature over its dark, more pessimistic side (Moss, 2001). For a glimpse into the life of a man who formulated a viewpoint of personality based on people's strengths, see "A Closer Look" on p. 227.

A Closer Look

The Life of Abraham H. Maslow

Abraham H. Maslow, the first of seven children, was born on April 1, 1908, in a Jewish district of Brooklyn, New York. His parents, who were Russian immigrants, owned a barrel-manufacturing company. As the business improved, the Maslows moved their family out of the slums and into a lower-middle-class neighborhood. In the new neighborhood, Maslow was the only Jewish boy and the target of much anti-Semitism. As a result, he spent much of his time alone reading books in the library. His relationship with his parents was also somewhat difficult. He talked about being afraid as a child of his father, and about his mother as probably being schizophrenic. Despite Maslow's strained relationships with his parents, he developed a very close relationship with his mother's brother. He attributed his mental stability to the care and attention he received from his uncle.

Abraham H. Maslow developed a viewpoint of personality that attempted to explain the motivation behind what makes great people great and good people want to be the best that they can possibly be.

After high school, Maslow was persuaded by his father to attend college to study law. Because he was not particularly interested in being a lawyer, Maslow's grades were not very good. He was also troubled by career uncertainty and his love for a woman of whom his parents disapproved. He dealt with these troubled times by leaving New York and enrolling at the University of Wisconsin. Shortly after moving there, Maslow (who was then 20) returned to New York to marry his childhood sweetheart, 19-year-old Bertha Goodman. The newlyweds then returned to Wisconsin. As an indication of the emotional difficulty of his early life, Maslow stated that he really did not start living until he married Bertha and moved to Wisconsin.

Maslow stayed at Wisconsin to earn his BA (1930), MA (1931), and PhD (1934). The educational training he received there emphasized the rigorous and objective scientific approach to the study of psychology that had become popular. His doctoral dissertation, which dealt with the sexual behavior of monkeys, was under the direction of the famous experimental psychologist Harry Harlow. Upon completing his PhD, Maslow returned to New York and accepted a position at Columbia University as a research assistant to Edwin L. Thorndike, another famous psychologist. Maslow also started teaching at Brooklyn College, where he stayed until 1951. During this time, he began to extend his early research on the establishment of dominance in monkey colonies to the study of dominance in humans.

Because many of Europe's leading psychologists, psychiatrists, and other intellectuals were settling in New York to escape the Nazis, Maslow was able to meet, interact with, and learn from such personality theorists as Karen Horney and Alfred Adler. Such a stimulating environment would be enough to affect most people's thinking, but Maslow reported that it was the birth of his first child that significantly affected his views. He proclaimed that all of his academic knowledge and training and scientific research with rats and monkeys did little to prepare him for the wonder and mysteries of an infant child. As a result, he shifted his attention away from the study of animals and began to study what he felt were the motivating forces behind personality out of a sincere desire to discover how to improve it.

In 1951, Maslow left Brooklyn College to accept a position at Brandeis University. He remained there until 1969. During that time, he continued to develop and refine his theory on the nature of human motivation, which attracted a considerable amount of recognition.

In 1967, Maslow was elected to the prestigious office of president of the APA. He left Brandeis University to become a resident fellow of the Laughlin Charitable Foundation in California, where he began a large-scale study applying his theory of human motivation and the philosophy of humanistic psychology to such topics as politics, economics, religion, and ethics. Because of all his efforts, he is considered a major force in the development of the humanistic movement in psychology (Moss, 2001).

Having had a history of heart trouble, Maslow died of a heart attack on June 8, 1970.

Basic Assumptions of Maslow's Perspective: Looking at the Positive Personality

Maslow believed the study of personality had a tradition of looking at the individual in somewhat negative terms: as being governed either by unconscious forces or by environmentally determined ones. By contrast, he proposed a positive viewpoint of the individual that has become known as the **third force** in psychology, with the psychodynamic emphasis on unconscious processes and the behaviorist emphasis on environmental controls on behavior being the two other forces. The emphasis of this third force has been to enhance people's dignity by studying the internal processes contributing to their self-directed self-enhancement.

A Positive View of the Individual

Like Rogers, Maslow viewed the individual as constantly striving for a sense of self-enhancement at a level of conscious awareness (Comer, 2007; Moss, 2001; Trull & Phares, 2001). He viewed people as basically good but somewhat weak in that they can easily fall victim to diversions that distract them from self-enhancement. For example, although going to school is an activity that reflects a desire for self-enhancement, any student would have little trouble listing occasions when he or she might have gotten distracted by going out with friends instead of studying for a test or working on a term paper in the library. Fortunately, most

students do eventually get back on track, even if it means staying up all night to do the required work. Thus, at the same time he recognized that they have faults, Maslow felt that people are basically good and motivated toward self-enhancement (Ellis, 1995; Raskin & Rogers, 2000).

An Emphasis on Investigating the Healthy Personality

Maslow felt the emphasis on studying clients in the context of psychotherapy resulted in a restricted view of people that revealed little about the characteristics of the healthy personality. As a result, he reasoned that to better understand emotionally healthy people, the emphasis should be on studying in detail those who best exemplify the emotionally healthy personality (Barone & Kominars, 1998; Moss, 2001). Much of Maslow's own research focused on an in-depth analysis of what he defined as "the best of the best individuals" in various disciplines, including Albert Einstein, Abraham Lincoln, and Ludwig van Beethoven.

The Motivational Nature of Personality and the Dynamic Satisfaction of Needs

Maslow viewed people as rarely being in a state of complete satisfaction. Instead, he believed that we are constantly being motivated to meet a variety of biological and psychological needs. The meeting of these needs was assumed to operate in a dynamic process rather than in isolation (Maddi, 1996; Reis & Patrick, 1996). For example, doing well in college will make it possible to obtain a comfortable salary to help meet basic biological needs for food and shelter; and it also meets the psychological needs of self-respect and gaining the respect of others.

The principal ideas examined in this section are presented in "Summing It Up: Basic Assumptions of Maslow's Motivational Perspective" on p. 229.

Basic Concepts of Maslow's Perspective: The Nature and Structure of Human Needs

The basic concepts of Maslow's viewpoint include his conceptualization of the nature and structure of human needs and their motivational impact on the individual. The principal objective of these needs is the motivation of the individual to reach a state of self-

Summing It Up *Basic Assumptions of Maslow's Motivational Perspective*

Basic Assumption	Description	Example
Positive View of the Person	Individuals are viewed as basically good and seeking self-enhancement while still having the potential to be distracted from this process of personal growth.	An individual stops at a doughnut shop after an exercise class and dieting all week, but promises to get back on the diet.
Emphasis on the Healthy Personality	To better understand personality, Maslow stressed looking at the most emotionally healthy individuals that could be found.	Knowledge of how to cope more effectively with stress in our everyday life has been enhanced by examining the successful coping strategies used by individuals who experienced severe stress, such as victims of natural disasters.
Motivational Nature of Personality	The process of motivation involves individuals constantly seeking to meet a variety of interrelated biological and psychological needs.	Wearing stylish clothes not only keeps a person warm (i.e., a biological need) but gains for the individual the recognition of friends (i.e., a psychological need).

actualization. For Maslow, the **state of self-actualization** involves people's attempts to reach their full potential by using their talents and abilities to the fullest extent while trying to achieve personal growth, satisfaction, and fulfillment. He organized human needs in a manner designed to promote the achievement of this state. Grouping the needs into two main categories, he then arranged them in a hierarchy of five needs.

The Categories of Needs: Deficiency and Being Needs

Maslow (1970b) made the following distinction between deficiency needs and being needs:

- **Deficiency needs** are the lower, more basic needs necessary for the survival of the individual, including hunger, thirst, and safety. The deficiency needs motivate the individual to engage in behavior designed to bring about their satisfaction.
- **Being needs** are the higher needs necessary for the achievement of a state of self-actualization, including those needs reflecting a desire for wisdom and a sense of aesthetics.

The being needs motivate the individual to engage in behavior designed to bring about their fulfillment (e.g., going to college or an art museum). Deficiency needs are characterized by a lack of something the individual is motivated to supply. Being needs are characterized by an ongoing motivational process of self-enhancement, not a deficiency in a need requiring only satisfaction. The lower needs are considered to be more potent and to have a greater influence on behavior than the higher ones. As a result of these features, the lower needs are also generally satisfied before the higher needs. When your stomach is making loud, grumbling noises, it is difficult to fully appreciate a Van Gogh painting. In this case, a quick trip to the snack bar will satisfy the hunger, making it possible to once again focus more attention on the higher aesthetic needs and pleasures. As this example illustrates, both types of needs are important in helping to motivate people in their attempts to achieve the state of self-actualization.

The Hierarchy of Needs: The Road to Self-Actualization

Maslow (1970b) organized human needs into five main groups in a hierarchical fashion. The logic of the

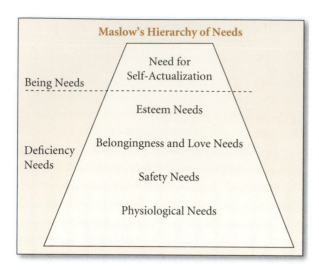

Maslow's Hierarchy of Needs

Need for Self-Actualization

Being Needs

Esteem Needs

Belongingness and Love Needs

Deficiency Needs

Safety Needs

Physiological Needs

Figure 6.3 Maslow's hierarchy of needs is organized with the lowest, most potent needs at the bottom and the highest, least potent needs at the top.

hierarchy of needs is that the needs at the lower end of the hierarchy exert more power in that they exert a greater sense of urgency to be satisfied than the needs at the next level. Progressing up the hierarchy of needs results in the individual coming closer to achieving the state of self-actualization (Schwartz, 2000). Figure 6.3 illustrates Maslow's hierarchical arrangement of needs.

Physiological Needs: The Most Basic Needs   At the bottom of the hierarchy are the most basic physiological needs. **Physiological needs** are those directly related to the survival of the individual. They include the need for food, water, sleep, and elimination. Such needs are extremely potent and when unfulfilled can dominate the life of the individual. For example, ideals like democracy and justice mean little to people who are on the brink of starvation. To what extent are people meeting these most basic of needs?

THE NEED FOR WATER   Although 75 percent of the world's surface is water, only 1 percent is readily usable by people around the world. Estimates indicate that about 1 billion people worldwide lack access to clean drinking water, and 40 percent of the world's population suffers regularly from serious water shortages (Noonoo, 2007). However, for individuals reading this book, access to usable water is probably no further than the bottle of water near your book or a short walk to a drinking fountain.

THE NEED FOR FOOD   While it is hard for many of us to imagine hunger as part of our daily life, this is not the case for many individuals around the world. The Food and Agricultural Organization of the United Nations (2006) estimated that in 2006 there were 854 million undernourished people worldwide, with 824 million people in the developing world being affected by chronic hunger. It also might surprise many of you that even in such a wealthy, industrious, and technologically advance culture as the United States, estimates indicate that in the same year approximately 22.7 million adults (10 percent of all adults) and 12.4 million children (16.9 percent of all children) were food insecure – struggling to meet their daily nutritional needs (Food Research and Action Center, 2006). On the other hand, it is clear that for many individuals around the world the basic need for food is being met in a more than adequate manner. The best example of this is the rising rate of obesity in adults and children in such diverse regions of the world as Europe, Asia, Africa, and especially the United States. The World Health Organization (2007) estimates that worldwide in 2007, there were approximately 1 billion overweight adults, with at least 300 million of them being obese. Estimates worldwide indicate that 22 million children under the age of five are overweight. Trends that seem to be contributing to this rising rate include: spending less time and energy obtaining food (e.g., going to the local grocery store for food vs. hunting and gathering), increased size of portions at restaurants and in pre-packaged foods (e.g., the "super-size" theme), increased consumption of high-fat, processed foods (e.g., soft drinks and fried foods), and a decrease in the amount of physical activity in our daily life (e.g., less exercising and more sedentary video gaming), to name just a few (Slentz et al., 2004; World Health Organization, 2007).

THE NEED FOR SLEEP   Like water and food, sleep also has its survival value in helping to restore both the body (e.g., rest muscles) and the mind (e.g., consolidate the memory of newly formed facts, such as the location of food sources and safe locations; Beuckmann & Yanagisawa, 2002; Gais & Born, 2004; Wagner et al., 2004). While most of you who are reading this book are getting enough water and food to meet those basic needs, chances are good that you are not meeting your need for sleep. It has been reported that college students in North America (Hicks, Fernandez, & Pelligrini, 2001) and Latin and South American countries

(Valencia-Flores et al., 1998) get less sleep than other people their own age. Possible factors contributing to this self-induced sleep loss include the academic demands placed on being a student combined with the responsibilities associated with job and family obligations and recreational activities, such as hanging out with friends, playing computer games, and surfing the Internet. Even short-term sleep deprivation can have serious consequences for individuals' survival (Gaba & Howard, 2002; Landrigan et al., 2004), including increases in mistakes made by medical personnel, auto accidents (D. Coleman, 1992; Dawson & Reid, 1997), and personal injury (Valent, Brusaferro, & Barbone, 2001).

For a firsthand look at the extent to which you are meeting these basic physiological needs, consider the material in "You Can Do It" below.

Maslow proposed that when physiological needs are routinely met, people can devote more of their energies to meeting the next level of needs – safety needs.

Safety Needs: The Desire for Stability **Safety needs** are those directly related to creating an environment for living that is free from the threat of danger. They include the need for order, predictability, and structure. For most people, safety needs are met by the dwellings in which they live and by the security and predictability they provide. No matter how hectic your day might have been, settling into an evening routine adds a sense of stability and security to your life. On the other hand, the trauma of being burglarized probably stems from the fact that the one place most people feel a sense of security has been violated. Just as routine seems to add to our sense of safety, as we will discuss next, changes in our life seem to create a threat to such a sense of security.

LIFE CHANGES AS A THREAT TO SAFETY NEEDS Without question, the terrorist attacks of 9/11 served as a universal and personal life-changing event. One of the major consequences of such catastrophic events is

You Can Do It

A Personal Look at the Bottom of the Hierarchy of Needs: Are You Meeting Your Physiological Needs?

What does it take to meet the physiological needs at the bottom of Maslow's hierarchy? To what extent are you meeting some of your major physiological needs? You can find out by comparing your efforts with the recommendations provided by some leading health organizations.

- *Water*. Are you drinking enough water each day? It is recommended by the Institute of Medicine that men should consume approximately 3.0 liters (about 13 cups) and women approximately 2.2 liters (about 9 cups) of water per day (www.mayoclinic.com/health/water/NU00283).

- *Food*. Are you getting enough to eat? You can assess the extent to which you are getting enough – or too much – to eat by assessing your **body mass index** (BMI), which is a numerical value used to determine whether your height is proportional to your weight, and as an index of your vulnerability to health risks (e.g., hypertension, heart attack, diabetes). A simple measure of your BMI is to divide your weight in kilograms (1 kilogram = 2.2 pounds) by the square of your height in meters (1 meter = 39.37 inches). Individuals with a BMI of 25 to 29.9 are considered to be overweight. Individuals with a BMI of over 30 are considered obese. More specific information about BMI calculators, as well as advice about weight loss, can be found at www.consumer.gov/weightloss/bmi.htm.

- *Sleep*. Are you getting enough sleep? It is recommended by the National Sleep Foundation that 7 to 8 hours of sleep a night is a healthy amount. More information about helping you to get the sleep you need can be found at www.sleepfoundation.org/site/c.huIXKjM0IxF/b.2417485/k.106/How_Much_Sleep_Do_We_Really_Need_Page_2.htm.

to alter dramatically the sense of safety, security, and predictability of our daily life. Among the variety of consequences of such traumatic events is a tendency for individuals to believe that the world is a more dangerous place and that other people cannot be trusted (Danieli, Engdahl, & Schlenger, 2004; Foa, Hembree, Riggs, Rauch, & Franklin, 2001).

On a less extreme basis, there is also evidence to suggest that an assortment of more common life changes can be sources of stress because they serve to disrupt daily or familiar routines (Holmes & Rahe, 1967; Rahe & Arthur, 1978). For example, such familiar life changes as getting engaged, pregnant, married, or divorced, getting hired or having your job terminated, purchasing a house or getting evicted, going on vacation, sustaining a personal injury or illness, or beginning college or graduating can all create a certain degree of distress because they all require some form of change in previously established routines. In support of the impact of life changes on individuals, research suggests that those individuals who experience more life changes (e.g., get divorced, purchase a house, change jobs, go on vacation) within a relatively short period of time (e.g., 9–18 months) tend to be more vulnerable to many kinds of physical (e.g., high blood pressure) and psychological problems (e.g., depression; Rahe, Veach, Tolles, & Murakami, 2000; Scully, Tosi, & Banning, 2000).

While life changes can serve as a source of disruption of familiar routine, you should know that it is not just the changes themselves that are critical, but certain characteristic features associated with them (Hobson & Delunas, 2001; F. Jones & Kinman, 2001). One such feature is the desirability of the change, with undesirable life changes creating more stress than desirable ones (McLean & Link, 1994; Turner & Wheaton, 1997). For example, while both involve changes in marital status, most individuals would probably consider getting married as a more positive and less distressful life change than getting a divorce, which most would probably consider as a negative and highly distressful life change.

A second feature affecting the impact of life changes on the individual is the extent to which the individual has control over them. The more perceived control individuals seem to have over the stressors in their life, the less negative impact such stressors seem to have on them (K. A. Christensen, Stephens, & Townsend, 1998; Krause & Shaw, 2000). There is considerable evidence to suggest that individuals who feel they have little or no control over the negative events

in their daily life appear to be more likely to experience physical and psychological problems. For example, research involving employees from the United States, Sweden, and the United Kingdom who had little or no control over their work environment (e.g., when they could take breaks) found they were more likely to experience heart disease and other health problems than were workers with a higher degree of control over their work environment (Bosma et al., 1997; Cheng, Kawachi, Coakley, Schwartz, & Colditz, 2000; Spector, 2002). On the other hand, individuals who were given information about their upcoming surgery and strategies for managing postoperative pain were found to report less distress, heal faster, and be discharged sooner after the surgery than individuals in a control group who were not given this special information (Egbert, Battit, Welch, & Bartlett, 1964), which is why it is standard practice in most hospitals today to help teach patients how to manage and control the pain associated with surgical procedures (Broadbent, Petrie, Alley, & Booth, 2003; Chamberlin, 2000). In a sense, the individuals with the special information about pain management experienced less distress as a result of having a greater sense of control over their pain.

In summary, while life changes can serve to disrupt our daily lives, having a sense of control and predictability serves to help us add a certain degree of safety and security to our daily lives. What are some of the routines you have in your life that help you to meet and maintain your safety needs?

Thus, by developing certain daily routines in our life, and order in our living environment, we are able to regularly meet these safety and security needs. The consistent satisfaction of safety needs allows us to begin considering the next cluster of needs – those for belongingness and love.

Belongingness and Love Needs: The Desire to Be with Others   **Belongingness and love needs** are directly concerned with the basic desire to feel accepted by and have meaningful interpersonal relationships with others. This category includes the need to feel a part of some reference group (e.g., family, neighborhood, a gang, religious group, or professional organization) and the ability to both receive and give love (e.g., establish meaningful friendships). Belonging to various social organizations (e.g., the Psychology Club, campus choir, intramural sports teams), community service groups (e.g., Habitat for Humanity, Big Brothers/Big Sisters, neighborhood recycling organization, volunteers at a local food pantry), and leisure organizations (e.g., health club membership, yoga class, book discussion group), as well as being a member of a family, gives us a sense of acceptance and belongingness and helps to meet this category of needs.

With the changing nature of the social structure in our society (e.g., high divorce rate, the constant transferring of families for business reasons, and urbanization) and technology (e.g., individuals spending more time alone on their computers at work and home), meeting these belonging needs has become more and more difficult, creating increases in feelings of loneliness and alienation (Kraut et al., 1998; Putnam, 1996, 2000). Maslow felt that failing to meet belongingness and love needs was at the core of most, if not all, forms of maladjustment. Indeed, there is considerable research to suggest that a reduced need for belonging is associated with a number of negative psychological and physical consequences, such as anxiety, depression, and mental illness (Baumeister & Leary, 1995). In addition, those who lack a sense of closeness and belonging to others tend to be more likely to engage in a variety of criminal and antisocial behaviors than do those who are a part of a social network (Baumeister & Leary, 1995; Shaver & Mikulincer, 2003). While a lack of feelings of belonging and the sense of being rejected and ostracized can have some negative consequences (Case & Williams, 2004; Pinel, Long, Landau, & Pyszczynski, 2004; Synder & Lopez, 2007), a solution to such ills can be found in social support.

THE VALUE OF SOCIAL SUPPORT   **Social support** is the network of friends and social contacts upon whom you can count on for help and support in times of need and distress (Demaray & Malecki, 2002). There is considerable evidence to suggest that social support serves to benefit both the mind (Kendler, Myers, & Prescott, 2005) and body (S. L. Brown, Nesse, Vinokur, & Smith, 2003). For example, it seems to serve as a buffer and reduces the negative impact of stress (Willis & Fegan, 2001). In support of such reasoning, those whose lives are isolated and lack intimacy seem to be at greater risk of depression in times of stress (Kendler et al., 2005; Nezlek, Hampton, & Shean, 2000). Individuals with reduced social support and feelings of loneliness tend to demonstrate less bodily capacity to deal with stress (e.g., fight off disease and illness) than do individuals who do not feel lonely (S. Cohen, 2002; Curtis, Groarke, Coughlan, & Gsel, 2004). On the other hand, individuals with social support tend to display a stronger bodily response to dealing with the physical consequences of stress (e.g., better recovery from illness; Spiegel & Fawzy, 2002; Taylor, 2006).

In addition to the benefits of receiving social support, there is also evidence to suggest that providing such support can be beneficial (Wills & Fegan, 2001). Finally, you should be aware that the value of social support is not just limited to being with other people. It has been reported that pet owners can see their pets as a source of social support, and that the support benefits associated with humans can indeed be produced by one's pet (Allen, Blascovich, & Mendes, 2002).

Once people are able to achieve a satisfactory sense of acceptance, they can devote some of their attention to meeting the fourth level of needs in the hierarchy – the esteem needs.

Esteem Needs: The Desire to be Recognized by Others   **Esteem needs** are concerned with the desire to have the respect of others and possess a sense of self-respect. Included in having the respect of others are achieving status and recognition within significant groups and being perceived as a worthy and able member of them. For example, when trying to meet this aspect of the esteem needs, it would not be enough simply to be a member of a community service group. You would demonstrate a caring for and an interest in the group by running for a position on the board of directors. Pursuing a seat on the board requires a sense of self-confidence and self-esteem. Being elected to the board reflects the confidence and esteem other members have for your abilities. Your ability to obtain and maintain the respect of others in a leadership capacity reflects the extent to which others perceive you as having the characteristic features associated with being an effective leader.

In addition to having the respect of others as an expression of the esteem needs is having respect for yourself. Included in possessing self-respect is having a level of self-esteem that reflects a feeling of confidence in your personal abilities to perform those activities associated with being a leader. Since leadership and self-esteem are important expressions of the esteem needs, we will discuss their characteristic features in more detail.

CHARACTERISTICS OF LEADERSHIP: THE WICS MODEL One expression of the esteem individuals have for others is to select them as leaders. What are the characteristics associated with being a leader? There is a variety of theories that discuss the characteristics of leaders (American Psychological Association, 2007; Antonakis, Cianciolo, & Sternberg, 2004; Kezar, Carducci, & Contreras-McGavin, 2006; Riggio, Murphy, & Pirozzolo, 2004). One influential theory is the WICS model (Sternberg, 2003a, 2003b, 2004, 2007, in press). The **WICS model of leadership** proposes that the three critical components are *w*isdom, *i*ntelligence, and *c*reativity, along with *s*ynthesis, and that one needs these three components working together (i.e., synthesized) to be a highly effective leader.

- *Creativity: Seeing old information in a new way.* Within the context of leadership, **creativity** is associated with the ability of the leader to take preexisting information and place it in a new context. This can be done in a variety of ways, such as extending the mission statement of the group to meet more contemporary concerns, or utilizing information from an older organization to solve a problem in a new group. For example, while the original mission of an Italian-American Association formed in the late 1800s in a large city might have been to help newly arriving immigrants adjust to the culture shock of coming to a new country, changes in immigration patterns over the last 100 years have made this mission less relevant today. However, to help keep the organization a vital and meaningful part of the community, the current president might change its mission to the preservation and promotion of the Italian culture for future generations, which is a more contemporary concern for many of the children and grandchildren of those initial immigrants. In a somewhat different example of creativity in leadership, an individual interested in forming an Ethiopian Immigrant Association might talk to the president of the well-established Italian-American Association about how to go about promoting the organization in the local ethnic community and identifying community officials and organizations that could be of some assistance to newly arriving individuals from Ethiopia. There is considerable evidence linking creative thinking with leadership success in contemporary organizations (Amabile, 1999) and throughout history (Simonton, 1988, 1994).
- *Intelligence: Using what you know in new ways.* Another critical characteristic of leadership is a form of intelligence referred as practical intelligence (Sternberg, 2007; Sternberg et al., 2000).

Practical intelligence involves possessing the skills and dispositions necessary to modify previously held knowledge in a purposeful manner and to develop and implement strategies based on this revised knowledge to help solve everyday problems in the context of changing environmental conditions. For example, from what she knows about the personal values of different groups in the community, the leader of an antigambling community organization might adapt the tone of her message from focusing on the moral concerns of gambling (e.g., gambling is sinful and will lead to moral decay) when speaking to church groups to focusing on its economic threats (e.g., money used for gambling will not be used to purchase services and goods in the community) when addressing the downtown merchants' association. In addition to speaking to local groups, she might take her message to the state capitol to lobby legislators to vote against gambling. In this setting, she might adopt a more power-assertive style by focusing on the number of voters associated with her organization that can be delivered in an upcoming election. Thus, effective leaders modify their preexisting knowledge and leadership style to fit environmental considerations (e.g., characteristics and location of the audience).

- *Wisdom: Working for the common good.* While creativity and intelligence are important dimensions of effective leadership, they are of little value if the leader is unwise (Sternberg, 2007). **Wisdom** is characterized by the ability to use one's intelligence, creativity, and knowledge in the context of one's values to meet the common good. To be successful, leaders must be able to meet their own needs, the needs of others, and the needs of other organizations. Successful leaders recognize the importance of aligning the interests of their group with the interests of other organizations, because, as Sternberg (2007, p. 38) notes, "no group operates in a vacuum." For example, the leader of the local Jamaican Community Center realizes that his group stands a better chance of gaining city funds for an ethnic festival if he also involves a variety of other local ethnic and service organizations, such as the German-American Society, the Irish-American Club, 100 Black Men, Hispanic-based churches, the Asian Cultural Center, and the Italian-American Heritage Museum. You should be aware that while wise leaders are usually charismatic, charismatic leaders are not necessarily wise (Sternberg, 2007), as can be seen from such charismatic figures as Nazi leader Adolf Hitler, Soviet Communist leader Joseph Stalin, Ugandan dictator Idi Amin, and Iraqi dictator Saddam Hussein.

- *Synthesis: Putting it all together.* The final component of the WICS model of leadership is synthesis. **Synthesis** is the process by which wisdom, intelligence, and creativity come together in a leader. As Sternberg (2007, p. 39) notes, "Truly good leadership is relatively rare because it requires a synthesis of all of the elements described above." A leader who lacks creativity might be able to maintain a business or organization but will not be able to expand and modify the operation to meet future changes and demands in the industry. For example, think of the individual whose company is in the business of repairing typewriters. A leader who is creative might be aware of changes (e.g., need to get into computer repair) and have a plan for responding to them (e.g., enroll the company's employees in the electronic repairs program at the local technical college) but still lack the intelligence to put the plan into action (e.g., generate an alternative source of income to live on while retraining, or seek government-sponsored student loans programs or local grants for starting a new small business), and so is not likely to be an effective leader. An individual leader who possesses both creativity and intelligence (e.g., gets the new computer repair business going) but lacks the wisdom to work with others (e.g., will not pay the dues for joining a professional organization of computer repair businesses) is not likely to survive in the increasingly global marketplace. No matter what the nature or purpose of the organization, a successful leader must be able to recognize that changes occurring in the environment will require a new way of thinking about the environment and the people in it (i.e., creativity), the development and implementation of novel strategies for responding to these changes (i.e., practical intelligence), and the ability to work with other organizations to help implement these strategies for the common good (i.e., wisdom). Thus, as you can see, when it comes to leadership, synthesis involves the ability to "put it all together."

To illustrate the concept of synthesis as it applies to leadership, consider a scenario that is being faced by more and more leaders in the business community. The president of a company recognizes that more and more ethnic minority individuals are migrating to the area and that these individuals will serve as not only an expansion of the company's traditional customer base but also potential employees. In response to these changes, the president works with the company's advertising coordinator to create new ads designed to appeal to these individuals. The president might also work with the company's human resources manager and the vice president of the local college to develop a program for sponsoring paid internships at the company for minority students in the college's marketing and management programs, with the idea of attracting these individuals as future employees. These people will use their increased employment earnings to purchase goods and services from local business, as well as their influence in the local ethnic community to have others do the same, thus stimulating the local economy and creating more jobs for both the traditional and newly arriving individuals in the area. As this example illustrates, the successful leader in this situation is able to combine – synthesize – all the elements of the WICS model to create a course of action that benefits all of the individuals involved.

In summary, many leaders will not develop or possess the WICS model characteristics in a sufficient degree to lead in the most effective manner. This is why leadership teams are important – they allow leaders to compensate for their weaknesses (Sternberg, 2007). In my own opinion, this may be the reason the first letter in the WICS acronym is "W." Possessing wisdom is probably the most important characteristic, because it helps leaders to be willing to work with other leaders who have the strengths to compensate for their weaknesses, as well as serving as a reminder that their leadership depends on their ability to work for the common good, not just their own personal needs. Now that you know about the characteristic features of leadership, let's turn our attention to the characteristic features of self-esteem.

CHARACTERISTICS OF SELF-ESTEEM: EVALUATING YOUR SELF-WORTH **Self-esteem** refers to your personal evaluation of your own sense of self-worth (Baumeister, Campbell, Krueger, & Vohs, 2003; Baumeister, Smart, & Boden, 1996; Mruk, 2006). A general or global sense of self-esteem refers to your overall evaluation of yourself. For example, in general you have a pretty favorable view of your self with respect to the attributes and abilities you possess. You can also have a more specific sense of self-esteem that is related to a particular attribute (e.g., being helpful) or ability (e.g., solving math problems) and how important that particular attribute or ability is to your sense of self. Attributes and abilities that are important to the individual have a greater impact on the individual's self-esteem than those that are not. For example, David is at the top of his class in math and the captain of the rugby team. However, he feels he is just awful at making conversation with individuals he meets at parties, particularly if the person is someone for whom he feels some attraction or is one of the more popular students at school. David's self-esteem is likely to be impacted in a negative way if he places a considerable emphasis on being able to gain the attention of others he finds attractive or values greatly being accepted by. On the other hand, his self-esteem is not likely to be affected if he places little emphasis on impressing this popular group of individuals and, instead, places more value on his skills in math and rugby and the friends he has made in these two areas of his life.

Thus, our self-esteem is determined by the attributes and abilities we possess and the significance we assign to them when evaluating our sense of self. Individuals with low self-esteem seem to place less value on those attributes and abilities they possess while individuals with high self-esteem seem to value them. However, what about individuals who have an overly exaggerated sense of themselves that does not seem to match their attributes and abilities? How do these individuals fit into our discussion of self-esteem? For some insights into this issue, see the information presented in "A Closer Look."

A Closer Look

Narcissism: The Dark Side of a Highly Positive Self-Evaluation

Is an individual who has a high opinion of himself or herself nothing more than a narcissist? A common point of misunderstanding is to confuse high self-esteem with narcissism. **Narcissists** are individuals

who have a grandiose and unrealistic sense of self and engage in constant attempts to draw to and keep the attention of others on themselves. As an example of a narcissist, think of the individual who dances wildly and tries to take over the microphone at a wedding reception. Additional characteristics of narcissists include their belief that they deserve special treatment (e.g., should be allowed to address an audience at a wedding reception) and their tendency to be highly sensitive to criticism, as well as react aggressively to this criticism when their beliefs about their sense of self are questioned or threatened (Kernis, 2003a, 2003b; Twenge & Campbell, 2003). Again, think of the individual who becomes belligerent and starts to make a scene when told by the host that she cannot go onto the stage to address the audience at the wedding reception.

It should be noted that such expressions of hostility by narcissists appear primarily when they are provoked (e.g., threats to their exaggerated sense of self-worth); when not provoked, narcissistic individuals are no more likely to express hostility and aggression than are non-narcissistic ones (e.g., Baumeister, Bushman, & Campbell, 2000; Twenge & Campbell, 2003). In support of this reasoning, it was reported that in response to either praise or criticism of an essay they wrote during a laboratory experiment, narcissistic individuals responded with exceedingly high levels of negative feelings and aggressive behavior towards those who criticized their work (Bushman & Baumeister, 1998). Additional support for the link between narcissism and aggression has been provided in a comparison of the self-esteem and narcissism scores of college males and male prisoners (Bushman & Baumeister, 2002). In this study, while the self-esteem scores of the college males and violent offenders were similar, the violent offenders tended to have significantly higher narcissism scores.

From these patterns of results, Baumeister and his colleagues (Baumeister, 1999; Baumeister et al., 1996) have proposed that individuals with narcissistic and hostile tendencies are likely to engage in a variety of expressions of interpersonal aggression, such as spouse abuse, bullying, rape, gang violence, hate crimes, and terrorism. This conceptualization of the relationship between an exaggerated self (i.e., excessive self-esteem) and aggressive behavior seems to shatter the myth that bullies, spouse abusers, and violent criminals are individuals with low self-esteem and can be treated by simply raising their self-esteem and making them feel good about themselves (Baumeister et al., 1996). A more effective treatment approach might include helping these individuals to develop more self-control, cultivate more realistic views of themselves, and be less sensitive to criticism.

CORRELATES OF SELF-ESTEEM: TO BE HAPPY AND SUCCESSFUL   One of the most consistent findings related to self-esteem is that of happiness – high self-esteem is associated with greater happiness while low self-esteem is associated with feelings of depression (Baumeister et al., 2003). It is easy to see how happy people would be more likely to foster the esteem of others. Individuals with high self-esteem are less likely to give up in response to failure than are those with low self-esteem (J. D. Brown & Dutton, 1995), perhaps because they are concerned with protecting their positive, successful image. Such a tendency to persist during trying times would certainly contribute to an individual being viewed in a favorable way by others in a group when it might be struggling to achieve a goal.

It has been found that individuals with high self-esteem tend to believe they possess a variety of interpersonal skills that make them more appealing and popular to others (e.g., have more friends), such as initiating relationships, being assertive when needed, providing emotional support to friends, and helping to resolve conflicts among individuals (Baumeister et al., 2003). However, such self-perceptions were not matched in this study by the more objective ratings of their interpersonal skills by others. When rated by others who knew them well (e.g., college roommates), individuals' level of self-esteem was correlated only with their ability to initiate new social contacts and friendships (e.g., walk up to someone at a party and start talking to them).

While there seems to be some degree of discrepancy between how interpersonally skillful individuals with high self-esteem think they are and how others view them, it may be that the confidence individuals with high self-esteem seem to have in their ability and willingness to approach and engage others is the critical element in their capturing the esteem of others. In a similar manner, while there is a positive relationship between a person's self-esteem and his or her self-rating of physical attractiveness, when considering the ratings of individuals' attractiveness made by others, the relationship

drops dramatically – there is little relationship between a person's self-esteem and how physically attractive others perceive them as being (Baumeister et al., 2003). But again, if a person perceives himself or herself as physically attractive, this will be critical in creating a willingness to approach others or assume that they are worthy of the affection and esteem of others.

So while self-esteem may not be objectively related to such factors as academic ability and interpersonal skills, having high self-esteem seems to play an indirect role by giving individuals the confidence to approach others, make social connections, and engage others in such a way that academic, career, and personal success, along with happiness, are the byproducts. So given the important role high self-esteem seems to play in being happy and successful, it is important to know what individuals might do to enhance it. To gain some insight into how you can enhance your own self-esteem, read the material in "Applications in Personality Psychology" on pp. 238–239.

Thus, gaining the respect of others through effective leadership and achieving and developing a sense of self-respect in the form of high self-esteem are two important factors associated with the meeting of esteem needs. People who are able to satisfy consistently the esteem needs can direct their motivation at the highest level of the hierarchy of needs – self-actualization.

Self-Actualization: Developing the Individual's Full Potential   Self-actualization involves the individual's desire to develop his or her abilities to their fullest potential (Batson & Strocks, 2004). Such development involves obtaining a deeper sense of one's own desires and abilities and maximizing their expression in an attempt to bring them together. As an example, for a young woman interested in acting, self-actualization would require participating in acting to the fullest extent of her ability. If she has only limited acting ability, this might involve acting in the local theater productions, as well as possibly attempting to direct some of the productions. If she has greater ability, self-actualization may involve moving to a large city and pursuing a full-time career in acting by devoting literally all of her time to this ambition.

For others, the expression of the self-actualization desire might involve designing clothes, working on cars, bodybuilding, or gardening. The point is that whatever the person feels is a vital part of his or her human nature should be pursued with the idea of doing it as well as can possibly be done. Such a

Applications in Personality Psychology

Enhancing Your Self-Esteem: Making a Good Person Even Better

Most students reading this book will have a relatively positive sense of self-esteem. After all, you must have a pretty solid self-esteem to go through all that is required to get into and stay in college these days. But as good as you probably are, with something like self-esteem, there is always room for improvement. Following are just a few recommendations that some psychologists have designed to help enhance your self-esteem (Mruk, 2006; Osborne, 1996; Rathus & Nevid, 2002).

1. *You control your own self-esteem.* Although a number of forces affect your self-esteem, you have to recognize that you are ultimately in control of how you feel about yourself. Following are several recommendations that will make it possible to take control of enhancing your own self-esteem.

2. *Controlling your own standards.* Decide for yourself how you want to be and what you really want to do. Avoid having others tell you that "you ought to get a better job," "you would feel better about yourself if you lost some weight," or "you are not trying hard enough." Part of developing a sense of control over your self-concept is having a sense of what you want for yourself. While you may seek others out as a source of information and for suggestions, learn to trust your own judgment about what is best for you.

3. *Accent the positive.* You have many fine qualities. Learn to accept and take responsibility for them. A characteristic of those with low self-esteem is that they tend to discount their role in positive events that happen to them. For example, when you receive a compliment on your appearance, don't automatically assume that the person was just being nice to you; assume that they meant it and that you really

do look nice. When you get a good grade on a test, learn to assume that it was a result of your intellectual ability and the effort you put into studying, not because the test was easy or you were lucky. Keep in mind that you would not have gotten this far in your educational development if you did not have certain positive characteristics, such as perseverance and intellect.

4. *Control your negative self-talk.* **Negative self-talk** refers to the tendency for people with low self-esteem to think and speak of themselves in unflattering terms. For example, they might describe themselves as unattractive, socially inept, and uninteresting. This negative self-talk is often based on the feedback they receive involving others. As an example, you might unfairly compare yourself to others who have much greater experience or ability, causing you to tell yourself that you really are not any good at tennis or giving speeches. You can also minimize negative self-talk by not tolerating people or situations that make you think and feel negatively about yourself. If it is not possible to change these external factors enough to make you feel better, simply stay away from them as much as possible. Life is too short to subject yourself to such unpleasantness.

5. *Set realistic standards for yourself.* By setting realistic standards for yourself, you can create a greater likelihood of experiencing success. But keep in mind that learning to establish a realistic standard might involve a certain degree of failure in the form of a trial-and-error process. It may not be realistic to work 25 hours a week, take care of your children, and manage a full load of courses with the expectation of maintaining a B+ average. However, you won't know until you try. After going to school under these conditions and getting a C+ average, you might have to adjust your standards. This might involve redefining success as getting Cs instead of Bs or working less and

taking fewer classes to maintain those Bs. The point is that there are many ways to define success. The key is to define one that is realistic for you.

6. *Learn to appreciate failure.* Learning to appreciate failure involves being able to see its value. The value of failure is that it can help to teach you what you did wrong in your attempts to go beyond what you normally do. Stepping outside of your comfort zone – what you find easy – helps you to test and expand your abilities. However, when going outside of your comfort zone, you increase your risk of failure because you are trying something new and different for you. Instead of being dejected by failure, think about what you did that did not seem to work in this case and what you might do differently when in that situation again. For example, you might have gotten a low grade on a class presentation because you stumbled over your speech when presenting it for the first time in front of others. To deal with this problem, you decide that for your next speech you will make it a point to not only practice it by yourself in front of a mirror but to practice it in front of a few friends when they gather in your room to play video games and in front of your family when you are at home this weekend. Your reasoning is that you want to practice your speech in front of other individuals before you actually deliver it to your classmates. Because you have practiced the speech in front of several different individuals, you are more likely to succeed when giving the speech in front of your classmates. The success you experience giving the speech this time in class will help to give you the confidence to extend your ability to speak in public to expressing your views on other matters related to your membership in the psychology club. Such verbal confidence to speak up during the meetings will likely lead others to nominate you to serve as an officer of the club.

As you can see, these recommendations are relatively straightforward and do not require a lot of sophisticated training in psychology. All they require is some desire on your part to make a good person like yourself even better.

sentiment was stated in an extremely eloquent manner by Maslow (1954) when he said: "A musician must make music, an artist must paint, a poet must write if he is ultimately to be at peace with himself. What a man can be he must be. This need we may call self-actualization" (p. 91; note that Maslow was referring to both men and women).

It is important to note that meeting the need of self-actualization is an ongoing process, not an absolute state of achievement (Polkinghorne, 2001). So the successful, full-time actor might continue to challenge himself by taking on different forms of artistic expressions, such as writing screenplays, producing movies, and teaching acting workshops in an effort to not only stretch all of his own acting skills but also help to improve the state of his craft and foster self-actualization in others by challenging the artistic expression of individuals who also hope to be successful actors. In addition, while the self-actualization need is at the highest level of the hierarchy, it is also the least

powerful. It is for this reason that Maslow felt that very few people are able to completely satisfy this need. For such a need to be achieved, the individual must be extremely motivated from within himself or herself. For example, although many may have the ability to be an Olympic figure skater or the heavyweight boxing champion of the world, very few have the internal desire required to devote the many years it takes to achieve such a goal. We will have more to say about the characteristics features of those exceptional individuals who Maslow felt were able to represent the essence of self-actualization in the next section.

A Final Comment on the Hierarchy of Needs: Some Points of Clarification Many people have some misunderstandings about the hierarchy of needs. First, although the needs are arranged hierarchically, this does not mean that a person must completely satisfy one group before moving on to the next level. Instead, the lower needs should be satisfied only to the extent

Summing It Up *Maslow's Hierarchy of Needs*

Description of Needs	Example
Physiological Needs: Those basic needs required for the survival of the individual	People are first and foremost concerned with having enough food, water, and rest.
Safety Needs: The desire of people to have stability, order, and predictability in their lives	By taking the same route to school each morning, a driver knows, for the most part, what to expect from the traffic.
Belongingness and Love Needs: The desire to be affiliated with others in a meaningful way	By wearing a t-shirt with the name of a club or organization on it, you can express your affiliation with others.
Esteem Needs: The desire for self-respect and the respect of others	You receive a sense of accomplishment and the praise of others after giving a successful campaign speech.
Self-Actualization: The highest of needs, motivating people to express significant aspects of their self to the fullest extent	Someone who enjoys playing tennis would subscribe to tennis magazines, attend tennis clinics, and take tennis lessons in an effort to continue to get better at the game.

that the individual has some relief from them and can devote more attention to the higher needs. The more relief a person has from lower needs, the more attention that person can give to the higher ones. For example, the less time a man has to spend concentrating on job security (i.e., threats to physiological and safety needs), the more time he has for personal sources of pleasure, such as practicing his saxophone to improve his musical ability (i.e., esteem needs), playing gigs with a local jazz band, and volunteering to teach jazz workshops at a local high school band camp (i.e., belongingness needs).

Second, because it is possible to experience more than one need at a time, it is also possible to satisfy more than one need at a time. For example, becoming the chairperson of a neighborhood block watch crime-prevention program involves the individual maximizing a sense of security (i.e., safety needs) but also obtaining status and recognition (i.e., esteem needs) within the neighborhood (i.e., belongingness and love needs).

Finally, even though the lowest needs are most powerful, they can be superseded by the higher ones. For example, an individual skips lunch (i.e., physiological need) to attend a club meeting or drive a friend to the airport (i.e., belongingness and love needs, respectively). More extreme examples of this are individuals who go on hunger strikes (e.g., Gandhi), often until death, or environmental activists who live in trees for

extended periods of time, forgoing the comforts of shelter, as a means of expressing their deep commitment to a particular cause, or the starving artist who would rather spend money on paints than on food. The concluding point to be made here is that the hierarchy of needs is not as cut and dried as many people might assume.

To conclude our discussion, the principal ideas examined in this section are presented in "Summing It Up: Maslow's Hierarchy of Needs" above.

Maslow's Study of Self-Actualizing Individuals: In Search of Excellence

Although Maslow was extremely interested in the nature and organization of human needs, he was particularly so in the self-actualization need. It is for this reason that he attempted to identify the characteristics of exceptional people in what is considered a groundbreaking study of self-actualization (Wertz, 2001). In the true tradition of studying the "best of the best," Maslow launched an ambitious study of self-actualizing people. He selected a relatively small number of subjects who he felt were operating at their maximum abilities. Among these were contemporary figures (e.g., Franklin D. Roosevelt and Sigmund Freud) and historical figures (e.g., Ludwig van Beethoven and Thomas

Jefferson). Using a clinical approach, Maslow collected information from a variety of sources. He conducted personal interviews with the subjects who were living at the time or with people who knew them well; and he analyzed historical and personal documents. In analyzing this information, he looked for characteristics shared by these people in their approach to work, interpersonal relationships, and life in general.

Some Self-Actualizing People: A "Who's Who" of the Best of the Best

People Maslow considered as coming closest to what he meant by self-actualization included the following:

- *Albert Einstein (1879–1955).* German physicist, formulator of the theory of relativity, and winner of the 1921 Nobel prize for physics
- *Eleanor Roosevelt (1894–1962).* U.S. diplomat, author, lecturer, and wife of President Franklin Delano Roosevelt
- *Jane Addams (1860–1935).* U.S. social worker, writer, and winner of the 1931 Nobel peace prize
- *William James (1842–1910).* U.S. psychologist and philosopher, and the father of psychology in the United States
- *Albert Schweitzer (1875–1965).* Alsatian physician and missionary in Africa
- *Aldous Huxley (1894–1963).* English novelist, essayist, and critic
- *Baruch Spinoza (1632–1677).* Dutch philosopher
- *Abraham Lincoln (1809–1865).* Sixteenth president of the United States
- *Thomas Jefferson (1743–1826).* U.S. architect, statesman, diplomat, and third president of the United States

Such a list reads like a "who's who" of the best of the best. However, more impressive than the names of these people are the characteristics they shared.

Characteristics of Self-Actualizing People: Some Common Threads of Excellence

While self-actualizing people can be found in all areas of life, Maslow (1970b) found that they seem to share certain characteristics, listed on the next page:

Two of the individuals Maslow considered to be self-actualizers: Albert Einstein and Eleanor Roosevelt

- *More accurate perception of reality.* Because they are secure in their needs, self-actualizing people can judge events in an unbiased, less defensive manner. For example, being secure in their sense of self, they can make decisions based on the issues at hand, rather than on some self-serving bias.

- *Greater acceptance of self and others.* Their realistic perception of the world makes it possible for self-actualizing people to see both the good and bad side of themselves and others. As a result, they tend to be more understanding and accepting. They also tend to view people more democratically, responding to the behavior rather than the personal characteristics of the individual. For example, they treat people fairly and equally, regardless of race, class, religion, or level of education.

- *Nonhostile sense of humor.* Their nonhostile sense of humor is characterized by a dislike for jokes that might be degrading to others. Self-actualizing people would not find jokes that feature the stereotypes of ethnic minorities funny. Instead, they prefer to laugh at themselves or at more philosophical or satirical forms of humor.

- *Being true to themselves.* Self-actualizing people tend to have a spontaneous, natural, and fresh approach to experiencing the world. They tend to say what they feel and feel what they are experiencing in a natural manner indicative of their inner self. Such naturalness also produces a high degree of spontaneity and freshness in their behavior. For example, a self-actualizing person might still be deeply moved by a scene from a favorite movie, even after seeing it many times, and express this feeling by crying openly in the theater.

- *Being other-centered rather than self-centered.* Self-actualizing people tend to demonstrate a concern for problems and issues that go beyond themselves and have the potential to affect many people. In the Adlerian sense, these people have a high degree of social interest. As an example, a self-actualizing student might be actively involved in organizations helping clients deal with homelessness or teenage pregnancy.

- *Autonomy in behavior and values.* Because they are motivated by the desire to fulfill their personal sense of self, self-actualizing people are less influenced by what others say or do. They also have a strong personal sense of ethics, which they use in deciding for themselves what is right and wrong. As a result, they tend to be nonconformists in their behavior and attitudes.

- *Being selective in their interpersonal relationships.* The autonomous nature of self-actualizing people creates in them a desire for privacy and detachment. Because they are inner-directed, they do not feel the need to be constantly around other people. As a result, they tend to have few friends. But the friendships they do develop tend to be very deep and rich. Self-actualizing people tend to seek out the friendship of other self-actualizers.

- *Being creative.* The creativity of self-actualizing people is not limited to such traditional forms as writing books or producing art; it is evident in the way they live their lives. For example, they might come up with creative solutions for the political bickering going on in the office, or with novel ideas for party games or inexpensive costumes. In short, they tend to have a unique perspective on things in all aspects of life.

- *Having peak experiences.* Their openness and naturalness in experiencing the world allow self-actualizing people to have a greater number of peak experiences. **Peak experiences** involve a heightened sense of wonder, awe, or ecstasy over an experience (Privette, 2001). For example, the tremendous sense of emotional elation you might feel when falling in love is a form of peak experience. Another example might be the sense of amazement you feel as a basketball player engages in a tremendous personal effort during the entire game to bring her teammates within three points of a last-minute victory over a highly favored opponent. In this sense, you are in awe because you know you have witnessed a truly great individual performance. Still another form of peak experience might be the overwhelming sense of pride and accomplishment an actor feels when delivering her lines during a scene in just the right fashion that it creates a dead silence in the theater. Maslow believed that we are all capable of having peak experiences, but self-actualizing people tend to have more of them and experience them to a greater degree than other people. To understand what is meant by a peak experience, try the exercise outlined in "You Can Do It" on p. 243.

You Can Do It

A Personal Look at Peak Experiences: Experiencing a Natural High

In his own attempt to understand the nature of peak experiences, Maslow (1962) used written descriptions of such experiences provided by college students. Polyson (1985) has developed a written exercise designed to help students gain a better understanding of the construct of peak experiences by looking for them in their own lives.

To examine possible peak experiences in your own life, write on a separate sheet of paper what you might consider such an experience. To help in this, "think of the most wonderful experience of your life: the happiest moments, ecstatic moments, moments of rapture, perhaps from being in love, or from listening to music or suddenly 'being hit' by a book or painting, or from some creative moment" (Maslow, 1962, p. 67).

To give you some point of reference, based on the written descriptions provided by his students, Polyson (1985) reports:

> Most of the peak experiences had occurred during athletic, artistic, religious, or nature experiences, or during intimate moments with a friend or family member. There were a number of peak experiences in which the students achieved an important personal goal or collective goal. There were also peak experiences in which the students overcame some adversity or danger or helped someone in need. (p. 212)

Thus, peak experiences are associated with very special moments in our lives when we are able to achieve an intense and unique feeling that can only be described as a "natural high."

Research on Peak Experiences: Objective Attempts to Investigate Subjective Experiences

Because the notion of peak experiences is probably the characteristic most closely associated with Maslow's concept of self-actualization, it has attracted the most research interest. In this regard, while it would seem that the subjective nature of peak experiences would make their investigation difficult, their study involves researchers using many of the standard research techniques (e.g., clinical interview and factor analysis) discussed throughout this book in an effort to find support for Maslow's ideas. For example, in support of his beliefs regarding the rarity of individuals being able to achieve self-actualization, it has been reported that only about 2 percent of individuals interviewed were classified as having peak experiences (Thomas & Cooper, 1977). Additional research has examined the distinguishing characteristics of peak experiences and variations of their nature.

Identifying the Distinguishing Characteristics of Peak Experiences   To identify the distinguishing features of peak experiences, Privette and her colleagues have studied them in a wide variety of individuals, including college students (Privette & Bundrick, 1987), exhibiting artists (Yeagle, Privette, & Dunham, 1989), realtors (Lanier, Privette, Vodanovich, & Bundrick, 1996), and individuals from different countries (Taiwanese vs. American; Privette, Hwang, & Bundrick, 1997), through the use of the **Experience Questionnaire** (Privette, 1984), which is designed to assess the unique and shared qualities of peak experiences and other intense, self-directed emotional experiences (Privette, 1983, 1984). Across this wide variety of individuals, peak experiences were found to be characterized by three distinguishing factors: fulfillment, significance, and spirituality (Privette, 2001; Privette & Bundrick, 1991).

- Fulfillment involves respondents describing peak experiences as intrinsically rewarding, providing an enduring positive feeling, and related positively to their own performance.
- Significance involves the respondents describing peak experiences as being turning points in their lives and featuring increases in personal understanding, expressions, and values.
- Spirituality involves respondents describing peak experiences as creating a sense of unity of self with the environment and a loss of time and space.

Flow: A Variation of Peak Experiences   A more recent attempt to investigate an emotional state similar to peak experiences (Batson & Stocks, 2004) comes from the work of Mihaly Csikszentmihalyi (pronounced *Chick-Sent-Me-High*; 1990, 1996, 1997; Csikszentmihalyi, Abuhamdeh, & Nakamura, 2005; Csikszentmihalyi & Nakamura, 1999) in his investigation of "flow." **Flow** is an emotional state characterized by becoming so involved in an activity that nothing else seems to matter. Its characteristic features include:

- *A clear sense of action.* While developing a new mathematical proof, a mathematician has a clear mental image of what the next three steps in the equation are going to be.
- *A blending of one's skills with the challenges of the activity.* A high-jumper knows the moment her feet leave the ground that she has made a record-breaking jump.
- *Exclusion of distractions from consciousness.* The basketball player blocks out all of the noise from the stands when attempting a critical basket.
- *Disappearance of self-consciousness.* An actor becomes so involved in the part he is playing that he "becomes" the character while on stage.
- *Distortion of time.* The time seems to "fly by" for a surgeon performing a delicate nine-hour operation.

Such intense emotional states are often associated with extreme activities reported by professionals when they describe their "peak performances." For examples, athletes talk about being "in the zone" when they describe extraordinary performances during a game. However, examples of flow can also be found in a variety of everyday experiences. Some everyday examples might be the intense emotional state you experience when you are totally engrossed in reading a great book or playing an exciting video game. Have you ever been so involved in these that you seem to lose track of time and block out all external sources of distractions while turning pages and reading as fast as you can, or feeling like your hands and fingers seem to be "at one" with the video controls? In these examples, the sense of pleasure experienced during the state of flow is associated with what seems like the effortlessness of the activity. Can you think of other examples of when you found yourself "going with the flow"?

Final Comments on the Study of Self-Actualizing People: Exceptional, But Not Perfect

You should be aware that included in this set of positive characteristics of self-actualizing people are some negative characteristics. Because they tend to be such emotionally strong people, they are capable of detaching themselves from those who they feel have done them wrong in a manner that might be described as cold, heartless, and ruthless. As you will recall, Freud severed his long-time friendships with Jung and Adler completely, never speaking to these individuals for the rest of his life. Like so many other people, some self-actualizers have been described as boring, silly, wasteful, and capable of temper outbursts. Finally, while self-actualizing people share certain characteristics that set them apart from most other people, it should be made clear that having these characteristics has little to do with intelligence and more to do with how the person chooses to live his or her life. Self-actualizing people tend to experience life to the fullest of their ability; and they search for excellence within themselves and in their experiences with other people and events in their lives. Thus, even while operating at their maximum potential, it should be made clear that self-actualizing people are not perfect.

Our discussion of Maslow's principal concepts is now complete. In the next section, we will examine some applications of them.

Applications of Maslow's Viewpoint: Using What is Known

As with most other profound theories, Maslow's views have been applied to a wide variety of areas, including psychotherapy (Boorstein, 2000; Maslow, 1970b), religion and spirituality (Elkins, 2001; Maslow, 1970a, 1976), education (Maslow, 1971, 1976), and stereotypes (Maslow, 1968, 1970b), as well as more recently to athletic performance (Privette, 2001) and consumer behavior and marketing (Hawkins, Mothersbaugh, & Best, 2007; Kahle, Homer, O'Brien, & Boush, 1997; Yalch & Brunel, 1996). A major application of Maslow's viewpoint has been to the world of work (Landy, 1989). In fact, an article by Maslow (1943) titled "A Theory of Human Motivation" was rated second among some 1,964 articles in a survey of significant contributions to the literature on management by Matteson (1974). In this section, we will explore the application of Maslow's viewpoint to the world of work and to personality assessment.

Maslow in the World of Work: "Working" Your Way Up the Hierarchy of Needs

Maslow felt that our needs should be met in all aspects of our lives. For many people, probably one of the most significant aspects of life, outside of family, is the world of work. In his own concern with human needs in the world of work, Maslow advocated what he called eupsychian management (Maslow, 1965/1998).

Applying Eupsychian Management: An Employee-Centered Approach The word **eupsychian** (pronounced "you-sigh-key-un") comes from *eu* meaning *good* (e.g., *euphoria*) and *psyche* meaning, basically, *mind* or *soul*. So *eupsychian* essentially means "having a good mind or soul" or "toward a good mind or soul." Maslow (1965) applied this concept to the world of work through what he called eupsychian management. **Eupsychian management** stresses that managers should concern themselves with becoming more aware of the needs of employees and creating a work environment designed to facilitate the satisfaction of these needs in their quest for self-actualization.

For example, let's say employees of a local factory have a high degree of job security and earn a substantial hourly wage (i.e., their physiological and safety needs are being met). If, however, they feel exploited by the company (i.e., their belongingness needs are not met) or are not sufficiently challenged by their job (i.e., their esteem needs are not met), both the workers and the company will suffer. Worker suffering might include increases in alcohol or drug abuse and various types of physical illnesses, such as ulcers and high blood pressure. The company suffers in that the decreased quality of products produced by such employees translates into loss of sales. The company also suffers because suffering workers will take more time off, which results in a loss of production, and the company's insurance costs to cover the medical needs of these suffering employees will rise.

Maslow suggested that one way to assess the extent to which employee needs are being met is to examine the nature of their complaints. When employees com- plain about the office being too crowded or noisy, he proposed that this should be a clue to management that safety needs are not being met. If they complain about office furnishings as being too drab or dehumanizing, this may be a sign that while their safety needs are met, their belongingness needs are not being satisfied. As employee complaints become more advanced in the nature of the need concerned, management can see that the employees are getting that much closer to being self-actualized. Thus, the point of eupsychian manage- ment is to listen to what employees are saying and act on this information in a manner that will help them to move up the hierarchy of needs within the world of work.

Criticisms of Maslow's approach to management emphasize that it has generated little empirical research (T. R. Mitchell & Daniels, 2003) and that the little research it has generated has yielded mixed results (Wahba & Bridwell, 1976). Although the amount of empirical research it has generated might be limited, others have pointed out that Maslow's concept of the hierarchy of needs has profoundly influenced our thinking in the area of management (Montuori & Purser, 2001). For example, in a survey of the biblio- graphical citations of the hierarchy of needs, Roberts (1972) noted over 200 listings after 1965 by over 140 authors in such diverse areas as organizational beha- vior and systems, teacher education, employee needs and expectations, leadership and management, political behavior, job performance, and psychological needs and satisfaction. "Synergy" – the term for developing a creative and mutually beneficial partnership among elements within an organization, such as workers and management – is a very popular contemporary idea that was introduced by Maslow (Montuori & Purser, 2001). Maslow's emphasis on searching for the higher purposes of organizations, other than profits, through corporate community involvement (e.g., sponsoring health fairs) and environmental concerns (e.g., invest- ing in alternative fuel sources) has now become a fea- ture of many contemporary organizations (Bunker & Alban, 1996; Emery & Purser, 1996; Porras & Collins, 1997). It is hard to dismiss something that has had the impact of Maslow's hierarchy of needs; but it should be judged on empirical evidence, not just its intuitive appeal. As an example, for still another area in which Maslow's ideas have been applied, consider the mater- ial in "At the Cutting Edge of Personality Psycho- logy: A Motivational Method of Mass Marketing" on pp. 246–247.

AT THE CUTTING EDGE OF PERSONALITY PSYCHOLOGY

A Motivational Method of Mass Marketing

Matching Motives and Merchandise: A Guide to Why We Buy

Among the forces that influence consumer decisions are motivation and personality (Berkowitz, Kerin, Hartley, & Rudelius, 2000). Because both of these forces are represented in Maslow's hierarchy of needs, his viewpoint can be used by marketing managers as "a macro theory designed to account for most human behavior in general terms" (Hawkins et al., 2007, p. 364). Marketers and others interested in trying to understand what drives consumers to make purchasing decisions have developed advertising campaigns for products based on their association with meeting certain need categories. What follows are some specific products and marketing examples arranged according to Maslow's hierarchy of needs.

- *Physiological needs.* Products designed to meet basic living requirements involving nutrition, rest, and health include food items, sleep products (e.g., mattresses, sleeping pills), exercise equipment, and medical-related supplies. *Marketing examples*: Band-Aid – "Blister-proof your feet"; Quaker Oats – "Eating oatmeal is good for your heart."
- *Safety needs.* Products designed to meet the needs of physical safety and security, stability, and familiarity include smoke detectors, insurance, retirement investments, seat belts, and burglar alarms. *Marketing examples*: Sleep Safe – "We've designed a travel alarm that just might wake you in the middle of the night – because a fire is sending smoke into your room. You see, ours is a smoke alarm as well as an alarm clock"; Revo cycling glasses – the caption under a photograph of a wrecked bike reads, "Should've worn Revo."

- *Belongingness and love needs.* Products designed to meet the needs of love, friendship, affiliation, and group acceptance include personal grooming products, group-identity clothing (e.g., college sweatshirt), and restaurants. *Marketing examples*: Olive Garden Restaurants – "Italians didn't invent sharing. They just made it impossible to resist"; Tums – "You are important. You are loved. You should take your calcium."
- *Esteem needs.* Products designed to meet the needs for status, self-respect, superiority, a sense of accomplishment, and feelings of usefulness to others include fancy cars, designer clothing, jewelry, expensive liquor, and stylish furniture. *Marketing examples*: Sheaffer – "Your hand should look as contemporary as the rest of you"; Cadillac – "Those long hours have paid off. In recognition, financial success, and in the way you reward yourself. Isn't it time you owned a Cadillac?"
- *Need for self-actualization.* Products designed to meet the need for self-fulfillment and promoting one's full potential include educational

Figure 6.4   Although this ad is for outdoor clothing, the central theme is an appeal to self-actualization needs and individuals striving to meet their full potential.

programs, hobbies, vacations, sports, and museums. *Marketing examples*: U.S. Army – "Be all you can be. Be an Army of One"; Outward Bound Schools – "Challenges, adventure, growth."

Such examples, as well as additional research (Yalch & Brunel, 1996), provide support for the validity of Maslow's viewpoint as an important tool in marketing. In addition, because more than one need category can be met by a specific product,

effective advertisements often operate at many different need categories. For example, although the brand of mountain climbing equipment and outdoor clothing being advertised in Figure 6.4 is designed primarily to meet the basic physiological (e.g., exercise) and safety (e.g., warmth and comfort) needs of outdoor enthusiasts, an additional appeal to consumers is the association of the brand with the motive for self-actualization implicit in scaling the side of a steep mountain or other outdoor activities that inspire individuals to seek their full potential.

The application of Maslow's viewpoint to various aspects of the world of work is proof of the usefulness of his ideas. Even more impressive is that such ideas seem to have global appeal. As an example, consider the cross-cultural examination of worker motivation from the perspective of Maslow's hierarchy of needs presented in "The Cultural Context of Personality Psychology."

Individuals from different cultural backgrounds seem to have similar motives for working.

The Cultural Context of Personality Psychology

A Global Perspective on Worker Motivation: A Cross-Cultural Look at Why We Work

In an attempt to investigate the cross-cultural nature of Maslow's need structure as it relates to worker motivation, Simcha Ronen (1994), of Tel Aviv University, obtained importance ratings of 14 specific work goals from workers in Canada, France, the United Kingdom, Germany, Japan, China, and Israel. An analysis of these ratings indicated that the goals could be classified into a 2-by-2 grid based on two general dimensions: individualism–collectivism and materialism–humanism. The individualism–collectivism dimension reflects the extent to which the emphasis is placed on recognizing the contributions of the individual

worker vs. the group of workers; the materialism–humanism dimension reflects the extent to which emphasis is placed on the financial success vs. personal satisfaction of work.

Maslow's physiological and safety need categories can be classified within this framework as reflecting materialistic collectivism, in that the goals of work are common to a group of paid employees who are working specifically toward financially quantifiable work goals to meet these basic needs (e.g., "I'm working to put food on the table and a roof over our heads"). Six of the fourteen work goals were included in this classification: *physical* (e.g., have good working conditions, such as good ventilation and lighting), *area* (e.g., live in a desirable area for you and your family), *time* (e.g., have a job that allows sufficient time for you to have a personal and family life), *security* (e.g., feeling that you are able to work for the company as long as you want to), *benefits* (e.g., have good fringe benefits), and *earnings* (e.g., have the opportunity for high earnings). An example of workers in this category might be those working on an assembly line, whose job might provide money to pay the bills but offer a minimal sense of personal satisfaction and stimulation.

Maslow's belongingness need category is classified as reflecting humanistic (nonmaterialistic) collectivism, which emphasizes the establishment of good interpersonal relationships at work (e.g., "I'm able to get along with others on the job."). Two of the fourteen work goals were included in this classification: *co-workers* (e.g., working with people who cooperate well with each other) and *manager* (e.g., having a good working relationship with your manager). An example of workers in this category might be co-workers who regularly eat lunch together and are members of the company soccer team.

Maslow's esteem need category is classified as reflecting materialistic individualism, which emphasizes personal achievement and recognition endowed by others (e.g., "I'm honored to be selected as employee of the month"). Three of the fourteen work goals were included in this classification: *recognition* (e.g., being able to receive recognition when you do a good job), *advancement* (e.g., the presence of opportunities for promotions to higher job levels), and *training* (e.g., having the opportunity to improve current skills or learn new ones). An example of workers in this category would be individuals who are elected by their co-workers to represent them on an employee grievance committee, and are given additional training on conflict resolution and negotiation practices in preparation for their new role.

Finally, Maslow's self-actualization need category is classified as reflecting humanistic (nonmaterialistic) individualism, which emphasizes working for personal satisfaction and self-expression (e.g., "I'm able to express my creativity through my work"). Three of the fourteen work goals were included in this classification: *autonomy* (e.g., freedom to adopt your own approach to doing your job), *skills* (e.g., the opportunity to use fully your skills and ability on the job), and *challenge* (e.g., the extent to which your work provides you with a sense of personal accomplishment). An example of a worker in this category might be an office manager who gets a personal sense of satisfaction from

her ability to introduce her own management style when solving work-related problems.

The significance of Ronen's work is that it provides evidence for a universal classification of worker needs. As our world of work becomes more global through increased opportunities to work with individuals from different countries, it is important to understand what motivates people around the world to work. Ronen's work is also reassuring because it suggests that there seems to be some common ground for such motivation, indicating that when it comes to work, no matter where we are in the world, we seem to do it for similar reasons.

Personality Assessment from Maslow's Viewpoint: The Assessment of Self-Actualization

The significance of the concept of self-actualization is also reflected in its application to personality assessment. Even though the concept is subjective and unique to each person, attempts have been made to develop objective measures for assessing an individual's degree of self-actualization (A. Jones & Crandall, 1986; Shostrom, 1975, 1977; Sumerlin & Bundrick, 1996, 1998).

The Personal Orientation Inventory An objective measure most often associated with assessing self-actualization is the Personal Orientation Inventory. The **Personal Orientation Inventory (POI)** was developed by Everett L. Shostrom (1963, 1964, 1975) as an objective means of measuring some of the behaviors and values related to Maslow's concept. The POI contains 150 items, arranged in pairs of opposing statements. From each pair, the individual is asked to select the statement that best describes him or her. The scoring of the POI involves assessing 2 major scales and 10 subscales. The major scales are Inner Directiveness (ID; i.e., autonomy) and Time Ratio (TR; i.e., orientation in the present and effective use of time). The 10 subscales consist of characteristics indicating self-actualization, including self-acceptance, spontaneity, synergy (i.e., flexibility in thinking), and capacity for intimate contact (Shostrom, 1963, 1964, 1975). To examine your own level of self-actualization, complete the exercise in "You Can Do It" on p. 249.

You Can Do It

The Assessment of Self-Actualization: Measuring Maximum Potential

Listed below is a sample of items similar to those in the POI. For each pair of items, select the alternative that seems to be most characteristic of how you feel.

1. (a) I do what others expect me to do.
   (b) I choose freely what I want to do.
2. (a) Jokes that make fun of others are not something I enjoy hearing.
   (b) Jokes that make fun of others are something I do enjoy hearing.
3. (a) It is my belief that people basically care about others.
   (b) It is my belief that people basically care about themselves only.
4. (a) Justifying my actions is something I must do in the pursuit of my own interests.
   (b) Justifying my actions is something I do not feel I must do in the pursuit of my own interests.
5. (a) The rules and standards of society guide the way I live my life.
   (b) The rules and standards of society are not always needed to guide the way I live my life.
6. (a) I need reasons to justify my feelings.
   (b) I do not need reasons to justify my feelings.
7. (a) Warm feelings are the only ones I feel free to express to my friends.
   (b) Both warm and hostile feelings are feelings I feel free to express to my friends.
8. (a) Being myself is the best way to continue to grow.
   (b) The only way to continue to grow is by setting my sights on a high-level goal that is socially approved.
9. (a) The anger people feel should always be controlled.
   (b) The anger people feel should be expressed honestly.
10. (a) Criticism can provide a welcomed opportunity for growth.
    (b) Criticism does not provide a welcomed opportunity for growth.

Interpretation

Give yourself one point each time your response agrees with the following scoring key: item 1 = b, 2 = a, 3 = a, 4 = b, 5 = b, 6 = b, 7 = b, 8 = a, 9 = b, 10 = a. The higher your score, the more consistent your responses are with the characteristic of self-actualization.

Adapted from Shostrom (1963).

Research Assessing the Validity of the POI The validity of the POI has been investigated by assessing how closely it correlates to other personality inventories that measure traits and values related to the characteristics of self-actualizing people. For example, the ID scale was correlated positively with inventories measuring self-esteem, faith in people, purpose in life, and empathy; but it was correlated negatively with rigidity, social anxiety, hopelessness, and narcissism (Leak, 1984). POI scales have also been correlated positively with tests of creativity (Braun & Asta, 1968), academic achievement (LeMay & Damm, 1968; Stewart, 1968), spirituality (Tloczynski, Knoll, & Fitch, 1997), and scores of sexual enjoyment among married couples (McCann & Biaggio, 1989). Supporting the notion of personal growth occurring within successful therapeutic experiences, greater increases in POI scores were found for people who participated in group therapy than for those who did not (Guinan & Foulds, 1970) and for individuals who have participated in other forms of therapeutic interventions (Duncan, Konefal, & Spechler, 1990).

Limitations of the POI include the apparent interrelatedness of the various scales (Hattie, 1981; Silverstein & Fisher, 1968, 1972) and findings inconsistent with Maslow's thinking (Maddi, 1996). Although there appear to be certain shortcomings, "the POI has shown impressive group differences following growth experiences and also impressive correlations with related trait measures" (Leak, 1984, p. 38). In fact, the amount of research on the POI is extensive. Over 700 studies were listed prior to 1979; in 1982, over 390 references were identified in a separate computer search of the POI literature (Hattie, Hancock, & Brereton, 1984). The POI is still the most widely used measure of self-actualization.

Our discussion of the applications of Maslow's viewpoint is complete. Evidence supporting the significance of his ideas, particularly the hierarchy of needs, is provided by the extent to which they are taught in different college courses and the diversity of their applications (Kahle et al., 1997). We will end our discussion of Maslow's viewpoint by considering some of its characteristic strengths and limitations.

Evaluating Maslow's Motivational Perspective: Strengths and Limitations

Characteristic Strengths

Here are some strengths of Maslow's motivational viewpoint:

- *An emphasis on the best of the best.* While many of the personality theorists discussed in this book developed viewpoints of personality based on their clinical work involving people with maladjusted personalities, Maslow took just the opposite approach. His approach was to learn about the healthy personality by studying the healthiest personalities he could find. His emphasis on studying the best of the best represents a welcome alternative in an attempt to better understand the operation of the healthy personality.
- *A realistic view of human nature.* Maslow maintained a relatively realistic view of human nature. He saw people as basically good and motivated in the direction of self-enhancement. But he also realized that such a process of self-enhancement did not just happen automatically; it required some desire and effort on the part of the individual. Maslow realistically pointed out that as the level of self-enhancement becomes higher, more personal effort and desire on the individual's part are required. His basic point was that

people will improve to the extent that they want to improve.

- *The impact of Maslow's ideas.* Because Maslow's hierarchy of needs makes so much intuitive sense, it is discussed in a wide variety of disciplines, from religion to work. It is also very easy for people to apply the needs hierarchy to their own lives as a means of explaining and understanding their own behavior. Thus, because it is something that can be easily used, the hierarchy of needs concept has been applied in various disciplines.

Summing It Up *Characteristic Strengths and Limitations of Maslow's Motivational Viewpoint*

Characteristic Strengths:

- *Studying the Best of the Best*: Rather than studying the maladjusted personality, Maslow focused on studying the most well-adjusted people he could find in his attempt to understand the nature and operation of personality.
- *Viewing Human Nature Realistically*: Maslow's view of human nature involved realizing that the process of personal growth required a sense of desire on the part of the individual, not just the assumption of an innate tendency toward personal growth.
- *The Impact of the Motivational Viewpoint*: The relatively intuitive nature of the hierarchy of needs concept has resulted in its discussion and application in a variety of areas.

Characteristic Limitations:

- *The Relative Untestability of the Motivational Viewpoint*: Because many of the principal components of the motivational viewpoint are stated in a rather ambiguous manner, testing the validity of the theory is difficult.
- *Subjectivity in the Judgment of Self-Actualization*: The determination of the characteristic features of self-actualizing individuals was based on Maslow's subjective judgment alone.
- *Lack of Supportive Empirical Evidence*: The amount of empirical evidence supporting Maslow's major concepts is rather limited and equivocal in nature.

Characteristic Limitations

Maslow's motivational viewpoint has the following limitations:

- *An almost untestable theory.* Central to Maslow's viewpoint is his hierarchy of needs. But much of what he said about this theoretical concept is rather ambiguous, with the exception of the ordering of the need categories. He was unclear about all of the needs that were included in each category. He also left unspecified the exact way these various needs could be satisfied. In short, many important questions about the hierarchy of needs remain unanswered – and the farther up the hierarchy you go, the more ambiguity you tend to find. Such ambiguity creates an almost untestable theory.

- *The subjective nature of self-actualization and self-actualizers.* Although Maslow defined the characteristics of the self-actualizing individual in a rather detailed and specific way, he selected these features primarily on his own subjective judgment, using little objective statistical analysis. The extent to which other researchers would come to the same conclusions as he did about what characteristics constitute the best of the best remains unanswered. In all fairness, however, the research on the POI does represent an attempt to objectively assess the concept of self-actualization.

- *Limited empirical research.* Because of the problems noted in the preceding two limitations, Maslow's viewpoint has generated very little empirical research. As noted earlier, the research that has been done seems to offer only minimal support for many of his principal concepts.

A summary of the principal ideas examined in this section is presented in "Summing It Up: Characteristics Strengths and Limitations of Maslow's Motivational Viewpoint" on p. 250.

Chapter Summary: Reexamining the Highlights

- *Carl Rogers's Phenomenological Viewpoint*

  - *Basic Assumptions of the Rogerian Viewpoint.* The basic assumptions of Rogers's viewpoint include an emphasis on the subjective experience of the individual, focusing on the importance of the here and now as the critical cause of behavior, having the actualizing tendency as the primary source of motivation, and considering the organismic valuing process as the basis of evaluating the value of subjective experience.

  - *Basic Concepts of the Rogerian Viewpoint.* The basic concepts of the viewpoint of personality proposed by Rogers include the phenomenal field, the process of subception, the self-concept as consisting of the organism and the self, and the states of congruence and incongruence.

  - *Self-Actualization.* The motivational process by which the actualizing tendency is expressed requires freedom and openness of experience. It is ongoing in nature, manifests itself uniquely in each person, and is holistic in its reaction.

  Personality Development. The process of personality development involves satisfying the need for positive regard from others and positive self-regard. Positive regard from others can be expressed in the form of unconditional or conditional positive regard. The need for positive self-regard can be altered by conditions of worth.

  - *The Nature of Personality Adjustment.* The fully functioning person reflects a high degree of personality adjustment and is characterized by congruence, incorporation of diverse information about the self, openness to experience, and trust in one's personal judgments. The maladjusted personality is characterized by distortions in awareness, denial, and rigid patterns of behavior.

  - *Applications of the Rogerian Viewpoint.* The most extensive applications of Rogers's viewpoint include person-centered therapy and the identification and development of the conditions necessary for an effective therapeutic experience. The application of the Rogerian viewpoint to personality assessment is best reflected by the

Q-Sort technique and its use to assess the outcome of psychotherapy.

– *Evaluating the Rogerian Viewpoint.* Characteristic strengths of the Rogerian viewpoint include its emphasis on research, the promotion of humanism, and the extensive impact of Rogers's ideas both inside and outside the field of personality psychology. Characteristic limitations include its emphasis on the subjective experience and self-report information, theoretical simplicity, and criticism of person-centered therapy as a therapeutic technique.

● *Maslow's Motivational Viewpoint*

– *Basic Assumptions of Maslow's Perspective.* The basic assumptions of Maslow's viewpoint include a rather positive and humanistic view of the individual, an emphasis on investigating the healthy personality, and perceiving the operation of personality to meet a combination of biological and psychological needs.

– *Basic Concepts of Maslow's Perspective.* The state of self-actualization involves the individual maximizing the satisfaction of personal needs. These needs are classified into deficiency needs and being needs and arranged into a hierarchy from most to least potent. The hierarchical arrangement includes physiological, safety, belongingness and love, esteem, and self-actualization needs.

– *Maslow's Study of Self-actualizing Individuals.* As identified by Maslow, characteristics of self-actualizers include a more accurate perception of reality, a greater acceptance of self and others, being true to themselves, having peak experiences, being other-centered and autonomous, having a limited number of very close personal friends, and being creative in everyday matters.

– *Applications of Maslow's Viewpoint.* Maslow's ideas have been extended to worker motivation with the philosophy of eupsychian management. However, research on the effectiveness of eupsychian management has produced mixed evidence. Applications of Maslow's ideas to personality assessment have focused on the development and validation of measures of self-actualization, such as the Personal Orientation Inventory.

– *Evaluating Maslow's Perspective.* Characteristic strengths of Maslow's viewpoint include his emphasis on studying the exceptionally healthy personality, his realistic view of human nature, and the diverse extension of his ideas. Characteristic limitations of Maslow's viewpoint include the untestable nature of many of his principal concepts, the subjective description of self-actualizers based only on his standards, and the limited amount of empirical research his ideas have generated.

Glossary

actualizing tendency   An internal inclination for continuous personal growth and development.

behaviorism   A school of thought in psychology that seeks to understand behavior by examining the environmental cues that serve to elicit specific behaviors.

being needs   A category of needs related to personal growth.

belongingness and love needs   A category of needs related to a basic desire to establish and maintain meaningful interpersonal relationships.

body mass index   A numerical index based on a ratio of your weight and height, associated with health problems.

conditional positive regard   Being accepted by others only to the extent that the individual meets certain conditions.

conditions of worth   Self-acceptance based on the conditions of acceptance by others.

congruence   A state of consistency between internal feelings and an individual's external perception of the self.

contact   A heightened and meaningful relationship between the client and therapist.

creativity   A leader's ability to utilize existing knowledge to address new challenges in diverse settings.

cultural responsiveness hypothesis   A belief that treatment effectiveness is increased when the therapist and client share similar ethnic and cultural characteristics.

deficiency needs   A category of needs related to basic survival.

e-therapy Any number of interactive therapies that are offered over the Internet to help individuals deal with a variety of emotional problems.

esteem needs A category of needs related to a basic desire to establish and maintain self-respect and the respect of others.

eupsychian The characteristic of possessing a good mind or soul.

eupsychian management An approach to worker motivation based on meeting both people's deficiency needs and their being needs.

Experience Questionnaire A self-report inventory designed to assess peak experiences.

flow An emotional state characterized by becoming so involved in a situation that nothing else seems to matter.

fully functioning person An individual characterized by a high degree of mental health and personality adjustment.

graduated practice A form of therapy used to help people overcome extreme fears.

hierarchy of needs A systematic arrangement of needs based on their potency and influence on the individual's behavior.

humanistic viewpoint A perspective of human nature emphasizing personal growth and the development of one's full potential.

ideal sort A Q-Sort technique in which the individual makes ratings of the self along various dimensions as he or she would like to perceive the self as being.

incongruence A state of inconsistency between internal feelings and an individual's perception of the self.

narcissist An individual with an exaggerated sense of self-worth and attention-seeking tendencies.

need for positive regard The desire to be accepted by others.

need for positive self-regard The desire to accept one's self.

negative self-talk Thinking or speaking of yourself in a self-demeaning manner.

organism The evaluative dimension of the self-concept.

organismic valuing process A personal standard by which actions are evaluated by their ability to promote self-enhancement.

peak experiences Moments of intense emotional reactions and self-awareness.

person-centered therapy A form of psychotherapy developed by Rogers to help treat an incongruent self-concept.

Personal Orientation Inventory (POI) An objective self-report method of personality assessment designed to measure self-actualization tendencies.

phenomenal field An individual's total sensory awareness at any given moment.

phenomenological perspective A viewpoint stressing that the subjective interpretation of events is the critical determinant of thoughts, feelings, and behavior.

physiological needs A category of needs whose satisfaction is required for basic survival.

practical intelligence The ability to modify one's knowledge in a purposeful manner to meet changing situational demands.

Q-Sort technique An assessment technique designed to measure various forms of congruence of the self-concept.

safety needs A category of need related to a basic desire for security and stability.

self The individual's sense of reference in the external environment.

self-actualization For Rogers, the source of motivation for self-enhancement; for Maslow, the tendency to develop one's potential to its fullest when meeting personal needs.

self-esteem An individual's overall evaluative sense of personal self-worth.

self–ideal sort A type of Q-Sort assessment technique measuring the degree of overlap in the perceptions of the real self and ideal self.

self-sort A Q-Sort technique in which the individual makes ratings of the self along various dimensions as he or she perceives the self as being now.

social support People and social groups that individuals can rely on to help them cope with problems.

state of self-actualization The utilization of a person's abilities to his or her full potential.

subception The process of formulating an affective reaction to an event before the event reaches total conscious awareness.

subjective experience A person's understanding of events from his or her own perception and interpretation of them.

synthesis A leader's ability to bring together the qualities of wisdom, intelligence, and creativity.

third force A movement in psychology emphasizing the study of those internal processes contributing to the enhancement and empowerment of the individual.

unconditional positive regard Being accepted by others without any limitations.

WICS model of leadership A theory suggesting that effective leaders possess the characteristics of wisdom, intelligence, and creativity and their synthesis.

wisdom The leadership ability to use one's knowledge and values to meet the needs of other members and organizations.

The Trait Viewpoint
Psychological Dispositions of Personality

7

Chapter Overview:
A Preview of Coming Attractions

In this chapter we will examine the trait viewpoint of personality. The trait viewpoint represents a dramatic shift away from an emphasis on the inner dynamics and processes of personality that captured the interest of Freud (e.g., the interaction of the id, ego, and superego), as well as those who reacted to him, to a greater emphasis on the objective assessment of observable behaviors to account for and predict individual differences in behavior (Nicholson, 2003). Such a shift began to take shape in the 1920s and 1930s as the development of viewpoints of personality moved out of clinical settings and into psychological laboratories. The sentiments of this shift are nicely illustrated by a statement made by Gordon Allport, an influential personality psychologist to be discussed in this chapter, when he wrote "The psychological problem [of personality] is strictly objective" and, he went on to say, "entirely consistent with the needs of laboratory procedures" (1922, pp. 11, 20). The essence of this statement is that the study of personality needed to follow the rules adopted by and be evaluated using the guidelines of other disciplines of science. Our presentation of the trait viewpoint begins with a discussion of the basic characteristics of traits. Next you will be introduced to the perspectives of Gordon W. Allport, Raymond B. Cattell, and Hans J. Eysenck. After considering the perspectives of these three theorists, we will explore some central issues associated with the consistency of the operational influence of traits and the nature of the structural organization of traits, with an emphasis on the Five-Factor Model.

Personality Traits: The Foundation of Personality

When you describe someone, you might describe them by their physical characteristics – "He's tall, about 6′2″, has brown eyes, and black hair." You might also describe someone by their personality characteristics – "She's honest, dependable, and outgoing." In both cases, when providing descriptions of an individual, we employ a series of adjectives. For personality psychologists, the adjectives used to describe someone's personality are referred to as traits. **Traits** are dimensions of personality that influence in a particular way a person's thoughts, feelings, and behaviors (Costa & McCrae, 2006; McCrae & Costa, 2003; Pervin, 2002; Wiggins, 1997; Winter, John, Stewart, Klohnen, & Duncan, 1998). They are also assumed to be a contributing factor to the consistency in the expression of such thoughts, feelings, and behavior across situations and over time (Fleeson, 2001; McAdams & Pals, 2006).

As you can see from this brief definition, traits go beyond the simple descriptive nature of adjectives. Throughout this chapter, you will see how traits are used to account for the expression of our own personality and the personalities of others in a number of different ways. As an example of the nature and operation of traits, suppose you are looking over the schedule of classes for the next semester, and you are considering enrolling in an Introduction to Principles of Economics course in order to fulfill a general educational requirement for graduation. As you look over the different sections of that course being offered, you do not recognize any of the instructors listed as teaching the course. In an attempt to help you make a decision about selecting a particular course section, you go to a website titled "Rate Your Professor" where students can provide their opinions of various instructors. As you read the opinions of other students for two of the professors who are teaching the course at timeslots that will fit well into your schedule, you notice that one professor is described by some students as being *interesting* (e.g., the lectures contain lots of everyday examples), *prompt* (e.g., feedback on exams and other assignments is provided at the next class meeting), and *demanding* (e.g., penalizes heavily when assignments are not turned in on time). The second professor tends to be described as *rigid* (e.g., talks only about the points listed in the PowerPoint slides), *self-centered* (e.g., frowns when

students disrupt the lecture by asking questions or making comments), and *undependable* (e.g., shows up for class late and is not in the office during posted office hours on a regular basis). In this example, the traits of the two professors are illustrated by the adjectives used by other students to describe them. Thus, the personality of each professor is reflected by the traits used to describe them. However, going beyond their descriptive nature, such traits are assumed to influence the way the professors will think (e.g., students should be seen, not heard), feel (e.g., seems to enjoy teaching), and behave (e.g., penalizes late assignments). As you ponder the traits used to describe the two professors, you are concerned not only with the descriptive nature of the traits, but, more importantly, with the way the expression of these sets of traits will influence the manner in which each professor will teach the course when you enroll in it next semester. In the language of the trait viewpoint, your concerns involve an understanding of the influence of the structural nature of the traits and the consistency of the expression of these sets of traits. In this case, the structural nature of the traits reflects how a combination of particular traits will influence the manner in which the professor teaches the course. For example, you might assume that an interesting but demanding professor will teach a course where students will enjoy what they are learning but be expected to do a lot of reading. On the other hand, you might assume that a rigid and self-centered professor might teach a course where students will just sit in class and take notes based on the lecture outline. The consistency of the expression of these traits reflects the extent to which you assume that the manner in which the professor has taught the course in the past will be similar to the way it will be taught next semester when you are enrolled in the course – the professor will be interesting and demanding next semester, too.

Thus, seeking to identify and understand the structural nature of the traits that comprise an individual's personality and determine the consistency of the expression of these traits are principal concerns that affect the decisions that we make on a day-to-day basis (e.g., "Is that insightful, charming job applicant going to behave the same way at work when hired for the job?"). The issues of trait structure and their consistency of operation are also major issues that we will explore in our discussion of the trait viewpoint of personality throughout this chapter. We will begin our examination of the trait viewpoint by considering some of the basic assumptions associated with it.

Basic Assumptions of the Trait Viewpoint

Although there are various trait viewpoints, they all tend to be guided by certain basic assumptions about personality traits (Wiggins, 1997). These include the principal assumptions that traits define the nature of personality, and, as a result, can be used to distinguish among individuals in the manner in which individual differences are expressed. A second basic belief is that such individual differences among individuals represent the operational influence different traits have on the variation in the style of expression of each individual's personality. For example, if we describe an individual as having the trait of introversion, we would expect that such a trait would influence the expression of his personality (e.g., leave noisy, crowded social events quickly) differently than someone that we might describe as having the trait of extraversion (e.g., seeks out noisy, crowded parties). Thus, as the fundamental element of personality, traits are used to describe and explain variations in the expression of personality. In this section, we will take a closer look at the basic beliefs associated with characteristic features of traits (Costa & McCrae, 1998; McCrae & Costa, 2003; Pervin, 2002; Wiggins, 1997).

Traits as the Basis of Individual Differences: Expressions of Uniqueness   A principal assumption of the trait viewpoint is that people differ in the degree to which they possess certain traits (Costa & McCrae, 1998, 2006; Funder, 1995; McCrae & Costa, 2003; Pervin, 2002). Individuals can differ in terms of the degree to which they possess a certain trait. For example, an individual who is high on the trait of dependability will have a different personality than an individual who is low on that trait. And this difference in the degree of dependability will express itself differently, in that the high-dependable individual will turn in assignments on time at work while the low-dependable individual will have a sporadic performance.

In addition, individuals can also differ in both the degree and the type of traits they possess. For example, a human resources manager at one company might have a personality that is characterized by being high on the trait of empathy and high on the trait of assertiveness, while a human resources manager at another company might have a personality that is characterized by being low on the trait of empathy and high on the trait of emotionality. Such variation in the degree and type of traits they possess would manifest itself in the different

approaches they might take to terminating employment. The high-empathic, high-assertive personnel manager might say in a kind but direct way, "I know this is going to make you feel bad, but it is my responsibility to tell you that your job is being terminated. I'm sorry to be the one to tell you." The low-empathic, high-emotional personnel manager might say in an uncaring, nervous manner, "I'm not really sure if this is the best way to say it, but your job is being terminated. Boy, that was really hard for me to say; I'm glad it's over." Thus, from the trait viewpoint, the expression of the uniqueness of an individual's personality is assumed to reflect the nature and degree of traits they possess (Johnson, 1997; Wiggins, 1997).

As an illustration of how this aspect of the trait viewpoint is expressed in everyday life, consider the exercise in "You Can Do It" on p. 258.

Traits as the Basis of Consistency: Expressions of Stability   Another principal assumption of the trait viewpoint is that behavior is influenced across a variety of situations in a manner consistent with the traits possessed by the individual (Fleeson, 2001; Funder, 1991; Johnson, 1997; Kenrick & Funder, 1988; Wiggins, 1997; Winter et al., 1998). For example, if an individual is very pushy about borrowing your class notes, parks in a handicapped zone without the right to, and smokes a cigarette in a nonsmoking section of the student activities center, we would probably assume that this person is very inconsiderate. From the trait viewpoint, the explanation of this tendency to behave in such an inconsiderate manner is that the individual's personality contains the trait of self-centeredness to a high degree. In a similar manner, we would expect the personnel manager with the high-empathy, high assertiveness personality to behave that way in other situations as well. For example, when asking for a refund at the department store, the individual might say, "While I certainly can see your position on the issue, and I know this is a difficult situation to place you in, I must request that you refund my money on this product because it did not meet my level of satisfaction based on the description in the ad."

Thus, an individual's personality is defined by the nature and the degree of the traits it consists of (e.g., high degree of self-centeredness and low degree of honesty). And that unique structure of these traits will then determine the individual's behavior in a consistent manner across a variety of situations (e.g., behaving selfishly and inconsiderately when talking in the theater, having

You Can Do It

How Do I Describe Thee? Let Me Count the Ways: An Everyday Example of Behaving Like a Trait Psychologist

Think of a friend you know well. After you have selected someone special, describe that person by writing in the space below those words or phrases that seem to capture his or her essential personality characteristics.

———————————————————

———————————————————

———————————————————

———————————————————

In a similar exercise with some of his students, the famous trait psychologist Gordon W. Allport found that the number of central traits used to describe the essential characteristics of an individual's personality was generally between 5 and 10, with an average of around 7. Does your description

support this hypothesis? As a further test of Allport's hypothesis, you might also ask a few of your friends to complete this exercise.

Using traits to describe our own personality and the personality of others is a very common activity. For example, you might use traits to describe yourself in a cover letter for a job (e.g., "I'm conscientious and dedicated") or in a personals ad in an online social network (e.g., "I'm spontaneous and outgoing"). You might also do the same when writing a letter of recommendation for a friend (e.g., "She's honest and diligent") or describing a supervisor at work to some friends, (e.g., "The night manager is insecure and hostile"). You would also be using your understanding of traits when looking at the personals ad of another individual online (e.g., "My friends say I have a great sense of humor, and I am an open-minded, uninhibited individual") to decide if you want to contact this person. Thus, using traits to describe yourself and others in everyday life is similar to how trait psychologists approach the study of personality.

more than 10 items in the express line at the supermarket, and showing up late for a study session). With this basic understanding of the nature and operation of traits, we now turn our attention to three of the major perspectives within the trait viewpoint.

Perspectives on the Trait Viewpoint: Theoretical Variations on Individual Differences in Personality

In this section, we will introduce you to the theoretical perspectives of Gordon W. Allport, Raymond B. Cattell, and Hans J Eysenck. This presentation will include a discussion of the basic assumptions, basic concepts, and applications associated with these three perspectives.

Allport's Personalistic Viewpoint: In Search of the Uniqueness of Individuals

Allport's theory of personality is **personalistic** in nature. **Personalism** is the psychology of the person (Allport, 1960). As a personalistic theorist, Allport emphasized trying to understand and explain the complexity and uniqueness of the total individual. His principal concern was to develop a theory of personality that would help to explain what makes each of us unique. Thus, he was trying to understand "real people" rather than the so-called average person who is supposed to represent what "most people" are like. For a more personal look at an individual who tried to promote personalism, consider the material in "A Closer Look" on p. 259.

A Closer Look

The Life of Gordon W. Allport

Gordon W. Allport is considered to be the founder of personality psychology in the United States.

Gordon W. Allport was born in Montezuma, Indiana, on November 11, 1897. He was the youngest, by some five years, of four sons. His father was a country doctor who turned to the study of medicine rather late in life (after a career in business and having three sons). Allport believed that he and his mother were his father's first patients.

Allport grew up and received his early education in Cleveland. Although describing himself as a "good routine student, but definitely uninspired and uncurious about anything beyond the usual adolescent concerns" (Allport, 1967, p. 5), he did graduate second in his high school class of 100. Not sure what to do after graduation, he followed the advice of his oldest brother, a Harvard graduate. Although Allport applied to Harvard late in the summer and just squeezed through the entrance exams, he succeeded in being admitted. On his first set of examinations, he received an array of Ds and Cs. However, by strengthening his efforts, he finished the first year with As.

After receiving his AB in 1919, majoring in economics and philosophy, Allport accepted a teaching position at Roberts College in Istanbul, Turkey, where he taught English and sociology. The year of teaching there was enjoyable for him and convinced him "that teaching was not such a bad career for me" (Allport, 1967, p. 7). His new-found enjoyment of teaching resulted in his accepting a fellowship for graduate study at Harvard.

On his return from Turkey, Allport stopped in Vienna to visit a brother who was working there. While there, Allport wrote a letter to Freud announcing that he was in Vienna and requesting a visit with the great psychoanalyst. Allport received a handwritten invitation from Freud to visit him at his office at a certain time.

Upon entering Freud's office, Allport found the great man sitting in silence, waiting for the younger man to state the purpose of his visit. Feeling uncomfortable with the silence, Allport began relating to Freud an incident he had observed on the streetcar en route to Freud's office. It involved a little boy who seemed to possess an intense fear of dirt and an extreme desire to avoid a "dirty man" sitting next to him.

When Allport finished the story, Freud asked, "And was that little boy you?" Allport realized that Freud's misunderstanding of his motivation for telling the story, which was to break the uncomfortable silence, was probably a result of the psychoanalyst's extensive contact with his clinical patients and their neurotic defenses. For Allport, this experience was significant; it taught him that psychoanalysis placed too much emphasis on the unconscious motivation of the individual and that more might be gained by studying the individual's surface motives (Allport, 1967; Elms, 1993).

Upon returning to Harvard, Allport continued his studies and completed the requirements for his PhD two years later in 1922. His doctoral dissertation, titled "An experimental study of the traits of personality *with application to the problem of social diagnosis*," is believed to be the first American dissertation concerned with personality traits. In addition, a course he taught at Harvard in 1924 and 1925, titled "Personality: Its Psychological and Social Aspects," is believed to be the first personality course to be offered at an American college.

In 1937, Allport published a textbook, which he said had been " 'cooking' in my head since my graduate days" (Allport, 1967, p. 15), titled *Personality: A Psychological Interpretation*. According to Allport, he wrote this book because he wanted to "give a psychological definition of the field of personality as I saw it" (Allport, 1967, p. 15). For almost 25 years, this classic textbook was more or less standard reading in the field of personality psychology. Some 24 years later, Allport (1961) revised the textbook to reflect new movements in the field of personality, as well as to update his ideas, and titled it *Pattern and Growth in Personality*.

Allport spent virtually all of his academic life, from 1924 to his death on October 9, 1967, on the faculty at Harvard. During his illustrious career, he made numerous significant contributions linking his research interests in personality and social psychology to issues and concerns having real social relevance. Such contributions included his work involving the evaluation of the radio as a powerful new form of mass communication in the 1920s and 1930s (Cantril & Allport, 1935), his study in the area of rumor analysis during World War II (Allport & Postman, 1947), his research on the problems of group conflict and prejudice (Allport, 1954), and his efforts to define and assess personal values (Allport, Vernon, & Lindzey, 1960). For his efforts, he received virtually every professional honor given by psychologists. Some of these honors included being elected president of the American Psychological Association, receiving the Gold Medal Award of the American Psychological Foundation, and receiving the American Psychological Association's award for distinguished scientific contributions. More information on the life of America's founder of personality psychology can be found in an autobiography (Allport, 1967) appearing in Boring and Lindzey's *A History of Psychology in Autobiography* or a book-length biography on Allport titled *Inventing Personality: Gordon Allport and the Science of Self-hood* (Nicholson, 2003).

Basic Assumptions of Allport's Definition of Personality

According to Allport (1961), "Personality is the dynamic organization within the individual of those psychophysical systems that determine his characteristic behavior and thought" (p. 28). To clarify his definition, Allport went on to discuss what he considered to be its key concepts:

- *Personality is a dynamic organization in a state of continuous growth.* The concept of "dynamic organization" stresses that although personality consists of an orderly system (i.e., an organization)

of components, the system is in a constant state of change and personal growth (i.e., a dynamic state). Within such a state, each experience that is encountered modifies or strengthens, even in the slightest way, various aspects of the individual's personality (Caspi & Roberts, 1999). For example, honesty in law-abiding students is strengthened when they read about dishonest students being disciplined for cheating.

- *Personality is psychophysical in nature as it combines the mind and body.* "Psychophysical" is a concept used by Allport to stress that personality consists of an integration of the capacities of the mind (i.e., *psycho-*, such as feelings, ideas, and beliefs, and the body (i.e., *-physical*), such as hormones and the nervous system. For example, the thrill-seeking personality exhibited by certain people has been linked to various biological characteristics (Geen, 1997; Pickering & Gray, 1999; Zuckerman, 1998, 2005; Zuckerman, Buchsbaum, & Murphy, 1980).

- *Personality is a determinant of behavior.* Allport uses the word *determine* to emphasize that personality serves as an activating and directive function in the individual's adaptive and expressive thoughts and behavior (Wiggins, 1997). Stated more simply, according to Allport (1961), "personality *is* something and *does* something" (p. 29).

- *Personality is an expression of each person's uniqueness.* The phrase "characteristic behavior and thought" refers to whatever people may do or think as they reflect on, adjust to, or strive to master their environment in a manner that is "unique" to (i.e., characteristic of) each person (Elms, 1993). For example, the way different people react and adjust to being turned down for a job reflects the characteristic nature of their personality.

In summary, Allport's definition of personality clarified the nature, operation, and purpose of the concept of personality as an expression of uniqueness.

Basic Concepts of Allport's Theory

The basic concepts of Allport's theory reflect the emphasis he placed on traits to help define and express each individual's unique personality. Allport's viewpoint focused on the classification and operation of traits.

Traits are the Basic Unit of Personality

For Allport, the trait is the basic unit of study for personality (Allport, 1958; Winter & Barenbaum, 1999). He defined a trait as "a neuropsychic structure having the capacity to render many stimuli functionally equivalent, and to initiate and guide equivalent (meaningfully consistent) forms of adaptive and expressive behavior" (Allport, 1961, p. 347). Thus, he assumed that traits are real within the individual and that they consistently guide the individual's thoughts and behavior across a variety of situations. For example, the extent to which Jack, a newspaper reporter, possesses the trait of aggressiveness will determine his behavior when charging the net in a game of tennis, honking the horn when cut off by another driver on the expressway, and being forceful when trying to get to the front of a crowd of other reporters to get a statement from a political candidate. Thus, the trait of aggressiveness influences Jack's behavior in a consistent manner across many different situations over time.

Common Traits and Personal Dispositions as Expressions of Uniqueness among People

Allport made a distinction between common traits and personal dispositions (or individual traits). The importance of this distinction has to do with attempts to understand the personality of an individual. **Common traits** refer to those traits possessed in varying degrees by all people. To study common traits, Allport emphasized the nomothetic approach. The **nomothetic approach** to the study of personality involves making comparisons of individuals or groups of individuals on certain common traits. For example, in the study of personality, comparing the common traits of shyness and anxiety, a researcher could compare the degree of shyness for Jack and Jill, two friends (i.e., different individuals), to see who is more shy or examine the level of anxiety in classes of college students (i.e., groups of individuals) to see if freshmen are more anxious than seniors. Allport noted that the utilization of the nomothetic approach to the study of common traits by comparing the personality of different people could be used for investigating the nature of personality and establishing general laws of behavior. Thus, common traits give us information involving comparisons between people rather than information about the personality of specific persons (Borkenau, 1993).

Personal dispositions are traits *unique* to the individual that create a personalized style of behavior. In this context, the term *unique* means that an individual's system of personal dispositions is specific to that person alone. To help understand how traits exert their influence on the expression of an individual's personality, the phrase *equalizing a variety of stimuli* means that the individual's unique system of personal dispositions interprets or perceives a wide variety of information in a similar (i.e., equalized) manner, resulting in a consistent pattern of behavior. Figure 7.1 illustrates how the personal disposition of self-consciousness results in the individual (John) interpreting all of these situations in a similar manner (i.e., threatening), which produces a pattern of consistency across his thoughts, feelings, and behaviors. Thus, Allport used the concept of personal dispositions to explain the uniqueness of each person and the consistency of the individual's behavior. To study personal dispositions and unique experiences, he recommended the idiographic approach to investigating the nature of personality. The **idiographic approach** to the study of personality is characterized by the detailed study of the expressions of a single individual in a variety of different ways in different situations. For example, to study the degree of aggressiveness of a particularly troubled teen, a counselor might examine the expression of aggressive comments the student

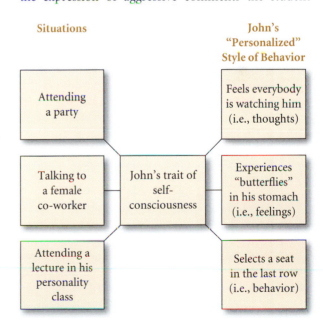

Situations		John's "Personalized" Style of Behavior
Attending a party		Feels everybody is watching him (i.e., thoughts)
Talking to a female co-worker	John's trait of self-consciousness	Experiences "butterflies" in his stomach (i.e., feelings)
Attending a lecture in his personality class		Selects a seat in the last row (i.e., behavior)

Figure 7.1   An example of John's trait of self-consciousness "equalizing" a variety of situations, resulting in a rather consistent pattern in his thoughts, feelings, and behavior.

includes in creative writing assignments and observations of this individual's aggressive behavior (e.g., teasing, bullying smaller classmates) during gym class.

Just as common traits and personal dispositions differ in their nature, so did the methods by which Allport felt they should be studied. To examine some of his research on common traits and personal dispositions based on the nomothetic and idiographic approaches, read "A Closer Look" below.

A Closer Look

Allport's Nomothetic and Idiographic Research

Allport was a master at letting the problem at hand define the method of study. He demonstrated great ingenuity in his research, making a major methodological distinction between the nomothetic and the idiographic approaches (Cohler, 1993; Lamiell, 1997; Winter & Barenbaum, 1999).

Allport used the nomothetic approach primarily when comparing the personalities of different people. The typical nomothetic study might involve having groups of people complete a survey, questionnaire, or personality test and then comparing the scores of people in the different groups. An example of Allport's research in the nomothetic tradition is his classic work on values. In this research, he and his colleagues (Allport et al., 1960) developed a personality test that assessed six basic values:

- Theoretical (e.g., discovering truth).
- Economic (e.g., being pragmatic).
- Aesthetic (e.g., seeking and appreciating beauty).
- Social (e.g., value helping others).
- Political (e.g., interested in power).
- Religious (e.g., desiring spiritual fulfillment).

Allport assumed that each person would combine these six values in a particular fashion to form a "philosophy of life." This philosophy of life would give meaning to the things people do and decisions they make. More will be said about Allport's work on values later in this chapter.

While the nomothetic approach was considered appropriate for studying and comparing groups, Allport did not consider it an appropriate method for studying the unique individual. As an alternative, he recommended the idiographic approach. The idiographic approach represents an in-depth analysis of a particular person. Some methods included in this approach are the examination of expressive behaviors (e.g., body movement and facial and vocal expressions), the case study method (discussed in Chapter 1), individualized questionnaires, and the content analysis of personal documents (e.g., letters and diaries). An example of Allport's research using the idiographic approach is the structural and content analysis of some 300 letters written by Jenny, a middle-aged woman, to a young, married couple over a period of 12 years (Allport, 1965). Following are two of Jenny's letters.

Sunday, March 4/34

Isabel, my dear:

It is quite evident that you have never been an indigent, aged female, or your splendid St. Patrick's Day box which arrived Saturday (March 3rd) would have been more wisely chosen, altho' certainly not with more kindly thought. Possibly you have never lived in one room. This house is largely made up of old women from 75 to 90 something; as a result it is kept unusually warm – very uncomfortably warm for me. I nearly faint in the dining room.

Whatever made you send me *a quart* of thick tomato juice? What did you suppose I could do with it? I always supposed tomato juice was an appetiser, to be taken before dinner, and frequently get it as such when I go to town. It is not appetisers we need here, it is something to eat. Yesterday I went to a restaurant on Broadway, and met 6 of our women, indigent females, all having something to eat. Our meals are a joke, or would be if we felt funny enough to see them that way. When the weather is severe and I cannot go out I lie awake until 3 or 4 am knowing I need food.

But could I get up to drink lukewarm thick tomato juice, or eat very salty crackers? If it were only plain crackers, sweet, wheat, graham, social tea, arrow root, but salt? And by the way, I have never seen them served anywhere – in what way are they used? They would probably be ok with a glass of beer if one had no pretzels or with cold meat. Had the sardines been in individual tins which contain 4 or 5 – I often buy them that way – but in such a large tin! I could not eat a whole tin at one sitting, and what could I do with what was left? My room is so hot. I have never eaten preserved meat of any kind – I couldn't. And the cheese is too soft for me.

I hope and pray you will be sensible and understand. Drop a line and say you're not vexed.

Lady M.

N.Y.C.
March 13/34

My dearest Girl:

Ah! I can breathe again – what a relief. You have written, and you are not blazing mad. The Gods are not so bad after all. You see, the letter was hardly out of my hand when I felt sorry for sending it – you might feel hurt, and be angry and the box wasn't worth that.

Lady M.

(Allport, 1965, pp. 116–117)

Note: From *Letters from Jenny*, by G.W. Allport, 1965, New York: Harcourt, Brace, and World.

To analyze Jenny's personality, Allport asked 36 people to read the letters and indicate what traits they believed Jenny possessed. The total number of traits listed by all of the judges was close to 200. However, Allport was able to group them into eight categories: suspiciousness, self-centered, autonomous dramatic, artistic, aggressive, cynical-morbid, and sentimental. The traits of suspiciousness, self-centered, and autonomous were identified as the most prominent traits of Jenny's personality.

In addition to providing a unique opportunity to investigate the study of traits, these letters are a fascinating glimpse into the lives of the individuals associated with them. But don't just take my word for it. Here is what Allport had to say about the letters: "I know of no other case material so rich and exciting and challenging for those who like to explore the mysteries of human nature, whether they be students of psychology or devotees of literature or simply observers of life" (Allport, 1965, p. x).

More about the letters and their analysis can be found in a brief book chapter titled "Gordon Allport and "Letters from Jenny" (Winter, 1993) and Allport's (1965) book *Letters from Jenny*.

Using Cardinal, Central, and Secondary Traits to Account for the Uniqueness of the Individual

Whereas personal dispositions were used to account for the unique variation among individuals, Allport (1961) used cardinal, central, and secondary traits to explain the unique variation *within* the individual (Cohler, 1993).

Cardinal traits represent the most significant and dominant features of the individual's personality, expressing themselves in virtually all aspects of behavior. For example, if someone is called a "social climber," it means that everything the individual does reflects his or her desire to "get ahead" (e.g., selection of friends and a spouse and organizations joined). Allport (1961, p. 365) referred to such a personal disposition as a "ruling passion" of life. Examples of cardinal traits are the pervasive sense of power so dominant in Hitler's personality and the pervasive sense of justice so dominant in the personality of Martin Luther King, Jr.

Not all people organize the nature of their personality around dominant cardinal traits. Instead, the personality of most people is defined by a set of central traits. **Central traits** are less pervasive and dominant than cardinal traits, but still highly characteristic of the individual's personality. Central traits might be exemplified in a letter of recommendation or in a description of an individual's most salient features. When describing a potential blind date to a friend, you might say that the individual is somewhat shy and slightly self-conscious when meeting people for the first time but really friendly and witty after getting to know them. For Allport, central traits described the "outstanding characteristics of the individual" (Allport, 1937, p. 338). In one study, Allport (1961, pp. 366–367) reported that the traits used to describe the essential features of an individual generally numbered between 5 and 10, with the average being 7.2 traits. As an example of this point, compare these results with the number of traits you used to describe the essential characteristics of a good friend in "You Can Do It" on p. 258.

Secondary traits are personal dispositions having a much more limited influence on the individual's behavior. Secondary traits tend to express themselves in the context of specific situations and circumstances. For example, the normally outspoken government official may become tongue-tied when being questioned in front of a congressional ethics committee.

The Proprium as the Core of Personality

If traits are considered the basic units of personality, then the proprium might be considered the core of personality for Allport (Maddi, 1996). For Allport (1955), the **proprium** includes all aspects of the individual's personality that are considered "personally" his or her own. In a general sense, the proprium helps the person define a sense of self (Cohler, 1993). It includes the vital and essential physical, psychological, and social aspects of life that are considered to be "part of you." For example, some people consider their car, house, or job as being vital to their sense of who they are. Other people have their room decorated with all of their personal belongings as an important reflection of their sense of individuality. Seeing someone at a party wearing the same outfit as yours might trigger a reaction such as "What is that person doing with *my* outfit on?" Thus, a key function of the proprium is that it helps to establish a unifying feeling of what is really a part of you.

As you can see, Allport was very concerned with viewing personality as an expression of the individual's uniqueness. In "The Cultural Context of Personality Psychology" below, Allport's concern's about the uniqueness of the individual is also found in his views regarding the impact of culture on personality.

The Cultural Context of Personality Psychology

The Impact of Culture on Personality as a Celebration of Diversity and Uniqueness: How Not to Lose Sight of the Trees in the Forest

"Culture shapes personality chiefly because it provides ready made, pretested solutions to many of life's problems" (Allport, 1961, p. 167). Allport's views on culture, like so many of his important ideas, reflect the distinction he made between the idographic and nomothetic approaches to studying personality. In discussing the impact of culture on personality, he distinguished between "real culture" and "the cultural construct." *Real culture* provides certain boundaries within which individuals have a wide range of freedom to express their personality (i.e., an idiographic feature). For example, in our culture, there is the general prescription that we wear clothes in public. However, as any trip to the mall or survey of fashion and style magazines will demonstrate, there is a tremendous amount of individual variation in the way people express their personality through the clothes they wear.

On the other hand, the *cultural construct* is a general description of a pattern of expression within a culture (i.e., a nomothetic feature). Such a description captures the characteristic features of the individuals of that particular culture. For example, the cultural construct of the United States is that we, as a collection of individuals, are democratic and tend to be technologically advanced. Yet many individuals within our culture endorse censorship and limitations on free speech or do not use computers or even know how to program their DVD. For Allport, the limitation of using the cultural construct approach to the study of personality is that it loses sight of the individual and does not seem to appreciate the uniqueness of individuals. As he stated, "The abstract cultural concept seems remote, even misleading, from the psychologist's view. No individual is a mirror image of the modal or average cultural pattern. We are molded by *real* culture and not by the anthropologist's distilled image of it. To apply this image directly to people is to falsify the diversity of personality found within any single culture" (Allport, 1961, p. 167). Such a statement reflected not only Allport's views about the cultural context of personality but, more importantly, how he hoped personality psychologists would study personality in the context of culture – seeking and celebrating the diversity of personality as an expression of the uniqueness of individuals. Thus, even when studying something as collectivistic in nature as the cultural influence on personality, Allport championed the study of the individual.

You Can Do It: Applying the Cultural Construct and Real Culture to Your Personality

You can begin to examine the cultural construct for yourself by considering some of the general descriptions that characterized the personality of individuals within your culture. Now consider the impact of real culture by thinking about how your personality is reflected within your culture by: (1) the way you drive within the prescribed laws of the road, (2) the nature of the movies you choose from the limited selection made available to you at the video store, and (3) the manner in which you decorate your personal living space from the restricted choice of items you see in the mall. Finally, how might your personality be different if you lived in another culture that offered alternatives that differ from those from which you currently choose?

Summing It Up *Definitions and Examples of the Basic Concepts of Allport's Viewpoint of Personality*

Basic Concept Defined	Example
Traits: The basic unit of personality serving to influence an individual's thoughts, feelings, and behavior in a consistent manner across a variety of situations.	Your trait of extraversion will determine your thoughts about going to social events, feelings about being invited to a party, and behavior at the party.
Common Traits: Traits possessed to some degree by all people and used to compare the personality of different individuals or groups of individuals.	Achievement motivation in groups of adolescents from developed and underdeveloped nations is compared by a personality psychologist.
Personal Dispositions: Traits unique to the individual that combine in a specific manner to produce a personal style of responding to a variety of stimuli.	Your traits of aggression and compassion combine in a way to produce a personal style of dealing with an annoying neighbor in a firm but considerate fashion.
Cardinal Traits: The most influential and pervasive features of the individual's personality.	Your sense of self-esteem serves to impact all aspects of your life, from choosing a career to purchasing a car.
Central Traits: The most outstanding and visible features of the individual's personality.	It is your sense of enthusiasm and intensity about life that others describe as the major features of your personality.
Secondary Traits: Features that impact the individual's behavior in a very limited number of circumstances.	Your normally passive style of behaving turns to one of aggression when loved ones are being threatened by a "street punk" while you are on vacation.
Proprium: The centerpiece of personality serving to help give the individual a sense of self.	What you define as "your" seat in "your" personality class reflects your individual sense of self.

In summary, the basic concepts proposed by Allport within his personalistic viewpoint were designed to help explain how each person is able to express his or her personality in a unique way. The principal ideas examined in this section are presented in "Summing It Up: Definitions and Examples of the Basic Concepts of Allport's Viewpoint of Personality" above.

In the next section, we will consider Allport's views on the operational dynamics of personality. Central to his views are the development of the proprium and the process of functional autonomy.

The Dynamics of Personality: Developmental and Motivational Processes of the Proprium

Something as complicated and detailed as a sense of who you are does not develop overnight. In an attempt to account for such a complicated developmental process, Allport (1961) outlined a lifelong pattern of development associated with the emergence of the seven aspects of the proprium. The unified development of each of these aspects results in the formation of a mature and healthy personality. More specifically, the emergence of the proprium involves a process of development ranging from the discovery of "I am" to "What shall I be?" With the development of each aspect of the proprium, individuals discover a little more about their unique self. Such a process is dynamic and continuous. Table 7.1 summarizes each aspect of proprium development.

Thus, proprium development is characterized as being a continuous and evolutionary process. Throughout life, the individual will continue to add to the development of his or her own sense of personal self-awareness and uniqueness.

Table 7.1   The Developmental Aspects of the Proprium

Aspect of Proprium Development	Specific Knowledge of the Self Acquired
Infancy (years 1 to 3):	
Bodily self (year 1)	I am separate from the environment. (e.g., I won't bite my own toe).
Self-identity (year 2)	I am separate from other individuals. (e.g., I am John).
Self-esteem (year 3)	I can manipulate and master my environment. (e.g., I can turn on the TV).
Childhood (years 4 to 12):	
Self-extension (years 4 to 6)	I can exist beyond my physical self. (e.g., This is my bike).
Self-image (years 4 to 6)	I see myself as being like this (e.g., I am good at naming my colors and afraid of the dark).
Self as a rational coper (years 6 to 12)	I can solve my problems by using my "brain" (I can think logically – e.g., I'll get my kite untangled by shaking the branches of the bush).
Adolescence (years 12 and above):	
Propriate striving (years 12 through adolescence)	What will I be in the future? (e.g., I will take accounting in high school to help get my college degree in business.)

Functional Autonomy: The Motivational Force behind Personality

The energy and motivational source behind the development and operation of the proprium are what Allport referred to as functional autonomy. Allport (1961) defines **functional autonomy** as "any acquired system of motivation in which the tensions involved are not the same as the antecedent tensions from which the acquired system developed" (p. 229). This concept simply means that in a mature adult, the motivation behind current actions is independent (autonomous) of early childhood motivation (Maddi, 1996).

As an example, think about why adults attend college (i.e., "go to school"). As children, people go to school because they "have to." But as mature adults, some people are still going to school, although for completely different and independent reasons (e.g., self- or career enhancement). "Functional autonomy" is Allport's way of saying that to understand the actions of the emotionally healthy and mature individual, we must look at present motives and future expectations and not just into the individual's "ancient past," as Freud proposed.

As a way of further clarifying this motivational concept, Allport (1961) described two levels of func-

tional autonomy: perseverative and propriate functional autonomy.

- **Perseverative functional autonomy** is a primitive motivational system that accounts for the expression of many repetitious behavior patterns and a desire for routine and familiarity. An example would be an office manager who refuses to use new, more efficient computerized equipment to run the office because of the comfort and security associated with running the office the "old way."

- **Propriate functional autonomy** represents a higher level of motivation that helps people to develop beyond their original level those aspects of their lives most significantly related to their sense of self-awareness (e.g., interests, abilities, values, and desires). For example, as a child Freida may originally be externally motivated to practice the piano because her parents tell her to. But as an adolescent, her practicing may be motivated by the sense of internal satisfaction and accomplishment she experiences when playing a musical piece well. Thus, the energy source for practicing the piano now comes from the sense of self-pride Freida develops as learning to be a better pianist becomes a vital part of her total sense of self.

Table 7.2   Six Characteristics of the Mature Personality

Characteristic*	Example
Extension of the sense of self. The mature individual is involved in activities outside of himself or herself.	By participating in community activities (e.g., volunteering to serve meals to the homeless), mature people are able to give of themselves to others.
Warm relating of the self to others. The mature individual is able to show compassion for the rights, needs, and values of others.	Mature people do not make jokes about another person at the expense of that individual's self-esteem.
Emotional security (self-acceptance). The mature individual is able to tolerate the frustrations of life without overreacting.	After going through a divorce, the mature individual does not jump immediately into another relationship just to make sure he or she is still able to be accepted by others.
Realistic perception, skills, and assignments. Mature people live in the "real world" and react to the problems of life rationally, not in a defensive or self-centered way.	After getting a low grade on a test, instead of just blaming the professor, the mature individual might reflect on how his or her study habits might have contributed to the poor test performance, in order to avoid such mistakes in the future.
Self-objectification: insight and humor. Mature people have a realistic self-image of what they can do and are not threatened by their weaknesses. They are also able to laugh at their weaknesses.	Realizing that he is not a very good tennis player, a mature individual is able to make a joke about his slipping and being hit by the ball on his "behind" as he tries to charge the net.
Unifying philosophy of life. Mature people have a clear sense of how they wish to live their lives.	A unifying philosophy of life for a mature individual might involve treating others as you would expect them to treat you, or operating on the assumption that all men and women are created equal and should be treated accordingly.

Note. *Note the similarity between the characteristics of Allport's view of the mature personality and Maslow's self-actualizing people discussed in Chapter 6 (pp. 240–244). Data from Allport (1961).

The proprium and functional autonomy operate dynamically in the developmental process of the emotionally healthy and mature individual. An overall level of an individual's maturity might be measured by the extent to which the person's motives are functionally autonomous. Table 7.2 is a more specific list summarizing the six major features Allport considered to be characteristic of a mature personality.

Personality Assessment from Allport's Viewpoint

In addition to trying to understand the uniqueness of the individual through the study of traits, Allport was interested in other psychological features that contribute to the unique expression of each person. In his attempt to identify other features that contribute to a person's psychological uniqueness, he examined human values. In this work, he viewed human values as an important expression of uniqueness through personal beliefs. The six categories of values he used were originally adapted from the work of the German philosopher Eduard Spranger (1928). Following are brief descriptions of the six categories of values:

- *Theoretical.* A desire to discover truth and systematize one's knowledge. An example of this type of value might be seen in the thinking of scientists and philosophers.
- *Economic.* A basic concern for what is useful and practical. Such a bottom-line philosophy might be seen in the thinking of people in the business world.
- *Aesthetic.* An appreciation of artistic beauty, harmony, and form for its own sake. This type of value might be dominant in the thinking of artists.
- *Social.* A basic concern for the well-being of other people. This type of thinking might be a dominant force in the lives of many teachers, social workers, and others in a variety of helping professions.

- *Political.* A basic interest in power related to any field, not just to politics. Such a value might be a guiding force in the thinking of a domineering spouse or an unscrupulous career-minded individual.
- *Religious.* A desire to unite the self with a higher sense of reality. Such spiritual awareness might be exemplified by people who regularly attend religious retreats and, to some degree, by those who take drugs to achieve a sense of expanded self-awareness.

The Study of Values Scale   To assess these six basic value categories, Allport and his colleagues developed a personality inventory they called the **Study of Values Scale** (Allport et al., 1960). This inventory consists of 45 forced-choice items, in which a response indicating each value is paired an equal number of times with each of the remaining five values. Here is a sample of items similar to those found in the Study of Values Scale (the values being compared are in parentheses and do not appear in the actual inventory):

Should great artists, such as Mozart or Leonardo da Vinci, be allowed to be selfish and ignore the feelings of others? a. yes; b. no (*artistic vs. social*)

Which of the two disciplines would you consider more important to further our understanding of mankind? a. mathematics; b. theology (*theoretical vs. religious*)

Assuming your ability and the salary were the same for each of these occupations, would you prefer to be a – a. mathematician; b. sales manager; c. clergyman; d. politician (*theoretical vs. economics vs. religious vs. political*)

The relative strength of each value for the individual is obtained by adding the number of times that person selects a particular value throughout the test. The more times the person selects a particular value (i.e., the higher the score), the more dominant the value is in his or her personality.

Research on the Study of Values Scale   Evidence supporting the validity of the values scale is demonstrated by comparing the scores of groups of people whose characteristics are known and from whom investigators would expect to find differences in certain values. For example, the religious dimension was the dominant value score for members of the clergy, while business students tended to score highest on the economic dimension (Allport et al., 1960).

Scores on the different value scales were also correlated with diverse behaviors from marijuana use (Weckowicz & Janssen, 1973; Weckowicz, Collier, & Spreng, 1977) to the speed with which people could perceive certain value-related words (Postman, Bruner, & McGinnies, 1948). For example, people scoring high on the economic scale might be able to perceive the word *dividend* sooner than those scoring high on the aesthetic scale.

Applications of Allport's Viewpoint: Using What Is Known

The utility of Allport's Study of Values Scale can be illustrated by considering its applications to two of life's most important issues: marriage and careers.

Marital Counseling

In discussing the various applications of the Study of Values Scale, Allport et al. (1960) noted that the assessment of values is helpful to marriage counselors, especially among the clergy, in preparing and counseling prospective marriage partners. In one of the first studies investigating marital compatibility, an early version of the Study of Values Scale was used to assess personality similarity in married couples (Schooley, 1936). "Veteran" couples, those who had been married from 5 to 20 years, showed more similarity in economic and religious values than "newlywed" couples, who had been married 4 years or less. But the veteran couples showed greater dissimilarity in theoretical and aesthetic values than the newlyweds. Thus, it seems that the key to longevity in marriage is for spouses to have a high degree of similarity on values about money (i.e., economic) and beliefs about how to live their daily lives (e.g., religion) and a low degree of similarity on values related to a concern for such abstract and ideal notions as the seeking of truth (i.e., theoretical) and beauty (i.e., aesthetic).

Such findings seem to be as true today as they were in the past. Similarity in religious and economic backgrounds and realistic expectations about marriage still seem to be some of the most important factors associated with long and successful marriages (Baron, Byrne, & Branscombe, 2006; R. S. Miller, Perlman, & Brehm, 2007; Murray & Holmes, 1997; Steinmetz, Clavan, & Stein, 1990). Similarly, a study of marital adjustment among nurses, based on the assessment of values, indicated that religious, economic, and theoretical values, in that order, were the ones most related to successful marital adjustment (Nimkoff & Grigg, 1958). In this same study, a greater emphasis on monetary issues (i.e., high economic value score) was the factor most highly related to a lack of marital adjustment.

Vocational Counseling

In the area of vocational counseling, the assessment of values has been used to help differentiate between various occupational groups (Braithwaite & Scott, 1991). In one study, students pursuing graduate training in clinical psychology were found to express values reflecting a love for people (i.e., high social value) to a greater degree than did students pursuing graduate training in other areas of psychology (Kelly & Fiske, 1950). Combining their general competitive nature with their occupational expectations of working in some type of community setting (e.g., physical education teachers or leaders of community recreation centers), males majoring in health and physical education at a college with a religious emphasis displayed peak scores in the political (e.g., competitiveness), social (e.g., working with people), and religious value categories (Seashore, 1947). In the same study, students majoring in the applied social sciences displayed peak scores in the social and religious value categories.

The utility of the Study of Values Scale in occupational and vocational counseling is enhanced by research suggesting the possibility that different vocational groups have distinctive value profiles (Allport et al., 1960). Overall, these studies seem to indicate that the assessment of values plays an important part in the process of vocational counseling.

Evaluating Allport's Personalistic Viewpoint: Strengths and Limitations

We will conclude our discussion of Allport's viewpoint of personality by considering its characteristic strengths and limitations.

Characteristic Strengths

Allport's personalistic viewpoint has the following strengths:

- *Versatility in the research methodologies employed.* As noted earlier, Allport was inclined to let the

nature of the problem dictate the methodology used to study it. As a result, few psychologists have demonstrated as much versatility in their research as he did. In a career of research spanning almost 50 years, he used investigative methods including surveys, questionnaires, case studies, content analysis, experimental methodology, and the analysis of personal documents (e.g., letters and diaries).

- *An emphasis on the "person" in personality.* Although Allport is classified as a trait theorist because of his extensive conceptual usage of traits in developing his viewpoint, he was also one of the first personality theorists to emphasize studying the uniqueness of the individual. Thus, consistent with Rogers and Maslow, Allport's personal philosophy reflected the belief that each person in his or her own right, functioning at a conscious level of awareness, is the most legitimate object of study in personality psychology.

Characteristic Limitations

Here are some limitations of Allport's personalistic viewpoint:

- *The invisibility of traits.* While traits played a central role in Allport's viewpoint, the concept of traits has certain limitations. Allport clearly assumed that traits existed, but his critics like to point out that no hard evidence exists to identify and locate a personality trait anywhere in the brain or rest of the body. His critics accuse him of building a theory around the invisible structure of the trait, which makes formulating and testing such a theory almost an empirical impossibility. In all fairness, the same criticism can be applied to other personality theorists (e.g., Freud's use of the ego and Rogers's use of the ideal self) and other areas of psychology (e.g., long-term memory, a concept used in the study of learning and memory).

- *Focusing on the discontinuity of development by failing to link the present with the past.* One major limitation noted in Allport's viewpoint has to do with his notion of functional autonomy and the emphasis it placed on the discontinuity of personality. His critics stressed that he tended to downplay, if not ignore, the relationship between personality development in childhood and in adulthood.

- *Too much emphasis on the individual created an "unscientific" approach to studying personality.* Allport has also been criticized for the emphasis he placed on studying the individual (i.e., idiographic approach) over trying to establish more general laws of behavior by studying groups of people (i.e., nomothetic approach). Studying groups of people to establish general laws of behavior is believed to be more consistent with what is considered the "scientific" approach to the study of personality. To be fair, Allport did spend a considerable amount of time studying groups of people in many different aspects of his research.

The principal ideas examined in this section are presented in "Summing It Up: Characteristic Strength and Limitations of Allport's Personalistic Viewpoint" below.

As the founder of the systematic study of personality in the United States, Allport's contributions are monumental and continue to influence contemporary thinking in personality psychology (Funder, 1991). His historical impact on contemporary thinking about trait psychology can be summarized by this simple but eloquent statement by Caspi (1998): "by and large, Allport had it right" (p. 312).

In the next section, we will examine another personality psychologist interested in the trait viewpoint by considering the work of Raymond Cattell. Going beyond simply discussing the nature of traits, Cattell's work focused on developing more precise methods of measuring and organizing the structural nature of traits.

Cattell's Structural Trait Viewpoint: The Search for Source Traits

"Science demands measurement! Measurement began in personality at the end of the Freudian, Jungian, and Adlerian phase of clinically derived theories" (R. B. Cattell, 1990, p. 101). To further appreciate this quotation from Raymond B. Cattell, you should know that he strongly rejected "armchair speculation" as a means of defining the nature of personality. As an alternative to such speculation, he favored what is best described as a "data-based" approach to defining the nature and operation of personality. He preferred to base his study of personality on empirical observations, which were then used to generate specific hypotheses to be confirmed or rejected by additional research. For a glimpse into the personal life of Raymond Cattell, read "A Closer Look" below.

A Closer Look

The Life of Raymond B. Cattell

Raymond B. Cattell was born on March 20, 1905, and raised in the Devonshire area of England. As a young boy, he read widely and was keenly interested in chemistry – he once made gunpowder in his "chemistry shed." At the tender age of 16, he entered London University, graduating with honors in physics and chemistry. Yet he decided not to pursue a career in these sciences: "A variety of circumstances conspired in my last year of work in the physical sciences to crystallize

Summing It Up *Characteristic Strengths and Limitations of Allport's Personalistic Viewpoint*

Characteristic Strengths:

- *A master of methodology.* Allport employed different methodologies in his study of personality.
- *Emphasis on the person.* Allport emphasized the study of the uniqueness of the person in personality psychology.

Characteristic Limitations:

- *The invisibility of traits.* There is a lack of evidence to document the actual physical existence of traits.
- *Discontinuity of development.* Functional autonomy emphasized the separate development of personality in childhood from that in adulthood.
- *Too much emphasis on the individual.* General laws of personality are not easily developed with Allport's emphasis on studying the individual.

Raymond B. Cattell's emphasis on a systematic and empirical approach to personality research did much to raise the scientific status of personality psychology. Cattell is also noted for applying his ideas to a variety of areas both inside and outside of personality psychology.

In 1929, after gaining his PhD from London University, Cattell found that his friends had been correct – there were no positions for those with a new doctorate in psychology. A succession of "fringe" jobs followed, but so did extreme poverty. But in 1937, E. L. Thorndike, a famous American psychologist, invited Cattell to come to America as a research associate for one year. Describing the departure from England as being as painful as a tooth extraction, Cattell consoled himself with the thought that it was only for one year and accepted the offer. However, the year at Columbia with Thorndike was followed by two years at Clark University and then a position at Harvard.

For Cattell, life really began at age 40. In 1945, he was invited to the University of Illinois. He also married Karen Schuettler, a mathematician who would assist him in his research in many ways, including being a subject. It was at the University of Illinois that most of Cattell's approach to personality blossomed in terms of both the development of his theory and research productivity. An example of his dedication is the truly impressive volume of research and other publications he produced: over 56 books and approximately 400 other publications. In recognition of his being "among a very small handful of people in this century who have most influenced the shape of psychology as a science" (American Psychological Association, 1997, p. 797), Cattell was awarded the American Psychological Association's prestigious Gold Medal Award for Life Achievement in Psychological Science in 1997.

After spending almost 30 years at the University of Illinois, Cattell retired and moved to Hawaii, where he became a member of the faculty at the University of Hawaii. He died at his home in Honolulu on February 2, 1998. More information on his life can be found in his autobiography, appearing in Lindzey's *A History of Psychology in Autobiography* (R. B. Cattell, 1974), and in Cattell's obituary (Horn, 2001).

that sense of a serious concern with social problems which had been awaiting germination in the five years since the war" (R. B. Cattell, 1974, p. 64). As a young lad, Cattell had seen soldiers, still in their blood-soaked bandages, coming back from the front lines. This experience was one of the turning points that would increase his concern with changing social conditions: "Gradually I concluded that to go beyond human irrationalities one had to study the workings of the mind itself . . . I realized that psychology was to be my life interest" (p. 64). His friends tried to persuade him against a career in psychology, agreeing with others' perceptions that it was a field for cranks. But he would not be dissuaded, even though prospects for gainful employment for psychologists were dismal at best.

As a graduate student at London University, Cattell studied with the eminent psychologist and statistician Charles Spearman, well known for his study of the structure of human intelligence and development of the early techniques of factor analysis – a technique that would play a crucial role in Cattell's career.

Basic Assumptions of Cattell's Definition of Personality

The basic assumptions of Cattell's viewpoint focus on using empirical measures to predict people's behavior. For Cattell, that which predicts behavior also defines personality.

Predicting the Person as the Principal Assumption of Personality

Cattell defined personality as "that which permits a prediction of what a person will do in a given situation" (1950, p. 2). His major objective was to be able to predict a person's behavior using information about his or her personality. Because Cattell's approach is based firmly on using empirical data – combined through a statistical formula – to predict behavior, he is credited with developing one of the first comprehensive trait theories of personality that relied strictly on the assessment and quantification of traits (Barone & Kominars, 1998).

Constructing a Definition of Personality Based on Three Types of Empirical Data

In defining and studying the nature of personality, Cattell used three primary sources of empirical data: L-data, Q-data, and T-data (R. B. Cattell, 1946, 1957; Wiggins, 2003; Winter & Barenbaum, 1999).

- **L-data** consist primarily of records of life events, located in such places as public records (e.g., a college transcript) or archives (e.g., a diary) and the ratings made by others (e.g., the contents of a personnel file).
- **Q-data** include self-ratings on questionnaires or personality tests (e.g., the six separate scores on Allport's values scale).
- **T-data** involve observations of an individual in a limited situation designed to assess some aspect of personality. Examples of T-data include measuring the time required to complete a complex set of hand–eye coordination tests or recording the amount of stuttering during a job interview.

Although these types of data are discussed individually, the ability to predict a person's behavior is increased by combining them. For example, in selecting candidates for jet pilot training school, Air Force trainers ask potential recruits to provide college transcripts (i.e., L-data), complete a variety of intelligence and personality tests (i.e., Q-data), and perform on a flight simulator (i.e., T-data) as a means of predicting how well they would perform under actual combat conditions. No matter how the three types of data are combined, Cattell believed that they are the data upon which you can begin to construct your definition of personality and predict the behavior of the individual.

Basic Concepts of Traits: Cattell's Structural Units of Personality

Like Allport, Cattell reflected the significance he placed on traits by the way he defined them. According to Cattell, "A trait may be defined as that which defines what a person will do when faced with a defined situation" (1979, p. 14). Thus, he used the individual's behavior to define traits. To account for the diverse nature of the personalities observed among people, he identified different categories of traits and the effects each has on behavior.

Surface and Source Traits: Creating Differences in Personality

The uniqueness of each person's personality is due to what Cattell conceptualized as surface and source traits (McAdams, 1997; Wiggins, 2003).

- **Surface traits** are related elements of behavior that, when empirically measured and intercorrelated, tend to cluster together. They are also the most visible evidence of a trait. For example, studying long hours, making sure all of the references in a term paper are correct, and showing up early to work might be considered visible evidence of the following surface traits: perseverance, conscientiousness, and punctuality, respectively. But surface traits are in turn controlled by underlying source traits.
- **Source traits** are responsible for the diversity seen in the personalities of those around us. In the preceding example, differences in perseverance, conscientiousness, and punctuality across individual students are explained by differences in the degree to which they possess the underlying source trait of ambitiousness.

Because of the major influence source traits have on behavior, Cattell maintained that the understanding of personality and the prediction of behavior are increased by studying how surface traits are collectively related to certain underlying source traits, instead of simply studying each behavioral element in isolation. For example, a greater understanding of people's personalities is gained by studying differences in the source trait of ambitiousness than by studying separately the surface traits of perseverance, conscientiousness, and punctuality.

Categorizing Traits: Conceptualizing the Similarities and Dissimilarities of Personality

In addition to the surface–source trait distinction, the depth of Cattell's conceptualization of traits is reflected in the detailed manner in which he categorized traits.

Common and Unique Traits   Cattell made the distinction between common and unique traits to account for the general nature of certain aspects of personality and the idiosyncratic nature of certain people's personalities.

- Like Allport, Cattell considered common traits to be certain traits assumed to be possessed by everyone to some degree. Examples of common traits are intelligence and anxiety.
- **Unique traits** are traits that are specific to one person and can take the form of peculiar interests (e.g., a friend who can watch reruns of *Seinfeld* for hours) or beliefs (e.g., an individual who believes children under the age of 18 should be banned from shopping malls). Unique traits are similar to what Allport defined as *personal dispositions*.

Ability, Temperament, and Dynamic Traits   The individual nature of personality is also reflected in what Cattell referred to as ability traits, temperament traits, and dynamic traits (McAdams, 1997; Pervin, 2002).

- **Ability traits** involve a person's skill in dealing with complex problem-solving situations (e.g., being insightful).
- **Temperament traits** reflect the general manner or style of an individual's behavior (e.g., being relaxed or intense).
- **Dynamic traits** relate to what is often referred to as motivation (e.g., expressing a desire to learn or being an underachiever).

Constitutional and Environmental-Mold Factors   Another way of categorizing traits involves considering the degree to which they are the result of biological or environmental factors.

- **Constitutional factors** are traits that are primarily dependent on biological factors. For example, an individual's degree of nervousness might be related to nervous system arousal level, which is a biologically determined characteristic.

- **Environmental-mold factors** are traits that are influenced primarily by environmental factors. For example, a person's degree of morality is highly influenced by such environmental factors as peer groups or family background.

Summing It Up *Cattell's Categorization of Traits*

Surface Traits vs. Source Traits:

- *Surface traits* are units of personality reflected in observable behaviors that tend to be interrelated. For example, calling up an employer for an interview, which reflects self-confidence, is related to talking to many people at a party, which reflects the surface trait of gregariousness.
- *Source traits* are the underlying units of personality responsible for the interrelatedness of surface traits. For example, self-confidence and gregariousness are related by the unifying influence of self-esteem.

Common Traits vs. Unique Traits:

- *Common traits* are assumed to be a part of everybody's personality. For example, everybody possesses self-confidence to some degree.
- *Unique traits* are assumed to be characteristics specific to each individual. For example, Jan is intensely interested in protecting the rights of animals.

Ability vs. Temperament vs. Dynamic Traits:

- *Ability traits* reflect your ability to solve problems (e.g., creativeness).
- *Temperament traits* reflect your general style of behavior (e.g., intense).
- *Dynamic traits* reflect your level of motivation (e.g., dedicated).

Constitutional Factors vs. Environmental-Mold Factors:

- *Constitutional factors* are traits having a primarily biological (i.e., nature) basis. For example, emotionality is a trait that reflects hormonal levels.
- *Environmental-mold factors* are traits having a primarily environmental (i.e., nurture) basis. For example, self-esteem is a trait that reflects parenting practices.

Of course, few traits are either–or. Most traits result from the intersection of biological and environmental factors.

Consistent with this point, Cattell determined what he called the nature–nurture ratio for many traits. The **nature–nurture ratio** represents the degree to which a trait is due to biological or environmental factors. For example, although intelligence is generally believed to be a biologically determined factor, it is possible to raise an individual's intelligence to some extent by placing the person in an environment that offers plenty of intellectual stimulation.

A summary of the major distinctions Cattell made among traits is presented in "Summing It Up: Cattell's Categorization of Traits" on p. 273.

With all of the different ways to categorize traits, students commonly ask, "How did Cattell identify the presence of these diverse traits?" To examine the technique he used to identify traits, read "A Closer Look" below.

A Closer Look

Factor Analysis: Cattell's Tool of the Trade

An important part of Cattell's work in personality is the statistical technique of **factor analysis**, a data-grouping and data-reduction technique based on the logic of the correlation coefficient (see Chapter 1). Factor analysis can be used to determine how a large number of surface traits can be clustered into a smaller number of groups related to specific source traits (Costa & McCrae, 1998; Wiggins, 2003).

The Process of Factor Analysis: A Step-by-Step Approach

The manner in which the researcher believes various surface traits will cluster is based on a specific theoretical framework or on previous knowledge of the operation of these surface traits. Factor analysis is used to determine the extent to which the researcher's ideas about the clustering of the surface traits are confirmed. Although there are many ways to perform a factor analysis, they all require the aid of a computer and usually involve the following basic steps:

1. *Data collection.* The first step in factor analysis is to collect data (e.g., L-, Q-, and T-data). For example, suppose information on some 500 students is obtained in the seven different situations listed in the "Measure" column of Table 7.3.
2. *Establishing an intercorrelation matrix.* An **intercorrelation matrix** summarizes the correlation coefficients between each measure of behavior with every other measure of behavior being investigated. Table 7.3 is an intercorrelation matrix illustrating the correlations among the seven measures of interest in our discussion. For example, in this table, item B, "nervous mannerisms of the hands," correlates .63 (i.e., strongly related) with item A, "butterflies in the stomach," while "number of captions" (item E) correlates .00 (i.e., unrelated) with "heart rate" (item D).

Table 7.3 The Intercorrelation Matrix for Seven Measures: An Example

Measure	A	B	C	D	E	F	G
A. "Butterflies in stomach' while talking to an attractive member of the opposite sex	–						
B. Nervous mannerisms of the hands during a job interview	.63	–					
C. Amount of rocking back and forth while giving a talk in class	.50	.55	–				
D. Rapid heart rate during exam	.72	.63	.61	–			
E. Number of captions written for a cartoon	.08	.03	.04	.00	–		
F. Number of uses suggested for common objects	.02	.15	.11	.68	.81	–	
G. Number of suggestions for activities the "gang" could engage in this weekend on a group date	.10	.00	.03	.72	.787	.68	–

Table 7.4 A Factor Matrix with Factor Loadings on Two Factors: An Example

Measure	Factor Loadings	
	Factor I	Factor II
A. "Butterflies"	.53	.03
B. Nervous mannerisms	.66	.10
C. Rocking	.61	.02
D. Heart rate	.72	.07
E. Captions	.00	.68
F. Uses for common objects	.09	.77
G. Activities suggested	.00	.73

3. *The identification of factors.* The third step in factor analysis is the identification of factors. A **factor** is defined as a cluster of related behavior measures. A **factor loading** is a numerical index of the extent to which each specific behavioral measure is related to each factor. Factor loadings are calculated with the aid of a computer and the statistical technique of factor analysis. The results of the factor analysis are summarized in a **factor matrix**, which is a listing of the factor loadings for each separate factor. As with a correlation coefficient, the higher the factor loading, the more a particular measure is related to the factor. Table 7.4 is an example of a factor matrix.

The factor matrix in Table 7.4 illustrates what might be likely to happen if the data in Table 7.3 were subjected to a factor analysis. The most striking feature of Table 7.4 is the extent to which the seven separate measures are grouped together into two separate clusters, or factors. This illustrates the data-reduction and data-grouping characteristics of factor analysis. More specifically, instead of the seven separate measures to consider in an attempt to understand the nature of the personality of the 500 students, a researcher now has only two factors.

4. *Naming factors.* The final step in a factor analysis involves naming the factors that have been identified in the factor matrix. In Table 7.4, Factor I has high factor loadings for "butterflies," "nervous mannerisms," "rocking," and "heart rate." Perhaps "anxiety" might be an appropriate label that would capture the essence of the underlying relationship among these four behavioral measures. Since

Factor II has loadings on "captions," "uses for common objects," and "activities suggested," perhaps "creativity" is a label that might capture the essence of the underlying relationship among these three behaviors. While the identification of factor structures is a rather empirical process, the naming of factors is more subjective.

The Yield of Factor Analysis Is "Real" Source Traits

For Cattell, the major purpose of factor analysis is to identify source traits. The source traits are then used to define the nature of personality and predict people's behavior. In support of this search, Cattell (1979) notes that certain source traits (i.e., factors) have been identified consistently regardless of the type of data used (e.g., questionnaire, personal records), have been found in many different cultures, and have been used to predict real-life behavior (e.g., academic achievement). However, you should be aware that the quality of the information that is a product of a factor analysis is only as good as the quality of the information that is put into in – "garbage in, garbage out," as the old saying goes. For example, if you use measures that are of questionable reliability and validity, such as people's self-report public ratings of their truthfulness, the factors that are revealed must also be called into question.

In summary, performing a factor analysis is a highly complicated mathematical process that requires a certain amount of training and experience. However, having an understanding of the "basic logic" of factor analysis that is presented here is enough to be able to comprehend the approach taken by Cattell in his attempt to identify source traits within his study of personality.

The Behavioral Specification Equation: A Formula for Predicting what People Will Do

As stated in his basic definition of personality, Cattell stressed that personality research can aid in the understanding of the individual because it can be used to *predict* behavior. To facilitate the prediction of behavior, he combined information (i.e., L-, Q-, and T-data) related to underlying source traits into the behavioral

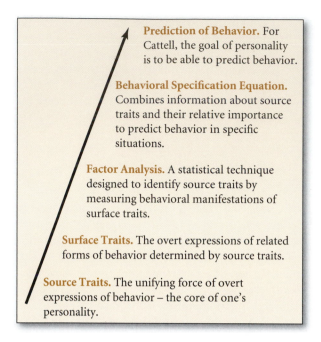

Prediction of Behavior. For Cattell, the goal of personality is to be able to predict behavior.

Behavioral Specification Equation. Combines information about source traits and their relative importance to predict behavior in specific situations.

Factor Analysis. A statistical technique designed to identify source traits by measuring behavioral manifestations of surface traits.

Surface Traits. The overt expressions of related forms of behavior determined by source traits.

Source Traits. The unifying force of overt expressions of behavior – the core of one's personality.

Figure 7.2   The basic concepts of Cattell's viewpoint are designed to achieve what he felt was the basic goal of personality psychology – to predict what an individual will do in a specific situation.

specification equation. The **behavioral specification equation** is a formula that combines information about traits, along with the degree of importance assigned to each type of information, in a mathematical manner for the purpose of predicting a particular behavior (McAdams, 1997).

In this section, we have explored the basic concepts of Cattell's viewpoint, his conceptualization and identification of source traits, and the utilization of source traits to predict behavior. Figure 7.2 summarizes the major points of this discussion and shows their interrelatedness.

Personality Assessment from Cattell's Viewpoint: Measurement of Source Traits

Cattell's passion for identifying and classifying source traits also manifests itself in the application of his viewpoint to personality assessment. The best-known of the many personality tests he developed is the **Sixteen Personality Factor Questionnaire**, or the **16PF** for short.

The 16PF   The 16PF (R. B. Cattell, Cattell, & Cattell, 1993; R. B. Cattell, Eber, & Tatsuoka, 1970) is a multidimensional personality inventory containing 185 questions designed to assess 16 different source traits. The questions are arranged in several types of forced-choice formats, illustrated by the three items presented here. These three items are similar to others measuring the "Social Boldness" factor (shy, timid vs. uninhibited) of the 16PF, which Cattell et al. (1993) identified by the letter *H*.

On social occasions I would rather:

a. come forward,
b. stay quietly in the background.

If I should suddenly become the focus of attention in a social situation, I would become slightly embarrassed.

a. yes,
b. no.

Having "stage-fright" in different social situations is something I have experienced:

a. quite often,
b. occasionally,
c. hardly ever.

The 16 source traits measured by the 16PF are presented in Table 7.5. The 16 traits are assigned letters in order of their contribution to the total personality structure. In other words, the traits near the top of the list have a greater influence on behavior than traits near the bottom. In addition, to indicate the types of behaviors controlled by each specific source trait, Table 7.5 includes a set of key words defining the principal characteristics of high- and low-scoring people.

Validity Research on the 16PF   With regard to such issues as reliability and validity, "the 16PF continues to be a be a leader among published personality tests" (Murphy & Davidshofer, 2005, p. 408). Along with a recently published supplement of updated norms (Maraist & Russell, 2002), much of the validation research on the 16PF involves the formulation of various behavioral specification equations that combine traits contained in it to distinguish between or predict the behavior of certain groups of people (R. B. Cattell & Cattell, 1995; Conn & Rieke, 1994; Oakes, Ferris,

Table 7.5   The Traits of the 16PF: A Listing and Description of the Basic Source Traits

Letter	Cattell's Label for the Factor	Description of High Score	Description of Low Score
A	Warmth	Warmhearted	Reserved
		Outgoing	Detached
		Easygoing	Critical
B	Reasoning	Bright	Dull
		High mental capacity	Low mental capacity
		Fast-learning	Poor judgment
C	Emotional Stability	Emotionally stable	Affected by feelings
		Mature	Easily upset
		Faces reality	Changeable
E	Dominance	Assertive	Obedient
		Aggressive	Easily led
		Competitive	Dependent
F	Liveliness	Enthusiastic	Serious
		Happy-go-lucky	Full of cares
		Talkative	Concerned
G	Rule-Consciousness	Conscientious	Disregards rules
		Persistent	Expedient
		Responsible	Undependable
H	Social Boldness	Adventurous	Shy
		Bold	Restrained
		Impulsive	Withdrawn
I	Sensitivity	Sensitive	Unsentimental
		Overprotected	Self-reliant
		Expects affection and attention	Keeps to the point
L	Vigilance	Jealous	Trusting
		Dogmatic	Understanding
		Suspicious	Ready to forget difficulties
M	Abstractedness	Imaginative	Practical
		Absent-minded	Conventional
		Interested in art, theory, basic beliefs	Concerned with immediate interests
N	Privateness	Worldly	Unpretentious
		Socially aware	Spontaneous
		Exact, calculating mind	Lacks self-insight
O	Apprehension	Apprehensive	Self-assured
		Insecure	Self-confident
		Troubled	Cheerful
Q1	Openness to Change	Experimenting	Not likely to change
		Analytic	Respects traditional values
		Free-thinking	Tolerant of old methods
Q2	Self-Reliance	Self-sufficient	Group dependent
		Resourceful	Is a "joiner"
		Prefers own decisions	Sound follower
Q3	Perfectionism	Controlled	Uncontrolled
		Exacting willpower	Follows own urges
		Compulsive	Careless of social rules
Q4	Tension	Tense	Relaxed
		Frustrated	Tranquil
		Driven	Composed

Note. Data from Cattell (1965); Karson & O'Dell (1976); Conn & Rieke (1994).

Martocchio, Buckley, & Broach, 2001). For example, Knowles (1966) used a previously established specification equation for identifying creativity in scientists to predict the subsequent academic achievement of incoming freshmen. The 16PF has also been used to examine the nature of entrepreneurship by examining the personality profiles of first- and second-generation entrepreneurs. The results suggests that first-generation entrepreneurs were (the letters of the source traits found in Table 7.5 are in parentheses) more suspicious (L+), assertive (E+), aloof (A−), imaginative (M+), and self-disciplined (Q3+) than the second-generation entrepreneurs (Fraboni & Saltstone, 1990). It seems that the second generation of entrepreneurs had lost some of the drive, ambition, and creativity characteristic of the entrepreneurial spirit of their predecessors. These studies suggest that a particular specification equation can be used to distinguish and predict the behavior of different groups of people.

The 16PF has also been used to identify the basic elements of personality associated with creativity. In one early study, Drevdahl and Cattell (1958) identified those traits on the 16PF that were found consistently among several samples of successful American and British artists. The personality of these successful artists included scoring high on the following 16PF source traits: being dominant (E+), radical (Q1+), emotionally sensitive (I+), strongly influenced by inner motivations (A−), and self-sufficient (Q2+). Low scores on the following 16PF source traits indicated that the personality characteristics of these artists also included being disregardful of rules (G−), natural and spontaneous in their behavior (N−), and somewhat detached (A−). The most striking feature of this study is the extent to which the same trait structure (e.g., being individualistic and free-thinking) was identified across several different groups of artists. This finding suggests that a common set of 16PF source traits can describe the basic personality of these successful artists. In a similar manner, more global aspects of creativity were found to be associated with the source traits of Dominance (E+), Social Boldness (H+), and Openness to Change (Q1+) (Rieke, Guastello, & Conn, 1994).

Many other interesting examples of studies documenting the validity of the 16PF, as well as additional information on its reliability, can be found in *The 16PF Fifth Edition Technical Manual* (Conn & Rieke, 1994).

Applications of Cattell's Viewpoint: Using What Is Known

The significant role of traits is illustrated further by the extent to which they are involved in the application of Cattell's viewpoint through the use of the 16PF. In this section, we will demonstrate the versatility of the 16PF by considering its applications to such diverse areas as the examination of marital relationships and the personality profiles of potential police profiles, members of the clergy, and suicide attempters.

Application of the 16PF to the Study of Marriage: Identifying Marital Stability and Compatibility

Do opposites attract? In a dating relationship, do people actively seek someone different from themselves to balance their own personality? Or is it better to be two similar peas in a pod? In an attempt to answer such difficult questions, Cattell and others applied their knowledge of traits and their assessment to the study of marriage.

The Study of Marriage Stability using the 16PF In 1967, Cattell and Nesselrode studied married couples they identified as either "stable" or "unstable." Stable couples were defined as those who took no steps toward dissolving the marriage. Unstable couples were defined as those who were separated or were undergoing marriage counseling. Cattell and Nesselrode hypothesized "that a positive correlation between husband and wife would be found over most of the personality factors for the normal group, but that negative, zero, or significantly lower positive correlations would be found for the unstable than for the normal couples" (p. 352). If their hypothesis were upheld, it would provide little support for the old saying that "opposites attract." As it turns out, their hypothesis was supported. Stable couples tended to have more highly correlated (i.e., similar) personality traits than unstable couples.

Assessing the Compatibility of Couples Using the 16PF The Cattell and Nesselrode study is a good example of how research can be useful in helping us to understand something as important as marriage. In a similar manner, Marry Russell and her colleagues (Madsen & Russell, 1982; Russell & Madsen, 1988; Russell & Robinson, 1995) have developed assessment instruments based on the 16PF to be used in couples counseling and therapy. One such instrument is the Couple's Counseling Report (Russell & Robinson, 1995). The **Couple's Counseling Report (CCR)** is a computer-generated interpretation comparing pairs of personality profiles based on the 16PF. With the aid of a trained counselor, the CCR is designed to examine individual and joint strengths and weaknesses found in the personalities of people in couples counseling, marriage counseling, and couples- and marriage-enhancement group therapy settings. The CCR can also be used to compare the personality patterns of people seeking marital counseling with the personality patterns of those experiencing successful marital adjustment. From these comparisons, the CCR provides information about the couple's personality patterns and their relationship that can be explored in greater detail during subsequent counseling sessions.

Will this marriage be a success? The Couple's Counseling Report is used in marriage counseling and marriage enhancement therapy to help marriages succeed.

A sample CCR comparing the paired profiles of a couple is presented in Table 7.6. In the table, the *F*s represent the scores obtained by the woman on the 16PF while the *M*s indicate the scores obtained by the man. The dotted lines between the *F*s and *M*s indicate the magnitude of the difference in their scores. Presented below is a summary interpretation of the couple's paired profiles:

> The couple's overall level of profile similarity is a score of 6, which reflects an average level of similarity. Their largest differences were on Factor E (Dominance), Factor O (Apprehension) and Factor N (Privateness). On the last quality, they are quite different; she tends to be more self-disclosing, while he tends to be more private. This difference, added to those mentioned above, may be related to both partners indicating that, if one area of the relationship could be changed to improve their satisfaction, it would be communication. (Wise & Elmore, 1996, p. 2)

The results of the paired profiles based on the 16PF is just one element of the overall CCR. Another part of the CCR is a written interpretation of the separate profiles. The interpretation is based upon research identifying personality traits related to adjustment and possible interpersonal difficulties. Following are some summaries of interpretations based on information from the counseling data section of the CCR for the couple whose personality profile is illustrated in Table 7.6.

> [His] orientation leans somewhat toward being domineering (Factor E = 7), and toward a preference for a structured and planful environment (Factor Q3 = 7). These qualities had manifested in his adoption of the role of "scheduler" and "assigner" of household chores. His perfectionistic tendencies (Factor Q3) played out in his self-assigned role of "quality control officer," characterized by strict and rigid evaluative criteria. In fact, adding his high-average level of tension and frustration (Factor Q4 = 7) to this picture, one might expect him to be somewhat demanding and rather easily disappointed by others.

> [She], with a tendency to be accommodating and deferential (Factor E = 3), tended to succumb to her husband's assigning, scheduling, and evaluation of household chores. Perhaps given her tendency to self-doubt (Factor O = 9) and her sense of trust that he was trying to improve their relationship (Factor L = 4), she accepted his criticism of her tolerance for disorder as valid. In fact, she was self-aware about her own preference for an unrestricted setting and lack of concern for precision or perfectionism (Factor Q3 = 3). (Wise & Elmore, 1996, p. 2)

Table 7.6   Assessing A Couple's Compatibility: A Sample CCR Profile

Trait			Score on Trait										
			1	2	3	4	5	6	7	8	9	10	
A	Warmth	Cool, reserved				M		F					Warm, easygoing
B	Reasoning	Concrete thinking								MF			Abstract thinking
C	Emotional Stability	Easily upset			F	M							Calm, stable
E	Dominance	Not assertive				F			M				Dominant
F	Liveliness	Sober, serious					F	M					Enthusiastic
G	Rule-Consciousness	Expedient				F	M						Conscientious
H	Social Boldness	Shy, timid		M	F								Venturesome
I	Sensitivity	Tough-minded					F		M				Sensitive
L	Vigilance	Trusting		M	F								Suspicious
M	Abstractedness	Practical							F		M		Imaginative
N	Privateness	Forthright	F						M				Shrewd
O	Apprehension	Self-assured					M			F			Self-doubting
Q1	Openness to Change	Conservative								F	M		Experimenting
Q2	Self-Reliance	Group-oriented	F			M							Self-sufficient
Q3	Perfectionism	Undisciplined				F		M					Self-disciplined
Q4	Tension	Relaxed				F		M					Tense-driven

Interpretation: The degree of personality similarity between these two people may be considered average.

Note. From Wise & Elmore (1996); Russel & Robinson (1995).

From what is known about these two people, how would you rate the likelihood of their creating a successful marital relationship? The value of the CCR is that it gives couples the opportunity before marrying or dissolving a relationship to become aware of personality factors in their relationships and the possible adjustments they may need to make in accommodating them.

Application of the 16PF to the Assessment of Police Officers: Identifying the Personality Profile of Police Officers

The application of the 16PF also includes various areas of law enforcement (Craig, 2005). One specific area is the evaluation of 16PF profiles for potential police officers. The selection of those individuals to be candidates for police academy training and, eventually, to be police officers is an important task because it is critical that the officers have the type of personality characteristics that will make it possible for them to be able to function effectively in a variety of situations involving many different types of individuals. To begin this process of evaluation, you must identify the pattern of personality traits associated with individuals working

as officers who have already successfully completed the officer training program.

For example, in an early study (Snibble, Fabricatore, & Azen, 1975), the 16PF results from the responses of 461 Los Angeles officers were examined. It was reported that the personality profiles of the officers indicated that they were bright and alert (High on Factor B: Reasoning) but somewhat interpersonally detached and reserved (Low on Factor A: Warmth). Such a combination of traits is important because the officers must be the voice of reason and stay neutral (e.g., emotionally detached) when dealing with highly emotional and irrational individuals reacting to emotionally charged situations (e.g., trying to remain calm while listening to the accusations by two intoxicated individuals involved in a domestic argument). They tended to be assertive (High on Factor E: Dominance), self-assured (Low on Factor O: Apprehension), realistic in their thinking (Low on Factor M: Abstractedness), and tough-minded and focused (Low on Factor I: Sensitivity). Such a combination of traits is important because the officers must often be responsible for taking control over a chaotic situation by focusing on the reality of the details of the situation (e.g., separating the disputing individuals before hearing their arguments against each other). Finally, the officers tended to be concerned about their image and reputation (Low on Factor Q1: Openness to Change) and rely on their own abilities (High on Factor Q2: Self-Reliance). Such a combination of traits is critical because the officers must rely on themselves to make decisions that will result in their behavior best upholding the tradition of protecting and serving all individuals equitably and fairly.

In a more recent study in this area of research (Zeidhlach, 2003), the scores on the 16PF for 246 police candidate applications from several states were compared to a sample of the normative scores from the general population. The pattern of results indicated that the biggest differences were that the applicants tended to score considerably higher than the general public on factors H: Social Boldness (e.g., adventurous) and Q3: Perfectionism (e.g., controlled) and lower on the factors of F: Liveliness (e.g., serious, concerned), O: Apprehension (e.g., self-assured, confident), and Q4: Tension (e.g., relaxed composed). Again, such a personality pattern seems to be consistent withthe idea that while being a police officer involves individuals who appear to be somewhat attracted to risk and adventure, it stills requires individuals who must be serious about what they do and composed and self-assured in the manner in which they do it. For example, even the most routine traffic stop has the potential to become a highly risky situation, if the driver decides to take off and leads the officer on a high-speed chase through heavy traffic. In this case, the officer must still be able to remain relatively calm and professional when dealing with this emotionally charged situation.

Finally, a summary of the results from published studies of law enforcement personnel indicates that when compared to the 16PF norms from the general population, the officers tended to be similar in warmth, rule-consciousness, vigilance, impulsivity, and shrewdness; slightly higher in intelligence, reasoning ability, perfectionism and organization, emotional stability, and dominance; and a bit lower in sensitivity and anxiety and tension (Craig, 2005). In short, what these results seem to suggest is that police officers possess personality characteristics similar to those of the general public but vary, to some extent, on those traits that are necessary for the successful performance of their duties. Such a personality profile is important because, while the officers must perform certain duties that are clearly different from what is expected of the general public, they must perform these duties within the context of the general public and, thus, must be able to relate to

them in a professional manner. The significance of the application of the 16PF in the process of assessing the personality profile of police officers is that as a highly reliable and valid measure of personality, the 16PF can help to identify the nature of the traits that are critical for performing this important aspect of community service, while reducing the potential for error in the assessment and selection process.

Application of the 16PF to the Assessment of Personality of Clergy Members: Identifying the Personality Characteristics of Clergy Members

Along the same lines, the 16PF has also been used to help identify the personality characteristics associated with individuals who are members of the clergy in comparison to males in the general population. Again, as with police officers, being able to identify the personality characteristics of individuals who are successful in the clergy is a critical factor in the future selection of those who will be admitted for religious training, and who will, eventually, be providing religious services to their communities. A recent study compared the responses to the 16PF of 580 male members of the Anglican clergy to normative responses of males in general (Musson, 2002). The results indicated the scores for the clergy were significantly different on 12 of the factors on the 16PF. Among the biggest differences were that members of the clergy scored *higher* than male members of the general public on the following three factors:

- *A: Warmth* (e.g., warmhearted, outgoing), which is consistent with the need for clergy members to be "people-centered," enabling them to be with others in their time of emotional and spiritual need, and also to be outgoing enough to be able to successfully recruit new members.
- *I: Sensitivity* (e.g., sensitive), which is consistent with the understanding and emotional support members of the clergy demonstrate when providing pastoral counseling and visitations.
- *Q1: Openness to Change* (e.g., analytical, free-thinking), which is necessary for members of the clergy to be able to be receptive to new ideas and make changes to improve their ministries.

Also among the biggest differences were that members of the clergy scored *lower* than male members of the general public on the following three factors. The parentheses give a brief description of a low score on the respective factor as seen in Table 7.5:

- *E: Dominance* (e.g., dependent), which is consistent with the need for members of the clergy when working with volunteers to be accommodating of their requirements and demonstrate a sense of appreciation of their efforts, since attracting and managing volunteers successfully is critical in the operation of their church and to help foster a sense of investment in the church by the volunteers.
- *F: Liveliness* (e.g., serious, concerned), which is consistent with the tendency for members of the clergy to be cautious in their attitudes about life and to be careful to think before they speak, since their thoughts and actions are the focal point for members of their church.
- *L: Vigilance* (e.g., trusting, understanding, ready to forget difficulties), which is critical because members of the clergy need to be able to see the goodness in others and view people as generally trustworthy.

While there were some clear differences in the personality profiles of the members of the clergy and male members of the general public, they were found to be similar on these three personality factors:

- *C: Emotional Stability* (e.g., faces reality), which implies that, like males in general, members of the clergy are relatively emotionally stable in their expectations and realistic in their ability to deal with life's problems, which helps them to be able to identify with the members of their church.
- *H: Social Boldness* (e.g., impulsive), which demonstrates that, like males in general, members of the clergy must be able to feel comfortable interacting with members of their church at a social level, as well as make members of their church feel comfortable interacting with them at this level.
- *Q2: Self-Reliance* (e.g., prefers own decisions), which implies that, like males in general, members of the clergy are able to find a balance between time spent alone in prayer and preparation and time spent with others providing pastoral care.

In summary, again, as with the personality profiles of police officers, while members of the clergy need to possess certain personality differences from the general public in order to perform their specific pastoral duties successfully, they must also possess certain personality characteristics that are similar to the general public's to make it possible for them to relate to members not only as parishioners but, just as importantly, as people, too.

The 16PF and the Assessment of Personality Profiles of Suicide Attempters

Another application of the 16PF includes the assessment of the personality profile of suicide attempters (Meyer & Deitsch, 1996). Attempters of suicide tend to score higher on factors Q4: Tension (e.g., tense, frustrated), O: Apprehension (e.g., insecure, troubled), I: Sensitivity (e.g., sensitive, expects affection and attention), and Q2: Self-Reliance (e.g., prefers own decisions), and lower on factors G: Rule-Consciousness (e.g., disregards rules, undependable), H: Social Boldness (e.g., restrained, withdrawn), and C: Emotional Stability (e.g., affected by feelings, easily upset). In addition, repeated attempters tended to score lower on factors Q3: Perfectionism (e.g., uncontrolled, follows own urges) and C: Emotional Stability (e.g., poor judgment) than first-time attempters, "indicating less stability and more impulsivity" (p. 318).

The importance of this application of the 16PF is that the identification of certain relevant personality characteristics is a critical element when attempting to assess the risk potential for suicide (i.e., the likelihood that the person will attempt suicide) by counselors working on suicide hot lines or at crisis intervention centers in their efforts to prevent individuals from committing suicide (Comer, 2007). It is estimated that 700,000 people from around the world commit suicide each year, with 31,000 in the United States, making suicide one of the leading causes of death in the world (S. E. Clark & Goldney, 2000; Stolberg, Clark, & Bongar, 2002). In addition, each year millions of other individuals attempt but do not succeed at suicide, with 600,000 of those individuals in the United States. Given the magnitude of such estimates, along with the pain and anguish such activities create for the family and loved ones of such victims, the use of the 16PF in this regard is probably one of its most significant applications I can think of.

This concludes our discussion of the applications of Cattell's trait theory and the 16PF. For more information on many other applications of the 16PF, read *Essentials of 16PF Assessment* (2003), authored by Heather Cattell, Cattell's daughter, and James Schuerger, a longtime associate of Cattell. We will end our discussion of Cattell's trait theory by considering its characteristic strengths and limitations.

Evaluating Cattell's Structural Trait Viewpoint: Strengths and Limitations

We will conclude our discussion of Cattell's viewpoint of personality by considering its characteristic strengths and limitations.

Characteristic Strengths

Here are some strengths of Cattell's structural trait viewpoint:

- *A quantitative approach.* One of Cattell's major strengths was the objectivity he used to study the nature of personality. Cattell believed that the best way to determine the structural nature of personality and predict behavior was to use quantitative methods, such as factor analysis, instead of armchair theorizing.
- *Cattell as a scientist.* The statistical technique of factor analysis and other techniques used by Cattell allowed him to study personality in a rather rigorous manner. Inconsistent with some of the less stringent approaches taken by other personality theorists, Cattell's commitment to rigorous research did much to earn him the label of "scientist" in every sense of the word.

Characteristic Limitations

Here are some limitations of Cattell's viewpoint:

- *The limitation of being too technical.* The statistical techniques that Cattell used to develop his structural trait viewpoint can be complicated and extremely technical. The language used to explain his viewpoint is also highly technical and not very appealing to the casual reader. For these reasons, Cattell's approach has not attracted the attention of many people outside of personality psychology. Given the emphasis personality psychologists place on the "scientific approach," it seems almost contradictory that Cattell should be criticized on the grounds of being "too technical."
- *An emphasis on identifying the universal personality while losing sight of the individual.* In his effort to establish a scientific approach to predicting behavior (e.g., the identification of 16 source traits), Cattell's research relies primarily on the study of large groups of people. Such an approach tends to reduce the study of personality to a consideration of the "average person." Cattell has been criticized for his attempt to define a universal set of source traits that seems to lose sight of the individual.

Our discussion of Cattell is now complete. In the next section, we will consider the trait perspective of Hans Eysenck, another individual who developed a very influential approach to the study of traits at a variety of levels.

Eysenck's Hierarchical Trait Viewpoint: A Type Theory of Traits

In addition to Allport and Cattell, a third individual has contributed significantly to the trait viewpoint of personality (Costa & McCrae, 2006; Pervin, 2002). Hans Eysenck's contributions have been in identifying fundamental dimensions of personality and their potential biological bases. For a glimpse into his life, read "A Closer Look" below.

A Closer Look

The Life of Hans J. Eysenck

Hans Jurgen Eysenck was born in Germany on March 4, 1916. His mother was an actress in films and his father an actor on the stage. Eysenck did not see much of his parents as a child; he was raised primarily by his grandmother. In reaction to the rise of Nazism and owing to his refusal to join the military at 18, he left Germany in 1934 and went to study in both France and England. In 1940, he received his PhD from the University of London while studying under the eminent psychologist Sir Cyril Burt. During World War II he served as a research psychologist at the Mill Hill Emergency Hospital, a psychiatric institution specializing in the treatment of patients suffering from combat stress. At the end of the war, Eysenck was named

Hans J. Eysenck was a personality researcher with a wide range of interests who was at the center of many important issues in psychology.

director of the Maudsley Hospital's new Institute of Psychiatry.

Eysenck demonstrated a most remarkable level of productivity – he published over 30 books and some 600 articles. Even more impressive is the diversity of topics about which he wrote. These include introversion–extraversion, biological bases of personality, learning theory, intelligence, genetics, smoking, criminal behavior, and sexuality. Some of his published works were co-authored with his second wife, Sybil B. G. Eysenck, and his son, Michael W. Eysenck. Eysenck was also at the center of many controversies in psychology. These include assessing the effectiveness of psychotherapy and the inheritability of intelligence. In recognition of his efforts, Eysenck received many prestigious awards, including the American Psychological Association's (APA) Award for Distinguished Contributions to Science (1988), APA's Presidential Citation for Outstanding Contributions to Psychology (1994), and the APA Division of Clinical Psychology's Centennial Award for Lifelong Contributions to Clinical Psychology (1996), to name just a few.

Eysenck died in London on September 4, 1997. More on his life can be found in a book-chapter-length autobiography (Eysenck, 1980), his obituary (Farley, 2000), and an autobiographical book titled *Rebel with a Cause* (Eysenck, 1996b).

Basic Assumptions of Eysenck's Definition of Personality

Like Cattell, Eysenck relied on factor analysis extensively to help identify the existence of the underlying dimensions of personality (Winter & Barenbaum, 1999). But unlike Cattell, Eysenck did not rely solely on factor analysis to define the outcome of personality structure. Instead, he started out with certain ideas about what he thought the dimensions of personality should look like and then used factor analysis to help identify the dimensions. He relied on the works of others, including Jung and the ancient Greek physicians Hippocrates and Galen, to help guide his thinking (L. A. Clark & Watson, 1999; Eysenck, 1967). Eysenck began with the fundamental idea that personality could be conceptualized as on two major dimensions (Brand, 1997). He then used factor analysis to test this idea. Figure 7.3 illustrates the nature of the two major dimensions of personality and the classification of various traits proposed by Eysenck.

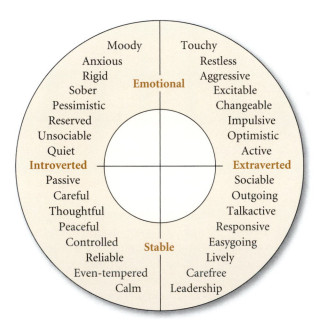

Figure 7.3   Eysenck's two major dimensions of personality and the classification of various personality traits
Source: Eysenck & Rachman (1965)

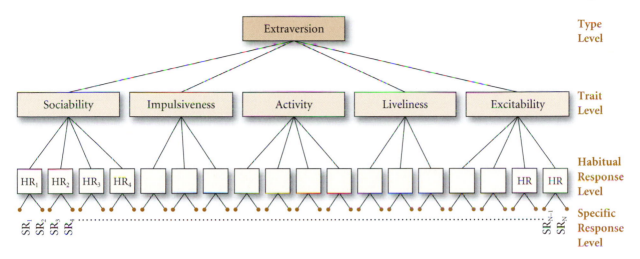

Figure 7.4 Eysenck's organization structure of personality traits
Source: Eysenck (1967)

Basic Concepts of Eysenck's Viewpoint: The Structure and Dynamics of Personality

Like Allport and Cattell, Eysenck demonstrated the significance he attributed to traits in the study of personality by the depth in which he described their structural organization and dynamics.

The Hierarchical Nature of Traits: From Specific Actions to General Types

Figure 7.4 illustrates Eysenck's view on the basic structural nature of personality (Contrada, Cather, & O'Leary, 1999; Eysenck, 1947, 1953, 1967, 1982, 1990; Eysenck & M. W. Eysenck, 1985). The hierarchical arrangement of personality started at the bottom with behaviors seen only in certain particular situations and went up to patterns of behavior that operate in a consistent manner across a wide variety of situations.

- *Specific response level.* At the bottom of the hierarchical structure are specific responses. **Specific responses** are particular actions observed in a particular situation. An example of specific response is when an individual smiles and extends a hand upon meeting someone new.
- *Habitual response level.* A **habitual response** is the repetition of the specific response across a number of situations. For example, if the individual smiles and extends a hand each time he or she

meets someone new, this pattern might then be defined as a habitual response to meeting someone new.
- *Trait level.* **Traits** are a collection of habitual responses. A person might be considered to have the trait of sociability if he or she also has the habitual response of going to parties, having many friends, and participating in group-type leisure activities (e.g., golf, cards).
- *Type level.* At the top of the hierarchy are personality types. A **type** is the interrelationship of many traits to create a general pattern of behavior that exerts a major influence on the individual's response style. Types are also the general dimensions around which Eysenck believed personality is organized. For example, if the individual is an extraverted type, he or she would probably select a career (e.g., sales or management) and elect to live in a location (e.g., in or near a big city) that makes possible the expression of the traits of sociability, impulsiveness, activity, liveliness, and excitability.

Thus, for Eysenck, personality is arranged in a hierarchical structure based on the degree of influence each trait level has on behavior.

Personality Dynamics: The Three Basic Personality Types

Eysenck described the dynamics of personality as involving the relationship of three basic types of traits.

The three basic types of personality he proposed are **extraversion–introversion** (E), **neuroticism** (N), and **psychoticism** (P; Eysenck, 1990; Eysenck & Eysenck, 1985). These dimensions are assessed using the Eysenck Personality Questionnaire (Eysenck & S. B. Eysenck, 1975, 1994).

Extraversion–Introversion   The extraversion–introversion dimension (E) comprises extraversion at one end of the continuum and introversion at the other end (Eysenck & S. B. Eysenck, 1975, 1994). Extraverted people like to be around other people, enjoy excitement, and are easygoing, optimistic, and adventurous. Introverted people like order and are introspective, emotionally controlled, calculating, and socially distant outside of having a few close friends. In addition to these overt differences, the two types differ in several other ways. Extraverts are more popular (Brown & Hendrick, 1971), happier (Lucas & Fujita, 2000), report more sexual behavior (Eysenck, 1976), acquire more sexual knowledge (Barnes, Malamuth, & Cheek, 1984) and sexual experience at a younger age (Schenk & Pfrang, 1986), take more risks (Arnaut, 2006) and have more accidents while driving (Shaw & Sichel, 1971), consume more alcohol (G. Edwards, Chandler, & Hensman, 1972), are better at reading the nonverbal behavior of others (Lieberman & Rosenthal, 2001), and are more likely to provide more social support to their spouse (Cutrona, Hessling, & Suhr, 1997), but are less creative (Eysenck, 1995; Simonton, 1999) than introverts. Extraversion was also found to be associated with greater stability of positive affect (e.g., favorable mood or positive outlook) throughout each day of the week (Larsen & Kasimatis, 1990) and over a 23-year period. (Charles, Reynolds, & Gatz, 2001), which may be explained by the greater tendency of extraverts to express positive affect (Silvia & Warburton, 2006), find more rewarding experiences in situations (Rusting, 1999), and recall pleasant memories (Rusting & Larsen, 1998) than introverts. Extraversion has also been linked with the tendency to find benefits in the face of adversity (Tennen & Affleck, 2003).

On a more covert level within the individual, extraverts seem to be less sensitive to stimulation (G. Wilson, 1978; Zuckerman, 2005), endure pain better (Eysenck & Eysenck, 1985), show more arousal later in the evening – from 9:00 p.m. to midnight – but less earlier in the day – from 7:00 a.m. to 4:00 p.m. (G. Wilson, 1990), and display faster reductions in cortical arousal (i.e., less electrical brainwave activity) to stimulation (Haier, Robinson, Braden, & Williams,

1984) than introverts. Many of these more covert differences between extraverts and introverts are due to differences in biological processes (Eysenck, 1967, 1970, 1990; Zuckerman, 2005). One of these biological processes is based on the notion that extraverts have certain brain structures that make them more sensitive to cues (e.g., loud music and lots of people laughing) and more likely to want to approach those environments (e.g., enter the building) associated with pleasure (Gray & McNaughton, 2000). The pleasure-seeking tendency of extraverts seems to suggests that while we may commonly assume that extraverts are "up for a party anytime" (i.e., attracted to any and all social situations), this seems to be true only when the social event is likely to be fun and enjoyable, thus a source of pleasure (Lucas, Diener, Grob, Suh, & Sho, 2000). Consistent with the pleasure-seeking tendency of extraverts, it was reported that they preferred nonsocial activities, such as going for a walk by themselves, *if they assumed the activity would be pleasurable* (Lucas & Diener, 2001).

More information on this and other biological and genetic processes are discussed in the next chapter dealing with the biological bases of personality.

Neuroticism   The neuroticism dimension (N) comprises emotional stability at one end of the continuum and emotional instability at the other (Eysenck & Eysenck, 1985). Emotionally stable people (those with low neuroticism scores) are characterized as carefree, even-tempered, and calm. Emotionally unstable people (those with high neuroticism scores) are characterized as touchy, restless, moody, and anxious. Emotionally unstable people are more sensitivity to odors (Larsson, Finkel, & Pedersen, 2000) and display greater reactions to stress (Maushammer, Ehmer, & Eckel, 1981), especially reoccurring stressors (Suls, Green, & Hillis, 1998), experience more severe depression (Harkness, Bagby, Joffe, & Levitt, 2002), and seem to require a longer period of readjustment following a stressful experience than emotionally stable people (Harvey & Hirschmann, 1980). As an example, while you might think that hearing that others are making progress with a similar medical condition would make cancer patients feel better, neurotic cancer patients didn't feel inspired by the progress being made by other cancer patients (Van der Zee, Buunk, & Sanderman, 1998).

Neurotic individuals have also been found to have trouble making distinctions within their present reality regarding stress-related bodily symptoms (e.g., headaches, nausea) and behaviors (e.g., criticized myself, felt overwhelmed) and negative feelings (e.g., distressed, irritable; Robinson & Clore, 2007). And although negative affect (e.g., unhappiness, less life satisfaction) was found to decrease with age, individuals with high neuroticism scores displayed less of a decrease across a 23-year period (Charles et al., 2001). In response to such negative affect, neurotic individuals also seem to be prone to engaging in risky behavior (e.g., alcohol consumption and unsafe sexual behavior) as a way to cope with aversive mood states (Cooper, Agocha, & Sheldon, 2000). As an indication of an overall low level of personal adjustment, neuroticism is associated with both poor self-esteem and decreased levels of life satisfaction (Heller, Watson, & Ilies, 2004; Watson, Suls, & Haig, 2002).

As shown in Figure 7.3, Eysenck combined the dimensions of extraversion and neuroticism to formulate a description of personality. Someone scoring more in the direction of extraversion and emotional stability might exhibit the personality traits of being responsive and easygoing; someone scoring more in the direction of the introversion and emotional instability dimensions might exhibit the personality traits of being sober and pessimistic. Thus, with Eysenck's system it is possible to describe various personality patterns and not just the extreme cases of general personality types.

Psychoticism The psychoticism dimension (P) comprises psychoticism at one end of the continuum and superego control (i.e., a sense of morality) at the other (Eysenck, 1990; Eysenck & S. B. G. Eysenck, 1976). Psychoticism is associated with the tendency to be impulsive, cold, not empathic, unconcerned about the rights and welfare of others, and antisocial. Individuals low in psychoticism are described as warm, sensitive, and concerned about others. A criticism of Eysenck's conceptualization of psychoticism has been that it is associated with more severe forms of personality pathology (e.g., schizophrenia; G. Claridge, 2006), and as such, it is less important as a dimension of personality in the study of the healthy personality (e.g., self-esteem) than in the study of the maladaptive personality (e.g., the mentally ill or criminal mentality).

For example, people scoring high on the P dimension displayed a pattern of sensory sensitivity and arousal to visual stimuli similar to that experienced by persons suffering from schizophrenia (G. S. Claridge, 1983; G. S. Claridge & Birchall, 1978; G. S. Claridge & Chappa, 1973). Eysenck (1995; Simonton, 1999) also proposed an interesting relationship between the continuum of creativity and psychoticism. Along the continuum of creativity, low levels of psychoticism were associated with an absence of creativity, but increased levels of psychoticism were associated with enhanced creativity. Putting this in the context of his study of the creative genius, Simonton (1999) notes that, "The genius emerges at the exalted level between creativity and madness" (p. 636).

This concludes our discussion of Eysenck's conceptualization of traits. A summary of the major points discussed in this is presented in "Summing It Up: The Basic

Summing It Up *The Basic Concepts of Eysenck's Hierarchical Trait Theory*

Hierarchical Nature of Traits. Eysenck organized traits on the basis of the nature of their expressed influence:

- *Specific responses.* Actions that exhibit an expressed influence in a particular situation. For example, someone yells when angry at work.
- *Habitual responses.* Actions that exhibit an expressed influence in a number of situations. For example, someone yells when angry at work and home.
- *Traits.* A collection of actions that exhibit an expressed influence in a number of situations and forms. For example, someone yells when angry and cries when frustrated.
- *Types.* A constellation of traits that exhibit an expressed influence in the form of a general style of behavior. For example, emotionality describes a general style of behavior characterized by yelling and crying.

Personality Dynamics. The dynamics of personality are based on the expression of the three major personality dimensions:

- *Extraversion–introversion.* Characterized by the degree of outward focus vs. inward focus of the individual's style of behavior. For example, extravert types prefer social activities while introvert types prefer solitary activities.
- *Neuroticism.* Characterized by the degree of emotional stability of the individual's style of behavior. For example, high neurotic types display a greater degree of emotional reaction to stress than do low neurotic types.
- *Psychoticism.* Characterized by the degree of impulsivity and emotional detachment from others. For example, a high degree of psychoticism is associated with more emotional disturbances than are the other two personality types.

Concepts of Eysenck's Hierarchical Trait Theory." In the next section, we will consider some of the many applications of Eysenck's viewpoint of personality.

Applications of Eysenck's Viewpoint: Using What Is Known

Eysenck remains one of the world's most renowned, influential, widely cited, and controversial psychologists; his work and ideas have permeated many of life's most important areas and issues (Nyborg, 1997). In this section, we consider the application of his viewpoint to organizational psychology, human sexuality, medicine, and criminality.

Organizational Psychology

Many applications of Eysenck idea's can be seen in the field of **organizational psychology** and the world of work (Furnham, 1997). In an investigation of job preferences, introverts preferred scientific and theoretical jobs, such as journalism, architecture, and the teaching of mathematics, while extraverts expressed more interests in jobs with a high degree of social contact, such as selling life insurance and social work (Bendig, 1963). In an interesting study of the job selection of would-be pilots (Jessup & Jessup, 1971), the personalities of the potential pilots were assessed early in their training course. The results indicated the failure rate was 67 percent for neurotic (high N scores) introverts, 37 percent for neurotic extraverts, 32 percent for stable (low N scores) extraverts, and only 14 percent for stable introverts. The high rate of failure for the neurotic introverts was attributed to their excessive level of cortical arousal (i.e., higher excitability). Since the training of pilots is expensive and their actions can have profound consequences for passenger safety, the ability to identify individuals with the best potential to become good pilots is extremely important.

In addition to career preferences and being able to select who is right for a job, another critical factor in the world of work is job satisfaction. In a study of job satisfaction (Furnham & Zacherl, 1986), individuals with high psychoticism scores (tough-minded) tended to demonstrate a lower level of job satisfaction by expressing less satisfaction with their supervisor, the nature of their work, and their co-workers than did individuals with low psychoticism scores (tender-minded). Individuals with high neuroticism scores (unstable neurotics) also tended to show a low degree of satis-

faction with the amount of work they were asked to do, their co-workers, and their pay. One possible explanation is that such individuals are less productive because they are less satisfied with their jobs.

Personality Correlates of Sexual Behavior

In the study of human sexuality, Eysenck investigated the relationship between personality factors and sexual attitudes and behaviors (G. D. Wilson, 1997), with much of this research summarized in Eysenck's (1976) book *Sex and personality*. For example, one of the best predictors of sexual experiences, especially for girls, was the smoking of cigarettes, which was also highly associated with extraversion (Schofield, 1968). Extraverts reported engaging in virtually all forms of sexual activity more than introverts, with the exception of masturbation, which should come as no surprise since masturbation is a solitary activity (Giese & Schmidt, 1968; Husted & Edwards, 1976). High neuroticism scores tended to be associated with higher rates of masturbation, greater desire for intercourse, and more spontaneous erections in men but less frequent orgasms and menstrual discomfort in women (Giese & Schmidt, 1968) and greater high-risk sexual behavior (e.g., "one-night stands," intercourse in exchange for drugs or money, unprotected intercourse; Cooper et al., 2000). Thus, for individuals high on N, males tended to experience more sexual tension and frustration while females tended to experience less sexual pleasure.

Personality Correlates of Cancer Patients

Another important area in which Eysenck's work has been applied is in the study of medicine (Nias, 1997). For example, in one of Eysenck's early studies, individuals suffering from lung cancer were found to have significantly lower neuroticism scores than noncancer patients (Kissen & Eysenck, 1962). This was found to be consistent with previous "observational evidence that cancer patients tended to be 'unassertive, compliant people, inexpressive of negative emotions like anger, fear, and anxiety'" (Nias, 1997, p. 92). Eysenck also investigated the relationship between stress and the personality profile of smokers, since both factors are believed to be associated with increased levels of cancer (Eysenck, 1991). The cancer-prone personality type tends to be seen in individuals who are likely to attach a considerable amount of emotionality to a highly valued object (e.g., car or house), person (e.g., peer group), occupation (e.g., actor), or whatever is viewed as the most important condition for their happiness and well-being. Such individuals become overly stressed when they are not able to achieve the desired source of satisfaction. Combining such a condition of stress with smoking produced a deadly combination, or what Eysenck considered "the cancer-prone type" (Eysenck, 1991, p. 55).

Crime and Personality

Eysenck's work on criminality focused on combining personality factors, biological processes, and principles of learning (Gudjonsson, 1997). He believed that criminality was associated with extraversion (E) and psychoticism (P) in that such individuals possessed a relatively low level of cortical arousal (i.e., "brain stimulation") and poor conditionability (i.e., learned associations more slowly). As a result, such individuals are less likely to develop a conditioned-response "conscience" (Eysenck, 1996a; Eysenck & Gudjonsson, 1989). More specifically, according to Eysenck, criminals are less likely to associate high levels of unpleasant arousal (e.g., guilt and anxiety) with criminal activities. It is the anticipated association of unpleasant feelings (i.e., one's conscience) with criminal actions that prevents most individuals from engaging in criminal activity.

The above is only a brief presentation of some of the many applications of Eysenck's viewpoint. More about the applications of Eysenck's work and ideas can be found in: *Smoking, Personality, and Stress: Psychosocial Factors in the Prevention of Cancer and Heart Disease* (Eysenck, 1991), *The Psychology of Politics* (Eysenck, 1998b), and *Intelligence: A New Look* (Eysenck, 1998a). To consider yet another but somewhat unusual application of Eysenck's viewpoint that is outside of the traditional realm of personality psychology, read "A Closer Look" below.

A Closer Look

The "Write" Stuff?: Eysenck's Analysis of Handwriting Analysis

It might be surprising to think that a man of Eysenck's scientific credibility would be interested in the study of **graphology**, or handwriting analysis. However, his initial interest in such a borderline aspect of science can be traced back to his student years in 1934 when he casually mentioned to a group of friends that he was a graphologist. He was not, of course, but he said so in his efforts to keep the attention of a certain young lady (Eysenck, 1957).

Although his initial efforts in the area of graphology may have stemmed from ulterior motives, Eysenck did use his keen sense of observation and considerable analytical skills to address this and other aspects of the pseudo-sciences that were being promoted to and uncritically accepted by many individuals, thus serving to undermine what he felt were the more scientific aspects of personality psychology. In one of his earliest studies on graphology, Eysenck (1948) had an experienced graphologist predict neuroticism on a 5-point scale for 176 neurotics and non-neurotics. The correlation between the psychographical predictions was extremely low ($r = -.02$) while the correlation bases on the personality test was rather high ($r = .73$). This led Eysenck to conclude: "The present study demonstrates that even with an imperfect criterion, short objective tests show much higher validity coefficients than does graphological analysis; this should seem to invalidate the claims of the graphologists" (p. 96).

Not willing to base a conclusion on a single study, Eysenck and some of his colleagues continued to investigate the claims of psychographology. In another study, Eysenck and Gudjonsson (1986) had a professional graphoanalyst propose answers to the items on a personality test for 99 randomly chosen adults based on handwriting samples. Consistent with previous results, the correlation between the scores based on the graphological sample and actual scores of test taken by the individual was, once again, extremely low ($r = .05$). Additional research demonstrated that graphologists were no better than nongraphologists in using handwriting samples to predict work performance (Neter & Ben-Shakhar, 1989) and match occupations (A. G. P. Edwards & Armitage, 1992). Finally, an analysis comparing over 100 graphological studies reached essentially the same conclusion as Eysenck did in 1986: that the correlation between the judgments of graphologists and reality is not big enough ($r = .12$) and reliable enough ($r = .42$) to be of any use (Dean, 1992).

In addition to the study of psychographology, Esyenck used his talents and commitment to scientific investigation to examine other aspects of what are considered the borderline sciences (Dean, Nias, & French,

1997), such as astrology (Eysenck & Nias, 1982) and parapsychology (Eysenck & Sargent, 1982, 1993), which is also discussed in detail in *Know Your Own Psi-Q* (Eysenck & Sargent, 1984).

Evaluating Eysenck's Viewpoint: Strengths and Limitations

We will conclude our discussion of Eysenck's viewpoint of personality by considering its characteristic strengths and limitations.

Characteristic Strengths

Here are some strengths of Eysenck's viewpoint:

- *Eysenck's emphasis on empiricism.* Like Cattell, Eysenck had as a principal strength his emphasis on developing the scientific perspective of personality psychology from empirical data. Eysenck relied heavily on factor analysis and other rather complicated statistical techniques to support his ideas.
- *Eclectic thinking.* Another of Eysenck's significant strengths was his eclectic thinking style and ability to integrate a variety of areas of knowledge within his viewpoint. His perspective on personality combined the study of genetics, biological and physiological processes, learning theory, and societal and cultural factors.

Characteristic Limitations

Here are some limitations of Eysenck's viewpoint:

- *Eysenck's emphasis on just three dimensions of personality.* A major criticism of Eysenck's approach centers on his assumption that personality can be reduced to just three principal types or factors. As discussed in the next section, a central issue in the study of traits is identifying the number of dimensions or factors necessary to describe personality. The research on this issue suggests that three factors are probably too few to describe the underlying structure of personality.
- *Concerns about the nature of Eysenck's dimensions of personality.* In a related matter, there are also

questions concerning the validity of the extraversion–introversion dimension as a single dimension. It has been suggested that this might be more accurately described as two separate dimensions of personality, such as sociability and impulsiveness.

Additional aspects of Eysenck's viewpoint of personality are discussed in the next chapter concerning the biological bases of personality. For more information about Eysenck's viewpoint, read *The Scientific Study of Human Nature: Tribute to Hans J. Eysenck at Eighty* (Nyborg, 1997).

Special Issues in the Study of Traits: The Consistency and Organization of Traits

Although only the trait theories of Allport, Cattell, and Eysenck are discussed in this chapter, many other people are working in the trait tradition today. Even though many of them do not offer their own definitions of traits, most "would probably agree that trait terms refer to stylistic consistencies in interpersonal behavior" (Hogan, DeSoto, & Solano, 1977, p. 256) and that traits are personality psychology's "unique and therefore defining characteristic" (A. H. Buss, 1989, p. 1378). The work of some of these people involves addressing issues related to the specific nature and operation of traits (D. M. Buss & Cantor, 1989; Cervone & Shoda, 1999a, 1999b; Costa & McCrae, 1998; McAdams, 1997; McCrae & Costa, 2003; Mischel & Shoda, 1998).

Two issues of central concern for contemporary personality psychologists working in the trait tradition involve the consistency of traits in influencing behavior and the structural organization of traits (Costa & McCrae, 1998, 2006).

The Issue of Cross-Situational Consistency: The Ability of Traits to Predict Behavior

As noted at the beginning of this chapter, trait theorists assume that traits exist and that people differ in the degree to which they possess certain traits. With the idea that traits exist comes the expectation that they should operate in a stable manner to influence an individual's behavior over time and across various situations. However, in discussing their own definition of traits as "dimensions of individual differences in tendencies to show consistent patterns of thoughts, feelings, and actions" (McCrae & Costa, 1990, p. 23), Paul T. Costa and Robert R. McCrae, two prominent trait personality psychologists (see pp. 299–300), note that "The most problematic part of that definition has been the phrase 'consistent patterns'" (Costa & McRae, 1998, p. 104). Their concerns about the ability of traits to manifest their existence and stable influence in a wide range of situations is often referred to as cross-situational consistency (Ickes, Snyder, & Garcia, 1997).

The Search for Cross-Situational Consistency: Traits as a Stabilizing Influence in Life

The basic assumption of **cross-situational consistency** is the stabilizing influence of traits on behavior over time and place. In other words, an individual's behavior is expected to be relatively consistent across a wide variety of situations (e.g., at work, school, and home) over the course of time due to the stabilizing impact of traits. For example, an extraverted individual was extremely outgoing last week at a party, is talkative today while attending a business conference, and is expected to be very friendly two months from now when on vacation. Although no one is expected to be perfectly consistent, people are expected to maintain their relative ranking across situations by exhibiting behaviors consistent with their level of endowment (e.g., high, medium, or low) of the trait. For example, attending a funeral will make even the most extraverted individual somewhat less sociable. But the individual high on the trait of extraversion will probably be more sociable (e.g., talk to more people) at the funeral home than will an individual low on the extraversion dimension.

Documenting a Lack of Cross-Situational Consistency: Classic and Contemporary Evidence

In this section, we will consider the evidence suggesting a lack of cross-situational consistency in behavior.

Some Classic Evidence Documenting a Lack of Cross-Situational Consistency

A classic example of research addressing the issue of cross-situational consistency is that of Hartshorne and May (1928). They investigated the cross-situational consistency of moral behavior (e.g., lying, cheating, cooperativeness) in more than 1,000 children across a variety of situations (e.g., home, school, party games, and athletic competitions). The results of this extensive research indicated that the average correlation between the moral behavior in any two situations was only about $r = +.30$. Such results suggest very little cross-situational consistency. Dudycha (1936) observed a similar pattern of results when studying punctuality of college students (e.g., arriving on time to class, social events, meals, and appointments) by examining more than 15,000 observations for over 300 college students. The average cross-situational correlation was calculated to be only $r = +.19$, which indicates a rather low degree of cross-situational consistency.

Some Contemporary Evidence Documenting a Lack of Cross-Situational Consistency

More contemporary evidence examining the issues of cross-situational consistency of behavior has been summarized by Mischel (1968) in his now-classic book titled *Personality and Assessment*. In this book, Mischel reviewed and summarized much of the past and present research on the ability of personality tests (i.e., trait measures) to predict behavior across a variety of situations, noting that there was little evidence to suggest that trait measures do a very good job of predicting behavior in different situations. Specifically, he noted that correlations between various personality tests (e.g., shyness) and observed behaviors (e.g., avoiding others at a party) rarely exceeded the magnitude of $r = .30$.

So consistent was this finding that Mischel (1968, p. 78) coined the phrase "personality coefficient" to describe it. **Personality coefficient** describes the correlation of around $r = .20$ to $.30$ that is typically found whenever attempts have been made to correlate a measure of a trait (e.g., aggressiveness) or other personality dimensions (e.g., an immediate sense of anger) assessed by personality tests with some observable behavior (e.g., number of hostile statements made in a group discussion). The inability of traits to predict behavior across situations has brought into question their overall value and importance (Kenrick & Funder, 1988).

In Support of Cross-Situational Consistency: Predicting Some of the People Some of the Time

In contrast to the early findings and conclusions about the inability of traits to predict behavior, contemporary research has documented a greater degree of cross-situational consistency than is represented by the personality coefficient. This research tends to make more realistic assumptions about the nature and operation of traits. It also uses more sophisticated research methodologies than simply calculating the correlation between the trait measure and behavior in various situations.

One of the more realistic assumptions made by contemporary researchers is that not everybody is equally consistent for each personality trait. As a test of this assumption, Bem and Allen (1974) had people indicate the extent to which they demonstrated consistency in behavior for the traits of friendliness and conscientiousness. Bem and Allen then selected groups of highly predictable and unpredictable people and obtained ratings of the individual's behavior across a number of situations related to being friendly and conscientious (e.g., sociability and promptness). The results indicated that the correlations between the trait of friendliness and the overall behavioral friendliness rating were $r = +.57$ for the predictable group and $r = +.27$ for the unpredictable group. For the trait of conscientiousness, the overall correlations were $r = +.45$ for the predictable group and $r = +.09$ for the unpredictable group.

This consistency between personality traits and behavior gets even larger when people are given the opportunity to select those specific traits for which they feel they are most consistent (Kenrick & Stringfield, 1980). Thus, as more realistic assumptions about traits are made (e.g., not all people are equally predictable) and more sophisticated procedures are employed (e.g., identifying predictable people and letting people select their predictable traits), there is considerable evidence to document cross-situational consistency in personality traits (A. H. Buss, 1989; Kenrick & Funder, 1988; Zuckerman et al., 1988).

Clarifying the Consistency Issue: Situational, Cognitive, and Aggregation Alternatives

With the impact of personality traits on behavior established, three general categories of approaches have been proposed to further clarify how traits might be used to help account for the cross-situational consistencies in behavior. These include the situational, cognitive, and aggregation alternatives.

The Situational Alternative: It's Not Only Who You Are but Where You Are That Counts

The situational alternative to the cross-situational consistency issue stresses that behavior occurs in a particular situation. The assumption here is that situational factors (e.g., posted rules) serve to modify behavior and create inconsistency across situations.

Situationism and External Constraints on Behavior
Situationism proposes that certain characteristics of the situation dictate what are acceptable or possible forms of behavior in a given situation (Bowers, 1973; Moos, 1973; Pettigrew, 1997; Price & Bouffard, 1974). For example, although an individual may be extremely talkative at school and parties, the formality of visiting a funeral home produces a much more somber display of behavior. In addition, posting a sign in a hallway at school that says "Quiet Please" might also produce uncharacteristic silence in this individual. Thus, the inconsistencies in the individual's degree of talkativeness are a result of the implicit (e.g., social customs) and explicit (e.g., instructions) constraints of the situation on behavior (Johnson, 1997; Pettigrew, 1997).

The Concept of Interactionism   An extension of the situational alternative is the concept of interactionism. **Interactionism** states that it is not the person (i.e., personality traits) or the situation (i.e., characteristics of the environment) independently but the interaction (i.e., combination) of these two factors that best explains and predicts the behavior of individuals (Bowers, 1973; Cervone & Mischel, 2002; Ekehammer, 1974; Endler, 1973, 1982; Higgins, 1990; Magnusson, 1999; Magnusson & Endler, 1977; McAdams, 1997; Ozer, 1986; Pervin, 1984). The logic behind interactionism is that the combination of personal and situational

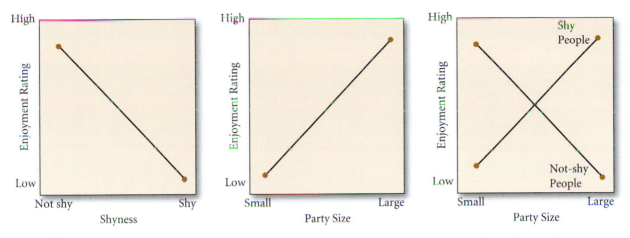

Figure 7.5 An example of interactionism: Enjoyment ratings of different-size parties by shy and not-shy people

components has a much greater effect than the two considered separately.

As an example of interactionism, consider how shy and not-shy people might rate their enjoyment of small (i.e., 20 people) or large (i.e., 75 people) social gatherings. If only the shyness of the individual (i.e., personality factor) is considered, the results might look like those in the left chart of Figure 7.5. If only the size of the party (i.e., situational factor) is considered, the results might look like those in the middle chart of Figure 7.5. But if both the personality and situational factors are considered, the results might look like those in the right chart of Figure 7.5. Shy people may prefer large parties because it might be easier for them to blend into the crowd and feel less self-conscious. On the other hand, less-shy people might prefer smaller parties where there is less competition for them to be the center of attention. Thus, by considering both situational and personality factors, researchers can achieve a more complete understanding of behavior than by considering these factors separately (Cervone & Mischel, 2002; Emmons & Diener, 1986; Emmons, Diener, & Larsen, 1985; Ickes et al., 1997).

While interactionism stresses the benefits of combining personality and situational factors, sometimes the effects of situational characteristics or the personality of the individual considered separately do a better job of predicting behavior and explaining cross-situational consistency (Diener & Larsen, 1984; Diener, Larsen, & Emmons, 1984; Sarason, Smith, & Diener, 1975). Sometimes the person–situation interactions are more complex than simply adding together the personalities

of the people and the characteristics of the situation, such as when there are also effects from biological (e.g., hormonal levels and brain functioning) and cognitive (e.g., beliefs and expectations) factors (Cervone & Mischel, 2002). Personality psychologists must consider more systematically when and why the characteristics of the situations, the personality of the individual, or the interaction of these two variables are most important (Buss, 1989; Diener & Larsen, 1984; Higgins, 1990; Magnusson & Endler, 1977; Mischel, 1973, 1984, 1985; Mischel & Shoda, 1995, 1998; Moskowitz, 1982; Pervin, 1999). Thus, because situational and personality factors considered alone tend to be equally moderately correlated with specific behaviors (Funder & Ozer, 1983; Mischel, 1968), the situational alternative proposes that cross-situational consistency can be better explained by considering both of these factors and their combination.

The Cognitive Alternative: Perceptions and Interpretations of Situations

The cognitive alternative to the cross-situational consistency issue stresses the role of cognitive factors in the perception and interpretation of situational cues that determine what behaviors will be performed. The basic assumption here is that the degree of cross-situational consistency will be determined by the extent to which there is consistency in the perception and interpretation of situational cues. The more likely different situations are perceived and interpreted as being similar, the greater the degree of behavioral consistency across these different situations.

Cognitive Factors as a Determinant of Behavior Consistency **Cognitive factors** refer to various mental processes that influence the thoughts people have about being in a particular situation and how they might respond to these thoughts (Cervone & Shoda, 1999b; Mischel, 1973, 1984, 1990; Mischel & Shoda, 1995, 1998, 1999). Examples of cognitive processes include the selective perception to certain cues in a situation (e.g., "Most people here are dancing"), the specific interpretation of these cues (e.g., "The people dancing seem to be having fun"), certain expectancies with regard to one's ability to perform specific behaviors (e.g., "I can dance just about as well as most of the people on the dance floor"), and specific beliefs with regard to the outcome of performing certain behaviors in that situation (e.g., "If I start dancing, I'll have a good time, too"). For most individuals, the behavior of others in a situation is a very powerful cue that can determine an individual's behavior (Lamm & Myers, 1978; Zimbardo, 1970). Even a very introverted person might start to yell and scream at a football game after being caught up in the excitement and emotion of the other fans. Thus, the inconsistency in behavior of this introverted person is due to the perception and interpretation of certain cues (e.g., screaming is perceived and interpreted as appropriate and desirable).

In their efforts to help explain inconsistency of behavior across different situations, Mischel and Shoda (1995, 1998, 1999) have introduced the concept of "if . . . then relations." The basic logic of **if . . . then relations** is to take into consideration the role of cognitive factors as mediating sources of influence when an individual decides what to do across different situations. For example, a very aggressive person may decide not to behave in an aggressive manner in certain situations, thus demonstrating a lack of consistency across situations. In such cases, the inconsistency in the individual's degree of aggressive behavior is a result of specific if . . . then relationships among the cognitive factors. For Mischel and Shoda, if you consider the role of cognitive factors, then such inconsistency in behavior is not really a form of inconsistency but of consistency in the manner in which the if . . . then relations are applied. In this case, the consistency of the if . . . then relations for this aggressive individual is: "*If* I perceive that aggressive behavior will result in a favorable outcome (e.g., I get my way), *then* I'll act aggressively. On the other hand, *if* I perceive that aggressive behavior will result in an unfavorable outcome (e.g., I could be beaten up), *then* I will not act aggressively." Thus, by considering the role of cognitive factors in the form of if . . . then relations, consistency can be found even in the inconsistency of behavior. More will be said about the role of cognitive factors in the expression of personality in Chapter 10.

Powerful vs. Weak Situations as Determinants of Cognitive Clarity To pinpoint more accurately the role of cognitive factors, Mischel (1973, 1984) described the power of situations to determine specific behaviors. The power of a situation is characterized by its cognitive clarity. Cognitive clarity is the extent to which everyone will perceive a particular situation in a similar manner and emit a similar response. A very powerful situation has a considerable amount of clarity and serves to minimize the contribution of personality traits (i.e., individualistic expression). On the other hand, a very weak situation is characterized by a high degree of ambiguity and makes possible a greater role for personality traits in influencing the response.

The power of a situation can be determined by such factors as its context (e.g., formal vs. informal; public vs. private), the amount of choice available to the individual (e.g., little vs. considerable), duration in the situation (e.g., brief vs. extensive), and the range of responses possible (e.g., narrow vs. broad; A. H. Buss, 1989). A very powerful situation might be one in which a military recruit is ordered by the drill instructor to hit other recruits as part of a hand-to-hand combat exercise. In this very formal, public, low-choice, and brief situation with a narrowly defined range of possible responses, even a very nonviolent individual will behave aggressively. A much weaker situation might be when the recruit is at home and is trying to decide what to do while on a two-week pass. Given this set of circumstances, the true nonviolent nature of the recruit's personality might result in the individual leaving a bar when a fight starts to break out. Thus, according to the cognitive alternative, inconsistency in behavior can be attributed to differences in the perception and interpretation of situational characteristics.

The Aggregation Alternative: "Adding up" the Consistency in Behavior

For Seymour Epstein (1979, 1980, 1983, 1984; Epstein & O'Brien, 1985; McAdams, 1997), the problem with trying to identify consistency in behavior has to do with the way personality psychologists have been looking for it. Personality psychologists have searched for consistency by examining single units of behavior as they relate to a particular personality trait. For example, suppose a researcher was investigating the degree of extraversion exhibited by a female college student in three different situations. If the researcher were to look at each of these situations separately, she or he might note that the student talks a lot to others at work, says nothing to others while riding on the bus, and talks only slightly to her classmates before class. Such evidence taken separately suggests a rather low degree of consistency between the trait of extraversion and her tendency to talk to others. But a more accurate picture of her consistency for the trait of extraversion might be obtained by combining all of the behaviors to form a more global index of social interaction.

Aggregation Research and Playing the Law of Averages   The logic of **aggregation research** is to document the stability of behavior by combining (i.e., aggregating) various measures of the behavior and determining an average level of its occurrence over time. A similar logic is applied when calculating a student's grade for a specific course. The grade for the course is determined not by a single test score but by a series of test scores obtained throughout the semester. The logic of aggregation is not a new idea by any means. As far back as 1910, the eminent psychologist Charles Spearman said, "Let each individual be measured several times with regard to any characteristics to be compared" (pp. 273–274).

Considerable evidence supports the ability of aggregation research to identify consistency in behavior (Cheek, 1982, Eaton, 1983; Epstein & O'Brien, 1985; Moskowitz & Schwarz, 1982; Rushton, Brainerd, & Pressley, 1983). This has also been found to be true for situations in which such consistency was thought to be lacking (Epstein & O'Brien, 1985). For example, the logic of aggregation research was applied to the data from the classic work of Hartshorne and May (1928) by combining several specific measures of honesty to form a more global index of it. With this procedure, the average correlation coefficient for predicting honesty across situations increased to $r = .73$, which represents a large increase from the average of only $r = .23$ when each measure of honesty was considered individually (Epstein, 1979). The intuitive nature of the aggregation alternative is also supported by evidence suggesting that people are aware of and employ the principles of aggregation when judging the cross-situational consistency of others in everyday life (Epstein & Teraspulsky, 1986).

The Act Frequency Approach to Confirming Consistency   Similar to aggregation research is the act frequency approach proposed by David Buss and Kenneth Craik (D. M. Buss, 1984, 1985; D. M. Buss & Craik, 1983, 1984, 1985; McAdams, 1997). The **act frequency approach** says that the nature and consistency of an individual's personality should be determined by calculating the frequency with which acts from a particular class of action occur. The more frequent the act, the more indicative that behavior is of the individual's personality and the greater the degree of behavioral consistency. For example, the degree of aggressiveness in an individual's personality would be determined by assessing the frequency and extent to which behaviors defined as aggressive are exhibited in different situations.

The aggregation alternative suggests that it is possible to find consistency in behavior across a variety of situations by adding up behaviors. But critics of both aggregation research (Mischel, 1984, 1985; Mischel & Peake, 1982) and the act frequency approach (Block, 1989; Mischel & Peake, 1982; Moser, 1989) do exist.

While the information presented in this section so far documents and helps to explain the consistency of personality across situations, an even more convincing case could be made by presenting evidence in support of this consistency being found in other cultures around the world. To examine this issue in more detail, see "A Closer Look."

A Closer Look

A Global Perspective on the Consistency Issue: Cross-Cultural Considerations in the Consistency of Personality

As awareness of the role of culture in the understanding of personality increases in its importance, it is critical to document the extent to which the degree of consistency of personality across situations identified for individuals in primarily Western cultures (e.g., the United States) in the previous research can be extended to non-Western cultures. An excellent example

The work of Shigehiro Oishi helps us to appreciate the role of culture while investigating the consistency of personality in a global perspective.

of research that attempts to examine cross-cultural considerations in the consistency issue is the work of Shigehiro Oishi, of the University of Virginia and his colleagues (Oishi, 2002; Oishi, Diener, Suh, & Lucas, 1999). In their efforts to provide additional support for and clarification of the cross-situational consistency of personality, Oishi and his colleagues (Oishi, Diener, Scollon, & Biswas-Diener, 2004) focus on the distinction between relative and absolute cross-situational consistency (Magnusson & Endler, 1977) within the context of cross-cultural comparisons.

Relative cross-situational consistency (RCSC) refers to the extent to which individuals demonstrate a certain degree of consistency from one situation to a variety of other situations. For example, a highly anxious individual would demonstrate a higher level of stress while taking a test and talking to others at a party than would a less anxious individual in those two situations. In a similar manner, cross-cultural considerations of RCSC would involve comparing the consistency of individuals from different cultural groups across a variety of situations. For the purposes of the consistency debate that is the focus of this section, the presence of a high degree of RCSC for the different cultural groups across a variety of situations would provide global support for the existence of stable personality traits. For example, if highly anxious individuals from both Cultures A and B demonstrate a high degree of stress across a variety of situations, this would suggest that the trait of anxiety operates in a similar manner

regardless of their culture, supporting the notion of cross-cultural consistency in personality.

Absolute cross-situational consistency (ACSC) refers to the extent to which individuals *within* a particular group demonstrate a similar degree of consistency across a variety of situations. For example, highly anxious individuals might show a very high degree of stress while taking a test but only a moderate degree of stress when talking to others at a party, while less anxious individuals might display a low degree of stress in both of these situations. In this case, the highly anxious individuals demonstrate a greater difference in their ACSC (e.g., more variability within their group) than do the less anxious. Thus, while the highly anxious individuals maintained their relative stability across situations in comparison to the less anxious individuals (i.e., they display higher levels of stress), these same highly anxious individuals display more inconsistency within their group across the two situations than do the less anxious. In the context of the consistency debate, the measure of ACSC can be interpreted as the extent to which the situation serves to influence an individual's behavior. When considering the role of culture, differences in the ACSC found in individuals from different cultures could then be attributed to the influence of culture (Oishi et al., 2004). For example, if performing well on a test is more important than talking to others in social situations for individuals in Culture A than in Culture B, you might see a greater degree of variability in the level of stress expressed by the individuals when taking a test in Culture A than in Culture B. In this case, it is the difference in the importance of test performance between the two cultures that accounts for the variability of the individuals in the two cultures, supporting the notion of the role of culture in the operation of personality.

To investigate the influence of culture in the consistency debate, Oishi and his colleagues (2004) examined the RCSC and ACSC for individuals from different cultures. They compared the affective responses across a variety of situations for a group of American (i.e., college students living in or near Urbana, Illinois), Hispanic (i.e., college students living in or near Fresno, California, who spoke Spanish at home), Japanese (i.e., college students living in or near Tokyo), and Indian (i.e., college students living in or near Calcutta) individuals. To assess their affective responses, the individuals were asked to engage in a mood time-sampling procedure for 7 day during their waking hours (e.g., 9:00 a.m. to 9:00 p.m. or 10:00 a.m. to 10:00 p.m.). During the

7 days, they were asked to record their feelings when signaled to do so randomly five times by either a handheld computer or a watch they wore on their wrist. The feelings of positive affect (PA) for which they were to rate were *affectionate, calm, happy, joy, pleasant,* and *proud,* while the feelings of negative affect (NA) were *guilt, irritation, sadness, unpleasant,* and *worry.* To assess cross-situational consistency, the individuals were also asked to indicate the nature of the situation by noting the person they were with when reporting their feelings. The six situational options were: alone or with a friend, classmate/co-worker, romantic partner, stranger, or family member.

The Influence of Culture on Personality Stability

The results indicated a high degree of RCSC for the four different cultures for both the measure of PA and of NA. The mean correlation coefficients for the PA and NA affective measures, respectively, across the six different situations were $rs = .61$ and .57 for the Americans, $rs = .40$ and .45 for the Hispanics, $rs = .52$ and .54 for the Japanese, and $rs = .51$ and .49 for the Indians. Such a pattern of results suggests that there is evidence to support the relative stability across a variety of situations for general measures of personality, and that the stability for these measures can be found for individuals across different cultures. Thus, the high degree of RCSC suggests that personality dimensions of PA and NA operate in a similar manner regardless of the culture, providing cross-cultural evidence for the stability of personality traits.

While these results do demonstrate a certain degree of cross-situational consistency across the cultures, you will also notice that the specific degree of consistency (i.e., magnitude of the correlation coefficients) is different for the various cultural groups. Such a pattern of results indicates that the degree of ACSC varied across the different cultures, implying that cultural factors may have had a greater influence for individuals from certain cultures in certain situations. For example, in comparison to the American individuals, the results indicated that the Japanese and Hispanic individuals displayed greater variability in PA when being with friends, while Indian individuals displayed more variability in NA when being with strangers than when being along. This suggests that for individuals within certain cultures, affective responses are more dependent on the nature of certain situations (e.g., being alone vs.

with friends vs. with a stranger) than for American individuals, whose affective responses tend to be less dependent on the situation and more dependent on the nature of their personality (e.g., being a happy individual). This cultural/situational specificity in the nature of the affective responses helps to explain the differences in the overall degree of cross-situational consistency for the different cultures noted previously, as well as providing support for the role of culture when attempting to understand the operation of personality.

Thus, the overall pattern of these results might be best summarized by saying that while individuals from different cultures tend to display personality stability across situations, certain individuals from certain cultures tend to show more stability in certain situations. While this may sound confusing, it simply means that when investigating personality stability, you have to consider both the person *and* the cultural context in which the person operates. Such considerations serve to help clarify our understanding of the consistency issue by putting it in a global context.

Interdependence vs. Independence Aspects of the Self-Concept: Cultural Considerations in Self-Expression

How can we rectify the pattern of these results, which seems to suggest that while there is consistency of personality across situations (i.e., RCSC), there seem to be differing patterns of variability among individuals in the different cultures (i.e., variation in ACSC)? Oishi and his colleagues (2004) help to clarify this pattern by discussing cultural differences in how individuals defined their sense of self in reference to others.

In their explanation, they discuss the distinction between interdependent and independent cultures (Markus & Kitayama, 1991, 1998). The **interdependent vs. independent cultures** distinction involves the extent to which an individual's sense of self and the nature of their expressive responses are influenced by their relationship to others. In interdependent cultures, individuals tend to define their sense of self and express their emotions by their relationship with others (e.g., friends vs. co-workers) to a greater degree than do individuals from independent cultures, whose sense of self and expressive responses are based less on their relationship with others and more on their personal tendencies (e.g., being a generally happy person). So highly happy individuals, regardless of their culture, would display more feelings of affection across situations than would less affectionate individuals (i.e., RCSC). But highly happy individuals from interdependent cultures would display more affection in certain situations (e.g., being with friends vs. being with co-workers) than would highly affectionate individuals from interdependent cultures, who might make less of a distinction between their relationships with friends and co-workers and display less of a difference in their level of affection toward these two (i.e., less of a difference in ACSC).

To apply this reasoning to the results of this research, it has been noted that Japanese, Hispanic, and Indian cultures are considered to reflect the characteristic features of interdependent cultures to a greater degree than does American culture, which is known for reflecting the characteristic features of an independent culture (Markus & Kitayama, 1991). So, as noted above, although Japanese, Hispanic, Indian, and American individuals all displayed a consistent pattern of experiencing more positive affect when being with friends than being alone, and more negative affect when being with strangers than being alone, the Japanese and Hispanic individuals showed a degree of greater positive affect while being with friends than when being alone, and the Indians showed a greater degree of negative affect while being with a stranger than when being alone, compared to the American individuals. The increased difference in the ACSC for the Japanese, Hispanic, and Indian individuals compared to the American individuals can be accounted for by examining differences in the degree of connectedness (i.e., interdependence of expressions of the self) found among these cultures. The intensification of positive affect while with friends and of negative affect while with strangers can be attributed to the greater emphasis placed in these cultures on a sense of connectedness to others – a greater degree of connectedness to friends in Japanese and Hispanic individuals, and a greater degree of disconnectedness to strangers in Indian individuals, compared to Americans. We will have more to say about the impact of interdependent vs. independent cultures when discussing the role of cultural influences on the expression of the self later in the textbook (see pp. 482–485).

The significance of this research is that it provides additional support documenting the global existence of the consistency of personality traits while at the same time highlighting the importance of culture in the expression of personality. As we have discussed many times before when noting cross-cultural considerations in the study of personality, an appreciation and under-

standing of how people are similar (i.e., RCSC), as well as being sensitive to cultural differences (i.e., ACSC), will be of considerable importance as changes in technology bring us into contact with people from around the world on a more frequent basis.

In conclusion, the research summarized in this section strongly suggests cross-situational consistency in the influence of personality traits on behavior. As a result, the original issue of whether traits affect cross-situational consistency seems to have transformed into issues related to developing more realistic assumptions about traits and research methodologies for assessing their influence (Mischel & Shoda, 1995, 1998, 1999). A summary of the major points discussed in this section is presented in "Summing It Up: Alternative Conceptualizations of Cross-Situational Consistency" on p. 299. In the next section, we will explore the classification of traits.

The Classification of Traits and the Five-Factor Model

We have seen that traits have been used to describe, predict, and understand behavior. But what is missing is a structure by which all of the many different personality traits studied by personality psychologists can be organized. The issue centers on the extent to which an organizing structure can be found and the nature of this structure. A central principle in the efforts to organize personality traits is the lexical approach (Allport & Odbert, 1936; Costa & McCrae, 2006; Goldberg, 1981; Saucier, 2003; Saucier & Goldberg, 1996, 1998, 2001). The **lexical approach** proposes that the use of personality traits in our language is based on the notion that they make a useful contribution by helping us to describe differences among individuals, and that the more words that are associated with a particular trait, the more important that trait is in the language. For example, *shy*, *quiet*, *withdrawn*, *avoidant*, *silent*, and *meek* are just a few of the many terms that might be associated with the trait of introversion. The ability to identify those personality traits that have emerged in our language because they help us to describe and understand individuals is a critical element in the ability to communicate and interact with individuals in our own culture and with those from different

Summing It Up *Alternative Conceptualizations of Cross-Situational Consistency*

The Situational Alternative. The degree of consistency in behavior is determined by situational factors.

- *Situationalism.* The degree of cross-situational consistency in behavior is determined by the situational constraints placed on the individual's behavior.
- *Interactionism.* A greater understanding of an individual's behavior is achieved when the characteristic features of the individual and the situation are combined instead of being considered individually.

The Cognitive Alternative. Consistency in behavior is determined not only by the situation the person is in but by how consistently information about the situation is processed.

- *Cognitive factors.* The manner in which situational cues are perceived and interpreted will influence the individual's behavior.
- *The relative strength of situations.* Powerful situations produce consistency because there is little ambiguity in how they are perceived. Responses to weak situations are more a function of the subjective perceptions of them by individuals, which produces more inconsistency and variability in responses across individuals.

The Aggregation Alternative. Evidence for cross-situational consistency can be achieved by combining observations from many different situations.

- *Aggregation research.* A method for assessing cross-situational consistency by averaging the level of occurrence of a particular class of behavior over time.
- *Act frequency approach.* A method for assessing cross-situational consistency by calculating the frequency at which a particular class of behavior occurs in different situations.

cultures (Robins, John, Caspi, Moffitt, & Stouthhamer-Loeber, 1996; Robins, John, & Caspi, 1998). For example, communicating with others from different cultures will be easier if the personality trait of *timidity* means the same thing in both cultures. In this next section,

we will look at the use of the lexical approach in the study of the personality structure of traits.

Classic Contributions to Classifying Traits that Made the Classification Process 900 Times Simpler

In one of the first attempts to identify and classify the number of personality traits, Allport and Odbert (1936) counted the number of words in the 1925 edition of *Webster's New International Dictionary*, which contained some 550,000 terms, that could be used to distinguish the behavior of one human being from another. Their research yielded some 18,000 terms! Upon further inspection, however, they determined that only about 4,500 of the terms met the criteria of personality traits (e.g., being causal and internal and having stable tendencies).

A few years later, Cattell used these 4,500 trait terms and added another 100 terms to reflect certain temporary states that could also be used to explain behavior (e.g., frightened). Using the technique of factor analysis, Cattell (1943) was able to organize these terms into 35 trait variable categories of words that seemed to be similar. In subsequent research, Cattell (1945) took the 35 trait variables and used factor analysis to reduce even further the organization of traits into 12 factor categories. Additional reanalysis and extensions of Cattell's work further simplified the structural organization of personality traits into 5 basic categories (Fiske, 1949; Tupes & Christal, 1961).

In a return to the work of Allport and Odbert (1936), Norman (1967) used the 1961 *Webster's Third New International Dictionary* to identify some 18,125 personality terms, and he was eventually able to reduce the list to 2,800 stable trait terms. These terms were then organized into 5 basic categories. Thus, through continued replications and refinements in techniques and procedures, the organizational nature of traits went from 4,500 individual terms to 5 basic factors. This represents a reduction of 90,000 percent, or 900 times, in the classification structure of traits.

Contemporary Contributions to Classifying Traits and the Validation of the Five-Factor Model

Although others had documented five factors in their attempt to identify the organizational nature of trait structures, it was Goldberg (1981) who coined the term the "Big Five." The **Five-Factor Model (FFM)** is

Table 7.7   The Big Five: Factor Labels and Characteristic Traits

Factor Label	Characteristic Traits
1. E-factor: Extraversion, energy, enthusiasm	Adventurous, assertive, dominant, quiet,* reserved,* retiring,* shy, sociable
2. A-factor: Agreeableness, altruism, affection	Cooperative, cruel,* generous, quarrelsome,* sympathetic, unfriendly*
3. C-factor: Conscientiousness, control, constraint	Careless,* deliberate, efficient, frivolous,* irresponsible,* precise
4. N-factor: Neuroticism, negative affectivity, nervousness	Anxious,* calm, contented, self-pitying,* stable, temperamental*
5. O-factor: Openness, originality, open-mindedness	Artistic, commonplace,* insightful, intelligent, narrow interests,* shallow*

Note. *These traits are negatively related to the factor. Adapted from John (1990).

a descriptive model used in analyzing and classifying terms used by people to describe themselves and others (Costa & McCrae, 2006; Digman, 1990; John, 1990; John & Srivastava, 1999; McCrae & Costa, 1999; Wiggins & Trapnell, 1997). Table 7.7 lists the Big Five factors and some characteristics associated with each one.

There is a considerable amount of evidence to document the presence of the FFM (Costa & Widiger, 1994; Digman, 1990; Goldberg, 1990, 1993; John, 1990; McCrae, 1989; McCrae & Costa, 2003; Wiggins, 1996). The presence of the FFM structure has been identified using various factor analysis techniques (Goldberg, 1990; John & Srivastava, 1999). In addition to its use with the classification of trait terms, the FFM structure has also been found in different forms of data, including the frequency of acts (Botwin & Buss, 1989), self vs. other ratings (Goldberg, 1990), and various questionnaires (Costa & McCrae, 1988a; McCrae & Costa, 1987, 2003; Peabody, 1987; Peabody & Goldberg, 1989). The ability of individuals to match personality adjectives with definitions of the five factors also provides support for the intuitive nature of the FFM (Sneed, McCrae, & Funder, 1998). Finally, as a significant feature in the study of evolutionary personality psychology (Figueredo et al., 2005), which will be discussed in more detail in Chapter 9, the FFM of personality is considered a central element within the adaptive process by which individuals have evolved (D. M. Buss, 1991).

The **NEO Personality Inventory** (**NEO-PI**; Costa & McCrae, 1985, 1992) is a widely used personality test designed to measure the five major dimensions of personality. The NEO-PI has been used to validate the existence of the FFM in other personality inventories

(Costa & McCrae, 1995) and their stability over extended periods of the life span (Costa & McCrae, 1994; McCrae, 1989; McCrae & Costa, 2003). The NEO-PI has also been used to investigate the FFM within attachment styles and romantic relationships (Shaver & Brennan, 1992), career decision making (Holland, 1996), and the tendency for academic success and juvenile delinquency in African-American and Caucasian adolescent boys (Robins et al., 1996). Finally, the FFM has also been incorporated into other aspects of personality, such as mood, needs, psychological types, heredity, and interpersonal behavior (John, 1990; McCrae & Costa, 2003; Wiggins, 1996), and mate selection and group formation based on evolutionary psychology (D. M. Buss, 1996). Taken together, this research does seem to "provide a good answer to the question of personality structure" (Digman, 1990, p. 436).

The FFM across the Life Span: Personality Changes in Response to Life Challenges

Another interesting aspect of the FFM is that while an individual's relative standing on these dimensions of personality remains stable over time (Caspi, Roberts, & Shiner, 2005; Roberts & DelVecchio, 2000), the majority of change in personality is most likely to occur during young adulthood (Caspi et al., 2005), and such changes in the five factors seem to reflect specific developmental tasks that occur across the life course. Specifically, additional support for the validity of the FFM is that the factors seem to reflect a degree of change across the life span in association with challenges that appear at various developmental stages throughout life, and that these changes in the personality factors seem to help the individuals meet these challenges more effectively.

In an important study demonstrating the nature of the changes in personality over the life course, Srivastava, John, Gosling, and Potter (2003) investigated overall life span trends for the Big Five Factors of personality. The participants in this study were 132,515 male and female individuals between the ages of 21 and 60 who were recruited over the World Wide Web and assessed along the Big Five Factors of personality. The overall pattern of results for this study indicated that changes in the Big Five Factors of personality of individuals across time tended to occur in a manner that facilitated the adjustment made by individuals to certain life challenges. For example, the results indicated that Conscientiousness, a trait associated with organization and discipline and with occupational and relationship success, tends to increase through the age range investigated in the study. Such a rise in Conscientiousness during young and middle adulthood is advantageous as individuals in this age group begin to focus their attention on the management of their careers, such as putting in extra time on certain projects with high visibility or considering a job change that has more career potential but will require more out-of-town travel, and the details associated with the responsibilities of adulthood during this time, such as making mortgage payments and planning for retirement and other family obligations (e.g., children's college funds). It makes sense that as the complexities of life increase over time, individuals need to become more conscientious to manage all of the details.

The trait of Agreeableness, associated with being warm, generous, and helpful, displayed the greatest degree of change for individuals during their 30s and continued to rise into their 60s. Such a "bump" in Agreeableness during the 30s makes sense as individuals begin to navigate complex interpersonal relationships that require them to be helpful, nurturing, and generous with their time and efforts, such as raising a family and negotiating social and emotional commitments among family members and co-workers. In such situations, it makes sense that individuals need to be more agreeable during this time, and continue to do so as the nature of their interpersonal relationships continues to grow, such as caring for grandchildren, taking on community leadership roles, and mentoring younger individuals at work seeking their advice.

The trait of Openness, which is associated with seeking novelty and change, displayed a pattern of slight decline as the age of the individuals increased. Such a decline across the life course may reflect the desire of individuals to devote more of their attention to a limited number of individuals, such as family members and close friends, and those activities that are more meaningful to them, such as hobbies and certain social causes (e.g., reducing pollution in their community). As they get older, it makes sense that individuals are more selective in how they spend the decreasing amount of time they have left in their lives, and that they choose to spend that time on only those activities that they know will bring them the most pleasure and satisfaction, instead of spending precious time experimenting with new experiences that may produce uncertain outcomes.

The trait of Neuroticism, which is associated with anxiety and negative affectivity, displayed a pattern that indicated that women tended to score higher than men in their early 30s, but that this difference tended to decrease over time. This previously observed gender difference in Neuroticism suggests that young women may have faced rather difficult social environments early in their life (Orenstein, 1994) as they responded to cultural shifts in sex roles. However, as they successfully adjusted to these changes and became more established in their lives over the years, this gender difference narrowed.

The trait of Extraversion, which is associated with sociability and the expression of positive affect, also displayed a pattern indicating that women tended to display slightly higher scores than men early in life, but that such a difference became smaller over time. This pattern seems to suggest that Extraversion is a trait that is relatively stable in terms of the role it plays across the life course. Such a pattern makes sense because no matter how old individuals become, it is still necessary for them to express positive emotions and seek out the company of others as they adjust to various developmental challenges across the life span.

Overall, such a pattern of results adds validity to the FFM by documenting its flexibility in response to the changing needs of individuals throughout their lives. While the five factors do demonstrate a certain degree of consistency over time, they are also flexible enough to display change as the challenges individuals experience across the life span require certain adjustments in their personality to be made. In a sense, the fact that the factors of the FFM are so responsive to the different developmental tasks suggests that they play an important role throughout the entire life course.

Cross-Cultural Expressions of the FFM: A Universal Trait Structure

In addition to evidence supporting its relative consistency across time, important evidence documenting the presence of the FFM is provided by research indicating that personality traits similar to the Big Five traits have been found in men and women across a number of different cultures and different races (Egger, De May, Derksen, & van der Staak, 2003; McCrae et al., 2004b; Paunonen, 2003). For example, support for the FFM has been found for personality trait terms in both Dutch (Brokken, 1978; De Raad, Mulder, Kloosterman, & Hofstee, 1988) and German (Angleitner & Ostendorf, 1989; Angleitner, Ostendorf, & John, 1990; McCrae et al., 2000). Using translations of American terminology, the FFM has also been documented with samples of Japanese, Chinese, and Philippine people (Bond, Nakazato, & Shiraishi, 1975; Katigbak, Church, & Akamine, 1996; McCrae, Zonderman, Costa, Bond, & Paunonen, 1995) and with samples of German, Russian, and Czechoslovakian individuals (McCrae, et al., 2004a; Ostendorf & Angleitner, 2004).

While demonstrating the existence of the FFM *within* a variety of different cultures by these separate studies provides supporting evidence for the FFM, even more convincing evidence comes from additional research that compares the existence and similarity of the FFM structure *across a large number of cultures within a single study*. To examine an example of some research that provides such cross-cultural comparison of the FFM, see "The Cultural Context of Personality Psychology."

The Cultural Context of Personality Psychology

A Cross-Cultural Comparison of the FFM: Documenting the Worldwide Presence of a Universal Trait Structure

Documenting the consistency of the existence of the FFM across a variety of different cultures provides some of the most compelling evidence for its universal nature.

The efforts of Robert R. McCrae and his colleagues (McCrae, 2002; McCrae et al., 2004a, 2004b) have done much to provide such supporting evidence. An outstanding example of this type of cross-cultural comparisons of the structural nature of the FFM is the research by McCrae and Antonio Terracciano, both of the National Institute of Mental Health, and 78 other members of the Personality Profiles of Cultures Project (PPCP). The PPCP is a collection of researchers from countries around the world who work together to examine issues in the study of personality from a cross-cultural perspective. In their research McCrae et al. (2005) collected data from individuals living in 50 cultures representing six contents. A list of the 50 different cultures represented in the present study can be seen in the first column of Table 7.8.

The participants were 11,985 college students who were asked to volunteer in a study of personality across cultures in which they were going to rate the personality characteristics of another individual. The volunteers were told that all of their responses would remain anonymous. The participants were randomly assigned to one of four conditions under which they were told to complete the NEO-PI-Revised (NEO-PI-R) for a particular target person. More specifically, the participants were instructed to:

> Please think of a *woman* [*man*] *aged 18–21* [*over age 40*] whom you know well. She [he] should be someone who is a native-born citizen of your country. She [he] can be a relative or a friend or neighbor – someone you like, or someone you do not like. She [he] can be a college student, but she [he] need not be.

The language in which the participants completed the NEO-PI-R for the target individual is listed in the second column of Table 7.8, while the number of participants from each culture is listed in the third column.

Establishing the Cross-Cultural Validity of the FFM: The Presence of a Universal Trait Structure

To establish the cross-cultural existence of the FFM, the ratings of the specific target person for the different cultures were compared to the pattern of results for an American normative sample listed in the NEO-PI-R manual (Costa & McCrae, 1992). The extent to which the ratings from the different cultures conformed to the specific FFM dimensions of the American normative sample can be seen by examining the congruence

Table 7.8   The FFM: A Cross-Cultural Comparison

Culture	Language[b]	Sample Size	Congruence Coefficients[a]					
			N	E	O	A	C	Total
Argentina	Spanish	204	.96	.96	.93	.93	.94	.94
Australia	English	206	.97	.95	.96	.95	.96	.95
Austria	German	158	.95	.92	.93	.96	.95	.94
Belgium	Flemish	247	.97	.93	.95	.95	.96	.95
Botswana	English	186	.88	.82	.53	.90	.89	.82
Brazil	Portuguese	597	.97	.96	.94	.95	.96	.96
Burkina Faso	French	207	.96	.92	.85	.94	.91	.92
Canada	English	133	.97	.93	.93	.95	.95	.94
Chile	Spanish	194	.96	.95	.97	.95	.94	.95
China	Chinese	177	.93	.93	.90	.95	.94	.93
Croatia	Croatian	191	.96	.96	.95	.95	.96	.95
Czech Republic	Czech	400	.95	.96	.96	.95	.96	.95
Denmark	Danish	153	.95	.92	.96	.94	.96	.94
Estonia	Estonian	298	.96	.97	.94	.92	.97	.95
Ethiopia	English	197	.89	.85	.82	.93	.96	.90
France	French	274	.97	.96	.96	.95	.95	.96
French Switzerland	French	265	.95	.94	.95	.96	.96	.95
German Switzerland	German	214	.97	.97	.96	.95	.96	.96
Germany	German	593	.98	.96	.96	.97	.97	.97
Hong Kong	Chinese	207	.96	.93	.92	.96	.95	.94
Iceland	Icelandic	199	.97	.94	.96	.96	.97	.95
India	Telugu	185	.93	.87	.80	.91	.92	.89
Indonesia	Indonesian	196	.94	.94	.84	.94	.96	.93
Italy	Italian	195	.95	.94	.96	.96	.95	.95
Japan	Japanese	191	.96	.96	.91	.93	.95	.94
Kuwait	Arabic	468	.97	.95	.86	.95	.95	.94
Lebanon	English	200	.96	.95	.88	.95	.95	.93
Malaysia	Malay	289	.92	.80	.82	.94	.93	.90
Malta	English	202	.98	.95	.93	.97	.94	.95
Mexico	Spanish	173	.96	.95	.89	.95	.95	.94
Morocco	English	171	.91	.85	.66	.89	.90	.85
New Zealand	English	200	.97	.93	.95	.95	.93	.94
Nigeria	English	184	.76	.66	.56	.88	.65	.71
Peru	Spanish	154	.96	.92	.88	.97	.92	.93
Philippines	Filipino	197	.97	.92	.89	.94	.93	.93
Poland	Polish	197	.97	.94	.93	.95	.93	.94
Portugal	Portuguese	198	.96	.97	.93	.95	.93	.94
Puerto Rico	Spanish	160	.95	.94	.93	.94	.96	.95
Russia	Russian	320	.94	.94	.94	.95	.95	.94
Serbia	Serbian	200	.97	.94	.97	.94	.94	.95
Slovakia	Slovakian	198	.96	.94	.95	.94	.95	.94
Slovenia	Slovene	209	.98	.97	.96	.95	.96	.96
South Korea	Korean	196	.97	.94	.89	.93	.95	.93
Spain	Spanish	200	.97	.93	.94	.95	.93	.94
Thailand	Thai	209	.94	.92	.83	.95	.93	.92
Turkey	Turkish	208	.95	.96	.94	.96	.95	.95
Uganda	English	166	.93	.88	.84	.91	.95	.90
United Kingdom: England	English	194	.97	.92	.97	.95	.94	.95
United Kingdom: Northern Ireland	English	106	.95	.94	.90	.97	.94	.94
United States	English	919	.97	.96	.96	.96	.97	.96

Note. [a]These are factor and total congruence coefficients comparing five Procrustes-rotated principal components in each sample with the American normative self-report structure (Costa & McCrae, 1992). [b]The language in which the NEO-PI-R was administered. Based on data from McCrae et al. (2005).

coefficients presented in columns four through eight in Table 7.8, while column nine lists the total for the congruence coefficients across the five dimensions for each culture. A complete explanation is well beyond the level of this textbook: all you need to know to is that the congruence coefficient is an index for comparing the factor structure of different data sets (e.g., ratings by individuals from different cultures) along the same measure (e.g., the NEO-PI-R) based on the technique of factor analysis (see pp. 274–275). For the sake of comparison, an index level of .85 or better suggests that the dimension has been successfully replicated in one group in comparison to another (Haven & ten Berge, 1977). In this particular case, the factor structure being compared is the dimensions of the FFM for the American normative sample with that of the 50 different cultures. As you can see in columns four through eight of Table 7.8, there is considerable evidence that the dimensions of the FFM were replicated in all but just a few cases (i.e., 94.4 percent), and those are indicated in boldface type. In addition, an inspection of column nine indicates that in only 2 (4 percent) of the 50 cultures did the total indices of congruence coefficients fail to reach .85. Such overwhelming evidence suggests that there is a high degree of cross-cultural consistency of the FFM, proving additional support for its validity.

While there is a high degree of consistency in the results of this research, there are a few exceptions. Botswana (.82) and Nigeria (.71) had total congruence coefficients of less than the acceptable standard of .85. The dimension of Openness failed to reach the acceptable standard for replication in 9 (18 percent) of the 50 cultures. Although the authors discussed a number of possible culturally based explanations (e.g., social norms) for these discrepancies in the results, the explanation receiving the most support had to do with the quality of the data being collected (e.g., items left blank, problems in the translation of items).

In conclusion, the research of McCrae, Terracciano, and the other members of the PPCP is important for a number of reasons. First, taken together, the pattern of the results suggests the universality of the trait viewpoint in general and the FFM in particular. Second, such commonality across cultures around the world can be interpreted as evidence supporting the biological basis of personality traits (Allik & McCrae, 2002), a topic to be discussed in more detail in the next chapter.

Narrative Identity and the FFM: A General Framework for Unique Life Stories

Going beyond just the identification of a basic trait structure, another form of evidence in support of the FFM comes from the study of narrative identities (McAdams, 2007; McAdams et al, 2004). A **narrative identity** is the development and formation of a personal sense of self that an individual creates by weaving together many different significant aspects and experiences of their life. In a sense, a narrative identity represents an individual's *life story*. "Narrative identity provides a person's life with some degree of unity, purpose, and meaning" (McAdams, 2007, p. 405). The establishment of a narrative identity can be done by asking individuals to describe in detail various aspects of their life (McAdams, 1993, 1999; Raggatt, 2000). For example, you might be asked to: describe the biggest problem or challenge you have had in your life and what you did to deal with it; list someone who had a major impact on your life and describe what that person was like and what he or she did; state the nature of some of the most personal issues or values that guide your life; describe your most valued possessions and indicate why they are so important to you.

In his research on narrative identities, Raggatt (2006) has identified a link between the self-descriptions (e.g., preserving, other-focused, frightened) individuals included in the responses used in the construction of their narrative identities and the corresponding characteristics associated with the dimensions of the FFM (e.g., assertive, co-operative, anxious). Specifically, individuals whose self-descriptions were expressed in terms of strength, confidence, optimism, and positive affect scored higher on the dimension of Extraversion than did those whose narrative identity did not include such terms. In comparison to those who scored low on the dimension of Neuroticism, individuals who score high on it tended to include self-descriptions such as sadness, depression, anger, and negative affect. Individuals whose self-descriptions tended to include such terms as artistic, creative, independent, and spiritual scored higher on the Openness dimensions than did those who did not use such self-descriptions. Scoring high on the agreeable dimensions was linked to individuals whose self-descriptions included making reference to love, nurturing, parenting, and family closeness. Surprisingly, no relationship between narrative identity self-descriptions and the dimension of Conscientiousness was identified, perhaps because aspects of the self involving success and achievement were not salient themes for this group of individuals (i.e., college students early in their career).

What is important is that, for the most part, the dimensions of the FFM were reflected in this expression of individuality. Going beyond just the classification of traits, the general nature of the FFM was validated through the use of highly personal and life-specific experiences and events expressed in the unique life stories found in these individuals' narrative identities. Thus, being able to provide a general framework for capturing the central themes in the *life stories* of individuals told *in their own words* is another example of the universal nature of the FFM.

The universal nature of the FFM has been demonstrated by its identification using a variety of methodological techniques, its presence in individuals in cultures around the world, and its ability to be integrated into the unique life stories of individuals. However, some of the most remarkable evidence documenting the universal nature of the FFM comes from research that has established its presence in animals! For a look at this innovative research, see "At the Cutting Edge of Personality Psychology."

AT THE CUTTING EDGE
OF PERSONALITY PSYCHOLOGY

An Analysis of the Personality Structure of Chimpanzees

"Monkeying Around" Around the World to Provide Interspecies Documentation of the FFM

As we have discussed so far, there is considerable evidence for the structural and operational consistency of the FFM. However, even more impressive evidence would be to document the structure and operation of the FFM in other species. Such evidence would suggest that the FFM transcends the boundaries of the human species, potentially reflecting a more universal expression of the nature of personality (Glossing, 2001). At the cutting edge of the topic of the interspecies expression of personality is the work of James E. King, of the University of Arizona, and his colleagues (King & Landau, 2003; Weiss, King, & Enns, 2002; Weiss, King, & Figueredo, 2000). In a pioneering studying, King and Figueredo (1997) examined the behavior of chimpanzees living in zoos and noted that they exhibited a pattern of behavior that could be characterized as expressing five categories of behavior similar to that of the FFM. The categories of behavior were: Surgency (i.e., Extraversion), Dependability (i.e., Conscientiousness), Agreeableness, Emotionality, and Openness. In addition to these five categories, they also identified a sixth chimpanzee-specific category they labeled Dominance.

While such results are interesting in and of themselves, a limitation of this research was that it was restricted to the observation of chimpanzees that have spent their entire lives in captivity under the primary care of humans. Such results do not tell us if the expression of the FFM, along with Dominance, exists in chimpanzees living in the wild. The identification of the expression of the FFM in those chimpanzees that, for the most part, have had little contact with humans would provide more convincing evidence that the FFM operates in more natural environments. In a sense, comparisons of the expression of the FFM in chimpanzees living in zoos with those living in more natural habitats can be considered as providing similar evidence to that demonstrating the cross-cultural and cross-national similarities in the human personality emphasized throughout this book.

Studying the Personality of Chimpanzees: "Monkeying Around" with the FFM

To investigate more thoroughly the universal expression of the FFM, King and Alexander Weiss, of the National Institute on Aging, and Kay H. Farmer, of the University of Stirling in Edinburgh, Scotland, examined the behavior of 117 chimpanzees living

It seems that the personality trait of affection is found in a variety of species in a number of different settings.

The work of James E. King is critical because it demonstrates that the presence and operation of the FFM can be generalized beyond humans, which is important in the establishment of a more universal expression of the structure of personality.

in three different regions of the world (King, Weiss, & Farmer, 2005). Seventy-four (26 males and 48 females) of the chimpanzees were living in nine zoos within the United States and Australia. Most of these chimpanzees were born in captivity and reared by their mothers. Forty-three (12 males and 31 females) of the chimpanzees were living in a wildlife chimpanzee sanctuary in the Republic of Congo. These chimpanzees were born in the wild and were subjected to a variety of early-life stress before arriving at the sanctuary. The differences in the habitat of the chimpanzees can be considered to represent two totally different environments, which is important in examining the extent to which the two groups may have developed different types of personalities in response to their different living conditions.

The chimpanzees living in the zoos were rated by a group of 35 individuals, with an average of 3.7 raters for each chimpanzee, who had known

their chimpanzees for an average of 6.5 years. The chimpanzees living in the wildlife sanctuary were rated by a group of 42 employees, with an average 16.2 raters for each chimpanzee, who had known their chimpanzees for an average of 6.9 months.

Creating a Chimpanzee Version of the FFM: Combining Human-Based Personality Adjective Descriptors

The chimpanzees were rated along 40 adjectival personality trait descriptors taken from a classification based on the Big Five dimensions of personality developed for use with humans (Goldberg, 1990) and adapted for use with primates (King & Figueredo, 1997). On the rating form, each descriptor was accompanied by a two- or three-sentence dictionary-like description for clarification. The raters were asked to rate the chimpanzee on a 7-point scale. A rating of "1" indicated that the rater believed the chimpanzee displayed a total absence or only slight amounts of the trait, while a rating of "7" indicated that the chimpanzee displayed extremely large amounts of the trait. The six separate personality factors dimensions were: Dominance, Extraversion, Dependability (i.e., Conscientiousness), Agreeableness, Emotionality, and Openness. For each individual rater of a chimpanzee, the values of the rating for each of the 40 different adjective descriptors were combined to create a total score for each of the six personality factors. The manner in which the specific adjective descriptors were combined to create a total score for each of the six personality factors is presented below.

Examiner and "Cross-Cultural" Consistencies of the FFM: Converging Pieces of Evidence

The extent to which the raters could agree on the expression of the six separate personality factors was assessed by examining the examiner reliability for the various raters of the different chimpanzees. As you will recall from the discussion of examiner reliability in Chapter 2 (see p. 44), the higher the index of the examiner reliability (i.e., the closer the correlation coefficient is to $r = 1.00$), the more confident we can feel that there is agreement

Personality Factor	Combination of Adjective Descriptors
Dominance	Dominant + Independent + Decisive + Intelligent + Persistent + Bullying + Stingy − Submissiveness − Dependent − Fearful − Timid − Cautious
Extraversion	Active + Playful + Sociable + Affectionate + Imitative + Friendly − Solitary − Lazy − Depressed
Dependability (Conscientiousness)	Predictable − Impulsive − Defiant − Reckless − Erratic − Irritable − Aggressive − Jealous − Disorganized
Agreeableness	Sympathetic + Helpful + Sensitive + Protective + Gentle
Emotionality	Excitable − Stable − Unemotional
Openness	Inventive + Inquisitive

among the judges with their ratings of the dimension in question. That is to say, the more we can assume that the different raters are seeing things in a similar manner. The results of the overall indices of examiner reliability across all of the raters for the chimpanzees in the zoos and wildlife sanctuary, respectively, for the six separate personality factors were: Dominance: $rs = .87$ vs. $.94$, Extraversion: $rs = .92$ vs. $.88$, Dependability: $rs = .83$ vs. $.91$, Agreeableness: $rs = .75$ vs. $.83$, Emotionality: $rs = .74$ vs. $.77$, and Openness: $rs = .83$ vs. $.86$. Such a pattern of results seems to suggest that there was a high degree of agreement among the raters across both groups of chimpanzees, even though the zoo raters had a lot more experience with their chimpanzees than did the wildlife sanctuary raters.

These results can be interpreted as providing evidence for the operation of the FFM, along with Dominance, appearing beyond that previously noted in humans, and for the operation of these factors in chimpanzees being so strong that it can be identified reliably by many different raters. In addition, finding such similarity between the two groups of chimpanzees living in such diverse environments can also be interpreted as providing "cross-cultural" support for the similarity in expression of these six personality factors, if we can assume that living in the two different residential environments can be viewed as different cultures that provide different daily experiences for the two groups of chimpanzees (e.g., dealing with natural predators). More specifically, compared to those living in the wildlife sanctuary, the chimpanzees living in the zoos: (1) were living

in a much more physically restrictive space, which meant that they were living much closer to each other (i.e., higher population density); (2) had fewer chimpanzees in each social group, which meant that they were operating in smaller groups; (3) were living in a highly artificial environment, which meant that they had less of an opportunity to express their natural abilities (e.g., hunt for food); (4) were existing in constant view of the general public; and (5) were reared by their natural mother in the rather tranquil zoo surroundings, instead of experiencing the highly varied, somewhat isolated, and often traumatic early-life environment associated with living in the wild. As you can see, such differences in living conditions could certainly be considered as creating two totally different physical and social cultural climates. The consistent presence and operation of these six personality factors in these two totally different cultures serves to illustrate the strength of their presence.

The work of James King and his associates is considered at the cutting edge because it provides some unique and powerful evidence supporting the universal expression of the FFM of personality. In addition, it serves to expand the boundaries of the study of personality psychology by linking it up with other significant considerations among all species, such as evolution. The consistency of the FFM within species across different environments and across various species suggests that the emergence of such a personality structure has evolutionary value (King et al., 2005), which is a point we will return to in the next chapter when we consider the recent emergence of the evolutionary perspective of personality.

Some Reservations Concerning the FFM

While there are many supporters of the FFM, it does have its critics (Livneh & Livneh, 1989; Waller & Ben-Porath, 1987). One criticism is that although the five factors are observed consistently, there seems to be no guiding explanation as to why they exist and how they came to be (Briggs, 1989; Hogan, 1996). Specifically, while the FFM describes the structure of personality, it does not explain the dynamic processes associated with the operation and development of personality (Block, 1995). For example, although a theoretical model based on the FFM has been proposed to account for the causal linkage of how such principles as learning, environmental influences, genetics, biological processes, and motivation explain the operation of personality (Costa & McCrae, 2006; McCrae & Costa, 1999, 2003), it leaves out many of the specific details of how these factors actually work.

Yet another criticism is that a Big Seven Model (Almagor, Tellegen, & Waller, 1995; Tellegen, 1993; Tellegen & Waller, 1987, in press; Waller & Zavala, 1993), which includes two additional evaluative dimensions, one positive and the other negative, provides a more complete description of personality variability and clinical emotional states than does the FFM (Waller & Zavala, 1993). The Big Seven Model also provides a more consistent representation of the way in which people commonly characterize personality than does the FFM (Tellegen, 1993), and has been found to be a better predictor of personality pathology than is the FFM (Simms, 2007). Cross-cultural research has also provided support for the Big Seven Model (Benet & Waller, 1995). But recent evidence seems to suggest that the dimensions of the FFM and Big Seven Model are actually quite similar and represent two different ways of organizing the structure of personality (Church, 1994). In a related point concerning the structure of the factors, another criticism of the FFM is that the five factors may not be as independent of each other as research seems to assume (Blackburn, Renwick, Donnelly, & Logana, 2004).

A final criticism of the FFM, as well as the Big Seven Model, is that such broad categorizations of people can increase the likelihood of losing sight of a major objective of personality psychology, which is understanding the uniqueness of the individual (Hogan, 1996; Lamiell, 1987, 1997) and accounting for an individual's behavior in specific situations (Epstein, 1996, 2007; Paunonen, 1998). The research in support of the

FMM is based on the study of populations (e.g., groups of students at a particular college or individuals from a particular culture), which is very different from studying the individual (Borsboom, Mellenbergh, & van Heerden, 2003; McAdams & Pals, 2006), a distinction made early in the study of personality by Allport.

Reconciling the Differences in the Support for and Reservations about the FFM   Probably the best way to reconcile the support for and reservations about the FFM is to remember that personality can be studied at many different levels. The FFM provides the overall structural organization of personality at the top. The study of specific dimensions of personality (e.g., shyness and achievement) starts from the bottom, laying the foundation upon which the FFM will rest and into which these specific dimensions of personality can be organized. Thus, not all trait personality psychologists have to study personality at the same level. But at some point, those working from the bottom up and those working from the top down will meet in the middle. This meeting in the middle will create a more complete understanding of personality from the trait perspective. A summary of the major points of discussion in this section is presented in "Summing It Up: The Classification of Traits" on p. 310.

Applications of the FFM: Using What Is Known

A principal feature of the FFM is its flexibility in application. In this section, we will consider the application of the FFM to personal and social concerns. We will begin by considering day-to-day applications of the FFM to our personal lives. Next, we will consider the application of the FFM to social concerns of disease and crime.

Day-to-Day Living: Everyday Correlates of the FFM

In this section we will consider how the FFM has been applied to such important day-to-day activities as work, school, leisure time, family life, and overall day-to-day happiness and health.

The World of Work and the FFM: Making a Living   Next to sleeping, probably the activity most of us would associate with our everyday life is going to work. The FFM has been linked to a variety of work-related features (De Fruyt & Mervielde, 1997). In

Summing It Up *The Classification of Traits*

The Lexical Approach to Trait Classification. The organization of personality traits based on their use in our language to:

- describe differences among individuals (e.g., Jake is shy vs. Sue is outgoing).
- assist in communication and interaction with others based on a similar meaning of traits when used by different groups of individuals (e.g., the bashful Chinese girl behaves in a similar manner to the bashful Peruvian boy).

Classic Contributions from 1936 to 1967. This classification of personality traits went from a list of some 4,500 separate trait-like terms to 5 general categories.

Contemporary Contributions from 1981 to the Present. The evidence supporting the FFM for the classification of personality traits includes:

- being found in different languages.
- being found using different factor analytic techniques.
- being found using different forms of data.
- being found using different questionnaires.
- being identified as relatively stable over time.
- being integrated into other aspects of personality.
- being found in different cultures.
- being useful in understanding an individual's unique sense of self through the analysis of narrative identities.

Reservations Concerning the FFM. Criticisms of the FFM include:

- the lack of specific details explaining the dynamic operation of the FFM trait structure.
- evidence suggesting the existence of more than five factors, such as Big Seven Model and the actual degree of independence of the factors in the FFM.
- the way it detracts from the study of the individual by focusing on general factors based on the study of groups.

terms of occupational interests, individuals classified as extraverts show a preference for occupations that are social and enterprising (e.g., sales), perhaps because they provide individuals with many opportunities to interact with others while making money. Those individuals classified as open to experience tend to display a preference for occupations that are more artistic and investigative in nature (e.g., advertising, consumer research), perhaps because such occupations allow them to explore in more detail why people behave the way they do and what can be done to influence those behavior patterns. In a more extreme sense of such artistic expression in occupational choice, sculptors (Caraca, Loura, & Martins, 2000) and rock musicians (Gillespie & Myors, 2000) tend to score higher than average on the Openness dimension of the FFM, perhaps because being able to achieve the level of creativity necessary to be successful in such competitive artistic careers requires these individuals to be open to trying new ideas or combining already existing ideas in novel ways (e.g., recording swing songs from the 1940s in a more contemporary musical style).

In addition to career choice, the FFM has also been linked to other occupational-related issues (Costa & McCrae, 2006). For example, the dimension of Neuroticism has been associated with job dissatisfaction (Judge, Heller, & Mount, 2002), perhaps because the overall negative mood and self-pitying attitude expressed by individuals high on Neuroticism makes it difficult for them to enjoy going to work. Mid-career shifts tend to be associated with individuals classified as Open to experience (McCrae & Costa, 1985), perhaps because such individuals are willing to examine and explore different areas of their personal interest that may require a career change. And when looking for work, individuals classified as extraverts display more effective job-seeking behaviors (e.g., asking others for job leads; Kanfer, Wanberg, & Kantrowitz, 2001), perhaps because their sense of assertiveness and enthusiasm makes them feel more optimistic about finding a job. Instead of working for someone, what about starting a new business? There is evidence to suggest that those individuals high on the Extraversion dimension are more likely to start new businesses than are those low in Extraversion (Baron & Markman, 2003), perhaps because being more adventurous and enthusiastic serves to encourage such individuals to strike out on their own. Finally, Conscientiousness tends to increase during young and middle adulthood when occupational and career development, along with family concerns, are central issues (Caspi et al., 2005), perhaps because it is during this time that careful and strategic decisions are made that can have serious long-term implications (e.g., career and salary advancement, pension and retirement benefits).

Academic Performance and the FFM: Making the Grade The FFM has been found to be associated with a number of indices of academic performance. For example, high Conscientiousness scores have been linked with students setting academic goals, as well as pursuing them, and getting better grades, while high scores on Neuroticism have be found to be associated with lower exam scores (Chamorro-Premuzic & Furnham, 2003; Judge & Ilies, 2002). A student's approach to learning has also been related to the FFM (Duff, Boyle, Dunleavy, & Ferguson, 2004). Specifically, students with high scores on Openness take a more comprehensive approach to learning that emphasizes a desire to know the material in more depth and acquire a full understanding of the topics. Such an approach might be characterized by the statement "Being able to apply what I am learning in this class to my other classes will help me understand the material better." On the other hand, Conscientiousness was associated with an approach to learning that was strategic and goal-directed. This might be characterized by the statement "What is it I have to know to get a good grade?" Outside of the classroom, students with high Agreeableness and Extraversion scores report being more satisfied with their intimate relationships, while those with high Neuroticism scores tend to be less satisfied (White, Hendrick, & Hendrick, 2004). In middle school, high Agreeableness scores were associated with both favorable student self-report and favorable teacher ratings of classroom behavior, while bullying was linked to low Agreeableness scores (Hair & Graziano, 2003), perhaps because those who are not able to get along with others (e.g., low Agreeableness scores) must use bullying as a means of relating to them.

Leisure Activities and the FFM: Expressions of Relaxation The FFM has also been found to be associated with the activities individuals engage in when they are not at work or at school but simply trying to relax, such as watching television and listening to music. For example, in a study of the use of mass media by adults, it was reported that individuals who scored higher on Extraversion and Agreeableness tended to display less mass-media use (e.g., print, radio, films), while individuals who scored high on Openness to Experience tended to watch less television (Finn, 1997). It is possible that because they want to be with others and are easy to get along with, extraverted and agreeable individuals are spending more time socializing with others than reading magazines or listening to the radio. And,

since individuals high on Openness to Experience tend to be more artistic and creative in their thinking, they might avoid watching television because of the lack of originality (e.g., all detective shows are about the same) and quality in programming (e.g., storylines in most situation comedies are rather predictable). In a similar manner, higher levels of television viewing were associated with lower scores on Agreeableness, Openness to Experience, and Conscientiousness (Persegani et al., 2002). It is possible that children who are less co-operative and friendly (e.g., low on Agreeableness) and less creative (e.g., low on Openness to Experience) are more likely to fill their time watching television, and that watching a lot of television may be associated with a deterioration in the child's ability to concentrate on reading (e.g., low on Conscientiousness).

With the invention of so many portable electronic recording devices, such as the iPod®, listening to music has become an ever-present activity, so it should come as no surprise that the FFM has also been found to be related to listening preferences (Rentfrow & Gosling, 2003). Individuals classified as agreeable tend to prefer pop and religious music, perhaps because both types of music are based on a sense of consensus with others – pop music is popular because lots of people like it and religious music is based on a communal set of spiritual beliefs. On the other hand, individuals classified as extraverted displayed a preference for rap and dance music, perhaps because such music facilitates social interaction – the high energy associated with these types of music serves as a catalyst for socializing with others. Classical music and jazz were musical styles preferred by individuals classified as open, perhaps because such music requires a more in-depth appreciation of its complex structure – the complex orchestral arrangements associated with classical music and the improvisational structure and wide range of styles characteristic of jazz. What type of music do you prefer, and what aspects of your personality do you feel influence your taste in music?

Family Life and the FFM: Home, Sweet Home We have examined how the FFM relates to such critical daily activities as work, school, and play. We would be remiss if we did not consider how the FFM relates to one of the most important daily activities – family life.

There is considerable evidence that the dimensions of the FFM relate to some of the most critical elements of family life. When considering the quality of a marriage, it has been noted that marital satisfaction has been found to be associated with individuals who are low on Neuroticism, high on Conscientiousness, and especially high on Agreeableness (McCrae, Stone, Fagan, & Costa, 1998). It is easy to see how being married to someone who is calm and not very anxious or temperamental, careful and responsible, and very cooperative, sympathetic, and affectionate would make for a happy marriage. On the other hand, it has been reported that both men and women who are likely to get a divorce are those who are high on the Neuroticism dimension, as well as men who are low on the dimension of Conscientiousness (Kelly & Conley, 1987), perhaps because of the infidelity and alcohol abuse associated with the characteristics of irresponsibility and lack of control and constraint. Finally, on one of the more tragic sides of family life, research indicates that abusive parents are likely to be narcissistic (i.e., low on Agreeableness) and lack impulse control (i.e., low on Conscientiousness; Wiehe, 2003).

Overall Daily Adjustment: Living the Good, Clean Life   Probably what most people want in their daily life is happiness and health. With regard to happiness, the FFM dimensions of Agreeableness, Extraversion, and Conscientiousness have all been found to be positively related to happiness (Lucas & Fujita, 2000; Peterson, 2006), perhaps because such individuals tend to have more friends and social support by being outgoing and friendly and taking strategic action to be more happy (e.g., taking time on the weekend to engage in hobbies and enjoy the company of others). On the other hand, Neuroticism has been found to be negatively associated with happiness (Lucas & Fujita, 2000), perhaps because the pervasive feelings of anxiety, negative affect, and nervousness make feeling happy difficult for neurotic individuals. In providing support for the stability of the FFM, Costa and McCrae (1988b) reported that on average an individual's level of happiness remained relatively stable over a 6-year period.

Dimensions of the FFM have also been found to be linked to living a more clean and healthy lifestyle. Conscientiousness has been found to associated with better eating habits, less use of alcohol and drugs, and less unsafe driving tendencies (Bogg & Roberts, 2004; Kersting, 2003; Markey, Markey, & Tinsley, 2003). Agreeableness has also been found to be related to safe driving tendencies, such as fewer number of tickets and accidents (Cellar, Nelson, & Yorke, 2000), perhaps because such individuals are more cooperative, friendly, and generous while sharing the road with others.

Happiness and health and the FFM are also linked by an important characteristic feature of a well-adjusted individual – forgiveness. In this regard, individuals high on Agreeableness and low on Neuroticism tend to be more forgiving (McCullough & Witvliet, 2002), perhaps because these individuals are associated with such characteristic traits as being cooperative, sympathetic, and generous. As a contributing factor to one's quality of life, forgiving individuals are less likely to experience depression, anger or hostility, and feelings of inadequacy and inferiority (Tangney, Fee, Reinsmith, Boone, & Lee, 1999) and are more likely to experience fewer negative psychophysiological reactions, such as increased blood pressure and heart rate (Witvliet, Ludwig, & Vander Laan, 2001) than are unforgiving individuals. Thus, the ability to forgive others can serve to make you both happier and healthier. Is there someone you might be able to forgive for a transgression against you? If you can, you will be a happier and healthier person for it.

Social Considerations of the FFM: Confronting and Responding to Problematic Behaviors

In addition to these everyday applications, the FFM has able been used to help us understand and respond to some serious social issues. In this section, we will consider the application of the FFM to help in the treatment and prevention of HIV and to understand the criminal behavior of drug abusers and sexual offenders.

The FFM and HIV/AIDS Prevention: Dealing with a Global Threat   During recent years, personality psychologists have offered their expertise in helping to address some important problematic behaviors (Hoyle, 2000), including violence and criminal behavior (Knueger, Caspi, & Moffitt, 2000), inmate recidivism (Clower & Bothwell, 2001), smoking (Zuckerman & Kuhlman, 2000), drinking (Cooper et al., 2000; Loukas, Krull, Chassin, & Carle, 2000; Zuckerman & Kuhlman, 2000), and high-risk sexual behaviors (Hoyle, Fejfar, & Miller, 2000). However, today, one of the most significant health issues worldwide is the pervasiveness of HIV/AIDS. Estimates by the World Health Organization indicate that approximately 39.5 million individuals are living with HIV/AIDS (World Health Organization, 2006). In the United States, the Center for Disease Control estimates that approximately 663,000 individuals are living with HIV/AIDS (Centers for Disease Control, 2006). While these numbers are staggering, keep in mind that they represent estimates of only the known cases – there are potentially many more cases of people who are unaware that they have HIV/AIDS.

Of particular interest to the discussion of the FFM is its use in the study of HIV/AIDS-risk-related behaviors (Costa, Masters, Herbst, Trobst, & Wiggins, 1998; Wiggins, Masters, Trobst, & Costa, 1998). For example, in one study (Trobst et al., 2000), the NEO-PI-R was administered to a group of 538 high-risk individuals living in the economically disadvantaged and impoverished Arkansas Delta Region, where the level of literacy is low and the rates of syphilis and substance abuse are high. The study participants were recruited from health clinics, substance abuse counseling programs, church groups, and public parks.

Individuals who denied the possibility of HIV infection had lower Openness to Experience (O) scores than did individuals who believed that they had some chance of being infected. Because individuals with low O scores, in general, do not entertain novel ideas (e.g., that people like themselves do have the potential to become HIV infected), do not experience particularly strong emotions (e.g., exhibit little fear about HIV infection), are not prone to analytical thinking (e.g., do not analyze the consequences of unprotected sex), and are less likely to consider altering long-held beliefs in response to new information (e.g., continue to believe they will not become HIV infected), such individuals create a belief system in which the reality of the *improbable likelihood of becoming HIV infected* is transformed into the *impossible likelihood of becoming HIV infected*. Such thinking has the potential to put these individuals at a greater risk of HIV infection. In addition, the researchers also examined the impact of a short-term (e.g., four brief sessions) intervention program designed to promote risk-reducing sexual behavior (e.g., the use of condoms, monogamous sexual relationships, and good communication skills). Data from 80 of the individuals who completed all four sessions indicated that increased condom use was associated with increased Conscientiousness (C) scores, suggesting that individuals low on Conscientiousness seem to be unmotivated by long-term rewards (e.g., a longer, healthier life) and are particularly vulnerable to problematic behaviors.

The pattern of these results has some important implications for public health programs addressing the problems associated with reducing and preventing HIV infection. The results suggest that public health professionals might improve treatment outcomes by tailoring their programs to fit the personality charac-

teristics of certain subcategories of individuals. For example, in addition to providing the same information about safe-sex practices to all individuals, public health professionals working with subgroups of individuals with low O scores might start such programs with lessons designed to promote critical thinking skills (Halpern, 1996), which could then be combined with the information on HIV prevention and the consequences of safe-sex practices. In a similar manner, public health professionals involved in behavior treatment programs designed to promote safe-sex practices working with subgroups of individuals with low C scores might begin with skills-training modules designed to teach the fundamental behavioral principles of self-regulation (e.g., delay of gratification and impulse control; Bandura, 1999; Baumeister, Heatherton, & Tice, 1994), which could then be incorporated with training modules teaching safe-sex behaviors. Finally, at a more general level, such research demonstrates the value of taking into consideration personality dimensions when addressing important issues that have an impact on our day-to-day living experiences.

Personality Profile of Drug Abusers: Assessment and Treatment Implications The FFM has been used to help identity the personality profiles of drug abusers and to develop drug treatment programs based on these profiles (Brooner, Schmidt, & Herbst, 1994). In one study, the scores on the five dimensions of the NEO-PI were compared for a group of 203 drug abusers and a normative sample of non-drug abusers (Costa & McCrae, 1989). The personality profiles of drug abusers tend to be characterized by higher scores on the Neuroticism dimension, particularly with regard to hostility, depression, and feelings of vulnerability, and lower scores on the Agreeableness and Conscientiousness dimensions than the profiles obtained from the normative sample of non-drug abusers. In addition, although the profile score for the drug abusers on the Extraversion dimension was similar to those of the non-drug-abusing sample, the drug abusers tended to demonstrate greater excitement-seeking tendencies, as measured within the Extraversion dimension. Consistent with the results of other studies (Alterman & Cacciola, 1991), the profiles of these drug abusers suggest that they are prone to high levels of emotional distress, interpersonal antagonism, and excitement seeking, and low levels of Conscientiousness.

The tendency of the drug abusers to have profiles characterized by a high degree of Neuroticism and a low degree of Agreeableness and Conscientiousness is critical because of the influence such features have on treatment planning and effectiveness. Researchers have noted that people who are disagreeable and unconscientious pose major problems for therapists (T. R. Miller, 1991). These people tend to be antagonistic and skeptical of the therapist, making it difficult for the client and therapist to establish an affiliation during treatment. In addition, while a high degree of emotional distress (i.e., Neuroticism) can serve as a source of motivation to enter and remain in treatment, the lack of Extraversion may be detrimental to the treatment process because effective treatment involves active involvement in the therapeutic process.

With this information in mind, it is important to establish reasonable therapeutic goals that may differ from those for other client populations. For example, because of the skepticism and antagonism of these drug abusers, more time might have to be allocated to the treatment program for trying to establish an emotional bond between the client and therapist. In addition, the high level of Neuroticism suggests that these people are bringing with them to the treatment setting a higher degree of emotional distress, which in turn will probably require longer treatment.

Personality Profile of Sex Offenders: A Forensic Evaluation   In an attempt to understand the personality makeup of sex offenders, the NEO-PI has been utilized as part of the forensic evaluation of incarcerated sex offenders. In one study, 99 male sex offenders (e.g., child molesters and exhibitionists) were given the NEO-PI as part of a forensic evaluation (Lehne, 1994). In comparison to the NEO-PI scores from a normative sample of non-sex offenders, the results indicated that, overall, the sex offender scores were higher on the Neuroticism dimension, which also included scoring higher on the anxiety, hostility, depression, self-consciousness, impulsiveness, and vulnerability facets of the Neuroticism dimension. But the sex offender scores were similar to the normative sample of non-sex offenders on the Extraversion, Openness to Experience, Agreeableness, and Conscientiousness dimensions of the NEO-PI. The only exception was that the sex offenders scored higher on the excitement-seeking facet of the Extraversion dimension.

This pattern of results suggests that, with the exception of the Neuroticism dimension and the excitement-seeking facet of the Extraversion dimension, the personality profiles of the sex offenders and non-sex offenders were very similar. Such results have some serious forensic implications. One implication has to do with the identification of sex offenders. Specifically, with the exception of expressing more of an excitement-seeking tendency, the sex offenders appear normal! This is an extremely important point because it helps to explain how these sex offenders are able to mingle in society and with their potential victims so successfully without being detected. For example, a child molester, with no previous history of arrest, who is very agreeable and extraverted would have little trouble gaining employment in a day-care center.

A second implication has to do with the treatment and rehabilitation of sex offenders. While sex offenders display a high degree of psychopathology, as indicated by their high scores on the Neuroticism dimension and all of its separate facets when compared to the non-sex offenders, it is the perverted sense of pleasure they seem to derive from their activities that makes them so difficult to treat and rehabilitate. An example of the manifestation of this deep-seated psychopathology is the intense arousal and pleasure (i.e., thrill-seeking excitement) of seeing the victim's reactions after an exhibitionist has exposed himself, or the arousal and excitement associated with stalking a child for molestation, that is most critical to such sex offenders (Comer, 2001). The fact that such behavior patterns exist in the face of some serious negative social and legal consequences is a statement about their powerful nature and resistance to treatment. In summary, it is the seemingly normal social nature of these sex offenders that makes it difficult to identify them prior to their committing crimes, but the deep-seated nature of their psychopathology that makes them so difficult to treat.

This concludes the discussion of applications of the FFM. Please note that even though only a few key applications were presented in this section, many more exist. Among those additional applications of the FFM are studies involving eating disorders (Ellis, 1994; Ghaderi & Scott, 2000; Heaven, Mulligan, Merrilees, Woods, & Fairooz, 2001), assessment of employee service performance (Stewart & Carson, 1995), the expression of spirituality (MacDonald, 2000), and the diagnosis of various personality disorders and treatment outcomes (L. A. Clark & Livesley, 1994; Harpur, Hart, & Hare, 1994; Katon et al., 2002; Trull, Widiger, & Burr, 2001; Trull, Widiger, Lynam, & Costa, 2003; Widiger & Trull, 1992), to name a few. This also concludes our discussion of the FFM. The magnitude of the contribution of the FFM can be seen from the following statement: "The new trait psychology heralded by the Big Five is arguably the most recognized contribution personality psychology has to offer today to the discipline of psychology as a whole and to the behavior and social sciences" (McAdams & Pals, 2006, p. 204). If you would like to know more about this truly comprehensive structure of personality traits, please read McCrae & Costa's (2003) *Personality in Adulthood: A Five-Factor Theory Perspective.*

Chapter Summary: Reexamining the Highlights

- *Personality Traits.* Traits are underlying psychological structures that predispose people to act in a particular manner, and, as a result, can be used to account for individual differences in and contribute to the consistency of behavioral expression across a variety of situations.

- *Allport's Personalistic Viewpoint*
  - *Basic Assumptions of Allport's Definition of Personality.* Allport viewed personality as being a dynamic organization within the person, psychophysical in nature, determining behavior, and contributing to the uniqueness of each person.
  - *Basic Concepts of Allport's Theory.* Traits are considered the basic unit of personality. They can be classified into common traits and personal dispositions. Cardinal, central, and secondary traits are used to account for the uniqueness expressed by each person. The proprium gives the individual a unifying sense of self.
  - *Dynamics of Personality.* Personality development is characterized by the emergence and integration of the separate aspects of the proprium. The source of motivation for personality is that of functional autonomy, which can be divided into preservative and propriate functional autonomy.
  - *Personality Assessment from Allport's Viewpoint.* Allport developed the Study of Values Scale, which assessed six categories of values: theoretical, economic, aesthetic, social, political, and religious.
  - *Applications of Allport's Viewpoint.* The classification and assessment of human values and their utilization in varied counseling settings represent a significant application of Allport's viewpoint of personality.

- *Evaluating Allport's Viewpoint.* Characteristic strengths of Allport's viewpoint include his utilization of various research methodologies and emphasis on studying the individual. Characteristic limitations include a failure to provide physical documentation concerning the existence of traits, the discontinuity of personality development, and an overemphasis on studying the individual at the expense of developing general laws of behavior.

- *Cattell's Structural Trait Viewpoint*
  - *Basic Assumptions of Cattell's Definition of Personality.* Cattell assumed that the principal function of personality was to help in predicting behavior. He used L-data, Q-data, and T-data as sources of empirical information to help in predicting behavior.
  - *Basic Concepts of Traits.* Traits are considered the basic units of personality and are reflected in the behavior of the individual. They are classified into surface and source traits, common and unique traits, and ability, temperament, and dynamic traits. Constitutional factors and environmental-mold factors are used to explain the contribution of inherited and environmental influences to personality traits. Factor analysis is the statistical technique used by Cattell to identify and classify traits. The behavioral specification equation is a formula he developed for predicting behavior from the relative contribution of various traits.
  - *Personality Assessment from Cattell's Viewpoint.* Cattell developed the Sixteen Personality Factor Questionnaire (16PF) to assess major source traits.
  - *Applications of Cattell's Viewpoint.* The Couple's Counseling Report (CCR) is an application of

the 16PF designed to assess the compatibility of individuals in a serious interpersonal relationship. Additional applications of the 16PF include the assessment of the personality profiles of police officers, members of the clergy, and attempters of suicide.

– *Evaluating Cattell's Viewpoint.* Characteristic strengths of Cattell's viewpoint include his quantitative and rigorous approach to the study of personality. Characteristic limitations are that it is too technical, and it overemphasizes understanding the global personality while losing sight of the individual.

● *Eysenck's Hierarchical Trait Viewpoint*

– *Basic Assumptions of Eysenck's Definition of Personality.* Eysenck assumed that two major dimensions serve as the underlying structure of personality.

– *Basic Concepts of Eysenck's Viewpoint.* Eysenck organized the hierarchical structure of personality to include specific responses, habitual responses, traits, and types.

– *Personality Dynamics.* The dynamics of personality involve the interrelationship of the personality types of extraversion–introversion, neuroticism, and psychoticism.

– *Applications of Eysenck's Viewpoint.* Areas of the application of Eysenck's viewpoint include organizational psychology, human sexuality, behavioral medicine, and criminality.

– *Evaluating Eysenck's Viewpoint.* Characteristic strengths of Eysenck's viewpoint include his empirical emphasis and the diversity of knowledge he tried to integrate within his viewpoint. Characteristic limitations include the rather limited number of factors he used to conceptualize personality and the validity of these factors.

● *Special Issues in the Study of Traits*

– *The Issue of Cross-Situational Consistency.* Cross-situational consistency assumes that personality traits provide a stabilizing influence on behavior over time and situations.

– *Documenting a Lack of Cross-Situational Consistency.* The personality coefficient summarized the tendency of personality measures to correlate around $r = .30$ with observable behavior.

– *In Support of Cross-Situational Consistency.* Increases in cross-situational consistency can be achieved by identifying consistent people and specific dimensions upon which they are highly consistent.

– *The Situational Alternative.* A greater understanding of cross-situational consistency can be achieved by considering the situation in which the behavior occurs. Situationism considers the constraints placed on behavior by the characteristics of the situation. Interactionism proposes that behavioral consistency is best understood by considering both the personality of the individual and the situation in which the behavior occurs.

– *The Cognitive Alternative.* Cognitive factors affect the way that we perceive and interpret situations. Powerful situations provide clear cues for behavior; weak situations allow for personality factors to determine individual responses.

– *The Aggregation Alternative.* Aggregation research documents cross-situational consistency by averaging the occurrence of behavior over time. The act frequency approach determines cross-situational consistency by calculating the number of times a particular class of behavior occurs.

● *The Five Factor Model (FFM) of Trait Classification*

– The lexical approach emphasizes the importance of traits based on their usefulness in helping us describe and understand expressions of individual differences.

– *Classic Contributions to Classifying Traits.* The number of trait-like terms used to describe behavior was reduced from some 4,500 terms to 5 basic factors.

– *Contemporary Contributions to Classifying Traits.* The FFM is used to describe the structural nature of the classification of traits. The five factors are Extraversion, Agreeableness, Conscientiousness, Neuroticism, and Openness, and are assessed using the NEO-Personality Inventory (NEO-PI). Evidence supporting this model has been found in different languages, using different factor analytic techniques and forms of data, in other aspects of personality, in a variety of cultures around the world, and within the unique expression of narratives identities.

– *Criticisms of the FFM.* One criticism of the FFM is that although it describes a basic trait structure, it does not explain why it exists. Another criticism is the identification of the Big Seven Model, which provides a more thorough explanation of personality. Still another is that the emphasis of the FFM on classifying individuals on the basis of these five broad factors does not make distinctions among more subtle dimensions of personality, and places less emphasis on promoting an understanding of the individual.

– *Reconciling the Differences.* The FFM is the general classification system by which the study of individual traits can be organized. Organizing a general classification system of traits and studying individual traits are both necessary for a complete understanding of personality from the trait viewpoint.

– *Applications of the FFM.* Applications of the FFM to day-to-day living include issues related to occupational choice and work satisfaction, academic performance, the utilization of leisure time, family relationships, and physical health and emotional well-being. Applications of the FFM to social concerns include issues related to HIV/AIDS prevention, drug abuse and its treatment, and the forensic evaluation of the personality profile of sex offenders.

Glossary

ability traits   Manifestations of the specific skills of an individual.

absolute cross-situational consistency   The extent to which individuals within a particular group maintain a degree of consistency in the expression of their personality across different situations.

act frequency approach   A procedure for estimating the consistency of behavior across situations by counting its occurrence over time.

aggregation research   A procedure for estimating the consistency of behavior across situations by averaging its occurrence over time.

behavioral specification equation   A procedure for combining trait information to predict behavior in specific situations.

cardinal traits   Traits having a dominant influence on the expression of an individual's personality.

central traits   Traits representing salient characteristic features of an individual's personality.

cognitive factors   Mental processes that determine the behavioral reactions to situations.

common traits   Traits possessed by all people to different degrees.

constitutional factors   Biologically determined traits.

Couple's Counseling Report (CCR)   An inventory, based on the 16PF, designed to assess marital compatibility.

cross-situational consistency   The assumption that traits stabilize behavior across a variety of situations.

dynamic traits   An individual's motivational source of behavior.

environmental-mold factors   Environmentally determined traits.

extraversion–introversion   A basic personality type identified by Eysenck and a dimension of the Five-Factor Model, characterized by varying degrees of sociability.

factor   The intercorrelation of a group of behavioral measures reflecting an underlying source trait.

factor analysis   A statistical procedure for identifying trait structures.

factor loading   The extent to which a specific behavioral measure is related to a certain factor.

factor matrix   The identification of different factors.

Five-Factor Model (FFM)   A model for describing the organizational structure of personality traits on five major dimensions.

functional autonomy   The motivational source in adulthood that is separated from the motivational sources in childhood.

graphology   The assessment of personality, and other personal information on an individual, from handwriting samples.

habitual response   Specific behaviors performed across a number of different situations.

idiographic approach   The study of the personal dispositions of an individual.

if . . . then relations   Specific patterns of cognitive factors that determine behavior in particular situations.

interactionism   The assumption that behavior is determined by a combination of personality and situational factors.

intercorrelation matrix   A summary of individual correlation coefficients used in factor analysis.

interdependent vs. independent cultures   A distinction between cultures based on the extent to which an individual's sense of self and self-expression are dependent on or independent of their relationship with others.

L-data   Forms of information about an individual that are a matter of public record.

lexical approach   The classification of traits based on the frequency of their use in our language and the number of other adjectives associated with them.

narrative identity   The creation of a sense of personal identity an individual develops by integrating significant life experiences.

nature–nurture ratio   An estimate of the extent to which a trait is determined by biological and environmental factors.

NEO Personality Inventory (NEO-PI)   An objective self-report personality inventory designed to measure the five major factors of personality.

neuroticism   A basic personality type identified by Eysenck and characterized by varying degrees of emotional stability.

nomothetic approach   The study of common traits by comparing the personality of different people.

organizational psychology   The study of principles of psychology applied to behavior in work settings.

personal dispositions   Traits that are unique to the individual.

personalism   An approach to psychology emphasizing the study of the person.

personalistic   With an emphasis on the understanding of the individual.

personality coefficient   The tendency for personality test scores and behavioral measures to be only moderately correlated.

perseverative functional autonomy   The motivational source for basic routine and repetitive behavior.

propriate functional autonomy   The motivational source for the development of a sense of self-awareness.

proprium   A psychological structure creating a sense of self in the individual's personality.

psychoticism   A basic personality type identified by Eysenck and characterized by varying degrees of personality pathology.

Q-data   Information about an individual obtained from questionnaires and personality inventories.

relative cross-situational consistency   The extent to which individuals maintain a degree of consistency in the expression of their personality across different situations.

secondary traits   Personal dispositions that influence an individual's behavior in very specific situations.

situationism   The tendency for behavior to be determined by the characteristics of the situation.

Sixteen Personality Factor Questionnaire (16PF)   A personality inventory used to assess major source traits.

source traits   Underlying psychological dispositions that influence behavior across a wide variety of situations.

specific responses   Behaviors observed in particular situations.

Study of Values Scale   A measure of the six basic human values identified by Allport.

surface traits   Interrelated forms of behavior serving as observable evidence for the presence of certain underlying traits.

T-data   Information about an individual obtained while observing the person in specific situations.

temperament traits   Manifestations of an individual's general behavioral style.

trait   A psychological construct assumed to predispose people to respond in a particular manner.

traits   For Eysenck, a set of related behaviors performed across a variety of situations.

type   For Eysenck, the grouping together of related traits.

unique traits   Traits specific to the particular individual.

The Biological Viewpoint
The Behavioral Genetics and Psychophysiological Perspectives on Personality

8

Chapter Overview:
A Preview of Coming Attractions

The biological viewpoint of personality assumes that certain biological factors influence the development and operation of personality. Among these are the constitutional, genetic, and psychophysiological factors. In this chapter we will discuss the theoretical formulations of these influences and examine a number of related applications. We begin by surveying some basic issues related to the biological viewpoint of personality.

Biological Processes in the Study of Personality: Some Basic Issues

The history of scientific perception of the role of biological processes in the study of personality is long and rich, dating back to some of the earliest views of personality. Before surveying this history, we will examine some of the basic issues associated with the biological viewpoint of personality. These include the nature–nurture controversy, the significance of heredity, limitations of genetic explanations of behavior, the logic of the biological viewpoint, and the biosocial interaction.

The Nature–Nurture Controversy: An Evolving Issue

A basic issue surrounding the biological perspective of personality – one that is evolving – is the nature–nurture controversy (Morf & Ayduk, 2005; Pervin, 2002). In its most fundamental form, the **nature–nurture controversy** concerns the extent to which personality and other complex behaviors are determined by biological factors vs. environmental ones. On the nature side of the argument is the assumption that various inherited biological factors (e.g., hormones and genetics) are the principal determinants of personality. On the nurture side is the assumption that environmental factors (e.g., parenting styles, socioeconomic status, educational opportunities, and sibling and peer relationships) and cognitive factors (e.g., perceptions, beliefs, and reasoning) are major determinants of personality. However, over time and with the accumulation of research into the nature–nurture controversy, the question "*How much nature vs. how much nurture?*" has evolved into "*How do nature and nurture interact?*" to determine personality. It became clear that nature was involved as a critical determinant of personality – in some instances as much as 50 percent of personality was determined by biological factors (Plomin, DeFries, McClearn, & McGuffin, 2001). The development of precise techniques for measuring these biological processes – along with the emergence of more sophisticated methodologies for examining how biological factors operate with family systems, social norms, and other environmental factors – has fostered this shift in emphasis on the role of nurture. To illustrate the evolution of the nature–

nurture controversy, we will examine recent conceptual developments involving the expanding influence of learning and experience (Hagan, 2005).

The Influence of Nature on Nurture: Learning in the Body   Nurture tends to emphasize the role of learning in response to environmental conditions, such as the lessons we learn from parents, the things we learn from interactions with peers, and the responses we learn from watching television. We learn, for example, how to resolve a playground argument through cooperation so that the game can continue. Such a lesson will come in handy later in adulthood during conflict at work or in a marriage. As important as this type of learning is, however, it occurs at a relatively superficial level. Such a superficial level fails to consider *how* nature plays a role in the process of learning at a much deeper level. At this deeper level are many forms of learning that take place in response to environmental demands.

Consider, for example, how your body's immune system keeps you from catching a cold every time a classmate or colleague sneezes. In response to new pathogens and other disease-producing bacteria, your system develops two strategies to combat them. Although each new pathogen poses a specific threat, the defense system developed by the immune system relies on two principles that it has come to associate with pathogens: first, that they, too, are made of proteins; and second, that these proteins are different from the proteins already located in the body. Thus, nature, as reflected in the operation of the immune system, can influence nurture by determining which proteins are to be attacked. Such a process suggests that learning takes place not only in the brain in response to external stimuli but also within bodily processes operating at the cellular level that does not involve the brain. This form of learning demonstrates how nature – the evolvement and operation of the immune system – can serve to influence nurture – learn which proteins are to be attacked. So the evolvement of the nature–nurture controversy has helped us to understand and appreciate that learning – a critical component of nature – takes place at both the level of the brain and the cellular level of the body.

The Influence of Nurture on Nature: The Body's Response to Experience   Proponents of the biological basis of personality emphasize how nature influences nurture, but many processes exist that illustrate how nurture influences nature. For example, as an individual's immune system develops defenses against biological threats to the body, the individual is busy trying to understand which environmental elements are protective. So as we learn that certain foods, such as apples and oranges, are rich sources of carbohydrates that can be of value to the immune system, there will be certain changes in the bodily systems as well. In response to this information, the body will develop sensory abilities to identify these foods and will develop a digestive system to break these foods down into their important nutritional elements. These types of bodily adaptations are a result of learning that will be stored as part of our genetic makeup, which is then passed along from generation to generation. For example, as part of our genetic makeup, we avoid eating foul-smelling apples and break down the stems of the apples into a form of waste that can be eliminated from the digestive system. Such information is passed along not only genetically, but also in the form of advice by parents, peers, and the media – all important elements of the process of nurture.

The impact of this type of learning goes well beyond the changes it produces in the various bodily processes. For example, in creating an environment that supports the changes created in the bodily process, we may develop social communities located near important resources (e.g., apple orchards, rivers, and lakes), develop rituals for reproducing, harvesting, and preparing these particular foods, and develop division-of-labor structures (e.g., farmers, transportation providers, sellers, consumers) to make such foods available to others (Richardson & Boyd, 2005). As our knowledge of these foods grows or they become scarce, we can learn to develop synthetic sources of them or learn to identify other food substitutes, which in turn will influence the nature of the bodily process associated with them. Thus, there are many ways that nurture influences the operation of nature.

The Role of Heredity: Estimates of the Influence of Biological Processes

When considering the nature–nurture controversy, declarations such as "The nature–nurture debate is over. The bottom line is everything is heritable, an outcome that has taken all sides of the nature–nurture debate by surprise" (Turkheimer, 2000, p. 160) can result in misunderstandings about the role of heredity and the influence of biological processes on personality. Although everything is heritable, this does not mean that all of your personality is determined by biological processes. What this statement actually means is that everything contains a hereditary component – certain biological contributions to physical and personality characteristics (Plomin et al., 2001).

Heredity is a mathematical estimate, based on many observations across individuals in a certain group, regarding genetically determined differences in certain physical (e.g., height), cognitive (e.g., memory), or personality (e.g., introversion) dimensions that can be attributed to differences in the nature of genetic makeup. Similarities and differences (i.e., variation) in genetic makeup are associated with how close individuals are biologically. For example, immediate family members have more in common with each other genetically than with distant relatives, and have even less in common with non-extended family members. Let us say we measured the height of and gave a test of extraversion to a large group of individuals attending a family reunion and estimated that 65 percent of the observed differences in height and 25 percent of the observed differences in extraversion scores were due to variation in genetic makeup (i.e., nature). By extrapolation we would conclude that, at least for the members of this particular family constellation, 35 percent of observed differences in height and 75 percent of observed differences in extraversion scores could be attributed to environmental factors (i.e., nurture). These might include lifestyle choices, such as diet and exercise, and social support systems such as entertaining others at home and volunteering in the community. Thus, when considering heritability, the issue is *to what degree* various dimensions are influenced by heredity. More specific to our concerns about personality, recent estimates of heritability of personality traits based on twin studies suggest that "30 to 50% (average 40%) of the variance in personality is due to genetic factors" (Zuckerman, 2005, p. 47) while the rest is due to environmental factors.

Another source of misunderstanding about heredity is that "Heredity is often treated as a fixed, universal statement of causation" (Zuckerman, 2005, p. 47). To counteract this myth, let us take a close look at the role of heredity within the biological viewpoint of personality (Zuckerman, 2005; Plomin et al., 2001). First, the logic of heredity is only appropriate for making statements about groups of individuals – not about a single individual. For example, it is appropriate to say that 25 percent of the estimated observed differences in the extraversion scores of family reunion attendees can be due to genetics; but the same cannot be said for "chatty old uncle Fred." His degree of extraversion reflects his unique genetic makeup and personal set of life experiences. Second, estimates of heredity from one group do not necessarily apply to other groups. For example, the estimates of heredity based on attendees of this particular family reunion could be quite different from estimates for the attendees of another family reunion at the same park the following weekend. The same can be said for nationalities (e.g., Chinese vs. Americans) and cultural factors (e.g., religious vs. nonreligious). Finally, estimates of heredity are not necessarily precise since they are subject to errors of reliability and validity (see Chapter 2, pp. 42–47) and require large sample sizes to form stable estimates. For example, because the measure of extraversion is less reliable than that of height, greater caution must be taken when forming conclusions about heritability of extraversion than when forming conclusions about heritability of height. In addition, such estimates based on a family reunion of 300 individuals would be more stable than those based on a family reunion of just 50 individuals. Thus, although heritability estimates play an important role in understanding the biological viewpoint of personality, they should be interpreted with caution.

Genetically Determined Does Not Equal Genetically Fixed: Affecting a Range of Possibilities

The U.S. Declaration of Independence states all men are created equal. In light of the role of biological processes in personality, literal interpretations of such a statement can be viewed as a source of controversy. Some may erroneously believe that endorsing the nature position acknowledges that some people are born more gifted (e.g., more intelligent or extraverted) and, as a result, will have a greater advantage than others. The major error in this type of reasoning is assuming that "genetically determined" means "genetically fixed" (Plomin et al., 2001).

Genetically determined refers to the notion that certain inborn biological factors combine with environmental factors to influence how an individual adjusts and responds to the events in his or her world. An individual born with very poor eyesight might not be able to be a fighter pilot or police officer. But with the right educational opportunities and encouragement from family members, he or she can become independent

and live a full life as a financial planner, for example. Another visually impaired individual who is pitied and coddled by his family might end up an extremely dependent, self-centered adult. As this example illustrates, biologically determined factors affect the possible range of opportunities available, rather than setting the individual on a "predetermined" course of action. Thus, nature and nurture both contribute significantly to the development and operation of personality (Wachs & Kohnstamm, 2001). We will examine evidence for this position throughout this chapter.

The Logic of the Biological Viewpoint: A Complementary and Supplementary Perspective

The emphasis of the biological viewpoint of the study of personality is to investigate how genetics, evolution, biochemistry, and bodily processes contribute to the operation and development of personality. However, the contributions made by such factors are not designed to supplant environmental, psychological, or cognitive explanations. Instead, both types of factors complement and supplement each other to yield a broad understanding of personality.

Consider how biological factors might contribute to the socially withdrawn behavior typically associated with the personality of introverts. Because introverts seem to show greater nervous system sensitivity and reactivity to lower levels of noise than do extraverts (Eysenck, 1990a; Stelmack, 1990), they may deal with loud noise at a party by being unsociable or by leaving the party prematurely. Thus, a more complete understanding of the characteristic feature of social withdrawal of introverts involves considering how biological (e.g., reactivity of the nervous system), environmental (e.g., noise level at the party), psychological (e.g., emotional discomfort), and cognitive (e.g., deciding to leave) factors operate together.

The Biosocial Interaction: A Unique Expression for a Complete Understanding of Personality

Recall the discussion of situational interactionism from Chapter 7, in which we said behavior was best understood by considering the individual's unique personality characteristics (e.g., specific combination of traits and beliefs) in combination with situational factors (e.g., party vs. employment setting). A corollary can be seen in the biological viewpoint of personality in what might be defined as a biosocial interaction. The basic assumption of a **biosocial interaction** is that personality can be best understood by considering the individual's unique biological characteristics (e.g., temperament and hormonal levels) within the context of social factors (e.g., family dynamics and cultural norms). Thus, both factors contribute to personality. Going beyond their relative and reciprocal contributions, it also implies that each factor may make a different contribution at different points in an individual's life (Plomin et al., 2001; Plomin & Nesselroade, 1990).

To exemplify, a child born with a biological temperament characterized by hypersensitivity might be overprotected by its parents and spend more time alone than playing with others. As a result of this social isolation, the child has less opportunity to acquire the social skills necessary to interact successfully with others. To cope with the lack of social skills and feelings of loneliness experienced as an adult, the person might join a singles club that advertises itself as being for "quiet and gentle

people." Thus, although this introverted person may be relatively shy and reserved most of the time, the quiet and gentle nature of this club allows the person to display a more socially expressive personality style. This example illustrates how biological factors (e.g., sensitivity of the nervous system) and environmental factors (e.g., a club for quiet and gentle people) operate reciprocally in a biosocial interaction to meet both the biological (e.g., desire for low stimulation) and emotional (e.g., desire to socialize) needs that make up the individual's personality.

In conclusion, the principal point to be made in this section is that people are social (i.e., nurture) and biological (i.e., nature) organisms. These two aspects of the individual do not operate independently; they operate interactively and reciprocally. The major objective of the biological viewpoint is to bring the studies of personality and biology together to enhance our understanding of personality, rather than to turn personality psychology into a biological analysis. A summary of the major points discussed in this section are presented in "Summing It Up: Basic Issues Associated with the

Summing It Up *Basic Issues Associated with the Biological Viewpoint of Personality*

Basic Issue	Examples
The Nature–Nurture Controversy. Addresses the degree to which inherited and environmental factors contribute to the expression of personality, as well as how both of these factors serve to influence each other.	To what degree does being born with an overly sensitive nervous system (i.e., nature) and growing up with a lack of opportunity to practice social skills (i.e., nurture) contribute to an individual's tendency to be a socially withdrawn adult?
The Role of Heredity. Addresses the extent to which the variation in the expression of a certain characteristic in a particular group of individuals can be attributed to genetic factors.	Joe, his sister Jamie, and their cousin Robbie are very outgoing and the life of any party they attend. To what degree is their social expressiveness due to a genetic influence on extraversion that runs in their family?
Genetic Determinism. Inherited factors help to determine – not fix – a range of possibilities for an individual's personality	The self-esteem of an individual born with a genetically based handicap will be influenced by treatment received from others, and not just by the handicap.
The Logic of the Biological Viewpoint. The consideration of biological factors in conjunction with psychological factors as determinants of personality, not as a replacement of them.	When trying to explain aggressiveness, personality researchers would examine family interactions as well as hormonal levels.
The Biosocial Interaction. The reciprocal operation of biological and social factors in determining personality.	An individual with an inherited tendency toward nervousness can feel outgoing when talking to a compassionate professor.

Biological Viewpoint of Personality." In the next section, we will take a historical look at some of the early perspectives on the role of biological process in the study of personality that set the stage for the more contemporary perspectives of the biological viewpoint of personality.

The Constitutional Perspective: The Early Roots of a Biological Basis of Personality

The notion of relating personality to various biological processes has a long and colorful history dating back to the ancient Greeks. In this section we place current approaches to **constitutional psychology** – the study of biological processes underlying human behavior – in a historical context. We begin by discussing some early attempts to identify the biological bases of personality.

Ancient Beginnings of the Biological Viewpoint of Personality: It's All Greek to Me

Some of the earliest attempts to identify the underlying biological bases of personality were made by the ancient Greeks. The great Greek physician and "father of medicine" Hippocrates (460?–377 BC) and – five centuries later – the Roman physician Galen (AD 130–200) were among the first to postulate a biological basis of personality. According to Hippocrates and Galen, different temperaments (i.e., personality types) were associated with the four basic body fluids, or **humors** – blood, black bile, yellow bile, and phlegm – and corresponded to the four basic cosmic elements of nature – air, earth, fire, and water, respectively. A person with too much blood had a **sanguine personality**, characterized by being hopeful and excitable. A person with too much black bile had a **melancholic personality**, characterized by sadness and depression. A person with too much yellow bile had a **choleric personality**, characterized by anger and irritability. A person with too much phlegm had a **phlegmatic personality**, characterized by calmness and apathy. The well-adjusted personality had a balance of all of the four basic humors.

Although only of historical interest today, the influence of this ancient theory is reflected in the contemporary biological viewpoint by investigations into the role of hormones in personality. In addition, recent research suggests a link between blood type and personality, as described in "A Closer Look."

A Closer Look

The Personality and Blood Type of Nations: A Contemporary Constitutional Cross-Cultural Comparison

The ancient humoral theory of personality linked differences in personality with variations in certain types of bodily fluids. More recently, a link between personality and blood type has been established. The personality of introversion is found more frequently among persons having the AB blood type, while the characteristic of emotionality is found more frequently among persons having the B blood type (Angst & Maurer-Groeli, 1974).

In an extension of these findings, Eysenck (1982) classified countries by the personality scores of thousands of people (Hofstede, 1976, 1980; Lynn, 1981) and assessed the percentage of persons having different blood types. His results indicate that countries classified as introverted by scoring low on extraversion (e.g., Egypt, France, and Japan) had a higher percentage of persons with AB blood type than did countries scoring high on extraversion (e.g., Australia, Canada, Greece, United Kingdom, United States, and Italy). Countries classified as emotional by scoring high on neuroticism (e.g., Egypt, West Germany, Japan, and Poland) had a higher percentage of persons with type B blood than countries scoring low on neuroticism (e.g., Australia, Italy, United States, and Sweden).

Because blood type is genetically determined, these results suggest that personality differences among nations and cultures may in part be due to biological and genetic factors. Thus, in addition to suggesting certain regional geographic and weather conditions (Pennebaker, Rime, & Blankenship, 1996) and cultural variations in norms and values (Triandis, 1996) as important determinants of cross-cultural differences in personality, personality psychologist also now include biological factors to account for cultural differences in personality.

The famous Greek philosopher Aristotle (384–322 BC) proposed understanding personality through **physiognomy**, or the inference of personality traits from physical features, particularly as they relate to the features of animals (Allport, 1937). For example, a person with a slender face and long nose might, like a fox, have a personality characterized by cleverness and deviousness (i.e., *sly as a fox*). Figure 8.1 illustrates the assumed relationship between physiognomic features and the four basic temperaments.

Some 2,000 years later, Italian criminologist Cesare Lombroso (1836–1909) theorized a relationship between facial features and criminal behavior. Because Lombroso believed that criminals represented a lower level of evolutionary development, he assumed they would possess characteristic features of this level of development, including squared jaws and protruding foreheads.

Although not considered seriously today, the physiognomic theme can be seen in the contemporary evolutionary perspective to be discussed in Chapter 9 (Buss, 2005). For example, symmetrical facial structure is preferred by women when considering a potential mate. According to this view, facial symmetry is associated with certain positive biological processes related to sexual reproduction, such as physical attractiveness,

better health, and sperm characteristics (Buss, 2008). In addition, a relationship between facial structure and an inhibited temperament (i.e., shyness) has been identified, with inhibited children having somewhat longer and narrower faces than uninhibited children (Kagan & Arcus, 1995).

Biological Viewpoints from the 19th Century

In the late 18th century, the German anatomist Franz Joseph Gail (1758–1828) and his student Johann Gaspar Spurzheim (1776–1832) developed **phrenology**, which proposed a relationship between the bumps and contours on a person's head and that person's personality and mental abilities. These bumps were believed to correspond to overly developed parts of the brain; and the attributes associated with them would dominate the individual's personality. A phrenologic mapping of the brain and listing of the corresponding affective and intellectual abilities are illustrated in Figure 8.2.

Although no scientific evidence was ever presented in support of phrenology, the relationship between brain functioning and personality has a contemporary corollary in the study of associations of specific personality characteristics with the measurement of electrical activity in particular parts of the brain (e.g., frontal or temporal area). In recent research, investigators have noted that heightened electrical activity in certain parts of the brain is associated with aggressiveness and violent behavior (Zuckerman, 2005), anxiety (Davidson, 2002), neuroticism (Canli et al., 2001), certain types of extroversion (Tran, Craig, & McIssac, 2001), and shyness and sociability (Schmidt, 1999). We will discover more about brain activity and personality later in this chapter.

Humor:	Black bile	Yellow bile	Phlegm	Blood
Temperament:	Melancholic	Choleric	Phlegmatic	Sanguine

Figure 8.1   Some illustrations of physiognomy and its relationship to the theory of humors
Source: Allport (1937, p. 68)

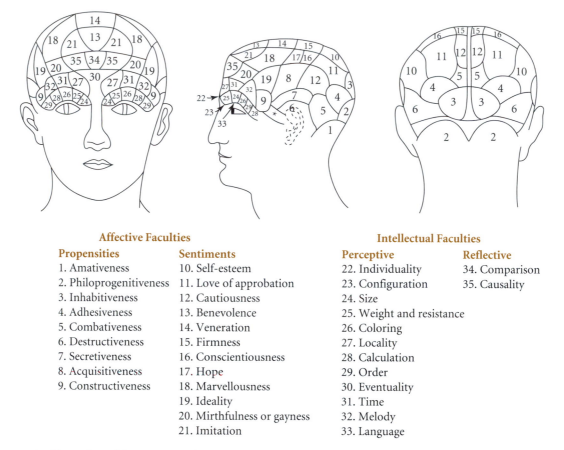

Affective Faculties

Propensities	Sentiments
1. Amativeness	10. Self-esteem
2. Philoprogenitiveness	11. Love of approbation
3. Inhabitiveness	12. Cautiousness
4. Adhesiveness	13. Benevolence
5. Combativeness	14. Veneration
6. Destructiveness	15. Firmness
7. Secretiveness	16. Conscientiousness
8. Acquisitiveness	17. Hope
9. Constructiveness	18. Marvellousness
	19. Ideality
	20. Mirthfulness or gayness
	21. Imitation

Intellectual Faculties

Perceptive	Reflective
22. Individuality	34. Comparison
23. Configuration	35. Causality
24. Size	
25. Weight and resistance	
26. Coloring	
27. Locality	
28. Calculation	
29. Order	
30. Eventuality	
31. Time	
32. Melody	
33. Language	

Figure 8.2 An illustration of the mapping of emotional and mental abilities as defined by phrenology
Source: Spurzheim (1834)

Biological Viewpoints from the Early 20th Century

Modern constitutional approaches to the study of personality include the work of the eminent German psychiatrist Ernst Kretschmer (Kretschmer, 1925) and, in the United States, William Sheldon, both of whom attempted to establish a relationship between an individual's physique and personality type. Through extensive research involving the ratings of over 4,000 people, Sheldon (1942, 1954) classified physiques (i.e., body types) by using three dimensions: endomorphy, mesomorphy, and ectomorphy. **Endomorphy** refers to a soft, round body structure (see the left panel in Figure 8.3). **Mesomorphy** refers to a hard, muscular body structure (see the middle panel in Figure 8.3). **Ectomorphy** refers to a linear, fragile body structure (see the right panel in Figure 8.3). Sheldon believed that physique is based not only on outward characteristics but also on the person's underlying bone structure. Consequently, he assumed that although body shape might change over time owing to illness, dieting, or exercise, the bone structure remains the same, which adds consistency to the body structure.

Sheldon (1942, 1954) classified individual physiques by a **somatotype rating**, or assessment of an individual's physique by using a three-digit number corresponding to the endomorphy, mesomorphy, and ectomorphy dimensions. In Figure 8.3, the first digit in the somatotype ratings under the drawings of the individuals indicates the extent to which the body is characteristic (i.e., 1 = *not characteristic* to 7 = *very characteristic*) of the endomorphy dimension. Similarly, the second digit reflects the mesomorphy dimension and the third digit reflects the ectomorphy dimension. Although there are 343 possible somatotype rating combinations with the

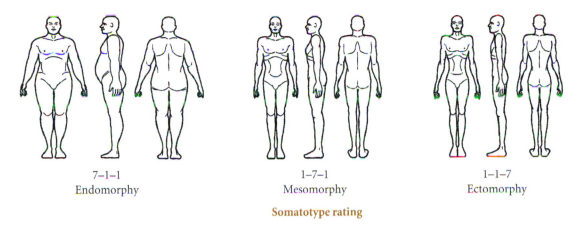

7–1–1	1–7–1	1–1–7
Endomorphy	Mesomorphy	Ectomorphy

Somatotype rating

Figure 8.3   Illustrations of Sheldon's dimensions of physique and somatotype ratings
Source: Adapted from Sheldon (1954)

three-digit system, Sheldon reported initially that he was able to identify only about 80 distinctively different somatotypes. But he increased his estimation to 267 with further refinements of his rating technique (Sheldon, Lewis, & Tenney, 1969). As a point of interest, you might take a moment to calculate your own somatotype rating.

To establish a link between body type and personality, Sheldon developed a personality test identifying three major dimensions of **temperament**: viscerotonia, somatotonia, and cerebrotonia.

- **Viscerotonia** consists of a cluster of traits relating to a love of food, comfort, people, and affection (e.g., the character of Bluto played by John Belushi in the classic movie *Animal House*).
- **Somatotonia** consists of a cluster of traits related to a high desire for physical adventure, risk-taking activities, and muscular activity (e.g., the character of Lara Croft played by Angelina Jolie in the *Tomb Raider* movies).
- **Cerebrotonia** consists of a cluster of traits related to emotional restraint, self-consciousness, and a preference for solitude and privacy (e.g., the character of Clark Kent, the public identity of Superman, played by Brandon Routh in *Superman Returns*).

Sheldon assumed that as with somatotype ratings, the three dimensions of temperament affect each person to a certain degree.

To establish the link between body type and personality, Sheldon (1942) calculated the correlations between somatotype ratings and temperament scores. The results indicate that the endomorphic body type correlates most strongly with the viscerotonia temperament rating ($r = +.79$); the mesomorphic body type correlates most strongly with the somatotonia temperament rating ($r = +.82$); and the ectomorphic body type correlates most strongly with the cerebrotonia temperament ($r = +.83$). The consistency and magnitude of these results support Sheldon's theory. A limitation of Sheldon's approach is that more systematic and controlled research failed to provide support for his proposed relationship between body type and personality (Eysenck, 1970).

Additional research assessing the relationship between somatotype and temperament ratings involving the school performance of children (Sanford et al., 1943), behavior of delinquent and nondelinquent boys (Glueck & Glueck, 1950, 1956), and performance of wartime pilots (Damon, 1955) also supports Sheldon's position. However, a major shortcoming of Sheldon's work is its assumption that body type causes temperament. The correlational nature of the research does not support such a conclusion. For example, the athletic activity of the somatotonic type may be reinforced by the cheers and praise of others, which are environmental factors.

This concludes our discussion of the constitution viewpoint of personality. Although the various constitutional theories may seem primitive by today's standards, the work of the early researchers set the stage for contemporary biological views of personality. For example, contemporary research in the study of temperament

Summing It Up *Explanations from the Constitutional Viewpoint*

Ancient Greeks. Explained individual differences in personality by focusing on the relationship between certain body fluids and an individual's physical features

- *Humors.* Variations in these four major body fluids were associated with certain personality types: *blood* with a sanguine personality (i.e., optimistic personality), *black bile* with a melancholic personality (i.e., a gloomy personality), *yellow bile* with a choleric personality (i.e., a hostile personality), and *phlegm* with a phlegmatic personality (i.e., an indifferent personality).
- *Physiognomy.* The association of certain physical features (e.g., shape of jaw) with certain personality characteristics (e.g., stern).
- *Contemporary Link.* Personality researchers are focusing on the link between hormones and personality charateristics. For example, do individuals with higher levels of the hormone testosterone engage in more aggressive behavior?

19th Century. Explained individual differences by focusing on the underlying structure of the brain being associated with certain mental abilities and personality characteristics.

- *Phrenology.* Bumps on certain places of the head (e.g., near the ears) were associated with certain personality characteristics (e.g., being a good listener).
- *Contemporary Link.* Personality researchers are focusing on the link between the measurement of the electrical activity in certain locations of the brain (e.g., right frontal region) with certain personality characteristic (e.g., being emotional). For example, do highly self-conscious individuals display more electrical brain activity when viewing socially threatening stimuli (e.g., someone being criticized in public) than individuals who are not self-consciousness?

Early 20th Century. Explained individual differences by focusing on a link between body structure and temperament (i.e., inherited personality types).

- *Ernst Kretschmer.* He made early attempts to establish a relationship between physique and personality.
- *William Sheldon.* He made systematic efforts to establish a relationship of the somatotype dimensions of endomorphy, mesomorphy, and ectomorphy with the temperament dimensions of viscerotonia, somatotonia, and cerebrotonia, respectively.
- *Contemporary Link.* Certain bodily features (e.g., hip-to-waist ratio; body-movement flexibility), as being associated with certain personality characteristics (e.g., femininity), are being investigated by the evolutionary viewpoint of personality (see Chapter 9). For example, are individuals with symmetrical (e.g., balanced) facial features seen as having more desirable personality characteristics (e.g., warmth) than those individuals with less balanced features (e.g., eyes too far from the nose)?

examines the contribution of the structure and development of personality, along with its interaction with culture, to help explain the enduring differences in the characteristics of individuals from different countries (Costa & McCrae, 2001). The role of structural features of the body, such as weight-to-height ratio, hip-to-waist ratio, and shoulder-to-hip ratio, along with personality characteristics, is currently being investigated in the context of the evolutionary perspective of personality (Sugiyama, 2005).

A summary of the major points of this section is presented in "Summing It Up: Explanations from the Constitutional Viewpoint" above. In the sections that follow we examine some contemporary biological

views of personality. We begin with a consideration of the behavioral genetics perspective.

The Behavioral Genetics Perspective: The Basic Biological Unit of Personality

The study of **behavioral genetics** attempts to determine the extent to which behavioral differences among people are due to genetic as well as environmental differences (Plomin et al., 2001). Similarly, the biological viewpoint of personality incorporates behavioral genetics to examine the extent to which various aspects of personality (Pervin, 2002), such as extraversion (Bouchard & Loehlin, 2001; Eysenck, 1990b) and sensation seeking (Zuckerman, 2005), are determined by genetic and environmental influences (Plomin, Chipuer, & Loehlin, 1990). Behavioral genetics research also examines the role of genetics in the structure of personality (Borkenau, Riemann, Angleitner, & Spinath, 2001; McCrae et al., 2000; Rowe, 1989) and personality consistency and variation during childhood (Leve, Kim, & Pears, 2005) and across the life span (Plomin & Nesselroade, 1990; Rowe, 1989).

The roots of behavioral genetics are found in the pioneering work of the Augustinian monk Gregor Mendel (1822–1884). Mendel's classic 1866 paper on qualitative traits of various species of pea plants, "Experiments in plant hybridization," was initially ignored, yet it set the framework for much contemporary research in behavior genetics. In this section we discuss some of the principal techniques used in this area of research and some of the basic findings.

Methodological Considerations in Behavioral Genetics: Tracking the Genetic Influence in Personality

A valuable research tool in studying the genetic bases of physical characteristics is selective breeding. In the **selective breeding experiment**, organisms (e.g., rats or flies) with certain characteristics (e.g., fur texture or eye color) are selected and bred to determine exactly how these characteristics are passed from one generation to the next. Because selective breeding of people to determine the transmission of personality traits is unethical, researchers using the behavioral genetics approach to studying personality must rely on other methods. Some of these methods include family studies, twin studies, adoption studies, and model fitting (Plomin et al., 2001).

Family Studies

In **family studies**, researchers examine family history to determine the extent to which certain personality characteristics occur more often among family members (e.g., mother, grandfather, third cousins) than in the general population. Proponents of these studies hold that the closer the relationship between the individuals (parent–child vs. stranger–child), the greater the shared genetic makeup and the more similar the personalities. For example, although the incidence of schizophrenia is only about 1 percent in the general population, it is almost 9 percent for children of schizophrenic parents and about 4 percent for the grandchildren of those suffering from schizophrenia (Gottesman, 1991).

Limitations of Family Studies A shortcoming of family studies is that because family members share not only genes but also a social environment, it is difficult to determine how much of the family similarity in personality is due to a common gene pool (nature) as opposed to a common home environment (nurture). Family studies are thus considered to provide the weakest type of evidence concerning the heritability of personality characteristics.

Twin Studies

Twins can be either identical or fraternal. **Identical twins**, also called **monozygotic twins** (MZ), develop from the same fertilized egg and share an identical genetic structure. **Fraternal twins**, also called **dizygotic twins** (DZ), develop from two separate fertilized eggs and are no more similar in their genetic structure than any two siblings.

Researchers in behavioral genetics using **twin studies** compare the personality similarity of identical twins with that of fraternal twins. Because identical and fraternal twins reared together share the same environment, any increase in similarity in personality between the identical twins can be attributed to genetic factors. The degree of similarity between any set of twins on any personality dimension is referred to as the **concordance rate**. In a cross-cultural study of extraversion involving twins from Canada and Germany (Jang, Livesley, Angleitner, Riemann, & Vernon, 2002), researchers found that identical twins showed a higher degree of personality similarity (concordance rate: mean correlation = .47) than fraternal twins (concordance rate: mean correlation = .21), replicating an earlier review of twin studies (Eysenck, 1990b).

Limitations of Twin Studies A limitation of twin studies is that the greater personality similarity found with identical twins can also be attributed to the possibility that because they look alike, identical twins are treated more similarly by their parents, siblings, other relatives, and teachers than are fraternal twins. This can

The study of twins using the methods of behavioral genetics research has done much to help us understand the relative contributions of biological and environmental factors to the expression of personality.

be interpreted as supporting evidence for an environmental contribution to personality. Supporters of the behavioral genetics position, however, argue that although identical twins are treated with greater similarity than fraternal twins, this special treatment is not a significant factor in the greater degree of personality and behavioral similarity seen in identical twins as opposed to in fraternal twins (Loehlin & Nichols, 1976; Morris-Yates, Andrews, Howie, & Henderson, 1990).

Adoption Studies

To avoid the confounding influence of environmental factors, noted previously, created when twins live in the same environment, behavioral geneticists also study twins reared in different environments as a result of adoption. In **adoption studies**, researchers compare a child's personality with those of his or her biological parents and adopted parents. Although the adopted child shares the social environment of the adopted parents, he or she shares the gene structure of the biological parents. Thus, if the child's personality resembles that of an adopted parent, the evidence is considered strong for an environmental influence. On the other hand, if the child's personality is more like that of a biological parent, this suggests a strong genetic influence.

Researchers also combine the logic of twin studies and adoption studies by comparing the adult personalities of identical twins who were separated at birth and raised in different families. Finally, there is the possibility that adults with their own children might also elect to adopt additional children. In such cases, it is also possible to compare the degree of similarity among the personalities of the biological children, the adopted children, and the parents to determine effects of the environment on people with different genetic makeups. The greater the similarity in personality between the adopted children and the biological children, the stronger the evidence for the environmental position.

Limitations of Adoption Studies   Biases in **selective placement**, or the procedures used by adoption agencies in selecting adoptive families and in assigning children to those families, are associated with adoption studies (Plomin et al., 2001). The suspicion here is that the information obtained from adoption studies may be based on the effects of being adopted into more favorable and affluent environments. Yet another bias is that adoption agencies tend to place children with parents who are similar in such dimensions as race, physical features, and intelligence. Thus, any contribution of the environment is maximized by creating a certain amount of similarity to the adopted parents from the beginning. However, research on such biases suggests that although they do have an impact when trying to assess intelligence, their effect is minimal when it comes to assessing personality variables (Loehlin, Willerman, & Horn, 1982; Plomin et al., 2001).

Model Fitting

Model fitting is a mathematical procedure for testing the proposed relationship among a variety of variables. In behavior genetics, a model is assembled reflecting the relative contribution of various genetic and environmental factors and comparing it with observed correlational relationships.

Figure 8.4 presents three models outlining the influence of shared environmental (E) factors (e.g., home of adopted parents) and genetic (G) factors (e.g., biological parents) on the personalities (P) of two adopted individuals. In Figure 8.4a, it is assumed that environmental factors are the only determinants of personality. In Figure 8.4b, it is assumed that genetic factors are the only determinants of personality. Figure 8.4c indicates that both environmental and genetic factors are important. These models are tested by calculating the separate correlational relationships (indicated by the arrows) and then comparing them statistically to determine which model comes closest to explaining the observed relationships. An excellent

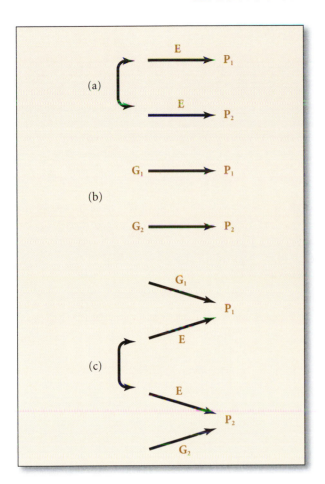

Figure 8.4 Three models outlining the influence of shared environmental factors (E) and genetic factors (G) on the personalities of two adopted people (P₁ and P₂)

example of model testing is the work of Michael Stallings and colleagues, who compared 1,287 twin pairs and tested 14 different models to determine the relative contribution of genetic and environmental factors to an assortment of personality dimensions (Stallings, Hewitt, Cloninger, Heath, & Eaves, 1996). Such a systematic comparison of many models helps us to develop a more complete understanding of how genetic and environmental factors influence a wide array of personality characteristics.

The major advantage of model fitting is that it enables researchers to combine variables from many different types of information, such as family, twin, and adoption studies (Plomin et al., 1990, 2001). For example, using model-fitting analysis to compare various twin (e.g., identical vs. fraternal twins reared together vs. reared apart) and adoption (nonadoptive

parents and offspring vs. adoptive parents and offspring) designs yielded heritability estimates of about 50 percent for extraversion and about 40 percent for neuroticism (Loehlin, 1992).

Limitations of Model Fitting A limitation of model fitting is that because it is primarily correlational, it cannot be used to determine definite causal influences of genetic or environmental factors. It can be used only in determining how well the model being proposed explains the observed relationships when compared to other models. In this regard, the model being tested is only as good as the theorist proposing it.

This concludes our discussion of some of the principal research methods associated with the behavior genetics perspective on the study of personality. A summary of the major points in this section is presented in "Summing It Up: Research Methods in Behavioral Genetics" on p. 332. In the next section, we will discuss some of the findings of the behavioral genetics perspective.

The Genetic Basis of Personality: Some Illustrative Evidence

In this section we consider a survey of behavioral genetics research to demonstrate the genetic contribution to personality. To do this, we will examine systematic research that uses the various research methods previously discussed (e.g., adoption studies, twin studies) to study different types of twin pairs (e.g., monozygotic vs. dizygotic) by comparing the strength of the correlations for these pairs of twins on various measures of personality to determine the degree of genetic influence on certain aspects of personality. In so doing we'll learn about the **index of heredity**, which expresses the amount of variability in personality measures that can be accounted for by a genetic contribution. The closer the index of heredity, designated by h^2, is to 1.00, the greater the genetic contribution. *As a cautionary note, please know that it is the author's intention that the nature and number of twin pairs and the numerical values for the index of heredity are presented for the purposes of comparison and to illustrate the relative genetic contribution to the various personality characteristic, and not with the intention that they are to be memorized.* Finally, although our consideration of personality characteristics is not exhaustive, it will illustrate the application of behavioral genetics research to the study of personality.

Summing It Up *Research Methods in Behavioral Genetics*

Method	Evidence	Example
Family Studies assess the genetic contribution to a particular personality characteristic by comparing its pervasiveness in groups of individuals who vary in their degree of family relatedness. *Caution*: Families share both similar genes and similar social environments.	The closer the individuals are genetically, the more similarity we would expect to see in the expression of the particular personality characteristic.	We see more similarity among brothers and sisters on the measure of anxiety than among third cousins, and even less among total strangers.
Twin Studies assess the genetic contribution to a particular personality characteristic by comparing its pervasiveness in groups of monozygotic (MZ) and dizygotic (DZ) twins. *Caution*: Problems are created by twins being treated alike because they look alike.	Since MZ twins share the same genetic structure, we would expect to see more similarity in the expression of the particular personality characteristic than in DZ twins.	The scores on an honesty test for each set of MZ twins were more similar than the scores for each set of DZ twins.
Adoption Studies assess the genetic contribution to a particular personality characteristic by comparing twins raised together with wins raised apart. *Caution*: Problems are created by the selective placement of adoptees into particular types of households.	Similarity on the personality characteristic of the twin to the adopted parents reflects an environmental influence, while similarity of the adopted twin to the biological parents reflects a genetic influence.	The scores for twins on a measure of aggressiveness were more similar to the scores for their biological parents than to the scores for their adopted parents.
Model Fitting assesses the genetic contribution to a particular personality characteristic by comparing the proposed influence of genetic and environmental factors within different configurations to the observed relationship of the results for each of these configurations. *Caution*: The proposed model is only as good as the theorist proposing it.	The closer the proposed specific configuration of the genetic and environmental factors is to the observed results, the more support there is for the specific model.	The model that came the closest for comparing a group of MZ and DZ adopted twin pairs with their same-sex half-sibling suggested that 59 percent of the variance in the measure of happiness was accounted for by genetic factors, while 18 percent was accounted for by parenting style and 23 percent was attributed to other undetermined external factors.

Happiness and Health: What We All Want

If you were to ask folks what they want most, they would probably say to be happy and healthy. To assess the genetic contribution to happiness and health, researchers examined the responses of 3,334 18- to 31-year-old Norwegian twins to separate measures of health and happiness, or what psychologists refer to as *subjective well-being* (Røysamb, Tambs, Reichborn-Kjennerud,

Neale, & Harris, 2003). The measure of perceived happiness (Røysamb, Harris, Magnus, Vittersø, & Tambs, 2002) included four questions, such as "When you think about your life at the present, would you say you are mostly satisfied, or mostly dissatisfied?" and "Are you usually happy or dejected?" The measure of perceived health (Bardage, Isacson, & Pedersen, 2001) involved a single item: "What is your health like, at present?" The twin pairs in the study were 526 monozygotic male (MZM) pairs, 397 dizygotic male (DZM) pairs, 777 monozygotic female (MZF) pairs, 655 dizygotic female (DZF) pairs, and 979 dizygotic unlike (e.g., brother and sister; DZU) pairs. The pattern of the correlations for the twin pairs on the measure of happiness was MZM = .41, MZF = .41, DZM = .24, DZF = .30, and DZU = .12, with an index of heredity of h^2 = .44 for the males and h^2 = .44 for the females. The pattern of the correlations for the twin pairs on the measure of perceived health was MZM = .36, MZF = .26, DZM = .17, DZF = .18, and DZU = .12, with an index of heredity of h^2 = .27 for the males and h^2 = .38 for the females.

This pattern suggests that almost half of an individual's level of happiness can be attributed to genetic factors, and is consistent with the idea that approximately 50 percent of chronic happiness is associated with a genetically determined happiness set point. **Happiness set point** is the central or expected value within an individual's general range of happiness during a particular period in life (Lyubomirsky, Sheldon, & Schkade, 2005), with another 40 percent being associated with intentional activity (e.g., exercising regularly, counting one's blessings, participating in meaningful causes), and the remaining 10 percent being associated with circumstantial factors (e.g., geographical residence, childhood trauma, marital status). Finally, the results also suggest that happiness and perceived health share a common genetic basis, supporting the idea that there may be an underlying link between how healthy people perceived themselves to be and the thoughts that people have about wanting to be both happy and healthy.

Loneliness: What We All Hope to Avoid

If you were to ask people what they do not want in life, they would probably say to be lonely. Human contact is of critical importance in that it is associated with normal development and a long and happy life when present (Cacioppo, Berntson, Sheridan, & McClintock, 2000) and a sense of social isolation and a lack of relational and collective connectedness when absent (Hawkley, Browne, & Cacioppo, 2005). Although certain situations can trigger feelings of loneliness, such as moving or the loss of a loved one, loneliness has also been conceptualized as a stable personality attribute that varies little across the life span until about age 80 (Pinquart & Sorensen, 2003).

In an attempt to understand its origins, researchers have looked at the heritability of loneliness. For example, in a series of studies examining the genetic contribution to loneliness in children, McGuire and Clifford (2000)

compared the loneliness scores of a group of 69 biologically related sibling pairs and a group of 64 unrelated pairs in adopted families, reporting that a significant amount (h^2 = 55 percent) of the variability of the loneliness scores could be accounted for by a genetic contribution. In a related study they compared the loneliness scores of 22 monozygotic (MZ) twins, 40 dizygotic (DZ) twins, and 80 full siblings at ages 9, 10, 11, and 12 to their schoolmates. Again, across the different ages a significant amount (h^2 = 48 percent) of the variability of the loneliness scores was accounted for by a genetic contribution. Additional support was found in a study that examined 8,387 adult twins (3,280 males and 5,107 females) through the Netherlands Twin Register, which gathers information on twins along a variety of personality and lifestyle measures (Boomsma, Willemsen, Dolan, Hawkley, & Cacioppo, 2005). The genetic contribution was significantly greater for the MZ twins (h^2 = 48 percent) than for the DZ twins (h^2 = 24 percent) when accounting for the variability of the loneliness scores.

The consistency of these results across the different age groups and different cultures suggests a genetic contribution to loneliness. Does such evidence suggest that lonely children are destined to be lonely adults? The answer is no. Although genetics may trigger the underlying dynamics that create the potential for individual differences during early development, "parental responses to heritable differences in their children may mediate the expression of genetic influence on adolescent development" (Loehlin, Neiderhiser, & Reiss, 2003, p. 386). Stated more simply, both nature and nurture contribute to the expression of loneliness.

Aggression and Hostility: Bad to the Bone

Aggressiveness is a basic personality characteristic. In an early meta-analysis of 24 studies investigating human aggression, Miles and Carey (1997) reported that approximately 50 percent of the variation in aggressive behavior could be accounted for by an overall genetic effect. Subsequent research has also documented the role of genetics in the expression of aggressive behavior. For example, in a cross-cultural study of anger and hostility using twin-study methodology, investigators examined the responses of 253 MZ and 207 DZ twin pairs from Canada, 526 MZ and 269 DZ twin pairs from Germany, and 134 MZ and 86 DZ twin pairs from Japan (Jang et al., 2001). A summary of the results indicated that the correlations for the MZ twins were higher than those for the DZ twins in Canada (rs = .50 vs. 24), Germany (rs = .44 vs. .18), and Japan (rs = .33 vs. 13), with a heredity index for the three countries of h^2 = .52 percent, h^2 = 52 percent, and h^2 = 40 percent, respectively.

Using the adoption method, Tellegen et al. (1988) reported a pattern of results that was consistent with a behavior genetics contribution involving the responses of 217 MZ and 114 DZ reared-together adult twin pairs and 44 MZ and 27 DZ reared-apart adult twin pairs. The results indicated that the correlation of the aggression scores for the MZ twins living together (r = .41) was greater than for the DZ twins living together (r = .18) and for the MZ twins living apart (r = .32), which was itself greater than for the DZ twins living apart (r = .09). When the genetic contribution to the aggression scores was assessed, the heredity index accounted for more of the variation in the aggression scores for the MZ twins vs. the DZ twins living together (h^2 = .46) and the MZ twins vs. DZ twins living apart (h^2 = .25).

Finally, an interesting set of studies examined the genetic contribution to various forms of aggression in male and female twins. In a study of 77 MZ and 21 DZ adult female twins reared together, researchers compared correlations on various measures of aggression, reporting that while there appeared to be basically no genetic contribution to the scores on the measure of direct assault – physical violence against others – (rs = .07[MZ] vs. .41[DZ], h^2 = .00), there was a genetic contribution to the scores on the measures of indirect assault – malicious gossip, temper tantrums – (rs = .40[MZ] vs. .01[DZ], h^2 = .40), verbal hostility – arguing, cursing, threatening, being overly critical – (rs = .41[MZ] vs. .06[DZ], h^2 = .40), and irritability – quick temper, rudeness – (rs = .28[MZ] vs. −.21[DZ], h^2 = .28; Cates, Houston, Vavak, Crawford, & Uttley, 1993). In a separate study comparing the correlations of 182 MZ and 118 DZ adult males twins, respectively, on these same measures of aggression, Coccaro, Bergeman, Kavoussi, and Seroczynski (1997) reported a genetic contribution to the scores on the measures of direct assault (rs = .50[MZ] vs. .19[DZ], h^2 = .50), indirect assault (rs = .42[MZ] vs. .02[DZ], h^2 = .42), verbal hostility (rs = .28[MZ] vs. .07[DZ], h^2 = .28), and irritability (rs = .39[MZ] vs. −.06[DZ], h^2 = .39). While both of these studies did find a moderate degree of heredity (i.e., .28 to .42) for the three less direct measures of hostility, results indicating the highest index of heredity for direct hostility in males but not for the females suggests the social expectation for females to exhibit fewer displays of physical aggression. It also suggests that

females may elect to express the genetic contribution of their aggression and hostility in more subtle, less overt ways (e.g., shunning others, spreading rumors).

Attitudes: What We Believe

In addition to personality characteristics, individuals also express their individuality through attitudes. In an attempt to assess the genetic contribution to individual attitudes, Olson, Vernon, Harris, and Jang (2001) surveyed 195 MZ (128 female pairs and 67 male pairs) and 141 same-sex DZ (97 female pairs and 44 male pairs) twin pairs regarding their attitude favorability (i.e., −3 = extremely unfavorable to 0 = neutral to +3 = extremely favorable) toward 30 different items covering a wide variety of topics. These included controversial issues (e.g., death penalty for murder, castration as punishment for sex crimes, easy access to birth control), personal activities, (e.g., reading books, exercising, wearing clothes that draw attention, roller-coaster rides), and social settings (e.g., big parties, loud music, public speaking, being the leader of groups). In addition, the participants were asked to indicate how important (0 = not important to 6 = extremely important) each of the attitudes was to them. Of the 30 attitude items, 26 yielded significant genetic effects, with the heredity indices for all the items ranging from h^2 = 0 to .58, with a median of h^2 = .35. The five items with the largest heredity indices (all greater than or equal to h^2 = .50) were attitudes toward reading books, abortion on demand, playing organized sports, roller-coaster rides, and the death penalty. The four items with the lowest heredity indices (h^2 = 0) were attitudes toward separate roles for men and women, playing bingo, easy access to birth control, and being assertive. In addition, the authors investigated the extent to which the heritability of an attitude was associated with its strength (importance), on the assumption that attitude strength would be associated with heritability (Tesser, 1993). Across all 30 items, there was a tendency for the index of heredity to be positively associated with the attitude item's rating of importance. These results suggest that heritable attitudes tend to be psychologically stronger.

The importance of this research is that although attitudes are learned, they embody a genetic component that seems to cut across a wide variety of attitudinal topics, ranging from personal to social to controversial issues. The linking of the index of heredity and attitudinal strength is an important finding with theoretical and practical implications. The theoretical implication is that although researchers noted a genetic influence on attitudes, considerable variance existed in the attitudinal measures accounted for by environmental factors, particularly for individuals who experienced the same family environment differently. In support of such reasoning, Plomin and Rende (1991) noted that, "Environmental factors important to development are experienced differently by children in the same family" (p. 179). These results suggest that personality psychologists should investigate more thoroughly how each sibling perceives, processes, and interprets the specific experiences that produce differences in attitudes. Such experiences might include the reading of magazines and newspapers found in the home, participation in family activities (e.g., watching a video together, family game night) or responsibilities (e.g., chores around the house), or discussions with family members on various political, social, and personal issues. A practical implication is that because attitudes with a large genetic component tend to be stronger than others, they may prove more difficult to change. This may help to explain why attitudes with a high degree of genetic influence and importance, such as those regarding the death penalty and abortion, are such change-resistant "hot-button" issues that contribute to religious and political divisiveness. It also helps to account for the critical influence such genetically based, psychologically potent attitudes have on many important intrapersonal choices we make, such as what programs we watch, what newspapers we read, what political candidates we vote for, and what products we buy; as well as on significant interpersonal decisions, such as who we will marry and have as friends and in which activities we elect to participate.

Adolescent Personality Adjustment: A Basic Personality Process

In addition to investigating the genetic contribution to individual personality characteristics, it is also possible to investigate several related characteristics of a more basic personality process to identify general patterns across these characteristics. A good example of this type of research is seen in the work of Loehlin et al. (2003) in their investigation of the genetic contribution to six characteristic features of the general process of adolescent adjustment. An interesting feature of this research was the nature of the family constellations and twin/sibling combinations used to assess genetic and environmental influences across the six characteristic features. The researchers implemented a nationwide random telephone campaign to identify a variety of prospective twin/sibling and family combinations. As

a condition of participation, families had to have lived together for at least 5 years and to have had a pair of same-sex children between the ages of 10 and 18 no more than four years apart in age. On those selection criteria, 702 families were identified.

Within these families, the researchers identified six different sibling constellations, which included intact and remarried families. The two twin constellations were MZ twins or DZ twins living in intact families. The third intact-sibling constellation was that of full siblings (SI), or two children born to parents who had not been previously married. There were also three sibling constellations created through remarriage. Full siblings in remarried families (SR) were two children born of the same two parents in a previous relationship and now living in the household with one remarried parent and new spouse (i.e., stepparent), but with no other siblings in the household from the spouse's previous relationship. However, such full siblings could also be half siblings (HS) in certain family constellations. HS might include children brought into the new family by one of the remarried spouses being siblings with the children of the spouse from a previous relationship, or two children born within the new marriage being siblings with the children of the spouse from a previous relationship also living in the household. Thus, HS in remarried families were a product of one parent bringing one child into a new marriage and having another child with the new spouse. Genetically unrelated siblings (US) were a product of each parent bringing a child from a previous marriage into the new marriage but having no children together. It should be noted that all of the half-sibling pairs in the Loehlin et al. (2003) study were maternal – a mother brought a child into a new marriage, and then had a child with the new husband.

The measures used in this research included the following six characteristic features of adolescent adjustment (Reiss, Neiderhiser, Hetherington, & Plomin, 2000): antisocial behavior (e.g., got into trouble at school, mean to others), autonomy (e.g., initiated activities, independently pursued leisure and work activities), cognitive agency (e.g., grades in several areas), depressive symptoms (e.g., felt depressed or sad during past three months), sociability (e.g., number of friends, activities in social organizations), and social responsibility (e.g., adherences to social norms, helping and sharing behavior). Ratings along the six measures of adolescent adjustment were obtained for each of the two adolescent members of the family. The data were gathered by 37 interview teams trained and supervised by a nationally represented survey

Table 8.1 Ratings on Six Dimensions of Adolescent Adjustment

Dimension	MZ	DZ	SI	SR	HS	US	h^2
Antisocial behavior	.81	.65	.46	.46	.47	.30	.58
Autonomy	.87	.73	.51	.68	.38	.60	.41
Cognitive agency	.87	.39	.35	.19	.23	.07	.86
Depression symptoms	.65	.25	.15	.24	.29	.27	.69
Sociability	.87	.74	.55	.53	.52	.35	.56
Social responsibility	.90	.63	.52	.35	.48	.27	.73
Mean correlation	.82	.57	.42	.40	.40	.31	
Number of pairs*	88–93	92–99	87–95	165–182	94–109	119–130	

Note. *Due to missing data, the number of pairs varies across the different sibling constellation. From Loehlin et al. (2003).

organization. The ratings included those provided by both the mother and the father and self-reported ratings by the adolescents.

According to the composite ratings of similarity for the six different sibling groups along the six dimensions of adolescent adjustment in Table 8.1, MZ twins, who share both genes and family environment, were always the most alike when compared to the other sibling groups for each of the six dimensions of adolescent adjustment. In addition, at an average of $r = .82$, the magnitude of their correlations was rather high and, with the exception of the depressive symptoms, displayed a high degree of similarity, all in the $rs = .80s$ and .90s. At the other end, the unrelated siblings (US) displayed the lowest degree of similarity. Their ratings were the lowest on four of the six dimensions, their average $r = .31$ being the lowest, and demonstrated the largest variability in their range of correlations – $rs = .07$ to .60. Consistent with much of the other research described in this section, the tendency of DZ twins to be less similar than MZ twins suggests the impact of genetics. The tendency for full siblings (SI and SR) to be less similar than DZ twins suggests the influence of environmental effects, since these two groups should be genetically similar, with similar environmental experiences. The tendency for full siblings and half siblings (HS) to not be very different – similar average $rs = .40$ and a similar range of variability – also suggests the influence of genetic factors inherited from the same mother. Finally, the index of heritability for each of the six dimensions of adolescent adjustments – hs ranging from .41 to .86 – also suggests a strong genetic influence. Such research is both interesting and important because it allows us to examine the consistency of the genetic influence across several characteristics on a

basic process of personality within the environmental context of a variety of intact and reconstructed family constellations.

As we have seen, a genetic component influences a number of personality characteristics. Other personality characteristics that seem to exhibit a genetic component are listed in Table 8.2. For a look at some recent behavior genetics research attempting to assess the genetic and environmental influences on religiousness, see "At the Cutting Edge" on p. 337.

Table 8.2 Summary of Correlations for Various Personality Dimensions in Identical Twins Reared Apart, Arranged by Strength of Correlation

Dimension	Correlation
Absorption (imagination)	.74
Stress reaction (neuroticism)	.70
Aggression	.67
Alienation	.59
Traditionalism (tendency to follow rules and authority)	.59
Social potency (a leader desiring to be the center of attention)	.57
Control (cautious, sensible)	.56
Sense of well-being	.49
Harm avoidance (takes low risks)	.45
Achievement (hard working, seeks mastery)	.38
Social closeness (intimate)	.15
Average	.54

Note. *Analyses of these data based on model-fitting techniques indicate 50 percent of the variability can be accounted for by inheritability. Adapted from Tellegen et al. (1988).

AT THE CUTTING EDGE

The Mixing of Genetics and Religion

Estimating the Genetic and Environmental Influences on Religiousness Over Time: Replication and Reconciliation

Conventional wisdom suggests that religion and politics should not be mixed. A similar argument might be made regarding the mixing of genetics and religion. However, that is just what Laura B. Koening, Matt McGue, Robert F. Krueger, and Thomas J. Bouchard, Jr. (2005) of the University of Minnesota-Twin Cities did as they investigated the genetic and environmental influences on religiousness. Previous research investigating the heritability of religiousness has yielded conflicting results, with some finding support for heritability (Bouchard et al., 2004) and others finding little support for it (Abrahamson, Baker, & Caspi, 2002). In attempting to reconcile such contradictory findings, Koening et al. suggested that age might be a moderating factor. In other words, the influence of genetic and environmental influences on religiousness might vary throughout the life span.

To test their idea, they obtained a sample of 169 MZ and 104 DZ male twins from the Minnesota Twin Registry. Average age of the study participants was 33 years. The general measure of religiousness consisted of nine items that respondents answered on a frequency-of-response scale that included "yes-no" and "never, weekly, daily, always, and don't know" options, depending on the item. In addition to an overall measure of religiousness, the nine items were also divided into two subscales: internal and external religiousness. The internal religiousness subscale contained five items: frequency of seeking guidance, help, or forgiveness through prayer; frequency of reading scripture or other religious material; frequency of deciding moral "dos" and "don'ts" for religious reasons; having friends with similar beliefs; and importance of religious faith in daily life. The internal religiousness subscale was designed to assess private aspects of religiousness that were assumed to be most susceptible to genetic/

heritable influences (e.g., personal dispositions). The external religiousness subscale contained four items: frequency of attending religious services; frequency of reviewing/discussing religious teachings with family; frequency of observing religious holidays; and membership in religious youth or study groups. The external religiousness subscale was designed to assess external/public aspects of religiousness that were assumed to be most susceptible to environmental influences (e.g., family religious practices).

Another novel element of this research was the nature of ratings provided by the twins. For each of the items on the religiousness scale, the twins provided current and retrospective ratings for themselves and their twin. The current ratings involved the individuals providing a set of ratings for themselves and their twin on their present (i.e., adult) views in response to the nine items. The retrospective ratings involved the individuals providing a set of ratings for themselves and their twin according to their past (i.e., when the individual/twin was young) views in response to the nine items. Thus, each individual provided four sets of ratings: current-self, current-twin, retrospective-self, and retrospective-twin ratings. It was assumed that by obtaining the retrospective and current ratings, it would be possible to examine the genetic and environmental influences on religiousness across time as moderated by age.

The retrospective rating of religiousness for the MZ pairs ($r = .69$) was similar to that of the DZ pairs ($r = .59$). On the other hand, the current rating religiousness for the MZ pairs ($r = .62$) was greater than that of the DZ pairs ($r = .42$). The similarity of both twin groups for the retrospective ratings of religiousness suggests low genetic and high environmental influences when the twins were young. However, when they got older, a larger genetic influence is indicated by the increased difference in the correlations. The pattern of results also suggests that while the MZ twins maintained a similarity over time ($rs = .69$ vs. .62), suggesting a genetic influence for the stability, the DZ twins became more dissimilar ($rs = .59$ vs. .42), suggesting environmental influences. Finally, estimates of the amount of variance accounted for in the ratings suggest a genetic influence accounting for more variance in the current ratings ($r = .44$) than in the retrospective ratings ($r = .12$) on religiousness. On the other hand, estimates suggest a greater shared environmental influence (e.g., similar family experiences) accounting for more variance in the retrospective ratings ($r = .56$) than in the current ratings ($r = .18$). The amount of variance accounted for by nonshared environmental factors (e.g., dissimilar experiences, along with measurement error) was very similar for both the retrospective ($r = .32$) and current ($r = .38$) ratings. Taken together, such a pattern of results indicates that there is a genetic contribution to religiousness that seems to express itself more strongly over time, while the environmental influence tends to have its greatest impact during youth and weakens over time.

We can get a further look at the genetic contribution to religiousness over time by examining the internal and external religiousness subscales. With respect to estimates of the amount of variance accounted for by genetic and shared environmental influences, the amount of variance accounted for by a genetic influence was greater for both the current internal ($r = .34$) and external ($r = .39$) subscale ratings of religiousness than for the retrospective internal ($r = .20$) and external ($r = .08$) subscale ratings. On the other hand, the amount of variance accounted for by the shared environmental influence was higher for the retrospective internal ($r = .44$) and external ($r = .53$) subscale ratings of religiousness than for the current internal ($r = .24$) and external ($r = .18$) subscale ratings. The degree of variance accounted for by the nonshared environmental influences was similar for both the current internal ($r = .42$) and external ($r = .43$) subscale ratings and for retrospective internal ($r = .36$) and external ($r = .39$) subscale ratings, suggesting that the impact of these factors is similar and does not change over time. Such a pattern of results suggests that the expression of religiousness during youth is more subject to influence by such environmental factors as the religious practices of one's parents and siblings, particularly with respect to the external expressions of religiousness (e.g., frequency of church attendance, discussions of religious teachings with family, and observations of religious holidays). However, as one gets older and moves away from the influence of parents and family, there is more of a genetic, internalized expression of one's religiousness (e.g., importance of religious faith in daily life, frequency of deciding moral "dos" and "don'ts" for religious reasons) that is less influenced by external influences.

Replicating and Rectifying the Results on Religiousness and Genetic and Environmental Influences

This research by Koening and her colleagues is critical for a number of reasons. First, it not only replicates previous research documenting the genetic contribution to religiousness, it also helps to rectify the conflicting results of previous research by demonstrating that this genetic influence is mediated by an age factor. Such findings imply that the increased influence of heritability on an individual's overall expression of religiousness may represent an increased importance of individual dispositional factors and a decreased importance of external factors over time. Specifically, these findings are consistent with the idea that important developmental changes begin to take place around the time adolescents leave the family environment (e.g., go away to college, enter military service, relocate for a job or personal adventure). During such periods of developmental transition, parents' influence (i.e., environmental factors) begins to weaken, as they can no longer monitor the child's behavior as in the past. For example, while growing up, children may not have much choice with regard to attending church, celebrating religious holidays, or discussing religious teachings with family members. However, when leaving home, individuals begin to decide for themselves the degree to which religion will be an important component of their lives.

Support for such reasoning is provided by the results for the internal and external subscale ratings of religiousness. The results for the external subscale, which represent more overt expressions of religiousness and are believed to be influenced to a greater degree by parents or other individuals, seem to exhibit more of an environmental influence and less of a genetic influence, particularly for the retrospective ratings for an individual's early years. On the other hand, the results for the internal subscale, which represent more individualized and deeper expressions of religiousness and are believed to be influenced to a greater degree by personal dispositions, seem to exhibit more of a genetic influence and less of an environmental influence, particularly with the passage of time. As the individual moves away from family influences, the personal, deeper aspects of their religiousness are expressed.

Although these results help us understand the extent to which genetic and environmental influences impact private and public aspects of religiousness over time, there are a few limitations to this research. First, because this included only male twins, additional research should include male and female participants. In addition, there are certain problems with using retrospective ratings due to potential memory and perceptual biases of the raters. Future research should attempt to replicate this research by looking at the religiousness ratings of the same sets of twins across time to reduce these potential biases.

This concludes our discussion of the behavioral genetics viewpoint of personality. If you would like to read more on the topics of behavior genetics, two books to consider are *Behavioral Genetics* (Plomin et al., 2001) and *Behavior Genetic Principles: Development, Personality, and Psychopathology* (DiLalla, 2004). In the next section, we will consider the psychophysiological perspective by looking at the operation of neurological activity and brain functioning as contributing factors in the expression of personality.

The Psychophysiological Perspective: Neurological and Cortical Considerations in the Study of Personality

The psychophysiological perspective attempts to investigate the extent to which underlying neurological activity and brain structures can help explain individual differences in personality. We begin by examining some of the techniques used in the assessment of these physiological processes and conclude by discussing examples of specific personality theories based on these physiological processes as well as the utilization of these assessment techniques.

Psychophysiological Assessment: Measuring Physiological Processes of Personality

Although a number of methods assess physiological processes in the study of personality (Eysenck, 1990a; Matthews, Deary, & Whiteman, 2003; Stern, Ray, & Quigley, 2001; Zuckerman, 2005), we will focus on the assessment of brain activity, bodily processes, and biochemical activity.

Assessment of Brain Activity: Getting Inside Your Head

Personality psychologists assess brain activity to examine which areas and structures of the brain are involved with various aspects of personality (see pp. 63–65). In so doing they record electricity in the brain and measure the rate of brain cell metabolism.

As the brain functions, it generates electrical activity that can be recorded by means of electrodes attached to a person's scalp with special adhesives that are painlessly removed when the recording is done. Researchers compare differences in the amount of recorded activity from the outer layer of the brain, as measured by electrodes placed at different scalp locations. As a particular area of the brain becomes more alert, active, and aroused, it generates an increased amount of electrical activity. The device that measures it is referred to as an **electroencephalograph** (EEG). Personality researchers might use EEG recordings to compare levels of brain arousal in nervous and less-nervous individuals. This information might help explain why the former prefer to avoid situations where there is a lot of noise. Similarly, personality researchers investigating the sensation-seeking personality might examine the degree to which one side of the brain is more active than the other in individuals whose behavior is characterized by the taking of many risks.

Another index of brain activity is the rate at which the brain metabolizes (i.e., breaks down) various energy-providing substances (e.g., sugar, oxygen). **Positron**

emission tomography (**PET**) is a diagnostic imaging tool that measures brain activity by assessing the rate of metabolism of brain cells in response to various forms of stimulation. With the PET technique, the individual is asked to inhale a non-toxic radioactive glucose (i.e., sugar-based) tracer substance that is taken in and used by brain cells when they are activated. As the cells in the individual's brain become more active, the rate at which the tracer substance is taken in and used increases. When the individual's head is placed in a scanning device, the location and rate of brain cell activity are visualized and a digital image of the brain is recreated that highlights those areas associated with increased activity in response to various forms of stimulation. For example, a PET scan might reveal that aggressive individuals display less activity in the part of the brain that is associated with higher-level reasoning. This finding might help explain why they tend to fight in the face of conflict instead of trying to reason and compromise.

Similar to the PET scan is the **functional magnetic resonance imaging** (**fMRI**) technique. A principal difference from the PET scan is the lack of use of the tracer substance. The fMRI assesses the degree of brain activity by measuring the rate of blood oxygen flow in brain cells, which increases as the cells become more active. With the fMRI, the individual's head is placed in a scanning device that measures the location and rate of blood oxygen flow and recreates a digital image of the brain on a computer screen, highlighting in different colors those areas associated with increased oxygen flow in response to various forms of stimulation. To try to understand the differences in the way happy and unhappy people cope with adversity, a personality researcher might use the fMRI technique to identify the location of those particular brain structures that are most active in happy people when confronted by stressful stimuli, as a means of trying to understand how they cope with adversity differently from unhappy people.

Assessment of Bodily Responses: Getting Under Your Skin

Another category of psychophysiological assessment is the measurement of responses associated with the autonomic nervous system (see p. 62). The **autonomic nervous system** (**ANS**) coordinates and regulates bodily responses to heightened emotional situations, regardless of whether the emotional state is positive or negative. For example, when you see an attractive or threatening person, your heart begins to pound, your muscles

tense up, and you start to perspire. All of these reactions are triggered by your ANS to help you deal with the heightened emotional situation. Personality psychologists utilize a number of measures associated with the ANS. One measure of ANS response is changes in heart rate assessed in response to a particular stimulus or to the average rate over a period of time. For example, a researcher studying shyness might investigate the changes in heart rate of shy and nonshy individuals as they are waiting to meet someone they previously identified as being attractive. Or a researcher developing a personality profile associated with coronary risk might instruct study participants to record their heart rate for 90 days with a portable, handheld monitor to determine what factors can predict elevated average heart rate and subsequent coronary difficulties.

The **electromyograph** (**EMG**) measures electrical activity associated with the tensing of muscles in response to various forms of stimulation. As with the EEG, the EMG involves placing electrodes on the skin to measure the degree of electrical activity even when no observable movement (e.g., raising a finger or bending an arm) is apparent. For example, a personality psychologist studying self-consciousness might place electrodes on the upper arm, forehead, and below the eyes of individuals who are high or low on the trait of self-consciousness while they are asked to imagine giving a speech in front of a large audience. In this way, degree of muscle tension could be assessed as a means of measuring stress reactions to being evaluated in public.

Electrodermal activity (**EDA**), another measure involving electrodes, allows researchers to determine electrical activity on the surface of the skin as affected by the trace amount of moisture (i.e., perspiration) resulting from activation of the sweat glands in response to emotional arousal. With EDA, electrodes are placed on the middle joint of the index and ring fingers and at the base of the palm near the extreme points of the wrist, because of the increased concentration of sweat glands in these locations. The increase in moisture in response to emotional arousal serves to reduce electrical activity on the skin. For example, as part of some additional research on self-consciousness, investigators might want to assess participants' stress reaction to watching others being evaluated during a public performance. In this research, the investigators might place electrodes on the fingers and palms of another group of high- and low-self-conscious individuals while they are asked to view a video of others giving a speech to a large audience. In this way, the participants' level of skin perspiration could be assessed as a means of measuring stress reactions to watching others being evaluated in public.

Pupil dilation is also used to determine ANS response. The **pupil**, which is the dark disk in the center of the eye that changes size to control the amount of light entering, helps us see more clearly. As part of the **pupil reflex**, the pupil contracts or expands as the amount of light decreases or increases, respectively. It also changes size in response to emotional arousal so as to increase the visibility of the emotionally triggering stimulus (e.g., a picture of a loved one or the image of an enemy). With **pupillography**, or the measurement of changes in the pupil, a videotape is made of the face of an individual while being presented with various stimuli (e.g., nudes, landscapes, scary snakes) under a consistent level of illumination. Changes in pupil size in reaction to the different stimuli are then analyzed by electronically measuring the videotaped images. For example, in attempting to validate scales measuring masculinity and femininity, an investigator might predict a positive correlation between masculinity scores and pupil dilation in response to viewing such traditional masculine stimuli as images of cars and contact sports, whereas femininity scores would be positively correlated with pupil dilation in response to viewing such traditional feminine stimuli as images of babies and kitchen appliances. Try pupillography for yourself in the "You Can Do It" feature opposite.

Assessment of Biochemical Activity: Going Beyond the Brain and the Body

Biochemical assessment involves examining various chemical substances in the brain and the body that influence thoughts, feelings, and behavior (see p. 63). This is accomplished by analyzing samples of various body fluids, including blood, urine, saliva, and cerebral spinal fluid. Neurotransmitters and hormones are among the chemical substances assessed.

Neurotransmitters are chemicals in the body used to help pass information between neurons and, eventually, to the brain and muscles. Neurotransmitters help coordinate a person's responses to external stimuli by triggering brain activity and causing muscle movement, or by reducing brain activity and inhibiting muscle movement. Imagine you are on a roller coaster. As your car ascends up the highest hill and you anticipate its impending descent, the neurotransmitter

You Can Do It

The "Eyes" Have It: Seeing Everyday Examples of Pupillography

In traditions dating back hundreds of years, people viewed the pupil of the eye as "the window of the soul," enabling merchants to determine how much customers were willing to pay for a piece of jewelry or livestock by "looking them in the eye." With pupil dilation considered an index of customer interest in the item and with larger pupils indicating greater interest, merchants would, consequently, set a higher asking price and be less willing to negotiate (Stern et al., 2001).

To discover how easily the pupil reflex is triggered, go into your bathroom, get in front of a mirror, turn off the lights, and close the blinds. It should be as dark as you can possibly make it. Now, while staring into the mirror, turn the light on. You will see your pupils get smaller "right before your eyes."

As a simple demonstration of the reactivity of pupil size in response to emotional arousal, get a few different types of magazines, such as ones on gardening, fashion, sports, and celebrity. While standing about an arm's length away, show a few friends the set of different magazine covers, making sure to vary the order of presentation for each friend. Look each person in the eye. Do you notice a change in the size of their pupils while staring into their eyes? Do you notice any changes in pupil size in reaction to the different magazine covers? Do you notice any certain "type" of friend responding in a particular way, such as a "sports-type" showing a strong reaction to the sports magazine cover or a "movie-type" showing a heightened response to seeing a highly attractive celebrity on the cover? Now, explain what you were doing and why. Finally, ask them to show the magazines to you while they look into your eyes. Discuss your reactions.

Do your results suggest that the pupil is "the window of the soul"? To conceal your desire and excitement, will you now begin to wear sunglasses when going to the mall, the appliance store, or the car dealership, or while playing poker?

Summing It Up *Techniques of Psychophysiological Assessment*

Technique	Example
Assessment of Brain Activity. The measurement of reactions in the brain to stimulation	
Electroencephalograph (EEG). The surface recording of electrical activity of areas of the brain following sensory stimulation	Surface EEG electrodes are attached to the upper front portion of the scalp to assess the electrical activity of the frontal portion of the brain and correlate the amount of activity in that region with scores on a 30-item personality inventory measuring impulsivity.
Positron Emission Tomography (PET). The measurement of the rate at which brain cells in a certain area utilize energy in response to various forms of sensory stimulation or mental activity	Personality researchers studying stress in military recruits record computerized images of PET measurements in response to decision making while under stress, to determine the difference in the brain cell activity of those individuals who score high or low on a leadership ability inventory.
Functional Magnetic Resonance Imaging (fMRI). The measurement of blood oxygen flow in various parts of the brain in response to various forms of sensory stimulation or mental activity	Personality researchers studying the reaction of highly competitive individuals compare fMRI recordings of these individuals while they are engaged in a chess game to examine how their brains react differently when they are winning or losing.
Assessment of Bodily Responses. The measurement of reactions associated with the autonomic nervous system	
Electromyography (EMG). The surface recording of electrical activity in muscles in response to sensory stimulation or mental activity	A researcher obtains EMG recordings of individuals with high and low self-esteem to assess their emotional reaction to receiving either positive or negative feedback.
Electrodermal Activity (EDA). The surface recording of electrical activity on the skin as expressed by trace amounts of moisture (i.e., perspiration)	A researcher assesses the EDA of individuals with high and low test anxiety in response to being given immediate feedback about whether they got each question right or wrong on a test.
Pupillography. The measurement of changes in the size of the pupil in response to various stimuli	To study the how males and females might respond differently to sexually explicit photographs, a researcher measures changes in pupil size in response to the photographs.
Assessment of Biochemical Activity. The measurement of chemical substances within the body and the brain in response to stimulation	
Neurotransmitters. The measurement of certain chemicals (e.g., acetylcholine and serotonin) released into the body to facilitate the operation of neurons	To study the biological basis of shyness, a researcher compares the level of serotonin in socially active and withdrawn children at 2 years, 5 years, and 7 years of age.
Hormonal Production. The measurement of certain hormones (e.g., testosterone and cortisol) released into the body in response to external stimuli and emotional reactions	A criminologist compares the level of testosterone for individuals convicted of violent crimes with those convicted of nonviolent crimes.

acetylcholine is released. Neurons tell your brain to be more attentive and your muscles to get ready to hold on tight. On the other hand, the neurotransmitter **serotonin** is related to brain activity that serves to put the brakes on behavior. Now imagine you are standing in line waiting to buy a ticket on the very scariest roller coaster. Suddenly you hear the screams of others on the ride. Quite possibly, your resolve to go on the ride and behaviors related to getting in the line (e.g., taking money out of your jacket to buy a ticket) may be inhibited by a boost of serotonin. To test the role of serotonin, a researcher investigating the personality trait of impulsivity might analyze the blood samples of participants to test the hypothesis that highly impulsive individuals have lower levels of serotonin than do less impulsive individuals.

Hormonal production refers to the release of various hormones into the nervous system in response to internal (e.g., increased heart rate) and external (e.g., sight of a threatening animal) stimuli. Among these hormones are testosterone and cortisol. In addition to its role during puberty in the development of such sex-linked masculine characteristics as body hair and lowering of the voice, release of **testosterone** is associated with heightened levels of aggressiveness both in males and in females. A researcher who is studying the relationship between aggressiveness and road rage might find that individuals with higher levels of testosterone in their saliva perceive everyday encounters, such as being cut off in traffic or tailgated, as a personal threat deserving of an aggressive response, such as yelling, honking the horn, or making threatening remarks. The hormone **cortisol** is released into the bloodstream in reaction to physical or psychological stress. For example, while studying at a nearby emergency center how well residents are coping with devastation caused by a recent hurricane, a researcher might find that individuals scoring the lowest on the personality measure of hardiness (e.g., the ability to respond well and recover from stressful situations) tended to have the highest levels of cortisol in their blood sample taken as part of the standard emergency evaluation for all individuals coming to the center.

A summary of the main points noted in this section are presented in "Summing It Up: Techniques of Psychophysiological Assessment" on p. 342. More information on these and other measures of psychophysiological assessment can be found in a book titled *Psychophysiological recording* (Stern et al., 2001). Next, we will illustrate how these physiological responses have been linked to the study of major dimensions of personality involving psychophysiological processes and cortical functioning, by examining Marvin Zuckerman's research on the personality dimension of sensation seeking, work based on Eysenck's dimension of extraversion–introversion, and the investigation of the personality dimensions of impulsivity and anxiety based on Jeffrey A. Gray's reinforcement sensitivity theory.

The Study of the Sensation-Seeking Personality: Seeking the Psychophysiological Bases of Thrill Seekers

Why do some people enjoy skydiving or driving fast cars, while others are more content to visit a museum? In this section, we will attempt to answer these questions by considering the psychophysiological basis of the sensation-seeking personality.

Defining the Sensation-Seeking Personality: The Specification of Thrill Seekers

For over 30 years, Marvin Zuckerman of the University of Delaware has been investigating the personality dimension of sensation seeking. As a trait of personality, **sensation seeking** is "defined by the need for varied, novel, and complex sensations and experiences and the willingness to take physical and social risks for the sake of such experience" (Zuckerman, 1979, p. 10). From this perspective, sensation seeking is not merely the search for stimulation but, rather, the achievement of unique and powerful internal sensory experiences as critical sources of arousal. For example, although watching television can stimulate your eyes and ears, you are not very likely to achieve any unique and powerful emotional sensation, since most of what is shown on television is rather similar (e.g., all detective shows are about the same). On the other hand, driving a car at 80 miles per hour with your eyes closed produces little external stimulation but a tremendous degree of internal stimulation owing to the risk and danger involved. This comparison points out that the decision to seek a very powerful level of internal sensation is a critical component of sensation seeking. Thus, sensation seeking can be considered the active search for experiences designed to produce unique and powerful internal sensations.

Marvin Zuckerman's study of the sensation-seeking personality has made a significant contribution to our understanding of the biological processes underlining personality.

The Sensation Seeking Scale: Assessing the Sensation-Seeking Personality

In investigating this dimension of personality, Zuckerman developed the **Sensation Seeking Scale** (**SSS**) for the purpose of assessing the degree to which people possess the trait of sensation seeking (Arnaut, 2006; Zuckerman, 1971). In its latest version, the SSS consists of 40 items arranged in a two-option, forced-choice format. The items are divided so that 10 of each are classified as falling into one of the four subscales: Thrill and Adventure Seeking, Experience Seeking, Disinhibition, and Boredom Susceptibility (Zuckerman, 1983, 2005).

- The *Thrill and Adventure Seeking* subscale measures the extent to which the individual expresses a desire to engage in activities of a physical nature involving speed, danger, novelty, and defiance of gravity (e.g., riding a motorcycle, parachuting, bungee jumping, or hang gliding).

You Can Do It

Are You A Thrill Seeker? Assessing Your Sensation-Seeking Tendency

To what extent are you a thrill seeker who shares a personality similar to the likes of such fictional characters as super-spy James Bond and tomb-raiding Lara Croft, or real-life individuals such as skateboarding daredevil Tony Hawk or famous Indy car driver Danica Patrick? Answer A or B for each of the six items listed below.

1. A. My preference would be for a job requiring a lot of travel.
   B. My preference would be for a job that required me to work in one location.
2. A. I would prefer to be indoors on a cold day.
   B. I am energized by being outdoors on a brisk, cold day.
3. A. Being a mountain climber is a frequent wish of mine.
   B. People who risk their necks climbing mountains are individuals I just can't understand.
4. A. I find body odors unpleasant.
   B. I find some of the earthy body smells pleasant.
5. A. Seeing the same old faces is something that bores me.
   B. I find comfort in the familiarity of everyday friends.
6. A. My preference would be to live in an ideal society where safety, security, and happiness are experienced by everybody.
   B. My preference would be to live in the unsettled days of our history.

Scoring

Each time your response agrees with the following answers, give yourself one point: 1–A, 2–B, 3–A, 4–B, 5–A, and 6–B. The higher your score, the more your responses reflect a tendency for sensation seeking. Please note that since only a very limited number of items were presented, these results are not meant to be an actual measure of sensation seeking.

Note. Adapted from Zuckerman (1971, 1979).

- The *Experience Seeking* subscale measures the extent to which the individual expresses a desire to engage in activities designed to produce novel experiences through travel, music, art, meeting unusual people, or following alternative lifestyles with other similar people (e.g., going to a nudist colony, taking mind-altering drugs, or listening to avant-garde music).

- The *Disinhibition* subscale measures the extent to which the individual seeks release through uninhibited social activities with or without the aid of alcohol (e.g., going to parties, sexual promiscuity, or high-stakes gambling).

- The *Boredom Susceptibility* subscale measures the extent to which the individual expresses displeasure at routine activities, repetitive experiences, and predictable people (e.g., an aversion to attending another company social function or seeing the same movie twice).

The presence of these four factors has also been identified in cross-cultural research using a Chinese sample (Wang et al., 2000). In addition to a score on the four separate subscales, a general measure of sensation seeking is obtained from the SSS by combining scores from the four subscales. Get a feel for your own level of sensation seeking by reading "You Can Do It" on p. 344.

Behavioral and Psychophysiological Correlates of Sensation Seeking: The Behavior and Body of Thrill Seekers

In this section, we will consider the behavior differences of high and low sensation seekers and the underlying physiological processes associated with these differences.

Behavioral Correlates of Sensation Seeking: What Sensation Seekers Do   High sensation seekers tend to engage in behavior involving greater risk and stimulation than that engaged in by low sensation seekers (Arnuat, 2006), and this tendency replicates across different cultures (Ang & Woo, 2003). For example, high sensation seekers tend to engage in physically dangerous activities – such as parachuting, motorcycle riding, scuba diving, and firefighting – to a greater degree than do low sensation seekers (Jack & Ronan, 1998; Zuckerman, Buchsbaum, & Murphy, 1980). On the road, high sensation seekers are more likely to drive while intoxicated and to break other traffic laws (e.g., by unsafe passing, not wearing a seatbelt, or speeding; Jonah, 1997; Jonah, Thiessen, & Au-Yeung, 2001). High

sensation seekers report participation in a greater variety of sexual activities with a greater number of partners at a younger age than do low sensation seeking individuals (Bratko & Butkovic, 2003; Raffaelli & Crockett, 2003; Zuckerman, 1979). High sensation-seeking scores are also associated with greater drug usage, gambling, and financial risk-taking behavior (McDaniel & Zuckerman, 2003; Wong & Carducci, 1991; Zuckerman, 1979). High sensation seekers also tend to be attracted to professions involving relatively high risks, such as crisis intervention worker, rape counselor, air traffic controller, police officer, psychologist, and other positions within the helping professions (Zuckerman, 1979). On the other hand, low sensation seekers are more likely to prefer somewhat less risky occupations, such as pediatric nurse, accountant, pharmacist, banker, or mortician. As you can see from even this relatively short list of the behavioral correlates of sensation seeking, high sensation seekers might be described as "living in the fast lane."

Psychophysiological Correlates of Sensation Seeking: Cortical and Neurological Activity of Sensation Seekers   In addition to the distinct behavioral differences between high and low sensation seekers, there is considerable evidence that high and low sensation seekers differ in their psychophysiological responses as well (Zuckerman, 2005). Some of the psychophysiological correlates of sensation seeking include brain functioning, neurotransmitters, and hormones.

CORRELATES OF BRAIN FUNCTIONING   When high sensation seekers are presented with a stimulus for the first time, they tend to respond with more brain activity than do low sensation seekers, but no differences are displayed between the two groups as the stimulation is repeated (Zuckerman, 2005). For example, when examining the orienting reflex to novel auditory and visual stimuli, researchers found that high sensation seekers respond with a greater degree of surface skin moisture (i.e., perspiration) than do low sensation seekers (Neary & Zuckerman, 1976; Zuckerman, 1989), although they found no difference in habituation to the stimuli. This suggests that while high sensation seekers initially become excited by exposure to a novel stimulus, they tend to get bored in a manner similar to that characteristic of low sensation seekers. In such situations, high sensation seekers might need to seek additional novel stimulation to a greater degree than do low sensation seekers. For example, high sensation seekers might be more likely to fall "head over heels" for someone right away, but as these feelings begin to level off, they might seek a new partner sooner than might low sensation seekers.

The search for an optimal level of arousal refers primarily to cortical arousal (i.e., the amount of electrical activity in the brain). Examination of the degree of cortical arousal seems to suggest that people respond with a style of **augmentation** (i.e., increasing their level of arousal) or reduction (i.e., reducing their level of arousal) to novel stimulation. Although the general level of sensation seeking is significantly correlated with cortical arousal (Brocke, Beauducel, John, Debener, & Heilemann, 2000; Zuckerman, Simons, & Como, 1988), the relationship seems to be strongest for people scoring high on the Disinhibition subscale of the SSS, who tend to respond to novel stimulation with a pattern of augmentation (Zuckerman, 1979, 1990). Recall that the Disinhibition subscale measures the extent to which people seek release through uninhibited social activities, such as dancing, going to concerts, or listening to loud music. For high sensation-seekers, such activities might be seen as a source of pleasure or enjoyment simply because they provide an increase in sensory arousal (Zuckerman, 2005). From this research on cortical arousal, it is clear that the basis of such uninhibited behavior might be the high levels of stimulation it provides, and that this desire for an increased level of stimulation may stem from the particular way the brains of high sensation seekers function – requiring more arousal. It is as if the brains of high sensation seekers require more stimulation to keep them stratified (i.e., maintain an increased level of contical arousal) and will direct these individuals to action to seek this level of satisfaction.

Correlates of neurotransmitters   A neurotransmitter found to be consistently related to sensation seeking is **monoamine oxidase (MAO)** (Zuckerman, 2005; Zuckerman et al., 1980). The basic function of MAO is to prevent other neurotransmitters responsible for initiating behaviors (e.g., moving your legs while running) from being released into the body. Thus, high levels of MAO would be associated with an inactive individual. Consistent with this reasoning, high sensation-seeking scores have been found to be negatively correlated with MAO level (Schooler, Zahn, Murphy, & Buchsbaum, 1978; Zuckerman, 1994; Zuckerman, Ballinger, & Post, 1984). Thus, it is possible that this low level of MAO in high sensation seekers makes it possible to maintain a higher level of

activity, as compared with individuals whose level of activity is reduced by the disinhibitive effects of MAO. That is to say, the tendency of high sensation seekers to engage in high-risk activities (e.g., drug use, gambling, extensive sexual behavior, reckless driving) may be due more to their inability to "put the brakes" on such behavior, as a result of MOA deficiency in their neurotransmitter system, than to a desire to seek excessive stimulation (Zuckerman, 1991).

Other neurotransmitters linked to sensation seeking include dopamine and serotonin (Zuckerman, 2005). **Dopamine** helps the brain control body movements. It is also involved in brain systems associated with responding to rewards and the motivation to approach attractive objects and people. Inappropriate utilization of dopamine by the brain can lead to **reward deficiency syndrome**, which is characterized by such outcomes as alcoholism, drug abuse, and pathological gambling (Blum, Cull, Braverman, & Comings, 1996). High sensation seekers tend to exhibit increased reactivity to dopamine-related stimulants, such as nicotine and amphetamines (e.g., excitatory drugs), suggesting a low level of dopamine in their neurological system (Zuckerman, 2005). It possible that sensation seekers tend to engage in such high-risk behaviors as gambling, drug use, smoking, drinking, and increased sexual activity as a way to seek rewards and pleasures to compensate for the low level of dopamine in their system. Serotonin, like MAO, is an inhibitory neurotransmitter responsible for putting the brakes on behavior, and, as you might expect, low levels of it are associated with high sensation seeking individuals.

Correlates of hormones   Testosterone is the hormone most often associated with sensation seeking (Zuckerman, 2005). On a positive note, increased testosterone is related to the expression of sociability, activity, and assertiveness (Daitzman & Zuckerman, 1980). On the negative side, it is associated with such tendencies as antisocial behavior, aggressiveness, and an increased number of sexual partners (Dabbs, 2000). When summarizing the relationship, Zuckerman (2005) notes that "high sensation seekers tend to have a very high level of testosterone whereas low sensation seekers have normal levels" (p. 198). Although not as consistently as testosterone levels, increases in the levels of the sex hormones androgen (a hormone involved in promoting growth of muscles and bones in both sexes) and estrogen (a hormone involved in regulation of the menstrual cycle) have also been linked with sensation

Summing It Up *Basic Principles of Sensation Seeking*

Principle	Example
Sensation Seeking. A desire for novel stimulation and the willingness to take risks to achieve it.	To achieve a heightened level of excitement in life, high sensation-seeking individuals are willing to tolerate more financial risk, personal discomfort, or physical injury.
Measurement of Sensation Seeking. The Sensation Seeking Scale assesses sensation-seeking tendencies along four dimensions: Thrill and Adventure Seeking, Experience Seeking, Disinhibition, and Boredom Susceptibility.	Thrill- and adventure-seeking individuals might like to drive at excessive speeds. Experience-seeking individuals might seek their thrills by eating exotic foods (e.g., insects). Disinhibited thrill seekers might seek excitement by engaging in risky social behavior (e.g., shoplifting for the fun of it). Boredom susceptibility thrill seekers might avoid routine by having 1,500 channels on their cable network and watching a variety of different shows.
Behavioral Correlates of Sensation Seeking. In comparison to low sensation seekers, the lifestyle of high sensation seekers is associated with greater risk in many vital areas of life.	High sensation seekers engage in physically dangerous activities, sexual behavior, drug use, and high-risk occupations to a greater degree than low sensation seekers.
Physiological Correlates of Sensation Seeking. High sensation seekers respond with more physiological arousal to stimulation, lower levels of monoamine oxidase and dopamine, and higher levels of testosterone than do low sensation seekers.	High sensation seekers might show a high degree of enthusiasm for a new hobby, impulsively buy lots of items in support of it (i.e., low level of monoamine oxidase), and compete more aggressively in it (i.e., high level of testosterone).

seeking (Daitzman & Zuckerman, 1980; Daitzman, Zuckerman, Sammelwitz, & Ganjam, 1978). The hormones androgen and testosterone have been found to be related to the sex drive and behavior in males and females. Although cultural factors also play a significant role, it is interesting to speculate about the role increased levels of these hormones might play in determining the intense level of emotional arousal associated with engaging in sexual behavior and high-risk activities. In addition to triggering sexual behavior and increasing the likelihood of approaching a potential partner (i.e., the influence of dopamine), it is possible that increased levels of these hormones serve to heighten the emotional experience associated with engaging in such behaviors, which would increase the likelihood that the individual will repeat them.

This concludes the discussion of the psychophysiological perspective as illustrated in the context of the personality dimension of sensation seeking. The main points in this section are presented in "Summing It Up:

Basic Principles of Sensation Seeking" above. For more information about the biological bases of sensation seeking, I recommended reading Chapter 5 in Zuckerman's (2005) *Psychobiology of Personality* and "Biosocial Bases of Sensation Seeking" (Zuckerman, 2006). In the next section, we will focus on the influence of brain structures on the expression of personality functioning.

The Study of Cortical Influences on Personality: Brain Functioning and Personality Processes

The study of cortical influences on personality focuses on the role of particular neurological structures in the brain and their impact on the expression of various aspects of personality (Matthews et al., 2003; Silvia & Warburton, 2006; Zuckerman, 2005). Two examples illustrating the relation between brain function and personality processes are the separate perspectives of Hans J. Eysenck and Jeffrey A. Gray.

Neurological Basis of Extraversion and Introversion: The Ascending Reticular Activating System and the Arousal Hypothesis

In addition to his work in classifying traits (see Chapter 7), Eysenck examined the biological bases of personality (Eysenck, 1967, 1990a). At the center of his biological perspective of personality is the neurological structure known as the ascending reticular activating system. As seen in Figure 8.5, the **ascending reticular activating system** (**ARAS**) is a collection of nerve fibers located at the base of the spinal cord and the lower portion of the brain. Its function is to help regulate the level of arousal in the brain to permit the individual to function most effectively. As indicated by the ascending arrows in Figure 8.5, brain arousal is increased when an individual is excited by music and conversation at a party or when concentrating intensely while studying for an important test. However, as indicated by the descending arrows, the brain may inform the ARAS to reduce the level of arousal under certain conditions – at bedtime, for example, when an individual is trying to fall asleep, or when being too excited interferes with the person's ability to answer questions on a test. Thus, depending on the feedback it receives from the brain, the ARAS can either increase or decrease the level of arousal.

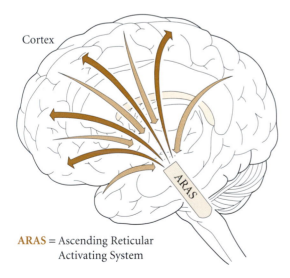

ARAS = Ascending Reticular Activating System

Figure 8.5 The location of the ARAS and the ascending and descending pathways of cortical arousal
Source: Adapted from Eysenck (1967, p. 231)

Linking Extraversion–Introversion with the ARAS through the Arousal Hypothesis

To establish a biological link with personality, Eysenck (1967) proposed that introverts have a lower threshold of arousal (or higher levels of activity) in the ARAS than do extraverts. Based on this relationship, a general formulation of the **arousal hypothesis** proposes that introverts should react with greater responsiveness than extraverts along physiological processes regulated by the ARAS. Because they are already somewhat more aroused (i.e., they have higher level of ARAS activity), introverts should react sooner and to a greater degree than extraverts to various forms of external stimulation.

Support for the Arousal Hypothesis: The Contrasting Arousal Styles of Extraverts and Introverts

There is a considerable amount of evidence to support the proposed relationship between extraversion–introversion and the ARAS formulated by the arousal hypothesis (Eysenck, 1990a; Matthews & Gilliland, 1999; Stelmack, 1990, 1997). For example, when using an EEG to measure cortical arousal, introverts exhibit more brainwave activity than do extraverts in response to stimulation (Gale, 1983; Knyazev, Slobodskaya, & Wilson, 2002). A similar pattern of results has been found using PET scans measuring cerebral blood flow (Johnson et al., 1999).

The expression of cortical arousal by introverts and extraverts seems to be influenced in a very interesting way by the level of stimulus intensity. As Figure 8.6a indicates, while introverts display a greater degree of skin conductance response (SCR) to moderately intense auditory stimulation than do extraverts, just the opposite is true at the high level of stimulus intensity (Stelmack, 1990, 1997; Wigglesworth & Smith, 1976). A similar pattern of results occurs when introverts and extraverts consume various drugs that serve as nervous system stimulants, such as caffeine (Smith, 1983) and nicotine (O'Connor, 1980, 1982; Figure 8.6b). On the other hand, because of their heightened level of arousal, introverts require a larger dose of a depressant drug (e.g., alcohol) to produce sedation effects than extraverts do (Shagass & Kerenyi, 1958). The lower level of cortical arousal found in extraverts is consistent with other research indicating that MAO levels are negatively related to extraversion (Zuckerman et al., 1984). Because

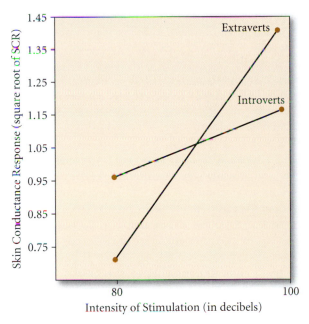

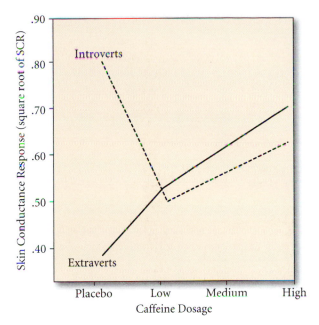

(a) Introverts respond more intensely to a moderate level of external stimulation, while extraverts respond more intensely to a high level of stimulation.

(b) The response intensity of introverts decreases as caffeine dosage increases; the opposite pattern of response occurs for extraverts.

Figure 8.6 The skin conductive response of extraverts and introverts in reaction to external auditory stimulation and caffeine
Source: Adapted from Stelmack (1990, pp. 296, 301)

a heightened level of arousal can interfere with task performance, particularly if the task is a difficult one, introverts have been observed to perform less effectively on a task of learning than do extraverts (McLaughlin & Eysenck, 1967). Finally, in addition to responding with greater intensity, introverts also tend to respond faster to external stimulation than do extraverts (Stelmack, 1985; Stelmack & Geen, 1992; Stelmack & Wilson, 1982). Such actions may represent an effort to reduce the aversive nature of excessive arousal. Thus, in support of the arousal hypothesis, extraverts and introverts appear to have contrasting styles of cortical arousal.

A Concrete Illustration of the Arousal Hypothesis: Let's Party

The preceding results provided converging evidence in support of the arousal hypothesis and the ARAS as a biological basis of the extraversion–introversion dimension. Now, as a more concrete example, consider how these results might be applied to the behavior

of introverts and extraverts at a party. In general, introverts may find parties more stressful than extraverts do. This may be because introverts' arousal level increases more quickly and to a greater degree than that of extraverts in response to the excessively stimulating music, conversation, and cigarette smoke found at many parties. This heightened reactivity may also inhibit their efforts to make conversation or think of witty things to say. To reduce such stimulus overload, introverts may leave the party early (respond faster) or avoid parties altogether (social avoidance).

Extraverts, on the other hand, may enjoy parties more because they have a greater tolerance for various sources of external stimulation (see Figure 8.6a), require less alcohol to experience reduced inhibitions (lower sedative threshold), and are predisposed to being more active owing to a generally lower MAO level. Although this explanation is only speculative, the general differences in the arousability and other corresponding biological processes can be used to help explain some of the variation in the behavior patterns exhibited by these two personality types.

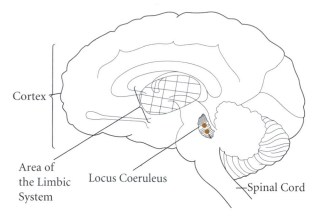

Cortex

Area of
the Limbic   Locus Coeruleus
System

Spinal Cord

Figure 8.7   This lateral view of the brain indicates the location of the locus coeruleus, limbic system, and cortex.

Reinforcement Sensitivity Theory: Cortical Links to the Push and Pull of Personality Types

Another cortical perspective focusing on the role of brain functioning in personality and personality processes is the **reinforcement sensitivity theory** of Jeffrey A. Gray (Corr, 2002; Gray, 1982, 1987, 1991, 1994a, 1994b; Gray & McNaughton, 2000). As seen in Figure 8.7, the structures involved in Gray's approach include those located in the lower, middle, and higher portions of the brain (Zuckerman, 2005). In the lower portion of the brain near the ARAS is the **locus coeruleus** (**LC**), a structure that helps to regulate an individual's sensitivity to novel stimuli or those associated with punishment (Redmond, 1985, 1987). In a sense, it operates like a warning signal that alerts an individual to avoid certain stimuli because they are associated with danger (i.e., punishment) or approach a novel stimulus with a certain degree of caution. The greater the intensity of the reaction of the LC, the more likely an individual is to approach (e.g., walk toward an attractive individual) or avoid (e.g., walk away from a verbal confrontation) a particular stimulus. In the midbrain is the **limbic system**, a collection of structures associated with emotional reactivity (e.g., pleasure and fear) and the formation, storage, and retrieval of memories linked to actions and events responsible for those emotions (e.g., remembering not to touch a hot pan on the stove). The **cortex** is part of the brain associated with higher mental functions, such as the control of motor behavior (e.g., walking, picking something up), verbal comprehension and behavior (e.g., formulating a meaningful thought and then saying it), abstract reasoning (e.g., generating or

connecting ideas), and sequential action (e.g., putting together a series of actions in a meaningful way), to name just a few.

Gray then relates these brain structures to the **Behavioral Approach System** (**BAS**) and the **Behavioral Inhibition System** (**BIS**). When activated, the BAS increases an individual's sensitivity to rewarding stimuli and helps to regulate behavior in the direction of approaching the stimuli. For example, when you hear your favorite song at a party, the BAS might involve the LC increasing your attention to the song – and the feelings and memories it triggers – above all of the other noise at the party. In this highly positive state, you begin to develop a plan of action, based on the operation of activities in the cortex, involving the following sequence: selecting someone to ask to dance (e.g., someone standing alone but moving to the music), thinking about how you are going to ask that person to dance (e.g., "You seem to be enjoying this song. It's one of my favorites, too. Would you like to dance?"), and executing the dance steps without stepping on your partner. On the other hand, an activated BIS increases an individual's sensitivity to punishing stimuli and helps to regulate behavior in the direction of the avoidance of the stimuli. For example, while walking in the mall, you see a former long-term romantic partner who terminated your relationship in a rather abrupt and unpleasant manner. In this case, the BIS might involve the LC increasing your attention to the individual and the associated unpleasant feelings and memories. In this distressed state, you begin to put together a plan of action to avoid confronting this person. This might involve locating the nearest exit and the quickest way to get there (e.g., "I need to turn around quickly and take the escalator to the next floor and go to the food court and to the exit.") or formulating an excuse to use to extract yourself from any conversation that may develop (e.g., "I'd love to talk, but I have an appointment in a few minutes. Good to see you"). Thus the BAS is like the green traffic light that signals when it is time to accelerate, while the BIS is like the red light that signals when it is time to stop.

Linking Brain Sensitivity Systems to Personality Dimensions: The Approach of Impulsive vs. the Avoidance of Anxious Individuals

In addition to outlining the two separate systems of behavioral sensitivity, Gray has also described how they are related to individual differences in personality. He and others (Corr, 2002; Gray, 1987; Pickering et al., 1997) have proposed that the BAS, which is associated with positive emotional states, is activated more easily in impulsive, extraverted individuals, while the BIS, which is associated with negative emotional states (e.g., punishment, threatening stimuli), is activated more easily in more anxious individuals. As a point of clarification of Gray's reinforcement sensitivity theory, it should be noted that he uses personality dimensions that are somewhat different from those used by Eysenck's theory. Gray's dimension of impulsivity is used to describe individuals who are high on extraversion and low on neuroticism (i.e., extraverts), while his dimension of anxiety is used to describe individuals who are high on neuroticism and low on extraversion (i.e., introverts).

Gray's conceptualization of cortical correlates of personality has received support using his own two dimensions of impulsivity and anxiety and Eysenck's two dimensions of extraversion and neuroticism, utilizing various measures of physiological arousal. For example, researchers found the brain activity of extraverts was stronger than that of introverts in association with rewarding and pleasant images (e.g., happy people), while in response to viewing negative images (e.g., upset people), brain activity was positively related to an individual's neuroticism score (Canli et al., 2001). As noted previously, extraverts, with their lower levels of cortical arousal, are more likely to seek (i.e., approach) social situations, be sensitive to and value environmental and social rewards, and experience positive feelings . Neurotic individuals, by contrast, with their generally heightened level of arousal, tend to become more easily upset by minor sources of stress, to respond with avoidance (i.e., the fight-or-flight response), and to experience negative emotions (Silvia & Warburton, 2006). Since the BAS and impulsivity are linked to the sensitivity of rewarding (e.g., pleasant) stimuli, and the BIS and anxiety are linked to the sensitivity of punishing (e.g., unpleasant) stimuli, along with the link of impulsivity with extraversion and anxiety with neuroticism, such a pattern of results provides support for Gray's perspective. More direct support comes from research by Corr (2002) indicating that high-anxiety/low-impulsive (i.e., neurotic) individuals show a stronger muscular physiological response to viewing unpleasant stimuli (e.g., mutilated bodies) than do low-anxiety/high-impulsive (i.e., extraverted) individuals.

Support for Gray's perspective has also been provided by researchers utilizing self-report measures assessing individual differences in the response strength of the BAS and BIS (Carver & White, 1994). For example, in a questionnaire designed to assess BIS functioning (e.g., fearfulness, anxiety, and risk avoidance), female mental patients with a history of anxiety-related disorders scored higher than a group of prostitutes, who were considered to be high risk takers (MacAndrew & Steele, 1991). In support of the BAS being associated with positive experiences, an individual's BAS self-report score was positively associated with the speed of learning a reward-based task but not with learning a punishment-based task (Zinbarg & Mohlman, 1998). Finally, in research looking at both BAS and BIS self-report measures, individuals with high BAS scores worked faster on a reasoning task in response to receiving rewards, while individuals with high BIS scores worked faster on the task in response to being punished (Larsen, Chen, & Zelenski, 2003). Such a collection of results suggests that BAS sensitivity is associated with positive feelings and rewards, while BIS sensitivity is associated with unpleasant feelings and punishment, in a manner consistent with those results using more direct physiological measures of BAS and BIS response sensitivity. However, some questions have been raised regarding the extent to which these two systems operate independently of each other (Carver, 2004). Additional information on Gray's perspective on the cortical process associated with the personality can be found in a book chapter titled "Jeffrey Gray's Contributions to Theories of Anxiety, Personality, and Psychopathology" (Fowles, 2006).

This concludes our discussion of the cortical perspective in the study of personality. A summary of the major points noted in this section is presented in "Summing It Up: Cortical Functioning and Personality Processes" on p. 352. For additional information comparing the perspectives of Eysenck and Gray, see an article titled "The Personality Theories of H. J. Eysenck and J. A. Gray: A Comparative Review" (Matthews & Gilliland, 1999), as well as a book chapter titled "Positive and Negative Affect: Bridging States and Traits" (Silvia & Warburton, 2006), for a discussion of other biologically oriented perspectives of personality addressing personality dimensions and emotional responses similar to those of Eysenck and Gray. In the next section, we will consider some of the applications of the biological viewpoint of personality.

Summing It Up *Cortical Functioning and Personality Processes*

Eysenck's Arousal Hypothesis	Gray's Reinforcement Sensitivity Theory
Basic Structure. The ascending reticular activating system (ARAS) helps to regulate arousal in the brain.	*Basic Structures.* The locus coeruleus (LC) controls an individual's response to stimuli associated with punishment and pleasure. The limbic system helps to regulate emotional reactivity and the processing of memories associated with such stimuli.
Basic Hypothesis. Because introverts have a higher level of arousal in the ARAS than do extraverts (e.g., more sensitive to noise at a crowded mall), they will respond with greater activity (e.g., shop faster) to reduce external arousal.	*Basic Hypotheses.* The Behavioral Approach System (BAS) controls an individual's behavior with respect to moving toward pleasurable stimuli (e.g., developing a plan to purchase a new car), while the Behavioral Inhibition System (BIS) controls an individual's behavior with respect to moving away from unpleasant or punishing stimuli (e.g., developing a course of action to avoid seeing your boss at a company party).
Basic Support for the Arousal Hypothesis. Introverts respond faster and with more cortical arousal and skin conductance to external stimulation than do extraverts.	*Basic Support for BAS and BIS Functioning.* Scores on the measure of BAS functioning are positively associated with performances on tasks involving the acquisition of rewards, while those measuring BIS functioning are associated with tasks involving the avoidance of punishment.

Applications of the Biological Viewpoint: Using What Is Known

Information from the biological viewpoint has been applied to several different important areas of contemporary life. In this section, we will consider selective applications based on the behavioral genetics and psychophysiological perspectives

Application of the Behavioral Genetics Perspective: Detection and Treatment of Genetic Dysfunction

Advances in the study of behavioral genetics have enabled scientists to assess prenatal development through the detection and treatment of disease and genetic defects in the fetus. Such early detection and treatment increase the likelihood of healthy prenatal and postnatal development. Three such prenatal approaches are genetic counseling, prenatal diagnosis, and gene therapy.

Genetic Counseling: Assessing Potential Problems Prior to a Pregnancy

Genetic counseling is designed to help couples determine the likelihood of genetic or other related biological defects in their offspring (Berk, 2006; Rathus, 2003). Genetic counselors obtain information about the couple's genetic family history, including information about diseases, birth defects, mental disorders, and causes of death of parents, siblings, grandparents, and other relatives. Sophisticated laboratory techniques evaluate the client's blood, skin tissue, urine, and sometimes fingerprints to obtain additional information about the possibility of certain diseases and genetic defects. From all of this information, the genetic counselor calculates the mathematical odds of a couple transmitting a genetic defect to their offspring. In addition to calculating genetic risks, genetic counselors also provide information to help potential parents deal more effectively with the knowledge of the potential genetic risks with a pregnancy. Counselors help dispel myths and misinformation about genetic diseases, and reduce feelings of anxiety and apprehension in a manner designed to support the decisions made by potential parents, rather than making the decisions for them (Plomin et al., 2001). If the risks of disease or genetic defect in the offspring are too high, a couple may decide to adopt children or consider artificial insemination (Berk, 2006).

Prenatal Diagnosis: Assessing Potential Problems During Pregnancy

In addition to genetic counseling before pregnancy, various medical techniques used during pregnancy can test the fetus for diseases and genetic defects (Berk, 2006; Rathus, 2003). With **amniocentesis**, at the 14th or 15th week of pregnancy a sample of amniotic fluid is obtained from the amniotic sac containing the fetus and is analyzed. With **chorionic villus sampling** (**CVS**), a small sample of tissue is taken from the placenta for analysis between the 9th and 14th week of the pregnancy. Both amniocentesis and CVS are associated with minimal risk to the fetus while testing for the potential of congenital (present before birth) defects.

In addition to permitting identification of the sex of the fetus, such techniques can assess genetic diseases and defects. These include Tay-Sachs disease (a fatal degenerative disease of the nervous system mostly afflicting Jews of Eastern European ancestry), sickle-cell anemia (a blood disorder found mostly among African-Americans), Down syndrome (a cause of mental retardation), and muscular dystrophy (a disease that produces progressive muscular deterioration), to name just a few.

Gene Therapy: Attempting Preemptive Genetic Strategies

Some of the most exciting work related to the behavioral genetics perspective is that of the Human Genome Project (HGP), an international program of research to uncover the chemical makeup of human genetic material (the genome). As part of the HGP, researchers are identifying the nature and function of the genome's chemical properties and are gathering information to improve our understanding of over 4,000 genetically related human disorders.

With this increased knowledge of the underlying properties and dynamics of the genome, paired with the ability to determine genetic risk and the presence of fetal genetic abnormalities, scientists are getting closer to correcting genetic problems in the fetus. In the emerging field of **gene therapy**, fetal genetic structures are altered through molecular manipulation (Banks, 2003; Berk, 2006; Carter & Schuchman, 2001). Examples of emerging genetic treatments include examining the genetic code of a fetus to assess the risk for a particular disease (e.g., depressive disorder), modifying the fetus's genetic code to prevent or cure certain diseases (e.g., enhance the ability of the immune system), and inserting foreign genes into the blood cells to help the body combat certain diseases (e.g., cancer). In addition to some potentially serious side effects (Relph, Harrington, & Pandha, 2004), the prospect of gene therapy has generated great controversy. Detractors contend that scientists should not be given the ability to "play God" and that genetic modification will lead to the alteration of our species in unknown and uncontrollable ways. Certainly, as efforts to develop gene therapy treatments continue, it is important that scientists continue to address the associated ethical and social concerns.

Fortunately, in 95 percent of cases in which the fetus is examined using prenatal diagnostic techniques, it is normal (Moore & Persaud, 2003). For some of the remaining cases, prenatal surgery or the injection of nutrients, vitamins, or hormones into the amniotic fluid can be used to treat genetically related diseases. For others, gene therapy holds some promise of a cure. However, some diseases have no known cure. In such cases, the parents must struggle with the decision to complete or terminate the pregnancy, raising critical ethical concerns. Among these are religious issues, the rights of the fetus to be born healthy, the rights of the parents, and the rights of society (e.g., reduce government healthcare costs by preventing birth defects).

Application of the Psychophysiological Perspective: Promoting Emotional and Occupational Satisfaction

Applications of the psychophysiological perspective focus on incorporating various biological processes to help address important personal and professional concerns. Two critical applications are the treatment of emotional problems and the examination of occupational choice and satisfaction.

Elevating Emotional Distress from the Psychophysiological Perspective: Treating Troubled Minds

An important application of the psychophysiological perspective is the treatment of emotional disorders using biological approaches. Although these biological approaches help alleviate suffering for many individuals, they are considered by some to be controversial. Such treatments of emotional disorders typically involve altering bodily processes (e.g., brain structures, neurotransmitters). Two biological treatments used in the treatment of emotional disorders are electroconvulsive therapy and psychopharmacotherapy.

Electroconvulsive Therapy: Treating Depression   One of the most controversial biologically based treatments is **electroconvulsive therapy** (**ECT**), also known as "shock" therapy. Although initially thought to be a cure for schizophrenia, as well other emotional disorders, ECT is most successful in treating certain forms of severe depression and suicidal behavior (Kring, Davison, Neale, & Johnson, 2007). An ECT session involves administering a very mild electric current of 70 to 130 volts to the forehead or temple region of the patient's head for a half second or less. This procedure produces a seizure similar to a grand-mal epileptic seizure. Prior to the session the patient receives a muscle relaxant to control the excessive movements of the body during the seizure. Moments after application of the electric current, the client is awake and remembers nothing about the treatment. Between six and twelve ECT sessions occur, with several days in between each treatment over a two- to four-week period, with a maximum of about twelve sessions within a year (Comer, 2007).

Use of ECT is controversial. Although its efficacy has been demonstrated in treating certain forms of depression and suicidal behavior (Sackeim & Lisanby, 2001), the process by which it works is unknown. One possible explanation is that the induced seizures stimulate the midbrain structures making up the reward system in the brain associated with the experience and expression of emotion (see pp. 341–343). This causes the release of certain neurotransmitters (e.g., dopamine and serotonin), elevating the client's mood, thoughts, and behavior (Depue & Iacono, 1989; Stockmeier, 2003). Another source of controversy involves the side effects of ECT. Depending on the procedure used (Sackeim & Lisanby, 2001), ECT recipients may have trouble remembering events occurring before and immediately after the treatment, although in most cases such memory loss goes after a few months (Calev et al., 1991; Calev, Gaudino, Squires, Zervas, & Fink, 1995; Glass, 2001). However, for some individuals, the effects of prolonged use of ECT may include memory loss, personality alteration, and permanent neurological changes (Rose, Wykes, Leese, Bindman, & Fleischmann, 2003; Taylor & Carroll, 1987). Because of these undesired effects and advances in the development and use of psychotropic drugs, the use of ECT has been declining since the 1950s (Comer, 2007). Today ECT is used primarily as a last resort after all other treatments have failed (Kring et al., 2007).

Psychopharmacotherapy: Mood-Altering Medications
The goal of **psychopharmacotherapy**, or the use of prescription medications as a therapeutic response to certain emotional disorders, is to restore a balance in the level of various neurotransmitters in the brain. For example, one possible biological explanation of depression is low serotonin levels (Flores et al., 2004). As was noted previously, serotonin is a neurotransmitter that helps inhibit emotional and behavioral reactions in response to threatening situations. For example, serotonin can help prevent individuals from becoming exceedingly anxious too easily (e.g., worrying too much about approaching an attractive person at a party) or overly depressed too often (e.g., becoming really sad and withdrawn each time your friends or co-workers disagree with you) in their everyday activities. To correct the imbalance in neurotransmitters, physicians frequently prescribe a class of drugs called *selective serotonin reuptake inhibitors* (*SSRIs*), which slow down the loss of serotonin in the nervous system. Among the SSRIs are Prozac (fluoxetine), Paxil (paroxetine), and Zoloft (sertraline). SSRIs can effectively treat depression while producing fewer of the potential side effects of older drugs previously used for this (Marangell, Silver, Goff, & Yudofsky, 2003). In addition, SSRIs have also been effective in individuals with generalized anxiety disorder (GAD) – pervasive and heightened feelings of anxiety not linked to a particular event. Another drug that is frequently prescribed to treat GAD is Buspar (buspirone), which tends to be slower acting – its effects taking one to three weeks to be realized but with fewer side effects (Ninan & Muntasser, 2004).

Like all medications, SSRIs have side effects. These include interference with sexual functioning, gastrointestinal complaints (e.g., constipation, diarrhea), nervousness, and headaches (Kring et al., 2007; Weiten, 2007). Such negative side effects can result in individuals stopping taking their prescribed SSRIs and, subsequently, a relapse (Herbert, 1995). A more serious concern is that SSRIs may increase the risk of suicide (Healy & Whitaker, 2003; Holden, 2004), although the results from research in this area are inconclusive (Gunnell & Ashby, 2004).

Another problem is the implication in the media that SSRIs are miracle drugs providing "quick fixes" for serious psychological problems. We have all seen television commercials portraying sad, lonely individuals who are too anxious to participate in social activities. In the next frame, the same individuals are suddenly surrounded by others and having fun, presumably after taking the prescribed medication. Although such ads may be persuasive, the fact is that while taking such drugs may provide relief from the symptoms of anxiety or depression, they do not teach the individual to solve the problems associated with such symptoms. For example, individuals may feel less anxious after taking a prescribed medication for feelings of excessive social anxiety. However, if they do not know how to approach others, start and maintain a conversation, enter into an ongoing conversation, ask someone out on a date, or behave on a date, just feeling less anxious will be of little value (Carducci, 2000). For this reason, psychopharmacotherapy is often more effective when combined with psychotherapy, in which clients gain insight into their problems and learn the cognitive skills to alter maladaptive behavior patterns. Thus, the best advice regarding such "miracle drugs" is "buyer beware."

Work and the Psychophysiological Perspective: Some Biological Contributions to Occupational Choice and Satisfaction

Next to sleeping, there is probably no single activity that people spend more time participating in than working. Certain biological dispositions are known to play a role in influencing vocational interests and job attitudes and satisfaction (Arvey, Bouchard, Segal, & Abraham, 1989; Plomin et al., 2001; Staw & Ross, 1985). For example, behavioral genetics research with monozygotic twins reared apart (average age at separation and reunion being .45 and 31.71 years, respectively) indicates "a significant genetic component to intrinsic job satisfaction as well as to general job satisfaction"

(Arvey et al., 1989, p. 190). This research also indicates that the jobs held by the twins were similar in their complexity level, motor skill requirements, and physical demands, suggesting "a genetic component in terms of the jobs that are sought and held by individuals" (Arvey et al., 1989, p. 190). When combining the evidence from twin and adoption studies, the results suggest that heredity accounts for approximately 35 percent of the variability in the expression of most vocational interests (Betsworth et al., 1994).

Testosterone level has been linked with occupational choice (Dabbs, 2000). In studies with both humans and animals, testosterone has been associated with a variety of characteristics such as dominance, aggression, persistence, and sensation seeking, to name just a few (Dabbs, 2000; Dabbs, de La Rue, & Williams, 1990; Zuckerman, 2005).

In relating testosterone to occupational choice (Dabbs, 2000), researchers have observed that women working in traditionally masculine occupations (e.g., lawyers, managers, technical workers) had higher testosterone levels than those working in traditionally feminine occupations (e.g., clerical workers, nurses, teachers, housewives; Purifoy & Koopmans, 1979; Schindler, 1979). For males, actors and professional football players were higher in testosterone than were physicians, professors, and firefighters, who were higher than salesmen and ministers (Dabbs et al., 1990). It is suggested that high-testosterone occupations are associated with the traditional masculine personality characteristics of competitiveness and dominance (Dabbs, 2000; Mazur, 1985; Mazur, Booth, & Dabbs, 1992), regardless of gender.

When comparing white-collar workers (e.g., professional and managerial, technical and sales) with blue-collar workers (e.g., precision production and repair, laborer and operator), along with unemployed individuals and farmers, farmers had the lowest testosterone levels, followed by white-collar workers. Blue-collar workers had the next highest level of testosterone, and unemployed workers had the highest. In accounting for these results, Dabbs (2000) notes that individuals with higher testosterone levels tend to be less educated and have more legal problems. High-testosterone individuals might have left school sooner because they were impatient and rambunctious. So the association of lower educational level with high testosterone level might explain the difference between those working in blue-collar jobs and those in white-collar jobs. Dabbs also notes that unemployed individuals may be "unable or unwilling to stay at the same job for very long" (Dabbs, 2000, p. 147).

The low testosterone level associated with farmers is counterintuitive, as farming has many of the characteristics associated with masculine-type occupations: It is physically challenging and highly dangerous work (e.g., accidents involving heavy machinery). Yet, as Dabbs (2000) notes, "Farmers have something in common with ministers, who are also low in testosterone. Both ministers and farmers have to be patient about things they cannot control. Ministers put up with sin and farmers put up with the weather" (p. 149). Similarly, Dabbs (2000) notes that those who tend to be attracted to the highly dangerous occupation of oil-field engineer – working on off-shore oil platforms in treacherous oceanic conditions – are highly educated and have a heightened level of testosterone. However, individuals who are the most satisfied by and successful at this type of work tend to have lower testosterone levels than those who are less fulfilled by their occupation. Like farmers and ministers, successful oil-field engineers must be patient and cautious for safety reasons. Oil-field engineers with a testosterone level that is too high are not likely to do well in such work because they may "feel restricted by the rules, supervision, and monitoring made necessary by safety concerns" (Dabbs, 2000, p. 141).

In more specific comparisons of individuals within particular occupations, missionaries, who work to build new congregations, were higher in testosterone than pastors, who work with existing congregations. Stand-up comedians, who succeed or fail alone, had higher testosterone levels than stage actors, who work with groups of other actors (Dabbs et al., 1990). For these typically low-testosterone occupations, increased levels of testosterone might be associated with greater success because such individuals are willing to stand out and take more social risks (e.g., "bomb" alone on stage; no one attending your new church).

In addition to examining the more traditional forms of occupational choice, we can also look at a somewhat less common occupation – being a soldier. Gimbel and Booth (1996) examined the testosterone levels and the nature of military service of Vietnam veterans, reporting that men who entered the army with low testosterone levels tended to be assigned to administrative and support positions, possibly owing to their higher educational level, as noted earlier. On the other hand, the high testosterone level of individuals sent into combat was positively associated with the intensity of

their combat experience, including the frequency of receiving enemy fire, encountering mines or booby traps, being ambushed, firing at the enemy, and seeing Americans or Vietnamese killed. Gimbel and Booth suggest that such high-testosterone soldiers were assigned to more combat duty than their low-testosterone counterparts because their commanders assumed that they would be better combatants. This assumption was based on the notion that characteristics associated with heightened testosterone – a tendency toward more violent behavior, physical strength, and less caution – are linked to characteristics of a good combat soldier.

The way biological factors operate with occupational choice and satisfaction is unclear. We do not know whether testosterone causes people to enter certain professions, or whether once individuals enter a particular occupation, their level of testosterone increases. It is also possible that people seek out occupations that are compatible with their genetic makeup (e.g., testosterone level). But their choice of occupations may be a function of their environment. For example, a female with high testosterone growing up in a family environment where nontraditional sex roles are supported but money is lacking may have fewer occupational choices than a similar individual whose family can afford to help her with college tuition. In these cases, the female in the former environment might seek employment in some technical field, while the female from the latter environment might elect to attend law school. Additional research needs to be done to explore the processes by which biological factors influence occupational choice and the dynamics by which it can contribute to job satisfaction (e.g., employee training, work assignments). If you would like to read more about the role of testosterone in occupational choice, read James Dabbs's (2000) highly engaging book titled *Heroes, Rogues, and Lovers: Testosterone and Behavior*.

This concludes our consideration of the applications of the biological viewpoint of personality. A summary of the major points discussed in this section is presented in "Summing It Up: Applications of the Biological Viewpoint" on p. 357.

The presentation of the biological viewpoint of personality is now complete. The study of the biological contributions to the operation and expression of personality involves some of the newest and most

Summing It Up *Applications of the Biological Viewpoint*

Application	Example
Behavioral Genetics Perspective:	
● *Assessment, Detection, and Treatment of Prenatal Genetic Disorders*	
Genetic counseling investigates family history for the potential likelihood of disease and genetic defects.	After her discussion with a genetic counselor, Ellen decided that she and her husband would adopt a child instead of running the risk of having a baby with the serious blood disease that runs in her family.
Amniocentesis and *chorionic villus sampling* are techniques for assessing the presence of certain diseases and genetic defects in the fetus.	Ashley was relieved that the results from the analyses of the sample of fluid and tissue taken from her amniotic sac indicated that her soon-to-be-born baby was a girl and showed no genetic disorders.
Gene therapy involves molecular manipulation of the chemical properties of the genetic structure of the fetus to treat genetic disorders.	After detecting a genetic disorder in the fetus during Karen's 10th-week prenatal exam, the doctor decided to facilitate the presence of certain cellular proteins by injecting her fetus with an experimental genetic material designed to trigger the production of the needed proteins.
Psychophysiological Perspective:	
● *Biological Treatment of Mental Disorders*	
Electroconvulsive therapy is the passing of a mild electrical current into the brain to induce a seizure for the purpose of treating certain forms of depression and suicidal behavior.	After being transported by an ambulance and admitted into the emergency unit of a local mental health center, a 22-year-old student was given ECT the following day to reduce his severe suicidal tendencies and repeated suicide attempts.
Psychopharmacotherapy is the use of prescription medication to treat various emotional disorders by affecting the level and influence of certain neurotransmitters on the functioning of the brain.	In addition to the ECT, the suicidal individual was also prescribed Paxil to balance out his level of serotonin and help him to be more receptive and responsive to his one-on-one therapy sessions.
● *Biological Contributions to Occupational Choice and Satisfaction*	
Research with twins suggests a potential genetic contribution to jobs sought and job satisfaction.	Although separated at birth, when they were united 35 years later, June and Sandy discovered that they were both firefighters.
The hormone testosterone has been linked to the type of and risk associated with career choice and military service, along with level of education.	After getting out of the military with two tours of heavy combat duty, Roger found working as a police officer more to his liking than his previous job as a dock supervisor for a shipping company.

exciting work currently being done in the field of personality psychology. If you would like more information on this topic, I would recommend that you consider reading *Biology of Personality and Individual Differences* (Canli, 2006). In the next chapter, we will examine the evolutionary viewpoint to the study of personality; a major emerging field in the psychology of personality.

Chapter Summary: Reexamining the Highlights

- *Biological Processes in the Study of Personality.* Some basic issues associated with the study of personality from the biological viewpoint include the nature–nurture controversy; the role of heredity; the limits of genetics in determining behavior; the role of the biological processes in conjunction with psychological, cognitive, and environmental processes; and the concept of biosocial interaction.

- *The Constitutional Perspective.* An initial biological approach to the study of personality was the constitutional prospective. Early constitutional approaches included humoral theories, physiognomy, and phrenology. Sheldon's approach attempted to link dimensions of physique (endomorphy, mesomorphy, and ectomorphy) with dimensions of temperament (viscerotonia, somatotonia, and cerebrotonia).

- *The Behavioral Genetics Perspective.* The study of behavioral genetics attempts to understand the extent to which personality dimensions are influenced by genetic and environmental factors and the processes by which such factors impact the operation and expression of these dimensions of personality.

  - *Methodological Considerations in Behavioral Genetics.* The study of genetic influences on behavior and personality characteristics involves family studies, twin studies, adoption studies, and model fitting.

  - *The Genetic Basis of Personality.* Using a variety of behavioral genetics research methods, as well the index of heredity to assess the degree of genetic influence, researchers have found considerable support for a significant genetic contribution to a variety of dimensions of personality, including happiness, loneliness, aggression, attitudes, and adolescent personality adjustment, to name just a few.

- *The Psychophysiological Perspective.* The study of psychophysiological processes involves attempts to understand the role of physiological process, neurological activity, and brain structures in the operation and expression of personality dimensions.

  - *Psychophysiological Assessment.* Methods for measuring physiological processes associated with personality include the assessment of brain activity in response to stimulation, bodily responses associated with the autonomic nervous system, and the biochemical activity related to the operation of neurotransmitters.

  - *The Study of the Sensation-Seeking Personality.* As an example of the psychophysiological approach, the study of sensation seeking attempts to explain the tendency to take risks to achieve novel stimulation. The tendency for sensation seeking is measured using the Sensation Seeking Scale and has been found to be correlated with risk-taking behaviors. Psychophysiological correlates of high sensation seeking include augmentation in cortical arousal, a lower level of the neurotransmitters monoamine oxidase, dopamine, and serotonin, and an excess of the hormone testosterone.

  - *The Study of Cortical Influences on Personality.* Cortical influences on personality illustrate how neurological structures within the brain impact the expression of various aspects of personality processes. The arousal hypothesis examines the neurological influence of the ascending reticular activating system as a psychophysiological basis for the expression of extraversion and introversion. Extraverts and introverts differ on several measures of arousal in a manner consistent with the arousal hypothesis. The reinforcement sensitivity theory proposes the coordination of certain brain structures in the underlying dynamics of the Behavioral Approach System (BAS), which controls an individual's sensitivity and approach to positive stimuli, and the Behavioral Inhibition System (BIS), which controls an individual's sensitivity to and avoidance of punishing stimuli, as cortical mechanisms in the operation and expression of personality. Cortical and self-report measures provide supporting evidence that the BAS influences expression of the characteristic features of impulsive, extraverted individuals, while the BIS influences expression of the characteristic features of anxious individuals.

- *Applications of the Biological Viewpoint*

  - *Application of the Behavioral Genetics Perspective.* The detection and treatment of prenatal genetic disorders include genetic counseling to calculate the assessed genetic risks associated with a potential pregnancy, amniocentesis and chorionic villus sampling to identify potential genetic problems within the fetus during the pregnancy, and gene therapy to treat genetic disorders through the molecular manipulation of certain chemical processes associated with specific fetal genetic structures.

  - *Application of the Psychophysiological Perspective.* Biological approaches to treating emotional

disorders involve altering bodily processes. Electroconvulsive therapy is used in treating certain forms of severe depression and suicidal behavior by inducing seizures in the brain. Psychopharamacotherapy involves the use of various groups of drugs, such as selective serotonin reuptake inhibitors, in the treatment of emotional disorders and can cause unwanted side effects. Biological factors associated with the study of vocational interests and job satisfaction include genetic evidence provided by twin studies, and level of testosterone as an indicator of the nature of occupational choice, degree of occupational risk, and amount of success of individuals within occupational areas.

Glossary

acetylcholine A neurotransmitter that energizes the neurological responses of the nervous system.

adoption studies A comparison of individuals with their biological and adopted parents to examine genetic transmission of various characteristics.

amniocentesis A procedure sampling fluid from the amniotic sac to screen for genetic defects and diseases in the fetus.

arousal hypothesis A proposed relationship between extraversion–introversion and the general level of arousal in the brain.

ascending reticular activating system (ARAS) A neurological structure that regulates the level of arousal in the brain.

augmentation The tendency to increase or intensify stimulation.

autonomic nervous system (ANS) A subdivision of the overall nervous system that is responsible for controlling bodily responses to positive or negative elevated emotional situations.

Behavioral Approach System (BAS) A neurological system that controls an individual's responsiveness and approach to positive stimuli.

behavioral genetics The assessment of behavioral differences due to genetic and environmental factors.

Behavioral Inhibition System (BIS) A neurological system that controls an individual's responsiveness to and avoidance of negative stimuli.

biosocial interaction The combined operation of biological and environmental factors to influence personality.

cerebrotonia A dimension of temperament characterized by emotional restraint.

choleric personality A tendency to be angry and irritable.

chorionic villus sampling (CVS) A procedure sampling tissue from the placenta to screen for genetic defects in the fetus.

concordance rate The extent to which sets of twins share certain characteristics.

constitutional psychology A viewpoint of psychology emphasizing bodily processes and characteristics to explain behavior.

cortex The portion of the brain responsible for the coordination and integration of cognitive, emotional, and behavioral functioning.

cortisol A hormone released into the bloodstream in response to stressful situations.

dizygotic twins Individuals who are fraternal twins.

dopamine A neurotransmitter involved in the regulation of body movement.

ectomorphy A dimension of physique characterized by frailness.

electroconvulsive therapy (ECT) A procedure for passing an electrical current into the brain to treat certain emotional disorders.

electrodermal activity (EDA) The electrical measurement of surface skin moisture as an index of emotional arousal.

electroencephalograph (EEG) The measurement of the amount of electrical activity at various locations in the brain.

electromyography (EMG) The measurement of electrical activity in muscles as an index of muscle tension.

endomorphy A dimension of physique characterized by softness and roundness.

family studies   The systematic investigation of family histories to assess the occurrence of certain individual characteristics.

fraternal twins   Two individuals conceived from different fertilized eggs who do not share the same genetic makeup.

functional magnetic resonance imaging (fMRI)   A technique for measuring brain activity by assessing the rate of oxygen flow to brain cells.

gene therapy   The alteration of the molecular structure of a gene to prevent and treat genetically related disorders.

genetic counseling   Advice given to people concerning their likelihood of having offspring with genetic defects and diseases.

genetically determined   Personality, behavioral, or physical characteristics appearing as a result of certain genes.

happiness set point   A genetically based value representing a central level of an individual's degree of happiness during a particular period of life.

heredity   The estimated percentage of the genetic contribution to particular physical, cognitive, behavior, or personality dimensions of a large group of individuals.

hormonal production   The creation, release, and termination of hormones within the nervous system to regulate emotions and behaviors in response to external stimuli.

humors   Fluids of the body, as defined by the ancient Greeks.

identical twins   Two people conceived from a single fertilized egg who share the same genetic makeup.

index of heredity   A statistical indication, ranging from 0.0 to 1.0, for describing the degree of genetic contribution to a personality dimension when studying twins.

limbic system   A collection of neurological structures located in the midbrain, responsible for processing information and controlling emotional and behavioral reactions linked to emotional experiences.

locus coeruleus (LC)   A neurological structure in the brainstem that controls the degree of responsiveness to novel or aversive stimuli.

melancholic personality   A tendency to be gloomy and sad.

mesomorphy   A dimension of physique characterized by high muscle tone.

model fitting   The comparison of various mathematical models to assess the proposed contribution of genetic and environmental factors to various characteristics.

monoamine oxidase   A neurotransmitter that inhibits actions.

monozygotic twins   Individuals who are identical twins.

nature–nurture controversy   The debate over the role of heredity vs. environmental factors as determinants of personality.

neurotransmitters   Chemicals used to send neurological information within the body.

phlegmatic personality   A tendency to be quiet and reserved.

phrenology   An early attempt to understand personality and mental abilities by relating them to the shape of a person's head.

physiognomy   An early attempt to understand personality by relating it to physical features of the person.

positron emission tomography (PET)   A technique for measuring brain activity by assessing the metabolic rate of brain cells.

psychopharmacotherapy   The treatment of emotional disorders with medication.

pupil   The dark center portion of the eye through which light enters.

pupil reflex   The reflexive increase and decrease of the opening of the pupil in response to the degree of stimulation by light.

pupillography   The recording of changes in the size of the pupil.

reinforcement sensitivity theory   A theory suggesting that two separate cortical structures that respond differently to cues for reward and punishment serve to influence approach and avoidance behavior, respectively.

reward deficiency syndrome   The inability of the brain to achieve a sense of pleasure and satisfaction, which can result in addictive behaviors in an attempt to achieve such pleasure and satisfaction.

sanguine personality   A tendency to be cheerful.

selective breeding experiment   The systematic breeding of organisms to study the genetic transmission of certain characteristics.

selective placement   Certain biases in the placement of children during the adoption process.

sensation seeking   A tendency for excessive, novel stimulation.

Sensation Seeking Scale (SSS)   A personality inventory to measure the sensation-seeking tendency.

serotonin   A neurotransmitter that reduces the level of neurological responses of the nervous system.

somatotonia   A dimension of temperament characterized by physical and risk-taking activities.

somatotype rating   A system for rating an individual's physique along the endomorphy, mesomorphy, and ectomorphy dimensions.

temperament   An inherited dimension of personality.

testosterone   A hormone, found in both sexes, associated with masculine physical characteristics and with behavior, particularly aggressiveness.

twin studies   The investigation of twins to study the genetic contribution to various individual characteristics.

viscerotonia   A dimension of temperament characterized by sociability.

The Evolutionary Viewpoint
Personality as an Adaptive Process

9

Chapter Overview:
A Preview of Coming AttractionsF

The foundation of the evolutionary viewpoint of personality is seen in the classic theory of evolution proposed by Charles Darwin (1859/1958), the works of contemporary biologist Edward O. Wilson (1975), and the field of evolutionary psychology. **Evolutionary psychology** attempts to understand human psychological processes and behavior on the basis of the theory of evolution. The evolutionary viewpoint of personality assumes that individual differences in the operation, development, and expression of personality are based on the principles of evolutionary psychology. In this chapter, we will discuss the basic processes, the basic expressions, and some applications of the evolutionary viewpoint of personality.

Linking Evolutionary Theory to the Study of Personality: Accounting for the Emergence of Variation in Physical and Psychological Characteristics

David M. Buss is a pioneer in the study of evolutionary psychology.

Much of our thinking regarding the evolutionary viewpoint of personality can be linked to the pioneering work of psychologist David Buss (2008) in his efforts to help explain, from the principles of classic evolutionary theory, how the universal expression of certain social behaviors (e.g., the emergence of leaders) and particular physical (e.g., physical strength) and personality (e.g., extraversion, cooperativeness) characteristics emerged together over time.

Classic evolutionary theory systematically explains the changes in the physical structures and features of organisms as they attempt to adapt and successfully adjust to environmental changes and challenges. For many animals this might have involved changes in their coloring or other external features. For example, as shifts in the earth resulted in more dirt entering a river and muddying the water, the coloring of a particular species of fish might have darkened over time so that it might become less visible to its predators. For humans living in cold, windy climates, changes might have occurred in eyelid shape and thickness (e.g., they might have become narrower and thicker). Similarly, in the study of personality psychology, as well as social psychology (Kenrick, Maner, & Li, 2005), developmental psychology (Bjorklund & Blasi, 2005), and cognitive psychology (Todd, Hertwig, & Hoffrage, 2005), the evolutionary perspective systematically explains the emergence of psychological characteristics that help organisms adapt successfully to environmental changes and challenges. For some animals, that might involve developing a timid temperament to avoid the attention of predators. Even within the specific species of these timid animals, there would be some individual variation in that the males of the species might be less timid than the females; their principal role might be to find food and shelter while the females stay in the shelter to take care of the young. For humans, that might involve developing a sense of cooperation (i.e., a social behavior), certain reasoning and problem-solving abilities (i.e., cognitive characteristics) – such as learning to hunt during the day and stay in a cave at night to reduce the likelihood of being surprised by a predator – and the trait of aggressiveness as a means of self-protection.

What is more, individual differences in these characteristics might provide some evolutionary advantages. For example, individuals who are less cooperative, better problem solvers, and more aggressive might be better able to serve as hunters for and protectors of the group. Other members of the group who are more cooperative, better at reasoning, and less aggressive might be better suited as leaders of the group. And as changes in the environment continue to emerge, we would expect to see changes in the nature of the physical and personality characteristics appearing in individuals operating in these environments. For example, as technological advances in the delivery of communications become more diverse and complicated, those individuals with the cognitive abilities (e.g., intelligence, creativity) and psychological characteristics (e.g., cooperativeness, trustworthiness) to adjust to these changes would emerge as leaders, while those individuals without them, such as those who relied on physical strength, would fade, resulting in a shift away from leadership based on physical (e.g., brute strength) characteristics to one based on cognitive (e.g., smarter) and psychological (e.g., more friendly) characteristics. Thus, from the viewpoint of evolutionary psychology, certain physical and psychological characteristics emerge and persist in their appearance and expression because they help individuals to adapt to changes in their environment.

Although an in-depth discussion of evolutionary theory is beyond the scope of this chapter, we will discuss some aspects of evolutionary psychology as they relate specifically to the study of personality. In the passages that follow we will begin by examining some basic considerations of evolutionary psychology (Beaulieu & Bugental, 2006; Tooby & Cosmides, 2005).

Basic Processes of the Evolutionary Viewpoint: Explanations of Essential Elements of Evolution

To examine the evolutionary perspective on personality, it would be helpful to have some basic information regarding several fundamental processes within evolutionary theory. These include survival and reproduction, natural selection, adaptive behavior, and the environment of evolutionary adaptedness.

Survival and Reproduction: The Basic Evolutionary Tasks

According to the evolutionary perspective, organisms evolve by passing their genetic and other biological characteristics to each succeeding generation. For such genetic transmission to occur, members of the current generation must be able to perform two basic evolutionary tasks: survival and reproduction. Survival involves being able to respond successfully to daily threats and environmental challenges. Examples of survival-related tasks involve finding food and shelter and defending against predators. Reproduction involves being able to mate successfully and produce offspring. Examples of reproduction-related tasks include being able to attract a sexual partner or partners, successfully mating, and providing for and protecting any resulting offspring. Throughout the remainder of the chapter, much of our discussion of the evolutionary perspective and its applicability to the study of personality will focus on factors that contribute to the successful completion of these two tasks.

Natural Selection: A Basic Element for Survival

Natural selection, a process of gradual changes occurring within organisms that result in an increased chance of survival and reproduction of the species, is critical to evolutionary theory. Specifically, the surviving members of each generation of a particular species pass along to their offspring whatever set of biological characteristics made survival possible. Because members of the species lacking those survival-related characteristics would have a decreased chance of survival, those weaker biological characteristics would not necessarily be passed along to the next generation. Even should these members of the species survive long enough to reproduce, they might pass along this set of substandard biological characteristics to their offspring, which would also have a decreased likelihood of survival. Thus, over successive generations, the process of natural selection would result in the continued development of those members of the species that possess survival-related characteristics, along with a gradual dying off of members who lack those characteristics. This attrition would gradually remove from the gene pool those nonsurvival-related biological characteristics, thus maximizing the likelihood of the survival of the species. For example, members of a species with the biological propensity for speed and cooperation could have a greater likelihood of survival because of their ability to outmaneuver and work together to protect themselves from their predators. Members that have only one or neither of these abilities would be less likely to survive. The fast, cooperative members would also be able to pass these survival-related characteristics along to their offspring. Thus, natural selection is nature's way of passing on to the next generation only those characteristics that increase the likelihood of survival.

Adaptive Behavior: A Basic Solution for Survival

An outcome of the process of natural selection is adaptive behavior. **Adaptive behavior** is behavior that has been repeated so often over the generations, due to its tendency to maximize the likelihood of the survival of the members of a current generation, that it has become part of the genetic makeup of a species. For example, as each successive generation of a species of deer learns to run quickly as a group, with the strongest members of the species positioning themselves at the back of the group to protect the group from predators, such a behavioral pattern will develop into a specific neurological circuit in the brain of the species and, over time, will become part of its genetic makeup. The value of such adaptive behavior is that it enables each succeeding generation to possess these highly successful and complex patterns of behavior without having to experience the slow and cumbersome trial-and-error process that made their development possible. Thus, adaptive behavior is nature's way of providing ready-made solutions to many of life's most persistent and difficult challenges.

The Environment of Evolutionary Adaptedness: The Basic Set of Conditions

When considering the evolutionary perspective in the context of contemporary issues, we must be mindful that many of its ideas and principles are based on the challenges that confronted our hunting-and-gathering ancestors, along with their corresponding adaptive responses, over a period of several thousand years. These responses became part of our own genetic makeup as a result. The systematic consideration of the responses of our hunting-and-gathering ancestors to constant environmental challenges as a valuable means of understanding contemporary behavior is formulated in what is termed the environment of evolutionary adaptedness. The idea behind the **environment of evolutionary adaptedness** (EEA) suggests that what is critical is being able to understand the general context involving both the problems our hunting-and-gathering ancestors had to solve and the enduring conditions under which they had to solve them.

EEA is not linked to a particular time and place, but rather encompasses a set of reliable environmental conditions requiring a consistent adaptive response that over time becomes part of the genetic makeup of the particular species. For example, as we will see when examining gender differences in personality from the evolutionary perspective in Chapter 12, the tendency for males to develop personality characteristics associated with being active, and for women to develop characteristics associated with being expressive and nurturing, had something to do with how our hunting-and-gathering ancestors dealt with the issues of survival and reproduction. Because their biological makeup confers

on them the capacity to give birth, women developed personality characteristics that were more conducive to caring for children in a stationary domestic setting. Males, on the other hand, developed biological characteristics associated with being physically active and personality characteristics associated with being more adventurous, as their adaptive response was to serve as the providers of food and protectors of the species.

Today these same environmental challenges – providing food and shelter for the family and caring for children and the home – exist, but with somewhat different adaptive responses. Adaptive responses now might include both the mother and father working outside the home while paying for day care, maid service, or personal assistance. Thus, the EEA suggests the value of the evolutionary perspective is to help us understand how individuals evolve by coming up with new adaptive responses to the fundamental challenges that have been confronting humans for many millennia.

As we have discussed in this section, the basics of evolutionary theory are linked to helping us understand how individuals developed physical features that are associated with increasing the likelihood of meeting the fundamental task of survival and reproduction. In a similar manner, the evolutionary viewpoint of personality has attempted to examine the personality characteristics associated with survival and reproduction. Systematic research in this important area of study has identified an interesting collection of personality characteristics that seem to be associated with increasing the probability of successfully completing these two critical evolutionary tasks. To see what some of these personality characteristics are, read "A Closer Look."

A Closer Look

Personality Correlates of Survival and Reproduction: Links to Longevity and a Legacy

As was noted earlier, the two fundamental evolutionary tasks were those involving survival and reproduction. Going beyond the more traditional use of evolutionary theory for the purpose of studying the physical characteristics associated with maximizing the odds for survival and reproduction (e.g., developing camouflage-type skin coloring), personality psychologists within the evolutionary viewpoint have also attempted to identify personality characteristics associated with the increased likelihood of those two basic tasks. Presented below is a summary of the research examining the personality correlates of survival and reproduction.

Personality Correlates of Survival: Links to Longevity

In the context of the basic evolutionary tasks, a critical concern is to consider those personality factors associated with survival. One way to consider the issue of survival is to examine the personality traits that seem simply to contribute to living longer. *Conscientiousness* is a personality factor related to longevity (Friedman, 2000; Friedman et al., 1993; Schwartz et al., 1995), with this relationship being more characteristic of females than of males. The logic, it seems, is that conscientious individuals are more likely to engage in health-promoting behaviors and to avoid health risks. A sense of *optimism* has been found to be related to having fewer physical symptoms and a better recovery time after surgery (Tucker & Friedman, 1996), which can be viewed as a being related to longevity. Individuals scoring high on the trait of sense of *coherence* about life report more positive physical and mental health (Ebert, Tucker, & Roth, 2002). Such individuals scoring high on coherence tend to view life as being understandable, manageable, and meaningful, while individuals scoring low on coherence tend to view life as being chaotic and out of control. It could be that having a sense of control regarding one's daily life results in less physical and mental stress. Finally, individuals scoring high on the trait of *subjective vitality*, suggesting a high level of overall well-being (i.e., positive feelings), reported fewer physical symptoms such as headaches and shortness of breath (Ryan & Frederick, 1997).

Just as some personality traits are positively associated with longevity, others are negatively associated with it. Among the later is the **Type D personality** (Denollet et al., 1996). Type D individuals tend to suppress emotional distress. Keeping emotions bottled up inside is associated with increases in the mortality of individuals with heart disease. Also negatively associated with longevity through its connection with heart disease and an assortment of unhealthy personal and behavioral characteristics is the **Hostile Type A personality** (Friedman, Hawley, & Tucker, 1994). Such individuals are more likely to experience greater distress than are non-Type A individuals when faced with day-to-day frustrations (e.g., waiting in line or at a red light). This causes a more intense physical stress reaction within the body and the immune system, which is exacerbated by the tendency to suppress such negative emotions (e.g., "fuming up" inside). Contributing to their physical distress, such individuals are more likely than others to abuse dangerous substances, such as tobacco, alcohol, or other drugs, and have interpersonal conflicts that tend to lead to a loss of social support and increases in physical distress and being involved in stressful situations. Neuroticism, with correlates of anxiety and hostility (Aldwin, Spiro, Levenson, & Cupertino, 2001), also has a negative association with coronary disease (Tucker & Friedman, 1996). Higher mortality risk across the life span has been linked to males with increased neurotic tendencies (e.g., mood instability) due to their tendency to engage in more risky behavior through aggressiveness, volatility, or hyperactivity (Friedman, 2000; Friedman et al., 1993; Schwartz et al., 1995).

Thus, on the upside, longevity seems to be associated with being careful (i.e., conscientious), having a positive outlook on life (i.e., being optimistic), being able to manage daily life (i.e., having a sense of coherence), and generally feeling good (i.e., having subjective vitality). On the downside, decreases in longevity seem to be associated with the bottling up of emotions (i.e., Type D personality), increased physical distress, loss of social support, and substance abuse (i.e., Hostile Type A personality), and anxiety and risky behavior (i.e., neuroticism). When it comes to physical health, it may pay to be conscientious and optimistic, and to have a good sense of coherence and vitality. Negative emotional reactions tend to produce increased emotional distress, which, in turn, leads to greater demands on the body's immune system and the facilitation of age-related conditions (e.g., the weakening of the heart; Kiecolt-Glaser, McGuire, Robles, & Glaser, 2002).

Personality Correlates of Reproductive Success: Links to Leaving a Legacy

From an evolutionary perspective, the study of successful reproduction has focused on the personality correlates of individuals with infertility disorders. When functionally infertile individuals (i.e., those for whom reproduction is possible but not occurring) were compared with organically infertile individuals (i.e., those not capable of reproduction), the functionally infertile individuals scored higher on measures of harm avoidance (Fasino et al., 2002). The researchers suggested that harm avoidance contributed to a lower fertility rate because it might have decreased the frequency, length, emotional involvement, and satisfaction of sexual intercourse. It also might have altered the level of sex-related hormones in response to environmental stress and relational distress. In addition, functionally infertile women scored lower on cooperativeness and self-directedness than did organically infertile women, while functionally infertile men scored lower on novelty seeking than did organically infertile men. Functional infertility in women also tends to be associated with higher scores of depression and anxiety (Wischmann, Stammer, Scherg, Gerhad, & Verres, 2001). For males, high scorers on the traits of self-confidence, extraversion, and social assertiveness had lower associated infertility rates (Hellhammer, Hubert, Phil, Frieschem, & Nieschlag, 1985).

Thus, for females, functional infertility seems to be associated with personality characteristics that promote the role of negative emotions associated with sex and reproduction (e.g., harm avoidance, depression, anxiety, and a lack of cooperation). On the other hand, increased functional reproductive ability for males seems to be associated with personality characteristics related to being able to approach potential sexual partners (e.g., self-confidence, assertiveness, extraversion, and seeking novelty). As we will see a few more times in this section, gender differences in factors related to sexual behavior have specific evolutionary purposes, as is seen in males' ability to approach and attract sexual mates and females' attempts to regulate their sexual behavior to a greater degree so as to improve the genetic quality of their offspring.

In conclusion, the systematic examination of those personality characteristics associated with survival and reproduction provides an important illustration of how research in the study of personality is incorporated into the evolutionary perspective, and the vital role this research can play in helping us understand the significant contribution made by personality factors to meeting critical evolutionary demands.

Summing It Up *Basic Processes of the Evolutionary Viewpoint*

Basic Process	Example
Survival and Reproduction. The two fundamental tasks that encompass the ability to deal successfully with the challenges of everyday life and to mate and procreate	Our hunting-and-gathering ancestors and contemporary individuals alike must deal with the challenges of trying to find a mate and raise a family in a safe and secure environment.
Natural Selection. The process by which systematic changes in the organism occur that are responsible for helping to achieve successfully the tasks of survival and reproduction, along with passing on to the next generation the genes that make these changes possible	Individuals who develop the greatest ability to solve problems, whether they involve trapping a deer for food or solving a software problem and getting a raise, will pass genes associated with those abilities to the next generation of individuals, which will make them more likely to solve the problems that they will face.
Adaptive Behavior. Behaviors that have been repeated successfully to solve daily challenges and become ingrained genetically in the organism's behavioral repertoire	Because the tendency for individuals to form social structures has met with so much evolutionary success, there is an innate tendency for individuals to organize socially, whether it is for a hunting party of our early ancestors or a local neighborhood block watch now.
The Environment of Evolutionary Adaptedness. The idea that many fundamental environmental challenges that faced our hunting-and-gathering ancestors are present today in somewhat different manifestations	Like their ancestors, mothers and fathers today struggle to find solutions by implementing technical advances (i.e., stone tools vs. new software) to maximize the success of protecting and providing for their offspring and themselves.

This concludes our discussion of the basic processes of the evolutionary viewpoint. The main points included in this section are presented in "Summing It Up: Basic Processes of the Evolutionary Viewpoint" on p. 366. In the next section, we will discuss how the evolutionary viewpoint of personality helps to account for one of the most important features in the study of personality psychology – the expression of individual differences in personality characteristics.

Accounting for the Emergence of Individual Differences in Personality: Vive La Différence

As we have stressed throughout this book, an important task in the study of personality psychology is to help explain the expression and value of individual differences in personality among us. In this section we will discuss how the evolutionary viewpoint of personality helps to account for the emergence of individual differences in personality and the expression of variation of the dimensions of the Big Five Model of personality.

The Evolutionary Value of Variation in Personality: Explanations of Individual Differences

In the spirit of addressing the critical task of explaining individual differences, and consistent with the principles of evolutionary psychology, the evolutionary viewpoint of personality psychology proposes that the emergence of particular personality characteristics and individual differences in these characteristics stems from the implementation of strategies for dealing with the survival and reproductive issues of the species (Buss, 2008; Figueredo et al., 2005). One obvious category of variability that has been examined from the evolutionary viewpoint of personality is the expression of gender differences in personality. For example, MacDonald (1998) has noted how certain sex differences in personality are related to tasks central to the basic issues of evolution. Specifically, males tend to be rated higher on characteristics linked with providing food and protection for the members of the species, such as sensation seeking, social dominance, and risk taking. On the other hand, females tend to be rated higher on traits

associated with love and nurturance, which are important to caregiving and ensuring the survival of offspring. Thus, such enduring gender differences in personality presumably have evolutionary significance for survival and reproduction (Buss, 1997, 2008). Later in this chapter, as well as in Chapter 12, we will consider gender differences in personality as an expression of variability in personality from the evolutionary perspective.

However, looking beyond basic gender differences in personality, another important concern in the study of the evolutionary viewpoint of personality is to account for individual differences in the expression of a particular personality trait or set of traits in the general population. For example, going beyond the obvious evolutionary development of gender differences in certain physical characteristics between men and women, such as height and strength, it is also important to account for the presence of variation among *all* of these individuals for these characteristics. For example, while men generally tend to be taller and physically stronger than women, there is a tremendous degree of variability for these two characteristics within the general population – not all men are equally tall and strong, and some women are taller and stronger than some men. The same can be said of attempting to account for such variability in personality. For example, while men are found to be generally more aggressive and dominant than women, not all men are equal in their degree of aggressiveness and dominance, and some women are more aggressive and dominant than some men. So in order to have a more complete understanding of personality, those individuals studying personality from the evolutionary viewpoint have also attempted to explain the expressions of individual differences in personality. Although there is a variety of factors to considered when attempting to account for individual differences in the personality from the evolutionary viewpoint (Figueredo et al., 2005), we will consider three sources of influence on the expression of variation of a particular personality trait or set of traits in the general population: its assessed value, the environmental context, and its relative frequency.

An Evolutionary Cost–Benefit Analysis: Assessing the Value of Variation

According to Daniel Nettle (2006a), of the University of Newcastle in the United Kingdom, the expression of individual differences in personality from the evolutionary viewpoint can be understood in the context of a cost–benefit analysis for the expression of a particular personality trait or set of personality traits. In general, a **cost–benefit analysis** involves examining what is lost (i.e., the cost) compared to what is gained (i.e., the benefit) by engaging in a specific course of action. When attempting to account for individual differences in personality, the cost–benefit analysis involves determining the survival and mating benefits vs. the costs of expressing a particular level of a personality trait. For example, the benefit of possessing a high degree of compassion might be that it will propel individuals in the general population to take care of each other. However, the cost of such a high degree of compassion is that while taking care of others, individuals spend less time and effort taking care of their own family members, thus reducing the possibility of successfully passing along one's genetic contribution to the next generation.

To solve this evolutionary dilemma, what is needed is a certain degree of variability in the trait of compassion within the general population. Individuals with a high degree of the trait of compassion will unselfishly help a wide variety of individuals less fortunate than themselves, even to the point of risking their own well-being. Good examples of such individuals would be Mother Teresa and others like her, who live among the poorest of the poor and expose themselves to an assortment of diseases and horrendous living conditions. Individuals with a moderate degree of compassion will be most concerned with helping members of their immediate families but will also be willing to help other members of their community. They might also be willing to help others in foreign countries through charity organizations that have special meaning to them, as long as they do not have to make too much of a personal sacrifice to offer such help to others. A good example of such individuals would probably be people like you and me. You exhibit your moderate degree of compassion by taking care of your family and close friends. You also probably express a willingness to help others outside of this intimate circle of individuals by volunteering some of your time or giving money to a community social agency associated with your school or sponsored by your employer, such as the local chapter of Big Brothers/Big Sisters, or an international relief organization, such as Doctors Without Borders.

With such variation in the trait of compassion, those select few who want to give of themselves to help others, even at the risk of their own peril, can do so through the support of many others who also want to help, but who do so at a reduced risk to themselves and those close to them. With such a solution, variation in the degree of the personality trait of compassion makes it possible for individuals to help those close to them (e.g., immediate family members) and other who are not (e.g., indigents living in a foreign country) while at the same time reducing personal risk and increasing the likelihood that they will pass along this trait of compassion to their genetic offspring. Thus, as this simple example illustrates, variation in personality exists within the individuals of the species because it contributes to the two fundamental evolutionary tasks: survival and reproduction.

The Environmental Context: The Value of Variation Based on Time and Place

While this cost–benefit analysis is essential to the evolutionary processes of survival and reproduction, to determine the value of the expression of variation in certain personality characteristics, you should realize that it does not operate in a vacuum. Such variation occurs within specific environmental constraints. And, like so many other important things in life, its value is determined by when and where it exists.

It's about Time: The Value of When Variation in Personality Occurs   The environmental consideration of time has to do with when the expression of variation of a particular trait or set of traits is operating. For example, when times are good and resources are plentiful and easy to obtain, people can be generous with such resources as their time, food, and money. If such a wealth of resources is extended over a long period of time (e.g., over successive generations), we might see a change in the expression of the trait of compassion in the general population. For example, we might see an overall increase in the level of compassion in the general population as it becomes easier to help provide for one's immediate family and assist with the concerns of others who are less fortunate. And within the general population, we might see a substantial increase in the trait of compassion for those individuals in the middle socioeconomic class if they believe these good times will continue for an extended period of time, making them feel they can afford to be more generous to those less fortunate than them. However, when times are hard and vital resources become scarce, individuals will become less generous with their support of others outside their immediate family. If such hard times continue for an extended period of time, we might see an overall

From the evolutionary viewpoint, what environmental context might produce such expressions of cooperation and compassion?

decrease in the expression of the trait of compassion in the general population. And within the general population, we might see a substantial decrease in the trait of compassion for those individuals in the upper socioeconomic class as they begin to hoard their resources as a protective strategy, in the belief that these hard times will continue. Thus, as these examples illustrate, you must consider the specific point in time when trying to account for the expression of variation of personality based on the evolutionary viewpoint.

Location, Location, Location: The Value of Where Variation in Personality Occurs   In addition to considering when the expression of variation of personality occurs, it is also important to take into consideration where it occurs. For example, in the northern part of a continent, there may be plenty of natural resources, so the individuals in the general population of this region might express the trait of compassion to a large degree. On the other hand, in the southern part of the continent, there may be a serious lack of resources, so the individuals in this region might express the trait of compassion to a lesser degree. If this disparity of regional resources continues for extended periods of time, we could expect to see considerable variation in the expression of the trait of compassion between the general populations of the two regions – the overall difference increases. Even within these specific regions, there might be different social customs that regulate the degree of generosity. For example, in the southern region, the upper class is expected to be the most generous, while in the northern region, individuals in the lower class are

expected to be the most generous. And if individuals remain in their specific socioeconomic class within their specific regions of the country for extended periods of time, we would also see the variation of the expression of the trait of compassion not only between these regions but within each one as well. Thus as these examples illustrate, you must also consider the nature of the specific location when trying to account for the expression of variation of personality from the evolutionary viewpoint.

Frequency-Dependent Selection: The Value of Variation Based on Frequency of Appearance

In addition to considerations of time and place, variation in the expression of personality is also a reflection of the process of frequency-dependent selection. **Frequency-dependent selection** involves the process by which the value of a particular characteristic feature increases or decreases as it appears relative to other characteristics within the species, and the impact such value has on mate-selection strategies. Specifically, when seeking a mate, as a particular characteristic becomes more frequent in a species, its value decreases, and as its frequency decreases within a species, its value increases. For example, as the number of individuals who possess a high degree of compassion increases, its high frequency becomes an evolutionary liability (i.e., passing on of one's genes), as we noted above. As a result, individuals will then begin to compete to mate with those who are low on the trait of compassion, thus making that level of the trait more valuable. However, as having a larger number of individuals low in the trait of compassion begins to produce an evolutionary threat to the survival of the species, it loses its value, and the competition for mating with those individuals who are high on the trait of compassion increases. Thus, the process of frequency-dependency selection helps to explain how the cost–benefit value of variation in the expression of a particular trait changes as its frequency of appearance within the population changes.

In summary, the evolutionary viewpoint of personality accounts for individual differences by examining the sources of influence that determine the value of the variation in the expression of personality traits within the general population in helping meet the basic evolutionary tasks of reproduction and the survival of the species. Next, we will consider how these sources of influence on individual differences can help us to understand the expression of the dimensions of the Five-Factor Model of personality.

The Five-Factor Model: Extending the Explanations of Individual Difference

As noted in Chapter 7, one of the most significant contemporary developments in the study of personality psychology has been the emergence of the Five-Factor Model (FFM) as a major framework for personality. The pervasive influence of the model has served to stimulate interest in extending the evolutionary explanations of individual differences to understanding the expression of variation of the dimensions of the FFM, particularly in the context of the evolutionary costs and benefits associated with such variation (Nettle, 2006a). We will now examine how the cost and benefits associated with the variation in the expression of each of the personality dimensions of the FFM of personality might serve to help meet the basic evolutionary tasks of survival and reproduction of the species.

Extraversion

The personality dimension of Extraversion is associated with such characteristics as sociability, warmth, and happiness. Variation in the expression of the trait of Extraversion is enhanced by the sexual behavioral pattern associated with individuals possessing a high degree of that trait. Specifically, Extraversion is associated with an increased number of sexual partners (Heaven, Fitzpatrick, Craig, Kelly, & Sebar, 2000; Nettle, 2005), which can lead to a greater likelihood of the transmission of the personality characteristic to future generations. Some of the evolutionary benefits of Extraversion include initiating social relationships with others (Buchanan, Johnson, & Goldberg, 2005), having a greater degree of social support (Franken, Gibson, & Mohan, 1990), being more physically active, and undertaking more exploratory behavior of one's environment (Chen, Burton, Greenberger, & Dmitrieva, 1999; Kircaldy, 1982). However, some of the evolutionary costs of Extraversion include a greater likelihood of being hospitalized due to illness or accidents (Nettle, 2005), engaging in criminal or antisocial behavior (Ellis, 1987), and being arrested (Samuels et al., 2004). In addition, because of their relationship turmoil, extraverts are also more likely to expose their offspring to the increased risks associated with step-parenting (Nettle, 2006a).

A cost–benefit analysis of the trait of Extraversion might suggest that during periods of social turmoil the value of individuals possessing a high degree of Extraversion would be their greater likelihood to initiate social contacts and deal well with novelty and uncertainty, while the value of individuals possessing a lower degree of Extraversion (i.e., introverts) during such times would be their greater likelihood of remaining injury-free and creating a more stable family environment. Such an example illustrates the evolutionary value of variation in the dimension of Extraversion.

Neuroticism

As a personality dimension, Neuroticism is associated with such emotions as fear, anxiety, sadness, and guilt. Some of the evolutionary costs associated with Neuroticism include impaired physical health due to chronic stress (Neeleman, Sytema, & Wadsworth, 2002), a strong predictor of psychiatric problems (Claridge & Davis, 2001), and related to relationship failure and social isolation (Kelly & Conley, 1987). However, some of the evolutionary benefits associated with Neuroticism include being overly cautious and attuned to danger (Nettle, 2006a).

A cost–benefit analysis might suggest that some degree of Neuroticism is of value in day-to-day living in that it helps individuals to be vigilant about their surroundings (e.g., driving in traffic) and worry about their performance on a variety of common tasks (e.g., studying for a test or doing your job at work). Thus, it seems like a good thing for folks to be a little neurotic, with the level of Neuroticism likely to decrease in the population during extended periods of environmental distress (e.g., when being extremely fearful and emotional is not very useful to others) and increase in times of extended environmental tranquility (e.g., preventing individuals from becoming too complacent).

Openness to Experience

Openness to Experience is a personality dimension associated with such characteristic features as being creative, seeking novelty of experiences and ideas, and having divergent interests. Some of the evolutionary benefits of Openness to Experience include an increase in creative ability (McCrae, 1987) and the heightened reproductive advantages of creative individuals to attract mates (Haselton & Miller, 2006) and have a greater number of sexual partners (Nettle & Clegg, 2006). A few of the costs associated with more extreme levels of Openness to Experience include a willingness to accept unusual ideas and beliefs that can range from a strong belief in supernatural and paranormal ideology (Charlton, 2005) to belief patterns linked to schizophrenia (Nettle, 2006b) and depression (Nowakowska, Strong, Santosa, Wang, & Ketter, 2005).

A cost–benefit analysis of variation in the trait of Openness to Experience might suggest an evolutionary value in the reproductive advantage of individuals possessing a high degree of this trait, as it would increase the presence of such characteristics as creativity and an appreciation of complex and novel ideas in the population. An evolutionary cost might be that individuals with an *extremely* high degree of the trait of Openness to Experience would increase a population's tendency to believe in ideas that have questionable validity (e.g., belief in the supernatural), resulting in both a decrease in critical thinking skills, and the pervasiveness of psychiatric disorders. However, the most advantageous evolutionary expression of variability in the trait of Openness to Experience would be to make sure that we have in the population some individuals with a low degree of Openness to Experience, who will help us to hold on to tradition and provide us with a link to our past, and some with a higher level of Openness to Experience, who will provide us with new and creative ways to see the world around us and act as role models and mentors for change and adaptation.

Conscientiousness

Attributes such as orderliness, self-control, and being efficient are characteristics associated with the personality dimension of Conscientiousness. Some of the evolutionary benefits associated with Conscientiousness include an increase in life expectancy due to the long-term adoption of and adherence to healthy behaviors and the avoidance of unhygienic risks (Friedman et al., 1995) and the ability to delay smaller immediate rewards in favor of greater future rewards (e.g., academic, professional, and financial success). Some of the evolutionary costs associated with certain characteristics associated with an elevated level of Conscientiousness, such as being overly moralistic, perfectionist, and excessively self-controlled, have been associated with the development of eating disorders, which are discussed later in this chapter, and an obsessive-compulsive personality disorder (Austin & Deary, 2000; Claridge & Davis, 2003). Another evolutionary cost is that because they tend

to forgo spontaneous, immediate short-term mating opportunities, highly conscientious individuals tend to reduce their likelihood of reproductive success (Schmidt, 2004).

A cost–benefit analysis of the dimension of Conscientiousness might suggest that the evolutionary value of individuals with a high degree of this trait would contribute to the population a tendency to a long life associated with exhibiting high moral values and characterized by productivity and financial success. The evolutionary costs might be that, due to their lowered level of reproductive success, they may not be contributing enough of these characteristics that are so beneficial to society, especially when there are harsh environmental conditions. As a point of concern, as technological advances make it easier and easier for individuals to obtain what they desire with ever-increasing speed, leading to less of a need to develop a sense of delay of gratification and self-control, the presence of the trait of Conscientiousness could be reduced in the general population. Such a reduction in the presence of the trait of Conscientiousness might lead to a drop in the level of productivity for individuals in the general population and a greater dependency of these individuals on others to provide them with the goods and services they desire. Expending less effort (i.e., burning fewer calories) on a day-to-day basis can lead to another threat to the survival of the species – obesity, which is discussed later in the chapter.

Agreeableness

Characteristics associated with Agreeableness include being trusting, generous, cooperative, and friendly. Evolutionary benefits of Agreeableness include being sympathetic to the emotional states of others (Baron-Cohen & Wheelwright, 2004), getting along with others, and avoiding interpersonal conflict and hostility (Caprara, Barbaranelli, & Zimbardo, 1996; Heaven, 1996; Suls, Martin, & David, 1998). Evolutionary costs linked to a high level of Agreeableness include such individuals being out-competed by those who are more selective in their level of Agreeableness (e.g., are competitive at work), such as achieving less financial and occupational status (Boudreau, Boswell, & Judge, 2001), and an extremely low level of Agreeableness being associated with antisocial personality disorder (Austin & Deary, 2000).

A cost–benefit analysis of the trait of Agreeableness might suggest that the evolutionary benefit of highly

Summing It Up *Evolutionary Influences on Individual Differences*

Explanation	Example
Accounting for the Emergence of Individual Differences. The personality characteristics that tend to emerge are those that have helped individuals meet the basic evolutionary tasks of survival and reproduction.	The personality traits of cooperativeness and aggressiveness continue to be expressed over generations because, in the right combination and the right circumstances, they have helped individuals to work together to protect their family and friends against threat.
Evolutionary Value of Variation in Personality. The value associated with the expression of the variation in those personality traits or set of traits that help meet the basic evolutionary tasks is determined by:	It is beneficial to have some individuals who are highly adventurous but also to have others who are overly cautious when trying to plan the investments of a company, depending on the fluctuations of the stock market.
Evolutionary Cost–Benefit Analysis. There are certain evolutionary advantages and disadvantages linked to having variation in a personality trait or group of personality traits among a group of individuals.	In order for the company to succeed, you need to have more assertiveness in your sales representatives than in your office staff, but more cooperativeness in your office staff than in your sales representatives, who spend more time working alone.
The Environmental Context. The value of variation of a specific trait or set of traits is determined by when and where it occurs.	When the company is doing well, managers are more generous with family-leave time for their employees. Managers in offices with fewer employees are less generous with family-leave time than are managers with more employees.
Frequency-Dependent Selection. The value of a trait or group of trait increases or decreases depending on its frequency in appearance relative to other traits or groups of traits.	As the number of assertive sales representatives increases in a company, those sales representatives who are also able to cooperate with others become more important to the company.
The Value of Variation in the FFM. An evolutionary cost–benefit analysis of the variation of the separate dimensions of the FFM is consistent with meeting the basic evolutionary tasks of survival and reproduction.	For companies to succeed, they need to have executives who are moderately agreeable, so as to be able to get along with but also discipline their employees, and marketing managers with a high degree of openness to experience, so as to develop new customer bases to maintain growth, along with everyone having a relatively low degree of neuroticism and high degree of conscientiousness.

agreeable individuals would be that they contribute the tendency to display an awareness of and sensitivity to the needs of others beyond one's immediate family members. The advantage of such a tendency would be that it fosters a sense of community that would provide social support in times of physical and social distress. The evolutionary costs of individuals with a low degree of Agreeableness might be that they contribute to the general population an increased sense of interpersonal hostility toward, a lack of trust in, and a

decreased willing to cooperate with others. The disadvantage of such a tendency would be that it creates an environment where each person would care only about the welfare of a very small group of individuals. Such a state of affairs is likely to be exacerbated when valuable resources (e.g., water, oil, land) become scarce. In addition, as Agreeableness increases in the general population to the extent that highly agreeable individuals begin to get cheated out of the resources they worked hard to obtain by others who do not obey the rules, these agreeable individuals will have to learn to become more skeptical of others, which will result in a subsequent decrease in Agreeableness in the general population as an adaptive response. Again, such a rise in skepticism will mostly likely produce a reduction in the trust of and willingness to cooperate with others. Thus, variation in Agreeableness will rise and fall in the general population as individuals learn to trust and work with others, but not to be too trusting and cooperative to the point that they are taken advantage of by others. In a sense, we need variation in the trait of Agreeableness to help "keep us on our guard."

This concludes our discussion of the emergence of individual differences and the sources of influence on the expression of variation in personality characteristics, including the dimensions of the FFM, from the evolutionary viewpoint. A summary of the main points noted in this section are presented in "Summing It Up: Evolutionary Influences on Individual Differences" on p. 372. In the next section, we will examine some basic strategic expressions for meeting the fundamental evolutionary task of survival and reproduction.

Basic Expressions of the Evolutionary Viewpoint: Strategic Efforts for Survival and Reproduction

Fundamental expressions of our attempts to meet the basic evolutionary tasks of survival and reproduction involve being able to mate successfully with other members of our species (Buss, 2005b). In this section, we will examine sexual selection and mate-retention strategies as two expressions of our attempts at successful mating, according to the principles of evolution. We will also examine the expressions of mate poaching as a basic threat to mate selection and retention, and jealousy as a basic reaction to such a threat.

Sexual Selection: The Evolutionary Making of a Mate

We have said that natural selection makes possible the development of physical changes and personality characteristics that increase the likelihood of survival and reproduction. A strategic expression linked to survival

and reproduction is that of sexual selection (Darwin 1859/1958). **Sexual selection** is the process by which an organism's characteristic features evolve to promote the possibility of successful mating. A basic assumption of this process is: "Traits that increase the probability of successful reproduction will tend to increase in frequency over time" (Kenrick, Sadalla, Groth, & Trost, 1990, p. 97). Sexual selection can be divided into two forms: epigamic selection (i.e., mate selection) and intrasexual competition (Figueredo et al., 2005). In **epigamic selection**, males and females select as mates those who possess specific characteristics that increase the likelihood of passing on their genes to the next generation. As a result, these favored characteristics will continue to evolve in the way they are expressed because those who express them most successfully will have more mating opportunities. For example, females of a particular species might prefer to mate with socially dominant males that display the most physical strength, while males might prefer to mate with females with soft, smooth, and clean skin and other physical features associated with good health. **Intrasexual competition** refers to interpersonal exchanges (e.g., forms of competition) between same-sex members of the species in which superior characteristics are demonstrated to prove that one member or another is a preferable mate and to increase its potential mating opportunities. For

What aspects of epigamic selection do you believe are expressed in this photograph?

example, males demonstrating the most strength and greatest ability to protect the females in their territory from other males will have more mating opportunities.

These two forms of sexual selection work together. For example, in females of a particular species of fish, a bright red coloring may develop on the stomach when they are at their hormonal peak for reproduction. Although this coloring may make them easy targets for predators and, thus, may work against the process of natural selection, it also signals clearly to the males that they are receptive to mating. The males' preference for mating with those females with bright red coloring is an example of epigamic selection. Males that have the best ability to see the changes in body coloring and that react fastest to these changes, while also having the strength to keep other males away, maximize their likelihood not only of mating and reproduction but also of passing along those characteristics (e.g., visual acuity, enhanced motor ability, social dominance, and physical strength) to the next generation, which in turn will promote survival and reproductive success. In this case, intrasexual competition among the male members of the species involves how well they see, how quickly they move, and how powerful they are.

Thus, not only do epigamic selection and intra-sexual competition work together, but natural selection and sexual selection also work together to increase the probability of survival and reproductive success. We next consider some of the physical and personality characteristics that are associated with sexual selection.

Physical and Personality Correlates of Sexual Selection: What We Want in a Mate

Now that you have a basic understanding of the process of sexual selection, we will consider what physical and personality characteristics are associated with sexual selection. In other words, "What do we want in a mate?" From an evolutionary point of view, we prefer individuals who possess the physical and personality characteristics associated with (1) the greatest likelihood of producing offspring with the best genetic composition and (2) the greatest potential to work with us to maximize our own survival and that of our offspring.

Physical Correlates of Sexual Selection: Health in Women, Strength in Men   The process of sexual selection is based on ability to attract a mate. The most visible cues available to demonstrate one's suitability

as a mate are physical features. In this section, we will consider those physical features individuals value and seem to prefer in a mate.

FEMALE MATE VALUE: A HEALTHY LOOK   According to the process of sexual selection, the principal physical characteristics associated with preference for a female mate tend to be linked with the ability to reproduce, such as age and health (Buss, 1992; Sugiyama, 2005). The logic is that sexual attractiveness is linked to age because there is a specific span of time – the time between menarche and menopause – during which females are most capable of reproduction. As a woman ages, she progressively loses her reproductive ability until she is no longer able to reproduce. In addition, healthy females are more likely than unhealthy females to become pregnant and reproduce.

A few of the physical characteristics associated with indices of health and sexual attractiveness in women include breast size and shape, movement patterns, hair quality, and overall body symmetry (Sugiyama, 2005). Breast size and shape are associated with age, health, and reproductive ability (Manning, Scutt, Whitehouse, & Leinster, 1997; Symons, 1979), with firm, high breasts being associated with youth and physical ability, and sagging breasts and a lack of fullness suggesting increased age and declining reproductive ability. Increased breast size is linked with attractiveness, perceived health, and sexual desirability (Grammer, Fink, Thornhill, Juette, & Runzal, 2002), particularly when associated with a low waist-to-hip ratio (i.e., small waist; Singh & Young, 1995). With respect to movement patterns, in one study involving ratings of pixilated images of women, respondents rated women who were able to make slow, more fluid movements as being more attractive, the assumption being that such movements provide information about age and agility (Grammer et al., 2002). In an examination of the hair samples of women between the ages of 13 and 73, younger women with a high reproductive value tended to have longer hair than did older women (Hinsz, Matz, & Patience, 2001). Ratings of overall body symmetry (i.e., the balanced development of both sides of the body) were found to be negatively associated with body mass index (i.e., body-fat level in proportion to height and weight) and overall reported number of medical conditions (Milne et al., 2003), suggesting that symmetry is linked with better health. Thus, as cues (e.g., loosening of the skin) associated with advanced age appear in females, their sexual attractiveness is decreased. Such reasoning helps to explain the attraction that men seem to have for youthful-looking women and the emphasis on beauty products (e.g., skin creams) and services (e.g., plastic surgery) designed to help women look younger.

MALE MATE VALUE: A LOOK OF STRENGTH   In addition to preferring a mate with high genetic quality, females also greatly value qualities related to a mate's ability to provide material resources for them, their offspring, and other adults (Gurven, Allen-Arave, Hill, & Hurtado, 2000; Kaplan, Hill, Lancaster, & Hurtado, 2000; Sugiyama & Chacon, 2000, 2005). Males who are perceived as being better able to provide these material resources tend to be more sexually attractive. For our early ancestors, such characteristics might have involved physical strength and the ability to hunt successfully and protect one's mate and offspring from predators. In comparison to males, females tend to be less concerned with youth and physical attractiveness in mates because males, unlike females, are able to reproduce from puberty to well into old age.

A few of the physical features associated with the ability to provide protection and material resources include height, body symmetry, and shoulder-to-hip ratio (Sugiyama, 2005). In contemporary populations, there tends to be a positive association between male height and health (Silventoinen, Lahelma, & Rahkonen, 1999) and reproductive success (Nettle, 2002). Preference for taller men has been demonstrated in response to personal ads and sperm donor selection, with taller men receiving more responses to their ads (Pawlowski & Koziel, 2002) and greater consideration by women as sperm donors (Scheib, Kristiansen, & Wara, 1997). Body symmetry in males is positively associated with being more muscular (Gangestad & Thornhill, 1997), being larger (Manning, 1995), and having a higher degree of testosterone-related facial cues (i.e., a more masculine-looking face) of dominance and reproductive health (Gangestad & Thornhill, 2003). Consistent with the basic principles of sexual selection, such a collection of "masculine features" seems to pay off in that women tend to find these traits desirable in terms of sexual partners (Greiling & Buss, 2000), particularly when in the most fertile phases of their ovulatory cycle (i.e., when their potential for pregnancy and reproduction is at its peak; Thornhill & Gangestad, 2003).

Women also tend to perceive as more attractive males with an "inverted-triangle torso" (e.g., moderately broad shoulders and chest), as long as they are not too muscular (Dijkstra & Buunk, 2001). Males with a favorable hip-to-shoulder ratio engaged in sexual intercourse at an earlier age and had more sexual partners (Hughes & Gallup, 2002), as well as being more physically and socially dominant and creating more feelings of jealousy in other males (Dijkstra & Buunk, 2001). Again, consistent with the principles of sexual selection, these masculine characteristics provide an epigamic selection advantage, in that such males are preferred by females as sexual partners, as well as an intrasexual competitive advantage, as they are seen by other males as a formidable source of competition.

GENDER DIFFERENCES IN MATE-VALUE ENHANCEMENT STRATEGIES: INCREASING INTRASEXUAL COMPETITIVENESS   It seems that males and females are aware of the physical characteristics that are preferred by the opposite sex in the process of sexual selection, and that they tend to engage in gender-specific behavioral strategies designed to produce such physical characteristics. For example, a recent investigation of sex differences in exercise behaviors and motivations revealed sex-appropriate strategies consistent with the evolutionary perspective (Jonason, 2007). Specifically, males reported spending more time and effort on exercise to increase and tone muscles in their upper body (i.e., chest) than did females. On the other hand, females reported spending more time and effort on exercise to reduce the size of their lower body (i.e., legs, hips, and buttocks) than did males. Males also reported a greater emphasis on gaining muscles when describing the focus of their exercise than did women. In just the opposite manner, females reported a greater emphasis on losing weight when describing the focus of their exercise than did males. Finally, although females spent slightly more effort on enhancing their abdomen than did males, this difference was not significant.

Such a pattern of behavior is consistent with the expression of strategies based on intrasexual competition. Recognizing the value women tend to place on the appearance of physical strength in their preferences for a mate, the focus of exercise by males is designed to increase their muscle mass and tone and enhance their chest-to-waist ratio – seeking that "inverted-triangle-torso" look. On the other hand, recognizing the value males place on the appearance of a healthy look in their preferences for mates, the focus of females' exercise is designed to lose weight and reduce the size of their lower body in an attempt to maintain a favorable hip-to-waist ratio, particularly as a means of enhancing the look of their breasts, and reduce their overall level of body fat, making them appear more healthy and feminine. Thus, while people may report that they are exercising to be in better shape, the "shape" that they are creating seems to be influenced, to some degree, by underlying process linked to the evolutionary perspective. Do you exercise? If so, what type of exercise do you do, and what is your motivation for doing so? Do you exercise to improve your health, be stronger, or look good to others?

Global consistency in mate value: International similarity in sexual selection   The tendency for males to focus on age and health in a mate, and the tendency of females to focus on the ability to provide material resources and protection in a mate, does not seem to be culturally specific. For example, in a widely cited study in which the characteristics of males and females from 37 different countries were examined, Buss found that, consistent with the process of sexual selection, males tend to place a greater emphasis on reproductive cues – age, health, and physical attractiveness – while females tend to place a greater emphasis on cues associated with the ability to provide material resources – educational level, socioeconomic status, and intelligence (Buss, 1989). More recent research in the Netherlands involving men and women aged 20 to 60 also tends to support such gender differences in mate values based on the principles of sexual selection (Buunk, Dukstra, Fetchenhauer, & Kenrick, 2002). Specifically, males preferred females who were more attractive than themselves, while females preferred males whose income, education, self-confidence, intelligence, dominance, and social position were greater than their own. Although these results suggest that females care more than males about material resources in terms of their preference for a mate, other research has documented that both men and women prefer to have a wealthy mate (Hanko, Master, & Sabini, 2004; Miller, Putcha-Bhagavatula, & Pedersen, 2002). Such preferences are not limited to contemporary mate preferences, as both George Washington and Thomas Jefferson saw the advantage of marrying wealthy widows (Wood, 2004).

Personality Correlates of Sexual Selection: Universal Preferences and Gender Differences   In addition to physical characteristics associated with mate value, personality correlates also exist that are related to sexual selection (Figueredo et al., 2005). In this section, we will examine the personality characteristics that seem to be generally more desirable in those individuals we would prefer as a mate, as well as gender differences in these preferred personality characteristics.

Consensual preferences in personality characteristics: A kind and committed mate   Consensual preferences in personality characteristics are preferences shared by men and women. Overall, both men and women across a variety of countries reported the characteristics they wanted most in a partner included being *kind*, *understanding*, and *intelligent* (Buss, 1985, 1989). In other research, Buss and Barnes (1986) found that *exciting personality* was also included with the traits of being kind, understanding, and intelligent. In creating a "top-10 list" of personality characteristics, they also noted that those 10 characteristics men and women most preferred in a partner included being: a *good companion*, *considerate*, *honest*, *affectionate*, *dependable*, *intelligent*, *kind*, *understanding*, *interesting to talk to*, and *loyal*.

It is easy to see how having a mate with these characteristics would contribute to the likelihood of a successful relationship. In taking care of each other and in nurturing their offspring, the individuals in that relationship would promote reproductive success, passing along to the next generation those genes and personality characteristics that would maximize the survival of the species. In addition, although males and females both expressed a preference for a mate with both masculine (e.g., being active and instrumental) and feminine (e.g., being nurturing and expressive) characteristics, the feminine characteristics were more important than the masculine ones (Green & Kenrick, 1994). Again, it is easy to see how such feminine characteristics would be important to promoting a successful relationship with a mate (e.g., expressing one's feelings) and the care of offspring (e.g., nurturing) in a manner consistent with the processes of sexual selection.

In an interesting twist to examining personality correlates of mate preference, Figueredo, Sefcek, and Jones (2004) asked individuals to rate the preferred personality characteristics of their ideal romantic partner along the lines of the personality characteristics included in the Big Five personality dimensions. These are Openness to Experience, Conscientiousness, Extraversion, Agreeableness, and Neuroticism (see pp. 299–300). The researchers then asked the respondents to rate their own personality characteristics along those same five dimensions. The romantic ideal and self-ratings correlated .81 for Openness to Experience, .36 for

Conscientiousness, .60 for Extraversion, .73 for Agreeableness, and .38 for Neuroticism. These results suggest that individuals prefer a romantic partner with personality characteristics similar to their own. In addition, the authors then calculated a difference score between the romantic-ideal ratings and self-ratings. These scores indicated that individuals preferred that their romantic ideal mate score significantly higher than themselves on Conscientiousness, Extraversion, and Agreeableness and lower than themselves on Neuroticism, with no difference being found for Openness to Experience. Thus, men and women both tend to want an ideal mate who is better than themselves on the positive characteristics – but not too much better, as evidenced by the correlations of similarity – and lower and somewhat different on the negative characteristics. It is easy to see how having such an ideal romantic partner would make for an ideal relationship.

GENDER-SPECIFIC PREFERENCES IN PERSONALITY CHARACTERISTICS We have said that males and females have consensual preferences in personality characteristics. Certain gender-specific preferences exist as well. For example, in an investigation of preferred personal characteristics in potential mates, Buss and Barnes (1986) reported that females ranked *considerate, honest, dependable, understanding, fond of children, well-liked by others, good earning capacity, ambitious and career orientated, good family background,* and *tall* higher than males. On the other hand, males ranked *physically attractive, good looking, good cook,* and *frugal* higher than females. This is consistent with our earlier statements about mate preferences being related to survival and reproduction. For males, physically attractive mates are associated with health, reproductive success, and culinary ability; and frugality is associated with the ability to provide the domestic skills necessary to care for the family in a manner that places the fewest demands on the male. For example, being a frugal cook eases demands on the male to provide food and other domestic resources. For females, ambitious and successful mates are associated with the ability to provide family necessities (e.g., food and shelter), while being kind, dependable, and fond of children are associated with the ability to provide care and protection for offspring and extended family. Additional research has supported this reasoning, noting that the personality traits of dominance and Agreeableness are related to females' perception that males scoring high on these two characteristic are more attractive (Jensen-Campbell,

Graziano, & West, 1995: Sadalla, Kenrick, & Vershure, 1987) and wealthier (Jensen-Campbell et al., 1995). Again, these results are consistent with notion that dominant and agreeable males are able to provide the necessary material resources for the family while also being easy to get along with as mates and members of the greater community.

This concludes our discussion of some of the fundamental processes associated with sexual selection. A summary of the major points discussed in this section is presented in "Summing It Up: Basic Expressions of Sexual Selection" on p. 378. In the next section, we will consider some of the basic responses associated with sexual selection by examining how individuals attempt to retain their mates and poach the mates of others, as well as their jealous reactions to threats to their relationships.

Mate-Retention Strategies: Protecting Your (Parental) Investment

In addition to being able to attract a mate with the preferred physical and personality characteristics, there is the related need to retain one's mate in the face of mating opportunities outside of the relationship (Campbell & Ellis, 2005). Such opportunities can pose threats to the relationship partners and their offspring. When a man has an extramarital relationship, he places the woman in his primary relationship at risk of losing material resources for herself and her offspring to the other woman and her resulting offspring. When a woman has an extramarital relationship, she creates for the man in her primary relationship the additional risk of losing material resources to offspring that are not genetically related to him at the expense of his genetically related offspring.

To maximize the possibility of retaining a mate and minimize the possibility of extramarital mating, men and women have developed specific mate-retention strategies. Buss and Shackelford (1997) reported that men tend to use displays of resources more than women do, while women tend to use appearance enhancement as a mate-retention tactic more than men do. For example, males might drive an expensive car and buy expensive gifts for potential mates as a display of their material resources. Females, on the other hand, might use cosmetics, figure-enhancing undergarments, and Botox injections to give themselves a more youthful

Summing It Up *Basic Expressions of Sexual Selection*

Basic Expression	Example
Sexual Selection. The process by which certain characteristics emerge because they are associated with successful mate selection and reproduction	Males developed more aggressive tendencies while women developed more compassionate tendencies because such characteristics made it possible to provide for and take care of their children, respectively.
Epigamic Selection. The emergence of certain characteristics because they tend to be preferred in the process of mate selection	Males developed more competitive tendencies while females developed more compassionate tendencies because such characteristics were seen as desirable by potential mates.
Intrasexual Competition. The competitive display between same-sex members of the species of those characteristics that will make them a desired mate	On the beach during vacation, the males race their boats to display their competitive nature while the females walk around in their bikinis to show how attractive they are.
Physical Correlates of Sexual Selection. The physical characteristics males and females prefer in their selection of potential mates	When writing a personal ad, males and females tend to list different physical qualities for potential respondents.
Female Mate Value. The expressed tendency for males to prefer females who appear to be healthy and possess characteristics related to successful reproductive ability	In his personals ad, William states he is "seeking someone who is fit, in proportion in height and weight, and in her late 20s and middle 30s."
Male Mate Value. The expressed tendency for females to prefer males who appear strong and possess those characteristics associated with an ability to provide material resources for the family	In her personals ad, Sue states she is "seeking someone who is college educated with a successful work history."
Personality Correlates of Mate Selection. The personality characteristics males and females prefer in their selection of potential mates	When writing a personals ad, males and females tend to list different personality characteristics for potential respondents.
Consensual Preferences in Personality Characteristics. The tendency of both males and females to prefer a mate who is kind, considerate and intelligent, and has an exciting personality	When writing their personals ad, both John and Jamie stated they were "seeking someone who is nice, understanding of the feelings of others, and educated but with a slight 'wild side.' "
Gender-Specific Preferences in Personality Characteristics. The tendency of females to prefer a mate who is family and career oriented, and of males to prefer a mate who is good looking, a good cook, and frugal	When writing her personals ad, Jessica stated she was "seeking someone with a successful work history who likes children," while Dave stated he was "seeking someone who is fit, likes to cook, and is financially conservative."

appearance. This study also reported that males' tendency to display resources as a mate-retention tactic was strongly associated with their partners' youthfulness and perceived attractiveness, while women's use of appearance-enhancing tactics was strongly associated with their mate's income and his effort to achieve status (e.g., working to earn money). Thus, such mate-retention tactics are highly consistent with the mate-preference characteristics noted previously – males value youth while females value material resources

– because they help to promote the success of the relationship, maximizing the probability of survival and reproduction. What mate-retention strategies have you used to help maintain a relationship, and how well did they work?

Mate Poaching: A Basic Threat to Mate Retention

In the context of our discussion of mate-retention strategies, maintaining a long-term relationship with a mate was assumed to ensure protection, resources, and care for the mates and their offspring. We now examine the threats to mate retention. These can come in the form of short-term mating behaviors, in which females mate with many males and males mate with many females. Such behaviors are typically brief, lack the exclusivity of long-term monogamous relationships, and involve long-term parenting responsibilities that typically are assumed by the female and her relatives (Schmitt, 2005). A common strategy associated with such short-term mating behavior is **mate poaching**, or "trying to attract someone who is already in a romantic relationship" (Schmitt & Buss, 2001, p. 894). The object of such poaching might be married, recently engaged, currently living with someone, or otherwise committed in an exclusive relationship.

In an examination of the pervasiveness of poaching among U.S. college students, Schmitt and Buss (2001) reported that approximately 60 percent of men and 40 percent of women had attempted short-term mate poaching and that nearly 80 percent of men and women reported that they had been targets of a mate-poaching attempt. In response, 50 percent of men and 35 percent of women reported having succumbed to such an attempt. Consequently, 15 percent of individuals in current relationships stated the current relationship was a direct result of poaching or having been poached, of which approximately 3 percent reported being a result of "co-poaching," in which both partners poached the other away from existing relationships.

Gender Differences in Poaching Strategies When seeking short-term mating opportunities, females prefer males with "good genes" over the potential to provide material resources (Schmitt, 2005). In this case, since the female does not expect the provision of a long-term commitment for material resources for herself and the offspring, and has the possibility of being saddled with all of the care, her goal is to secure and pass along to her offspring the best collection of genes to maximize

their survival, increased mate value, and eventual reproductive ability. By contrast, when a female seeks a mate for a long-term commitment, the male's ability and willingness to provide material resources and a desire to protect and care for his mate and their offspring are essential qualities For males seeking short-term mating opportunities, sexual accessibility is slightly preferred over physical symmetry. Specifically, women who are likely to consent quickly to sex are viewed as especially good candidates for short-term mating opportunities (Schmitt & Buss, 2001). On the other hand, males tend to have greater success when poaching by implementing a strategy that involves displays of status and resource-related tactics (e.g., buying gifts; Schmitt, 2002), since such a strategy is designed primarily to attract a mate for the short term and not necessarily for making a long-term commitment to the relationship and any offspring such mating may produce. This pattern of results suggests that from an evolutionary point of view, short-term mating and poaching tactics seem to have an adaptive value that differs from that stemming from tactics promoting long-term mating commitments.

The consistent nature of these results suggests that poaching is a pervasive phenomenon and that gender differences have emerged that reflect evolutionary adaptations. Going beyond such general patterns and gender differences, additional research has examined specific individual differences in the personality characteristics associated with those involved in poaching (Schmitt & Buss, 2001). For a worldwide look at the personality correlates of mate poachers and their targets, consider the material presented in "The Cultural Context of Personality Psychology."

The Cultural Context of Personality Psychology

Personality Correlates of Mate Poachers and Their Targets: A Global Perspective

As part of the International Sexual Deception Project, David P. Schmitt of Bradley University, along with 121 researchers at universities around the world, investigated mate poaching by surveying 16,954 participants from 53 nations. In all, 5 continents, 28 languages, and 12 islands were represented (Schmitt et al., 2004). The 53 nations were categorized into the 10 world regions listed in Figure 9.1. In this research, collaborators from a global perspective administered a survey in which individuals responded to questions about their poaching activities. These included their attempts to attract someone already in a romantic relationship, their success in such attempts, attempts by others to attract them into a short-term sexual relationship, and others' successes in luring them into such a relationship.

In addition to responding to the poaching-related survey items, the participants also responded to two personality inventories, including the Big Five Inventory (BFI) of personality traits (Benet-Martínez & John, 1998). The five dimensions of personality assessed by the BFI, with a sample item for each dimension, are: Extraversion "I see myself as someone who is outgoing, sociable"), Agreeableness ("I see myself as someone who is helpful and unselfish with others"), Conscientiousness ("I see myself as a reliable worker"), Neuroticism ("I see myself as someone who worries a lot"), and Openness ("I see myself as someone who is curious about many different things"). In addition to assessing general personality characteristics with the BFI, aspects of participants' sexual attributes were assessed using the Sexy Seven Measure (Schmitt & Buss, 2000). The Sexy Seven Measure requires participants to rate themselves in comparison with others they know along six rating scales: Sexual Attractiveness (including facets of beauty and seduction), Relationship Exclusivity (whether one is promiscuous and adulterous), Gender Orientation (masculinity and femininity), Sexual Restraint (abstinence and prudishness), Erotophilic Disposition (expressing obscenity, indecency, and lust), Emotional Investment (love and romance), and Sexual Orientation (homosexuality and heterosexuality).

Pervasiveness of Mate Poaching Around the World

One of the most dramatic findings of this cross-cultural investigation of poaching was its global pervasiveness. As is shown at the bottom of Figure 9.1, approximately 57 percent of men and 35 percent of women all around the world admitted to having attempted to attract someone else's partner, with the percentage of males exceeding the females in all 10 world regions. In other results, 10 percent of the individuals indicated

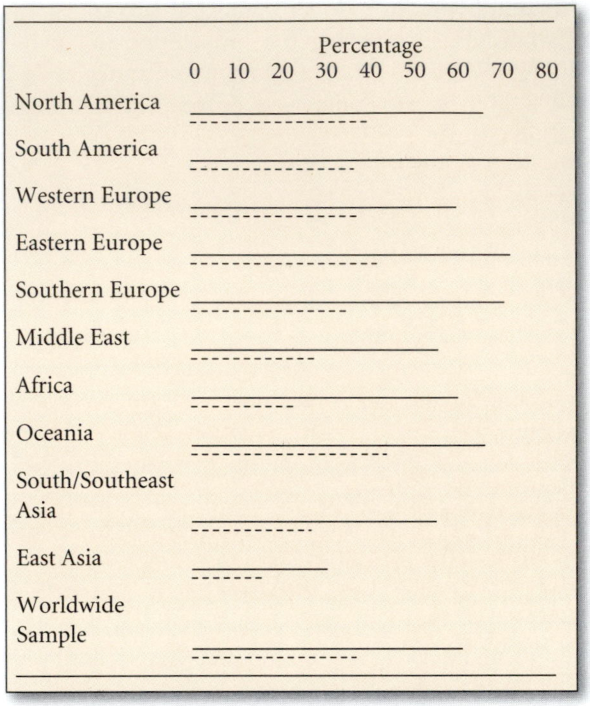

Figure 9.1   The percentage of males (—) and females (---) from 10 different world regions indicating that they had attempted mate poaching for the purpose of short-term mating.
Source: Adapted from Schmitt et al. (2004)

that their current romantic relationship was a result of mate poaching, while 3 percent reported that their current relationship was a result of mutual attempts at poaching each other away from a previous partner (Schmitt et al., 2004).

Universal Personality Correlates of Poaching

Even more dramatic than the universality of poaching was the specialized set of personality characteristics that characterized poachers and their targets across the 10 different world regions.

Personality Correlates of Mate Poachers

Around the world, individuals who attempted to poach the mates of others described themselves as extraverted, meaning active, assertive and talkative, and disagreeable (low Agreeableness score), meaning not generous, not gentle, and not empathic. However, the relation between attempts at poaching and Extraversion was stronger for males than for females, while the relationship between mate poaching and disagreeableness was stronger for females than for males. On measures of the Sexy Seven, the results were much stronger and consistent for both men and women across all 10 world regions. Specifically, attempts at mate poaching both by males and by females were strongly associated with being sexually unfaithful (i.e., lower scores on Relationship Exclusivity) and possessing an Erotophilic Disposition (i.e., scoring high in lust, perversion, and indecency).

Personality Correlates of Successful Mate Poachers

Around the world, those individuals who successfully poached the mates of others tended to score high on the dimension of Openness to Experience and Sexual Attractiveness, and to score lower on the measure of Relationship Exclusivity. Successful mate poachers also tended to describe themselves as sexually unrestrained. Having an Erotophilic Disposition was found to be more globally associated with being a successful mate poacher for women than for men. In 9 of the 10 world regions, the exception being South America, having an Erotophilic Disposition was found to be associated with women who were successful poachers. On the other hand, only in North America, Western and Eastern Europe, and East Asia was having an erotiphilic disposition found to be associated with males who were successful poachers. Such a pattern of results is consistent with our earlier statement that women demonstrating greater sexual willingness are viewed as highly successful at attracting short-term mating opportunities and are preferred for sexual accessibility by males seeking short-term mating opportunities. The tendency for successful mate poachers around the world to be attractive supports the evolutionary notion that for short-term mating opportunities women seek "good genes," which are demonstrated most visibly by "good looks," while males seek a "youthful, healthy look," which is associated with attractiveness, for both short-term and long-term mating opportunities.

Personality Correlates of Targets of Mate Poachers

The targets of mate poaching attempts around the world, regardless of whether they are male or female, also possess certain personality characteristics. Specific-

ally, they tend to be extraverted, open to experience, sexually attractive, sexually unfaithful, and erotophilic. Being extraverted and open to experience is associated with a greater likelihood of increased risk-taking behavior, including a willingness to be involved with multiple sexual relationships (Zuckerman, 1994). Again, given the expressed preferences for attractiveness in mating opportunities, it should come as no surprise that individuals who describe themselves as attractive should be targets of mate-poaching attempts. Being unfaithful and displaying a heightened degree of sexuality (e.g., being willing to talk openly about sex and sexual deviancy) appear to serve as universal cues of attraction for would-be mate poachers. Thus, just as animals in the wild look for certain cues (e.g., a limp or a deer wandering away from the herd) to indicate which will be the easiest prey, mate poachers around the world look for certain personality characteristics in potential targets.

Personality Correlates of Targets Successfully Poached Away

When considering the personality characteristics associated with individuals who reported that they were successfully poached away from their partner, researchers found that only two characteristics showed a clear and dramatic pattern across all 10 regions of the world. Specifically, individuals who were successfully poached away from their partner reported themselves to be less sexually faithful (i.e., low Relationship Exclusivity score) and more erotophilic (i.e., high score on the Erotophilic Disposition). This personality pattern suggests that individuals with a diminished view of sexual fidelity and a heightened sense of expressed sexuality are those who are most easily poached away from another partner.

In summary, mate poaching is a universal phenomenon, as are the personality characteristics of those who poach and are targets of poachers. Poachers tend to be extraverted and disagreeable, while their targets tend to be extraverted and open to experience (e.g., risk takers) and describe themselves as sexually attractive. Although the personality characteristics of the individuals involved in the various degrees of poaching vary to some degree, individuals who are most likely to attempt poaching and are most successful at it – and individuals who are targets of and have succumbed to mate-poaching attempts – tend to share two characteristics: They tend to be unfaithful (low on Relationship

Exclusivity) and they possess an Erotophilic Disposition. This universal combination seems to suggest that there are critical psychological components in the process of mate poaching. Their universal presence also prompts such questions as "Why their universal presence? What evolutionary purpose do they serve?" These and many other questions are only the beginning for future research into the personality dynamics of mate poaching. What other questions do you think should be addressed by this research?

Jealousy: A Basic Reaction to Mate Poaching

Jealousy is a response that can be triggered in reaction to real or imagined threats to the relationship by a rival (Campbell & Ellis, 2005). From an evolutionary perspective, individuals with an increased sense of vigilance to rivals have a greater likelihood of successful reproduction than those with a lower sense of vigilance (Buss, 2000). Although the frequency and intensity of jealousy do not differ in men and women (Buss, 2000; Shackelford, LeBlanc, & Drass, 2000), gender differences in triggers for jealousy do exist (Buss, 2000). These differences tend to correspond to the differing relationship goals for males and females, as seen through the lens of the evolutionary perspective (Campbell & Ellis, 2005). For males, the objective is to provide protection and material resources to their offspring to increase the likelihood of their genes surviving into the next generation. However, since providing protection and material resources for the offspring of a rival would be an extra burden (e.g., having to work extra hours) and create additional risks (e.g., health risks from overexertion), males who are sensitive to the cues of sexuality infidelity (e.g., rivals who are flirtatious and friendly) will have an evolutionary advantage by reducing the likelihood of being subjected to such additional physical burdens and risks (Haselton & Buss, 2000; Haselton, Nettle, & Andrews, 2005).

For females, on the other hand, since there is no uncertainty as to whether or not she is the mother of her offspring, the principal relationship goal is to secure a mate with the ability to provide protection and material resources. This goal would be jeopardized if her mate shifted his resources to an outside emotional relationship. Under such conditions, females who are less trusting of males' commitment in relationships and who are especially sensitive to infidelity cues will have an evolutionary advantage by reducing the likelihood of being abandoned and losing those much-needed resources to a romantic rival (Haselton & Buss, 2000).

Extensive supporting research indicates that gender differences in jealousy are expressed along the lines of those suggested by gender-specific relationship goals proposed by the evolutionary perspective (Buss, 2000). In a frequently cited study conducted by Buss and colleagues (Buss, Larsen, Westen, & Semmelroth, 1992), men and women were asked to imagine being in a close relationship and then to imagine their partner becoming involved with someone else. When asked to indicate what type of involvement would be most troubling, men said that imagining their partner enjoying passionate sexual intercourse with another person was the most bothersome, whereas women said the development of a deep emotional relationship with another person. Consistent with these self-report ratings, males displayed an increase in their pulse rate and tension in facial muscles associated with furrowing of their brow when imagining their partner having sex with another individual. These physiological measures were less pronounced when males imagined their partner had developed an emotional relationship with someone else. Women, on the other hand, displayed greater physiological reactions to the scenario involving their partner's emotional rather than sexual involvement with another individual.

In addition, men are less likely than women to forgive a partner for sexual rather than emotional infidelity; and men are more likely to terminate a relationship as a result of sexual rather than emotional infidelity (Shackelford, Buss, & Bennet, 2002). Cross-cultural research from Germany, the Netherlands, and Korea has documented the tendency for males to be more distressed than females in response to sexual infidelity (Buunk, Angleitner, Oubaid, & Buss, 1996). From an evolutionary perspective, men display more jealousy in response to sexual infidelity since such threats tend to place on them additional demands to provide for offspring that are not theirs, while women tend to display more jealousy in response to emotional infidelity since such threats tend to place on them additional demands to maintain the relationship, in an attempt to avoid the loss of the material resources that men provide to them and their offspring within that relationship. Are your experiences with jealousy consistent with those proposed by the evolutionary perspective?

This concludes our discussion of mate-retention strategies, mate poaching, and jealous reactions as associated with the process of sexual selection. A summary of the major points discussed in this section is presented in "Summing It Up: Basic Expressions of Mate Retention, Mate Poaching, and Jealousy."

Our presentation of the basic principles and fundamental patterns of expression based on the evolutionary viewpoint of personality is complete. If you would like more information about the evolutionary perspective and the topics discussed in this section, consider reading David Buss's textbook titled *Evolutionary*

Summing It Up *Basic Expressions of Mate Retention, Mate Poaching, and Jealousy*

Basic Expression	Example
Mate-Retention Strategies. Males tend to demonstrate their resources while females tend to emphasize the enhancement of their physical appearance.	Bill tries to keep his girlfriend happy by buying her lots of expensive gifts, while Julie tries to keep her boyfriend happy by going to the gym and watching what she eats.
Mate Poaching. Both males and females may attempt to attract an individual away from an already-existing romantic relationship.	Jamie was approached by a man at work to have an affair while her husband was out of town on business.
Gender Differences in Mate-Poaching Strategies. The mate-poaching activities of males and females reflect the expected duration of their relationship with the target of the poaching.	Julie began flirting with her best friend's boyfriend while her husband was away on business; David began to flirt with his best friend's girlfriend after he had fallen in love with her.
Female Mate-Poaching Strategies. Females wanting a long-term commitment seek to poach a male for his ability to provide material resources, but seek good physical features when seeking to poach a male for a short-term relationship.	Sara is thinking about having an affair with a married senior partner with the hopes of eventually marrying him, while Judy is thinking about going away for the weekend with the good-looking guy who works in the technology support department.
Male Mate-Poaching Strategies. Males seeking to poach a female tend to focus on her sexual accessibility and physical features and use the display of material resources to attract her.	David approached the attractive account manager at the firm about going away with him to his beach house while her fiancé was out of town on business.
Jealousy. Although they do not tend to differ in the frequency with which they experience jealousy, males and females tend to react differently to the real or imagined threats to a relationship by another individual.	Jake became jealous when he found out his wife was having an affair, while Reese began feeling jealous when she saw her husband talking with an attractive woman at a wedding reception.
Jealousy in Males. Males tend to exhibit feelings of jealousy in response to the real or imagined sexual transgressions of their partner.	Ian became jealous when he found out that his wife was having sex with their neighbor's husband, while Tony became jealous when he suspected that his wife might be having sex with his neighbor's husband.
Jealousy in Females. Females tend to exhibit feelings of jealously in response to the real or imagined emotional transgressions of their partner.	Ellen became jealous when her husband told her he had fallen in love with a woman at work, while Debbie became jealous when she began to suspect that her husband might be falling in love with a female co-worker.

Psychology: The New Science of the Mind (2008), which is an excellent overview of the field of evolutionary psychology, as well as two other books by Buss titled *The Evolution of Desire: Strategies for Human Mating* (2003) and *The Dangerous Passion: Why Jealousy is as Necessary as Love and Sex* (2000). In the next section, we will examine some applications of the evolutionary viewpoint.

Applications of the Evolutionary Viewpoint: Using What Is Known

Information from the evolutionary viewpoint has been applied to several different important areas of contemporary life. In this section, we will consider the application of the evolutionary perspective to some issues of personal and social concern. Specifically, we will examine the application of the evolutionary perspective to the topic of consumer behavior and to the behavioral problems of eating disorders and sexual harassment.

Consumer Behavior: Putting Your Money Where Your Evolutionary Principles Are

As the influence of evolutionary psychology in areas outside of the traditional sciences continues to increase (Saad & Gill, 2000), interest is growing in the application of these principles to consumer behavior (Bagozzi & Nataraajan, 2000; Lynn, Kampschroeder, & Perriera, 1998; Saad, 2005, 2007; Saad & Gill, 2000). A framework for applying evolutionary psychology to consumer behavior is the consideration of gender differences in the underlying principles of sexual selection noted previously. We have said that males seek attractive, youthful-looking mates, and they display material resources (or the potential for providing them) to attract such mates. Females, meanwhile, seek mates who are able to provide and share material resources; to attract them, they attempt to achieve and maintain a healthy, youthful appearance. Guided by such basic differences in mate selection, we will examine how consumer behavior can be understood by applying principles of evolutionary psychology to the purchase of cosmetic products, to financial management, and to leisure-time pursuits.

Consumer Spending on Cosmetic Products: Attempts at Achieving Attractiveness

With respect to the emphasis on physical appearance for women as a means of increasing their mate potential, researchers have noted that women devote more consumer time and energy than men to appearance-related attitudes and behaviors, including fashion concerns, body consciousness, dieting frequency and restrictive dieting, cosmetic surgery attitudes, sunbathing frequency, and tanning salon usage (Burton, Netemeyer, & Lichtenstein, 1994). In addition, in an examination of 1998 statistics from the American Academy of Cosmetic Surgeons that involved 4,879,464 cosmetic procedures in the United States, Saad and Gill (2000) reported that the number of cosmetic procedures performed on females (3,892,139 or approximately 80 percent) was approximately four times that for males (987,325 or approximately 20 percent). Of these procedures, females were more likely to have the following performed: chemical peel (827,640 or 86.69 percent), sclerotherapy (vein surgery) (410,450 or 94.67 percent), breast surgery (105,237 or 89.66 percent), liposuction surgery (312,487 or 83.81 percent), facial surgery (581,993 or 76.54 percent), and all other procedures (1,637,368 or 88.63 percent). The only category in which this trend did not appear was for the cosmetic procedure of hair transplant or restoration, with males (192,999 or 91.92 percent) far exceeding the number performed on females (16,964 or 8.08 percent). Even with less extreme procedures, women accounted for 48 percent ($8,651 million) of the yearly total sales of $18,058 million of cosmetic products for such appearance-enhancement products as color cosmetics (e.g., face makeup, eye makeup, lip color, nail color, and other related produces, such as applicators, organizers, etc; $5,352 million or 30 percent) and women's fragrances (e.g., perfumes, colognes, and fine fragrance ancillary products; $3,209 million or 18 percent). Thus, consistent with the principles of sexual selection, females tend to spend more money than males do on appearance-enhancement products.

Consumer Decisions Related to Money Management: Risky Business

Although women tend to place more emphasis on looking good, men tend to place more emphasis on the acquisition and display of their status and ability to

You Can Do It

Doing "Risky Business": Will You Stick Your Neck Out to Get Ahead?

Indicate whether or not you would be willing to engage in each of the 10 acts listed below by responding "yes" or "no."

_____ 1. Take a sick day to go on an interview for a better-paying job

_____ 2. Look for a better-paying job on your employer's computer during company time

_____ 3. Falsify information during a job interview for a better-paying job

_____ 4. Save money by taking supplies home from work to use for your school assignments

_____ 5. Pad your expense account with an extra $50.00

_____ 6. Falsify information on your income tax form to save $500.00

_____ 7. Engage in the use of "insider trading" information in the purchase of stocks

_____ 8. Falsify information on a loan application for a new car

_____ 9. Use electronic transfer procedures to take $20,000 from your employer

_____ 10. Make a profit of $100,000 from the sale of marijuana

Now ask a few of your male and female friends to respond to these items. To what extent were you willing to engage in some "risky business" to get ahead financially? How did you compare to your male and female friends? Are your results consistent with the principles based on the evolutionary perspective discussed in the text?

---

provide material resources. Both are motivated by a need to increase their mate value within the process of sexual selection. On this fundamental principle of evolutionary psychology, males can be assumed to be willing to take greater risks than females to achieve material resources. Consistent with this reasoning, researchers have found that males engage in more risky financial decision making than do females (Powell & Ansic, 1997) and that single females hold less of their wealth in risky assets (e.g., stocks) than do single males (Jianakoplos & Bernasek, 1998). Finally, males are more willing than females to engage in unethical behaviors at work to acquire additional financial resources (Betz, O'Connell, & Shepard, 1989). Specifically, males were more willing than females to claim an extra $50 on their travel expenses (39.3 percent vs. 19.6 percent), buy stock with inside information (50.0 percent vs. 31.3 percent), transfer $20,000 by computer from their employer (12.3 percent vs. 4.0 percent), and make $100,000 from a marijuana deal (17.5 percent vs. 2.0 percent). It is interesting to note that as the dollar value of the risk increased, so did the difference in the ratio of males to females who would be willing to engage in the risky, unethical financial behavior. These results suggest that the tendency for males to be more concerned with material resources is reflected in their increased willingness to take more risks to achieve financial success. How much risk are you willing to take to achieve increased financial success? What about your friends? To find out, try the activity presented in "You Can Do It" above.

Consumption in Leisure Pursuits: Spending in Your Spare Time

An old saying suggests "time is money." If this is true, males can increase their mate-selection value through the way they spend money in their spare time. Away from their jobs, they can engage in high-risk intrasexual activities that demonstrate aggressiveness and competitiveness as a secondary index of their ability to acquire and provide material resources. A manifestation of such intrasexual expression can be the degree of risk associated with the consumer-related pursuits in their leisure-time activities. From a summary of gender differences in leisure activity pursuits, Saad & Gill (2000) reported that a substantially greater number of males than females participated in the more risky outdoor activities of windsurfing (63 percent vs. 37 percent), power boating (60 percent vs. 40 percent), hunting (79 percent vs. 21 percent), snowmobiling (63 percent vs. 37 percent), motorcycling (72 percent vs. 28 percent), and snowboarding (67 percent vs. 33 percent). Gender differences were much smaller in the less risky leisure pursuits of canoeing (55 percent vs. 45 percent), bicycle riding (52 percent vs. 48 percent), and roller-blading (53 percent vs. 47 percent). Thus, while such high-risk activities may not be directly related to formal social status (e.g., being the president of a bank), engaging in them – which often involves consumer-related expense (e.g., a power boat or motor-cycle vs. a bicycle or rollerblades) – can serve as a marker of status and can further demonstrate a male's

potential for providing material resources . Thus, even in their leisure time, males seem to be willing to take more risks and spend more money to improve their mate-selection value in a manner consistent with the principles of sexual selection.

In this section, we have seen how the principles of sexual selection can be used to influence consumer decisions about how we look, manage our money, and spend money while we play. However, we do not just spend money on ourselves. We also spend money on others, frequently by buying gifts. Are our gifting decisions also consistent with the principles of sexual selection, or do they follow other rules? To find out, read "At the Cutting Edge of Personality Psychology."

AT THE CUTTING EDGE OF PERSONALITY PSYCHOLOGY

An Evolutionary Analysis of Tactical Fiscal Allocation

Sexual Selection and the Ritual of Gift-Giving: The Trojan Horse Effect

According to ancient legend, Greek warriors presented the citizens of Troy with a huge wooden horse full of hidden Greek soldiers. The warriors' hope was that once the horse was inside the city walls, the hidden soldiers would emerge in the cover of darkness, open the gates to let the rest of their army in, and take over the city of Troy while its citizens slept. The lesson of this story is to be wary of gifts from others because, rather than stemming from simple kindness, they may be based on ulterior motives. In this regard, marketing researchers Gad Saad of Concordia University and Tripat Gill of Case Western Reserve University (2003) applied the principles of sexual selection to examine gender differences in the motives of the ritual of gift-giving.

In this research, undergraduate students completed a survey about various tactical and situational motives for gift-giving. The tactical motives were: displaying financial resources, creating a good impression, as a means of seduction, showing affection, displaying long-term interest, and displaying generosity. The

situational motives were: the occasion demanding it, reconciliation after a fight, and to reciprocate. To assess their gift-giving motives, the participants indicated the frequency that each reason was a critical factor when making the decision to give a gift to their partner. To assess the accuracy of their perceptions of their partner's gift-giving motives, the participants indicated, to the best of their knowledge, the frequency each of the reasons given was a critical factor in their partner's decision to give a gift to them. All responses were made on a five-point scale ranging from 1 ("never") to 5 ("always").

In addition, Saad and Gill tested another evolutionary principle suggesting that investment would be greater (i.e., more money would be spent on gifts) in individuals who were genetically similar (e.g., relatives) than those who were dissimilar (e.g., teachers). To assess the relationship between gift-giving and genetic similarity, the respondents were given a list of potential gift recipients who varied in their genetic similarity, and were asked to indicate how much money they would spend on gifts for each individual. Those with a high degree of genetic similarity included mother, father, and older or younger sister or brother. Those with moderate genetic similarity included aunt, uncle, niece, nephew, grandmother, grandfather, half-brother, and half-sister. Those with the lowest degree of similarity included stepmother, stepfather, stepbrother, stepsister, close friend, romantic partner, teacher, boyfriend's parents, and child for whom the individuals babysat.

His vs. Her Motives for Gift-Giving: Gender Differences in the Presentation of Presents

Males were more likely than females to use five of the six tactical motives when offering gifts to their romantic partners, with the motive "to create a good impression" being the strongest. The only exception was that males and females were equally likely to use the tactical motive of "displaying generosity" as a gift-giving strategy. On the other hand, males and females did not differ in the frequency of their use of the three situational motives.

These results are consistent with the evolutionary explanation of gift-giving as a romantic courtship strategy in that males display resources (e.g., give gifts) as a strategy to achieve short-term mating opportunities and to demonstrate their interest in a long-term mating commitment (Schmitt & Buss, 1996). They are also consistent with the work of Belk and Coon (1993), in which males reported believing that gift-giving can be used as a form of exchange for sexual favors, and that gift-giving was reduced when they had achieved a "victory" in securing a long-term commitment (e.g., when the women professed their love). In addition, these researchers reported that although women are as likely to give a gift to a man or woman, men tend to give gifts primarily to women, providing further support for the evolutionary explanation of gift-giving. The lack of gender differences in the use of situational motives for gift-giving suggests that males and females employ these motives equally in response to the dictates of social norms (e.g., for a birthday) and to maintain balance in a relationship in response to a specific event (e.g., as a peace offering after a fight, or as part of a mutual gift-giving exchange such as an anniversary gift). Thus, although males are more likely to give gifts to attract a partner (e.g., display financial resources, make a good impression, as a means of seduction, show affection, and display long-term interest), both males and females use gift-giving equally to demonstrate a sense of generosity and similar level of commitment to maintaining the relationship as

equal partners within it (e.g., display balance and equality in their investment to each other).

His vs. Her Perceptions of Gift-Giving Motives: Gender Differences in Looking a Gift Horse in the Mouth

With respect to participants' perceptions of why they give gifts versus why their partners give them gifts, there were clear gender differences. For five of the six tactical motives, males believed their partners give gifts for the same reasons they give gifts to their partners, the exception being the motive of "displaying long-term interest." In this case, males perceived their partners were using this motive to a greater degree than they themselves used it. On the other hand, females perceived their partner as using five of the six tactical motives to a greater degree in giving gifts to them than they themselves used when giving gifts to their partner, the exception being "displaying generosity." In this case, females perceived that they used this motive to a greater degree when giving gifts than their partner did. With respect to the three situational motives, males and females did not differ in their perceptions of the extent to which they and their partners used these motives when giving gifts to each other.

These results suggest that within the courtship process, women tend to be aware that males are likely to use a variety of tactical motives to attract them. Males, by contrast, lack this awareness, suggesting that "they have not learned to read the signals in this type of gift-giving exchange" (Saad & Gill, 2003, p. 779). From an evolutionary perspective, females may have developed a greater ability to detect the gift-giving motives of males because it protects them from being attracted to and mating with males who are insincere or not committed to a long-term relationship. Why? The consequences of doing so would be more severe for the female, who would bear most of the responsibility for any offspring that result from such mating. At the very least there would be the initial cost of time associated with the nine-month pregnancy, and at the very most there might be complete responsibility for the welfare of the child without any material support from the male. By contrast, little genetic risk is associated with the male's ability to perceive the gift-giving motives of women. If a man is misled into mating with a woman by her gift-giving strategies, at the very least a principal advantage is the increased probability of the successful transmission of his genes to the next generation through any offspring that are produced (Saad & Gill, 2003).

Resource Allocation and the Role of Genetic and Interpersonal Closeness: Gift-Giving to Family, Friends, and Lovers

No gender differences were noted in the amount of money one would be willing to spend and the individual on whom it would be spent. However, with respect to the relation between an individual's genetic similarity and the amount of money a participant would spend on a gift for that individual, the results indicated partial support of the evolutionary perspective. Specifically, although participants were willing to spend more on gifts for highly genetically similar individuals (e.g., mother, father, siblings; average of $73.12) than on moderately similar ones (e.g., grandmother, grandfather, aunt, half-sibling; average of $19.03) or those with a low degree of genetic similarity (e.g., stepmother, stepfather, stepsister; average of $18.56), they also were willing to spend the most (average of $106.43) on their partner, with whom they had no genetic similarity. Similarly, they were willing to spend more on a gift for a friend (average of $46.34) and individuals in the "other" category (average of $27.03), with whom they lack genetic similarity, than on those with whom they have a moderate or low degree of similarity.

These results suggest that the primary motive for gift-giving by the college-aged participants is based on reproductive fitness – passing one's genes along to the next generation – to a greater degree than non-reproductive fitness – taking care of others who are genetically close. This makes perfectly good sense,

given that college students are operating in their principal mate-seeking period (Saad & Gill, 2003) with the limited resources typical of this stage. In other words, college students must allocate their gift-giving resources to their maximum advantage, which means spending the most on gifts for individuals who offer the greatest opportunity for reproductive success. The tendency to spend more on gifts for a friend and others (e.g., girlfriend's parents) than on those with a moderate or low level of genetic similarity may reflect the influence of "perceived similarity" or interpersonal closeness to a greater degree than genetic similarity or biological closeness. Indeed, when Saad and Gill asked the participants to provide ratings of their "perceived relatedness" to the list of individuals (e.g., parents, partner, nephew, friend, teacher) along a 100-point scale (0 = completely unrelated to 100 = extremely closely related), a significant positive association ($r = .48$) was seen between the perceived closeness with the individual and the amount of money the participant would be willing to spend on the next gift for that individual. This provides support for an evolutionary explanation of allocation of resources to those individuals who matter the most from both a genetic (e.g., parents) and reproductive (e.g., romantic partner) perspective.

Such research provides a closer look at the application of the evolutionary perspective to a ritual of consumer behavior that we all engage in on a routine basis. Take a few moments to reflect on the motives for your own gift-giving behavior and on the recipients of your gifts. How well do such findings fit into your past, present, and future gift-giving tendencies? How well do they fit with those of family and friends? To find out, do a little of your own research by asking them.

The application of evolutionary psychology to individual differences in consumer behavior can help us understand the underlying dynamics of how and why we manage our money the way we do. In the next section, we will turn our attention to the application of the evolutionary viewpoint to understanding a problem of a more personal concern that also involves consumption, but in this case it is the problematic consumption of food in the form of certain eating disorders.

Eating Disorders: The Evolutionary Perspective on Eating Too Much and Eating Too Little

Two pervasive problems associated with food consumption involve either eating too much or eating too little. In this section. we will explore how principles from the evolutionary explanations can help us understand the underlying dynamics associated with eating too much, resulting in obesity, and eating too little, resulting in anorexia nervosa and bulimia.

Obesity: Applying Ancient Wisdom to a Contemporary Problem

Although **obesity** is technically not considered an eating disorder, it has become a major public health concern. Estimates indicate that approximately 60 percent of the U.S. population is considered overweight and 27 percent is considered obese (Koretz, 2001). Contributing to this problem is that during the past 15 years, obesity has risen by 30 percent in adults and 100 percent in children (Kring, Davison, Neale, & Johnson, 2007), with an estimated health cost of approximately $117 billion in the year 2000 alone (USDHHS, 2001).

The general approach to understanding obesity has been to focus on problems of overweight people who consume excessive food. From an evolutionary perspective, the question is not "What is wrong with fat people?" but "Why are we vulnerable to obesity?" (Nesse, 2005, p. 915). The evolutionary-based response to this question is that brain mechanisms controlling our eating behavior were developed when the circumstances of food consumption were very different from what they are today. For our ancient hunting-and-gathering ancestors living on the African savanna, the consequence of eating too little food was lethal; a lack of energy and weakness due to the intake of an insufficient amount of calories led to vulnerability to predators. And even when there was plenty of food, obesity was not likely for our distant ancestors, because food options were limited (e.g., one ate only those items in immediate proximity), the caloric content of such food (e.g., roots, fruits, and nuts) was low, and the amount of effort and energy (i.e., calories burned) to obtain the food was considerable (Eaton, Shostak, & Konner, 1988). In this environment, eating as much possible had an evolutionary advantage.

The same brain mechanisms for regulating eating behavior remain with us today, but now the number of available choices is tremendous, the calories contained in much of the processed food we eat are considerable, and the amount of effort (i.e., calories burned) we have to exert to obtain this high-caloric food is extremely low, and dropping all the time as home delivery and drive-through services for more food choices increasingly become available (Kopelman, 2000). In addition, the amount of money spent to advertise high-calorie, high-fat foods, particularly from fast-food restaurants, is astronomical. The 2001 combined advertising budget for Pepsi and Coke, for example, was approximately $3 billion (Brownell & Horgen, 2003). By contrast, the National Cancer Institute's advertising budget to promote a more healthy dietary style was only $2 million (Nestle, 2002). This contrast becomes even more striking when you realize that the $3-billion advertising budget to promote less healthy food choices was for just two companies. Imagine what it probably is when you begin to include the many fast-food chains, candy companies, and alcohol products!

These phenomena do not excuse obesity, nor do they reduce the personal responsibility of obese individuals, but they do help to explain how evolutionary principles can be used to help understand and possibly solve the problem. The crux of the matter is that our hunting-and-gathering ancestors ate foods with fewer calories while burning off more calories each day. Similarly, any contemporary physician or health professional would advise you to control your weight by eating more healthy foods and exercising more each day. So it seems that such ancient wisdom can apply to the contemporary problem of obesity.

Anorexia Nervosa and Bulimia: A Conflict of Ancient Mate Preferences and Contemporary Media Influences

The most common eating disorders are anorexia nervosa and bulimia (APA, 2000). **Anorexia nervosa** is characterized by an intense fear of being overweight, the refusal to maintain a normal body weight, excessive efforts through dieting and exercise to lose weight and keep it off, and the perception of being fat even when emaciated. **Bulimia** is characterized by a binge–purge cycle in which the individual periodically eats a considerable amount of typically high-caloric foods (i.e., binges) and then induces vomiting or consumes laxatives to facilitate the expulsion of this food (i.e., purges). Both anorexia nervosa and bulimia are much more pervasive in females than males (APA, 2000; Kring et al., 2007), with approximately 90 to 95 percent of all cases occurring in females, particularly young females between 14 and 21 years of age (APA, 2000).

The evolutionary explanation of these two eating disorders is based on the emphasis placed on the physical attractiveness of females in the mate-selection process and is viewed as a variation in an array of other potential mating strategies (e.g., wearing makeup, dressing seductively) to achieve a sense of attractiveness (Surby, 1987; Voland & Voland, 1989). Such a strategy expressed as an eating disorder is likely to be fostered in large societies where the competition for potential mates is enhanced and where media representations tend to promote images of real bodies as being inadequate or undesirable (Nesse, 2005). One need not look far in youth-oriented, highly competitive U.S. society to see that the bodies of women presented in magazines, on television, and in the movies do not represent those of "real" women seen in the general population. Although the pervasiveness of eating disorders in women is consistent with the preferred physical characteristics of females by males and mate-attraction, -retention, and -poaching strategies employed by females, the vulnerability to such disorders is also influenced by biological (e.g., hormonal imbalances), social (e.g., family interaction patterns, child abuse), cognitive (e.g., beliefs about one's body and control over one's life), personality (e.g., perfectionism, neuroticism, low self-esteem), and cultural (e.g., industrial vs. nonindustrial economies) factors, to name a few (Kring et al., 2007).

Sexual Harassment: A Conflict of Ancient Mate Preferences and Contemporary Social and Legal Concerns

In addition to seeking potential mates at parties, dances, and bars, males and female seek short- and long-term mating opportunities at work. As in other contexts, however, sexual strategies may backfire when seeking mating opportunities with co-workers. From both an emotional and legal perspective, a particularly unpleasant type of disagreement in the workplace can be in the form of sexual harassment. **Sexual harassment**, or unwanted and unsolicited sexual attention from others in the workplace (Terpstra & Cook, 1985), can range from conspicuous staring at a co-worker and sexual innuendos, to making overtly suggestive comments and repeatedly seeking social contact, to trying to kiss, hug, or touch the person's breasts, buttocks, or genital area. From an evolutionary perspective, sexual harassment can be viewed as a mate-selection strategy for seeking a short-term sexual relationship, but it can also involve the exercise of power by the harasser and the expectations of a long-term romantic relationship with the victim(s). An understanding of sexual harassment from an evolutionary perspective can be achieved by considering the characteristics of the victim, her reac-

tions to such unwelcome advances, and the conditions under which the harassment occurs (Buss, 2008).

Victims of sexual harassment tend to be female and perpetrators tend to be male. Given that women experience more distress in response to such unwelcome sexual advances (Buss, 2003; Rotundo, Nguyen, & Sackett, 2001), it seems reasonable, as a result, that they would be more likely than males to file complaints following harassment (Buss, 2008). In addition, consistent with males' mating values, the victims are disproportionately young, physically attractive, and single – all characteristics that would be held in high regard as mate values in the sexual selection process for males. In support of such reasoning, researchers found that women between the ages of 20 and 35 representing 43 percent of the workforce filed 72 percent of sexual harassment complaints. In contrast, women over the age of 45 representing 28 percent of the workforce filed only 5 percent of harassment complaints (Studd & Gattiker, 1991). However, the degree of distress experienced by women following unwelcome sexual advances seems to depend on the status of the harasser in a manner consistent with the preferred mating values of females, based on a male's ability to provide material resources. Buss (2003) asked college-age women how upset they would be by a male's repeated requests for a date despite their persistent refusal. As a test of the evolutionary preference of females for males with an increased potential for material resources, the occupational status of the persistent male was varied from low (e.g., garbage collector) to high (e.g., rock star). As the status of the male making the persistent, unwelcome advances increased, the level of distress decreased. Specifically, the females anticipated being most upset by repeated requests made by garbage collectors (4.32), cleaning men (4.19), gas station attendants (4.13), and construction workers (4.09) and least upset by repeated requests made by graduate students (2.80), successful rock stars (2.71), and premedical students (2.65). Similarly, when college-aged women were asked how flattered they would feel at an outright sexual proposition by males whose occupational status varied, the women suggested that the higher the status of the male, the more flattered they would be.

Thus, in accordance with the processes associated with sexual selection, the greater willingness of males to seek casual sexual encounters without commitment, particularly with young, physically attractive females in their prime reproductive years, can help to explain why certain males might use sexual harassment as a mate-selection strategy targeting certain females. On the other hand, the resulting distress experienced by females reflects an adaptive response for preventing mating with an unwelcome partner, along with all of the potential costs associated with such mating (e.g., emotional distress, sexually transmitted disease, unwanted pregnancy), particularly if the partner is perceived as having a reduced capacity (i.e., low occupational status) for providing material resources. Although the evolutionary perspective does provide an explanation of the underlying dynamics of such mistreatment of women, it should not be viewed as an excuse to dismiss the responsibility of the perpetrators of sexual harassment, nor should it be viewed as justification for blaming victims of such harassment.

This concludes our discussion of the applications of the evolutionary viewpoint. A summary of the major points discussed in this section is presented in "Summing It Up: Applications of the Evolutionary

Summing It Up *Applications of the Evolutionary Viewpoint*

Application	Example
Evolutionary Considerations of Consumer Behavior:	
Cosmetic Products. Females tend to spend more on cosmetic products as a sexual selection strategy to enhance their physical appearance.	Judy and all of her friends have decided to get Botox injections to remove the wrinkles in their faces when each of them turns 40 next year.
Money Management. Males tend to engage in more financial risk as a sexual selection strategy to enhance the display of their material resources.	Elliot puts all of his money in a new, high-risk tech stock in the hopes of making money to buy a new luxury car.
Leisure Pursuits. Males tend to spend more on leisure activities that involve heightened levels of risk as a sexual selection strategy to demonstrate their dominance and competitiveness.	Steve spends a lot of money on a new speedboat in the hopes of having the fastest boat on the lake and impressing all of the females coming to the resort this season.
Evolutionary Considerations of Eating Disorders:	
Problem of Obesity. The consumption of too much food is a result of the evolution of brain mechanisms that emerged during ancestral times when food was scarce and required the exertion of many calories to obtain it.	Obesity is on the rise because while we are programmed to eat lots of food, much of our food is high in calories (e.g., fast food) and requires little effort to obtain (e.g., drive-throughs).
Problems of Anorexia Nervosa and Bulimia. The consumption of too little food and the refusal to maintain a healthy weight by females are consistent with sexual section strategies designed to project a youthful appearance.	The local hospital reported seeing more cases of teenage girls with eating disorders as the female celebrity pop stars, actresses, and models appearing on the cover of magazines became younger and thinner.
Evolutionary Considerations of Sexual Harassment:	
The tendency for victims to be young females and perpetrators to be males is consistent with the mate preferences and short-term mating strategies of males, based on sexual selection.	At the regional meeting of human resources managers, it was reported that most of the victims of sexual harassment were single, female, college summer interns.
The nature of the reactions by females tends to be consistent with preferences for mates with greater potential for providing material resources.	At the legal seminar on sexual harassment, it was reported that the victims are more likely to file a grievance against an hourly employee than against an executive.

Viewpoint." However, you should be aware that this presentation has not been exhaustive. The principles of evolutionary psychology have also been applied to other such diverse areas as literature (Carroll, 2005), the law and legal system (Jones, 2005), human resources management (Colarelli, 2003), and marketing (Saad, 2007), to name just a few. In the next section, we will provide an evaluation of the evolutionary viewpoint.

Evaluating the Evolutionary Viewpoint: Strengths and Limitations

In this section, we will provide an evaluation of the evolutionary viewpoint by considering some of its characteristic strengths and limitations.

Characteristic Strengths

Here are some of the characteristic strengths of the evolutionary viewpoint:

- *A new view*: *Innovation through evolution.* The evolutionary viewpoint represents a major theoretical development in the study of personality. For example, as noted at the beginning of this chapter, it offers a new perspective on the fundamental issue in the study of personality psychology – the nature of variation in the expression of individual differences in personality. It also offers a new perspective on some other principal concerns in the study of personality, such as helping to explain the emergence of the FFM as the major structural organization of personality (Chapter 7) and the existence of certain gender differences in personality (Chapter 12).
- *A common thread: Bringing it together.* The evolutionary viewpoint offers a framework for linking many of the other viewpoints in the study of personality. For example, the operation of unconscious processes (Chapters 3 and 4) emphasized by Freud (e.g., life and death instincts) and Jung (e.g., archetypes) is consistent with the automatic expression of certain behavioral patterns characteristic of adaptive behavior based on the principle of natural selection. The operation of the continuous actualizing processes (Chapter 6)

emphasized by Rogers and Maslow can be considered psychological extensions of the ongoing biological and physical enhancements to individuals based on the principles of evolution. Finally, the importance of interpersonal relationships and concerns for developing a sense of social connectedness (Chapters 4 and 5) emphasized by Adler (e.g., social interest), Horney (e.g., social security), and Erikson (e.g., intimacy vs. isolation) have as their bases the formation of (e.g., mate selection and retention) and threats to (e.g., mate poaching and jealousy) such social bonds based on evolutionary principles of sexual selection.

- *A tradition of excellence: Theoretical and empirical benefits.* The evolutionary viewpoint places the study of personality firmly within the broader historical context of the study of evolution and serves to link it to a tradition of scientific investigation. Specifically, from a theoretical basis, personality psychologists have been able to use the principles of evolution developed in other scientific disciplines to guide their thinking in the development of ideas and formation of hypotheses to be tested. From an empirical basis, the scientific tradition provides an important standard by which the quality of the research done on personality from the evolutionary viewpoint can be judged. For example, from extensive research in evolutionary biology investigating the mating patterns of animals, hypotheses can be tested regarding the nature of the physical (e.g., youthful) and personality (e.g., dominant) characteristics humans would seek in potential mates and the strategies males (e.g., buying gifts) and females (e.g., cosmetic surgery) would employ to attract and retain them. Confidence in the results of such research in the study of personality psychology is increased by its consistency with the findings in some of the other, more established scientific disciplines.

Characteristic Limitations

Here are some of the characteristic limitations of the evolutionary viewpoint:

- *Too much speculation: Creating past scenarios to fit the present data.* It has been suggested that the evolutionary viewpoint is based on speculating about what our hunting-and-gathering ancestors had to do and then linking such speculation to support the findings of the current research. Specifically, while there are physical artifacts (e.g., skeletal remains and stone bowels) that we can use to speculate about these ancestors' physical size and lifestyle, we have no records of what their personalities were like. For example, it has been speculated that Agreeableness has emerged as a major dimension of personality because our prehistoric ancestors had to be agreeable in order to survive, yet there are no physical artifacts to show that Agreeableness was a critical factor.

- *A consistency in evolutionary challenges: Do things really remain the same?* The evolutionary viewpoint assumes that the challenges of our hunting-and-gathering ancestors form the bases of the challenges we face today, and that the basic nature of their responses to those ancient challenges form the foundation of how we respond to contemporary challenges. For example, our ancestors increased their proficiency in being mobile because they were constantly searching for sources of food and avoiding predators, and so developed small and more accurate weapons that were easier to carry from one hunting ground to another and use in their defense against predators. Yet today we continue to increase our efforts to be more mobile, but such mobility has little to do with securing food or providing protection from predators. For example, cell phones are getting smaller and smaller and have more and more capabilities, but their increased mobility has, little to do securing food or providing protection from predators, and much more to do with their entertainment and social status value.

- *On being unfalsifiable: Can evolution be disproved?* As a general explanation of all forms of behavioral responses, the evolutionary viewpoint has been accused of being a theory that cannot be disproved, since any behavior that exists must be present because it serves an adaptive purpose. For example, why do people drive while listening to music and eating fast food? Well, from

an evolutionary viewpoint, it could be said that as technology becomes more pervasive and advanced, it will require that people be able to incorporate it into their daily lives, and those who are not able to learn to do this will fall further and further behind and eventually, so the theory goes, will not be able to adapt and survive, and thus will be removed from the population of those individuals who were able to adapt to the changes. What about those folks who drive while talking on their cell phone and text messaging? It seems the evolutionary viewpoint has an explanation for that as well. A student speculated while discussing this issue in class, "Those jerks will have accidents, and hopefully will not survive, and that will be nature's way of getting those fools out of the gene pool who try to take technology too far too fast." As you can see, the evolutionary viewpoint can provide explanations for about anything. The result is that the issue of being unfalsifiable now becomes: How can we formulate specific hypotheses based on the highly developed principles of evolution so that they can be tested using well-established methods of science to determine the validity of these explanations? And as was noted previously, one of the strengths of the evolutionary viewpoint is its long-standing tradition of being linked with scientific excellence.

This concludes our discussion of the evaluation of the evolutionary viewpoint of personality. A summary of the major points noted in this section is presented in "Summing It Up: Evaluating the Evolutionary Viewpoint" on p. 394.

Our presentation of the evolutionary viewpoint of personality is now complete. For more information about this perspective, an excellent source is a book chapter titled "Evolutionary Personality Psychology" (Figueredo et al., 2005). For more information about evolutionary psychology, an outstanding source is *The Handbook of Evolutionary Psychology* edited by David Buss (2005a), which includes comprehensive coverage of the major topics in the field.

Summing It Up *Evaluating the Evolutionary Viewpoint*

Characteristic Strengths:

- *A New View.* The evolutionary viewpoint represents a major new theoretical approach to addressing many of the significant issues in the study of personality psychology. For example, addressing the issue of gender differences in personality from the evolutionary viewpoint, it is adaptive to have some males be less aggressive than other males but also for the females to be more nurturing and less aggressive than most of the males, to maximize survival and reproduction of the general population.

- *A Common Thread.* The evolutionary viewpoint helps to link together the concepts and processes from different theoretical perspectives. For example, the unconscious operation of the archetype of the persona and the conscious expression of social interest are the results of the evolutionary value of the agreeableness dimension of the FFM.

- *A Tradition of Excellence.* The evolutionary viewpoint is guided by a scientific framework and the proven standards of the evolutionary tradition. For example, from the relationship between the size of their territorial space and the mating behavior of male primates in the wild that was reported in a zoology journal, a personality psychologist predicts that males with the biggest houseboats on the lake will have the most dates over the summer.

Characteristic Limitations:

- *Too Much Speculation.* Evidence in support of the evolutionary viewpoint is based on many assumptions regarding the personality of our hunting-and-gathering ancestors. For example, without any physical evidence, we assume that variation in the personality trait of novelty seeking between males and females served to help our ancestors survive on the plains of Africa.

- *Consistency in Evolutionary Challenges.* The idea that the environmental challenges faced by our ancient ancestors are similar in nature to the environmental challenges we face today has been questioned. For example, although individuals have always been concerned with meeting the challenges of seeking shelter as protection from the elements, the nature and size of houses being built today seem to be more about status than seeking protection from the elements.

- *On Being Unfalsifiable.* The evolutionary explanations for the expressions of any behavior are provided in such a way that they cannot be proven wrong. For example, the preference some people have for eating thin-crust vs. thick-crust pizza must have an evolutionary reason for being, because such a difference exists.

Chapter Summary: Reexamining the Highlights

- *Linking Evolutionary Theory to the Study of Personality*

    - *Basic Logic.* The evolutionary viewpoint uses principles of classic and contemporary evolutionary theory to understand the operation and expression of personality dimensions.

- *Basic Processes of the Evolutionary Viewpoint*

    - *Survival and Reproduction.* The two fundamental tasks in the process of evolution are the attraction of potential mates and the transmission of genetic and biological characteristics to the offspring resulting from successful mating.

    - *Natural Selection.* Gradual changes in the physical characteristics of organisms that increase the likelihood of survival and reproduction of the species are a result of natural selection.

    - *Adaptive Behavior.* Responses to environmental challenges that result in survival and reproductive success are repeated and incorporated into the neurological circuits in the brain, forming the basis of genetic behavioral patterns.

    - *The Environment of Evolutionary Adaptedness.* While the nature of the environmental conditions and adaptive behaviors may change over time, the basic evolutionary tasks – successful survival and reproduction – remain the same.

- *Accounting for the Emergence of Individual Differences in Personality*

  - *The Evolutionary Value of Variation in Personality.* The evolutionary viewpoint proposes that individual differences in personality emerge because the variability in certain personality traits among individuals increases the likelihood of survival and reproduction within a general population. Some of the factors that contribute to the emergence of such variability include the associated costs and benefits of the variation in a particular trait or group of traits, the particular point in time and location in which the variation of the trait or group of traits occurred, and the increase or decrease in value associated with the trait or group of traits based on its frequency of appearance within the general population relative to other traits or groups of traits.

  - *The Five-Factor Model.* A cost–benefit analysis of the value of potential variation in the separate dimensions of the FFM supports their contribution to the fundamental evolutionary tasks of survival and reproduction and helps to account for the pervasiveness of this model as a major framework for the study of individual differences in personality.

- *Basic Expressions of the Evolutionary Viewpoint*

  - *Sexual Selection.* Characteristic features appear and evolve because they increase the likelihood of attracting the most desirable mates and of successful reproduction. Physical features associated with sexual selection include a healthy, youthful look for females and a look of physical strength for males. Personality correlates of sexual selection for both sexes include kindness, the quality of being understanding, intelligence, and an exciting personality. Mate preferences of females include a mate who is ambitious and family-oriented; mate preferences for males include a mate who is frugal and a good cook.

  - *Mate-Retention Strategies.* Strategies for mate retention by males include displays of resources; strategies by females involve attempts to enhance and preserve a more youthful appearance.

  - *Mate-Poaching Strategies.* Strategies for mate poaching by males are characterized by displays of resources and preferences for youthful-looking partners; strategies for females are characterized by suggestions of their sexual accessibility and a preference for physically healthy males.

  - *Jealousy.* Both males and females experience feelings of jealousy in reaction to the mate-poaching efforts of others. Males display jealous reactions in response to sexual infidelity by their mate, whereas females display jealousy in response to emotional infidelity by their mate.

- *Applications of the Evolutionary Viewpoint*

  - *Consumer Behavior.* Principles of the evolutionary viewpoint have been applied to consumer spending. Consistent with the process of sexual selection, females tend to devote more fiscal resources to the purchase of cosmetic products and services designed to enhance their attractiveness, while males tend to display greater risks in their fiscal management engage in more risky and expensive leisure activities in an attempt to display their ability to acquire and provide material resources.

  - *Eating Disorders.* Explanations for eating disorders based on principles of evolutionary psychology include vulnerability to obesity because of the environmental needs and dietary practices of our hunting-and-gathering ancestors, and the heightened occurrence of anorexia nervosa and bulimia in young females as a variant appearance-enhancement strategy in the process of sexual selection fostered by youth-oriented, image-conscious media.

  - *Sexual Harassment.* Explanations for sexual harassment based on principles of evolutionary psychology suggest that the tendency for the victims of such harassment to be young females and the perpetrators to be males reflects a variant pattern consistent with male mate-preference characteristics and mate-retention strategies, whereas the reaction of women to such harassment reflects a pattern consistent with female mate-preference characteristics.

- *Evaluating the Evolutionary Viewpoint*

  - *Characteristic Strengths.* Characteristic strengths of the evolutionary viewpoint include its representing a major theoretical development for addressing some of the most important issues in the study of personality, an ability to integrate in its basic principles many other viewpoints of personality, and its link with the scientific tradition associated with the study of evolution.

– *Characteristic Limitations.* Characteristic limitations of the evolutionary viewpoint include its use of speculation about our ancient ancestors to support current findings, calling into question the extent to which the historic environmental challenges and behavioral responses to those challenges can serve as a basis for explaining our responses to contemporary environmental challenges, and the idea of its being a viewpoint that is difficult to prove wrong.

Glossary

adaptive behavior   Repetitive behavior in response to environmental challenges that eventually becomes genetically transmitted.

anorexia nervosa   An eating disorder associated with a preoccupation with being overweight and a dangerous level of weight loss.

bulimia   An eating disorder associated with the cyclical consumption of large quantities of food, followed by self-induced expulsion of the food.

cost–benefit analysis   The making of a decision based on a consideration of the advantages and disadvantages of taking a particular course of action.

environment of evolutionary adaptedness (EAA)   The adaptive responses to environmental challenges confronting our ancient ancestors, which form the bases of the adaptive responses by contemporary individuals to current manifestation of those earlier environmental challenges.

epigamic selection   The tendency of males and females to choose as mates those who display specific characteristics that will result in the most successful genetic transmission.

evolutionary psychology   The application of classic and contemporary principles of evolutionary theory to the study of psychological principles and processes.

frequency-dependent selection   The impact on mate selection of the value of a particular characteristic as determined by its relative frequency of appearance in the general population in comparison to other characteristics.

Hostile Type A personality   A personality style associated with a heightened response of hostility to everyday sources of frustration, and with heart disease.

intrasexual competition   The competitive display by same-sex members of a species of characteristics used to attract potential mates.

mate poaching   Specific efforts designed to attract an individual who is already in a romantic relationship.

natural selection   The systematic changes that occur in organisms in response to the challenges of nature and increase the organisms' chances of survival.

obesity   A health problem associated with being excessively overweight.

sexual harassment   Repeated unwelcome attention of a sexual nature, which produces feelings of discomfort.

sexual selection   The selection of mates for the purpose of maximizing successful reproduction.

Type D personality   A personality style linked with the suppression of emotional distress and with heart disease.

The Social-Cognitive Viewpoint
Cognitive Processes and Personality

Chapter Overview:
A Preview of Coming Attractions

Cognitive processes are the mental processes by which people give meaning and respond to events and experiences (Barker, 2001; Cantor, 1990; Cantor & Zirkel, 1990; Cervone & Shoda, 1999; Fiske & Taylor, 2008; Kazdin, 2001; Moskowitz, 2005; Pervin, 2002; Williams & Cervone, 1998; Winter & Barenbaum, 1999). For example, people with violence-prone personalities tend to perceive hostility in the actions of others and view aggression as an appropriate, as well as a rewarding, response (Berkowitz, 1993; Geen, 1995; Krahé, 2001; Strack & Deutsch, 2007). On the other hand, people with a high need to evaluate events and experiences demonstrate a chronic tendency to analyze them by means of discussion and debate (Jarvis & Petty, 1996). Even in international politics (Tetlock, 2007), the possession of certain beliefs about the perceived motives of particular governmental leaders (e.g., hostile vs. cooperative) by other world leaders can serve to influence political action (e.g., boycotts vs. foreign aid).

In this chapter we will consider some basic assumptions of the social-cognitive viewpoint of personality. We'll focus on the social-cognitive perspectives of Julian Rotter, Albert Bandura, and Walter Mischel, three influential contemporary social-cognitive personality theorists. We will discuss the basic concepts and processes of personality adjustment described by each theorist, along with some real-world applications of their respective perspectives.

Basic Assumptions of the Social-Cognitive Viewpoint: The Role of Cognitive Processes in Personality

The social-cognitive viewpoint emphasizes the role of cognitive processes in the study of personality (Pervin, 2002; Sternberg & Grigorenko, 1997; Williams & Cervone, 1998). In the study of personality, such **cognitive processes** might include the nature of the mental strategies people use to organize information about themselves and others, the decision-making strategies we use in self-regulation of our behavior, and the subjective evaluation of the consequences of various actions in response to a given situation (Cervone & Shoda, 1999). For example, as a law student, Kathy's level of self-confidence is determined by how cogent she perceives her classroom comments are in comparison to those of the other students (i.e., by mentally organizing information about herself and others), whether she believes joining a study group or seeking the aid of a tutor will help her do better in class (i.e., by subjectively evaluating various actions), and the amount of time she spends studying each night (i.e., by self-regulating her behavior). Thus, the major characteristic of the social-cognitive viewpoint is its emphasis on our mental processes and how they can be used to influence the nature of our thoughts, feelings, and behavior within our day-to-day interpersonal activities.

At the core of the social-cognitive viewpoint are the following four basic assumptions:

- The significance of the personal perspective.
- The presence of a need for cognition.
- People's desire to seek further understanding and clarification of their personal world.
- The significance of subjective probabilities.

The Significance of the Personal Perspective: The Importance of Perceptions and Beliefs

An important assumption of the social-cognitive viewpoint is the significance attributed to an individual's perceptions and beliefs about events and the impact such cognitive processes have on the individual's feelings and behavior. The logic of this assumption is that much of what we do, feel, and think is related to our perceptions and beliefs (Isen, Niedenthal, & Cantor, 1992; Trope & Liberman, 1996). For example, a shy person decides not to talk to others at a party because he may assume that what he has to say is not interesting and that others are more amusing than he is. In this example, the shy person withdraws from others as a result of the beliefs (i.e., his contribution is not interesting) and perceptions (i.e., others are more amusing) he has about himself and others. In another example, when trying to determine whether to stay at a boring but secure job or to quit, a female sales manager might decide that she is not likely to look for a more exciting job as long as she has her present one. As a result, she decides to quit her job without having another one waiting for her. While many people may not consider this a systematic approach to career planning, from her personal perspective, this is the most "logical" course of action.

Thus, like the view of Carl Rogers (see Chapter 6), the social-cognitive viewpoint assumes that to truly understand personality, the nature and structure of the person's perceptions and belief system must be considered. This is in sharp contrast to the learning viewpoints, which emphasize external or environmental factors as the primary regulators of personality.

The Presence of a Need for Cognition: The Desire to Think

Rather than simply viewing individuals as passively responding to their environment, the social-cognitive viewpoint describes people as actively seeking information in a direct attempt to give meaning to their experiences and cope with the demands placed on them, particularly in the presence of causal uncertainty (Weary & Edwards, 1994). Once this information is obtained, each individual processes it to determine the most meaningful course of action from his or her personal perspective (Cantor & Harlow, 1994; Cantor & Zirkel, 1990; Gollwitzer & Moskowitz, 1996; Williams & Cervone, 1998).

Yet people differ in their **need for cognition**, which refers to the amount of time and effort an individual is willing to put forth when processing information to prepare a course of action in response to external stimuli (Cacioppo & Petty, 1982; Cacioppo, Petty, Feinstein, & Jarvis, 1996; Cacioppo, Petty, & Morris,

1983). For example, when trying to decide which liquid diet program is likely to be most effective for its cost, an individual with a high need for cognition would read the claims made in the advertising brochures more closely than would an individual with a low need for cognition, who may simply skim through the claims and focus on the photographs in the brochures.

People with a high need for cognition tend to be willing to engage in considerable cognitive processing while analyzing information, even when there is no extrinsic reward (e.g., money or recognition) for doing so (Petty, Cacioppo, & Kasmer, 1985).

For some firsthand experience with the way the need for cognition is assessed, read "You Can Do It."

You Can Do It

The Need for Cognition Scale: "I Think, Therefore I Am Having Fun"

The Need for Cognition Scale (NCS) is a 45-item instrument assessing the expressed desire people have for engaging in and enjoying various cognitive activities (e.g., problem solving, seeking to understand something, having a desire to know). The following is a subset of items adapted from those in NCS (Cacioppo & Petty, 1982). Try it yourself by using the response format described.

Instructions

Indicate the extent to which you agree or disagree with each of the 10 statements presented below by using the following scale:

- **A.** Very strong agreement
- **B.** Strong agreement
- **C.** Moderate agreement
- **D.** Slight agreement
- **E.** Neither agreement nor disagreement
- **F.** Slight disagreement
- **G.** Moderate disagreement
- **H.** Strong disagreement
- **I.** Very strong disagreement

_____ 1. I really like to work on issues that involve generating new solutions to problems.

_____ 2. It does not excite me very much to learn new ways of thinking.

_____ 3. I would rather work on a task that is intellectually difficult and significant than one that is only moderately important but does not require me to think too much.

_____ 4. Instead of making an effort to try to figure out why things happen the way they did, I would rather let things just happen.

_____ 5. It makes me proud when I reflect on the way I reason about things.

_____ 6. I do not like the idea of having to think abstractly.

_____ 7. I would really like it if my life were filled with puzzles that I had to solve.

_____ 8. Instead of thinking about long-term projects, I would rather think about small projects on a daily basis.

_____ 9. I find it fun to think about a problem even if my efforts do not provide a solution to it.

_____ 10. I do not find thinking a fun activity.

Scoring

The scoring for items 1, 3, 5, 7, and 9 is A = +4, B = +3, C = +2, D = +1, E = 0, F = −1, G = −2, H = −3, and I = −4. For items 2, 4, 6, 8, and 10, the scoring is reversed (e.g., A = −4, B = −3, etc.). Add the numbers corresponding to your responses together. The higher the score, the more your style of thinking reflects that of a higher need for cognition.

Adapted from Cacioppo and Petty (1982).

For details about some research assessing the validity of the NCS, read "A Closer Look."

A Closer Look

Validation Research on the NCS: Confirming the Desire to Think

In some of the earliest research into the development of the NCS, John T. Cacioppo and Richard E. Petty (1982) conducted a series of four studies to examine how NCS scores were related to certain personality, cognitive, and affective measures.

In the initial validation study, Cacioppo and Petty compared the NCS scores for a group of university faculty members with a group of assembly line workers. As expected, the group of faculty members scored much higher on the NCS than did the group of assembly line workers. In a second study involving over 400 college students, NCS scores were positively correlated with solving spatial ability problems (e.g., finding an embedded figure hidden within other figures) and were not related to experiencing test anxiety (Cacioppo & Petty, 1982). In a third study, Cacioppo and Petty examined the relationship between NCS scores and those on a measure of the personality dimension of dogmatism (i.e., the degree to which an individual is open- or closed-minded in his or her thinking). As you might expect, higher NCS scores were associated with more open-minded thinking (e.g., less dogmatism).

In the final study in this series, college students identified from their NCS scores as having either a high or low need for cognition were asked to perform either the simple or complex version of a number-circle task. In the simple version, students were asked to circle all of the 1s, 5s, and 7s found in three pages of a notebook containing 3,500 random numbers on each page. In the complex version, students were asked to circle all of the 3s, any 6 preceded by a 7, and every other 4 found in three pages of a notebook containing 3,500 random numbers on each page. Although the students did not enjoy the tedious number-circling task much, the high-need-for-cognition students enjoyed the complex version more than the simple version; and just the opposite pattern of enjoyment was found for the low-

need-for-cognition students. Thus, even with a boring task that involves a mental challenge, people high in the need for cognition will manage to find some fun and enjoyment in it simply because they like to think.

In a separate set of two studies, Cacioppo, Petty, and Morris (1983) also demonstrated that people with a high need for cognition not only spend more time thinking but also are better able to evaluate the quality of what they are thinking about than people with a low need for cognition. In addition to spending more time thinking about arguments contained in persuasive messages, people with a high need for cognition evaluated strong arguments more favorably than weak arguments, while people with a low need for cognition evaluated the weak arguments more favorably than the strong arguments. In addition, the judgments of others by individuals who were low in the need for cognition were more influenced by stereotypes than were those of individuals high in the need for cognition (Crawford & Skowronski, 1998).

Taken together, the results of these and other studies (Cacioppo et al., 1996; Chaiken, 1987; Lassiter, Briggs, & Bowman, 1991; Lassiter, Briggs, & Shaw, 1991) tend to support the validity of the NCS in its ability to identify people who differ in the amount of time spent thinking, quality of thinking, and degree of enjoyment derived from thinking. Adding to the cross-cultural validity of the NCS, such tendencies are also found when comparing individuals from different ethnic backgrounds (Culhane, Morera, & Watson, 2006).

In addition to the need for cognition, you should be aware that there is a variety of individual-difference dimensions of cognitive processing being investigated within the social-cognitive viewpoint of personality. These other cognitive processes, along with instruments to assess them, include the need to evaluate – "the extent to which individuals engage in evaluative responding" (Jarvis & Petty, 1996, p. 172), the need for precision – "a preference for engaging in a relatively fine-grained mode of processing" (Viswanathan, 1997, p. 717), the need for closure – "the extent to which a person, faced with a decision or judgment, desires *any* answer, as compared with confusion and ambiguity" (Neuberg, Judice, & West, 1997, p. 1396), and the need and ability to achieve cognitive structure – "the preference to use cognitive structuring as a means to achieve certainty" (Y. Bar-Tal, Kishon-Rabin, & Tabak, 1997, p. 1158), to name just a few.

Correlates of the Need for Cognition: Examples of the Desire to Think in Daily Life   The importance of the need for cognition construct, as well as the versatility of the NCS, can also be seen from the fact that it is involved in so many important aspects of our daily lives. Here is a summary of some of these correlates.

CONSUMER CORRELATES OF THE NEED FOR COGNITION
Since there is a variety of cognitive processes associated with the decision to purchase products, it should come as no surprise that the need for cognition has been found to be related to consumer behavior. When faced with wide variety of consumer choices, individuals with high scores on the NCS were better able to employ systematic reasoning to evaluate more carefully the positive and negative attributes of the various product alternatives than were individuals with low NCS scores, who tended to experience in such situations what might be described as information overload (Lin & Wu, 2006). In a similar manner, individuals with high NCS scores were better able to analyze the more subtle features in advertisements than were individuals with low NCS scores (Brennan & Bahn, 2006). This pattern of results is significant because, as the number of products and the variety of the options available with these products increases – just think about all of the styles, features, options, and plans available for cell phones – the differences among these products will become more subtle. And as the number of products and their available options increase, the likelihood of such information overload occurring in our everyday life, along with the negative emotional consequences associated with it, such as feelings of anxiety, exhaustion, and confusion, will also increase (B. Schwartz, 2004).

Individuals with high NCS scores are more analytical not only in their thinking about products, but in their thinking about the services others provide. As an indication of their increased analytical skills, individuals with high NCS scores were less influenced by the prior information about a trainer (i.e., being effective vs. ineffective) than were individuals with low scores when evaluating the quality of the trainer's performance and the amount they learned from the training (Towler & Dipboye, 2006).

ACADEMIC CORRELATIONS OF NEED FOR COGNITION
Two broad area of interests for psychologists are activities that have a more analytic and scientific emphasis (e.g., conducting research and writing articles for publication) versus those that have a more practical and applied emphasis (e.g., working in a clinic conducting psychotherapy sessions with individual clients). Research on undergraduate psychology majors interested in pursuing graduate work in psychology has demonstrated that high scores on the NCS were more positively associated with a focus on a career involving research activities and academic ideas than with a focus on more practical and applied activities (Leong, Zachar, Conant, & Tolliver, 2007). While attending graduate school is associated with obtaining a certain degree of academic success, academic underachievement is considered a lack of academic success. In this regard, since academic success is associated with a desire to engage in thinking and other academic activities, it should come as no surprise that low NCS scores were found to be associated with academic underachievement in male and female teenage students (Preckel, Holling, & Vock, 2006).

INQUISITIVENESS CORRELATES OF NEED FOR COGNITION
Inquisitive individuals satisfy their curiosity by searching for answers from a variety of sources, and the need for cognition has been found to be related to the use of many of these sources. For example, working on the assumption that it requires more cognitive involvement to obtain information from the newspaper than from watching television, it has been reported that individuals with high NCS scores demonstrated a stronger relationship between political knowledge obtained and used from reading the newspaper than did individuals with low NCS scores (Liu & Eveland, 2005). In the search for life satisfaction, individuals who had high NCS and religiosity scores, even when having increased doubts about their religious beliefs, had higher life satisfaction scores than did those who were less religious and had low NCS scores (Gauthier, Christopher, Walter, Mourad, & Marek, 2006). It seems that, bolstered by one's faith, being willing to engage in the cognitive challenges of pondering and reconciling one's religious beliefs and doubts can serve to impact one's sense of life satisfaction. Finally, looking at the skies and stars above for answers to a wide variety of personal issues has a long history. For example, humans have stared at the stars seeking points of navigation to help them find their way over land and sea, plotted astrological charts based on the alignment of the stars and planets to help them find answers to personal and professional issues in their lives, and looked through powerful telescopes into space to investigate the origins of the universe and the possibility of other

life forms elsewhere to help them find their place in the universe. Given the diversity and complexity of the cognitive challenges looking up at the stars and skies can present, it should come as no surprise that scores on the NCS are positively related to a strong interest in or psychological attachment to the night sky and night-sky watching (Kelly, 2005).

As you can see, the need for cognition has many interesting correlates. For a look at some recent research on the need for cognition that involves a significant contemporary health issue, see "At the Cutting Edge of Personality Psychology."

AT THE CUTTING EDGE OF PERSONALITY PSYCHOLOGY

Designing a Better Informational HIV-Prevention Campaign

The Need for Cognition and the Battle Against AIDS: How Best to Tell People to Use a Condom

Without question, one of the most important health issues in the world today is addressing the AIDS epidemic. A critical component in the battle against AIDS is the idea that providing people with information about the spread and prevention of HIV would influence their attitudes and behavior regarding safe sex. To help address the issue, Andrea Carnaghi, of the University of Padova in Italy, and her colleagues (Carnaghi, Cadinu, Castelli, Kiesner, & Bragantini, 2007) are incorporating the characteristic features of the need for cognition into their efforts to develop safe-sex message campaigns designed to increase people's knowledge about HIV transmission and their motivation to use condoms.

Carnaghi and her colleagues found that individuals with a high need for cognition are more likely to satisfy their desire to process information at a deeper level by reading the newspaper for news than watching television when compared to individuals with a low need for cognition, who tend to rely more on watching television than reading the newspaper (Ferguson, Chung, & Weigold, 1986; Liu & Eveland, 2005). From this, the researchers reasoned that safe-sex messages presented in a written format would have a greater impact on individuals with a high need for cognition than that same information presented to them in a visual format, and that just

the opposite would be true for individuals with a low need for cognition. In addition, Carnaghi and colleagues incorporated other research on attitude change in the area of HIV-prevention programs, suggesting that the intention of individuals to use a condom is positively related to having favorable attitudes about condom use and having friends with favorable attitudes about condom use (Albarracin, Fishbein, Johnson, & Mullerleile, 2001).

The participants were 56 male and 52 female high school students who had the permission of their parents and granted their own permission to participate in this study, which took place in a classroom setting. The participants were told that this study was concerned with looking at issues in their everyday lives, including sex-related issues such as safe sex. In the first part of the study, the participants completed a packet of information that included the NCS. Next, they were presented with some information concerning safe-sex behavior. The information discussed such issues as how one could be infected by the virus (e.g., vaginal sex, and oral sex with a male or female partner, are risky behaviors), how one could prevent oneself from being infected (e.g., using a male or female condom when having oral sex), which sexual behaviors are safe (e.g., kissing is a safe sexual habit), and when one should be tested for AIDS (e.g., three months after having unprotected sex). The classes of students were randomly assigned to one of three information-format conditions. For the students in the written-text condition, the information was presented in a pamphlet containing written text without any pictures. In the comic-strip condition, the information was presented in a sequence of 16 different pictures in which students in a classroom asked questions (e.g., "When should one get tested after having unprotected sex?") and teachers provided them with the appropriate answers. In a control condition, students did not receive any safe-sex information. Finally, the participants were asked to complete a series of questionnaires. The attitudinal index assessed their knowledge of HIV transmission (e.g., "Is it risky to have oral sex without a condom?") and their attitudes towards condom use (e.g., safe vs. chancy; useful vs. risky). The normative index assessed their shared normative beliefs (i.e., the attitudes of peers and friends) related to condom use (e.g., "My friends think a condom should be used when having sexual intercourse") and motivation to comply with the previously mentioned normative beliefs (e.g., "I generally do what my friends want me to do").

Overall, the results were consistent with the researchers' assumption regarding the impact the need for cognition would have on the processing of safe-sex information in the written vs. comic-strip formats. Participants with a high level of need for cognition displayed greater scores on the attitude measure, which assessed both knowledge of HIV transmission and views on condom use, than did individuals with a low level. This is consistent with the research we noted previously indicating that individuals with a high need for cognition display a deeper level of information comprehension than do those with a low level. More importantly, the results also indicated that individuals with a high level of need for cognition displayed greater scores on the attitude measure in response to the written format than did individuals with a low level or those receiving no information. On the other hand, individuals with a low level of need for cognition scored higher on the attitude measure in response to the comic-strip format than did individuals with a high level and those receiving no information. A similar pattern of results was observed for the normative index. Specifically, individuals with a high level of need for cognition displayed higher scores on the normative index in response to the written format than did individuals with a low level and those receiving no information. In just the opposite fashion, individuals with a low level of need for cognition

displayed greater scores on the normative index in response to the comic-strip format than did individuals with a high level and those receiving no information.

A More Realistic Approach to Developing and Distributing Persuasive Messages on Condom Use: The Consideration of Personality, Social, and Technological Factors

The research by Carnaghi and her colleagues is considered important for a number of reasons. It provides additional empirical research to support the construct validity of the need for cognition and the NCS while addressing a critical public heath issue. It demonstrates that to improve the impact of informational campaigns, we must consider both personality and social variables. The incorporation of the personality variable of the need for cognition helps to remind us that "one size does not fit all" when it comes to developing persuasive messages designed to change people's attitudes and behavior – people with different personality characteristics have different needs, and these needs are met in different ways. It also recognizes another important characteristic of the human condition, namely that "no man or woman is an island." People do not operate in a vacuum – they are influenced by the people around them. So if you want people to change their attitudes and behavior on important issues, you must consider the social variable of normative influences (e.g., the role of peers) as a motivating factor. Such considerations represent a more realistic approach to the complexity of changing attitudes and behavior.

In addition to helping us better understand how to design more effective safe-sex messages, Carnaghi and her colleges offer suggestions for addressing strategic issues associated with the distribution of these messages. For example, in the present research, the individuals were pre-selected according to their scores on the NCS prior to receiving variations in the safe-sex information. In the real world, it is not likely that public health workers would be able to pre-select individuals prior to presenting them with either the written or pictorial versions of the safe-sex information. To deal with this issue, Carnaghi and colleagues suggest that it would be more effective to have both formats available on display so that individuals would be free to select the one more appealing to them. In a related manner, since the need for cognition is associated with level of education, public health educators might also elect to vary the format according to the education level of the audience. For example, it might prove more effective to present the safe-sex information in the comic-strip version to those individuals in junior high and the first years of high school, but in the written format to those in the advanced grades of high school and in college. Finally, since educational levels vary around the world, it might be more effective to distribute safe-sex information in the comic-strip format to those regions where the educational level is low.

With more and more individuals using the Internet as a source of information, another important implication of this research has to do with the presentation of safe-sex information there. Research indicates that the need for cognition is related to preferences individuals have about websites (Amichai-Hamburger, Kaynar, & Fine, 2007). Individuals with a low level of need for cognition prefer more interactive websites and seem to be influenced by the site's appearance more than individuals with a high level, who tend to view the Internet as more of a source of information and are less influenced by the aesthetic qualities of the site. In this regard, public health workers looking to distribute safe-sex information over the Internet should also consider how they display such information on their website when linking it to other sites. As an example, for those websites with more of a visual emphasis, such as social network (e.g., photographs of potential dates) and recreational (e.g., photographs of vacation locations) sites, a visual format for providing the safe-sex information might prove more appealing to users. On the other hand, for those websites with more of an informational emphasis, such as fact-seeking (e.g., online encyclopedias) or academic (e.g., databases of scientific articles) sites, the written format for providing the safe-sex information might prove more appealing to users.

As you can see, this research by Carnaghi and her colleagues is considered "at the cutting edge" because it makes contributions to our understanding of the need for cognition at so many levels – theoretical, individual, and social – and attempts to provide some assistance in dealing with one of today's most pressing global health issues.

A Desire to Understand and Clarify One's Personal World: The Pursuit of Precision

Another basic assumption of the social-cognitive viewpoint is that people are motivated to make their understanding of their personal world more accurate and precise. That is to say, we assess the outcome of our actions to determine the present effectiveness and future viability of these actions. For example, suppose a student believes that cramming is a very effective method for getting a good grade on a test. But if the student crammed for a test and got a D, she would probably then have to reconsider the validity of this hypothesis when studying for the next test. In this case she may decide that cramming is still a good idea, but that the cramming session must start earlier in the evening. For the next test, she decides to start cramming at 8:00 p.m., instead of at midnight after coming home from a movie, as she did for the previous test. The point to be made here is that although you may not agree with the cramming method, this individual does. And from her viewpoint, she will continue to seek information (e.g., cramming longer) that will help to maintain the accuracy of this belief. Thus, regardless of our beliefs, the social-cognitive viewpoint assumes that we are motivated to determine the accuracy and utility of these beliefs.

The Nature and Value of Subjective Probabilities: Playing the Odds

Earlier we discussed the significance of the personal world as a powerful determinant of behavior. A variety of cognitive processes contributes to the individual's view of his or her personal world. One of these processes is the subjective determination of probability that a particular course of action will produce a desired

Summing It Up *Basic Assumptions of the Social-Cognitive Viewpoint*

Basic Assumption	Example
The Significance of the Personal View. To understand an individual's behavior, we must take into consideration his or her perceptions and beliefs.	After losing his job, an individual might become depressed because he believes he will never be able to find another good job.
The Presence of a Need for Cognition. Individuals vary in the extent to which they enjoy and put forth effort related to thinking.	While some individuals will work on word puzzles for the fun of it, others will do so only if they must.
A Desire for Accuracy in Understanding. Individuals examine the outcome of their hypotheses and modify them depending on the nature of their consequences.	After pleasantly asking for her money back and failing to get the desired outcome, the customer decides to see whether pounding on the counter and demanding to see the manager works more effectively than the gentle approach.
The Nature and Value of Subjective Probabilities. Individuals use their past experiences to determine the likelihood that a particular behavior will result in a desired consequence, thus having to avoid simply guessing about what to do.	The next time she is in a situation where she has to ask for a refund, the odds are that she will probably start by pounding on the counter before asking quietly and calmly.

outcome (Plante, 2005). The logic here is that from our experiences, each of us begins to develop "odds" that in a particular situation, each different course of action will result in a specific outcome or set of consequences (Olson, Roese, & Zanna, 1996). After considering the various response alternatives, as well as their respective outcomes, we decide what course of action to take.

For example, while riding on a bus, a shy man observes that the people who are most likely to carry on successful conversations with total strangers seem to know something about current events. As a result, he decides to read the current issue of *Time*, *Newsweek*, and *People* before going to a singles dance that weekend. From what happens at the dance, the man will then establish new odds about the effectiveness of keeping up with current events in helping him to meet new people. This revised subjective probability will then influence his behavior in other social situations, such as starting conversations with people while riding on a bus or waiting in line at the cinema.

Thus, from the social-cognitive viewpoint, the subjective probabilities we establish for certain courses of actions are influenced by the interaction between what we perceive as being the right course of action and the nature of the change it produces in our world. Thus, rather than viewing the individual as passively reacting

to the environment, the social-cognitive viewpoint sees the individual as "playing the odds" by actively calculating the subjective probability of a course of action, based on both internal (e.g., personal experiences) and environmental (e.g., the present outcome) factors.

This concludes the discussion of the basic assumptions of the social-cognitive viewpoint. A summary of these is presented in "Summing It Up: Basic Assumptions of the Social-Cognitive Viewpoint" above.

In the next section, we will consider the social learning theory of Julian Rotter, one of the pioneers in the social-cognitive viewpoint of personality.

Rotter's Social Learning Theory: The Role of Expectancies in Understanding Personality

Julian Rotter has spent almost 50 years developing and refining his social learning theory of personality (Rotter, 1993). A cornerstone of his theory is the emphasis he gives to how our experiences (i.e., learning) and our perceptions and beliefs about the present situation (i.e., cognitive processes) are interrelated in determining our individual responses to life's challenges. Rotter also emphasizes the relationship between scientific research and clinical applications in the development of his social learning theory of personality (Trull & Phares, 2001). For a glimpse into the life of this influential personality theorist, read "A Closer Look."

A Closer Look

The Life of Julian B. Rotter

Julian Rotter was born in 1916 in Brooklyn, New York. During his youth, he spent a considerable amount of time in the Avenue J Library in Brooklyn, demonstrating a particular fondness for fiction. During his junior year in high school, while searching the library stacks for something new to read, he came across some books by Freud and Adler (Rotter, 1982, 1993). He became so engrossed with his new-found interest in psychoanalytical thought that by his senior year, he was interpreting the dreams of his high school friends. As a senior in high school, he wrote a thesis titled "Why We Makes Mistakes" and dreamed of having a career in psychology.

For almost 50 years, Julian Rotter has made many significant contributions to personality theory, personality assessment, and psychotherapy.

Rotter pursued psychology during his undergraduate years at Brooklyn College, but he took it only as an elective. Because the climate of the Great Depression offered few career opportunities in psychology, and the college did not have a formal psychology department, he could not major in psychology. Instead, he selected chemistry, a more practical major that promised a greater likelihood of a job after college. Even so, he took more courses in psychology than chemistry. One of his teachers was Solomon Ash, whose classic research on conformity and group influence would eventually make him an influential social psychologist.

In addition to taking courses from Ash, Rotter had the opportunity to meet Alfred Adler. In his junior year at Brooklyn College, Rotter learned that Adler was teaching at the Long Island College of Medicine, where he was a professor of medical psychology. Rotter attended some of Adler's lectures and several of his clinical demonstrations. While still in college, Rotter got to know Adler personally. Rotter attended monthly meetings of the Society of Individual Psychology at Adler's home, where Adler spoke on individual psychology. In response to Adler's passionate lectures, the young Rotter became even more convinced that his future would be in psychology. Although Adler's influence on Rotter had begun when he read Adler's books during high school, it did not end with these lectures. Some 40 years later, Rotter stated that Adler had been "a strong influence on my thinking. I was and continue to be impressed by his insights into human nature" (Rotter, 1982, p. 1).

Rotter graduated from Brooklyn College in 1937. Inspired by Adler and encouraged by two of his undergraduate professors, Rotter decided to pursue graduate study in psychology at the University of Iowa. He arrived at the university with enough money to last a few weeks. However, the chair of the psychology department was able to obtain a research assistantship for Rotter, giving him enough money to survive. At the University of Iowa, he took a seminar in social psychology taught by the noted and very influential social psychologist Kurt Lewin. Lewin was famous for his work on how people use personal and environmental factors to determine their perceptions of and reactions to the world around them. The critical importance of personal and situational variables in the interpretation of events and as determinants of action were to become central features of Rotter's own theory of personality.

In 1938, Rotter received his MA and moved to Massachusetts to attend Worcester State Hospital, at that time a major training and research center in clinical psychology. At Worcester, he participated in one of the first-ever internships in clinical psychology; he also met Clara Barnes, his future wife. Hoping to be one of the first clinical psychologists, Rotter left Worchester to attend Indiana University, where in 1941 he received his PhD in clinical psychology; he was married to Clara that same year.

After receiving his PhD, Rotter wanted an academic position. But he soon discovered that the warnings he had been given since his days at Brooklyn College about Jews not being able to obtain academic jobs, regardless of their credentials, were now becoming reality. He accepted a position at Norwich State Hospital as a clinical psychologist. At Norwich, his responsibilities included the training of interns and assistants from the University of Connecticut and Wesleyan University. In 1942, he was drafted into the army. He spent the next three years as a military psychologist, where he served as a consultant, helped with officer candidate selection, and – among his many contributions – developed a method for reducing the incidence of going absent without leave (AWOL).

After his military service, Rotter returned briefly to Norwich State Hospital. But he soon discovered that the shortage of clinical psychologists after World War II created a need for his services sufficient to overcome the anti-Semitism that had once prevented him from obtaining an academic position. He had many universities from which to select. He soon accepted a position at Ohio State University in the clinical psychology program, from which Carl Rogers had recently departed. Like Rogers before him, Rotter combined his emphasis on scientific research with the application of his ideas within the clinical setting to help build a clinical psychology program rated among the best in the country. He became the director of the clinical psychology program in 1951.

During his stay at Ohio State University, Rotter formulated and, along with a group of outstanding graduate students, tested and developed the basic framework of his social learning theory. The culmination of this work was his classic textbook titled *Social Learning and Clinical Psychology* (Rotter, 1954). Although he was happy and extremely productive at Ohio State, Rotter was quite disturbed by the political climate created in the midwest by the Communist-baiting Senator Joe McCarthy. As a result, Rotter left Ohio State in 1963 and moved to the University of Connecticut. He retired in 1987 from his faculty position there, but continues to refine his theory, conduct research, supervise the training of clinical psychology graduate students, and see clients in his private practice as a clinical psychologist.

A significant characteristic of Rotter's distinguished career has been his emphasis on training clinical psychologists to be both researchers and practicing clinicians. In addition, throughout his career, he has been active in many professional associations, serving as president of the Eastern Psychological Association, as well as president of Division 8: Personality and Social Psychology and Division 12: Clinical Psychology of the American Psychological Association (APA). He also served as a member of the Educational and Training Board of the APA, the APA Council, and the United States Public Health Service Training Committee. In recognition of his many significant contributions throughout his lifetime of work, he received the prestigious APA Distinguished Scientific Contribution Award in 1988. More information on his life can be found in a chapter he wrote titled "Expectancies," which appears in *The History of Clinical Psychology in Autobiography* (Walker, 1993).

Basic Assumptions of Rotter's Social Learning Theory: Combining Experience with Expectations

At the foundation of Rotter's social learning perspective are four basic assumptions. These are learning from meaningful experiences, the reciprocal nature of life experience, the motivational nature of personality, and the role of expectancies (Rotter, 1954, 1982, 1990; Rotter, Chance, & Phares, 1972; Rotter & Hochreich, 1975).

Learning from Meaningful Experiences: Live and Learn

Rotter's first assumption is that personality is developed from the individual's interaction with the environment. In other words, people learn by adjusting their perceptions and expectations on the basis of meaningful experiences with their environment. As a result, according to Rotter, if you want to predict how an individual is going to behave, you need to know something about the person's experiences. For example, a student's decision to study by cramming all night before the exam probably depends considerably on the extent to which such a pattern has been successful in the past. If it was not successful, the student is likely to formulate another strategy, such as studying a little each night. Thus, Rotter believes that we learn from living and adjust our behavior accordingly.

The Reciprocal Nature of Life Experience: A Mixing of the Old and New

A second assumption of Rotter's perspective emphasizes the interactive nature of new and old experiences. Rotter believes that our reactions to new experiences are influenced to a certain degree by our old experiences, and the perceptions we have of our old experiences are influenced by our new experiences. For example, your reaction to the first few weeks of college was probably influenced to a tremendous degree by the experiences you had in high school (e.g., both situations involve using basic learning skills). On the other hand, once you established the feel for what college is all about, you began to see how much different it is from high school (e.g., a greater amount of freedom to select what you want to study and when you want to study it). Thus, for Rotter, the nature of personality development is not simply a list of our experiences, but the outcome of a process of the reciprocal influence of these old and new experiences.

The Motivational Nature of Personality: In Search of Rewards

Rotter also assumes that behavior is goal directed. More specifically, he believes that we are motivated to maximize reward and minimize punishment. For example, from the experiences you had in high school, you conclude that taking notes in class will maximize the probability of obtaining good grades. But from the feedback from your first test, if your technique for taking notes is not very good, you will probably need to go to the student resource center to upgrade your skills. On this assumption, Rotter suggests that we modify our behaviors according to our experiences to maximize success in achieving a desired outcome (e.g., getting better grades).

The Role of Expectancies: The Effect of Anticipation on Rewards

Although the emphasis Rotter places on rewards and punishments might make him sound like a learning theorist espousing principles of operant conditioning (i.e., learning that focuses on the consequences of behavior), his position on the role of expectancies clearly separates his perspective from traditional learn-

ing perspectives. More specifically, he assumes that the importance an individual gives to a reward is determined not only by its nature (e.g., $5,000) but also by the expectancies the person has about the possibility of obtaining the reward (e.g., 1 chance in 50 million). Thus, when trying to understand and predict the behavior of an individual with any degree of success, Rotter believes you have to know not only the nature of the reward but the extent to which the person feels he or she can obtain it.

A reward is of little motivational value if the individual perceives the likelihood of getting it to be very low. For example, one of the reasons many school-age children living in ghettos might not spend much time studying is that their expectations of such behavior making a difference in their life are very low. What we can take from this example is not whether higher education leads to better-paying jobs – we already know it does – but how these children anticipate the likelihood of receiving such rewards. Thus, Rotter's emphasis on the importance of an individual's expectancies about reward outcome illustrates quite clearly the cognitive nature of his social learning theory.

In summary, the basic assumptions of Rotter's social learning theory tend to emphasize combining experience with expectancies as important factors in understanding the nature of personality. A summary of these assumptions is presented in "Summing It Up: Basic Assumptions of Rotter's Social Learning Theory" on p. 409.

Basic Concepts of Rotter's Social Learning Theory: The Specifics for Predicting Behavior

Social learning theory outlines four basic concepts used to help explain and predict behavior. These are behavior potential, expectancy, reinforcement value, and the psychological situation, as well as their combination into the basic formula for predicting behavior (Rotter, 1954, 1982; Rotter & Hochreich, 1975).

Behavior Potential: What Are My Options?

Rotter believes that we have various options when it comes to the way we respond to the events in our life. The term he uses to describe this state of affairs is *behavior potential*. **Behavior potential** refers to the likelihood of a specific behavior occurring in a particular situation as a means of achieving a specific goal. The higher

Summing It Up *Basic Assumptions of Rotter's Social Learning Theory*

Basic Assumption	Example
Learning from meaningful experience involves the view that learning is based on adjusting your perceptions in response to experiences within the environment.	To build up your self-confidence about giving your first sales presentation, practice in front of a mirror and then in front of a few friends to gain some meaningful experience.
The reciprocal nature of life experience states that old and new life experiences influence each other to form the basis of our perceptions.	While your past experiences have led you to believe that traffic officers love only to give speeding tickets, you change your view when one stops to give you a ride after you have run out of gas on the interstate.
The motivational nature of personality is that of guiding the individual to maximize reinforcement and minimize punishment.	Practicing your presentation not only builds your confidence but also maximizes the probability of impressing your boss and minimizes the possibility of embarrassing yourself in front of your peers.
The role of expectancies is that they influence behavior by determining the beliefs we have about the likelihood of receiving certain reinforcements.	The extent to which you are willing to risk raising your hand in class to answer a question is largely determined by the expectancies you have about receiving recognition from your peers for knowing the right answer.

the probability of a behavior occurring in a given situation, the greater its behavior potential is said to be. For example, when studying for a test, you might choose one of these options: studying your notes, studying the chapter summaries and definitions, or looking for similarities between the book and the notes. On the basis of what others have told you about how this professor tests, you decide to study only the notes. In this example, studying the notes has a higher behavioral potential than the other two alternatives. But in another class, on the basis of what you have heard about another professor, studying the similarities between the notes and book has the greatest behavior potential. Thus, the more you know about what options are available to an individual, the greater your chances of understanding and predicting that person's behavior.

Expectancy: What Are the Odds?

For Rotter, what we decide to do is influenced not only by the alternatives available to us but also by what we think will happen if we engage in that behavior (Rotter, 1993). The term he uses to explain the subjective nature of what we think will happen is *expectancy*. **Expectancy** refers to an individual's subjective belief that if he or she behaves in a particular manner in a specific situation, certain reinforcements will occur. For exam-

ple, when deciding to study only your class notes for a test, you are saying that you "expect" to get a better grade in this class by studying the notes rather than the material in the book. You need to keep in mind that expectancies represent subjective perceptions of the situation. In reality, studying the notes may not be the best approach. However, because you believe this to be the case, studying the notes has a greater behavior potential for you than studying the material in the book.

Understanding expectancy also gives us a better understanding of why people behave in ways that seem maladaptive to us. For example, a very lonely person might make no attempt to seek others out at social gatherings because she simply assumes (e.g., maintains a high expectancy) that she will be rejected. Expectancies can also be considered by examining the extent to which the individual uses them in various situations:

- *Specific expectancies* refers to the subjective beliefs an individual has about a particular course of action producing a desired outcome in a specific situation. For example, you would be demonstrating a specific expectancy if you believed that studying only the notes would get you a good grade in your history class, but not in your personality course.

- *Generalized expectancies* refers to subjective beliefs an individual might possess that are applied to a variety of situations. For example, you would be demonstrating a generalized expectancy if you assumed that studying only the class notes would get you good grades in all of your courses this semester.

While specific and generalized expectancies are discussed separately, you should realize that they also influence each other. What starts out as a generalized expectancy may develop into a specific expectancy based on experience. For example, when you start college, you may assume that all you need to do is take good notes in all of your classes and study only the notes for the test. But after your first set of midterms, you discover that this strategy works with some professors but not with others. As a result of these experiences, you begin to tailor your expectations so that the nature of your studying behavior is specific to each particular professor.

On the other hand, specific expectancies can also turn into generalized expectancies based on experience. For example, after studying only the class notes for this particular professor's freshman survey course in history, you now take an advanced course from her and study the same way. If you are successful, your expectancies will be generalized; you may conclude that for any course you take from this instructor, all you need to do is have a good set of class notes.

The value of generalized expectancies is that they make adjusting to new situations easier, if the behavior is appropriate. The value of specific expectancies is that they enable us to adjust our behavior to the situation at hand. As you can imagine, people who are not able to employ generalized and specific expectancies successfully are bound to have problems in coping with life. For example, a man who continues to use the same approach in asking women to dance, even though they constantly turn him down, is going to be very lonely – assuming that he is actually trying to get a dance partner. Thus, for Rotter, expectancy means asking yourself "What are the odds of getting what I want with this course of action?"

Reinforcement Value: What Do You Want?

For Rotter, what people want in life is represented by the term *reinforcement value*. **Reinforcement value** refers to the expressed preference an individual has for one source of reinforcement over others, given that all of them are equally available. For example, suppose Cheng, a college student, has had friends arrange three blind dates for him. One woman is a history major, one a biology major, and one a Spanish major. His selection of the woman who is the history major would indicate that she has a higher reinforcement value than the other two women. In this case, the reinforcement value might be the possibility of establishing a meaningful relationship.

Reinforcement value is determined by a number of factors. One is the expectancy that the reinforcement will meet your needs and objectives. For example, in this case, since Cheng has a history minor, he probably expects to have more in common with the history major than with the other two women. Reinforcement value is also based on the relative choices available. Suppose another friend says that a woman in his tennis club would also be willing to go out with Cheng on a blind date. Given this additional option, and his passion for tennis, Cheng may select the tennis player instead of the history major. Thus, the value we place on what we want is determined not only by expectations we have for selecting it but also by what other choices are available.

The Psychological Situation: Reinforcement in Context

Rotter realized that what is valued in one situation or context may not be valued in another. As a result, he proposed the notion of the **psychological situation**, which refers to any aspect of the specific situation to which the individual is responding.

Suppose that during his blind date with the tennis player, Cheng discovers that she is top-ranked in their area. On knowing this, he becomes tense and nervous due to his own competitive nature. In this context, his reaction is determined by the fact that his perception of the situation changes once he begins to focus on the woman's great tennis ability rather than on the other interests they have in common.

The subjective nature of the way people perceive a situation is the reason Rotter refers to it as psychological. His point is that we are influenced not only by the objective cues in a situation (e.g., Cheng's date is a good tennis player.) but also by the psychological reactions they trigger in each of us (e.g., Cheng feels inferior because of his date's tennis ability). Thus, our responses are determined not only by our expectations and reinforcement values but also by the subjective perception of the cues that are available to us in a particular situation.

The Basic Formula: Combining the Specifics to Predict Behavior

To help predict the nature of an individual's behavior in a particular situation, Rotter combines the concepts we have just discussed. His **basic formula** states that the behavior potential (BP) in a specific situation (S1) is a function (f) of the expectancy (E) of the occurrence of a certain reinforcement (RVa) following a particular behavior (x). The basic formula might also be expressed in the following way:

$$BP_{S1} = f(E_{RVa} + RV_{x, S1})$$

Stated more simply, the basic formula proposes that the likelihood of your performing a particular behavior in a given situation is a function of the expectancy you have that this behavior will produce a reinforcement that is desirable to you. For example, suppose that you are bored and want to have some fun. You could go to a party or a newly released movie. According to the basic formula, in this context, your decision would be based on your perception of which activity would be more enjoyable. Thus, Rotter's belief is that we can predict behavior more accurately if we know the specifics of the situation, including the choices available, what the person hopes to obtain, what the person believes is the likelihood of obtaining it, and the subjective perception of cues in the situation.

This concludes the discussion of the basic concepts of Rotter's social learning theory of personality. A summary of these concepts is presented in "Summing It Up: Basic Concepts of Rotter's Social Learning Theory" below. In the next section, we will examine how Rotter conceptualizes the nature of personality adjustment.

Summing It Up *Basic Concepts of Rotter's Social Learning Theory*

Basic Concept	Example
Behavior potential is the probability of a particular behavior occurring in a specific situation.	The probability of you wearing a suit to a job interview is higher than that of you wearing cut-off jeans and a t-shirt.
An *expectancy* is a belief that an individual has that a particular behavior will lead to a specific reinforcement in a given situation.	You have the belief that wearing a suit to a job interview has a greater likelihood of producing a job offer than does wearing cut-off jeans and a t-shirt.
Specific expectancies are beliefs related to a specific situation.	You believe that your dark blue suit is the best choice for the job interview with the bank but not for the interview with the marketing research firm.
Generalized expectancies are beliefs related to a wider range of situations.	As a general rule, you believe that having well-styled hair leads to making a more favorable impression than messy hair.
Reinforcement value is your expressed interest in one particular reinforcer over others.	All things considered, you would rather get a job offer from the marketing research firm than the bank.
The *psychological situation* includes all of the cues found in the environment that influence the response of the individual.	The information you read about a company in their brochure suggests to you that you should wear your conservative dark blue suit to the interview.
The *basic formula* is an equation that combines reinforcement value and expectancies to predict behavior potential in a specific psychological situation.	The suit you decide to wear (behavior potential) to this particular job interview (psychological situation) is influenced by how much you want the job (reinforcement value) and how much you believe wearing the suit will help you get it (expectancy).

Personality Adjustment: The General Nature of Coping

Rotter's basic formula is designed to predict behavior in specific situations, but determining the nature of personality adjustment involves considering behavioral responses on a more general level. In this regard, Rotter defined certain personality processes that are associated with successful and unsuccessful personality adjustment.

Freedom of Movement and Need Value: Having What It Takes to Get What You Want

Do you have what it takes to get what you want? **Freedom of movement** refers to the expectancy an individual has about a set of behaviors being able to achieve a group of related reinforcements. **Need value** is the average value an individual places on this group of related reinforcements. For example, you may assume that taking good notes, keeping up on your reading assignments, asking questions in class, and studying regularly are behaviors having a high probability of helping you to obtain a group of rewards after graduating from college that might include a stimulating job, a fancy car, and stylish clothes.

Successful personality adjustment requires that the individual has the skills necessary (i.e., high freedom of movement) to obtain those things he or she wants so much (i.e., need value). On the other hand, unsuccessful personality adjustment is characterized by not having the required skills (i.e., low freedom of movement) necessary to obtain the rewards an individual desires, or disproportional need values that are too high (e.g., you expect every person you meet at the party to like you) or too low (e.g., beating by a wide margin at tennis someone who is clearly a lot worse than you will neither give you much satisfaction in this achievement nor be much of a source of pride in your tennis ability).

As you would imagine, not being able to get what you really want could lead to such maladaptive behavior as defensiveness, the manipulation of others, or excessive fantasizing. For example, an individual who will not admit to his lack of study skills is likely to blame others (e.g., the instructors are unfair, or other students cheat) in a defensive manner for his lack of academic success. He might also engage in manipulative behavior by borrowing notes or copying other students' answers to the test. Finally, in a more serious sense, the individual may spend more time fantasizing about living the good life than actually doing what it takes (i.e., studying) to get what is desired. Thus, as they relate to personality adjustment, freedom of movement and need value involve having what it takes to get what you want.

Minimal Goal Level: What Is the Least You Will Settle For?

When considering what different people believe is reinforcing, Rotter found it valuable to introduce the term **minimal goal level**, which he defined as the lowest level within a category of reinforcements an individual will consider as being reinforcing. For example, when you are considering job offers, you might tell yourself that you will not work for anything less than $23,000 a year. In this example, $23,000 represents your minimal goal level. The same can be said for the student who believes that anything less than an A is an unacceptable grade. In this case, the minimal goal level is an A.

It is important to note that minimal goal level is a relative term. For example, while one student might be perfectly willing to work for $20,000 a year, given the salary expectations for people with his college degree, another individual with a different college degree would not even acknowledge a job offer paying less than $28,000 per year. From the experiences of this author when passing back exams, it is interesting to note the reactions students have due to the variations in their minimal goal levels. For example, some students feel happy, almost relieved, when they receive a C; others are visibly upset with themselves because they only received a B+. Thus, different people have different minimal goal levels in the same situation.

Successful personality adjustment is associated with having the freedom of movement necessary to achieve the minimal goal level you have set for yourself. For example, expecting only As makes sense if you have the set of studying skills and motivation (i.e., high freedom of movement) that makes such demands on yourself possible.

On the other hand, personality maladjustment is most likely to occur when an individual does not have the freedom of movement to obtain the minimal goal level set for himself or herself. For example, an individual might become easily depressed if he is constantly turned down for jobs because he lacks the necessary educational requirements and relevant experience. Thus, an individual's level of adjustment is related to the extent to which the person sets realistic expectations for what he or she is able to achieve – and willing to settle for.

Generalized Expectancies and Personality Adjustment: The Appropriate and Inappropriate Generalization of Expectancies

In addition to being used to help predict behavior in a specific situation, generalized expectancies also have implications for understanding personality adjustment from the social learning perspective. People with a high degree of personality adjustment are able to determine when a certain course of action will lead to the expected reward and when it will not. People with a low degree of personality adjustment are not able to make such discriminations and tend to overextend the nature of their generalized expectancies.

For example, suppose that Peter receives rejection letters from the first five companies to which he has sent job applications. As a result of these five rejections, he becomes depressed and decides to stop sending out job applications because of the overextended generalized expectancy he now has that "nobody is ever going to hire him." The maladjusted nature of Peter's generalized expectancies is that he has overgeneralized the possibility of rejection from these five companies to all companies. Thus, the degree of personality adjustment is also reflected by the appropriateness of the generalization of a person's expectancies.

This concludes the discussion of personality adjustment from the social learning perspective. A summary of the principal ideas discussed in this section is presented in "Summing It Up: Processes of Personality Adjustment from Rotter's Social Learning Theory" below.

As a practicing clinical psychologist, Rotter has been extremely concerned with helping people overcome problems of personality adjustment. In the next section, we will explore how the basic principles of social learning theory are utilized by Rotter in his

Summing It Up *Processes of Personality Adjustment from Rotter's Social Learning Theory*

Personality Processes	Successful Adjustment	Unsuccessful Adjustment
Freedom of movement involves the extent to which you believe you possess the abilities to achieve a group of related reinforcements having a certain average level of worth referred to as their *need value*.	Experiencing the sense of esteem from realizing that you have the physical, mental, and emotional ability to compete successfully with your co-workers for an upcoming promotion, salary increase, and bonus	The feelings of nervousness you experience from realizing that you do not have the necessary career experiences to compete with you co-workers for that promotion, salary, and bonus you want so much
Minimal goal level is the least amount of a particular reinforcement category that you will accept as being worthwhile.	The sense of satisfaction you experience when you achieve the basic career goals you set for yourself two years ago	The sense of disappointment you might experience when you realize that you are far from achieving the basic career goals you set for yourself two years ago
The relationship between *generalized expectancies and personality adjustment* involves being able to assess correctly the degree of utility of your expectancies.	As a manager, knowing that the generalized expectancy of company involvement includes working overtime in the evenings and some weekends but not playing on the union employees' softball team	Getting so caught up in "company activities" that your participation in all of these events begins to affect your performance as a manager

own unique form of psychotherapy and other assorted applications.

Applications of Rotter's Social Learning Theory: Using What is Known

As a scientist and practitioner, Rotter has not only been interested in testing his theoretical ideas, but also very concerned with finding useful applications for them (Trull & Phares, 2001). He and others have found many important applications for his ideas. In this section, you will read about applications of his social learning theory to psychotherapy, personality assessment, and marital satisfaction and adjustment to divorce.

Psychotherapy: Therapy as a Learning Process for Modifying Maladaptive Cognitive and Behavior Patterns

Rotter (1970, 1978; Rotter & Hochreich, 1975) views psychotherapy as a learning process involving the modification of maladaptive cognitive and behavioral patterns. In this regard, inappropriate cognitions and behaviors are not only eliminated but replaced with more constructive and adaptive alternatives that are taught to the client during the course of psychotherapy. For example, a client may be depressed because he has the faulty cognition that after being downsized from his job, he now believes that he will never find another job that will be as good. As a result of the faulty cognition, he has stopped looking for another job. The early emphasis Rotter placed on the identification and modification of faulty cognitions as a principal component in the therapeutic process has served to set the stage for the development of some of the more contemporary and influential forms of psychotherapy that also focus on the role of maladaptive cognitions and their modification (Ellis, 2008; Lazarus, 2008).

As in other learning situations, clients enter therapy with very different attitudes, motives, and experiences. As a result, a characteristic of social learning psychotherapy is the flexibility required on the part of the therapist. For example, for some clients, the therapist may have to work one-on-one to help them focus on clarifying their goals; other clients may require working in a group therapy setting in order to acquire certain interpersonal skills. For still others, a combination of treatment techniques, including behavior therapy and

family therapy, might be what is required. Thus, rather than trying to fit the client's problem into a specific therapeutic technique, Rotter believes that the nature of the client's problem should dictate the type of therapeutic technique to be used. In the true social-cognitive tradition, social learning psychotherapy can be construed as a problem-solving process that involves trying to determine the optimal way for the client to adopt more rational cognitions (e.g., "I can find another job, if I update my skills") and learn those behaviors that will bring the greatest likelihood of obtaining rewards (e.g., enrolling in computer training courses at the community college to update his skills).

The Basic Goal: Increasing Freedom of Movement
The goal of psychotherapy from the perspective of social learning theory is to help increase the client's freedom of movement. Enhancing freedom of movement increases the client's likelihood of achieving the minimal goal level for those reinforcements that contribute to greater life satisfaction (Rotter & Hochreich, 1975). Rotter does not specify a particular set of techniques for achieving this objective; instead, he takes a more problem-solving approach. This approach relies on the therapist developing an individualized treatment program designed to help the client obtain the necessary cognitive and behavior changes to produce more freedom of movement. Depending on the degree of the client's personality maladjustment, the treatment program may involve teaching the client how to explore new alternatives for goal attainment, focus on the consequences of his or her behavior, or develop a more appropriate system for generalizing expectancies, to name just a few. Regardless of its nature, the basic goal of social learning therapy is to increase the client's freedom of movement.

Techniques for Teaching: Some Examples of Social Learning Therapy Some people may be experiencing emotional problems because they have set minimal goal levels that are too high. In such cases, social learning therapy would involve helping the client to establish a more realistic minimal goal level. For example, a female bank executive might be creating an excessive amount of tension for herself because she feels she must personally do all of the work in her office to achieve complete acceptance by her male peers. In this case, the therapist would work with her on possibly lowering the goals she has set for herself by helping her to understand that it is not a sign of failure or weakness to delegate some of the less important work to her staff. This example demonstrates how freedom of movement can be increased by altering the cognitions held by the client.

Sometimes the minimal goal level set by a client is realistic, but he or she may lack the skills necessary to achieve it. The therapist would then work with the client to identify and help acquire the necessary skills. For example, suppose that Paul, a sales representative, has developed feelings of depression because of his inability to close sales after his group presentations. In this case, the therapist might ask the client to participate in group therapy. By working within the group, the therapist might determine that when talking to a group, Paul rarely makes eye contact and tends to talk nonstop, or until someone interrupts him. After identifying these shortcomings, the therapist then works with Paul on how to make eye contact and summarize points that will stimulate questions, both of which can be practiced in the process of group therapy. This example demonstrates how freedom of movement can be increased by learning more adaptive skills.

The maladaptive use of generalized expectancies by clients is another common problem addressed during social learning therapy. For example, after being turned down by several women he has asked out for dates, a client may develop the generalized expectancy that he is an unworthy person. In this case, the therapist may help the client to focus on his positive characteristics during one-on-one therapy sessions and then involve him in group therapy where he can experience a more general level of acceptance by the other group members. The therapist may then recommend that the client join a local volunteer organization as a means of extending his generalized expectancies of being accepted by others. But the therapist would also help the client to determine the limitations of his expectancies by helping him to realize that he does not have to be liked by everyone and to recognize which type of people seem to like him and which do not. Making such discriminations will help the client to minimize those situations in which he is going to be rejected. Thus, learning how to use generalized expectancies more appropriately can also lead to an increase in freedom of movement.

Since an individual's emotional problems might also be caused by his or her relationship with significant others (e.g., spouse, parents, teachers, or children), social learning therapy might require involving these people in therapy as well. For example, a female client's low self-esteem may be due to her inability to tell her parents that she wants to make her own decisions about college and a career. In this case, the parents may be asked to attend the therapy sessions so that the dynamics of the total family situation might be examined more closely. It could be that the control the parents are exerting on the adult daughter may be a result of their own loneliness and unhappiness. As a result, the therapist might have all of them work on developing more effective communication patterns to express their needs, rather than trying to control each other with emotional tactics. Thus, helping all of the family members learn to communicate more effectively gives them greater freedom of movement not only as individuals but also as a family unit.

As you can see from these examples, psychotherapy from the perspective of social learning theory involves trying to identify the therapeutic technique that will best help the client achieve a greater degree of freedom of movement. Because of the variety of techniques necessary and the emphasis on helping the client to learn new skills and alternatives, a successful social learning therapist must also be an effective problem solver and teacher (Trull & Phares, 2001). In the next section, you will see how the eclectic nature of social learning theory has also been utilized in its application to personality assessment.

Personality Assessment: The Measurement of Generalized Expectancies

In developing a comprehensive theory of personality, Rotter also applied the basic principles of social learning theory to the area of personality assessment. More specifically, he developed two measures of personality that are designed to assess generalized expectancies: the Interpersonal Trust Scale and the Internal vs. External Control of Reinforcement Scale.

The Interpersonal Trust Scale: Identifying Suspicious Minds   As conceptualized by Rotter (1967, 1971, 1980), **interpersonal trust** is a generalized expectancy held by an individual that the words and promises of others can be relied on when there is no evidence for believing otherwise. The Interpersonal Trust Scale (Rotter, 1967, 1971) is designed to assess the extent to which an individual possesses this generalized expectancy. The trust scale is a 40-item forced-choice questionnaire containing 25 trust items and 15 filler items. People respond to each item by indicating the extent of their agreement. Here is a sample of trust items from the scale:

> Most people can be counted on to do what they say they will do.
> Most elected officials are really sincere in their campaign promises.
> In dealing with strangers, one is better off to be cautious until they have provided evidence that they are trustworthy.

Consistent with the proposed notion of interpersonal trust, research shows that people with high trust scores are less likely to lie, cheat, steal, and be unhappy. They are more prone to give people a second chance, respect the rights of others, and be sought out as friends than are people with low trust scores (Phares & Chaplin, 1997; Rotter, 1980). In one rather interesting study, people scoring low on the trust scale tended to view the Warren Commission Report on the assassination of President Kennedy as part of a cover-up conspiracy (Hamsher, Geller, & Rotter, 1968).

Low-trusting people also demonstrated their sensitivity to negative stimuli related to trustworthiness by more quickly recognizing negative words (e.g., *deceitful, malicious*) than positive (e.g., *sincere, truthful*) and neutral words (e.g., *slender, healthy*) when presented with the words for just a fraction of a second. High-trusting people showed no difference in their ability to respond to the three categories of words (Gurtman & Lion, 1982). Finally, when contacted by researchers to serve as participants in a study, high-trusting people asked fewer questions (e.g., "How did you get my name?" "What is the experiment about?") than did low-trusting subjects. Thus, this body of research, as well as other works (Rotter, 1971, 1980; Wrightsman, 1991), seems to provide evidence that supports the Interpersonal Trust Scale in identifying suspicious minds.

The Internal-External Control of Reinforcement Scale: Where Do You Believe Your Reinforcements Come From?   The **Internal-External Control of Reinforcement Scale** (**I-E Scale**; Rotter, 1966) is designed to measure the extent to which an individual holds the generalized expectancy that reinforcements in life are controlled by internal factors (e.g., what you do) or external factors (e.g., luck, fate, or the power of others). The I-E Scale contains 29 statement pairs, 6 of which are filler pairs, presented in a forced-choice format. For each pair of statements, the person is asked to select one that best represents his or her belief about the operation of events in the world. In each item pair, one statement reflects belief in internal control of reinforcement (e.g., what you get out of life depends on how much you put into it) and one reflects belief in external control of reinforcement (e.g., it's not what you do but who you know that determines what you get out of life). People who tend to express a belief reflecting a generalized expectancy of an internal locus of control are referred to as "internals," while those who express an external locus of control are referred to as "externals" (Cohen & Swerdlik, 2005; Phares, 2001; Wallston, 2001). To sample the I-E Scale for yourself, answer the questions in "You Can Do It" on p. 417.

Validation Research on the I-E Scale: A Tradition of Support Continues   The topic of internal versus external control of reinforcement is currently one of the most studied variables in psychology and the other social sciences (Lefcourt, 1992; Phares, 2001; Rotter, 1990). As of 1990, Rotter's original monograph on internal-external control had been cited in other texts more than 4,700 times, "a number far in excess of any other article for the same period of time" (Rotter, 1990, p. 492). It is also interesting to note that the current research on locus of control continues at approximately the same pace as it did over 30 years ago (Rotter, 1990). Such longevity implies that the locus of control concept continues to stimulate new ideas and areas of research.

As you might imagine, trying to summarize all the research validating the I-E Scale and internal-external control of reinforcement construct would be next to impossible in the limited space available in this section. However, to illustrate the diverse uses of the I-E Scale, here is a sample of some of the validation research:

- *Information processing and I-E.* Since internals believe they have a greater degree of influence over what happens to them, it is expected that they would pay more attention to – and retain more – information that would be useful to them later (Strickland, 1979; Wallston, 2001). Consistent with this logic, hospitalized tuberculosis patients identified as internals retained more information about their condition than those identified as externals (Seeman & Evans, 1962). A similar pattern of results was found for prisoners with regard to retaining information related to achieving parole successfully (Seeman, 1963).

You Can Do It

The I-E Scale: Measuring One of the Most Studied Variables in Personality Psychology

Of the different scales for assessing personality that he developed, Rotter is probably most associated with the I-E Scale. The following 10 items are a sample of the response pairs found in the I-E Scale (Rotter, 1966). For each pair of statements, select the one that best represents your opinion.

1. a. Many of the unhappy things in people's lives are partly due to bad luck.
   b. People's misfortunes result from the mistakes they make.
2. a. One of the major reasons why we have wars is because people don't take enough interest in politics.
   b. There will always be wars, no matter how hard people try to prevent them.
3. a. Without the right breaks one cannot be an effective leader.
   b. Capable people who fail to become leaders have not taken advantage of their opportunities.
4. a. In the case of the well-prepared student there is rarely if ever such a thing as an unfair test.
   b. Many times exam questions tend to be so unrelated to course work that studying is really useless.
5. a. Who gets to be the boss often depends on who was lucky enough to be in the right place first.
   b. Getting people to do the right thing depends upon ability; luck has little to do with it.
6. a. Becoming a success is a matter of hard work; luck has little to do with it.
   b. Getting a good job depends mainly on being in the right place at the right time.
7. a. It is hard to know whether or not a person really likes you.
   b. How many friends you have depends on how nice a person you are.
8. a. With enough effort we can wipe out political corruption.
   b. It is difficult for people to have much control over the things politicians do in office.
9. a. Sometimes I can't understand how teachers arrive at the grades they give.
   b. There is a direct connection between how hard I study and the grades I get.
10. a. People are lonely because they don't try to be friendly.
    b. There's not much use in trying to please people; if they like you, they like you.

Scoring

Each time you selected "a" for items 1, 3, 5, 7, and 9, give yourself one point; each time you selected "b" for items 2, 4, 6, 8, and 10, give yourself one point. Add up the number of points. The higher your score, the more your responses reflect belief in an external control of reinforcement. Because only a small sample of items was presented, however, do not consider this an extremely accurate measure of your locus of control.

When making decisions, internals tend to give reasons based more on previously learned information than externals do, even though both originally had equal access to the information (Phares, 1968). Individuals with an internal locus of controlled also tended to make better use of economic information and more profitable financial choices than did those with an external locus of control (Plunkett & Buehner, 2007).

- *Taking responsibility and I-E.* The belief that they have some control over the events in their lives seems to result in internals taking more action than externals (Rahim, 1997). For example, among sexually active single college females, internals were more likely to be practicing some form of birth control than were externals (MacDonald, 1970). It has also been reported that participation in civil rights demonstrations and other forms of political actions tended to be associated with an internal locus of control (Abramowitz, 1973; Gore & Rotter, 1963; Strickland, 1965). In just the opposite manner, female survivors of acquaintance rape reported greater belief in external forces, such as luck, chance, and powerful others, playing a more important role in the outcome of their lives than did women who had not been assaulted (McEwan, de Man, & Simpson-Housley, 2005), suggesting that the victims of assault believed that they did not have control over such violent events in their lives. In a somewhat different area, individuals with an internal locus of control expecting to earn a professional degree expressed less of a desire to borrow money to finance their education than did individuals with an external locus of control (Trent, Lee, & Owens-Nicholson, 2006). Thus, internals not only believe that they can make a difference in their lives but also tend to take action to make such changes possible.

- *Assigning responsibility and I-E.* In addition to assuming more responsibility, individuals with internal locus of control orientations are also more likely to assign more responsibility to others for their actions. In an interesting twist on the I-E concept, jurors with high internal scores tend to hold defendants more responsible for their predicaments, especially when the evidence is ambiguous (Phares & Wilson, 1972). Such perceptions could lead jurors with an internal locus of control to support more harsh sentences than those with external locus of control scores, who are more likely to attribute the criminal acts to forces outside of the defendant's control (Wrightsman, Nietzel, & Fortune, 1998). For example, prospective jurors with an internal locus of control are more likely to support the death penalty (Butler & Moran, 2007), which can be viewed as the ultimate expression of holding individuals responsible for their actions.
- *Academic achievement and I-E.* The tendency of internals to take more action than externals also translates into greater academic success. In research with college students, internals tend to study more, perform better on tests, and get better grades than externals do (Nord, Connelly, & Daignault, 1974; Prociuk & Breen, 1975). Students with an internal locus of control also tended to score better on tests even under conditions designed to undermine their performance

(Cadinu, Maass, Lombardo, & Frigerio, 2006). Even for children, internal locus of control scores were found to be positively related to scores in science for children ranging in age from 4 to 8 years old (Martin et al., 2007). In a 26-year follow-up study, it was reported that internal locus of control scores for boys and girls at age 10 predicted educational attainment in those individuals as adults (Flouri, 2006). Thus, from elementary students to graduate students, there seems to be a rather consistent relationship between internality and academic success (D. Bar-Tal & Bar-Zohar, 1977; Findley & Cooper, 1983; Lefcourt, 1982). Some possible reasons for the greater academic success of internals are that they appear to be better than externals at planning and working toward long-term goals, such as a grade that may be two months away or an advanced degree that may take five years to obtain (Lefcourt, 1982). Internals are also better than externals at establishing reachable goals for themselves (Gilmor & Reid, 1978, 1979). For example, while an external might decide to take four courses per semester with a 35-hour-per-week work schedule, an internal might more realistically decide to take just two courses. In support of this reasoning, in addition to their academic work, students with an internal locus of control demonstrated enhanced career decision-making skills (Milar & Shevlin, 2007). Finally, associated with all of this academic success is the finding that students with an internal locus of control tend to be happier (Ye, She, & Wu, 2007).

- *Health behavior and I-E.* Individuals also vary in the extent to which their locus of control serves to influence a variety of health-related behaviors, with those having an internal locus of control taking more responsibility for their health. In support of this reasoning, internal locus of control was positively associated with individuals taking action (e.g., remembering to take their medication and keeping track of their pills) designed to increase hypertension medication adherence (Hong, Oddone, Dudley, & Bosworth, 2006). In addition, women who had an internal locus of control maintained a stronger belief that they could reduce their risk of breast cancer (Rowe, Montgomery, Duberstein, & Bovbjerg, 2005). Finally, individuals with an internal locus of control with respect to their health displayed greater cardiac coping ability after completing a stressful video-game task (Weinstein & Quigley, 2006), as well as exhibited a tendency to respond to adversity with strategies that involved taking action (Leontopoulou, 2006). In just the opposite manner, individuals who were experiencing chronic illness and had external locus of control scores related to their health (e.g., assuming doctors have control over their health status) and a reduced belief in their ability to help themselves tended to report a high degree of emotional distress in relation to their illness (Shelly & Pakenham, 2004), suggesting that they might have given up hope of getting better. Individuals with an external locus of control also tended to be absent from work more due to sickness (Selander, Marnetoft, Åkerström, & Asplund, 2005). Finally, as a more extreme health issue, adolescent suicide risk was associated with more external locus of control (W. P. Evans, Owens, & Marsh, 2005). From a developmental perspective, it has been reported that as children get older, they become less external in their beliefs regarding controlling the outcome of their health status (Malcarne, Drahota, & Hamilton, 2005), which seems to correspond to the developmental changes in the complexity of their cognitive abilities.

● *Addictive behavior and I-E.* A number of studies have documented the relationship between alcohol consumption and I-E (Brannon & Feist, 2000; Goggin, Murray, Malcarne, Brown, & Wallston, 2007). For example, high school and college students with high external locus of control scores tended to drink more in a variety of situations, both pleasant and unpleasant (Jih, Sirgo, & Thomure, 1995). In addition, external locus of control scores were found to be associated with a high degree of alcoholism (L. B. Clements, York, & Rohrer, 1995), while internal locus of control scores predicted the degree of abstinence from drinking for alcoholics participating in alcohol abuse treatment programs (Koski-Jannes, 1994). Internet addiction – spending an excessive amount of time online – has also been linked to an external sense of locus of control (Chak & Leung, 2004). Thus, individuals who demonstrate addictive behaviors seem to assume that these are beyond their personal control.

Some interesting evidence validating the I-E Scale also comes from its application to the world of work, as described in "Applications in Personality Psychology" below.

Applications in Personality Psychology

The I-E Scale in the World of Work: Making Your Locus of Control Pay Off

Numerous studies have been conducted in industry to determine the role of locus of control in worker behavior (Schultz & Schultz, 1998). In a study using female factory workers, Giles (1977) found that internals who were dissatisfied with their jobs were more likely to volunteer for a job enrichment program than externals were. In a related finding, a survey of over 3,000 workers in six countries indicated that an internal locus of control was associated with greater work involvement (Reitz & Jewell, 1979).

When it comes to using pay incentives to increase performance, as you might expect, internals respond with greater performance than that of externals (Spector, 1982). As a result of this tendency, another suggested application of the I-E Scale involves using it in the personnel selection process to help identify internals for jobs with incentive systems (e.g., sales or piecework pay schedules; Lawler, 1971).

The belief that internals have in making a difference in their world of work, as reflected in greater job involvement and performance, does seem to have some positive consequences in terms of career advancements and promotion. In a 5-year longitudinal study conducted on a national sample of some 4,330 people, investigators reported that internals made greater job progress than did externals (Valecha, 1972). In addition, although there are some specific exceptions, internals have been found to be generally more satisfied with their jobs (Spector, 1982) and to show a higher degree of business ethics (Baehr, Jones, & Nerad, 1993). Finally, in response to losing their job, those who attributed the loss of their job to internal factors (e.g., did not work hard enough; lack of skills) were less likely to find jobs than those who attributed their unemployment to external factors beyond their control (e.g., downturn in the economy; Prussia, Kinicki, & Bracker, 1993).

In an extremely interesting study, Carl Anderson (C. R. Anderson, 1977) examined the relationship between the locus of control of business owners and their financial recovery following a flood (caused by Hurricane Agnes) that destroyed almost all of the businesses in a small Pennsylvania community in 1972. Anderson followed the problem-solving strategies and financial recovery of 90 business owners over a period of $3^{1}/_{2}$ years following the flood. Externals were found to use more emotion-directed coping strategies (e.g., withdrawal or hostility) and fewer problem-solving coping methods (e.g., task-oriented strategies) and to perceive their circumstances as being more stressful than internals did. The most noteworthy finding of this analysis, however, was the more favorable credit rating of the internal business owners in comparison to the externals at the end of the $3^{1}/_{2}$ years. From the results of this study, it was concluded that "the task-oriented coping behaviors of internals are apparently associated with a more successful solution of the problems created by the stressful event, since the performance of the internals' organizations is higher" (Anderson, 1977, p. 450).

When it comes to the world of work, believing that you can make a difference seems to pay off. This can be the case for employees and business owners alike.

The few areas of research described here are a very limited sampling of the research validating the I-E Scale. As you will learn in the next section, the I-E Scale has also been used in addressing a number of significant personal and social issues.

Applying Locus of Control to Matrimony and Divorce

The locus of control construct and I-E Scale have been used in various important applications, including helping to understand how people cope with and recover from unpleasant human conditions such as war, natural disasters, illness, and disease; treating alcoholism; studying the implications for child-rearing practices; studying the personalities and performances of athletes; and promoting health-related behaviors, to name just a few (Brannon & Feist, 2000; Lefcourt, 1982, 1983, 1984, 1992; Lefcourt & Davidson-Katz, 1991; LeUnes & Nation, 1989; Snyder & Forsyth, 1991). The application of locus of control to issues related to marriage and divorce is especially noteworthy and is featured in this section.

Locus of Control and the World of Matrimony: Understanding Marital Interaction and Satisfaction   In looking at how couples resolve marital conflict, researchers have discovered that husbands with an internal locus of control behave more assertively than do husbands with an external locus of control; however, assertiveness is not related to the locus of control of the wives (Doherty & Ryder, 1979). In observing the ways that couples try to communicate in marital problem solving, researchers discovered that external husbands respond with more verbal and physical aggression than do internal husbands, while external wives resort to more indirect forms of communication, such as teasing and kidding around, than do internal wives (Winkler & Doherty, cited in Doherty, 1983b). These results seem to suggest that because they believe that their direct (e.g., assertive) forms of communication have no effect, external husbands and wives must resort to less mature forms of communication when trying to resolve marital conflicts.

Additional research indicates that internal husbands and wives are more aware of and sensitive to potential marital problems than are external spouses, more willing to discuss them openly, and more likely to use problem-solving strategies that involve trying to understand and alter the conditions that were the source of grievance for their spouses (P. C. Miller, Lefcourt, Holmes, Ware, & Saleh, 1986). One possible reason for this pattern of response to marital problems is the rather active and direct problem-solving orientation of internals. Because internal spouses perceive themselves as more responsible for the outcome of their marriage and view marital outcomes as being controllable by their actions, they are much more likely than externals to be willing to engage in problem-solving coping strategies (e.g., open discussion of the problem or carrying out alternatives; P. C. Miller et al., 1986). In addition, because externals seem to feel rather uncomfortable with adopting problem-solving methods for dealing with stress, they tend to employ emotion-focused methods (e.g., suppression; Parkes, 1984; Strentz & Auerbach, 1988). In the case of marital problems, since external spouses feel that they have less control over their marital outcome, they are probably more likely to employ an emotion-focused method of coping, such as suppression (i.e., ignoring the problem), and assume that the problem will simply work itself out.

Because locus of control is related to how effectively couples settle their marital conflicts, you would also expect it to be related to marital satisfaction. In support of this reasoning, internality has been found to be positively associated with marital satisfaction (P. C. Miller, 1981; P. C. Miller et al., 1986) and marital intimacy (P. C. Miller, 1981). Research also seems to suggest that marital dissatisfaction is highest in those marriages where there is considered discrepancy in the locus of control of the spouses, such as the wife being more external than her husband (Doherty, 1981; Mlott & Lira, 1977). The explanation for this relationship seems to be that while these external wives may need a high degree of outward, expressive support, they tend to be married to men who are critical, impatient, and not creative, and who they perceive as not being intellectual or outgoing (Doherty, 1981, 1983b). These internal husbands tend to be married to women who are aggressive, selfish, and talkative, and they described their wives as being aggressive and trying. Couples with little difference in their locus of control scores seem to experience the least marital dissatisfaction (Doherty, 1981). In short, couples in the more-external-wife or more-internal-husband marriages have nothing good to say about each other, which would certainly contribute to their high degree of marital dissatisfaction.

Locus of Control and Understanding Adjustment to Divorce: When Breaking up Is Hard (and Not so Hard) to Do When marital dissatisfaction is high, ending the relationship becomes very likely. If this is the case, what is the relationship between locus of control and divorce? In one study involving over 904 people from a national probability sample, divorced people were found to have higher internal scores on the I-E Scale than those who were married or had never been married (Doherty, 1980). While it might be tempting to conclude that internal people are more likely to get a divorce, the data do not support this conclusion. In a study involving people from a national probability sample whose I-E scores were obtained twice over a 9-year period, the results generally indicated no statistical relationship between the scores of those staying married and those who split up (Doherty, 1983a).

An alternative explanation for the relationship between divorce and internality suggests that successful coping with the rigors of a divorce may produce a stronger belief in people's personal control over their lives (Doherty, 1983a). To test this explanation, in 1969 William Doherty obtained the I-E scores from a national probability sample of 5,393 women, ages 30–44. He later obtained I-E scores from these women in 1972 and 1977. When examining the relationship between I-E score and marital status, once again Doherty found that locus of control was not related to subsequent likelihood of getting a divorce during the period from 1969 to 1977. But the I-E scores for those who were divorced during the period from 1967 to 1972 were significantly more external than for those who stayed married (see Figure 10.1). Just the opposite pattern was observed for the period from 1972 to 1977: those who stayed married became more external than those who were divorced (see Figure 10.1). If we assume that rapid movement toward externality is an undesirable experience, then the pattern of results suggests that "divorce has a short-term negative effect on the average woman but that this negative effect does not endure because those who divorce become indistinguishable later from those who remain married" (Doherty, 1983a, p. 838).

In a related study, Helen Barnet (1990) examined the level of pre- and post-divorce stress in a sample of 107 divorced men and women, who had been married on average 10 years (with a range from 1 to 25 years). The survey questions examined how long it took them to decide to get a divorce, the stress due to the divorce, their adjustment to the divorce, and their locus of

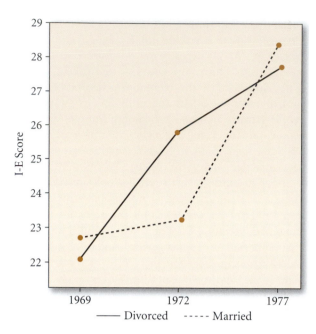

Figure 10.1 Changes in the scores on the locus of control scale for groups of married and divorced women over a 9-year period: The higher the score, the more external the orientation
Source: Doherty (1983a)

control score. The results indicated that internals displayed more pre-divorce decision stress but less post-divorce decision stress than did externals. In addition, internals displayed less overall stress than did externals. It seems that because they feel a greater sense of control, the increased level of pre-divorce decision stress found in internals may be due to their experiencing more agony over the decision to get a divorce. But thinking more about and agonizing more over the decision to get a divorce may have contributed to the internals experiencing less post-divorce decision stress and greater overall adjustment to the divorce than externals did.

Thus, when considering the relationship between locus of control and divorce, it seems that divorced people, particularly internals, experience an immediate crisis period. Their long-term reaction, however, might be more accurately described as a recovery period characterized by a greater sense of personal control. To examine another interesting application of locus of control, see "The Cultural Context of Personality Psychology" opposite as an illustration of how locus of control has been used to help understand the reactions of individuals to a major geopolitical event.

The Cultural Context of Personality Psychology

Anticipatory Anxiety and the Hong Kong Shift: Locus of Control as a Mediator of the Experience of Uncertainty

One of the most significant geopolitical events to occur during the last part of the 20th century took place on July 1, 1997. On this date, Hong Kong shifted from being a dependent territory of the British, as it had been for the previous 150 years, to become a Special Administrative Region of the People's Republic of China. Because Hong Kong residents were well aware that this change was going to take place on a specific date, the anticipation of such a monumental geopolitical shift was expected to be a source of considerable emotional apprehension. As evidence of the degree of anticipatory anxiety created, in a poll of a large and representative sample of Hong Kong Chinese, more than 50 percent surveyed indicated they were considering leaving the territory (DeGolyer, 1995). This anticipatory anxiety was also used to help explain the marked increase in divorce petitions, from 3,700 to 8,100, between 1983 and 1992 (R. Schwartz & Chung, 1996), which could not be accounted for by actual marriage rates or population increases alone (*Hong Kong Annual Digest of Statistics*, 1993, p. 20).

In an attempt to help understand the potential psychological impact of this shift in territory, Robin Goodwin, of Bristol University in the United Kingdom, and Catherine Tang, of the Chinese University of Hong Kong, investigated the role of locus of control in mediating the perceptions of threat and uncertainty brought on by the shift in territory. In their investigation, Goodwin and Tang (1998) surveyed 403 married individuals (198 males and 205 females) living in Hong Kong.

As expected, an individual's locus of control score was found to be an important predictor of how much of a perceived threat the territorial shift in 1997 would be – the more external the individual's locus of control, the greater the perceived threat of the territorial shift. In addition, an individual's locus of control score, along with the extent to which family and friends

Summing It Up *Applications of Rotter's Social Learning Theory*

Psychotherapy: Therapy as a Learning Process:

- *The Basic Goal.* To Rotter, the purpose of psychotherapy is to help the client develop greater freedom of movement as a means of increasing the likelihood of the individual being able to obtain those reinforcements he or she desires.
- *Techniques of Psychotherapy.* Unlike most psychotherapies, social learning therapy involves utilizing a variety of techniques and procedures to deal with the specific problems of adjustment clients bring to therapy, including the following:
  - *Minimal goal levels* that are too high can create anxiety and tension. *Treatment*: altering the nature of the client's cognitions (e.g., goals), so that expectations become more realistic and the likelihood of achieving desired reinforcements increases.
  - *Lacking the specific skills* necessary to achieve realistic minimal goal levels can lead to depression. *Treatment*: helping the client to acquire the necessary verbal and behavioral skills by working individually with the therapist or in group therapy.
  - The *faulty generalization of expectancies* can lead to feelings of despair. *Treatment*: helping the client to learn when and where the expectancies are appropriate, to increase the client's freedom of movement.
  - *Faulty communication* with significant others can lead to problems of adjustment. *Treatment*: enhancing communication effectiveness with significant others during the process of family and group therapy.

Personality Assessment: Measuring Generalized Expectancies:

- The *Interpersonal Trust Scale* measures the extent to which individuals believe what they are told by others.
- The *Internal-External Control of Reinforcement Scale (I-E Scale)* assesses the extent to which an individual believes the reinforcements in life are controlled by personal factors (i.e., internal orientation) or by forces outside of the person's control (i.e., external orientation).

Applications of Locus of Control to Matrimony and Divorce. The I-E Scale has been used to understand how locus of control is related to marital interaction and communication patterns and adjustment to divorce.

expressed anxiety about the shift, was also associated with a negative impact on the individual's relationship with his or her spouse. Goodwin and Tang reasoned that the perceived threat of the territorial shift was greatest for those individuals who felt that little could be done to control their life events after it. This increased level of anticipated stress, in turn, seemed to produce an increased level of day-to-day stress that was creating difficulties for these individuals with their spouses. Such a pattern of results is consistent with previous research indicating that psychological adaptation to stressful events is generally superior for those with a high internal locus of control (Rice, 1992). The significance of this research by Goodwin and Tang is that it demonstrates how personality factors, such as locus of control, can be helpful in understanding the process by which individuals evaluate, interpret, and adapt to major cultural transitions as well as day-to-day events.

This concludes the discussion on the applications of Rotter's social learning viewpoint. A summary of the major points discussed in this section is presented in "Summing It Up: Applications of Rotter's Social Learning Theory" above.

Evaluating Rotter's Social Learning Theory: Strengths and Limitations

Our discussion of Rotter's social learning theory concludes with a summary of its characteristic strengths and limitations.

Characteristic Strengths

Here are some strengths of Rotter's social learning theory:

- *Inclusion of cognitive variables: Looking beyond behavior.* Rotter has been a true pioneer in the social-cognitive viewpoint of personality. In addition to acknowledging the significance of cognitive factors in personality, he has developed a theory of personality that specifies explicitly what the factors are (e.g., reinforcement value) and how they are related to each other (e.g., the basic formula) to predict behavior in specific situations. His use of generalized expectancies also represents an extension of the use of cognitive variables to predict behavior in a broader sense. Thus, Rotter's use of cognitive variables involves looking far beyond just behavior to predict behavior.

- *Emphasis on research: Verification of constructs.* Because of his affiliation with major research universities, Rotter has always been very concerned with the validation of his theory through basic and applied research. Research on social learning theory has been stimulated by the fact that the theory's basic concepts can be easily measured. For example, the effectiveness of social learning therapy can be verified by noting the extent to which a client lists a greater number of alternative courses of action as the therapy progresses. The ease with which such generalized expectancies as locus of control and interpersonal trust can be measured has also contributed to the tremendous amount of research that has been done to verify social learning theory. Thus, the clarity with which the basic concepts are stated has contributed to the large amount of research done on social learning theory.

Characteristic Limitations

Here are some limitations of Rotter's social learning theory:

- *On being too cognitive: Ignoring the objective situation.* Social learning theory has been criticized for placing too much emphasis on the cognitive side of the individual. For example, critics from the more traditional learning viewpoint have expressed displeasure with the emphasis social learning theory has put on subjective perceptions by the individual. For example, social learning theory tends to rely on such subjective concepts as reinforcement value and specific and generalized expectancies at the expense of attention to objective environmental factors (e.g., the

situational conditions under reinforcement and punishment are delivered). Thus, social learning theory has been criticized by traditional learning theorists as being too subjective.

- *More on being too cognitive: A theory with no feeling.* From the more humanistic viewpoint, social learning theory has been criticized as placing too much emphasis on the cognitive side of human nature at the expense of the emotional side. For example, such basic emotions as anxiety are not found anywhere in the language of social learning theory. In its defense, social learning theory uses such terms as high reinforcement value and low freedom of movement to describe situations in which an individual would experience what might be considered feelings of anxiety. Thus, while social learning theory has been criticized as lacking a concern for emotions, it actually chooses to consider emotional expressions in more objectively stated terms.

In the next section, we consider the perspective of Albert Bandura, another contemporary social-cognitive personality theorist who shares Julian Rotter's emphasis on cognitive factors and systematic validation research.

Bandura's Social-Cognitive Theory: Outlining the Reciprocal Nature of Personality

When describing the basic nature of his social-cognitive theory, Albert Bandura notes that "people are neither driven by inner forces nor automatically shaped and controlled by external stimuli. Rather, human functioning is explained in terms of a model of triadic reciprocality in which behavior, cognitive and other personal factors, and the environment all operate as interacting determinants of each other" (Bandura, 1986, p. 18). Bandura believes that to understand an individual, you have to consider the synergism of how what people do affects what they believe and what they believe affects what they do, and how what people both think and do is interrelated with the situation in which they find themselves (e.g., their present physical location or the subculture or society in which they live). Such comprehensiveness characterizes Bandura's approach to his theorizing, research, and applications of his social-cognitive theory. For a glimpse into the life of one of the world's best known and respected psychologists, read "A Closer Look."

A Closer Look

The Life of Albert Bandura

Albert Bandura was born on December 4, 1925, and grew up in the beautiful but cold and rugged region of northern Alberta, Canada. Like many other children growing up in a small village, he attended the same school from elementary school through high school.

Albert Bandura is one of personality psychology's most innovative and influential thinkers. His work has made significant contributions to our understanding of the process of observational learning, the impact of media violence on the behavior of children, and psychotherapy.

But because of a shortage of teachers and resources, he and many of his classmates were almost required to teach themselves. The summer after his graduation, he worked on the Alaskan Highway, which was built during World War II to connect the United States with the Alaskan territory. During that time, the young Bandura came into contact with a variety of co-workers with an assortment of psychopathologies and rather "colorful" pasts, including parole violators, debtors, and ex-husbands trying to avoid paying alimony. His observations of and interactions with these people sparked his interest in clinical psychology.

After graduating from high school, Bandura entered the University of British Columbia. In addition to clinical psychology, he developed a strong interest in learning theory. In 1949, after only three years in college, he received a BA degree in psychology. When selecting a graduate school, he followed his interest in learning theory and entered the University of Iowa, which at that time was one of the premier midwestern centers for the study of learning, under the leadership of the influential learning theorist Kenneth W. Spence.

Although he was interested in clinical psychology, Bandura, under Spence's influence, became exposed to the rigor of experimental research and gained firsthand experience with Spence's theoretical conceptualization of learning, which was a dominant force in psychology at that time. Bandura received his MA degree in 1951 and his PhD in clinical psychology in 1952 from the University of Iowa.

In addition to being educated by a major figure in psychology, attending the University of Iowa changed Bandura's life in another important way – he met his future wife. Bored with his reading assignments, he decided one day to play some golf with a friend. On the course, Bandura and his friend were playing behind a female twosome. Eventually the male and female twosomes became a foursome. One of the women in the twosome was Virginia Varns, whom Bandura would soon marry.

After leaving the University of Iowa, Bandura accepted a one-year clinical internship at the Wichita Guidance Center. In 1953, at the end of his internship in Wichita, he accepted a position as an instructor at Stanford University in Palo Alto, California, where he has remained for all but one year of his academic career.

At Stanford, Bandura began what was to turn into an extremely distinguished career. His early research and publications involved clinical psychology, including the Rorschach test, the interactive processes underlying psychotherapy, and the role of family patterns in the development of aggression in children. Working with Richard Walters, his first graduate student at Stanford, Bandura developed a program of rigorous research investigating the role of the modeling process in the development of aggression in children. He expanded his research in modeling to include the role of observational learning in personality development (e.g., sex-role development), social issues (e.g., television violence), and psychotherapy. His most recent research focuses on the influence of the self as a determinant and regulator of behavior.

Although he began as only a lecturer, Bandura later served as the chairman of Stanford's exceptional psychology department, where he held the distinguished title of David Starr Jordan Professor of Social Science in Psychology. For his voluminous scholarly research contribution to psychology, he has received numerous awards, including the prestigious Guggenheim Fellowship and the Distinguished Contribution Award from the Division of Clinical Psychology (Division 12) of the American Psychological Association in 1972. In 1974, he was elected to the distinguished position of president of the American Psychological Association. In 1980, he received the extremely prestigious Award for Distinguished Scientific Contribution from the American Psychological Association, as well as the Distinguished Contribution Award from the Society for Research on Aggression. He also received the James McKeen Cattell Award for outstanding contributions to psychology in 1977, and he was elected to Fellow status of the American Academy of Arts and Sciences in 1980. In recognition of his sustained efforts and contributions, he received the American Psychological Association's Award for Lifetime Contributions to Psychology in 2004.

Bandura is still at Stanford University, where he continues to conduct a great deal of research, refine his theory, and teach both undergraduate and graduate courses. More information about his life can be found in a brief biography appearing in the *American Psychologist* (American Psychological Association, 1981) or in a book titled *Albert Bandura, the Man and His Ideas – a Dialogue*, by Richard I. Evans (1989).

Basic Assumptions of Bandura's Social-Cognitive Theory: Linking Cognitive Processes and Social Factors

In his social-cognitive theory, Bandura has developed a perspective on personality that combines the contemporary emphasis on cognitive processes with the study of the individual in the context of social factors (e.g., certain situational cues, specific social norms, and broader societal and economical conditions). This helps us understand how these elements work together to influence an individual's decision to engage in a particular course of action in order to induce change in the person's environment, either immediate (e.g., get a noisy person in a theater to be quite) or extended (e.g., participate in an anti-war demonstration to foster greater world peace; Bandura, 1986, 1999b, 2001, 2006). Foundational assumptions of this eclectic approach are the self system and triadic reciprocal causation.

The Self System: Subjective Filters of Objective Stimuli

Like other social-cognitive theorists, Bandura does not believe that the individual simply reacts to the objective stimuli in the environment as a robot might. Instead, Bandura suggests that the individual processes information about the stimuli in the environment through a self system (Bandura, 1978, 1986). The **self system** is a set of cognitive functions within the individual that help in the perception and evaluation of the environment and regulation of behavior. For example, when you see a sign that says the speed limit is 65 mph, your speed is determined by several cognitive processes operating within your self system, including the extent to which you perceive others around you as speeding, your evaluation of the likelihood of getting caught speeding today, and how much of a hurry you are in to get to your destination (e.g., level of motivation). Thus, as in traditional learning theory, Bandura recognizes the influence of environmental stimuli in determining behavior (e.g., punishment in the form of a ticket for speeding), but conceptualizes this influence as being filtered through a series of cognitive processes (e.g., the perceived likelihood of being caught speeding). In this manner, he acknowledges the significant contribution made by both learning and cognitive theories.

Triadic Reciprocal Causation: Reacting to the Reaction of Others Reacting to Your Reactions

In addition to the cognitive processes operating on environmental stimuli, Bandura assumes that the environment itself operates on the self system. **Triadic reciprocal causation** (Bandura 1999a, 1999b), previously referred to as *reciprocal determinism* (Bandura, 1978, 1986), is the term he uses to describe the back-and-forth influence between the environment and the self system on the regulation of behavior (Bandura, 1978, 1986). For example, if you are generally a speeder and go 65 mph in a 55-mph zone, but then enter a 65-mph zone, you are probably going to increase your speed to around 70 or 75 mph. In this case, the new speed limit sign serves as an external stimulus that influences your driving behavior. In response to the increased number of speeders on this stretch of road, the highway patrol may increase their surveillance of it. In this case, the behavior of the highway patrol is influenced by the behavior of the speeders. With the belief that you are more likely to get caught, based on your perception of more patrol officers in the area, you then reduce your speed. Once again, as the number of speeders is reduced, the highway patrol will shift its emphasis to another stretch of road. As this example illustrates, the behavior of both the highway patrol and speeders is influenced reciprocally by their separate but interrelated sets of perceptions and beliefs based on environmental cues.

Thus, while other cognitive theorists discussed the systematic interrelationship between cognitive and environmental factors in the behavior of the person, Bandura introduced the idea of combining the separate systems (e.g., the speeders and the highway patrol) to demonstrate more realistically the reciprocal manner in which behavior in the "real world" is determined. To help clarify the notion of reciprocal determinism, Figure 10.2 is a graphic illustration of the speeder–highway patrol example.

With the assumptions of the self system and reciprocal determinism, Bandura has been able to acknowledge the influence of both external stimuli and cognitive process. By incorporating these two assumptions, he has brought together the learning and cognitive viewpoints in a manner that realistically explains the operation of behavior. The next section describes some major concepts and processes of his social cognitive theory.

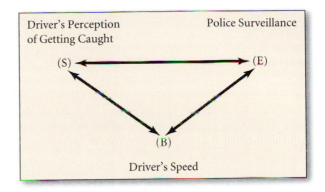

Figure 10.2   According to triadic reciprocal causation, behavior (B) is a result of the interrelatedness of the individual's self system (S) and the nature of the cues found in the environment (E).

Basic Concepts and Processes of Bandura's Social-Cognitive Theory: Imitation, Expectations, and Regulation

Next we will discuss the basic concepts and processes involved in Bandura's viewpoint.

Observational Learning: Learning by Looking

Although his training in learning theory was very traditional, Bandura's position on observational learning clearly places him outside the category of a traditional learning theorist. He has argued that the learning of most of the more significant and complex aspects of behavior is not based solely on principles of operant and classical conditioning, but on observational learning (Bandura, 1977b, 1986, 1997, 1999a, 1999b).

For Bandura, **observational learning** involves acquiring complex behaviors by watching, hearing about, or reading about the behavior of others. His reasoning is that much of the behavior that plays a significant role in our everyday living is too complex and costly to be learned on the basis of the trial-and-error method involved in the more traditional methods of learning. For example, falling in love is a behavior that cannot be explained by basic principles of learning. Instead, we rely on what we see in the movies, read in books, or hear from our family and friends to help us know when we are in love and how then to behave. In a more global sense, it is difficult to explain how we transmit such complex phenomena as language, social norms, and cultural traditions without acknowledging the contribution that observing others plays in the acquisition of these important aspects of all of our lives. In a more pragmatic sense, observational learning is also the logic behind many of the self-help videos, books, and seminars that seem to be so popular today.

The Distinction between Learning and Performance: Knowing vs. Doing   One point related to observational learning that separates Bandura from the traditional learning theorists is the distinction he makes between learning and performance. Proponents of the more traditional learning viewpoints believe that a behavior has to be performed before it can be confirmed that it has been learned. In sharp contrast, from the social-cognitive viewpoint, a behavior does not necessarily need to be performed in order to imply that it is learned. In many cases, simply observing someone doing something is enough to learn how to do it.

For example, although most 10-year-old children have not done so, most of them probably know what it would take to start the family car, put it in gear, and back it out of the driveway. The same is probably true for adults regarding what we may have learned from the movies about firing a gun, stopping a bullet wound from bleeding, indirectly trying to bribe a police officer, or participating in unconventional sexual practices. The point is that you do not have to perform a behavior to demonstrate that you have learned it. In fact, it is probably better that we do not attempt many of the behaviors (e.g., bribing a police officer) that we actually know how to perform.

The Role of Vicarious Reinforcement: Direct vs. Vicarious Payoffs   Another point of deviation of the social-cognitive theory from traditional learning viewpoints is the role played by reinforcement (Bandura, 1986, 1999a, 1999b). From the traditional learning viewpoint, behavior is strengthened or weakened to the extent that a certain behavior is followed by a reinforcer. Bandura disagrees; he assumes that simply observing someone being rewarded or punished for a particular behavior is enough to increase the likelihood of the observer performing a certain behavior.

For example, most of us do not have to be put in jail to know that shooting someone will lead to punishment. We have learned to expect punishment from

reading about and seeing on the news what happens to those who have done so. On the other hand, if we know of people who get away with cheating on their income tax, we are more likely to cheat as well. The point is that increasing or decreasing the likelihood of a behavior being performed can be influenced not only by actually experiencing the consequences but also by developing certain expectancies about the consequences solely from watching what happens to others. Thus, it is not really necessary to have had a payoff in order to engage in a behavior; just seeing that it might pay off seems to be enough.

The Processes of Observational Learning: The Essentials of Learning by Looking   In addition to suggesting that observational learning does take place, Bandura (1969, 1977b, 1986, 1999a, 1999b) has also specified four basic processes, divided into four stages, that are involved if such learning is to occur: attentional processes, retention processes, motor reproduction processes, and motivational processes.

- *Stage one: Can I have your attention, please?* Attentional processes influence observational learning by determining to what the individual is going to attend. For observational learning to occur, the individual must not only be aware of what the model is doing but also be able to determine what aspects of the behavior are the most relevant. For example, when watching a professional tennis match in an attempt to improve your serve you must concentrate on how high the professionals toss the ball and the arch in their backs, not the color of their tennis outfits. Part of what is involved in discussing attentional processes is considering what factors influence them. Factors such as the age, sex, attractiveness, status, and competence of the model, as well as the motivational state of the observer, all influence the degree of attentional processes. It is for this reason that advertisers hire celebrities to endorse their products; these are the types of people to whom we are most likely to attend.

- *Stage two: Run that by me again, please.* Retention processes influence observational learning by determining the extent to which the individual remembers the model to which he or she was attending. Retention processes are important because in many cases, a person might have only a limited amount of contact with the model and must rely on a memory of what was observed. Bandura asserts that retention processes involve both visual and verbal dimensions. The visual dimension involves being able to generate and maintain a mental image of what was done by the model. The verbal dimension involves being able to describe what was done in words. For example, while you have a mental picture of what the tennis pro looked like while serving, you probably can describe the action by saying something like, "She tossed the ball up slowly about two feet, arched her back about twenty degrees, and bent her elbow slightly as she brought her arm directly over her head when making the serve." The verbal description provides a more concrete set of cues that can be recalled at a later date than the mental image, which tends to fade rather rapidly.

- *Stage three: Try doing that again, please.* Motor reproduction processes involve transforming the information about the model that has been attended to and visually and verbally coded into overt behavior. For example, as a beginning tennis player, you might go to the park with a bucket of tennis balls and begin practicing your serve while telling yourself to "toss the ball slowly about two feet in the air." Transforming the visual and verbal information into actual behavior may not be as simple as it sounds, with the first few serves possibly going right into the net. But with some patience and practice, the motor reproductions soon get smoother and smoother. Without the previously coded information obtained through observation, however, learning to serve would involve a lot of guesswork and trial-and-error behavior.

- *Stage four: What will it take for you to do this?* Motivational processes involve providing the desire to perform those behaviors that have been acquired through the process of observational learning. It is at this point that the distinction between learning and performance comes into play. As noted earlier, the types of factors that influence the performance of learned behaviors include observing the consequences for the model (e.g., did the tennis pro make the serve?), the expectancies of the observer (e.g., will practice improve your serve?), and the motivational level of the observer (e.g., you'll receive a lot of recognition from your peers). While the motiva-

tional processes have been discussed as the last stage in observational learning, you should realize that they play a significant role during each of the stages. For example, if you do not really care too much about improving your serve, you may in fact spend more time looking at the color of the tennis players' outfits than their serving techniques.

You have examined some factors and processes that are involved in observational learning. As you can see, combining the general notion of observational learning – along with its four basic processes – with those basic principles of the more traditional learning viewpoints does a good job of explaining some of the more complex and significant aspects of social behavior. For some rather significant examples of observational learning, as well as the consequences of the process, read "A Closer Look."

A Closer Look

The Observational Learning of Sex and Violence: What You See Is What You Do – Sometimes

One of the more significant implications of Bandura's emphasis on observational learning is the possibility of learning various forms of antisocial behavior from models that appear on television or in motion pictures. A serious concern has been the impact of media sex and violence on viewer behavior.

Watching Violence in the Media: Modeling Aggressive Behavior

One of the earliest research attempts to investigate the issue of media violence on children's behavior was a series of classic studies known as the "Bobo doll studies," because they used a 5-foot-tall, inflatable plastic clown doll called Bobo. In these studies (Bandura & Walters, 1963), nursery school children were exposed to aggressive or nonaggressive models and then observed for their own level of aggressiveness during free-play periods.

Figure 10.3 The top row illustrates the aggressive behavior of the adult model against the Bobo doll. The second and third rows illustrate the children modeling the aggressive behavior.

In the aggressive model condition, the children were exposed to an adult who acted very aggressively while playing with the Bobo doll. The aggressive adult model hit the doll with a toy wooden hammer, kicked it, sat on it, and punched it while saying such things as "Kick him" or "Sock him in the nose" (see Figure 10.3). Children in the control model condition were exposed to an adult model who played quietly and passively with other toys in the room. Later, the children were placed in the room containing the Bobo doll and other toys and observed through a one-way mirror for 20 minutes in an attempt to note how similar their behavior would be to that of the model they had seen. As predicted from the social-cognitive theory, those children who had observed the aggressive model behaved more aggressively than those who had observed the quiet, passive model. In fact, the aggressive behavior of the children resembled that of the aggressive model in many cases (see Figure 10.3).

Results similar to those of the "Bobo studies" have been found in other studies (Berkowitz, 1993; Liebert & Schwartzberg, 1977; Liebert, Sprafkin, & Davidson,

1989; Wood, Wong, & Chachere, 1991). For example, children exposed to excerpts from an actual television show containing a high degree of violence (*The Untouchables*) demonstrated a greater willingness to inflict what they believed was pain upon another child than did children who were exposed to excerpts from an arousing but nonviolent track race (Liebert & Baron, 1972).

Similar results have also been obtained with aggressive behaviors in more natural settings (Eron, 1987; Parke, Berkowitz, Leyes, West, & Sebastian, 1977) and across a variety of different cultures (Botha, 1990). For example, groups of institutionalized delinquent boys were exposed to aggressive commercials every night for a week, while others in the institution were exposed to neutral commercials. The results of this study indicated that the boys exposed to the aggressive commercials engaged in more physical and verbal aggression, even in the presence of institutional staff members, than did those exposed to the neutral commercials (Leyens, Camino, Parke, & Berkowitz, 1975). In another study (Josephson, 1987), young boys exposed to a modified version of a highly violent television show (e.g., a SWAT team killing a group of snipers) displayed more aggressive behavior during a game of floor hockey than did boys exposed to an exciting but nonviolent television program (e.g., a motorcross bike race featuring many exciting stunts). In a more dramatic fashion, the techniques used to kill individuals in violent fictional motion pictures have been observed to be used in murders in real life (C. A. Anderson, 1997).

Finally, you should be aware that, as well as observing consistent effects from brief exposures to media violence during laboratory studies (Bushman & Huesmann, 2001), research monitoring the viewing habits of individuals over many years suggests that the more violent television programs the individuals watched as children, the higher their level of aggression was found to be as teenagers and adults, including being more likely to be arrested for violent crimes (C. A. Anderson & Bushman, 2002; Huesmann & Eron, 1984, 1986; Huesmann, Moise-Titus, Podolski, & Eron, 2003). In addition, such exposure effects on aggressive behavior are not limited to viewing violent television or films but extend to the viewing of violence in news programs and the violent lyrics in popular songs (C. A. Anderson, Carnagey, & Eubanks, 2003) and violent video games (C. A. Anderson, 2004; C. A. Anderson et al., 2004; Schutte, Malouff, Post-Gorden, & Rodasts, 1988).

Consistent with Bandura's social-cognitive theory, recent theoretical developments designed to help explain how exposure to media violence leads to aggressive behavior suggest that a combination of cognitive and situational factors plays a role (C. A. Anderson et al., 2004; C. A. Anderson & Bushman, 2001; Bushman & Anderson, 2002). Specifically, continued exposure to media violence creates a knowledge base related to aggression, such as observing how to behave aggressively (e.g., seeing fighters hitting each others with chairs and bottles), developing certain expectations about the outcomes of such aggressive behavior (e.g., seeing violent criminals driving expensive cars and wearing extravagant jewelry – violence pays!), and fostering normative beliefs about aggressive behavior (e.g., it's acceptable to use violence to get what you want). With such a knowledge base, individuals are more inclined to engage in aggressive behavior when these aggressive cognitions are activated by specific events. For example, a group of teenagers who are regular viewers of violent movies and video games may attack another kid in the park who has a set of designer tennis shoes, popular sports jersey, and handheld video game that the group want. They attack the kid because they have developed the belief that if the situation is right (e.g., three against one, with no other witnesses around), they can use a specific aggressive tactic they saw in a movie (e.g., distract the kid by pretending to be arguing with each other) to get the desired items (e.g., the expectation that aggression will lead to a favorable outcome).

Watching Sex in the Media: Modeling Sexual Behavior

Some evidence also indicates that certain aspects of sexual behavior may be modeled from the media (Shaffer, 1999). For example, in one study (Bryant, 1985), adolescents and adults were interviewed to determine what their reactions were the first time they viewed X-rated films and magazines. The results indicated that almost 70 percent of the males and 40 percent of the females surveyed expressed a desire to imitate the sexual activity portrayed in the films. Of more importance was the finding that about 30 percent of the males and 20 percent of the females actually did imitate the activity portrayed in the film the first time they were exposed to it. But this disinhibition effect seems to be rather short-lived, lasting only about 24 hours. For example, in one study (Mann, Berkowitz, Sidman, Starr, & West, 1974), 66 married couples were shown erotic or nonerotic films once a week for a month. One group of couples were exposed to the erotic movies for the first two weeks of the month, then the nonerotic films for the second two weeks; another group was exposed to the nonerotic films for the first two weeks. A third group viewed only nonerotic films for the entire month. During the month, all of the couples were asked to monitor their rate of sexual intercourse. The results of this study indicated that during the initial exposure to the erotic films, there was a tendency for the couples to increase the likelihood of sexual intercourse on the movie nights. Thus, there was little carry-over effect of the erotic films to the next day, suggesting that the modeling behavior may have been rather weak. These results are consistent with other research indicating that both males and females reported increases in their frequency of masturbation only within a 24-hour period of watching sexually explicit slides and movies (Schmidt & Sigusch, 1970). Thus, while the initial effect of viewing erotic material may trigger some modeling, in the long run, the novelty seems to wane and people settle into a previously established pattern of sexual behavior.

Watching Sex and Violence in the Media: Modeling Violence against Women

Another area of research on modeling that combines the themes of sex and aggression concerns itself with the role of violence against women in pornography (Baron & Richardson, 1994; Geen, 1998; McAnulty & Burnette, 2001). A common theme in the pornographic literature involves a man physically overpowering a woman, forcing her to have sex that she initially finds unpleasant but then comes to enjoy (Monk-Turner & Purcell, 1999). There is consistent evidence that exposing males to such pornographic literature increases the aggression they exhibit toward women (Donnerstein, 1980; Malamuth & Briere, 1986). More important, males who maintain the belief that the females enjoy the violent sex that is portrayed in pornography are much more likely to admit to the possibility of committing a rape if no one would know and they could get away with it without punishment (Malamuth, 1984). This notion is supported by the finding that when a group of sex offenders was surveyed, 33 percent of the rapists reported looking at pornographic literature as part of their preparation for committing the crime (Marshall, 1985). Thus, there is some evidence that in a small percentage of males, modeling may play a role in developing and helping to maintain certain attitudes linking sex and violence against women that may contribute to rape.

More generally, another quite significant finding is that after prolonged exposure to pornography involving violence against women, both males and females developed more calloused attitudes and less emotional sensitivity toward the victims of such activities (Intons-Peterson & Roskos-Ewoldsen, 1989; Linz, Donnerstein, & Penrod, 1984, 1988; Zillmann & Bryant, 1984). They felt less sympathy toward the rape victim, perceived violent crimes against women as being less serious, and expressed more agreement with rape myths (e.g., women really want this type of treatment). Fortunately, there is also research to suggest that such negative attitudes can be mitigated through dispelling these beliefs prior to exposure to such callous depictions of women (Linz, Fuson, & Donnerstein, 1990).

As you can see, the role of modeling as a process in acquiring behavior and attitudes has some very important social implications. In a related topic, other research focuses on the developmental and interpersonal effects of exposure to chronic real-life community violence on young children (Osofsky, 1995).

Thus, observational learning explains the process by which people acquire behavior by imitating what we see others doing. But the performance of this behavior is influenced by various other factors, including beliefs about our ability to execute it and the expected outcome it will produce.

Self-Efficacy: What Do You Think You Can Do?

Observational learning provides a means by which an individual has the opportunity to acquire a particular skill or behavior pattern. But, as noted earlier, simply knowing how to do something is not enough to guarantee that you will perform the behavior. To explain more completely the relationship between what we know and what we do, Bandura utilizes the concept of self-efficacy (Bandura, 1977a, 1977b, 1982, 1986, 1989a, 1991b, 1997, 1999a, 1999b; Rokke & Rehm, 2001).

Self-efficacy refers to a person's perceived belief that he or she can execute a specific behavior in an attempt to cope with a particular situation. For example, your decision to go out on the dance floor is a function of the belief that you have in your ability to execute the dance steps and movements successfully enough so that you do not embarrass yourself or your partner. Judgments of self-efficacy determine not only whether you decide on a course of action but also how long you will persist and the extent to which you will prepare for it (Bandura, 1989b, 1997; Multon, Brown, & Lent, 1991; Rokke & Rehm, 2001). For example, if you perceive yourself to be a good dancer, you will probably stay out on the dance floor longer than someone who might not consider himself to be a good dancer.

A concept related to self-efficacy is that of outcome expectation (Bandura, 1986). **Outcome expectations** are the consequences an individual believes will follow the performance of a particular act. For example, a man might believe that if he dances well, he will receive a lot of attention and recognition from his peers. Bandura (1986) summarizes the relationship between self-efficacy and outcome expectations in the following manner: "In social, intellectual, and physical pursuits, those who judge themselves highly efficacious will expect favorable outcomes, self-doubters will expect mediocre performances of themselves and negative outcomes" (p. 392). Thus, if you view yourself as being a good dancer, and believe that dancing well will bring you social recognition, you are much more likely to engage in such behavior than those who do not perceive themselves as being good dancers or believe that dancing will not produce favorable consequences. It is for this reason that a defining characteristic of individuals who are entrepreneurs – people who start new businesses – is a high level of self-efficacy (Markman, Balkin, & Baron, 2005). It stands to reasons that entrepreneurs would not risk the personal and financial costs of starting a new business if they did not believe they had the skills to be successful.

The Influence of Self-Efficacy: Affecting Thoughts, Feelings, and Behavior   Self-efficacy influences not only people's behavior (Stajkovic & Luthans, 1998) but also their thoughts and emotions (Brutus & Ryan, 1998). For example, if you believe that being a good dancer is important because of the attention and popularity it will bring you, and if you also believe you are not a good dancer and will never be one no matter how hard you try, you are likely to feel depressed. Such a combination of beliefs and emotions may cause you to not even try to improve your dancing ability. As you might expect, this pattern of self-efficacy is often characteristic of people who experience problems of personality adjustment and psychopathology (Bandura, 1986, 1997; Rokke & Rehm, 2001). For example, individuals in treatment programs for substance abuse who doubt their ability (i.e., low self-efficacy) to succeed in their efforts to overcome their addiction generally do not do well (Ilgen, McKellaar, & Tiet, 2005). In a similar manner, individuals who are trying to quit smoking but do not have much confidence in their ability to do so tend to relapse within weeks of quitting (Gwaltney, Shiffman, Balabanis, & Paty, 2005).

Factors Influencing Self-Efficacy: What You Hear, See, Do, and Feel Makes a Difference   Because of the importance of self-efficacy, it is important to know some of the factors that might influence it (Bandura, 1977a, 1986, 1997, 1999a, 1999b).

- The *verbal persuasion* of others concerning your ability to perform the particular course of action. An example of this might be your friends saying, "Go ahead and go out there. You can dance just as well as all of those other people."
- *Vicarious experience*, or simply watching someone else perform the action successfully. Seeing that others who are enjoying themselves dancing are no better at it than you are may be just what is needed to get you out of your chair and onto the dance floor.
- *Performance accomplishments*, or simply having performed the behavior successfully in the past – probably the most powerful factor. You are more likely to get up and dance if you had a good time and received positive feedback from your friends the last two times you were out on the dance floor.
- *Emotional arousal*, or the degree of anxiety you feel in a particular situation that tells you how well you are performing a specific behavior. For example, if you feel very self-conscious and nervous while on the dance floor, you are probably going to assume that it is due to people evaluating you negatively because you are not dancing very well. As a result, you are probably less likely to dance again in the near future.

Although each of these factors is discussed individually, you should realize that in most cases, they operate together to help determine self-efficacy. For example, while your friends may tell you that you dance well enough, and you see that others dance no better than you, your feelings of self-consciousness may be too powerful and keep you sitting in your chair just tapping your feet. Thus, your level of self-efficacy is based on a combination of information obtained from external (e.g., what we see or others tell us) and internal sources (e.g., our personal thoughts, emotions, and direct experience).

As part of the self-system, Bandura conceptualizes self-efficacy as a subjective mediating process of behavior that is determined by both personal (e.g., beliefs) and external factors (e.g., feedback from others). The concept of self-efficacy also reflects his emphasis on considering both person and environment when attempting to explain and understand the dynamics of personality.

Self-Regulation: Doing What You Want to Do

In the more traditional learning perspective, behavior is governed by its consequences. This view suggests that our behavior is regulated by external rewards and punishments, but it ignores the role played by the individual in regulating his or her own behavior. In a more realistic view of the individual, Bandura also proposes the notion of self-regulation of behavior (Bandura, 1977b, 1978, 1986, 1989b, 1991b, 1997, 1999a, 1999b). **Self-regulation** involves the process by which the individual establishes and acts upon a set of internally derived standards and expectations. Included in the process of self-regulation are ethical and moral beliefs, standards of excellence, judgments of competency in comparison to the behavior of others, and past performance. For example, whether you decide to stop and try to help an injured person at the scene of an accident depends on the extent to which you feel doing so is the "right" thing to do, you believe that you can make a difference if you do intervene, you assume there are others present who are more qualified to help (e.g., medical personnel) than you, or you have been helpful in other situations.

Self-Reward and Self-Punishment: The Consequences of Self-Regulation

At the base of the process of self-regulation are self-reward and self-punishment. When you meet the standards you have set for yourself, you give yourself a pat on the back or feel an increase in your sense of self-worth. As a result, you may try even harder in the future. This often occurs regardless of external consequences. For example, you would assist the accident victim even though the person could not give you any monetary reward, or even though no news reporters were around to put your picture in the paper. As another example, a runner in a marathon may get a sense of reward just for finishing the race. On the other hand, when you fail to meet your own standards, you may blame yourself for not pushing hard enough and feel a personal sense of failure. For example, when you do not get the grade you thought you would, you vow to study even harder for the next test. The point is that it is overly simplistic to assume that only external rewards regulate behavior. Instead, Bandura (1991a, 1991b, 1999a, 1999b) proposes that self-regulation is selectively activated on the basis of internal standards of evaluation (e.g., self-efficacy or moral convictions) and environmental conditions (e.g., the presence of other bystanders). And, as you might expect, individuals with a high sense of self-regulation – those who can operate within their own goals and personal standards – are much more likely to experience success in a variety of important areas of life, including work, school,

and interpersonal relationships, to name just a few (Baumeister, Heatherton, & Tice, 1994; Baumeister, Schmeichel, & Vohs, 2007; Tangney, Baumeister, & Boone, 2004)

The Role of Learning: From Where Do these Standards for Self-Regulation Come?

Like so many other aspects of our behavior, personal standards of self-regulation are learned through the traditional processes of classical and operant conditioning and observational learning (Bandura, 1977b, 1986). For example, when you fail to meet the expectations of your boss, she may tell you to work harder. As a result, for the next couple of weekends, you regulate your behavior to spend more time working on your assigned report instead of playing tennis. If such behavior does lead to reward, you then come to associate hard work with rewards. You might also observe others being praised by the boss for all the extra time they put in on their reports over the weekend.

Similar processes of learning occur through our interactions with other significant people in our lives, such as parents, siblings, friends, and teachers. Thus, the standards we acquire from others, to some extent, form the basis of our self-regulatory systems. But understand that it is the individual, and the individual alone, who is responsible for activating the self-regulation system. Thus, regardless of the origin of self-regulating systems, their importance in determining behavior cannot be ignored.

Personality Maladjustment: Maladaptive Modeling, Unrealistic Self-Evaluations, and Inefficacy

According to social cognitive theory, three contributing factors to personality maladjustment are maladaptive modeling, dysfunctional self-evaluations, and perceived inefficacy.

Maladaptive Modeling: Looking but Not Learning Anything

As with other more traditional learning theories, social-cognitive theory assumes that personality maladjustment is a result of faulty learning. But in a departure from more traditional learning theories, Bandura (1968) also believes that maladaptive behavior can be learned by exposure to models displaying maladaptive behavior. For example, consider teenagers who see that their parents simply complain about the difficulties they are facing in life instead of taking some kind of action to improve the situation. Such

Summing It Up *Basic Concepts of Bandura's Social-Cognitive Theory*

Observational learning is the process by which we learn complex behavior patterns from watching others, instead of on a trial-and-error basis. Characteristic features of observational learning include the following:

- *The distinction between learning and performance.* In the context of observational learning, we do not necessarily have to perform a behavior as proof that we have learned it.
- *The role of vicarious reinforcement.* The process of observing someone being reinforced is enough to influence the likelihood of a particular behavior being performed; direct reinforcement and punishment are not the only determinants of learning.
- *The process of observational learning.* Observational learning is facilitated when the individual: (1) is paying attention to the model, (2) employs visual (e.g., mental images) and verbal (e.g., descriptions) retention strategies, (3) practices the behavior observed, and (4) is motivated to perform the behavior.

Self-efficacy involves the expectations an individual has about his or her ability to perform those behaviors necessary to cope effectively with specific situations, and involves the following features and processes:

- *The influence of self-efficacy.* Self-efficacy can affect your thoughts (e.g., what will you do?), feelings (e.g., emotions based on your expectations and abilities), and behavior (e.g., actions you perform).
- *Factors influencing self-efficacy.* The beliefs you have about what you can do are determined by what others tell you, what others are doing, and past experience with actually performing a specific or related behavior.

Self-regulation is the set of internal standards (e.g., moral, social, and personal) you employ to help guide the nature and extent of your behavior and to form the basis for self-rewards and self-punishment.

Personality maladjustment can be determined, to some extent, by observing others demonstrating faulty or inappropriate behaviors during *maladaptive modeling, dysfunctional self-evaluations* involving unrealistic expectations, and *perceived inefficacy* characterized by self-doubt concerning your abilities.

---

teenagers will probably model this passive coping strategy when confronted with major problems in their own lives as well.

Dysfunctional Self-Evaluations: Unrealistic Expectations   A category of cognitive processes that can contribute to personality maladjustment is dysfunctional self-evaluations (Bandura, 1977b). **Dysfunctional self-evaluations** involve the failure to establish an effective standard for self-rewards and self-punishments. An example of dysfunctional self-evaluation might be a female executive who sets such high standards for herself that she is never able to experience the satisfaction of doing work that is good enough. Self-evaluation that lacks self-reward but is excessive in self-punishment is probably going to contribute to feelings of depression.

Perceived Inefficacy: Having Self-Doubts   Feelings of anxiety and depression can also be triggered by perceived inefficacy (Bandura, 1977b; Bandura, Pastorelli, Barbaranelli, & Caprara, 1999). **Perceived inefficacy**

involves the feeling that you cannot deal effectively with important events (Bandura, 1982). For example, an individual who perceives himself as not having anything interesting to say may feel helpless at parties and other social gatherings and may spend much of his time alone and depressed.

This concludes our discussion of the basic concepts of Bandura's social-cognitive theory. A summary of these concepts is presented in "Summing It Up: Basic Concepts of Bandura's Social-Cognitive Theory" above. We will now turn our attention to some of its applications.

Applications of Bandura's Social-Cognitive Theory: Using What Is Known

Although there are many applications of Bandura's social-cognitive theory and other related cognitive perspectives, the common thread in the applications featured in this section is the emphasis on the modification of behavior and cognitions through modeling and changes in self-efficacy. The three areas used to illustrate the diversity of these applications are therapeutic modeling, cognitive therapy, and self-defense training.

Social-Cognitive Therapeutic Intervention: Promoting Self-Efficacy and Behavior Change through Modeling

Bandura believes that psychotherapy must go beyond simply talking to clients about their problem. He believes that the therapeutic process should be a learning experience resulting in a change in the client's behavior. In his approach to therapeutic intervention, Bandura (1961, 1986, 1995, 1997, 2004; Plante, 2005; Rokke & Rehm, 2001) promotes combining fundamental principles of learning with his own specific concerns for promoting self-efficacy as a critical element in changing behavior. A critical component in his approach to therapeutic intervention is the use of modeling to help clients acquire new skills and a sense of increased confidence (Bandura, 1977a, 1986, 1997, 2004; Wilson, 2000).

Modeling Techniques of Therapeutic Intervention: Facilitating the Acquisition of Competencies and Confidence   In its most basic form, the therapeutic use of modeling involves the client observing various models, either live or via videotape, participating in some desired behavior that results in favorable consequences (Comer, 2007; Nietzel, Bernstein, & Milich, 1994; Trull & Phares, 2001). For example, an individual with low self-esteem might watch a film or observe a live model receiving a refund after making a request to the sales clerk in a very assertive manner.

In **mastery modeling**, the client is assisted by the therapist or live model in performing the desired behavior (Bandura, 1986, 1988, 1997). Although similar to role playing, mastery modeling involves breaking down the desired behavior into subskills and progressively more difficult behaviors. Guiding the client step by step through the problematic behavior increases the client's likelihood of experiencing continuous progress and success. For example, working with an excessively shy client, the therapist might "walk through" the steps of how to approach a stranger at a social gathering in order to initiate and maintain a conversation. In this case, the therapist might first work with the client on making eye contact and smiling when being introduced to

someone new at a party. Next, the therapist might show the client how to ask questions in order to keep a conversation going. Finally, the therapist might show the client how to end conversations but leave open the opportunity for future interactions (e.g., asking for a date). Thus, by systematically arranging what needs to be learned and how to learn it most effectively, the therapist is much more likely to help the client experience success and acquire a sense of self-efficacy.

For therapy to be successful, Bandura believes that therapists have to create in clients a sense of confidence that they can succeed. This is facilitated by demonstrating what people need to do through modeling techniques and offering them the opportunity to practice these skills (R. I. Evans, 1989). An interesting application of modeling technique presents videotaped models of parents using various behavior modification techniques, in order to help parents watching these videos use these same techniques more effectively with their own children. Increasing the competencies and confidence of parents to use these techniques resulted in improved performances by the children at home and at school (Webster-Stratton, 1992). But as you will find in reading "Applications in Personality Psychology" on p. 437, one of the most frequent and successful therapeutic applications of social-cognitive theory has been in the treatment of phobias (Bandura, 1986, 1997; Kazdin, 2001; Nevid, Rathus, & Greene, 2000; Pull, 2005; Wolfe, 2005).

Cognitive-Behavioral Therapy: Learning to Think and Behave Better

The emphasis given to the role of cognitive factors in the therapeutic process led to the development of what are called cognitive-behavioral therapies (Beck & Weishaar, 2008; Dobson & Dozois, 2001; P. Grant, Young, & DeRubeis, 2005; Hollon & Beck, 2004; Leahy, 2006). **Cognitive-behavioral therapies** have as their basis the development of techniques designed to modify cognitions and the effects they have on behavior. Major approaches to cognitive therapy include Ellis's rational-emotive therapy (Dryden & Ellis, 2001; Ellis, 1962, 1980, 1987, 2008) and Beck's cognitive therapy (Beck, 1976; Beck & Weishaar, 2008; DeRubeis, Tang, & Beck, 2001; Hollon & Beck, 2004).

A good example of this approach is the cognitive-behavioral therapies developed by Donald Meichenbaum (Meichenbaum, 1977, 1985; Rokke & Rehm, 2001). The major objective of Meichenbaum's approach to

Applications in Personality Psychology

Curing Phobias: Overcoming What Scares You

How can you overcome what scares you? A classic example of social-cognitive learning therapy involved the treatment of people suffering from snake phobias who answered a newspaper ad placed by Bandura and his colleagues (Bandura, Blanchard, & Ritter, 1969). These phobic people were divided into four groups. In the live model/participation group, the people watched a model handle the snake and were then guided through the actual handling of the snake by the therapist. In the symbolic modeling group, the people simply watched a film showing adults and children handling a snake. In the systematic desensitization group, the people were taught relaxation training while watching the film. Finally, a control group received no special training or treatment at all. The degree to which all of the people would approach and/or handle the snake was recorded before and after treatments were given. As can be seen in Figure 10.4, the treatment program involving the people observing a live model and then being guided through snake handling proved to be the most effective.

The effectiveness of modeling to reduce a fear of dogs (Bandura, Grusec, & Menlove, 1967), as well as a fear of medical and dental procedures (Melamed & Siegel, 1975; Melamed, Hawes, Heiby, & Glick, 1975), has also been documented. In addition to the treatment of phobias, including social phobia (Rodebaugh, Holaway, & Heimberg, 2004; Turner,

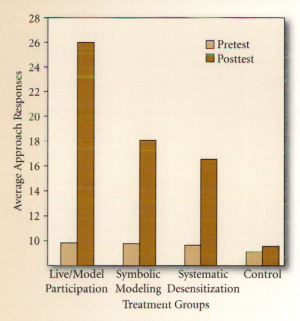

Figure 10.4 The average number of approach responses for clients receiving different treatments for a snake phobia
Source: Bandura et al. (1969).

Beidel, & Cooley-Quille, 1995), modeling has been used to treat various other clinical problems, including obsessive-compulsive disorder, antisocial behavior, social withdrawal, narcissistic personality disorder, and early infantile autism, to name just a few (Kim, 2005; Mellon & Grossman, 2005; Rosenthal & Steffek, 1991).

cognitive-behavior therapy is to help clients handle anticipated stressors by teaching them new coping responses (e.g., relaxation training) while making them aware of the way negative self-statements influence their behavior. For example, a woman who has recently experienced the end of a long-standing love affair might now express the negative self-statement that "No one else will ever love me." As a result, she may not try to establish another relationship. After making

the client aware of the effects of her negative self-statements, the cognitive-behavioral therapist then begins to replace them with more appropriate and realistic self-statements and teach the client more effective responses to coping with the stress of meeting new people. The therapist might instruct the client to engage in a relaxation exercise if she becomes anxious while attending a social gathering. The therapist might also help the client replace the negative self-statements with others, such as "Not everybody I meet is going to like me right away," or "If I don't meet someone I like here today, I'll try someplace else." Some of the many important applications of Meichenbaum's work have been in the area of behavioral medicine, such as helping individuals to be better able to manage their pain (Turk, Meichenbaum, & Genest, 1983) and comply with their medical treatments (Meichenbaum & Turk, 1987). Thus, the major goal of Meichenbaum's cognitive-behavioral therapy is very consistent with Bandura's emphasis on developing competencies and confidence during the therapeutic process.

Self-Defense Training: Enhancing Empowerment through Self-Efficacy

As was noted earlier, sexual assault against women is a serious social problem. This is particularly true on college campuses, where it has been reported that one in four college women surveyed reported being victims of rape or attempted rape, with 85 percent of rapes on campus being by acquaintances (/www. psu.edu/ouic/orientation100/T10/sexassult.html). In a rather unusual application of social-cognitive theory, Elizabeth Ozer and Bandura (1990) incorporated the principles of mastery modeling and self-efficacy into a self-defense program designed to help women learn to defend themselves successfully against unarmed sexual assailants. In this program, mastery modeling was used to teach women the necessary self-protective skills to escape the hold of or disable an assailant. The skills included eye strikes, biting, kicks, foot stomps, and elbow, knee, and palm strikes, as well as how to deliver these defensive behaviors to vital parts of the body such as the eyes, head, throat, knees, and groin. Since many sexual assaults involve throwing the woman to the ground, the women were also taught safe ways to fall and how to strike the assailant while being pinned on the ground.

Graduated Mastery: The Process for Ensuring Success   To ensure mastery of the skills and increase self-efficacy, the skills were taught to the women in a graduated manner through simulated assaults. The simulated assaults were carried out by a male assistant wearing a heavily padded headpiece and specifically designed protective body gear. At first, the women watched as the instructor delivered the blows in the simulated assault. Next, each woman was guided through the self-protection maneuvers by the instructor. Finally, each woman participated in a series of simulated assaults depicting various situations, such as a frontal assault, while lying down, being thrown to the ground, and being pinned down. To increase the reality of the assaults, as well as to help increase a sense of confidence and mastery, the simulated assaults were structured so that the assailant gradually increased the amount of the force and constraint of the assault as each woman began to acquire more skill in delivering the self-protective blows. While each woman in the program participated in the simulated assaults, the rest of the class remained active vicariously by watching the assaults and shouting out the most effective defensive blows for disabling the assailant.

In addition to the physical defense skills, mastery modeling was used to teach the women attitudinal and verbal techniques for halting potential assaultive encounters. For example, through modeling and simulated reenactments, the women were taught how to project a sense of confidence, speak assertively when dealing with unwelcome advances, issue stern verbal warnings if the unwelcome advance continued, and yell to frighten off an attacker. Cognitive restructuring was also included as part of this program; specifically, the women were taught how viewing themselves as defenseless could be a barrier to their self-protection and freedom of movement.

The Outcome of Mastery Modeling: Increased Self-Efficacy in Self-Protection   To assess the effectiveness of the self-defense mastery modeling program, Ozer and Bandura (1990) surveyed the women before their participation in the course, right after completing it, and again six months later. In comparison to their views before participating in the program, the women completing it expressed a greater sense of confidence in their ability to protect themselves, viewed themselves as less vulnerable to assault, and demonstrated greater freedom of movement by their willingness to attend more recreational, social, and cultural activities. Thus, the findings indicated that these women certainly benefited as a result of their participation in this program based on the principles of social-cognitive theory.

A summary of the principal ideas discussed in this section is presented in "Summing It Up: Applications of Bandura's Social-Cognitive Theory" on p. 439. This concludes the discussion of applications based on the social-cognitive theory.

Summing It Up *Applications of Bandura's Social-Cognitive Theory*

Social-cognitive therapy relies on observational learning as its primary method of helping clients acquire more adaptive patterns of behavior. Incorporated into this method are:

- *Mastery modeling.* This involves the client watching others perform successfully the more adaptive behavior patterns, or being assisted by the therapist in performing more adaptive behaviors first learned during therapeutic modeling.
- *Curing phobias.* This is one of the most frequent disorders treated using social-cognitive therapy.

Cognitive-behavioral therapy emphasizes the modification of self-defeating beliefs and ideas and helps clients handle anticipated stressors by teaching them new coping responses.

Self-defense training for women based on principles of mastery modeling and enhanced self-efficacy promotes self-protection skills against sexual assault, empowerment, and increased freedom of movement.

Evaluating Bandura's Social-Cognitive Theory: Strengths and Limitations

Presented in this section is a summary of the characteristic strengths and limitations of Bandura's social-cognitive theory.

Characteristic Strengths

Here are some strengths of Bandura's social-cognitive theory:

- *Identifying the importance of modeling and self-efficacy: Taking a realistic look at behavior.* A major strength of Bandura's theory is the realistic view he takes of behavior. Going beyond traditional learning viewpoints, his use of such concepts as observational learning, mastery modeling, and self-efficacy makes it possible to more realistically explain how many complex patterns of behavior are acquired and the reasons they may

or may not be performed (e.g., an individual's lack of self-confidence).

- *An emphasis on research: An appreciation of systematic evaluation.* There is an emphasis on scientific research in Bandura's theory. Whether it involves testing basic concepts of his theory or applying these concepts to a variety of settings, he continues to emphasize the importance of systematic evaluation of his ideas.
- *A concern for social relevance: Putting his ideas to work.* In addition to his theoretical work, Bandura has actively applied his theory to issues of social relevance. His work in the area of aggression modeling has contributed significantly to what we know about the impact of media violence on children's aggressive behavior. The treatment of phobias and other problems of personality adjustment has been enhanced by developments in social-cognitive theory. Most recently, Bandura has begun to examine the role of self-efficacy in the development of educational programs designed to promote self-control over behaviors that carry the risk of the person contracting AIDS (Bandura, 1990) and in the treatment of eating disorders and alcohol and substance abuse (Bandura, 1997), as well as encouraging individuals to serve as agents of personal and social change (Bandura, 2002, 2006).

Characteristic Limitations

Here are some limitations of Bandura's social-cognitive theory:

- *On ignoring the unconscious: Concentrating too much on cognition.* While Bandura has done much to increase our awareness of cognitive variables in the study of personality, he has been criticized for ignoring some of the more complex psychological components of personality. For example, he has been criticized for putting too much emphasis on the conscious aspects of cognitive processes while ignoring unconscious dynamic processes. Like Rotter, Bandura has also been criticized for developing a theory of personality that places little emphasis on the emotional components of personality.
- *Overlooking the developmental component of personality: A theory with no growing pains.* Bandura's viewpoint has also been criticized because it

does not give much attention to the developmental aspects of personality. For example, he discusses principles of modeling as if they occur the same way for children and adults.

This concludes the presentation of Bandura's social-cognitive theory. More information about his ideas can be obtained by reading some of his recent articles in which he discusses the general development of his social-cognitive perspective (Bandura, 2001, 2004) and its applications to various social issues (Bandura, 2002, 2006), along with his classic book titled *Social Foundations of Thought and Action: A Social-Cognitive Theory* (Bandura, 1986).

Mischel's Cognitive-Affective System Theory: A Personalistic Cognitive Perspective

The final perspective to be considered in this chapter is one proposed by Walter Mischel. Like Rotter and Bandura, he is a contemporary personality theorist who has been quite influential in promoting a more cognitive view of personality. For a glimpse into the life of Mischel, read "A Closer Look."

A Closer Look

The Life of Walter Mischel

Walter Mischel was born on February 22, 1930, not too far from Freud's office in Vienna. With the Nazi invasion of Austria, Mischel's family left Vienna in 1938 to avoid Nazi persecution and moved to the United States. The Mischel family spent two years living in various parts of the United States before settling in Brooklyn in 1940.

Upon completing secondary school, Mischel was to attend college on a scholarship. However, before he could start college, his father became ill. Mischel had to delay going to school in order to earn money for his

Walter Mischel has been at the center of some of contemporary personality psychology's most heated controversies, as well as a central figure in the cognitive viewpoint of personality.

family. During that time, he held several odd jobs (including working as a stock boy, as an elevator operator, and in a garment factory), but he continued to pursue his interest in art and psychology by attending New York University. While he fueled his interest in painting and sculpture by spending time in Greenwich Village, he was rather turned off by his psychology classes, which tended to emphasize the study of learning in animals (e.g., the laboratory rat and pigeon) that was so popular in psychology then. Mischel saw little relevance of this type of psychology to everyday problems. His early interest in personality psychology was in what he read about Freudian psychoanalysis as an undergraduate student, which, at the time, seemed to have some relevance to his desire to understand people.

Upon graduating from college, Mischel decided to pursue clinical psychology and entered the MA program at the City College of New York. While working on his master's degree, he held a job as a social worker in the Lower East Side of New York, working with troubled teens and helping the poor and the elderly. It was during this time as a social worker that he came to the conclusion that the writings of Freud and the use of projective tests were of little help in understanding the real-life problems of people living in the slums. As a result, Mischel began to search for a more practical and empirically based approach to psychology. This research led him to Ohio State University, where he became a student of Julian Rotter.

Mischel received his PhD in clinical psychology in 1956 from Ohio State University under Rotter, and spent the years from 1956 to 1958 in the Caribbean, studying religious cults that practiced spirit possession and investigating the cross-cultural nature of delay of gratification. In his research, he examined the beliefs, fantasies, and behavior of people while they were in possessed and normal states, in an effort to determine why some people prefer immediate rewards but others do not.

After working in the Caribbean, Mischel spent the next two years on the faculty of the University of Colorado before taking a position at Harvard University. At Harvard, he benefited from his interactions with such eminent personality psychologists as Gordon Allport, David McClelland, and Henry A. Murray, further developing his interest in personality processes and personality assessment. While at Harvard, Mischel met and married Harriet Nerlove, also a psychologist. In 1962, the couple and their three children moved to California, where Mischel accepted a position at Stanford University. At Stanford, he came into close contact with Albert Bandura. After more than 20 years at Stanford, Mischel accepted a faculty position at Columbia and returned to New York City in 1983, where he continues to be active as a teacher and researcher.

In much of his early work, Mischel attempted to evaluate the effectiveness of personality traits and psychodynamic concepts to predict behavior. He summarized this work in his very influential textbook titled *Personality and Assessment* (1968). Recently, however, he has devoted more attention to integrating personality psychology with cognitive psychology by considering individual differences in the way people process information as a major determinant of their behavior (Mischel, 1973, 1977, 1979, 1984, 1990, 1999, 2000, 2004; Mischel & Morf, 2003; Mischel & Shoda, 1995, 1999).

Over the years, Mischel has been a leading figure in promoting a more critical look at the nature of personality theories and personality assessment. For his efforts, he has won not only the respect of many personality psychologists but also the 1978 Distinguished Scientist Award from the Clinical Psychology Division of the American Psychological Association (APA), the APA's award for Distinguished Scientific Contribution in 1982, and the Society of Experimental Social Psychologists' Distinguished Scientist Award in 2000. In 2004, he received the distinct honor of being elected to the National Academy of Sciences. He is also the author of a highly successful undergraduate personality psychology textbook (Mischel, Smith, & Shoda,

2008). More information about the life of Walter Mischel can be found in a biography appearing in the *American Psychologist* (American Psychological Association, 1983).

Basic Concepts of Mischel's Cognitive-Affective Perspective: Cognitive-Affective Units

At the core of Mischel's viewpoint is what he refers to as cognitive-affect units (also referred to previously as *cognitive social learning person variables* or *cognitive person variables*; Mischel, 1973, 1990, 1999; Mischel, Cantor, & Feldman, 1996; Mischel & Shoda, 1995, 1999). **Cognitive-affective units** are certain personal qualities that influence how the individual processes information about the environment and that generate complex patterns of behaviors in reaction to it. For example, your decision to apply for a job will depend on, among other things, how you interpret the job description and how qualified you feel. Mischel (1999, 2000, 2004; Mischel & Shoda, 1995, 1999) lists five such units: encodings, expectancies and belief, affects, goals and values, and competencies and self-regulatory plans.

Encoding Strategies: How You Put the Pieces Together

Encodings refer to the different strategies people use to organize, store, and transform the information they receive or possess. For example, a trained detective might see the information at a crime scene differently than a professional photographer. Differences in encoding strategies are determined by such factors as attention, level of motivation, personal values, and training, to name just a few. The point is that the same information can mean different things to different people because of the way each encodes it.

Expectancies and Beliefs: The Outcomes

What people decide to do is most often influenced by what they believe their actions will produce. For Mischel, there are three types of expectancies.

- **Behavior-outcome expectancies** refer to the relationship an individual perceives between a particular behavior and the specific outcome it is likely to produce. For example, you believe that if you dress appropriately, you will make a favorable impression on the interviewer.

- **Stimulus-outcome expectancies** refer to the tendency for people to use certain pieces of information in their environment to predict future outcomes. For example, the failure of the interviewer to shake your hand at the end of the interview may be viewed as a sign that you probably will not be offered the job.
- **Self-efficacy expectancies** refer to an individual's beliefs that he or she can perform the behavior that will produce a desired outcome. For example, the confidence you feel about having a favorable interview will depend on how effectively you believe you will be able to answer the questions you are likely to be asked.

Affects: Your Feelings Affecting Your Thoughts and Behaviors

Affects refer to feelings and emotional reactions that serve to influence our thinking and actions. For example, seeing a humorous movie will produce an uplifting emotional state. In such a state, you are more likely to overlook the carelessness of another driver who cuts you off in your traffic lane. On the other hand, receiving a negative evaluation by your supervisor will produce an unpleasant emotional state. In this state, you are more likely to perceive a careless driver as reckless and to respond by honking your horn and yelling at the person. These examples illustrate how situational factors can influence our thoughts and behaviors. However, individual differences also exist in people's general affective states that may stem from biological and temperamental factors (Plomin, DeFries, McClearn, & McGuffin, 2001). For example, someone with an overly reactive nervous system (i.e., a highly sensitive person) may perceive many social situations as too loud, and, therefore, emotionally unpleasant. As a result, the individual may elect to leave such situations early, avoid them altogether, or select more quiet and sedate atmospheres in which to socialize with others.

Goals and Values: What Do You Prefer?

Goals and values refer to the preferences we have for certain objects or outcomes over others. For example, the extent to which you select a high-paying, boring job over a low-paying, stimulating one reflects the greater value you give to money over intellectual challenges. An individual with a greater value for stimulation might make just the opposite decision. Thus, much of the variety we see in human behavior is a reflection of the tremendous differences in people's goals and subjective values (Dweck, Higgins, & Grant-Pillow, 2003; Dweck & Molden, 2005; H. Grant & Dweck, 1999).

Competencies and Self-Regulatory Systems and Plans: Knowing What You Can Do and How You Can Get What You Want

Competencies refer to what the individual knows and can do. Cognitive competencies refer to the amount and types of information an individual possesses. For example, a professional basketball coach possesses information that is quite different from that of the average fan. Behavioral competencies refer to differences in abilities to perform certain actions. For example, a professional basketball player is better able to generate certain complex behavior patterns on the court than the average street-ball player. Competencies are determined by several factors, including age, health, psychological maturity and adjustment, strength, intelligence, and training.

Self-regulatory systems and plans refer to the internal processes that the individual uses to control the nature of his or her behavior.

- **Self-regulatory systems** are internal standards we use to guide our behavior. For example, because of your strong beliefs against nuclear arms, you turn down the opportunity to attend an interview with an engineering firm that specializes in nuclear defense contracts.
- **Self-regulatory plans** include the specific course of action you may decide to take in order to achieve a desired outcome. Such plans are a critical part of how people cope with life's problems (S. M. Miller, Shoda, & Hurley, 1996). For example, you might decide that in order to get a job, you need a new suit. As a result, your plan of action might include looking through magazines to see what is in style and then seeking out clothing stores that carry the latest suits. Another person's plan might include seeking the advice of a career counselor.

Thus, like Rotter's and Bandura's, Mischel's approach to understanding personality is to acknowledge that our

Summing It Up *Basic Concepts of Mischel's Cognitive-Affective System Theory*

Cognitive-affective units are characteristic qualities of the individual that serve to influence how he or she interprets, processes, and reacts to cues encountered in the environment. There are five such units:

- *Encodings* include a variety of strategies you can use to manipulate the information you receive or possess.
- *Expectancies and beliefs* are responses based on the beliefs you have about the relationship between what you do and what you think will happen (i.e., *behavior-outcome expectancies*), what you assume from cues in the environment (i.e., *stimulus-outcome expectancies*), and your ability to perform the desired behavior successfully (i.e., *self-efficacy expectancies*).
- *Affects* are emotional reactions that serve to influence your thoughts and behavior in different situations.
- *Goals and values* are your expressed desires for certain types of reinforcers over others and the impact these preferences have on your behavior.
- *Competencies and self-regulatory systems and plans* refer to the nature, extent, and quality of the information and behavioral skills you believe you possess and include the internal standards and code of behavior (i.e., *self-regulatory systems*) and specific courses of action (i.e., *self-regulatory plans*) you use to help determine your behavior in conjunction with environmental cues.

behavior is governed by both cognitive and situational factors (S. M. Miller et al., 1996; Mischel, 1999, 2000, 2004; Mischel & Shoda, 1999).

A summary of the major ideas discussed in this section is presented in "Summing It Up: Basic Concepts of Mischel's Cognitive-Affective System Theory" above. Next we will explore Mischel's construct of personality processes.

Basic Processes of Mischel's Cognitive-Affective Perspective: Delay of Gratification and Conditions of Behavioral Consistency

Two important personality processes Mischel uses to help explain personality and predict behavior are the ability to delay gratification and the matching of cognitive-affective units with situational demands.

Delaying Gratification: The Expression and Consequences of "Willpower"

One important personality process studied by Mischel is delay of gratification and the consequences it has on behavior. (Metcalfe & Mischel, 1999; Mischel, 1990; Mischel & Ayduk, 2002, 2003; Mischel et al., 1996; Mischel & Rodriguez, 1993; Mischel, Shoda, & Rodriguez, 1992).

Expressing Delay of Gratification: Showing Willpower **Delay of gratification** is the tendency to forgo a smaller but immediate reward for a larger reward in the future. In his study of delay of gratification in children and adolescents, Mischel has been concerned with the factors affecting the ability to delay gratification and the strategies people can use to help increase this delay. A typical example of Mischel's research on delay of gratification involves giving children the choice of receiving a smaller reward (e.g., cracker) immediately for the asking or a larger reward (e.g., several pieces of candy) later. Delay of gratification is made more difficult if the rewards are present and visible to the child (Mischel & Ebbesen, 1970), and if the child is thinking about how crunchy the cracker is or how sweet the candy tastes (Mischel & Baker, 1975).

Increasing Delay of Gratification: It's All in Your Head – Well, Most of It Is Mischel and his colleagues found that the ability to delay gratification is increased in children through the use of various behavior (e.g., playing with one's shoe) and cognitive (e.g., thinking of fun things) strategies that take the child's mind off the desired object and help pass the time (Mischel & Ayduk, 2003; Mischel et al., 1996; Mischel, Ebbesen, & Zeiss, 1972; Mischel, Shoda, & Rodriguez, 1989; Moore, Mischel, & Zeiss, 1976; Peake, Hebl, & Mischel, 2002; Rodriguez, Mischel, & Shoda, 1989). For example, having the children think about the reward in front of them as something else (e.g., the pieces of candy as being small stones) increases delay of gratification.

More realistically, for adults who are trying to delay their gratification and not eat between meals, various behavior strategies might include dusting the furniture or clearing out the closet; cognitive strategies might involve thinking about a party you'd like to have or fantasizing about a loved one. In commenting on his delay of gratification research, Mischel notes, "Thus what is in the children's head – not what is physically in front of them – determines their ability to delay" (Mischel, 1993, p. 457). To help you resist temptation, keep this important piece of information in mind the next time you find yourself being confronted with the desire to light up your next cigarette while trying to stop smoking, snack between meals while on your diet, or get up to watch television instead of doing your homework.

Consequences of Delaying Gratification: The Interpersonal and Academic Benefits of Willpower
Mischel has noted the importance of delay of gratification as a core component of successful personality adjustment (Mischel, 1990; Mischel & Ayduk, 2003, 2004; Mischel et al., 1996; Mischel et al., 1989, 1992; Mischel & Rodriguez, 1993; Rodriguez et al., 1989). A lack of delay of gratification can be implicated in a variety of addictive and antisocial behaviors. For example, in a study of adolescents in a summer residential treatment facility, the inability to delay gratification was associated with aggressiveness (Rodriguez et al., 1989).

On the other hand, the ability to delay gratification is associated with a number of favorable consequences for adolescents. Mischel and his colleagues examined the academic and social competencies of adolescents whose ability to delay gratification was first assessed when they were in preschool. In comparison to those adolescents who demonstrated a lack of delay of gratification when measured in preschool, those who exhibited an ability to delay gratification had higher Scholastic Aptitude Test (SAT) scores and were rated by their parents as being more mature, better able to cope with stress and frustration, more likely to respond to and use reason, and more likely to think and plan ahead (Shoda, Mischel, & Peake, 1990). At the interpersonal level, the ability to delay gratification seems to serve as a long-term buffer against *rejection sensitivity* – the tendency to experience feelings of anxiety when anticipating being rejected by others. Specifically, in a 20-year follow-up, preschoolers vulnerable to rejection sensitivity but who were assessed at that time to have a high ability to delay gratification showed a greater degree of interpersonal functioning as adults by demonstrating higher self-esteem and self-worth and greater coping ability than those individuals who displayed high rejection sensitivity and low delay of gratification back in preschool (Ayduk et al., 2000). Although the process of self-regulation has been associated with certain stress reactions (Muraven, Tice, & Baumeister, 1998), developing the ability to delay gratification does seem to have some very favorable consequences (Mischel & Ayduk, 2003; Mischel et al., 1996). An interesting application of Mischel's research on delay of gratification is presented in "Applications in Personality Psychology."

Applications in Personality Psychology

A Penny Saved is a Penny Delayed: Teaching Delaying Gratification to Kids is a Sound Investment

An interesting application of Mischel's research on delay of gratification has been to help teach children about money skills, particularly that of saving money. In an article appearing in *The Wall Street Journal*, Jonathan Clements (1999) writes about the importance of delay of gratification by noting, "This self-control is critically important, and not just when it comes to saving money. We also need sufficient resolve to stick with our stock-market investments, despite the frequent turmoil, so that we can enjoy the long-term rewards." In an effort to help parents, Clements interviewed Walter Mischel for advice on how to foster delay of gratification in their children as a money-saving skill. Here are some tips offered by Mischel:

- *Deliver on promises.* Parents must be consistent and follow through with the promises they make to reward children who show delay of gratification. For example, if a parent promises the child a bonus in her allowance (e.g., the child can select a second movie at the video store this weekend) if the child's room is cleaned up within an hour after dinner instead of waiting until just before going to bed, the parents must make good on that promise at the end of the week. As Mischel notes, "Unless the children learn to believe that it's worth the wait, they won't do it."
- *Be realistic.* Set realistic standards for the degree of delay that is expected of the child. For example, it may be appropriate to tell a 12-year-old that if he cleans his room each weekend for the next seven months before his birthday, he will receive that electric guitar he has been looking at in the mall's music store. On the other hand, expecting a 5-year-old child to wait seven months for that new toy she has seen at the mall may be too much to ask. In this case, the parent might promise that the child will be able to check out a favorite video this weekend if she puts her clothes in the hamper each time she is given a bath.
- *Make it fun.* Parents should help to make the process of learning to delay gratification pleasant. "The process itself should become rewarding for a child," Mischel notes. For example, if a child has to clean up her room each night an hour before bedtime all week to receive her allowance, her parents can let her do the cleaning while listening to her favorite songs on the compact disk player as loud as she wants.
- *Be a good example.* Children are more likely to be good savers if they see their parents saving regularly and find saving money to be worthwhile and enjoyable. For example, parents might have a "vacations savings jar" in the kitchen where they put bank deposit slips from money being saved for the family vacation. The parents can talk with their children about the fun activities they might do on their vacation each time a deposit slip is placed in the jar.
- *Combine instant and delayed gratification.* It is difficult to teach children delay of gratification if you do not combine it with instant gratification. For example, parents might allow their child to keep half her allowance for pocket money to be spent as the child wishes but also offer to match the other half of the allowance that is being saved by the child. This procedure will allow the child to obtain some instant gratification for her efforts but also reap the benefits of delaying gratification.

Although this advice was offered by Mischel to help teach children to save money, much of it can easily be applied to your own life, if you are like so many other individuals who just cannot seem to find a way to save enough money.

Perception and Prediction of Behavioral Consistency: The Matching of Conditions and Competencies

Mischel and his colleagues have also been interested in using cognitive-affective units to help explain and predict the behavioral consistency of people across situations (Mischel, 1990, 1999, 2004; Mischel & Morf, 2003; Miscel & Shoda, 1995, 1998, 1999). A central theme of this work has been the application of what Mischel refers to as "if . . . then" relations (Mischel, 1999). The logic of **"if . . . then" relations** involves the analysis of situations, on the basis of the cognitive-affective units, to determine the nature of the behavior to be performed in these various situations. The degree of behavioral consistency across situations is determined by the extent to which the "if . . . then" analysis of different situations calls for a similar behavior to be displayed (Mischel, 1999, 2004; Mischel & Morf, 2003; Mischel & Shoda, 1995, 1998, 1999; Shoda, Mischel, & Wright, 1989, 1993a, 1993b, 1994). For example, "Joking Jackie," a stand-up comic, is an individual who is skilled at making people laugh. Jackie will be more likely to demonstrate consistency in this behavior across those situations where this skill is perceived by her as appropriate (e.g., at comedy clubs, on television appearances, at parties, while on a date, or sitting at the dinner table with friends) than in those situations where such behavior is deemed inappropriate or less important (e.g., riding in an elevator, dining with her manager during a business luncheon, or visiting a funeral home). Although Jackie's behavior may appear inconsistent, if we apply the logic of Mischel's "if . . . then" relations to its analysis, we will see a high degree of consistency. Specifically, Jackie is consistent in the expression of her humorous behavior across those situations where she views such actions as appropriate and perceives that she has the ability to perform such behavior effectively. She is also consistent in her lack of expression of humorous behavior across those situations where she views it as inappropriate or unimportant. The point to be made here is that understanding how Jackie applies the logic of "if . . . then" relations when deciding what to do in different sets of situations gives us a more comprehensive picture of her personality and how it serves to foster consistency in her behavior.

But a problem can develop when we make assumptions regarding the "if . . . then" relations of others. If we perceive someone as having a particular characteristic that supposedly reflects a critical aspect of the individual's personality, we might expect to see this characteristic reflected in the person's behavior across a wide variety of situations, and we might be surprised if we do not see it being demonstrated. For example, fans of Jackie may be disappointed when they accidentally meet her in an elevator and she does not speak to them, much less saying something funny. In this situation, the fans' perception of inconsistency in Jackie's behavior is due to their reasoning that "if" Jackie is funny around people, "then" she should be funny in any and all social situations where people are present. But Jackie's own expectancies regarding riding in an elevator on her day off are different from the expectations of being on stage or at a party with friends, and, therefore, she may not feel it is necessary to be funny. As a result of this interaction, the fans may now think of Jackie as being a real snob and not as funny the next time they see her on television.

You can most likely think of some examples from your own life when the "if . . . then" perceptions of you by others (e.g., parents, teachers, or friends) were different from your own, as well as the inter-

personal difficulties these differences produced. Thus, by considering both the cognitive-affective units (e.g., encoding strategies and expectancies and beliefs) and situational demands on these cognitive-affective units, Mischel has demonstrated how you can gain a better understanding of yourself and those around you.

A summary of the principal ideas discussed in this section is presented in "Summing It Up: Basic Processes of Mischel's Cognitive-Affective System Theory."

Summing It Up *Basic Processes of Mischel's Cognitive-Affective System Theory*

Delay of Gratification. This is the tendency to forgo a smaller but immediate reward for a larger reward that is postponed. For example, instead of watching television now, Roger decides to study for his psychology test so as to earn a higher grade in the class at the end of the semester.

- *Increasing Delay of Gratification.* Behavioral and cognitive strategies designed to divert the individual's attention away from the immediate reward serve to increase the ability to delay gratification. For example, by going to the library and concentrating on his reading assignment, Roger is able to avoid watching television and study for a longer period of time.
- *Consequences of the Ability to Delay Gratification.* The ability to delay gratification is associated with a variety of favorable consequences from coping with stress to increased academic achievement. For example, because he was able to put in the study time, instead of watching television, Roger did very well on his tests and made the Dean's List that semester.

The Prediction of Behavioral Consistency. This is enhanced when the characteristic features of the individual match the demands of the situation through the use of "if . . . then relations", matching conditions and competencies. For example, Joan is a competitive individual and, if the situation requires competitiveness, she is going to demonstrate this tendency in those work and leisure activities that demand competitiveness.

Applications of Mischel's Cognitive-Affective Perspective: Using What Is Known

In this section, we will discuss the application of Mischel's cognitive-affective system perspective to the process of personnel selection and to adjustment to college life.

Personnel Selection: The Matching of Employee Competencies with Employment Conditions

As mentioned previously, Mischel and his colleagues (Mischel, 2000, 2004; Shoda et al., 1989, 1993a, 1993b, 1994) have noted the importance of matching personal competencies of the individual with situational demands to improve the prediction of cross-situational consistency in behavior. An excellent application of this logic is the process of **personnel selection**.

In the process of personnel selection, information from various psychological tests and other sources (e.g., letters of reference, interviews, and school records) is used to help make hiring decisions and predict job performance (Cohen & Swerdlik, 2005; Murphy & Davidshofer, 2005; Riggio, 2000). Personnel managers use various psychological tests to assess the specific cognitive, social, and self-regulatory competencies of individuals for the purpose of matching them with the specific situational demands of the position outlined in the job description.

For example, a personnel manager for a company that sells industrial solvents and cleaners has identified the following situational demands for people working as field sales representatives:

- Have the cognitive competencies to retain a considerable amount of knowledge about the different products sold by the company.
- Be able to calculate estimates in helping customers determine how much of the company's products they might need.
- Possess the social competencies to make conversation and establish rapport with different types of customers.
- Possess sufficient self-regulatory competencies to be able to work without being monitored directly by a supervisor.

In selecting the sales representative, the personnel manager might use a general intelligence test to measure memory and mathematical abilities defined as important cognitive competencies. To measure the social competencies of potential sales representatives, the personnel manager might administer a social skills test (Riggio, 1986), which supposedly measures an individual's ability to assess a social situation and modify his or her behavior accordingly. Self-regulatory competencies might be assessed by administering any number of **integrity tests**, such as the Applicant Potential Inventory (Jones, Brasher, & Huff, 2002) or the Personnel Selection Inventory (London House, 1980), which attempt to measure such behavior as employee theft of money, supplies, or time (i.e., taking unscheduled breaks or days off), work values, customer relations, and drug avoidance.

Thus, by defining what the company feels are the important situational demands to be made on their sales representatives, and then having the personnel manager select people who are most likely to possess the necessary cognitive, social, and self-regulatory competencies, the company is predicting that these competencies will be demonstrated consistently across a variety of situations involving customer–sales representative interactions. Stated more directly, in the company's eyes, matching competencies of the sales representatives with the situational demands of selling in the field will produce customer satisfaction and big profits for the company.

Coping with Life Tasks: Meeting the Challenges of College Life

Social Intelligence: Knowledge for Day-to-Day Problem Solving Similar to Mischel's emphasis on cognitive social learning person variables and cognitive processes in the study of personality is the emphasis on social intelligence proposed by Nancy Cantor, of Syracuse University, and John Kihlstrom, of the University of California, Berkeley (Cantor, 1990; Cantor & Kihlstrom, 1985, 1987, Norem, 2000). **Social intelligence** refers to the skills, abilities, and knowledge people bring to various social situations. It can include knowledge about what to say and do that has been acquired over time through experience in similar circumstances (e.g., it is appropriate to be witty at parties but quiet and polite at funerals), knowledge about specific events and people (e.g., Uncle Joe does not like salt on his food), and knowledge about strategies for forming impressions of others in order to explain and predict their behavior (e.g., the way she looked away makes me think she is lying and can't be trusted).

The work on life tasks by Nancy Cantor and Julie Norem helps us to understand how college students cope with academic stress. Such research illustrates the importance of applying what we know about personality psychology to help individuals deal with real-life concerns.

Life Tasks: The Significant Issues in Day-to-Day Living   An important application of social intelligence is its use in helping people to deal with what Cantor and Kihlstrom refer to as life tasks (Cantor, 1990, 1994; Cantor & Harlow, 1994; Cantor & Kihlstrom, 1985, 1987; Cantor & Zirkel, 1990; Norem, 2000; Sanderson & Cantor, 1999). **Life tasks** are defined as the problems people see themselves as working on in a particular period of life transition. Life tasks come in various forms, but are characterized by the significance each person attributes to them, as illustrated by the amount of time and energy devoted to the tasks and the extent to which they dominate daily life (Cantor & Malley, 1991; Cantor et al., 1991; Cantor, Zirkel, & Norem, 1993; Sanderson & Cantor, 1999). For example, a life task for an adolescent might involve struggling to be accepted by peers through experimentation in dress and after-school activities. A life task for a middle-aged single parent returning to school might include trying to develop a strategy for dealing with child care and finding enough time to study. For an elderly individual, life tasks might involve trying to deal with the increased amount of free time now available as a result of being retired or coping with the death of a spouse. The significance of these life tasks, along with the strategies designed to deal with them, is also illustrated by the extent to which they continue throughout the life of the individual (Harlow & Cantor, 1996). For example, to deal with her desire to make more friends, a high school student might develop a strategy that involves participating in a variety of school-related activities. As an adult who has relocated to a new city, she might deal with this same issue by employing a similar strategy that includes participating in a variety of community events. In late adulthood, she might deal with her adjustment to moving into a nursing home by attending many of the social events held in the nursing home's recreational center.

Optimism and Defensive Pessimism Strategies: The Bright and the Dark Side of Coping with Academic Anxiety   In her own work on life tasks, Nancy Cantor and her colleagues have focused on various issues facing college students during this significant period of transition, including dealing with independence (Zirkel, 1992; Zirkel & Cantor, 1990), academic performance (Cantor, Norem, Niedenthal, Langston, & Brower, 1987), friendships (Langston & Cantor, 1989), and romantic intimacy (Cantor, Acker, & Cook-Flannagan, 1992; Cantor & Sanderson, 1998; Sanderson & Cantor, 1995, 1997).

For example, in a two-year longitudinal study of how college students cope with the life task of academic stress, it was noted that the students utilized two somewhat different coping strategies (Cantor et al., 1987). One group of students used a strategy characterized by optimism. The strategy of optimism is characterized by an "illusory glow" – generating positive thoughts as an attempt to make themselves feel better when distressed (Norem, 1989; Norem & Illingworth, 1993). That is, students using the optimistic strategy tended to view academic tasks as difficult and challenging but not something that would overwhelm them. They did not view themselves as overly anxious or out of control before having to perform academically (e.g., take a test, turn in a paper, or give a speech). They were able to avoid a sense of failure by setting realistically high goals for themselves based on past success. Finally, as a means of maintaining a positive sense of self-image, they tended to assume control over their academic successes (e.g., "I studied hard") while denying having control over their academic failures (e.g., "The professor's questions were too picky"). Thus, "optimists" used a number of encoding strategies (e.g., seeing themselves as in control) and stimulus-outcome expectancies (e.g., setting goals on the basis of past success) to cope effectively with the life tasks associated with academic stress.

A second group of students used a strategy described as defensive pessimism (Norem & Cantor, 1986a, 1986b; Norem & Illingworth, 1993). Students using the defensive pessimism strategy had a history of academic success but guarded against threats to their self-esteem by setting unrealistically low expectations for themselves and creating "worst-case scenarios." For example, they tended to feel anxious and reported a lack of control with respect to their performance in academic situations.

What is most interesting about these two different strategies for coping with life tasks in academic settings is that they seem to be successful for both groups. The optimists tend to deal with their academic anxieties by "looking on the bright side." The defensive pessimists tend to use "worst-case scenarios" to motivate themselves to deal with their academic anxiety. The point is that different people use different – but equally effective – strategies to deal with significant life tasks (Norem, 1998; Spencer & Norem, 1996). For an examination of some important recent developments in the study of optimism and pessimism, consider "At the Cutting Edge of Personality Psychology" below.

A summary of the principal points noted in this section is presented in "Summing It Up: Applications of Mischel's Cognitive-Affective System Theory" on p. 450.

AT THE CUTTING EDGE OF PERSONALITY PSYCHOLOGY

The Positive Side of Pessimistic Thinking

Strategic Approaches of Optimists and Pessimists: Seeing the Glass as Both Half Full and Half Empty

The old saying goes that the optimist sees the glass as half full while the pessimist sees it as half empty. Although there is some truth in that saying, for Julie Norem, of Wellesley College, a leading researcher in the field of optimism and pessimism, the issue has more to do with how optimists and pessimists respond to the amount of water in the glass. In recent research, Norem and others have focused on trying to identify and understand the strategies used by optimists and pessimists to deal with the challenges of their lives (Norem, 2000, 2001; Norem & Illingworth, 2004; Sanna, Chang, Carter, & Small, 2006). Two of the critical strategies she has identified are coping imagery and relaxation imagery.

Coping Imagery: Fantasizing about Failing and Finding a Solution   The strategy favored by the defensive pessimists is one of **coping imagery**, which is characterized by a two-step process. First, the individual forms a mental image of something going wrong during the performance of a particular activity. Second, the individual imagines fixing or recovering from whatever has happened. With this strategy, defensive pessimists can harness the anxiety they typically experience as a result of their pessimistic outlook and channel it into thinking about what they can do to prevent such a catastrophe from occurring. In a sense, by developing a worse-case scenario, defensive pessimists are able to

express their characteristic pessimistic doomsday perspective (i.e., "The glass is half empty") while taking a course of defensive action (i.e., thinking about how to prevent the negative consequence from happening) that allows them to maintain an optimistic perspective (i.e., "The glass is half full"). As an example, a college student might imagine being on a job interview where she is asked a series of question about her career plans, which she proceeds to fumble over in her answers. In response to this imagined worst-case scenario, the student then proceeds to imagine over and over these and other possible questions that she might be asked during her interview next week. Each time she replays the scene in her head, she tries to correct any mistakes she made during her previous mental image of the interview.

Relaxation Imagery: Looking on the Bright Side, and Away from the Bad Side, of the Street The strategy favored by the strategic optimist is relaxation imagery. **Relaxation imagery** is also characterized by a two-step process. The first step involves the individual focusing his or her attention away from the anxiety-provoking activity or performance. The second step involves the individual focusing on relaxing completely. With this strategy, anxiety is used as a source of avoidance that will drive the individual to think more pleasant, relaxing thoughts. In a sense, by developing a favorable-case scenario, strategic optimists are allowed to express their optimistic perspective ("The glass is half full") during their relaxation imagery while avoiding any negative, anxiety-provoking thoughts (i.e., thinking about how difficult the activity or performance is) characteristic of a pessimistic perspective (i.e., "The glass is half empty"). As an example, a college student who is preparing to give a presentation in his history class would not think about how nervous he feels about the upcoming speech, but would try to relax himself as he reviews his notes at home the day before the presentation.

So, the next time you are confronted with a life challenge where you have to decide whether the glass is half full or half empty, think about Julie Norem's research. Remember, it is not about how you perceive the water in the glass but, more importantly, the strategy you adopt in response to that perception. Specifically, if you see the glass as being half full, use the relaxation imagery strategy. If you see the glass as half empty, use the coping imagery strategy.

Summing It Up *Applications of Mischel's Cognitive-Affective System Theory*

Personnel Selection. This uses the logic of matching the competencies of the individual with the demands of the job. For example, when hiring new medical staff, those nurses with psychological test scores indicating the greatest ability to tolerate stress will be assigned to the emergency room for three shifts a week.

Social Intelligence and the Solving of Life Tasks. Social intelligence is the ability to resolve successfully a variety of life tasks appearing in the form of significant personal and social challenges. For example, a student might use his ability to tell jokes to help overcome his loneliness during his first few weeks at college, while a newly divorced parent might use her organizational skills to start a single-parents' support group.

Evaluating Mischel's Cognitive-Affective Perspective: Strengths and Limitations

Our discussion of Mischel's Cognitive-Social Perspective will conclude with a summary of its characteristic strengths and limitations.

Characteristic Strengths

The basic strength of Mischel's perspective is his attempt to integrate several of the major viewpoints in personality. His emphasis on cognitive-affective units to account for individual differences is consistent with that of the trait viewpoint. The significance he gives to behavior-outcome and stimulus-outcome relationships utilizes concepts from the learning tradition. His use of subjective values and expectancies is consistent with the social learning theories of Rotter and Bandura. Finally, the use of encoding strategies is very characteristic of the cognitive viewpoint. Because of such integration, Mischel can be viewed as a real "builder of bridges" in the study of personality. Another strength of hiss perspective is the emphasis he gives to the use of empirical research to validate and develop his ideas.

Characteristic Limitations

A basic limitation of Mischel's perspective is that, with only a few exceptions (e.g., encoding strategies), it is not really that much different from the perspectives of Rotter and Bandura. In addition, while Mischel emphasizes the significance of such cognitive person variables as encoding strategies, he does not specify them in any detail; they simply exist and influence behavior. Be aware, however, that the use of cognitive-affective units is a perspective of personality that is still evolving. As Mischel continues to develop and refine his theory, he will become more specific about the details that distinguish it from other cognitive perspectives.

Chapter Summary: Reexamining the Highlights

- *Basic Assumptions of the Social-Cognitive Viewpoint.* The social-cognitive viewpoint emphasizes the role of cognitive processes in the study of personality. The basic assumptions of the social-cognitive viewpoint include the significance of the personal perspective, the presence of a need for cognition, a desire on people's part to seek further understanding and clarification of their personal world, and the significance of subjective probabilities.

- *Rotter's Social Learning Theory*
  - *Basic Assumptions of Rotter's Social Learning Theory.* Four basic assumptions of Rotter's social learning theory are people learning from meaningful experiences, the reciprocal nature of life experience, the goal-directed motivational nature of personality, and the role of expectancies.
  - *Basic Concepts of Rotter's Social Learning Theory.* Four basic concepts used by social learning theory to explain and predict behavior are behavior potential, expectancies, reinforcement value, and the psychological situation, as well as their combination into the basic formula.
  - *Personality Adjustment.* The processes of personality adjustment include freedom of movement and need value, minimal goal level, and generalized expectancies in problem solving.
  - *Applications of Rotter's Social Learning Theory.* The basic goal of *psychotherapy* is to increase the client's freedom of movement. Some techniques for achieving this goal include altering cognitions,

teaching more adaptive interpersonal skills, modifying maladaptive generalized expectancies, and participating in group or family therapy. In *personality assessment*, the Interpersonal Trust Scale assesses an individual's degree of trust in others, while the Internal-External Control of Reinforcement Scale (I-E Scale) assesses the extent to which an individual believes life's rewards are influenced more by internal or external forces. In *applications of locus of control to matrimony and divorce*, the I-E Scale has been used examine marital interaction and satisfaction, as well as the process of adjusting to divorce.

  - *Evaluating Rotter's Social Learning Theory.* Characteristic strengths of Rotter's social learning theory include its inclusion of cognitive variables and emphasis on research; characteristic limitations include too great an emphasis on cognitive variables at the expense of external forces and affective reactions.

- *Bandura's Social-Cognitive Theory*
  - *Basic Assumptions of Bandura's Social-Cognitive Theory.* The influence of the self system and the role of triadic reciprocal causation are two principal assumptions of Bandura's theory.
  - *Basic Concepts and Processes of Bandura's Social-Cognitive Theory.* Basic concepts used by Bandura to explain the nature and operation of personality involve observational learning, including the role of vicarious reinforcement and the effects of

media violence, the nature and influence of self-efficacy, and the process of self-regulation. The processes of personality maladjustment include maladaptive modeling, dysfunctional self-evaluations, and perceived inefficacy.

– *Applications of Bandura's Social-Cognitive Theory.* Therapeutic interventions based on social-cognitive theory include the use of various modeling techniques and cognitive modification. Self-defense training programs based on principles of mastery modeling and self-efficacy help to empower women against physical assault.

– *Evaluating Bandura's Social-Cognitive Theory.* Characteristic strengths of Bandura's theory include its rather realistic view of the role of modeling and self-efficacy as determinants of behavior, emphasis on empirical research, and relevance to a variety of social issues. Some of its characteristic limitations are an overemphasis on cognitive processes at the expense of unconscious processes and a lack of emphasis on personality development.

● *Mischel's Cognitive-Affective System Theory*

– *Basic Concepts of Mischel's Cognitive-Affective Perspective.* Mischel relies on the role of cognitive-affective units in the study of personality, which include encoding strategies, expectancies and beliefs, affects, goals and values, and competencies and self-regulatory plans.

– *Basic Processes of Mischel's Cognitive-Affective Perspective.* The process of delay of gratification and conditional determinants of behavioral consistency, as well as those factors affecting them, are important basic concepts of Mischel's theory.

– *Applications of Mischel's Cognitive-Affective Perspective.* The process of personnel selection illustrates important aspects of Mischel's emphasis on understanding the conditional determinants of behavioral consistency. The study of social intelligence as it applies to coping with life tasks illustrates the utility of cognitive-affective units.

– *Evaluating Mischel's Cognitive-Affective Perspective.* Characteristic strengths of Mischel's theory include his attempt to integrate various theoretical perspectives and emphasis on systematic research. Characteristic limitations include its similarity to other cognitive viewpoints and a rather limited explanation of the operational nature of the cognitive variables he discusses.

Glossary

affects Emotional reactions that affect an individual's thoughts and actions.

basic formula A formula utilizing expectancies and reinforcement values to predict behavior in specific situations.

behavior-outcome expectancies An individual's beliefs about the relationship between specific actions and outcomes.

behavior potential The probability of performing a particular behavior.

cognitive-affective units A set of internal factors that influence an individual's perceptions of events and behavior.

cognitive-behavioral therapies A group of therapeutic approaches designed to modify maladaptive cognitions and behavior patterns.

cognitive processes Mental activities involving the manipulation and modification of information.

competencies An individual's beliefs about his or her abilities.

coping imagery A strategy favored by defensive pessimists that involves thinking about what could go wrong and then thinking about what could be done to avoid this possibility.

delay of gratification The refusing of a smaller but immediate reward for a larger but postponed reward.

dysfunctional self-evaluations Maladaptive strategies for administering self-rewards and punishment.

encodings Strategies for processing and categorizing information.

expectancy The belief that a particular behavior will produce a specific outcome.

freedom of movement The belief that certain related actions will result in a set of desired outcomes.

if . . . then relations Specific patterns of cognitive factors that determine behavior in particular situations.

integrity tests   A category of psychological tests designed to assess and predict employee antisocial behavior.

Internal-External Control of Reinforcement Scale (I-E Scale)   A personality inventory designed to measure the generalized expectancies about the source of reinforcements.

interpersonal trust   A generalized belief in the word of others.

life tasks   A significant problem, or category of activities, during a specific period of life requiring a considerable amount of time and energy from an individual.

mastery modeling   A technique for acquiring new behaviors by observing others or with their assistance.

minimal goal level   The lowest value assigned to a reinforcer.

need for cognition   A desire to engage in thinking, reasoning, and other mental activities.

need value   The average value assigned to a specific collection of reinforcers.

observational learning   Acquiring information and skills by watching the behavior of others.

outcome expectations   The assumed outcome following specific behaviors.

perceived inefficacy   Assumed feelings of self-doubt.

personnel selection   The systematic selection of employees to maximize worker satisfaction and productivity.

psychological situation   All aspects of the environment that produce a response in an individual.

reinforcement value   The expressed preference for one reinforcer over others.

relaxation imagery   A strategy favored by optimists that involves avoiding thinking about the source of anxiety and focusing on trying to relax.

self-efficacy   An individual's self-perceived level of skill.

self-efficacy expectancies   An individual's belief about having the skills to obtain certain desired outcomes.

self-regulation   The use of internal standards for governing behavior.

self-regulatory plans   Specific strategies for obtaining specific outcomes.

self-regulatory systems   Internally generated rules for governing behavior.

self system   An organizational framework by which external stimuli are personalized.

social intelligence   The personal abilities that help people to cope with social situations.

stimulus-outcome expectancies   An individual's beliefs that certain stimuli are associated with specific outcomes.

triadic reciprocal causation   The interrelatedness of personal and environmental factors to influence behavior.

Selected Topics in the Study of Personality Psychology

Part III

In Part II, a survey of the major viewpoints of personality psychology was presented. The approach of Part II was to present a discussion of various topics (e.g., personality development and adjustment), issues (e.g., consistency of behavior), and applications (e.g., business and therapeutic implications) in the context of each viewpoint. Such an approach makes it possible to appreciate the complexity of personality and the diversity in viewpoints used to help understand this complex nature. In Part III, our focus will shift from the different viewpoints of personality to some selected topics in the study of personality. These topics were selected because they have a rich tradition in the study of personality psychology, they address some very important personal and social issues, and they have been the source of some interesting applications. Thus, while the focus of Part III has changed, the principal objective remains the same – to demonstrate to you the importance of the study of personality psychology in our everyday living experiences.

The Self-Concept
The Core of Personality

11

Chapter Overview:
A Preview of Coming Attractions

No concept comes closer to encompassing the core of personality psychology than that of the self. Its significance is evident in the attention it has been given not only by such masters as Freud, Jung, and Rogers and other such eminent psychologists as William James and Kurt Koffka, but also by a number of great social thinkers including sociologists Charles H. Cooley, George Herbert Mead, and Erving Goffman (Hermans, 1996). In fact, renowned personality psychologist Gordon Allport (1961) described the self as "some kind of core in our being" (p. 110) and proclaimed that the study of the self would expand and flourish in the coming decades (Allport, 1943). As Allport predicted, the self continues to hold a "center-stage position in psychology" (Banaji & Prentice, 1994, p. 297). As an objective measure of Allport's prophecy, researchers identified more than 31,000 publications on the self during the course of two recent decades (Ashmore & Jussim, 1997). A more recent survey of personality psychologists indicated that 43 percent of the researchers reported that they are involved in the study of the self-concept (Robins, Tracy, & Sherman, 2007). According to expert Roy F. Baumeister, "The self is one of the most actively researched topics in all of psychology" (Baumister, 1999, p. 1). Or, stated more succinctly, "The literature on the self is enormous" (Robins, Tracy, & Trzesniewski, 2008, p. 423).

This chapter will explore several different aspects of the self. We start by considering how the self-concept is defined and when it begins to develop. Next we will discuss historical changes in the self throughout history. We will then examine the personal/private and social/public dimensions of the self-concept. Finally, we will examine the cultural influences on the self.

Fundamentals of the Self-Concept: Its Definition and Origin

What does the term *self-concept* mean to you? Is it the same as *self-esteem?* What is its relationship to *identity?* Our discussion of self-concept will begin with two fundamental issues. First, we will describe what self-concept is, as well as what it is not. Next, we will consider its origin and emergence. We begin by considering the way personality psychologists use this term and differentiate it from related terms.

Self-Concept, Self-Esteem, and Identity

Self-concept refers to a person's belief about himself or herself (Baumeister, 1991, 1995; Brown, 1998; Higgins & May, 2001; Hoyle, Kernis, Leary, & Baldwin, 1999). Within the self-concept are the individual's assessment of his or her physical characteristics and personality attributes. Beliefs about physical characteristics might include the extent to which you believe your height and weight are proportional, your hair is too curly or too short, and your face is too round or too thin. Beliefs about personality attributes might include the extent to which you perceive yourself as being friendly, assertive, active, emotional, and sensitive to the needs of others. Other information included as part of the self-concept might be related to how smart you think you are, your interests (e.g., "I like baseball and hip hop but not in-line skating"), and your political beliefs (e.g., "I believe in strong local government") and religious beliefs (e.g., "I believe there is a supreme being"). Your assessment of these attributes is often based on a comparison with those of others around your (e.g., friends, co-workers, classmates, teammates; Mussweiler & Strack, 2000). In short, your self-concept is what you know and believe about yourself relative to what you observe about others.

Self-concept should not be confused with self-esteem. **Self-esteem** refers to a person's overall *evaluation* of himself or herself (Baumeister, 1991; Brown, 1998; Buss, 1995, 2001; Harter, 1999). Specifically, given what you know about yourself, how does that knowledge make you feel about yourself? Do you feel good about yourself (i.e., do you have high self-esteem) or bad about yourself (i.e., do you have low self-esteem)?

Your self-esteem can also be linked to a specific aspect of self-concept if that aspect is integral to your definition of who you are. For example, if being a successful business owner is significant to your self-concept, the fact that you neglect your family while running that business is of little relevance to your self-esteem, as long as your business is successful. Thus, self-esteem can be based on either a specific aspect (e.g., a particular ability) of self-concept or on a more global view of the self. We will consider self-esteem in greater detail in the next chapter.

Personal **identity**, by contrast, refers to the objective, physical, social, and personal characteristics and attributes that help distinguish a person from others (Baumeister, 1991; Buss, 1995, 2001; Hoyle et al., 1999). Many elements help each of us establish our own personal identity; among the most salient is a person's name. Objectively, such items as a social security number, a telephone number, a personalized license plate, and an e-mail address all distinguish you from other people and, therefore, contribute to your identity.

Physically, identity can be defined through gender (i.e., anatomy), hairstyle (e.g., a five-inch pink mohawk), clothing (e.g., wearing colorful ties), and permanent bodily modifications (e.g., a tattoo, pierced nose or tongue). Socially, identity can be defined by family, political affiliation (e.g., "Bill is a Democrat"), nationality, (e.g., "Gino is Italian"), geographic location (e.g., "Donna is a northeasterner"), group membership (e.g., "Brutus is a member of the Hell's Angels motorcycle club"), religious affiliation (e.g., "Harold is a Mormon"), sexual orientation (e.g., "Susan is a lesbian"), and occupation (e.g., "Alice is an accountant"), to name just a few.

From a personal perspective, internal beliefs and philosophy are also critical to a person's sense of identity. In fact, because people tend to conform to external social pressures, such internal beliefs might tell us more about a person than would the various public expressions of that person's identity. For example, although an office manager might wear an "Equality in the Workplace Now!" t-shirt for a unity day celebration at the office, at home this same person might complain vehemently about all the special treatment given to certain minority groups.

Identity conflict, occurring when aspects of an individual's public and private identities do not match, can be a source of much emotional discomfort. For example, with respect to gender identity, a biological male may view himself psychologically as a woman trapped in a man's body. Thus, like self-esteem, personal

Summing It Up *Some Points of Clarification in Defining the Self-Concept*

Term	Characterized by	Example
Self-Concept	Beliefs about physical features and personality characteristics	Carlos sees himself as tall and liberal in his political views.
Self-Esteem	General self-evaluation	Whitney is down on herself because of her inability to find a more satisfying job.
Identity	Distinction between self and others	Carly's involvement in Students for World Peace is an important aspect of how she sees herself.

identity is a component of self-concept that can be expressed in various ways.

As you can see from this brief discussion of self-concept, a variety of elements contribute to who you are. A summary of the major points discussed in this section is presented in "Summing It Up: Some Points of Clarification in Defining the Self-Concept" above. At what age do you learn you are you? This and related questions are considered in the next section.

Origin and Onset of the Self-Concept: When You Learn You Are You

If you have ever spent time watching a baby playing, you may have wondered, "Is the baby aware of who it is?" or "Does the baby realize that he or she is a distinct and separate entity? If so, when does a baby first make this realization?" To help answer such questions, in the late 1870s the great biologist Charles Darwin (1877) observed that around 9 months of age a child would recognize an image of himself or herself in the mirror. Research indicates that the initial signs of a sense of self seem to appear at about 6 months of age, emerging gradually and becoming more refined over a period of a year or so (Damon & Hart, 1982, 1988; Lewis, Sullivan, Stranger, & Weiss, 1989). When placed in front of a mirror, children at around 6 months of age will reach out and try to touch their image as if it were another child.

At this point you may ask, "How do we actually know that the child really recognizes herself in the mirror and is not just reaching out to touch someone else who is willing to do exactly as she does?" To answer this question, researchers dabbed some red rouge on the noses of children and then placed them in front of a mirror. At around 15 to 18 months of age, upon seeing the rouged nose each of the children would touch his or her own nose, rather than its reflected image in the mirror. (Gallup & Suarez, 1986). Additional research suggests that while some children display self-recognition around 15 to 17 months, it is not until between 18 and 24 months that a majority of children do so (Lewis & Brooks-Gunn, 1979). Thus, between 18 and 24 months of age, most children have some sense of what their face should look like and are curious about any variations of it. In addition, just prior to their second birthday, children display a certain degree of distress when they are unable to imitate the behavior of adults playing with a toy, suggesting that children are aware that their actions do not match those of the adults (J. Kagan, 1998). Such a reaction implies that the children are making a distinction between themselves and others, which would require a sense of self.

A child's initial recognition of his or her facial appearance is the basis of a blossoming sense of self-concept. Soon after, children are able to identify themselves and others with respect to gender and age, but not necessarily numerical age (e.g., "I'm little but my uncle is old," rather than "I'm 3 years old and my uncle is 47"; Baumeister, 1991; Kaplan, 2000; Shaffer & Kipp, 2007). By school age, children are able to define their sense of self by group membership (e.g., belonging to a certain family group or classroom), psychological traits, and abilities (e.g., "I can kick a ball hard, but I cannot stay inside the lines while coloring"; Lefrancois, 2001).

From about 6 to 12 years of age, children begin to refine their sense of self by comparing their personal characteristics and abilities to those of other children (Kaplan, 2000). For example, a young child's sense of self might hinge on whether she can ride a bike, whereas an older child's sense of self might depend on the extent to which he can ride his bike faster or farther than others can (Damon & Hart, 1982). Such comparisons with other children can result in a greater sense of self-consciousness, which increases considerably around 12 to 13 years of age (Baumeister, 1991; Kaplan, 2000; Tice, Buder & Baumeister, 1985).

By around age 8 to 10 years, the child's self-concept is quite stable and becomes a measure by which the sense of self can be compared to others. During adolescence, the self-concept begins to go beyond just the considerations of physical characteristics to include more abstract inner qualities and characteristics, such as traits, moral values, personal beliefs, and ideologies (Shaffer & Kipp, 2007). Given the significance of the self-concept in helping us to define who we are, you might be wondering if humans are the only species with a self-concept. Do animals have a sense of self? If so, how could you measure it? For some answers to these questions, read "A Closer Look" below.

the chimps and dyed one ear and one eyebrow of each chimp a bright red. After recovering from the anesthetic, the chimps again observed themselves in the mirror. Upon doing so, the animals began to touch themselves on the painted ear and eyebrow. Such behavior indicated that they did recognize themselves and were curious about their altered appearance. Similar results using the mirror/dye test have been observed for orangutans, but not for other lower primates (e.g., rhesus monkeys and macaques) or lower animals (e.g., dogs and rats; Gallup & Suarez, 1986).

Whereas at least some animals have a sense of self-consciousness (i.e., they are aware of changes to their bodies), they lack the second critical component that must be present before a sense of **self-recognition** can be inferred – the ability to be self-reflective (Gergen, 1971; Sedikides & Skowronski, 1997). Specifically, animals are not self-reflective in that they demonstrate no knowledge of their traits, thoughts, feelings, or behaviors. Thus, although they do seem to have distinctive personalities (i.e., differences in temperament) in that some are playful while others are aggressive, they do not have a sense of self. But for people who really love their pets, these results are not all that important. They love a pet for who it is, not for what the pet thinks it is.

A Closer Look

Do Animals Have a Sense of Self?

If you are an animal lover, you will surely admit that your pet dog, cat, or parrot has a distinct personality. But would you go so far as to say that it has a self-concept? To answer this intriguing question, work on the onset of the self-concept in children has been extended to address this issue for different species of animals (Povinelli & Prince, 1998; Suddendorf & Whiten, 2001).

In some classic research to study this possibility, Gallup (Gallup, 1977; Gallup & Suarez, 1986) used a variation of the mirror test described above to investigate the extent to which various animals have a self-concept. In a chimpanzee study (Gallup, 1977), the animals first observed themselves in a mirror as a baseline measure. Next, the researcher anesthetized

Beyond being just an interesting issue, the comparative analysis of self-recognition of humans and various species of animals helps us to answer other fascinating questions. For example, by comparing the similarities and differences in the brain structures of organisms with an enhanced sense of self-recognition and of those without it, it is possible to identify the neurological structure associated with the sense of self. Stated more directly, the issue is: Where is the self located in the brain? To consider this fascinating question, read "At the Cutting Edge of Personality Psychology" on p. 461.

Thus far we have discussed what the self-concept is, what it is not, when it emerges, who possesses it, and where it is located. Next we will explore the changes in conceptualization of the self-concept throughout history. Such information will help us to put into context our views of the self-concept today and how they have developed.

AT THE CUTTING EDGE OF PERSONALITY PSYCHOLOGY

In Search of the Self

Where is the Sense of Self Located? Getting Inside Your Own Head

Where is your sense of self located? We can start looking for the answer to this question by comparing the brains of individuals demonstrating a sense of self-recognition in response to the mirror test, and those that do not demonstrate it. In this regard, a critical difference is in the timing of the maturation of the prefrontal cortex. As discussed above, a majority of infants begin to demonstrate a sense of self in response to the mirror test around 18 to 24 months of age (Suddendorf & Whiten, 2001), which is approximately when the prefrontal cortex begins to mature in stature and function (Robins, Norem, & Cheek, 1999). Figure 11.1 illustrates the difference in the prefrontal cortex of various organisms.

In a more systematic search for the location of the self, University of Toronto psychologist Fergus I. M. Craik and colleagues (Craik et al., 1999) used positron emission tomography (PET) scans, which track blood flow through the brain, to measure the amount of brain activity in reaction to judgments about the self in comparison to other judgment tasks. Participants were asked to make judgments of particular trait adjectives (e.g., "stubborn") under four different conditions: "self" rating ("How well does the adjective describe you?"), "other" rating ("How well does this adjective describe [name of a famous person inserted]?"), "general" evaluative task ("How socially desirable is the trait described by the adjective?") and "syllable-rating" task ("How many syllables does this trait adjective contain?"). The "other," "general," and "syllable" ratings were used as a basis of comparison for the "self" rating.

Results indicated that information processing about the self in the form of self-ratings was located primarily in the prefrontal cortex, with the most striking pattern appearing in the right side of the frontal cortex, a finding that has also been identified measuring electrical brainwave activity (Velichkovsky, Klemm, Dettmar, & Volke, 1996) and a variety of

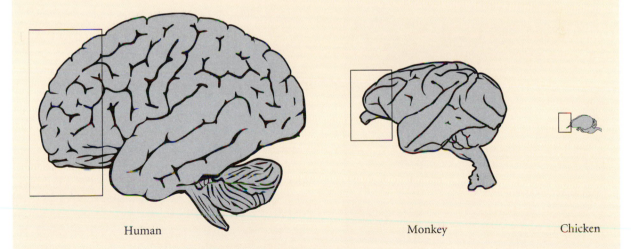

Human   Monkey   Chicken

Figure 11.1 The higher the organism is on the evolutionary scale, the greater the degree of development of the prefrontal cortex.

other techniques, such as PET and functional magnetic resonance imaging (fMRI; Gusnard, 2006) and comparisons of individuals with brain injury and frontal lobe dysfunction (Klein & Kihlstrom, 2002). This research, along with other evidence (Klein, Loftus, & Kihlstrom, 1996; Robins et al., 1999; Tulving, 1993), suggests that the self is located in the prefrontal cortex, along with many other complex psychological processes that make it possible for you to express your unique sense of self. Examples of such processes are memory, planning, reasoning, and abstract thought (Hugdahl, 2001), along with the subsequent displays of such complex emotions as pride, shame, embarrassment, and anxiety (Zillmer & Spiers, 2001) resulting from your own self-reflection.

Changes in the Concept of the Self through History

In this chapter, the definitions offered for the various components of the self reflect a contemporary view of the self (Baumeister, 1986a, 1987, 1995, 1997, 1999). However, the self has not always been perceived this way. Florida State University psychologist Roy F. Baumeister has traced the changes in the Western concept of the self throughout Western history and has noted the factors influencing these changes. In this section, we review the concept of the self through history (Baumeister, 1986a, 1987, 1995, 1999).

Late Medieval Period (1000s through 1400s): You Are What You Do

During the late medieval period, knowledge of the self was not considered very important. There was little concern for introspection and self-reflection about personal behavior. More emphasis was placed on the spiritual soul, on what happens after death, and on the population's collective salvation than on people's self-knowledge and understanding. For the most part, the sense of self was linked to a person's place in the social hierarchy, which was based on the services that person provided (e.g., "Hans the blacksmith") or the details of his or her family background (e.g., "Countess Maria of York"). Thus, an individual's sense of self was equated with what she or he did – in other words, with the social or public self.

Early Modern Period (1500s through early 1700s): Examining the Inner Self of Others

Toward the end of the late medieval period, social mobility increased (e.g., commoners gained access to the aristocracy through marriage) and the social hierarchy began to weaken. As a result, emphasis on the sense of self as reflected by birth status or occupation began to decrease.

At the same time, emphasis on the private self began to increase. During the 1500s, people believed that a hidden aspect of the self resided inside each person that was quite different from the individual's public image. Also during this time, people were concerned with the notion that people's public behavior did not

Roy F. Baumeister has made many significant contributions to the study of the self, including his intriguing analysis of how the concept of the self has changed in response to religious, philosophical, economic, and technical changes throughout history.

necessarily reflect their private beliefs and values. In this social setting Shakespeare wrote his great works describing the moral conflict between the public behavior and private desires of his characters that we still find so enjoyable and relevant today. But the emphasis during this period was on knowing the inner self of others, rather than one's own private self.

Puritan Era (late 1500s to late 1600s): The Beginnings of a Concern for Self-Awareness

During the Puritan era, the focus shifted from trying to know others to trying to know one's self. This shift in emphasis can be explained in the context of the Puritan doctrine of *predestination*, which proposed that people were destined either to heaven or to hell. As you can imagine, because people wanted to know the direction of their fate, they began to look within themselves for signs that offered a clue to their destination. The Puritans thought one possible clue might be the degree of success achieved in their public life. The Puritan emphasis on work as the road to salvation was thus used to maximize the direction of a person's fate towards going to heaven. During this time, such terms as *self-awareness* and *consciousness* began to be used with the meanings they still have today (Whyte, 1960).

Romantic Era (late 1700s and early 1800s): Fulfilling the Hidden Self

The Romantic era was characterized by a sense of conflict between the individual and society. The source of the conflict was a shift from the prevailing view of the Puritan-era society that an individual's fate was predetermined to the emerging view of the Romantic era that individuals were in charge of their own destiny (Baumeister, 1999). Specifically, the unique destiny of each person was now emphasized; his or her task was to discover what that predetermined destiny was and to fulfill it. This concern for self-discovery led to an increased emphasis on self-knowledge and exploration of the hidden self. The idea of the hidden self reflected the notion of what we might consider today as "personality" (i.e., characteristics within the individual), which began to replace social rank and social roles as the central aspect of the self.

In contrast to individual salvation occurring in the afterlife as described in the Puritan era, people in the Romantic era emphasized individual fulfillment while on earth. This took the form of a rich inner life, "focused on work, especially creative arts, and inner passion, especially love" (Baumeister, 1987, p. 167). The focus during the Romantic era on personal fulfillment through living a "rich, full life" based on individual passions and creative efforts sounds very much like the concept of self-actualization proposed by Carl Rogers and Abraham Maslow (see Chapter 6).

Victorian Era (approximately 1830 to early 1900s): The Emergence of Freud's Ideas

During the Victorian era, the emphasis on individuality continued to grow. But the excessively high moral standards brought about by the influence of the conservative reign of Queen Victoria made such self-examination by Victorians difficult. As a result, a tendency developed for the Victorians to become self-deceptive and deny certain aspects of their personality (Houghton, 1957). During this time people were anxious that others would be able know their private thoughts and wishes by looking at their clothes or other assorted behavioral subtleties. In reaction to their fears of unintentionally revealing the private self, people's urban clothing styles became more modest in appearance (Sennett, 1974). In fact, many Victorian women who had the choice simply refused to be seen in public during daylight for fear of being looked at by others (Sennett, 1974).

During this time, Freud proposed his psychosexual stages to describe the intrapsychic conflicts involving people's desires and societal constraints (see Chapter 3). He also began to describe the serious consequences of excessive self-deception (i.e., neuroses), occurring when people failed to successfully resolve their intrapsychic conflicts. Thus, the Romantic emphasis on the expression of the individual's desires, conflicting with the realities of a restrictive Victorian society, created the right psychological climate for Freud's ideas.

Early 20th Century (1900 to 1940s): The Alienated Self

During the early part of the 20th century, Freud had a tremendous influence on how people began to perceive the self. He emphasized the significance of the hidden, unconscious aspects of the self (i.e., the id) while devaluing the conscious aspects of the self. Thus he proposed that, because of an assortment of psychological threats and defenses, complete self-knowledge was not possible.

Another general characteristic of the view of the self during the early 1900s was the sense of alienation people began to feel as they perceived self-sufficiency becoming increasingly obsolete. The demise of family-owned farms and of small neighborhood businesses (e.g., mom-and-pop groceries), along with the economic depression produced by the 1929 stock market crash, helped create this sense of alienation. The increasing presence of assembly-line work, which offered little opportunity for individual self-expression or personal identification and satisfaction with the product being made, also contributed to feelings of alienation. People began to experience a loss of their sense of personal identity as they became more dependent on society.

Late 20th Century through Early 21st Century: The Search for Uniqueness in a Collective Society

After World War II and during the latter part of the 20th century, although an ever-increasing bureaucracy of government programs and corporate industrialization continued to foster a sense of self characterized by alienation, people began to assert their sense of individuality, searching for their own "special place" in society. Such a shift was brought about, in part, by advances in mass communication, such as the growing ownership of televisions and mass marketing, that triggered "new ideas about how people could possibly live in a world of mass media and mass production, while yet finding individuality and satisfaction, [and] began to point the way toward a less dismal view" (Baumeister, 1999, p. 4). The contemporary view of self emphasizes each person's uniqueness. Thus, this view also emphasizes self-exploration and self-discovery as a means of finding personal uniqueness within this collective atmosphere. Phrases like "getting in touch with yourself" or "finding out who I really am" reflect this late 20th-century view of the self.

People pursued self-exploration and self-discovery through such means as hallucinogenic drugs during the 1960s, encounter groups during the 1970s, and personal growth seminars during the 1980s. The resurgence of interest in Native American Indian rituals and Eastern religions as part of the New Age spiritual movement during the 1990s, and the continued proliferation of self-help books and nonprint media in the early 2000s, are signs of a contemporary view of the self that is unlike those from 50 years ago – and extremely unlike those from some 500 years ago. Thus, as Baumeister (1987) eloquently summarizes the contemporary state of the self, "Recent trends suggest that the individual has accepted the state of being immersed in and dependent on society and is struggling to find meaning and fulfillment within those limitations" (p. 171).

As we have seen in this section, the self has evolved over time in a manner that is linked to many different historical factors and influences, including religious, sociological, psychological, and economic ones. A summary of the major points noted in this section is presented in "Summing It Up: Views of the Self through History" on p. 465. For more information on the historical developments of the concept of the self, read an article titled "How the Self Became a Problem: A Psychological Review of Historical Research" (Baumeister, 1987) and the book titled *Identity: Cultural Change and the Struggle for the Self* (Baumeister, 1986a).

Dimensions of the Self-Concept: The Internal and External Sense of Self

At the turn of the century, William James, the founder of psychology in America, described two different aspects of the self: the spiritual self and the social self (James, 1890). For James, the *spiritual self* refers to an inner or personal sense of self – the thoughts and feelings that help define your sense of self. The *social self*, on the other hand, refers to an external or public sense of self obtained through the recognition of others. As an indication of its importance, the distinction between the personal and public aspects of the self has gone through many psychological and sociological variations but has managed to survive more than 100 years (Brown, 1998; Buss, 2001; Cheek, 1989; Hogan & Cheek, 1983; Hoyle et al., 1999). In this section, we will explore some contemporary views of the public and private dimensions of the self-concept.

Discussions of the self include distinguishing between private and public aspects (Brown, 1998; Buss, 2001; Davis & Franzoi, 1991). **Private self-awareness** refers to an awareness of those aspects of the self that are

Summing It Up *Views of the Self through History*

Time Period	View of the Self	Example
Late Medieval (1000s through 1400s)	A sense of self was determined by one's occupation or social position.	People might be identified as "David the carpenter" or "the duke of York."
Early Modern (1500s through early 1700s)	A sense of self reflected one's public behavior and an interest in the inner self of others.	While Sara is careful to behave conservatively in public, she spends a lot of time thinking about the king's true motives for sending soldiers to the New World to "save the souls of the savages."
Puritan Era (late 1500s to late 1600s)	Individuals engaged in self-reflection to find a sign of their fate after death.	Being successful and living a good life were signs of going to heaven in the afterlife.
Romantic Era (late 1700s and early 1800s)	Individuals searched their inner self to help find their unique destiny.	Raul's passion for painting influenced his decision to be an artist, instead of a baker like his father and brother.
Victorian Era (approximately 1830 to early 1900s)	High moral standards prevented Victorian individuals from expressing their true inner self and fostered self-deception.	Frances channeled her sexual desires into her charitable activities at the mission.
Early 20th Century (1900 to 1940s)	A sense of alienation from the self increased as mass-production technology replaced self-sufficiency.	The sense of pride Alice once received from her hand-crafted vases was lost when she went to work on an assembly line.
Late 20th Century through Early 21st Century	Individuals seek to find a sense of uniqueness as an ever-increasing bureaucracy fosters a sense of collectivism.	Frank wears a nose ring and 5-inch blue Mohawk to express his individuality at work as a data processor.

hidden from the public, such as our thoughts, feelings, desires, dreams, fantasies, and attitudes. **Public self-awareness** refers to an awareness of those aspects of the self that can be viewed by others, such as public statements, overt expressions of emotion, and appearance. In this section, we will examine contemporary topics in personality research that illustrate the distinction between the private/internal and public/external aspects of the self-concept. This presentation will include the topics of public and private self-consciousness, objective self-awareness, the control-theory model of the self, self-monitoring, and identity orientations. It is to these topics that you will next turn your attention.

Self-Consciousness: Private and Public Perspectives on the Self

Self-consciousness is a personality trait that refers to an individual's tendency to be attentive to his or her sense of self (Buss, 2001; Davis & Franzoi, 1991; Hoyle et al., 1999). Research on the topic of self-consciousness has been triggered by the work of Michael Scheier, of Carnegie Mellon University; Charles Carver, of the University of Miami; and Arnold Buss, of the University of Texas at Austin. In their work, Scheier, Carver, and Buss (Buss, 1980, 1995, 2001; Carver & Scheier, 1981a) have proposed both private and public aspects of self-consciousness.

Private self-consciousness refers to a tendency to be in a constant state of internal self-analysis and reflection. For example, people who are very privately self-conscious regularly try to figure themselves out, examine their motives, and generally focus on such internal aspects as thoughts, fantasies, and emotions. The guiding principle of people who are privately self-conscious might be "Get in touch with thoughts and feelings."

Public self-consciousness refers to a state of knowledge-seeking that is characterized by an external self-analysis regarding public appearance. People who are publicly self-conscious are very concerned with their personal attributes and social behavior, including how they look, what they say, what they do, and the general impression they make on others. The guiding principle of people who are publicly self-conscious might be "It's better to look good than to feel good." Thus, while privately self-conscious people are more internally focused on their sense of self, publicly self-conscious people are more externally focused on their sense of self.

Measuring Public and Private Self-Consciousness: The Self-Consciousness Scale

Like any other significant personality dimension, public and private self-consciousness vary from one person to another. Such individual differences in self-consciousness can be assessed using the Self-Consciousness Scale (SCS; Fenigstein, Scheier, & Buss, 1975; Scheier & Carver, 1985). The SCS is designed to assess the extent to which people:

- Are generally preoccupied with their past, present, and future behavior.
- Display inner sensitivity to their feelings.
- Are able to recognize their positive and negative attributes.
- Possess introspective tendencies.
- Are able to visualize the self.
- Are aware of the impression they make on others.
- Are concerned with the evaluations others have of them.

The original and most-used version of the SCS consists of 10 items measuring private self-consciousness (i.e., the extent to which an individual habitually engages in internal self-analysis and examination) and 7 items measuring public self-consciousness (i.e., the

extent to which an individual habitually engages in external self-analysis and examination). People are asked to respond to each item on a five-point, fixed-format scale ranging from 0 (extremely uncharacteristic [not like me]) to 4 (extremely characteristic [very much like me]). Following is a subset of items from the SCS:

> Private self-consciousness items:
> I'm always trying to figure myself out.
> I sometimes have the feeling that I'm off somewhere watching myself.
> I'm aware of the way my mind works when I work through a problem.
> Public self-consciousness items:
> I'm concerned about my style of doing things.
> I usually worry about making a good impression.
> One of the last things I do before leaving the house is look in the mirror.

Correlates of Self-Consciousness

People who score high in private or public self-consciousness reflect specific patterns of thoughts, feelings, and behaviors that are characterized by the utilization of either an internal or external reference, respectively, as the point of focus for their sense of self. The following subsections describe some characteristics of privately self-conscious and publicly self-conscious people.

Characteristics of Private Self-Consciousness: Matching an Internal Sense of Awareness with Your Actions and Feelings People who score high in private self-consciousness match an internal sense of awareness with their actions and feelings. Because such individuals are less concerned with the impression they make on others than are people who are low in private self-consciousness, you would expect the former to behave in ways that reflect their true internal feelings and beliefs. Research supports this reasoning. When college students were tested to measure aggressiveness and were subsequently given the opportunity to deliver electric shocks to others as part of a psychology experiment, the very privately self-conscious students demonstrated a closer relationship between their aggressive scores and their aggressive behavior. In other words, students with high aggression scores delivered more shocks while students with lower aggression scores delivered fewer shocks (Scheier, Buss, & Buss, 1978).

Similarly, when college students were asked to complete a self-report questionnaire on altruism and then were subsequently given the opportunity to help another individual, the students who were very privately self-conscious demonstrated a closer relationship between their self-report level of altruism and their actual tendency to help (e.g., highly altruistic people offered more help) than did students who were less privately self-conscious (Smith & Shaffer, 1986). As another measure of their increased sense of self-awareness, high privately self-conscious participants were much less likely to change their attitudes and opinions in response to external sources of information than were low privately self-conscious people (Scheier, Carver, & Gibbons, 1979; Carver & Scheier, 1981b).

People high in private self-consciousness also demonstrate a greater sense of emotional awareness than do people who score low in private self-consciousness. For example, when men were shown slides of nude women and slides of atrocities (e.g., dead bodies piled up) and then asked to give their emotional reaction to these slides, people high in private self-consciousness offered more extreme reactions than did those scoring low in it (Scheier & Carver, 1977). Specifically, high privately self-conscious people rated the nude slides as more emotionally pleasant and the atrocity slides as more unpleasant than did low privately self-conscious individuals.

Other research indicates that high privately self-conscious people exhibit more laughter in response to humorous material (Porterfield et al., 1988), show more aggressive behavior when made angry by others (Scheier, 1976), and display more bodily symptoms (e.g., increased heart rate, muscle tension) in reaction to external stressors (e.g., time pressures; Frone & McFarlin, 1989) than do low privately self-consciousness individuals. Finally, in addition to responding with more extreme emotional reactions, privately self-conscious people are more likely to consume greater amounts of alcohol in response to personal failure (Hull & Young, 1983) and negative life events (Hull, Young, & Jouriles, 1986) than are less privately self-conscious people. Apparently, high privately self-conscious people use the alcohol to help reduce the emotional intensity of the unpleasant events brought on as a result of their increased sense of personal self-awareness.

Consistent with this reasoning, when keeping a diary of their daily moods, individuals high in private self-consciousness reported more negative moods at work and at home, as well as when involved in negative social interactions, than did those low in private self-consciousness (Flory, Raikkonen, Matthews, & Qwens, 2000). This pattern may reflect the tendency of individuals high in private self-consciousness to ruminate (i.e., to obsessively ponder or contemplate) to a greater extent (Trapnell & Campbell, 1999). For example, a student high in public self-consciousness who answers a question incorrectly when called upon in class will probably spend the rest of the afternoon ruminating over the mistake, thus creating a sense of misery. As a result, she may go home that evening and drink to deal with the event.

Characteristics of Public Self-Consciousness: Seeking an External Sense of Awareness for Your Beliefs and Actions   Whereas privately self-conscious people are more focused on their internal sense of self, publicly self-conscious people are more focused on seeking an external sense of awareness for their beliefs and actions. Thus, you would expect people high in public self-consciousness to be more concerned about and aware of their physical appearance than are those who are low in public self-consciousness. Along these lines, you would predict that high publicly self-conscious people would use more makeup to enhance their physical appearance and social interactions than would low publicly self-conscious people. In support of this reasoning, researchers noted that high publicly self-conscious women wore more makeup (e.g., lipstick, eye shadow) than did low publicly self-conscious women to an experimental situation in which they were forewarned that their pictures would be taken (L. C. Miller & Cox, 1982). In a similar concern for their physical appearance, men scoring on high public self-consciousness displayed a heightened concern about losing their hair (Franzoi, Anderson, & Frommelt, 1990).

Consistent with this emphasis on the external sense of self, high publicly self-conscious people are judged to be more physically attractive by other participants (L. C. Miller & Cox, 1982; Turner, Gilliland, & Klein, 1981), react more quickly when asked to rate their physical features (Turner et al., 1981), are better than low publicly self-conscious people at predicting the impression they will make on others (Tobey & Tunnell, 1981), and are more aware of how much they use expressive gestures, such as moving their hands and arms when talking (Gallaher, 1992) . Among the additional evidence supporting the significance attached to their public image is that high scorers on public self-consciousness also attached greater importance to discrepancies from their ideal level of physical attractiveness (Cash & Szymanski, 1995) and endorsed the belief that physical appearance plays an important role in one's life (Cash & Labarge, 1996) more than did low scorers.

People who score high in public self-consciousness also demonstrate this tendency toward an external sense of self when interacting with others. Compared with low-scoring publicly self-conscious people, high scorers are more likely to assume personal responsibility for how much others like or dislike them and for the feelings they create in others (Fenigstein, 1979, 1984), are more conforming to external norms (Froming & Carver, 1981), are more likely to change their attitudes in the direction of their public behavior over private beliefs (Scheier & Carver, 1980), are more likely to express a preference for national-brand products with a more favorable public image than for bargain-brand products (Bushman, 1993), and are more concerned about making a good impression than about doing what is fair or morally right (Greenberg, 1983; Kernis & Reis, 1984).

Finally, high publicly self-conscious people tend to exhibit a tendency toward thoughts of paranoid ideation (e.g., "I am suspicious of overly friendly people," "Someone has it in for me"; Buss & Perry, 1992; Fenigstein & Vanable, 1992). Such paranoid ideation is an extreme example of a normal tendency to focus on the self as a social object, rather than being equivalent to paranoia in a psychopathologic sense (Buss, 1995, 2001). Again, what we see in this list of behaviors is the tendency of people high in public self-consciousness to place more emphasis on external factors than on internal awareness when interacting with others.

Objective Self-Awareness: A Case of Situationally Induced Self-Consciousness

In addition to individual differences in the trait of self-consciousness, situational conditions can also induce public self-consciousness. Some of these situational conditions include receiving too much attention from others, as when standing in front of an audience, or receiving too little attention, as when being ignored at a party (Buss, 1995, 2001). In both cases, you begin to focus more attention on your sense of self as a social object when you feel scrutinized and evaluated by others.

Creating a Sense of Increased Self-Reflection

A number of situational conditions are known to increase an individual's sense of private self-consciousness. For example, filming or taping people with a camera, videotape recorder, or tape recorder can amplify certain characteristics of private self-consciousness, such as self-analysis and self-reflection.

One of the simplest and most interesting ways to increase a person's sense of private self-consciousness is to place him or her in front of a mirror. According to Duval and Wicklund (S. Duval & Wicklund, 1972), placing people in front of a mirror increases their private self-consciousness by creating a state of **objective self-awareness**, a condition in which people are made more aware of their internal feelings and beliefs (T. S. Duval & Silvia, 2001; Silvia & Gendolla, 2001). When people feel more objectively self-aware (e.g., because of seeing their reflection in a mirror, having their voice tape-recorded, or being in front of a video camera), they are also more aware of any discrepancy between their internal feelings and beliefs and their external behavior (Davis & Franzoi, 1991; S. Duval & Wicklund, 1972; T. S. Duval & Silvia, 2002; Silvia & Gendolla, 2001).

Coping with Increases in Objective Self-Awareness

The increased awareness of this discrepancy between internal feelings and beliefs and external behavior creates a state of uneasiness that people try to reduce or eliminate (Silvia & Gendolla, 2001) through escape or reconciliation. The first way of coping with this discrepancy is to avoid situations that make you feel self-aware. For example, people who were led to believe that they had "failed" to do well on an IQ test spent less time sitting in a waiting room that contained a mirror facing them than did people in the same room without the mirror (Duval, Wicklund, & Fine, described in S. Duval & Wicklund, 1972). Apparently, it was more comforting for some of these people to leave after a failure than to have to look at themselves in the mirror. Similarly, when asked to write about their own mortality, individuals placed in front of a mirror spent less time in their cubicle doing so than when the mirror was not present (Arndt, Greenberg, Simon, Pyszczynski, & Solomon, 1998).

The second way of coping with the discrepancy created by an increased sense of objective self-awareness is to make your external behavior more consistent with your internal standards. For example, people who favored the use of punishment delivered more electric shocks to others when they were supposedly given the opportunity to do so while sitting facing a mirror than did people with similar internal beliefs who were not facing a mirror (Carver, 1975). In a similar manner, people show a greater degree of similarity between their self-reported rating of sociability and their observed sociability when given the opportunity to interact with others when a mirror is present than when the mirror is absent (Pryor, Gibbons, Wicklund, Fazio, & Hood, 1977). When faced with the pressure to conform to the attitudes of others, the people in the presence of a mirror were more likely to "stick to their guns" and stay with their own internal beliefs than were people with no mirror present (Carver, 1977).

As an indication of a greater sense of self-reflection, patients in a Veterans Administration hospital recalled their medical history more accurately when placed in front of a mirror than did people not exposed to the mirror (Gibbons et al., 1985). In a similar manner, psychiatric patients who responded to questions regarding their feelings of anxiety, hostility, and depression in front of a mirror reported more intense negative feelings than did people who answered the same questions in the absence of the mirror (Gibbons et al., 1985). Thus, all of these studies indicate that when confronted with an increased sense of objective self-awareness as a result of being exposed to a mirror, people are much more likely to behave in a manner that is consistent with their internal feelings and beliefs than are people who are not exposed to the mirror. This pattern of results is very consistent with the high degree of self-analysis and self-reflection characteristic of privately self-conscious people (Buss, 1995, 2001).

From the research just described, it is clear that creating a sense of self-awareness through the use of a mirror can help people to bring their external behavior more in line with their internal feelings and beliefs. Use this information to your advantage by trying the procedures described in "Applications in Personality Psychology" below.

Applications in Personality Psychology

Mirror, Mirror on the Wall: Using Objective Self-Awareness as a Study Aid

If you must study this evening, why not use what you know about objective self-awareness to help yourself study more? Instead of studying the way you normally do, place a small mirror in front of you. The logic here is that having the mirror there will make more salient the internal beliefs you have about your desire to study. Ideally, being in front of the mirror will make it more likely that you will bring your external behavior of studying in line with the internal desire regarding the need to study, and, as a result, you may spend more time studying.

A Tip to Remember

Remember that the mirror may make you feel uncomfortable if your external behavior is not meeting your increased awareness of your internal standards. In this case, you may feel uncomfortable if you know you have to study, but you see yourself in the mirror not studying (e.g., daydreaming or doodling). Be aware that you may try to deal with this uneasiness by altering your internal standards (e.g., telling yourself that it's not really all that important that you study tonight) or leaving the situation (e.g., getting up to call a friend, watching some television, or going to a movie). Instead of avoiding this situation, try telling yourself that this is a new study procedure for you, and that it may just take a little time for you to feel comfortable using it.

Try using the mirror as a study aid for the next couple of weeks, and record the amount of time you spend studying. If this works for you, don't forget to share it with a friend.

The Control-Theory Model of the Self: Finding Common Ground between the Trait of Self-Consciousness and the State of Objective Self-Awareness

Although we have discussed the trait of self-consciousness and the state of self-awareness separately in this chapter, the control-theory model of the self, proposed by Charles Carver and Michael Scheier (1981a, 1990, 1998, 1999a, 1999b), attempts to unify this body of research and other aspects of self-control and self-regulation. The **control-theory model** (**CTM**) proposes that people regulate their behavior by making a series of comparisons against preexisting standards, until the behavior matches the standards. In the CTM, self-focused attention helps to determine the nature of the preexisting standard to be used. If the self-focus of attention is inward, the individual is likely to use a preexisting internal standard of comparison (e.g., personal beliefs, attitudes, and desires). On the other hand, if the self-focus of attention is outward, the individual is likely to use a preexisting external standard of comparison (e.g., the views expressed by others).

The Self-Focused Attention Feedback Loop

According to the CTM, a feedback loop exists comprising attention, comparison, action, reexamination, and termination. Self-focused *attention* increases the likelihood of a person making a *comparison* between a current state (e.g., what the person is thinking or doing) and a preexisting standard (e.g., a desire or personal attitude). If there is a discrepancy between the current state and the preexisting standard, the person then takes *action* to reduce or eliminate this difference. After taking action, the person then compares the present state with the standard, engaging in *reexamination* to determine whether the discrepancy still exists. If it does, additional action is taken and the comparison is made again. Once the discrepancy has been eliminated, *termination* occurs; the person stops this sequence until another instance of self-focused attention makes salient this new discrepancy between the current state and the preexisting standard.

For example, suppose that a woman is approached on the street by a news reporter, who asks about her views on capital punishment. Being confronted in this

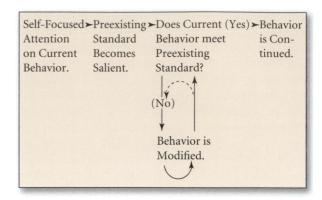

Figure 11.2 According to the control-model theory, self-focused attention creates a feedback loop that results from continuously comparing modifications in behavior to a preexisting standard. When the behavior meets the preexisting standard, the loop is broken.

manner is likely to create a state of self-focused attention that will prompt the woman to examine her views on capital punishment. If she says she is in favor of capital punishment (i.e., a preexisting standard), she will continue to present her views (i.e., external action) to the reporter until she feels that her statements reflect her actual views (i.e., the preexisting standard). As illustrated in Figure 11.2, the CTM is based on a feedback loop that involves an attempt to regulate current behavior so that it is consistent with some preexisting standard.

CTM and Private Self-Focused Attention

The CTM can be used to explain the behavior of people who are made privately self-aware by situational circumstances (e.g., being placed before a mirror) or who are high in the trait of private self-consciousness (e.g., have a high SCS score). The CTM predicts that because of their increased tendency to engage in a greater degree of self-analysis and self-reflection, such people are more likely to use an internal standard of comparison to regulate their behavior (Carver & Scheier, 1981a, 1998, 1999a, 1999b).

For example, a college student who is getting ready for school may be looking at herself in the mirror while listening to a radio talk-show host discuss the issue of using capital punishment as a method of crime prevention. In this situation, she is very likely to reflect on and analyze her personal views in deciding how she will vote in the next state referendum to reinstate the death penalty. In a similar manner, as he listens to this same radio program in his car while driving to school, an accountant high in private self-consciousness is also very likely to engage in the process of self-analysis and self-reflection in deciding how he is going to vote on this issue. In these two cases, the state of private self-awareness and the trait of private self-consciousness are both likely to promote the use of an internal standard of comparison when regulating behavior.

CTM and Public Self-Focused Attention

The CTM also helps to explain the behavior of people who are made publicly self-aware by situational circumstances (e.g., being in the presence of others who will be judging them) or who are high in the trait of public self-awareness (e.g., have a high SCS score). The CTM predicts that these people are likely to use an external standard of comparison to regulate their behavior, because of their tendency to view the self as a social object that is subject to the scrutiny of others

(Buss, 1995, 2001; Carver & Scheier, 1981a, 1998; Davis & Franzoi, 1991). For example, to decide how to vote about the issue of increasing the gasoline tax in the next election, while one person might use a conversation he had with others about this issue (i.e., a situationally induced state of public self-awareness), another person high in the trait of public self-consciousness might use what she read in the student newspaper (i.e., a tendency of publicly self-conscious people to rely on the views of others).

The private and public aspects of the self thus can be viewed from the perspective of individual differences in self-consciousness or from the situationally induced state of objective self-awareness; and both of these aspects of self-focused attention can be linked with the CTM of the self.

A summary of the principal points discussed in this section is presented in "Summing It Up: Dimensions of

Summing It Up *Dimensions of the Self-Concept: Private and Public Self-Consciousness*

Concept	Definition	Example
Private Self-Awareness	An awareness of the internal aspects of the self	Sally senses that she is becoming more anxious as she begins her speech.
Public Self-Awareness	An awareness of one's overt actions and features	Sue is worried that her audience seems bored with her speech.
Private Self-Consciousness	Individual differences in the tendency to engage in self-reflection based on internal sources of reference	Bill tries to make sure that his views about fairness are reflected in his treatment of all his customers.
Public Self-Consciousness	Individual differences in the tendency to engage in self-analysis based on external sources of reference	Bob makes sure that his comments in the meeting reflect what everyone else believes.
Self-Consciousness Scale (SCS)	A personality test that assesses individual differences in private and public self-consciousness	Items from the SCS: "I reflect on myself a lot (private SC)," "I'm self-conscious about the way I look" (public SC).
Objective Self-Awareness	A situationally induced sense of self-consciousness	Joan feels her anxiety rising as she looks into a mirror while waiting to deliver her speech.
Control-Theory Model (CTM)	A model of behavior using a feedback loop based on a preexisting standard to regulate the actions of self-conscious and objectively self-aware individuals	While John uses his own values to decide what to say, Julie uses the opinions of others.

the Self-Concept: Private and Public Self-Consciousness" on p. 471. For more information related to the topics of public and private dimensions of the self, read *Self-Consciousness and Social Anxiety* (Buss, 1980), *On the Self-Regulation of Behavior* (Carver & Scheier, 1998), *Self-Awareness and Causal Attributions: A Dual-Systems Theory* (T. S. Duval & Silvia, 2001), or *Public Self and Private Self* (Baumeister, 1986b). The information in this section illustrates how individuals attempt to reconcile the personal and public dimensions of the self-concept while dealing with a variety of everyday situations. In the next section, we will discuss a dimension of the self-concept that does just the opposite – helps individuals to present a public self that is different from the private self while interacting with others.

Self-Monitoring: The Public Appearance and Private Reality of the Self-Concept

In addition to the dimensions of self-consciousness and objective self-awareness, another interesting relationship that has received considerable attention is that between the public appearance and the private realities of the self (Osborne, 1996; Snyder, 1987). The public appearance of the self is the image we present to others through our words and deeds in various social situations. The private reality of the self represents our true feelings and beliefs. For example, while you may be really bored with the conversation at a party (i.e., private beliefs), you continue to nod your head, maintain eye contact, and ask questions to give the public impression of being interested. Just as the construct of self-consciousness captures the relationship between the real and ideal aspects of the self-concept, the construct of **self-monitoring** links the relationship between the public appearances and private realities of the self-concept. In this section, you will consider the nature, measurement, and applications of the self-monitoring aspect of the self-concept.

The Nature of Self-Monitoring: Putting Your Best Personality Forward

Much of what we know about the construct of self-monitoring is based on the research of Mark Snyder. According to Snyder (1987), people vary in the extent to which they monitor or regulate the nature of the public appearance they present to others during their social and interpersonal relationships.

High self-monitors are people who are able to control to a great degree the image they present to others, regardless of how they might actually be feeling or thinking. Research indicates that high self-monitors are less likely to behave in ways that agree with their true attitudes and more likely to publicly express an attitude that they really do not believe (Zanna & Olson, 1982). An example of a high self-monitor might be a politician who agrees with and is friendly toward whomever he or she happens to be speaking to at the time, regardless of how he or she really feels about these people.

Low self-monitors are people who are less concerned with determining the nature of the situation and generating a public appearance that matches it. Because they are more concerned with expressing their true feelings and behavior, regardless of the social situation, they tend to display more consistent behavior than do high self-monitors. In support of this reasoning, research indicates that people identified as low self-monitors tend to express public opinions that are consistent with their private beliefs (McCann & Hancock, 1983; Mellema & Bassili, 1995). An example of low self-monitors might be political protesters who say what they really believe despite the threat of arrest.

The Measurement of Self-Monitoring: The Self-Monitoring Scale

The Self-Monitoring Scale is used to identify people who are considered high and low self-monitors (Snyder, 1974). The **Self-Monitoring Scale** is an objective self-report inventory containing 25 true–false self-descriptive statements that assess the extent to which people feel they are able to use social cues to regulate and control their behavior to look, do, and say what is considered appropriate for any given situation. People who are high self-monitors would tend to endorse items on the Self-Monitoring Scale such as, "In different situations and with different people, I often act like very different persons." On the other hand, people who are low self-monitors would tend to endorse items such as, "I have trouble changing my behavior to suit different people and different situations" (Snyder, 1987, pp. 16–17). To get some firsthand experience with assessing your own level of self-monitoring, try "You Can Do It" on p. 473.

You Can Do It

Identifying Interpersonal Actors: Assessment of Self-Monitoring

For each of the following six items, answer "true" or "false" to indicate whether or not the item describes you.

1. I find it hard to imitate the behavior of other people.
2. I guess I put on a show to impress or entertain people.
3. In a group of people, I am rarely the center of attention.
4. I have considered being an entertainer.
5. I am not particularly good at making other people like me.
6. I sometimes appear to others to be experiencing deeper emotions than I actually am.

Scoring

If you answered "false" to items 1, 3, and 5, give yourself one point. If you answered "true" to items 2, 4, and 6, give yourself one point. Now add the total number of points you have received. The higher your score, the more you express opinions characteristic of high self-monitoring.

Interpretation

High self-monitors perceive themselves as being able to convincingly produce whatever self-presentation image seems appropriate for the present situation. They also perceive themselves to be good actors in social situations. On the other hand, low self-monitors see themselves as not being skillful enough actors to present themselves in any other way than "being themselves" (Snyder, 1987). Be aware that most people are not exclusively high or low self-monitors, but typically fall somewhere in the middle when responding to the complete set of items on the Self-Monitoring Scale. Also be aware that there is some disagreement regarding what is being measured by the Self-Monitoring Scale (Briggs & Cheek, 1988; Briggs, Cheek, & Buss, 1980; Osborne, 1996).

To Be or Not to Be . . . a High or Low Self-Monitor: Which Is Better?

The construct of self-monitoring represents a particular style of interacting with others – nothing more. Neither a high self-monitoring nor a low self-monitoring style is better than the other (Osborne, 1996; Ross, 1992; Snyder, 1987). Rather than a separate construct, self-monitoring must be considered as part of a more general pattern of events occurring during social interactions (Karoly, 1993). In addition to simply being able to monitor a given situation, people must assess what the behavioral alternatives are in that situation, how well they believe they can perform any of these behaviors, and the likelihood of which behavior will produce the greatest reward. An individual may be good at monitoring what behaviors are appropriate for the situation, but may not be able to perform any of them well. In certain situations, a high self-monitoring and a low self-monitoring individual might behave in a similar manner just by leaving the scene after realizing that neither has what it takes to operate successfully.

Putting Self-Monitoring in Perspective: A Combination of Personality Characteristics

Rather than trying to decide whether high or low self-monitoring is better than the other, what is more important is how the self-monitoring construct is combined with other personality characteristics in an individual's total personality. For example, a high self-monitoring individual who possesses a low degree of guilt feelings might be someone to avoid. Such an individual would probably be the prototypical "con artist," doing or saying whatever is needed without worrying about the consequences for others. On the other hand, a high self-monitoring individual with a high degree of empathy might be just the person you want to be around if you are distressed. In such a situation, you would want someone to respond by being sensitive to your needs and presenting a comforting demeanor, even if that person was also distressed. A low self-monitoring individual with a high degree of hostility might be prone to expressing these feelings of hostility without regard to the surrounding situation.

While it may not be possible, nor is it necessary, to pass judgment about the nature of high and low self-monitors, this construct is of some value in understanding important aspects of our behavior. In the next section, you will consider some applications of the self-monitoring construct.

Applications of Self-Monitoring: Using What Is Known

One way to determine the value of a construct in personality psychology is to consider how extensively it has been applied to various issues in our everyday living experiences. On this measure, the construct of self-monitoring has demonstrated a rather large degree of utility. In this section, you will learn how self-monitoring has been applied to the areas of advertising, consumer behavior, and career counseling.

Advertising: The "Soft" vs. the "Hard" Sell Two approaches taken to the advertising of products involve the "hard sell" and the "soft sell" (Fox, 1984). The soft sell is based on images consumers may be able to project as a result of using a particular product. Ads that stress using a particular brand of toothpaste to give you sex appeal or drinking a certain type of beer to make you a "party animal" are soft-sell ads. In contrast, the hard sell is an approach to advertising that involves stressing the quality, merits, and functional value of the product. Ads that stress buying a particular watch because it lasts a long time or the soft-drink taste-test challenges that attempt to persuade consumers to base their decision on the taste quality of the drinks are hard-sell ads. Thus, the soft sell stresses a public image for the consumer while the hard sell stresses the inherent features of the product.

As applied to self-monitoring, it has been found that high self-monitors evaluate image-oriented ads more favorably than product-oriented ads, while low self-monitors exhibit just the opposite pattern (DeBono & Packer, 1991; Snyder & DeBono, 1985b). High self-

monitors were also willing to pay more for a product if its ads stressed image rather than product quality, but low self-monitors were willing to pay more for quality than image.

The same response pattern was true for ads designed to get consumers not to engage in a particular behavior. In this case, the behavior the ads were trying to reduce was smoking. The image-oriented ads stressed "Bad breath, yellow teeth, smelly clothes . . . is smoking worth it?" while the health-quality-oriented ads stressed "Coughing, shortness of breath, sore throat . . . is smoking really worth it?" As you might expect by now, high self-monitors indicated the image-oriented ads to be more favorable and effective than the health-quality-oriented ads, while low self-monitors indicated just the opposite pattern (Snyder, Nettle, & DeBono, 1985). When asked to select ads that could be used to persuade others to be nonsmokers, once again, high self-monitors selected the image-quality ads while low self-monitors expressed a greater interest in using the health-quality-image ads. The pattern of these results makes it clear that high self-monitors respond to the soft sell while low self-monitors respond to the hard sell. To further explore this phenomenon for yourself, read "Applications in Personality Psychology" on p. 475.

Consumer Behavior: Choosing Form vs. Function In addition to the types of advertisements (e.g., image vs. quality) we are exposed to, part of the decision to purchase a product involves certain decisions by the consumer. In discussing the role of self-monitoring in consumer decisions, Snyder (1987) distinguishes between form and function. Consumer decisions made on the basis of form emphasize the outward characteristics of the product, not its inherent characteristics. For example, buying a sleek, flashy, imported sports car – even if it does not perform as well as less expensive domestic passenger cars – or drinking a premium beer offering higher status – even if it does not really taste any better than most of the less expensive beers – are decisions based on form. Consumer decisions made on the basis of function emphasize the inherent characteristics of the product. For example, buying the "generic" brand of beer because it is cheaper and tastes about as good as the "premium" brand, or buying clothes based on durability rather than "trendiness," are decisions based on function.

Linking self-monitoring to the form vs. function aspects of consumer behavior, Snyder (1987) suggests

Applications in Personality Psychology

Hard Sell, Soft Sell, and Self-Monitoring: The Linking of Personality Psychology and Advertising

To examine the extent to which others you know might respond differently to image-oriented and quality-oriented ads, have them select from the following four ads the two they believe to be the most effective.

Each time they select one of the image ads, give them 3 points; each time they select one of the quality ads, give them 1 point. Now add up their total points. Next have them answer the self-monitoring questions in "You Can Do It" on p. 473. According to what you have read so far, there should be some relationship between their score for this exercise and their self-monitoring score. Is there?

Adapted from Jones (1994).

that high self-monitors are more likely to base their consumer decisions on form, while low self-monitors are more likely to base their decisions on function. In support of this reasoning, it was discovered that low self-monitors are more likely to agree (i.e., 59 percent)

with the statement "I think generic products are just as good as name-brand products" to a greater degree than are high self-monitors (i.e., 42 percent; Snyder & DeBono, 1984). In another study, the subjects were asked to read one of two car performance test reports that they

Summing It Up *The Nature and Applications of Self-Monitoring*

Concept	Definition	Example
The Nature of Self-Monitoring	The tendency for individuals to control the nature of their public behavior	Some individuals put on a happy act even when they feel tired.
High Self-Monitoring Individuals	Individuals who tend to display public behavior that is dictated by the particular situation, regardless of their true feelings	While at the office party, Paul acts interested when his boss tells him the same boring stories about his vacation.
Low Self-Monitoring Individuals	Individuals who tend to display public behavior that is more in line with their true feelings and attitudes, regardless of the particular situation	While sitting in class, Jane is bored and reminds the instructor that she is repeating the same stories she talked about last week.
Self-Monitoring Scale	A single-dimension personality test consisting of 25 items that assesses the degree to which individuals express self-monitoring tendencies	Actors would score high on the Self-Monitoring Scale.
Some Applications of Self-Monitoring:		
Advertising	High self-monitors are more responsive to advertisements emphasizing the projection of a certain image (e.g., being popular) while low self-monitors are more responsive to advertisements emphasizing the quality of the product (e.g., durability).	As a high self-monitor, Julia is more persuaded by the glamorous actress in the ad for the toothpaste. As a low self-monitor, Jesse is more interested in the claims in the ad of the toothpaste's effectiveness in reducing reducing cavities.
Consumer Behavior	High self-monitors tend to make consumer decisions based on the overt features of the product (e.g., bright and bold colors) while low self-monitors tend to emphasize the inherent characteristics of the product (e.g., the guarantee).	As a high self-monitor, Judy buys shoes that are in style, even if they are not made very well. As a low self-monitor, Jackie looks for clothes that are well made, even if they are not the most stylish.
Career Counseling	High self-monitors tend to require more specific information (e.g., amount of vacation time and sales bonuses) when considering a job offer, as well as actively seek more information (e.g., reading company literature) when looking for a job, than do low self-monitors.	As a high self-monitor, Josh reads the employment ads in the local paper and visits the websites of various companies but focuses on only the starting salary and health benefits when looking for a job. As a low self-monitor, Abe talks to a career counselor about finding a job where it will be possible for him to fulfill his desire to help people with their personal problems.

thought were from *Consumer Reports*. In both cases, the car was described as being of average performance. But for some of the subjects, the picture attached to the report was of the very stylish Pontiac Fiero; the other report had a picture of the rather boxy-looking Volkswagen Rabbit. The results of this study indicated that even though there was no difference in the performance reports of the cars, high self-monitors rated the Fiero more favorably and judged it to be of higher quality. On the other hand, low self-monitors rated the

Rabbit more favorably and judged it to be of higher quality (Snyder & DeBono, 1985a). In considering the decision-making process that produced such results, it could be that high self-monitors equate looks with quality while low self-monitors may view flashy packaging as a way of covering up product weaknesses (Snyder, 1987).

Career Counseling: Self-Monitoring in the Workplace

One of the most important issues you are probably going to face during your college years is deciding what you want to do once you graduate. Seeking career counseling is one approach to this issue. One factor that might influence your decision about a job is the job description. For example, is the nature of the job clearly stated in detail (e.g., you will be required to work two weekends a month, entertaining clients in your home) or vaguely stated (e.g., you will be required to work some weekends)? In one study, it was reported that high self-monitors were more likely to accept a job only if they were given a high degree of detail about what they would be expected to do, while low self-monitors gave an equal preference for the job whether it was described in detail or quite vaguely (Snyder & Gangestad, 1982). This difference may reflect the tendency of high self-monitors to want to know as much as possible about the situation beforehand in order to present the most appropriate public appearance.

In addition to wanting to know specific details about a job, high self-monitors also seem to be rather specific in the strategies they use when seeking employment. High self-monitors were found to engage in such activities as setting a precise job goal, taking job interview training, and using reference groups to gain organizational contacts to a greater extent than were low self-monitors (Latham, 1985). Once again, the idea seems to be that high self-monitors are more likely to seek specific information that makes it possible to structure the situation so that they can present the most "appropriate" public self.

Finally, when deciding which applicant should receive a job offer, high self-monitors were found to base their personnel decisions to a greater extent on the physical appearance of the applicants than did low self-monitors, who tended to base their decisions on the personality disposition of the applicants (Snyder, Berscheid, & Matwychuk, 1988). From such research, it seems that when making personnel decisions, high self-monitors are more likely "to judge a book by its cover" than are low self-monitors. Thus, whether it involves making career decisions for themselves or

others, high self-monitors tend to rely more on the public presentation of the self than low self-monitors do.

This concludes the discussion of self-monitoring. A summary of the principal points discussed in this section is presented in "Summing It Up: The Nature and Applications of Self-Monitoring" on p. 476. If you would like to know more about the construct of self-monitoring, read Mark Snyder's (1987) award-winning book *Public Appearances/Private Realities: The Psychology of Self-Monitoring*. In the next section, we will consider the private and public dimensions of the self as based on identity orientation.

Identity Orientations: Personal and Social Determinants of the Self

Another approach to the conceptualization of the private and public dimensions of the self is the identity orientation framework proposed by Jonathan Cheek of Wellesley College (Banaji & Prentice, 1994; Brown, 1998; Robins, Norem, & Cheek, 1999). **Identity orientation** refers to the extent to which people focus their attention and effort on their internal characteristics or external environment when defining their identity (Cheek, 1989; Cheek, Tropp, Chen, & Underwood, 1994; Sampson, 1978).

Jonathan Cheek's work on aspects of identity helps us understand how our sense of identity can influence such important decisions as occupational choices and leisure-time activities.

Personal and Social Identity Orientations: Internal and External Points of Reference for a Sense of Self

Identity orientations are labeled as personal, social, and collective. A *personal* identity orientation describes a sense of self within an individual that reflects more of an internal emphasis, based on self-knowledge and self-evaluation. People with this orientation focus on their emotions, thoughts, ideas, beliefs, and personal goals to define their sense of self. Thus, personal identity reflects a more private sense of self. On the other hand, a *social* identity orientation describes a sense of self within an individual that reflects more of an external emphasis, based on interactions with and the reactions of others. People with such an orientation focus on what others say about them, or how others treat them in defining their sense of self. Thus, social identity reflects a more public sense of self (e.g., concerns about your popularity and reputation). A *collective* identity orientation describes a sense of self within an individual that reflects more of a communal emphasis, based on a sense of belonging to a larger social group. For example, individuals with such an orientation focus on their ethnic heritage (e.g., "I'm French-Canadian"), religious affiliation, occupation, or country of citizenship when defining their sense of self. Thus, collective identity reflects a sense of self based on group membership.

The Aspects of Identity Questionnaire: Measuring Identity Orientations

To help assess people's identity orientations, Cheek and colleagues developed the Aspects of Identity Questionnaire (Cheek & Briggs, 1981, 1982; Cheek et al., 1994; Cheek, Underwood, & Cutler, 1985). The most recent version of the questionnaire consists of 35 items, to which people are asked to respond on a 5-point, forced-choice format. Of the items, 10 assess an individual's tendency toward a personal identity orientation, 7 toward a social identity orientation, and 8 toward a collective identity orientation, and 10 are fillers (e.g., items that are included in the test but not scored, to help disguise the test's true purpose). For some first-hand experience with assessing identity orientations, answer the questions in "You Can Do It" opposite.

You Can Do It

Examining Your Identity Orientation: How Do You Define Your Sense of Self?

Instructions

Score each of the 12 items below, using this scale:

1 = Not important to my sense of who I am
2 = Slightly important to my sense of who I am
3 = Somewhat important to my sense of who I am
4 = Very important to my sense of who I am
5 = Extremely important to my sense of who I am

_____ **1.** My emotions, thoughts, and feelings
_____ **2.** The reactions of others to what I say or do
_____ **3.** My sense of belonging to the community in which I live
_____ **4.** My moral values and personal standards
_____ **5.** The impression I make on others with my mannerisms
_____ **6.** My race or ethnic heritage
_____ **7.** My private self-evaluations and personal opinions of myself
_____ **8.** How popular I am with other people
_____ **9.** My religious affiliation
_____ **10.** The personal goals and hopes I have for myself in the future
_____ **11.** How attractive other people find me
_____ **12.** The nature of my political commitment to certain causes and issues

Scoring

The extent to which your answers reflect a personal identity orientation can be examined by totaling your responses to items 1, 4, 7, and 10. The extent to which answers reflect a social identity orientation can be examined by totaling your responses to items 2, 5, 8, and 11. The extent to which your answers reflect a collective identity orientation can be examined by totaling your responses to items 3, 6, 9, and 12. The higher your score for each set of items, the more your responses reflect that particular orientation.

Note: These are a subset of modified Aspects of Identity Questionnaire items, adapted from Cheek et al. (1994).

For ease of presentation, we have considered the personal, social, and collective identity orientations separately in this section. However, Cheek (1989; Cheek et al., 1994) notes that although these three orientations may be considered as independent dimensions, a person's sense of self can reflect any or all of them to varying degrees. For example, since Jane is a very introspective person, her sense of self may be based primarily on a personal identity orientation. On the other hand, since Jackie is more of a social butterfly, her sense of self may be defined more by a social identity orientation. Julia, who prides herself on being somewhat independent but also still feels some need for the regard of others, might define her sense of self to a high degree on the basis of the personal identity orientation but to a moderate degree on that of the social identity orientation. Finally, Judy's sense of self is influenced both by a social identity associated with her occupation as an accountant and by a collective identity associated with her ethnic heritage, evidenced through active participation in a neighborhood-based Italian-American Association. There can also be conflicts when the various aspects of identity conflict with each other. For example, Justine may feel conflicted when deciding how to respond to some remarks made by a group of her friends (social identity) that go against her political beliefs (collective identity). Thus, as you might expect, the amount of balance or conflict among the aspects of identity "may have a significant impact on the self-concept processes and social behavior of an individual" (Cheek, 1989, p. 277). With this important point in mind, we will next consider some consequences of identity orientation.

Expressions of Identity Orientation: Personality Correlates of Personal, Social, and Collective Identity

Identity orientation has an impact on an individual's personality and other dimensions of self-concept. Although research has not demonstrated gender differences for collective identity orientation (Cheek et al., 1994), a tendency for females to score slightly higher than males on the personal identity and social identity orientations has been reported (Lapsley, Rice, & Fitzgerald, 1990).

Developmental differences in identity orientation have also been reported. In one study, older adults demonstrated a greater tendency toward social identity, whereas younger college students displayed a greater tendency toward personal identity (Leary, Wheeler, & Jenkins, 1986). Such a pattern of results is consistent with Erikson's belief (see Chapter 5) that young adulthood is associated with establishing a personal identity, whereas middle adulthood is associated with having a social identity established within a community (e.g., generativity). Also consistent with Erikson's viewpoint are the findings indicating that personal identity orientation is positively correlated with identity achievement and negatively correlated with identity diffusion, while social identity is related to establishing your identity through group identification, such as clubs or community actions organizations (Berzonsky, Trudeau, & Brennan, 1988). Such a pattern suggests that with a sense of identity achieved, individuals are able to incorporate their individual identity with the social identity of others, just as Erikson noted. In addition to these developmental correlates, socioeconomic correlates of identity orientation exist. Adolescents from higher socioeconomic backgrounds scored higher on personal identity, while those from lower socioeconomic backgrounds scored higher on collective identity (Reddy & Gibbons, 1995).

Personal Correlates of Identity Orientation   Personal, social, and collective identity orientations are associated with somewhat different sets of personality characteristics (Berzonsky, 1994; Cheek & Busch, 1982; Cheek et al., 1994; Cutler, Lennox, & Wolfe, 1984; Dollinger, Preston, O'Brien, & DiLalla, 1996; Forman & Crandall, 1986; Hogan & Cheek, 1983; Johnson, 1987; Wink, 1997). A personal identity orientation tends to be associated with a sense of independence, a lack of concern for social appropriateness, and a need for uniqueness. On the other hand, a social identity orientation tends to be associated with tendencies toward conformity, concerns for social appropriateness, and a desire to help others. Collective identity seems to be associated with a preference for social order (e.g., emphasis on politeness and respect for traditions) and a sense of self that involves a heightened commitment to others (e.g., try to respect the decisions made by the group; Wink, 1997). In the United States, such a pattern is particularly true for individuals of Asian, Chinese, and Korean descent, whose cultures tend to emphasize collective relationships, when compared to individuals of European descent (Cheek et al., 1994; Wink, 1997). In support of the collective identity orientation reflecting a communal sense of self, individuals expressing a collective identity orientation tended to describe themselves as members of an ethnic group, to rank ethnicity as a highly central aspect of their sense of self, and to downplay the role of uniqueness as central to their self-concept (Tropp, 1992).

With respect to emotional reactions, social identity orientation is associated with high self-esteem following successful interactions with others (McKillop, Berzonsky, & Schlenker, 1992). However, social identity is also associated with a susceptibility to experiencing shame, which reflects a concern for the public exposure of personal faults or the failure to meet external standards of morality. Personal identity is associated with a susceptibility to experiencing guilt, which reflects a concern for an individual's own conscience or internal moral standards (Cheek & Hogan, 1983). Finally, as an expression of patriotism, individuals high on collective identity orientation rated the United States more favorably following a national failure in response to crises involving other countries than did individuals low in collective identity (Kowalski & Wolfe, 1994).

Identity Orientation and Self-Consciousness Personal and social identity orientations also are related to other measures of self-concept, such as public and private self-consciousness. As discussed previously, given that private self-consciousness reflects a more internal emphasis on the self whereas public self-consciousness reflects a more external emphasis on the self, you would expect personal identity scores to be positively related to private self-consciousness, and social identity scores to be positively related to public self-consciousness. Such a pattern of results has been found in a number of studies (Britt, 1993; Cheek & Briggs, 1982; Cutler et al., 1984; Hogan & Cheek, 1983; Lamphere & Leary, 1990; Penner & Wymer, 1983; Schlenker & Weigold, 1990).

Occupational and Recreational Preferences and Identity Orientation: Personal and Social Identity Orientations for Work and Play

Next to eating and sleeping, two other important parts of our lives involve what we do for a living and how we spend our free time. Because work and play are such important aspects of our lives, you would expect them to be important to our sense of self. As a result, you would also expect identity orientation to play a role in the occupational and recreational choices people make.

Identity Orientation and Occupational Choice In their analysis of job characteristics, Leary, Wheeler, and Jenkins (1986) proposed that certain occupations offer greater personal rewards (e.g., self-fulfillment) whereas other occupations offer greater social rewards (e.g., social status). From this distinction, they proposed a relationship between identity orientation and occupational preference. In support of their reasoning, they found that people with a high sense of personal identity expressed a preference for occupations that emphasized personally relevant job outcomes involving self-fulfillment and personal growth. These people expressed a preference for occupations that offered a chance to be creative, a job consistent with personal values, an opportunity to use their abilities to their fullest, the possibility to reach personal goals in life, and the opportunity to have a great deal of input.

On the other hand, people with a high sense of social identity expressed a preference for occupations that emphasized socially relevant job outcomes. These people expressed a preference for occupations that offered social status, high pay, the opportunity to be well known in their field, recognition from others, the possibility of forming friendships with co-workers, and an active social life.

In a similar manner, women who had a stronger sense of personal self-definition were more likely to take more active roles in social and career initiatives, such as starting and leading organizations, than were women with a more social sense of self-definition (Jenkins, 1996). Women with a stronger sense of social self-definition tended to choose more traditional female careers, report more career indecision and compromise, and experience more role conflict (e.g., home vs. work role conflicts).

Identity Orientation and Recreational Choice In their analysis of recreational activities, Leary, Wheeler, and Jenkins (1986) proposed that people engage in individual and team sports for different reasons. Individual sports, which do not require a teammate (e.g., jogging and swimming), offer the individual complete control over the activity and can be enjoyed for their intrinsic rewards (e.g., the satisfaction of improving your running time). On the other hand, sports requiring teammates (e.g., volleyball, baseball, or soccer) offer the individual a chance to work with others and provide interpersonal rewards (e.g., praise, friendship, and companionship).

From this distinction, Leary et al. proposed a relationship between identity orientation and recreational sport preference. In support of their reasoning, they found that people with a high sense of personal identity participated in more individual sports and expressed more personal reasons for doing so (e.g., personal enjoyment, self-satisfaction, and a desire to be physically fit). People with a high sense of social identity participated in more team sports and expressed more interpersonal reasons for doing so (e.g., for the enjoyment of competing with others, to make others notice how physically fit they were, and to increase the possibility for interacting with others).

In related findings, research has shown that, out of an increased concern for one's public appearance and the belief that having a tan enhances one's attractiveness, individuals who tended to engage in sunbathing and use tanning beds, with their increased risk for skin cancer, have a high social identity orientation. On the other hand, while having a personal identity orientation was not associated with sunbathing or use of tanning booths, individuals with a personal identity orientation tended to use sunscreen while exposed to the sun (Leary & Jones, 1993). Thus, individuals with a social identity orientation were more willing to take risks for the sake of being more attractive to others than were individuals with a personal identity orientation, who were more concerned with self-protection than with enhancing their social status through physical appearance.

Thus, as a critical dimension of the self-concept, identity orientation is associated with other relevant personality characteristics and important aspects of the individual's life, such as occupational choice and recreational preferences. A summary of principal ideas discussed in this section is presented in "Summing It Up: Dimensions of the Self-Concept: Personal,

Summing It Up *Dimensions of the Self-Concept: Personal, Social, and Collective Identity Orientations*

Concept	Definition	Example
Personal Identity Orientation (PIO)	A sense of identity based on internal or private standards	Diane's sense of self is based on a desire to be the best accountant she can be.
Social Identity Orientation (SIO)	A sense of identity based on external or public standards	Pat's sense of self is based on a desire to have people show approval of her ideas.
Collective Identity Orientation (CIO)	A sense of identity based on belonging to a larger social group	Greg's sense of self is based on his commitment to his community's environmental preservation society.
Aspects of Identity Questionnaire (AIQ)	A personality test that assesses individual differences in personal, social, and collective identity orientations	Items from the AIQ: "My emotions and feelings are important to who I am (PIO)"; "My attractiveness to others is important to who I am (SIO)"; "My religous affiliation is important to who I am (CIO)."
Occupational Preferences	Individuals with a PIO prefer occupations that offer personal satisfaction, while those with an SIO prefer occupations that offer social recognition	Jill wants a job that will allow her creativity to be to be expressed, while Jack wants a job with a fancy company car.
Recreational Preferences	Individuals with a PIO prefer recreational activities that offer personal satisfaction, while those with an SIO prefer activities that offer social interaction	Hans likes to walk because it improves his health, while Rose plays volleyball because she gets to be with others and demonstrate her skill.

Social, and Collective Identity Orientations" on p. 481. For more information on the topic of identity orientations, read a book chapter by Jonathon Cheek (1989) titled "Identity Orientations and Self-Interpretation" or visit the "Identity Orientation" website at www. wellesley.edu/Psychology/Cheek/jcheek.html.

This concludes our discussion of private and public dimensions of the self-concept. To help place this discussion in some context, think back on Freud's constructs of the id and superego (see Chapter 3), Adler's concepts of the creative self and social interest (see Chapter 4), Jung's views on unconsciousness/the shadow and consciousness/the persona (see Chapter 4), Erikson's view of identity and generativity (see Chapter 5), and Maslow's emphasis on belonging needs and esteem needs (see Chapter 6). With respect to establishing a solid self-concept, all of these constructs serve as reminders of the significance of incorporating not only one's own personal/private needs but also social expectations and requirements. For more information about the public and private dimensions of the self-concept, read either or both of the articles titled "The Dynamic Self-Concept: A Social Psychological Perspective" (Markus & Wurf, 1987) and "The Self in Social Context" (Banaji & Prentice, 1994). However, private needs and public expectations are not the only factors determining self-concept. In the next section, we will consider views of the self from around the world.

Cultural Dimensions of the Self: Views from Around the World

In an extension of the concept of the personal/private aspects (e.g., your tendency to be introspective) and social/public aspects (e.g., your reputation) of the self, Harry Triandis of the University of Illinois (1989, 1995, 1996, 1997, 2001) proposed the concept of the collective self to account for the influence of culture as a determinant of one's identity. The **collective self** refers to an individual's membership in certain social groups. Social groups that contribute to the collective self and social identity include those based on family ties, ethnic identity, religious affiliation, geographic region, and cultural heritage (Baumeister, 1995; Buss,

1995, 2001; Pennebaker, Rimé, & Blankenship, 1996; Pervin, 2002). In addition to simply creating a sense of belonging to a particular group, the degree of collective identification (e.g., being a member of a welder's union) has also been shown to be critical in determining the extent to which individuals are willing to take social action (e.g., going on strike for better working conditions) on behalf of the group (Simon et al., 1998) on the basis of their perception of the beliefs of high-ranking members of the group (e.g., union president and local union stewards; Ybarra & Trafimow, 1998).

Cultural Influences on the Self: East vs. West

In this section, we will delineate the differences between Eastern and Western cultural influences on the self. First, we will discuss the characteristics of collective and individualistic cultures and their differential impact on the nature and expression of the sense of self. Next, we will focus on the independent self and interdependent self as manifestations of that cultural impact.

Collective Cultures: Promoting a Strong Public Image

Variations in cultures have different effects on the private, public, and collective aspects of the self (Triandis, 1989, 1995, 1996, 1997, 2001). **Collective cultures**, such as that of Japanese society, place considerable emphasis on the public and communal aspects of the self and less emphasis on the private aspects of the self and individual self-expression. These cultures are described as "tight" societies because of the high expectations they place on people to conform to societal values, roles, and norms (Carpenter, 2000; Triandis, 2001).

In tight societies, individuals promote a strong outward image by cultivating a well-developed public and collective self and by paying scant attention to the private self. For example, even though she may not like studying economics, a young Japanese college student may pursue a career as an economist to fulfill the wishes of elder members of her family. In her culture, it is more important to maintain a proper public image and sense of honor for the family than to express personal desires. The same is true of various religious groups that have tight or rigid guidelines regarding the behavior of women. For example, in certain

Muslim communities, young girls and women must remain veiled or modest in their expression, and in very observant communities girls and women are prohibited from attending school at all.

Individualistic Cultures: Promoting Expressions of Uniqueness

By contrast, **individualistic cultures,** as exemplified by American society, place more emphasis on individual expression and the private self than on the public self (Triandis, 1989, 1995, 1996, 1997, 2001). These cultures can be described as "complex" because people have considerable societal flexibility to join many different groups and exercise a wide range of choices in the expression of various social roles.

In complex cultures, the collective and public selves are weaker in comparison to the private self, which is given considerable freedom of expression. For example, although many American parents expect their children to go to college, college students are free to choose a major that reflects their personal needs and interests. Although complex cultures allow for greater personal expression and promote a more favorable sense of subjective well-being (Diener, Diener, &

Diener, 1995), they also appear to foster more identity problems and confusion (Baumeister, 1995; Katakis, 1984). It may be that greater freedom of choice and expression produces more confusion.

The impact of collective and individualistic cultures on the sense of self can be illustrated by comparing the nature and expression of the independent self and the interdependent self, which we will consider next.

Independent Self and Interdependent Self: Cultural Influences on the Expression of the Self

With which of these two proverbs do you agree most?

> The squeaky wheel gets the grease.
> The nail that stands out gets pounded down.

The first sentence reflects the view of American culture, with its emphasis on individuality and the expression of unique talents and abilities (Trafimow, Triandis, & Goto, 1991). The second sentence, on the other hand, reflects the view of Japanese culture, with its emphasis

The work of Hazel Rose Markus and Shinobu Kitayama makes it possible to understand the role culture plays in the development and expression of personality. Such cross-cultural investigations are extremely important as advances in electronic technology and travel make it easier for people from different parts of the world to come together.

on the individual's membership in a collective network of social relationships. These statements also illustrate some basic differences in the way these two cultures influence the expression of the self. A bicultural team of researchers refers to these expressions as the independent self and the interdependent self (Cross & Markus, 1999; Markus & Kitayama, 1991; Markus, Kitayama, & Heiman, 1996).

The Independent Self

"I've got to be me." As reflected in these words from an old tune sung by Sammy Davis, Jr., American culture emphasizes the independent self. The **independent self** is a sense of the self as a person's unique feelings, beliefs, and motives that are separate from the social context. Americans tend to think of themselves as being independent and free to act on personal views and desires.

According to Kitayama (1992), this comes from the tendency in Western cultures to teach children to be independent of others. As evidence of this tendency, the increasing influence of individualism in the United States is associated with "increases in self-focus (narcissism) and a decrease in norm adherence" (Roberts & Helson, 1997, p. 641). For example, greater frequency of individuals talking on cell phones while in a movie in a theater is an example of an increase in self-focus (e.g., "I have to take my call, regardless of the circumstances") and a decrease in norm adherence (e.g., minimizing your conversation in a movie theater to be courteous toward others).

The Interdependent Self

"There is no *I* in *team*." These words from the author's high school football coach reflect the emphasis found in non-Western cultures on the interdependent self. The **interdependent self** is a sense of the self as belonging to a group or unit that has an important influence on the individual's behavior. In Japanese culture, people define and develop a meaningful sense of self in the context of social relationships, rather than through independent actions and achievements. Instead of focusing on unique self-expression, the interdependent self emphasizes considering the consequences of actions on the feelings and views of others and the desirability of blending in with them. For example, in Japanese culture, getting fired from a job would bring shame and embarrassment to one's family; in America, it would be more likely to be construed as a personal failure. Examine some manifestations of independent and interdependent self-expression in "The Cultural Context of Personality Psychology."

The Cultural Context of Personality Psychology

Independent vs. Interdependent Self-Expression

Cultural emphases on an independent self or an interdependent self can influence thoughts, feelings, and behaviors (Cross & Markus, 1999; Kashima, Yamaguchi et al., 1995; Triandis, 1996, 1997, 2001). To illustrate this point, following are some differences in self expression between an independent and interdependent sense of self:

- *Expressions of Pride.* Americans take pride in their individual accomplishments, whereas the Japanese take pride in knowing their efforts helped their group to be successful (Ouchi, 1981), and in some cultures, such as those of certain regions in India, expressions of pride are considered undesirable and to be regulated (Menon & Shweder, 1994).
- *Sources of Self-Esteem.* Competitive behavior is linked to high self-esteem in cultures promoting an independent sense of self, whereas cooperative behavior is linked to high self-esteem in cultures promoting an interdependent sense of self (S. Kagan & Knight, 1979).
- *Feelings of Shame and Guilt.* Because of their emphasis on public aspects of the self, collective cultures promote greater feelings of shame and guilt than do individualistic cultures (Buss, 2001; Heine, Lehman, Markus, & Kitayama, 1999; Lutwak, Razzino, & Ferrari, 1998; Mosquera, Manstead, & Fisher, 2000).
- *Feelings of Happiness.* In a survey of nations that included three fourths of the world's population, individualism was consistently associated with happiness (Diener et al., 1995).

- *Beliefs about Personal Uniqueness.* In Western cultures, people see themselves as being unique and view others as being more similar to them. In Eastern cultures, people perceive themselves as being very similar to others and view others as being unique (Kitayama, Markus, Tummala, Kurokawa, & Kato, 1990).

- *Beliefs about Responsibility.* In Western cultures, people are more likely to hold someone personally responsible for his or her own behavior (e.g., "Dale is really clumsy"). People in Eastern cultures, however, are more likely to attribute the cause of an individual's behavior to situational factors (e.g., "Pat slipped on the wet floor"; Chiu, Morris, Hong, & Menon, 2000; Choi, Nisbett, & Norenzayan, 1999; Masuda & Nisbett, 2001; J. G. Miller, 1984; Nisbett, Peng, Choi, & Norenzayan, 2001; Norenzayan & Nisbett, 2000).

- *Explanations for Personal Success.* In Western cultures, people assume personal responsibility for their success through self-enhancement (e.g., "I worked really hard for my raise"). People in Eastern cultures, on the other hand, perceive their success in a self-effacing manner and as being due to situational factors (e.g., "I received my raise because my boss is a generous person"; Lee & Seligman, 1997; Takata, 1987; Yik, Bond, & Paulhus, 1998). This East–West difference in the pattern for promoting self-enhancement was also found when individuals were evaluating groups to which they belong, not just within themselves (Heine & Lehman, 1997). For example, individuals in Western cultures perceive others as more personally responsible for their success (e.g., "She put in a lot of overtime") while those in Eastern cultures perceive the success of others as being due to situational factors (e.g., working for a supportive company).

- *Explanations for Personal Failures.* In Western cultures, people are likely to downplay personal responsibility for their failures in a manner that protects their self-image (e.g., "I did not get a raise because my boss dislikes me and is cheap"). In Eastern cultures, however, people explain their failures by elevating others' personal attributes (e.g., "I did not get the raise because I did not work as hard as my co-workers"; Heine et al., 1999; Lee & Seligman, 1997; Shikanai, 1978). In fact, this tendency for individuals from collective cultures to take less credit for success and more

responsibility for failure may contribute to increased feelings of depression and loneliness (Anderson, 1999).

- *Optimism and Success.* Because of their tendency to assume more responsibility for success and less responsibility for failure, Westerners (e.g., Americans) tend to be more optimistic than Easterners (e.g., mainland Chinese; Lee & Seligman, 1997).

- *Expression of Emotions.* In Western cultures, people are more likely to experience emotions related directly to a personal sense of self, such as pride (e.g., "I did a great job") or frustration (e.g., "I was cheated out of a raise"), to a greater degree than are people in Eastern cultures (Eid & Diener, 2001; Markus & Kitayama, 1991). More than people from individualistic cultures, people from collective cultures tend to base their emotional expression on assessments of social worth and shifts in relative social worth, which emphasize the relatedness of the person to others (Mesquita, 2001).

- *Assertiveness and Independence.* Expressions of assertiveness and independence are more characteristic of people from individualistic cultures (e.g., Australia and the United States) than collective cultures (e.g., Japan and Korea; Kashima et al., 1995).

As this summary illustrates, there are some very definite influences of culture on the sense of self. Can you think of other ways in which your culture might have shaped your personality?

In this section as well as in the preceding "The Cultural Context of Personality Psychology," we have seen the impact of culture on a person's sense of self. However, transportation technology has made the world a smaller place by making international destinations more accessible. People now have the opportunity to change their cultural context simply by traveling to different parts of the world. Thus, an American banker may be working in Japan or a Pakistani college student may be studying in Germany. How do people cope with such changes in cultural context? Consider the research addressing this phenomenon in "A Closer Look" on p. 486.

A Closer Look

Coping with Shifts in Cultural Context at College

Advances in transportation technology now make it much more likely that people from varying cultures will visit other parts of the world for business or pleasure. However, because new environments can challenge the basic meaning of a person's identity, shifts in cultural context can be stressful (Breakwell, 1986; Roysircar-Sodowsky & Maestas, 2000), particularly if they occur for an extended time (e.g., immigration to a new country).

A widespread shift in cultural context occurs in countries all over the world every autumn, as students from diverse cultural and ethnic backgrounds leave home for the foreign land known as college. This transition from living at home to living away at college is stressful for most students, and some may feel as though they are strangers in a strange land. It can be especially stressful for those whose sense of identity is threatened when they discover they are among an ethnic or racial minority on campus.

Adjusting to college is never easy. Kay Deaux (pictured above) and Kathleen Ethier are helping explain what strategies students use to help make a successful transition from ethnic majority status in their own neighborhoods to ethnic minority status on campus. Such information will help all of us to cope more effectively with major transitions throughout our lives.

To help understand the psychological and social dynamics of such shifts in cultural context, Kay Deaux, of the City University of New York Graduate School and University Center, and Kathleen Ethier, of Yale University, investigated how Latinos maintain their sense of ethnic identity when they experience a dramatic shift in the context of their culture.

Strength of Pre-College Ethnic Identity and Adjustment to College

These researchers (Deaux, 1993, 1996; Ethier & Deaux, 1990, 1994) investigated the way Hispanic students maintained their identity as they transitioned from living at home to living away at college. Deaux and Ethier reported that the minority status of Hispanic people on predominantly white college campuses was a serious source of stress owing to difficulties in maintaining a sense of ethnic identity and self-esteem (Ethier & Deaux, 1990, 1994). An important predictor of success in maintaining ethnic identity was the strength of study participants' ethnic identity before going to college (Ethier & Deaux, 1994). Factors in the students' home life that were relevant to a sense of ethnic identity included the language spoken in the home, the ethnic composition of the neighborhood, and the percentage of friends in the same ethnic group. Students with a strong sense of ethnic identity before going away to college showed the least amount of stress in response to maintaining their ethnic identity while at college. Students with a weak pre-college sense of ethnic identity experienced decreases in self-esteem and perceived being away at college as threatening.

Remooring as a Strategy for Maintaining Ethnic Identity

Ethier and Deaux noted that students with a strong sense of ethnic identity before coming to college maintained that identity by becoming involved with Hispanic activities at college (e.g., club meetings, lectures, or courses) and establishing new friendships with other Hispanic students. These new activities and friends helped replace the sources of support for ethnic identity back home. The researchers called this successful strategy *remooring*.

Such a pattern of action is consistent with those of other ethnic minorities, such as Italian, German, Chinese, Jewish, and Irish immigrants, as they migrated to the United States from their countries of origin over the decades. Thus, most metropolitan cities have their own "Little Italy" or "Chinatown," where immigrants from these countries gather together to minimize the stress of coming to a new country and to help preserve their ethnic heritage in a new location. The same type of remooring occurs when people join a church or synagogue upon moving to a new city. Religious affiliation can be a significant component of personal identity. Affirming one's religious affiliation in this way can minimize the stress of moving to a new town. A similar pattern of remooring might occur in people for whom other aspects of their identity are significant. For example, someone with a passion for playing chess or restoring antique cars might also attempt to establish ties with people having similar interests when moving to a new part of the country.

The implication of this research is that whatever is important to an individual's sense of identity (Deaux & Perkins, 2001), be it ethnicity, social interests, or sexual preference, finding others who share a similar sense of identity is important for coping with stress and maintaining this sense of identity when moving to a new location (Frable, Wortman, Joseph, Kirscht, & Kessler, 1997). This is an especially important lesson to remember as our society becomes increasingly mobile and we face a greater likelihood of having to "pick up and go" because a job commitment demands that we move to a different part of the country – or even

a different country. To consider how you might apply research on the remooring strategy to your own life, see "Applications in Personality Psychology" below.

In this section, we have examined how different cultures influence the personalities of the people living in them; and we have considered some coping strategies associated with the stress of leaving one's culture. A summary of the main points discussed in this section is presented in "Summing It Up: Cultural Influences on the Self" on p. 488. For more influences on cultural influences on personality, read the following chapters "The Cultural Constitution of Personality" (Cross & Markus, 1999), "Cross-Cultural Perspectives on Personality" (Triandis, 1997), "Cross-National Prevalence of Collectivism" (Triandis & Trafimow, 2001), and "Social Identification" (Deaux, 1996), or the books *Individualism and Collectivism* (Triandis, 1995) and *Handbook of Cross-Cultural and Multicultural Personality Assessment* (Dana, 2000).

This concludes our survey of the meaning, origins, historical changes, dimensions, and cultural influences of the self-concept. As we have seen, the self-concept

Applications in Personality Psychology

Personalizing the Strategy of Remooring

Can remooring help you to cope with the stress of college life and the possible threats to your own identity? If you are stressed and have not already started to connect with others with similar interests, consider doing so. A good place to start is by going to the psychology department to see if there is a psychology club, or to the student activities office for a list of clubs and organizations on campus. After finding out what groups or clubs are on your

campus, attend a meeting or two to see which of them meet your own needs for developing and maintaining a sense of ethnic, social, and personal identity.

Avoid using the excuse that you are too busy or don't have time for this activity. As noted in "A Closer Look" above, remooring reduces stress and promotes positive self-esteem. Such outcomes will not only increase your likelihood of achieving success at college (Gardner & Jewler, 2001; Jewler, Gardner, & Owens, 1993) but also make remooring worth your while in the long run.

Summing It Up *Cultural Influences on the Self*

Concept	Definition	Example
Collective Self	A sense of identity linked to group membership (e.g., ethic, religious, or cultural)	Gino is a member of the local Italian-American Association.
Collective Cultures	Cultures that emphasize the public aspects of the self over personal aspects	In some cultures, saving face for one's family is more important than personal happiness.
Individualistic Cultures	Cultures that emphasize the personal aspects of the self over public aspects	In some cultures, one's occupational choice is based more on personal interests than on the expectations of family members.
Independent Self	A sense of self based on an individual's personal feelings and beliefs separate from the social context	In the United States, individuals are encouraged to express their political views, even though such views might be different from those of family members neighbors, or co-workers.
Interdependent Self	A sense of self based on an individual's group membership in a social context	Some cultural constraints are so powerful that they influence considerably many critical expressions of the self, including how the individual can dress, who the individual will marry, and what music or reading materials can be read or listened to in the individual's spare time.

is extremely complex and influences many important aspects of a person's thoughts, feelings, and behavior. If you would like to know more about the self-concept, read any of the following books: Abraham Tesser, Richard B. Felson, and Jerry M. Suls's (2000) *Psychological Perspectives on Self and Identity*, Susan Harter's (1999) *The Construction of the Self: A Developmental Perspective*, Jonathon D. Brown's (1998) *The Self*, Arnold H. Buss's (2001) *Psychological Dimensions of the Self*, and Christopher J. Mruk's (2006) *Self-Esteem Research, Theory, and Practice: Toward a Positive Psychology of Self-Esteem*. In the next chapter, we continue our exploration of the self-concept by focusing on one of its most important components – gender identity.

Chapter Summary: Reexamining the Highlights

● *Fundamentals of the Self-Concept*

  – *Self-Concept, Self-Esteem, and Identity. Self-Concept* refers to beliefs an individual has about himself or herself. *Self-esteem* refers to an individual's overall evaluation of himself or herself. *Identity* refers to definitions an individual uses to help distinguish himself or herself from others.

  – *The Origin and Onset of the Self-Concept.* Children begin to explore an image of themselves in the mirror at around 6 months of age, and by about 18 to 24 months of age, a majority of children demonstrate a solid sense of self. Their sense of self continues to grow as they compare themselves to others at about 6 to 12 years of age, which creates increased self-consciousness.

- *Changes in the Concept of the Self through History.* Historical views of the self reflect various social, economic, religious, and psychological factors. During the late medieval period, the self was defined primarily by a person's social position. The early modern period emphasized knowing the inner self of others, while the Puritan era emphasized an early concern for self-awareness. The Victorian era promoted a view of the self characterized by deception and denial. The early 20th century was characterized by a view of the self reflecting a sense of alienation brought on by the industrial age. The period of the late 20th and early 21st centuries is characterized by a view of the self that is seeking a sense of uniqueness in a collective society.

- *Dimensions of the Self-Concept*
  - *Self-Consciousness. Private self-awareness* refers to those aspects of the self hidden from the public, while *public self-awareness* refers to those aspects of the self that can be viewed by others. Self-consciousness is the tendency to be aware of your sense of self. *Private self-consciousness* refers to the tendency of an individual to be self-reflective; *public self-consciousness* refers to a tendency to engage in self-analysis regarding a person's public image. The Self-Consciousness Scale (SCS) is used to measure individual differences in the traits of private and public self-consciousness. The behavior of people who score high in the trait of private self-consciousness reflects internal standards, while the behavior of people high in the trait of public self-consciousness reflects external standards.

  - *Objective Self-Awareness.* Objective self-awareness is the sense of heightened self-consciousness created by situational conditions. Private self-awareness is a situationally induced tendency toward internal self-analysis, while public self-awareness is a situationally induced tendency for external self-analysis. Coping with objective self-awareness involves leaving those situations that create these feelings of objective self-awareness, or attempting to make overt behavior more consistent with internal standards.

  - *The Control-Theory Model (CTM) of the Self.* The CTM links the personality traits of self-consciousness and the state of objective self-awareness. According to the CTM, people regulate their behavior against a preexisting standard. For privately self-conscious people and those in a state of private self-awareness, this preexisting standard is internal. For publicly self-conscious people and those in a state of public self-awareness, the preexisting standard is external.

  - *Self-Monitoring.* The personality dimension of self-monitoring reflects an individual's ability to regulate overt appearances in response to various situations. High self-monitors are more likely to regulate their overt appearance in response to external situations, while low self-monitors are more likely to regulate their overt behavior in response to personal beliefs. The personality dimension of self-monitoring is assessed with the Self-Monitoring Scale. The evaluation of your degree of self-monitoring must include the extent to which you are able to generate appropriate responses, as well as to monitor what responses are appropriate. When applied to advertising, high self-monitors are more likely to respond to soft-sell appeals based on the public image the product can create for the individual, while low self-monitors are more likely to respond to hard-sell appeals based on the merits of the product. As applied to consumer behavior, high self-monitors are more likely to make consumer decisions based on the form or outward appearance of the product, while low self-monitors are more likely to make consumer decisions based on the functional aspects of the product. As applied to career-decision making, high self-monitors are more likely to prefer employment positions with a clear job description, seek more job-related information, and emphasize appearances in performance evaluations than are low self-monitors.

  - *Identity Orientations.* Identity orientation refers to the extent to which people focus on internal or external environments in defining their identity. A personal identity orientation characterizes people who use self-knowledge and self-analysis to define their identity. A social identity orientation characterizes people who use their interactions with others to define their identity. A collective identity orientation characterizes people who use their communal membership of larger groups to define their identity. Personal, social, and collective identity orientations are assessed using the Aspects of Identity Questionnaire. Personality, occupational, and recreational correlates of a personal identity orientation reflect a desire for independence and uniqueness, while correlates of a social identity orientation reflect a tendency toward conformity and a concern for social appropriateness.

● *Cultural Dimensions of the Self*
  – Collective cultures emphasize the public aspects of the self and conformity to social norms, roles,

and values. Individualistic cultures emphasize individuality and the expression of the private self. The independent self is the sense of self defined as a unique expression of the individual's thoughts and feelings independent of a social context, while the interdependent self is the sense of self defined primarily in the context of social relationships.

Glossary

collective cultures   Cultures that emphasize the public expression of the self over the personal concerns of the individual.

collective self   A sense of self determined by group membership.

control-theory model (CTM)   An explanation for the regulation of behavior based on an internal preexisting standard.

high self-monitors   People whose behavior tends to reflect situational demands.

identity The sense of self that sets you apart from others.

identity conflict   The emotional discomfort created when there is a mismatch between an individual's public and private identities.

identity orientation   The extent to which individuals use an external or an internal frame of reference in defining their sense of self.

independent self   A sense of self separate from any group membership.

individualistic cultures   Cultures that emphasize the true sense of self in terms of how the person really is over public concern for self-expression.

interdependent self   The sense of self determined by an individual's meaningful relationship with others in a group.

low self-monitors   People whose behavior tends to reflect personal beliefs.

objective self-awareness   An increased awareness of internal aspects of the self.

private self-awareness   An awareness of the internal aspects of the self.

private self-consciousness   The increased tendency to engage in internal self-examination.

public self-awareness   An awareness of the external aspects of the self.

public self-consciousness   The increased tendency to engage in external self-examination.

self-concept   Beliefs you have about yourself.

self-consciousness   The tendency for each person to focus on a sense of self.

self-esteem   Your general evaluation of your sense of self.

self-monitoring   A personality dimension expressing the tendency for an individual's behavior to reflect personal beliefs vs. situational demands.

Self-Monitoring Scale   A personality test assessing individual differences in self-monitoring.

self-recognition   Being able to recognize oneself in a mirror or photograph.

Gender Identity and Personality

A Special Topic in the Study of the Self-Concept

12

Chapter Overview:
A Preview of Coming Attractions

In this chapter, we expand our understanding of the self-concept by studying a special topic in the study of the self – gender. Our study of gender and personality will begin with a consideration of the various processes by which we acquire our sense of gender identity. Next we will examine some of the consequences of such an identity by focusing on gender differences in personality and sex-role stereotypes. Finally, we will explore the concept of androgyny as an illustration of the way personality psychologists continue to develop, refine, and expand their vision of gender as the views of gender continue to evolve within our society and around the world. Needless to say, the study of gender and personality is enhanced by the richness and diversity of issues it attempts to address, many of which will be discussed in this chapter. As with all of the other topics considered up to this point, this presentation is supported by systematic research and amplified by compelling applications.

Gender Identity: The Most Pervasive Aspect of the Self-Concept

Probably the most pervasive aspect of what people consider to be a sense of self is that of gender identity. **Gender identity** refers to the individual's private experience of being a male or female (A. H. Buss, 2001; Mealey, 2000; Money & Ehrhardt, 1972; Smith, 2007). More specifically, it represents the overt expressions of behavior and attitudes held by individuals toward their status of being male or female (LaFrance, Paluck, & Brescoll, 2004). For example, a female professional basketball player may perceive herself as displaying a sense of competitiveness and aggressiveness on the court that is characteristic of that displayed by male professional basketball players; however, at the same time she knows that her status as a female professional athlete is rated below that of males, as reflected by the lower salary she receives for her efforts. We begin our consideration of this fascinating topic by considering the various explanations of gender identity proposed by personality psychologists.

Theories of Gender Identity: Developing a Sense of Being Male and Female

As is the case for other important and complex topics in the field of psychology, the development of a sense of being male or female has been explained in several ways. In this section we will explore psychological, social, biological, and evolutionary explanations.

Psychological Explanations of Gender Identity: The Processes of Identification, Observation, and Categorization

Psychological explanations of gender identity focus on various psychological processes in accounting for the acquisition of gender identity. These processes include identifying with same-sex others, receiving and observing rewards for gender-appropriate behavior, categorizing attitudes and activities along gender lines, and processing information according to gender.

Psychoanalytic Theory: The Importance of Identification

Traditional psychoanalytic theory proposes that, like all other significant aspects of personality development, gender identity takes place very early in life. More specifically, during the phallic stage (ages 3 to 6 years), boys resolve their Oedipal complexes and girls resolve their Electra complexes by successfully identifying with the same-sex parent (see p. 95 for a review). With identification comes the internalization of the attitudes, characteristics, and beliefs of the same-sex parent. Much of which is internalized has to do with what is considered masculine and feminine. For example, in identifying with his father, a little boy washes his bike in imitation of his father washing the family car; or a little girl might imitate her mother going to the office each day by having her "mommy doll" go to work.

While still relying on the dynamics of identification, contemporary psychoanalytic views on gender identity include more of an emphasis on the nature and dynamics of culture and the analysis of the changing roles of men and women in contemporary society (Bell, 2004; Benjamin, 1998; Chodorow, 1999a, 1999b). For example, as an increasing number of women are entering traditional male areas of work and politics, and men are slowly entering more traditional female spheres of parenting and domestic work, children now have a much wider range of characteristic features to incorporate during the process of identification. In addition, more attention is being devoted to post-Oedipal development and the ability to develop a more comprehensive sense of gender identity that involves a more complete expression of one's sense of self than the more simplistic, dichotomous classification of "boy" or "girl" appearing in childhood, and beyond the confines of the more rigid and traditional categorization of masculine or feminine identity in adulthood. For example, in contemporary society, the emotionally healthy male and female can display such features as assertiveness and independence and warmth and passivity, depending on the nature of the situation, instead of acting only within the confines of "what a man or a woman does."

Thus, as we have seen with so many other areas of personality, the psychoanalytic viewpoint of gender identity has evolved to include the role of culture and development across the life span. Or, as Bell (2004) states so eloquently, "For contemporary theorists, the development and experience of gender continues throughout life and is not finished following the Oedipal period" (p. 162).

Social-Cognitive Theory: The Acquisition and Regulation of Gender-Linked Behavior

The social-cognitive theory of gender development is based on Albert Bandura's social-cognitive viewpoint of personality discussed in Chapter 10 (see pp. 361–373). Similar to Bandura's general viewpoint on personality (Bandura, 2001, 2002), central to the social-cognitive theory of gender development are the processes by which children acquire information about what is considered gender-appropriate behavior and how they then learn to regulate the performance of that behavior (Bandura & Bussey, 2004; Bussey & Bandura, 1999, 2004). In this section, we will discuss the process of acquisition and self-regulated gender-related behavior according to social-cognitive theory.

Acquisition of Gender-Appropriate Behavior: Learning What Boys and Girls Will Do   The basic processes by which children acquire information about gender-appropriate behavior, according to social-cognitive theory, include modeling influences, enactive experience, and direct tutelage.

MODELING   According to the social-cognitive theory and other theories of gender development (Martin, Ruble, & Szkrybalo, 2002, 2004), a critical element in the process of the acquisition of gender behavior is that of modeling. Through the process of observational learning, children gain information about their own gender identity and what behaviors are considered appropriate for it (Bandura, 1989, 1999, 2001, 2002; Bussey & Bandura, 2004). Children observe that certain behaviors done by certain people lead to rewards, while others lead to punishment. For example, by watching television or reading storybooks, children learn that males are more likely to have important roles, make critical decisions, and be rewarded for taking action, while females are more likely to be rewarded for seeking help and behaving more passively and working at "feminine occupations" (e.g., being a nurse or waitress; Liebert & Sprafkin, 1988; Smith, 2007; Sternglanz & Serbin, 1974; Weitzman, Eifler, Hokada, & Ross, 1972). Not surprisingly, therefore, children who watch

more than 25 hours of television per week express more strongly stereotyped views of men and women than do those who watch less television (McGhee & Frueh, 1980). The good news is that as more women appear on television in less stereotyped roles, such as detectives or executives, what children will learn about gender roles will change. In support of this reasoning, it has been demonstrated that children who regularly watch non-sexist programs do hold less stereotypical views of men and women (Rosenwasser, Lingenfelter, & Harrington, 1989; Smith, 2007).

Of particular importance to this process of observational learning is that children pay more attention to same-sex models than to opposite-sex models (Bussey & Bandura, 1984), suggesting once again the importance of identification. A critical factor in this process of same-gender modeling is the consistency of the behavior exhibited by the male and female models (Bussey & Bandura, 2004). Specifically, as the percentage of same-sex models performing a behavior increases, the likelihood of a same-sex child modeling that behavior increases (Bussey & Perry, 1982; Perry & Bussey, 1979). The everyday implications of these results is that the more consistently television programs, motion pictures, and video games portray males as authoritative while portraying females as dependent or emotional, the more likely it is that such behavioral patterns will be modeled by the children who watch them. On the other hand, the more consistently the media present males and females in less stereotypical and more egalitarian ways, the more likely it is that we will see changes not only in the behavior of boys and girls but also, by extension, in the men and women these children grow up to be. As a way of applying this information to your own life, to what extent do you think there is consistency in the gender-stereotypical presentation of men and women in the media, where you work, or at your school?

ENACTIVE EXPERIENCE   A second process involved in the acquisition of gender-related behavior is that of enactive experience. **Enactive experience** is the process by which children acquire information regarding gender-appropriate behavior by the reactions it produces in others. The range of enactive experience can vary from explicit reactions, such as the verbal praise of parents, teachers, or coaches for engaging in gender-appropriate behavior, to more subtle, less direct reactions, such as other kids on the playground giving the "silent treatment" to a boy or girl for engaging in "sissy play" or "tomboy behavior," respectively. In addition, certain individuals are more concerned about and reactive in their response to gender-linked behavior than others are. For example, researchers have found that fathers react more negatively than mothers when their sons engage in feminine toy play (Idle, Wood, & Desmarais, 1993). Thus, children pick up on, weigh, evaluate, and integrate this diverse range of information regarding their actions and the reactions they produce in others to develop guidelines for gender-related behavior.

DIRECT TUTELAGE AND DIRECT TUITION   The reactions people display in response to the gender-related behavior of others involve the opinions they have regarding what is appropriate behavior for individuals of each sex in our society. **Direct tutelage** is the process by which children are instructed as to what is considered gender-appropriate behavior by others, such as parents, teachers, coaches, siblings, and friends. Although there is a variety of ways by which individuals can attempt to convey what they consider gender-appropriate behavior, an important process is that of direct tuition (Bandura, 1989; Shaffer, 2002). **Direct tuition** involves parents and other individuals directly attempting to influence the child's behavior by using rewards and punishments. For example, researchers have observed that for children as young as 20 months, parents respond differently according to the sex of the toddler by encouraging gender-appropriate play and reacting negatively to cross-sex behavior (Fagot, 1977; Fagot & Leinbach, 1989), with fathers being more likely than mothers to encourage gender-appropriate behavior and discourage behavior that is considered more for the other sex (Leve & Fagot, 1997; Lytton & Romney, 1991) In such cases, girls were reinforced for dancing, asking for assistance, and playing with dolls, while boys were punished for playing with dolls and reinforced for playing with trucks and blocks.

Another form of direct tuition is expressed by the toys and furnishings parents buy for toddlers. The rooms of young boys typically contain outer-space toys, sporting equipment, and toy vehicles, while the rooms of young girls contain dolls, domestic toys, and floral furnishings and ruffles (MacKinnon, Stoneman, & Brody, 1984; Pomerleau, Bolduc, Malcuit, & Cossette, 1990). What is most interesting about these findings is that such direct tuition by parents occurs even before the children have acquired a basic sense of gender identity and clear preference for male and female activities (Fagot & Hagan, 1991). As children get older

and start to socialize with other children at school, the same process of direct tuition can occur when the children are teased by their peers for doing things that involve acting like a "sissy" or gaining acceptance for doing what everybody else is doing, such as young girls wearing makeup to school.

Regulators of Gendered Behavior: Learning When to Do What Boys and Girls Will Do   In addition to describing how children acquire the knowledge of what is considered gendered behavior, social-cognitive theory also describes how children learn to decide how to regulate for themselves the expression of their gendered behaviors.

EXPECTED OUTCOMES   One critical factor in the self-regulation of gendered behavior is the expected outcome such behavior is most likely to produce. Building on previous experience involving modeling influences, the enactive reactions of others, and direction tuition, children begin to develop a sense of what consequences certain gendered behaviors are likely to elicit. From such anticipated outcomes, they then make decisions to perform those socially sanctioned gender-appropriate behaviors that lead to the likelihood of rewards (e.g., praise from parents and peer acceptance) and avoid performing those behaviors that lead to the likelihood of punishment (e.g., being scolded by parents and teased or rejected by peers). Thus, initially, children's regulation of gendered behavior is determined by the expected outcomes of such behaviors according to gender-linked social sanctions operating outside of them.

REGULATORY SELF-SANCTIONS   As children gain more and more experience with being able to anticipate the outcomes their gendered behavior is likely to produce, they begin to develop **regulatory self-sanctions**. The development of regulatory self-sanctions represents a shift from the determinants of gendered behavior that operate outside of individuals (e.g., parents, peers, and socially sanctioned standards) to a greater influence exerted from the development of a set of internal personal standards (Bandura, 1986; Bussey & Bandura, 2004). The development of a set of internal standards for gendered behavior provides two important functions: direction and motivation (Bussey & Bandura, 2004). Regulatory self-sanctions provide direction with regard to helping the child to decide which gendered behavior is most appropriate within the social-situational context, such as the gender ratio of the group (e.g., same-sex vs. mixed-sex) or ongoing activity (e.g., reading in the classroom vs. being in the playground during a structured activity vs. playing at home after school), to name just a few. The sense of personal accomplishment that will go along with the child's ability to self-select the appropriate gendered behavior, coupled with the sense of personal disapproval for failing to do so, serves as the source of motivation for behaving in ways that meet the child's personal standards. As children mature and the developmental process of gender identity continues through adolescence and into adulthood, there is a complex interaction between the influence of the gender-linked social sanctions of society and the more internal, personal regulatory self-sanctions of individuals on the pattern of sex-role behavior exhibited by them.

PERCEIVED SELF-EFFICACY   A third element in the process of the regulation of gendered behavior is the development of a sense of perceived self-efficacy in one's ability to engage in those patterns of gendered behaviors appropriate for the social-situational context (e.g., going to a dance), as well as for life's other tasks (e.g., parenting) and challenges (e.g., dealing with retirement). A strong sense of perceived self-efficacy serves to influence the extent to which individuals will motivate themselves and persevere in face of difficulties in their efforts to express what they believe to be gender-appropriate behavior despite gender-linked social sanctions. For example, a young girl's decision to try out for the school's boys' wrestling team and another girl's decision to try out for the school's cheerleading squad represent each of these girls' perceived sense of self-efficacy regarding their abilities to succeed in activities that each one considers an appropriate part of her gender identity. Thus, as this example illustrates, what individuals consider an appropriate part of their gender identity is a combination of internal and external influences.

In summary, although the value of the social-cognitive view of gender is debated (Martin et al., 2002, 2004), a characteristic feature of this view is the way it attempts to account for both the acquisition and the regulation of gendered behavior. Accounting for both the acquisition and regulation of gendered behavior is achieved by considering the underlying processes associated with the complex set of societal influences and personal standards, as well as their interaction, that help us understand how children establish a sense of gender identity and how this process continues across the life span. Next we will consider the cognitive perspectives on gender development.

Cognitive Perspectives on Gender Development: Creating Consistency in the Classification of Cognitions

We saw in Chapter 10 that the cognitive perspectives emphasize how thoughts and beliefs help us interpret and make sense of everyday experiences and determine our reactions to them. In a similar manner, the cognitive perspectives on gender development attempt to help us understand how individuals develop ideas and beliefs regarding their gender identity (e.g., "Am I a boy or a girl?") and the extent to which these ideas and beliefs impact the way individuals view themselves and others with respect to gender (e.g., gender stereotypes). They also help us understand the way such ideas and beliefs influence gendered behavior decisions (e.g., whether to play with trucks or dolls) and the treatment of others (e.g., whether to disregard boys as playmates while playing with dolls; Martin, 2000; Martin et al., 2002, 2004). In this section, we will consider two of the most influential cognitive perspectives on gender development: cognitive-development theory and gender schema theory.

Carol Lynn Martin's research in the area of cognitive-development theory has done much to explain the role of cognitive process in the development of gender identity.

Cognitive-Development Theory: Consistency in Categorization Is Critical **Cognitive-development theory (CDT)** assumes that gender identity occurs as a result of children's ability to categorize what is considered masculine and feminine and then to behave in a way that is consistent with their gender. A critical component of CDT is **gender constancy** (Martin, 2000; Martin et al., 2002), by which the child understands that one's sex remains the same and does not change over time or in different situations. The development of gender consistency is typically expressed in three stages, with each stage representing a different level of understanding (Martin et al., 2002; Slaby & Frey, 1975).

Stage 1, *gender identity*, represents the extent to which children realize that they are either a boy or girl. For example, a 2-year-old girl volunteers that she is a girl but her male cousin is a boy. Stage two, *gender stability*, reflects children's realization that their gender will not change over time. For example, a 4-year-old preschooler knows that he is a boy now and will still be a boy when in kindergarten next year. Stage three, *gender consistency*, reflects children's recognition that changes in gender-related physical appearances or activities do not alter their perception of being a boy or girl. For example, a 6-year-old girl playing with her brother's trucks knows that doing so does not make her a boy or that a male television character dressed up like a woman in a comedy sketch is still a man. Thus, increases in gender constancy help children to strengthen their self-categorization of gender.

Just as children pass through a series of stages in their development of gender constancy, CDT also proposes that they will pass through a series of stages that involve acquiring the ability to perform increasingly complex cognitive functions, and that such increases in cognitive abilities will be reflected in their beliefs about and behavioral expressions of gender constancy for themselves and others (Kohlberg, 1966; Maccoby, 1990; Martin, 2000; Martin et al., 2002). For example, at around 2 or 3 years, young children acquire the ability to use symbols to stand for other objects. As an example, a rock can stand for a truck for a young boy to use in the sand or as a pillow on which a young girl's doll can rest its head. At around the age of 5 or 6, children begin to develop not only the ability to define whether they are male or female but also the ability to group other pieces of information into categories that are for "boys" and "girls." For example, children of this age might say that a boy's bike should have a horn but not a white wicker basket. Keep in mind that although children as young as 2 years are able to classify themselves as either a boy or girl, they do not yet have a clear sense of what is included in this category. For example, a 2-year-old child might assume that if you are a girl and cut your hair short or wear a tie, you are now a boy. In this example, the child exhibits a sense of gender identity but lacks an understanding of gender stability and gender consistency. Thus, what is critical here is the ability not only to label but also to categorize in a consistent manner along gender lines.

According to CDT, as gender constancy strengthens in children, they appreciate the value of and prefer attitudes and activities from the category that is consistent with their gender identity, as well as individuals within that category (e.g., an in-group of other boys who like to play football). At the same time, they tend to devalue attitudes, activities, and individuals not in that category (e.g., an out-group of girls playing with dolls and boys who play with dolls; Cameron, Alvarez, Ruble, & Fuligni, 2001). The logic is that *because I am a boy, I will do boy things; because I am a girl, I will do girl things*. These gender-type preferences and behaviors are reinforced when children model the same-sex parent and receive praise and rewards for acting like a "little man" or "little lady" (Martin et al., 2002, 2004).

Thus, identification according to CDT is viewed as the end result of the process of gender identity, rather than as the starting point, as suggested by psychoanalytic theory. Critics of CDT contend that the process of gender identity is already underway well before the child begins to demonstrate the ability to categorize objects and events along the lines of gender stability and gender consistency (Bandura & Bussey, 2004). For example, children as young as three already show preferences for gender-appropriate activities (Bussey & Bandura, 1992). However, supporters of CDT point out that such low-level expressions of gender identity may simply represent the child displaying learned parental preferences. (Martin et al., 2002, 2004). For example, little girls learn that they get a smile and words of encouragement (e.g., "You are such a good mommy to your doll") from parents when playing with a doll offered to them by parents, and that "gender identity and labeling are organizers and promoters of gender development, not that they are the only means by which gender-typed behavior might be exhibited" (Martin et al., 2004, pp. 704–705). Such a view suggests that there is more to gender development than simply gender identity of "I am a boy; I am a girl." With this point in mind, we will now look at gender schema theory, which builds on the categorization of "I am a boy" or "I am a girl" to account for gender development.

Gender Schema Theory: An Information-Processing Approach   Like CDT, gender schema theory uses an information-processing approach in proposing that people use categories based on what they consider to be masculine and feminine to help establish their gender identity and understand their lives and the lives of others (Bem, 1981, 1983, 1987, 1993; Martin, 1991, 2000; Martin & Halverson, 1981, 1987; Martin et al., 2002). The critical difference between the two theories is the role of gender schemas.

A **gender schema** is an individual's cluster of beliefs and expectancies with regard to being male and female that influences the type of information which he or she attends to, recalls, and elaborates (Martin et al., 2002). According to gender schema theory, the establishment of gender motivates children to begin organizing their experiences and interactions with others into gender schemas (Bem, 1981, 1993; Hyde, 2004; Martin, 1991, 2000; Martin & Halverson, 1983, 1987). Two important motivational processes guiding the systematic organization of gendered information are the operation of schema-directed memory and the maintenance of gender-linked cognitive consistency (Martin et al., 2002).

The operation of **schema-directed memory** involves the process by which children are motivated to pay attention to and remember gender-linked information about same-sex, self-relevant activities (e.g., to pay attention to what other boys do in the playground or recall what the male characters did in a video), which, in turn, increases the likelihood of their ability to perform behaviors consistent with gender norms supported by various cultural norms that are consistent with their gender-identity classification (e.g., "I am a boy") and the gender-linked activities supported by those various cultural influences (e.g., "Boys are supposed to play with trucks. As a boy, I play with trucks at the day-care center"). Maintaining such gender-linked cognitive consistency strengthens the nature of gender schemas. In addition, as you can see, there is a reciprocal and supportive relationship between the motivational operation of schema-directed memory and gender-linked cognitive consistency. For example, knowing and remembering what girls are supposed to do (e.g., play with dolls) will make it easier for girls to engage in that behavior (e.g., select a doll from a box of toys at the day-care center), which, in turn, strengthens the

knowledge and memory of what to do in the future (e.g., request a doll for a birthday present).

To facilitate and strengthen the formation of gender schemas, children develop certain classification systems that help them to decide what gender-linked information is worthy of their attention and what information can be disregarded. In developing this system of classification, children develop an **in-group/out-group schema** to classify the extent to which certain objects (e.g., a bat or doll), roles (e.g., teacher or police officer), and behaviors (e.g., fighting or crying) are for "boys" or "girls." Children also develop an **own-sex schema**, or a set of thoughts and beliefs about their own gender and the way they will express these with respect to themselves and in their interaction with others. For example, if a boy learns that playing baseball is for boys (in-group schema) but sewing is for girls (out-group schema), the information-processing nature of gender schema theory assumes that he will be more motivated to seek, attend to (e.g., watch the way major leaguers hold the bat), recall (e.g., try to imitate a major leaguer when he is playing baseball), and elaborate on (e.g., decorate his room with posters of his favorite players) information related to baseball than to information on sewing.

Support for the information-processing influence of gender schema theory has been reported in research utilizing both children and adults (Deaux & LaFrance, 1998; Martin, 2000). For example, in one illustrative study (Martin & Halverson, 1983), 5- to 6-year-old children were shown 16 pictures in which a child was depicted as engaging in a gender-consistent action (e.g., a boy playing with a truck) or gender-inconsistent action (e.g., a girl chopping wood). When tested a week later, the children were better able to recall, and with greater confidence, those pictures in which gender-consistent actions were depicted than those of gender-inconsistent actions. In addition, the children also demonstrated a tendency to err in the direction of gender consistency (e.g., recall that it was a *boy* chopping wood). In another interesting study (Martin, Eisenbud, & Rose, 1995), 4- and 5-year-old boys and girls were shown some unfamiliar, gender-neutral toys (e.g., spinning bells, magnet stand), were told that the toys were "for boys" or "for girls," and then were asked whether they and other boys and girls would like them. The children expressed a clear preference for those toys labeled consistent with their gender and felt that others of their gender would express a similar preference. In addition, even toys that were highly attractive were seen as less attractive when they were labeled as being for the other gender. So what children remember, forget, and value seems to be classified on the basis of maintaining gender consistency.

In a study involving adults (Bem, 1981), participants were shown a random list of 61 masculine- or feminine-related words from four categories: proper names (e.g., Henry, Deborah), animals (e.g., gorilla, butterfly), verbs (e.g., hurling, blushing), and clothing (e.g., trousers, bikini). The adults were then given 8 minutes to recall the words in *any* order they could. In support of gender schema theory, the participants with the strongest gender schemas, such as highly masculine males and very feminine females, tended to recall the words in clusters based on their gender relatedness. For example, masculine males tended to recall word clusters having a "masculine theme" (Henry, trousers, hurling, and gorilla) while feminine females tended to recall word clusters having a "feminine theme" (bikini, butterfly, Deborah, and blushing). Non-sex-typed men and women, who supposedly possessed a weaker gender schema, did not display the clustering of gender-related items.

In yet another study, Frable and Bem (1985) had adults listen to 5-minute taped conversations of six separate people. In the "gender condition" of the study, the participants were told that they would be listening to three men and three women. In the "race condition" of the study, they were told they would be listening to three blacks and three whites. While they were listening to the taped conversation of each target person, a picture of that person was projected on the wall. After hearing all six of the conversations, the participants were given a photograph of each person and a written transcript of all of the conversations and then asked to match the conversation with the person. One of the most interesting results of this study was the tendency for those participants who supposedly had a very strong gender schema (i.e., masculine men and feminine women) to make more "opposite-sex errors" than "same-sex errors" when matching the target persons with the appropriate transcript. Specifically, masculine men were more likely to confuse which female target person said what than which male said what, while feminine females were more likely to confuse which male target person said what than which female target person said what. To put it more simply, the traditional masculine males tended to view all the females alike, while the traditional females tended to view all the males alike. What is equally interesting is that the same

pattern of errors *was not* made for those masculine males and feminine females in the "race condition" of the study. Taken together, these studies tend to demonstrate the information-processing impact of gender schemas on how people attend to (e.g., which female or male said what), recall (e.g., remembering gender-related word clusters), and elaborate on (e.g., reconstructing gender-consistent memories for actions observed) information in a manner consistent with gender schema theory. In summary, these studies using both children and adults illustrate how gender schemas can serve to influence how individuals process gender-linked information about themselves and others. However, you should also know that gender schemas can serve to influence how individuals treat others (Brehm, Kassin, & Fein, 2005; Goodwin & Fiske, 2001), and that such treatment can have some serious consequences. As an example, to examine how gender schemas can play a role in the mistreatment of women, read "A Closer Look."

A Closer Look

The Treatment of Women as Sex Objects: A Gender-Schematic Interpretation

The mistreatment of women has long been associated with their depiction as sex objects in pornographic materials (Slade, 2000). Because of the serious consequences of such depiction, including sexual violence (Felson, 2002) and sexual harassment (Strauss, 2003), it is important to develop an understanding of the underlying dynamics associated with this phenomenon.

In an ingenious study, Doug McKenzie-Mohr, of Wilfrid Laurier University, and Mark Zanna, of the University of Waterloo, examined the role of pornography as a trigger for sexist thinking and behavior in males with a strong gender schema (McKenzie-Mohr & Zanna, 1990). In this study, 30 males classified as gender schematic (expressing very traditional masculine characteristics) and 30 males classified as gender aschematic (expressing a combination of masculine and feminine characteristics) were asked to participate in three independent experiments.

Priming Sexist Thinking Using Pornography

The first of the three experiments involved the men viewing a 15-minute video. The subjects in the "sexually primed" condition were asked to watch a 15-minute pornographic video depicting a heterosexual couple engaging in various sexual acts. In the "control" condition, the subjects were asked to watch a 15-minute video of a question-and-answer period from the Canadian House of Commons.

Assessing Behavioral Sexism

After viewing the video, each man was escorted into a separate room, where he was interviewed by a female investigator as part of the second study on adjustment to college. In this session, the female interviewer asked each subject a series of questions relating to making the transition from high school to college. During the interview, the female interviewer used a standard set of questions (e.g., "Was going to college what you expected it to be?") and behaved toward them in a neutral and professional manner.

Assessing Cognitive Sexism

After the subject answered the questions, the interview was ended and he was escorted to a third room, where another male experimenter welcomed him to the third study, which supposedly was a study about memory. In this third study, the subject was given 5 minutes to recall everything he could about the female in the second experiment and the room in which the interview was conducted. After this free-recall task, the individual was placed in front of a computer terminal and asked to respond to a series of seven questions about the female interviewer (e.g., "What color was her hair?") and seven questions about the interview room (e.g., "What color were the walls in the room?"). In addition to assessing the subject's responses to these questions, the computer also measured how long it took to respond to the questions. It should be noted that in the debriefing session conducted after the third study, none of the men indicated that they believed the three studies were related.

Behavioral Sexism in Gender-Schematic Males

The results of this study support the hypothesis that gender-schematic males exposed to pornographic mater-

ial would respond to women in a more sexist manner. Specifically, those males with a traditional male gender schema who viewed the pornographic material were rated by the female interviewer as being more sexually motivated and spending more time looking at her body than were the other three groups of males she encountered. You should note that the female interviewer was not aware of the gender-schematic classification of the subjects or of whether they viewed the pornographic material. This is an important methodological point because it rules out the possibility of the female's ratings of the males being influenced by her expectations of them. In addition, a measure of how close these men positioned their chairs to the female interviewer indicated that the gender-schematic males who viewed the pornographic material sat closer to the female interviewer than did the other three groups of males.

Demonstrating Cognitive Sexism in Gender-Schematic Males

When given the opportunity to recall information about the female experimenter, those schematic males who viewed the pornographic material tended to recall more information about her physical features (e.g., physical appearance and attire) than did males in the other three groups. This tendency to recall physical features of the female was particularly strong during the first minute of the 5-minute free-recall task for males in the schematic/pornography group.

While those males in the schematic/pornography group were very quick in their recall of information about the physical features of the female interviewer, they recalled much less about what she really had said during the interview and what the interview was about than did the other three groups. Finally, it should be noted that the males in the schematic/pornography group tended to take less time to recall the information about the physical features of the female interviewer than did the rest of the groups. Thus, these males appeared to be paying more attention to her body and appearance than what she actually said.

Implications for Understanding Sexism

These results are important because they illustrate how males with rather traditional gender schemas perceive and react to women in a rather sexist manner. One important implication of this research is that the processing of gender-schematic information that is sexist in nature, such as focusing on a woman's body or what she is wearing, can prevent the individual from focusing on what the woman is actually saying or doing. For example, if a male personnel director views a female co-worker as a sexual object, her on-the-job performance may be overlooked and her continued employment jeopardized. It also has implications for how sexual intent and the refusal of sexual advances (e.g., rape) may be perceived by men (Felson, 2002; Shotland & Hunter, 1995).

Another important implication of this research suggests that a potentially harmful effect of pornography is that it can trigger gender-based schematic thoughts and behaviors that are sexist in nature and detrimental to women. Finally, as a point of clarification, research in personality assessment is being done to develop a means of measuring individual differences in hostile sexism toward women (Glick & Fiske, 1996), as well as identifying institutional characteristics most likely to involve a high incidence of sexual harassment (Paludi & Paludi, 2000, 2003a). The identification of hostile sexism in certain males, as well as certain types of institutions, will make it easier to develop and direct programs designed to reduce such sexism. If you would like to read more on the dynamics of and consequences associated with the treatment of women as sex objects, consider reading Richard B. Felson's (2002) *Violence and Gender Reexamined* and Michele and Carmen Paludi's (2003b) *Academic and Workplace Sexual Harassment: A Handbook of Cultural, Social Science, Management, and Legal Perspectives.*

Although the cognitive perspective on gender identity has produced some interesting and supportive research, it is not without its critics. Concerns have been raised regarding the integration of the two major elements of the cognitive perspective – CDT and schema theory – as well as the emergence of different variations of self-schema theory (Bandura & Bussey, 2004). Other concerns involve the extent to which an understanding of gender permanency is able to predict expressed preferences for gender-linked activities and stereotypical knowledge (Evans, Metindogan, & Carter, 2003). In addition to cognitive processes, the question of the degree to which other underlying motivations and external social and cultural factors contribute to gendered development and the expression of gendered behavior has been raised (Bandura & Bussey, 2004).

Integrating the Psychological Processes: Bringing Them All Together Although each of these four general explanations – the psychoanalytic, social-cognitive, cognitive-developmental, and gender schema – has been discussed separately, the processes of gender identity, like so many other psychological processes, rarely operate individually. Instead, they tend to operate in conjunction with each other. That is, identifying with specific models helps the individual to focus his or her attention on certain attitudes and behaviors. These are organized according to social roles, based on the skills necessary to perform them, and categorized according to gender, which makes them easier to organize, remember, and reproduce later. Receiving rewards or observing similar others receiving rewards makes the likelihood of expressing these attitudes or performing these behaviors much more likely. Thus, while each explanation emphasizes a slightly different psychological process, it is possible to integrate them.

Social Role Theory: A Hierarchy of Role Distribution and the Consequences for Gender It Creates

As is true for social-cognitive theory, in **social role theory** the processes of observation and sex differences are critical to the development of gendered behavior and gender identity (Eagly et al., 2004). And, like cognitive theories, social role theory also considers the beliefs that people have about the classification of behavior along gendered lines (Eagly et al., 2004). However, what distinguishes social role theory is the belief that the observation and classification of gendered behaviors have their origins in the sexual division of labor and a hierarchy of social status associated with this division of labor (Eagly, 1987, 1997; Eagly, Wood, & Diekman, 2000; Eagly et al., 2004; Wood & Eagly, 2002). In this division of labor, men are most often found in the role of resource provider, which involves performing work outside the home and being paid more for that work than women are. On the other hand, women tend to be most often found in the role of domestic caregiver, which involves performing more domestic activities while working in the home and being paid less than men are. Thus, in this hierarchy of role distribution, men are more likely to be found in the higher-status social roles while women are more likely found in the lower-status ones. With the placement in the higher-status

The work of Alice Eagly and Wendy Wood on social role theory has done much to help point out the influence of social status as expressed in the division of labor when examining gender identity.

social roles comes decision-making power, authority, and access to resources (Eagly et al., 2000).

According to social role theory, the distribution of more men in the high-status role of "breadwinner" (i.e., resource provider) and more women in the lower-status role of "homemaker" (i.e., domestic caregiver) provides a clear basis for the development of gender-role expectations of what men and women are supposed to do and the skills necessary to do it. For example, in a traditional family, the male is the breadwinner and is expected to exhibit a set of behaviors, such as being instrumental, decisive, and dominant, that eventually become stereotypical of the male role. On the other hand, the typical female is the homemaker and is expected to exhibit a set of behaviors, such a being other-focused, nurturing, and subordinate, that eventually become stereotypical of the female role. And, because of the central role of the family, children begin to develop a sense of the characteristic features associated with being male or female. This process of socialization that begins in the home during early childhood is extended and strengthened throughout childhood and adolescence, as boys and girls tend to self-select those activities and experiences that are supported by social agencies outside of the family, such as peers, teachers, and coaches.

In adulthood, the socialization process continues and the gender-based division of labor along social roles continues as men and women make personal and professional choices. For example, in addition to adopting an other-focused, nurturing orientation at home as caregivers, women extend this orientation to their occupational choices in many female-dominated occupations, such as teacher, nurse, and social worker. The expectations associated with gender are again strengthened by personal decisions involving self-regulation and a desire to maintain gender-consistent behavior within social (e.g., family and friends) and economical (e.g., employment opportunities) constraints. Thus, according to social role theory, it is the nature of the distribution of men and women in the hierarchy of family and occupational roles that forms the basis of gendered behavior.

Evidence supporting social role theory is diverse. Anthropological evidence suggests that this division of labor is accounted for by physical sex differences, especially women's reproductive activities of pregnancy and lactation and the physical strength of men (Eagly et al., 2000; Eagly et al., 2004; Wood & Eagly, 2002). For example, the reproductive and childcare activities of women tend to restrict their participation in activities that involve speed, uninterrupted periods of activity, and long-distance travel away from home. On the other hand, to the extent to which obtaining resources involves speed and strength, men generally have the advantage over women.

Occupational evidence from labor statistics indicates that although a majority of women are in the workforce, men and women tend to be employed in different areas of occupations, with more men than women in those occupations that yield high levels of income and status (e.g., U.S. Department of Labor, Bureau of Labor Statistics, 2004). Societal evidence suggests that stereotypical beliefs that operate in the workplace create somewhat different expectations for men than for women (Eagly & Karau, 2002). For example, in contrast to female managers, male managers are expected to be more self-confident, assertive, firm, and analytical (Heilman, Block, Martell, & Simon, 1989).

Psychological evidence suggests that men and women tend to act in a manner consistent with the social roles they are assigned. For example, in a rather interesting study undertaken to demonstrate the operation of social role theory, men and women were assigned to the role of a supervisor (i.e., high social status), a co-worker (i.e., equal social status), or supervisee (i.e., low social status; Moskowitz, Suh, & Desaulniers, 1994). Both men and women when assigned to the supervisor role tended to display more dominance. When assigned to the role of supervisee, both men and women tended to display more submissiveness. An interesting twist in this study was that the individuals were reassigned to different social roles throughout the study, which in turn affected their behavior. Specifically, reversing the role assignments from supervisor to supervisee tended to produce less dominance and more submissiveness, while reversing the role assignment from supervisee to supervisor tended to produce less submissiveness and more dominance. Such a pattern of results, as suggested by social role theory, implies that characteristic features displayed by men and women are, in part, due to the roles they are assigned and the status associated with those roles.

In summary, the evidence from many different perspectives and viewpoints in support of social role theory suggests that certain physical differences between men and women, the restrictions in the nature of the social roles these differences create for them, and, most importantly, the value society assigns to the roles combine with the distribution ratio of men and women in the hierarchy of social roles to provide a framework from which individuals within society seek others to observe and model their behavior on to help them formulate their gender identity. Such a set of events also implies that, as technical advances minimize the value of the physical differences between the work that can be done by men and women, and as more and more women are being found in positions of authority in industry and the government, the nature of the distribution of men and women in the social role hierarchy will change, which will be associated with a shift in the views we have about men and women, what they can do, and how they should behave. Over time, the impact of this shift will be reflected in the nature of gender identity developed by children, which will provide a greater and more equal range of social, educational, and occupational opportunities for both boys and girls and men and women. For more information on social role theory of gender identity, read a book chapter titled "Social Role Theory of Sex Differences and Similarities: Implications for the Partner Preferences of Men and Women" (Eagley et al., 2004). Next, we will consider biological explanations of gender identity.

Biological Explanations of Gender Identity Chromosomes, Hormones, and Hermaphroditism

The biological explanations of gender identity have focused on those biological processes within the individual that determine the internal and external physical nature of each person's sex. A distinction is made between internal and external because, as we will see, there are certain people who have the sexual organs of one sex internally but the physical appearance of the other (Hyde & DeLamater, 2003; Mealey, 2000). The biological considerations to be discussed include chromosomes, hormones, and hermaphroditism (Smith, 2007).

Sex Chromosomes: The Building Blocks of Gender Identity **Chromosomes** are genetic structures found within each cell. Each cell in the human body contains a set of 23 pairs of chromosomes. One pair of these chromosomes determines the gender of the individual. A chromosome pair XX designates a female individual and determines the development of the cells of the body in the appropriate physical direction. A chromosome pair XY designates a male individual and determines the development of the cells of the body in the appropriate physical direction. Part of the development determined by these chromosomes is the development of gonads and their production of various sex hormones (Hines, 2004).

Hormones: The Substances of Gender Identity
Hormones are chemical substances secreted within the body by a system of glands referred to as the **endocrine system**. The **gonads** are the sexual glands that secrete the hormones that regulate sexual development. For males, the gonads are the **testes**; for females, the gonads are the **ovaries**. For males, the major sex hormones are **androgen** and **testosterone**; for females, the sex hormones are **estrogen** and **progesterone** (Hyde & DeLamater, 2003). During fetal development, the presence of these hormones influences the development of **primary sexual characteristics** that include the major reproductive organs within the individual. During puberty, the presence of these hormones determines the appearance of **secondary sexual characteristics** that for females involves the development of breasts, broadening of hips, growth of body hair, and other changes in body shape; and for males involves deepening of the voice and the presence of facial and body hair (Mealey, 2000). In addition, there is also evidence to suggest that these hormones are associated with personality characteristics. For example, aggression is a personality characteristic typically associated with masculine behavior, and there is evidence to suggest that increased levels of the male hormone testosterone in both men and women are associated with greater levels of aggression (Lippa, 2005) and antisocial behavior (Dabbs & Dabbs, 2000) when compared to men and women with more gender-appropriate levels of testosterone; however, this pattern is not always consistent (Hines, 2004). On the other hand, nurturance is a personality characteristic associated with feminine behavior, and there is evidence to suggest that increased levels of testosterone are associated with decreased interest in an assortment of nurturing behaviors among girls, including reduced interests in dolls, babysitting, and other aspects of child care, including plans to have children (Hines, 2002). Thus, while these sex hormones have been discussed separately, you should realize that males and females produce both types of sex hormones. And what seems to be critical, as the evidence suggests, is the amount that is produced.

Hermaphroditism: A Biosocial Interaction for Deciding Gender While the discussion of chromosomes

and hormones might lead you to believe that the development of gender identity from a biological perspective is pretty straightforward, this is not always the case (Money, 1987). A good example of this appears in what is known as hermaphroditism. **Hermaphroditism** is a biological condition in which the individual possesses the sexual characteristics of both genders. For example, the individual may have a penis but also ovaries and breasts. Other related conditions include **pseudohermaphroditism** (or an intersex individual) in which some aspects of the individual's biological sex do not match up with their physical sexual characteristics, or they have ambiguous genitals (Mealey, 2000).

The major concern in such cases is whether the individual is to be classified as a male or female. As it turns out, the critical factor is when such a classification is made and how the child is raised. More specifically, in such cases, a decision is made as to whether the child is to be labeled a girl or boy. This decision is typically made after consulting with the parents and a staff of genetic counselors, medical doctors, and mental health professionals.

After the decision is made, depending on the case, there may be some surgery to create the appropriate external organs, (e.g., construction of a vagina) and hormonal treatment to stimulate appropriate primary and secondary sex characteristics (e.g., the development of breasts at puberty). The individual is then raised with the assigned gender identity (e.g., put in dresses, called "Mary," and given dolls).

It is recommended that if such gender assignment is to be done, it should occur before the age of 18 months. After that time, the child may have already established a gender identity and may suffer some severe psychological trauma (Ehrhardt, 1985; Money & Ehrhardt, 1972). You should realize, however, that there is some disagreement regarding this conclusion (Diamond, 1982, 1996, 1999; Diamond & Sigmundson, 1997; Imperato-McGinley, Peterson, Gautier, & Sturla, 1979; Wisniewski et al., 2000). As an example, the book titled *As Nature Made Him: The Boy Who Was Raised as a Girl* (Colapinto, 2000) describes the highly compelling and emotionally disturbing real-life story of a boy who, because of a botched operation to his penis for a urinary problem in infancy, was raised as a girl.

Integrating Biological Explanations with Cultural and Psychological Factors: Bringing Them All Together
The integration of the biological explanations involving chromosomes and hormones is relatively straightforward:

Chromosomes trigger the release of certain hormones that, in turn, trigger the development of certain physical features. But the presence of hermaphroditism poses some problems of integration. To account for the process of gender identity on the basis of the assignment of gender involves considering the biological explanations together with cultural and psychological ones. The work with hermaphrodites illustrates just how important cultural (e.g., cultural stereotypes) and psychological (e.g., the process by which these stereotypes are taught to children) factors are when combined with biological factors in the process of the acquisition of one's gender. Once again, you can see that something as significant and complex as gender identity involves many factors and a not-so-simple explanation. For more information on the biological explanations of gender identity, consider reading a book chapter by Melissa Hines (2004) on the impact of early hormone environment on gender-related behavior, and John Money and Anke Ehrhardt's (1972) classic book titled *Man and Woman, Boy, and Girl*. In the next section, we will consider the evolutionary psychology perspective of gendered behavior.

The Evolutionary Perspective of Gendered Behavior: Responding to Adaptive Problems with Successful Strategies for Survival of the Species

As you recall from Chapter 9 (see pp. 361–373), evolutionary psychology is the study of the way psychological processes and social behavior have emerged to help individuals resolve various adaptive problems – those for which individuals must develop successful strategies in order to reproduce and survive – over the course of time (D. M. Buss, 2004, 2005). Successfully resolving adaptive problems of survival and reproduction is based on the principle of natural selection. Through natural selection, the fittest members of a species, which have developed the most successful strategies in response to adaptive problems, survive to pass along their genes, which contain the biological information upon which these successful strategies are stored, to the next generation though successful reproduction. Facilitating the process of successful reproduction, as you will recall, is the principle of sexual selection by which, in most cases, male members of a species compete with each other for the mating oppor-

tunities with the females, while the female members choose only to mate with certain male members of the species. Finally, there is the principle of parental investment in which parents exhibit behaviors designed to increase the likelihood of their offspring surviving and passing along those genes containing the successful adaptive strategies to the next generation.

Gendered Behavior as an Evolutionary Response: Men and Women Adapting for the Good of the Species
As applied to the understanding of gendered behavior, evolutionary psychology has utilized these principles as the underlying explanation to account for the systematic differences in complex social behavior patterns and psychological processes that have been characteristic of men and women for generations (Mealey, 2000; G. F. Miller, 1998; Silverman & Choi, 2005).

As an example, consider how sexual strategies theory (D. M. Buss & Schmitt, 1993; Schmitt, 2005) might account for gender differences in aggressiveness and nurturance. Specifically, the increased levels of aggressiveness and instrumental behaviors that are more characteristic of males than females have evolutionary value because they make it possible for males to demonstrate their ability to protect and provide for those females they desire most as mates, as well as any offspring such mating might produce. In humans, such aggressiveness and instrumental behavior might be expressed in highly aggressive business practices that produced increased levels of wealth, which can then be seen as an index of a male's ability to provide for his family. On the other hand, the heightened level of nurturance and emotional expressiveness that is more characteristic of females than of males has evolutionary value because this makes it possible for females to provide the care and attention needed to maximize the likelihood that the infants will survive into adulthood and be able to pass on the genes of the parents to the next generation. In humans, such nurturing and emotionally expressive behaviors are encouraged and reinforced in our society by advertisements geared toward women that emphasize the importance of maintaining a safe and clean household environment for their children and spouse (i.e., the provider and protector). Thus, from the evolutionary perspective, the typical family of the male working outside the home and the female staying home to take care of the family supposedly is not based on superficially imposed stereotypical attitudes about men and women, but is the result of a long and systematic evolutionary process involving natural selection and sexual selection, adapted to accommodate the social and environmental changes that are occurring, and will continue to occur, in society by the creation of new technologies and alterations in such standard social institutions as the family and the nature of work. A good example of such changes and the development of successful strategies to deal with such adaptive problems associated with family life and work is that the development of computer technology has made it possible for more businesses to offer flextime, which makes it possible for parents to work outside the home as well as work from home, but adapt their work schedule to respond to the special needs of their families.

Another interesting evolutionary link between gendered behavior and the formation and maintenance of the family is the possible explanation of the orgasm of the human female as the development of a successful evolutionary strategy to the adaptive problem of the survival of young offspring (Barash, 1982). As stated above, the survival of young offspring in humans is maximized by the successful pairing of a male and female, along with the complementary skills each possesses. The development of any element that increases the likelihood of a permanent, monogamous pairing of a mother and father would be a successful solution to an adaptive problem and be favored in the evolutionary process. It has been suggested that the evolutionary development of the female orgasm is a critical element in helping to maintain this parental union. Specifically, the female orgasm, along with the human female's ability to demonstrate continued interested in sexual activity during all phases of her menstrual cycle, has evolved as a means of helping to ensure the possibility of keeping together the parents, along with, as noted previously, their complementary set of evolutionarily successful skills – the male providing protection and resources and the female providing nurturing care of the infant and domestic support. Another possible explanation for the adaptive function of the female orgasm is that it serves to position the internal structure of the vagina to retain a greater amount of sperm, thus increasing the likelihood of conception with a partner with the highest genetic quality (T. K. Shackelford, Pound, Goetz, & LaMunyon, 2005). Thus, given that female orgasm is thought to exist in few, if any, other species, the evolutionary significance given to the orgasm of the human female, along with the proposed reasoning for its development, is that it is considered to be a successful strategy to an important adaptive problem. Can you think of another possible explanation for its existence?

As you can see, the evolutionary psychology perspective on gendered behavior incorporates biological, psychological, and societal influences to help explain how humans, as well as other species, have developed in response to a variety of adaptive problems. An outcome of such adaptive responses over time has been the development of patterns of social behavior and personality characteristics associated with each gender that has made it possible for the human species to create a social environment that is in the best interest of all its members. As cultural and societal changes and technological advances appear to create new challenges to individuals, it is safe to say that from an evolutionary psychology perspective, adjustments in behavior patterns and personality characteristics of men and women will reflect the adaptive responses to these challenges.

Additional information discussing the evolutionary psychology perspective on gendered behavior and personality can be found in a book chapter titled "Sex Roles as Adaptations: An Evolutionary Perspective on Gender Differences and Similarities" (Kenrick, Trost, & Sundie, 2004) and in "Chapter 3: Evolution of Sex and Sex Differences" in a book by Linda Mealey (2000) titled *Sex Differences: Development and Evolutionary Strategies*. Finally, for an alternative viewpoint on the evolutionary perspective of gender identity from a feminist sociobiology viewpoint, see a rather interesting book titled *Mother Nature: Maternal Instincts and How They Shaped the Human Species* (Hrdy, 1999).

Integration of Explanations: Incorporating the Psychological, Social, Biological, and Evolutionary Perspectives of Explanations of Gender Identity

We conclude our discussion with an attempt to integrate the various perspectives on gender identity to demonstrate their collective contribution to our understanding. The *biological perspective* involves chromosomes triggering the release of certain hormones that, in turn, trigger the development of certain bodily characteristics associated with being male and female. But, as the presence of hermaphroditism indicates, there is more to the process than just the biological nature of the individual – the assignment of gender involves considering the biological influences together with social and psychological ones. The *evolutionary perspective* explains the systematic development of the physical characteristics of males and females that are expressed in gendered behavior and personality characteristics that help to promote the survival of individuals. *Social role theory* incorporates the presence of these physical features and personality characteristics in a social context by considering how such gender differences help create gender-role expectations associated with what men and women are supposed to do in a particular society to help that society flourish. On the basis of such social expectations, the *cognitive perspectives* help to account for how individuals organize and mentally structure this information along gender lines to help guide their decisions regarding their expression of behavior consistent with their gender identity. The *psychoanalytic* and *social-cognitive theories* help to account for how such psychological processes as identification, modeling, and the use of reinforcement (e.g., praise from parents and acceptance of peers) and punishment (e.g., criticism of parents and rejection by peers), along with the nature of the reactions of other significant social agents (e.g., teachers and coaches) and the nature of the messages presented in the media regarding the consequences of supporting or violating these gender-role expectations, are involved in the acquisition, maintenance, and transmission of gendered behavior, gender differences in personality, and sex-role stereotypes. Thus, once again, as has been demonstrated throughout our study of personality, you can see that something as significant and complex as gender identity and gendered behavior involves many factors interacting together and a not-so-simple explanation.

Gender identity is a complex process that requires a number of theoretical perspectives in order to appreciate and understand fully its nature, dynamics, and consequences, all of which will be explored in more detail throughout the rest of this chapter. For more information on this topic, consult the following sources: a book by Janet Shibley Hyde (2004) titled *Half the Human Experience: The Psychology of Women* (see "Chapter 2: Theoretical Perspectives") and "Part II: Theoretical Approaches" in a book titled *The Developmental Social Psychology of Gender* (Eckes & Trautner, 2000). This concludes our discussion of theories of gender identity. To help you organize and study this diverse material, a summary of the major ideas discussed in this section is presented in "Summing It Up: Theories of Gender Identity" on p. 507. In the next section, you will consider some consequences of gender identity by examining gender differences in personality and behavior and sex-role stereotypes.

Consequences of Gender Identity: Gender Differences in Personality and Gender-Role Stereotypes

One consequence of differences in gender identity is that the members of each gender might somehow develop certain characteristic personality features or be perceived as possessing these features. The characteristics that develop as a result of gender identity are considered gender differences in personality. The characteristics and abilities that members of one gender are assumed to possess are considered gender-role stereotypes (Hyde, 2004; S. E. Taylor, Peplau, & Sears, 2003). In this section, you will consider the nature of gender differences in personality and perceived gender-role stereotypes as consequences of gender identity.

Gender Differences in Personality: How Do Males and Females Differ?

How do males and females differ? As a consequence of gender identity, males and females are subjected to various biological, psychological, evolutionary, societal, and cultural factors that have an impact on their personality development (D. M. Buss, 1995; Eckes & Trautner, 2000; Hyde, 2004; Kashima et al., 1995; Pomerantz, Fei-Yin Ng, & Wang, 2004). In this section, we will examine some potential differences in personality that this diversity of factors may produce, as well as some issues related to the magnitude and measurement of these differences (Eagly, 1995; Hyde, 2005; Kimball, 2001; Lippa, 1995). Whenever possible, an explanation is given for why such differences exist. The gender differences in personality to be discussed in this section include aggression, expressions of emotional and physical intimacy, social influence, emotional expressiveness, self-evaluation and expectations, happiness and depression, and cognitive functioning.

Aggression: Gender Differences in Hurting

One of the more consistent findings has been that males behave more aggressively than females (Baron &

Summing It Up *Theories of Gender Identity*

Explanation	Example
Psychological:	
Psychoanalytic Theory. Gender identity occurs through the process of identification during which the child internalizes the attitudes and values of the same-sex parent.	By acting like "mommy," the little girl begins to learn how females behave in our society.
Social-Cognitive Theory. Gender identity occurs through the process of the child observing what others of the same sex are doing, receiving instructions from others regarding what is gender-appropriate behavior, receiving reinforcement when such behavior is performed, and learning to self-regulate the expression of gender-appropriate behavior in order to receive such reinforcement.	By watching wrestling with his father, being told by his coach that he needs to be more aggressive on the soccer field, and receiving praise from his father, coach, and teammates when he plays aggressively on the field, the little boy begins to act more aggressively not only on the soccer field but also while playing with others in the playground during recess.
Cognitive Perspectives. Gender identity occurs through the process by which children classify activities and behaviors as being for either boys or girls, while developing schemas for helping them to observe, recall, and relate their actions in a manner that is consistent with their own gender labeling.	"Because playing with trucks is for boys, and I'm a boy, I'd rather play with trucks than skip rope."
Social Role Theory. Gender identity is based on the notion that there is a historical pattern of a division of labor that is based on males being providers and women being domestic caregivers, and that with the social roles reflected in this division of labor, males tend to occupy higher-status roles while women then to occupy the lower-status ones. This leads to the expectation that males and females are to display a pattern of behavior consistent with their social roles.	In a hospital setting, males are more likely to be found in the high-status position of physicians and expected to display a pattern of behavior that is authoritative and instrumental, while females are more likely to be found in the lower-status position of nurses and to display a more subservient and nurturing pattern of behavior.
Biological:	
Sex Chromosomes. Gender identity occurs through the presence of chromosomes that determine the extent to which the cells in the body develop into the physical structures of a male or female.	The presence of the XX chromosome pair makes possible the development of a vagina and ovaries in females.
Hormones. Gender identity occurs through the presence of hormones, which are the chemical substances that regulate the development of primary and secondary sex characteristics.	The secretion of male hormones triggers the development of facial hair for males and breasts for females during adolescence.
Hermaphroditism. Because a hermaphrodite possesses the primary sex characteristics of both sexes, gender identity occurs through the process of deciding on what sex the child will be raised as, and using corrective surgery to create the appropriate external genitals and other physical features.	After determining to raise a child hermaphrodite as a boy, male hormones are injected at adolescence to make sure that such features as facial hair and upper-torso development occur.
Evolutionary Perspective. Gender identity is based on the evolution of males and females developing different patterns of behavior that help the species procreate and survive, including males exhibiting a pattern of aggressive behavior because it allows them to provide food and protection for other members of the species and attract the most desirable mating partners, while females exhibit a pattern of nurturing behavior because it ensures the necessary care and attention required for infants to reach adulthood.	The father works overtime on a regular basis to surpass his sales quotas in order to receive a bonus and promotion, which will make it possible for the mother to stay home with the children and move the family to a safer neighborhood with better schools, which will increase the likelihood of the children getting into a better college and having an improved standard of living and higher quality of life.

Richardson, 1994; Hyde, 2004, 2005; Krahé, 2001; Maccoby & Jacklin, 1974). This difference has been found in animals (Archer, 1988; Berkowitz, 1993; Harlow & Suomi, 1971; Krahé, 2001) and in many different cultures (Shaffer, 2002; Whiting & Pope, 1974). Specifically, a number of meta-analyses reviewing over a 100 studies of aggression conclude that males are more aggressive than females both physically and verbally (Eagly & Steffen, 1986; Hyde, 1986; Knight, Fabes, & Higgins, 1996). Developmentally, this difference tends to show up relatively early (Krahé, 2001) and at all age levels, including with individuals in their seventies and eighties (Walker, Richardson, & Green, 2000). In addition, males show a greater tendency than females to perform aggressive acts and be the target of such aggression (Bogard, 1990; Harris, 1992, 1994), to demonstrate aggression against others when the other individuals have *not* provoked them (Bettencourt & Miller, 1996), to exhibit aggression and other forms of antisocial behavior reflective of mental health problems (Rosenfield, Vertefuille, & McAlpine, 2000), and to be arrested for violent crimes such as murder and non-negligent manslaughter, aggravated assault, and all other sorts of violent crimes (Federal Bureau of Investigation, 1997; Krahé, 2001;). However, an emerging trend is the rise in violent crimes committed by young females, as suggested by FBI statistics indicating that "the number of girls 10 to 17 arrested for aggravated assault has doubled over the last 20 years. The number of boys arrested for weapons possession rose 22 percent between 1983 and 2003, while the number of girls increased by a whopping 125 percent. Today, one in three juveniles arrested for violent crimes is female" (Scelfo, 2005, p. 66).

While some of these differences can be explained as a result of hormonal levels, such as testosterone (Glaude, 1991; Krahé, 2001; Zuckerman, 2005), and evolutionary dynamics (A. Campbell, 2005; Felson, 2002; Krahé, 2001), they are more likely explained by the processes of the social role model involving principles of learning, modeling, and social expectations (Baron & Richardson, 1994; Krahé, 2001). In most cultures, boys are encouraged to engage in more physical activity, and it is possible that this increased level of physical activity also carries over into their aggressive behavior. There is also evidence that while girls may not be as physically aggressive as boys, they are more capable of engaging in passive or indirect aggressive behaviors than boys are (Brodzinsky, Messer, & Tew, 1979; A. Campbell, 2005; Green, Richardson, & Lago, 1996; Harris, 1992;

Krahé, 2001; Österman et al., 1998), with such a trend being observed in several different countries (Österman et al., 1998; Owens, Shute, & Slee, 2000). In this case, indirect aggression might involve ignoring another individual, calling names, gossiping, or excluding another child from an activity. Thus, this difference in aggression appears to be a consequence of gender identity. Be aware, however, that the size of this difference is not as large as popular belief might suggest, and that it is determined by several factors, including the type of aggression studied, method of study, age of the subjects studied, and various other cultural considerations (A. H. Buss, 1995; Eagly, 1987; Krahé, 2001; Shaffer, 2002).

Expressions of Emotional and Physical Intimacy: Gender Differences in Love, Romance, Mate Selection, Sexuality, and Jealousy

Some of the most interesting gender differences are observed in the context of how men and women express some of the most intimate emotional and physical aspects of human nature. Along these lines, we will now consider gender differences in the expression of love, romance, mate selection, sexual behavior, and jealousy.

Gender Differences in Love and Romance: Matters of the Heart Consistent with research looking at various types of emotions, the research on gender differences

While both of these individuals seem to be enjoying this romantic dinner, gender differences in attachment indicate that men and women seem to experience love and jealousy differently. Are your experiences with love and jealousy consistent with the results reported in the text?

in love has generally reported that although women tend to experience stronger emotions than men do in response to feelings of love, there do not appear to be any major differences between men and women on more specific measures to assess various aspects of love and attachment styles (R. S. Miller, Perlman, & Brehm, 2007). However, gender differences in the experience of love begin to appear when researchers go beyond the scores on love scales and ask people about their feelings and experience associated with love (R. S. Miller et al., 2007). Specifically, compared to men, women report being in love more frequently and having more intense romantic feelings (Dion & Dion, 1973), as well as more vivid memories of past romantic partners (Harvey, Flanary, & Morgan, 1986). In addition, while females tend to view love as more rewarding than do males, they also tend to report more experience with loving someone without being loved in return (Dion & Dion, 1975).

Researchers have also examined gender differences in romance. When examining scores on scales of romanticism, several studies have indicated that men tend to score higher than women do (Sprecher & Metts, 1989). For example, men, to a greater degree than women, tend to believe that it is possible to "fall in love at first sight," which helps to explain why men tend to fall in love faster than women (Hatfield & Sprecher, 1986). On the other hand, in contrast to men, woman tend to be more pragmatic about love (Hendrick, Hendrick, & Dicke, 1998) and more cautious about love in terms of being more selective about with whom they fall in love, feeling passion at a slower rate, and limiting their feelings of love to those partners who have higher intelligence, status, and resources (D. M. Buss, 1998; Kenrick et al., 2004; L. C. Miller & Fishkin, 1997). Such a behavior pattern is consistent with the evolutionary and social role perspectives on gender noted previously in this chapter, which suggest that women attempt to seek resources linked to parental investment, social status, and power when considering potential mates (Schmitt, 2005).

Gender Differences in Mate Selection: Looking for Love, or at Least Genetic Transmission   As we discussed in Chapter 9, the evolutionary perspective suggests that when seeking a potential mate, men tend to focus on the physical attractiveness of potential mates while females tend to center on the potential mate's status and resources (Fletcher, Tither, O'Loughlin, Friesen, & Overall, 2004; Schmitt, 2005; Sugiyama, 2005). For

males, the youthful and healthy-looking features of a female are viewed as signs of increased breeding potential, which increases the likelihood that the male's genes would be passed on to the next generation (D. M. Buss, 1994, 1998, 2004). Some of the physical features that have been found to influence males' attachment to females include long, shiny hair (Etcoff, 1999; Hinsz, Matz, & Patience, 2001), symmetrical facial features (i.e., having mirror-image features on the left and right side of the face; Hughes, Harrison, & Gallup, 2002), and symmetrical body (i.e., having a balanced-looking body on both sides; Manning, Koukourakis, & Brodie, 1997; Scutt, Manning, Whitehouse, Leinster, & Massey, 1997). It has been reported that, to maximize the likelihood of selecting a mate with the highest potential for status and resources, females tend to prefer males who are higher in income, education level, self-confidence, intelligence, dominance, and social status than they are (Buunk, Dukstra, Fetchenhauer, & Kendrick, 2002). However, you should be aware that others have proposed, from culture-based research (L. C. Miller, Putcha-Bhagavatula, & Pedersen, 2002), that *both* men and women have expressed a preference for a wealthy mate (Hanko, Master, & Sabini, 2004).

Gender Differences in Sexuality: The How and Why of Expressions of Physical Intimacy   There is considerable evidence to document gender differences in sexuality (Baumeister & Tice, 2001; Hyde, 2005; Peplau & Garnets, 2000). In one meta-analysis that reviewed 177 studies of gender differences in sexuality, the biggest gender difference identified was the incidence of masturbation (Oliver & Hyde, 1993), with the difference varying across time, from 92 percent of men vs. 58 percent of women when asked if they hade ever masturbated (Kinsey, Pomeroy, & Martin, 1948; Kinsey, Pomeroy, Martin, & Gebhard, 1953) to 63 percent for males vs. 42 percent for females when asked if they had masturbated in the last year (Laumann, Gagnon, Michael, & Michaels, 1994). In this same review, the second biggest gender difference was in terms of sexual attitudes, in that men tended to be much more approving of casual sex (i.e., nonmarital sex with no emotional commitment between the partners – "a one-night stand") than females did (Oliver & Hyde, 1993).

Consistent with this finding and across a variety of ethnic groups, it was reported that Caucasian (76 percent), African-American (77 percent), & Hispanic (78 percent) females were more likely than Caucasian (53 percent), African American (43 percent), and Hispanic (57 percent) males to indicate that they would have sex with someone only if they were in love with that person (Mahay, Laumann, & Michaels, 2000). Along these lines, as well as across 52 different nations, males express a desire to have, on the average, 13 different sexual partners over the next 30 years of their lifetime, while females expressed a desire to have, on the average, only 2.5 sexual partners over this same period (Schmitt et al., 2003). In a similar manner, when asked "Ideally, how many different sexual partners would you like to have within the next month?" over 23 percent of males but only 3 percent of females from North America indicated that they would like to have more than one partner in the next month (Schmitt et al., 2003). Such a pattern of results suggests that males and females have very different standards for both long-term and short-term expressions of sexual behavior, as well as different reasons for doing so (Schmitt, 2005). When having sex, males are more likely to experience an orgasm during sexual intercourse with their partner than females are (79 percent of males vs. 29 percent of females), but this difference is reduced during masturbation (80 percent of males vs. 60 percent of females; Laumann et al., 1994).

In terms of the reasons for having sex, in general, females are more likely to report a desire to express affection, gain intimacy, and seek a mate with characteristics (e.g., ambition and kindness) indicating the capacity to provide long-term provisional care for the females and their offspring in a committed relationship, while males are more likely to report the variety of sexual experience, the seeking of physical gratification, and reproductive characteristics (e.g., the female's youth and physical attractiveness; Hatfield, Sprecher, Pillemer, Greenberger, & Wexler, 1989; R. S. Miller et al., 2007; Schmitt, 2005). However, you should know that when it comes to engaging in casual sex, males and females express similar reasons for doing so, including sexual desire, experimentation, and the attractiveness of the partner. In terms of the outcome of having sex, females tend to express the belief that it might increase the probability of a long-term commitment with the sexual partner, while males tend to express the belief that it might increase their status with their male peers and the increased likelihood of genetic transmission to the next generation (Regan & Dreyer, 1999; Schmitt, 2005). Finally, a review of the relevant research suggests that males tend to have a greater sex drive than women, including males reporting more frequent

feelings of sexual arousal and spending more time thinking and fantasizing about sex than females do (Baumeister & Tice, 2001), but that, in general, gender differences in sexual satisfaction appear to be close to zero (Hyde, 2005).

Thus, while there are some clear gender differences in sexuality, you should realize that there are substantial individual differences among males and females when it comes to sexual behavior (Bailey, Kirk, Zhu, Dunne, & Martin, 2000). And, of course, something as complicated as gender and sexuality has many different explanations, including biological, hormonal, cultural, social, and evolutionary ones, to name just a few (Hyde & DeLatamer, 2003).

Gender Differences in Jealousy: Reactions to Threats of Sexual vs. Emotional Infidelity   Threats to one's love or romantic interest can produce feelings of jealousy in both men and women (D. M. Buss, 2000; L. Campbell & Ellis, 2005), and these feelings have shown a consistent gender difference. One approach to the study of gender differences in this area has looked at the responses of men and women to various measures of jealousy. The assessment of gender differences on jealousy scales indicates that while there are no differences between men and women on global measures of jealousy (White & Mullen, 1989), males tend to experience their jealousy along a cognitive component – having thoughts about others being attracted to their partner – and females along an affective component – expressing strong feelings about others being attracted to their partner (Carmickle & Carducci, 1993). In addition, expressions of jealousy in females tend to be related more to the expectation that it would be difficult to replace their current relationship, while expressions of jealousy for males are related more to a threat to their self-esteem (White, 1981a, 1981b). In a summary of how men and women cope differently with their feelings of jealousy, it was reported that men were more likely than women to leave relationships, while women were more likely than men to try to preserve the existing relationships (R. S. Miller et al., 2007).

Another area of research has examined the nature of those situations that are likely to arouse feelings of jealousy. Researchers have looked at how males and females would respond to a situation in which the partner has engaged in sexual infidelity versus the partner becoming seriously emotionally involved with someone else. A basic finding of this research is that males display much more jealousy and distress in response to sexual infidelity than do females, who tend to show a greater degree of jealousy and distress in response to emotional infidelity (D. M. Buss, Larsen, Semmelroth, & Westen, 1992; L. Campbell & Ellis, 2005; Pietrzak, Laird, Stevens, & Thomson, 2002). This basic finding has also been identified in a variety of different cultures (Buss et al., 1999; Buunk, Angleitner, Oubaid, & Buss, 1996). Although there are alternative explanations provided for this pattern of results (DeSteno & Salovey, 1996; DeSteno, Bartlett, Salovey, & Braverman, 2002), based on the evolutionary perspective (D. M. Buss, 2000; L. Campbell & Ellis, 2005) the explanation for these gender differences in jealousy is that, for a male, a sexual infidelity by his mate represents a serious threat to the possibility that she might have a pregnancy by another male, which would pose a threat to the possibility of his genes being passed along to the next generation. For a female, since there is no doubt that she is the mother of her offspring, the fact that her mate is engaging in sexual infidelity with another female is not the real threat. The most pressing evolutionary threat is that if her mate becomes emotionally involved with other woman, she runs the risk of losing her mate's resources, time, commitment, and parental investment as a result of him devoting all of them to the other woman.

As you can see, there are some rather interesting patterns of gender differences in a variety of expressions of emotional and physical intimacy. How do these finding compare to your own experiences?

Social Influence: Gender Differences in Going Along and Getting Along

With social influence, the basic assumption has been that females are more likely to be influenced by others than are males along the lines of being more easily persuaded, more suggestible, and more conforming, as well as more willing to work with others. This conclusion is based on earlier research comparing the degree of social influence of men and women in various situations (Crutchfield, 1955; Eagly & Carli, 1981). But a closer look at this area of research involving a meta-analysis of 145 different studies reveals that there were a number of other factors that could have been used to account for these gender differences in social influence (Eagly, 1987; Eagly & Carli, 1981). For example, in some of these studies, the tasks used were more familiar to males than to females at that time (e.g., economic or business issues).

As a more valid test of gender differences, subsequent research was conducted (Sistrunk & McDavid, 1971) involving tasks that favored either males (e.g., identifying tools) or females (e.g., identifying kitchen utensils) or neither (e.g., identifying celebrities). The results of this research indicated females conformed more than males to the male-familiar tasks, males conformed more than females to the female-familiar tasks, and both were equally conforming in the neutral tasks. These and similar results (Carli & Bukatko, 2000; Eagly, 1987; Eagly & Carli, 1981) suggest that gender differences in conformity may have more to do with cultural expectations than with underlying abilities of men and women.

In terms of attempts to influence others, a recent survey of this research indicates that men tend to exert more social influence than women do in gender-neutral tasks (Carli & Bukatko, 2000). In addition, it was reported that men tend to be more resistant to attempts to influence them by women than women are to such attempts by men. A key element in these gender differences in social influence is the extent to which individuals listen to men and women. For example, it has been reported that when men and women were interacting in the same group, information provided by the men was six times more likely to have an influence on the group than was *identical* information provided by the women in the group (Propp, 1995). The information provided by the women was basically ignored. Such gender differences in social influence tend to be explained by differences in leadership attainment – men tend to emerge as leaders to a greater degree than women do, which is due, in part, to their increased degree of group participation (Eagly & Karau, 1991). However, as an interesting side note, men tend to be more influenced by women when they stand to gain by the influence. For example, men are more likely to be influenced by a competent woman than by a less competent woman when her ideas can help them achieve some goal, such as obtaining money or some other reward (S. Shackelford, Wood, & Worchel, 1996).

In terms of getting along with others during group interactions, men tend to exhibit a higher percentage of direct disagreement and other forms of negative social behaviors (e.g., expressions of hostility and tension) than women do, while women tend to exhibit a higher percentage of positive social behaviors (e.g., showing agreement and attempting to maintain good relationships among group members; Carli, 1981; Carli & Bukatko, 2000). In addition, both men and women tend to be more warm and cooperative when interacting

Summing It Up *Gender Differences in Personality: Aggression, Expressions of Emotional and Physical Intimacy, and Social Influence*

Personality Characteristic	Evidence	Example
Aggression	Males tend to display more overt physical aggression than females do, but males and females display equal amounts of passive or indirect aggression.	When angry, a young boy might punch a peer in the playground, while a young girl might try to keep the peer out of a game of tag with other girls.
Expressions of Emotional and Physical Intimacy:		
Love and Romance	Compared to men, women tend to report being in love more frequently, having more romantic feelings, and finding love more rewarding, but also having more experiences of loving someone without being loved in return and having more pragmatic views about love.	Although Jack and Jill have been dating for several months, and Jill really likes Jack and the time they spend together, her past experiences tell her that she should be cautions about telling him that she is falling in love with him.
Mate Selection	Males tend to focus on the physical features (e.g., attractiveness and youthfulness) of potential mates, while females tend to focus on status and resources (e.g., income and education).	When placing a personals ad in the local paper, Ed, who is 40, says he is looking for someone between the ages of 25 and 35 with proportional height and weight dimensions, while Cathy, who is also 40, says she is looking for someone who likes to travel and attend cultural events.
Sexuality	Compared to women, men tend to have more casual attitudes regarding sexual behavior, a greater likelihood of experiencing an orgasm during sex, and greater sex drive, but a similar level of sexual satisfaction.	Although both Brad and Jennifer are happy with their sex lives at college, Brad tends to be having a wider range of sexual experiences with more individuals than Jennifer does.
Jealousy	Males tend to experience jealousy over the possibility of their partner having sex with someone else, while females tend to experience jealousy over their partner having strong feelings for someone else.	Roger is jealous because his girlfriend might be having an affair with one of her co-workers, while Tina is jealous that her boyfriend might be falling in love with one of his co-workers.
Social Influence	While females tend to be more conforming on masculine-related tasks, males tend to be more conforming on feminine-related tasks; no differences between males and females in conformity tends are found on neutral tasks.	While playing Trivial Pursuit, Sue is more like to go along with Dave's answers on questions of sports, while Dave is more likely to go along with Sue's answers about food-related topics; they tend to argue the most when the topic is motion picture celebrities.

with women (Carli, 1989, 1990). However, just as with social influence, gender differences in group interaction also depend on the degree of expertise and experience with the task (Carli & Bukatko, 2000). More specifically, when interacting with others on a stereotypically feminine task, females show more task behavior (e.g., providing information, directions, and answers) and less positive social behavior, while men show more positive social behavior and less task behavior than for masculine tasks (Yamada, Tjosvold, & Draguns, 1983).

In summary, whether it is going along or getting along, gender differences in social influence are much smaller and more complicated that people typically would believe, and are mediated by the individual's degree of experience, expertise, and status (Baron, Byrne, & Branscombe, 2006).

A summary of the gender differences discussed in this section is presented in "Summing It Up: Gender Differences in Personality: Aggression, Expressions of Emotional and Physical Intimacy, and Social Influence" on p. 512.

Emotional Expressiveness: Gender Differences in the Freedom to Feel

The gender stereotype associated with emotional expressiveness is that women are more emotional than men (L. R. Brody & Hall, 2000; Hyde 2004), with this stereotype found in the United States and in other countries (Fischer & Manstead, 2000). It is a common sex-role stereotype that boys do not cry and men do not show their feelings. Along these lines, gender differences in emotional expressiveness solidify rather early. For example, by the time they are 11 or 12 years of age, girls indicate that they are more comfortable than boys about expressing their emotions openly (Fuchs & Thelen, 1988). Reflecting this basic difference, research on gender differences in emotional expressiveness indicates that girls and women characterize their emotions as deeper and more intense than do boys and men (Diener, Sandvik, & Larsen, 1985).

Although boys and men seem to demonstrate less emotional expressiveness, this does not mean that they experience less intense emotions than girls or women do. In most previous studies using self-report measures of emotionality, girls are shown to be more fearful, timid, and anxious than boys are (Block, 1976). But studies that use direct observation of behavioral responses to threatening stimuli often find no gender differences in fearfulness (Maccoby & Jacklin, 1974). In a more

specific sense, recent research suggests that the degree of emotional expressiveness in women may be influenced by the extent to which they possess "certain female gender role traits" (Bromberger & Matthews, 1996, p. 591). Thus, gender differences in emotional expressiveness tend to be less robust than expected and influenced by the individual's particular personality characteristics, such as confidence level. For example, a female rock climber who is very confident of her abilities will be less fearful when climbing up the side of a steep cliff than will a male with little confidence and experience in such situations.

Variations in the Level, Experience, and Regulation of Emotional Expressiveness: Gender Differences in "Facing up" to and Controlling the Expression of Emotions Gender differences in emotional expression are exhibited at various levels (L. R. Brody & Hall, 2000; Kring & Gordon, 1998). For example, women tend to demonstrate more facial expression of their emotions than men do, with the exception of anger, which men tend to demonstrate more through their facial expression than women do. On the other hand, men tend to exhibit more physiological expression, such as higher levels of skin conductance (e.g., "sweating"), than women do. Such a pattern of results is consistent with the gender stereotype that while women express their emotions, men to hide the them, in a sense, by keeping them "under their skin." When it comes to the use of emotional words, whether in conversation or in written expressions (e.g., notes or letters), both girls and women use more emotional words than do boys and men (L. R. Brody & Hall, 2000; Goldschmidt & Weller, 2000).

In addition to being more emotionally expressive than men at a number of different levels, women tend to experience their emotions more intensely, show a higher degree of awareness of their emotions, and process their emotions in their memory in greater detail than men do (Barrett, Lane, Sechrest, & Schwartz, 2000; L. R. Brody & Hall, 2000; Seidlitz & Diener, 1998), with this basic pattern of results being consistent for boys and girls (Diener et al., 1985). As an example of the range of intensity with which women experience their emotions, females tend to experience both happiness and sadness more intensely than males do (L. R. Brody & Hall, 2000).

In addition to gender differences in emotional expression, there are gender differences in the way that males and females react to their emotions, and these reactions also demonstrate the tendency for females to respond in a more socially appropriate manner than males do. For example, when it comes to the expression of anger, young girls are more likely to pout and sulk, while boys are more likely to display physical expressions, such as hitting or kicking (Buntaine & Costenbader, 1997). And, when trying to get over their feelings of anger, girls are more likely to try to talk about their feelings or spend quiet time alone, while boys tend to engage in more physical activities. When it comes to responding to being disappointed, girls tended to mask their feelings of disappointment by expressing more positive feelings than negative feelings by comparison with boys (T. L. Davies, 1995). Such a pattern of emotional reactions based on social appropriateness can be seen in adults, as well. For example, when examining how individuals respond to marital conflict, it has been found that women tend to prefer to keep talking about and continue to work on resolving the conflict, while men are more likely to simply withdraw from the discussion (Brehm, Miller, Perlman, & Campbell, 2002; Levenson, Carstensen, & Gottman, 1994). Thus, girls and women tend to be more able to express and control their emotions in a more socially appropriate manner than boy and men are.

Accounting for Gender Differences in Emotional Expression: Looking Beyond Just Family and Friends   How do we explain these patterns of emotional expression highlighting the difference between males and females? As you might expect, the possible explanations are many and include evolutionary processes, influence of the family, impact of peers, and adherence to social roles.

Survival of the fittest   Some of the earliest (Spencer, 1897, 1902) and most recent (D. M. Buss, 2003) explanations of gender difference in emotional expressiveness involve evolutionary processes and the survival of the species (Shields, 2005). In such explanations, the expression of anger and suppression of fear have evolved in response to men's competition with other men for resources necessary for survival (e.g., shelter, food, and mating partners). Today, according to the evolutionary explanation, the basic processes still remain but reflect a more contemporary social context. For example, men still are more likely to express anger and suppress fear than women are in order to compete successfully with other males; the principal difference is the nature of the resources for which they now compete (e.g., higher-status jobs, better neighborhoods, and prestigious cars).

All in the family   Probably the most powerful influence on the development of gender differences in emotional expressiveness is that of parents. Starting at birth, parents begin to influence the emotional expressiveness of their children in a manner that is consistent with gender stereotypes. In a summary of how parents begin to influence the emotional expression of their children, it was noted that at birth and for the first year of life, mothers exhibit greater variety of emotions and more intense facial expressions of emotionality when interacting with their daughters than with their sons; mothers are more likely to talk to their daughters about emotions than with their sons and to use more positive than negative emotional words when doing so; and mothers are more likely to encourage their sons, rather than their daughters, to respond to angry situations with anger and retaliation (Hyde, 2004). Such a pattern of parental interaction seems to encourage girls, from a very early age, to be more emotionally expressive than boys. If you combine this pattern with parents modeling such behaviors in their own lives (e.g., the way husbands and wives communicate with each other in front of their children), the degree of parental influence can become even stronger.

The power of peers   Outside the family, a critical influence is that of peers. Peers can serve to promote gender stereotypes by offering or withholding various forms of social rewards and punishments (e.g., friendship, rejection, teasing). For example, in one study of elementary school children, the most popular boys were those who suppressed their emotions, while the popular girls were verbally expressive and highly sensitive to the feelings of other (Adler, Kless, & Adler, 1992). The children who tended to violate sex-role stereotypes (e.g., girls who were not sensitive or boys who were) were less popular and treated more harshly by their peers (e.g., boys who cried were called "sissies"). Children are also more likely to control the expression of their emotions in the presence of their peers than with their parents, because they fear the possibility of ridicule and rejection by their peers (Zeman & Garber, 1996).

Society and sex-role preparation   Beyond the family and peers, society also plays a role in the perpetuation of gender differences in emotional expression by helping to prepare boys and girls for the culturally defined roles they are likely to play in adulthood (L. Brody, 1999). For example, as noted previously, the roles for men tend to focus on employment, the establishment of resources, and the acquisition of power and status. In such a context, males would need to project those emotions that would help them achieve this power and status, such as anger, contempt, and pride, while suppressing those emotions that might suggest weakness or vulnerability, such as fear, anxiety, and feelings of uncertainty. On the other hand, as noted previously, the roles for women tend to focus on caregiving (e.g., teachers and nurses) and caretakers (e.g., mothers). In such a context, women would need to exhibit not only those emotions that project a sense of warmth, compassion, and empathy but, at the same time, those emotions that suggest a sense of vulnerability and weakness (e.g., fear, sadness, and anxiety) that is consistent with the lower status associated with such roles. Thus, once again, we see that the gender differences in emotional expressiveness, as well as their acquisition and promotion, seem to be linked to the differential roles and the power and status associated with these roles occupied by men and women.

There is, however, some evidence to suggest that such trends can be modified by parental involvement (L. Brody, 1999). It has been demonstrated that girls with fathers who are more involved in their lives express less fear and sadness than do girls with less-involved fathers, and boys with fathers who are more involved in their lives express more warmth and fear than do boys with less-involved fathers. Such a pattern of results is consistent with the work of others who feel that the fathers' involvement tends to be crucial in the modification of sex-role stereotypes for the next generation (Chodorow, 1978) and that it is critical for men to become more involved in the childcare process (Hyde, 2004). It is possible that when men bring their social status to the process of caregiving and involvement in the lives of their children, it makes engaging in such behavior (i.e., behavior inconsistent with society's expected gender roles) easier for others to accept, more likely to be modeled by others, and more likely to contribute to the changing of stereotypical behavior patterns for both adults (e.g., encouraging men to be more involved in the childcare process) and their children (e.g., encouraging girls to be less fearful and boys to be more warm and caring).

Self-Evaluation and Expectations: Gender Differences in Self-Esteem and Self-Confidence

Self-esteem is the general degree of positive evaluation individuals have of themselves. Supported by numerous popular-press books, such as *Reviving Ophelia*

(Pipher, 1994), and an assortment of news and media reports, the general stereotypical assumption is that girls have lower self-esteem than boys. In an attempt to assess the nature of gender differences in self-esteem, several researchers have conducted extensive meta-analyses comparing various studies examining the extent of these differences (Kling, Hyde, Showers, & Buswell, 1999; Major, Barr, Zubek, & Babey, 1999). One of these meta-analyses, which included 216 different samples involving 97,000 individuals, examined the nature of the difference in self-esteem between males and females in various age groups (Kling et al., 1999). The pattern of results indicated that in elementary school (ages 7 to 10) boys displayed slightly better self-esteem than girls did, that the difference increased slightly for those in middle school years (ages 11 to 14), and that it reached its peak for those in high school. However, for those in adulthood (ages 23 to 59), the difference became closer to what is was in elementary school, and it almost disappeared completely for those individuals over 60 years of age. Thus, although boys and men tend to display a higher degree of self-esteem than girls and females do, with the difference varying throughout the life cycle but reaching a peak during the adolescent years, the actual differences are smaller than one would expect.

While the gender difference seems to be smaller than expected, the tendency for it to reach its peak in adolescence is somewhat troubling. As noted previously, adolescent girls generally show lower self-esteem than boys (Quatman & Watson, 2001), and there seem to be a number of possible explanations for this (Rathus, 2006). One explanation focuses on physical changes associated with adolescence, since physical appearance contributes more to the development of self-esteem during adolescence that any other factor (Galliher, Rostosky, & Hughes, 2004). In general, because girls tend to develop physically sooner than boys, they may express more dissatisfaction with the bodily changes brought upon by the onset of puberty (Hoffmann, 2002). In support of this explanation, it was noted that early-maturing girls – girls who experience the bodily changes associated with puberty sooner than most of their female peers – tend to have a more difficult time with their self-esteem (Kaplan, 2004). Perhaps such difficulties might be due to the additional attention given by others, the increased sense of self-consciousness brought on by their bodies looking more mature than those of their peers, and the tendency for physical appearance to be more important for girls than for boys during this time.

Another possible explanation focuses on the different messages adolescent boys and girls receive during this time period, which emphasize instrumental and achievement tendencies for boys but passivity, nurturing, and appearance- or body-oriented tendencies for girls (Dacey, Kenny, & Margolis, 2000; Rathus, 2006). Still another possible explanation focuses on the tendency for boys to be more outspoken about their sense of competencies, while girls have a tendency to be more modest (Kaplan, 2004), when reflecting on the actual gender differences in self-esteem noted. Again, rather than focusing on any single explanation, it is probably best to consider a combination of the explanations proposed.

Somewhat associated with self-esteem is **self-confidence**, which is an individual's self-assessment of his or her ability to be successful at a particular task. While there is a tendency for women to be less self-confident than men are, the extent of this self-confidence is mediated by the nature of the task involved (Hyde, 2004). For example, when they feel the task is gender-appropriate (e.g., judgments of fashion), females do not display less self-confidence than men. When given clear and unambiguous feedback on the level of their task performance, the self-confidence of females is similar to that of men. It seems that in the absence of such feedback, woman tend to be more modest in their expectations of success. Another critical factor is the presence of other individuals and the extent to which the others are being evaluated. Specifically, in the presence of others who are also being compared with each other, women tend to give lower estimates of self-confidence than if they are performing alone or do not anticipate being evaluated. Again, it seems that woman tend to display more gender-appropriate, socially accepted behavior by being more modest and less achievement oriented in the presence of others when being compared to them. However, when removing the presence of others and the prospects of evaluation eliminates these constraints of having to maintain gender-appropriate behaviors, self-confidence in women tends to rise.

Such a pattern of results has considerable implications for the career aspirations of women. Since there is a tendency for masculine-related careers (e.g., lawyer, engineer) to pay more than feminine-related careers (e.g., teacher, nurse), having less confidence about masculine-related careers can affect the confidence women have regarding entering these careers and their expectations of success in them, thereby possibly reducing their income potential and the quality-of-life items associated with that potential (e.g., health benefits, retirement plan). In addition, because women tend to exhibit a sense of modesty in underestimating their level of confidence and achievement in masculine-oriented careers, women may also be more likely to minimize the contribution they feel they make, and expect and settle for less compensation for their efforts. As you can see, gender differences in self-confidence can have some considerable, lifelong implications.

A final consideration related to gender differences in self-confidence has to do with the semantic way in which this topic has been considered (Hyde, 2004). The interpretation of the results of the lack of self-confidence in women is that they *underestimate* their abilities and expectations for success. However, it is possible to provide an alternative explanation that would suggest that instead of the females underestimating their abilities and expectations, the males display a tendency to *overestimate* their abilities and expectations of success. What is most interesting when considering such an explanation is that it suggests that there is a gender bias in the basic way questions and explanations of gender difference in personality are proposed.

Joy and Sadness: Gender Differences in Happiness and Depression

If you ask people what they want out of life, chances are they will tell you: to be happy, healthy, and wealthy. When it comes to happiness, there is considerable evidence to suggest that men and women are similar in their level of self-reported happiness (Diener, 2000; Myers & Diener, 1995) and that this trend seems to be consistent across a variety of cultures (Haring, Stock, & Okun, 1984; Michalos, 1991). And as a side note, just in case you are wondering, beyond what it takes to live comfortably (e.g., $50,000 a year for a family of four in the United States), an increasing level of wealth does not necessarily correlate with a corresponding level of happiness (Chatzky, 2003; Myers, 2000; Shaughnessy, 2005).

In contrast to the gender equality associated with happiness, the picture for depression is much different. There is considerable and consistent evidence to suggest that women are two to three times more likely to experience depression than men are (Comer, 2007; Davison, Neale, & Kring, 2004). However, while girls and women are three times more likely than boys and men to attempt suicide, boys and men are four to five times more likely to actually kill themselves (Davison et al., 2004; National Center for Injury Prevention and Control, 2004; Rathus, 2006). The principal reason for this difference is that boys and men tend to use much more lethal and rapid methods (e.g., shoot themselves) while girls and women are more likely to use slower-acting methods (e.g., taking sleeping pills or tranquilizers) that increase the likelihood of someone rescuing them (Joseph, Reznik, & Mester, 2003; Lubell, Swahn, Crosby, & Kegler, 2004; Skogman, Alsén, & Öjehagen, 2004).

How do we account for gender differences in depression? In a survey of possible explanations and contributing factors, Hyde (2004) notes a number of possibilities. One factor is that females tend to engage in a more negative and pessimistic style of thinking by holding themselves more personally responsible for negative events in their lives (e.g., "I did not get the job interview because I am not smart enough"). Such a tendency to self-blame can set the stage for feelings of depression. Another possibility is that girls and women have a more negative body image than boys and men do, which serves to contribute to feelings of depression. Although both boys and girls are likely to experience being harassed by their peers in school, girls are much more likely to react with greater intensity (e.g., feeling more embarrassed, less self-confident, more self-conscious), which is likely to lead to feelings of depression. Such harassment in school is likely to be experienced by adolescent girls who experience puberty, and all of the corresponding visible bodily changes, earlier than their male and female peers. Violence against women, such as sexual harassment, physical abuse, or rape, is yet another contributing factor associated with increased depression in women. Finally, there is poverty, as evidenced by the increasing number of women, many of them single mothers, living below the poverty line. Certainly, all of the stress associated with these women living in poverty contributes to their increased level of depression. As you can see, depression is complex and not easily explained. If you or someone you know is depressed, contact your school's counseling center or go to the National Institute for Mental Health website at www.nimh.nih.gov and click on "Depression" under "Health Information" for information and suggestions for assistance.

A summary of the gender differences discussed in this section is presented in "Summing It Up: Gender Differences in Personality: Emotional Expressiveness, Self-Evaluation and Expectations, and Joy and Sadness" on p. 518.

Cognitive Functioning: Gender Differences in Reading, Writing, and Arithmetic

Who are smarter: boys and men or girls and women? Overall, there appears to be no major differences between males and females on tests measuring general intelligence in either the past (Miles, 1935; Terman & Miles, 1936) or the present (Halpern, 2000, 2003, 2004; Unger & Crawford, 1992). This is probably because test developers make every attempt to avoid such biases in performance (Halpern, 2000; Terman & Merrill, 1937). However, there are some basic differences in cognitive functions that have been reported between males and females that will be discussed in this section.

Verbal Abilities: Gender Differences in Reading and Writing   Forgive the pun, but when we "talk" about verbal abilities, we are referring to various skills, such as reading, spelling, grammar, oral comprehension, writing, and word fluency. Taken together, there is evidence to suggest that females, as a group, tend to outperform males on various measures of verbal ability (Halpern, 2000, 2003, 2004; Hyde & Linn, 1988; Maccoby & Jacklin, 1974; Tavris, 1992). As an example, such gender differences in verbal ability seem to show up rather early in the developmental process, as girls generally tend to acquire their language faster, say their first word sooner, and develop larger vocabularies than boys (Rathus, 2006). In contrast, boys are more likely to be dyslexic and have other reading problems, such as reading below their grade level (Halpern, 2004).

How do we account for these gender differences in verbal abilities? One explanation focuses on early parenting practices that indicate that parents spend more time talking to, smiling at, demonstrating more emotional expressiveness to, and focusing more on emotions when talking to their infant daughters than with their infant sons (Martin et al., 2002; Powlishta, Sen, Serbin, Poulin-Dubois, & Eichstedt, 2001). In contrast, parents, especially fathers, are more likely to engage in rough-and-tumble play with their sons than with daughters (Eccles, Freedman-Doan, Frome, Jacobs, & Yoon, 2000; Fagot, Rodgers, & Leinbach, 2000). Because of this early emphasis on language ability for girls, it has been suggested that they are more likely to rely on verbal skills as they interact with others,

Summing It Up *Gender Differences in Personality: Emotional Expressiveness, Self-Evaluation and Expectations, and Joy and Sadness*

Personality Characteristic	Evidence	Example
Emotional Expressiveness	While males tend to self-report less emotional expression, more objective measures show no gender differences.	While Rick does not say he is afraid of getting on the roller coaster, his heart is really pounding in his chest.
Variation in Emotional Expression	Compared to males, females tend to demonstrate more facial expressions of their emotions, with the exception of aggression, display more verbally and experience more intensely their emotions, and express their emotions in a more socially acceptable manner.	When being told that money is missing from her register, Diane's face becomes flushed as she tries to explain her side of the accusation, while she continues to become even more upset and states that she will be filing a formal grievance with the personnel office. When presented with a similar accusation, Greg throws his nametag on the manager's desk, says "You're all a bunch of liars" and storms out of the room.
Accounting for Gender Differences in Emotional Expression	Explanations accounting for gender differences in emotional expression include: an evolutionary survival value; differences in parental encouragement of emotional expression by their sons and daughters; the rewards and punishments provided by peers for emotional expressiveness; and the societal expectations placed on men and women regarding the appropriateness of emotional expressiveness.	Buster expresses his feelings of frustration to his boss for not being selected the new district manager. His reaction is based on: the belief that if he lets his boss treat him this way, his advancement in the company will be stalled; his father telling him as a kid that a man always stands up for himself; his memory of the status he received as a kid for standing up to bullies on the playground; and the social roles that say that a true man does not tolerate injustices to himself or others.
Self-Evaluation and Expectations: Self-Esteem	Males tend to display a slightly higher level of self-esteem than girls, with it peaking during adolescence and this difference being due, in part, to the variations in physical development occurring during adolescent and the concern over body image for girls.	As a group, adolescent girls tend to experience bodily changes to a greater degree than boys, which can produce enhanced feelings of self-consciousness and lower self-esteem.
Self-Confidence	Women tend to display lower levels of self-confidence when performing non-gender-appropriate tasks and there is the possibility of them being evaluated, which tends to reflect their more modest and less achievement-focused expression of self-presentation.	In contrast to high ratings of her self-confidence when performing tasks related to her profession as a baker, Linda's rating of self-confidence dropped when asked and being judged, as part of a personnel training session, to select the appropriate tools to make specific auto repairs.
Joy and Sadness	While men and women display an equal degree of happiness, women tend to exhibit a higher level of depression than men, which may be attributed to a more pessimistic style of thinking, less than equal treatment in various aspects of society, and negative economic factors experienced more by women than men.	Sheila has been feeling more depressed over the last several months because she believes that her failure to get a promotion at work, which is starting to have a significant impact on her family, is due to her lack of assertiveness during management meetings as a result of the office director's response to comments made by women managers.

which will help to further develop skills (Halpern & LaMay, 2000).

Although it has been suggested that sex differences in brain function might be helpful in explaining these gender differences (Hines, 2004), there is evidence to suggest cultural factors also play a role. For example, it has been noted that gender differences in reading ability tend to be related to the extent to which a culture considers reading a masculine, feminine, or gender-neutral activity (Goldstein, 2005). For example, in Nigeria and England, where reading is considered a masculine activity, boys typically demonstrate a greater reading ability than girls do, while in the United States and Canada, where reading is considered more of a feminine activity, girls tend to demonstrate a greater reading ability than boys do. Thus, as with so many of the personality characteristics we have discussed so far, cultural factors, such as parental practices and gender stereotyping, tend to play an important in gender differences in verbal abilities.

This emphasis on cultural factors to help account for gender differences in verbal ability also helps to explain what is referred to as the "**paradox of achievement**" (Adelman, 1991). Specifically, although it is documented that women generally demonstrate superior scores on verbal ability, most of the critically acclaimed writers are males; and other high-status professions where a high degree of verbal ability is critical, such as careers as lawyers, politicians, and journalists, also tend to be dominated by males. Adelman (1991) has discussed the potential economical loss to the United States as the superior educational achievements of women are being compensated to a much smaller degree than those of males. In discussing some possible reasons for the paradox, Halpern (2000) has suggested that it is possible that such tests of verbal ability do not measure heightened levels of creativity, that women fail to use their talents as frequently as men, or that different standards are used to judge the quality of writing done by men and women. Still another culturally based reason proposed is that, until recently, women were educated differently than men (e.g., less emphasis on career or professional development), and when they were educated, the emphasis on their duties associated with family and domestic responsibility left little time to write. In support of her reasoning, Halpern notes that several outstanding female writers, including Dickenson and the Brontë sisters, were single women with other means of financial support. Thus, once again we see the critical role culture plays in the development, expression, and consequences, including financial (Hyde, 2005), of gender-related social behavior.

Mathematical Abilities: Gender Differences in Arithmetic In just the opposite of the pattern for verbal abilities, in the United States males tend to demonstrate a greater mathematical ability than females do (Halpern, 2004; Leahey & Guo, 2001). Although in elementary school, girls tend to do better in math than boys (Hyde, Fennema, & Lamon, 1990), by high school girls tend to lose their lead. This difference in mathematical ability is reflected in the fact that males are significantly overrepresented in comparison to females in SAT Math Scores above 600 (Benbow & Stanley, 1980; Dorans & Livingston, 1987; Stanley & Benbow, 1982; Tavris, 1992) and that this ratio has remained stable for over 20 years (Benbow, 1988). In addition, there is evidence to suggest that females have been highly underrepresented in the highest levels of competitive mathematical achievement. One analysis of the 144 winners of the U.S.A. Mathematical Olympiad contest featuring high school students during a period from 1972 to 1990 indicated only 2 were females (Stanley, 1990). More recently and globally, the results from the 49th International Mathematical Olympiad in 2008 indicate that just 1 of the 47 gold medals was awarded to a female while only 9 of the 101 silver medals and 7 of

While both the boys and girls in this classroom show an eagerness to respond, research on gender differences in cognitive functioning reports girls demonstrating higher verbal abilities than boys, while boys demonstrate better mathematical and spatial abilities than girls. Such differences have been attributed to different classroom (e.g., responses by teachers) and cultural (e.g., encouraging boys to pursue math and science) expectations. Do you see the men and women in your classes being treated equally?

the 120 bronze medals were awarded to females (International Mathematical Olympiad, 2008).

How do we account for such gender differences? As with gender differences in verbal ability, there is a variety of explanations that combine biological, psychological, and cultural factors (Anderman et al., 2001; Fredricks & Eccles, 2002; Halpern, 2004; Watt & Bornholt, 2000), but there is a pattern in these explanations that reflects the tendency for individuals in the U.S. to have different expectations of mathematical ability for boys and girls, and for these expectations to result in boys and girls being treated differently at home and at school. For example, at home, girls receive less encouragement from their parents for studying math, parents are more likely to buy math and science books for boys than for girls, and parents tend to believe that boys are better at math than girls. At school, teachers tend to spend more time on math with boys than with girls, girls receive less support from their peers for studying math than boys do, and females in high school and college tend to take fewer math courses than males do, as well as being less likely to pursue careers in math and related fields, even when they perform well in these courses. Another barrier is that in math and science classrooms, a few males are allowed to dominate class discussion while the females remain silent and/or are ignored by the teacher (Eccles, 1989).

As a result of such experiences, from a psychological perspective, by junior high school, students begin to see math as being associated with the male domain (Correll, 2001; Watt & Bornholt, 2000), with males being more likely to view math as being of some use in their life (Fredricks & Eccles, 2002) and developing a positive self-concept regarding math, while girls are more likely to experience anxiety associated with math (Osborne, 2001). In support of such an explanation, it was reported that girls performed more poorly on a difficult math test when they were told, prior to taking the test, that it had been shown to produce sex differences in its results, thus possibly creating increased levels of anxiety about taking the test (O'Brien & Crandell, 2003). Thus, if just simply being told that a math test produced sex differences was enough to lower the performance of females, it is easy to see how receiving such messages from parents, teachers, and other cultural agents can have a detrimental effects on the sense of efficacy and the career and professional aspirations of women in the fields of math and science. A good example of such a detrimental statement was the one made in January 2005 by Harvard president Lawrence Summers while addressing the National Bureau of Economic Research when he commented that the lack of women in math and science was due in part to "issues of intrinsic aptitude" (Rimer & Healy, 2005, A-1). His statements sent shockwaves throughout the academic community and across the country. In response to such statements, as well as to what you have read in this section, what are your thoughts on gender differences in mathematical ability and the possible explanations for these differences?

Visual-Spatial Abilities: Gender Differences in Mental Manipulation Related to the superior performance in mathematics by males is their increased performance in the area of visual-spatial ability (Delgado & Prieto, 2004). **Visual-spatial ability** refers to the ability to mentally rotate and manipulate objects and images "in your head." As you would expect, the ability to rotate mental and abstract images and information would be valuable for such areas as mathematics and the sciences and for professions such as engineering, architecture, and the arts, all of which, by no coincidence, tend to be dominated by males.

What accounts for gender differences in visual-spatial abilities? From an evolutionary perspective, it has been suggested that because males needed to define and protect their territory, they developed a genetic tendency to be able spatially to define and recall that home territory from many different locations and directions (Ecuyer-Dab & Robert, 2004). Another explanation suggests that because reading is considered a feminine activity, visual-spatial ability, like mathematical ability, is considered a masculine activity and is associated with a variety of masculine-related activities, such as playing football, baseball, and basketball, hunting, building, and flying airplanes, to name just a few activities (Halpern, 2004). Still another explanation focuses on the nature of toys and early childhood activities, in that toys for boys, such as Lego, building blocks, and tool sets, provide more opportunity for boys to develop their spatial ability. In addition to being able to travel further away from home to play, which reflects the evolutionary explanations, the play of boys tends to involve throwing balls and other objects through space, which provides other opportunities to develop and practice visual-spatial abilities (Halpern, 2004). In total, all of these explanations seem to suggest that the gender differences in visual-spatial abilities reflect the tendencies of boys to be given more opportunity to

Summing It Up *Gender Differences in Personality: Cognitive Functioning*

Personality Characteristic	Evidence	Example
General Intelligence	There are no major gender differences on measures of general intelligence.	In the results of the intelligence test taken by high school seniors, there was no significant difference between the scores for the male and female students.
Verbal Abilities of Reading and Writing	Women tend to score higher on measures of verbal ability, such as reading and writing.	In the results of the examinations in the series of English and literature classes for high school seniors, the female students tended to outperform the male students.
Accounting for Gender Differences in Verbal Abilities	Explanations accounting for gender differences in verbal abilities include: preferential responses by parents when talking to their infant daughters; early emphasis on language ability for girls; and cultural expectations.	Sue's parents tended to smile more at her than at her brother when she was learning to talk, and bought her more books for gifts when she was growing up. She was also fortunate to grow up in a country that encourages the development of verbal abilities in young girls and women.
Mathematical Abilities	In general, males tend to score higher on measures of mathematical ability.	The dean of the math department at the local university was concerned about what could be done to increase the number of female math majors.
Accounting for Gender Differences in Mathematical Abilities	Explanations include differing cultural expectations and differential treatment of males in schools encouraging their abilities and interest in mathematics.	Paul and the rest of his male classmates were much more likely to be called on in their math class when raising their hands in class than were Ester and her female classmates.

engage in those activities that foster the development of enhanced visual-spatial ability than girls are.

A summary of the gender differences discussed in this section is presented in "Summing It Up: Gender Differences in Personality: Cognitive Functioning" above. If you would like more information on the topics discussed in this section, I would suggest reading a book by Diane Halpern, a leading authority on sex differences in cognitive abilities, titled *Sex Differences in Cognitive Abilities* (2000), or two of her recent articles titled "Sex Differences in Cognitive Abilities" (2003) and "A Cognitive-Process Taxonomy for Sex Differences in Cognitive Abilities" (2004).

This concludes the discussion on gender differences in personality. If you would like to read more about gender differences in personality, see Table 1 in an article by Janet Shibley Hyde (2005), one of the foremost experts on gender differences and similarities, titled "The Gender Similarities Hypothesis," which summarizes the references for many articles on psychological gender differences. Next, you will consider some of the sex-role stereotypes that appear as a consequence of gender identity.

Sex-Role Stereotypes: How Do the Perceptions of Males and Females Differ?

Sex-role stereotypes are biased beliefs about the behavioral attributes assumed to be associated with being male or female. An example of this type of bias might involve not allowing women to be major league umpires because of a belief that they are not capable of handling the stress and tension of major league competition as well as men do. When acted upon, such sex-role stereotypes can result in people being treated unfairly in ways that can range from not being given credit for what they have done to job discrimination and sexual harassment. In this section, you will consider the consequences of sex-role stereotypes for men and women in three different areas: performance evaluation, explanations for successful performance, and the perception of personality characteristics.

Judgment of Work Quality: Being Just as Good is Not Being Good Enough for Females

One of the more pervasive sex-role stereotypes that has been documented is the tendency for work to be judged as being of better quality if it was done by men than by women, even if the work is *identical*. For example, in one of the first studies to document this tendency, Philip Goldberg (1968) collected articles from various fields (e.g., law, art, business, dietetics, literature) and had people read and then rate the quality of the articles. Half of the subjects read articles that were supposedly written by a male author, while the other half read articles that were supposedly written by a female author. The results were very consistent and extremely clear: regardless of the field and the sex of the individual doing the rating, identical articles written by males were judged as being of higher quality than those written by females.

Such findings triggered a flurry of other studies designed to identify the extent to which such evaluative biases could be found in other areas. Some of the other early studies reporting similar results were found in the judgment of job applicant résumés (Dipboye, Fromkin, & Wiback, 1975), evaluation of job grievances (Rosen & Jerdee, 1975), making of personnel decisions (Rosen & Jerdee, 1974), and ratings of academic intelligence (Lao, Upchurch, Corwin, & Grossnickle, 1975). Consistent with this early research, in some more recent studies, it was noted that leadership behavior when performed by females is perceived less favorably than similar behavior performed by males (Eagly & Karau, 2000, 2002; Ridgeway & Bourg, 2004) and that women managers are evaluated less favorably than male managers are (Rudman & Glick, 1999). Such a gender bias was even found with university faculty members in that women were evaluated more unfavorably than men were

when being considered for an entry-level faculty position (Steinpreis, Anders, & Ritzke, 1999).

In addition to identifying the nature of these gender biases in evaluation of work-related performance, subsequent research also identified the conditions under which the work of females was considered more favorably than that of males. In one early but important study, it was noted that the performance of a woman tended to be evaluated more favorably than that of a male under conditions when the woman's performance was unexpected or out of the ordinary (Abramson, Goldberg, Greenberg, & Abramson, 1977). For example, if individuals are told that the woman is a successful surgeon, her work is evaluated more favorably than that of a male surgeon described in the same way. What seems to occur in this case is that the individuals are rating the work of this particular female as being superior to that of this particular male. That is to say, there must be something about this out-of-the-ordinary woman that makes her work superior, not something about women in general.

Since Goldberg's (1968) initial findings, systematic analysis of research on gender-based evaluation biases indicates that they are more complex than first perceived (Graves, 1999). For example, a subsequent examination of more than 100 studies in this area of research indicates that several important factors must be considered when trying to understand the nature and dynamics of gender differences in performance evaluation (Top, 1991). One factor is the gender typing of the task. Men seem to receive the evaluation advantage for masculine jobs (e.g., manager), while women receive the evaluation advantage for feminine jobs (e.g., office assistant). For gender-neutral jobs, men and women receive similar evaluations (Glick, Zion, & Nelson, 1988). Gender biases are also less likely to occur when additional information is provided to the evaluator regarding the individual's abilities (Pazy, 1992; Steinpreis et al., 1999). Females also tend to receive less favorable ratings when there is an imbalance in the male–female ratio in the particular occupation that favors males (Fiske, Bersoff, Borgida, Deaux, & Heilman, 1991). Females also tend to be judged less favorably than males when using objective measures (e.g., being selected for membership on a team vs. not being selected) as opposed to subjective measures (e.g., ratings of ability or skill that are open to interpretation), suggesting that gender biases may be hidden in the subjective ratings but exhibited in the more concrete, objective ones (Biernat & Vescio, 2002). Finally, the bias toward giving males more respect (e.g., being viewed favorably and as having worth) than females has also been identified as a mediating factor in the gender-based evaluation bias of the potential of female applicants (L. M. Jackson, Esses, & Burris, 2001). Thus, unless other information is presented, such as information about the nature of a task or an individual's ability, one consequence of sex-role stereotyping is for the work of women to be rated lower than identical work done by men, creating a situation for women when "being just as good is not being good enough."

Explanations of Successful Performance: Skillful Men, Lucky Women

Another form of sex-role stereotyping that has been consistently identified is in the way people explain the successful performance of men and women. In the early work on this issue, it was noted that the successful performance of males on various tasks tends to be attributed to their ability and effort, while the successful performance of females tends to be attributed to luck (Deaux, 1982; Deaux & Emswiller, 1974; Garland & Price, 1977; Unger & Crawford, 1992). This tendency is particularly true when the task is considered masculine in its orientation (e.g., the identification of tools). But even when the task is considered feminine in its orientation (e.g., the identification of household objects), females are rated as being only slightly more skillful than males (Deaux & Emswiller, 1974). A similar gender bias in the attributions of sports performance has also been identified in boys and girls (LeUnes & Nation, 1989). Thus, when it comes to evaluating success, it is assumed that males are successful because of their superior skill and all the hard work they have put in, while females are perceived as less skillful and more lucky. This pattern of results has also been identified in a more recent analysis that investigated some 58 separate studies over a 20-year period (Swim & Sanna, 1996).

The consequences of such sex-role stereotyping can have a negative impact on women in the world of work. For example, because of the way their work is evaluated, women may come to expect lower starting salaries than men, and may expect to achieve a lower salary at the height of their careers than men (L. A. Jackson, Gardner, & Sullivan, 1992; Major & Konar, 1984), particularly when they compare themselves with other females instead of to their more highly paid male peers (Bylsma, Major, & Cozzarelli, 1995; Major,

1989). Because of such expectations, competent female employees may actually be undermining their own careers by assuming that such salaries are fair and, thus, settling for lower salaries (L. A. Jackson et al., 1992; L. A. Jackson & Grabski, 1988). Consistent with this reasoning is the finding that the higher the starting salaries people requested, the higher their actual salary (Major, Vanderslice, & MacFarlin, 1985). In a related manner, another factor that has been associated with the decreased amount paid to women in response to their evaluation of their work is that women, in comparison to men, are more likely to make career decisions that involve commitment to family (e.g., deciding not to put in overtime hours at the office) and that can work against career advancement and increased compensation (Steil, McGann, & Kahn, 2001).

Fortunately, efforts are being made to take action that attempts to reduce such biases in the judgment of the performance of women and in the financial compensation for their efforts. For example, it has been noted that by having raters focus more on the actual work of the individual rather than on gender, such biases in the evaluation of job performance can be reduced (Izraeli, Izraeli, & Eden, 1985). In addition, many U.S. states have put forth legislative action that mandates that men and women be paid equally for jobs that are comparable in responsibility, education requirements, required experience, and management level (Hyde, 2004).

The Perceived Personality Traits of Men and Women: Competent Males, Warm and Expressive Females

The reason that men are evaluated more favorably may have something to do with the personality traits believed to be possessed by men and women and the value given to these traits. For example, in a classic study on gender stereotypes, individuals were asked to indicate the traits they considered most characteristic of men and of women (Rosenkrantz, Vogel, Bee, Broverman, & Broverman, 1968). Those traits believed to be most characteristic of males included being ambitious, independent, objective, dominant, active, and self-confident. On the other hand, some of the traits considered most characteristic of females included being gentle, talkative, interested in their own appearance, sensitive to the feelings of others, and able to express feelings of tenderness. Table 12.1 is a more complete list of the traits believed to reflect the personalities of men and women. Thus, while males were perceived as possessing

Table 12.1   Some Favorable Stereotypical Traits for Men and Women: Competency vs. Warmth–Expressiveness Characteristics

Favorable Traits for Men Characterized by Competency	Favorable Traits for Women Characterized by Warmth and Expressiveness
Very aggressive	Very talkative
Very independent	Very tactful
Almost always hides emotions	Very gentle
Very objective	Aware of the feelings of others
Very active	Interested in own appearance
Very competitive	Very neat in habits
Very logical	Very quiet
Very self-confident	Very strong need for security
Very ambitious	Expresses tender feelings

Note. From Broverman et al. (1972).

Table 12.2   An Updated Summary of Some Gender-Related Stereotypical Personality Traits

Masculine Characteristics	Feminine Characteristics
Accomplished	Aware of other's feelings
Active	Devoted to others
Aggressive	Emotional
Competent	Fashionable
Competitive	Friendly
Decisive	Follower
Independent	Gentle
Leader	Helpful to others
Never gives up	Kind/Polite
Nonconforming	Sensitive
Self-confident	Understanding
Stable	Warm
Stands up to pressure	Weak
Strong	
Tough/Coarse	

Note. Adapted from Davies et al. (2005); Deaux & Kite (1993); Eagly & Mladinic (1994); Fiske et al. (2002); Spence & Buckner (2000); & Twenge (1999).

personality traits reflecting competency, females were perceived as possessing personality traits characterized as being warm and expressive. This pattern of results was found to be consistent regardless of socioeconomic class, religion, age, education, and marital status of the subjects (Broverman, Vogel, Broverman, Clarkson, & Rosenkrantz, 1972), both then and 15 years later in some related research (Martin, 1987).

It could be argued that the list of stereotypical gender-related traits presented in Table 12.1 is outdated, since the research it is based on was conducted almost 40 years ago and a generation of social change and progress with regard to the perceptions of women has passed. However, as can be seen in Table 12.2, more recent investigations of gender-related stereotypical traits reveal a pattern similar to those noted previously of men being perceived as possessing traits associated with competency and action, while women are perceived as possessing traits associated with warmth and emotional expression (L. R. Brody & Hall, 2000; P. G. Davies, Spencer, & Steele, 2005; Deaux & Kite, 1993; Eagly & Mladinic, 1994; Fiske, Cuddy, Glick, & Xu, 2002; Spence & Buckner, 2000; Twenge, 1999).

The pattern of results of Tables 12.1 and 12.2 suggests that the stereotypical gender-related traits appear to have remained relatively stable and consistent over the past 40 years. In addition to looking at the perception of gender-related stereotypical traits across time, another interesting question would be to examine such

perceptions across cultures. As an example of an attempt to address this issues, consider the information presented in "The Cultural Context of Personality Psychology."

The Cultural Context of Personality Psychology

Perceptions of Gender Differences in the Personality Traits Across 50 Different Cultures: It's a Small World After All

In one of the most ambitious efforts to date designed to investigate gender-related stereotypical traits, Robert R. McCrae and Antonio Terracciano of the National Institute on Aging in the Department of Health and Human Services, and 78 other members of the Personality Profiles of Cultures Project (2005), which has representatives from 50 different cultures, collected data from men and women around the world on the perceived personality traits of men and women. The personality traits used for comparison were based on those contained in the Revised NEO-Personality Inventory (NEO-PI-R), which was discussed in Chapter 7 (see pp. 298–300). Recall that the NEO-PI-R is a self-report objective measure of personality that contains 240 items, including six items for each of the five basic personality factors: Neuroticism (N: negative activity, nervousness), Extraversion (E: energetic, enthusiastic), Openness to Experience (O: originality, open-mindedness), Agreeableness (A: altruistic, affectionate), and Conscientiousness (C: controlled, constrained). In this cross-cultural research, male and female college students from the 49 different cultures listed in the first column of Table 12.3 were instructed to "think of a man [woman] you know well" and then asked to rate that person along the items contained in the NEO-PI-R. In making their ratings, the participants were randomly assigned to one of four different rating conditions. The participants were assigned to rate either a male or female target within an age group between 18 and 21 or over 40. This procedure produced ratings for 11,852 target individuals across the 49 cultures! And, as you can imagine, because of the considerable volume of data produced from this study, only a few of the highlights of the results from this study will be presented here.

One of the most interesting findings of this research was "the universality of sex differences across methods, age groups, and cultures" (McCrae et al., 2005, p. 554). More specifically, when examining individually the specific traits that make up the five major factors, men were rated higher than women on such traits as Assertiveness (E3), Excitement Seeking (E5), and Ideas (O5). In contrast, women were rated higher than men on such traits as Anxiety (N1), Vulnerability (N6), Esthetics (O2), Feelings (O3), and Tender-mindedness (A6). Consistent with the pattern of results presented in Tables 12.1 and 12.2, an examination of the results for these traits will reveal a pattern that reflects a picture of males as being characterized around the world as strong and competent and females as being characterized as emotionally expressive and warm.

In addition to examining specific traits, the researchers also wanted to examine the cross-cultural perceptions of men and women in the context of the five major personality factors contained in the NEO-PI-R, in a manner that reflected patterns identified previously in other cross-cultural research involving gender differences in self-perceptions of personality traits based on men and women from various cultures (Costa, Terracciano, & McCrae, 2001). To do this, the authors employed the Neuroticism (N) and Agreeableness (A) factors as they are typically measured, because all of the traits that comprise these two factors tend to display a pattern of results that are consistent in a direction showing women displaying higher scores than men (Costa et al., 2001). However, for the other factors, the authors created three new indices that summarized gender differences among traits within these three factors based on previous research involving self-perceptions (Costa et al., 2001). For the sake of consistency with the N and A factors used in the study, the authors created the three new feminine composite indices to reflect a feminine (F) response style and gender differences in a direction that would predict greater scores for females than males. The three composite indices were: F-Extraversion/Introversion (F-Ex/In), F-Openness/Closedness (F-Op/Cl) and F-Conscientiousness/Unconscientiousness (F-Co/Un). The F-Extraversion/Introversion (F-Ex/In) composite index was created by combining the perceived ratings of the female and male target scores for the traits of Warmth (E1) + Gregariousness (E2) + Positive Emotions (E6) – Assertiveness (E3) – Excitement Seeking (E5) ratings and then dividing the total by five. As you can see, the F-Ex/In composite rating could be considered scored in the feminine direction because it emphasizes a style of interaction that reflects a more comforting and collectivistic form of social interaction. The F-Openness/Closedness (F-Op/Cl) composite factor was created by adding the perceived ratings of the female and male target scores for the traits of Esthetics (O2) + Feelings (O3) + Actions (O4) – Ideas (O5) and then dividing the total by four. The F-Op/Cl composite could be considered scored in the feminine direction because it emphasizes actions in the form of the expression of feelings. Finally, the F-Conscientiousness/Unconscientiousness (F-Co/Un) composite factor was created by combining the perceived ratings of female and male target scores for the traits of Dutifulness (C2) + Order (C3) – Competence (C1) and dividing the total by three. The F-Co/Un composite is considered scored in the feminine direction because it emphasizes commitment to others while removing the trait of competence, which is typically associated with males.

Although there is a considerable amount of information presented in Table 12.3, it is actually fairly

Table 12.3 A Cross-Cultural Comparison of the Perceptions of the Personality: Mean Differences in the Perception Between Women and Men in 49 Cultures on NEO-PI-R Factors or Composites

Culture	N	A	F-Ex/In	F-Op/Cl	F-Co/Un
Nigeria	.00	.00	−.04	.00	.00
India	.13	.13	−.05	−.03	.07
Botswana	.08	.06	−.01	.13	.03
Ethiopia	.13	−.02	.01	.15	.05
Russia	.25*	−.02	.14**	.19**	.11*
Puerto Rico	.23	.11	.09	.20*	.05
Uganda	.30	.23	.13	.00	.08
Morocco	.16	.26	.20*	.08	.11
Mexico	.33*	.17	.10	.26**	.05
Croatia	.49**	.03	.17**	.13*	.17**
Indonesia	.40**	.22	.15*	.21**	.08
Peru	.57***	.16	.06	.21*	.13
Malaysia	.36**	.39**	.17**	.13*	.17**
Kuwait	.48***	.31**	.19***	.09	.16**
Thailand	.41**	.31*	.15*	.13*	.24***
Philippines	.52***	.32*	.11	.25**	.04
Serbia	.54***	.10	.19**	.34***	.11
China	.56***	.33*	.19*	.13	.12
Brazil	.59***	.25**	.11**	.26***	.15***
Chile	.48**	.27	.21**	.23**	.18**
Poland	.42**	.29*	.22***	.27***	.18**
Portugal	.45**	.31*	.19**	.11	.33***
Italy	.55***	.22	.22**	.23**	.19**
Argentina	.20	.46**	.39***	.30***	.10
Malta	.67***	.24	.21**	.14	.20**
Japan	.70***	.11	.21**	.38***	.09
Lebanon	.39**	.34*	.23***	.34***	.19**
United States	.59***	.29***	.23***	.30***	.09**
France	.48***	.39**	.17**	.33***	.21***
Turkey	.46**	.49**	.25***	.35***	.06
Hong Kong	.51***	.41**	.22***	.22**	.26***
Burkina Faso	.59***	.46**	.25***	.20**	.12*
Slovakia	.68***	.29*	.16*	.23***	.30***
South Korea	.48**	.50***	.26***	.40***	.08
Slovenia	.29	.53***	.34***	.45***	.11
Germany	.54***	.50***	.28***	.32***	.13**
Estonia	.56***	.49***	.25***	.39***	.15**
Iceland	.57***	.45**	.20**	.37***	.22***
Belgium	.52***	.47***	.33***	.36***	.14*
Spain	.64***	.45**	.26***	.28***	.20**
United Kingdom: Northern Ireland	.66**	.43*	.19*	.30**	.25**
Denmark	.70***	.35*	.23**	.36***	.20**
Australia	.76***	.42**	.19**	.36***	.17**
New Zealand	.54***	.50***	.33***	.40***	.11
French Switzerland	.79***	.42**	.28***	.22**	.33***
German Switzerland	.80***	.49**	.37***	.42***	.10
Austria	.67***	.54**	.40***	.42***	.21*
Czech Republic	.70***	.64***	.34***	.48***	.34***
United Kingdom: England	.78***	.84***	.43***	.28***	.20**

Note. N = Neuroticism, A = Agreeableness, F-Ex/In = Feminine Extraversion/Introversion, F-Op/Cl = Feminine Openess/Closedness, F-Co/Un = Feminine Conscientiousness/Unconscientiousness. * $p < .05$. ** $p < .01$. *** $p < .001$. Adapted from McCrae et al. (2005).

simple to read. The numerical values in the table represent a calculated difference score that basically reflects the rating for the female target minus the rating for the male target for those individuals performing the ratings within each culture. The positive numbers reflect those factors in which female targets were perceived as having a higher score than male targets, while a negative score reflects those factors in which male targets had a higher score than female targets. The closer to zero the difference score is, the smaller the perceived gender difference on the factor. Because of the nature of the calculation of the difference score, the maximum value of the difference score is 1, either plus or minus.

In the results presented in Table 12.3, there appear to be some highly consistent patterns. First of all, the pattern tends to reflect a predominance of positive numbers, with only six negative difference scores, which represents only about 2.4 percent of the scores reported. Such a pattern reflects an interesting global consensus regarding the perception of the personality structure of females and males. Second, the preponderance of positive scores reflects the tendency for the factors to be selected and constructed to emphasize a feminine response style, which would be predicted from previous cross-cultural research using self-perception ratings (Costa et al., 2001). Regardless, the important point to note in this pattern is that there seems to be considerable agreement across the cultures regarding the perceived personality traits of men and women. Another interesting pattern is that the magnitude of the perceived sex differences is relatively small, with very few difference scores approaching .80. Still another interesting pattern is the consistency of the magnitude of the differences for the five factors within and across the various cultures. More specifically, those cultures that have small sex differences tended to have small sex differences across all of the five factors, while those cultures that tended to have large sex differences tended to have large sex differences across all five of the factors.

Finally, and probably the most interesting of all, there is a pattern reflecting the rankings of the cultures in terms of the overall magnitude of their difference scores combined across all five of the factors. An inspection of the ranking of the cultures in the extreme left column of Table 12.3 indicates that Asian and African cultures tend to make up the top third of the countries with the smallest gender differences, while Western European countries tend to make up the bottom third

of the countries having the greatest gender differences. The United States, ranked 28th, is about in the middle. In addition, a closer examination of the pattern of results for the United States seems to suggest that here, women are perceived as much more neurotic (negative activity, nervousness) than men, moderately more extraverted (energetic, enthusiastic), open to experience (originality, open-mindedness), and agreeable (altruistic, affectionate) than men, and about equal to men in conscientiousness (controlled, constrained). Are these perceptions consistent with the men and women you know?

Thus, there appears to be general agreement within each culture regarding the nature of the perceived personality characteristics of men and women around the world, and some differences across cultures. Such differences probably reflect the cultural norms that help to give each culture its unique identity, just as the use of indigenous spices helps to give a special ethnic twist on the preparation of common food items, such as potatoes or bread. However, a critical point to remember is that even with all of the variation, the magnitude of these differences, overall, is not that large. Such a pattern of similarity across the different cultures suggests, as the Disney World tune goes, that, in the end, "It's a small world after all." People seem to be much more alike around the world in their perceptions of men and women than they are different.

Accounting for the Global Consensus in the Perceived Personality Traits of Men and Women: A Description Based on the Prescription for the Perception of Gender-Related Personality Traits   As you can see, there seems to be some consensus regarding the gender-stereotypical personality traits associated with men and women that seem to be consistent across time and across cultures. Such consistency prompts the question "What accounts for it?" One possible explanation is based on a fundamental characteristic feature of gender stereotypes in comparison to other stereotypes. Specifically, gender stereotypes tend to be *prescriptive* in nature rather than just *descriptive* (Brehm et al., 2005). They are prescriptive in that they represent what a majority of individuals in a particular culture believe men and women *should* be like, as opposed to being merely descriptive in terms of what a majority believe men and women *are* like. The prescriptive nature of gender stereotypes places additional pressure on individuals to conform to them, and increases the perceiver's resistance against information and behavior that is inconsistent with these prescriptive stereotypes (Cuddy, Norton, & Fiske, 2005; Prentice & Carranza, 2002; Rudman & Glick, 2001). For example, in the world of work, women from around the world are much more likely than men to be found in occupations that involve "taking care of others" such as clerical occupations (e.g., secretaries, bookkeepers), sales occupations (e.g., salespeople, real estate agents), or service occupations (e.g., caregivers, cooks, hairdressers; Brehm, Kassin, & Fein, 2005). Such a state of affairs is due to women being described as "warm and nurturing," which, when universally accepted, results in women being prescribed work in those occupations that are characterized by "taking care of others," and that typically pay much less than the work prescribed to men, which tends to involve more professional (e.g., lawyer, dentist), technical (e.g., architect, computer system analyst), and administrative/managerial (e.g., CEO) occupations. As you can see, the nature of the work prescribed to men tends to be characterized by "taking action," having higher status, and paying more than the work prescribed to females. For more about how gender stereotypes impact men and women in the world of work, read "A Closer Look" below.

Research indicates that sex discrimination in the workplace exists when it is believed that only individuals of a particular gender possess the physical and personality characteristics that are required for a particular job. The female construction worker in this photograph is an example of an individual performing work that is inconsistent with sex-role stereotypes, thus helping to break down certain sex-role stereotypes about what work men and women can do and should be given the opportunity to perform.

A Closer Look

The Role of Sex-Role Stereotypes and Sex Discrimination in the Hiring and Promoting of Women: The Matching of Job and Gender Stereotypes

Another serious implication of sex-role stereotypes is in the area of sex discrimination in hiring and promotion decisions (Hyde, 2004). A basic problem seems to be that certain jobs are perceived to require a specific set of skills that are believed, on the basis of sex-role stereotypes, to be associated with one gender or the other. For example, the job of nurse is believed to require personality traits involving warmth and nurturance, which are generally assumed to be characteristic of women. On the other hand, the job of executive is typically associated with an individual possessing the personality traits of aggressiveness and competitiveness, which are generally assumed to be characteristic of men. The resulting bias this creates in the hiring and promotion process is the assumption that one gender is more suited for certain jobs than the other because of the traits it is believed to possess. With such issues in mind, let's take a closer look at some illustrative research examining the impact of sex-role stereotypes on the hiring and promotion process, and some possible solutions to the biases they create.

Sexual Discrimination in the Hiring Process: The Role of Gender-Related Information

To investigate the operation of sex-role stereotypes and some ways of reducing sex discrimination in the hiring process, a highly illustrative study by Glick, Zion, and Nelson (1988) sent upper-level managers and business professionals a résumé from which they were asked to anonymously evaluate an applicant for three different jobs: sales manager for a heavy machinery company (considered a traditionally masculine job), dental receptionist/secretary (considered a traditionally feminine job), and administrative assistant in a bank (considered a gender-neutral job). The applicant was described as either a male (e.g., "Ken Norris") or female (e.g., "Kate Norris"). The extent to which the applicant possessed certain personality traits was introduced by the gender-related nature of his or her previous experience, as listed in the résumé. Masculine work experience included working in a sporting goods store and being captain of the men's or women's varsity basketball team. Feminine work experience included working in retail sales at a jewelry store and being captain of the pep squad. Gender-neutral work experience included working in retail sales at a shoe store and being captain of the men's or women's varsity swim team.

The results indicated that providing the gender-related information on the résumé did have an equalizing influence on the evaluation of the applicants. For example, male and female applicants with masculine-related job experience were seen as equally masculine, while male and female applicants with feminine-related job experience were seen as equally feminine. The results also indicated that both the male and female applicants were more likely to be interviewed for the masculine job when they had the masculine-related work experience than when they had feminine-related work experience. On the other hand, they were both more likely to be interviewed for the feminine job when they had feminine-related work experience than when they had masculine-related work experience. But when both males and females were seen as having similar gender-related experience, it was the match between the gender of the individual and the gender-relatedness of the job that seemed to be the most powerful factor in determining the applicant's likelihood of being interviewed.

What conclusions can we draw from this research? On the positive side, providing information about work experience indicating that the individual does possess the type of gender-related personality traits that seem to be appropriate for the gender-related nature of the job can increase the likelihood of being considered for the job. On the negative side, however, an applicant who is seen as having the right personality (e.g., masculine traits) but the wrong gender (e.g., being a female) for the stereotyped nature of the job (e.g., masculine) may lose out to the individual who is not only perceived as having the right personality traits (e.g., masculine) but also happens to be the right gender (e.g., male). Thus, sex discrimination in hiring seems to be influenced by a matching process that involves both sex-role stereotypes about people and sex-role stereotypes about jobs. Fortunately, as more legal action is taken against those who simply look at gender as the basis of their hiring decisions, less sex discrimination in hiring will take place.

Sexual Discrimination in the Promoting Process: The Role of Gender-Related Personality Traits in Departmental Assignments

When it comes to the promotion of women in business, there is evidence to suggest that the role of perceived stereotyped personality traits also comes into play, as women managers tend to be discriminated against by being kept in positions that seem to rely on commonly held gender-related stereotypes. Specifically, since women tend to be perceived as warm and sensitive while men tend to be perceived as ambitious, self-reliant, and aggressive, they tend be assigned to positions that reflect these traits. For example, in a study involving 1,940 male and 175 female directors from 130 companies that examined how committee assignments were made, it was noted that male directors were much more likely than female directors to be assigned to powerful and prestigious committees such as the compensation, executive, and finances ones. On the other hand, female directors were much more likely to be assigned to the less powerful and prestigious public affairs committee (Billimoria & Piderit, 1994). In the corporate world of work, areas such as public affairs, public relations, and human resources are all considered aspects of business that rely more on social skills and social sensitivity, which are considered "soft skills" or "people skills," than general leadership skills, which are considered "dominant skills."

The implication of such assignments is that they impact the nature of the promotions and career paths of individuals. Specifically, in one study of 338 managers over a 10-year period, the power status of the department into which managers entered determined the progress rate of their promotions and salary increases (Sheridan, Slocum, Buda, & Thompson, 1990). Those individuals who entered more powerful departments at the beginning of their corporate career tended to progress more rapidly than those who began by entering less powerful ones. Since women tend to be located in the less powerful departments, they tend to be trapped in career paths that result in less recognition and compensation. And, as was noted earlier (see p. 523), even when women do succeed in those career areas outside of traditional gender boundaries (e.g., management), their successful performance is more likely to be perceived as being due to luck rather than internal, stable, personal attributes (e.g., skillful leadership ability). And, as you might suspect, attributing an individual's performance to "luck" over "ability" will also negatively affect the nature of an individual's career in terms of being selected, promoted, and compensated in a fair and equitable manner.

What can be done to minimize such gender discrimination in the departmental assignment and promotion of women? According to Laurie Larwood (Larwood, Szwajkowski, & Rose, 1988a, 1988b; Trentham & Larwood, 1998) of the University of Nevada, Reno, what seems to be critical is for the client or president of the company to make a public statement against such discriminatory practices. It seems that managers tend to operate on the perceived norms of the corporate culture. If the message from the corporate leaders tends to be one of fairness, managers are more likely to protect their own self-interest by following this corporate philosophy of gender-fair practices in the hiring, assigning, and promoting of employees.

While the results of the research contained here suggest that there are certain gender-related biases in the processes of hiring and promoting women, fortunately there are also some specific suggestions for dealing with such biases. For more information on ways to deal with and reduce sex discrimination in the world of work, see the chapter titled "Preventing Sex Discrimination in Hiring" in a book titled *Fair, Square and Legal: Safe Hiring, Managing and Firing Practices to Keep You and Your Company Out of Court* (Weiss, 2004).

Ambivalent Sexism: A Double-Edged Sword that Works Against Women at Home and in the World of Work

In addition to the workplace discrimination, another problem created by the stereotypical traits associated with women is **ambivalent sexism** (Glick & Fiske, 2001; Glick et al., 2000). Ambivalent sexism is composed of two basic components: hostile sexism and benevolent sexism. *Hostile sexism* is characterized by negative feelings and the resentment of women because of their perceived values and abilities to challenge the power of men. Examples of some of the beliefs that reflect such hostile sexism might include: women seek special treatment that they do not deserve; women enjoy teasing men by seeming sexually available and then rejecting their sexual advances; women try to take power that they should not have away from men. *Benevolent sexism* is characterized by positive feelings and chivalrous attitudes toward women that lead to the patronizing belief that women need and deserved to be protected. Examples of some of the beliefs that reflect such benevolent sexism might include: women have higher moral standards than men; in times of danger, women should be rescued and protected before men; the lives of men are incomplete without women.

Although these two forms of sexism present two totally different views of women, ratings on the two separate components tend to be positively correlated (Glick et al., 2000). Strong endorsement of one form of sexism is associated with strong endorsement of the other form, with men displaying a tendency to report higher hostile sexism scores than women do, while women display a tendency to report higher benevolent sexism scores than men do. In addition, there seems to be some cross-cultural consistency in these patterns of the expression of ambivalent sexism. Specifically, in a study involving some 15,000 individuals from 19 different countries across 6 continents, this pattern of a positive correlation between the two forms of sexism and the gender differences was also observed around the world (Glick et al., 2000). It was also noted that those countries with the greatest degree of economic and political disparity between men and women tended to display the highest degree of both hostile and benevolent sexism! What this means is women seem to have the least power in those countries where they are both revered and protected and also disrespected and not trusted.

These seemingly paradoxical views of women tend to create problems for them both at home and in the world of work, in that these contrasting perceptions of the traits and values that they possess tend to create prescribed social roles for them. The benevolent sexism characterization of women as being caring while needing to be cared for and protected places them in the subordinate domestic categories of homemaker or caregiver and the less prestigious professional categories of salesperson, office assistant, or human relations director, all of which involve taking care of others, such as spouses and children at home or customers and co-workers at work, while at the same time being taken care of by those in more powerful positions, such as the male "breadwinner" at home or the male CEO at the office. On the other hand, the characterization of women based on hostile sexism as trying to take the power away from men also works against women, both at home, by them being perceived as "career women" who are neglecting their families and taking jobs away from men who are trying to support their families, and in the world of work, as getting promotions and special treatment because they are women, while also being rated more negatively and less feminine when they display masculine behaviors, such as being competitive and assertive, that are often rewarded when they are displayed by men.

An example of the negative consequences of the backlash associated with the perceived threat of benevolent sexism is the recent work of John T. Jost of New York University and Aaron C. Kay of Stanford University. In their work, Jost and Kay (2005) examined how the threat of benevolent sexism can increase support for endorsing the status quo in gender-related treatment of men and women in contemporary society, which tends to reflect, as we have noted throughout this section, the unequal treatment of women in comparison to men. As part of the program of research on this issue, male and female participants were first presented with some information suggesting that women or men made better managers. After receiving this information, the participants were asked to judge the ambiguity of a series of statements that were supposedly going to be used in another, unrelated study. These statements contained information that reflected the instrumental nature of males (e.g., "In general, males are more rational than women," "In general, men are more self-reliant than women") or the social nature of women (e.g., "In general, women are more cooperative than men," "In general, women are more sensitive than men"). It should be noted that the participants were not asked to indicate the extent to which they agreed or disagreed with these statements,

but only to indicate the extent to which the statements were "ambiguously worded." After reading and rating the ambiguity of the statements, the participants were asked to indicate their agreement with a series of statements that reflected their support of the current state of gender-related treatment of males and females in the United States (e.g., "In general, relations between men and women are fair," "Most policies relating to gender and the sexual division of labor serve the greater good").

The results indicated that when presented with the information that women were better managers while also being reminded of the instrumental features of males, the participants showed greater support for the current state of gender-related treatment of males and females than did those participants who were told that men were better managers. When presented with the information that men were better managers and also reminded of the social features of women, the participants showed greater support for the current state of gender-related treatment of males and females than did those participants who were told that women were better managers. What this pattern of results means is that when reminded of the threat women pose to men (i.e., hostile sexism), you can maintain support for the status quo in gender-related treatment of keeping women in their place (i.e., benevolent sexism) by reminding folks of the instrumental nature of men. On the other hand, you can also maintain support for the status quo by letting folks know that men are better at running things (e.g., better managers) and reminding them of the social role nature of women (e.g., caring for others). Presented in this way, ambivalent sexism is a double-edged sword that can promote discrimination against women in the workplace while also serving to maintain a social system of gender-related treatment that promotes the continuation of the stereotypical perception of the personality traits of men and women, which only serves to strengthen the nature and the negative consequences of ambivalent sexism.

Stereotype Threat: The Negative Impact of the Self-Acceptance of Sex-Role Stereotypes

Another issue associated with the sex-role stereotypes is stereotype threat. **Stereotype threat** is a situation where individuals in a group begin to accept the stereotyped beliefs others have about them, and the self-fulfilling impact such beliefs can have on their performance.

According to Claude Steele, a pioneering researcher in this area, the situational presence of a stereotype threat can serve as a disruptive force by serving to undermine the stigmatized individuals' performance and aspirations with respect to certain aspects of their life and sense of social identity (P. G. Davies, Spencer, Quinn, & Gerhardstein, 2002; Steele, 1997; Steele & Aronson, 1995; Steele, Spencer, & Aronson, 2002). An example of the operation of such a stereotype threat might be when the stereotype beliefs about the leadership ability of women result in a female applicant beginning to doubt her management skills and to start answering in short sentences while avoiding eye contact during an interview with a group of seven male executives. It is the impact of the stereotype threat that makes it so detrimental.

The Dynamics of Stereotype Threat: Setting the Stage for Stereotype Threat   For the stereotype threat to have these disruptive effects, Steele suggests that two conditions must be present (Steele et al., 2002). First, it is required that the individuals have some knowledge of the stereotypes associated with their stigmatized social identities. Examples of this type of knowledge might be African-Americans being aware of stereotypes that associate them with being intellectually inferior and aggressive; women being aware that they are perceived as emotional, bad at math, and lacking the ability to be leaders; and males knowing that they are viewed as lacking emotional sensitivity (Crocker, Major, & Steele, 1998; Leyens, Désert, Croizet, & Darcis, 2000). Second, it is required that the stigmatized individuals have knowledge that they run the risk of being personally reduced to those stereotypes in those particular situations. Examples of this type of outcome might be an African-American student running the risk being perceived as not being very smart after making a mistake while doing a homework assignment on the board in front of other non-African-American students; a female account manager being perceived as incompetent after stumbling over the sales figures in a business presentation; or a male client being judged as callous by other members of a divorce-survival group for refusing to share his feelings with them. Thus, since all individuals have some aspect of their social identity that can be stigmatized by the presence of negative stereotypes in one situation or the other, no group of individuals is immune from the impact of stereotype threat.

As noted previously, because of the pervasiveness of the potential negative impact on the performance and aspirations on many different groups of individuals, Steele and his colleagues have attempted to identify those conditions that contribute to the creation of the disruptive state of the stereotype threat among stigmatized groups, along with creating strategies for reversing the negative consequences of stereotype threat. In this regard, one condition that has been identified is the extensive exposure of sex-role stereotypes presented in television commercials and the consequences of such pervasive exposure. Specifically, it has been suggested that the highly pervasive nature of television commercials can make them a major venue in which gender stereotypes can be formed, strengthened, and activated (Lavine, Sweeney, & Wagner, 1999). As a specific example, a recent study by Davies, Spencer, Quinn, and Gerhardstein (2002) demonstrated that exposing males and females to feminine gender-stereotypical commercials prior to their performing a math test served to activate such gender stereotypes as females being irrational, emotional, indecisive, and weak, to name a few, for both male and female participants, and that the stereotypical commercials also served to create a condition of stereotype threat in females, as the results indicated a negative impact on the performance of the female participants on the math test but not on the performance of the male participants. Going a step further in the study of the impact of stereotype threat is the material presented in "At the Cutting Edge of Personality Psychology" on p. 533.

Removing Stereotype Threat: Clearing the Air and Weakening the Glass Ceiling   Steele (1997, 2002; Markus et al., 2002; Steele et al., 2002) talks about conditions of identity safety being able to remove "the threat in the air" created by stereotype threats to women in leadership positions. Such a threat in the air is created as women begin to search their environment for cues that indicate the extent to which their gender identity will be targeted by those around them and serve as a barrier to their advancement and success by what some have called "the glass ceiling" – an invisible barrier of discrimination that prevents women from entering into the upper levels of management and leadership positions in the corporate world (Lyness & Thompson, 2000; Morrison & Von Glinow, 1990). Such explicit cues might include a sexist comment by a male co-worker, being the only woman in a management meeting, or a pattern of staffing where most of the subordinate positions are occupied by women, as well as more subtle cues such as not being invited

AT THE CUTTING EDGE OF PERSONALITY PSYCHOLOGY

Media Influences on the Activation of Stereotype Threat and the Leadership Potential of Women

Sexist Commercials and the Activation of Aspirations of Avoidance of Leadership Responsibilities in Women: Getting Women Out of the Driver's Seat

Going beyond just the impact of the stereotype threat on the performance of certain stigmatized groups, such as feminine gender-stereotype commercials activating stereotype threats that impact negatively the performance of females on certain tasks, Steele has proposed that such stereotype threats can also impact negatively the specific aspirations among stigmatized groups (Steele, 1992, 1997; Steele & Aronson, 1995; Steele et al., 2002). More specifically, in some of his most recent research, Steele and his colleagues (P. G. Davies et al., 2005) have looked at how activating a condition of stereotype threat

Claude Steele's work on the nature and dynamics of stereotype threat, and effective responses to it, illustrates some of the everyday examples of the impact of gender stereotypes.

through exposure to feminine gender-stereotypical television commercials could impact the leadership aspirations of women that would lead them to avoid leadership roles and responsibilities in favor of less threatening, subordinate roles.

In this research, Paul G. Davies of the University of California, Los Angeles, Steven J. Spencer of the University of Waterloo, and Claude Steele (2005, Study 1) of Stanford University had male and female participants view a set of television commercials that included nonfeminine or feminine gender-stereotypical information supposedly as part of an experiment on long-term memory for details in television commercials. In the nonfeminine stereotypical condition, the participants viewed four neutral, nonfeminine stereotypical commercials advertising products that were supposedly gender-neutral. The gender-neutral products being advertised in these commercials included a cell phone, a gas station, a pharmacy, and an insurance company. In the feminine stereotypical condition, the participants viewed the original four nonfeminine stereotypical commercials interspersed with two additional gender-stereotypical commercials. One of the gender-stereotypical commercials was an advertisement for an acne product that illustrated a young woman who was so overjoyed about being a consumer of the acne product that she was shown jumping on her bed with joy. The second gender-stereotypical commercial illustrated a young college co-ed dreaming of becoming the homecoming queen. For methodological purposes, it should be noted that none of the six commercials made any reference to leadership.

After watching the commercials in their respective conditions, the participants were told that 20 minutes would need to pass before testing their long-term memory for the details of the commercials. So to pass the time, the participants were asked to volunteer for a second experiment investigating various leadership styles. At this point, the participants were asked to read a statement noting that as part of their participation in this research project on leadership strategies, they were to indicate whether they wanted to take the role as leader or problem solver in groups that would be formed to solve a series of complex problems, and that there would be one leader selected for each group. In the description, it was noted that while both the leaders and problem solvers would be given written descriptions of the complex problems, only the leaders would be given the solutions, and that it would be the leaders' responsibility to guide the problem solvers to the correct solution without explicitly telling them how to solve the problems. It was also noted that, according to previous research, effective leaders possessed excellent interpersonal skills while good problem solvers were good team players and had excellent communication skills. After reading the description, the participants were asked to indicate on a seven-point scale, from 1 (no interest) to 7 (strong interest), the extent to which they were interested in assuming the leader and problem-solver roles. After indicating their interest in the two roles, the participants were informed of the true nature of their participation and had any questions they might have answered.

The results indicated that while the nature of the commercials did not affect the extent to which the male participants expressed a desire to be leaders or problem solvers, this was not the case for the women. Specifically, in the neutral, nonfeminine gender-stereotypical commercial condition, like the male participants, the female participants did not express a preference for either the leader or the problem-solver role. On the other hand, in the feminine gender-stereotypical commercial condition, the female participants expressed a significantly greater preference for the problem-solver role and a significantly lesser preference for assuming the leader role. Thus, as expected, activating a stereotype threat through feminine gender-stereotypical commercials served to reduce the leadership aspirations of the females but not the males.

Identity-Safe Environments: Reducing the Impact of Stereotype Threat

In the discussion of these results, Steele and his associates noted that women seemed to respond to the information in the feminine gender-stereotypical commercial by utilizing a strategy of reducing their leadership aspirations, in order to avoid being placed in the spotlight created by stereotype threat to their leadership ability. While it is critical to be able to identify those conditions that create the presence of gender-related stereotype threat to females, as well as documenting the negative impact on their performance and aspirations, it is also important to be able to identify those conditions that can help to alleviate such effects. In response to such an important challenge, Steele has proposed the creation of **identity-safe environments**. Environments that create identity safety involve letting stigmatized individuals know that their stigmatized social identities based on stereotypes (e.g., women are emotional, African-Americans are intellectually deficient, males are lacking emotional sensitivity) are not endorsed, nor are they a barrier to their success in a particular aspect of their lives (e.g., being accepted into a college, being interviewed for a job, being promoted at work), and assuring the individuals that they are welcome, supported, and valued regardless of their background (Markus, Steele, & Steele, 2002; Steele, 2002; Steele et al., 2002).

In their efforts to reduce the negative impact of gender-related stereotype threat on the leadership aspirations of women through the creation of an identity-safe environment, in this research, Davies, Spencer, and Steele (2005, Study 2) had male and female participants view the same two sets of commercials utilized in Study 1. In addition to the two previously established commercial conditions, they included a third commercial condition that created an identity-safe environment. In this identity-safe condition, the participants viewed the set of six commercials that included the two feminine gender-stereotypical commercials followed by some written information that served to discount the presence of the sex-role stereotype threat created by this set of commercials.

In many ways the procedures of Study 2 were very similar to those in Study 1, with a few critical modifications. Specifically, after viewing one of the sets of commercials, the participants were asked to engage in two different tasks to help pass the time before their long-term memory for the details of the commercials was tested. The first was a word-recognition task involving the participants being exposed to a series of letter combinations flashed on a screen, during which time the speed at which the participants would indicate whether the letter combination was a word or nonword was measured. In actuality, all of the 15 sets of letters composed words characterizing female stereotypes, such as gullible, irrational, weak, gentle, kind, and indecisive. The word-recognition task was included to assess the extent to which gender stereotypes were activated by the gender-stereotypical or non-gender-stereotypical commercial condition. After completing the word-recognition task, as in Study 1, the participants were then asked to participate in a task involving leadership strategies. After agreeing to do so, the participants either read the same statement involving the description of leaders and problem solvers noted in Study 1 or a slightly modified version. The modified version was identical to the version used in Study 1 but contained one additional sentence designed to create the identity-safe condition: "There is a great deal of controversy in psychology surrounding the issue of gender-based differences in leadership and problem-solving ability; however, our research has revealed absolutely no gender differences in either ability on this particular task." After reading one of the two versions of the leadership-task description, the participants were asked to indicate their degree of interest in assuming the leadership and problem-solver roles on a scale ranging from 1 (no interest) to 7 (strong interest). Again, after indicating the rating of interest for the two roles, the actual nature of the research was explained and any questions raised by the participants were answered. In summary, the male and female participants in Study 2 were exposed to one of three conditions: the set of non-gender-stereotypical commercials *without* the identity-safety sentence, the set of gender-stereotypical commercials *without* the identity-safety sentence, and the set of gender-stereotypical commercials *with* the identity-safety sentence. Please note that the first two commercial conditions

were identical to those two commercial conditions in Study 1.

Just as in Study 1, since the material in the feminine gender-stereotypical commercials did not create a stereotype threat to the identity of the male participants, the rate of the recognition of the feminine-stereotypical words and the role preference by the male participants were not affected by the nature of the commercial conditions. However, a stereotypical bias in the word-recognition task was greater for the female participants who viewed either of the two sets of feminine gender-stereotypical commercials than for those female participants exposed to the non-gender-stereotypical set. More importantly, as found in Study 1, the female participants who viewed the feminine gender-stereotypical commercials without the identity-safety sentence expressed a significantly greater preference for the problem-solver role and a significantly lesser preference for the leadership role than did the female participants who viewed the non-gender-stereotypical commercials without the identity-safety sentence or the gender-stereotypical commercials with the identity-safety sentence displayed. Within the latter two groups, the female participants did not differ in their expressed preference for the leader or problem-solver roles. Thus, it is critical to note that the presence of the identity-safety sentence served to offset the negative impact of the stereotype threat to the leadership ability created by the feminine gender-stereotypical commercials.

The research by Davies, Spencer, and Steele (2005) is considered "at the cutting edge" because it was the first to demonstrate (1) that stereotype threat can serve to go beyond creating deficiencies in performance by also affecting the aspirations of stigmatized individuals; (2) that feminine gender-stereotypical commercials can create a stereotype threat that can impact the leadership aspirations of women; and, most importantly, (3) that creating the conditions of identity safety can offset the impact of such a stereotype threat to the leadership aspirations of women.

to lunch or other unofficial activities (e.g., a golf outing on the weekend) with male colleagues, to name just a few. Rest assured that such threats in the air and the presence of a glass ceiling are real, as evidenced by recent surveys of Fortune 500 companies that indicate that women hold only 4 percent of all leadership positions and a mere 0.6 percent of all CEO positions. Such a threat in the air is aggravated by the threat created in the airwaves as television commercials continue to promote feminine-related gender stereotypes. Given that the average American watches over 35 hours of television per week, which translates to over 37,000 commercials per year, it does not take much reasoning to realize the critical impact such a pervasive medium can have on the way men and women are perceived (Bretl & Cantor, 1988).

In summary, while the picture painted of this state of affairs appears cloudy and bleak, the important work by Steele and his colleagues provides hope that it is possible to "clear the air," most notably the airwaves, of the impact stereotype threats have on women's leadership aspirations by creating environments characterized

Summing It Up *Sex-Role Stereotypes: Differences in the Perception of the Personality of Men and Women*

Sex-Role Stereotype	Consequence	Example
Judgment of Work Quality. Males have skills superior to women.	Even when similar in quality, work done by women tends to be rated lower than the same work done by men.	Although their departments have equal levels of productivity, Julie's monthly departmental evaluations tend to be lower than Brad's.
Explanations of Successful Performance. Successful performances by males tend to be attributed to the effort exerted and skills possessed, while the success of women is attributed to luck.	Women are perceived as being less skillful and industrious than males and, as a result, tend to be paid less for their work.	In their monthly performance evaluations, Gordon gets high marks for his leadership skills, while Sue is told she is fortunate to have such good support staff in her office.
Perceived Personality Traits of Men and Women. The traits possessed by males are perceived as being more positive and valued more by our society.	Women around the world are associated with being warm, nurturing caregivers, while men are perceived as being competent and instrumental.	At the volunteer center, women volunteers are assigned to kitchen duty more often than are men, who are more likely to be assigned to be group discussion leaders.
Ambivalent Sexism. Women are perceived as needing to be protected and are also resented for their abilities to challenge men.	Women have the least power in those countries where they are both protected and disrespected.	Helen is given the title of assistant vice-president but not invited to the all-male golf outings where many company decisions are made.
Stereotype Threat. You or a group to which you belong may be aware of and accept certain stereotype beliefs about yourself.	The acceptance of the stereotype beliefs begins to affect your performance in a manner consistent with the beliefs.	Kate begins to doubt her leadership ability, and, as a result, she begins to avoid making personnel decisions, which lowers the productivity of her department.
Reducing the Impact of Stereotype Threat. Identity-safe environments can be created that make it clear that the stereotype threats are not endorsed.	Environments free of stereotype threats create a sense of welcome and belonging for all individuals.	The personnel department at Joan's company initiated a company-wide campaign denouncing sexist behavior in the workplace.

by identity safety. Just as it takes the collective effort of all individuals to clear the air of environmental pollutants so that we all can live and breathe easier, it is also important for every one of us to do what we can do, as Steele suggests, to remove the "threat in the air" by creating an identity-safe environment that will make it possible for all individuals to feel welcome and achieve their aspirations.

This concludes the discussion of sex-role stereotypes. A summary of the material discussed in this section is presented in "Summing It Up: Sex-Role Stereotypes: Differences in the Perception of the Personality of Men and Women" on p. 536. In the next section, the discussion of sex roles goes one step further by considering the notion of androgyny.

Androgyny: The Blending of Masculinity and Femininity

To this point, the discussion of various topics and issues related to sex-roles stereotypes has centered on the distinction between masculinity and femininity. However, a third dimension has been introduced that has contributed to a more complete understanding of sex roles. The concept is that of androgyny (Hyde, 2004).

Defining Androgyny

Broken down, the word **androgyny** means "man" (in Greek, *andros*) and "woman" (*gyne*). The concept of androgyny is most closely associated with the work of Sandra Lipsitz Bem of Cornell University and Janet Spence of the University of Texas at Austin. In their original conceptualization of androgyny, masculinity and femininity were considered two separate dimensions, and androgyny a combination of the two.

An individual who possesses and exhibits many masculine traits and behaviors but few feminine characteristics would be considered a **masculine sex-typed** individual. For example, an aggressive, emotionless office manager, either a man or woman, would be considered masculine sex-typed. An individual who possesses and exhibits many feminine traits and behaviors but few masculine characteristics would be considered a **feminine sex-typed** individual. For example, a compassionate, gentle office manager, either a man or a woman, would be considered feminine sex-typed. On the other hand, an

Sandra Lipsitz Bem has done important work on the assessment, dynamics, and expression of androgyny.

androgynous individual is one who is described as possessing and exhibiting both masculine and feminine personality traits and behaviors, depending on what is most appropriate for the specific situation (Bem, 1974, 1975, 1985, 1993; Lippa, 2005). For example, an androgynous office manager would be assertive with an employee who is consistently late for work but also show compassion for the employee who is having difficulties on the job because of some domestic problem. Thus, androgyny is conceptualized as the blending of masculinity and femininity within the individual.

Behavioral and Personality Correlates of Androgyny: A Question of Flexibility, Self-Regard, and Adjustment

Because they possess both masculine and feminine characteristics, androgynous people have been found to behave in a more flexible and adaptive manner (Bem, 1974, 1975; Chen, 2005; Jose & McCarthy, 1988; Prager & Bailey, 1985; Shaffer, Pegalis, & Cornell, 1991). For example, sex-typed masculine, sex-typed feminine, and androgynous people were observed in a situation that involved demonstrating the masculine attribute of independence by resisting social pressure in the ratings of cartoons, or in one that involved the feminine attribution of nurturance during a 10-minute interaction with a 5-month-old baby (Bem, 1978). The results of this study indicated that the masculine sex-typed and androgynous subjects were more independent in the social pressure situation than were feminine-typed people. On the other hand, the feminine sex-typed and androgynous subjects were more nurturing than were the masculine sex-typed people when interacting with the baby.

These results are consistent with the notion of greater role adaptability being associated with androgynous people. Androgynous people have also been found to demonstrate their flexibility by performing well in a wide range of tasks and games stereotypically associated with their own sex and the opposite sex. Sex-typed people, on the other hand, tend to perform well and prefer tasks and games stereotypically associated with their own sex (Bem & Lenney, 1976; Bem, Martyna, & Watson, 1976).

In interpersonal situations, some evidence also supports the androgyny advantage. In both childhood and adolescence, androgynous people are perceived by their peers as more likeable and better adjusted than classmates who are traditionally sex typed (Boldizar, 1991; Major, Carnevale, & Deaux, 1981). Androgynous men and women are also more comfortable with their sexuality (Garcia, 1982) and more satisfied interpersonally (Rosenzweig & Daley, 1989) than are sex-typed people. When meeting for the first time, heterosexual couples that included an androgynous individual expressed a greater liking for each other than did couples that included the more traditional masculine sex-typed male and the feminine sex-typed female, casting doubt on the old saying "opposites attract" (Ickes & Barnes, 1978).

The advantages of androgyny have also been documented in several real-life settings. For example, androgynous college students were found to receive more honors and awards, date more, and have a lower incidence of childhood illness than low sex-typed masculine and high sex-typed feminine students (Spence, Helmreich, & Stapp, 1975). In a study of Israeli soldiers, masculine and androgynous soldiers received more positive evaluations from fellow officers than did feminine sex-typed soldiers (Dimitrovsky, Singer, & Yinon, 1989). This greater role flexibility and behavioral success may be due to the tendency of androgynous people to be less likely to organize information, including information about themselves, in terms of gender and sex-role stereotypes (Bem, 1983). The logic of androgynous people seems to be to classify information and events on the basis of people rather than on

gender stereotypes (Bem, 1983, 1985; Fiske & Taylor, 1991).

While the results of the behavioral correlates of androgyny seem to favor clearly the androgynous individual, the results for the personality correlates are less conclusive. For example, research indicates that androgyny is associated with higher levels of psychosocial development (Waterman & Whitbourne, 1982) and self-esteem (O'Connor, Mann, & Bardwick, 1978; Spence et al., 1975). However, the relationship with self-esteem seems to be the strongest for masculine and androgynous individuals for both adolescents and adults and across a number of different ethnic groups, including Hispanic-Americans, African-Americans, Asian-Americans, and Anglo-Americans (Bem, 1977; Stein, Newcomb, & Bentler, 1992). Androgynous people are perceived by themselves and others as being better adjusted than masculine and feminine sex-typed people (Bem, 1985; Flaherty & Dusek, 1980; Major et al., 1981; O'Heron & Orlofsky, 1990; Orlofsky & O'Heron, 1987). Other research, however, suggests that androgynous people do not exhibit higher self-esteem or better adjustment than other people (Lubinski, Tellegen, & Butcher, 1981; M. C. Taylor & Hall, 1982; Whitley, 1983). In fact, these studies suggest that it is the possession of "masculine traits" by the sex-typed masculine and androgynous people that contributes most to the expressions of the highest level of self-regard and overall adjustment (Allgood-Merten & Stockard, 1991; Lippa, 2005; Markstrom-Adams, 1989; M. C. Taylor & Hall, 1982; Whitley, 1988).

One possible reason for this contradiction in the results is that while the notion of androgyny may be psychologically appealing, in reality sex-typed masculine characteristics (e.g., aggressiveness, competitiveness, and independence) are valued more and associated more with what our individualistic, achievement-striving, competitive society values and labels as being part of the personality of successful people (e.g., leaders in business and government; Whitley, 1988). Thus, those who possess and exhibit masculine characteristics are much more likely to receive social recognition and, therefore, feel better about themselves. On the other hand, those individuals with high femininity scores tend to show a greater degree of adjustment in such areas of interpersonal relationships as being a good friend (Antill, 1983; Kurdeck & Schmitt, 1986) and being empathetic (Spence & Helmreich, 1978), which are the kinds of traits you would want in your good friends or romantic partner (Lippa, 2005). So, when it comes to looking at sex-type categorization and degree of adjustment, it seems that masculinity, in particular, and androgyny are related to what is good for society – competitive achievement – while femininity seems to be good for the heart and soul – social support and love.

The Changing Face of Androgyny: Moving Beyond Gender-Linked Sex Roles

The concept of androgyny did much to help develop our thinking about the nature of masculinity and femininity. However, as with so many other important ideas, further examination of the concept of androgyny also brought changes in the way we view it (Lippa, 2005; Maccoby, 1998). Specifically, more recent thinking on the conceptualizations of masculinity and femininity has proposed a much deeper look at these two concepts. For example, one challenge to the concept of androgyny is that it tends to preserve the notion that there are still separate masculine and feminine qualities, while simply giving people the permission to possess both sets of qualities. Such an approach still tends to link an individual's personal attributes to a sex-linked standard (e.g., assertiveness is masculine). In contrast, some of the early challenges to the concept of androgyny (Garnets & Peck, 1979) proposed the concepts of masculinity, femininity, and androgyny should be more about "sex-role transcendence," meaning that an individual's attributes and preferences are not associated with gender but rather placed in more descriptive categories that reflect the nature of the behavioral pattern of the individuals, regardless of their sex. As an example, the self-perceived ratings of such personal characteristics as being active, decisive, and self-confident could be labeled as an index of "agency" or "instrumentality" instead of the more gender-linked "masculinity." In a similar manner, the self-perceived rating of such personal characteristics as being emotional, kind, and nurturing could be labeled as an index of "communion" or "expressivity" instead of the more gender-linked "femininity" (Helgeson, 2003; Spence & Buckner, 2000). As you can see, such an approach moves beyond gender-linked sex roles and focuses only on the more neutral descriptions of the nature of the behavior pattern.

In addition to being a more gender-neutral system of classifying personal attributes, this approach also takes into consideration the more complex and expansive manner in which people view masculinity and femininity to include not only personality characteristics (e.g., decisive, nurturing) but also physical features, primary (e.g., reproductive organs) and secondary (e.g., facial hair) sexual characteristics, and social (e.g., community volunteer) and occupational (e.g., sale representative) roles. Elements contained in each of these different categories are not necessarily located within the single category of masculinity or femininity but may also be combined in different ways for different individuals (Helgeson, 2003; Spence & Buckner, 2000). For example, one woman might consider herself masculine in her personality at work (e.g., decisive, active) while feminine in her personality at home when interacting with her children (e.g., nurturing, emotional), feminine in her physical appearance (e.g., petite), and androgynous within her social (e.g., wife and mother) and occupational (e.g., police officer) roles. On the other hand, a man might consider himself both masculine and feminine in his personality at work (e.g., assertive and competitive, patient and compassionate), while feminine in his personality at home when interacting with his children (e.g., nurturing, emotional), masculine in his physical appearance (e.g., beard), and androgynous within his social (e.g., husband and father) and occupational (e.g., florist) roles. As these examples illustrate, the manifestation of both masculinity and femininity can operate throughout the daily life of each individual, creating a pattern of behavior that helps to define the individual's unique personality.

An example of this changing view of androgyny that focuses more on the gender-neutral descriptive categories of instrumentality and expressiveness is the work of Andrea E. Abele of the University of Erlangen in Germany. In her work, Abele (2000) has focused on gender and career-related processes, such as career self-efficacy (e.g., personal belief about having the skills to do one's job), career motivation (e.g., personal satisfaction, income, and success), and career development (e.g., movement up the career ladder) as they relate to constructs of instrumentality and expressiveness. The results of her research indicate that individuals high on instrumentality displayed a greater degree of career self-efficacy and higher income. In addition, career progress seems to enhance instrumentality to a greater degree in women when they have a position consistent with their educational background than for men. On the other hand, men tend to show a decrease in instrumentality when they are in a position that is inconsistent with their educational background, while women do not. Stated more directly, "Women become more

Summing It Up *Conceptual, Behavioral, and Personality Correlates of Androgyny*

Conceptual Correlates:

- *Masculine sex-typed individuals* are characterized by the expression of traits and behaviors typically associated with males in our society (e.g., independence and competitiveness). For example, the local college basketball coach was successful because of her strong desire to win and her ability to stand up to the pressure of the local boosters to weaken her recruiting standards.
- *Feminine sex-typed individuals* are characterized by the expression of traits and behaviors typically associated with females in our society (e.g., gentle and expresses feelings). For example, in the ad for the receptionist position, the company stated it was looking for someone who was warm and pleasant and likes to help others.
- *Androgynous individuals* are characterized by the expression of traits and behaviors typically associated with both males and females in our society (e.g., ambitious and tactful). For example, the most effective psychotherapists are those who show compassion and sensitivity toward their clients but know how to be assertive when setting and enforcing treatment guidelines.

Behavioral Correlates:

- *Independence.* Androgynous and masculine sex-typed individuals display more behavioral independence (e.g., expressing their own opinion) than do feminine sex-typed individuals. For example, while playing Trivial Pursuit, if they feel they have the correct answer, androgynous and masculine individuals would be less likely to change their mind when pressed to do so by the other members of their team than would feminine sex-typed individuals.
- *Nurturance.* Androgynous and feminine sex-typed individuals display more nurturing behavior (e.g., comforting others) than do masculine sex-typed males. For example, after hearing that a friend received some bad news, feminine sex-typed and androgynous individuals would spend more time talking with the friend on the phone discussing the situation than would masculine sex-typed individuals.
- *Flexibility.* While masculine and feminine sex-typed individuals tend to perform best on tasks preferred by their own sex, androgynous individuals demonstrate a greater degree of flexibility, performing well on both male- and female-preferred tasks (e.g., fixing cars or baking cakes). For example, while trying to hold down two jobs in the summer to earn money to pay for tuition, the androgynous individual was successful working as both a florist arranging flowers and a dockworker loading freight on trucks.
- *Information Processing.* Sex-typed individuals tend to organize information the on basis of sex-role stereotypes (e.g., what males and females are expected to do) to a greater degree than do androgynous individuals. For example, when making volunteer assignments for the company picnic, the sex-typed supervisors tended to assign the female employees to make baked goods while the male employees were assigned to do the grilling of the food.

Personality Correlates:

- *Personality Adjustment.* There is a tendency for androgynous individuals to be perceived as more adjusted than sex-typed individuals. For example, while conducting job interviews, the personnel manager noticed that the androgynous-scoring individuals tended to come across better during the interviews than did the masculine- and feminine sex-typed-scoring individuals.
- *Self-Concept.* Sex-typed masculine and androgynous individuals tend to report a more favorable self-image, since the masculine traits they possess tend to be valued more in our achievement-oriented society, while sex-typed feminine individuals tended to be rated more favorably in terms of traits more relevant to interpersonal relationships. For example, when asked to rate how well they thought they did on the interview for the supervisor's position, masculine sex-typed and androgynous individuals reported more self-confidence than did feminine sex-typed individuals, who tended to report more confidence for the less prestigious staff coordinator's position.

Reconceptualizing Androgyny. Attempts have been made to replace the sex-linked terminology of masculinity and femininity with the more behaviorally linked descriptive terminology of agency and instrumentality and communion and expressivity, respectively. For example, regardless of their gender, the successful candidate for the administrative position will be an individual who demonstrates the ability to act in a clear and decisive manner while being able to work with others and communicate effectively.

instrumental with more career success but not less instrumental with less career success. Men become less instrumental with less career success but not more instrumental with more career success" (Abele, 2000, p. 383). Taken together, the results of this research demonstrate how it is possible to study complex social processes (e.g., career development) and gender without having to rely on more traditional sex-linked descriptions of personal attributes stereotypically linked to men and women. Specifically, there is no need for the concept of androgyny because there is no distinction to be made between masculinity, femininity, and the blending and balancing of the two; there is only a discussion of how these two gender-neutral descriptive personality categories serve to influence each individual's beliefs and behavior.

This concludes our discussion on the concept of androgyny. The major points of the material discussed in this section are presented in "Summing It Up: Conceptual, Behavioral, and Personality Correlates of Androgyny" on p. 540. If you would like to read more about this topic, an excellent summary can be found in a book chapter titled "Masculinity and Femininity: Gender within Gender" in a book by Richard A. Lippa (2005) titled *Gender, Nature, and Nurture*.

This concludes our discussion of gender identity. As you can see from the diverse nature of the topics covered in this chapter, gender identity is a principal feature of personality, and one that serves to impact some of the most important aspects of our everyday lives and the lives of those around us. If you would like more information on the topic of gender and gender identity, three outstanding resources are *The Psychology of Gender* (Eagly, Beall, & Sternberg, 2004), *Gender, Nature, and Nurture* (Lippa, 2005), and the *Handbook of the Psychology of Women and Gender* (Unger, 2001).

Chapter Summary: Reexamining the Highlights

- *Theories of Gender Identity*
  - *Psychological Explanations of Gender Identity.* The psychological explanations of gender identity include psychoanalytic theory and its emphasis on identifying with same-sex others; social-cognitive theory and the role of enactive experience (e.g., the influence of others), observational learning, self-regulation of gendered behavior (e.g., anticipated outcomes, regulatory self-sanctions, and perceived self-efficacy); and the cognitive perspectives, which include CDT, with its emphasis on the strengthening of gender identity through the categorization and incorporation of activities based on gender, and gender schema theory, based on attending to, storing, and recalling information consistent with being a male or female.
  - *Social Role Theory.* The social role theory of gender identity proposes that differences in gendered behavioral roles are a result of the social division of labor and the status associated with those behaviors, with the behavior of men being associated with higher social status (e.g., leaders)

  and social reward (e.g., recognition and increased compensation), and the behavior of women being associated with performing those behaviors that have lower social status (e.g., caregiver) and social reward (e.g., lack of prestige and decreased compensation).

  - *Biological Explanations of Gender Identity.* Biological explanations of gender identity include chromosomal and hormonal influences and the interaction of biological and psychological factors in the expression of hermaphroditism.

  - *Evolutionary Perspective of Gendered Behavior.* The evolutionary psychology perspective proposes that gendered behaviors and personality characteristics have developed in response to the tasks of reproduction and survival of the species, with males taking on those behaviors and personality characteristics associated with providing resources (e.g., food) and protection (e.g., aggressiveness), while females take on those behaviors and personality characteristics associated with domestic activities (e.g., cooking) and caregiving (e.g., nurturing).

- *Integration of Explanations*. Biological processes provide the basis for the physical differences between males and females, while the evolutionary explanation provides an account of how these differences in behavior and personality characteristics developed, the social role theory provides an account of the hierarchical organization of these differences, and the psychological explanations offer an account of those processes associated with the individualized categorization and expression of such differences.

● *Consequences of Gender Identity*

- *Gender Differences in Personality*. One consequence of gender identity is the impact on gender differences in personality along such personality dimensions as aggression (e.g., physical, verbal, and indirect), expressions of emotional and physical intimacy (e.g., love, romance, mate selection, sexuality, and jealousy), social influence (e.g., conformity and disagreement), emotional expressiveness (e.g., verbal and covert), self-evaluation and expectations (e.g., self-esteem and self-confidence), joy and sadness (e.g., happiness and depression), and cognitive functioning (e.g., verbal, mathematical, and visual-spatial abilities).

- *Sex-Role Stereotypes*. Another consequence of gender identity is the presence of sex-role stereotypes and their effects on the judgment of work quality (i.e., males' work being judged superior), explanations of successful performance (i.e., skillful men, lucky women), and the cross-cultural perceived personality traits of men and women (i.e., males as competent, woman as warm and expressive). *Ambivalent sexism* is characterized by the expression of the opposing views of hostile sexism (i.e., the resentment of women) and benevolent sexism (i.e., women deserve and need to be protected), which results in women being relegated to more subordinate and caregiver roles (e.g., office assistant) and lower social status. *Stereotype threat* is the condition where a specific group of individuals (e.g., women) begins to believe certain stereotypes associated with their group (e.g., women are not good at being leaders) and such beliefs begin to affect negatively the behavior of individuals in the group (e.g., a female does not apply for a supervisor's position at work). This threat can be reduced by the presence of identity-safe environments in which there is official denunciation of the stereotype beliefs.

● *Androgyny*

- *Defining Androgyny*. The personality dimension of androgyny is the expression of both masculine and feminine personality traits and behaviors.

- *Behavioral and Personality Correlates of Androgyny*. Androgynous individuals demonstrate a greater degree of sex-role flexibility and interpersonal satisfaction and, along with masculine sex-typed individuals, self-regard, which has been linked to the possession of masculine traits.

- *The Changing Face of Androgyny*. More recent conceptualizations of androgyny rely less on gender-linked characterizations of masculinity and femininity and more on gender-free descriptions of behavior patterns (e.g., agency and expressivity).

Glossary

ambivalent sexism   A belief system composed of hostile sexism – the belief that women are not to be trusted because of their abilities to challenge the authority of males – and benevolent sexism – the belief that women are to be protected.

androgen   A hormone that regulates sexual development in males.

androgynous   An individual who demonstrates both masculine and feminine traits and behaviors.

androgyny   A combination of masculinity and femininity together.

chromosomes   Structures within cells that contain genetic information.

cognitive-development theory (CDT)   The viewpoint of gender identity based on the classification of behaviors into masculine and feminine categories.

direct tuition   The use of rewards or punishment to influence behavior.

direct tutelage   The process of receiving direct instruction from others regarding what is considered gender-appropriate behavior.

enactive experience   The process of acquiring information about gender-appropriate behavior by the reactions others provide to that behavior.

endocrine system The glands regulating the release of hormones into the body.

estrogen A hormone that regulates sexual development in females.

feminine sex-typed An individual who demonstrates traditional feminine traits and behaviors.

gender constancy The understanding that gender remains constant across time and situations.

gender identity The awareness of one's gender.

gender schema A collection of personal assumptions about the beliefs and behaviors possessed by each gender.

gonads A gland that secretes hormones which regulate sexual development.

hermaphroditism The presence of both masculine and feminine sex characteristics within the same individual.

hormones Chemical substances, produced by and secreted into the body, that influence mood and behavior.

identity-safe environments Conditions created to deal with stereotype threats by letting stigmatized individuals know they are welcomed and valued.

in-group/out-group schema A set of assumptions about which ideas, beliefs, or behaviors go together and which do not with regard to a particular group of individuals.

masculine sex-typed An individual who demonstrates traditional masculine traits and behaviors.

ovaries The gonads of females.

own-sex schema A set of assumptions about which beliefs and behaviors are appropriate for a person's own gender.

paradox of achievement The situation in which women demonstrate high verbal skills but exhibit a low success rate in those high-status professions in which such skills are critical.

primary sexual characteristics The presence of specific organs and hormones that make reproduction possible.

progesterone A hormone that regulates sexual development in females.

pseudohermaphroditism An individual whose genitals are ambiguous or do not match up with the person's biological sex.

regulatory self-sanctions The development of a personal set of standards that determine the decision to perform gendered behavior.

schema-directed memory The motivation to attend to and recall information and activities associated with a gender schema.

secondary sexual characteristics A collection of body changes that indicate gender-specific sexual maturation.

self-confidence An individual's assessment of his or her ability to be successful in a particular task.

self-esteem An individual's overall sense of personal self-worth.

sex-role stereotypes Assumptions about the behaviors, beliefs, and traits associated with a particular gender.

social role theory A theory of gendered behavior and identity based on the classification and social ranking of gendered behavior.

stereotype threat The condition in which a group of individuals comes to believe certain stereotypes about the group, which begins to have a negative impact on the behavior of those individuals.

testes The gonads of males.

testosterone A hormone that regulates sexual development in males.

visual-spatial ability The ability to mentally rotate and manipulate objects and visualize the change in their images without having to draw them out.

Anxiety
An All-Encompassing Intrapersonal Process of Personality

13

Chapter Overview:
A Preview of Coming Attractions

Although the concept of anxiety has been mentioned in previous chapters, it was typically treated only as a secondary point of discussion. In this chapter, the concept of anxiety is the primary focus of attention. You will start by considering its core dimensions and the different ways in which they manifest themselves. Then you will learn about the various theoretical viewpoints that have been proposed to explain the nature and dynamics of anxiety. In the next section, you will examine some different types of anxiety, including the distinction between anxiety as a state and anxiety as a trait, the nature and dynamics of test anxiety, and the characteristics and causes of anxiety disorders. At the end of this chapter on anxiety, you will consider two areas of application: (1) examining how anxiety has been applied to the world of advertising, and (2) using what is known to help understand and overcome shyness. Thus, in the course of this discussion, you will be exposed to the conceptual, theoretical, and practical sides of anxiety.

Anxiety as an Intrapersonal Personality Process: The Influence of Personality on the Person

In this chapter, anxiety is conceptualized as an intrapersonal personality process. An **intrapersonal personality process** is a specific dimension of personality that is rather encompassing in the effect it has on the individual. The term *intrapersonal* is used because the major effect such a dimension has is primarily within (i.e., "intra") the individual (i.e., "personal"). Anxiety is considered a personality process because, in and of itself, it has specific dynamics that affect the individual differently than other separate dimensions of personality. A personality process is considered encompassing because, as a separate dimension of personality, it influences many different aspects of life. For example, anxiety affects aspects of your life ranging from the thoughts and feelings you have about yourself to the perceptions and reactions you have about the people and products around you. In addition, some of the more specific and serious effects of anxiety include affecting an individual's feelings of pessimism and daily mood (Räikkönen, Matthews, Floy, Owens, & Gump, 1999), abuse of alcohol (Stewart, Samoluk, & MacDonald, 1998), and sense of marital satisfaction (Caughlin, Huston, & Houts, 2000), as well as being identified as increasing an individual's vulnerability to physical illness (Suinn, 2001). Because the major effect anxiety has as a personality dimension is primarily within the individual, such an effect can be easily conceptualized as "the effect of personality on the person."

The Dimensions of Anxiety: Affecting Your Body, Mind, and Actions

One reason that anxiety has such a profound effect on you whenever it appears is that it manifests itself in so many different ways. For example, when you become anxious, you seem to feel it in the form of "butterflies" in your stomach, a sense of "impending doom" in your mind, and a noticeable increase in the clumsiness and awkwardness of your voice while giving a speech to a large group of people. This section devotes some attention to the three specific dimensions of anxiety: the physiological, cognitive, and behavioral dimensions of anxiety.

The Physiological Dimension of Anxiety: The Building of Butterflies in Your Stomach

Whenever you experience an anxiety-provoking situation, your body responds by triggering its sympathetic nervous system. The **sympathetic nervous system (SNS)** is that aspect of your nervous system that takes over your body to help it prepare to cope with the threat presented in the situation (Carlson, 2001). For example, some of the reactions in your body triggered by the SNS involve increasing your heart rate, blood pressure, and respiration, all of which are designed to get more blood and oxygen to the muscles in your body. As your muscles get more oxygen, they become stronger and better able to deal with the threatening situation. The SNS also causes various hormones, such as adrenaline, to be released into the bloodstream, which make you more resistant to and better able to cope with the stress. The SNS dilates (i.e., enlarges) the pupils in your eyes, so that you can better see the source of the threat.

While some reactions are triggered by the SNS, other systems are turned off by it in times of stress and anxiety. For example, the SNS minimizes the functioning of your digestive and sexual systems in response to anxiety-provoking situations, since eating or having sex would probably not be very useful when attempting to cope with the stress. Thus, the physiological dimension of the anxiety involves your body responding in numerous ways to anxiety-provoking situations (Brown, Tomarken, Loosen, Kalin, & Davidson, 1996; Räikkönen et al., 1999; Rosen & Schulkin, 1998; Suinn, 2001). In a more subjective sense, it is these dramatic changes in your body that contribute to those feelings of butterflies in your stomach.

The Cognitive Dimension of Anxiety: The Closing of Your Mind

In addition to causing changes in your body, anxiety causes changes in your mind, or more specifically the cognitive processes that occur in your mind (Fiske,

Morling, & Stevens, 1996; McNally, 1998). For example, when you are confronted with an anxiety-provoking situation, your thoughts often become confused and unrelated. You might have experienced such a state of events when you found it difficult to remember what you were going to say next when giving a speech, or when you started to say something from the middle of your speech at the beginning. Your thoughts might also become stereotyped and repetitive when you are anxious. You might not be able to think of a novel answer and simply give the old standby response of "I don't know" when confronted by a traffic officer as to why you were doing 70 mph in a 55-mph speed zone.

In the presence of anxiety, your ability to recall information from your memory also becomes impaired. You have probably experienced the situation in which you couldn't remember an answer to a question when you were rushing to finish it as time was running out during a test, only to have the answer jump out at you while you were driving home from school after the test. Thus, the cognitive dimension of anxiety involves the influence it has on your ability to think effectively in anxiety-provoking situations (Leary & Kowalski, 1995; McIlroy, Bunting, & Adamson, 2000; McNalley, 1998). As you can see, the general effect of the cognitive dimension of anxiety is almost literally the closing of your mind.

The Behavioral Dimension of Anxiety: Fumbling, Fighting, or Fleeing

While the physiological and cognitive dimensions of anxiety are private signals of anxiety to you, the behavioral dimension of anxiety is a public signal to others that you are experiencing anxiety. The behavioral dimension of anxiety is characterized by three response categories: disturbances in the fluency of behavior, attack, and avoidance.

One category of behavioral response to an anxiety-provoking situation is a disturbance in the fluency of behavior. A characteristic of this category is otherwise smooth movements becoming disjointed and awkward when experiencing anxiety. For example, when experiencing anxiety while giving a speech, some signs of such a breakdown in the fluency of behavior might include trembling, shifting your weight from one foot to the other, fidgeting with your hair or clothing, and the cracking or changing of the pitch in your voice, as

well as those beads of perspiration that may form on your forehead. Regardless of their specific nature, one of the behavioral consequences is for you to begin fumbling around.

The other two behavioral categories of anxiety can be conceptualized into a **fight-or-flight reaction** pattern (Cannon, 1929). The basic logic underlying the fight-or-flight reaction is that when confronted with an anxiety-provoking situation, an individual responds by either attacking (i.e., fighting) the situation or avoiding (i.e., fleeing from) it. Suppose that you receive an extremely low grade on a test in your psychology class and begin to feel anxious because you now run the risk of receiving a below-passing grade for the course. You might "attack" this anxiety-provoking situation by launching into a verbal campaign designed to get the professor to feel sorry for you and to change your grade on the test. On the other hand, another student in the class might cope with this threatening situation by avoiding the issue and going to the nearest video store and checking out three movies to help him escape for awhile. The point is that sometimes we respond to an anxiety-provoking situation by fighting it, and at times we elect to take flight from it (Raffety, Smith, & Ptacek, 1997).

Combining the Dimensions of Anxiety: The Manifest Anxiety Scale (MAS)

One consequence of these three dimensions of anxiety is that they can be combined to create vast differences in the level of anxiety that people experience. One of the most widely used measures of these individual differences in the level of anxiety is the **Manifest Anxiety Scale** (**MAS**; J. A. Taylor, 1953). A sample of items from the MAS is presented in "You Can Do It" on p. 548.

In support of the validity of the MAS in assessing individual differences in anxiety, people scoring high on the MAS reported experiencing a greater level of anxiety when confronted with a threatening situation (Hodges & Spielberger, 1969) and displayed a tendency to interpret ambiguous stimuli as having emotionally negative meaning (Terry & Burns, 2001) than those scoring low on the MAS, as well as demonstrating a pattern of learning consistent with the drive viewpoint of anxiety (see pp. 550–551; Aiken, 2003).

As you can see, the physiological, cognitive, and behavioral dimensions of anxiety involve a wide variety

You Can Do It

Selected Items from the MAS: Assessing Physiological, Cognitive, and Behavioral Dimensions of Anxiety

The Manifest Anxiety Scale (MAS) contains 50 true–false items and is designed to measure individual differences in anxiety. Included in the MAS are items indicating the physiological, cognitive, and behavioral dimensions of anxiety. Here are some representative MAS items for you to examine.

Physiological Dimension of Anxiety

T   F   I have very few headaches. (False)
T   F   I sweat very easily even on cool days. (True)

Cognitive Dimension of Anxiety

T   F   I cannot keep my mind on one thing. (True)
T   F   I find it hard to keep my mind on a task or job. (True)

Behavioral Dimension of Anxiety

T   F   I am more sensitive than most other people. (True)
T   F   I am usually calm and not easily upset. (False)

Scoring

Agreement with the choice in parentheses indicates a response characteristic of an anxious person.

of systems, processes, and responses that manifest themselves in the body, mind, and actions of the individual. The next section focuses on the theoretical viewpoints of anxiety. But before reading further, you should realize that while the preceding examples focus on the negative effects of anxiety on behavior, believe it or not, anxiety can actually improve the quality of your performance. For example, if you become anxious about the possibility of getting a below-passing grade in a psychology class, you might respond to this threat by attacking your books and studying much harder than

you have done in the past. Read "A Closer Look" below to consider the conditions under which anxiety can help or hinder your performance.

A Closer Look

The Yerkes-Dodson Law: Using Anxiety to Your Advantage

The **Yerkes-Dodson Law** is a principle of motivation that outlines the relationship between motivation and performance (Geen, 1995; Rathus & Nevid, 2002). In its simplest sense, a fundamental point of the Yerkes-Dodson Law is that motivation or arousal may be viewed as existing on a continuum, ranging from very low to extremely high levels of excitement. As can be seen in Figure 13.1, at the very low end of the continuum, the individual is viewed as being underaroused or undermotivated (e.g., asleep, drowsy, or bored). At the very high end, the individual is viewed as being extremely aroused and overly motivated (e.g., in a

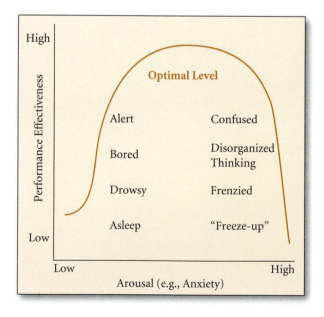

Figure 13.1   The "inverted-U" relationship of the Yerkes-Dodson Law, describing the relationship between different levels of arousal and performance effectiveness

state of frenzy). Within this framework, anxiety is conceptualized as a form of arousal.

Another fundamental principle of the Yerkes-Dodson Law is that arousal affects performance in what is described as an "inverted-U pattern" (see Figure 13.1). At the very low end, your performance is believed to be hindered by a low level of anxiety (arousal) because you become inattentive and careless. Examples of this level might be missing your exit on the expressway because you were tired or misreading a test question because you just didn't really care that much about it. At the very high end, your level of performance is also believed to be hindered by an extremely high level of anxiety (arousal) because you become disorganized and flustered. An example of this would be when you become so anxious during a test that your mind goes "completely blank" and you end up getting a low grade on the test.

Between these two extremes is a moderate level of arousal, defined as the **optimal level of arousal** because it maximizes the quality of your performance. At this optimal level of arousal, you are aroused or motivated enough that you force yourself to concentrate more intensely on the task at hand, but are not so motivated that you are overwhelmed by your level of arousal.

Examples of this level might be the tremendous sense of concentration and determination that goes along with a moderate increase in the level of anxiety you experience while trying to maneuver your car through the scene of a traffic accident, or when you are trying to recall a game-winning question while playing Trivial Pursuit.

Thus, the lesson to be learned here is to try to establish what your optimal level of anxiety is so that you can use anxiety to your advantage. This might involve trying to calm yourself down or "psyching" yourself up.

As you can see from this discussion of the basic dimensions of anxiety, the nature of the impact anxiety has on the individual involves the characteristic features of the separate dimensions of anxiety, the combination of these basic dimensions interacting together, and the overall level of anxiety. A summary of the major points presented in this section is presented in "Summing It Up: The Three Dimensions of Anxiety" below. In the next section, you will examine the major theoretical viewpoints of anxiety.

Summing It Up *The Three Dimensions of Anxiety*

Dimension	Definition	Example
Physiological	The sympathetic nervous system and other neurological and hormonal processes designed to help prepare your body to cope with threatening situations are activated.	During a job interview, you begin to breathe deeper in order to increase the ability of your muscles to withstand the stress of the interview.
Cognitive	When confronted with an anxiety-provoking situation, your ability to organize and recall information becomes impaired.	When worrying about the impression you have made on a prospective employer, you forget her name at the end of the interview.
Behavioral	The presence of anxiety produces behavioral patterns characterized by awkwardness, defensiveness, and withdrawal.	During the interview, you begin to wriggle in your chair and avoid making eye contact.
Manifest Anxiety Scale (MAS)	The scale provides a measure of anxiety based on items assessing the three basic dimensions of anxiety.	Individuals with a high score on the MAS will display more features of anxiety during the interview than will those with a low score.

Theoretical Viewpoints of Anxiety: Anxiety as a Warning Signal, Acquired Response, Driving Force, and Element of Survival

Something as complex as anxiety is not easily explained. As a result, a number of theoretical viewpoints have been proposed to help explain the nature of anxiety. This section focuses on four of them: the psychodynamic, learning, drive, and evolutionary viewpoints of anxiety.

The Psychodynamic Viewpoint: Anxiety as a Signal of Danger

In one of the earliest formulations of anxiety, Freud (1926/1959), as you will recall from Chapter 3 (p. 86), conceptualized anxiety as a warning signal to the ego that some threatening unconscious impulse is on the verge of breaking through and manifesting itself in the individual's conscious awareness (Josephs, 1994). Using this warning signal, the ego can then take evasive action by employing any one of several defense mechanisms. For example, suppose you were taking a test and were not sure of the answer to one question. In such a situation, you might be tempted to take a look at the test of the person sitting near you. However, as you think about this possibility, you start to feel a little anxious because of the prospect of getting caught. As a result, instead of cheating, you simply close your eyes and try even harder to concentrate on recalling the answer to the question. In this case, the feeling of anxiety was enough to prevent you from cheating and the possibility of getting caught and suffering an even greater threat to your ego by being labeled a cheater. Thus, from the psychodynamic viewpoint, anxiety is viewed as a warning signal to keep you out of danger.

The Learning Viewpoint: The Acquisition of Anxiety

From the learning viewpoint, anxiety is conceptualized as a learned response to certain stimuli that signals to the organism the imminent onset of an unpleasant event, along with the anticipation of possible suffering (Mowrer, 1950, 1960). Although from both the psychodynamic and learning viewpoints anxiety is seen as a signal of impending danger, the learning viewpoint has extended our understanding of anxiety by more thoroughly explaining the underlying process by which the response of anxiety actually comes to serve as a warning signal (Emmelkamp & Scholing, 1994).

The fundamental explanation of this process is based on classical conditioning (Kring, Davison, Neale, & Johnson, 2007). The logic of **classical conditioning** is that certain emotionally neutral stimuli can acquire the aversive consequences. For example, suppose you know that whenever employees get fired at work, they typically get a phone call around 4:30 p.m. As a result, you and your co-workers begin to get a feeling of intense anxiety each time the phone rings late in the afternoon. In this case, your anxiety caused by a late-afternoon phone call is an acquired response used to signal the aversive possibility of being fired. Your anxiety in this situation can be considered an acquired response because, as you look back, it was only after starting to work for this company that you began to "fear the phone."

You are now probably saying something like, "Come on! Can we really learn to fear a phone and/or other harmless objects on the basis of classical conditioning?" To find out, try for yourself the demonstration in "You Can Do It" on p. 551.

Thus, from the learning viewpoint, anxiety is an acquired response that serves as a warning signal for the onset of a potentially threatening stimulus and the possibility of suffering by the organism. The process by which such responses are acquired is based on classical conditioning.

The Drive Viewpoint: Anxiety as a Driving Force

Somewhat different from the psychodynamic and learning viewpoints of anxiety is the drive viewpoint (Geen, 1995; Hull, 1943; Purdy, Markham, Schwartz, & Gordon, 2001; Spence, 1956). According to this viewpoint, anxiety is a motivating force that fits into a more general formula for predicting the likelihood of a particular behavior being performed. Here is the basic formula proposed by drive theory:

$$E = D \times H$$

The Conditioning of Anxiety: Acquiring an Aversion to Air in the Blink of an Eye

For this demonstration, you will need a willing subject (i.e., a good friend), a tube of toothpaste, and a toothbrush. For the sake of your friendship, before doing the demonstration, brush your teeth to make sure you have fresh breath! To start, have your friend sit comfortably in front of you. Sit facing your friend and position your face about 12 inches from his or her face. Next, with your hand to your side and out of the view of your friend, snap your fingers and immediately afterwards blow a small puff of air into his or her face. Repeat this about 20 or 30 times. (Now you know the importance of the toothpaste and toothbrush.) The next part of the demonstration involves testing for the conditioning of the anxiety response. To do this, while sitting in the same position, now snap your finger but do not blow the puff of air into your friend's face. What you should see now is your friend blinking his or her eyes to the sound of your fingers snapping. In this case, the eye blinking is a conditioned anxiety response to the sound of your fingers snapping, which was used to signal the aversive stimulus of a puff of air into the eyes. As you can see from this very simple demonstration, it is possible to acquire an aversion to air in the blink of an eye.

Excitatory Potential: What Are You Likely to Do?   In this formulation, *E* refers to the **excitatory potential** of a response, which represents the likelihood of a particular response being performed by an individual. An example of this would be the likelihood of you turning your steering wheel in the proper direction when your car starts into a spin.

Drive Level: How Motivated Are You to Do It?   *D* refers to the **drive level** within the individual, which represents the extent to which the individual is motivated to perform a particular behavior. Within this basic formula, anxiety is considered to fall into the category

of drive level. For example, as you become more anxious when your car begins to go into a spin, the amount of force you use to press on your brakes increases, causing your tires to squeal as you begin to skid, as well as spin.

Habit Strength: How Well Do You Do It?   *H* refers to the **habit strength** of a response, which represents how well a response has been learned by an individual. The habit strength of a response is also further conceptualized into dominant and nondominant responses:

- A **dominant response** is one that has been performed routinely and is done very well. An example of this would be the many times you place your foot on the brake pedal of your car whenever you are confronted with a threatening situation while driving.
- A **nondominant response** is one that has not been performed very often and is not done very well. An example of this would be the rare situation in which you must turn your car in the direction of a skid to get out of it safely.

Combining $E = D \times H$: Putting It All Together   According to the formula, the basic relationship between habit strength and drive level is that any experience that raises the drive (i.e., anxiety) level increases the habit strength of a behavior, which in turn increases the excitatory potential. According to this relationship, dominant behaviors become even stronger in habit strength while nondominant behaviors become even weaker. This is the reason that, as your level of anxiety increases, you are much more likely to "stomp" on your brakes when your car starts to go into a spin rather than turn your steering wheel in the direction of the spin, which is what you are supposed to do. On the other hand, a professional race-car driver, because of many years of practicing what to do in a spin, has turning into the spin, rather than braking, as the dominant response in this anxiety-provoking situation. Thus, the role of anxiety in the drive viewpoint is to increase the likelihood of the dominant response occurring.

The Evolutionary Viewpoint: Anxiety + Adaptation = Survival

From the perspective of evolutionary psychology, the role of anxiety is to create a state of emotional distress in response to the possibility of a threat that serves to prompt us to make the necessary changes in our thinking, behavior, and physiological processes to deal adaptively with the source of threat (D. M. Buss, 2004; Neese, 2005; Neese & Williams, 1994). For example in combat, the threat of being killed by an enemy creates a state of emotional distress that triggers an anxiety-evoked pattern of adaptation designed to maximize the likelihood of survival. Such adaptive changes might include thinking about how and where the enemy might be likely to stage an attack and developing a strategy to offset it. The adaptive changes would also include engaging in the necessary behaviors to initiate a counteractive response, which might including attempting to get to the location of the attack before the enemy for a surprise strike. Finally, adaptive changes in physiological responses would probably include the release of certain hormones into the body that would make it possible for the troops to stay awake for the extended period of time, suppress their desire for food, increase their tolerance of pain, and produce the additional energy necessary to help them think clearly and execute the plan successfully. Thus, although a costly response (e.g., wear and tear on the body, the time and expenses of staging a surprise attack), such an anxiety-evoked pattern of adaptation increases the chances of survival and makes possible the transmission of genetically linked processes associated with success by the survivors to their offspring. In a more subtle sense, buckling up your seatbelt in response to the state of mild distress that comes from the possibility of not surviving an accident is a more pedestrian example of the survival value of anxiety from the evolutionary viewpoint. Thus, from the evolutionary viewpoint, the purpose of anxiety is to stimulate adaptive actions that promote survival.

Integrating the Viewpoints of Anxiety: Describing Different Aspects of Anxiety

Although this chapter has presented the different theoretical viewpoints of anxiety separately, you should not view them as opposing viewpoints. Instead, they should be integrated according to their ability to help explain different aspects of the total nature of anxiety. For example, the psychodynamic viewpoint describes the basic purpose of anxiety – it serves as a warning signal of impending danger. The learning viewpoint describes the underlying process by which anxiety becomes a warning signal of this impending danger –

it is an acquired response based on the process of classical conditioning. The drive viewpoint provides a basic description of how anxiety affects behavior – it intensifies dominant responses. Finally, the evolutionary viewpoint describes how certain cognitive, behavioral, and physiological processes become adaptive responses to the signal of anxiety – it promotes the survival of the individual. Thus, when combined, the different viewpoints of anxiety provide a more thorough explanation of the total nature of anxiety than any one viewpoint considered separately.

This concludes the discussion of the theoretical viewpoints of anxiety. A summary of the principal ideas examined in this section is presented in "Summing It Up: Theoretical Viewpoints of Anxiety" on p. 553. Now that you have a basic understanding of the various dimensions and theoretical viewpoints of anxiety, the next section focuses on some different types of anxiety.

Types of Anxiety: An Abundance of Anxieties

As you might expect, something as complex and pervasive as anxiety does not come in one single form or at one level. This section focuses on three types of anxiety. First, you will learn about the very important conceptual distinction between anxiety as a state and anxiety as a trait. Next, you will focus on the nature, dynamics, and measurement of test anxiety, as well as some suggestions for overcoming test anxiety. Finally, you will consider the nature and dynamics of anxiety disorders, a type of anxiety that can be very debilitating to those who experience it.

State vs. Trait Anxiety: Threatening Places and Anxious Faces

There is one distinction that differentiates between two different types of anxiety: anxiety as a state and anxiety as a trait (R. J. Cohen & Swerdlik, 2001; Martens, Vealey, & Burton, 1990; Spielberger, 1966, 1972).

State Anxiety: Transitory Tension

All of us have experienced a brief period of time when we have felt very uneasy. In this regard, **state anxiety** refers to the temporary emotional change that you

Summing It Up *Theoretical Viewpoints of Anxiety*

Viewpoint of Anxiety	Examples of Anxiety
Psychodynamic Viewpoint. Anxiety serves as a warning signal that unacceptable unconscious impulses are about to enter conscious awareness.	You begin to feel anxious when you consider keeping the $20 bill you saw someone drop on the ground.
Learning Viewpoint. Anxiety is a conditioned emotional response to a stimulus that signals the possibility of a danger to the individual.	After almost being hit by a red van, you begin to feel anxious each time you see a red van pass you on the road.
Drive Viewpoint. Anxiety is a driving force that serves to increase the likelihood of a well-learned response being performed.	Your feelings of anxiety serve to improve your presentation of a speech you spent many hours rehearsing.
Evolutionary Viewpoint. Anxiety creates a state of emotional distress that serves to prompt a pattern of adaptation to a threat in order to maximize survival.	In response to the feeling of distress created by the treat of an oncoming car weaving through traffic, you honk your horn, tap on your brakes, and steer in the opposite direction.
Integrating the Viewpoints. Anxiety is a signal of impending danger acquired by the process of conditioning that triggers action by the individual.	The feelings of anxiety you experience as you see the mailbox where you were almost bitten by a dog last week causes you to cross over to the other side of the street.

experience when confronted with a threatening situation. State anxiety is said to fluctuate and vary in its intensity over time and to be triggered by specific stimuli (R. J. Cohen & Swerdlik, 2001; Martens et al., 1990; Spielberger, 1972). An example of state anxiety would be the state of emotional uneasiness you feel when waiting to get the results back from your first major test in a particular class. On the other hand, as a result of doing well on all of the previous tests, toward the middle of the semester, your state of emotional uneasiness is not as high while you are waiting to get back your third test. As you are returning to your car after class, however, you notice a large dog eating part of a discarded hamburger that was thrown next to your car. Noticing you, the dog growls in an effort to protect its meal, at which point you begin to experience the onset of a rather intense state of emotional uneasiness. As this example illustrates, your level of state anxiety varies from situation to situation, as well as from moment to moment. Thus, a characteristic of state anxiety is its transitory nature.

Trait Anxiety: Always-Anxious Individuals

While state anxiety is considered a response to a situation, trait anxiety is considered a characteristic of the individual. Trait anxiety refers to the fact that some people are simply more anxious than others. More specifically, **trait anxiety** describes individual differences in the tendency to perceive a wide range of situations as threatening and respond to them with anxiety reactions – that is, with state anxiety (R. J. Cohen & Swerdlik, 2001; Martens et al., 1990; Spielberger, 1972). When used to describe anxious people, this definition attributes two major characteristics to them: the range of anxiety reactions and the intensity of anxiety response.

People with high trait anxiety tend to respond more anxiously to a wider range of situations than do people with low trait anxiety. For example, people with high trait anxiety might perceive making a decision about changing jobs, applying for new jobs, and going on job interviews as situations that trigger high levels of anxiety, while people with low trait anxiety might only perceive going on interviews as being an anxiety-provoking situation. People with high trait anxiety also tend to respond with more intense anxiety reactions to threatening situations than do people with low trait anxiety. For example, while waiting for a job interview, people with high trait anxiety will be more anxious than will people with low trait anxiety. Thus, the two characteristics of trait anxiety include perceiving more situations as anxiety provoking and responding with a greater degree of anxiety to these situations, or, stated more simply, as being "always anxious."

Measuring State and Trait Anxiety: The Assessment of Two Types of Anxiety Together

While state and trait anxiety have been discussed as separate types of anxiety, keep in mind that they can operate together. For example, while all of the passengers may experience anxiety when the plane begins to bounce around due to wind turbulence (i.e., state anxiety), some passengers might experience more anxiety than others (i.e., trait anxiety).

To assess these two types of anxiety together, Charles Spielberger and his colleagues have developed the **State-Trait Anxiety Inventory** (**STAI**; Spielberger, Gorsuch, & Lushene, 1970; Spielberger & Rickman, 1990). The STAI consists of two 20-item scales arranged in a fixed format. The 20 items comprised by the state-anxiety portion of the STAI are designed to assess the *present feelings* of the individual (e.g., "I feel calm"). In contrast, the 20 items comprised by the trait-anxiety portion of the STAI are designed to assess how the individual *generally feels* (e.g., "I lack self-confidence"). The ability to conceptualize and accurately assess anxiety into state and trait categories has been the impetus of some rather interesting and significant research (Spielberger, 1972; Spielberger & Rickman, 1990). To examine some of this research, as well as the STAI itself, read "A Closer Look."

A Closer Look

Mixing Athletics with Academics: Research on State and Trait Anxiety Using the STAI

As stated previously, the STAI contains items assessing both how the individual currently feels and how the individual feels in general. Following are sample items from both the state-anxiety and trait-anxiety portions of the STAI, along with their basic instructions.

Assessing State and Trait Anxiety: A Sample of STAI Items

State-Anxiety Items   For each of the following items, circle the number under the statement on the right that best indicates how you feel at this moment.

	Not at all	Somewhat	Moderately so	Very much so
1. I feel tense	1	2	3	4
2. I feel content	1	2	3	4
3. I feel nervous	1	2	3	4

Trait-Anxiety Items   For each of the following items, circle the number under the statement on the right that best indicates how you generally feel.

	Almost never	Sometimes	Often	Almost always
1. I wish I could be as happy as others seem to be.	1	2	3	4
2. I become tense and upset when I think about my concerns.	1	2	3	4
3. I tire quickly.	1	2	3	4

Note. Adapted from Spielberger et al. (1970).

Scoring

Calculate your state-anxiety score and your trait-anxiety scores separately by adding together the value of the numbers you have circled for each set of items. The higher your scores, the greater your level of state and trait anxiety.

Illustrative Research with the STAI: The Similarity of Athletes and Academics

Separate state- and trait-anxiety scores can be obtained when using the STAI. Some interesting research in this area involves using both of them together.

Anxiety in Athletics   Coaches speak of "Wednesday All-Americans" as people who perform well at practice during the week but cannot live up to their capabilities on game day because of the debilitating effects of anxiety (Smith & Smoll, 1990). Yet these same coaches

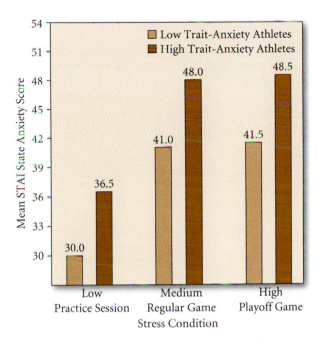

Figure 13.2 Mean STAI state anxiety scores for high and low trait-anxiety athletes as a function of the stress condition
Source: Adapted from Klavora (1975).

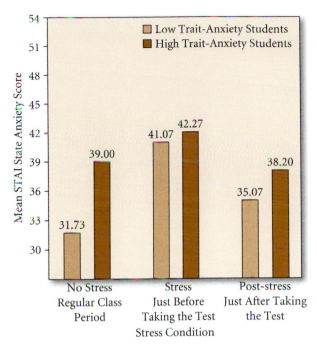

Figure 13.3 Mean STAI state anxiety scores for high and low trait-anxiety students as a function of the stress condition
Source: Adapted from Kendall et al. (1976).

also talk about how anxiety can increase performance for some people on game day. A key to this paradoxical effect of anxiety may have something to do with individual differences in anxiety levels across athletes. For example, in one rather novel use of the STAI, Peter Klavora (1975) assessed the trait-anxiety levels of several hundred Canadian high school football and basketball players. Using athletes' trait-anxiety scores, he classified the athletes into high and low trait-anxiety groups. He then measured their state anxiety before a regular practice, a regular season game, and a playoff game. As can be seen in Figure 13.2, overall, the high-anxiety athletes displayed a greater level of anxiety than did low-anxiety athletes, and this pattern was seen across all the different situations.

Anxiety in Academia   In another study, college students were asked to complete the STAI several times throughout a course, including just before taking an examination that was worth one-third of their final grade and right after taking this examination (Kendall, Finch, Auerbach, Hooke, & Mikulka, 1976). Once again, on the basis of their trait-anxiety scores, the

students were divided into high and low trait-anxiety groups. Figure 13.3 shows that the high trait-anxiety students, like the high trait-anxiety athletes, displayed more anxiety before, during, and after the test than did low trait-anxiety students.

Although the research just discussed studied two rather different samples of people, the patterns of the results are very similar; they illustrate the two major characteristics of trait anxiety discussed earlier (see pp. 553–554):

- Anxious people respond with anxiety to a wider range of situations (e.g., at practice, a regular game, and a playoff game; before, during, and after an examination).
- Anxious people respond with an overall greater intensity of anxiety.

Thus, whether you are talking about athletics or academics, the nature and dynamics of state and trait anxiety seem to operate in a rather similar manner.

Summing It Up *State and Trait Anxiety*

Type of Anxiety or Measure	Impact on the Individual	Example
State Anxiety. The type of transitory anxiety you normally experience when exposed to a threatening situation	A temporary increase in the level of anxiety occurs in response to situations perceived as potentially dangerous.	There is a temporary increase in your level of arousal as you see a police car start flashing its lights in your rearview mirror, and a sense of relief as it passes you by.
Trait Anxiety. A heightened level of anxiety characteristic of normal individuals who might be described as "anxious"	The "anxious individual" perceives many situations as threatening and responds to them with increased anxiety.	A candidate's already high level of arousal makes it difficult for her to sleep well, navigate the heavy rush-hour traffic in the new city, and make her presentation with noise coming from the next room.
State-Trait Anxiety Inventory (STAI). An objective self-report measure assessing both state anxiety and trait anxiety	Individuals can receive a score for both their current level of anxiety and their persistent level of anxiety.	An overly anxious individual with a high trait anxiety score becomes even more anxious when stuck in an elevator between floors.

This concludes the discussion of the state-trait theory of anxiety. A summary of the main points discussed in this section is presented in "Summing It Up: State and Trait Anxiety" above. As you can now see, this conceptualization makes it possible to view anxiety not only as a transitory emotional response to threatening situations but also as a pervasive behavioral pattern characteristic of people who seem to be anxious all of the time. In the next section, you will consider the type of anxiety that probably has the most relevance to you as a student – test anxiety.

Test Anxiety: Turmoil during Testing

For students, few things are more frustrating than the experience of test anxiety, especially if you have spent time studying diligently. To get a better understanding of test anxiety, in this section you will find some information concerning its assessment and dynamics, as well as some suggestions to help you minimize it.

The Assessment of Test Anxiety: Tabulating Testing Turmoil

When studying test anxiety, researchers have found it helpful to classify people into high and low test-anxiety groups. One of the most extensively used inventories for assessing test anxiety is the Text Anxiety Scale (Sarason, 1972, 1980a, 1980b). The **Test Anxiety Scale** (**TAS**) includes 37 items, written in a true–false format, designed to assess responses related specifically to testing situations. Thus, unlike the generalized level of anxiety exhibited across a variety of situations measured by the MAS or the trait-anxiety dimension of the STAI, the TAS measures state-anxiety responses to the perceived threat and stress related to situations involving taking tests. In this regard, test anxiety is considered a much more specific type of anxiety. To get some idea of how relevant the concept of test anxiety is to you, answer the questions presented in "You Can Do It" on p. 557.

A Fundamental Finding: Tests as Ego Threats

A basic finding of research using the TAS is that when the test has some degree of ego involvement (i.e., the results are important to the individual), high test-anxiety subjects perform more poorly on a variety of tasks than do low test-anxiety subjects. For example, when told the task they were going to perform was a measure of their intelligence, high test-anxiety subjects performed worse than did low test-anxiety subjects (Sarason & Palola, 1960). In other research, high test-anxiety subjects performed worse than did low test-

You Can Do It

Measuring Test Anxiety: Assess Your Level Using an Excerpt from the Test Anxiety Scale

Test Anxiety Scale

For each of the 12 items presented here, circle one letter to indicate whether the statement is true (T) or false (F) for you.

T   F   1. While taking an important exam, I find myself thinking of how much brighter the other students are than I am.

T   F   2. During tests, I find myself thinking of the consequences of failing.

T   F   3. Getting a good grade on one test doesn't seem to increase my confidence on the second.

T   F   4. After taking a test, I always feel I could have done better than I actually did.

T   F   5. When taking a test, I believe that my emotional feelings do not interfere with my performance.

T   F   6. During a course examination, I frequently get so nervous that I forget facts I really know.

T   F   7. I seem to defeat myself while working on important tests.

T   F   8. I would rather write a paper than take an examination for my grade in a course.

T   F   9. On examinations I take the attitude, "If I don't know it now, there's no point worrying about it."

T   F   10. Thoughts of doing poorly interfere with my performance on tests.

T   F   11. I seldom feel the need for "cramming" before an exam.

T   F   12. The university should recognize that some students are more nervous than others about tests and that this affects their performance.

Scoring

Each time your response matches the following answer key, give yourself one point.

Answer Key

1 T; 2 T; 3 T; 4 T; 5 F; 6 T; 7 T; 8 T; 9 F; 10 T; 11 F; 12 T

Interpretation

The higher your score, the greater degree of test anxiety you tend to experience during test situations. However, since the items here represent only an excerpt from the full scale, you should not consider your score to be an accurate assessment of your actual level of test anxiety.

Note. This is an excerpt from the full scale. From Sarason (1980a).

anxiety subjects when told that they were being observed by people behind a one-way mirror (Ganzer, 1968) or when another person was performing the same task in their presence (Pederson, 1970). In these examples, having inferences made about your intelligence, being watched by someone else, or having yourself compared to others all seem to be threats to some people's egos.

On a more personal note, for readers who scored high on the TAS, these findings help to explain why you experience test anxiety while taking a test in class. During a test in class, an inference is being made about your intelligence (i.e., you are being graded), someone is observing you (i.e., the instructor or teaching assistant is watching you take the test), and others are performing the task at the same time (i.e., other students are taking the test in the room and you compare yourself to them). Thus, the experience of test anxiety tends to manifest itself whenever the testing situations present some perceived threat to the individual's ego.

Now that you have some idea of how to identify the people who experience test anxiety, the next step is to consider its underlying dynamics.

The Underlying Dynamics of Test Anxiety: Differences in the Personalities of People with High and Low Test Anxiety

You are already familiar with one of the most fundamental differences between high and low test-anxiety people: high test-anxiety people perceive tests as posing a greater threat to their ego than do low test-anxiety people. But some other important differences in the underlying dynamics operating within high and low test-anxiety people also increase our basic understanding of test anxiety and its effects (Sarason & Sarason, 1990). In this section, you will consider some of these additional differences in the underlying dynamics by grouping them into three major categories: behavioral, evaluative, and cognitive differences.

Differences in Behavioral Responses to Test Anxiety: What Are You Doing During the Test?

High and low test-anxiety people differ in their overt and covert behavior during testing situations. At the overt level, high test-anxiety people were found to take longer on problem-solving tasks than were low test-anxiety people (K. Holroyd, Westbrook, Wolf, & Badhorn, 1978; Sarason, 1973). An example of this is the highly anxious student who is the last one to finish the test because he keeps going over his answers "just to make sure." High test-anxiety people seem to feel they are experiencing more intense emotional reactions during the testing situation than low test-anxiety people are. For example, when asked to indicate their level of physiological arousal, high test-anxiety subjects indicated they were experiencing more arousal (e.g., increased heartbeat and skin perspiration) than low test-anxiety subjects were (K. A. Holroyd & Appel, 1980).

At the covert level, however, when the actual measures of physiological responses are recorded from the subjects during testing situations, the evidence seems to indicate that high and low test-anxiety subjects tend to experience *very similar* levels of physiological arousal (K. A. Holroyd & Appel, 1980; K. Holroyd et al., 1978). Thus, while high test-anxiety people may believe they are experiencing a greater degree of anxiety than low test-anxiety people are, their levels of anxiety are actually the same. So it is the perceived level of physiolo-

gical arousal experienced by the high test-anxiety people that is distracting them, not the actual level of arousal.

Differences in the Evaluation of Test Performance: How Did You Do on the Test?

Like most of us, people with test anxiety are concerned with their performance on the test. But unlike most of us, people with high test anxiety tend to evaluate their performance differently than people with low test anxiety. This difference is reflected in how they view their potential performance before they actually take the test (K. Holroyd et al., 1978; Sarason & Stoops, 1978). High test-anxiety people tend to evaluate their performance on a test as being poor regardless of how well they actually performed. For example, even if they seemed to know the answers to the test and finished it before many of their classmates, people with high test anxiety would still believe that they did not do very well. On the other hand, people with low test anxiety tend to evaluate their performance by how well they actually did on the test. In this case, people who finish quickly would evaluate their performance as favorable, while people who seem to have difficulty with the test would, justifiably, evaluate their performance as not being very good. Thus, a major difference between people with high and low test anxiety seems to be in how they evaluate their performance.

Don't Remind Me How Well I Did on the Test, Please

The information in the preceding section seems to suggest that people with high test anxiety do not respond to their own subjective, self-assessed performance feedback about how well they are doing while taking a test. Although they might not have confidence in their own subjective assessment of their test performance, you would think that providing them with an external and objective source of feedback about their performance during the test might enhance their performance on the rest of the test. That is to say, high test-anxiety individuals might be encouraged about their performance if they were given some outside feedback about how they might be doing during the test instead of just having to rely on their own pessimistic assessment of their performance. As logical as this idea might seem, it apparently does not work (Ray, Katahn, & Snyder, 1971).

For example, in one trial of this possibility, people classified as having high or low test anxiety were asked to perform a task (Mandler & Sarason, 1952). Midway through the testing situation, some people from each group were interrupted and given feedback on their performance, while the remaining people were not interrupted to be given feedback. As honorable as their intentions might have been, these researchers found that providing the feedback during the interruption resulted in a *decrease* (i.e., slower times) in the performance of high test-anxiety subjects but an *increase* (i.e., faster times) in the performance of low test-anxiety subjects on the rest of the test. This pattern of results is summarized in Figure 13.4. Thus, high test-anxiety subjects seemed to perform better when they were not given feedback than when they were given feedback. The reason for this seems to be that anything that reminds high text-anxiety people that they are being tested hinders their performance (Mandler & Sarason, 1952). Reminding high test-anxiety people that they are taking a test focuses their attention on the testing situation itself and the anxiety reactions it is producing, thus decreasing their performance.

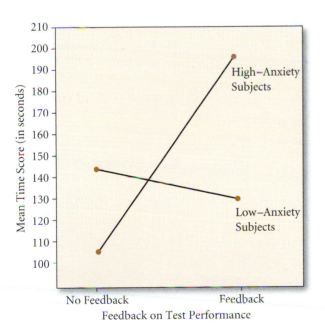

Figure 13.4   Mean time scores for high and low test-anxiety subjects as a function of feedback on test performance
Source: Mandler & Sarason (1952).

Differences in Cognitive Processes: What's Going through Your Head during the Exam?

High and low test-anxiety people tend to differ in certain cognitive processes that are critical during the testing situation (Geen, 1980). Specifically, they differ in their attention and utilization of task-relevant information, response to success and failure, and response to physiological arousal.

I Should've Seen That!   One difference in cognitive processes has to do with the attention to and utilization of information required to perform a particular task correctly. High test-anxiety people tend to ignore information on the test that could help them perform better (Geen, 1976). For example, relevant information such as test instructions or critical information provided in a mathematical word problem are much more likely to be ignored or overlooked by high test-anxiety people than by low test-anxiety people. We have all had this experience at one time or another; it typically elicits responses such as "Darn it! I should've seen that on the test" when the instructor returns the test.

Fueling Future Failure   High and low test-anxiety people also tend to differ in their responses to previous success and failure. Following failure on one task, high-anxiety people tended to perform more poorly than other high-anxiety people who did not experience failure, while low-anxiety people performed better after failure than other low-anxiety people who did not experience previous failure (Sarason, 1957). Such early failure for those high in anxiety seems to increase the number of self-deprecating thoughts (e.g., "I'm so stupid"), which results in the lowering of their expectations and overall motivation to succeed in the future (Mandler, 1972; Spiegler, Morris, & Liebert, 1968). Thus, for high-anxiety people, failing seems to fuel future failure.

What Are You Worrying About?   The final difference in cognitive processes involves the way that people high and low in test anxiety respond to the physiological reactions occurring within the body during times of stress. As noted earlier, people with high and low test anxiety tend to experience increased levels of physiological arousal during testing situations. But it has been noted that high test-anxiety people tend to respond to this anxiety by labeling it in a more negative affective manner, and then spending more time worrying about it, than low test-anxiety people do (Sarason, 1972). For example, the highly anxious individual might produce a line of reasoning something like this: "My high level of excitement is because I am worrying about my performance on the test." Thus, high test-anxiety people tend to label their physiological arousal during an exam as something to worry about.

Putting It All Together: Designing Your Own Despair

The picture painted of high test anxiety seems to be one of people who tend to exaggerate the level of their anxiety, evaluate their performance more negatively, and cloud their minds with disruptive thoughts about the test. From this perspective, it should be very clear that engaging in this pattern of behavior is surely designed to create a sense of despair that would make you feel extremely upset about the prospect of taking a test.

Although you now have a complete understanding of the assessment and dynamics of test anxiety, knowing all about it is not enough for those of you who experience it; you want to know how to reduce it. For some helpful hints on how to reduce your anxiety, read "Applications in Personality Psychology" below.

Applications in Personality Psychology

Six Simple Steps for Overcoming Test Anxiety: Pinpointing the Problems and Practicing the Solutions

Because test anxiety is such a problem for many people, many personality psychologists and other professionals have spent a considerable amount of effort to develop strategies for overcoming it (Kanar, 2001; Sapp, 1999; Sarason, 1980b; Sarason & Sarason, 1990; Zeidner, 1998). Here are six simple steps designed to help you overcome your test anxiety (Rathus & Nevid, 2002).

Step 1: Pinpointing Situations That Trigger Test Anxiety

The first thing you must do is to begin to identify those situations that trigger your test anxiety. Here are a few examples of some situations that typically trigger feelings of test anxiety.

1. Waiting for the professor to give you the test.
2. Answering a few questions and then starting to feel unsure about your answers.
3. Changing some of your answers because you feel unsure due to the anxiety.
4. Being completely baffled by one of the questions.
5. Looking around and seeing that everybody else seems to be working as if they know what they are doing.
6. Handing in the test.
7. Hearing some people outside of the classroom talk about their answers to the test as you are walking away afterwards.

Although these situations may not be the exact ones that trigger test anxiety in you, they can be used as a starting point to generate situations that are a bit more relevant to you.

Step 2: Pinpointing Self-Defeating Thoughts

The next step involves pinpointing the specific thoughts in the situations identified in Step 1 that seem to trigger test anxiety. This is done by using your active imagination. Get comfortable and close your eyes. Now, concentrate on being in each of the situations. Imagine the sights and sounds involved in the situation. After you have conjured up the physical details of the situation, start examining some of the thoughts that might be racing through your mind while in that test-anxiety situation. Try to pinpoint any of these self-defeating thoughts that might be triggering your feelings of anxiety. They are called **self-defeating thoughts** because the anxiety that they generate seems to prevent you from concentrating on answering the test questions. To help you in identifying your own self-defeating thoughts, some of them are presented in the following table, under the heading of "Self-Defeating Thoughts."

Self-Defeating Thoughts vs. Rational Thinking: Some Illustrative Examples

Self-Defeating Thoughts	Rational Thinking
"I should have studied more. I'm not prepared enough to pass the test."	"I've done as much studying as I can. All that is left to do now is take the test."
"There's not going to be enough time for me to finish the test. I'm going to run out of time, I just know it."	"Don't start to rush. Just take one question at a time and answer all those I can first, then go back to those that might require more time."
"I can't answer this question. Now I am going to blow the whole test."	"It's only one question. The grade for the whole test does not rest on this one question."
"Look at all of those people leaving before me. They all must be really smart."	"Just because people are leaving does not mean they are going to get a better grade. I'll just work at my own pace. This is a test, not a race."
"Why do I feel like such a loser after I hand in the test?"	"The test is over. There's no sense worrying about it now. I feel pretty good."

Step 3: Practicing Rational Thinking

As just noted, the problem with self-defeating thoughts is that they get in the way of concentrating on the test. To overcome this problem, you should begin to generate rational thoughts as alternatives to these self-defeating thoughts. Some examples of rational thinking as alternatives to certain self-defeating thoughts are presented in the table column titled "Rational thinking." The primary purpose of rational thinking is to help you eliminate self-defeating thoughts and minimize the interfering anxiety they create, thus allowing you to focus more of your attention on taking the test.

Step 4: Practicing Rational Test Taking

As with trying to learn any other new form of behavior, in learning to overcome your test anxiety, you must practice doing it. And the best way to do this is to create situations that are as close to the actual testing situation as possible. For example, when studying for a test, do not just study your notes; write out test questions and try to answer them. When answering these questions, set some time limits so that you can get used to organizing your thoughts and working under pressure. While taking the practice test, if you start to experience self-defeating thoughts, practice replacing them with the rational alternatives you generated in the previous step. Again, as with anything else, the more you practice, the easier you will find it is to perform these rational behaviors. And the more you practice them, the more likely they are to become a dominant response in your test-taking repertoire.

Step 5: Practicing the Process of Overlearning

In order for you to feel more comfortable with the material you are studying for a test, as well as the rational test-taking behaviors, it is a good idea to overlearn the material. **Overlearning** involves going over the material you have already mastered again and again. Rehearsing information again and again makes it easier to recall when you need it and less likely to be interfered with by other distractions, such as anxiety.

Step 6: Practicing Self-Reward

Because tests are associated with the unpleasant experience of anxiety, it would be beneficial to associate them with something more pleasant. As you will recall from Chapter 10, it is possible to replace negative associations with pleasant ones by using the process of classical conditioning. This is done by associating taking tests with as many pleasant and positive emotions and experiences as possible. For example, as you replace a self-defeating thought with a rational alternative, concentrate on how good it makes you feel. Pat yourself on the back for being able to use the relaxation technique to calm yourself down during the test. During the test, do not punish yourself by focusing on those questions about which you are unsure. Instead, make yourself feel good by focusing your attention on all of the material that you are able to answer with some degree of ease and confidence. Finally, once the test is over, let it be over. Do not continue to punish yourself with thoughts of what you should have done.

Instead, reward yourself by doing something enjoyable. Although this may sound strange, if you get really good at the process of practicing self-reward, you may find that you will actually enjoy taking tests because of the favorable emotions and events that you have come to associate with them.

As you can see from these six simple steps, the process of overcoming test anxiety is relatively straightforward. All it requires is some practice.

Summing It Up *The Assessment, Dynamics, and Overcoming of Test Anxiety*

Assessment of Test Anxiety. Anxious reactions associated with stimuli and situations specifically related to taking tests, as a result of tests being perceived as a threat to the individual's ego, are measured. For example, because of your perceived inability to answer two questions on your geography test, you begin to feel nervous and upset while taking the test.

Dynamics of High and Low Test-Anxiety Individuals. Individuals high and low in test anxiety differ in their behavioral (e.g., estimated level of their anxiety), evaluative (e.g., rating of their performance), and cognitive (e.g., nature of their thoughts) responses to the testing situation. For example, because highly anxious individuals taking a test are more likely to perceive their level of anxiety as being higher than low-test anxiety individuals are, they are more likely to rate their performance more negatively and, as a result, tend to express more self-defeating thoughts.

Overcoming Test Anxiety. Overcoming test anxiety involves replacing self-defeating thoughts with more rational thinking during the testing situation, overlearning the test material, learning to relax, and associating the testing situation with rewards. For example, to help reduce her test anxiety, the first-year law student tried to concentrate on the questions she was able to answer, since she felt well prepared after spending the entire weekend studying. When her exams were over, she spent the rest of the week watching old movies and playing tennis.

This concludes the discussion of test anxiety. A summary of the principal points discussed in this section is presented in "Summing It Up: The Assessment, Dynamics, and Overcoming of Test Anxiety" opposite. If you would like to learn more about test anxiety, read *Test Anxiety: Theory, Research, and Applications*, edited by Irwin G. Sarason (1980b), one of the foremost authorities on test anxiety. It is full of helpful strategies for controlling test anxiety. Two other informative resources are: *Test Anxiety: Applied Research, Assessment, and Treatment Interventions* (Sapp, 1999) and *Test Anxiety: The State of the Art* (Zeidner, 1998).

The discussion of the various types of anxiety will focus next on anxiety disorders, a type of anxiety reaction that is rather extreme and can disturb a person's entire life.

Anxiety Disorders: Anxiety of Pathological Proportions

To this point in the chapter, you have been examining the types of anxiety that are familiar to everyone, because we have all probably experienced them to some degree. For example, we have all had experience with being in a state of anxiety, known someone who seems to be the "anxious type," or experienced test anxiety at one time or another. Some types of anxiety are well within what you might consider normal levels. But this section introduces another type of anxiety, one that is considered abnormal. This type is referred to as anxiety disorder (Barlow, 2002; Comer, 2007; Griez, et al., 2001).

Anxiety Disorders: A Matter of Degree

Like the anxiety that is considered a normal part of life, anxiety that is defined as abnormal is also characterized by nervousness, fear, apprehension, perspiration, muscle tension, rapid heartbeat, and debilitating effects on behavior. But anxiety is considered to be abnormal when its level of intensity begins to interfere with personal goals or interpersonal relationships and causes a great degree of fear and/or pain. At such a level of intensity, the anxiety is considered an anxiety disorder. Thus, an **anxiety disorder** is characterized by a level of anxiety being experienced by the individual that is more intense, frequent, and debilitating than normal anxiety (Diagnostic and Statistical Manual of Mental Disorders, 2000; Nevid, Rathus, & Greene, 2003; Stein & Hollander, 2002).

Although extreme in nature, anxiety disorders are relatively common. For example, it has been estimated that at any given time, about 19 percent of the general adult population suffer from some type of an anxiety disorder (Comer, 2007; Kessler & Zhao, 1999). In fact, as you read about anxiety disorders in this section, you will probably be surprised at how much you already know about them as a result of their appearance in your everyday conversation. However, the cost of such pervasiveness of anxiety disorders in the United States is staggering – at least $42 billion each year in healthcare expenses, lost wages, and lost productivity (Dozois & Westra, 2004; Greenberg et al., 1999; Greenberg et al., 1999). The anxiety disorders discussed in this section are panic disorder, generalized anxiety disorder, obsessive-compulsive disorder, and phobic disorder.

Panic Disorder: Having an "Anxiety Attack" A **panic disorder** is characterized by a sudden, very brief, but extremely intense feeling of fear, doom, uneasiness, and panic that creates a sense of terror within the individual. This sense of panic is so strong that it literally causes the individual to "freeze up" to the point where taking any action is almost impossible. Lasting anywhere from just a few seconds to an hour or more, this "anxiety attack" is unpredictable. That is to say, the individual can begin to experience this high level of anxiety without the presence of any external threat. For example, you have probably heard stories of people freezing up when their car gets stuck on the train tracks. While the emotional state probably resembles that of a panic disorder, it would not be considered an anxiety disorder because the oncoming train does represent something about which you really should be feeling anxious.

Generalized Anxiety Disorder: The Experience of Chronic Anxiety A **generalized anxiety disorder** is characterized by a chronic feeling of apprehension, worry, uneasiness, and nervousness that lasts for at least one month and often for several months or more. While the level of anxiety is not intense enough to render the individual completely immobile, as is the case with the panic disorder, the constant pressure of the anxiety is enough to affect the emotional and motivational state of the individual to the point where just trying to maintain everyday living activities becomes a chore. As an example of what it is like to experience a generalized anxiety disorder, think about what it would be like to feel the level of test anxiety you experience before a very important exam all day long, day in and day out for months.

Obsessive-Compulsive Disorder: Uncontrollable Thoughts and Behavior An **obsession** is characterized by a persistent preoccupation with a particular thought, idea, or feeling that the individual seems unable to control. The thought, feeling, or idea typically involves a rather bizarre or irrational theme, such as drowning one's child while bathing it. Anxiety is created because the individual is unable to stop such thoughts from recurring and/or worries about the possibility of actually executing them. You have probably had some experience with a minor obsession, such as wondering whether you turned off the iron when you left your house to go on vacation. An obsession becomes pathological when the anxiety associated with it begins to interfere with the individual's daily ability to function.

A **compulsion** is characterized by an irresistible urge to perform a particular act or course of action again and again. The behavior triggered by the compulsion is typically extremely rigid and must follow certain rules developed by the individual. The anxiety is created when the individual fails to carry out the act in the previously specified manner. But if the act is performed in the prescribed manner, the anxiety is reduced and the person feels much better. Because it eliminates the anxiety, the compulsive behavior becomes much more likely to be performed again each time the anxiety reappears. For example, a lawyer may develop a hand-washing compulsion because she believes germs are all over her office. As a result, she must wash her hands constantly to relieve the anxiety associated with the germs. Again, you have probably had some experience with minor compulsions yourself, such as walking around a ladder or getting up out of bed to make sure you turned off the stove. As with more extreme compulsions, you immediately begin to feel much better after walking around the ladder or getting up to check the stove.

Phobic Disorder: Unrealistic Fears   A **phobic disorder** (or phobia) is characterized by feelings of fear and anxiety that are out of proportion to the actual danger present in the situation. There are three basic types of phobic disorders: agoraphobia, social phobia, and simple phobia.

- **Agoraphobia** is the fear of being alone or being in a public place, with the feeling that if something should go wrong, no one will be able to help you. As a result, people suffering from agoraphobia often may be limited to their home environment and/or require constant companionship, resulting in a very restricted existence.
- **Social phobia** involves an irrational fear and avoidance of social situations where the individual must interact with others, usually fearing the possibility of humiliation or embarrassment. The most common example of this type of phobia is the excessive anxiety people feel over having to speak in public, resulting in the person being willing to do almost anything to avoid such situations.
- A **simple phobia** is characterized by excessive anxiety triggered by an irrational fear of a particular object or situation. The anxiety appears when the feared stimulus is present, and is eliminated if the stimulus can be avoided. The individual suffering from a phobic disorder will spend a considerable amount of energy and effort trying to organize his or her life around avoiding the fear stimulus. For example, an individual suffering from **ailurophobia** (fear of cats) may spend most of his time at home for fear of encountering a cat while outside.

As Table 13.1 demonstrates, it seems that almost anything can be the source of a phobic reaction, including, as in the case of Sean "P. Diddy" Combs, a phobia of clowns (see p. 565).

Explaining Anxiety Disorders: From Unconscious Conflict and Faulty Learning to Self-Defeating Thoughts and the Biology of the Brain

How is it that someone could develop **ergasiophobia** (the fear of writing) or go around with the compulsion

Table 13.1   Some Examples of Exotic Phobias

Name of Phobia	Object of Phobia
Acarophobia	Insects
Androphobia	Men
Aphephobia	Being touched
Arachnephobia	Spiders
Chrematophobia	Money
Erotophobia	Sex
Gynephobia	Women
Hypnophobia	Sleep
Keraunophobia	Lightning
Linonophobia	String
Monophobia	Being alone
Parthenophobia	Virgins
Phantasmophobia	Ghosts
Ponophobia	Work
Spectrophobia	Mirrors
Trichophobia	Hair
Triskaidekaphobia	Thirteen
Zelophobia	Jealousy

Note. Adapted from Fann & Goshen (1973).

of having to touch each wall in a room before feeling comfortable in it? As it turns out, explaining the cause of anxiety disorders is not an easy task. Four of the primary explanations of anxiety disorders are based on the psychodynamic, learning, cognitive, and neurological viewpoints (Comer, 2007; Kring et al., 2007; Nevid et al., 2003; Wolman & Stricker, 1994).

Psychodynamic Explanation: Manifestations of Unresolved Conflicts

According to the psychodynamic viewpoint, anxiety disorders are a result of an unresolved unconscious conflict that is now manifesting itself in the form of the anxiety disorder (J. M. Jackson, 1994). As an example of a generalized anxiety disorder, an individual who has never expressed his anger at his parents for forcing him to go to college might spend his entire college career feeling anxious over his desire to quit school. An obsessive thought of harming her child held by a devoted mother may reflect the unconscious resentment she may actually feel about having to take care of the baby rather than pursuing her own personal goals. From the psychodynamic viewpoint, the treatment of anxiety disorders typically involves helping the individual gain insight into and resolve the unconscious conflicts.

"Keep out the clowns." According to a news report, music entertainer Sean "P. Diddy" Combs has an irrational fear of clowns, known as "coulrophobia," which manifests itself in his reportedly including a "no-clowns clause" in his performance contacts.

Learning Viewpoint: Learning of a Faulty Nature

According to the learning viewpoint, anxiety disorders are a result of faulty learning. For example, on one very hot day, a veteran may experience a panic disorder for what seems to be no apparent reason. This panic reaction may reflect the feelings of intense anxiety he had while in the hot jungles of Vietnam many years ago. Thus, through the process of classical conditioning, the individual may have come to associate very hot days with intense fear of a debilitating nature.

In another example, as a result of reading about and seeing plane crashes on the news, an individual may develop **aviophobia** (the fear of flying) and now comes to associate the sight of a plane with the possibility of crashing. Further, when the person stays off planes, the anxiety is reduced, thereby – on principles of operant conditioning – reinforcing the avoidance behavior. In a similar manner, because engaging in the compulsive behavior of washing one's hands reduces the feelings of anxiety, the compulsive behavior is reinforced and is much more likely to appear again.

The treatment of anxiety disorders from the learning viewpoint typically involves learning new emotional associations and more effective behavior patterns (Nevid et al., 2003). This might involve helping the individual to replace the feelings of anxiety with more favorable or appropriate emotions using the process of systematic desensitization. The maladaptive avoidance behavior pattern of a phobic disorder and the ritualistic behavior characteristic of a compulsive disorder are replaced utilizing behavior modification programs to help the individual acquire new, more adaptive behavior patterns. For a look at a recent development in the treatment of phobic disorders based on the learning viewpoint, read "At the Cutting Edge of Personality Psychology" on p. 566.

Cognitive Viewpoint: Endorsing Self-Defeating Thought Patterns and Beliefs

The cognitive viewpoint proposes that anxiety disorders are a result of a set of thought patterns and beliefs that increase the individual's sense of fear. One pattern is that some individuals with anxiety disorders tend to overestimate the amount of fear associated with various anxiety-provoking situations. As an example, an individual might overestimate the amount of pain to be experienced when visiting the dentist, thus

Virtual Reality Therapy

The Taming of Fears with Technology: When a Simulated Experience Produces Real Results

Virtual reality technology uses high-speed computers with large memory storage capacities to create simulations of real-life experiences. In such simulations, individuals put on special goggles that make it possible for them to change completely the visual image of the environment in a manner that would be similar to a turn of the head or rotation of the body in the real world. In addition, when special gloves and headphones are worn, the simulated experience includes the sounds and feel of interacting with the stimulus, including being able to manipulate items in the simulated environment by handling them. The realism created by the capacity of virtual technology can increase the individual's participation in the simulated environment and enhance the person's ability to be immersed in the virtual experience.

One of the most recent developments in the treatment of phobic disorders has been to incorporate virtual reality technology into the process of systematic desensitization in what is known as virtual reality therapy (Mueller, 2002; Winerman, 2005). In **virtual reality therapy** (**VRT**), phobic individuals are exposed to the phobic object (e.g., spiders) or situation (e.g., flight in an airplane) at gradually increasing levels of threat while having the opportunity to become accustomed to the stimuli. The validity of the VRT experienced has been documented in that individuals show the same physiological changes, such as increased heart rate and sweat, that are experienced in the actual environment (Goleman, 1995).

For example, in a VRT program for a fear of flying, phobic individuals received graduated exposure in a virtual airplane that involved sitting in the virtual airplane as well as taxiing, taking off, landing, and flying in both calm and turbulent weather. In support of the VRT program, those phobic individuals who participated in the program showed fewer symptoms of anxiety and lower scores on self-reported measures of fear of flying than did similar individuals on a waiting list who did not receive the VRT. At the end of their VRT, individuals displayed a decrease in their self-report ratings of anxiety from the level at the beginning of their departing flight to the end of their returning flight on an actual commercial flight of one and a half hours in duration (Rothbaum, Hodges, Smith, Lee, & Price, 2000).

In addition to being used in the treatment of specific phobias, VRT has been used in the treatment of posttraumatic stress disorder, eating disorders, and pain management (Anderson, Rothbaum, & Hodges, 2001). A principal advantage of treating an individual with VRT is that, in certain instances, it is more cost effective and less time consuming than placing them in actual environments. For example, it would be less expensive to treat individuals with a fear of flying in a virtual airplane than having to take them to the airport, purchase tickets, and fly great distances. One negative side effect of VRT is cyber-sickness, in which the individual experiences symptoms similar to motion sickness: headaches, nausea, sweating (Mueller, 2002). However, these symptoms, which serve as evidence of the degree of realism created in the simulated environment, can be minimized by limiting the amount of time in the virtual world.

avoiding such visits and creating the possibility of eventual tooth decay and disease. Another pattern might involve self-defeating or irrational beliefs in the face of an anxiety-provoking situations. For example, an individual with a hand-washing compulsion might believe that if she does not wash her hands 75 times a day, she will be fired from her job as a lab assistant. Some individuals with anxiety disorders may possess a set of beliefs that involve an oversensitivity to certain environmental cues. For example, an individual with generalized anxiety disorder may perceive the fluctuations in the stock market as a sign that the country is falling on unstable times and that there will be little opportunity for him to feel secure. Still another pattern is for some individuals with anxiety disorders to misinterpret bodily sensations. For example, individuals prone to panic attacks may misinterpret an increase in heart rate and arousal due to the noise of a passing subway train as a sign that they are about to lose control of their emotions or "go crazy" in public. Finally, some individuals with anxiety disorders tend to express low self-efficacy expectations in their ability to handle or cope with certain situations. For example, an individual with social phobia believes she is terrible at giving speeches, so she experiences a heightened sense of anxiety and "freezes up" when asked to speak in front of others at a business meeting. Thus, as you can see, from the cognitive viewpoint anxiety disorders have as their basis a set of self-defeating thoughts and beliefs that result in individuals perceiving and interpreting events in their lives in an overly threatening manner, which creates feelings of intense anxiety.

In response to such self-defeating thoughts and beliefs, the treatment of anxiety disorders involves cognitive therapy (Beck & Weishaar, 2000). Although there are many different techniques, cognitive therapy has as its goal "correcting the errors and biases in the information processing and modifying the core beliefs that promote faulty conclusions" (Beck & Weishaar, 2000, p. 243). For example, an individual with social phobia fears going to parties because she feels everyone will be judging her and evaluating everything she says and does. During cognitive therapy, the therapist would help her to realize and modify the errors in such thinking that produce the intense level of anxiety. For example, the therapist may help her to realize that people are more likely to be concerned about what they are saying and doing than about her, and that she should not expect to be perfect at the party but focus more on just trying to be nice when interacting with others. For an individual with panic disorder, the cognitive therapist would help the person realize that the increased arousal experienced during rides on the subway is not to be misinterpreted as an internal cue that he is losing control of his emotions but as a normal reaction to the noise, movement, and crowds associated with riding public transport during peak hours of operations. Thus, cognitive therapy is designed to address directly those patterns of self-defeating thoughts and beliefs that

serve to create the individual's excessive feelings of anxiety.

Neurological Viewpoint: An Overly Aroused Brain

The neurological viewpoint proposes the role of various neurotransmitters as a contributing factor to anxiety disorders. One neurotransmitter that has received considerable attention in the study of anxiety disorders is **gamma-aminobutyric acid** (**GABA**). GABA is a neurotransmitter found in the brain. Its purpose is to prevent neurons in the brain from overly exciting other nearby neurons (Rains, 2002). In a sense, GABA operates like the brakes on your car. If the car starts to move too quickly (e.g., if going down a hill or the accelerator pedal gets stuck), you can step on the brakes to bring it under control. When there is an inadequate amount of GABA in the brain, neurons can fire out of control, which can bring about seizures in more extreme cases and feelings of emotional arousal and anxiety in more moderate cases. In support of the role of GABA in anxiety reactions is the use of a family of drugs know as **benzodiazepines**, which includes such well-known drugs as Valium and Xanax, used to treat anxiety disorders. Benzodiazepines work by making the neurons more sensitive to GABA, thus increasing its calming (e.g., inhibitory) effects. To continue our automotive analogy, the taking of benzodiazepines is like adjusting your brakes so they are more sensitive and respond more quickly to any pressure you place on them.

This concludes the discussion of anxiety disorders. A summary of the major principles discussed in this section is presented in "Summing It Up: The Classification and Explanation of Anxiety Disorders" on p. 568. In the author's experience, most students find anxiety disorders a fascinating topic and will want to learn more about them. For more information, read *Anxiety* (1998), by Stanley Rachman, a world authority on anxiety disorders. This relatively short (i.e., 192 pages) book provides an easy-to-read and thorough presentation of the types, theories, dynamics, and treatment of anxiety disorders. Two somewhat more extensive books on the topic of anxiety are *Anxiety Disorders: An Introduction to Clinical Management and Research* (Griez et al., 2001) and *Anxiety and Its Disorders: The Nature and Treatment of Anxiety and Panic* (Barlow, 2002)

Summing It Up *The Classification and Explanation of Anxiety Disorders*

Classification of Anxiety Disorders

Panic Disorder. An acute, intense feeling of anxiety that can appear unexpectedly and serve to immobilize the individual.

Generalized Anxiety Disorder. A chronic and pervasive sense of uneasiness that can make everyday functioning difficult, but not impossible.

Obsessive-Compulsive Disorder. An *obsession* is the sense of anxiety that is created by the persistent occurrence of a rather unacceptable thought (e.g., harming a loved one) that the individual fears may actually be executed. A *compulsion* is the sense of anxiety created by an uncontrollable urge to carry out repeatedly a particular course of action (e.g., repeatedly checking to see if the stove is off).

Phobic Disorder. The sense of anxiety created by the unrealistic and excessive fear of being isolated in a public place (i.e., agoraphobia), possible humiliation (i.e., social phobia), or a specific object (i.e., simple phobia).

Explanations of Anxiety Disorders

Psychodynamic Explanation. Anxiety disorders are a result of unconscious conflicts that appear in the form of pathological behavior, such as the avoidance of certain objects (i.e., simple phobia) or a constant sense of apprehension (i.e., generalized anxiety disorder).

Learning Explanation. Anxiety disorders are a result of faulty learning involving inappropriate associations, such as pairing the sight of a snake with feelings of extreme uneasiness (i.e., simple phobia), or erroneous assumptions about the consequences of behavior, such as bad luck being avoided by walking around a ladder (i.e., compulsion).

Cognitive Explanation. Anxiety disorders are a result of individuals maintaining a set of thoughts and beliefs that serve to foster a sense of intense fear, such as overestimating the amount of fear associated with an object or situation (e.g., developing a simple phobia about riding on a bus), endorsing self-defeating or irrational beliefs (e.g., an individual with obsessive-compulsive disorder feels safe only after checking the locks on the door four times before going to bed), being overly sensitive to situational cues (e.g., an individual may have a panic attack in response to the sound of a car backfiring), misinterpreting bodily sensations (e.g., an individual with generalized anxiety disorders focuses too much attention on small changes in his heart rate), and espousing low self-efficacy expectations (e.g., an individual with agoraphobia assumes that she will not reach the exit fast enough while attending a movie).

Neurological Explanation. Anxiety disorders are a result of an imbalance of neurotransmitters (e.g., GABA) in the brain that creates increased levels of arousal. They can be treated by drugs (e.g., benzodiazepines) that serve to reestablish the balance of neurotransmitters to regulate the level of emotional arousal

Some Closing Remarks on the Types of Anxiety: Covering the Full Range of Intensity

In this chapter's discussion of the types of anxiety, you have considered three types covering a range that varies in the intensity level of the anxiety and the effect it has on behavior. We began with a discussion of the fundamental distinction between state and trait anxiety at a basic level of intensity and its effect on behavior in general. Next you examined the experience of anxiety at a somewhat more intense level in the form of test anxiety and its effect on test-taking behavior. Finally, you read about the experience of anxiety at its most intense level and with its most debilitating effect on behavior, in the form of anxiety disorders. Such a wide-ranging discussion should remind you how complex and pervasive an emotion anxiety is in our lives, and as a subject of study for personality psychologists. This presentation on anxiety ends with a discussion of the specific applications of anxiety in the public world of advertising and the personal world of shyness.

The Application of Personality Psychology: Using What Is Known

In this section, we will discuss two applications based on the study of anxiety. First, we will discuss the role of anxiety in advertising through the use of fear appeals. Then we will consider the role of anxiety in social situations by examining the topic of shyness.

Anxiety in Advertising: Motivating You with Misery

Fear appeals create a sense of uncertainty, unpleasantness, and unpredictability in people. The ad presented in Figure 13.5 is an example of what is called a fear appeal in advertising. **Fear appeals** are ads designed to motivate people to change their attitudes about or buy a particular product by creating anxiety (Berkowitz, Kerin, Hartley, & Rudelius, 2000; Peter & Olson, 2002). Whether it is an ad about life insurance, dental hygiene, shoplifting, smoking, drinking and driving, drug abuse, bad breath, or waxy buildup on your kitchen

Figure 13.5 An ad illustrating the use of fear appeals in advertising

floor, the use of anxiety in fear appeals is based on the tendency for anxiety to be aroused by events that are uncertain, unpleasant, and unpredictable. An example of a fear appeal based on anxiety would be a life insurance commercial on television depicting a woman questioning (i.e., uncertainty) how she is going to be able to take care of her children adequately (i.e., unpleasantness) after the unexpected death of her husband (i.e., unpredictability).

The Role of Anxiety in Advertising: Bringing You Down, then Picking You Up

The basic principle upon which anxiety is used in advertising can be summarized in a two-step process. The first step involves the advertisement creating a sense of anxiety, either by utilizing the anxiety that is already present in most people (e.g., fear of rejection) or by creating a state of anxiety (e.g., you could die prematurely). The second step involves providing a message (e.g., "our mouthwash reduces plaque") or a course of action (e.g., "act now and receive our bonus coverage") designed to reduce the anxiety. Thus, the basic role of anxiety in advertising is to make you feel uneasy so the product being advertised can make you feel good. In short, the basic process is designed to bring you down, and then pick you up.

Creating Anxiety through Positive and Negative Appeals: To Use, or Not to Use – That Is the Question

The use of fear appeals to create anxiety in advertisements generally takes one of two forms: positive or negative appeals (Aaker & Myers, 1982; Kotler & Armstrong, 1994; Wheatley & Oshikawa, 1970). **Positive appeals** are designed to *reduce* the viewer's anxiety about "buying and using" the product or service. For example, a commercial for homeowner's insurance might emphasize the positive aspects of buying and using the product, such as its low cost in comparison to other investments, the quickness of service provided, and the friendliness of the insurance agents. By highlighting all the positive aspects of this product, the commercial minimizes the viewer's anxiety about buying insurance.

On the other hand, **negative appeals** are designed to *increase* the viewer's anxiety about "not using" the product or service. For example, in a somewhat different approach, another commercial for homeowner's insurance might emphasize the negative aspects of not buying the insurance, such as losing all of your possessions in a fire, or not being able to rebuild your house to the pre-fire standards because of increased costs of building materials. Thus, by highlighting all the negative aspects of the absence of the product, the commercial maximizes the viewer's anxiety about not buying the insurance. Now that the anxiety has been created, the next step involves trying to reduce it.

Reducing the Anxiety in Advertising: Creating Competence and Stressing Support

To help you cope with the anxiety created by the uncertainty, unpleasantness, and unpredictability in these positive and negative fear appeals, advertisers typically use two basic procedures to help viewers achieve relief (D. Cohen, 1981).

- One procedure is to increase the viewers' sense of mastery of or confidence in the anxiety-provoking situation. For example, a deodorant commercial might show how an individual will feel much more confident and in control under the pressure of a big business meeting knowing that he or she will not have to worry about "those embarrassing perspiration stains."
- The other procedure involves securing reassurance or support from others. For example, a commercial for toothpaste might have an actor playing the role of a dentist and reassuring the viewers that the product will help to kill the germs that cause bad breath and tooth decay. Commercials against drinking and driving might show a group of friends providing social support for another friend who decides not to drive home after realizing he or she has had too much to drink.

Because anxiety can be such a powerful motivator, fear appeals are quite popular with advertisers. Just how popular are they? To find out, try for yourself the exercise in "You Can Do It" on this page.

Thus, the role of anxiety in advertising is to create a sense of uneasiness, by employing either positive or negative appeals, and to present ways to minimize this anxiety. Now that you have some understanding of the role anxiety plays in advertising, the next step is to consider how it works. To do this, the discussion turns to the underlying dynamics of anxiety in advertising.

You Can Do It

The Abundance of Anxiety in Advertising: Pinpointing Positive and Negative Appeals

Now that you have a basic understanding of the difference between positive and negative fear appeals, you can begin to see just how pervasive such appeals are by scanning commercials on television and the radio and/or advertisements in newspapers, magazines, or billboards. When you find such appeals, first determine whether they are positive or negative. Then decide whether the message is designed to foster anxiety and then to reduce it. After analyzing the fear appeal ads you have identified, you might present them to some of your friends to see whether they can, without any prior knowledge of the role of anxiety in advertising, explain what the ad is trying to do and how it goes about it. Chances are they will be able to tell you that the ad is trying to "scare" them into doing something, but they will probably not be aware of the subtleties by which these ads are designed to have their influence: first scaring you, then reassuring you. It's possible that one of the reasons that these ads are so popular is that most people are unaware of just how such ads operate. Before you leave, make sure you explain to your friends what is going on in these ads.

The Dynamics of Anxiety in Advertising: Combining the Right Ingredients

The successful utilization of anxiety in advertising is like trying to bake bread. What is most critical in both cases is knowing not only what ingredients to use but also just how much of each to use. In this section, you will examine the "ingredients" that go into the successful use of anxiety in advertising. This discussion covers the specific dynamics created by anxiety as a stimulus and a drive, the level of anxiety created, and the effect of a concrete recommendation.

Anxiety as a Stimulus and Drive: The Push and Pull of Anxiety in Advertising

As a complex emotional reaction, anxiety can create both positive and negative consequences. To understand fully the dynamics of anxiety in advertising, you have to first consider the role anxiety plays as a stimulus and drive (Aaker & Myers, 1982).

Anxiety as a Stimulus: Triggering Uneasiness　As a stimulus, anxiety can trigger a variety of negative reactions that can reduce the effectiveness of the advertisement to change the attitudes or purchasing behavior of the viewers. Such reactions include withdrawing your attention from the message (e.g., you get up and leave the room or change the channel), developing hostility and dislike for the source of the message (e.g., saying to yourself, "That guy in the commercial is such a jerk"), or generating defensive thoughts (e.g., thinking to yourself, "Getting cancer from smoking won't happen to me"). All of these negative reactions interfere with the viewer's ability to process the message that is being communicated by the advertiser, and thus reduce the likelihood of its effectiveness to change attitudes and behaviors.

Anxiety as a Drive: Energizing Behavior　On the other hand, anxiety can also act as a drive, motivating and energizing the individual into action. In this capacity, anxiety tends to increase the viewer's dominant response to the message in the commercial. For example, if you are already buying toothpaste, the anxiety created in a commercial for "Smile Bright" toothpaste can increase the likelihood of your buying this particular brand the next time you are shopping. Thus, if the person is responding attentively to the commercial, the anxiety created can actually energize the individual into taking action.

The Level of Anxiety Aroused in Advertising: Moderation is the Key

At this point, you are probably wondering how it is that anxiety can be used effectively in advertising if it pushes people away by creating defensiveness as a stimulus but, at the same time, pulls people into action as a drive. The answer to this paradox is that while anxiety as a stimulus tends to have the negative effect of causing viewers to pay less attention to the commercial, anxiety as a drive tends to have the more positive effect of

motivating viewers to take action. The key to this rather contradictory state of affairs, however, is the level of anxiety created by the advertisement. If the level of anxiety is too high, it will trigger negative and defensive reactions (Aronson, Wilson, & Akert, 2002). If the level of anxiety is too low, it will not stimulate a drive strong enough to cause the individual to take action. What is required is a moderate level of anxiety that is strong enough to create some concern within the individual and energize him or her into action, but not so strong that it triggers uneasiness, defensiveness, and withdrawal (Baumeister & Bushman, 2008; Berkowitz et al., 2000; Myers, 2008).

The Recommendation: Make it Concrete

Once the fear appeal has created a moderate level of anxiety in the individual, the effectiveness of the advertisement is increased when a concrete recommendation for reducing the anxiety is included as part of the message to the viewer (Aronson et al., 2002). For example, an advertisement for life insurance might show the individual calling the insurance company to reduce the anxiety that was created concerning not having enough insurance coverage for his family in the event of accidental death. The point is that by recommending to the individual a specific course of action that is designed to reduce the level of anxiety, the advertisement is going to cause the individual to develop more favorable attitudes about the product or service being advertised (S. E. Taylor, Peplau, & Sears, 2000).

As you can see, there is a lot more to the use of anxiety in advertising than simply trying to scare the person with a fear appeal. Those using anxiety in advertising must consider the reactions such anxiety is likely to create, the level of anxiety created, and the recommendations designed to reduce this anxiety. Figure 13.6 summarizes the major points discussed in this section.

Anxiety in Social Situations: Understanding and Overcoming Shyness

Understanding Shyness: The Components and Types of Shyness

Shyness is conceptualized as a syndrome of affective, cognitive, and behavioral components characterized by social anxiety and behavioral inhibition resulting from

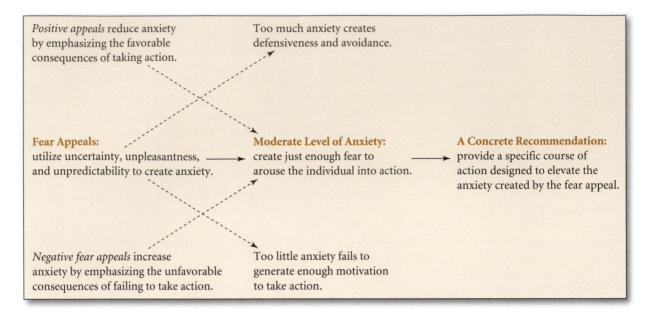

Positive appeals reduce anxiety by emphasizing the favorable consequences of taking action.

Too much anxiety creates defensiveness and avoidance.

Fear Appeals: utilize uncertainty, unpleasantness, and unpredictability to create anxiety.

Moderate Level of Anxiety: create just enough fear to arouse the individual into action.

A Concrete Recommendation: provide a specific course of action designed to elevate the anxiety created by the fear appeal.

Negative fear appeals increase anxiety by emphasizing the unfavorable consequences of failing to take action.

Too little anxiety fails to generate enough motivation to take action.

Figure 13.6 The successful application of anxiety in advertising involves three ingredients: (1) a fear appeal (either positive or negative) designed to create (2) a moderate level of anxiety, followed by (3) a concrete recommendation for a course of action to reduce the anxiety.

the feeling that others are evaluating you (A. H. Buss, 1995; Carducci, 2000a; Carducci & Zimbardo, 1995; Leary & Kowalski, 1995; Zimbardo, 1977).

- The affective component of shyness reflects the anxiety, muscle tension, increased heart rate, upset stomach, and an assortment of other psychophysiological reactions experienced by shy people.
- The cognitive component of shyness reflects the excessive sense of self-consciousness (e.g., "Everybody is staring at me"), negative self-appraisal (e.g., "What I said was so stupid"), and irrational belief system (e.g., "Nobody at the party will find me interesting") characteristic of the way that shy people think about themselves.
- The behavioral component of shyness is expressed by behavioral inhibition (e.g., not speaking to others at a party) and social avoidance (e.g., avoiding eye contact or standing in the corner during a group discussion).

Thus, shyness is not just one or two symptoms but an all-encompassing collection of characteristics that manifests itself in the mind, body, and behavior of shy people.

The Pervasiveness of Shyness: If You're Shy, You're Not Alone   Although most shy people feel they are more shy than other people (Carducci & Clark, 1996), shyness is a self-reported characteristic of personality that is expressed by over 40 percent of those surveyed (Carducci & Clark, 1996; Carducci & Stein, 1988; Zimbardo, 1977). Only about 7 percent of Americans surveyed indicate that they have never experienced shyness in their entire life (Zimbardo, 1977). Thus, shyness is a pervasive phenomenon; if you are shy, you are not alone. In fact, as can be seen in Figure 13.7, some of the world's most famous public figures are shy.

Types of Shyness: The Shades of Shyness   An important development in the understanding of shyness is that shy people are not all the same; there are different types

Figure 13.7 Some of the world's most famous entertainers and public figures are shy. So if you are shy, you are in some pretty good company.

of shyness. **Publicly shy** people express distress as a consequence of more overt manifestations of their shyness, such as being too quiet, behaving awkwardly, and failing to respond appropriately in social situations (e.g., not acknowledging a compliment; Pilkonis, 1977). **Privately shy** people express distress as a consequence of more covert manifestations of their shyness, such as through intense psychophysiological arousal (e.g., pounding heart, muscle tension, and anxiety reactions; Pilkonis, 1977). **Socially anxious shy** people express distress as a consequence of more cognitive manifestations of their shyness, such as being excessively self-conscious (e.g., "Do my clothes fit right?") and overly concerned about being evaluated socially by others (e.g., "I wonder what she thinks of my comment?"; Carducci & Clark, 1994; Melchior & Cheek, 1990). Thus, while shy people tend to experience all of the affective, cognitive, and behavioral components of shyness, some experience one of the components more than others, which helps to explain the different types of shyness. Finally, while there seems to be some commonality to the experience of shyness, this experience is influenced by cultural factors. For an examination of the cross-cultural perspective on shyness, read "The Cultural Context of Personality Psychology."

The Cultural Context of Personality Psychology

Shyness in the East and West: Cultural Differences and Similarities

Although shyness has been found to be a universal experience, its pervasiveness varies across cultures (Gudykunst & Ting-Toomey, 1988; Zimbardo, 1986). In several studies, shyness has been found to be more pervasive in individuals from Asian countries (e.g., Japan, China, and Thailand) than in the United States (T. Jackson, Flaherty, & Kosuth, 2000). In attempting to understand the cultural context of shyness, one recent explanation has focused on how common personality factors associated with shyness might be experienced differently by shy individuals within different cultures (T. Jackson et al., 2000). Specifically, according to the self-presentation theory of shyness (Arkin,

Lake, & Baumgardner, 1986; T. Jackson, Towson, & Narduzzi, 1997), concerns about disapproval (i.e., being rejected) and perceived deficits in interpersonal skills (e.g., being critical of one's ability to respond appropriately in social situations), along with reduced self-esteem, are critical factors associated with shyness. Adding the cultural component to the self-presentation theory of shyness would suggest that those personality factors associated with shyness would be experienced to a greater degree in Asian cultures, which tend to be more collectivist and place greater restraints on individual expression, than in the United States, which tends to be more individualistic and allow for greater ease and tolerance of individual expression (see pp. 482–485 for a more detailed discussion of individualist vs. collectivistic cultures).

In support of this reasoning, recent research has reported that perceived interpersonal competence deficits and heightened expectations of rejection were the strongest predictors of shyness for both Asian and American individuals (T. Jackson et al., 2000). Furthermore, in support of cultural differences in the intensity of experience of these two critical factors associated with shyness, Asian individuals tend to be more sensitive to rejection (Yamaguchi, Kuhlman, & Sugimori, 1995) and more self-critical (Kitayama, Markus, Matsumoto, & Norasakkunkit, 1997) than American individuals.

In addition to providing a greater understanding of the underlying dynamics of shyness, including this cultural component has implications for the treatment of shyness. Ishu Ishiyama, of the University of British Columbia in Vancouver, has proposed the use of Morita therapy for helping individuals deal with their shyness. As a "culturally fit" therapy that is consistent with Japanese values and social structure, **Morita therapy**, which is based in the Buddhist perspective, focuses on "changing the inner attitudes and beliefs for greater adjustment and effectiveness without altering the symptoms" (Ishiyama, 1987, p. 547). As it applies to the counseling of shy individuals, Morita therapy would emphasize that shy individuals be more accepting of the symptoms of their shyness (e.g., "It's OK to have feelings of anxiety and uncertainty") and less critical of their actions (e.g., worry less about whether or not an opening line was funny enough). Such principles are quite consistent with addressing the heightened sense of the perceived interpersonal competence deficits and increased sense of rejection as critical factors identified by the self-presentation model of shyness and intensified in the Eastern cultural context. Finally, because these two critical factors are also observed in shy individuals in Western cultures, Morita therapy has also been found to be effective in treating shy individuals in the West (Ishiyama, 1985, 1986).

Thus, our understanding of shyness, as well as its treatment, is enhanced by considering both personality factors and cultural dynamics. Such an approach illustrates clearly the value of investigating the cultural context of personality psychology.

What Shy People Do to Deal with Their Shyness: Limitations and Liabilities While it might be tempting to conclude that shy individuals simply accept their fate and react passively to their shyness, this is not the case. Recent research indicates that shy individuals exhibit a variety of strategies to deal with their shyness (Carducci, 2000b). Unfortunately, many of the self-selected strategies utilized by shy individuals to deal with their shyness tend to be limited in their effectiveness. For example, the most common self-selected strategy used by shy individuals is "forced extraversion," in which shy individuals report forcing themselves to go to social situations, such as parties, bars, shopping malls, and art receptions, in the hopes of meeting others. However, a limitation of this strategy is that just showing up is not enough. Specifically, being in social situations means being social, such as approaching others and initiating and maintaining conversations, which are tasks many shy individuals find difficult (Carducci, Ragains, Kee, Johnson, & Duncan, 1998), as expressed by this shy individual: "I have tried to overcome my shyness by being around new people as much as possible and getting involved in the conversation, however, after a few seconds, I become quiet. I have a problem keeping the conversation flowing" (Carducci, 2000b, p. 175).

Another self-selected strategy identified is that of "liquid extraversion," in which shy individuals consume alcohol or other nonprescription drugs to make themselves feel more relaxed in social settings. However, limitations of this strategy are that it does not really address the underlying cognitive (e.g., feeling self-conscious) and behavior (e.g., not knowing how to promote the flow of conversation) components of shyness and, while there may be some immediate benefits (e.g., feeling less aroused and anxious), the subsequent consequences can range from personal disappointment to the development of a drinking problem (Carducci & McLeish, 2000), as expressed by this shy individual: "I do like drinking with my friends, but I notice that I tend to indulge myself in alcohol to feel more loose and more talkative when it comes to meeting my boyfriend's friends. But when I see them sober, I feel like such a loser because they just saw me the other night as a happy talkative drunk" (Carducci, 2000b, p. 178).

Although these and other self-selected strategies used by shy individuals seem to be of limited utility, it should be made clear that there are many other more constructive strategies that shy individuals can utilize to deal successfully with their shyness. In the next section, you will consider some of these strategies.

Tips for Overcoming Shyness: Addressing the Multidimensional Nature of Shyness

This section presents a number of suggestions for overcoming shyness. Taken from a variety of sources (Carducci, 1999; 2000a, 2005; Carducci & Zimbardo, 1995; Cheek, 1989; Leary & Kowalski, 1995; Zimbardo, 1977), these suggestions require no complicated treatment procedures. All they require is a desire on the part of the individual to become less shy.

Start with Self-Awareness: Which Shy Type Are You? Because each person experiences his or her shyness in a unique way, the place to start when trying to overcome shyness is to gain some understanding of your own shyness. Begin by looking at what situations seem to make you feel shy, and why. For example, do you become shy when meeting new people, interacting at a social gathering, or speaking to someone to whom you find yourself attracted? Try to understand whether your shyness manifests itself cognitively (e.g., excessive self-consciousness or self-deprecating statements), affectively (e.g., overriding feelings of anxiety), or behaviorally (e.g., failure to speak to others at social gatherings).

You might also try to understand how these three different aspects of shyness might interact with each other in your experience of shyness. For example, consider the following situation where the affective and cognitive components of shyness interact to produce avoidant behavior: You are at a party and assume others are evaluating you. As a result, you begin to experience feelings of intense anxiety, which makes it difficult for you

to think of anything to say to others. Such lack of involvement in the ongoing conversation makes you perceive yourself as socially incompetent and not very interesting. As a consequence, you leave the party. Since leaving the party reduces the feelings of anxiety, making you feel good, leaving becomes a strategy you are more likely to use in the future.

Thus, you can begin to overcome your shyness by examining the nature of your shyness.

Overcome the Affective Component of Shyness: Eliminate Excessive Emotions If your shyness manifests itself primarily through affective reactions, such as excessive levels of anxiety, a racing heart, and butterflies in the stomach, then such symptoms need to be brought under control. There is a variety of simple relaxation techniques you can use to reduce your level of psychophysiological arousal. Simple breathing exercises involve inhaling and exhaling deeply and slowly and focusing your attention on the nature of your breathing. Taking the attention away from the physiological symptoms of your shyness and focusing on the nature of your breathing will help you relax. Another relaxation technique involves tightening and loosening your muscles, such as squeezing your hands into a tight fist and then letting go, to reduce some of the tension you are experiencing. The important point is that it is very difficult for you to think or act appropriately if you are overly anxious, as indicated by the Yerkes-Dodson Law (see pp. 548–549).

As a word of caution, do not resort to alcohol or other drugs as a means of reducing your level of arousal. The principal reason is that after the short-term effects of the alcohol or drugs have worn off, the level of anxiety is going to return. You'll be right back where you started, but now you'll also have a hangover.

Overcome the Behavioral Deficits of Shyness: Practice What to Say and Do A common problem with shy people is that they fail to respond appropriately in social situations. If your problem of shyness is manifested as behavioral deficits, there is a variety of strategies you can develop to help you learn to respond more appropriately and effectively. Here are four recommendations:

1. *Start with very, very small talk and simple actions: Getting your feet wet.* Shy people often report that they have trouble talking with people they have just met, particularly those people to whom

they might feel attracted. A strategy for helping shy people to overcome this inhibition is to start with relatively nonthreatening situations and very small talk. Nonthreatening situations might include malls, museums, political rallies, or sporting events where you will have the opportunity to interact with a lot of people for a relatively brief period of time. In such interactions, you can start by smiling and saying something simple like "hello" to as many people as you care to make eye contact with and who will smile at you. Asking for simple directions, giving an unexpected compliment, or offering assistance (e.g., offer to hold a door) are three very simple ways to practice talking with people. Thus, the point here is to get used to talking with others.

2. *Develop conversation skills: How to keep talking.* Shy people who have mastered the art of small talk can take the next step by developing their conversational skills (Carducci, 1999). The trick to successful conversation is to *have something to say.* There are a number of very simple strategies that shy people can employ to make sure they have something to say. You can start by reading the newspaper or magazines or listening to information-based radio programs to keep up on the type of current events other people are most likely to be talking about. An important advantage of such information sources is that they also give you the type of in-depth, "behind-the-headlines" analysis that is the basic substance of much social conversation. Shy people can also do their part to help keep the conversation going by asking open-ended questions that require more than a yes or no answer (e.g., "What do you think of . . . ?").

3. *Rehearse what you are going to say: Practice makes perfect.* Shy people who want to increase their confidence in the art of making conversation can prepare a "script" ahead of time, based on events that are most likely to be the topic of conversation at the social gathering, and rehearse it in the privacy of their own home in front of the mirror. For example, a shy individual going to a political rally might practice expressing his or her views on the political issues that are most likely to be brought up by others attending the rally.

4. *Perform social graces: Give (kindness) and you shall receive (kindness).* Performing social graces

is a safe way to facilitate social interactions. The performance of social graces might include giving a compliment or offering to get someone some refreshments as you are getting some for yourself. Shy people can maximize their likelihood of successful social interactions by looking for others who might appear shy, such as an individual who is standing or sitting alone and would welcome the opportunity to interact with someone.

Planning and rehearsing for social interactions with others might sound a bit trite and artificial. But because shy people manifest their shyness in the form of behavior deficits when interacting with others, what they need is to acquire new social and conversational skills. And the best way to acquire and develop such skills is still to define what the skills are and to practice them beforehand in a comfortable environment.

Overcome the Cognitive Deficits of Shyness: Getting Your Mind Right   For those individuals whose shyness is expressed primarily through negative thoughts about themselves, the key to overcoming their shyness is to change the way they think about themselves. Such change is more difficult than it sounds, because it is not easy to change the thoughts an individual may have had about himself or herself since early childhood. Here are six strategies for reducing the cognitive component of shyness:

1. *Reduce your sense of self-consciousness: The whole world is not looking at you.* Since self-consciousness is a principal cognitive component for many shy people, it is very helpful for such shy people to realize that most people are far more interested in how they look or what they are doing than what anyone else is doing or saying. As an example, realize that if you are dancing on the dance floor, others who are dancing are more interested in how they are doing than how you are doing. And those people who are in their seats around the dance floor are probably wishing they had the courage to be out on the dance floor, and are not just thinking about how well or poorly you are dancing. Thus, for shy people, realizing that other people care more about themselves than about you will make interacting in social situations much more tolerable.

2. *Focus on your social successes: Stop whipping yourself.* Shy people tend to be overly self-critical

of their performance in social situations. In their view, they are never outgoing enough or witty enough to be satisfied with themselves. To help overcome their shyness, shy people can begin to minimize the anxiety such expectations create by focusing on their strengths, and not only on what they perceive as their weaknesses. For example, rather than being upset with herself for not using the jokes she practiced at home, this shy person should focus on the fact that at the party, she did give a few compliments, carried on a conversation with several new people, and was approached by others. Thus, focusing on the reactions of others to what she did or said, rather than on the negative statements about herself, will shift her focus of attention to others and make her feel less self-conscious.

3. *Avoid overgeneralizations: It may not be your fault.* A mistake many shy people make is to overgeneralize their social misfortunes in one context to another and often unrelated social context. Such a tendency magnifies the negativity of the experience and degree to which the shy individual feels personally responsible. For example, after one individual excuses himself while talking to Judy, a shy individual, she now assumes that no one else at the party will want to talk to her and decides to leave. Leaving the party early only guarantees that no one else will be able to talk to her. Another error in this situation is in Judy's assumption that the other person excused himself because he found her boring. But the other individual could have excused himself because he had someone else to meet. Thus, the point is to avoid overgeneralizing social misfortunes and your responsibility for them.

4. *Avoid perfectionism: Nobody's perfect.* Part of the exaggerated sense of self-criticism experienced by shy people is based on the excessive expectations they have for themselves. Their jokes have to be absolutely funny and their remarks insightful and witty. In short, shy people tend to set standards that are impossible to maintain. A simple strategy for overcoming the cognitive component of shyness is for shy people to set more realistic standards for themselves. It's not necessary to be the life of the party in order to categorize your performance as a social success. In some cases, simply talking to four new people at a party might be the mark of a successful performance. Thus, shy people can reduce the misery they create for themselves by being less perfectionist and more realistic.

5. *Learn to take rejection: No one is liked by everyone.* Rejection is one of the risks that accompanies engaging in social interactions. A key to overcoming shyness is not to take rejection personally. There may be a variety of reasons that someone is rejected by someone else, none of which may have anything at all to do with the person being rejected. For example, one person may not like what the shy person is wearing, and another person may be bored with the entire social situation, not just with her conversation with the shy individual. The point is that sometimes you can control the reactions of others (e.g., by wearing stylish clothes) and at other times you cannot. What's important is that shy people make a realistic attempt to socialize with others. If it doesn't work out and rejection results, simply select someone else and start all over again.

6. *Find your comfort zone; Do what fits you.* Not all social situations are for everyone. For example, some shy people might be uneasy in a bar or nightclub where physical attractiveness and stylish dress are critical predictors of social success. In other situations, extensive knowledge of politics, art, or murder mysteries might be the key to success. Shy people should seek out those situations that are most consistent with their temperament and interests. It is easier for shy people to overcome or manage their sense of social anxiety and self-consciousness by finding situations in which they feel reasonably comfortable. Volunteering for different organizations is a good strategy for shy people to use in an attempt to find various places where they might feel comfortable. In most cases, being a volunteer requires a low level of skills, offers the possibility of meeting many different types of people, and is easy to terminate if the experience does not turn out to be what was expected. Thus, overcoming shyness can be helped by seeking out an assortment of volunteer experiences as a means of meeting new people, practicing social skills in different situations, and helping to find those social situations that are the most comfortable.

As you can see, there is a variety of strategies for coping with shyness. If you would like more information on this topic, read Bernardo J. Carducci's *Shyness: A Bold New Approach* (2000a) or *The Shyness Workbook: 30 Days to Dealing Effectively with Shyness* (2005), Philip G. Zimbardo's (1977) *Shyness: What It Is, What to Do about It*, or Jonathan M. Cheek's (1989) *Conquering Shyness: The Battle Anyone Can Win*. All of these books provide sound advice for overcoming shyness.

This concludes the discussion on shyness. Your understanding of shyness should be enhanced now that you know about the multidimensional aspects of how shy people experience and manifest their shyness, as well as what shy people can do to overcome their shyness. For more information on the general topic of shyness, read *Shyness: Development, Consolidation and Change* (Crozier, 2000) or *Shyness: Perspectives on Research*

and Treatment (Jones, Cheek, & Briggs, 1986). These books provide scholarly coverage of the topic of shyness and its treatment.

Some Closing Remarks: A Statement of Reiteration

This concludes the discussion of anxiety. As you may now realize, anxiety is truly a distinct dimension of personality, characterized by many different dimensions and dynamics. It seems to exist in levels of intensity on a spectrum ranging from normal to pathological proportions. Because the sphere of its influence seems almost unlimited, as noted earlier, anxiety is considered an "all-encompassing intrapersonal process of personality."

Chapter Summary: Reexamining the Highlights

- *Anxiety as an Intrapersonal Personality Process.* Anxiety consists of a physiological, cognitive, and behavioral dimension. Individual differences in anxiety can be assessed with the Manifest Anxiety Scale (MAS).

- *Theoretical Viewpoints of Anxiety*
  - *The Psychodynamic Viewpoint.* The psychodynamic viewpoint conceptualizes anxiety as a warning signal used to indicate the possible expression of certain unacceptable unconscious impulses.
  - *The Learning Viewpoint.* The learning viewpoint conceptualizes anxiety as a conditioned response to certain stimuli. The conditioned anxiety signals the impending aversive stimuli.
  - *The Drive Viewpoint.* The drive viewpoint conceptualizes anxiety as a motivating force that triggers the individual into taking action. The likelihood of a specific response occurring is determined by the strength of the response and level of motivation.
  - *The Evolutionary Viewpoint.* From the evolutionary viewpoint, the role of anxiety is to create a state of emotional distress that serves to prompt the person to develop an adaptive response to the source of threat. The adaptive response serves to improve the individual's likelihood of survival.

  - *Integrating the Viewpoints of Anxiety.* The different viewpoints of anxiety can be integrated to explain the purpose, acquisition, and influence of anxiety.

- *Types of Anxiety*
  - *State vs. Trait Anxiety.* State anxiety is a temporary change in anxiety in response to an external threat. Trait anxiety is an enduring characteristic of the individual's personality. State and trait anxiety can be assessed with the State-Trait Anxiety Inventory (STAI).
  - *Test Anxiety.* Test anxiety is an excessive emotional response to activities associated with taking tests. Test anxiety can be assessed with the Test Anxiety Scale (TAS). People with high and low test anxiety differ in what they do in response to the test, how they evaluate their test performance, and what they think about during the test.
  - *Anxiety Disorders.* Anxiety disorders are characterized by a level of anxiety that is excessive in response to the external threat. They include panic disorder, generalized anxiety disorder, obsessive-compulsive disorder, and phobic disorder. The psychodynamic viewpoint explanation of anxiety disorders is based on their manifestation as unresolved conflicts, while the

learning viewpoint explanation emphasizes the process of conditioning. The cognitive viewpoint explanation of anxiety disorders is based the individual maintaining a set of beliefs that serves to create a sense of fear, while the neurological viewpoint explains anxiety disorders as being due to an imbalance of neurotransmitters in the brain that contributes to a sense of arousal and emotional distress.

● *The Application of Personality Psychology*

– *Anxiety in Advertising.* A fear appeal is a form of advertising that utilizes anxiety as a means of motivating the consumer into action. Positive appeals emphasize how the use of the product will reduce the consumer's anxiety, while negative appeals emphasize how failure to use the product will increase the consumer's anxiety. The successful use of fear appeals involves an ad that creates a moderate level of anxiety, which is followed by a specific recommendation designed to reduce the consumer's anxiety and reinforce acting upon the recommendation.

– *Anxiety in Social Situations.* Shyness consists of an affective, cognitive, and behavioral component. Three types of shyness are public, private, and socially anxious shyness. While the self-selected strategies employed by shy individuals to deal with their shyness seem to have limited utility, successfully overcoming shyness involves incorporating different strategies corresponding to the three different dimensions of shyness.

Glossary

agoraphobia   An irrational fear of open spaces.

ailurophobia   An irrational fear of cats.

anxiety disorder   A category of mental disorders characterized by excessive anxiety reactions that interfere with daily living.

aviophobia   An irrational fear of flying.

benzodiazepines   A category of drugs used for the treatment of anxiety disorders.

classical conditioning   A form of learning based on the repeated pairing of a neutral stimulus with an emotionally charged stimulus so that the neutral stimulus begins to evoke an emotional response when presented alone.

compulsion   An uncontrollable desire to perform a specific behavior.

dominant response   A well-learned, easily performed response.

drive level   The degree to which an individual is motivated to perform a specific action.

ergasiophobia   An irrational fear of writing.

excitatory potential   The likelihood of a response being emitted.

fear appeals   An approach to advertising that creates anxiety to motivate the consumer into action.

fight-or-flight reaction   The tendency to either engage a threatening stimulus directly or flee from it.

gamma-aminobutyric acid (GABA)   A major neurotransmitter in the brain whose purpose is to help keep under control the operation of neurons.

generalized anxiety disorder   A chronic sense of unexplained feelings of anxiety.

habit strength   The extent to which a response has been learned.

intrapersonal personality process   A dimension of personality that influences many aspects of an individual's thoughts, feelings, and behavior.

Manifest Anxiety Scale (MAS)   A personality test measuring individual differences in anxiety.

Morita therapy   A Far Eastern culturally based therapy that emphasizes acceptance of one's feelings and actions.

negative appeals   Advertisements designed to create anxiety if the advertised product is not utilized.

nondominant response   A novel response that is performed with some difficulty.

obsession   The presence of an intrusive, recurring thought.

optimal level of arousal   The degree of arousal that results in the best performance by the individual.

overlearning   The continued rehearsal of a well-established behavior.

panic disorder   The unexpected onset of acute anxiety.

phobic disorders   A group of mental disorders characterized by irrational fears that interfere with daily living.

positive appeals   Advertisements designed to reduce anxiety if the advertised product is utilized.

privately shy   The distress of shyness expressed as a consequence of covert reactions.

publicly shy   The distress of shyness expressed as a consequence of overt actions.

self-defeating thoughts   Personal beliefs about your abilities that interfere with your performance.

shyness   Perceived distress as a consequence of excessive self-consciousness and a lack of social skills.

simple phobia   An irrational fear of certain objects or situations.

state anxiety   Anxiety in response to an external threat.

State-Trait Anxiety Inventory (STAI)   A personality inventory for assessing an individual's specific and general feelings of anxiety.

social phobia   An irrational fear of being evaluated.

socially anxious shyness   The distress of shyness expressed as a consequence of ineffective thoughts and beliefs.

sympathetic nervous system (SNS)   A portion of the nervous system that is activated in response to stressful events.

Test Anxiety Scale (TAS)   A personality inventory for assessing individual differences in test anxiety.

trait anxiety   The degree of variation exhibited across people in their personal level of anxiety.

virtual reality therapy (VRT)   The use of simulated environments created by virtual reality technology to help individuals gradually overcome their fears and stress reactions to specific objects and situations.

Yerkes-Dodson Law   A principle of motivation that explains the "inverted-U" relationship between motivation and performance.

References

Chapter 1

Aiken, L. R. (2003). *Psychological assessment and testing* (11th ed.). Boston: Allyn & Bacon.

Aiken, L. R., & Groth-Marnat, G. (2006). *Psychological testing and assessment* (12th ed.). New York: Pearson/Allyn & Bacon.

Alge, B. J., Gresham, M. T., Heneman, R. L., Fox, J., & McMasters, R. (2002). Measuring customer service orientation using a measure of interpersonal skills: A preliminary test in a public service organization. *Journal of Business and Psychology, 16*, 467–476.

Allport, G. W. (1937). *Personality: A psychological interpretation.* New York: Henry Holt.

Allport, G. W. (1961). *Pattern and growth in personality.* New York: Holt, Rinehart & Winston.

American Psychological Association. (1977). *Standard for providers of psychological services.* Washington, DC: Author.

American Psychological Association. (1981a). Ethical principles of psychologists. *American Psychologist, 36*, 633–638.

American Psychological Association. (1981b). Specialty guidelines for the delivery of services. *American Psychologist, 36*, 639–685.

American Psychological Association. (1982). *Ethical principles in the conduct of research with human participants.* Washington, DC: Author.

American Psychological Association. (1990). Ethical principles of psychologists (Amended June 2, 1989). *American Psychologist, 45*, 390–395.

American Psychological Association. (1992a). APA continues to refine its ethics code. *The APA Monitor, 23*, 38–42.

American Psychological Association. (1992b). Ethical principles of psychologists and code of conduct. *American Psychologist, 47*, 1597–1611.

American Psychological Association. (2002). *Ethical principles of psychologists and code of conduct* (Revision effective date: June 1, 2003). Retrieved from www.apa.org/ethics/code2002.html.

American Psychological Association's Committee on Animal Research and Ethics (CARE). (2002). *Guidelines for ethical conduct in the care and use of animals.* Retrieved from www.apa.org/science/anguide.html.

American Psychological Association's Ethics Committee. (1997/2002). *APA statement on services by telephone, teleconferencing, and Internet: A statement by the Ethics Committee of the American Psychological Association.* Retrieved from www.apa.org/ethics/stmnt01.html.

Arbisi, P. A., & Seime, R. J. (2006). Use of the MMPI-2 in medical settings. In J. N. Butcher (Ed.), *MMPI-2: A practioner's guide* (pp. 273–299). Washington, DC: American Psychological Association.

Archer, J. (2004). Sex differences in aggression in real-world settings: A meta-analytic review. *Review of general psychology, 8*, 291–322.

Avis, J. M., Kudisch, J. D., & Fortunato, V. J. (2002). Examining the incremental validity and adverse impact of cognitive ability and conscientiousness on job performance. *Journal of Business and Psychology, 17*, 87–105.

Azar, B. (2002). Searching for genes that explain our personalities. *Monitor on Psychology, 35*, 44–46.

Barnes, G. E., Murray, R. P., Patton, D., Bentler, P. N., & Anderson, R. E. (2000). *The addiction-prone personality.* New York: Kluwer Academic.

Baumrind, D. (1971). Current patterns of parental authority. *Developmental Psychology Monographs, 80*(1, Pt. 2), 1–103.

Benjamin, J., Ebstein, R., & Belmaker, R. (Eds.). (2002). *Molecular genetics and the human personality.* Washington, DC: American Psychiatric Publishing.

Berkowitz, L. (2005). On hate and its determinants: Some affective and cognitive influences. In R. J. Sternberg (Ed.), *The psychology of hate* (pp. 155–183). Washington, DC: American Psychological Association.

Blanck, P. D., Bellack, A. S., Rosnow, R. L., Rotheram-Borus, M. J., & Schooler, M. J. (1992). Scientific rewards and conflicts of ethical choices in human subjects research. *American Psychologist, 47*, 959–965.

Block, J. (1971). *Lives through time.* Berkeley, CA: Bancroft.

Block, J. (1993). Studying personality the long way. In D. C. Funder, R. D. Parke, C. Tomlinson-Keasey, & K. Widaman (Eds.), *Studying lives through time* (pp. 9–41). Washington, DC: American Psychological Association.

Block, J. (1995). A contrarian view of the five-factor approach to personality description. *Psychological Bulletin, 117*, 187–215.

Bond, R., & Smith, P. B. (1996). Culture and conformity: A meta-analysis of studies using Asch's (1952b, 1956) line judgment task. *Psychological Bulletin, 119*, 111–137.

Bradsher, K. (2000, July 23). Would Freud have driven an SUV or a minivan? *The Courier-Journal*, D1, D4.

Brandstätter, H. (1997). Becoming an entrepreneur – a question of personality structure? *Journal of Economic Psychology, 18*, 157–177.

Brislin, R. W., & Lo, K. D. (2006). Culture, personality, and people's uses of time: Key interrelationships. In J. C. Thomas & D. L. Segal (Eds.), *Comprehensive handbook of personality and psychopathology: Vol. 1. Personality and everyday functioning* (pp. 44–61). Hoboken, NJ: John Wiley.

Bröder, A. (1998). Deception can be acceptable. *American Psychologist, 53*, 805–806.

Bullock, M. (2002). Doing our work: The latest on research and IRBs. *Psychological Science Agenda, 15,* 12.

Butcher, J. M., Ones, D. S., & Cullen, M. (2006). *Personnel screening with the MMPI-2.* In J. N. Butcher (Ed.), *MMPI-2: A practitioner's guide* (pp. 381–406). Washington, DC: American Psychological Association.

Canli, T. (Ed.). (2006). *Biology of personality and individual differences.* New York: Guilford Press.

Carducci, B. J., & Wong, A. S. (1998). Type A and risk taking in everyday money matters. *Journal of Business and Psychology, 12,* 355–359.

Carlson, R. (1971). Where is the person in personality research? *Psychological Bulletin, 75,* 203–219.

Carlson, R. (1984). What's social about social psychology? Where's the person in personality research? *Journal of Personality and Social Psychology, 47,* 1304–1309.

Caspi, A. (2000). The child is the father of the man: Personality correlates from childhood to adulthood. *Journal of Personality and Social Psychology, 78,* 158–172.

Caspi, A., & Roberts, B. W. (1999). Personality continuity and change across the life course. In L. A. Pervin & O. P. John (Eds.), *Handbook of personality: Theory and research* (2nd ed., pp. 300–326). New York: Guilford Press.

Caspi, A., & Roberts, B. (2001). Personality development across the life course: The argument for change and continuity. *Psychological Inquiry, 12,* 46–66.

Cattell, R. B. (1950). *Personality: A systematic, theoretical, and factual study.* New York: McGraw-Hill.

Cohen, R. J., & Swerdlik, M. E. (2002). *Psychological testing and assessment: An introduction to tests and measurement* (5th ed.). Boston: McGraw-Hill.

Cole, S. W., Kemeny, M. E., & Taylor, S. E. (1997). Social identity and physical health: Accelerated HIV infection in rejection-sensitive gay men. *Journal of Personality and Social Psychology, 72,* 320–336.

Comer, R. J. (2001). *Abnormal psychology* (4th ed.). New York: Worth.

Commier, A. (Ed.). *Historic World Leaders.* Detroit: Gale Research.

Contrada, R. J., & Guyll, M. (2001). On who gets sick and why: The role of personality and stress. In A. Baum, T. R., & J. E. Singer (Eds.), *Handbook of health psychology* (pp. 59–84). Mahwah, NJ: Erlbaum.

Coomes, M. (2002, August 11). U r what you drive. *The Courier-Journal,* pp. H1–H2.

Coopersmith, S. (1967). *Antecedents of self-esteem.* San Francisco: Freeman.

Costa, P. T., Jr., & McCrae, R. R. (1997). Longitudinal stability of adult personality. In R. Hogan, J. Johnson, & S. Briggs (Eds.), *Handbook of personality psychology* (pp. 269–290). San Diego, CA: Academic Press.

Craig, R. J. (2005). *Personality-guided forensic psychology.* Washington, DC: American Psychological Association.

Cross, S. E., & Markus, H. R. (1999). The cultural constitution of personality. In L. A. Pervin & O. P. John (Eds.), *Handbook of personality: Theory and research* (2nd ed., pp. 378–396). New York: Guilford Press.

Danner, D. D., Snowdon, D. A., & Friesen, W. V. (2001). Positive emotions in early life and longevity: Findings from the nun study. *Journal of Personality and Social Psychology, 80,* 804–813.

Darbonne, A. R. (1969). Suicide and age: A suicide note analysis. *Journal of Consulting and Clinical Psychology, 33,* 46–50.

DeAngelis, T. (2002). A bright future for PNI. *Monitor on Psychology, 33,* 446–50.

DiLalla, L. F. (Ed.). (2004). *Behavioral genetics principles: Perspectives in development, personality, and psychopathology.* Washington, DC: American Psychological Association.

Eagly, A. H., & Steffen, V. J. (1986). Gender and aggressive behavior: A meta-analytic review of the social psychological literature. *Psychological Bulletin, 100,* 309–330.

Eder, R. A., & Mangelsdorf, S. C. (1997). The emotional basis of early personality development. In R. Hogan, J. Johnson, & S. Briggs (Eds.), *Handbook of personality psychology* (pp. 209–240). San Diego, CA: Academic Press.

Elms, A. C. (1976). *Personality and politics.* New York: Harcourt Brace Jovanovich.

Elms, A. C. (1994). *Uncovering lives: The uneasy alliance of biography and psychology.* New York: Oxford University Press.

Emler, N., & Cook, T. (2001). Moral integrity in leadership: Why it matters and why it may be difficult to achieve. In B. W. Roberts & R. Hogan (Eds.), *Personality psychology in the workplace* (pp. 277–298). Washington, DC: American Psychological Association.

Epley, N., & Huff, C. (1998). Suspicion, affective responses, and educational benefits as a result of deception in psychological research. *Personality and Social Bulletin, 24,* 759–768.

Figueredo, A. J., Sefcek, J. A., Vasquez, G., Brumbach, B. H., King, J. E., & Jacobs, W. J. (2005). Evolutionary personality psychology. In D. M. Buss (Ed.), *The handbook of evolutionary psychology* (pp. 851–877). Hoboken, NJ: John Wiley.

Flin, R. (2001). Selecting the right stuff: Personality and high-reliability occupations. In B. W. Roberts & R. Hogan (Eds.), *Personality psychology in the workplace* (pp. 253–275). Washington, DC: American Psychological Association.

Funder, D. C. (2001). *The personality puzzle* (2nd ed.). New York: Norton.

Funder, D. C., Parke, R. D., Tomlinson-Keasey, C., & Widaman, K. (Eds.). (1993). *Studying lives through time: Personality and development.* Washington, DC: American Psychological Association.

Furnham, A. (2001). Personality and individual differences in the workplace: Person–organization–outcome fit. In B. W. Roberts & R. Hogan (Eds.), *Personality psychology in the workplace* (pp. 223–251). Washington, DC: American Psychological Association.

Gatchel, R. J., & Weisberg, J. N. (Eds.). (2000). *Personality characteristics of patients with pain.* Washington, DC: American Psychological Association.

Goldstein, M. D. (1998). Forming and testing implicit personality theories in cyberspace. *Teaching of Psychology, 25,* 216–220.

Graham, K. E., McDaniel, M. A., Douglas, E. F., & Snell, A. F. (2002). Biodata validity decay and score inflation with faking: Do item attributes explain variance across items? *Journal of Business and Psychology, 16,* 573–592.

Gross, R. T., & Duke, P. (1980). The effect of early versus late physical maturation on adolescent behavior. In I. Litt (Ed.), *Symposium on adolescent medicine: The pediatric clinics of North America, 27*, 71–78.

Guilford, J. P. (1959). *Personality*. New York: McGraw-Hill.

Hall, C. S., Lindzey, G., & Campbell, J. B. (1998). *Theories of personality* (4th ed.). New York: John Wiley.

Halverson, C. F., Jr., & Wampler, K. S. (1997). Family influence on personality development. In R. Hogan, J. Johnson, & S. Briggs (Eds.), *Handbook of personality psychology* (pp. 241–267). San Diego, CA: Academic Press.

Handler, L., & Clemence, A. J. (2003). Educational and training in psychological assessment. In J. R. Graham & J. A. Naglieri (Eds.), *Handbook of psychology: Vol. 10. Assessment psychology* (pp. 181–209). Hoboken, NJ: John Wiley.

Hayslip, B., Jr., Neumann, C. S., Louden, L., & Chapman, B. (2006). Developmental stage theories. In J. C. Thomas & D. L. Segal (Eds.), *Comprehensive handbook of personality and psychopathology: Vol. 1. Personality and everyday functioning* (pp. 115–141). Hoboken, NJ: John Wiley.

Holmes, R. M., & Holmes, S. T. (2002). *Profiling violent crimes: An investigative tool* (3rd ed.). Thousand Oaks, CA: Sage.

Hoyle, R. H., Fejfar, M. C., & Miller, J. D. (2000). Personality and sexual risk taking: A quantitative review. *Journal of Personality, 68*, 1202–1231.

Hyde, J. S. (1984). How large are gender differences in aggression? A developmental meta-analysis. *Developmental Psychology, 20*, 722–736.

Hyde, J. S. (1986). Gender differences in aggression. In J. S. Hyde & M. C. Linn (Eds.), *The psychology of gender: Advances through meta-analysis* (pp. 51–66). Baltimore: Johns Hopkins University Press.

Hyde, J. S. (2005). The gender similarities hypothesis. *American Psychologist, 60*, 581–592.

Kaplan, P. S. (2000). *A child's odyssey* (3rd ed.). Belmont, CA: Wadsworth/Thomson Learning.

Kendall, P. C., & Norton-Ford. J. D. (1982). *Clinical psychology: Scientific and professional dimensions*. New York: John Wiley.

Koocher, G. P., & Keith-Spiegel, P. (1998). *Ethics in psychology: Professional standards and cases* (2nd ed.). New York: Oxford University Press.

Krueger, R. F., Caspi, A., & Moffitt, T. E. (2000). Epidemiological personology: The unifying role of personality in population-based research on problem behaviors. *Journal of Personality, 68*, 967–998.

Lamiell, J. T. (1997). Individuals and the difference between them. In R. Hogan, J. Johnson, & S. Briggs (Eds.), *Handbook of personality psychology* (pp. 117–141). San Diego, CA: Academic Press.

Lanyon, R. I., & Goodstein, L. D. (1997). *Personality assessment* (3rd ed.). New York: John Wiley.

Leenaars, A. A. (1989). *Suicide notes: Predictive clues and patterns*. New York: Human Sciences.

Lester, D., & Linn, M. (1998). The content of suicide notes written by those using different methods of suicide. *Perceptual and Motor Skills, 87*, 722.

Levy, L. H. (1970). *Conceptions of personality*. New York: Random House.

Lewis, M. (1999). On the development of personality. In L. A. Pervin & O. P. John (Eds.), *Handbook of personality: Theory and research* (2nd ed., pp. 327–346). New York: Guilford Press.

Mazlish, B. (1973). *In search of Nixon*. Baltimore: Penguin.

McAdams, D. P. (1992). The Five-Factor Model of personality: A critical appraisal. *Journal of Personality, 60*, 329–361.

McAdams, D. P. (1997). A conceptual history of personality psychology. In R. Hogan, J. Johnson, & S. Briggs (Eds.), *Handbook of personality psychology* (pp. 3–39). San Diego, CA: Academic Press.

McClelland, D. C. (1951). *Personality*. New York: Dryden Press.

Megargee, E. I. (2006). *Use of the MMPI-2 in correctional settings* In J. N. Butcher (Ed.), *MMPI-2: A practioner's guide* (pp. 327–360). Washington, DC: American Psychological Association.

Midlarsky, E., Jones, S. F., & Corley, R. P. (2005). Personality correlates of heroic rescue during the Holocaust. *Journal of Personality, 73*, 907–934.

Millon, T., & Grossman, S. D. (2006). Goals of a theory of personality. In J. C. Thomas & D. L. Segal (Eds.), *Comprehensive handbook of personality and psychopathology: Vol. 1. Personality and everyday functioning* (pp. 3–22). Hoboken, NJ: John Wiley.

Mischel, W. (1999). *Introduction to personality* (6th ed.). Forth Worth, TX: Harcourt Brace College.

Nass, C., & Lee, K. M. (2001). Does computer-synthesized speech manifest personality? Experimental tests of recognition, similarity-attraction, and consistency-attraction. *Journal of Experimental Psychology: Applied, 7*, 171–181.

Nelson, R. J. (Ed.). (2006). *Biology of aggression*. New York: Oxford University Press.

Neuman, G. A., & Kickul, J. R. (1998). Organizational citizenship behaviors: Achievement orientation and personality. *Journal of Business and Psychology, 13*, 263–279.

Nicol, A. A. M., & Paunonen, S. V. (2002). Validity evidence for the different items styles of overt honesty measures. *Journal of Business and Psychology, 16*, 431–445.

Ones, D., & Viswesvaran, C. (2001). Personality at work: Criterion-focused occupational personality scales used in personnel selection. In B. W. Roberts & R. Hogan (Eds.), *Personality psychology in the workplace* (pp. 63–92). Washington, DC: American Psychological Association.

Ortmann, A., & Hertwig, R. (1998). The question remains: Is deception acceptable? *American Psychologist, 53*, 806–807.

Papalia, D. E., Olds, S. W., & Feldman, R. D. (2001). *Human development* (8th ed.). Boston: McGraw-Hill.

Pervin, L. A. (1990). *Handbook of personality: Theory and research*. New York: Guilford Press.

Pervin, L. A. (2002). *Current controversies and issues in personality* (3rd ed.). New York: John Wiley.

Pervin, L. A., & John, O. P. (2001). *Personality: Theory and research* (8th ed.). New York: John Wiley.

Plomin, R. (Ed.). (2002). *Behavioral genetics in the postgenomic era*. Washington, DC: American Psychological Association.

Plomin, R., & Crabbe, J. (2002). DNA. *Psychological Bulletin, 126*, 806–828.

Roberts, B. R., & Caspi, A. (2003). The cumulative continuity model of personality development: Striking a balance between continuity and change in personality traits across the life course. In D. M. Staudinger & U. Lindenberger (Eds.), *Understanding human developmental lifespan psychology in exchange with other disciplines* (pp. 183–214). Dordrecht, Netherlands: Kluwer.

Rogers, R. W. (1980). *Subjects' reactions to experimental deception*. Unpublished manuscript, University of Alabama.

Rosenthal, R. (1966). *Experimenter effects in behavior research*. New York: Appleton-Century-Crofts.

Rosenthal, R. (1969). Interpersonal expectations: Effects of the experimenter's hypothesis. In R. Rosenthal & R. L. Rosnow (Eds.), *Artifacts in behavioral research* (pp. 181–277). New York: Academic Press.

Runyan, W. K. (2006). Psychobiography and the psychology of science: Understanding relations between the life and work of individual psychologists. *Review of General Psychology, 10*, 147–162.

Sales, B. D., & Folkman, S. (Eds.). (2000) *Ethics in research with human participants*. Washington, DC: American Psychological Association.

Schmidt, F. L., & Hunter, J. E. (1998). The validity and utility of selection methods in personnel psychology: Practical and theoretical implications of 85 years of research findings. *Psychological Bulletin, 124*, 262–274.

Schulze, R., Holling, H., & Böhning, D. (Eds.). (2003). *Meta-analysis: New developments and applications in medical and social sciences*. Cambridge, MA: Hogrefe & Huber.

Shaffer, D. R., & Kipp, K. (2007). *Developmental psychology: Childhood and adolescence* (7th ed.). Belmont, CA: Thomson Learning.

Simonton, D. K. (1999). Creativity and genius. In L. A. Pervin & O. P. (Eds.), *Handbook of personality: Theory and research* (2nd ed., pp. 629–652). New York: Guilford Press.

Smith, S., & Richardson, D. (1983). Amelioration of deception and harm in psychological research: The important role of debriefing. *Journal of Personality and Social Psychology, 44*, 1075–1082.

Sommers, J. A., Schell, T. L., & Vodanovich, S. J. (2002). Developing measures of individual differences in organizational revenge. *Journal of Business and Psychology, 17*, 207–222.

Sommers-Flanagan, J., & Sommers-Flanagan, R. (2004). *Counseling and psychotherapy theories in context and practice: Skills, strategies, and techniques*. Hoboken, NJ: John Wiley.

Stirman, S. W., & Pennebaker, J. W. (2001). Words used in the poetry of suicidal and nonsuicidal poets. *Psychosomatic Medicine, 63*, 517–522.

Stritzke, W. G. K., Nguyen, A., & Durkin, K. (2004). Shyness and computer-mediated communication: A self-presentation theory perspective. *Media Psychology, 6*, 1–22.

Therivel, W. A (1998). Creative genius and the GMA theory of personality: Why Mozart and not Salieri? *Journal of Personality and Social Behavior, 13*, 201–234.

Timmerman, T. A. (1997). A closer look at the personality characteristics of outplaced executives. *Journal of Business and Psychology, 12*, 55–66.

Torgerson, C. (2003). *Systematic reviews and meta-analysis*. London: Continuum International.

Trull, T. J., & Phares, E. J. (2001). *Clinical psychology: Concepts, methods, and profession* (6th ed.). Belmont, CA: Wadsworth/Thomson Learning.

Tuckman, J., Kleiner, R., & Lavell, M. (1959). Emotional content of suicide notes. *American Journal of Psychiatry, 116*, 59–63.

Turner, S. M., DeMers, S. T., Fox, H. R., & Reed, G. M. (2001). APA's guidelines for test user qualifications: An executive summary. *American Psychologists, 56*, 1099–1112.

Von Emster, G. R., & Harrison, A. A. (1998). Role ambiguity, spheres of control, burnout, and work-related attitudes of teleservice professionals. *Journal of Social Behavior and Personality, 13*, 375–385.

Webley, P., Burgoyne, C. B., Lea, S. E. G., & Young, B. M. (2001). *The economic psychology of everyday life*. Philadelphia, PA: Taylor & Francis.

Wiggins, J. S. (1999). In defense of traits. In R. Hogan, J. Johnson, & S. Briggs (Eds.), *Handbook of personality psychology* (pp. 95–115). San Diego, CA: Academic Press.

Winter, D. C., & Barenbaum, N. B. (1999). History of modern personality theory and research. In L. A. Pervin & O. P. John (Eds.), *Handbook of personality theory and research* (2nd ed., pp. 3–27). New York: Guilford Press.

Wong, A., & Carducci, B. J. (1991). Sensation seeking and finicial risk taking in everyday money matters. *Journal of Business and Psychology, 5*, 525–530.

Wrightsman, L. S. (2001). *Forensic psychology*. Belmont, CA: Wadsworth.

Wrightsman, L. S., Greene, E., Nietzel, M. T., & Fortune, W. H. (2002). *Psychology and the legal system* (5th ed.). Belmont, CA: Wadsworth.

Zillmer, E. A., Harrower, M., Ritzler, B. A., & Archer, R. P. (1995). *The quest for the Nazi personality: A psychological investigation of Nazi war criminals*. Hillsdale, NJ: Erlbaum.

Zuckerman, M. (2006). Biosocial bases of sensation seeking. In T. Canli (Ed.), *Biology of personality and individual differences* (pp. 37–59). New York: Guilford Press.

Chapter 2

Adler, T. (1993). Separate gender norms on tests raise questions. *APA Monitor, 24*, 6.

Adorno, T. W., Frenkel-Brunswick, E., Levinson, D. J., & Sanford, R. N. (1950). *The authoritarian personality*. New York: Harper & Row.

Aiken, L. R. (2003). *Psychological testing and assessment* (11th ed). Boston: Pearson Education.

Aiken, L. R., & Groth-Marnat, G. (2006). *Psychological testing and assessment* (12th ed.). New York: Pearson/Allyn & Bacon.

Ambady, N., Chiao, J. Y., Chiu, P., & Deldin, P. (2006). Race and emotion: Insights from a social neuroscience perspective. In J. T. Cacioppo, P. S. Visser, & C. L. Pickett (Eds.), *Social neuroscience: *People thinking about thinking people* (pp. 209–227). Cambridge, MA: MIT Press.

American Psychological Association. (1981). Ethical principles of psychologists. *American Psychologists, 36,* 633–638.

American Psychological Association. (1986). *American Psychological Association guidelines for computer-based tests and interpretation.* Washington, DC: Author.

American Psychological Association. (1990). Ethical principles of psychologists (Amended June 2, 1989). *American Psychologists, 45,* 390–395.

American Psychological Association. (1999). *The Standards for Educational and Psychological Testing.* (Effective date June 1, 2003.) Retrieved from www.apa.org/science/standards.html.

American Psychological Association. (1992). APA continues to refine its ethics code. *The APA Monitor, 23,* 38–42.

American Psychological Association. (2000). Test security: Protecting the integrity of test. *American Psychologist, 54,* 1078.

American Psychological Association. (2002). *Ethical principles of psychologists and code of conduct* (Effective date June 1, 2003). Retrieved from www.apa.org/ethics/code2002.html.

American Psychological Association, Committee on Professional Standards and Committee on Psychological Tests and Assessment. (1986). *Guidelines for computer-based tests and interpretations.* Washington, DC: Author.

Anastasi, A., & Urbina, S. (1997). *Psychological testing* (7th ed.). Upper Saddle River, NJ: Prentice Hall.

Aron, A., Fisher, H., Mashek, D. J., Strong, G., Li., H., & Brown, L. L. (2005). Reward, motivation, and emotional systems associated with early-stage intense romantic love. *Journal of Neurophysiology, 94,* 327–337.

Association of Test Publishers. (1996). *Model guidelines for preemployment integrity testing programs.* Washington, DC: Author.

Atlis, M. M., Hahn, J., & Butcher, J. N. (2006). Computer-based assessment with the MMPI-2. In J. M. Butcher (Ed.), *MMPI-2: A practitioner's guide.* Washington, DC: American Psychological Association.

Beck, A. T., Brown, G., Berchick, R. J., Stewart, B. L., & Steer, R. A. (1990). Relationship between hopelessness and ultimate suicide: A replication with psychiatric outpatients. *American Journal of Psychiatry, 147,* 190–195.

Benjamin, J., Ebstein, R. P., & Belmaker, R. H. (Eds.). (2002). *Molecular genetics and the human personality.* Washington, DC: American Psychiatric Publishing.

Brannon, L., & Feist, J. (2000). *Health psychology: An introduction to behavior and health* (4th ed.). Belmont, CA: Wadsworth/Thomson Learning.

Breiter, H. C., Gollub, R. L., Weisskoff, R. M., Kennedy, D. N., Makris, N., Berke, J. D., et al. (1997). Acute effects of cocaine on human brain activity and emotion. *Neuron, 19,* 591–611.

Briggs, S. R., & Cheek, J. M. (1988). On the nature of self-monitoring: Problems with assessment, problems with validity. *Journal of Personality and Social Psychology, 54,* 663–678.

Briggs, S. R., Cheek, J. M., & Buss, A. H. (1980). An analysis of the self-monitoring scale. *Journal of Personality and Social Psychology, 38,* 679–686.

Burger, J. M. (2004). *Personality* (6th ed.). Belmont, CA: Wadsworth/Thomson Learning.

Burns, R. C. (1987). *Kinetic-House-Tree-Person (K-HT-P).* New York: Brunner/Mazel.

Butcher, J. N. (1990). *Assessing patients in psychotherapy: Use of the MMPI-2 for treatment planning.* New York: Oxford University Press.

Butcher, J. N. (2003). *The Minnesota Report: Adult clinical system – revised* (4th ed.). Minneapolis: Regents of the University of Minnesota.

Butcher, J. N. (Ed.). (2006). *MMPI-2: A practitioner's guide.* Washington, DC: American Psychological Association.

Butcher, J. N., Dahlstrom, W. G., Graham, J. R., Tellegen, A., & Kaemmer, B. (1989). *Minnesota Multiphasic Personality Inventory-2 (MMPI-2): Manual for administration and scoring.* Minneapolis: University of Minnesota Press.

Butcher, J. N., Mosch, S. C., Tsai, J., & Nezami, E. (2006). Cross-cultural applications of the MMPI-2. In J. N. Butcher (Ed.), *MMPI-2: A practitioner's guide* (pp. 505–537). Washington, DC: American Psychological Association.

Cacioppo, J. T., Berntson, G. G., & Crites, Jr. (1996). Social neuroscience: Principles of psychophysiological arousal and response. In E. T. Higgins & A. W. Kruglanski (Eds.), *Social psychology: Handbook of basic principles* (pp. 72–101). New York: Guilford Press.

Cacioppo, J. T., Ernst, J. M., Burleson, M. H., McClintock, M. K., Malarkey, W. B., Hawkley, L. C., et al. (2002). Lonely traits and concomitant physiological processes: The MacArthur social neuroscience studies. In J. T. Cacioppo, G. G. Bertson, R. Adolphs, C. S. Carter, R. J. Davidson, M. K. McClintock, et al. (Eds.), *Foundations in social neuroscience* (pp. 839–852). Cambridge, MA: MIT Press.

Cacioppo, J. T., Visser, P. S., & Pickett, C. L. (Eds.). (2006). *Social neuroscience: People thinking about thinking people.* Cambridge, MA: MIT Press.

Canli, T. (Ed.). (2006). *Biology of personality and individual differences.* New York: Guilford Press.

Carducci, B. J. (2000). *Shyness: A bold new approach.* New York: HarperCollins.

Carducci, B. J. (2005). *The shyness workbook: 30 days to dealing effectively with shyness.* Champaign, IL: Research Press.

Carducci, B. J., & Webber, A. W. (1979). Shyness as a determinant of interpersonal distance. *Psychological Reports, 44,* 1075–1078.

Cascio, W. F. (2003). Changes in workers, work, and organizations. In W. C. Borman, D. R. Ilgen, & R. J. Klimoski (Eds.), *Handbook of psychology: Vol. 12. Industrial and organizational psychology* (pp. 401–422). Hoboken, NJ: John Wiley & Sons.

Cash, T. F., & Pruzinsky, T. (Eds.). (1990). *Body images: Development, deviance, and change.* New York: Guilford Press.

Coggins, M. H., Pynchon, M. R., & Dvoskin, J. A. (1998). Integrating research and practice in federal law enforcement: Secret Service applications of behavioral science expertise to protect the president. *Behavioral Sciences and the Law, 16,* 51–70.

Cohen, R. J., & Swerdlik, M. E. (2002). *Psychological testing and assessment: An introduction to tests and measurement* (5th ed.). Boston: McGraw-Hill.

Comer, R. J. (2007). *Abnormal psychology* (6th ed.). New York: Worth.

Costa, P. T., Jr., & McCrae, R. R. (1992). *Revised NEO Personality Inventory (NEO-PI-R) and NEO Five-Factor Inventory (NEO-FFI) professional manual.* Odessa, FL: Psychological Assessment Resources.

Costa, P. T., Jr., & McCrae, R. R. (1998). The Revised NEO Personality Inventory (NEO-PI-R). In S. R. Briggs, J. M. Cheek, & E. M. Donahue (Eds.), *Handbook of adult personality inventories.* New York: Plenum.

Craig, R. J. (2005). *Personality-guided forensic psychology.* Washington, DC: American Psychological Association.

Cronbach, L. J., & Meehl, P. E. (1955). Construct validity in psychological tests. *Psychological Bulletin, 52,* 281–302.

Dabbs, J. M. (2000). *Heroes, rogues, and lovers: Testosterone and behavior.* New York: McGraw-Hill.

Dahlstrom, W. G., & Welsh, G. S. (1960). *An MMPI handbook: A guide to use in clinical practice and research.* Minneapolis: University of Minnesota Press.

Dahlstrom, W. G., Welsh, G. S., & Dahlstrom, L. E. (1972). *An MMPI handbook: Vol. 1. Clinical interpretation* (rev. ed.). Minneapolis: University of Minnesota Press.

Dahlstrom, W. G., Welsh, G. S., & Dahlstrom, L. E. (1975). *An MMPI handbook: Vol. 2. Research applications* (rev. ed.). Minneapolis: University of Minnesota Press.

Davidson, R. J., & Irwin, W. (2002). The functional neuroanatomy of emotion and affective style. In J. T. Cacioppo, G. G. Bertson, R. Adolphs, C. S. Carter, R. J. Davidson, M. K. McClintock, et al. (Eds.), *Foundations in social neuroscience* (pp. 473–490). Cambridge, MA: MIT Press.

Diener, E. (2000). Subjective well-being: The science of happiness and a proposal for a national index. *American Psychologist, 55,* 34–43.

Drumheller, P. M., Eicke, F. J., & Scherer, R. F. (1991). Cognitive appraisal and coping of students varying in stress level during three stages of a college examination. *Journal of Social Behavior and Personality, 6,* 237–254.

Edwards, A. L. (1954). *Manual for the Edwards Personal Preference Schedule.* New York: Psychological Corporation.

Edwards, A. L. (1959). *Edwards Personal Preference Schedule.* New York: Psychological Corporation.

Elliot, R., Newman, J. L., Longe, O. A., & Deakin, J. F. (2003). Differential response patterns in the striatum and orbitofrontal cortex to financial reward in humans: A parametric functional magnetic resonance imagining study. *Journal of Neuroscience, 23,* 303–307.

Eysenck, H. J. (1990). Biological dimensions of personality. In L. A. Pervin (Ed.), *Handbook of personality: Theory and research* (pp. 244–276). New York: Guilford Press.

Fisher, H. E. (1998). Lust, attraction, and attachment in mammalian reproduction. *Human Nature, 9,* 23–52.

Frank, L. K. (1939). Projective methods for the study of personality. *Journal of Psychology, 8,* 389–413.

Gable, M., & Topol, M. T. (1991). Machiavellian managers: Do they perform better? *Journal of Bussiness and Psychology, 5,* 355–365.

Geen, R. G. (1997). Psychophysiological approaches to personality. In R. Hogan, J. Johnson, & S. Briggs (Eds.), *Handbook of personality psychology* (pp. 387–414). San Diego, CA: Academic Press.

Geer, J. H. (1965). The development of a scale to measure fear. *Behavior Research and Therapy, 3,* 45–53.

Gilbert, D. G., Gilbert, B. O., Johnson, S., & McColloch, M. A. (1991). Electrocortical and electrodermal activity differences between aggressive adolescents and controls. *Journal of Social Behavior and Personality, 6,* 403–410.

Girodo, M. (1991). Personality, job stress, and mental health in undercover agents. *Journal of Social Behavior and Personality, 6,* 375–390.

Gladding, S. T. (2003). *Counseling: A comprehensive profession* (5th ed.). Upper Saddle River, NJ: Pearson Education.

Goodman-Delahunty, J., Forsterlee, L., & Forsterlee, R. (2005). Dealing with the guilty offender. In N. Brewer & K. D. Williams (Eds.), *Psychology and the law: An empirical perspective* (pp. 445–482). New York: Guilford Press.

Gough, H. G. (1957). *California psychological inventory.* Palo Alto, CA: Consulting Psychologists Press.

Gough, H. G. (1987). *California psychological inventory: Administrator's guide.* Palo Alto, CA: Consulting Psychologists Press.

Graham, J. R. (1990). *MMPI-2: Assessing personality and pathology.* New York: Oxford University Press.

Graham, J. R. (2006). *MMPI-2: Assessing personality and pathology* (4th ed.). New York: Oxford University Press.

Granhag, P. A., & Vrij, A. (2005). Deception detection. In N. Brewer & K. D. Williams (Eds.), *Psychology and law: An empirical perspective* (pp. 43–92). New York: Guilford Press.

Gray-Little, B. (2002). The assessment of psychopathology in racial and ethic minorities. In J. M. Butcher (Ed.), *Clinical personality assessment: Practical approaches* (2nd ed., pp. 171–189). New York: Oxford University Press.

Gray-Little, B., & Kaplan, D. A. (1998). Interpretation of psychological tests in clinical and forensic evaluations. In J. Sandoval, C. L. Frisby, K. F. Geisinger, J. D. Scheuneman, & J. R. Grenier (Eds.), *Test interpretation and diversity: Achieving equity in assessment* (pp. 141–178). Washington, DC: American Psychological Association.

Gross, J. J. (1999). Emotion and emotion regulation. In L. A. Pervin & O. P. John (Eds.), *Handbook of personality: Theory and research* (2nd ed., pp. 525–552). New York: Guilford Press.

Groth-Marnat, G. (1990). *Handbook of psychological assessment* (2nd ed.). New York: John Wiley.

Groth-Marnat, G. (2003). *Handbook of psychological assessment* (electronic book version, 4th. ed.). Hoboken, NJ: John Wiley.

Handler, L., & Clemence, A. J. (2003). Educational and training in psychological assessment. In J. R. Graham & J. A. Naglieri (Eds.), *Handbook of psychology: Vol. 10. Assessment psychology* (pp. 181–209). Hoboken, NJ: John Wiley.

Hansen, C. P. (1991). Personality characteristics of the accident-involved employee. In J. W. Jones, B. D. Steffy, & D. W. Bray (Eds.), *Applying psychology in business: The handbook for managers and human resource professionals* (pp. 801–812). Lexington, MA: Lexington Books.

Hatfield, E., & Sprecher, S. (1986). Measuring passionate love in intimate relationships. *Journal of Adolescence, 9,* 383–410.

Hathaway, S. R., & McKinley, J. C. (1940). A multiphasic personality schedule (Minnesota): I. Construction of the schedule. *Journal of Psychology, 10,* 249–254.

Hathaway, S. R., & McKinley, J. C., (1943). *Manual for the Minnesota multiphasic personality inventory.* New York: Psychological Corporation.

Hathaway, S. R., & Meehl, P. E. (1951). *An atlas for the clinical use of the MMPI.* Minneapolis: University of Minnesota Press.

Herrington, J. D., Mohanty, A., Koven, N. S., Fisher, J. E., Stewart, J. L., Banich, M., et al. (2005). Emotion-modulated performance and activity in left dorsolateral refrontal cortex. *Emotion, 5,* 200–207.

Hollon, S. D., & Kendall, P. C. (1980). Cognitive self-statements in depression: Development of an Automatic Thoughts Questionnaire. *Cognitive Therapy and Research, 4,* 383–395.

Hough, L. M., & Furnham, A. (2003). Use of personality variables in work settings. In W. C. Borman, D. R. Ilgen, & R. J. Klimoski (Eds.), *Handbook of psychology: Vol. 12. Industrial and organizational psychology* (pp. 131–169). Hoboken, NJ: John Wiley.

Ito, T. A., Larsen, J. T., Smith, N. K., & Cacioppo, J. T. (2002). Negative information weighs more heavily on the brain: The negativity bias in evaluative categorizations. In J. T. Cacioppo, G. G. Bertson, R. Adolphs, C. S. Carter, R. J. Davidson, M. K. McClintock, et al. (Eds.), *Foundations in social neuroscience* (pp. 575–597). Cambridge, MA: MIT Press.

Jones, J. W., & Terris, W. (1983). Predicting employees' theft in home improvement centers. *Psychological Reports, 52,* 187–201.

Jones, J. W., & Terris, W. (1991). Personnel selection to control employee theft and counterproductivity. In J. W. Jones, B. D. Steffy, & D. W. Bray (Eds.), *Applying psychology in business: The handbook for managers and human resource professionals* (pp. 851–861). Lexington, MA: Lexington Books.

Jones, J. W., & Wuebker, L. (1984, April). *Development and validation of the Safety Locus of Control (SLC) Scale.* Paper presented at the American Industrial Hygiene Association Research Conference, Upper Midwest Section, Roseville, MN.

Kleinmuntz, B. (1982). *Personality and psychological assessment.* New York: St. Martin's Press.

Koocher, G. P., & Rey-Casserly, C. M. (2003). Ethical issues in psychological assessment. In J. R. Graham & J. A. Naglieri (Eds.), *Handbook of psychology: Vol. 10. Assessment psychology* (pp. 165–180). Hoboken, NJ: John Wiley.

Kring, A. M., Davison, G. C., Neale, J. M., & Johnson, S. L. (2007). *Abnormal psychology* (10th ed.). Hoboken, NJ: John Wiley.

Lanyon, R. I., & Goodstein, L. D. (1997). *Personality assessment.* New York: John Wiley.

Larsen, R. J., Diener, E., & Cropanzano, R. S. (1987). Cognitive operations associated with individual differences in affect intensity. *Journal of Personality and Social Psychology, 53,* 767–774.

LeDoux, J. E. (2002). Fear and the brain: Where have we been, and where are we going? In J. T. Cacioppo, G. G. Bertson, R. Adolphs, C. S. Carter, R. J. Davidson, M. K. McClintock,

et al. (Eds.), *Foundations in social neuroscience* (pp. 411–423). Cambridge, MA: MIT Press.

Lieberman, M. D., & Eisenberger, N. I. (2006). A pain by any other name (rejection, exclusion, ostracism) still hurts the same: The role of dorsal anterior cingulated cortex in social and physical pain. In J. T. Cacioppo, P. S. Visser, & C. L. Pickett (Eds.), *Social neuroscience: People thinking about thinking people* (pp. 167–187). Cambridge, MA: MIT Press.

Lindzey, G. (1961). *Projective techniques and cross-cultural research.* New York: Appleton-Century-Crofts.

Matthews, G., Deary, I. J., & Whiteman, M. C. (2003). *Personality traits* (2nd ed.). New York: Cambridge University Press.

Messick, S. (1995). Validity of psychological assessment: Validation of inferences from person's responses and performances as scientific inquiry into score meaning. *American Psychologist, 50,* 741–749.

Mitchell, J. P., Mason, M. F., Macrae, C. N., & Banaji, M. R. (2006). Thinking about others: The neural substrates of social cognition. In J. T. Cacioppo, P. S. Visser, & C. L. Pickett (Eds.), *Social neuroscience: People thinking about thinking people* (pp. 63–82). Cambridge, MA: MIT Press.

Morgan, C. D., & Murray, H. A. (1935). A method for investigating fantasies: The Thematic Apperception Test. *Archives of Neurology and Psychiatry, 34,* 289–306.

Murphy, K. R., & Davidshofer, C. O. (2005). *Psychological testing: Principles and applications* (6th ed.). Upper Saddle River, NJ: Pearson Education.

Murray, C. B., Kaiser, R., & Taylor, S. (1997). The O. J. Simpson verdict: Predictors of beliefs about innocence or guilt. *Journal of Social Issues, 53,* 455–475.

Murray, H. A. (Ed.). (1938). *Explorations in personality.* New York: Oxford University Press.

Murray, H. A. (1943). *Thematic Apperception Test.* Cambridge, MA: Harvard University Press.

Myers, D. G. (1992). *The pursuit of happiness: Who is happy – and why.* New York: Morrow.

Myers, D. G. (2000). The funds, friends, and faith of happy people. *American Psychologist, 55,* 56–67.

Nevid, J. S., Rathus, S. A., & Greene, B. (2000). *Abnormal psychology in a changing world* (4th ed.). Upper Saddle River, NJ: Prentice Hall.

Nyborg, H. (Ed.). (1997). *The scientific study of human nature: Tribute to Hans J. Eysenck at eighty.* New York: Pergamon.

O'Brien, W. H., McGrath, J. J., & Haynes, S. N. (2003). Assessment of psychopathology with behavioral approaches. In J. R. Graham & J. A. Naglieri (Eds.), *Handbook of psychology: Vol. 10. Assessment psychology* (pp. 509–529). Hoboken, NJ: John Wiley.

Okazaki, S., Kallivayalil, D., & Sue, S. (2002). Clinical personality assessment with Asian Americans. In J. M. Butcher (Ed.), *Clinical personality assessment: Practical approaches* (2nd ed., pp. 135–153). New York: Oxford University Press.

Osborne, R. E. (1996). *Self: An eclectic approach.* Boston: Allyn & Bacon.

Otten, K. L. (2004). An analysis of a classwide self-monitoring approach to improve the behavior of elementary students with severe emotional and behavioral problems [abstract].

Dissertation Abstracts International: Section A: Humanities and Social Sciences, 65, 893.

Pilkonis, P. A. (1977). The behavioral consequences of shyness. *Journal of Personality, 45,* 596–611.

Pine, D. S. (2005). Editorial: Where have all the clinical trials gone? *Journal of Child Psychology and Psychiatry, 46,* 449–450.

Plante, T. G. (2005). *Contemporary clinical psychology* (2nd ed.). Hoboken, NJ: John Wiley.

Plomin, R., & Caspi, A. (1999). Behavior genetics and personality. In L. A. Pervin & O. P. John (Eds.), *Handbook of personality: Theory and research* (pp. 251–276). New York: Guilford Press.

Plomin, R., DeFries, J. C., McClearn, G. E., & McGuffin, P. (2001). *Behavioral genetics* (4th ed.). New York: Worth.

Pope, K. S., Butcher, J. M., & Seelen, J. (2000). *The MMPI, MMPI-2, and the MMPI-A in court: A practical guide for expert witnesses and attorneys* (2nd ed.). Washington, DC: American Psychological Association.

Puce, A., & Perrett, D. (2004). Electrophysiology and brain imagining of biological motion. In C. D. Frith & D. M. Wolpert (Eds.), *The neuroscience of social interaction: Decoding, imitiating, and influencing the actions of others* (pp. 1–21). New York: Oxford University Press.

Raine, A., Lencz, T., Bihrle, S., & LaCasse, L. (2000). Reduced prefrontal gray matter volume and reduced autonomic activity in antisocial personality disorder. *Archives of General Psychiatry, 57,* 119–127.

Reynolds, C. R., & Ramsey, M. C. (2003). Bias in psychological assessment: An empirical review and recommendations. In J. R. Graham & J. A. Naglieri (Eds.), *Handbook of psychology: Vol. 10. Assessment psychology* (pp. 67–93). Hoboken, NJ: John Wiley.

Riggio, R. E. (2002*). Introduction to industrial/organizational psychology* (4th ed.). Old Tappan, NJ: Prentice Hall.

Riordan, C. A., Johnson, G. D., & Thomas, J. S. (1991). Personality and stress at sea. *Journal of Social Behavior and Personality, 6,* 391–409.

Rorschach, H. (1942). *Psychodiagnostics.* Berne, Switzerland: Huber.

Rotter, J. B. (1954). *Social learning and clinical psychology.* Englewood Cliffs, NJ: Prentice Hall.

Rotter, J. B., Lah, M. I., & Rafferty, J. E. (1992*). Rotter incomplete sentences blank: Manual* (2nd ed.). San Antonio, TX: Psychological Corporation.

Rotter, J. B., & Rafferty, J. E. (1950). *Manual for the Rotter incomplete sentences blank, college form.* New York: Psychological Corporation.

Rowe, D. C. (1997). Genetics, temperament, and personality. In R. Hogan, J. Johnson, & S. Briggs (Eds.), *Handbook of personality* (pp. 367–386). San Diego, CA: Academic Press.

Sackett, P. R., & Wanek, J. E. (1996). New developments in the use of measures of honesty, integrity, conscientiousness, dependability, trustworthiness, and reliability for personnel selection. *Personnel Psychology, 46,* 613–627.

Schmitt, N., Cortina, J. M., Ingerick, M. J., & Wiechmann, D. (2003). Personnel selection and employee performance. In W. C. Borman, D. R. Ilgen, & R. J. Klimoski (Eds.), *Handbook*

of psychology: Vol. 12. Industrial and organizational psychology (pp. 77–105). Hoboken, NJ: John Wiley.

Sherry, P. (1991). Person–environment fit and accident prediction. *Journal of Business and Psychology, 5,* 411–416.

Sinha, R. (2006). Sex differences in brain functional magnetic resonance imagining response to stress. In T. Canli (Ed.), *Biology of personality and individual differences* (pp. 203–222). New York: Guilford Press.

Slora, K. B., Joy, D. S., & Terris, W. (1991). Personnel selection to control employee violence. *Journal of Business and Psychology, 5,* 417–426.

Small, D. M., Zatorre, R. J., Dagher, A., Evans, A. C., & Jones-Gotman, M. (2001). Changes in brain activity related to eating chocolate: From pleasure to aversion. *Brain, 124,* 1720–1733. University Press.

Snyder, M. (1974). The self-monitoring of expressive behavior. *Journal of Personality and Social Psychology, 30,* 526–537.

Snyder, M. (1987). *Public appearances/private realities: The psychology of self-monitoring.* New York: Freeman.

Stafford, K. O., & Ben-Porath, Y. S. (2002). Assessing criminal responsibility. In J. N. Butcher (Ed.), *Clinical personality assessment: Practical approaches* (pp. 452–465). New York: Oxford

Stern, R. M., Ray, W. J., & Quigley, K. S. (2001). *Psychophysiological recording* (2nd ed.) New York: Oxford University Press.

Szondi, L. (1944). *Schicksalsanalyse.* Basel, Switzerland: Benno/Schwabe.

Taylor, S. E., Klein, L. C., Lewis, B. P., Gruenewald, T. L., Gurung, R. A. R., & Updegraff, J. A. (2002). Biobehavioral responses to stress in females: Tend-and-befriend, not fight-or-flight. In J. T. Cacioppo, G. G. Bertson, R. Adolphs, C. S. Carter, R. J. Davidson, M. K. McClintock, et al. (Eds.), *Foundations in social neuroscience* (pp. 661–693). Cambridge, MA: MIT Press.

Terris, W., & Jones, J. W. (1985). Psychological factors related to employees' theft in the convenience story industry. In W. Terris (Ed.), *Employee theft: Research, theory, and applications* (pp. 25–47). Park Ridge, IL: London House Press.

Thompson, A. E. (1986). An object relational theory of affect maturity: Applications to the Thematic Apperception Test. In M. Kissen (Ed.), *Assessing object relations phenomena* (pp. 207–224). Madison, CT: International Universities.

Tooby, J., & Cosmides, L. (2005). Conceptual foundations of evolutionary psychology. In D. M. Buss (Ed.), *The handbook of evolutionary psychology* (pp. 5–67). Hobooken, NJ: John Wiley.

Trull, T. J., & Phares, E. J. (2001). *Clinical psychology: Concepts, methods, and profession* (6th ed.). Belmont, CA: Wadsworth/Thomson Learning.

Velásquez, R. J., Maness, P. J., & Anderson, U. (2002). Culturally competent assessment of Latino clients: The MMPI-2. In J. M. Butcher (Ed.), *Clinical personality assessment: Practical approaches* (2nd ed., pp. 154–170). New York: Oxford University Press.

Viglione, D. J., & Rivera, B. (2003). Assessing personality and psychopathology with projective methods. In J. R. Graham &

J. A. Naglieri (Eds.), *Handbook of psychology: Vol. 10. Assessment psychology* (pp. 531–552). Hoboken, NJ: John Wiley.

Walters, G. D., Revella, L., & Baltrusaitis, W. J., II. (1990). Predicting parole/probation outcome with the aid of the Lifestyle Criminality Screening form. *Psychological Assessment, 2,* 313–316.

Westen, D., Barends, A., Leigh, J., Mendel, M., & Silbert, D. (1988). *Manual for dimensions of object relations and social cognition from interview data.* Unpublished manuscript, University of Michigan.

Wolpe, J., & Lang, P. J. (1964). A fear survey schedule for use in behavior therapy. *Behavior Research and Therapy, 2,* 27–34.

Wrightsman, L. S., Greene, E., Nietzel, M. T., & Fortune, W. H. (2002). *Psychology and the legal system* (5th ed.). Belmont, CA: Wadsworth.

Zillmer, E. A., Harrower, M., Ritzler, B. A., & Archer, R. P. (1995). *The quest for the Nazi personality: A psychological investigation of Nazi war criminals.* Hillsdale, NJ: Erlbaum.

Zimbardo, P. G. (1974). *Stanford survey on shyness.* Unpublished survey, Department of Psychology, Stanford University.

Zimbardo, P. G. (1977). *Shyness: What it is, what to do about it.* Reading, MA: Addison Wesley.

Zuckerman, M. (1991). *Psychobiology of personality.* New York: Cambridge University Press.

Zuckerman, M. (1994). *Behavioral expression and biosocial bases of sensation seeking.* New York: Cambridge University Press.

Zuckerman, M. (1995). Good and bad humors: Biochemical bases of personality and its disorders. *Psychological Science, 6,* 325–332.

Zuckerman, M. (1997). The psychobiological basis of personality. In H. Nyborg (Ed.), *The scientific study of human nature: Tribute to Hans J. Eysenck at eighty* (pp. 3–16). New York: Pergamon.

Zuckerman, M. (1998). Psychobiological theories of personality. In D. F. Barone, M. Hersen, & V. B. Van Hasselt (Eds.), *Advanced personality* (pp. 123–154). New York: Plenum.

Zuckerman, M. (2005). *Psychobiology of personality* (2nd ed, rev. and updated). New York: Cambridge University Press.

Chapter 3

Abrams, R. L., & Greenwald, A. G. (2000). Parts outweigh the whole (word) in unconscious analysis of meaning. *Psychological Science, 11,* 118–124.

Adler, J., Underwood, A., & Bain, M. (2006). Freud in our midst. *Newsweek, 147,* 42–49.

Ainsworth, M. D. S. (1979). Infant–mother attachment. *American Psychologist, 34,* 932–937.

Ainsworth, M. D. S., Blehar, M. C., Waters, E., & Wall, S. (1978). *Patterns of attachment: A psychological study of the strange situation.* Hillsdale, NJ: Erlbaum.

Alford, C. F. (1998). Freud and violence. In A. Elliot (Ed.), *Freud 2000* (pp. 61–87). New York: Routledge.

Anooshian, L. J., & Seibert, P. S. (1996). Conscious and unconscious retrieval in picture recognition: A framework for exploring gender differences. *Journal of Personality and Social Psychology, 70,* 637–645.

Apter, A., Plutchik, R., Sevy, S., Korn, M., Brown, S., & van Praag, H. (1989). Defense mechanism in risk of suicide and risk of violence. *American Journal of Psychiatry, 146,* 1027–1031.

Arlow, J. A. (1995). Psychoanalysis. In R. J. Corsini & D. Wedding (Eds.), *Current psychotherapies* (5th ed., pp. 15–50). Itasca, IL: F. E. Peacock.

Arlow, J. A. (2000). Psychoanalysis. In R. J. Corsini & D. Wedding (Eds.), *Current psychotherapies* (6th ed., pp. 16–53). Itasca, IL: F. E. Peacock.

Arnould, E., Price, L., & Zinkhan, G. (2002). *Consumers.* Boston: McGraw-Hill.

Aronson, E., Wilson. T. D., & Akert, R. M. (2002). *Social psychology* (4th ed.). Upper Saddle River, NJ: Prentice Hall.

Ball, J. D., & Peake, T. H. (2006). Brief psychotherapy in the U.S. Military. In C. H. Kennedy & J. A. McNeil (Eds.), *Military psychology: Clinical and operational applications* (pp. 61–73). New York: Guilford Press.

Baumeister, R. F., Dale, K., & Sommer, K. L. (1998). Freudian defense mechanisms and empirical findings in modern social psychology: Reaction formation, projection, displacement, undoing, isolation, sublimation, and denial. *Journal of Personality, 66,* 1061–1081.

Belsky, J., Spritz, B., & Crnic, K. (1996). Infant attachment security and affective-cognitive information processing at age 3. *Psychological Science, 7,* 111–114.

Bem, S. L. (1989). Genital knowledge and gender constancy in preschool children. *Child Development, 60,* 649–662.

Benjamin, L. T., Jr., & Dixon, D. N. (1996). Dream analysis by mail: An American woman seeks Freud's advice. *American Psychologist, 51,* 461–468.

Ben-Shakhar, G., Bar-Hillel, M., Bilu, Y., & Shefler, G. (1998). Seek and ye shall find: Test results are what you hypothesize they are. *Journal of Behavioral Decision Making, 11,* 235–249.

Berkowitz, E. N., Kerin, R. A., Hartley, S. W., & Rudelius, W. (2000). *Marketing* (6th ed.). Boston: Irwin/McGraw-Hill.

Berstell, G., & Nitterhouse, D. (1997). Looking "outside the box." *Marketing Research, 9,* 4–13.

Bibring, E. (1954). Psychoanalysis and the dynamic psychotherapies. *Journal of the American Psychoanalytic Association, 2,* 745–770.

Blum, G. S. (1949). A study of the psychoanalytic theory of psychosexual development. *Genetic Psychology Monograph, 39,* 3–99.

Blum, G. S. (1950). *The Blackey Pictures and manual.* New York: Psychological Corporation.

Blum, G. S. (1968). Assessment of psychodynamic variables by the Blacky Pictures. In P. McReynolds (Ed.), *Advances in psychological assessment: Vol. 1* (pp. 150–168). Palo Alto, CA: Science and Behavior Books.

Bornstein, R. F. (1996). Psychoanalytic research in the 1990s: Reclaiming what is ours. *Bulletin of the Psychoanalytic Research Society, 5,* 3–4.

Bornstein, R. F., & Masling, J. M. (Eds.). (1998a). *Empirical perspectives on the psychoanalytic unconscious.* Washington, DC: American Psychological Association.

Bornstein, R. F., & Masling, J. M. (Eds.). (1998b). *Empirical studies of the therapeutic hour.* Washington, DC: American Psychological Association.

Bowlby, J. (1982). Attachment and loss: Retrospect and prospect. *American Journal of Orthopsychiatry, 52,* 664–678.

Boyer, L. B., De Vos, G. A., & Boyer, R. M. (1989). Crisis and continuity in the personality of a shaman. In G. A. De Vos & L. B. Boyer, *Symbolic analysis cross-culturally: The Rorschach Test* (pp. 378–437). Berkeley: University of California Press.

Bragg, M., & Gardiner, R. (1999). *On giants' shoulders: Great scientists and their discoveries from Archimedes to DNA.* New York: John Wiley.

Brannon, L. A., & Brock, T. C (1994). The subliminal persuasion controversy. In S. Shavitt & T. C. Brock (Eds.), *Persuasion: Psychological insights and perspectives* (pp. 279–293). Needham Heights, MA: Allyn & Bacon.

Braum, K. A., Ellis, R., & Loftus, E. F. (2002). Make my memory: How advertising can change our memories of the past. *Psychology & Marketing, 19,* 1–23.

Brenner, C. (1955). *An elementary textbook of psychoanalysis.* New York: International Universities Press.

Brenner, C. (1973). *An elementary textbook of psychoanalysis* (rev. ed.). Madison, CT: International Universities Press.

Bretherton, I. (1985). Attachment theory: Retrospect and prospect. In I. Bretherton & E. Waters (Eds.), Growing points of attachment theory and research. *Monographs of the Society for Research in Child Development, 50* (1–2, Serial No. 209), 3–35.

Breuer, J. B., & Freud, S. (1955). Studies in hysteria. In *Standard edition: Vol. 2.* London: Hogarth Press. (Original work published 1895)

Bronstein, C. (Ed.). (2001). *Introduction to Kleinian psychoanalysis: A contemporary perspective.* London: Whurr.

Brown, J., & Richards, B. (1998). The humanistic Freud. In A. Elliot (Ed.), *Freud 2000* (pp. 233–261). New York: Routledge.

Butcher, J. N., Nezami, E., & Exner, J. E. (1998). Psychological assessment in cross-cultural settings. In S. Kazarian & D. R. Evans (Eds.), *Cultural clinical psychology: Theory, research, and practice* (pp. 61–105). New York: Oxford University Press.

Calabrese, M. L. (1998). *Object relations as they relate to adult attachment, intimacy, and self-esteem [Abstract]. Dissertation Abstracts International: Section B: The Sciences and Engineering, 59,* 3050.

Calabrese, M. L., Farber, B. A., & Westen, D. (2005). The relationship of adult attachment constructs to object relational patterns of representing self and others. *Journal of American Academy of Psychoanalysis and Dynamic Psychiatry, 33,* 513–530.

Camara, W., Nathan, J., & Puente, A. (1998). *Psychological tests usage in professional psychology: Report to the APA Practice and Science Directorates.* Washington, DC: American Psychological Association.

Cashdan, S. (1988). *Object relations theory: Using the relationship.* New York: Norton.

Cassidy, J., Kirsh, S. J., Scolton, K. L., & Parke, R. D. (1996). Attachment and representations of peer relationships. *Developmental Psychology, 32,* 892–904.

Chaplin, S. (2000). *The psychology of time and death.* Ashland, OH: Sonnet Press.

Chodorow, N. J. (1989). *Feminism and psychoanalytic theory.* New Haven, CT: Yale University Press.

Chu, J. A. (2000). "Memories of childhood abuse: Disassociation, amnesia, and collaboration": Reply. *American Journal of Psychiatry, 157,* 1348–1349.

Cohen, R. J., & Swerdlik, M. E. (1999). *Psychological testing and assessment: An introduction to tests and measurement* (4th ed.). Mountain View, CA: Mayfield.

Cohen, R. J., & Swerdlik, M. E. (2005). *Psychological testing and assessment: An introduction to tests and measurement* (6th ed.). Boston: McGraw-Hill.

Connolly, M. B., Crits-Cristoph, P., & Barber, J. P. (2000). Transference patterns in the therapeutic relationships in supportive-expressive psychotherapy for depression. *Psychotherapy Research, 10,* 356–372.

Contrada, R. J., & Guyll, M. (2001). On who gets sick and why: The role of personality and stress. In A. Baum, T. A. Reverson, & J. E. Singer (Eds.), *Handbook of health psychology* (pp. 59–84). Mahwah, NJ: Erlbaum.

Costanzo, K. M. (1996). *The connection between object relations, social support, social adjustment, and health.* Unpublished master's thesis, Harvard University, Cambridge, Massachusetts.

Craib, I. (2001). *Psychoanalysis: A critical introduction.* Cambridge, UK: Polity.

Craig, R. J. (1990). *Current utilization of psychological tests at diagnostic practicum sites.* Paper presented at the Annual Meeting of the Society for Personality Assessment, San Diego, CA.

Cramer, P. (2000). Defense mechanisms in psychology today: Further processes for adaptation. *American Psychologist, 55,* 637–646.

Cramer, P. (2001). The unconscious status of defense mechanism. *American Psychologist, 56,* 762–763.

Cramer, P. (2006). *Protecting the self: Defense mechanisms in action.* New York: Guilford Press.

Crenson, M. (1999, November 1). Science is taking the guesswork out of dreaming. *The Salt Lake Tribune,* p. A1.

Crews, F. (1996). The verdict on Freud [Review of *Freud evaluated: The complete arc*]. *Psychological Science, 7,* 63–68.

Crits-Christoph, P. (1992). The efficacy of brief dynamic psychotherapy: A meta-analysis. *The American Journal of Psychiatry, 149,* 151–158.

Cross, D. G., Sheehan, P. W., & Khan, J. A. (1982). Short- and long-term follow-up of clients receiving insight oriented therapy and behavior therapy. *Journal of Consulting and Clinical Psychology, 50,* 103–112.

Cummings, N. A. (1986). The dismantling of our health system: Strategies for the survival of psychological practice. *American Psychologist, 41,* 426–431

Davanloo, H. (1999). Intensive short-term dynamic psychotherapy-central dynamic sequence: Phase of challenge. *International Journal of Short-Term Dynamic Psychotherapy, 13,* 237–262.

Dawes, R. (1994). *House of cards: Psychology and psychotherapy built on myth.* New York: Free Press.

DeFleur, M. L., & Petranoff, R. M. (1959). A television test of subliminal persuasion. *Public Opinion Quarterly, 23,* 170–180.

Democrats smell a rat. (2000, September 13). *ABC News Online*. Retrieved September 13, 2000, from http://abcnews.go.com/sections/politics/DailyNews/gopad0000912.html.

De Vos, G. A., & Boyer, L. B. (1989). *Symbolic analysis cross-culturally: The Rorschach Test*. Berkeley: University of California Press.

Dichter, E. (1949). A psychological view of advertising effectiveness. *Journal of Marketing, 14*, 61–66.

Dichter, E. (1960). *The strategy of desire*. Garden City, NJ: Doubleday.

Dichter, E. (1964). *Handbook of consumer motivations*. New York: McGraw-Hill.

Dijksterhuis, A., Aarts, H., & Smith, P. K. (2005). The power of the subliminal: On subliminal persuasion and other potential applications. In R. R. Hassin, J. S. Uleman, & J. A. Bargh (Eds.), *The new unconscious* (pp. 77–106). New York: Oxford University Press.

Dixon, N. F. (1971). *Subliminal perception: The nature of a controversy*. London: McGraw-Hill.

Dixon, N. F. (1981). *Preconscious processing*. Chichester, UK: John Wiley.

Domhoff, G. W. (1999). Drawing theoretical implications from descriptive empirical findings on dream content. *Dreaming, 9*, 201–210.

Domhoff, G. W. (2003). *The scientific study of dreams: Neural network, cognitive development, and content analysis*. Washington, DC: American Psychological Association.

Drassinower, A. (2003). *Freud's theory of culture: Eros, loss, and politics*. Lanham, MD: Rowman & Littlefield.

Druckman, D., & Bjork, R. A. (Eds.). (1991). *In the mind's eye: Enhancing human performance*. Washington, DC: National Academy Press.

Eisenberger, N. I., & Lieberman, M. D. (2005). Broken hearts and broken bones: The neurocognitive overlap between social pain and physical pain. In K. D. Williams, J. P. Forgas, & W. von Hipple (Eds.), *The social outcast: Ostracism, social exclusion, rejection, and bullying* (pp. 109–127). New York: Cambridge University Press.

Elliott, A. (1999a). Freud, feminism, and postmodernism. In A. Elliott (Ed.), *Freud 2000* (pp. 88–109). New York: Routledge.

Elliott, A. (Ed.). (1999b). *Freud 2000*. New York: Routledge,

Elms, A. (2005). Freud as Leonardo: Why the first psychobiography went wrong. In W. T. Schultz (Ed.), *Handbook of psychobiography* (pp. 210–222). New York: Oxford University Press.

Engelman, E. (1976). *Berggrasse 19: Sigmund Freud's home and offices, Vienna 1938*. Chicago: University of Chicago Press.

Erdberg, P., & Exner, J. E., Jr. (1984). Rorschach assessment. In G. Goldstein & M. Hersen (Eds.), *Handbook of psychological assessment* (pp. 332–347). New York: Pergamon.

Erdelyi, M. H. (1985). *Psychoanalysis: Freud's cognitive psychology*. New York: W. H. Freeman.

Erdelyi, M. H. (2001). Defense processes can be conscious and unconscious. *American Psychologist, 56*, 761–762.

Exner, J. E., Jr. (1991). *The Rorschach: A comprehensive system: Vol. 2 Interpretation* (2nd ed.). New York: John Wiley.

Exner, J. E., Jr. (1993). *The Rorschach: A comprehensive system: Vol. 1. Basic foundations* (3rd ed.). New York: John Wiley.

Exner, J. E., Jr. (2002). *The Rorschach: A comprehensive system: Vol. 1* (4th ed.). New York: John Wiley.

Eysenck, H. J. (1978). An exercise in megasilliness. *American Psychologist, 33*, 517.

Fancher, R. E. (2000). Snapshots of Freud in America, 1899–1999. *American Psychologist, 55*, 1025–1028.

Fisher, S., & Greenberg, R. P. (1996). *Freud scientifically reappraised: Testing the theories and therapy*. New York: John Wiley.

Foxall, G. R., & Goldsmith, R. E. (1988). Personality and consumer research: Another look. *Journal of the Market Research Society, 30*, 111–125.

Frank, L. K. (1939). Projective methods for the study of personality. *Journal of Psychology, 8*, 389–413.

Frank, R. (1999). *Luxury fever: Why money fails to satisfy in an era of excess*. New York: Free Press.

Freud, A. (1936). *The ego and the mechanisms of defense*. New York: International Universities Press.

Freud, S. (1910). The origin and development of psychoanalysis. *American Journal of Psychology, 21*, 181–218.

Freud, S. (1953a). The interpretation of dreams. In *Standard edition: Vols. 4 and 5*. London: Hogarth Press. (Original work published 1900)

Freud, S. (1953b). Three essays on the theory of sexuality. In *Standard edition: Vol. 7*. London: Hogarth Press. (Original work published 1905)

Freud, S. (1955). Beyond the pleasure principle. In *Standard edition: Vol. 18*. London: Hogarth Press. (Original work published 1920)

Freud, S. (1957a). On narcissism. In *Standard edition: Vol. 14*. London: Hogarth Press. (Original work published 1914)

Freud, S. (1957b). On the history of the psychoanalytic movement. In *Standard edition: Vol. 14*. London: Hogarth Press. (Original work published 1914)

Freud, S. (1957c). Instincts and their vicissitudes. In *Standard edition: Vol. 14*. London: Hogarth Press. (Original work published 1915)

Freud, S. (1959). Inhibitions, symptoms, and anxiety. In *Standard edition: Vol. 20*. London: Hogarth Press. (Original work published 1926)

Freud, S. (1960a). Psychopathology of everyday life. In *Standard edition: Vol. 6*. London: Hogarth Press. (Original work published 1901)

Freud, S. (1960b). Jokes and their relation to the unconscious. In *Standard edition: Vol. 8*. London: Hogarth Press. (Original work published 1905)

Freud, S. (1961). The ego and the id. In *Standard edition: Vol. 19*. London: Hogarth Press. (Original work published 1923)

Gabbard, G. O. (2000). *Psychodynamic psychiatry in clinical practice* (3rd ed.). Washington, DC: American Psychiatric Press.

Gallo, P. S. (1978). Meta-analysis — A mixed meta-phor? *American Psychologist, 33*, 515–517.

Garchik, L. (1996, April 1). Personals: Madison Avenue is a place where dreams come true. *The Courier-Journal*, D-4.

Gay, P. (1999, March). Sigmund Freud. *Time, 153*, 66–69.

Geen, R. G. (1995). *Human motivation: A social psychological approach*. Belmont, CA: Wadsworth.

Gerow, J. R. (Ed.). (1988). Psychology 1923–1988 [Special Issue]. *Time*.

Glaser, J., & Kihlstrom, J. F. (2005). Compensatory automaticity: Unconscious volition is not an oxymoron. In R. R. Hassin, J. S., Uleman, & J. A. Bargh (Eds.), *The new unconscious* (pp. 171–195). New York: Oxford University Press.

Glassman, N. S., & Andersen, S. (1999). Activating transference without awareness: Using significant-other representations to go beyond the subliminally given information. *Journal of Personality and Social Psychology, 77,* 1146–1162.

Goldfried, M. R., Greenberg, L. S., & Marmar, C. (1990). Individual psychotherapy: Process and outcome. *Annual Review of Psychology, 41,* 659–688.

Grauwe, K. (1987, June 20). *The Bern meta-analysis of outcome studies: Dynamic vs. non-dynamic therapies.* Paper presented at the meeting of the Society for Psychotherapy Research, Ulm, Germany.

Gray-Little, B. (1995). The assessment of psychopathology in racial and ethnic minorities. In J. N. Butcher (Ed.), *Clinical personality assessment* (pp. 140–157). New York: Oxford University Press.

Greenwald, A. G., & Draine, S. G. (1997). Do subliminal stimuli enter the mind unnoticed? Test with a new method. In J. D. Cohen & J. W. Schooler (Eds.), *Scientific approaches to consciousness* (pp. 83–108). Mahwah, NJ: Erlbaum.

Greenwald, A. G., Draine, S. C., & Abrams, R. L. (1996). Three cognitive markers of unconscious semantic activation. *Science, 275,* 1699–1701.

Greenwald, A., McGhee, D., & Schwartz, J. (1998). Measuring individual differences in implicit cognition: The implicit association. *Journal of Personality and Social Psychology, 74,* 1464–1480.

Greenwald, A. G., Nosek, B. A., & Banaji, M. R. (2003). Understanding and using the implicit association test: I. An improved scoring algorithm. *Journal of Personality and Social Psychology, 85,* 197–216.

Greenwald, A. G., Spangenberg, E. R., Pratkanis, A. R., & Eskenazi, J. (1991). Double-blind test of subliminal self-help audiotapes. *Psychological Science, 2,* 119–122.

Hall, C. S. (1954). *A primer of Freudian psychology.* Cleveland, OH: World.

Hassin, R. R., Uleman, J. S., & Bargh, J. A. (Eds.). (2005). *The new unconscious.* New York: Oxford University Press.

Hawkins, D. I., Best, R. J., & Coney, K. A. (2001). *Consumer behavior: Building marketing strategy* (8th ed.). Boston: McGraw-Hill.

Heart, S. H., & McDaniel, S. W. (1982). Subliminal stimulation: Marketing applications. In J. U. McNeal & S. W. McDaniel (Eds.), *Consumer's behavior: Classical and contemporary dimensions* (pp. 165–175). Boston: Little, Brown.

Hedegard, S. (1969). *A molecular analysis of psychological defenses.* Unpublished doctoral dissertation, University of Michigan.

Henry, W. P., Strupp, H. H., Schacht, T. E., & Gaston, L. (1994). Psychodynamic approaches. In A. E. Bergin & S. L. Garfield (Eds.), *Handbook of psychotherapy and behavior change* (4th ed., pp. 467–508). New York: John Wiley.

Hepworth, J. T., & West, S. G. (1988). Lynching and the economy: A time-series reanalysis of Hovland and Sears (1940). *Journal of Personality and Social Psychology, 55,* 239–247.

Hobson, J. A. (1997). Dreaming as delirium: A mental status analysis of our nightly madness. *Seminar in Neurology, 17,* 121–128.

Hobson, J. A. (2002). *Dreaming: An introduction to the science of sleep.* Oxford: Oxford University Press.

Holmes, D. S. (1974). Investigations of repression: Differential recall of material experimentally or naturally associated with ego threat. *Psychological Bulletin, 81,* 632–653.

Horgan, J. (1996, December). Why Freud isn't dead. *Scientific American,* pp. 106–111.

Hovland, C. I., & Sears, R. (1940). Minor studies of aggression: Correlation of lynching with economic indices. *Journal of Psychology, 9,* 301–310.

Howes, C., Hamilton, C. E., & Philipsen, L. (1998). Stability and comorbidity of child–caregiver and child–peer relationships. *Current Directions in Psychological Science, 69,* 418–426.

Hoyt, M. F. (1995). Brief psychotherapies. In A. S. Gurman & S. B. Messer (Eds.), *Essential psychotherapies: Theory and practice* (pp. 441–487). New York: Guilford Press.

Hunsley, J., & Bailey, J. M. (1999). The clinical utility of the Rorschach: Unfilled promises and uncertain future. *Psychological Assessment, 11,* 266–277.

Hunsley, J., Lee, C. M., & Wood, J. M. (2003). Controversial and questionable assessment techniques. In S. O. Lilienfeld & S. J. Lynn (Eds.), *Science and pseudoscience in clinical psychology* (pp. 39–76). New York: Guilford Press.

Jacobsen, T., & Hofmann, V. (1997). Children's attachment representations: Longitudinal relations to school behavior and academic competency in middle childhood and adolescence. *Developmental Psychology, 33,* 703–710.

Jahoda, M. (1977). *Freud and the dilemmas of psychology.* London: Hogarth Press.

Jones, E. (1953, 1955, 1957). *The life and work of Sigmund Freud* (Vols. 1–3). New York: Basic Books.

Judd, C. M., Blair, I. V., & Chapleau, K. M. (2004). Automic stereotypes vs. automatic prejudice: Sorting out the possibilities in the Payne (2001) weapons paradigm. *Journal of Experimental Social Psychology, 40,* 75–81.

Kaufman, J. C., & Sexton, J. D. (2006). Why doesn't the writing cure help poets? *Review of General Psychology, 10,* 268–282.

Kazdin, A. E. (1982). Symptom substitution, generalization, and response covariation: Implications for psychotherapy outcome. *Psychological Bulletin, 91,* 349–365.

Kennedy, C. H., & McNeil, J. A. (2006). A history of military psychology. In C. H. Kennedy & J. A. McNeil (Eds.), *Military psychology: Clinical and operational applications* (pp. 1–17). New York: Guilford Press.

Kernberg, O. (1975). *Borderline conditions and pathological narcissism.* New York: Jason Aronson.

Kernberg, O. (1976). *Objects relations theory and clinical psychoanalysis.* New York: Jason Aronson.

Kernberg, O. (1984). *Severe personality disorder: Psychotherapeutic strategies.* New Haven, CT: Yale University Press.

Kihlstrom, J. F. (1990). The psychological unconscious. In L. A. Pervin (Ed.), *Handbook of personality: Theory and research* (pp. 445–464). New York: Guilford Press.

Kihlstrom, J. F. (1999). The psychological unconscious. In L. A. Pervin & O. John (Eds.), *Handbook of personality:*

Theory and research (2nd ed., pp. 424–442). New York: Guilford Press.

Kimeldorf, C., & Geiwitz, P. J. (1966). Smoking and the Blacky orality factors. *Journal of Projective Techniques, 30,* 167–168.

Kivlighan, D. M. J. (2002). Transference, interpretation, and insight: A research-practice model. In G. S. Tryon (Ed.), *Counseling based on process research: Applying what we know* (pp. 166–196). Boston: Allyn & Bacon.

Klein, D. (1980). Psychosocial treatment of schizophrenia or psychosocial help for people with schizophrenia? *Schizophrenia Bulletin, 6,* 122–130.

Klein, M. (1937). *The psycho-analysis of children* (2nd ed.). London: Hogarth Press.

Klein, M. (1948). *Contributions to psycho-analysis, 1921–1945.* London: Hogarth Press.

Klopfer, B., & Davidson, H. H. (1962). *The Rorschach technique: An introductory manual.* New York: Harcourt, Brace & World.

Knapp, S. L., & VandeCreek, L. D. (2000). Recovered memories of childhood abuse: Is there an underlying professional consensus? *Professional Psychology: Research and Practice, 31,* 365–371.

Kofman, S. (1985). *The enigma of woman: Women in Freud's writing.* Ithaca, NY: Cornell University Press.

Kohut, H. (1971). *The analysis of the self.* New York: International University Press.

Kohut, H. (1977). *The restoration of the self.* New York: International University Press.

Kohut, H. (1984). *How does analysis cure?* Chicago: University of Chicago Press.

Koss, M. P., Butcher, J. N., & Strupp, H. H. (1986). Brief psychotherapy methods in clinical research. *Journal of Consulting and Clinical Psychology, 54,* 60–67.

Koss, M. P., & Shiang, J. (1994). Research on brief psychotherapy. In A. E. Bergin & S. L. Garfield (Eds.), *Handbook of psychotherapy and behavior change* (4th ed., pp. 664–700). New York: John Wiley.

Kotler, P., & Armstrong, G. (1994). *Principles of marketing* (6th ed.). Englewood Cliffs, NJ: Prentice Hall.

Krajick, K. (1990, July 30). Sound too good to be true? Behind the boom in subliminal tapes. *Newsweek, 116,* 60–61.

Krueger, J. (1996). Personal beliefs and cultural stereotypes about racial characteristics. *Journal of Personality and Social Psychology, 71,* 536–548.

Kunst-Wilson, W., & Zajonc, R. (1980). Affective discrimination of stimuli that cannot be recognized. *Science, 207,* 557–558.

Lambert, M. J., Bergin, A. E., & Garfield, S. L. (2004). Introduction and historical overview. In M. J. Lambert (Ed.), *Bergin and Garfield's psychotherapy and behavior change* (pp. 3–15). New York: John Wiley.

Lepore, S. J., & Smyth, J. M. (Eds.). (2002). *The writing cure: How expressive writing promotes health and emotional well-being.* Washington, DC: American Psychological Association.

Lerner, P. M. (1996a). Current perspectives on psychoanalytic Rorschach assessment. *Journal of Personality Assessment, 67,* 450–461.

Lerner, P. M. (1996b). The interpretive process in Rorschach testing. *Journal of Personality Assessment, 67,* 494–500.

Lerner, P. M. (1998). *Psychoanalytic perspectives on the Rorschach.* Hillsdale, NJ: Analytic Press.

Leuzinger-Bohleber, M., & Target, M. (Eds.). (2002). *Outcome of psychoanalytic treatment.* London: Whurr.

Levenson, H. (2003). Time-limited dynamic psychotherapy: An integrationist perspective. *Journal of Psychotherapy Integration, 13,* 300–333.

Lieberman, J. D., & Greenberg, J. (1999). *Cognitive-experiential self-theory and displaced aggression.* Unpublished manuscript, University of Arizona.

Lieberman, M. D., & Eisenberger, N. I. (2006). A pain by any other name (rejection, exclusion, ostracism) still hurts the same: The role of dorsal anterior cingulated cortex in social and physical pain. In J. T. Cacioppo, P. S. Visser, & C. L. Pickett (Eds.), *Social neuroscience: People thinking about thinking people* (pp. 167–187). Cambridge, MA: MIT Press.

Lieberman, M. D., Eisenberger, N. I., Crockett, M. J., Tom, S. M., Pfeifer, J. H., & Way, B. M. (in press). Putting feelings into words: Affect labeling disrupts amygdale activity to affective stimuli. *Psychological Science.*

Lilienfeld, S. O., Wood, J., & Garb, H. N. (2000). The scientific status of projective techniques. *Psychological Science in the Public Trust, 1,* 27–66.

Loftus, E. F. (2003). Make-believe memories. *American Psychologists, 58,* 867–873.

Luborsky, L. (1997). The core conflictual relationship theme: A basic formulation method. In T. D. Ellis (Ed.), *Handbook of psychotherapy case formation* (pp. 58–83). New York: Guilford Press.

Luborsky, L., & Crits-Christoph, P. (1996). *Understanding transference: The core conflictual relationship theme method* (2nd ed.). Washington, DC: American Psychological Association.

Luborsky, L., & Crits-Christoph, P. (1998). *Understanding transference: The core conflictual relationship theme method* (2nd ed.). Washington, DC: American Psychological Association.

Luborsky, E. B., O'Reilly-Landry, M., & Arlow, J. A. (2008). Psychoanalysis. In R. J. Corsini & D. Wedding (Eds.), *Current psychotherapies* (8th ed., pp. 15–62). Belmont, CA: Thomson Higher Education.

Luborsky, L., & Spence, D. P. (1978). Quantitative research on psychoanalytic therapy. In S. L. Garfield & A. E. Bergin (Eds.), *Handbook of psychotherapy and behavior change: An empirical analysis* (2nd ed., pp. 331–368). New York: John Wiley.

Lutgendorf, S., & Ullrich, P. (2002). Journaling about stressful events: Effects of cognitive processing and emotional expression. *Annuals of Behavioral Medicine, 24,* 244–250.

Mahler, M. S. (1968). *On human symbiosis and the vicissitudes of individuation: Infantile psychosis.* New York: International Universities.

Mahler, M. S., Pine, F., & Bergman, A. (1975). *The psychological birth of the human infant: Symbiosis and individuation.* New York: Basic Books.

Martin, L. C. L., & Fabes, R. A. (2001). The stability and consequences of young children's same-sex peer interactions. *Developmental Psychology, 37,* 431–446.

McConnell, J. V., Cutler, R. L., & McNeil, E. B. (1958). Subliminal stimulation: An overview. *American Psychologist, 13,* 229–242.

McCullough, L., Winston, A., Farber, B. A., Porter, F., Pollack, J., Laikin, M., et al. (1991). The relationship of patient–therapist interaction to outcome in brief psychotherapy. *Psychotherapy, 28,* 525–533.

McCullough, M. E., & vanOyen Witvliet, C. (2002). The psychology of forgiveness. In C. R. Snyder & S. J. Lopez (Eds.), *Handbook of positive psychology* (pp. 446–458). New York: Oxford University Press.

McDowell, C., & Acklin, M. W. (1996). Standardizing procedures for calculating Rorschach interrater reliability: Conceptual and empirical foundations. *Journal of Personality Assessment, 66,* 308–320.

McGregor, I. (2003). Defensive zeal: Compensatory convection about attitudes, values, goals, groups, and self-definition in the face of personal uncertainty. In S. J. Spencer, S. Fein, M. P. Zanna, & J. M. Olsen (Eds.), *Motivated perception: The Ontario Symposium: Vol. 9* (pp. 73–92). Mahwah, NJ: Erlbaum.

McGregor, I. (2004). Zeal, identity, and meaning: Going to extremes to be one self. In J. Greenberg, S. L. Koole, & T. Pyszczynski (Eds.), *Handbook of experimental existential psychology* (pp. 182–199). New York: Guilford Press.

McNally, R. J. (2003). *Remembering trauma.* Cambridge, MA: Belknap Press/Harvard University Press.

McNally, R. J., Clancy, S. A., Barrett, H. M., & Parker, H. A. (2005). Reality monitoring in adults reporting repressed, recovered, or continuous memories of childhood sexual abuse. *Journal of Abnormal Psychology, 114,* 147–152.

McWilliams, N. (2004). *Psychoanalytic psychotherapy*: A practitioner's guide. New York: Guilford Press.

Meloy, J. R., Hansen, T. L., & Weiner, I. B. (1997). Authority of the Rorschach: Legal citations during the past 50 years. *Journal of Personality Assessment, 69,* 53–62.

Merikle, P., & Skanes, H. E. (1992). Subliminal self-help audiotapes: A search for placebo effects. *Journal of Applied Psychology, 77,* 772–776.

Messer, S. B., & Kaplan, A. H. (2004). Outcomes and factors related to efficacy of brief psychodynamic therapy. In D. P. Charman (Ed.), *Core processes in brief psychodynamic psychotherapy: Advancing effective practice* (pp. 103–118). Mahwah: Erlbaum.

Mestel, R. (2003a, May 19). Rorschach lore and the test's legacy. *Los Angeles Times,* p. F5.

Mestel, R. (2003b, May 19). Rorschach tested. *Los Angeles Times,* pp. F1, F5.

Mikulincer, M. (1998a). Adult attachment style and affect regulations: Strategic variations in self-appraisals. *Journal of Personality and Social Psychology, 75,* 420–435.

Mikulincer, M. (1998b). Adult attachment style and individual differences in functional versus dysfunctional experiences of anger. *Journal of Personality and Social Psychology, 74,* 513–524.

Mollon, P. (2001). *Releasing the self: The healing legacy of Heinz Kohut.* London: Whurr.

Monahan, J. L., Murphy, S. T., & Zajonc, R. B. (2000). Subliminal mere exposure: Specific, general, and diffuse effects. *Psychological Science, 10,* 419–422.

Monin, B., & Norton, M. I. (2003). Perceptions of fluid consensus: Uniqueness bias, false consensus, false polarization, and pluralistic ignorance in a water conservation crisis. *Personality and Social Psychology Bulletin, 29,* 559–567.

Moore, T. E. (1982). Subliminal advertising: What you see is what you get. *Journal of Marketing, 46,* 38–47.

Moore, T. E. (1992). Subliminal perception: Facts and fallacies. *Skeptical Inquirer, 16,* 273–281.

Moore, T. E. (1995). Subliminal self-help auditory tapes: An empirical test of perceptual consequences. *Canadian Journal of Behavioural Science, 27,* 9–20.

Moran, P. W. (2000). The adaptive practice of psychotherapy in the managed care era. *Psychiatric Clinics of North America, 23,* 383–402.

Morf, C. C., & Rhodewalt, F. (1993). Narcissism and self-evaluation maintenance: Explorations in object relations. *Personality and Social Psychology Bulletin, 19,* 668–676.

Mosher, L. R., & Keith, S. J. (1979). Research on the psychosocial treatment of schizophrenia. *American Journal of Psychiatry, 136,* 623–631.

Moskowitz, G. B. (2001). Preconscious control and compensatory cognition. In G. B. Moskowitz (Ed.), *Cognitive social psychology: The Princeton symposium on the legacy and future of social cognition* (pp. 334–358). Mahwah, NJ: Erlbaum.

Moskowitz, G. B. (2005). *Social cognition: Understanding self and others.* New York: Guilford Press.

Moskowitz, G. B., Gollwitzer, P. M., Wasel, W., & Schaal, B. (1999). Preconscious control of stereotypic activation through chronic egalitarian goals. *Journal of Personality and Social Psychology, 77,* 167–184.

Murphy, K. R., & Davidshofer, C. O. (2005). *Psychological testing: Principles and applications* (6th ed.). Upper Saddle River, NJ: Prentice Hall.

Murphy, S. T., & Zajonc, R. B. (1993). Affect, cognition, and awareness: Affecting priming with optimal and suboptimal stimulus exposures. *Journal of Personality and Social Psychology, 64,* 723–739.

Murray, B. (2002). Writing to heal. *Monitor on Psychology, 33,* 54–55.

Myers, D. G. (2005). *Social psychology* (8th ed.). Boston: McGraw-Hill.

Neuberg, S. L. (1988). Behavioral implications of information presented outside of awareness: The effects of subliminal presentation of trait information on behavior in the prisoner's dilemma game. *Social Cognition, 6,* 207–230.

Newman, L. S. (2001). Coping and defense: No clear distinction. *American Psychologist, 56,* 760–761.

Niederhoffer, K. G., & Pennebaker, J. W. (2002). Sharing one's story: On the benefits of writing or talking about emotional experience. In C. R. Snyder & S. J. Lopez (Eds.), *Handbook of positive psychology* (pp. 573–583). New York: Oxford University Press.

Nikles, C. D., II, Brecht, D. L., Klinger, E., & Bursell, A. L. (1998). The effects of current-concern- and nonconcern-related waking suggestions on nocturnal dream content. *Journal of Personality and Social Psychology, 75,* 242–255.

Nolen, I. S., & Nolen, P. (2002). *Object relations and integrative psychotherapy: Tradition and innovation in theory and practice.* London: Whurr.

O'Connor, A. (2004, March 23). Dreams ride on Freud's royal road, study finds. *New York Times*, p. F5.

Olson, M. A., & Fazio, R. H. (2001). Implicit attitude formation through classical conditioning. *Psychological Science, 12*, 413–417.

Packard, V. (1957). *The hidden persuaders.* New York: Pocket Books.

Payne, B. K. (2001). Prejudice and perception: The role of automatic and controlled processes in misperceiving a weapon. *Journal of Personality and Social Psychology, 81*, 181–192.

Pederson, W. C., Gonzeles, C., & Miller, N. (2000). The moderating effect of trivial triggering provocation on displaced aggression. *Journal of Personality and Social Psychology, 78*, 913–947.

Pennebaker, J. W. (1997a). *Opening up: The healing power of expressing emotions.* New York: Guilford Press.

Pennebaker, J. W. (1997b). Writing about emotional experiences as a therapeutic process. *Psychological Science, 8*, 162–166.

Pennebaker, J. W. (2002). What our words can say about us: Toward a broader language. *Psychological Science Agenda, 15*, 8–9.

Perry, J. C., & Cooper, S. H. (1986). A preliminary report on defenses and conflicts associated with borderline personality disorder. *Journal of the American Psychoanalytic Association, 34*, 863–893.

Perry, J. C., & Cooper, S. H. (1989). An empirical study of defense mechanisms: I. Clinical interview and life vignette ratings. *Archives of General Psychiatry, 46*, 444–460.

Pesant, N., & Zadra, A. (2004). Working with dreams in therapy: What do we know and what should we do? *Clinical Psychology Review, 24*, 489–512.

Peter, J. P., & Olson, J. C. (2002). *Consumer behavior and marketing strategy* (6th ed.). Boston: McGraw-Hill.

Petrie, K. J., Booth, R. J., & Pennebaker, J. W. (1998). The immunological effects of thought suppression. *Journal of Personality and Psychology, 75*, 1261–1272.

Petrie, K. J., Booth, R., Pennebaker, J. W., Davison, K. P., & Thomas, M. (1995). Disclosure of trauma and immune response to Hepatitis B vaccination program. *Journal of Consulting and Clinical Psychology, 63*, 787–792.

Petrie, K. J., Fontanilla, I., Thomas, M. G., Booth, R. J., & Pennebaker, J. W. (2004). Effect of written emotional expression on immune function in patients with human immunodeficiency virus infection: A randomized trial. *Psychosomatic Medicine, 66*, 272–275.

Piotrowski, C. (1996a). The Rorschach in contemporary forensic psychology. *Psychological Reports, 78*, 458.

Piotrowski, C. (1996b). Use of the Rorschach in forensic practice. *Perceptual and Motor Skills, 82*, 254.

Piper, W. E., Azim, F. A., Joyce, S. A., & McCallum, M. (1991). Transference interpretations, therapeutic alliance and outcome in short-term individual psychotherapy. *Archives of General Psychiatry, 48*, 946–953.

Plante, T. G. (2005). *Contemporary clinical psychology* (2nd ed.). Hoboken, NJ: John Wiley.

Plutchik, R. (1998). Emotions, diagnoses and ego defenses: A psychoevolutionary perspective. In W. Flack & J. D. Laird (Eds.), *Emotions in psychopathology: Theory and research* (pp. 367–379). New York: Oxford University Press.

Porter, F. A. (1987). *The immediate effects of interpretation on patient response in short-term dynamic psychotherapy.* Unpublished doctoral dissertation, Columbia University, New York.

Pratkanis, A. R. (1992). The cargo-cult science of subliminal persuasion. *Skeptical Inquirer, 16*, 260–272.

Pratkanis, A. R., Eskenazi, J., & Greenwald, A. G. (1994). What you expect is what you believe (but not necessarily what you get): A test of the effectiveness of subliminal self-help audiotapes. *Basic and Applied Social Psychology, 15*, 251–276.

Pyszczynski, T., Greenberg, J., & Solomon, S. (1999). A dual-process model of defense against conscious and unconscious death-related thoughts: An extension of terror management theory. *Psychological Review, 106*, 835–845.

Quintar, B., Lane, R. C., & Goeltz, W. B. (1998). Psychoanalytic theories of personality. In D. F. Barone, M. Hersen, & V. B. Van Hasselt (Eds.), *Advanced personality* (pp. 27–55). New York: Plenum.

Rath, T. (2006). *Vital friends: The people you can't afford to live without.* Washington, DC: Gallup Organization.

Ricks, M. H. (1985). The social transmission of parental behavior: Attachment across generations. In I. Bretherton & E. Waters (Eds.), Growing points of attachment theory and research. *Monographs of the Society for Research in Child Development, 50* (1–2, Serial No. 209), 211–227.

Rock group not liable for deaths. (1990, September 10). *National Law Journal*, p. 33.

Rorschach, H. (1942). *Psychodiagnostics: A diagnostic test based on perception* (P. Lemkau & B. Kronenberg, Trans.). Berne, Switzerland: Huber. (1st German ed. published 1921; U.S. distributor, Grune & Stratton.)

Runyan, W. M. (2006). Psychobiography and the psychology of science: Understanding relations between the life and work of individual psychologists. *Review of General Psychology, 10*, 147–162.

Runyon, K. E. (1980). *Consumer behavior and the practice of marketing* (2nd ed.). Columbus, OH: Merrill.

Russek, L. G., & Schwartz, G. E. (1997). Perceptions of parental caring predict health status in midlife: A 35-year follow-up of the Harvard Mastery of Stress Study. *Psychosomatic Medicine, 59*, 144–149.

Rychlak, J. F. (1981). *Introduction to personality and psychotherapy: A theory-construction approach* (2nd ed.). Boston: Houghton Mifflin.

Sagarin, B. J., Rhoads, K. V. L., & Cialdini, R. B. (1998). Deceiver's distrust: Denigration as a consequence of undiscovered deception. *Personality and Social Psychology Bulletin, 24*, 1167–1176.

Sayers, J. (2000). *Kleinians: Psychoanalysis inside out.* Cambridge, UK: Polity.

Schaller, M. (1997). The psychological consequences of fame: Three tests of the self-conscious hypothesis. *Journal of Personality, 65*, 291–309.

Scharf, J. S., & Scharf, D. (1998). *Object relations individual therapy.* New York: Jason Aronson.

Schoell, W. F., & Guiltinan, J. P. (1995). *Marketing: Contemporary concepts and practices* (6th ed.). Englewood Cliffs, NJ: Prentice Hall.

Schwartz, S. (2000). *Abnormal psychology: A discovery approach.* Mountain View, CA: Mayfield.

Shaffer, D. R., & Kipp, K. (2007). *Developmental psychology: Childhood and adolescence* (7th ed.). Belmont, CA: Thomson Higher Education.

Shedler, J., Mayman, M., & Manis, M. (1993). The illusion of mental health. *American Psychologist, 48,* 1117–1131.

Silverman, L. H. (1976). Psychoanalytic theory: "The reports of my death are greatly exaggerated." *American Psychologist, 31,* 621–637.

Silverman, L. H. (1980). A comprehensive report of studies using the subliminal psychodynamic activation method. *Psychological Research Bulletin, 20,* 1–22.

Silverman, L. H. (1982). A comment on two subliminal psychodynamic activation studies. *Journal of Abnormal Psychology, 91,* 126–130.

Silverman, L. H., Ross, D. L., Adler, J. M., & Lustig, D. A. (1978). Simple research paradigm for demonstrating subliminal psychodynamic activation: Effects of Oedipal stimuli on dart-throwing accuracy in college males. *Journal of Abnormal Psychology, 87,* 341–357.

Slatcher, R. B., & Pennebaker, J. W. (2006). How do I love thee? Let me count the words: The social effects of expressive writing. *Psychological Science, 17,* 660–664.

Slone, R. B., Staples, F. R., Cristol, A. H., Yorkston, N. J., & Whipple, K. (1975). *Short-term analytically oriented psychotherapy versus behavior therapy.* Cambridge, MA: Harvard University Press.

Smith, E. R., & De Coster, J. (2000). Dual models in social and cognitive psychology: Conceptual integration and links to underlying memory systems. *Personality and Social Psychology Review, 4,* 108–131.

Smith, K. H., & Rogers, M. (1994). Effectiveness of subliminal messages in television commercials: Two experiments. *Journal of Applied Psychology, 79,* 866–874.

Smith, M. L., & Glass, G. V. (1977). Meta-analysis of psychotherapy outcome studies. *American Psychologist, 32,* 752–760.

Smith, M. L., Glass, G. V., & Miller, T. I. (1980). *The benefits of psychotherapy.* Baltimore: Johns Hopkins University Press.

Smith, T. W., & Gallo, L. C. (2001). Personality traits as risk factors for physical illness. In A. Baum, T. A. Reverson, & J. E. Singer (Eds.), *Handbook of health psychology* (pp. 139–173). Mahwah, NJ: Erlbaum.

Snyder, C. R., Higgins, R. L., & Stucky, R. (1983). *Excuses: Masquerades in search of grace.* New York: Wiley-Interscience.

Sommers-Flanagan, J., & Sommers-Flanagan, R. (2004). *Counseling and psychotherapy theories in context and practice: Skills, strategies, and techniques.* Hoboken, NJ: John Wiley.

Sroufe, L. A., & Fleeson, J. (1986). Attachment and the construction of relationships. In W. W. Hartup & Z. Rubin (Eds.), *Relationships and development* (pp. 51–71). Hillsdale, NJ: Erlbaum.

St. Clair, M. (2004). *Object relations and self psychology: An introduction* (4th ed.). Belmont, CA: Thomson/Wadsworth.

Stepansky, P. E. (Ed.). (1988). *The memories of Margaret S. Mahler.* New York: Free Press.

Stirman, S. W., & Pennebaker, J. W. (2001). Word use in the poetry of suicidal and non-suicidal poets. *Psychosomatic Medicine, 63,* 517–523.

Stone, I. (1971). *The passions of the mind.* Garden City, NY: Doubleday.

Stone, M. (1985). Shellshock and psychologists. In W. F. Bynum, R. Porter, & M. Shepherd (Eds.), *The anatomy of madness: Vol. 2* (pp. 242–247). London: Tavistock.

Strack, F., & Deutsch, R. F. (2004). Reflective and impulsive determinants of social behavior. *Personality and Social Psychology Bulletin, 8,* 220–247.

Strahan, R. F. (1978). Six ways of looking at an elephant. *American Psychologist, 33,* 693.

Strean, H. S. (1994). *Essentials of psychoanalysis: Vol. 2.* New York: Brunner/Mazel.

Strupp, H. H., & Binder, J. L. (1984). *Psychotherapy in a new key: A guide to time-limited dynamic psychotherapy.* New York: Basic Books.

Strupp, H. H., Fox, R. E., & Lessler, K. (1969). *Patients view their psychotherapy.* Baltimore: Johns Hopkins University Press.

Stuart, S., & Noyes, R., Jr. (1999). Attachment and interpersonal communication in somatization. *Psychosomatics, 40,* 34–43.

Svartberg, M., & Stiles, T. C. (1991). Comparative effects of short-term psychodynamic psychotherapy: A meta-analysis. *Journal of Consulting and Clinical Psychology, 59,* 704–714.

Tamir, M., Robinson, M. D., Clore, G. L., Martin, L. L., & Whitaker, D. J. (2004). Are we puppets on a string? The contextual meaning of unconscious expressive cues. *Personality and Social Psychology Bulletin, 30,* 237–249.

Tangney, J. T., & Mashek, D. J. (2004). In search of the moral person: Do you have to feel really bad to be good? In J. Greenberg, S. L. Koole, & T. Pyszczynski (Eds.), *Handbook of experimental extistential psychology* (pp. 156–166). New York: Guilford Press.

Taylor, S. E. (2006). *Health psychology* (6th ed.). Boston: McGraw-Hill.

Taylor, S. E., Dickerson, S. S., & Klein, L. C. (2002). Toward a biology of social support. In C. R. Snyder & S. J. Lopez (Eds.), *Handbook of positive psychology* (pp. 556–569). New York: Oxford University Press.

Teixeira, M. A. (1992). Psychoanalytic theory and therapy in the treatment of manic-depressive disorders. *Psychoanalysis and Psychotherapy, 11,* 162–177.

Theus, K. T. (1994). Subliminal advertising and the psychology of processing unconscious stimuli: A review. *Psychology and Marketing, 11,* 271–290.

Thomas, A. K., Bulevich, J. B., & Loftus, E. F. (2003). Exploring the role of repetition and sensory elaboration in the imagination inflation effect. *Memory & Cognition, 31,* 630–640.

Time capsule (2000). *Monitor on Psychology, 31,* 10.

Tolson, J. (1999). The bible of dreams turns 100. *U.S. News Online.* Retrieved from www.usnews/issue/991108/dreams/htm.

Trappey, C. (1996). A meta-analysis of consumer choice and subliminal advertising. *Psychology and Marketing, 13,* 517–530.

Trull, T. J., & Phares, E. J. (2001). *Clinical psychology: Concepts, methods, and profession* (6th ed.). Belmont, CA: Wadsworth/Thomson.

Vaillant, G. E. (1977). *Adaptation to life.* Boston: Little, Brown.

Vaillant, G. E. (Ed.). (1986). *Empirical studies of ego mechanisms of defense.* Washington, DC: American Psychiatric Press.

Vaillant, G. (Ed.). (1992). *Ego mechanisms of defense: A guide for clinicians and researchers.* Washington, DC: American Psychiatric Association Press.

Vaillant, G. E., & Drake, R. E. (1985). Maturity of defenses in relation to DSM-III Axis II personality disorder. *Archives of General Psychiatry, 42,* 597–601.

Values and Life Styles Program (1989). *Descriptive materials for the VALS2 segmentation system.* Menlo Park, CA: SRI International.

Vernon, P. E. (1935). Recent work on the Rorschach test. *Journal of Mental Science, 81,* 894–920.

Verschueren, K., & Marcoen, A. (1999). Representations of self and socioemotional competence in kindergarteners: Differential and combined effects of attachment to mother and father. *Child Development, 70,* 183–201.

Viglione, D. J., & Rivera, B. (2003). Assessing personality and psychopathology with projective methods. In J. R. Graham & J. A. Naglieri (Eds.), *Handbook of psychology: Vol. 10. Assessment psychology* (pp. 531–552). New York: John Wiley.

Vivian, J. (1993). *The media of mass communication.* Boston: Allyn & Bacon.

Waters, E., & Cummings, E. M. (2000). A secure base from which to explore close relationships. *Child Development, 71,* 164–172.

Watkins, C. E., Jr., Campbell, V. L., & Manus, M. (1990). Personality assessment training in counseling psychology programs. *Journal of Personality Assessment, 55,* 380–383.

Wegner, D. M., Wenzlaff, R. M., & Kozak, M. (2004). Dream rebound: The return of suppressed thoughts in dreams. *Psychological Science, 15,* 232–236.

Weinberger, D. A. (1995). The construct validity of the repressive coping style. In J. L. Singer (Ed.), *Repression and dissociation: Implications for personality theory, psychopathology, and health* (pp. 337–386). Chicago: University of Chicago Press.

Weinberger, J., & Westen, D. (2001). Science and psychodynamics: From arguments about Freud to data. *Psychological Inquiry, 12,* 129–166.

Weiner, I. B. (1997). Current status of the Rorschach Inkblot Test. *Journal of Personality Assessment, 68,* 5–19.

Weiner, I. B. (1998). *Principles of Rorschach interpretation.* Mahwah, NJ: Erlbaum.

Weiner, I. B., Exner, Jr., J. E., & Sciara, A. (1996). Is the Rorschach welcome in the courtroom? *Journal of Personality Assessment, 67,* 422–424.

Weir, W. (1984, October 15). Another look at subliminal "facts." *Advertising Age,* p. 46.

Wenzlaff, R. M., & Bates, D. E. (2000). The relative efficacy of concentration and suppression strategies of mental control. *Personal and Social Psychology Bulletin, 26,* 1200–1212.

Westen, D. (1990). Psychoanalytic approaches to personality. In L. A. Pervin (Ed.), *Handbook of personality: Theory and research* (pp. 21–65). New York: Guilford Press.

Westen, D. (1991). Social cognition and object relations. *Psychological Bulletin, 3,* 429–455.

Westen, D. (1998). The scientific legacy of Sigmund Freud: Toward a psychodynamically informed psychological science. *Psychological Bulletin, 124,* 333–371.

Westen, D. (2005). Implications of research in cognitive neuroscience for psychodynamic psychotherapy. In G. O. Gabbard, J. S. Beck, & J. Holmes (Eds.), *Oxford textbook of psychotherapy* (pp. 443–448). New York: Oxford University Press.

Westen, D., & Gabbard, G. O. (1999). Psychoanalytic approaches to personality. In L. A. Pervin & O. P. John (Eds.), *Handbook of personality: Theory and research* (2nd ed., pp. 57–101). New York: Guilford Press.

Westen, D., & Heim, A. K. (2003). Disturbances of self and identity in personality disorders. In M. R. Leary & J. P. Tangney (Eds.), *Handbook of self and identity* (pp. 643–664). New York: Guilford Press.

Westen, D., & Shedler, J. (1999). Revising and assessing Axis II, Part II: Developing a clinically and empirically valid assessment method. *American Journal of Psychiatry, 156,* 258–272.

Wilhelm, R. (1956). Are subliminal commercials bad? *Michigan Business Review, 8,* 26.

Winerman, L. (2006, October). Taking the pain away. *Monitor on Psychology, 37,* 35.

Wood, J. M., Nezworski, M. T., Lilienfeld, S. O., & Garb, H. N. (2003). *What's wrong with the Rorschach? Science confronts the controversial inkblot test.* San Francisco: Jossey-Bass.

Zajonc, R. B. (1980). Feeling and thinking: Preferences need no inferences. *American Psychologist, 35,* 151–175.

Zeanah, C. H., & Zeanah, P. D. (1989). Intergenerational transmission of maltreatment: Insights from attachment theory and research. *Psychiatry, 52,* 177–196.

Zillmer, E. A., & Spiers, M. V. (2001). *Principles of neuropsychology.* Belmont, CA: Wadsworth/Thomas Learning.

Chapter 4

Adler, A. (1927). *Practice and theory of individual psychology.* New York: Harcourt, Brace & World.

Adler, A. (1929a). *The science of living.* New York: Greenberg.

Adler, A. (1929b). *Problems of neurosis.* London: Kegan Paul.

Adler, A. (1930). Individual psychology. In C. Murchison (Ed.), *Psychologies of 1930* (pp. 395–405). Worcester, MA: Clark University Press.

Adler, A. (1931). *What life should mean to you.* Boston: Little, Brown.

Adler, A. (1935). The fundamental views of individual psychology. *International Journal of Individual Psychology, 1,* 5–8.

Adler, A. (1939). *Social interest.* New York: Putnam.

Adler, A. (1956a). The study of organ inferiority and its physical compensation. In H. L. Ansbacher & R. R. Ansbacher (Eds.), *The individual psychology of Alfred Adler.* New York: Harper. (Original work published 1907)

Adler, A. (1956b). The psychology of hermaphroditism in life and in neurosis. In H. L. Ansbacher & R. R. Ansbacher (Eds.), *The individual psychology of Alfred Adler*. New York: Harper. (Original work published 1910)

Adler, A. (1956c). The meaning of life. In H. L. Ansbacher & R. R. Ansbacher (Eds.), *The individual psychology of Alfred Adler*. New York: Harper. (Original work published 1933)

Allen, J., & Brock, A. (2002). *Health care communication using personality type: Patients are different*. Philadelphia: Taylor & Francis.

Altus, N. C. (1966). Birth order and its sequelae. *Science, 151*, 44–49.

Andrews, H. F. (1990). Helping and health: The relationship between volunteer activity and health-related outcomes. *Advances, 7*, 25–34.

Arnau, R. C., Green, B. A., Rosen, D. H., Gleaves, D. H., & Melancon, J. G. (2003). Are Jungian preferences really categorical? *Individual Differences, 34*, 233–251.

Baltes, P. B., Glück, J., & Kunzman, U. (2002). Wisdom: Its structure and function in regulating successful life span development. In C. R. Snyder & S. J. Lopez (Eds.), *Handbook of positive psychology* (pp. 327–347). New York: Oxford University Press.

Baron, R. A., & Byrne, D. (2000). *Social psychology: Understanding human interaction* (9th ed.). Boston: Allyn & Bacon.

Belmont, L., & Marolla, F. A. (1973). Birth order, family size, and intelligence. *Science, 182*, 1096–1101.

Belsky, J., Gilstrap, B., & Rovine, M. (1984). The Pennsylvania infant and family development project, I: Stability and change in mother–infant and father–infant interaction in a family setting at one, three, and nine months. *Child Development, 55*, 692–705.

Bennet, E. A. (1983). *What Jung really said*. New York: Schocken Books.

Blake, J. (1989). Number of siblings and educational attainment. *Science, 245*, 32–36.

Bonner, M. A. (1989). *The Myers-Briggs type indicator as an aid to instructional design in interior design and apparel merchandising*. Unpublished master's thesis, Indiana University, Bloomington, IN.

Boroson, W. (1973). First born – fortune's favorite? In *Readings in human development* (pp. 192–196). Guilford, CT: Dushkin.

Bottome, P. (1957). *Alfred Adler: A portrait from life* (3rd ed.). New York: Vanguard Press.

Breland, H. M. (1974). Birth order, family configuration, and verbal achievement. *Child Development, 45*, 1011–1019.

Brislin, R. W., & Lo, K. D. (2006). Culture, personality, and people's use of time: Key interrelationships. In J. C. Thomas & D. L. Segal (Eds.), *Comprehensive handbook of personality and psychopathology: Vol. 1. Personality and everyday functioning* (pp. 44–61). Hoboken, NJ: John Wiley.

Cann, D. R., & Donderi, D. C. (1986). Jungian personality typology and the recall of everyday and archetypal dreams. *Journal of Personality and Social Psychology, 50*, 1021–1030.

Capraro, R. M., & Capraro, M. M. (2002). Myers-Briggs Type Indicator score reliability across studies: A meta-analytical reliability generalization study. *Educational and Psychological Measurement, 62*, 590–602.

Capretz, L. F. (2003). Personality types in software engineering. *International Journal of Human-Computer Studies, 58*, 207–214.

Carlson, R. (1980). Studies of Jungian typology: II. Representations of the personal world. *Journal of Personality and Social Psychology, 38*, 801–810.

Carlson, R., & Levy, N. (1973). Studies of Jungian typology: I. Memory, social perception, and social action. *Journal of Personality, 41*, 559–576.

Carlyn, M. (1977). An assessment of the Myers-Briggs Type Indicator. *Journal of Personality Assessment, 41*, 461–473.

Carr, M. (2006). How managers and non-managers differ in their MBTI personality type. *People Management, 12*, 48.

Clary, E. G., Snyder, M., Ridge, R. D., Copeland, J., Stukas, A. A., Haugen, J., & Miene, P. (1998). Understanding and assessing the motivations of volunteers: A functional approach. *Journal of Personality and Social Psychology. 74*, 1516–1530.

Clary, E. G., Snyder, M., Ridge, R. D., Miene, P., & Haugen, J. (1994). Matching messages to motives in persuasion: A functional approach to promoting volunteerism. *Journal of Applied Social Psychology, 24*, 1129–1149.

Cohen, R. J., & Swerdlik, M. E. (2005). *Psychological testing and assessment: An introduction to tests and measurement* (6th ed.). Boston: McGraw-Hill.

Corneau, H. (1980). An examination of the relationship between sex, birth order, and creativity. *Creative Child and Adult Quarterly, 5*, 251–258.

Crandall, J. E. (1975). A scale for social interest. *Journal of Individual Psychology, 31*, 187–195.

Crandall, J. E. (1980). Adler's concept of social interest: Theory, measurement, and implications for adjustment. *Journal of Personality and Social Psychology, 39*, 481–495.

Crandall, J. E. (1981). *Theory and measurement of social interest: Empirical tests of Alfred Adler's concept*. New York: Columbia University Press.

Crandall, J. E. (1984). Social interest as a moderator of life stress. *Journal of Personality and Social Psychology, 47*, 164–174.

Crandall, J. E., & Putman, E. L. (1980). Social interest and psychological well-being. *Journal of Individual Psychology, 36*, 156–168.

Darley, J. M., & Aronson, E. (1966). Self-evaluation vs. direct anxiety reduction as determinants of the fear-affiliation relationship. *Journal of Experimental Social Psychology Supplement, 1*, 66–79.

Dawes, R. (2004). Time for critical empirical investigation of the MBTI. *European Business Forum, 18*, 88–89.

Descouzis, D. (1989). Pyschological types of tax preparers. *Journal of Psychological Types, 17*, 36–38.

Dimond, R. E., & Munz, C. (1968). Ordinal position of birth and self-disclosure in high school students. *Psychological Reports, 21*, 829–833.

Ellenberger, H. F. (1970). *The discovery of the unconscious: The history and evolution of dynamic psychiatry*. New York: Basic Books.

Ernst, C., & Angst, J. (1983). *Birth order: Its influence on personality*. New York: Springer.

Eysenck, H. J. (1990). Biological dimensions of personality. In L. A. Pervin (Ed.), *Handbook of personality: Theory and research* (pp. 244–276). New York: Guilford Press.

Eysenck, H. J., & Cookson, D. (1969). Personality in primary school children: 3. Family background. *British Journal of Educational Psychology, 40*, 117–131.

Falbo, T., & Polit, D. F. (1986). Quantitative review of the only child literature: Research evidence and theory development. *Psychological Bulletin, 100*, 176–189.

Forer, L. (1976). *The birth order factor*. New York: McKay.

Furtmuller, C. (1964). Alfred Adler: A biographical essay. In H. L. Ansbacher & R. R. Ansbacher (Eds.), *Superiority and social interest* (pp. 311–393). Evanston, IL: Northwestern University Press.

Glass, D. C., Neulinger, J., & Brim, O. G. (1974). Birth order, verbal intelligence, and educational aspiration. *Child Development, 45*, 807–811.

Goldenberg, I., & Goldenberg, H. (1995). Family therapy. In R. J. Corsini & D. Wedding (Eds.), *Current psychotherapies* (5th ed., pp. 356–385). Itasca, IL: F. E. Peacock.

Hammer, A. L. (Ed.). (1996). *MBTI applications: A decade of research on the Myers-Briggs Type indicator*. Palo Alto, CA: Consulting Psychological Press.

Harris, I. D. (1964). *The promise seed: A complete study of eminent first and later sons*. New York: Free Press.

Harris, J. R. (2006). *No two alike: Human nature and human individuality*. New York: Norton.

Helson, R. (1978). Dimensions and patterns in writings of critics. *Journal of Personality, 46*, 348–361.

Helson, R. (1982). Critics and their texts: An approach to Jung's theory of cognition and personality. *Journal of Personality and Social Psychology, 43*, 409–418.

Heppner, P. P., & Lee, D. (2002). Problem-solving appraisal and psychological adjustment. In C. R. Snyder & S. J. Lopez (Eds.), *Handbook of positive psychology* (pp. 288–298). New York: Oxford University Press.

Hetherington, E. M., & Feldman, S. E. (1964). College cheating as a function of subject and situational variables. *Journal of Educational Psychology, 55*, 212–218.

Hilton, I. (1967). Differences in the behavior of mothers toward first and later born children. *Journal of Personality and Social Psychology, 7*, 282–290.

Hirsh, S. K., & Kise, J. A. G. (2006). *Work it out: Using personality type to improve team performance* (rev. ed.). Mountain View, CA: Davis-Black.

Hoffman, L. W. (1991). The influence of the family environment on personality: Accounting for sibling differences. *Psychological Bulletin, 2*, 187–203.

Hopcke, R. H. (1989). *A guided tour of the collected works of C. G. Jung*. Boston: Shambhala.

Howarth, E. (1980). Birth order, family structure, and personality variables. *Journal of Personality Assessment, 44*, 299–301.

Hoyenga, K. B., & Hoyenga, K. T. (1984). *Motivational explanations of behavior*. Monterey, CA: Brooks/Cole.

Ickes, W., & Turner, M. (1983). On the social advantages of having an older, opposite-sex sibling: Birth order influences in mixed-sex dyads. *Journal of Personality and Social Psychology, 45*, 210–222.

Jung, C. G. (1907). On the psychological relations of the association experiment. *Journal of Abnormal Psychology, 7*, 247–255.

Jung, C. G. (1953a). The psychology of the unconscious. In *The collected works of C. G. Jung: Vol. 7*. Princeton: Princeton University Press. (Original work published 1943)

Jung, C. G. (1953b). The relations between the ego and the unconscious. In *The collected works of C. G. Jung: Vol. 7*. Princeton: Princeton University Press. (Original work published 1945)

Jung, C. G. (1959a). The archetypes and the collective unconscious. In *The collected works of C. G. Jung: Vol. 9, Part I*. Princeton: Princeton University Press. (Original work published 1936)

Jung, C. G. (1959b). The concept of the collective unconscious. In *The collected works of C. G. Jung: Vol. 9, Part I*. Princeton: Princeton University Press. (Original work published 1936)

Jung, C. G. (1959c). The shadow. In *The collected works of C. G. Jung: Vol. 9, Part II*. Princeton: Princeton University Press. (Original work published 1948)

Jung, C. J. (1959d). Psychological aspects of the mother archetype. In *The collected works of C. G. Jung: Vol. 9, Part I*. Princeton: Princeton University Press. (Original work published 1954)

Jung, C. G. (1959e). Concerning the archetypes, with special reference to the anima concept. In *The collected works of C. G. Jung: Vol. 9, Part I*. Princeton: Princeton University Press. (Original work published 1954)

Jung, C. G. (1959f). Conscious, unconscious, and individuation. In *The collected works of C. G. Jung: Vol. 9, Part 1*. Princeton: Princeton Univeristy Press. (Original work published 1939)

Jung, C. G. (1960a). A review of the complex theory. In *The collected works of C. G. Jung: Vol. 8*. Princeton: Princeton University Press. (Original work published 1934)

Jung, C. G. (1960b). On psychic energy. In *The collected works of C. G. Jung: Vol. 8*. Princeton: Princeton University Press. (Original work published 1948)

Jung, C. G. (1960c). The stages of life. In *The collected works of C. G. Jung: Vol. 8*. Princeton: Princeton University Press. (Original work published 1931)

Jung, C. G. (1960d). The transcent function. In *The collected works of C. G. Jung: Vol. 8*. Princeton: Princeton University Press. (Original work published 1916)

Jung, C. G. (Ed.). (1964). *Man and his symbols*. New York: Doubleday.

Jung, C. G. (1966). Two essays on analytical psychology. In *The collected works of C. G. Jung: Vol. 7*. Princeton: Princeton University Press. (Original work published 1917)

Jung, C. G. (1969). General aspects of dream psychology. In *The collected works of C. G. Jung: Vol. 8*. Princeton: Princeton University Press. (Original work published 1916)

Jung, C. G. (1971). Psychological types. In *The collected works of C. G. Jung: Vol. 6*. Princeton: Princeton University Press. (Original work published 1921)

Jung, C. G. (1973a). The reaction time ratio in the association experiment. In *The collected works of C. G. Jung: Vol. 2.* Princeton: Princeton University Press. (Original work published 1905)

Jung, C. G. (1973b). The psychological diagnosis of evidence. *In The collected works of C. G. Jung: Vol. 2.* Princeton: Princeton University Press. (Original work published 1909)

Kaufmann, Y. (1989). Analytical psychotherapy. In R. J. Corsini & D. Wedding (Eds.), *Current psychotherapies* (4th ed., pp. 119–152). Itasca, IL: F. E. Peacock.

Kennedy, R. B., & Kennedy, D. A. (2004). Using the Myers-Briggs Type Indicator in career counseling. *Journal of Employing Counseling, 41*, 38–44.

Levesque, L. C. (2001). *Breakthrough creativity: Achieving top performance using eight creative talents.* Palo Alto, CA: Davies-Black.

Locke, E. A. (2002). Setting goals for life and happiness. In C. R. Snyder & S. J. Lopez (Eds.), *Handbook of positive psychology* (pp. 299–312). New York: Oxford University Press.

Lopez, S. J., Prosser, E. C., Edwards, L. M., Magyar-Moe, J. L., Neufeld, J. E., & Rasmussen, H. N. (2002). Putting positive psychology in a multicultural context. In C. R. Snyder & S. J. Lopez (Eds.), *Handbook of positive psychology* (pp. 700–714). New York: Oxford University Press.

Maddi, S. R. (1996). *Personality theories: A comparative analysis* (6th ed.). Pacific Grove, CA: Brooks/Cole.

McCall, R. B. (1984). Developmental changes in mental performance: The effect of the birth of a sibling. *Child Development, 55*, 1317–1321.

McCaulley, M. H. (2000). Myers-Briggs Type Indicator: A bridge between counseling and consulting. *Consulting Psychology Journal: Practice and Research, 52*, 117–132.

McDanel, P. W. (2005). The impact of personality as measured by the Myers-Briggs Type Indicator on the negative perceptions of students of accounting [abstract]. *Dissertation Abstracts: International Section A: Humanities and Social Sciences, 66*, 461.

Miller, N., & Maruyama, G. (1976) Ordinal position and peer popularity. *Journal of Personality and Social Psychology, 33*, 123–131.

Monte, C. F. (1987). *Beneath the mask: An introduction to theories of personality* (3rd ed.). New York: Holt, Rinehart and Winston.

Morris, L. W. (1979). *Extraversion and introversion: An interactional perspective.* New York: Hemisphere.

Mosak, H. H. (1995). Adlerian psychotherapy. In R. J. Corsini & D. Wedding (Eds.), *Current psychotherapies* (5th ed., pp. 51–94). Itasca, IL: F. E. Peacock.

Mosak H. H., & Maniacci, M. P. (1999). *A primer of Adlerian psychology: The analytic-behavioral-cognitive psychology of Alfred Adler.* Philadelphia, PA: Brunner/Mazel.

Myers I. B. (1962). *The Myers-Briggs Type Indicator manual.* Palo Alto, CA: Consulting Psychologists Press.

Myers, I. B. (1980). *Introduction to type* (3rd ed.). Palo Alto, CA: Consulting Psychologists Press.

Myers, M. B., & McCaulley, M. H. (1985). *Manual: A guide to the development and use of the Myers-Briggs Type Indicator.* Palo Alto, CA: Consulting Psychologists Press.

Myers, I. B., McCaulley, M. H., Quenk, N. L., & Hammer, A. L. (1998). *Manual: A guide to the development and use of the Myer-Briggs Type Indicator.* Palo Alto, CA: Consulting Psychologists Press.

Nisbett, R. E. (1968). Birth order and participation in dangerous sports. *Journal of Personality and Social Psychology, 8*, 351–353.

Omoto, A. M. (1998). Responding to the HIV epidemic: Current research on volunteerism and its implications. *Psychology and AIDS Exchange, 25*, 3–11.

Omoto, A. M., & Malsch, A. M. (2005). Psychological sense of community: Conceptual issues and connections to volunteerism-related activism. In A. M. Omoto (Ed.), *Processes of community change and social action* (pp. 83–103). Mahwah, NJ: Erlbaum.

Omoto, A. M., & Snyder, M. (2002). Considerations of community: The context and process of volunteerism. *American Behavioral Scientist, 45*, 846–867.

Omoto, A. M., Snyder, M., & Martino, S. C. (2000). Volunteerism and the life course: Investigating age-related agendas for action. *Basic and Applied Social Psychology, 22*, 181–197.

Owyang, W. N. (1971). Ordinal position, frustration, and the expression of aggression [abstract]. *Dissertation Abstracts International, 31*, 6243B.

Pervin, L. A. (Ed.). (1992). Recent theoretical contributions on views of the self. *Psychological Inquiry, 3*.

Peterson, F., & Jung, C. G. (1907). Psychophysical investigations with the galvanometer and insane individuals. *Brain, 30*, 143–182.

Piotrowski, C., & Armstrong, T. (2002). Convergent validity of the Key Point pre-employment measure with the MBTI. *Psychology and Education: An Interdisciplinary Journal, 39*, 49–50.

Pittenger, D. J. (1993). The utility of the Myers-Briggs Type Indicator. *Review of Educational Research, 63*, 467–488.

Ricksher, C., & Jung, C. G. (1908). Further investigations on the galvanic phenomenon and respiration in normal and insane individuals. *Journal of Abnormal Psychology, 2*, 189–217.

Ring, K., Lipinski, C. E., & Braginsky, D. (1965). The relationship of birth order to self-evaluation, anxiety reduction, and susceptibility to emotional contagion. *Psychological Monographs, 79*, (Whole No. 603).

Rothbart, M. K. (1971). Birth order and mother–child interaction in an achievement situation. *Journal of Personality and Social Psychology, 17*, 113–120.

Rule, W. R. (2006a). The earliest recollection: A clue to present behavior. In W. R. Rule and M. Bishop, *Adlerian lifestyle counseling* (pp. 3–14). New York: Routledge.

Rule, W. R. (2006b). Introduction. In W. R. Rule and M. Bishop, *Adlerian lifestyle counseling* (pp. 3–14). New York: Routledge.

Rule, W. R., & Bishop, M. (2006). *Adlerian lifestyle counseling: Practice and research.* New York: Routledge.

Rule, W. R., & Comer, A. T. (2006). Family constellation and birth order variables related to vocational choice of dentistry. In W. R. Rule and M. Bishop, *Adlerian lifestyle counseling* (pp. 255–263). New York: Routledge.

Schachter, S. (1959). *The psychology of affiliation: Experimental studies of the sources of gregariousness.* Stanford, CA: Stanford University Press.

Schachter, S. (1963). Birth order, eminence, and higher education. *American Sociological Review, 28,* 757–767.

Searleman, A., Porac, C., & Coren, S. (1989). Relationship between birth order, birth stress, and lateral preferences: A critical review. *Psychological Bulletin, 105,* 397–408.

Snyder, C. R., & Lopez, S. J. (Eds.). (2002) *Handbook of positive psychology.* New York: Oxford University Press.

Snyder, M., & Omoto, A. N. (2000). Doing good for self and society: Volunteerism and the psychology of citizen participation. In M. Van Vugt, M. Snyder, T. R. Tyler, & A. Biel (Eds.), *Cooperation in modern society: Promoting the welfare of communities, states and organizations* (pp. 127–141). London: Routledge.

Snyder, M., & Omoto, A. M. (2004). Volunteer organizations: Theoretical perspectives and practical concerns. In R. E. Riggio & S. S. Orr (Eds.), *Improving leadership in nonprofit organizations* (pp. 163–179). San Francisco: Jossey-Bass/John Wiley.

Snyder, M., Omoto, A. M., & Crain, A. L. (1999). Punished for their good deeds: Stigmatization of AIDS volunteers. *American Behavioral Scientist, 42,* 1175–1192.

Snyder, M., Omoto, A. M., & Lindsay, J. J. (2004). Sacrificing time and effort for the good of others: The benefits and costs of volunteerism. In A. G. Miller (Ed.), *The social psychology of good and evil* (pp. 444–468). New York: Guilford Press.

Sommers-Flanagan, J., & Sommers-Flanagan, R. (2004). *Counseling and psychotherapy theories in context and practice: Skills, strategies, and techniques.* Hoboken, NJ: John Wiley.

Stewart, A. E. (2004). Can knowledge of client birth order bias clinical judgment? *Journal of Counseling and Development, 82,* 167–176.

Stricker, L. J., & Ross, J. (1964). Some correlates of a Jungian personality inventory. *Psychological Reports, 14,* 623–643.

Sulloway, F. J. (1990). *Orthodoxy and innovation in science: The influence of birth order in a multivariate context.* Paper presented at the meeting of the American Association for the Advancement of Science, New Orleans, LA, 16 February.

Sulloway. F. J. (1996). *Born to rebel: Birth order, family dynamics, and creative lives.* New York: Pantheon Books.

Sweeney, T. J. (1995). Foreword. In M T. Burke & J. G. Miranti (Eds.), *Counseling: The spiritual dimension* (pp. vii–viii). Alexandria, VA: American Counseling Association.

Taylor, S. E., Dickerson, S. S., & Klein, L. C. (2002), Toward a biology of social support. In C. R. Snyder & S. J. Lopez (Eds.), *Handbook of positive psychology* (pp. 556–569). New York: Oxford University Press.

Thompson, V. D. (1974). Family size: Implicit policies and assumed psychological outcomes. *Journal of Social Issues, 30,* 93–124.

Tieger, P. D., & Barron-Tieger, B. (2001). *Do what you are: Discover the perfect career for you through the secrets of personality type.* Boston: Little, Brown.

Toman, W. (1993). *Family constellation: Its effects on personality and social behavior* (4th ed.). New York: Springer.

Vacha-Haase, T., & Thompson, B. (2002). Alternative ways of measuring counselees' Jungian psychological-type preferences. *Journal of Counseling and Development, 80,* 173–179.

Varvel, T., Adams, S. G., Pridie, S., & Ruiz Ulloa, B. (2004). Team effectiveness and individual Myers-Briggs Personality Dimensions. *Journal of Management Engineering, 20,* 141–146.

Vowler, J. (2004, March 16). Creative thinking makes top team. *Computer Weekly,* p. 40.

Ward, C. D., Castro, A., & Wilcox, A. H. (1974). Birth-order effects in a survey of mate selection and parenthood. *Journal of Social Psychology, 94,* 57–64.

Warren, R. (1966). Birth order and social behavior. *Psychological Bulletin, 65,* 38–49.

Wilhelm, R., & Jung, C. G. (1931). *The secret world of the golden flower.* New York: Harcourt, Brace & World.

Winter, D. G., & Barenbaum, N. B. (1999). History of modern personality theory and research. In L. A. Pervin & O. P John (Eds.), *Handbook of personality: Theory and research* (2nd ed., pp. 3–27). New York: Guilford Press.

Zajonc, R. B. (1975, January). Dumber by the dozen. *Psychology Today,* 37–43.

Zajonc, R. B. (1976). Family configuration and intelligence. *Science, 192,* 227–236.

Zajonc, R. B., & Markus, G. B. (1975). Birth order and intellectual development. *Psychological Review, 82,* 74–88.

Zimbardo, P., & Formica, R. (1963). Emotional comparison and self-esteem as determinants of affiliation. *Journal of Personality, 31,* 141–162.

Zweigenhaft, R. L. (1975). Birth order, approval-seeking, and membership in Congress. *Journal of Individual Psychology, 31,* 205–210.

Chapter 5

Arlow, J. A. (1995). Psychoanalysis. In R. J. Corsini & D. Wedding (Eds.), *Current psychotherapies* (5th ed., pp. 15–50). Itasca, IL: F. E. Peacock.

Arnett, J. J. (2000). Emerging adulthood: A theory of development from the late teens through the twenties. *American Psychologist, 55,* 469–480.

Bai, M., Bagley, S., Johnson, S., & Levy, S. (1999, May 3). Death at Columbine High. *Newsweek, 133,* 23–39.

Baumeister, R. F. (1997). Identity, self-concept, and self-esteem. In R. Hogan, J. Johnson, & S. Briggs (Eds.), *Handbook of personality psychology* (pp. 681–710). San Diego, CA: Academic Press.

Beck, A. T. (1999). *Prisoners of hate: The cognitive basis of anger, hostility, and violence.* New York: HarperCollins.

Beck, A. T., & Weishaar, M. E. (1995). Cognitive therapy. In R. J. Corsini & D. Wedding (Eds.), *Current psychotherapies* (5th ed., pp. 229–261). Itasca, IL: F. E. Peacock.

Bell, L. C. (2004). Psychoanalytic theories of gender. In A. H. Eagly, A. E. Beall, & R. J. Sternberg (Eds.), *The psychology of gender* (2nd ed., pp. 145–168). New York: Guilford Press.

Bellew-Smith, M., & Korn, J. H. (1986). Merger intimacy status in adult women. *Journal of Personality and Social Psychology, 50,* 1186–1191.

Bergman, M., Akin, S. B., & Felig, P. (1990). Understanding the diabetic patient from a psychological dimension: Implications for the patient and the provider. *American Journal of Psychoanalysis*, *50*, 25–33.

Berkowitz, E. N., Kerin, R. A., Hartley, S. W., & Rudelius, W. (2000). *Marketing* (6th ed.). Boston: Irwin/McGraw-Hill.

Booth, P. B., & Lindaman, S. L. (2000). Theraplay for enhancing attachment in adopted children. In H. G. Kaduson & C. Schaefer (Eds.), *Short-term play therapy for children* (pp. 194–227). New York: Guilford Press.

Bornstein, R. F. (2006). The complex relationship between dependency and domestic violence: Converging psychological factors and social forces. *America Psychologist*, *61*, 595–606.

Brannon, L., & Feist, J. (2000). *Health psychology: An introduction to behavior and health* (4th ed.). Belmont, CA: Wadsworth/Thomson Learning.

Buss, D. M. (1999). *Evolutionary psychology: The new science of the mind*. Boston: Allyn & Bacon.

Carver, C. S., & Scheier, M. F. (2002). Optimism. In C. R. Snyder & S. J. Lopez (Eds.), *Handbook of positive psychology* (pp. 231–243). New York: Oxford University Press.

Chandler, M J., Lalonde, C. E., Sokol, B. W., & Hallett, D. (2003). Personal persistence, identity development, and suicide. *Monographs of Society for Research in Child Development*, *68* (No. 2, Serial No. 273).

Cocores, J. (1987). Co-addiction: A silent epidemic. *Psychiatry Letter*, *5*, 5–8.

Cohen, J. B. (1967). An interpersonal orientation to the study of consumer behavior. *Journal of Marketing Research*, *4*, 270–278.

Constantinople, A. (1969). An Eriksonian measure of personality development in college students. *Developmental Psychology*, *1*, 357–372.

Costa, P. T., Jr., & McCrae, R. R. (1997). Longitudinal stability of adult personality. In R. Hogan, J. Johnson, & S. Briggs (Eds.), *Handbook of personality psychology* (pp. 269–290). San Diego, CA: Academic Press.

Cretser, C. A., & Lombardo, W. K. (1999). Examining codependency in a college population. *College Student Journal*, *33*, 629–637.

de St. Aubin, E. (1998). Truth against the world: A psychobiographical explanation of generativity in the life of Frank Lloyd Wright. In D. P. McAdams & E. de St. Aubin (Eds.), *Generativity and adult development: How and why we care for the next generation* (pp. 391–427). Washington, DC: American Psychological Association.

Dillon, M., & Wink, P. (2004). American religion, generativity, and the therapeutic culture. In E. de. St Aubin & D. P. McAdams (Eds.), *The generative society* (pp. 153–174). Washington, DC: American Psychological Association.

Dweck, C. S. (2001). Caution – praise can be dangerous. In K. L. Frieberg (Ed.), *Human development 01/02* (29th ed., pp. 105–109). Guilford, CT: Dushkin/McGraw-Hill.

Elms, A. (2005). Freud as Leonardo: Why the first psychobiography went wrong. In W. T. Schultz (Ed.), *Handbook of psychobiography* (pp. 210–222). New York: Oxford University Press.

Engel, J. F., Blackwell, R. D., & Miniard, P. W. (1993). *Consumer behavior* (7th ed.). Fort Worth, TX: Dryden Press.

Erikson, E. H. (1950). *Childhood and society*. New York: Norton.

Erikson, E. H. (1958). *Young man Luther: A study in psychoanalysis and history*. New York: Norton.

Erikson, E. H. (1963). *Childhood and society* (2nd ed.). New York: Norton.

Erikson, E. H. (1968). *Identity, youth, and crisis*. New York: Norton.

Erikson, E. H. (1969). *Gandhi's truth*. New York: Norton.

Erikson, E. H. (1970). Autobiographic notes on the identity crisis. *Daedalus*, *99*, 730–759.

Erikson, E. H. (1974). *Dimensions of a new identity*. New York: Norton.

Erikson, E. H. (1975). *Life history and the historical movement*. New York: Norton.

Erikson, E. H., Erikson, J. M., & Kivnick, H. Q. (1986). *Vital involvement in old age*. New York: Norton.

Farver, J. A., M., Kim, Y. K., & Lee-Shin, Y. (2000). Within cultural differences: Examining individual differences in Korean American and European American preschoolers' social pretend play. *Journal of Cross-Cultural Psychology*, *31*, 583–602.

Fehr, B., & Sprecher, S. (2004, July). *Compassionate love: Conceptual, relational, and behavioral issues*. Paper presented at the meeting of the International Association of Relationship Research, Madison, WI.

Fromm, E. (1941). *Escape from freedom*. New York: Rinehart.

Fromm, E. (1947). *Man for himself*. Greenwich, CT: Fawcett Books.

Fuller, J. A., & Warner, R. M. (2000). Family stressors as predictors of codependency. *Journal of Social, Genetic, and General Psychology Monographs*, *26*, 5–22.

Gay, P. (1988). *Freud: A life for our time*. New York: Norton.

Gladding, S. T. (2003). *Counseling: A comprehensive profession* (5th ed.). Old Tappam, NJ: Prentice Hall.

Goencue, A., Mistry, J., & Mosier, C. (2000). Cultural variations in the play of toddlers. *International Journal of Behavioral Development*, *24*, 321–329.

Hamon, S. A. (1987). Some contributions of Horneyan theory to enhancement of the Type A behavior construct. *The American Journal of Psychoanalysis*, *47*, 105–115.

Harris, M. A., & Lustman, P. J. (1998). The psychologist in diabetes care. *Clinical Diabetes*, *16*, 91–93.

Hart, H. M. (1998). Generativity and social involvement [abstract]. *Dissertation Abstracts International*, *58*, (11–B), 6257.

Hart, H. M., McAdams, D. P., Hirsch, B. J., & Bauer, J. (2001). Generativity and social involvement among African American and white adults. *Journal of Research in Personality*, *35*, 208–230.

Harter, S. (2002). Authenticity. In C. R. Snyder & S. J. Lopez (Eds.), *Handbook of positive psychology* (pp. 382–394). New York: Oxford University Press.

Hartmann, H. (1958). *Ego psychology and the problem of adaptation*. New York: International Universities Press.

Hartmann, H. (1964). *Essays on ego psychology: Selected problems in psychoanalytic theory*. New York: International Universities Press.

Hawkins, D. I., Best, R. J., & Coney, K. A. (2001). *Consumer behavior: Building marketing strategy* (8th ed.). Boston: Irwin/McGraw-Hill.

Helson, R., Pals, J., & Solomon, M. (1997). Is there adult development distinctive to women? In R. Hogan, J. Johnson, & S. Briggs (Eds.), *Handbook of personality psychology* (pp. 291–314). San Diego, CA: Academic Press.

Hopkins, J. R. (1995). Erik Homburger Erikson (1902–1994). *American Psychologist, 50,* 796–797.

Horney, K. (1937). *The neurotic personality of our time.* New York: Norton.

Horney, K. (1939). *New ways in psychoanalysis.* New York: Norton.

Horney, K. (1942). *Self-analysis.* New York: Norton.

Horney, K. (1945). *Our inner conflicts.* New York: Norton.

Horney, K. (1950). *Neurosis and human growth.* New York: Norton.

Horney, K. (1967). *Feminine psychology.* New York: Norton.

Hyffamn, J. R. (1989). Young man Johnson. *The American Journal of Psychoanalysis, 49,* 251–265.

Irvine, L (1999). *Codependent for evermore: The invention of self in a twelve-step group.* Chicago: University of Chicago Press.

Jabin, N. (1987). Attitudes toward disability: Horney's theory applied. *The American Journal of Psychoanalysis, 47,* 143–153.

Kassarjian, H. H. (1971). Personality and consumer behavior: A review. *Journal of Marketing Research, 8,* 409–418.

Kelly, S. A., Brownell, C. A., & Campbell, S. E. (2000). Mastery motivation and self-evaluative affect in toddlers: Longitudinal relations with maternal behavior. *Child Development, 71,* 1061–1071.

Kernan, J. B. (1971). The CAD instrument in behavioral diagnosis. *Proceedings, Second Annual Conference, Association for Consumer Research,* 307–312.

Kring, A. M., Davision, G. C., Neale, J. M., & Johnson, S. L. (2007). *Abnormal psychology* (10th ed.). Hoboken, NJ: John Wiley.

Lachman, M. E. (2004). Development in midlife. *Annual Review of Psychology, 55,* 305–331.

Loeber, R., & Stouthamer-Loeber, M. (1998). Development of juvenile aggression and violence: Some common misconceptions and controversies. *American Psychologist, 53,* 242–249.

Lyon, D., & Greenberg, J. (1991). Evidence of codependency in women with an alcoholic parent: Helping out Mr. Wrong. *Journal of Personality and Social Psychology, 61,* 435–439.

Marcia, J. E. (1966). Development and validation of ego identity status. *Journal of Personality and Social Psychology, 3,* 551–558.

Marcia, J. E. (1980). Identity in adolescence. In J. Adelson (Ed.), *Handbook of adolescent psychology* (pp. 157–187). New York: John Wiley.

Marcia, J. E., & Friedman, M. L. (1970). Ego identity status in college woman. *Journal of Personality, 38,* 249–263.

Marcia, J. E., Waterman, A. S., Matteson, D. R., Archer, S. L., & Orlofsky, J. L. (1993). *Ego identity: A handbook for psychosocial research.* New York: Springer.

Marks, S. G., & Koepke, J. E. (1994). Pet attachment and generativity among young adults. *Journal of Psychology, 128,* 641–650.

Martsolf, D. S., Sedlak, C. A., & Doheny, M. O. (2000). Codependency and related health variables. *Archives of Psychiatric Nursing, 14,* 150–158.

McAdams, D. P. (1997). The three voices of Erik Erikson. *Contemporary Psychology, 42,* 575–578.

McAdams, D. P. (1999). Personal narratives and the life story. In L. A. Pervin & O. P. John (Eds.), *Handbook of personality: Theory and research* (2nd ed., pp. 478–500). New York: Guilford Press.

McAdams, D. P., & de St. Aubin, E. (1992). A theory of generativity and its assessment through self-report, behavior acts, and narrative themes in autobiography. *Journal of Personality and Social Psychology, 62,* 1003–1015.

McAdmans, D. P., & de St. Aubin, E. (Eds.). (1998). *Generativity and adult development: How and why we care for the next generation.* Washington, DC: American Psychological Assoiation.

McAdams, D. P., de St. Aubin, E., & Logan, R. L. (1993). Generativity among young, midlife, and older adults. *Psychology and Aging, 8,* 221–230.

McAdams, D. P., & Logan, R. L. (2004). What is generativity? In E. de St. Aubin, D. P. McAdams, & T. C Kim (Eds.), *The generative society* (pp. 15–31). Washington, DC: American Psychological Association Books.

McClelland, D. C., Atkinson, J. W., Clark, R. A., & Lowell, E. L. (1953). *The achievement motive.* East Norwalk, CT: Appleton-Century-Crofts.

McGregor, I. (2004). Zeal, identity, and meaning: Going to extremes to be one self. In J. Greenberg, S. L. Koole, & T. Pyszczynski (Ed.), *Handbook of experimental existential psychology* (pp. 182–199). New York: Guilford Press.

McGregor, I., Zanna, M. P., Holmes, J. G., & Spencer, S. J. (2001). Compensatory conviction in the face of personal uncertainty: Going to extremes to be yourself. *Journal of Personality and Social Psychology, 80,* 472–488.

Mealey, L. (2000). *Sex differences: Development and evolutionary strategies.* San Diego, CA: Academic Press.

Mikulincer, M., & Shaver, P. R. (2005). Attachment, security, compassion, and altruism. *Current Directions in Psychological Science, 14,* 34–38.

Miller, R. S., Perlman, D., & Brehm, S. S. (2007). *Intimate relationships* (4th ed.). New York: McGraw-Hill.

Mosak, H. H. (1995). Adlerian psychotherapy. In R. J. Corsini & D. Wedding (Eds.), *Current psychotherapies* (5th ed., pp. 51–94). Itasca, IL: F. E. Peacock.

Munson, J. M., & Spivey, W. A. (1982). The factor validity of an inventory assessing Horney's interpersonal response traits of compliance, aggression, and detachment. *Educational and Psychological Measurement, 42,* 889–898.

Murry, J. P., Jr., Latovicka, J. L., & Austin, J. R. (1997). The value of understanding the influence of lifestyle trait motivations on consumer beliefs. In L. R. Kahle & L. Chiagouris (Eds.), *Values, lifestyles, and psychographics* (pp. 45–68). Mahwah, NJ: Erlbaum.

Mussweiler, T., Gabriel, S., & Bodenhausen, G. V. (2000). Shifting social identities as a strategy for deflecting threatening social comparisons. *Journal of Personality and Social Psychology, 79,* 398–409.

Myers, D. G. (2000). *The American paradox: Spiritual hunger in an age of plenty*. New Haven, CT: Yale University Press.

Nevid, J. S., Rathus, S. A., & Greene, B. (2000). *Abnormal psychology in a changing world* (5th ed.). Upper Saddle River, NJ: Prentice Hall.

Noerager, J. P. (1979). An assessment of the CAD – A personality instrument developed specifically for marketing research. *Journal of Marketing Research*, 16, 53–59.

Ochse, R., & Plug, C. (1986). Cross-cultural investigation of the validity of Erikson's theory of personality development. *Journal of Personality and Social Psychology*, 50, 1240–1252.

Paris, B. J. (Ed.). (1989). Introduction: Interdisciplinary applications of Horney. *American Journal of Psychoanalysis*, 49, 181–188.

Paris, B. J. (1994). *Karen Horney: A psychoanalyst's search for self-understanding*. New Haven, CT: Yale University Press.

Peter, J. P., & Olson, J. C. (1999). *Consumer behavior and marketing strategy* (5th ed.). Boston: Irwin/McGraw-Hill.

Peterson, B. E., Smirles, K. A., & Wentworth, P. A. (1997). Generativity and authoritarianism: Implications for personality, political involvement, and parenting. *Journal of Personality and Social Psychology*, 72, 1202–1216.

Pratt, M. W., Danso, H. A., Arnold, M. L., Norris, J., & Flyer, R. (2001). *Journal of Personality*, 69, 89–120.

Pratt, M. W., Norris, J. E., Arnold, M. L., & Filyer, R. W. L. (1999). Generativity and moral development as predictors of value-socialization narratives for young persons across the life span: From lessons learned to stories shared. *Psychology of Aging*, 14, 414–426.

Pride, W. P., & Ferrell, O. C. (1993). *Marketing: Concepts and strategies* (8th ed.). Boston: Houghton Mifflin.

Putnam, R. D. (2000). *Bowling alone: The collaspe and revival of American community*. New York: Simon & Schuster.

Pyszczynski, T., Solomon, S., & Greenberg, J. (2003). *In the wake of 9/11: The psychology of terror*. Washington, DC: American Psychological Association.

Quinn, S. (1988). *A mind of her own: The life of Karen Horney*. Reading, MA: Addison Wesley.

Rachman, S. (2004). *Anxiety* (2nd ed.). New York: Psychology Press.

Rendon, D. (1987). Understanding social roles from a Horneyan perspective. *American Journal of Psychoanalysis*, 47, 131–142.

Roberts, B. W., Walton, K. E., & Viechtbauer, W. (2006). Patterns of mean-level change in personality traits across the life course: A meta-analysis of longitudinal studies. *Psychological Bulletin*, 132, 1–25.

Roemer, W. W. (1986). Leary's circle matrix: A comprehensive model for the statistical measurement of Horney's clinical concepts. *American Journal of Psychoanalysis*, 46, 249–262.

Roemer, W. W. (1987). An application of the interpersonal models developed by Karen Horney and Timothy Leary to Type A-B behavior patterns. *American Journal of Psychoanalysis*, 47, 116–130.

Rossi, A. S. (Ed.). (2001). *Caring and doing for others*. Chicago: University of Chicago Press.

Rubins, J. L. (1978). *Karen Horney: Gentle rebel of psychoanalysis*. New York: Dial.

Runyan, W. M. (Ed.). (1988a). *Psychology and historical interpretation*. New York: Oxford.

Runyan, W. M. (1988b). Progress in psychobiography. *Journal of Personality*, 56, 295–236.

Runyan, W. M. (1997). Studying lives: Psychobiography and the conceptual structure of personality psychology. In R. Hogan, J. Johnson, & S. Briggs (Eds.), *Handbook of personality psychology* (pp. 41–69). San Diego, CA: Academic Press.

Runyan, W. M. (2006). Psychobiography and the psychology of science: Understanding relations between the life and work of individual psychologists. *Review of General Psychology*, 10, 147–162.

Sayer, J. (1991). *Mothers of psychoanalysis: Helene Deutsch, Karen Horney, Anna Freud, Melanie Klein*. New York: Norton.

Schaef, A. (1986). *Codependence: Misunderstood-mistreated*. Minneapolis, MN: Winston Press.

Schultz, W. T. (Ed.). (2005). *Handbook of psychobiography*. New York: Oxford University Press.

Schwartz, B. (2004). *The paradox of choice: Why more is less*. New York: HarperCollins.

Schwartz, S. (2000). *Abnormal psychology: A discovery approach*. Mountain View, CA: Mayfield.

Shaffer, D. R., & Kipp, K. (2007). *Developmental psychology: Childhood and adolescence* (7th ed.). Belmont, CA: Thomson Higher Education.

Sheldon, K. M., & Kasser, T. (2001). Getting older, getting better? Personal striving and psychological maturity across the life span. *Developmental Psychology*, 37, 491–501.

Solomon, S., Greenberg, J., & Pyszczynski, T. (2004). The cultural animal: Twenty years of terror management theory and research. In J. Greenberg, S. L. Koole, & T. Pyszczynski (Eds.), *Handbook of experimental existential psychology* (pp. 13–34). New York: Guilford Press.

Sommers-Flanagan, J., & Sommers-Flanagan, R. (2004). *Counseling and psychotherapy theories in context and practice: Skills, strategies, and techniques*. Hoboken, NJ: John Wiley.

Sprecher, S., & Fehr, B. (2005). Compassionate love for close others and humanity. *Journal of Social and Personal Relationships*, 22, 629–651.

Stewart, A. J., & Vandewater, E. A. (1999). "If I had to do it over again . . .": Midlife review, midcourse corrections, and women's well-being in midlife. *Journal of Personality and Social Psychology*, 76, 270–283.

Strachan, M. W. J., Deary, I. J., Ewing, F. M. E., & Frier, B. M. (2000). Recovery of cognitive function and mood after severe hypoglycemia in adults with insulin-treated diabetes. *Diabetes Care*, 23, 305–311.

Strozier, C., & Offer, D. (Eds.). (1985). *The leader: Psycho-historical essays*. New York: Plenum.

Taylor, S. E. (2006). *Health psychology* (6th ed.). New York: McGraw-Hill.

Trull, T. J., & Phares, E. J. (2001). *Clinical psychology* (6th ed.). Belmont, CA: Wadsworth.

U.K. Prospective Diabetes Study Group (1999). Quality of life in type 2 diabetic patients is affected by complications but not by intensive policies to improve blood glucose or blood pressure control (UKPDS 37). *Diabetes Care*, 22, 1125–136.

Valsiner, J., & Lawrence, J. A. (1997). Human development in culture across the life span. In J. W. Berry, P. R. Dasen, & T. S. Saraswathi (Eds.), *Handbook of cross-cultural psychology: Vol. 2. Basic process and human development* (2nd ed., pp. 69–106). Boston: Allyn & Bacon.

Vandewater, E. A., Ostrove, J. M., & Stewart, A. J. (1997). Predicting women's well-being in midlife: The importance of personality development and social role involvements. *Journal of Personality and Social Psychology, 72,* 1147–1160.

Waite, R. G. L. (1977). *The psychopathic god: Adolf Hitler.* New York: Basic Books.

Walaskay, W., Whitbourne, S. K., & Nehrke, M. F. (1983–1984). Construction and validation of an ego-integrity status interview. *International Journal of Aging and Human Development, 18,* 61–72.

Waters, E., & Cummings, E. M. (2000). A secure base from which to explore close relationships. *Child Development, 71,* 164–172.

Wells, W. D., & Beard, A. D. (1973). Personality and consumer behavior. In S. Ward & T. S. Robertson (Eds.), *Consumer behavior: Theoretical sources* (pp. 141–199). Englewood Cliffs, NJ: Prentice Hall.

Westen, D., & Gabbard, G. O. (1999). Psychoanalytic approaches to personality. In L. A. Pervin & O. P. John (Eds.), *Handbook of personality: Theory and research* (2nd ed., pp. 57–101). New York: Guilford Press.

Westkott, M. (1986a). *The feminist legacy of Karen Horney.* New Haven, CT: Yale University Press.

Westkott, M. (1986b). Historical and developmental roots of female dependency. *Psychotherapy, 23,* 213–220.

Westkott, M. (1989). Female relationship and the idealized self. *American Journal of Psychoanalysis, 49,* 239–250.

Whitbourne, S. K., Zuschlag, M. K., Elliot, L. B., & Waterman, A. S. (1992). Psychosocial development in adulthood: A 22-year sequential study. *Journal of Personality and Social Psychology, 63,* 260–271.

Zucker, A. N., Ostrove, J. M., & Stewart, A. J. (2002). College-educated women's personality development in adulthood: Perceptions and age differences. *Psychology and Aging, 2,* 236–244.

Zuckerman, M. (2000). Optimsim and pessisim: Biological foundations. In E. C. Chang (Ed.), *Optimism and pessimism: Implications for theory, research, and practice* (pp. 169–188). Washington, DC: American Psychological Association.

Chapter 6

Allen, K., Blascovich, J., & Mendes, W. B. (2002). Cardiovascular reactivity in the presence of pets, friends, and spouses: The truth about cats and dogs. *Psychosomatic Medicine, 64,* 727–739.

Amabile, T. M. (1999). How to kill creativity. In *Harvard Business Review on breakthrough thinking* (pp. 1–28). Boston: Harvard Business School Press.

American Psychological Association (2007). Leadership [Special issue]. *American Psychologist, 62*(1).

Antonakis, J., Cianciolo, A., & Sternberg, R. J. (Eds.). (2004). *The nature of leadership.* Thousand Oaks, CA: Sage.

Axline, V. M. (1947). *Play therapy.* Boston: Houghton Mifflin.

Barone, D. F., & Kominars, K. D. (1998). Introduction to personality study. In D. F. Barone, M. Hersen, & V. B. Van Hasselt (Eds.), *Advanced personality* (pp. 3–24). New York: Plenum.

Batson, C. D., & Stocks, E. L. (2004). Religion: Its core psychological functions. In J. Greenberg, S. L. Koole, & T. Pyszczynski (Eds.), *Handbook of experimental existential psychology* (pp. 141–155). New York: Guilford Press.

Baumeister, R. F. (1999). The nature and structure of the self: An overview. In R. F. Baumeister (Ed.), *The self in social psychology* (pp. 1–20). Ann Arbor, MI: Edwards Bros.

Baumeister, R. F., Bushman, B. J., & Campbell, W. K. (2000). Self-esteem, narcissism, and aggression: Does violence result from low self-esteem or from threat to egotism? *Current Directions in Psychological Science, 9,* 26–29.

Baumeister, R. F., Campbell, J. D., Krueger, J. I., & Vohs, K. D. (2003). Does high self-esteem cause better performance, interpersonal success, happiness, or healthier lifestyles? *Psychological Science in the Public Interest, 4,* 1–44.

Baumeister, R. F., & Leary, M. R. (1995). The need to belong: Desire for interpersonal attachments as a fundamental human motivation. *Psychological Bulletin, 117,* 497–529.

Baumeister, R. F., Smart, L., & Boden, J. M. (1996). Relation of threatened egotism to violence and aggression: The dark side of high self-esteem. *Psychological Review, 103,* 5–33.

Bem, D. J., & Allen, A. (1974). On predicting some of the people some of the time: The search for cross-situational consistencies in behavior. *Psychological Review, 81,* 506–520.

Bem, D. J., & Funder, D. C. (1978). Predicting more of the people more of the time: Assessing the personality of situations. *Psychological Review, 85,* 485–501.

Berkowitz, E. N., Kerin, R. A., Hartley, S. W., & Rudelius, W. (2000). *Marketing* (6th ed.). Boston: Irwin/McGraw-Hill.

Beuckmann, C. T., & Yanagisawa, M. (2002). Orexins: From neuropeptide to energy homeostasis and sleep/wake regulation. *Journal of Molecular Medicine, 80,* 329–342.

Block, J. (1971). *Lives through time.* Berkeley, CA: Bancroft Books.

Bohart, A. C., & Greenberg, L. S. (Eds.). (1997). *Empathy reconsidered: New directions in psychotherapy.* Washington, DC: American Psychological Association.

Boorstein, S. (2000). Transpersonal psychotherapy. *American Journal of Psychotherapy, 54,* 408–423.

Bosma, H., Marmot, M. G., Hemingway, H., Nicholson, A. C., Brunner, E., & Stansfeld, S. A. (1997). Low job control and risk of coronary heart disease in Whitehall II (prospective cohort) study. *British Medical Journal, 314,* 558–565.

Braun, J., & Asta, P. (1968). Intercorrelations between the Personal Orientation Inventory and the Gordon Personal Inventory scores. *Psychological Reports, 23,* 1197–1198.

Broadbent, E., Petrie, K. J., Alley, P. G., & Booth, R. J. (2003). Psychological stress impairs early wound repair following surgery. *Psychosomatic Medicine, 65,* 865–869.

Brown, J. D., & Dutton, K. A. (1995). The thrill of victory, the complexity of defeat: Self-esteem and people's emotional reactions to success and failure. *Journal of Personality and Social Psychology, 68,* 712–722.

Brown, S. L., Nesse, R. M., Vinokur, A. D., & Smith, D. M. (2003). Providing social support may be more beneficial than receiving it: Results from a prospective study of morality. *Psychological Science, 14,* 320–327.

Brown, S. R. (1968). Bibliography on Q technique and its methodology. *Perceptual and Motor Skills, 26,* 587–61.

Bunker, B. B., & Alban, B. I. (1996). *Large group change.* San Francisco: Jossey-Bass.

Bushman, B. J., & Baumeister, R. F. (1998). Threatened egotism, narcissism, self-esteem, and direct and displaced aggression: Does self-love or self-hate lead to violence? *Journal of Personality and Social Psychology, 75,* 219–229.

Bushman, B. J., & Baumeister, R. F. (2002). Does self-love or self-hate lead to violence? *Journal of Research in Personality, 36,* 543–545.

Butler, J. M. (1968). Self-ideal congruence in psychotherapy. *Psychotherapy: Theory, Research, and Practice, 5,* 13–17.

Butler, J. M., & Haigh, G. V. (1954). Changes in the relation between self-concepts and ideal concepts consequent upon client-centered counseling. In C. R. Rogers & R. Dymond (Eds.), *Psychotherapy and personality change: Co-ordinated research studies in the client-centered approach* (pp. 55–75). Chicago: University of Chicago Press.

Case, T. I., & Williams, K. D. (2004). Ostracism: A metaphor for death. In J. Greenberg, S. L. Koole, & T. Pyszczynski (Eds.), *Handbook of experimental existential psychology* (pp. 336–351). New York: Guilford Press.

Caspi, A., & Roberts, B. W. (1999). Personality continuity and change across the life course. In L. A. Pervin & O. P. John (Eds.), *Handbook of personality: Theory and research* (2nd ed., pp. 300–326). New York: Guilford Press.

Cassel, R. N. (1958). *The leadership Q-sort test: A test of leadership values.* Murfreesboro, TN: Psychometric Affiliate.

Chamberlin, J. (2000). Easing children's psychological distress in the emergency room. *Monitor on Psychology, 31,* 40–42.

Cheng, Y., Kawachi, I., Coakley, E. H., Schwartz, J., & Colditz, G. (2000). Association between psychosocial work characteristics and health functioning in American woman: Prospective study. *British Medical Journal, 320,* 1432–1436.

Christensen, H., Griffiths, K., Groves, C., & Korten, A. (2006). *Australian and New Zealand Journal of Psychiatry, 40,* 59–62.

Christensen, H., Griffiths, K. M., & Jorm, A. F. (2004). Delivering interventions for depression by using the Internet: Randomised controlled trial. *British Medical Journal, 328,* 265.

Christensen, K. A., Stephens, M. A. P., & Townsend, A. L. (1998). Mastery in women's multiple roles and well-being: Adult daughters providing care to impaired parents. *Health Psychology, 17,* 163–171.

Cohen, R. J., & Swerdlik, M. E. (2005). *Psychological testing and assessment: An introduction to tests and measurements* (6th ed.). Boston: McGraw-Hill.

Cohen, S. (2002). Psychological stress, social network, and susceptibility to infection. In H. G. Koenig & H. J. Cohen (Eds.), *The link between religion and health: Psychoneuroimmunology and the faith factor* (pp. 101–123). New York: Oxford University Press.

Coleman, D. (1992). Why do I feel so tired? Too little, too late. *American Health, 11,* 43–46.

Coleman, H. L. K., Wampold, B. E., & Casali. S. L. (1995). Ethnic minorities' ratings of ethnically similar and European-American counselors: A meta-analysis. *Journal of Counseling Psychology, 42,* 55–64.

Comer, R. J. (2007). *Abnormal psychology* (6th ed.). New York: Worth.

Csikszentmihalyi, M. (1990). *Flow: The psychology of optimal experience.* New York: HarperCollins.

Csikszentmihalyi, M. (1996). *Creativity: Flow and the psychology of discovery and invention.* New York: HarperCollins.

Csikszentmihalyi, M. (1997). *Finding flow.* New York: Basic Books.

Csikszentmihalyi, M., Abuhamdeh, S., & Nakamura, J. (2005). Flow. In A. J. Elliot & C. S. Dweck (Eds.), *Handbook of competence and motivation* (pp. 598–608). New York: Guilford Press.

Csikszentmihalyi, M., & Nakamura, J. (1999). Emerging goals and the self-regulation of behavior. In R. S. Wyer, Jr. (Ed.), *Advances in social cognition: Vol. 12* (pp. 107–118). Mahwah, NJ: Erlbaum.

Curtis, R., Groarke, A. M., Coughlan, R., & Gsel, A. (2004). The influence of disease severity, perceived stress, social support, and coping in patients with chronic stress: A 1-year follow-up. *Psychology, Health, and Medicine, 9,* 456–475.

Danieli, Y., Engdahl, B., & Schlenger, W. E. (2004). The psychological aftermath of terrorism. In F. M. Moghaddam & A. J. Marsella (Eds.), *Understanding terrorism: Psychological roots, consequences, and interventions* (pp. 223–246). Washington, DC: American Psychological Association.

Dawson, D., & Reid, K. (1997). Fatigue, alcohol, and performance impairment. *Nature, 388,* 235.

Demaray, M. K., & Malecki, C. K. (2002). Critical levels of perceived social support associated with student adjustment. *Social Psychology Quarterly, 17,* 213–241.

DeMulder, E. K., Denham, S., Schmidt, M., & Mitchell, J. (2000). Q-sort assessment of attachment security during the preschool years: Links from home to school. *Developmental Psychology, 36,* 274–282.

Duan, C., Rose, T. B., & Kraatz, A. (2002). Empathy. In G. S. Tryon (Ed.), *Counseling based on process research: Applying what we know* (pp. 197–231). Boston: Allyn & Bacon.

Duncan, R. C., Konefal, J., & Spechler, M. M. (1990). Effect of neurolinguistic programming training on self-actualization as measured by the Personal Orientation Inventory. *Psychological Reports, 66,* 1323–1330.

Egbert, L. D., Battit, G. E., Welch, C. E., & Bartlett, M. K. (1964). Reduction of post-operative pain by encouragement and instruction of patients: A doctor–patient rapport. *New England Journal of Medicine, 270,* 825–827.

Elkins, D. N. (2001). Beyond religion: Toward a humanistic spirituality. In K. J. Schneider, J. F. T. Bugental, & J. F.

Pierson (Eds.), *The handbook of humanistic psychology: Leading edges in theory, research, and practice* (pp. 201–212). Thousands Oaks, CA: Sage.

Ellinwood, C. G., & Raskin, N. J. (1993). Client-centered/humanistic psychotherapy. In T. R. Kratochwill & R. J. Morris (Eds.), *Handbook of psychotherapy with children and adolescents* (pp. 258–287). Boston: Allyn & Bacon.

Ellis, A. (1995). Rational emotive behavior therapy. In R. J. Corsini & D. Wedding (Eds.), *Current psychotherapies* (5th ed., pp. 162–196). Itasca, IL: F. E. Peacock.

Emery, M., & Purser, R. (1996). *The search conference.* San Francisco: Jossey-Bass.

Foa, E. B., Hembree, E. A., Riggs, D., Rauch, S., & Franklin, M. (2001). *Common reactions to trauma.* Retrieved from www.ncptsd.org/facts/diasters/fs_foa_jandout.html.

Food and Agricultural Organization (FAO) of the United Nations (2006). State of food insecurity in the world 2006: Undernourishment around the world. In *The Millennium Development Goals Report 2006.* New York: FAO United Nations.

Food Research and Action Center (2006). Hunger in the U.S.: Hunger and food insecurity in the United States. Washington, DC: U.S. Department of Agriculture. Retrieved from *www.frac.org/4/6/2007.*

Funder, D. C., & Block, J. (1989). The role of ego-control, ego-resiliency, and IQ in delay of gratification in adolescents. *Journal of Personality and Social Psychology, 57,* 1041–1050.

Funder, D. C., Block, J. H., & Block, J. (1983). Delay of gratification: Some longitudinal personality correlates. *Journal of Personality and Social Psychology, 44,* 1198–1213.

Funder, D. C., Parke, R. D., Tomlinson-Keasey, C., & Widaman, K. (Eds.). (1993). *Studying lives through time: Personality and development.* Washington, DC: American Psychological Association.

Gaba, D. M., & Howard, S. K. (2002). Fatigue among clinicians and the safety of patients. *New England Journal of Medicine, 347,* 1249–1255.

Gais, S., & Born, J. (2004). Low acetylcholine during slow-wave sleep is critical for declarative memory consolidation. *Proceedings of the National Academy of Sciences, 101,* 2140–2144.

Greenberg, L., Elliott, R., & Lietaer, G. (1994). Research on experiential psychotherapies. In A. E. Bergin & S. L. Garfield (Eds.), *Handbook of psychotherapy and behavior change* (4th ed., pp. 509–539). New York: John Wiley.

Greenberg, L., Watson, J. C., & Lietaer, G. (Eds.). (1998). *Handbook of experiential psychotherapy.* New York: Guilford Press.

Greening, T. (2001). Becoming authentic: An existential-humanistic approach to reading literature. In K. J. Schneider, J. F. T. Bugental, & J. F. Pierson (Eds.), *The handbook of humanistic psychology: Leading edges in theory, research, and practice* (pp. 143–152). Thousands Oaks, CA: Sage.

Gregory, R. J. (2007). *Psychological testing: History, principles, and applications* (5th ed.). Boston: Pearson Education.

Griffiths, K. M., & Christensen, H. (2006). Review of randomized controlled trials of Internet interventions for mental disorders and related conditions. *Australian Psychological Society, 10,* 16–29.

Guinan, J. F., & Foulds, M. L. (1970). Marathon group: Facilitator of personal growth? *Journal of Counseling Psychology, 17,* 145–149.

Hattie, J. (1981). A four-stage factor analytic approach to studying behavioral domains. *Applied Psychological Measurement, 5,* 77–88.

Hattie, J., Hancock, P., & Brereton, K. (1984). The relationship between two measures of self-actualization. *Journal of Personality Assessment, 48,* 17–25.

Hawkins, D. I., Mothersbaugh, B. L., & Best, R. J. (2007). *Consumer behavior: Building marketing strategy* (10th ed.). Boston: McGraw-Hill/Irwin.

Hicks, R. A., Fernandez, C., & Pelligrini, R. J. (2001). The changing pattern of sleep habits of university students: An update. *Perceptual and Motor Skills, 93,* 648.

Hobson, C. J., & Delunas, L. (2001). National norms and life-event frequencies for the revised Social Readjustment Rating Scale. *International Journal of Stress Management, 8,* 299–314.

Holmes, T. H., & Rahe, R. H. (1967). The Social Readjustment Scale. *Journal of Psychosomatic Research, 11,* 213–218.

Jacobs, M. K., Christensen, A., Snibbe, J. R., Dolezal-Wood, S., Huber, A., & Polterok, A. (2001). A comparison of computer-based versus traditional individual psychotherapy. *Professional Psychology: Research and Practice, 32,* 92–96.

Jackson, D. N., & Messick, S. (1958). Content and style in personality assessment. *Psychological Bulletin, 55,* 243–252.

Jones, A., & Crandall, R. (1986). Validation of a short index of self-actualization. *Personality and Social Psychology Bulletin, 12,* 63–73.

Jones, F., & Kinman, G. (2001). Approaches to studying stress: In F. Jones & J. Bright (Eds.), *Stress: Myth, theory and research* (pp. 17–44). Harlow, UK: Pearson Education.

Kahle, L. R., Homer, P. M., O'Brien, R. M., & Boush, D. M. (1997). Maslow's hierarchy and social adaptation as alternative accounts of value structures. In L. R. Kahle & L. Chiagouris (Eds.), *Values, lifestyles, and psychographics* (pp. 111–135). Mahwah, NJ: Erlbaum.

Kasser, T., & Sheldon, K. M. (2004). Nonbecoming, alienated becoming, and authentic becoming. In J. Greenburg, S. L. Koole, & T. Pyszcznski (Eds.), *Handbook of experiential existential psychology* (pp. 480–493). New York: Guilford Press.

Kendler, K. S., Myers, J., & Prescott, C. A. (2005). Sex differences in the relationship between social support and risk for major depression: A longitudinal study of opposite-sex twin pairs. *American Journal of Psychiatry, 162,* 250–256.

Kernis, M. H. (2003a). Optimal self-esteem and authenticity: Separating fantasy from reality. *Psychological Inquiry, 14,* 83–89.

Kernis, M. H. (2003b). Toward a conceptualization of optimal self-esteem. *Psychological Inquiry, 14,* 1–26.

Kezar, A. J., Carducci, R., & Contreras-McGavin, M. (2006). *Rethinking the "L" word in higher education: The revolution of research and leadership.* San Francisco: Jossey-Bass.

Krause, N., & Shaw, B. A. (2000). Role-specific feelings of control and mortality. *Psychology and Aging, 15,* 617–626.

Kraut, R., Patterson, M., Lundmark, V., Kiesler, S., Mukopadhyay, T., & Scherlis, W. (1998). Internet paradox: A social technology that reduces social involvement and psychological well-being? *American Psycholgist, 53*, 1017–1031.

Lakin, M. (1998). Carl Rogers and the culture of psychotherapy. In G. A. Kimble & M. Wertheimer (Eds.), *Portraits of pioneers in psychology: Vol. 3* (pp. 245–258). Washington, DC: American Psychological Association.

Lambert, M. J., Bergin, A. E., & Garfield, S. L. (2004). Introduction and historical overview. In M. J. Lambert (Ed.), *Bergin and Garfield's handbook of psychotherapy and behavior change* (5th ed., pp. 3–15). New York: John Wiley.

Lambert, M. J., & Hill, C. E. (1994). Assessing psychotherapy outcome and processes. In A. E. Bergin & S. L. Garfield (Eds.), *Handbook of psychotherapy and behavior change* (4th ed., pp. 72–113). New York: John Wiley.

Landau, B. M. (2001). Psychotherapy online in 2001: For psychotherapists new to the Internet. *Journal of Mental Imagery, 25*, 65–82.

Landrigan, C. P., Rothschild, J. M., Cronin, J. W., Kaushal, R., Burdick, E., Katz, et al. (2004). Effect of reducing interns' work hours on serious medical errors in intensive care units. *New England Journal of Medicine, 351*, 1838–1848.

Landy, F. J. (1989). *Psychology of work behavior* (4th ed.). Pacific Grove, CA: Brooks/Cole.

Lange, A., van de Ven, J. P., Schrieken, B., & Smith, M. (2004). "Interapy" burnout: Prevention and therapy of burnout via the Internet. *Verhaltenstherapie, 14*, 190–199.

Lanier, L. S., Privette, G., Vodanovich, S., & Bundrick, C. M. (1996). Peak experiences: Lasting consequences and breadth of occurrences among realtors, artists, and a comparison group. *Journal of Social Behavior and Personality, 11*, 781–791.

Lanyon, R. I., & Goodstein, L. D. (1997). *Personality assessment* (3rd ed.). New York: John Wiley.

Leak, G. K. (1984). A multidimensional assessment of the validity of the Personal Orientation Inventory. *Journal of Personality Assessment, 48*, 37–41.

LeMay, M., & Damm, V. (1968). The Personal Orientation Inventory as a measure of self-actualization of underachievers. *Measurement and Evaluation in Guidance, 1*, 110–114.

Maddi, S. R. (1996). *Personality theories: A comparative analysis* (6th ed.). Pacific Grove, CA: Brooks/Cole.

Maslow, A. H. (1943). A theory of human motivation. *Psychological Review, 50*, 370–396.

Maslow, A. H. (1954). *Motivation and personality*. New York: Harper & Row.

Maslow, A. H. (1962). *Toward a psychology of being*. Princeton, NJ: Van Nostrand.

Maslow, A. H. (1965). *Eupsychian management: A journal*. Homewood, IL: Irwin-Dorsey Press.

Maslow, A. H. (1968). *Toward a psychology of being* (2nd ed.). New York: Van Nostrand Reinhold.

Maslow, A. H. (1970a). *Religions, values, and peak experiences*. Columbus: Ohio State University.

Maslow, A. H. (1970b). *Motivation and personality* (2nd ed.). New York: Harper & Row.

Maslow, A. H. (1971). *The farther reaches of human nature*. New York: Viking.

Maslow, A. H. (1976). *Religions, values, and peak experiences*. New York: Penguin.

Maslow, A. H. (1998). *Maslow on motivation*. New York: John Wiley. (Original work published 1965)

Matteson, M. T. (1974). Some reported thoughts on significant management literature. *Academy of Management Journal, 17*, 386–389.

McCann, J. T., & Biaggio, M. K. (1989). Sexual satisfaction in marriage as a function of life meaning. *Archives of Sexual Behavior, 18*, 59–72.

McCrae, R. R., Costa, P. T., & Busch, C. M. (1986). Evaluating comprehensiveness in personality systems: The California Q-Set and the Five-Factor Model. *Journal of Personality, 54*, 430–446.

McGaw, W. H., Rice, C. P., & Rogers, C. R. (1973). *The steel shutter*. La Jolla, CA: Film Center for Studies of the Person.

McLean, D. E., & Link, B. G. (1994). Unraveling complexity: Strategies to refine concepts, measures, and research designs in the study of events and mental health. In W. R. Avison & I. H. Gotlib (Eds.), *Stress and mental health: Contemporary issues and prospects for the future* (pp. 15–38). New York: Plenum.

Meador, B. D., & Rogers, C. R. (1973). Client-centered therapy. In R. J. Corsini (Ed.), *Current psychotherapies* (pp. 119–166). Itasca, IL: F. E. Peacock.

Merluzzi, T. V., Glass, C. R., & Genest, M. (Eds.). (1981). *Cognitive assessment*. New York: Guilford Press.

Mischel, W. (1972). Direct versus indirect personality assessment: Evidence and implications. *Journal of Consulting and Clinical Psychology, 38*, 319–324.

Mischel, W. (1981). Metacognition and the rules of delay. In J. H. Flavell & L. Ross (Eds.), *Social cognitive development: Frontiers and possible futures* (pp. 240–271). New York: Cambridge University Press.

Mitchell, K. M., Bozarth, J. D., & Krauft, C. C. (1977). A reappraisal of the therapeutic effectiveness of accurate empathy, nonpossessive warmth, and genuineness. In A. S. Gurman & A. M. Razin (Eds.), *Effective psychotherapy: A handbook of research* (pp. 482–502). New York: Pergamon.

Mitchell, T. R., & Daniels, D. (2003). Motivation. In W. C. Borman, D. R. Ilgen, & R. J. Klimoski (Eds.), *Handbook of psychology: Vol. 12. Industrial organizational psychology* (pp. 225–254). Hoboken, NJ: John Wiley.

Montuori, A., & Purser, R. (2001). Humanistic psychology in the workplace. In K. J. Schneider, J. F. T. Bugental, & J. F. Pierson (Eds.), *The handbook of humanistic psychology: Leading edges in theory, research, and practice* (pp. 635–644). Thousands Oaks, CA: Sage.

Morris, R. J., & Suckerman, K. R. (1974). The importance of the therapeutic relationship in systematic desensitization. *Journal of Consulting and Clinical Psychology, 42*, 148.

Mortley, J., Wade, J., & Enderby, P. (2004). Superhighway to promoting a client–therapist partnership: Using the Internet to deliver word-retrieval computer therapy, monitored remotely with minimal speech and language therapy. *Aphasiology, 18*, 193–211.

Moss, D. (2001). The roots and genealogy of humanistic psychology. In K. J. Scheider, J. F. T. Bugental, & J. F. Pierson (Eds.), *The handbook of humanistic psychology: Leading edges in theory, research, and practice* (pp. 5–20). Thousand Oaks, CA: Sage.

Mruk, C. J. (2006). *Self-esteem research, theory, and practice: Toward a positive psychology of self-esteem* (3rd ed.). New York: Springer.

Nevid, J. S., Rathus, S. A., & Greene, B. (2000). *Abnormal psychology in a changing world* (4th ed.). Upper Sadle River, NJ: Prentice Hall.

Nezlek, J. B., Hampton, C. P., & Shean, G. D. (2000). Clinical depression and day-to-day social interaction in a community sample. *Journal of Abnormal Psychology, 109,* 11–19.

Noonoo, J. (2007, July 2/9). The dry facts about water. *Newsweek,* p. 49.

Orlinsky, D. E., Rønnestad, M. H., & Willutzki, U. (2004). Fifty years of psychotherapy process-outcome research: Continuity and change. In M. J. Lambert (Ed.), *Bergin and Garfield's handbook of psychotherapy and behavior change* (5th ed., pp. 307–389). New York: John Wiley.

Osborne, R. E. (1996). *Self: An eclectic approach.* Boston: Allyn & Bacon.

Ozer, D. J., & Gjerde, P. F. (1989). Patterns of personality consistency and change from childhood through adolescence. *Journal of Personality, 57,* 483–507.

Patterson, C. H. (2000). *Person-centered approach and client-centered therapy: Essential readers.* Ross-on-Wye, UK: PCCS Books.

Pinel, E., Long, A. E., Landau, M. J., & Pyszczynski, T. (2004). I-sharing, the problem of existential isolation, and their implications for interpersonal and intergroup phenomena. In J. Greenberg, S. L. Koole, & T. Pyszczynski (Eds.), *Handbook of experimental existential psychology* (pp. 352–368). New York: Guilford Press.

Polkinghorne, D. E. (2001). The self and humanistic psychology. In K. J. Schneider, J. F. T. Bugental, & J. F. Pierson (Eds.), *The handbook of humanistic psychology: Leading edges in theory, research, and practice* (pp. 81–99). Thousand Oaks, CA: Sage.

Polyson, J. (1985). Students' peak experiences: A written exercise. *Teaching of Psychology, 12,* 211–213.

Porras, J. C., & Collins, J. I. (1997). *Built to last.* New Yorker: HarperCollins.

Privette, G. (1983). Peak experience, peak performance, and flow: A comparative analysis of positive human experiences. *Journal of Personality and Social Psychology, 45,* 1361–1368.

Privette, G. (1984). *Experience Questionnaire.* Pensacola: University of West Florida.

Privette, G. (2001). Defining moments of self-actualization: Peak performance and peak experience. In K. J. Schneider, J. F. T. Bugental, & J. F. Pierson (Eds.), *The handbook of humanistic psychology: Leading edges in theory, research, and practice* (pp. 161–180). Thousand Oaks, CA: Sage.

Privette, G., & Bundrick, C. M. (1987). Measurement of experience: Construct and content validity of the experience questionnaire. *Perceptual and Motor Skills, 65,* 315–332.

Privette, G., & Bundrick, C. M. (1991). Peak experience, peak performance, and flow: Correspondence of personal descriptions and theoretical constructs. *Journal of Social Behavior and Personality, 6,* 169–188.

Privette, G., Hwang, K. K., & Bundrick, C. M. (1997). Cross-cultural measurement of experience: Taiwanese and American peak performance, peak experience, misery, failure, sport and average events. *Perceptual and Motor Skills, 84,* 1459–1482.

Putnam, R. D. (1996). The strange disappearance of civic America. *The American Prospect, 24,* 34–46.

Putnam, R. D. (2000). *Bowling alone: The collapse and revival of American community.* New York: Simon & Schuster.

Rabasca, L. (2000). Taking telehealth to the next step. *Monitor on Psychology, 31,* 36–37.

Rahe, R. H., & Arthur, R. H. (1978). Life change and illness studies. *Journal of Human Stress, 4,* 2–15.

Rahe, R. H., Veach, T. L., Tolles, R. L., & Murakami, K. (2000). The stress and coping inventory: An educational and research instrument. *Stress Medicine, 16,* 199–208.

Raskin, N. J., & Rogers, C. R. (1989). Person-centered therapy. In R. J. Corsini & D. Wedding (Eds.), *Current psychotherapies* (4th ed., pp. 155–194). Itasca, IL: F. E. Peacock.

Raskin, N. J., & Rogers, C. R. (1995). Person-centered therapy. In R. J. Corsini & D. Wedding (Eds.), *Current psychotherapies* (5th ed., pp. 128–161). Itasca, IL: F. E. Peacock.

Raskin, N. J., & Rogers, C. R. (2000). Person-centered therapy. In R. J. Corsini & D. Wedding (Eds.), *Current psychotherapies* (6th ed., pp. 133–167). Itasca, IL: F. E. Peacock.

Raskin, N. J., Rogers, C. R., & Witty, M. C. (2008). Person-centered therapy. In R. J. Corsini & D. Wedding (Eds.), *Current psychotherapies* (8th ed., pp. 141–186). Belmont, CA: Thomson-Brooks/Cole

Rathus, S. P., & Nevid, J. S. (2002). *Psychology and the challenges of life: Adjustment in the new millennium* (8th ed.). New York: John Wiley.

Reis, H. T., & Patrick, B. C. (1996). Attachment and intimacy: Component processes. In E. T. Higgins & A. W. Kruglanski (Eds.), *Social psychology: Handbook of basic principles* (pp. 523–563). New York: Guilford Press.

Riggio, R. E., Murphy, S. E., & Pirozzolo, F. J. (2002). *Multiple intelligence and leadership.* Mahwah, NJ: Erlbaum.

Roberts, T. B. (1972). *Maslow's human motivation needs hierarchy: A bibliography.* De Kalb: Northern Illinois University.

Rochlen, A. B., Zack, J. S., & Speyer, C. (2004). Online therapy: Review of relevant definitions, debates, and current empirical support. *Journal of Clinical Psychology, 60,* 269–283.

Rogers, C. R. (1939). *The clinical treatment of the problem child.* Boston: Houghton Mifflin.

Rogers, C. R. (1942a). *Counseling and psychotherapy.* Boston: Houghton Mifflin.

Rogers, C. R. (1942b). The use of electrically recorded interviews in improving psychotherapeutic techniques. *American Journal of Orthopsychiatry, 12,* 429–434.

Rogers, C. R. (1951). *Client-centered therapy: Its current practice, implications, and theory.* Boston: Houghton Mifflin.

Rogers, C. R. (1952). Communication: Its blocking and facilitation. *ECT: A Review of General Semantics, 9,* 83–88.

Rogers, C. R. (1957). The necessary and sufficient conditions of therapeutic personality change. *Journal of Consulting Psychology, 21,* 95–103.

Rogers, C. R. (1958). A process conception of psychotherapy. *American Psychologist, 13,* 142–149.

Rogers, C. R. (1959). A theory of therapy, personality, and interpersonal relationship, as developed in the client-centered framework. In S. Koch (Ed.), *Psychology: A study of a science: Vol. 3. Formulations of the person and the social context* (pp. 184–256). New York: McGraw-Hill.

Rogers, C. R. (1961). *On becoming a person: A therapist's view of psychotherapy.* Boston: Houghton Mifflin.

Rogers, C. R. (1964). The concept of the fully functioning person. *Psychotherapy: Theory, Research, and Practice, 1,* 17–26.

Rogers, C. R. (1967). Autobiography. In E. G. Boring & G. Lindzey (Eds.), *A history of psychology in autobiography: Vol. 5* (pp. 341–384). New York: Appleton-Century-Crofts.

Rogers, C. R. (1969). *Freedom to learn.* Columbus, OH: Merrill.

Rogers, C. R. (1970). *Carl Rogers on encounter groups.* New York: Harper & Row.

Rogers, C. R. (1972). *Becoming partners: Marriage and its alternatives.* New York: Delacorte.

Rogers, C. R. (1974). In retrospect: Forty-six years. *American Psychologists, 29,* 115–123.

Rogers, C. R. (1977). *Carl Rogers on personal power.* New York: Delacorte.

Rogers, C. R. (1980). *A way of being.* Boston: Houghton Mifflin.

Rogers, C. R. (1982, August). Nuclear war: A personal response. *American Psychological Association Monitor, 7,* 6–7.

Rogers, C. R. (1983). *Freedom to learn for the 80's.* Columbus, OH: Merrill.

Rogers, C. R. (1986a). Client-centered therapy. In I. L. Kutash & A. Wolf (Eds.), *Psychotherapist's casebook: Therapy and technique in practice* (pp. 197–208). San Francisco: Jossey-Bass.

Rogers, C. R. (1986b). The Rust workshop: A personal overview. *Journal of Humanistic Psychology, 26,* 23–45.

Rogers, C. R. (1987). Inside the world of the Soviet professional. *Journal of Humanistic Psychology, 27,* 277–304.

Rogers, C. R., & Dymond, R. F. (Eds.). (1954). *Psychotherapy and personality change: Co-ordinated research studies in the client-centered approach.* Chicago: University of Chicago Press.

Rogers, C. R., & Ryback, D. (1984). One alternative to nuclear planetary suicide. In R. F. Levant & J. M. Shlien (Eds.), *Client-centered therapy and the person-centered approach: New directions in theory* (pp. 400–422). New York: Praeger.

Rogers, C. R., & Sanford, R. C. (1985). Client-centered psychotherapy. In H. I. Kaplan, B. J. Sadock, & A. M. Friedman (Eds.), *Comprehensive textbook of psychiatry* (4th ed., pp. 1374–1388). Baltimore: Williams & Walkins.

Ronen, S. (1994). An underlying structure of motivational need taxonomies: A cross-cultural confirmation. In H. C. Triandis, M. D. Dunnettee, & L. M. Hough (Eds.), *Handbook of industrial and organizational psychology: Vol. 4* (2nd ed., pp. 241–269). Palo Alto, CA: Consulting Psychologists Press.

Rosen, L. (2005). "Online therapy" is excellent e-primer. *National Psychologist, 14,* 16.

Schofield, W. (1964). *Psychotherapy: The purchase of friendship.* Englewood Cliffs, NJ: Prentice Hall.

Schwartz, S. (2000). *Abnormal psychology: A discovery approach.* Mountain View, CA: Mayfield.

Scully, J. A., Tosi, H., & Banning, K. (2000). Life checklists: Revisiting the social readjustment rating scale after 30 years. *Educational and Psychological Measurement, 60,* 864–876.

Shaver, P. R., & Mikulincer, M. (2003). The psychodynamics of social judgments: An attachment theory perspective. In J. P. Forgas, K. D. Williams, & W. von Hippel (Eds.), *Responding to the social world: Implicit and explicit processes in social judgments and decisions* (pp. 85–114). New York: Cambridge University Press.

Shostrom, E. (1963). *Personal Orientation Inventory (POI): A test of self-actualization.* San Diego, CA: Educational and Industrial Testing Service.

Shostrom, E. (1964). An inventory for the measurement of self-actualization. *Educational and Psychological Measurement, 24,* 207–218.

Shostrom, E. L. (1975). *Personal Orientation Inventory.* San Diego, CA: Educational and Industrial Testing Service.

Shostrom, E. L. (1977). *Manual for the Personal Orientation Dimensions.* San Diego, CA: Edits.

Silverstein, A. B., & Fisher, G. (1968). Is item overlap responsible for a "built-in" factor structure? *Psychological Reports, 23,* 935–938.

Silverstein, A. B., & Fisher, G. (1972). Item overlap and the "built-in" factor structure of the Personal Orientation Inventory. *Psychological Reports, 31,* 491–494.

Simonton, D. K. (1988). Creativity, leadership, and chance. In R. J. Sternberg (Ed.), *The nature of creativity: Contemporary psychological perspectives* (pp. 386–426). New York: Cambridge University Press.

Simonton, D. K. (1994). *Greatness: Who makes history and why?* New York: Guilford Press.

Slentz, C. A., Duscha, B. D., Johnson, J. L., Ketchum, K., Aiken, L. B., Samsa, G. P., et al. (2004). Effects of the amount of exercise on body weight, body comparison, and measures of central obesity: STRRIDE – A randomized controlled study. *Archives of Internal Medicine, 164,* 31–39.

Smith, D. (1982). Trends in counseling and psychotherapy. *American Psychologist, 37,* 802–809.

Snyder, C. R., & Lopez, S. J. (2007). *Positive psychology: The scientific and practical explorations of human strength.* Thousand Oaks, CA: Sage.

Sommers-Flanagan, J., & Sommers-Flanagan, R. (2004). *Counseling and psychotherapy theories in context and practice: Skills, strategies, and techniques.* Hoboken, NJ: John Wiley.

Spector, P. E. (2002). Employee control and occupational stress. *Current Directions in Psychological Science, 11,* 133–136.

Spiegel, D., & Fawzy, F. I. (2002). Psycholosocial interventions and prognosis in cancer. In H. G. Koenig & H. J. Cohen (Eds.), *The link between religion and health: Psychoneuroimmunology and the faith factor* (pp. 84–100). New York: Oxford University Press.

Stephenson, W. (1953). *The study of behavior.* Chicago: University of Chicago Press.

Stephenson, W. (1980). Newton's fifth rule and Q methodology: Application to educational psychology. *American Psychologist*, *35*, 882–889.

Sternberg, R. J. (2003a). WICS: A model of leadership in organizations. *Academy of Management Learning and Education, 2*, 386–401.

Sternberg, R. J. (2003b). *Wisdom, intelligence, and creativity synthesized*. New York: Cambridge University Press.

Sternberg, R. J. (2004). WICS: A model of educational leadership. *The Educational Forum*, *68*, 108–114.

Sternberg, R. J. (2007). A systems model of leadership: WICS. *American Psychologist*, *62*, 34–42.

Sternberg, R. J. (in press). The WICS approach to leadership: Stories of leadership and the structures and processes that support them. *The Leadership Quarterly*.

Sternberg, R. J., Forsythe, G. B., Hedlund, J., Horvath, J., Snook, S., Williams, W. M., et al. (2000). *Practical intelligence in everyday life*. New York: Cambridge University Press.

Stewart, R. A. C. (1968). Academic performance and components of self-actualization. *Perceptual and Motor Skills*, *26*, 918.

Stubbs, J. P., & Bozarth, J. D. (1994). The dodo bird revisited: A qualitative study of psychotherapy efficacy research. *Journal of Applied and Preventive Psychology*, *3*, 109–120.

Sue, S. (1988). Psychotherapeutic services for ethnic minorities: Two decades of research findings. *American Psychologist*, *43*, 301–308.

Sue, S., Fujino, D. C., Hu, L. T., Takeuchi, D. T., & Zane, D. T. (1991). Community mental health services for ethnic minority groups: A test of the cultural responsiveness hypothesis. *Journal of Consulting and Clinical Psychology*, *59*, 533–540.

Sumerlin, J. R., & Bundrick, C. M. (1996). Brief Index of Self-Actualization: A measure of Maslow's model. *Journal of Social Behavior and Personality*, *11*, 253–271.

Sumerlin, J. R., & Bundrick, C. M. (1998). Revision of the Brief Index of Self-Actualization. *Perceptual and Motor Skills*, *87*, 115–125.

Taylor, S. E. (2006). *Health psychology* (6th ed.). New York: Mcgraw-Hill.

Thomas, L. E., & Cooper, P. E. (1977, September). *The mystic experience: Can it be measured by structured question?* Paper presented at the American Sociological Association, Chicago.

Thorne, B., & Lambers, E. (Eds.). (1998). *Person-centered therapy: A European perspective*. London: Sage.

Tloczynski, J., Knoll, C., & Fitch, A. (1997). The relationship among spirituality, religious ideology, and personality. *Journal of Psychology and Theology*, *25*, 208–213.

Truax, C. B., & Mitchell, K. M. (1971). Research on certain therapist interpersonal skills in relation to process and outcome. In A. E. Bergin & S. L. Garfield (Eds.), *Handbook of psychotherapy and behavior change: An empirical analysis* (pp. 299–344). New York: John Wiley.

Trull, T. J., & Phares, E. J. (2001). *Clinical psychology: Concepts, methods, and profession* (6th ed.). Belmont, CA: Wadsworth.

Tudor, K., & Worrall, M. (2006). *Person-centered therapy: A clinical philosophy*. New York: Routledge.

Turner, J. R., & Wheaton, B. (1997). Checklist measures of stressful life events. In S. Cohen, R. C. Kessler, & U. L. Gordon (Eds.), *Measuring stress: A guide for health and social scientists* (pp. 29–58). New York: Oxford University Press.

Twenge, J. M., & Campbell, W. K. (2003). Isn't it fun to get the respect that we're going to deserve? Narcissism, social rejection, and aggression. *Personality and Social Psychology Bulletin*, *29*, 261–272.

Tyler, L. E. (1961). Research explorations in the realm of choice. *Journal of Consulting Psychology*, *8*, 195–202.

Valencia-Flores, M., Castana, V. A., Campos, R. M., Rosenthal, L., Resendiz, M., Vergara, P., et al. (1998). The siesta culture concept is not supported by the sleep habits of Mexican students. *Journal of Sleep Research*, *7*, 21–29.

Valent, F., Brusaferro, S., & Barbone, F. (2001). A case-crossover study of sleep and childhood injury. *Pediatrics*, *107*, 23.

Wagner, R. D., Rilling, J. K., Smith, E. E., Sokolik, A., Casey, K. L., Davidson, R. J., et al. (2004). Placebo-induced changes in fMRI in the anticipation and experience of pain. *Science*, *303*, 1162–1167.

Wahba, M. A., & Bridwell, L. G. (1976). Maslow reconsidered: A review of research on the need hierarchy theory. *Organizational Behavior and Human Performance*, *15*, 212–240.

Watson, J. C., & Greenberg, L. S. (1998). Humanistic and experiential theories of personality. In D. F. Barone, M. Hersen, & V. B. Van Hasselt (Eds.), *Advanced personality* (pp. 81–102). New York: Plenum.

Wertz, F. J. (2001). Humanistic psychology and the qualitative research tradition. In K. J. Schneider, J. F. T. Bugental, & J. F. Pierson (Eds.), *The handbook of humanistic psychology: Leading edges in theory, research, and practice* (pp. 81–99). Thousand Oaks, CA: Sage.

Westen, D., & Gabbard, G. O. (1999). Psychoanalytical approaches to personality. In L. A. Pervin & O. P. John (Eds.), *Handbook of personality: Theory and research* (2nd ed., pp. 57–101). New York: Guilford Press.

Westen, D., & Shedler, J. (1999). Revising and assessing Axis II, Part II: Toward an empirically based and clinically useful classification of personality disorder. *American Journal of Psychiatry*, *156*, 273–285.

Williams, S. K., Jr. (1978). The Vocational Card Sort: A tool for vocational exploration. *Vocational Guidance Quarterly*, *26*, 237–243.

Willis, T. A., & Fegan, M. F. (2001). Social networks and social support. In A. Baum, T. A. Revenson, & J. E. Singer (Eds.), *Handbook of health psychology* (pp. 209–234). Mahwah, NJ: Erlbaum.

Winter, D. G., & Barenbaum, N. B. (1999). History of modern personality theory and research. In L. A. Pervin & O. P. Oliver (Eds.), *Handbook of personality: Theory and research* (2nd ed., pp. 3–27). New York: Guilford Press.

Wittenborn, J. R. (1961). Contributions and current status of Q methodology. *Psychological Bulletin*, *58*, 132–142.

Wong, P. T. P. (2006). Existential and humanistic theories. In J. C. Thomas & D. L. Segal (Eds.), *Comprehensive handbook of personality and psychotherapy: Vol. 1. Personality and everyday functioning* (pp. 192–211). Hoboken, NJ: John Wiley.

World Health Organization (2007). *Obesity and overweight.* Retrieved from www.who.int/dietphysicalactivity/publications/facts/obesity/en.

Yalch, R., & Brunel, F. (1996). Need hierarchies in consumer judgments of product design. In K. P. Corfman & J. G. Lynch (eds.), *Advances in consumer research: Vol. 23* (pp. 405–410). Provo, UT: Association for Consumer Research.

Yeagle, E., Privette, G., & Dunham, F. (1989). Highest happiness: An analysis of artists' peak experience. *Psychological Reports, 65,* 315–332.

Yufit, R. I. (1988). *Manual of procedures – Assessing suicide potential: Suicide assessment team.* (Available from Robert I. Yufit, PhD, Department of Psychiatry and Behavioral Sciences, Division of Clinical Psychology, Northwestern University Medical School, Chicago, IL).

Zane, N., Hall, G. C. N., Sue, S., Young, K., & Nunez, J. (2004). Research on psychotherapy with culturally diverse populations. In M. J. Lambert (Ed.), *Bergin and Garfield's handbook of psychotherapy and behavior change* (5th ed., pp. 767–804). New York: John Wiley.

Zur, O. (2007). *Boundaries in psychotherapy: Ethical and clinical expectations.* Washington, DC: American Psychological Association.

Chapter 7

Allik, J., & McCrae, R. R. (2002). A five-factor theory perspective. In R. R. McCrae & L. Allik (Eds.), *The Five-Factor Model of personality across cultures* (pp. 303–322). New York: Kluwer Academic/Plenum.

Allport, G. W. (1922). *An experimental study of traits of personality with application to the problem of social diagnosis.* Unpublished doctoral dissertation, Harvard University.

Allport, G. W. (1937). *Personality: A psychological interpretation.* New York: Henry Holt.

Allport, G. W. (1954). *The nature of prejudice.* Cambridge, MA: Addison Wesley.

Allport, G. W. (1955). *Becoming: Basic considerations for a psychology of personality.* New Haven, CT: Yale University Press.

Allport, G. W. (1958). What units shall we employ? In G. Lindzey (Ed.), *Assessment of human motives* (pp. 239–260). New York: Holt, Rinehart & Winston.

Allport, G. W. (1960). *Personality and social encounter: Selected essays.* Boston: Beacon Press.

Allport, G. W. (1961). *Pattern and growth in personality.* New York: Holt, Rinehart & Winston.

Allport, G. W. (1965). *Letters from Jenny.* New York: Harcourt, Brace & World.

Allport, G. W. (1967). Autobiography. In E. G. Boring & G. Lindzey (Eds.), *A history of psychology in autobiography: Vol. 5* (pp. 1–25). New York: Appleton-Century-Crofts.

Allport, G. W., & Odbert, H. S. (1936). Trait-names: A psycholexical study. *Psychological Monographs, 47* (No. 211).

Allport, G. W., & Postman, L. (1947). *The psychology of rumor.* New York: Holt.

Allport, G. W., Vernon, P. E., & Lindzey, G. (1960). *Study of values* (3rd ed.). Boston: Houghton Mifflin.

Almagor, M., Tellegen, A., & Waller, N. G. (1995). The Big-Seven Model: A cross-cultural replication and further exploration of the basic dimensions of natural language trait descriptors. *Journal of Personality and Social Psychology, 69,* 300–307.

Alterman, A. I., & Cacciola, J. S. (1991). The antisocial personality disorder diagnosis in substance abusers: Problems and issues. *Journal of Nervous and Mental Disease, 179,* 401–409.

American Psychological Association (1997). Gold Medal Award for Life Achievement in Psychological Science. *American Psychologist, 52,* 797–799.

Angleitner, A., & Ostendorf, F. (1989, July). *Personality factors via self- and peer-ratings based on a representative sample of German trait-descriptive terms.* Paper presented at the First European Congress of Psychology, Amsterdam.

Angleitner, A., Ostendorf, F., & John, O. P. (1990). Towards a taxonomy of personality descriptors in German: A psycholexical study. *European Journal of Personality, 4,* 89–118.

Arnaut, G. Y. (2006). Sensation seeking, risk taking, and fearlessness. In J. C. Thomas & D. L Segal (Eds.), *Comprehensive handbook of personality and psychotherapy: Vol. 1. Personality and everyday functioning* (pp. 322–341). Hoboken, NJ: John Wiley.

Bandura, A. (1999). Social cognitive theory of personality. In L. A. Pervin & O. P. John (Eds.), *Handbook of personality: Theory and research* (2nd ed., pp. 154–196). New York: Guilford Press.

Barnes, G. E., Malamuth, N. M., & Cheek, J. V. (1984). Personality and sexuality. *Personality and Individual Differences, 5,* 159–172.

Baron, R. A., Byrne, D., & Branscombe, N. R. (2006). *Social psychology* (11th ed.). Boston: Allyn & Bacon.

Baron, R. A., & Markman, G. D. (2003). Beyond social capital: The role of entrepreneurs' social competence in their financial success. *Journal of Business Venturing, 19,* 221–240.

Barone, D. F., & Kominars, K. D. (1998). Introduction to personality study. In D. F. Barone, M. Hersen, & V. B. Van Hasselt (Eds.), *Advanced personality* (pp. 3–24). New York: Plenum.

Baumeister, R. F., Heatherton, T. F., & Tice, D. M. (1994). *Losing control: How and why people fail to self-regulate.* San Diego, CA: Academic Press.

Bem, D. J., & Allen, A. (1974). On predicting some of the people some of the time: The search for cross-situational consistencies in behavior. *Psychological Review, 81,* 506–520.

Bendig, A. W. (1963). The relation of temperament traits of social extraversion and emotionality to vocational interest. *Journal of General Psychology, 69,* 287–296.

Benet, V., & Waller, N. G. (1995). The Big Seven factor model of personality description: Evidence for its cross-cultural generality in a Spanish sample. *Journal of Personality and Social Psychology, 69,* 701–718.

Blackburn, R., Renwick, S. J. D., Donnelly, J. P., & Logana, C. (2004). Big Five or Big Two? Superordinate factors in the NEO Five Factor Inventory and the Antisocial Personality Questionnaire. *Personality and Individual Differences, 37,* 957–970.

Block, J. (1989). Critique of the act frequency approach to personality. *Journal of Personality and Social Psychology, 56,* 234–245.

Block, J. (1995). Going beyond the five factors given: Rejoinder to Costa and McCrae (1995) and Goldberg and Saucier (1995). *Psychological Bulletin, 117,* 226–229.

Bogg, T., & Roberts, B. W. (2004). Conscientiousness and health-related behaviors: A meta-analysis of the leading behavioral contributions to morality. *Psychological Bulletin, 130,* 887–919.

Bond, M. H., Nakazato, H., & Shiraishi, D. (1975). Universality and distinctiveness in dimensions of Japanese person perception. *Journal of Cross-Cultural Psychology, 6,* 346–357.

Borkenau, P. (1993). To predict some of the people more of the time: Individual traits and the prediction of behavior. In K. H. Craik, R. Hogan, & R. N. Wolfe (Eds.), *Fifty years of personality psychology* (pp. 237–249). New York: Plenum.

Borsboom, D., Mellenbergh, G. J., & van Heerden, J. (2003). The theoretical status of latent variables. *Psychological Review, 110,* 203–219.

Botwin, M. D., & Buss, D. M. (1989). Structure of act-report data: Is the Five-Factor Model of personality recaptured? *Journal of Personality and Social Psychology, 56,* 988–1001.

Bowers, K. S. (1973). Situationism in psychology: An analysis and critique. *Psychological Review, 80,* 307–336.

Braithwaite, V. A., & Scott, W. A. (1991). Values. In J. P. Robinson, P. R. Shaver, & L. S. Wrightsman (Eds.), *Measures of social psychological attitudes: Vol. 1. Measures of personality and social psychological attitudes* (pp. 661–753). San Diego, CA: Academic Press.

Brand, C. R. (1997). Hans Eysenck's personality dimensions: Their number and nature. In H. Nyborg (Ed.), *The scientific study of human nature: Tribute to Hans J. Eysenck at eighty* (pp. 17–35). New York: Pergamon.

Briggs, S. R. (1989). The optimal level of measurement for personality constructs. In D. M. Buss & N. Cantor (Eds.), *Personality psychology: Recent trends and emerging directions* (pp. 246–260). New York: Springer.

Brokken, F. B. (1978). *The language of personality.* Meppel, Netherlands: Krips.

Brooner, R. K., Schmidt, C. W., Jr., & Herbst, J. H. (1994). Personality trait characteristics of opioid abusers with and without comorbid personality disorders. In P. T. Costa, Jr., & T. A. Widiger (Eds.), *Personality disorders and the five-factor model of personality* (pp. 131–148). Washington, DC: American Psychological Association.

Brown, S. R., & Hendrick, C. (1971). Introversion, extroversion and social perception. *British Journal of Social and Clinical Psychology, 10,* 313–319.

Buss, A. H. (1989). Personality as traits. *American Psychologist, 44,* 1378–1388.

Buss, D. M. (1984). Toward a psychology of person–environment (PE) correlation: The role of spouse selection. *Journal of Personality and Social Psychology, 84,* 361–377.

Buss, D. M. (1985). The act frequency approach to the interpersonal environment. In R. Hogan & W. H. Jones (Eds.), *Personality in perspective: A research annual: Vol. 1* (pp. 173–200). Greenwich, CT: JAI.

Buss, D. M. (1991). Evolutionary personality psychology. *Annual Review of Psychology, 42,* 459–491.

Buss, D. M. (1996). Social adaptation and five major factors of personality. In J. E. Wiggins (Ed.), *The Five Factor Model of personality: Theoretical perspectives* (pp. 180–207). New York: Guilford Press.

Buss, D. M., & Cantor, N. (Eds.). (1989). *Personality psychology: Recent trends and emerging directions.* New York: Springer.

Buss, D. M., & Craik, K. H. (1983). The act frequency approach to personality. *Psychological Review, 90,* 105–126.

Buss, D. M., & Craik, K. H. (1984). Acts, dispositions, and personality. In B. A. Maher & W. B. Maher (Eds.), *Progress in experimental personality research: Normal personality processes: Vol. 13* (pp. 241–301). New York: Academic Press.

Buss, D. M., & Craik, K. H. (1985). Why not measure that trait? Alternative criteria for identifying important dispositions. *Journal of Personality and Social Psychology, 48,* 934–946.

Cantril, H., & Allport, G. (1935). *The psychology of radio.* New York: Harper.

Caraca, M. L., Loura, L., & Martins, C. (2000). Personality characteristics in sculptors and scientific researchers. *Analise Psicologica, 18,* 53–58.

Caspi, A. (1998). Personality development across the life course. In N. Eisenberger (Ed.), *Handbook of child psychology: Vol. 3. Social, emotional, and personality development* (pp. 311–388). New York: John Wiley.

Caspi, A., & Roberts, B. W. (1999). Personality continuity and change across the life course. In L. A. Pervin & O. P. John (Eds.), *Handbook of personality: Theory and research* (2nd ed., pp. 300–326). New York: Guilford Press.

Caspi, A., Roberts, B. W., & Shiner, R. L. (2005). Personality development: Stability and change. *Annual Review of Psychology, 56,* 453–484.

Cattell, H. E. P., & Schuerger, J. M. (2003). *Essentials of 16PF assessment* (5th ed.). Hoboken, NJ: John Wiley.

Cattell, R. B. (1943). The description of personality: Basic traits resolved into clusters. *Journal of Abnormal and Social Psychology, 38,* 476–506.

Cattell, R. B. (1945). The description of personality: Principles and findings in a factor analysis. *American Journal of Psychology, 58,* 69–90.

Cattell, R. B. (1946). *Description and measurement of personality.* Yonkers-on-Hudson, NY: World.

Cattell, R. B. (1950). *Personality: A systematic, theoretical, and factual study.* New York: McGraw-Hill.

Cattell, R. B. (1957). *Personality and motivation structure and measurement.* Yonkers-on-Hudson, NY: World.

Cattell, R. B. (1974). Autobiography. In G. Lindzey (Ed.), *A history of psychology in autobiography: Vol. 6* (pp. 59–100). New York: Appleton-Century-Crofts.

Cattell, R. B. (1979). *Personality and learning theory.* New York: Springer.

Cattell, R. B. (1990). Advances in Cattellian personality theory. In L. A. Pervin (Ed.), *Handbook of personality: Theory and research* (pp. 101–110). New York: Guilford Press.

Cattell, R. B., Cattell, A. K., & Cattell, H. E. (1993). *Sixteen Personality Factor Questionnaire, Fifth Edition*. Champaign, IL: Institute for Personality and Ability Testing.

Cattell, R. B., & Cattell, H. E. (1995). Personality structure and the new fifth edition of the 16PF. *Educational and Psychological Measurement, 55*, 926–937.

Cattell, R. B., Eber, H. W., & Tatsuoka, M. M. (1970). *Handbook for the Sixteen Personality Factor (16PF)*. Champaign, IL: Institute for Personality and Ability Testing.

Cattell, R. B., & Nesselroade, J. R. (1967). Likeness and completeness theories examined by Sixteen Personality Factor measures by stably and unstably married couples. *Journal of Personality and Social Psychology, 7*, 351–361.

Cellar, D. F., Nelson, Z. C., & Yorke, C. M. (2000). The Five-Factor Model and driving behavior: Personality and involvement in vehicular accidents. *Psychological Reports, 86*, 454–456.

Centers for Disease Control and Prevention (2006). *HIV/AIDS Surveillance Report,* Vol. *18* (pp. 1–55). Atlanta: U.S. Department of Health and Human Services, Centers for Disease Control and Prevention; 2008:[1–55]. Retrieved November 13, 2008, from www.cdc.gov/hiv/topics/surveillance/resources/reports/.

Cervone, D., & Mischel, W. (2002). Personality science. In D. Cervone & W. Mischel (Eds.), *Advances in personality science* (pp. 1–26). New York: Guilford Press.

Cervone, D., & Shoda, Y. (1999a). Beyond traits in the study of personality coherence. *Current Directions in Psychological Science, 8*, 27–32.

Cervone, D., & Shoda, Y. (1999b). Social-cognitive theories and the coherence of personality. In D. Cervone & Y. Shoda (Eds.), *The coherence of personality: Social-cognitive bases of consistency, variability and organization* (pp. 3–33). New York: Guilford Press.

Chamorro-Premuzic, T., & Furnham, A. (2003). Personality predicts academic performance: Evidence from two longitudinal university samples. *Journal of Research in Personality, 37*, 319–338.

Charles, S. T., Reynolds, C. A., & Gatz, M. (2001). Age-related differences and change in positive and negative affect over 23 years. *Journal of Personality and Social Psychology, 80*, 136–151.

Cheek, J. M. (1982). Aggregation, moderator variables, and the validity of personality tests: A peer-rating study. *Journal of Personality and Social Psychology, 43*, 1254–1269.

Church, A. T. (1994). Relating the Tellegen and Five-Factor Models of personality structure. *Journal of Personality and Social Psychology, 67*, 898–909.

Claridge, G. (2006). Biological models and issues. In S. Strack (Ed.), *Differentiating normal and abnormal personality* (pp. 137–164). New York: Springer.

Claridge, G. S. (1983). The Eysenck psychoticism scale. In J. P. Butcher & C. D. Spielberger (Eds.), *Advances in personality assessment: Vol. 2* (pp. 71–114). Hillsdale, NJ: Erlbaum.

Claridge, G. S., & Birchall, P. M. J. (1978). Bishop, Eysenck, Block, and psychoticism. *Journal of Abnormal Psychology, 87*, 604–668.

Claridge, G. S., & Chappa, H. J. (1973). Psychoticism: A study of its biological nature in normal subjects. *British Journal Social and Clinical Psychology, 12*, 175–187.

Clark, L. A., & Livesley, W. J. (1994). Two approaches to identifying the dimensions of personality disorders: Convergence on the Five-Factor Model. In P. T. Costa, Jr., & T. A. Widiger (Eds.), *Personality disorders and the Five-Factor Model of personality* (pp. 261–277). Washington, DC: American Psychological Association.

Clark, L. A., & Watson, D. (1999). Temperament: A new paradigm for trait psychology. In L. A. Pervin & O. P. John (Eds.), *Handbook of personality: Theory and research* (2nd ed., pp. 399–423). New York: Guilford Press.

Clark, S. E., & Goldney, R. D. (2000). The impact of suicide on relatives and friends. In K. Hawton & K. van Heeringen (Eds.), *The international handbook of suicide and attempted suicide* (pp. 467–484). Chichester, England: John Wiley.

Clower, C. E., & Bothwell, R. K. (2001). An exploratory study of the relationship between the Big Five and inmate recidivism. *Journal of Research in Personality, 35*, 231–237.

Cohler, B. J. (1993). Describing lives: Gordon Allport and the "science" of personality. In K. H. Craik, R. Hogan, & R. N. Wolfe (Eds.), *Fifty years of personality psychology* (pp. 131–146). New York: Plenum.

Comer, R. J. (2001). *Abnormal psychology* (4th ed.). New York: Worth.

Comer, R. J. (2007). *Abnormal psychology* (6th ed.). New York: Worth.

Conn, S. R., & Rieke, M. L. (Eds.). (1994). *The 16PF fifth edition technical manual*. Champaign, IL: Institute for Personality and Ability Testing.

Contrada, R. J., Cather, C., & O'Leary, A. (1999). Personality and health: Dispositions and processes in disease susceptibility and adaptation to illness. In L. A. Pervin & O. P. John (Eds.), *Handbook of personality: Theory and research* (2nd ed., pp. 576–604). New York: Guilford Press.

Cooper, M. L., Agocha, V. B., & Sheldon, M. S. (2000). A motivational perspective on risky behaviors: The role of personality and affect regulatory processes. *Journal of Personality, 68*, 1059–1088.

Costa, P. T., Jr., Masters, H. L., III, Herbst, J. H., Trobst, K. K., & Wiggins, J. S. (1998, March). *Neuroticism and lack of conscientiousness as potential predisposing factors for HIV infection*. Paper presented at the Annual Convention of the Society for Behavioral Medicine, New Orleans.

Costa, P. T., Jr., & McCrae, R. R. (1985). *The NEO Personality Inventory manual*. Odessa, FL: Psychological Assessment Resources.

Costa, P. T., Jr., & McCrae, R. R. (1988a). From catalog to classification: Murray's needs and the Five-Factor Model. *Journal of Personality and Social Psychology, 55*, 258–265.

Costa, P. T., & McCrae, R. R. (1988b). Personality in adulthood: A six-year longitudinal study of self-report and spouse ratings on the NEO Personality Inventory. *Journal of Personality and Social Psychology, 54*, 853–863.

Costa, P. T., Jr., & McCrae, R. R. (1989). *The NEO-PI/NEO-FFI manual supplement*. Odessa, FL: Psychological Assessment Resources.

Costa, P. T., Jr., & McCrae, R. R. (1992). *NEO PI-R: Professional manual*. Odessa, FL: Psychological Assessment Resources.

Costa, P. T., Jr., & McCrae, R. R. (1994). Set like plaster? Evidence for the stability of adult personality. In T. F. Heatherton & J. L. Weinberger (Eds.), *Can personality change?* (pp. 21–40). Washington, DC: American Psychological Association.

Costa, P. T., Jr., & McCrae, R. R. (1995). Primary traits of Eysenck's P-E-N system: Three- and five-factor solutions. *Journal of Personality and Social Psychology, 69*, 308–317.

Costa, P. T., & McCrae, R. R. (1998). Trait theories of personality. In D. F. Barone, M. Hersen, & V. B. Van Hasselt (Eds.), *Advanced personality* (pp. 103–121). New York: Plenum.

Costa, P. T., & McCrae, R. R. (2006). Trait and factor theories. In J. C. Thomas & D. L. Segal (Eds.), *Comprehensive handbook of personality and psychotherapy: Vol. 1. Personality and everyday functioning* (pp. 96–114). Hoboken, NJ: John Wiley.

Costa, P. T., Jr., & Widiger, T. A. (Eds.). (1994). *Personality disorders and the Five-Factor Model of personality*. Washington, DC: American Psychological Association.

Craig, R. J. (2005). *Personality-guided forensic psychology*. Washington, DC: American Psychological Association.

Cutrona, C. E., Hessling, R. M., & Suhr, J. A. (1997). The influence of husband and wife personality on marital social support interactions. *Personal Relationships, 4*, 379–393.

Dean, G. A. (1992). The bottom line: Effect size. In B. L. Beyerstein & D. F. Beyerstein (Eds.), *The write stuff: Evaluations of graphology* (pp. 269–341). Buffalo, NY: Prometheus.

Dean, G. A., Nias, D. K. B., & French, C. C. (1997). Graphology, astrology, and parapsychology. In H. Nyborg (Ed.), *The scientific study of human nature: Tribute to Hans J. Eysenck at eighty* (pp. 511–542). New York: Pergamon.

De Fruyt, F., & Mervielde, I. (1997). The Five-Factor Model of personality and Holland's RIASEC interest types. *Personality and Individual Differences, 23*, 87–103.

De Raad, B., Mulder, E., Kloosterman, K., & Hofstee, W. K. (1988). Personality-descriptive verbs. *European Journal of Personality, 2*, 81–96.

Diener, E., & Larsen, R. J. (1984). Temporal stability and cross-situational consistency of affective, behavioral, and cognitive responses. *Journal of Personality and Social Psychology, 47*, 871–883.

Diener, E., Larsen, R. J., & Emmons, R. A. (1984). Person X situation interactions: Choice of situations and congruence response models. *Journal of Personality and Social Psychology, 47*, 580–592.

Digman, J. M. (1990). Personality structure: Emergence of the Five-Factor Model. *Annual Review of Psychology, 41*, 417–440.

Drevdahl, J. E., & Cattell, R. B. (1958). Personality and creativity in artists and writers. *Journal of Clinical Psychology, 14*, 107–111.

Dudycha, G. J. (1936). An objective study of punctuality in relation to personality and achievement. *Archives of Psychology, 204*, 1–319.

Duff, A., Boyle, E., Dunleavy, K., & Ferguson, J. (2004). The relationship between personality approach to learning and academic performance. *Personality and Individual Differences, 36*, 1907–1920.

Eaton, W. O. (1983). Measuring activity level with actometers: Reliability, validity, and arm length. *Child Development, 54*, 720–726.

Edwards, A. G. P., & Armitage, P. (1992). An experiment to test the discriminating ability of graphology. *Personality and Individual Differences, 13*, 69–74.

Edwards, G., Chandler, C., & Hensman, C. (1972). Drinking in a London suburb: I. Correlates of normal drinking. *Journal of Studies in Alcohol, 33* (Suppl. No. 6), 69–93.

Egger, J. I. M., De May, H. R. A., Derksen, J. J. L., & van der Staak, C. P. E. (2003). Cross-cultural replication of the Five-Factor Model and comparison of the NEO-PI-R and the MMPI-2 Psy-5 scales in a Dutch psychiatric sample. *Psychological Assessment, 15*, 81–88.

Ekehammer, B. (1974). Interactionism in personality from a historical perspective. *Psychological Bulletin, 81*, 1026–1048.

Ellis, C. G. (1994). Bulimia nervosa within the context of maladaptive personality traits. In P. T. Costa, Jr., & T. A. Widiger (Eds.), *Personality disorders and the Five-Factor Model of personality* (pp. 205–209). Washington, DC: American Psychological Association.

Elms, A. C. (1993). Allport's *personality* and Allport's personality. In K. H. Craik, R. Hogan, & R. N. Wolfe (Eds.), *Fifty years of personality psychology* (pp. 39–55). New York: Plenum.

Emmons, R. A., & Diener, E. (1986). A goal-affect analysis of everyday situational choices. *Journal of Research in Personality, 20*, 309–326.

Emmons, R. A., Diener, E., & Larsen, R. J. (1985). Choice and avoidance of everyday situations and affect congruence: Two models of reciprocal interactionsism. *Journal of Personality and Social Psychology, 51*, 815–826.

Endler, N. S. (1973). The person versus the situation – a pseudo issue? A response to Alker. *Journal of Personality, 41*, 287–303.

Endler, N. S. (1982). Interactionism: A personality model, but not yet a theory. In M. M. Page (Ed.), *Nebraska symposium on motivation* (pp. 155–200). Lincoln: University of Nebraska Press.

Epstein, S. (1979). The stability of behavior: I. On predicting most of the people much of the time. *Journal of Personality and Social Psychology, 37*, 1097–1126.

Epstein, S. (1980). The stability of behavior: II. Implications for psychological research. *American Psychologist, 35*, 790–806.

Epstein, S. (1983). Aggregation and beyond: Some basic issues on the prediction of behavior. *Journal of Personality, 51*, 360–392.

Epstein, S. (1984). The stability of behavior across time and situations. In R. A. Zucker, J. Aronoff, & A. I. Rabin (Eds.), *Personality and the prediction of behavior* (pp. 209–268). New York: Academic Press.

Epstein, S. (1996). Commentary: Recommendations for the future development of personality psychology. *Journal of Research in Personality, 30*, 435–446.

Epstein, S. (2007). Problems with McAdams and Pal's (2006) proposal of a framework for an integrative theory of personality. *American Psychologist, 62,* 59–60.

Epstein, S., & O'Brien, E. J. (1985). The person–situation debate in historical and current perspective. *Psychological Bulletin, 98,* 513–537.

Epstein, S., & Teraspulsky, L. (1986). Perception of cross-situational consistency. *Journal of Personality and Social Psychology, 50,* 1152–1160.

Eysenck, H. J. (1947). *Dimensions of personality.* London: Routledge & Kegan Paul.

Eysenck, H. J. (1948). Neuroticism and handwriting. *Journal of Abnormal and Social Psychology, 43,* 94–96.

Eysenck, H. J. (1953). *The structure of personality.* New York: John Wiley.

Eysenck, H. J. (1957). *Sense and nonsense in psychology.* Harmondsworth, UK: Penguin.

Eysenck, H. J. (1967). *The biological basis of personality.* Springfield, IL: Charles C Thomas.

Eysenck, H. J. (1970). *The structure of human personality* (3rd. ed.). London: Methuen.

Eysenck, H. J. (1976). *Sex and personality.* London: Open Books.

Eysenck, H. J. (1980). Autobiography. In G. Lindzey (Ed.), *A history of psychology in autobiography: Vol. 7* (pp. 153–187). San Francisco: Freeman.

Eysenck, H. J. (1982). Development of a theory. In C. D. Spielberger (Ed.), *Personality, genetics and behavior* (pp. 1–38). New York: Praeger.

Eysenck, H. J. (1990). Biological dimensions of personality. In L. A. Pervin (Ed.), *Handbook of personality: Theory and research* (pp. 244–276). New York: Guilford Press.

Eysenck, H. J. (1991). *Smoking, personality, and stress: Psychosocial factors in the prevention of cancer and coronary heart disease.* New York: Springer.

Eysenck, H. J. (1995). *Genius: The natural history of creativity.* Cambridge, UK: Cambridge University Press.

Eysenck, H. J. (1996a). Personality and crime: Where do we stand? *Psychology, Crime, and Law, 2,* 143–152.

Eysenck, H. J. (1996b). *Rebel with a cause.* Somerset, NJ: Transaction.

Eysenck, H. J. (1998a). *Intelligence: A new look.* Somerset, NJ: Transaction.

Eysenck, H. J. (1998b). *The psychology of politics.* Somerset, NJ: Transaction.

Eysenck, H. J., & Eysenck, M. W. (1985). *Personality and individual differences: A natural science approach.* New York: Plenum.

Eysenck, H. J., & Eysenck, S. B. (1975). *Manual of the Eysenck Personality Questionnaire.* San Diego, CA: Educational and Industrial Testing Service.

Eysenck, H. J., & Eysenck, S. B. (1994). *Manual of the Eysenck Personality Questionnaire.* San Diego, CA: Educational and Industrial Testing Service.

Eysenck, H. J., & Eysenck, S. B. G. (1976). *Psychoticism as a dimension of personality.* London: Hodder & Stoughton.

Eysenck, H. J., & Gudjonsson, G. (1986). An empirical study of the validity of handwriting analysis. *Personality and Individual Differences, 7,* 263–264.

Eysenck, H. J., & Gudjonsson, G. H. (1989). *The causes and cures of criminality.* New York and London: Plenum.

Eysenck, H. J., & Nias, D. K. B. (1982). *Astrology: Science and superstition?* London: Temple Smith.

Eysenck, H. J., & Rachman, S. (1965). *The causes and cures of neurosis: An introduction to modern behavior therapy based on learning theory and the principle of conditioning.* London: Routledge & Kegan Paul.

Eysenck, H. J., & Sargent, C. L. (1982). *Explaining the unexplained: Mysteries of the paranormal.* London: Weidenfeld and Nicolson.

Eysenck, H. J., & Sargent, C. L. (1984). *Know your own Psi-Q.* New York: World Almanac.

Eysenck, H. J., & Sargent, C. L. (1993). *Explaining the unexplained: Mysteries of the paranormal* (2nd ed.). London: Prion.

Farley, F. (2000). Hans J. Eysenck (1916–1997). *American Psychologist, 55,* 674–675.

Figueredo, A. J., Sefcek, J. A., Vasquez, G., Brumbach, B. H., King, J. E., & Jacobs, W. J. (2005). Evolutionary personality psychology. In D. M. Buss (Ed.), *The handbook of evolutionary psychology* (pp. 851–877). Hoboken, NJ: John Wiley.

Finn, S. (1997). Origins of media exposure: Linking personality traits to TV, radio, print, and film use. *Communication Research, 24,* 507–529.

Fiske, D. W. (1949). Consistency of the factorial structures of personality ratings from different sources. *Journal of Abnormal and Social Psychology, 44,* 329–344.

Fleeson, W. (2001). Toward structure- and process-integrated view of personality: Traits as density distributions of states. *Journal of Personality and Social Personality, 80,* 1011–1027.

Fraboni, M., & Saltstone, R. (1990). First and second generation entrepreneur typologies: Dimensions of personality. *Journal of Social Behavior and Personality, 5,* 105–113.

Funder, D. C. (1991). Global traits: A neo-Allportian approach to personality. *Psychological Science, 2,* 31–39.

Funder, D. C. (1995). On the accuracy of personality judgment: A realistic approach. *Psychological Review, 102,* 652–670.

Funder, D. C., & Ozer, D. J. (1983). Behaviors as a function of the situation. *Journal of Personality and Social Psychology, 44,* 107–112.

Furnham, A. (1997). Eysenck's personality theory and organizational psychology. In H. Nyborg (Ed.), *The scientific study of human nature: Tribute to Hans J. Eysenck at eighty* (pp. 462–490). New York: Pergamon.

Furnham, A., & Zacherl, M. (1986). Personality and job satisfaction. *Personality and Individual Differences, 7,* 453–455.

Geen, R. G. (1997). Psychophysiological approaches to personality. In R. Hogam, J. Johnson, & S. Briggs (Eds.), *Handbook of personality psychology* (pp. 387–414). San Diego, CA: Academic Press.

Ghaderi, A., & Scott, B. (2000). The Big Five and eating disorders: A prospective study in the general population. *European Journal of Personality, 14,* 311–323.

Giese, H., & Schmidt, A. (1968). *Studenten sexualitat.* Hamburg: Rohwolt.

Gillespie, W., & Myors, B. (2000). Personality and rock musicians. *Psychology and Music, 28,* 154–165.

Glossing, S. D. (2001). From mice to men: What can we learn about personality from animal research. *Psychological Bulletin, 127*, 45–86.

Goldberg, L. R. (1981). Language and individual differences: The search for universals in personality lexicons. In L. Wheeler (Ed.), *Review of personality and social psychology: Vol. 2* (pp. 141–165). Beverly Hills, CA: Sage.

Goldberg, L. R. (1990). An alternative "description of personality": The Big-Five factor structure. *Journal of Personality and Social Psychology, 59*, 1216–1229.

Goldberg, L. R. (1993). The structure of phenotypic personality traits. *American Psychologist, 48*, 26–34.

Gray, J. A., & McNaughton, N. (2000). *The neuropsychology of anxiety: An enquiry into the functions of the septo-hippocampal system* (2nd ed.). New York: Oxford University Press.

Gudjonsson, G. H. (1997). Crime and personality. In H. Nyborg (Ed.), *The scientific study of human nature: Tribute to Hans J. Eysenck at eighty* (pp. 142–164). New York: Pergamon.

Haier, R. J., Robinson, D. L., Braden, W., & Williams, D. (1984). Evoked potential augmenting-reducing and personality differences. *Personality and Individual Differences, 5*, 293–301.

Hair, E. C., & Graziano, W. G. (2003). Self-esteem, personality and achievement in high school: A prospective longitudinal study in Texas. *Journal of Personality, 71*, 971–994.

Hall, C. S., Lindzey, G., & Campbell, J. B. (1998). *Theories of personality* (4th ed.). New York: John Wiley.

Halpern, D. F. (1996). *Thought and knowledge: An introduction to critical thinking* (3rd ed.). Mahwah, NJ: Erlbaum.

Harkness, K. L., Bagby, R. M., Joffe, R. T., & Levitt, A. (2002). Major depression, chronic minor depression, and the Five-Factor Model of personality. *European Journal of Personality, 16*, 271–281.

Harpur, T. J., Hart, S. D., & Hare, R. D. (1994). Personality and the psychopath. In P. T. Costa, Jr., & T. A. Widiger (Eds.), *Personality disorders and the Five-Factor Model of personality* (pp. 149–173). Washington, DC: American Psychological Association.

Hartshorne, H., & May, M. A. (1928). *Studies in the nature of character: Vol. 1. Studies in deceit.* New York: Macmillan.

Haven, S., & ten Berge, J. M. F. (1977). Tucker's coefficient of congruence as a measure of factorial invariance: An empirical study. *Heymans Bulletin 290 EX.* Groningen, Netherlands: University of Groningen.

Harvey, F., & Hirschmann, R. (1980). The influence of extraversion and neuroticism on heart rate responses to aversive stimuli. *Personality and Individual Differences, 1*, 97–100.

Heaven, P., Mulligan, K., Merrilees, R., Woods, T., & Fairooz, Y. (2001). Neuroticism and conscientiousness as a predictor of emotional, external, and restrained eating behaviors. *International Journal of Eating Disorders, 30*, 161–166.

Heller, D., Watson, D., & Ilies, R. (2004). The role of the person versus the situation in life satisfaction: A critical examination. *Psychological Bulletin, 130*, 574–600.

Higgins, E. T. (1990). Personality, social psychology, and person–situation relations: Standards and knowledge activation as a common language. In L. A. Pervin (Ed.), *Handbook of personality: Theory and research* (pp. 301–338). New York: Guilford Press.

Hogan, R. (1996). A socioanalytic perspective on the Five-Factor Model. In J. E. Wiggins (Ed.), *The Five-Factor Model of personality: Theoretical perspectives* (pp. 163–179). New York: Guilford Press.

Hogan, R., DeSoto, C. B., & Solano, C. (1977). Traits, tests, and personality research. *American Psychologist, 32*, 255–264.

Holland, J. L. (1996). Exploring careers with a typology: What we have learned and some new directions. *American Psychologist, 51*, 397–406.

Horn, J. (2001). Raymond Bernard Cattell (1905–1998). *American Psychologist, 56*, 71–72.

Hoyle, R. H. (Ed.). (2000). Personality processes and problem behavior [Special issue]. *Journal of Personality, 68* (6).

Hoyle, R. H., Fejfar, M. C., & Miller, J. D. (2000). Personality and sexual risk taking: A quantitative review. *Journal of Personality, 68*, 1203–1231.

Husted, J. R., & Edwards, A. E. (1976). Personality correlates of male sexual arousal and behaviour. *Archives of Sexual Behavior, 7*, 149–156.

Ickes, W., Snyder, M., & Garcia, S. (1997). Personality influences on the choice of situations. In R. Hogan, J. Johnson, & S. Briggs (Eds.), *Handbook of personality psychology* (pp. 165–195). San Diego, CA: Academic Press.

Jessup, G., & Jessup, H. (1971). Validity of Eysenck's Personality Inventory in pilot selection. *Occupational Psychology, 45*, 111–123.

John, O. P. (1990). The "Big Five" factor taxonomy: Dimensions of personality in the natural language and in questionnaires. In L. A. Pervin (Ed.), *Handbook of personality: Theory and research* (pp. 66–100). New York: Guilford Press.

John, O. P., & Srivastava, S. (1999). The Big Five trait taxonomy: History, measurement, and theoretical perspectives. In L. A. Pervin & O. P. John (Eds.), *Handbook of personality: Theory and research* (2nd ed., pp. 102–138). New York: Guilford Press.

Johnson, J. A. (1997). Units for analysis for the description and explanation of personality. In R. Hogan, J. Johnson, & S. Briggs (Eds.), *Handbook of personality psychology* (pp. 73–93). San Diego, CA: Academic Press.

Judge, T. A., Heller, D., & Mount, M. K. (2002). Five-factor model of personality and job satisfaction: A meta-analysis. *Journal of Applied Psychology, 87*, 530–541.

Judge, T. A., & Ilies, R. (2002). Relationship of personality to performance motivation: A meta-analytic review. *Journal of Applied Psychology, 87*, 797–807.

Kanfer, R., Wanberg, C. R., & Kantrowitz, T. M. (2001). Job search and employment: A personality-motivational analysis and meta-analytic review. *Journal of Applied Psychology, 86*, 837–855.

Karson, S., & O'Dell, J. W. (1976). *A guide to the clinical use of the 16PF.* Champaign, IL: Institute for Personality and Ability Testing.

Katigbak, M. S., Church, A. T., & Akamine, T. X. (1996). Cross-cultural generalizability of personality dimensions: Relating indigenous and imported dimensions in two cultures. *Journal of Personality and Social Psychology, 70*, 99–114.

Katon, W., Russo, J., Frank, E., Barrett, J., Williams, J. W., Jr., Oxman, T., et al. (2002). Predictors of nonresponse to treatment in primary care patients with dysthymia. *General Hospital Psychiatry, 24*, 20–27.

Kelly, E. L., & Conley, J. J. (1987). Personality and compatibility: A prospective analysis of marital stability and marital satisfaction. *Journal of Personality and Social Psychology, 52*, 27–40.

Kelly, E. L., & Fiske, D. W. (1950). The prediction of success in the VA training program in clinical psychology. *American Psychologist, 5*, 395–406.

Kenrick, D. T., & Funder, D. C. (1988). Profiting from controversy: Lessons from the person–situation debate. *American Psychologist, 43*, 23–24.

Kenrick, D. T., & Stringfield, D. O. (1980). Personality traits and the eye of the beholder: Crossing some traditional philosophical boundaries in the search for consistency in all of the people. *Psychological Review, 87*, 88–104.

Kersting, K. (2003). What exactly is creativity? *Monitor on Psychology, 34*, 40–41.

King, J. E., & Figueredo, A. J. (1997). The Five-Factor Model plus Dominance in chimpanzee personality. *Journal of Research in Personality, 31*, 257–271.

King, J. E., & Landau, V. I. (2003). Can chimpanzee (*Pan troglodytes*) happiness be estimated by human raters? *Journal of Research in Personality, 37*, 1–15.

King, J. E., Weiss, A., & Farmer, K. H. (2005). A chimpanzee (*Pan troglodytes*) analogue of cross-national generalization of personality structure: Zoological parks and an African sanctuary. *Journal of Personality, 73*, 389–410.

Kissen, D. M., & Eysenck, H. J. (1962). Personality in male lung cancer patients. *Journal of Psychosomatic Research, 6*, 123–137.

Knowles, R. T. (1966). *A pilot study of the relationship between a "creative" personality pattern and scholastic achievement.* Unpublished manuscript, Ball State Teacher's College, Muncie, Indiana.

Knueger, R. F., Caspi, A., & Moffitt, T. E. (2000). Epidemiological personality: The unifying role of personality in population-based research on problem behaviors. *Journal of Personality, 68*, 967–998.

Lamiell, J. T. (1987). *The psychology of personality: An epistemological inquiry.* New York: Columbia University Press.

Lamiell, J. T. (1997). Individuals and the difference between them. In R. Hogam, J. Johnson, & S. Briggs (Eds.), *Handbook of personality psychology* (pp. 117–141). San Diego, CA: Academic Press.

Lamm, H., & Myers, D. G. (1978). Group-induced polarization of attitudes and behavior. In L. Berkowitz (Ed.), *Advances in experimental social psychology* (pp. 145–195). New York: Academic Press.

Larsen, R. J., & Kasimatis, M. (1990). Individual differences in entertainment of mood to the weekly calendar. *Journal of Personality and Social Psychology, 58*, 164–171.

Larsson, M., Finkel, D., & Pedersen, N. L. (2000). Odor identification: Influences of age, gender, cognition, and personality. *Journal of Gerontology: Psychological Sciences, 55*, 304–310.

Lehne, G. K. (1994). The NEO-PI and the MCMI in the forensic evaluation of sex offenders. In P. T. Costa, Jr., & T. A. Widiger (Eds.), *Personality disorders and the Five-Factor Model of personality* (pp. 175–188). Washington, DC: American Psychological Association.

Lieberman, M. D., & Rosenthal, R. (2001). Why introverts can't always tell who likes them: Multitasking and nonverbal decoding. *Journal of Personality and Social Psychology, 80*, 294–310.

Livneh, H., & Livneh, C. (1989). The Five-Factor Model of personality: Is evidence of its cross-measure validity premature? *Personality and Individual Differences, 10*, 75–80.

Loukas, A., Krull, J. L., Chassin, L., & Carle, A. C. (2000). The relation of personality to alcohol abuse/dependence in a high-risk sample. *Journal of Personality, 68*, 1153–1175.

Lucas, R. E., & Diener, E. (2001). Understanding extraverts' enjoyment of social situations: The importance of pleasantness. *Journal of Personality and Social Psychology, 81*, 343–356.

Lucas, R. E., Diener, E., Grob, A., Suh, E. M., & Shao, L. (2000). Cross-cultural evidence for the fundamental features of extraversion. *Journal of Personality and Social Psychology, 79*, 452–446.

Lucas, R. E., & Fujita, F. (2000). Factors influencing the relation between extraversion and pleasant affect. *Journal of Personality and Social Psychology, 79*, 1039–1056.

MacDonald, D. A. (2000). Spirituality: Description, measurement, and relation to the Five Factor Model of personality. *Journal of Personality, 68*, 153–197.

Maddi, S. R. (1996). *Personality theories: A comparative analysis* (6th ed.). Pacific Grove, CA: Brooks/Cole.

Madsen, D. H., & Russell, M. T. (1982). *Marriage counseling report.* Champaign, IL: Institute for Personality and Ability Testing.

Magnusson, D. (1999). Holistic interactionism: A perspective for research on personality development. In L. A. Pervin & O. P. John (Eds.), *Handbook of personality: Theory and research* (2nd ed., pp. 219–247). New York: Guilford Press.

Magnusson, D., & Endler, N. S. (Eds.). (1977). *Personality at the crossroads: Current issues in interactional psychology.* Hillsdale, NJ: Erlbaum.

Maraist, C. C., & Russell, M. T. (2002). *16PF Fifth Edition norm supplement.* Champaign, IL: Institute for Personality and Ability Testing.

Markey, C. N., Markey, P. M., & Tinsley, B. J. (2003). Personality, puberty, and preadolescent girls' risky behaviors: Examining the predictive value of the Five-Factor Model of personality. *Journal of Research in Personality, 37*, 405–419.

Markus, H. R., & Kitayama, S. (1991). Culture and the self: Implications for cognition, emotion, and motivation. *Psychological Review, 98*, 224–253.

Markus, H. R., & Kitayama, S. (1998). The cultural psychology of personality. *Journal of Cross-Cultural Psychology, 29*, 63–87.

Maushammer, C., Ehmer, G., & Eckel, K. (1981). Pain, personality and individual differences in sensory evoked potentials. *Personality and Individual Differences, 2*, 335–336.

McAdams, D. P. (1993). *The stories we live by: Personal myths and the making of the self.* New York: Morrow.

McAdams, D. P. (1997). A conceptual history of personality psychology. In R. Hogan, J. Johnson, & S. Briggs (Eds.),

Handbook of personality psychology (pp. 3–39). San Diego, CA: Academic Press.

McAdams, D. P. (1999). Personal narratives and the life story. In L. A. Pervin & O. P. John (Eds.), *Handbook of personality: Theory and research* (2nd ed., pp. 478–500). New York: Guilford Press.

McAdams, D. P. (2007). *The person: A new introduction to personality psychology* (4th ed.). Hoboken, NJ: John Wiley.

McAdams, D. P., Anyidoho, N. O., Brown, C., Huang, Y. T., Kaplan, B., & Machado, M. (2004). Traits and stories: Links between dispositional and narrative features of personality. *Journal of Personality, 72*, 761–784.

McAdams, D. P., & Pals, J. L. (2006). A new Big Five: Fundamental principles for an integrative science of personality. *American Psychologist, 61*, 204–217.

McCrae, R. R. (1989). Why I advocate the Five-Factor Model: Joint factor analyses of the NEO-PI with other instruments. In D. M. Buss & N. Cantor (Eds.), *Personality psychology: Recent trends and emerging directions* (pp. 237–245). New York: Springer.

McCrae, R. R. (2002). NEO-PI-R data from 36 cultures: Further intercultural comparisons. In R. R. McCrae & J. Allik (Eds.), *The Five-Factor Model of personality across cultures* (pp. 105–125). New York: Kluwer Academic/Plenum.

McCrae, R. R., & Costa, P. T., Jr. (1985). Openness to experience. In R. Hogan & W. H. Jones (Eds.), *Perspectives in personality: Vol. 1* (pp. 145–172). Greenwich, CT: JAI Press.

McCrae, R. R., & Costa, P. T., Jr. (1987). Validation of the five-factor model of personality across instruments and observers. *Journal of Personality and Social Psychology, 52*, 81–90.

McCrae, R. R., & Costa, P. T., Jr. (1990). *Personality in adulthood.* New York: Guilford Press.

McCrae, R. R., & Costa, P. T., Jr. (1999). A five-factor theory of personality. In L. A. Pervin & O. P. John (Eds.), *Handbook of personality: Theory and research* (2nd ed., pp. 139–153). New York: Guilford Press.

McCrae, R. R., & Costa, P. T., Jr. (2003). *Personality in adulthood: A Five-Factor theory perspective* (2nd ed.). New York: Guilford Press.

McCrae, R. R., Costa, P. T., Jr., Hřebíčková, M., Urbánek, T., Martin, T. A., Oryol, V. E., et al. (2004a). Age differences in personality traits across cultures: Self-report and observer perspectives. *European Journal of Personality, 18*, 143–157.

McCrae, R. R., Costa, P. T., Jr., Martin, T. A., Oryol, V. E., Rukavishnikov, A. A., Senin, I. G., et al. (2004b). Consensual validation of personality traits across cultures. *Journal of Research in Personality, 38*, 179–201.

McCrae, R. R., Costa, P. T., Jr., Ostendorf, F., Angleitner, A., Hřebíčková, M., Avia, M. D., et al. (2000). Nature over nurture: Temperament, personality, and lifespan development. *Journal of Personality and Social Psychology, 78*, 173–186.

McCrae, R. R., Stone, S. V., Fagan, P. J., & Costa, P. T., Jr. (1998). Identifying causes of disagreement between self-report and spouse ratings of personality. *Journal of Personality, 66*, 285–313.

McCrae, R. R., Terracciano, A., & 78 Members of the Personality Profiles of Cultures Project. (2005). Universal features of personality traits from the other's perspective: Data from 50 cultures. *Journal of Personality and Social Psychology, 88*, 547–561.

McCrae, R. R., Zonderman, A. B., Costa, P. T., Jr., Bond, M. H., & Paunonen, S. (1996). Evaluating replicability of factors in the revised NEO Personality Inventory: Confirmatory factor analysis versus procrustes rotation. *Journal of Personality and Social Psychology, 70*, 552–566.

McCullough, M. E., & Witvliet, C. V. O. (2002). The psychology of forgiveness. In C. R. Snyder & S. J. Lopez (Eds.), *Handbook of positive psychology* (pp. 446–458). New York: Oxford University Press.

Meyer, R. G., & Deitsch, S. E. (1996). *The clinician's handbook: Integrated diagnostics, assessment, and intervention in adult and adolescent psychopathology* (4th ed.). Boston: Allyn & Bacon.

Miller, R. S., Perlman, D., & Brehm, S. S. (2007). *Intimate relationships* (4th ed.). New York: McGraw-Hill.

Miller, T. R. (1991). The psychotherapeutic utility of the five-factor model of personality: A clinician's experience. *Journal of Personality Assessment, 57*, 415–433.

Mischel, W. (1968). *Personality and assessment.* New York: John Wiley.

Mischel, W. (1973). Toward a cognitive social learning reconceptualization of personality. *Psychological Review, 80*, 252–283.

Mischel, W. (1984). Convergences and challenges in the search for consistency. *American Psychologist, 39*, 351–364.

Mischel, W. (1985). Looking for personality. In S. Koch & D. E. Leary (Eds.), *A century of psychology as a science* (pp. 515–526). New York: McGraw-Hill.

Mischel, W. (1990). Personality dispositions revisited and revised: A view after three decades. In L. A. Pervin (Ed.), *Handbook of personality: Theory and research* (pp. 111–134). New York: Guilford Press.

Mischel, W., & Peake, P. K. (1982). Beyond deja vu in the search for cross-situational consistency. *Psychological Review, 89*, 730–755.

Mischel, W., & Shoda, Y. (1995). A cognitive-affective system theory of personality: Reconceptualizing situations, dispositions, dynamics, and invariance in personality structure. *Psychological Review, 102*, 246–268.

Mischel, W., & Shoda, Y. (1998). Reconciling processing dynamics and personality dispositions. *Annual Review of Psychology, 49*, 229–258.

Mischel, W., & Shoda, Y. (1999). Integrating disposition and processing dynamics within a unified theory of personality: The cognitive-affective personality system. In L. A. Pervin & O. P. John (Eds.), *Handbook of personality: Theory and research* (2nd ed., pp. 197–218). New York: Guilford Press.

Moos, R. H. (1973). Conceptualizations of human environments. *American Psychologist, 28*, 652–665.

Moser, K. (1989). The act-frequency approach: A conceptual critique. *Personality and Social Psychology Bulletin, 15*, 73–83.

Moskowitz, D. S. (1982). Coherence and cross-situational generality in personality: A new analysis of an old problem. *Journal of Personality and Social Psychology, 43*, 754–768.

Moskowitz, D. S., & Schwarz, J. C. (1982). Validity comparisons of behavior counts and ratings by knowledgeable informants. *Journal of Personality and Social Psychology, 42,* 518–528.

Murphy, K. R., & Davidshofer, C. O. (2005). *Psychological testing: Principles and applications* (6th ed.). Upper Saddle River, NJ: Pearson Education.

Murray, S. L., & Holmes, J. G. (1997). A leap of faith: Positive illusions in romantic relationships. *Personality and Social Psychology Bulletin, 23,* 586–604.

Musson, D. J. (2002). Personality of male Anglican clergy in England: Revisited using the 16PF5. *Mental Health, Religion, and Culture, 5,* 195–206.

Neter, E., & Ben-Shakhar, G. (1989). The predictive validity of graphological inferences: A meta-analytic approach. *Personality and Individual Differences, 10,* 737–745.

Nias, D. K. B. (1997). Psychology and medicine. In H. Nyborg (Ed.), *The scientific study of human nature: Tribute to Hans J. Eysenck at eighty* (pp. 92–108). New York: Pergamon.

Nicholson, I. A. M. (2003). *Inventing personality: Gordon Allport and the science of self-hood.* Washington, DC: American Psychological Association.

Nimkoff, M. F., & Grigg, C. M. (1958). Values and marital adjustment of nurses. *Social Forces, 37,* 67–70.

Norman, W. T. (1967). *2,800 personality trait descriptors: Normative operating characteristics for a university population.* Ann Arbor: Department of Psychology, University of Michigan.

Nyborg, H. (Ed.). (1997). *The scientific study of human nature: Tribute to Hans J. Eysenck at eighty.* New York: Pergamon.

Oakes, D. W., Ferris, G. R., Martocchio, J. J., Buckley, M. R., & Broach, D. (2001). Cognitive ability and personality predictors of training program skill acquisition and job performance. *Journal of Business and Psychology, 15,* 523–548.

Oishi, S. (2002). Experiencing and remembering of well-being: A cross-cultural analysis. *Personality and Social Psychology Bulletin, 28,* 1398–1406.

Oishi, S., Diener, E., Scollon, C. N., & Biswas-Diener, R. (2004). Cross-situational consistency of affective experiences across cultures. *Journal of Personality and Social Psychology, 86,* 460–472.

Oishi, S., Diener, E., Suh, E., & Lucas, R. E. (1999). Value as a moderator in subjective well-being. *Journal of Personality, 67,* 157–184.

Orenstein, P. (1994). *Schoolgirls: Young women, self-esteem, and the confidence gap.* New York: Doubleday.

Ostendorf, F., & Angleitner, A. (2004). *NEO-Persönlichkeitsinventar, revidierte Form, NEO-PI-R nach Costa und McCrae* [Revised NEO Personality Inventory, NEO-PI-R of Costa and McCrae]. Göttingen, Germany: Hogrefe.

Ozer, D. J. (1986). *Consistency in personality.* New York: Springer.

Paunonen, S. V. (1998). Hierarchical organization of personality and prediction. *Journal of Personality and Social Psychology, 74,* 538–556.

Paunonen, S. V. (2003). Big Five factors of personality and replicated predictions of behavior. *Journal of Personality and Social Psychology, 84,* 411–424.

Peabody, D. (1987). Selecting representative trait adjectives. *Journal of Personality and Social Psychology, 52,* 59–71.

Peabody, D., & Goldberg, L. R. (1989). Some determinants of factor structures from personality-trait descriptors. *Journal of Personality and Social Psychology, 57,* 552–567.

Persegani, C., Russo, P., Carucci, C., Nicolini, M., Papeschi, L. L., & Trimarchi, M. (2002). Television viewing and personality structure in children. *Personality and Individuals Differences, 32,* 977–990.

Pervin, L. A. (1984). *Current controversies and issues in personality* (2nd ed.). New York: John Wiley.

Pervin, L. A. (1999). Epilogue: Constancy and change in personality theory and research. In L. A. Pervin & O. P. John (Eds.), *Handbook of personality: Theory and research* (2nd ed., pp. 689–704). New York: Guilford Press.

Pervin, L. A. (2002). *Current controversies and issues in personality* (3rd. ed.). New York: John Wiley.

Peterson, C. (2006). *A primer in positive psychology.* New York: Oxford University Press.

Pettigrew, T. F. (1997). Personality and social structure. In R. Hogan, J. Johnson, & S. Briggs (Eds.), *Handbook of personality* (pp. 417–438). San Diego, CA: Academic Press.

Pickering, A. D., & Gray, J. A. (1999). The neuroscience of personality. In L. A. Pervin & O. P. John (Eds.), *Handbook of personality: Theory and research* (2nd ed., pp. 277–299). New York: Guilford Press.

Postman, L., Bruner, J. S., & McGinnies, E. (1948). Personal values as selective factors in perception. *Journal of Abnormal and Social Psychology, 43,* 142–154.

Price, R. H., & Bouffard, D. L. (1974). Behavioral appropriateness and situational constraint as dimensions of social behavior. *Journal of Personality and Social Psychology, 30,* 579–586.

Raggatt, P. (2000). *The Personality Web Protocol – Questionnaire Form.* Townsville, Queensland: James Cook University.

Raggatt, P. (2006). Putting the Five-Factor Model into context: Evidence linking Big Five traits to narrative identity. *Journal of Personality, 74,* 1321–1347.

Rentfrow, P. J., & Gosling, S. D. (2003). The do re mi's of everyday life: The structure and personality correlates of music preferences. *Journal of Personality and Social Psychology, 84,* 1236–1256.

Rieke, M. L., Guastello, S. J., & Conn, S. R. (1994). Leadership and creativity. In S. R. Conn & M. L. Rieke (Eds.), *The 16PF Fifth Edition technical manual* (pp. 183–212). Champaign, IL: Institute for Personality and Ability Testing.

Roberts, B. W., & DelVecchio, W. F. (2000). The rank-order consistency of personality traits from childhood to old age: A quantitative review of longitudinal studies. *Psychological Bulletin, 126,* 3–25.

Robins, R. W., John, O. P., & Caspi, A. (1998). The typological approach to studying personality. In R. B. Cairns, J. Kagan, & L. Bergman (Eds.), *The individual in developmental research: Essays in honor of Marian Radke-Yarrow* (pp. 135–160). Beverly Hills, CA: Sage.

Robins, R. W., John, O. P., Caspi, A., Moffitt, T. E., & Stouthhamer-Loeber, M. (1996). Resilient, overcontrolled, and undercontrolled boys: Three replicable personality types. *Journal of Personality and Social Psychology, 70,* 157–171.

Robinson, M. D., & Clore, G. L. (2007). Traits, states, and encoding speed: Support for a top-down view of neuroticism/state relations. *Journal of Personality, 75,* 95–120.

Rushton, J. P., Brainerd, C. J., & Pressley, M. (1983). Behavioral development and construct validity: The principle of aggregation. *Psychological Bulletin, 94,* 18–38.

Russell, M. T., & Madsen, D. H. (1988). *Marriage counseling report user's guide.* Champaign, IL: Institute for Personality and Ability Testing.

Russell, M. T., & Robinson, R. P. (1995). *16PF(R) Fifth Edition Couple's Counseling Report.* Champaign, IL: Institute for Personality and Ability Testing.

Rusting, C. L. (1999). Interactive effects of personality and mood on emotion-congruent memory and judgment. *Journal of Personality and Social Psychology, 77,* 1073–1086.

Rusting, C. L., & Larsen, R. J. (1998). Personality and cognitive processing of affective information. *Personality and Social Psychology Bulletin, 24,* 200–213.

Sarason, I. G., Smith, R. E., & Diener, E. (1975). Personality research: Components of variance attributed to the person and the situation. *Journal of Personality and Social Psychology, 32,* 199–204.

Saucier, G. (2003). Factor structure of English-language personality type-nouns. *Journal of Personality and Social Psychology, 85,* 695–708.

Saucier, G., & Goldberg, L. R. (1996). The language of personality: Lexical perspectives on the Five-Factor Model. In J. S. Wiggins (Ed.), *The Five-Factor Model of personality: Theoretical perspectives* (pp. 21–50). New York: Guilford Press.

Saucier, G., & Goldberg, L. R. (1998). What is beyond the Big Five? *Journal of Personality, 66,* 495–524.

Saucier, G., & Goldberg, L. R. (2001). Lexical studies of indigenous personality: Premises, products, and prospects. *Journal of Personality, 69,* 847–880.

Schenk, J., & Pfrang, H. (1986). Extraversion, neuroticism, and sexual behavior: Interrelationships in a sample of young men. *Archives of Sexual Behavior, 15,* 449–455.

Schofield, M. (1968). *The sexual behaviour of young people.* Harmondsworth, UK: Penguin.

Schooley, M. (1936). Personality resemblances among married couples. *Journal of Abnormal and Social Psychology, 31,* 340–347.

Seashore, H. G. (1947). Validation of the study of values for vocational groups at the college level. *Educational and Psychological Measurement, 7,* 757–763.

Shaver, P. R., & Brennan, K. A. (1992). Attachment styles and the "Big Five" personality traits: Their connections with each other with romantic relationship outcomes. *Personality and Social Psychology Bulletin, 18,* 536–545.

Shaw, L., & Sichel, H. (1971). *Accident proneness.* New York: Pergamon.

Silvia, P. J., & Warburton, J. B. (2006). Positive and negative affect: Bridging states and traits. In J. C. Thomas & D. L Segal (Eds.), *Comprehensive handbook of personality and psychotherapy: Vol. 1. Personality and everyday functioning* (pp. 268–284). Hoboken, NJ: John Wiley.

Simms, L. J. (2007). The Big Seven Model of personality and its relevance to personality pathology. *Journal of Personality, 75,* 65–94.

Simonton, D. K. (1999). Creativity and genius. In L. A. Pervin & O. P. John (Eds.), *Handbook of personality: Theory and research* (2nd ed., pp. 629–652). New York: Guilford Press.

Sneed, C. D., McCrae, R. R., & Funder, D. C. (1998). Lay conceptions of the Five-Factor Model and its indicators. *Personality and Social Psychology Bulletin, 24,* 115–126.

Snibble, H. M., Fabricatore, J., & Azen, S. P. (1975). Personality patterns of White, Black, and Mexican-American patrolmen as measured by the Sixteen Personality Factor Questionnaire. *American Journal of Community Psychology, 3,* 221–226.

Spearman, C. (1910). Correlation calculated from faulty data. *British Journal of Psychology, 3,* 271–295.

Spranger, E. (1928). *Types of men: The psychology and ethics of personality.* New York: Johnson Reprint.

Srivastava, S., John, O. P., Gosling, S. D., & Potter, J. (2003). Development of personality in early and middle age: Set like plaster or persistent change? *Journal of Personality and Social Psychology, 84,* 1041–1053.

Steinmetz, S. K., Clavan, S., & Stein, K. F. (1990). *Marriage and family realities: Historical and contemporary perspectives.* New York: Harper & Row.

Stewart, G. L., & Carson, K. P. (1995). Personality dimensions and domains of service performance: A field investigation. *Journal of Business and Psychology, 9,* 365–378.

Stolberg, R. A., Clark, D. C., & Bongar, B. (2002). Epidemiology, assessment, and management of suicide in depressed patients. In I. H. Gotlib & C. L. Hammen (Eds.), *Handbook of depression* (pp. 581–601). New York: Guilford Press.

Suls, J., Green, P., & Hillis, S. (1998). Emotional reactivity to everyday problems, affective inertia, and neuroticism. *Personality and Social Psychology Bulletin, 24,* 127–136.

Tangney, J. P., Fee, R., Reinsmith, C., Boone, A. L., & Lee, N. (1999, August). *Assessing individual differences in the propensity to forgive.* Paper presented at the annual meeting of the American Psychological Association, Boston.

Tellegen, A. (1993). Folk concepts and psychological concepts of personality and personality disorder. *Psychological Inquiry, 4,* 122–130.

Tellegen, A., & Waller, N. G. (1987, August). *Re-examining basic dimensions of natural language trait descriptors.* Paper presented at the 95th annual convention of the American Psychological Convention, New York.

Tellegen, A., & Waller, N. G. (in press). *Exploring personality through test construction: Development of the Multidimensional Personality Questionnaire (MPQ).* Minneapolis: University of Minnesota Press.

Tennen, H., & Affleck, G. (2003). Benefit-finding and benefit-reminding. In C. R. Snyder & S. J. Lopez (Eds.), *Handbook of positive psychology* (pp. 584–597). New York: Oxford University Press.

Trobst, K. K., Wiggins, J. S., Costa, P. T., Jr., Herbst, J. H., McCrae, R. R., & Masters, H. L., III (2000). Personality psychology and problem behavior: HIV risk and the Five-Factor Model. *Journal of Personality, 68*, 1233–1252.

Trull, T. J., Widiger, T. A., & Burr, R. (2001). A structured interview for the assessment of the Five Factor Model of personality: Facet level relations to the Axis II personality disorders. *Journal of Personality, 69*, 175–198.

Trull, T. J., Widiger, T. A., Lynam, D. R., & Costa, P. T., Jr. (2003). Borderline personality disorder from the perspective of general personality functioning. *Journal of Abnormal Psychology, 112*, 193–202.

Tupes, E. C., & Christal, R. C. (1961). *Recurrent personality factors based on trait ratings* (Tech. Rep. No. ASD-TR-61–97). Lackland Air Force Base, TX: U.S. Air Force.

Van der Zee, K. V., Buunk, B., & Sanderman, R. (1998). Neuroticism and reactions to social comparison information among cancer patients. *Journal of Personality, 66*, 175–194.

Waller, N. G., & Ben-Porath, Y. (1987). Is it time for clinical psychology to embrace the Five-Factor Model of personality? *American Psychologist, 42*, 887–889.

Waller, N. G., & Zavala, J. D. (1993). Evaluating the Big Five. *Psychological Inquiry, 4*, 131–134.

Watson, D., Suls, J., & Haig, J. (2002). Global self-esteem in relation to structural models of personality and affectivity. *Journal of Personality and Social Psychology Bulletin, 83*, 185–197.

Weckowicz, T. E., Collier, G., & Spreng, L. (1997). Field dependence, cognitive functions, personality traits, and social values in heavy cannabis users and nonuser controls. *Psychological Reports, 41*, 291–302.

Weckowicz, T. E., & Janssen, D. V. (1973). Cognitive functions, personality traits, and social values in heavy marijuana smokers and nonsmoker controls. *Journal of Abnormal Psychology, 81*, 264–269.

Weiss, A., King, J. E., & Enns, R. M. (2002). Subjective well-being is heritable and genetically correlated with dominance in chimpanzees (*Pan troglodytes*). *Journal of Personality and Social Psychology, 83*, 1141–1149.

Weiss, A., King, J. E., & Figueredo, A. J. (2000). The heritability of personality factors in chimpanzees (*Pan troglodytes*). *Behavior Genetics, 30*, 213–221.

White, J. K., Hendrick, S. S., & Hendrick, C. (2004). Big Five personality variables and relationships constructs. *Personality and Individual Differences, 37*, 1519–1530.

Widiger, T. A., & Trull, T. J. (1992). Personality and psychopathology: An application of the Five-Factor Model. *Journal of Personality, 60*, 363–393.

Wiehe, V. R. (2003). Empathy and narcissism in a sample of child abuse perpetrators and a comparison sample of foster parents. *Child Abuse and Neglect, 27*, 541–555.

Wiggins, J. S. (Ed.). (1996). *The Five-Factor Model of personality.* New York: Guilford Press.

Wiggins, J. S. (1997). In defense of traits. In R. Hogan, J. Johnson, & S. Briggs (Eds.), *Handbook of personality psychology* (pp. 95–115). San Diego, CA: Academic Press.

Wiggins, J. S. (2003). *Paradigms of personality assessment.* New York: Guilford Press.

Wiggins, J. S., Masters, H. L., III, Trobst, K. K., & Costa, P. T., Jr. (1998, March). *Personality determinants of high-risk behavior in an HIV-negative sample.* Paper presented at the Annual Convention of the Society for Behavioral Medicine, New Orleans.

Wiggins, J. S., & Trapnell, P. D. (1997). Personality structure: The return of the Big Five. In R. Hogan, J. Johnson, & S. Briggs (Eds.), *Handbook of personality psychology* (pp. 737–765). San Diego, CA: Academic Press.

Wilson, G. (1978). Introversion/extroversion. In H. London & J. E. Exner (Eds.), *Dimensions of personality* (pp. 217–261). New York: John Wiley.

Wilson, G. (1990). Personality, time of day, and arousal. *Personality and Individual Differences, 11*, 153–168.

Wilson, G. D. (1997). Sex and personality. In H. Nyborg (Ed.), *The scientific study of human nature: Tribute to Hans J. Eysenck at eighty* (pp. 165–188). New York: Pergamon.

Winter, D. G. (1993). Gordon Allport and "Letters from Jenny." In K. H. Craik, R. Hogan, & R. N. Wolfe (Eds.), *Fifty years of personality psychology* (pp. 147–163). New York: Plenum.

Winter, D. G., & Barenbaum, N. B. (1999). History of modern personality theory and research. In L. A. Pervin & O. P. John (Eds.), *Handbook of personality: Theory and research* (2nd ed., pp. 3–27). New York: Guilford Press.

Winter, D. G., John, O. P., Stewart, A. J., Klohnen, E. C., & Duncan, L. E. (1998). Traits and motives: Toward an integration of two traditions in personality research. *Psychological Review, 105*, 230–250.

Wise, S. R., & Elmore, R. T. (1996). Co-therapy for couples. *Insight, 2*(2). Champaign, IL: Institute for Personality and Ability Testing.

Witvliet, C. V. O., Ludwig, T., & Vander Laan, K. (2001). Granting forgiveness or harboring grudges: Implications for emotion, physiology, and health. *Psychological Science, 121*, 117–123.

World Health Organization (2006). *Global AIDS epidemic continues to grow.* Retrieved November 13, 2008, from www.who.int/hiv/mediacentre/news62/en/index.html.

Zeidhlach, D. (2003). *Critical thinking and personality dispositions.* Unpublished doctoral dissertation, Argosy University, Illinois School of Professional Psychology, Chicago.

Zimbardo, P. G. (1970). The human choice: Individuation, reason, and order versus deindividuation, impulse, and chaos. In W. J. Arnold & D. Levine (Eds.), *Nebraska symposium on motivation, 1969* (pp. 237–307). Lincoln: University of Nebraska Press.

Zuckerman, M. (1998). Psychobiological theories of personality. In D. F. Barone, M. Hersen, & V. B. Van Hasselt (Eds.), *Advanced personality* (pp. 123–154). New York: Plenum.

Zuckerman, M. (2005). *Psychobiology of personality* (2nd ed., rev. and updated). New York: Cambridge University Press.

Zuckerman, M., Buchsbaum, M. S., & Murphy, D. L. (1980). Seeking and its biological correlates. *Psychological Bulletin, 88*, 187–214.

Zuckerman, M., Koestner, R., DeBoy, T., Garcia, T., Maresca, B. C., & Sartoris, J. M. (1988). To predict some of the people some of the time: A reexamination of the moderator variable approach in personality theory. *Journal of Personality and Social Psychology, 54*, 1006–1019.

Zuckerman, M., & Kuhlman, D. M. (2000). Personality and risk-taking: Common biosocial factors. *Journal of Personality, 68*, 999–1029.

Chapter 8

Abrahamson, A. C., Baker, L. A., & Caspi, A. (2002). Rebellious teens? Genetic and environmental influences on social attitudes of adolescents. *Journal of Personality and Social Psychology, 83*, 1392–1408.

Allport, G. W. (1937). *Personality: A psychological interpretation.* New York: Henry Holt.

Ang, R. P., & Woo, A. (2003). Influence of sensation seeking on boys' psychosocial adjustment. *North American Journal of Psychology, 5*, 121–136.

Angst, J., & Maurer-Goeli, Y. A. (1974). Blutgruppen und Persönlichkeit. *Archiv für Psychiatrie und Nervenkrankheiten, 218*, 291–300.

Arnaut, G. Y. (2006). Sensation seeking, risk-taking, and fearlessness. In J. C. Thomas & D. L. Segal (Eds.), *Comprehensive handbook of personality and psychopathology: Vol. 1. Personality and everyday functioning* (pp. 322–341). Hoboken, NJ: John Wiley.

Arvey, R. D., Bouchard, T. J., Segal, N. L., & Abraham, L. M. (1989). Job satisfaction: Environmental and genetic components. *Journal of Applied Psychology, 74*, 187–192.

Banks, D. (2003). Proteomics: A frontier between genomics and metabolomics. *Chance, 16*, 6–7.

Bardage, C., Isacson, D., & Pedersen, N. L. (2001). Self-rated health as a predictor of mortality among persons with cardiovascular disease in Sweden. *Scandinavian Journal of Public Health, 29*, 13–22.

Berk, L. E. (2006). *Child development* (7th ed.). Boston: Pearson Education.

Betsworth, D. G., Bouchard, T. J., Jr., Cooper, C. R., Grotevant, H. D., Hansen, J. I. C., Scarr, S., et al. (1994). Genetic and environmental influences on vocational interests assessed using adoptive and biological families and twins reared apart and together. *Journal of Vocational Behavior, 44*, 263–278.

Blum, K., Cull, J. G., Braverman, E. R., & Comings, D. E. (1996). Reward deficiency syndrome. *American Scientist, 84*, 132–146.

Boomsma, D., Willemsen, G., Dolan, C. V., Hawkley, L. C., & Cacioppo, J. T. (2005). Genetic and environmental contributions to loneliness in adults: The Netherlands Twins Register Study. *Behavior Genetics, 35*, 745–752.

Borkenau, P., Riemann, R., Angleitner, A., & Spinath, F. (2001). Genetic, and environmental influences on observed personality: Evidence from the German Observational Study of Adult Twins. *Journal of Personality and Social Psychology, 80*, 655–668.

Bouchard, T. J., & Loehlin, J. C. (2001). Genes, evolution, and personality. *Behavior Genetics, 31*, 243–273.

Bouchard, T. J., Jr., Segal, N. L., Tellegen, A., McGue, M., Keys, M., & Krueger, R. F. (2004). Genetic influence on social attitudes: Another challenge to psychology from behavior genetics. In L. DiLalla (Ed.), *Behavior genetic principles: Development, personality, and psychopathology* (pp. 89–104). Washington, DC: American Psychological Association Press.

Bratko, D., & Butkovic, A. (2003). Family study of sensation seeking. *Personality and Individual Differences, 35*, 1559–1570.

Brocke, B., Beauduecel, A., John, R., Debener, S., & Heilemann, H. (2000). Sensation seeking and affective disorders: Characteristics in the intensity dependence of acoustic evoked potentials. *Neuropsychobiology, 41*, 24–30.

Buss, D. M. (Ed.). (2005). *The handbook of evolutionary psychology.* Hoboken, NJ: John Wiley.

Buss, D. M. (2008). *Evolutionary psychology: The new science of the mind* (3rd ed.). Boston: Pearson Education/Allyn & Bacon.

Cacioppo, J. T., Berntson, G. G., Sheridan, J. F., & McClintock, M. K. (2000). Multi-level integrative analysis of human behavior: Social neuroscience and the complementing nature of social and biological approaches. *Psychological Bulletin, 126*, 829–843.

Calev, A., Gaudino, E. A., Squires, N. K., Zervas, I. M., & Fink, M. (1995). ECT and non-memory cognition: A review. *British Journal of Clinical Psychology, 34*, 505–515.

Calev, A., Nigal, D., Shapira, B., Tubi, N., Chazan, S., Ben-Yehuda, Y., et al. (1991). Early and long-term effects of electroconvulsive therapy and depression on memory and other cognitive functions. *Journal of Nervous and Mental Diseases, 179*, 526–533.

Canli, T. (Ed.). (2006). *Biology of personality and individual differences.* New York: Guilford Press.

Canli, T., Zhao, Z., Desmond, J. E., King, E., Gross, J., & Gabrieli, J. D. E. (2001). An fMRI study of personality influences on brain reactivity to emotional stimuli. *Behavioral Neuroscience, 115*, 33–42.

Carducci, B. J. (2000). *Shyness: A bold new approach.* New York: HarperPerennial.

Carter, J. E., & Schuchman, E. H. (2001). Gene therapy of neurodegenerative disease: Fact or fiction? *British Journal of Psychiatry, 178*, 392–394.

Carver, C. S. (2004). Negative affects deriving from the behavioral approach system. *Emotion, 4*, 3–22.

Carver, C. S., & White, T. L. (1994). Behavioral inhibition, behavioral activation, and affective responses to impeding reward and punishments: The BIS/BAS scales. *Journal of Personality and Social Psychology, 67*, 319–333.

Cates, D. S, Houston, B. K., Vavak, C. R., Crawford, M. H., & Uttley, M. (1993). Heritability of hostility related emotions, attitudes, and behavior. *Journal of Behavioral Medicine, 18*, 237–256.

Coccaro, E. F., Bergeman, C. S., Kavoussi, R. J., & Seroczynski. A. D. (1997). Heritability of aggression and impulsivity: A twin study of the Buss-Durkee aggression scales in adult male twins. *Biological Psychiatry, 41*, 273–284.

Comer, R. J. (2007). *Abnormal psychology* (4th ed.). New York: Worth.

Corr, P. J. (2002). J. A. Gray's reinforcement sensitivity theory: Tests of the joint subsystem hypothesis of anxiety and impulsivity. *Personality and Individual Differences, 33*, 511–532.

Costa, P. T., & McCrae, R. R. (2001). A theoretical context for adult temperament. In T. D. Wachs & G. A. Kohnstamm (Eds.), *Temperament in context* (pp. 1–21). Mahwah, NJ: Erlbaum.

Dabbs, J. M., Jr. (2000). *Heroes, rogues, and lovers: Testosterone and behavior.* New York: McGraw-Hill.

Dabbs, J. M., Jr., de La Rue, D., & Williams, P. M. (1990). Testosterone and occupational choice: Actors, ministers, and other men. *Journal of Personality and Social Psychology, 59,* 1261–1265.

Daitzman, R., & Zuckerman, M. (1980). Disinhibitory sensation seeking personality and gonadal hormones. *Personality and Individual Differences, 1,* 103–110.

Daitzman, R., Zuckerman, M., Sammelwitz, P., & Ganjam, V. (1978). Sensation seeking and gonadal hormones. *Journal of Biosocial Sciences, 10,* 401–408.

Damon, A. (1955). Physique and success in military flying. American *Journal of Physical Anthropology, 13,* 217–252.

Davidson, R. J. (2002). Anxiety and affective style: Role of prefrontal cortex and amygdala. *Biological Psychiatry, 51,* 68–80.

Depue, R. A., & Iacono, W. G. (1989). Neurobehavioral aspects of affective disorders. *Annual Review of Psychology, 40,* 457–492.

DiLalla, L. (Ed.). (2004). *Behavior genetic principles: Development, personality, and psychopathology.* Washington, DC: American Psychological Association Press.

Eysenck, H. J. (1967). *The biological basis of personality.* Springfield, IL: Charles Thomas.

Eysenck, H. J. (1970). *The structure of human personality.* London: Methuen.

Eysenck, H. J. (1982). The biological basis of cross-cultural differences in personality: Blood group antigens. *Psychological Reports, 51,* 531–540.

Eysenck, H. J. (1990a). Biological dimensions of personality. In L. A. Pervin (Ed.), *Handbook of personality: Theory and research* (pp. 244–276). New York: Guilford Press.

Eysenck, H. J. (1990b). Genetic and environmental contributions to individual differences: The three major dimensions of personality. *Journal of Personality, 58,* 245–261.

Flores, B. H., Musselman, D. L., DeBattista, C., Garlow, S. J., Schatzberg, A. F., & Nemeroff, C. B. (2004). Biology of mood disorders. In A. F. Schatzberg & B. Nemeroff (Eds.), *Textbook of psychopharmacology* (3rd ed., pp. 717–763). Washington, DC: American Psychiatric Publishing.

Fowles, D. C. (2006). Jeffrey Gray's contributions to theories of anxiety, personality, and psychopathology. In T. Canli (Ed.), *Biology of personality and individual differences* (pp. 7–34). New York: Guilford Press.

Gale, A. (1983). Electroencephalographic studies of extraversion–introversion: A case study in the psychophysiology of individual differences. *Personality and Individual Differences, 4,* 371–380.

Gimbel, C., & Booth, A. (1996). Who fought in Vietnam? *Social Forces, 74,* 1137–1157.

Glass, R. M. (2001). Electroconvulsive therapy. *Journal of the American Medical Association, 285,* 1346–1348.

Glueck, S., & Glueck, E. (1950). *Unraveling juvenile delinquency.* New York: Harper & Row.

Glueck, S., & Glueck, E. (1956). *Physique and delinquency.* New York: Harper & Row.

Gottesman, I. I. (1991). *Schizophrenia genesis: Origins of madness.* New York: Freeman.

Gray, J. A. (1982). *The neuropsychology of anxiety: An enquiry into the function of the septohippocampal system.* New York: Oxford University Press.

Gray, J. A. (1987). The neuropsychology of emotion and personality. In S. M. Stahl, S. D. Iverson, & E. C. Goodman (Eds.), *Cognitive neurochemistry* (pp. 171–190). Oxford: Oxford University Press.

Gray, J. A. (1991). Neurosystems, emotion, and personality. In J. Madden, IV (Ed.), *Neurobiology of learning, emotion, and affect* (pp. 273–306). New York: Raven Press.

Gray, J. A. (1994a). Personality dimensions and emotion systems. In P. Ekman & R. J. Davidson (Eds.), *The nature of emotion: Fundamental questions* (pp. 329–331). New York: Oxford University Press.

Gray, J. A. (1994b). Three fundamental emotion systems. In P. Ekman & R. J. Davidson (Eds.), *The nature of emotion: Fundamental questions* (pp. 243–247). New York: Oxford University Press.

Gray, J. A., & McNaughton, N. (2000). *The neuropsychology of anxiety: An enquiry into the functions of the septohippocampal system* (2nd ed.). Oxford: Oxford University Press.

Gunnell, D., & Ashby, D. (2004). Antidepressants and suicide: What is the balance of benefit and harm? *British Medical Journal, 329,* 34–38.

Hagan, E. H. (2005). Controversial issues in evolutionary psychology. In D. M. Buss (Ed.), *The handbook of evolutionary psychology* (pp. 145–173). Hoboken, NJ: John Wiley.

Hawkley, L. C., Browne, M. W., & Cacioppo, J. T. (2005). How can I connect with thee? Let me count the ways. *Psychological Science, 16,* 798–804.

Healy, D., & Whitaker, C. (2003). Antidepressants and suicide: Risk–benefit conundrums. *Journal of Psychiatry and Neuroscience, 28,* 28.

Herbert, J. D. (1995). An overview of the current status of social phobia. *Applied and Preventive Psychology, 40,* 39–51.

Hofstede, G. (1976). *Nationality and organizational stress.* Brussels: European Institute for Research in Management.

Hofstede, G. (1980). *Culture's consequences: International differences in work-related values.* London: Sage.

Holden, C. (2004). FDA weighs suicide risk in children on antidepressants. *Science, 303,* 745.

Jack, S. J., & Ronan, K. R. (1998). Sensation seeking among high- and low-risk sports participants. *Personality and Individual Differences, 25,* 1063–1083.

Jang, K. L., Hu, S., Livesley, W. J., Angleitner, A., Riemann, R., Ando, J., et al. (2001). Covariance structure of neuroticism and agreeableness: A twin and molecular genetic analysis of the role of the serotonin transporter gene. *Journal of Personality and Social Psychology, 81,* 295–304.

Jang, K. L., Livesley, W. J., Angleitner, A., Riemann, R., & Vernon, P. A. (2002). Genetic and environmental influences on the covariance of facets defining the domains of the Five-Factor Model of personality. *Personality and Individual Differences, 33*, 83–101.

Johnson, D. L., Wiebe, J. S., Gold, S. M., Andreason, N. C., Hichwa, R. D., Watkins, G. L., et al. (1999). Biological bases of extraversion: A positron emission tomographical study. *American Journal of Psychiatry, 156*, 252–257.

Jonah, B. A. (1997). Sensation seeking and risky driving: A review and synthesis of the literature. *Accident Analysis and Prevention, 29*, 651–665.

Jonah, B. A., Thiessen, R., & Au-Yeung, E. (2001). Sensation seeking, risky driving, and behavior adaptation. *Accident Analysis and Prevention, 33*, 679–684.

Kagan, J., & Arcus, D. (1995). Temperament and craniofacial variation in the first two years. *Child Development, 66*, 1529–1540.

Koening, L. B., McGue, M., Krueger, R. F., & Bouchard, T. J., Jr. (2005). Genetic and environmental influences on religiousness: Findings for retrospective and current religiousness ratings. *Journal of Personality, 73*, 471–488.

Knyazev, G. G., Slobodskaya, H. R., & Wilson, G. D. (2002). Psychological correlates of behavioral inhibition and activation. *Personality and Individual Differences, 33*, 647–660.

Kretschmer, E. (1925). *Physique and character*. New York: Harcourt.

Kring, A. M., Davison, G. C., Neale, J. M., & Johnson, S. L. (2007). *Abnormal psychology* (10th ed.). Hoboken, NJ: John Wiley.

Larsen, R. J., Chen, B., & Zelenski, J. (2003). *Response to punishment and reward in the emotion Stroop paradigm: Relations to BIS and BAS*. Unpublished manuscript.

Leve, L. D., Kim, H. K., & Pears, K. C. (2005). Childhood temperament and family environment as predictors of internalizing and externalizing trajectories from ages 5 to 17. *Journal of Abnormal Child Psychology, 33*, 505–520.

Loehlin, J. C. (1992). *Genes and environment in personality development*. Newbury Park, CA: Sage.

Loehlin, J. C., Neiderhiser, J. M., & Reiss, D. (2003). The behavior genetics of personality and the NEAD study. *Journal of Research in Personality, 37*. 373–387.

Loehlin, J. C., & Nichols, R. C. (1976). *Heredity, environment, and personality: A study of 850 sets of twins*. Austin: University of Texas Press.

Loehlin, J. C., Willerman, L., & Horn, J. M. (1982). Personality resemblances between unwed mothers and their adopted-away offspring. *Journal of Personality and Social Psychology, 42*, 1089–1099.

Lynn, R. (1981). Cross-cultural differences in neuroticism, extraversion and psychoticism. In R. Lynn (Ed.), *Dimensions of personality* (pp. 263–286). London: Pergamon.

Lyubomirsky, S., Sheldon, K. M., & Schkade, D. (2005). Pursuing happiness: The architecture of sustainable change. *Review of General Psychology, 9*, 111–131.

MacAndrew, C., & Steele, T. (1991). Gray's behavioral inhibition system: A psychometric examination. *Personality and Individual Differences, 12*, 157–171.

Marangell, L. B., Silver, J. M., Goff, D. C., & Yudofsky, S. C. (2003). Psychopharmacology and electroconvulsive therapy. In R. E. Hales & S. C. Yudofsky (Eds.), *Textbook of clinical psychiatry* (4th ed., pp. 1047–1150). Washington, DC: American Psychiatric Publishing.

Matthews, G., Deary, I. J., & Whiteman, M. C. (2003). *Personality traits*. New York: Cambridge University Press.

Matthews, G., & Gilliland, K. (1999). The personality theories of H. J. Eysenck and J. A. Gray: A comparative review. *Personality and Individual Differences, 26*, 583–626.

Mazur, A. (1985). A biosocial model of status in face-to-face primate groups. *Social Forces, 64*, 377–402.

Mazur, A., Booth, A., & Dabbs, J. M., Jr. (1992). Testosterone and chess competition. *Social Psychology Quarterly, 55*, 70–77.

McCrae, R. R., Costa, P. T., Ostendorf, F., Angleitner, A., Hrebickova, M., Avia, M. D., et al. (2000). Nature over nurture: Temperament, personality, and lifespan development. *Journal of Personality and Social Psychology, 78*, 173–186.

McDaniel, S. R., & Zuckerman, M. (2003). The relationship of impulsive sensation seeking and gender to interest and participation in gambling activities. *Personality and Individual Differences, 35*, 1385–1400.

McGuire, S., & Clifford, J. (2000). Genetic and environmental contributions to loneliness in children. *Psychological Science, 11*, 487–491.

McLaughlin, R. J., & Eysenck, H. J. (1967). Extraversion, neuroticism and paired-associate learning. *Journal of Experimental Research in Personality, 2*, 128–132.

Mendel, G. J. (1866). Versuche ueber Pflanzenhybriden. *Verhandlungen des Naturforschunden Vereines Bruenn, 4*, 3–47.

Miles, D. R., & Carey, G. (1997). Genetic and environmental architecture of human aggression. *Journal of Personality and Social Psychology, 72*, 207–217.

Morf, C. C., & Ayduk, O. (Eds.). (2005). *Current directions in personality psychology*. Upper Saddle River, NJ: Pearson/Prentice Hall.

Moore, K. L., & Persaud, T. V. N. (2003). *Before we are born* (6th ed.). Philadelphia: Saunders.

Morris-Yates, A., Andrews, G., Howie, P., & Henderson, S. (1990). Twins: A test of the equal environments assumption. *Acta Psychiatrica Scandinavica, 81*, 322–326.

Neary, R. S., & Zuckerman, M. (1976). Sensation seeking trait and state anxiety and the electrodermal orienting reflex. *Psychophysiology, 13*, 205–211.

Ninan, P. T., & Muntasser, S. (2004). Buspiron and gepirone. In A. F. Schatzberg & C. B. Nemeroff (Eds.), *Textbook of psychopharmacology* (3rd ed., pp. 391–404). Washington, DC: American Psychiatric Publishing.

O'Connor, K. (1980). The CNV and individual differences in smoking behavior. *Personality and Individual Differences, 1*, 57–72.

O'Connor, K. (1982). Individual differences in the effect of smoking on frontal-central distribution of the CNV: Some observations on smokers' control of attentional behavior. *Personality and Individual Differences, 3*, 271–285.

Olson, J. M., Vernon, P. A., Harris, J. A., & Jang, K. L. (2001). The heritability of attitudes: A study of twins. *Journal of Personality and Social Psychology, 80*, 845–860.

Pennebaker, J. W., Rime, B., & Blankenship, V. E. (1996). Stereotypes of emotional expressiveness of Northerners and Southerners: A cross-cultural test of Montesquieu's hypotheses. *Journal of Personality and Social Psychology, 70*, 372–380.

Pervin, L. A. (2002). *Current controversies and issues in personality* (3rd ed.). New York: John Wiley.

Pickering, A. D., Corr, P. J., Powell, J. H., Kumari, V., Thornton, J. C., & Gray, J. A. (1997). Individual differences in reactions to reinforcing stimuli are neither black nor white: To what extent are they Gray? In H. Nyborg (Ed.), *The scientific study of human nature: Tribute to Hans. J. Eysenck at eighty* (pp. 36–67). New York: Pergamon.

Pinquart, M., & Sorensen, S. (2003). Risk factors for loneliness in adulthood and old age – a meta-analysis. In S. P. Shohov (Ed.), *Advances in psychological research: Vol. 19* (pp. 111–143). Hauppauge, NY: Nova Science.

Plomin, R., Chipuer, H. M., & Loehlin, J. C. (1990). Behavior genetics and personality. In L. A. Pervin (Ed.), *Handbook of personality: Theory and research* (pp. 225–243). New York: Guilford Press.

Plomin, R., DeFries, J. C., McClearn, G. E., & McGuffin, P. (2001). *Behavioral genetics* (4th ed.). New York: Worth.

Plomin, R., & Nesselroade, J. R. (1990). Behavioral genetics and personality change. *Journal of Personality, 58*, 191–220.

Plomin, R., & Rende, R. (1991). Human behavioral genetics. *Annual Review of Psychology, 42*, 161–190.

Purifoy, F. E., & Koopmans, L. H. (1979). Androstenedione, testosterone, and free testosterone concentration in women of various occupations. *Social Biology, 26*, 179–188.

Raffaelli, M., & Crockett, L. J. (2003). Sexual risk taking in adolescence: The role of self-regulation and attraction to risk. *Developmental Psychology, 39*, 1036–1046.

Rathus, S. A. (2003). *Voyages: Childhood and adolescence.* Belmont, CA: Wadsworth.

Redmond, D. E., Jr. (1985). Neurochemical basis for anxiety and anxiety disorders: Evidence from drugs which decrease human fear and anxiety. In A. H. Tuna & J. D. Maser (Eds.), *Anxiety and the anxiety disorder* (pp. 533–555). Hillsdale, NJ: Erlbaum.

Redmond, D. E., Jr. (1987). Studies of locus coeruleus in monkeys and hypothesis for neuropsychopharmacology. In H. Y. Meltzer (Ed.), *Psychopharmacology: The third generation of progress* (pp. 967–975). New York: Raven Press.

Reiss, D., Neiderhiser, J. M., Hetherington, E. M., & Plomin, R. (2000). *The relationship code: Deciphering genetic and social influences on adolescent development.* Cambridge, MA: Harvard University Press.

Relph, K., Harrington, K., & Pandha, H. (2004). Recent developments and current status of gene therapy using viral vectors in the United Kingdom. *British Medical Journal, 329*, 839–842.

Richardson, P. J., & Boyd, R. (2005). *Not by genes alone: How culture transformed evolution.* Chicago: University of Chicago.

Rose, D., Wykes, T., Leese, M., Bindman, J., & Fleischmann, P. (2003). Patients' perspectives on electroconvulsive therapy: Systematic review. *British Medical Journal, 326*, 1363–1365.

Rowe, D. C. (1989). Personality theory and behavioral genetics: Contributions and issues. In D. M. Buss & N. Cantor (Eds.), *Personality psychology: Recent trends and emerging directions* (pp. 294–307). New York: Springer.

Røysamb, E., Harris, J., Magnus, P., Vittersø, J., & Tambs, K. (2002). Subjective well-being: Sex-specific effects of genetic and environmental factors. *Personality and Individual Differences, 32*, 211–223.

Røysamb, E., Tambs, K., Reichborn-Kjennerud, T., Neale, M. C., & Harris, J. R. (2003). Happiness and health: Environmental and genetic contributions to the relationship between subjective well-being, perceived, and somatic illness. *Journal of Personality and Social Psychology, 85*, 1136–1146.

Sackeim, H. A., & Lisanby, S. H. (2001). Physical treatments in psychiatry: Advances in electroconvulsive therapy, transcranial magnetic stimulation, and vagus nerve stimulation. In M. W. Weissman (Ed.), *Treatments of depression: Bridging the 21st century* (pp. 151–174). Washington, DC: American Psychiatric Publishing.

Sanford, R. N., Adkins, M. M., Miller, R. B., Cobb, E. A., et al. (1943). Physique, personality, and scholarship: A cooperative study of school children. *Monographs of the Society for Research in Child Development, 8* (1, Serial No. 34).

Schindler, G. L. (1979). Testosterone concentration, personality patterns, and occupational choice in women [abstract]. *Dissertation Abstracts International, 40*, 1411A. (University Microfilms No. 79–19,403)

Schmidt, L. A. (1999). Frontal brain electrical activity in shyness and sociability. *Psychological Science, 10*, 316–320.

Schooler, C., Zahn, T. P., Murphy, D. L., & Buchsbaum, M. S. (1978). Psychological correlates of monoamine oxidase in normals. *Journal of Nervous and Mental Disease, 166*, 177–186.

Shagass, C., & Kerenyi, A. B. (1958). Neurophysiological studies of personality. *Journal of Nervous and Mental Diseases, 126*, 141–147.

Sheldon, W. H. (with the collaboration of Stevens, S. S.). (1942). *The varieties of temperament: A psychology of constitutional differences.* New York: Harper & Row.

Sheldon, W. H. (with the collaboration of Dupertuis, C. W., & McDermott, E.). (1954). *Atlas of men: A guide for somatotyping the adult male at all ages.* New York: Harper & Row.

Sheldon, W. H., Lewis, N. D. C., & Tenney, A. M. (1969). Psychotic patterns and physical constitution: A thirty-year follow-up of thirty-eight hundred psychiatric patients in New York State. In D. V. Siva Sankar (Ed.), *Schizophrenia: Current concepts and research* (pp. 838–912). New York: PJD Publications.

Silvia, P. J., & Warburton, J. B. (2006). Positive and negative affect: Bridging states and traits. In J. C. Thomas & D. L. Segal (Eds.), *Comprehensive handbook of personality and psychopathology: Vol. 1. Personality and everyday functioning* (pp. 268–284). Hoboken, NJ: John Wiley.

Smith, B. D. (1983). Extraversion and electrodermal activity: Arousability and the inverted-U. *Personality and Individual Differences, 4*, 411–420.

Spurzheim, J. G. (1834). *Phrenology, or the doctrine of mental phenomena.* Boston: Marsh, Capen, and Lynons.

Stallings, M. C., Hewitt, J. K., Cloninger, C. R., Heath, A. C., & Eaves, L. J. (1996). Genetic and environmental structure of the Tridimensional Personality Questionnaire: Three or four temperament dimensions? *Journal of Personality and Social Psychology, 70,* 127–140.

Staw, B. M., & Ross, J. (1985). Stability in the midst of change: A dispositional approach to job attitudes. *Journal of Applied Psychology, 70,* 469–480.

Stelmack, R. M. (1985). Extraversion and auditory evoked potentials: Some empirical and theoretical considerations. In D. Papakostopoulos, S. Butler, & I. Martin (Eds.), *Experimental and clinical neuropsychophysiology* (pp. 238–255). Lancaster: Medical and Technical Publications.

Stelmack, R. M. (1990). Biological bases of extraversion: Psychophysiological evidence. *Journal of Personality, 58,* 293–311.

Stelmack, R. M. (1997). The psychophysics and psychophysiology of extraversion and arousal. In H. Nyborg (Ed.), *The scientific study of human nature: Tribute to Hans J. Eysenck at eighty* (pp. 388–403). New York: Pergamon.

Stelmack, R. M., & Geen, R. G. (1992). The psychophysiology of extraversion. In A. Gale & M. W. Eysenck (Eds.), *Handbook of individual differences: Biological perspectives* (pp. 227–254). New York: John Wiley.

Stelmack, R. M., & Wilson, K. G. (1982). Extraversion and the effects of frequency and intensity on the auditory brainstem evoked response. *Personality and Individual Differences, 3,* 373–380.

Stern, R. M., Ray, W. J., & Quigley, K. S. (2001). *Psychophysiological recording* (2nd ed.). Oxford: Oxford University Press.

Stockmeier, C. A. (2003). Involvement of serotonin in depression: Evidence from postmortem and imaging studies of serotonin receptors and the serotonin transporter. *Journal of Psychiatric Research, 37,* 357–373.

Sugiyama, L. S. (2005). Physical attractiveness in adaptationist perspective. In D. M. Buss (Ed.), *The handbook of evolutionary psychology* (pp. 292–343). Hoboken, NJ: John Wiley.

Taylor, J. R., & Carroll, J. L. (1987). Current issues in electroconvulsive therapy. *Psychological Reports, 60* (3, Part 1).

Tellegen, A., Lykken, D. T., Bouchard, T. J., Jr., Wilcox, K., Segal, N., & Rich, S. (1988). Personality similarity in twins reared apart and together. *Journal of Personality and Social Psychology, 54,* 1031–1039.

Tesser, A. (1993). The importance of heritability in psychological research: The case of attitudes. *Psychological Review, 100,* 129–142.

Tran, Y., Craig, A., & McIssac, P. (2001). Exrtraversion–introversion and 8–13 Hz waves in frontal cortical regions. *Personality and Individual Differences, 30,* 205–215.

Triandis, H. C. (1996). The psychological measurement of cultural syndromes. *American Psychologist, 51,* 407–415.

Turkheimer, E. (2000). Three laws of behavior genetics and what they mean. *Current Directions in Psychological Science, 9,* 160–164.

Wachs, T. D., & Kohnstamm, G. A. (Eds.). (2001). *Temperament in context.* Mahwah, NJ: Erlbaum.

Wang, W., Wu, Y.-X., Peng, Z.-G., Lu, S.-W., Yu, L., Wang, G.-P., et al. (2000). Test of sensation seeking in a Chinese sample. *Personality and Individual Differences, 28,* 169–179.

Weiten, W. (2007). *Psychology: Themes and variations* (7th ed.). Belmont, CA: Thomson/Wadsworth.

Wigglesworth, M. J., & Smith, B. D. (1976). Habituation and dishabituation of the electrodermal orienting reflex in relation to extraversion and neuroticism. *Journal of Research in Personality, 10,* 437–445.

Wong, A., & Carducci, B. J. (1991). Sensation seeking and financial risk taking in everyday matters. *Journal of Business and Psychology, 5,* 525–530.

Zinbarg, R. E., & Mohlman, J. (1998). Individual differences in the acquisition of affectivity valenced associations. *Journal of Personality and Social Psychology, 74,* 1024–1040.

Zuckerman, M. (1971). Dimensions of sensation seeking. *Journal of Consulting and Clinical Psychology, 36,* 45–52.

Zuckerman, M. (1979). *Sensation seeking: Beyond the optimal level of arousal.* Hillsdale, NJ: Erlbaum.

Zuckerman, M. (Ed.). (1983). *Biological bases of sensation seeking, impulsivity, and anxiety.* Hillsdale, NJ: Erlbaum.

Zuckerman, M. (1989). Personality in the third dimension: A psychobiological approach. *Personality and Individual Differences, 10,* 391–418.

Zuckerman, M. (1990). The psychophysiology of sensation seeking. *Journal of Personality, 58,* 313–345.

Zuckerman, M. (1991). *Psychobiology of personality.* New York: Cambridge University Press.

Zuckerman, M. (1994). *Behavioral expression and biosocial bases of sensation seeking.* New York: Cambridge University Press.

Zuckerman, M. (2005). *Psychobiology of personality* (2nd ed., rev. and updated). New York: Cambridge University Press.

Zuckerman, M (2006). *Biosocial bases of sensation seeking.* In T. Canli (Ed.), *Biology of personality and individual differences* (pp. 37–59). New York: Guilford Press.

Zuckerman, M., Ballinger, J. C., & Post, R. M. (1984). The neurobiology of some dimensions of personality. *International Review of Neurobiology, 25,* 391–436.

Zuckerman, M., Buchsbaum, M. S., & Murphy, D. L. (1980). Sensation seeking and its biological correlates. *Psychological Bulletin, 88,* 187–214.

Zuckerman, M., Eysenck, S. B. G., & Eysenck, J. J. (1978). Sensation seeking in England and America: Cross-cultural, age, and sex comparisons. *Journal of Consulting and Clinical Psychology, 46,* 139–149.

Zuckerman, M., Simons, R. F., & Como, P. G. (1988). Sensation seeking and stimulus intensity as modulators of cortical, cardiovascular, and electrodermal response: A cross-modality study. *Personality and Individual Differences, 9,* 361–372.

Chapter 9

Aldwin, C. M., Spiro, A., III, Levenson, M. R., & Cupertino, A. P. (2001). Longitudinal findings from the normative aging study: III. Personality, individual health trajectories, and mortality. *Psychology and Aging, 16,* 450–465.

APA (American Psychiatric Association). (2000). *Diagnostic and statistical manual of mental disorders (DSM-IV-TR)* (4th ed., rev.). Washington, DC: Author.

Austin, E. J., & Deary, I. J. (2000). The "four As": A common framework for normal and abnormal personality? *Personality and Individual Differences, 28,* 977–995.

Bagozzi, R. P., & Nataraajan, R. (2000). The year 2000: Looking forward. *Psychology and Marketing, 17,* 1–11.

Baron-Cohen, S., & Wheelwright, S. (2004). The empathy quotient: An investigation of adults with Asperger syndrome or high functioning autism, and normal sex differences. *Journal of Autism and Developmental Disorders, 34,* 163–175.

Beaulieu, D. A., & Bugental, D. B. (2006). Evolutionary theories. In J. C. Thomas & D. L. Segal (Eds.), *Comprehensive handbook of personality and psychopathology: Vol. 1. Personality and everyday functioning* (pp. 158–172). Hoboken, NJ: John Wiley.

Belk, R. W., & Coon, G. S. (1993). Gift giving as agapic love: An alternative to the exchange paradigm based on dating experiences. *Journal of Consumer Research, 20,* 393–417.

Benet-Martínez, V., & John, O. P. (1998). Los Cinco Grandes across cultures and ethnic groups: Multitrait-multimethod analysis of the Big Five in Spanish and English. *Journal of Personality and Social Psychology, 75,* 729–750.

Betz, M., O'Connell, L., & Shepard, J. M. (1989). Gender differences in proclivity for unethical behavior. *Journal of Business Ethics, 8,* 321–324.

Bjorklund, D. F., & Blasi, C. H. (2005). Evolutionary developmental psychology. In D. M. Buss (Ed.), *The handbook of evolutionary psychology* (pp. 828–850). Hoboken, NJ: John Wiley.

Boudreau, J. W., Boswell, W. R., & Judge, T. A. (2001). Effects of personality on executive career success in the United States and Europe. *Journal of Vocational Behavior, 58,* 53–58.

Brownell, K. D., & Horgen, K. B. (2003). *Food fight: The inside story of the food industry: America's obesity crisis, and what can be done about it.* Chicago: Contemporary Books.

Buchanan, T., Johnson, J. A., & Goldberg, L. R. (2005). Implementing a five-factor personality inventory for use on the Internet. *European Journal of Psychological Assessment, 21,* 115–127.

Burton, S., Netemeyer, R. G., & Lichtenstein, D. R. (1994). Gender differences for appearance-related attitudes and behaviors: Implications for consumer welfare. *Journal of Public Policy and Marketing, 13,* 60–75.

Buss, D. M. (1985). Human mate selection. *American Psychologist, 73,* 47–51.

Buss, D. M. (1989). Sex differences in human mate preferences: Evolutionary hypotheses tested in 37 cultures. *Behavioral and Brain Sciences, 12,* 1–49.

Buss, D. M. (1992). Mate preference mechanism: Consequences for partner choice and intrasexual competition. In J. Barkow, L. Cosmides, & J. Tooby (Eds.), *The adapted mind: Evolutionary psychology and the generation of culture* (pp. 556–79). New York: Oxford University Press.

Buss, D. M. (1997). Evolutionary foundations of personality. In R. Hogan (Ed.), *Handbook of personality psychology* (pp. 317–344). London: Academic Press.

Buss, D. M. (2000). *The dangerous passion: Why jealousy is as necessary as love and sex.* New York: Free Press.

Buss, D. M. (2003). *The evolution of desire: Strategies for human mating* (rev. ed.). New York: Basic Books.

Buss, D. M. (Ed.). (2005a). *The handbook of evolutionary psychology.* Hoboken, NJ: John Wiley.

Buss, D. M. (2005b). Mating. In D. M. Buss (Ed.), *The handbook of evolutionary psychology* (pp. 251–254). Hoboken, NJ: John Wiley.

Buss, D. M. (2008). *Evolutionary psychology: The new science of the mind* (3rd ed.). Boston: Pearson Education/Allyn & Bacon.

Buss, D. M., & Barnes, M. (1986). Preferences in human mate selection. *Journal of Personality and Social Psychology, 50,* 559–570.

Buss, D. M., Larsen, R. J., Westen, D., & Semmelroth, J. (1992). Sex differences in jealousy: Evolution, physiology, and psychology. *Psychological Science, 3,* 251–255.

Buss, D. M., & Shackelford, T. K. (1997). From vigilance to violence: Mate retention tactics in married couples. *Journal of Personality and Social Psychology, 72,* 346–361.

Buunk, B., Angleitner, A., Oubaid, V., & Buss, D. M. (1996). Sexual and cultural differences in jealousy: Tests from the Netherlands, Germany, and the United States. *Psychological Science, 7,* 359–363.

Buunk, B. P., Dukstra, P., Fetchenhauer, D., & Kenrick, D. T. (2002). Age and gender differences in mate selection criteria for various involvement levels. *Personal Relationships, 9,* 271–278.

Campbell, L., & Ellis, B. J. (2005). Commitment, love, and retention. In D. M. Buss (Ed.), *The handbook of evolutionary psychology* (pp. 419–442). Hoboken, NJ: John Wiley.

Caprara, G. V., Barbaranelli, C., & Zimbardo, P. (1996). Understanding the complexity of human aggression: Affective, cognitive and social dimensions of individual differences. *European Journal of Personality, 10,* 133–155.

Carroll, J. (2005). Literature and evolutionary psychology. In D. M. Buss (Ed.), *The handbook of evolutionary psychology* (pp. 931–952). Hoboken, NJ: John Wiley.

Charlton, L. (2005). *Schizotypy, personality, and paranormal belief.* Unpublished manuscript, University of Newcastle, UK.

Chen, C., Burton, M., Greenberger, E., & Dmitrieva, J. (1999). Population migration and the variation of dopamine D4 receptor (DRD4) allele frequencies around the globe. *Evolution and Human Behavior, 20,* 309–324.

Claridge, G., & Davis, C. (2001). What's the use of neuroticism? *Personality and Individual Differences, 31,* 383–400.

Claridge, G., & Davis, C. (2003). *Personality and psychological disorders.* London: Arnold.

Colarelli, S. M. (2003). *No best way: An evolutionary perspective on human resource management.* Westport, CT: Praeger.

Darwin, C. (1958). *The origin of species* (6th ed.). New York: New American Library. (Original work published 1859)

Denollet, J., Sys, S. U., Stroobant, N., Rombouts, H., Gillebert, T. C., & Brutsaert, D. L. (1996). Personality as independent predictor of long-term mortality in patients with coronary health disease. *Lancet, 347,* 417–421.

Dijkstra, P., & Buunk, B. P. (2001). Sex-differences in the jealousy-evoking nature of a rival's body build. *Evolution and Human Behavior, 22,* 335–341.

Eaton, S. B., Shostak, M., & Konner, M. (1988). *The Paleolithic prescription.* New York: Harper & Row.

Ebert, S. A., Tucker, D. C., & Roth, D. L. (2002). Psychological resistance factors as predictors of general health status and physical symptom reporting. *Psychology, Health, and Medicine, 7,* 363–375.

Ellis, L. (1987). Relationships of criminality and psychopathy with eight apparent manifestations of sub-optimal arousal. *Personality and Individual Differences, 8,* 905–925.

Fasino, S., Garzaro, L., Peris, C., Amianto, F., Piero, A., & Daga, G. A. (2002). Temperament and character in couples with fertility disorders: A double-blind, controlled study. *Fertility and Sterility, 77,* 1233–1240.

Figueredo, A. J., Sefcek, J., & Jones, D. N. (2004). *Ideal romantic partner: Absolute or relative preferences in personality?* Manuscript in preparation.

Figueredo, A. J., Sefcek, J. A., Vasquez, G., Brumbach, B. H., King, J. E., & Jacobs, W. J. (2005). Evolutionary personality psychology. In D. M. Buss (Ed.), *The handbook of evolutionary psychology* (pp. 851–877). Hoboken, NJ: John Wiley.

Franken, R. E., Gibson, K. J., & Mohan, P. (1990). Sensation seeking and disclosure to close and casual friends. *Personality and Individual Differences, 11,* 829–832.

Friedman, H. S. (2000). Long-term relations of personality and health: Dynamisms, mechanisms, tropisms. *Journal of Personality, 68,* 1089–1107.

Friedman, H. S., Hawley, P. H., & Tucker, J. S. (1994). Personality, health, and longevity. *Current Directions in Psychological Science, 3,* 37–41.

Friedman, H. S., Tucker, J. S., Schwartz, J. E., Martin, L. R., Tomlinson-Keasey, C., Wingard, D. L., et al. (1995). Childhood conscientiousness and longevity: Health behaviors and cause of death. *Journal of Personality and Social Psychology, 68,* 696–703.

Friedman, H. S., Tucker, J. S., Tomlinson-Keasey, C., Schwartz, J. E., Wingard, D. L., & Criqui, M. H. (1993). Does childhood personality predict longevity? *Journal of Personality and Social Psychology, 65,* 176–185.

Gangestad, S. W., & Thornhill, R. (1997). Human sexual selection and developmental stability. In J. A. Simpson & D. T. Kenrick (Eds.), *Evolutionary social psychology* (pp. 169–195). Hillsdale, NJ: Erlbaum.

Gangestad, S. W., & Thornhill, R. (2003). Fluctuating asymmetry, developmental instability, and fitness: Toward model-based interpretation. In M. Polak (Ed.), *Developmental instability: Causes and consequences* (pp. 62–80). New York: Oxford University Press.

Grammer, K., Fink, B., Thornhill, R. R., Juette, A., & Runzal, G. (2002). Female faces and bodies: N-dimensional feature space and attractiveness. In G. Rhodes & L. A. Zebrowitz (Eds.), *Facial attractiveness: Evolutionary, cognitive, and social perspectives* (pp. 91–126). Westport, CT: Greenwood.

Green, B. L., & Kenrick, D. T. (1994). The attractiveness of gender-typed traits at difference relationship levels: Androgyn-ous characteristics may be desirable after all. *Personality and Social Psychology Bulletin, 20,* 244–253.

Greiling, H., & Buss, D. M. (2000). Woman's sexual strategies: The hidden dimension of extra-pair mating. *Personality and Individual Differences, 28,* 929–963.

Gurven, M., Allen-Arave, W., Hill, K., & Hurtado, A. M. (2000). Signaling generosity among the Ache of Paraguay. *Evolution and Human Behavior, 21,* 263–282.

Hanko, K., Master, S., & Sabini, J. (2004). Some evidence about character and mate selection. *Personality and Social Psychology Bulletin, 30,* 732–742.

Haselton, M. G., & Buss, D. M. (2000). Error management theory: A new perspective on biases in cross-sex mind reading. *Journal of Personality and Social Psychology, 78,* 81–91.

Haselton, M. G., & Miller, G. F. (2006). Women's fertility across the life cycle increases the short-term attractiveness of creative intelligence. *Human Nature, 17,* 50–73.

Haselton, M. G., Nettle, D., & Andrews, P. W. (2005). The evolution of cognitive bias. In D. M. Buss (Ed.), *The evolutionary psychology handbook* (pp. 724–746). Hoboken, NJ: John Wiley.

Heaven, P. L. (1996). Personality and self-reported delinquency: Analysis of the "Big Five" personality dimensions. *Personality and Individual Differences, 20,* 47–54.

Heaven, P. L., Fitzpatrick, J., Craig, F. L., Kelly, P., & Sebar, G. (2000). Five personality factors and sex: Preliminary findings. *Personality and Individual Differences, 28,* 1133–1141.

Hellhammer, D. H., Hubert, W., Phil, C., Freischem, C. W., & Nieschlag, E. (1985). Male infertility: Relationships among gonadotropins, sex steroids, seminal parameters, and personality attitudes. *Psychosomatic Medicine, 47,* 58–66.

Hinsz, V. B., Matz, D. C., & Patience, R. A. (2001). Does women's hair signal reproductive potential? *Journal of Experimental Social Psychology, 37,* 166–172.

Hughes, S. M., & Gallup, G. G. (2002). Sex differences in morphological predictors of sexual behavior. *Evolution and Human Behavior, 24,* 173–178.

Jensen-Campbell, L. A., Graziano, W. G., & West, S. G. (1995). Dominance, prosocial orientation, and female preference: Do nice guys finish last? *Journal of Personality and Social Psychology, 68,* 427–440.

Jianakoplos, N. A., & Bernasek, A. (1998). Are women more risk averse? *Economic Enquiry, 36,* 620–630.

Jonason, P. K. (2007). An evolutionary perspective on sex differences in exercise behaviors and motivations. *Journal of Social Psychology, 147,* 5–14.

Jones, O. D. (2005). Evolutionary psychology and the law. In D. M. Buss (Ed.), *The handbook of evolutionary psychology* (pp. 953–974). Hoboken, NJ: John Wiley.

Kaplan, H., Hill, K., Lancaster, J. J., & Hurtado, A. M. (2000). A theory of human life history evolution: Diet, intelligence, and longevity. *Evolutionary Anthropology, 9,* 156–185.

Kelly, E., & Conley, J. (1987). Personality and compatibility: A prospective analysis of marital stability and marital satisfaction. *Journal of Personality and Social Psychology, 52,* 27–40.

Kenrick, D. T., Maner, J. K., & Li, N. P. (2005). Evolutionary social psychology. In D. M. Buss (Ed.), *The handbook of evolutionary psychology* (pp. 803–827). Hoboken, NJ: John Wiley.

Kenrick, D. T., Sadalla, E. K., Groth, G., & Trost, M. R. (1990). Evolution, traits, and the stages of human courtship: Qualifying the parental investment model. *Journal of Personality, 58*, 97–116.

Kiecolt-Glaser, J. K., McGuire, L., Robles, T. F., & Glaser, R. (2002). Emotion, morbidity, and mortality: New perspectives from psychoneuroimmunology. *Annual Review of Psychology, 53*, 83–107.

Kircaldy, B. D. (1982). Personality profiles at various levels of athletic participation. *Personality and Individual Differences, 3*, 321–326.

Kopelman, P. G. (2000). Obesity as a medical problem. *Nature, 404*, 635–643.

Koretz, G. (2001, January 15). Extra pounds, slimmer wages. *Business Week*, p. 28.

Kring, A. M., Davison, G. C., Neale, J. M., & Johnson, S. L. (2007). *Abnormal psychology* (10th ed.). Hoboken, NJ: John Wiley.

Lynn, M., Kampschroeder, K., & Perriera, T. (1998). *Evolutionary perspectives on consumer behavior: An introduction.* Paper presented at Advances in Consumer Research, Twenty-Sixth Annual Conference of the Association for Consumer Research, Montreal, Canada.

MacDonald, K. B. (1998). Evolution, culture, and the Five-Factor Model. *Journal of Cross-Cultural Psychology, 29*, 119–149.

Manning, J. T. (1995). Fluctuating asymmetry and body weight in men and women: Implications for sexual selection. *Ethology and Sociobiology, 16*, 145–153.

Manning, J. T., Scutt, D., Whitehouse, G. H., & Leinster, S. J. (1997). Breast asymmetry and phenotypic quality in women. *Evolution and Human Behavior, 18*, 2223–2236.

McCrae, R. (1987). Creativity, divergent thinking, and openness to experience. *Journal of Personality and Social Psychology, 52*, 1258–1265.

Miller, L. C., Putcha-Bhagavatula, A., & Pedersen, W. C. (2002). Men's and women's mating preference: Distinct evolutionary mechanisms? *Current Directions in Psychological Sciences, 11*, 88–93.

Milne, B. J., Belsky, J., Poulton, R., Thomson, W. M., Caspi, A., & Kieser, J. (2003). Fluctuating asymmetry and physical health among young adults. *Evolution and Human Behavior, 24*, 53–63.

Neeleman, J., Sytema, S., & Wadsworth, M. (2002). Propensity to psychiatric and somatic ill-health: Evidence from a birth cohort. *Psychological Medicine, 32*, 793–803.

Nesse, R. M. (2005). Evolutionary psychology and mental health. In D. M. Buss (Ed.), *The handbook of evolutionary psychology* (pp. 903–927). Hoboken, NJ: John Wiley.

Nestle, M. (2002). *Food politics: How the food industry influences nutrition and health.* Berkeley: University of California Press.

Nettle, D. (2002). Women's height, reproductive success and the evolution of sexual dimorphism in modern humans. *Proceedings of the Royal Society of London. Series B: Biological Sciences, 269*, 1919–1923.

Nettle, D. (2005). An evolutionary approach to the extraversion continuum. *Evolution and Human Behavior, 26*, 363–373.

Nettle, D. (2006a). The evolution of personality variation in humans and other animals. *American Psychologist, 61*, 622–631.

Nettle, D. (2006b). Schizotypy and mental health amongst poets, visual artists, and mathematicians. *Journal of Research in Personality, 40*, 876–890.

Nettle, D., & Clegg, H. (2006). Schizotypy, creativity and mating success in humans. *Proceedings of the Royal Society of London. Series B: Biological Sciences, 273*, 611–615.

Nowakowska, C., Strong, C. M., Santosa, C. M., Wang, P. W., & Ketter, T. A. (2005). Temperamental commonalities and differences in euthymic mood disorder patients, creative controls, and healthy controls. *Journal of Affective Disorders, 85*, 207–215.

Pawlowski, B., & Koziel, S. (2002). The impact of traits offered in personal advertisements on response rates. *Evolution and Human Behavior, 23*, 139–149.

Powell, M., & Ansic, D. (1997). Gender differences in risk behavior in financial decision-making: An experimental analysis. *Journal of Economic Psychology, 18*, 605–628.

Rotundo, M., Nguyen, D. H., & Sackett, P. R. (2001). A meta-analytic review of gender differences in perceptions of harassment. *Journal of Applied Psychology, 86*, 914–922.

Ryan, R. M., & Frederick, C. (1997). On energy, personality, and health: Subjective vitality as a dynamic reflection of well-being. *Journal of Personality, 65*, 529–565.

Saad, G. (2005). *Applications of evolutionary psychology in consumer behavior.* Mahwah, NJ: Erlbaum.

Saad, G. (2007). *The evolutionary bases of consumption.* Mahwah, NJ: Erlbaum.

Saad, G., & Gill, T. (2000). Applications of evolutionary psychology in marketing. *Psychology and Marketing, 17*, 1005–10034.

Saad, G., & Gill, T. (2003). An evolutionary psychology perspective on gift giving among young adults. *Marketing and Psychology, 20*, 765–784.

Sadalla, E. K., Kenrick, D. T., & Vershure, B. (1987). Dominance and heterosexual attraction. *Journal of Personality and Social Psychology, 52*, 730–738.

Samuels, J., Bienvenu, O. J., Cullen, B., Costa, P. T., Eaton, W. W., & Nestadt, G. (2004). Personality dimensions and criminal arrest. *Comprehensive Psychiatry, 45*, 275–280.

Scheib, J. E., Kristiansen, A., & Wara, A. (1997). A Norwegian note on sperm donor selection and the psychology of female mate choice. *Evolution and Human Behavior, 18*, 143–149.

Schmidt, D. (2004). The Big Five related to risky sexual behaviour across 10 world regions: Differential personality associations of sexual promiscuity and relationship infidelity. *European Journal of Personality, 18*, 301–319.

Schmitt, D. P. (2002). A meta-analysis of sex differences in romantic attraction: Do rating contexts affect tactic effectiveness judgments? *British Journal of Social Psychology, 41*, 387–402.

Schmitt, D. P. (2005). Fundamentals of human mating strategies. In D. M. Buss (Ed.), *The handbook of evolutionary psychology* (pp. 258–291). Hohoken, NJ: John Wiley.

Schmitt, D. P., & Buss, D. M. (1996). Strategic self-promotion and competitor derogation: Sex and context effects on the perceived effectiveness of mate attraction tactics. *Journal of Personality and Social Psychology, 70*, 1185–1204.

Schmitt, D. P., & Buss, D. M. (2000). Sexual dimensions of person description: Beyond or subsumed by the Big Five? *Journal of Research in Personality, 34*, 141–177.

Schmitt, D. P., & Buss, D. M. (2001). Human mate poaching: Tactics and temptations for infiltrating existing mateships. *Journal of Personality and Social Psychology, 34*, 894–917.

Schmitt, D. P., & 121 Members of the International Sexuality Deception Project (2004). Patterns and universals of mate poaching across 53 nations: The effects of sex, culture, and personality on romantically attracting another person's partner. *Journal of Personality and Social Psychology, 86*, 560–584.

Schwartz, J. E., Friedman, H. S., Tucker, J. S., Tomlinson-Keasey, C., Wingard, D. L., & Criqui, M. H. (1995). Sociodemographics and psychosocial factors in childhood as predictors of adult mortality. *American Journal of Public Health, 85*, 1237–1245.

Shackelford, T. K., Buss, D. M., & Bennet, K. (2002). Forgiveness or breakup: Sex differences in response to a partner's infidelity. *Cognition and Emotion, 16*, 299–307.

Shackelford, T. K., LeBlanc. G. J., & Drass, E. (2000). Emotional reactions to infidelity. *Cognition and Emotion, 14*, 643–659.

Silventoinen, K., Lahelma, E., & Rahkonen, O. (1999). Social background, adult body-height and health. *International Journal of Epidemiology, 28*, 911–918.

Singh, D., & Young, R. K. (1995). Body weight, waist-to-hip ratio, breasts, and hips: Role in judgments of female attractiveness and desirability for relationships. *Ethology and Sociobiology, 16*, 483–507.

Studd, M. V., & Gattiker, U. E. (1991). The evolutionary psychology of sexual harassment in organizations. *Ethology and Sociobiology, 12*, 249–290.

Sugiyama, L. S. (2005). Physical attractiveness in adaptationist perspective. In D. M. Buss (Ed.), *The handbook of evolutionary psychology* (pp. 292–343). Hoboken, NJ: John Wiley.

Sugiyama, L. S., & Chacon, R. (2000). Effects of illness and injury on foraging among the Yora and Shiwiar: Pathology risk as adaptive problem. In L. Cronk, N. A. Chagnon, & W. Irons (Eds.), *Human behavior and adaptation: An anthropological perspective* (pp. 371–395). New York: Aldine.

Sugiyama, L. S., & Chacon, R. (2005). Juvenile responses to household ecology among the Yora of Peruvian Amazonia. In B. Hewlett & M. Lamb (Eds.), *Hunter-gatherer childhoods: Evolutionary, developmental, and cultural perspectives* (pp. 237–261). New York: Aldine.

Suls, J., Martin, R., & David, J. P. (1998). Person–environment fit and its limits: Agreeableness, neuroticism, and emotional reactivity to interpersonal conflicts. *Personality and Social Psychology Bulletin, 24*, 88–89.

Surby, M. K. (1987). Anorexia nervosa, amenorrhea, and adaptation. *Ethology and Sociobiology, 8*, 47–61.

Symons, D. (1979). *The evolution of human sexuality*. New York: Oxford University Press.

Terpstra, D. E., & Cook, S. E. (1985). Complainant characteristics and reported behaviors and consequences associated with formal sexual harassment charges. *Personnel Psychology, 38*, 559–574.

Thornhill, R., & Gangestad, S. W. (2003). Do women have evolved adaptation for extra-pair copulation? In E. Voland & K. Grammer (Eds.), *Evolutionary aesthetics* (pp. 341–368). Heidelberg, Germany: Springer.

Todd, P. M., Hertwig, R., & Hoffrage, U. (2005). Evolutionary cognitive psychology. In D. M. Buss (Ed.), *The handbook of evolutionary psychology* (pp. 776–802). Hoboken, NJ: John Wiley.

Tooby, J., & Cosmides, L. (2005). Conceptual foundations of evolutionary psychology. In D. M. Buss (Ed.), *The handbook of evolutionary psychology* (pp. 5–67). Hoboken, NJ: John Wiley.

Tucker, J. S., & Friedman, H. S. (1996). Emotion, personality, and health. In C. Magai & S. J. McFadden (Eds.), *Handbook of emotion, adult development, and aging* (pp. 307–326). San Diego, CA: Academic Press.

USDHHS (U.S. Department of Health and Human Services). (2001). *The Surgeon General's call to action to prevent and decrease overweight and obesity*. [Rockville, MD]: U.S. Department of Health and Human Services. Public Health Service, Office of the Surgeon General. Available from U.S. GPO, Washington.

Voland, E., & Voland, R. (1989). Evolutionary biology and psychiatry: The case of anorexia nervosa. *Ethology and Sociobiology, 10*, 223–240.

Wilson, E. O. (1975). *Sociobiology*. Cambridge, MA: Harvard University Press.

Wischmann, T., Stammer, H., Scherg, H., Gerhard, I., & Verres, R. (2001). Psychosocial characteristics of infertile couples: A study by the Heidelberg Fertility Consultation Service. *Human Reproduction, 16*, 1753–1761.

Wood, G. S. (2004, April 12). Pursuits of happiness. *The New Republic*, 38–42.

Zuckerman, M. (1994). *Behavioral expression and biosocial bases of sensation seeking*. New York: Cambridge University Press.

Chapter 10

Abramowitz, S. I. (1973). Internal-external control and social-political activism: A test of the dimensionality of Rotter's I-E Scale. *Journal of Consulting and Clinical Psychology, 40*, 196–201.

Albarracin, D., Fishbein, M., Johnson, B. T., & Mullerleile, P. A. (2001). Theories of reasoned action and planned behavior as models of condom use: A meta-analysis. *Psychological Bulletin, 127*, 142–161.

American Psychological Association. (1981). Awards for distinguished scientific contributions: 1980. Albert Bandura. *American Psychologist, 36*, 27–34.

American Psychological Association. (1983). Awards for distinguished scientific contributions: 1982. Walter Mischel. *American Psychologist, 38*, 9–14.

Amichai-Hamburger, A., Kaynar, O., & Fine, A. (2007). The effects of need for cognition on Internet use. *Computers in Human Behavior, 23*, 880–891.

Anderson, C. A. (1997). Effects of violent movies and trait hostility on hostile feelings and aggressive thoughts. *Aggressive Behaviors, 23*, 161–178.

Anderson, C. A. (2004). An update on the effects of playing violent video games. *Journal of Adolescence, 27,* 113–122.

Anderson, C. A., Berkowitz, L., Donnerstein, E., Huesmann, L. R., Johnson, J. D., Linz, D., et al. (2004). The influence of media violence on youth. *Psychology in the Public Interest, 4,* 81–110.

Anderson, C. A., & Bushman, B. J. (2001). Effects of violent video games on aggressive behavior, aggressive cognition, aggressive affect, physiological arousal, prosocial behavior: A meta-analytic review of the scientific literature. *Psychological Science, 12,* 353–359.

Anderson, C. A., & Bushman, B. J. (2002). Media violence and the American public revisited. *American Psychologist, 57,* 27–51.

Anderson, C. A., Carnagey, N. L., & Eubanks, J. (2003). Exposure to violent media: The effects of songs with violent lyrics on aggressive thoughts and feelings. *Journal of Personality and Social Psychology, 84,* 960–971.

Anderson, C. R. (1977). Locus of control, coping behaviors and performance in a stress setting: A longitudinal study. *Journal of Applied Psychology, 62,* 446–451.

Ayduk, O., Mendoza-Denton, R., Mischel, W., Downey, G., Peake, P. K., & Rodriguez, M. (2000). Regulation and the interpersonal self: Strategic self-regulation for coping with rejection sensitivity. *Journal of Personality and Social Psychology, 79,* 776–792.

Baehr, M. E., Jones, J. W., & Nerad, A. J. (1993). Psychological correlates of business ethics orientation in executives. *Journal of Business and Psychology, 7,* 291–308.

Bandura, A. (1961). Psychotherapy as a learning process. *Psychological Bulletin, 58,* 143–159.

Bandura, A. (1968). A social learning interpretation of psychological dysfunctions. In P. London & D. Rosenhan (Eds.), *Foundations of abnormal psychology* (pp. 293–344). New York: Holt, Rinehart & Winston.

Bandura, A. (1969). *Principles of behavior modification.* New York: Holt, Rinehart & Winston.

Bandura, A. (1977a). Self-efficacy: Toward a unifying theory of behavioral change. *Psychological Review, 84,* 191–215.

Bandura, A. (1977b). *Social learning theory.* Englewood Cliffs, NJ: Prentice Hall.

Bandura, A. (1978). The self system in reciprocal determinism. *American Psychologist, 33,* 344–358.

Bandura, A. (1982). Self-efficacy mechanism in human agency. *American Psychologist, 37,* 122–147.

Bandura, A. (1986). *Social foundations of thought and action: A social cognitive theory.* Englewood Cliffs, NJ: Prentice Hall.

Bandura, A. (1988). Perceived self-efficacy: Exercise of control through self-belief. In J. P. Dauwalder, M. Perrez, & V. Hobi (Eds.), *Annual series of European research in behavior therapy: Vol. 2* (pp. 27–59). Lisse, Netherlands: Swets & Zeitlinger.

Bandura, A. (1989a). Human agency in social cognitive theory. *American Psychologist, 44,* 1175–1184.

Bandura, A. (1989b). Regulation of cognitive processes through perceived self-efficacy. *Development Psychology, 25,* 729–735.

Bandura, A. (1990). Perceived self-efficacy in the exercise of control over AIDS infection. *Evaluation and Program Planning, 13,* 9–17.

Bandura, A. (1991a). Social cognitive theory of moral thought and action. In W. M. Kurtiness & J. L. Gewirtz (Eds.), *Handbook of moral behavior and development: Vol. 1. Theory* (pp. 45–103). Hillsdale, NJ: Erlbaum.

Bandura, A. (1991b). Social cognitive theory of self-regulation. *Organization Behavior and Human Decision Processes, 50,* 248–287.

Bandura, A. (Ed.). (1995). *Self-efficacy in changing societies.* New York: Cambridge University Press.

Bandura, A. (1997). *Self-efficacy: The exercise of control.* New York: Freeman.

Bandura, A. (1999a). Social cognitive theory of personality. In D. Cervone & Y. Shoda (Eds.), *The coherence of personality: Social-cognitive bases of consistency, variability, and organization* (pp. 185–241). New York: Guilford Press.

Bandura, A. (1999b). Social cognitive theory of personality. In L. A. Pervin & O. P. John (Eds.), *Handbook of personality: Theory and research* (2nd ed., pp. 154–196). New York: Guilford Press.

Bandura, A. (2001). Social cognitive theory: An agentic perspective. *Annual Review of Psychology, 52,* 1–26.

Bandura, A. (2002). Environmental sustainability by socio-cognitive deceleration of population growth. In P. Schmuch & W. Schultz (Eds.), *The psychology of sustainable development* (pp. 209–238). Dordrecht, Netherlands: Kluwer.

Bandura, A. (2004). Swimming against the mainstream: The early years from chilly tributary to transformative mainstream. *Behaviour Research and Therapy, 42,* 613–630.

Bandura, A. (2006). Toward a psychology of human agency. *Perspectives on Psychological Science, 1,* 164–180.

Bandura, A., Blanchard, E. B., & Ritter, B. (1969). Relative efficacy of desensitization and modeling approaches for inducing behavioral, affective, and attitudinal changes. *Journal of Personality and Social Psychology, 13,* 173–199.

Bandura, A., Grusec, J. E., & Menlove, F. L. (1967). Some social determinants of self-monitoring reinforcement systems. *Journal of Personality and Social Psychology, 5,* 449–455.

Bandura, A., Pastorelli, C., Barbaranelli, C., & Caprara, G. V. (1999). Self-efficacy pathways to childhood depression. *Journal of Personality and Social Psychology, 76,* 258–269.

Bandura, A., & Walters, R. (1963). *Social learning and personality development.* New York: Holt, Rinehart & Winston.

Barker, L. M. (2001). *Learning and behavior: Biological, psychological, and sociological perspectives* (3rd ed.). Upper Saddle River, NJ: Prentice Hall.

Baron, R. A., & Richardson, D. R. (1994). *Human aggression* (2nd ed.). New York: Plenum.

Barnet, H. S. (1990). Divorce stress and adjustment model: Locus of control and demographic predictors. *Journal of Divorce, 13,* 93–109.

Bar-Tal, D., & Bar-Zohar, Y. (1977). The relationship between perception of locus of control and academic achievement. *Contemporary Educational Psychology, 2,* 181–199.

Bar-Tal, Y., Kishon-Rabin, L., & Tabak, N. (1997). The effect of need and ability to achieve cognitive structuring on cognitive structuring. *Journal of Personality and Social Psychology, 73,* 1158–1176.

Baumeister, R. F., Heatherton, T. F., & Tice, D. M. (1994). *Losing control: How and why people fail at self-regulation.* San Diego, CA: Academic Press.

Baumeister, R. F., Schmeichel, B. J., & Vohs, K. D. (2007). Self-regulation and the executive function. In A. W. Kruglanski & E. T. Higgins (Eds.), *Social psychology: Handbook of basic principles* (2nd ed., pp. 516–539). New York: Guilford Press.

Beck, A. T. (1976). *Cognitive therapy and the emotional disorders.* New York: International Universities Press.

Beck, A. T., & Weishaar, M. E. (2008). Cognitive therapy. In R. J. Corsini & D. Wedding (Eds.), *Current psychotherapies* (8th ed, pp. 263–294). Belmont, CA: Thomson Higher Education.

Berkowitz, L. (1993). *Aggression: Its causes, consequences, and control.* New York: McGraw-Hill.

Botha, M. (1990). Television exposure and aggression among adolescents: A follow-up study over 5 years. *Aggressive Behavior, 16,* 361–380.

Brannon, L., & Feist, J. (2000). *Health psychology: An introduction to behavior and health.* Belmont, CA: Wadsworth/ Thomson Learning.

Brennan, I., & Bahn, K. D. (2006). Literal versus extended symbolic messages and advertising effectiveness: The moderating role of need for cognition. *Psychology and Marketing, 23,* 273–295.

Brutus, S., & Ryan, A. M. (1998). A new perspective on preferential treatments: The role of ambiguity and self-efficacy. *Journal of Business and Psychology, 13,* 157–178.

Bryant, J. (1985, September). *Testimony on the effects of pornography: Research findings.* Paper presented at the U.S. Justice Department Hearings, Houston.

Bushman, B. J., & Anderson, C. A. (2002). Violent video games and hostile expectations: A test of the general aggression model. *Personality and Social Psychology Bulletin, 28,* 1679–1686.

Bushman, B. J., & Huesmann, L. R. (2001). Effects of televised violence on aggression. In D. Singer & J. Singer (Eds.), *Handbook of children and the media* (pp. 223–254). Thousand Oaks, CA: Sage.

Butler, B., & Moran, G. (2007). The impact of death qualification, belief in a just world, legal authoritarianism, and locus of control on venirepersons' evaluation of aggravating and mitigating circumstances in capital trials. *Behavior Sciences and the Law, 25,* 57–68.

Cacioppo, J. T., & Petty, R. E. (1982). The need for cognition. *Journal of Personality and Social Psychology, 42,* 116–131.

Cacioppo, J. T., Petty, R. E., Feinstein, J., & Jarvis, W. B. G. (1996). Dispositional differences in cognitive motivation: The life and times of individuals varying in need for cognition. *Psychological Bulletin, 119,* 197–253.

Cacioppo, J. T., Petty, R. E., & Morris, K. J. (1983). Effects of need for cognition on message evaluation, recall, and persuasion. *Journal of Personality and Social Psychology, 45,* 805–818.

Cadinu, M., Maass, A., Lombardo, M., & Frigerio, S. (2006). Stereotype threat: The moderating role of locus of control beliefs. *European Journal of Social Psychology, 36,* 183–197.

Cantor, N. (1990). From thought to behavior: "Having" and "doing" in the study of personality and cognition. *American Psychologist, 45,* 735–750.

Cantor, N. (1994). Life task problem solving: Situational affordances and personal needs. *Personality and Social Psychology Bulletin, 20,* 235–243.

Cantor, N., Acker, M., & Cook-Flannagan, C. (1992). Conflict and preoccupation in the intimacy life task. *Journal of Personality and Social Psychology, 63,* 644–655.

Cantor, N., & Harlow, R. E. (1994). Social intelligence and personality: Flexible life task pursuit. In R. J. Sternberg & P. Ruzgis (Eds.), *Personality and intelligence* (pp. 137–168). New York: Cambridge University Press.

Cantor, N., & Kihlstrom, J. F. (1985). Social intelligence: The cognitive basis of personality. In P. Shaver (Ed.), *Review of personality and social behavior: Vol. 6* (pp. 15–33). Beverly Hills, CA: Sage.

Cantor, N., & Kihlstrom, J. F. (1987). *Personality and social intelligence.* Englewood Cliffs, NJ: Prentice Hall.

Cantor, N., & Malley, J. (1991). Cognition in close relationships. In G. J. O. Fletcher & F. D. Fincham (Eds.), *Cognition in close relationships* (pp. 101–125). Hillsdale, NJ: Erlbaum.

Cantor, N., Norem, J., Langston, C., Zirkel, S., Fleeson, W., & Cook-Flannagan, C. (1991). Life tasks and daily life experience. *Journal of Personality, 59,* 425–451.

Cantor, N., Norem, J. K., Niedenthal, P. M., Langston, C. A., & Brower, A. M. (1987). Life tasks, self-concept ideals, and cognitive strategies in a life transition. *Journal of Personality and Social Psychology, 53,* 1178–1191.

Cantor, N., & Sanderson, C. A. (1998). Social dating goals and the regulation of adolescent dating relationships and sexual behavior: The interaction of goals, strategies, and situations. In J. Heckhausen & C. Dweck (Eds.), *Motivation and self-regulation across the life span* (pp. 185–215). New York: Columbia University Press.

Cantor, N., & Zirkel, S. (1990). Personality, cognition, and purposive behavior. In L. A. Pervin (Ed.), *A handbook of personality: Theory and research* (pp. 135–164). New York: Guilford Press.

Cantor, N., Zirkel, S., & Norem, J. K. (1993). Human personality: Asocial and reflexive? *Psychological Inquiry, 4,* 273–277.

Carnaghi, A., Cadinu, M., Castelli, L., Kiesner, J., & Bragantini, C. (2007). The best way to tell you to use a condom: The interplay between message and individuals' level of need for cognition. *AIDS Care, 19,* 432–440.

Cervone, D., & Shoda, Y. (1999). Social-cognitive theories and the coherence of personality. In D. Cervone & Y. Shoda (Eds.), *The coherence of personality: Social-cognitive bases of consistency, variability, and organization* (pp. 3–33). New York: Guilford Press.

Chaiken, S. (1987). The heuristic model of persuasion. In M. P. Zanna, J. M. Olson, & C. P. Herman (Eds.), *Social influence: The Ontario Symposium: Vol. 5* (pp. 3–40). Hillsdale, NJ: Erlbaum.

Chak, K., & Leung, L. (2004). Shyness and locus of control as predictors of Internet addiction and Internet use. *Cyber-Psychology and Behavior, 7,* 559–570.

Clements, J. (1999, March 9). Teaching your children to save well. *The Wall Street Journal*, p. C1.

Clements, L. B., York, R. O., & Rohrer, G. E. (1995). The interaction of parental alcoholism and alcoholism as a predictor of drinking-related locus of control. *Alcoholism Treatment Quarterly*, *12*, 97–110.

Cohen, R. J., & Swerdlik, M. E. (2005). *Psychological testing and assessment: An introduction to tests and measurements* (6th ed.). Boston: McGraw-Hill.

Comer, R. J. (2007). *Abnormal psychology* (6th ed.). New York: Worth.

Crawford, M. T., & Skowronski, J. J. (1998). When motivated thought leads to heightened bias: High need for cognition can enhance the impact of stereotypes on memory. *Personality and Social Psychology Bulletin*, *24*, 1075–1088.

Culhane, S. E., Morera, O. F., & Watson, P. J. (2006). The assessment of factorial invariance in need for cognition using Hispanic and Anglo samples. *Journal of Psychology*, *140*, 53–67.

DeGolyer, M. E. (1995, September). *What is politics in Hong Kong?* Unpublished report for the Hong Kong Transition Project, Baptist University, Hong Kong.

DeRubeis, R. J., Tang, T. Z., & Beck, A. T. (2001). Cognitive therapy. In K. S. Dobson (Ed.), *Handbook of cognitive-behavioral therapies* (2nd ed., pp. 349–392). New York: Guilford Press.

Dobson, K. S., & Dozois, D. J. (2001). Historical and philosophical bases of the cognitive-behavioral therapies. In K. S. Dobson (Ed.), *Handbook of cognitive-behavioral therapies* (2nd ed., pp. 3–39). New York: Guilford Press.

Doherty, W. J. (1980). Divorce and belief in internal versus external control of one's life: Data from a national probability sample. *Journal of Divorce*, *3*, 391–401.

Doherty, W. J. (1981). Locus of control difference and marital dissatisfaction. *Journal of Marriage and the Family*, *43*, 369–377.

Doherty, W. J. (1983a). Impact of divorce on locus of control orientation in adult women: A longitudinal study. *Journal of Personality and Social Psychology*, *44*, 834–840.

Doherty, W. J. (1983b). Locus of control and marital interaction. In H. M. Lefcourt (Ed.), *Research with the locus of control construct: Developments and social problems: Vol. 2* (pp. 155–183). New York: Academic Press.

Doherty, W. J., & Ryder, R. G. (1979). Locus of control, interpersonal trust, and assertive behavior among newlyweds. *Journal of Personality and Social Psychology*, *37*, 2212–2220.

Donnerstein, E. (1980). Aggressive erotica and violence against women. *Journal of Personality and Social Psychology*, *39*, 269–277.

Dryden, W., & Ellis, A. (2001). Rational emotive behavior therapy. In K. S. Dobson, (Ed.), *Handbook of cognitive-behavioral therapies* (2nd ed., pp. 295–348). New York: Guilford Press.

Dweck, C. S., Higgins, E. T., & Grant-Pillow, H. (2003). Self-systems give unique meaning to self variables. In M. R. leary & J. P. Tangney (Eds.), *Handbook of self and identity* (pp. 239–252). New York: Guilford Press.

Dweck, C. S., & Molden, D. C. (2005). Self-theories: Their impact on competence motivation and acquisition. In A. J. Elliot & C. S. Dweck (Eds.), *Handbook of competence and motivation* (pp. 122–140). New York: Guilford Press.

Ellis, A. (1962). *Reason and emotion in psychotherapy*. New York: Lyle Stuart.

Ellis, A. (1980). Rational emotive therapy and cognitive behavior therapy: Similarities and differences. *Cognitive Therapy and Research*, *4*, 325–340.

Ellis, A. (1987). The impossibility of achieving consistently good mental health. *American Psychologist*, *42*, 364–375.

Ellis, A. (2008). Rational emotive behavior therapy. In R. J. Corsini & D. Wedding (Eds.), *Current psychotherapies* (8th ed., pp. 187–222). Belmont, CA: Thomson Higher Education.

Eron, L. D. (1987). The development of aggressive behavior from the perspective of a developing behaviorism. *American Psychologist*, *42*, 435–442.

Evans, R. I. (1989). *Albert Bandura, the man and his ideas – a dialogue*. New York: Praeger.

Evans, W. P., Owens, P., & Marsh, S. C. (2005). Environmental factors, locus of control, and adolescent suicide risk. *Child and Adolescent Social Work Journal*, *22*, 301–319.

Ferguson, M., Chung, M., & Weigold, M. (1985). *Need for cognition and the medium dependency components of reliance and exposure*. Paper presented at the meeting of the International Communication Association, Honolulu, HI.

Findley, M. J., & Cooper, H. M. (1983). Locus of control and academic achievement: A literature review. *Journal of Personality and Social Psychology*, *44*, 419–427.

Fiske, S. T., & Taylor, S. E. (1991). *Social cognition* (2nd ed.). New York: McGraw-Hill.

Fiske, S. T., & Taylor, S. E. (2008). *Social cognition: From brains to culture* (4th ed.). New York: McGraw-Hill.

Flouri, E. (2006). Parental interest in children's education, children's self-esteem and locus of control, and later educational attainment: Twenty-six year follow-up of the 1970 British birth cohort. *Bristish Journal of Educational Psychology*, *76*, 41–55.

Gauthier, K. J., Christopher, A. N., Walter, M. I., Mourad, R., & Merek, P. (2006). Religiosity, religious doubt, and the need for cognition: Their interactive relationship with life satisfaction. *Journal of Happiness Studies*, *7*, 139–154.

Geen, R. G. (1995). Human aggression. In A. Tesser (Ed.), *Advanced social psychology* (pp. 383–417). New York: McGraw-Hill.

Geen, R. G. (1998). Aggression and antisocial behavior. In D. T. Gilbert, S. T. Fiske, & G. Lindzey, *The handbook of social psychology: Vol. 2* (4th ed., pp. 317–356). Boston: McGraw-Hill.

Giles, W. F. (1977). Volunteering for job enrichment: A test of expectancy theory predictions. *Personnel Psychology*, *30*, 427–435.

Gilmor, T. M., & Reid, D. W. (1978). Locus of control, prediction, and performance on university examinations. *Journal of Consulting and Clinical Psychology*, *46*, 565–566.

Gilmor, T. M., & Reid, D. W. (1979). Locus of control and causal attribution for positive and negative outcomes on university examinations. *Journal of Research in Personality*, *13*, 154–160.

Goggin, K., Murray, T. S., Malcarne, V. L., Brown, S. A., & Wallston, K. A. (2007). Do religious and control cognitions predict risky behavior? I. Development and validation of the

Alcohol-related God Locus of Control Scale for adolescents. *Cognitive Therapy and Research*, *31*, 111–122.

Gollwitzer, P. M., & Moskowitz, G. B. (1996). Goal effects on action and cognition. In E. T. Higgins & A. W. Kruglanski (Eds.), *Social psychology: Handbook of basic principles* (pp. 361–399). New York: Guilford Press.

Goodwin, R., & Tang, C. (1998). The transition to uncertainty? The impacts of Hong Kong 1997 on personal relationships. *Personal Relationships*, *5*, 183–190.

Gore, P. M., & Rotter, J. B. (1963). A personality of social action. *Journal of Personality*, *31*, 58–64.

Grant, H., & Dweck, C. S. (1999). A goal analysis of personality and personality coherence. In D. Cervone & Y. Shoda (Eds.), *The coherence of personality: Social-cognitive bases of consistency, variability, and organization* (pp. 345–371). New York: Guilford Press.

Grant, P., Young, P. R., & DeRubeis, R. J. (2005). Cognitive and behavioral therapies. In G. O. Gabbard, J. S. Beck, & J. Holems (Eds.), *Oxford textbook of psychotherapy* (pp. 15–25). New York: Oxford University Press.

Gurtman, M. B., & Lion, C. (1982). Interpersonal trust and perceptual vigilance for trustworthiness descriptors. *Journal of Research in Personality*, *16*, 108–117.

Gwaltney, C. J., Shiffman, S., Balabanis, M. H., & Paty, J. A. (2005). Dynamic self-efficacy and outcome expectancies: Prediction of smoking lapse and relapse. *Journal of Abnormal Psychology*, *114*, 661–675.

Hamsher, J. H., Geller, J. D., & Rotter, J. B. (1968). Interpersonal trust, internal-external control, and the Warren Commission Report. *Journal of Personality and Social Psychology*, *9*, 210–215.

Harlow, R. E., & Cantor, N. (1996). Still participating after all these years: A study of life task participation in later life. *Journal of Personality and Social Psychology*, *71*, 1235–1249.

Hollon, S. D., & Beck, A. T. (2004). Cognitive and cognitive-behavioral therapies. In M. J. Lambert (Ed.), *Bergin and Garfield's handbook of therapy and behavior change* (5th ed., pp. 447–492). New York: John Wiley.

Hong Kong Annual Digest of Statistics. (1993). Hong Kong: Government Information Services.

Hong, T. B., Oddone, E. Z., Dudley, T. K., & Bosworth, H. B. (2006). Medication barriers and anti-hypertensive medication adherence: The moderating role of locus of control. *Psychology, Health, and Medicine*, *11*, 20–28.

Huesmann, L. R., & Eron, L. D. (1984). Cognitive processes and the persistence of aggressive behavior. *Aggressive Behavior*, *10*, 243–251.

Huesmann, L. R., & Eron, L. D. (1986). *Television and the aggressive child: A cross-national comparison*. Hillsdale, NJ: Erlbaum.

Huesmann, L. R., Moise-Titus, J., Podolski, C., & Eron, L. D. (2003). Longitudinal relations between children's exposure to TV violence and their aggressive and violent behavior in young adulthood: 1977–1992. *Developmental Psychology*, *39*, 201–221.

Ilgen, M., McKellar, J., & Tiet, Q. (2005). Abstinence self-efficacy and abstinence 1 year after substance use disorder treatment. *Journal of Consulting and Clinical Psychology*, *73*, 1175–1180.

Intons-Peterson, M. J., & Roskos-Ewoldsen, B. (1989). Mitigating the effects of violent pornography. In S. Gubar & J. Hoff (Eds.), *For adult users only: The dilemma of violent pornography* (pp. 218–239). Bloomington: Indiana University Press.

Isen, A. M., Niedenthal, P. M., & Cantor, N. (1992). An influence of positive affect on social categorization. *Motivation and Emotion*, *16*, 65–78.

Jarvis, W. B. G., & Petty, R. E. (1996). The need to evaluate. *Journal of Personality and Social Psychology*, *70*, 172–194.

Jih, C-S., Sirgo, V. I., & Thomure, J. C. (1995). Alcohol consumption, locus of control, and self-esteem of high school and college students. *Psychological Reports*, *76*, 851–857.

Jones, J. W., Brasher, E. E., & Huff, J. W. (2002). Innovations in integrity-based personnel selection: Building a technology-friendly assessment. *International Journal of Selection and Assessment*, *10*, 87–97.

Josephson, W. L. (1987). Television violence and children's aggression: Testing the priming, social script, and disinhibition predictions. *Journal of Personality and Social Psychology*, *53*, 882–890.

Kazdin, A. E. (2001). *Behavior modification in applied settings* (6th ed.). Pacific Grove, CA: Brooks/Cole.

Kelly, W. E. (2005). Some cognitive characteristics of night-sky watchers: Correlations between social problem-solving, need for cognition, and noctcaelador. *Education*, *126*, 328–333.

Kim, E. (2005). The effect of the decreased safety behaviors on anxiety and negative thoughts in social phobics. *Journal of Anxiety Disorders*, *19*, 69–86.

Koski-Jannes, A. (1994). Drinking-related locus of control as a predictor of drinking after treatment. *Addictive Behaviors*, *19*, 491–495.

Krahé, B. (2001). *The social psychology of aggression*. Philadelphia: Taylor & Francis.

Langston, C. A., & Cantor, N. (1989). Social anxiety and social constraint: When making friends is hard. *Journal of Personality and Social Psychology*, *56*, 649–661.

Lassiter, G. D., Briggs, M. A., & Bowman, R. E. (1991). Need for cognition and the perception of ongoing behavior. *Personality and Social Psychology Bulletin*, *17*, 156–160.

Lassiter, G. D., Briggs, M. A., & Slaw, R. D. (1991). Need for cognition, causal processing, and memory for behavior. *Personality and Social Psychology Bulletin*, *17*, 694–700.

Lawler, E. E. (1971). *Pay and organizational effectiveness: A psychological view*. New York: McGraw-Hill.

Lazarus, A. A. (2008). Multimodal therapy. In R. J. Corsini & D. Wedding (Eds.), *Current psychotherapies* (8th ed., pp. 368–401). Belmont, CA: Thomson Higher Education.

Leahy, R. L. (Ed.). (2006). *Contemporary cognitive therapy: Theory, research, and practice*. New York: Guilford Press.

Lefcourt, H. M. (1982). *Locus of control: Current trends in theory and research* (2nd ed.). Hillsdale, NJ: Erlbaum.

Lefcourt, H. M. (Ed.). (1983). *Research with the locus of control construct: Developments and social problems: Vol. 2*. New York: Academic Press.

Lefcourt, H. M. (Ed.). (1984). *Research with the locus of control construct: Extensions and limitations: Vol. 3*. Orlando, FL: Academic Press.

Lefcourt, H. M. (1992). Durability and impact of the locus of control concept. *Psychological Bulletin, 112,* 411–414.

Lefcourt, H. M., & Davidson-Katz, K. (1991). Locus of control and health. In C. R. Snyder & D. R. Forsyth (Eds.), *Handbook of social and clinical psychology: The health perspective* (pp. 246–266). New York: Pergamon.

Leong, F. T. L., Zachar, P., Conant, L., & Tolliver, D. (2007). Career specialty preferences among psychology majors: Cognitive processing styles associated with scientist and practitioner interests. *The Career Development Quarterly, 55,* 328–338.

Leontopoulou, S. (2006). Resilience of Greek youth at an educational transition point: The role of locus of control and coping strategies as resources. *Social Indicators Research, 76,* 95–126.

LeUnes, A. D., & Nation, J. R. (1989). *Sports psychology: An introduction.* Chicago: Nelson-Hall.

Leyens, J., Camino, L., Parke, R. D., & Berkowitz, L. (1975). Effects of movie violence on aggression in a field setting as a function of group dominance and cohesion. *Journal of Personality and Social Psychology, 32,* 346–360.

Liebert, R. M., & Baron, R. A. (1972). Some immediate effects of televised violence on children's behavior. *Development Psychology, 6,* 469–475.

Liebert, R. M., & Schwartzberg, N. S. (1977). Effects of mass media. *Annual Review of Psychology, 28,* 141–173.

Liebert, R. M., Sprafkin. J. N., & Davidson, E. S. (1989). *The early window: Effects of television on children and youth* (3rd ed.). New York: Pergamon.

Lin, C., & Wu, P. (2006). The effect of variety on consumer preferences: The role of need for cognition and recommended alternatives. *Social Behavior and Personality, 34,* 865–876.

Linz, D., Donnerstein, E., & Penrod, S. (1984). The effects of multiple exposure to filmed violence against women. *Journal of Communication, 34,* 130–137.

Linz, D., Donnerstein, E., & Penrod, S. (1988). Effects of long-term exposure to violent and sexually degrading depictions of women. *Journal of Personality and Social Psychology, 55,* 758–768.

Linz, D., Fuson, I. A., & Donnerstein, E. (1990). Mitigating the negative effects of sexually violent mass communications through pre-exposure briefings. *Communication Research, 17,* 641–674.

Liu, Y., & Eveland, W. P., Jr. (2005). Education, need for cognition, and campaign interest as moderators of news effects on political knowledge: An analysis of the knowledge gap. *Journalism and Mass Communication Quarterly, 82,* 910–929.

London House. (1980). *Personal Selection Inventory (PSI).* Park Ridge, IL: London House Press.

MacDonald, A. P. (1970). Internal-external locus of control and the practice of birth control. *Psychological Reports, 27,* 206.

Malamuth, N. M. (1984). Aggression against women: Cultural and individual causes. In N. M. Malamuth & E. Donnerstein (Eds.), *Pornography and sexual aggression* (pp. 19–52). Orlando, FL: Academic Press.

Malamuth, N. M., & Briere, J. (1986). Sexual violence in the media: Indirect effects on aggression against women. *Journal of Social Issues, 42,* 75–92.

Malcarne, V. L., Drahota, A., & Hamilton, N. A. (2005). Children's health-related locus of control beliefs: Ethnicity, gender, and family income. *Children's Health Care, 34,* 47–59.

Mann, J., Berkowitz, L., Sidman, J., Starr, S., & West, S. (1974). Satiation on the transient stimulating effect of erotic films. *Journal of Personality and Social Psychology, 30,* 729–735.

Markman, G. D., Balkin, D. B., & Baron, R. A. (2005). Inventors and new venture information: The effects of general self-efficacy and regretful thinking. *Entrepreneurship Theory and Practice, 27,* 149–165.

Marshall, W. L. (1985, September). *The use of pornography by sex offenders.* Paper presented at the U.S. Justice Department Hearings, Houston.

Martin, S., Meyer, J. A., Nelson, L., Baldwin, V., Ting, L., & Sterling, D. (2007). Locus of control, self-control, and family income as predictors of young children's mathematics and science scores. *Perceptual and Motor Skills, 104,* 599–610.

McAnulty, R. D., & Burnette, M. M. (2001). *Exploring human sexuality: Making healthy decisions.* Boston: Allyn & Bacon.

McEwan, S. L., de Man, A. F., & Simpson-Housley, P. (2005). Acquaintance rape, ego-identity achievement, and locus of control. *Social Behavior and Personality, 33,* 587–592.

Meichenbaum, D. H. (1977). *Cognitive-behavior modification: An integrative approach.* New York: Plenum.

Meichenbaum, D. H. (1985). *Stress inoculation training.* New York: Pergamon.

Meichenbaum, D., & Turk, D. (1987). *Facilitating treatment adherence.* New York: Plenum.

Melamed, B. G., Hawes, R. R., Heiby, E., & Glick, J. (1975). The use of filmed modeling to reduce uncooperative behavior of children during dental treatment. *Journal of Dental Research, 54,* 797–801.

Melamed, B. G., & Siegel, L. J. (1975). Reduction of anxiety in children facing hospitalization and surgery by use of filmed modeling. *Journal of Consulting and Clinical Psychology, 43,* 511–521.

Mellon, T., & Grossman, S. D. (2005). Psychotherapy for narcissistic personality disorder. In G. O. Gabbard, J. S. Beck, & J. Holems (Eds.), *Oxford textbook of psychotherapy* (pp. 279–289). New York: Oxford University Press.

Metcalfe, J., & Mischel, W. (1999). A hot/cool-system analysis of delay of gratification: Dynamics of willpower. *Psychological Review, 106,* 3–19.

Milar, R., & Shevlin, M. (2007). The development and factor structure of a career locus of control scale for use with school pupils. *Journal of Career Development, 33,* 224–249.

Miller, P. C. (1981). *The construct validation of the Marital Locus of Control Scale.* Unpublished master's thesis, University of Waterloo, Ontario.

Miller, P. C., Lefcourt, H. M., Holmes J. G., Ware, E. E., & Saleh, W. E. (1986). Marital locus of control and marital problem solving. *Journal of Personality and Social Psychology, 51,* 161–169.

Miller, S. M., Shoda, Y., & Hurley, K. (1996). Applying cognitive-social theory to health-protective behavior: Breast self-examination in cancer screening. *Psychological Bulletin, 119,* 70–94.

Mischel, W. (1968). *Personality and assessment.* New York: John Wiley .

Mischel, W. (1973). Toward a cognitive social learning reconceptualization of personality. *Psychological Review, 80,* 252–283.

Mischel, W. (1977). On the future of personality assessment. *American Psychologist, 32,* 246–254.

Mischel, W. (1979). On the interface of cognition and personality: Beyond the person–situation debate. *American Psychologist, 34,* 740–754.

Mischel, W. (1984). On the predictability of behavior and the structure of personality. In R. A. Zucker, J. Aronoff, & A. I. Rabin (Eds.), *Personality and the prediction of behavior* (pp. 269–305). New York: Academic Press.

Mischel, W. (1990). Personality dispositions revisited and revised: A view after three decades. In L. A. Pervin (Ed.), *Handbook of personality: Theory and research* (pp. 111–134). New York: Guilford Press.

Mischel, W. (1993). *Introduction to personality* (5th ed.). Fort Worth, TX: Harcourt Brace Jovanovich.

Mischel, W. (1999). Personality coherence and dispositions in a cognitive-affective personality (CAPS) approach. In D. Cervone & Y. Shoda (Eds.), *The coherence of personality: Social-cognitive bases of consistency, variability, and organization* (pp. 37–60). New York: Guilford Press.

Mischel, W. (2000). A cognitive-affective system theory of personality: Reconceptualizing situations, dispositions, dynamics, and invariance in personality structure. In E. T. Higgins & A. W. Kruglanski (Eds.), *Motivational science: Social and personality perspectives* (pp. 150–176). New York: Psychology Press.

Mischel, W. (2004). Toward an integrative science of the person. *Annual Review of Psychology, 55,* 1–22.

Mischel, W., & Ayduk, O. (2002). Self-regulation in a cognitive-affective personality system: Attentional control in the service of the self. *Self and Identity, 1,* 113–120.

Mischel, W., & Ayduk, O. (2003). Willpower in a cognitive-affective processing system. In R. F. Baumeister & K. D. Vohs (Eds.), *Handbook of self-regulation: Research, theory, and applications* (pp. 99–129). New York: Guilford Press.

Mischel, W., & Baker, N. (1975). Cognitive appraisals and transformations in delay behavior. *Journal of Personality and Social Psychology, 31,* 254–261.

Mischel, W., Cantor, N., & Feldman, S. (1996). Principles of self-regulation: The nature of willpower and self-control. In E. T. Higgins & A. W. Kruglanski (Eds.), *Social psychology: Handbook of basic principles* (pp. 329–360). New York: Guilford Press.

Mischel, W., & Ebbesen, E. B. (1970). Attention in delay of gratification. *Journal of Personality and Social Psychology, 16,* 329–337.

Mischel, W., Ebbesen, E. B., & Zeiss, A. R. (1972). Cognitive and attentional mechanisms in delay of gratification. *Journal of Personality and Social Psychology, 21,* 204–218.

Mischel, W., & Morf, C. C. (2003). The self as a psycho-social dynamic processing system: A meta-perspective on a century of the self in psychology. In M. L. Leary & J. P. Tangney (Eds.), *Handbook of self and identity* (pp. 15–43). New York: Guilford Press.

Mischel, W., & Rodriguez, M. L. (1993). Psychological distance in self-imposed delay of gratification. In R. R. Cocking & K. A. Renninger (Eds.), *The development and meaning of psychological distance* (pp. 109–121). Hillsdale, NJ: Erlbaum.

Mischel, W., & Shoda, Y. (1995). A cognitive-affective system theory of personality: Reconceptualizing situations, dispositions, dynamics, and invariance in personality structure. *Psychological Review, 102,* 246–268.

Mischel, W., & Shoda, Y. (1998). Reconciling processing dynamics and personality dispositions. *Annual Review of Psychology, 49,* 229–258.

Mischel, W., & Shoda, Y. (1999). Integrating dispositions and processing dynamics within a unified theory of personality: The cognitive-affective personality system. In L. A. Pervin & O. P. John (Eds.), *Handbook of personality: Theory and research* (2nd ed., pp. 197–218). New York: Guilford Press.

Mischel, W., Shoda, Y., & Rodriguez, M. L. (1989). Delay of gratification. *Science, 244,* 933–937.

Mischel, W., Shoda, Y., & Rodriguez, M. L. (1992). Delay of gratification in children. In G. Loewenstein & J. Elster (Eds.), *Choice over time* (pp. 147–164). New York: Russell Sage Foundation.

Mischel, W., Smith, R. E., & Shoda, Y. (2008). *Introduction to personality: Toward an integration* (8th ed.). Hoboken, NJ: John Wiley.

Mlott, S. R., & Lira, F. T. (1977). Dogmatism, locus of control, and life goals in stable and unstable marriages. *Journal of Clinical Psychology, 33,* 142–146.

Monk-Turner, E., & Purcell, H. C. (1999). Sexual violence in pornography: How prevalent is it? *Gender Issues, 17,* 58–68.

Moore, B., Mischel, W., & Zeiss, A. R. (1976). Comparative effects of the reward stimulus and its cognitive representation in voluntary delay. *Journal of Personality and Social Psychology, 34,* 419–424.

Moskowitz, G. B. (2005). *Social cognition: Understanding self and others.* New York: Guilford Press.

Multon, K. D., Brown, S. D., & Lent, R. W. (1991). Relation of self-efficacy beliefs to academic outcomes: A meta-analytic investigation. *Journal of Consulting Psychology, 38,* 30–38.

Muraven, M., Tice, D. M., & Baumeister, R. F. (1998). Self-control as limited resource: Regulatory depletion patterns. *Journal of Personality and Social Psychology, 74,* 774–789.

Murphy, K. R., & Davidshofer, C. O. (2005). *Psychological testing: Principles and applications* (6th ed.). Upper Saddle River, NJ: Pearson.

Neuberg, S. L., Judice, T. N., & West, S. G. (1997). What the Need for Closure Scale measures and what it does not: Toward differentiating among related epistemic motives. *Journal of Personality and Social Psychology, 72,* 1396–1412.

Nevid, J. S., Rathus, S. A., & Greene, B. (2000). *Abnormal psychology in a changing world* (4th ed.). Upper Saddle River, NJ: Prentice Hall.

Nietzel, M. T., Bernstein, D. A., & Milich, R. (1994). *Introduction to clinical psychology* (4th ed.). Englewood Cliffs, NJ: Prentice Hall.

Nord, W. R., Connelly, F., & Daignault, G. (1974). Locus of control and aptitude test scores as predictors of academic success in graduate school. *Journal of Educational Psychology*, *66*, 956–961.

Norem, J. K. (1989). Cognitive strategies as personality: Effectiveness, specificity, flexibility, and change. In D. M. Buss & N. Cantor (Eds.), *Personality psychology: Recent trends and emerging directions* (pp. 45–60). New York: Springer.

Norem, J. K. (1998). Should we lower our defenses about defense mechanism? *Journal of Personality*, *66*, 895–917.

Norem, J. K. (2000). Defensive pessimism, optimism, and pessimism. In E. C. Chang (Ed.), *Optimism and pessimism: Implications for theory, research, and practice* (pp. 77–100). Washington, DC: American Psychological Association.

Norem, J. K. (2001). *The positive power of negative thinking: Using defensive pessimism to harness anxiety and perform at your peak*. New York: Basic Books.

Norem, J. K., & Cantor, N. (1986a). Anticipatory and post hoc cushioning strategies: Optimism and defensive pessimism in "risky" situations. *Cognitive Therapy and Research*, *10*, 347–362.

Norem, J. K., & Cantor, N. (1986b). Defensive pessimism: "Harnessing" anxiety as motivation. *Journal of Personality and Social Psychology*, *51*, 1208–1217.

Norem, J. K., & Illingworth, K. S. S. (1993). Strategy-dependent effects of reflecting on self and tasks: Some implications of optimism and defensive pessimism. *Journal of Personality and Social Psychology*, *65*, 822–835.

Norem, J. K., & Illingworth, K. S. S. (2004). Mood and performance among defensive pessimists and strategic optimists. *Journal of Research in Personality*, *38*, 351–366.

Olson, J. M., Roese, N. J., & Zanna, M. P. (1996). Expectancies. In E. T. Higgins & A. W. Kruglanski (Eds.), *Social psychology: Handbook of basic principles* (pp. 211–238). New York: Guilford Press.

Osofsky, J. D. (1995). The effects of exposure to violence on young children. *American Psychologist*, *50*, 782–788.

Ozer, E. M., & Bandura, A. (1990). Mechanisms governing empowerment effects: A self-efficacy analysis. *Journal of Personality and Social Psychology*, *58*, 472–486.

Parke, R. D., Berkowitz, L., Leyes, J. P., West, S. G., & Sebastian, R. J. (1977). Some effects of violent and nonviolent movies on the behavior of juvenile delinquents. In L. Berkowitz (Ed.), *Advances in experimental social psychology: Vol. 10* (pp. 135–172). New York: Academic Press.

Parkes, K. R. (1984). Locus of control, cognitive appraisal and coping in stressful episodes. *Journal of Personality and Social Psychology*, *46*, 655–668.

Peake, P., Hebl, M., & Mischel, W. (2002). Strategic attention development in waiting and working situations. *Developmental Psychology*, *38*, 313–326.

Pervin, L. A. (2002). *Current controversies and issues in personality* (3rd ed.). New York: John Wiley.

Petty, R. E., Cacioppo, J. T., & Kasmer, J. (1985, May). *Effects of need for cognition on social loafing*. Paper presented at the meeting of the Midwestern Psychological Association, Chicago.

Phares, E. J. (1968). Differential utilization of information as a function of internal-external control. *Journal of Personality*, *36*, 649–662.

Phares, E. J. (2001). Locus of control. In W. E. Craighead & C. B. Nemeroff (Eds.), *The Corsini encyclopedia of psychology and behavioral science: Vol. 2* (pp. 889–891). Hoboken, NJ: John Wiley.

Phares, E. J., & Chaplin, W. E. (1997). *Introduction to personality* (4th ed.). New York: Longman.

Phares, E. J., & Wilson, K. G. (1972). Responsibility attribution: Role of outcome severity, situational ambiguity, and internal-external control. *Journal of Personality*, *40*, 392–406.

Plante, T. G. (2005). *Contemporary clinical psychology* (2nd ed.). Hoboken, NJ: John Wiley.

Plomin, R., DeFries, J. C., McClearn, G. E., & McGuffin, P. (2001). *Behavioral genetics* (4th ed.). New York: Worth.

Plunkett, H., & Buehner, M. J. (2007). The relation of general and specific locus of control to intertemporal monetary choice. *Personality and Individual Differences*, *42*, 1233–1242.

Preckel, F., Holling, H., & Vock, M. (2006). Academic underachievement: Relationship with cognitive motivation, achievement motivation, and conscientiousness. *Psychology in the Schools*, *43*, 401–411.

Prociuk, T. J., & Breen, L. J. (1975). Defensive externality and academic performance. *Journal of Personality and Social Psychology*, *31*, 549–556.

Prussia, G. E., Kinicki, A. J., & Bracker, J. S. (1993). Psychological and behavioral consequences of job loss: A covariance structure using Weiner's (1985) attribution model. *Journal of Applied Psychology*, *78*, 382–394.

Pull, C. B. (2005). Current status of virtual reality exposure therapy in anxiety disorders. *Current Opinion in Psychiatry*, *18*, 7–14.

Rahim, M. A. (1997). Relationships of stress, locus of control, and social support to psychiatric symptoms and propensity to leave a job: A field study with managers. *Journal of Business and Psychology*, *12*, 159–174.

Reitz, H. J., & Jewell, L. N. (1979). Sex, locus of control, and job involvement: A six-country investigation. *Academy of Management Journal*, *22*, 72–80.

Rice, P. L. (1992). *Stress and health* (2nd ed.). Pacific Grove, CA: Brooks/Cole.

Riggio, R. E. (1986). Assessment of basic social skills. *Journal of Personality and Social Psychology*, *51*, 649–660.

Riggio, R. E. (2000). *Introduction to industrial/organizational psychology* (3rd ed.). Upper Saddle River, NJ: Prentice Hall.

Rodebaugh, T. L., Holaway, R. M., & Heimberg, R. G. (2004). The treatment of social anxiety disorder. *Clinical Psychology Review*, *24*, 883–908.

Rodriguez, M. L., Mischel, W., & Shoda, Y. (1989). Cognitive person variables in the delay of gratification of older children at risk. *Journal of Personality and Social Psychology*, *57*, 358–367.

Rokke, P. D., & Rehm, L. P. (2001). Self-management therapies. In K. S. Dobson (Ed.), *Handbook of cognitive-behavioral therapies* (2nd ed., pp. 173–210). New York: Guilford Press.

Rosenthal, T. L., & Steffek, B. D. (1991). Modeling methods. In F. H. Kanfer & A. P. Goldstein (Eds.), *Helping people change* (4th ed., pp. 70–121). New York: Pergamon.

Rotter, J. B. (1954). *Social learning and clinical psychology.* Englewood Cliffs, NJ: Prentice Hall.

Rotter, J. B. (1966). Generalized expectancies for internal versus external control of reinforcement. *Psychological Monographs, 80* (1, Whole No. 609).

Rotter, J. B. (1967). A new scale for the measurement of interpersonal trust. *Journal of Personality, 35,* 651–665.

Rotter, J. B. (1970). Some implications of a social learning theory for the practice of psychotherapy. In D. J. Levis (Ed.), *Learning approaches to therapeutic behavior change* (pp. 208–241). Chicago: Aldine.

Rotter, J. B. (1971). Generalized expectancies for interpersonal trust. *American Psychologist, 26,* 443–452.

Rotter, J. B. (1978). Generalized expectancies for problem solving and psychotherapy. *Cognitive Therapy and Research, 2,* 1–10.

Rotter, J. B. (1980). Interpersonal trust, trustworthiness, and gullibility. *American Psychologist, 35,* 1–7.

Rotter, J. B. (1982). *The development and applications of social learning theory: Selected papers.* New York: Praeger.

Rotter, J. B. (1990). Internal versus external control of reinforcement: A case history of a variable. *American Psychologist, 45,* 489–493.

Rotter, J. B. (1993). Expectancies. In C. E. Walker (Ed.), *The history of clinical psychology in autobiography: Vol. 2* (pp. 273–284). Pacific Grove, CA: Brooks/Cole.

Rotter, J. B., Chance, J. E., & Phares, E. J. (1972). *Applications of a social learning theory of personality.* New York: Holt, Rinehart & Winston.

Rotter, J. B., & Hochreich, D. J. (1975). *Personality.* Glenview, IL: Scott, Foresman.

Rowe, J. L., Montgomery, G. H., Duberstein, P. R., & Bovbjerg, D. H. (2005). Health locus of control and perceived risk for breast cancer in healthy women. *Behavioral Medicine, 31,* 33–40.

Sanderson, C. A., & Cantor, N. (1995). Social dating goals in late adolescence: Implications for safer sexuality. *Journal of Personality and Social Psychology, 68,* 1121–1134.

Sanderson, C. A., & Cantor, N. (1997). Creating satisfaction in steady dating relationships: The role of personal goals and situational affordances. *Journal of Personality and Social Psychology, 73,* 1424–1433.

Sanderson, C. A., & Cantor, N. (1999). A life task perspective on personality coherence: Stability versus change in tasks, goals, strategies, and outcomes. In D. Cervone & Y. Shoda (Eds.), *The coherence of personality: Social-cognitive bases of consistency, variability, and organization* (pp. 372–392). New York: Guilford Press.

Sanna, L. J., Chang, E. C., Carter, S. E., & Small, E. M. (2006). The future is now: Prospective temporal self-appraisals among defensive pessimists and optimists. *Personality and Social Psychology Bulletin, 32,* 727–739.

Schmidt, G., & Sigusch, V. (1970). Sex differences in responses to psychosexual stimulation by film and slides. *Journal of Sex Research, 6,* 268–283.

Schutte, N. S., Malouff, J. M., Post-Gorden, J. C., & Rodasts, A. L. (1988). Effect of playing video games on children's aggressive and other behavior. *Journal of Applied Social Psychology, 18,* 454–460.

Schultz, D., & Schultz, S. E. (1998). *Psychology and work today: An introduction to industrial and organizational psychology* (7th ed.). Upper Saddle River, NJ: Prentice Hall.

Schwartz, B. (2004). *Paradox of choice: Why more is less.* New York: HarperCollins.

Schwartz, R., & Chung, R. (1996). Anticipating stress in the community: Worries about the future of Hong Kong. *Anxiety, Stress, and Coping, 9,* 163–178.

Seeman, M. (1963). Alienation and social learning in a reformatory. *American Journal of Sociology, 69,* 270–284.

Seeman, M., & Evans, J. (1962). Alienation and learning in a hospital setting. *American Sociological Review, 27,* 772–782.

Selander, J., Marnetoft, S., Åkerström, B., & Asplund, R. (2005). Locus of control and regional differences in sickness absence in Sweden. *Disability and Rehabilitation, 27,* 925–928.

Shaffer, D. R. (1999). *Developmental psychology: Childhood and adolescence* (5th ed.). Pacific Grove, CA: Brooks/Cole.

Shelly, M., & Pakenham, K. I. (2004). External health locus of control and general self-efficacy: Moderators of emotional distress among university students. *Australian Journal of Psychology, 56,* 191–199.

Shoda, Y., Mischel, W., & Peake, P. K. (1990). Predicting adolescent cognitive and self-regulatory competencies from preschool delay of gratification: Identifying diagnostic conditions. *Developmental Psychology, 26,* 978–986.

Shoda, Y., Mischel, W., & Wright, J. C. (1989). Intuitive interactionism in person perception: Effects of situation–behavior relations on dispositional judgments. *Journal of Personality and Social Psychology, 56,* 41–53.

Shoda, Y., Mischel, W., & Wright, J. C. (1993a). The role of situational demands and cognitive competencies in behavior organization and personality coherence. *Journal of Personality and Social Psychology, 65,* 1023–1035.

Shoda, Y., Mischel, W., & Wright, J. C. (1993b). Links between personality judgments and contextual behavior patterns: Situation–behavior profiles of personality prototypes. *Social Cognition, 4,* 399–429.

Shoda, Y., Mischel, W., & Wright, J. C. (1994). Intra-individual stability in the organization and patterning of behavior: Incorporating psychological situations into the idiographic analysis personality. *Journal of Personality and Social Psychology, 65,* 1023–1035.

Snyder, C. R., & Forsyth, R. D. (Eds.). (1991). *Handbook of social and clinical psychology: The health perspective.* New York: Pergamon.

Spector, P. E. (1982). Behavior in organizations as a function of employee's locus of control. *Psychological Bulletin, 91,* 482–497.

Spencer, S. M., & Norem, J. K. (1996). Reflection and distraction: Defensive pessimism, strategic optimism, and performance. *Personality and Social Psychology Bulletin, 22,* 354–365.

Stajkovic, A. D., & Luthans, F. (1998). Self-efficacy and work-related performance: A meta-analysis. *Psychological Bulletin, 124,* 240–261.

Sternberg, R. J., & Grigorenko, E. L. (1997). Are cognitive styles still in style? *American Psychologist, 52,* 700–712.

Strack, F., & Deutsch, R. (2007). The role of impulse in social behavior. In A. W. Kruglanski & E. T. Higgins (Eds.), *Social psychology: Handbook of basic principles* (2nd ed., pp. 408–431). New York: Guilford Press.

Strentz, T., & Auerbach, S. M. (1988). Adjustment to the stress of simulated captivity: Effects of emotion-focused versus problem-focused preparation on hostages differing in locus of control. *Journal of Personality and Social Psychology, 55,* 652–660.

Strickland, B. R. (1965). The prediction of social action from a dimension of internal-external control. *Journal of Social Psychology, 66,* 353–358.

Strickland, B. R. (1979). Internal-external expectancies and cardiovascular functioning. In L. C. Perlmuter & R. A. Monty (Eds.), *Choice and perceived control* (pp. 221–231). Hillsdale, NJ: Erlbaum.

Tangney, J. P., Baumeister, R. F., & Boone, A. L. (2004). High self-control predicts good adjustment, less pathology, better grades, and interpersonal success. *Journal of Personality, 72,* 271–322.

Tetlock, P. E. (2007). Psychology and politics: The challenges of integrating levels of analysis in social science. In A. W. Kruglanski & E. T. Higgins (Eds.), *Social psychology: Handbook of basic principles* (2nd ed., pp. 888–912). New York: Guilford Press.

Towler, A., & Dipboye, R. L. (2006). Effects of trainer reputation and trainees' need for cognition on training outcomes. *Journal of Psychology, 140,* 549–564.

Trent, W. T., Lee, H. S., & Owens-Nicholson, D. (2006). Perceptions of financial aid among students of color: Examining the role(s) of self-concept, locus of control, and expectations. *American Behavioral Scientist, 49,* 1739–1759.

Trope, Y., & Liberman, A. (1996). Social hypothesis testing: Cognitive and motivational mechanisms. In E. T. Higgins & A. W. Kruglanski (Eds.), *Social psychology: Handbook of basic principles* (pp. 239–270). New York: Guilford Press.

Trull, T. J., & Phares, E. J. (2001). *Clinical psychology* (6th ed.). Belmont, CA: Wadsworth/Thomson Learning.

Turk, D. C., Meichenbaum, D., & Genest, M. (1983). *Pain and behavioral medicine: A cognitive-behavioral perspective.* New York: Plenum.

Turner, S. M., Beidel, D. C., & Cooley-Quille, M. R. (1995). Two-year follow-up of social phobia treated with social effectiveness therapy. *Behaviour Research and Therapy, 33,* 553–555.

Valecha, G. K. (1972). Construct validation of internal-external locus of reinforcement related to work-related variables. *Proceedings of the 80th Annual Convention of the American Psychological Association, 7,* 455–456.

Viswanathan, M. (1997). Individual differences in need for precision. *Personality and Social Psychology, 23,* 717–735.

Walker, C. E. (1993). *The history of clinical psychology in autobiography: Vol. 2.* Pacific Grove, CA: Brooks/Cole.

Wallston, K. A. (2001). Conceptualization and operationalization of perceived control. In A. Baum, T. A. Revenson, & J. E. Singer (Eds.), *Handbook of health psychology* (pp. 49–58). Mahwah, NJ: Erlbaum.

Weary, G., & Edwards, J. A. (1994). Individual differences in causal uncertainty. *Journal of Personality and Social Psychology, 67,* 308–318.

Webster-Stratton, C. (1992). Individually administered videotape parent training: "Who benefits?" *Cognitive Therapy and Research, 16,* 31–52.

Weinstein, S. E., & Quigley, K. S. (2006). Locus of control predicts appraisals and cardiovascular reactivity to a novel active coping task. *Journal of Personality, 74,* 911–931.

Williams, S. L., & Cervone, D. (1998). Social cognitive theories of personality. In D. F. Barone, M. Hersen, & V. B. Van Hasselt (Eds.), *Advanced personality* (pp. 173–207). New York: Plenum.

Wilson, G. T. (2000). Behavior therapy. In R. J. Corsini & D. Wedding (Eds.), *Current psychotherapies* (pp. 205–240). Itasca, IL: F. E. Peacock.

Winter, D. G., & Barenbaum, N. B. (1999). History of modern personality theory and research. In L. A. Pervin & O. P. John (Eds.), *Handbook of personality: Theory and research* (2nd ed., pp. 3–27). New York: Guilford Press.

Wolfe, B. E. (2005). The application of the integrative model of specific anxiety disorders. In B. E. Wolfe (Ed.), *Understanding and treating anxiety disorders: An integrative approach to healing the wounded self* (pp. 125–153). Washington, DC: American Psychological Association.

Wood, W., Wong, F. Y., & Chachere, J. G. (1991). Effects of media violence on viewers' aggression in unconstrained social interaction. *Psychological Bulletin, 109,* 371–383.

Wrightsman, L. S. (1991). Interpersonal trust and attitudes toward human nature. In J. P. Robinson, P. R. Shaver, & L. S. Wrightsman (Eds.), *Measures of personality and social psychological attitudes: Vol. 1* (pp. 373–412). San Diego, CA: Academic Press.

Wrightsman, L. S., Nietzel, M. T., & Fortune, W. H. (1998). *Psychology and the legal system* (4th ed.). Pacific Grove, CA: Brooks/Cole.

Ye, M., She, Y., & Wu, R. (2007). The relationship between graduated students' subjective well-being and locus of control. *Chinese Journal of Clinical Psychology, 15,* 63–65.

Zillmann. D., & Bryant, J. (1984). Effects of massive exposure to pornography. In N. M. Malamuth & E. Donnerstein (Eds.), *Pornography and sexual aggression* (pp. 115–138). Orlando, FL: Academic Press.

Zirkel, S. (1992). Developing independence in a life transition: Investing the self in the concerns of the day. *Journal of Personality and Social Psychology, 62,* 506–521.

Zirkel, S., & Cantor, N. (1990). Personal construal of life tasks: Those who struggle for independence. *Journal of Personality and Social Psychology, 58,* 172–185.

Chapter 11

Allport, G. W. (1943). The ego in contemporary psychology. *Psychological Bulletin, 50,* 451–478.

Allport, G. W. (1961). *Pattern and growth in personality.* New York: Holt, Rinehart & Winston.

Anderson, C. A. (1999). Attributional style, depression, and loneliness: A cross-cultural comparison of American and Chinese students. *Personality and Social Psychology Bulletin, 25,* 482–499.

Arndt, J., Greenberg, J., Simon, L., Pyszczynski, T., & Solomon, S. (1998). Terror management and self-awareness: Evidence that morality salience provokes avoidance of the self-focused state. *Personality and Social Psychology Bulletin, 24,* 1216–1227.

Ashmore, R. D., & Jussim, L. (1997). Toward a second century of the scientic analysis of the self and identity. In R. Ashmore & L. Jussim (Eds.), *Self and identity: Fundamental issues* (pp. 3–19). New York: Oxford University Press.

Banaji, M. R., & Prentice, D. A. (1994). The self in social context. *Annual Review of Psychology, 45,* 297–332).

Baumeister, R. F. (1986a). *Identity: Cultural change and the struggle for self.* New York: Oxford University Press.

Baumeister, R. F. (Ed.). (1986b). *Public self and private self.* New York: Oxford University Press.

Baumeister, R. F. (1987). How the self became a problem: A psychological review of historical research. *Journal of Personality and Social Psychology, 52,* 163–176.

Baumeister, R. F. (1991). Self-concept and identity. In V. J. Derlega, B. A. Winstead, & W. H. Jones (Eds.), *Personality: Contemporary theory and research* (pp. 349–380). Chicago: Nelson-Hall.

Baumeister, R. F. (1995). Self and identity: An introduction. In A. Tesser (Ed.), *Advanced social psychology* (pp. 50–97). New York: McGraw-Hill.

Baumeister, R. F. (1997). Identity, self-concept, and self-esteem: The self lost and found. In R. Hogan, J. Johnson, & S. Briggs (Eds.), *Handbook of personality psychology* (pp. 681–710). San Diego, CA: Academic Press.

Baumeister, R. F. (1999). The nature and structure of the self: An overview. In R. F. Baumeister (Ed.), *The self in social psychology* (pp. 1–20). Philadelphia, PA: Psychology Press.

Berzonsky, M. D. (1994). Self-identity: The relationship between process and content. *Journal of Research in Personality, 28,* 453–460.

Berzonsky, M. D., Trudeau, J. V., & Brennan, F. X. (1988, March). *Social-cognitive correlates of identity status.* Paper presented at the second biennial meeting of the Society for Research on Adolescence, Alexandria, VA.

Breakwell, G. (1986). *Coping with threatened identities.* London: Methuen.

Briggs, S. R., & Cheek, J. M. (1988). On the nature of self-monitoring: Problems with assessment, problems with validity. *Journal of Personality and Social Psychology, 54,* 663–678.

Briggs, S. R., Cheek, J. M., & Buss, A. H. (1980). An analysis of the self-monitoring scale. *Journal of Personality and Social Psychology, 54,* 679–686.

Britt, T. W. (1993). Metatraits: Evidence relevant to the validity of the construct and its implications. *Journal of Personality and Social Psychology, 65,* 554–562.

Brown, J. D. (1998). *The self.* Boston: McGraw-Hill.

Bushman, B. J. (1993). What's in a name? The moderating role of public self-consciousness on the relation between brand label and brand preference. *Journal of Applied Psychology, 78,* 857–861.

Buss, A. H. (1980). *Self-consciousness and social anxiety.* San Francisco: Freeman.

Buss, A. H. (1995). *Personality: Temperament, social behavior, and the self.* Boston: Allyn & Bacon.

Buss, A. H. (2001). *Psychological dimensions of the self.* Thousand Oaks: CA: Sage.

Buss, A. H., & Perry, M. (1992). The Aggression Questionnaire. *Journal of Personality and Social Psychology, 63,* 452–459.

Carpenter, S. (2000). Effects of cultural tightness and collectivism on self-concept and causal attributions. *Cross-Cultural Research, 34,* 38–56.

Carver, C. S. (1975). Physical aggression as a function of objective self-awareness and attitudes toward punishment. *Journal of Experimental Social Psychology, 11,* 510–519.

Carver, C. S. (1977). Self-awareness, perception of threat, and the expression of reactance through attitude change. *Journal of Personality, 45,* 501–512.

Carver, C. S., & Scheier, M. F. (1981a). *Attention and self-regulation: A control-theory approach to human behavior.* New York: Springer.

Carver, C. S., & Scheier, M. F. (1981b). Self-consciousness and reactance. *Journal of Research in Personality, 15,* 16–29.

Carver, C. S., & Scheier, M. F. (1990). Principles of self-regulation: Action and emotion. In E. T. Higgins & R. M. Sorrentino (Eds.), *Handbook of motivational and cognitive foundations of social behavior: Vol. 2* (pp. 3–52). New York: Guilford Press.

Carver, C. S., & Scheier, M. F. (1998). *On the self-regulation of behavior.* New York: Cambridge University Press.

Carver, C. S., & Scheier, M. F. (1999a). Stress, coping, and self-regulation. In L. A. Pervin & O. P. John (Eds.), *Handbook of personality: Theory and research* (2nd ed., pp. 553–575). New York: Guilford Press.

Carver, C. S., & Scheier, M. F. (1999b). Themes and issues in the self-regulation of behavior. In R. S. Wyer, Jr. (Ed.), *Advances in social cognition: Vol. 12* (pp. 1–105). Mahwah, NJ: Erlbaum.

Cash, T. F., & Labarge, A. S. (1996). The psychology of cosmetic surgery. *Cognitive Therapy and Research, 20,* 37–50.

Cash, T. F., & Szymanski, M. L. (1995). The development and validation of the Body-Image Ideals Questionnaire. *Journal of Personality Assessment, 64,* 466–477.

Cheek, J. M. (1989). Identity orientations and self-interpretation. In D. M. Buss & N. Cantor (Eds.), *Personality psychology: Recent trends and emerging directions* (pp. 275–285). New York: Springer.

Cheek, J. M., & Briggs, S. R. (1981, August). *Self-consciousness, self-monitoring, and aspects of identity.* Paper presented at the meeting of the American Psychological Association, Los Angeles.

Cheek, J. M., & Briggs, S. R. (1982). Self-consciousness and aspects of identity. *Journal of Research in Personality, 16,* 401–408.

Cheek, J. M., & Busch, C. M. (1982, April). *Self-monitoring and the inner-outer metaphor: Principled versus pragmatic self?* Paper presented at the meeting of the Eastern Psychological Association, Baltimore.

Cheek, J. M., & Hogan, R. (1983). Self-concepts, self-presentations, and moral judgments. In J. Suls & A. G. Greenwald (Eds.), *Psychological perspectives on the self: Vol. 2* (pp. 249–273). Hillsdale, NJ: Erlbaum.

Cheek, J. M., Tropp, L. R., Chen, L. C., & Underwood, M. K. (1994, August). *Identity orientations: Personal, social, and collective aspects of identity*. Paper presented at the meeting of the American Psychological Association, Los Angeles.

Cheek, J. M., Underwood, M. K., & Cutler, B. L. (1985). *The Aspects of Identity Questionnaire (III)*. Unpublished manuscript, Wellesley College.

Chiu, C., Morris, M. W., Hong, Y., & Menon, T. Y. (2000). Motivated cultural cognition: The impact of implicit cultural theories on dispositional attribution varies as a function of need for closure. *Journal of Personality and Social Psychology, 78*, 247–259.

Choi, I., Nisbett, R. E., & Norenzayan, A. (1999). Causal attribution across cultures: Variation and universality. *Psychological Bulletin, 125*, 47–63.

Craik, F. I. M., Moroz, T. M., Moscovitch, M., Stuss, D. T., Winocur, G., Tulving, E., et al. (1999). In search of the self: A positron emission tomography study. *Psychological Science, 10*, 26–34.

Cross, S. E., & Markus, H. R. (1999). The cultural constitution of personality. In L. A. Pervin & O. P. John (Eds.), *Handbook of personality: Theory and research* (2nd ed., pp. 378–396). New York: Guilford Press.

Cutler, B. L., Lennox, R. D., & Wolfe, R. N. (1984, August). *Reliability and construct validity of the Aspects of Identity Questionnaire*. Paper presented at the meeting of the American Psychological Association, Toronto, Canada.

Damon, W., & Hart, D. (1982). The development of self-understanding from infancy through adolescence. *Child Development, 53*, 841–864.

Damon, W., & Hart, D. (1988). *Self-understanding in childhood and adolescence*. Cambridge, UK: Cambridge University Press.

Dana, R. H. (Ed.). (2000). *Handbook of cross-cultural and multicultural personality assessment*. Mahwah, NJ: Erlbaum.

Darwin, C. (1877). A biographical sketch of an infant. *Mind, 2*, 285–294.

Davis, M. H., & Franzoi, S. L. (1991). Self-awareness and self-consciousness. In V. J. Derlega, B. A. Winstead, & W. H. Jones (Eds.), *Personality: Contemporary theory and research* (pp. 311–347). Chicago: Nelson-Hall.

Deaux, K. (1993). Reconstructing social identity. *Personality and Social Psychology Bulletin, 19*, 4–12.

Deaux, K. (1996). Social identification. In E. T. Higgins & A. W. Kruglanski (Eds.), *Social psychology: Handbook of basic principles* (pp. 777–798). New York: Guilford Press.

Deaux, K., & Perkins, T. S. (2001). The kaleidoscopic self. In C. Sedikides & M. B. Brewer (Eds.), *Individual self, relational self, collective self* (pp. 299–313). Philadelphia, PA: Psychology Press.

DeBono, K. G., & Packer, M. (1991). The effects of advertising appeal on perceptions of product quality. *Personality and Social Psychology Bulletin, 17*, 194–200.

Diener, E., Diener, M., & Diener, C. (1995). Factors predicting the subjective well-being of nations. *Journal of Personality and Social Psychology, 69*, 851–864.

Dollinger, S. J., Preston, L. A., O'Brien, S. P., & DiLalla, D. L. (1996). Individuality and relatedness of the self: An autophotographic study. *Journal of Personality and Social Psychology, 71*, 1268–1278.

Duval, S., & Wicklund, R. A. (1972). *A theory of objective self-awareness*. New York: Academic Press.

Duval, T. S., & Silvia, P. J. (2001). *Self-awareness and causal attributions: A dual-systems theory*. Boston: Kluwer Academic.

Duval, T. S., & Silvia, P. J. (2002). Self-awareness, probability of improvement, and the self-serving bias. *Journal of Personality and Social Psychology, 82*, 49–61.

Eid, M., & Diener, E. (2001). Norms for experiencing emotions in different cultures: Inter- and intranational differences. *Journal of Personality and Social Psychology, 81*, 869–885.

Ethier, K. A., & Deaux, K. (1990). Hispanics in ivy: Assessing identity and perceived threat. *Sex Roles, 22*, 427–440.

Ethier, K. A., & Deaux, K. (1994). Negotiating social identity when contexts change: Maintaining identification and responding to threat. *Journal of Personality and Social Psychology, 67*, 243–251.

Fenigstein, A. (1979). Self-consciousness, self-attention, and social interaction. *Journal of Personality and Social Psychology, 37*, 75–86.

Fenigstein, A. (1984). Self-consciousness and the overprotection of the self as a target. *Journal of Personality and Social Psychology, 47*, 860–870.

Fenigstein, A., Scheier, M. F., & Buss, A. H. (1975). Public and private self-consciousness: Assessment and theory. *Journal of Consulting and Clinical Psychology, 43*, 522–527.

Fenigstein, A., & Vanable, P. A. (1992). Paranoia and self-consciousness. *Journal of Personality and Social Psychology, 62*, 129–138.

Flory, J. D., Raikkonen, K., Matthews, K. A., & Owens, J. F. (2000). Self-focused attention and mood during everyday social interactions. *Personality and Social Psychology Bulletin, 26*, 875–883.

Forman, B. D., & Crandall, J. E. (1986). Social interest, irrational beliefs, and identity. *Individual Psychology, 42*, 26–34.

Fox, S. (1984). *The mirror makers*. New York: Morrow.

Frable, D. E. S., Wortman, C., Joseph, J., Kirscht, J., & Kessler, R. (1997). Predicting self-esteem, well-being, and distress in a cohort of gay men: The importance of cultural stigma and personal visibility. *Journal of Personality, 65*, 599–624.

Franzoi, S. L., Anderson, J., & Frommelt, S. (1990). Individual differences in men's perception of and reactions to thinning hair. *Journal of Social Psychology, 130*, 209–219.

Froming, W. J., & Carver, C. S. (1981). Divergent influences of private and public self-consciousness in a compliance paradigm. *Journal of Research in Personality, 15*, 159–171.

Frone, M. R., & McFarlin, D. B. (1989). Chronic occupational stressors, self-focused attention, and well-being: Testing a cybernetic model of stress. *Journal of Applied Psychology, 74*, 876–883.

Gallaher, P. (1992). Individual differences in non-verbal behavior: Dimensions of style. *Journal of Personality and Social Psychology, 63*, 133–145.

Gallup, G. G. (1977). Self-recognition in primates: A comparative approach to the bidirectional properties of conscious. *American Psychologist, 32*, 329–338.

Gallup, G. G., Jr., & Suarez, S. D. (1986). Self-awareness and the emergence of mind in humans and other primates. In J. Suls & A. G. Greenwald (Eds.), *Psychological perspectives on the self: Vol. 3* (pp. 3–26). Hillsdale, NJ: Erlbaum.

Gardner, J. N., & Jewler, A. J. (2001). *Your college experience: Strategies for success* (4th ed.). Belmont CA: Wadsworth.

Gergen, K. J. (1971). *The concept of the self.* New York: Holt, Rinehart & Winston.

Gibbons, F. X., Smith, T. W., Ingram, R. E., Pearce, K., Brehm, S. S., & Schroeder, D. J. (1985). Self-awareness and self-confrontation: Effects of self-focused attention on members of a clinical population. *Journal of Personality and Social Psychology, 48*, 662–675.

Greenberg, J. (1983). Self-image versus impression-management in adherence to distributive justice standards. *Journal of Personality and Social Psychology, 44*, 5–19.

Gusnard, D. A. (2006). Neural substances of self-awareness. In J. T. Cacioppo, P. S. Visser, & C. L. Pickett (Eds.), *Social neuroscience: People thinking about people* (pp. 41–62). Cambridge, MA: MIT Press.

Harter, S. (1999). *The construction of the self: A developmental perspective.* New York: Guilford Press.

Heine, S. J., & Lehman, D. R. (1997). The cultural construction of self-enhancement: An examination of group-serving biases. *Journal of Personality and Social Psychology, 72*, 1268–1283.

Heine, S. J., Lehman, D. R., Markus, H. R., & Kitayama, S. (1999). Is there a universal need for positive self-regard? *Psychological Review, 106*, 766–794.

Hermans, H. J. (1996). Voicing the self: From information processing to dialogical interchange. *Psychological Bulletin, 119*, 31–50.

Higgins, E. T., & May, D. (2001). Individual self-regulatory functions: It's not "we" regulation, but it's still social. In C. Sedikides & M. B. Brewer (Eds.), *Individual self, relational self, and collective self* (pp. 47–67). Philadelphia, PA: Psychological Press.

Hogan, R., & Cheek, J. M. (1983). Identity, authenticity, and maturity. In T. R. Sarbin & K. E. Scheibe (Eds.), *Studies in social identity* (pp. 339–357). New York: Praeger.

Houghton, W. E. (1957). *The Victorian frame of mind: 1830–1870.* New Haven, CT: Yale University Press.

Hoyle, R., Kernis, M. H., Leary, M. R., & Baldwin, M. W. (1999). *Selfhood: Identity, esteem, regulation.* Boulder, CO: Westview Press.

Hugdahl, K. (2001). *Psychophysiology.* Cambridge, MA: Harvard University Press.

Hull, J. G., & Young, R. D. (1983). Self-consciousness, self-esteem, and success–failure as determinants of alcohol consumption in male social drinkers. *Journal of Personality and Social Psychology, 4*, 1097–1109.

Hull, J. G., Young, R. D., & Jouriles, E. (1986). Applications of the self-awareness model of alcohol consumption: Predicting patterns of use and abuse. *Journal of Personality and Social Psychology, 51*, 790–796.

James, W. (1890). *The principles of psychology: Vol. 1.* New York: Holt.

Jenkins, S. R. (1996). Self-definitions in thought, action, and life path choices. *Personality and Social Psychology Bulletin, 22*, 99–111.

Jewler, A. J., Gardner, J. N., & Owens, H. F. (1993). Keys to success. In A. J. Jewler & J. N. Gardner (Eds.), *Your college experience: Strategies for success* (pp. 1–22). Belmont, CA: Wadsworth.

Johnson, J. A. (1987). Influence of adolescent social crowds on the development of vocational identity. *Journal of Vocational Behavior, 31*, 182–199.

Jones, M. (1994). Linking dispositions and social behavior: Self-monitoring and advertising preferences. *Teaching of Psychology, 21*, 160–161.

Kagan, J. (1998). Is there a self in infancy? In M. Ferrari & R. J. Sternberg (Eds.), *Self-awareness: Its nature and development* (pp. 137–147). New York: Guilford Press.

Kagan, S., & Knight, G. P. (1979). Cooperation–competition and self-esteem: A case of cultural relativism. *Journal of Cross-Cultural Psychology, 10*, 457–467.

Kaplan, P. S. (2000). *A child's odyssey: Child and adolescent development* (3rd ed.). Belmont, CA: Wadsworth/Thomson Learning.

Karoly, P. (1993). Mechanisms of self-regulation: A systems view. *Annual Review of Psychology, 44*, 23–52.

Kashima, Y., Yamaguchi, S., Kim, U., Choi, S., Gelfand, M. J., & Yuki, M. (1995). Culture, gender, and self: A perspective from individualism–collectivism research. *Journal of Personality and Social Psychology, 69*, 925–937.

Katakis, C. D. (1984). *The three identities of the Greek family.* Athens, Greece: Kedros.

Kernis, M. H., & Reis, H. T. (1984). Self-consciousness, self-awareness, and justice in reward allocation. *Journal of Personality, 52*, 58–70.

Kitayama, S. (1992). Some thoughts on the cognitive-psychodynamic self from a cultural perspective. *Psychological Inquiry, 3*, 41–44.

Kitayama, S., Markus, H., Tummala, P., Kurokawa, M., & Kato, K. (1990). *Cultural and self-cognition.* Unpublished manuscript.

Klein, S. B., & Kihlstrom, J. F. (2002). On bridging the gap between social-personality psychology and neuropsychology. In J. T. Cacioppo, G. G. Berntson, R. Adolphs, C. S. Carter, R. J. Davidson, M. K. McClintock, et al. (Eds.), *Foundations in social neuroscience* (pp. 47–68). Cambridge, MA: MIT Press.

Klein, S. B., Loftus, J., & Kihlstrom, J. F. (1996). Self-knowledge of an amnesic patient: Toward a neuropsychology of personality and social psychology. *Journal of Experimental Psychology: General, 125*, 250–260.

Kowalski, R. M., & Wolfe, R. (1994). Collective identity orientations, patriotism, and reactions to national outcomes. *Personality and Social Psychology Bulletin, 20*, 533–540.

Lamphere, R. A., & Leary, M. R. (1990). Private and public self-processes: A return to James's constituents of the self. *Personality and Social Psychology Bulletin, 16*, 717–725.

Lapsley, D. K. Rice, K. G., & Fitzgerald, D. P. (1990). Adolescent attachment, identity, and adjustment to college: Implications for the continuity of adaptation hypothesis. *Journal of Counseling and Development, 68*, 561–565.

Latham, V. M. (1985, May). *The role of personality in the job-search process*. Paper presented at the annual meeting of the Midwestern Psychological Association, Chicago.

Leary, M. R., & Jones, J. L. (1993). The social psychology of tanning and sunscreen use: Self-presentation motives as a predictor of health risk. *Journal of Applied Social Psychology, 23*, 1390–1406.

Leary, M. R., Wheeler, D. S., & Jenkins, T. B. (1986). Aspects of identity and behavioral preference: Studies of occupational and recreational choice. *Social Psychology Quarterly, 49*, 11–18.

Lee, Y., & Seligman, M. E. P. (1997). Are Americans more optimistic than the Chinese? *Personality and Social Psychology Bulletin, 23*, 32–40.

Lefrancois, G. R. (2001). *Of children: An introduction to child and adolescent development* (9th ed.). Belmont, CA: Wadsworth/Thomson Learning.

Lewis, M., & Brooks-Gunn, J. (1979). *Social cognition and the acquisition of the sense of self*. New York: Plenum.

Lewis, M., Sullivan, M. W., Stranger, C., & Weiss, M. (1989). Self-development and self-conscious emotions. *Child Development, 60*, 146–156.

Lutwak, N., Razzino, B. E., & Ferrari, J. R. (1998). Self-perceptions and moral affect: An exploratory analysis of subculture diversity in guilt and shame emotions. *Journal of Social Behavior and Personality, 13*, 333–348.

Markus, H. R., & Kitayama, S. (1991). Culture and the self: Implications for cognition, emotion, and motivation. *Psychological Review, 98*, 224–253.

Markus, H. R., Kitayama, S., & Heiman, R. J. (1996). Culture and "basic" psychological principles. In E. T. Higgins & A. W. Kruglanski (Eds.), *Social psychology: Handbook of basic principles* (pp. 857–913). New York: Guilford Press.

Markus, H. R., & Wurf, E. (1987). The dynamic self-concept: A social psychological perspective. *Annual Review of Psychology, 38*, 299–337.

Masuda, T., & Nisbett, R. E. (2001). Attending holistically versus analytically: Comparing the context sensitivity of Japanese and Americans. *Journal of Personality and Social Psychology, 81*, 922–934.

McCann, C. D., & Hancock, R. D. (1983). Self-monitoring in communicative interactions: Social cognitive consequences of goal-directed message modification. *Journal of Experimental Social Psychology, 19*, 109–121.

McKillop, K. J., Berzonsky, M. D., & Schlenker, B. R. (1992). The impact of self-presentations on self-beliefs: Effects of social identity and self-presentational context. *Journal of Personality, 60*, 789–808.

Mellema, A., & Bassili, J. N. (1995). On the relationship between attitudes and values: Exploring the moderating effects of

self-monitoring and self-monitoring schematicity. *Personality and Social Psychology Bulletin, 9*, 885–892.

Menon, U., & Shweder, R. A. (1994). Kali's tongue: Cultural psychology and the power of shame in Orissa, India. In S. Kitayama & H. R. Markus (Eds.), *Emotion and culture: Empirical studies of mutual influence* (pp. 241–284). Washington, DC: American Psychological Association.

Mesquita, B. (2001). Emotions in collectivist and individualist contexts. *Journal of Personality and Social Psychology, 80*, 68–74.

Miller, J. G. (1984). Culture and the development of everyday social explanation. *Journal of Personality and Social Psychology, 46*, 961–978.

Miller, L. C., & Cox, C. L. (1982). For appearances' sake: Public self-consciousness and makeup use. *Personality and Social Psychology Bulletin, 8*, 748–751.

Mosquera, P. M. R., Manstead, A. S. R., & Fisher, A. H. (2000). The role of honor-related values in the elicitation, experience, and communication of pride shame, and anger: Spain and the Netherlands compared. *Personality and Social Psychology Bulletin, 26*, 833–844.

Mruk, C. J. (2006). *Self-esteem research, theory, and practice: Toward a positive psychology of self-esteem*. New York: Springer.

Mussweiler, T., & Strack, F. (2000). The "relative self": Informational and judgmental consequences of comparative self-evaluation. *Journal of Personality and Social Psychology, 79*, 23–38.

Nisbett, R. E., Peng, K., Choi, I., & Norenzayan, A. (2001). Culture and systems of thought: Holistic versus analytical cognition. *Psychological Review, 108*, 291–310.

Norzenzayan, A., & Nisbett, R. E. (2000). Culture and causal cognition. *Current Directions in Psychological Science, 9*, 132–135.

Osborne, R. E. (1996). *Self: An eclectic approach*. Boston: Allyn & Bacon.

Ouchi, W. G. (1981). *Theory Z: How American business can meet the Japanese challenge*. New York: Avon Books.

Pennebaker, J. W., Rimé, B., & Blankenship, V. E. (1996). Stereotypes of emotional expressiveness of northerners and southerners: A cross-cultural test of Montesquieu's hypotheses. *Journal of Personality and Social Psychology, 70*, 372–380.

Penner, L. A., & Wymer, W. E. (1983). The moderator variable approach to behavioral predictability: Some of the variables some of the time. *Journal of Research in Personality, 17*, 339–353.

Pervin, L. A. (2002). *Current controversies and issues in personality* (3rd ed.) New York: John Wiley.

Porterfield, A. L., Mayer, F. S., Dougherty, K. G., Kredich, K. G., Kronberg, M. M., Marsee, K. M., et al. (1988). Private self-consciousness, canned laughter, and responses to humorous stimuli. *Journal of Research in Personality, 22*, 409–423.

Povinelli, D. J., & Prince, C. G. (1998). When self met other. In M. Ferrari & R. J. Sternberg (Eds.), *Self-awareness: Its nature and development* (pp. 37–107). New York: Guilford Press.

Pryor, J. B., Gibbons, F. X., Wicklund, R. A., Fazio, R. H., & Hood, R. (1977). Self-focused attention and self-report validity. *Journal of Personality, 45*, 513–527.

Reddy, R., & Gibbons, J. L. (1995). *Socio-economic contexts and adolescent identity development in India*. Paper presented at the annual meeting of the Society for Cross-Cultural Research, Savannah, GA.

Roberts, B. W., & Helson, R. (1997). Changes in culture, changes in personality: The influence of individualism in a longitudinal study of women. *Journal of Personality and Social Psychology, 72*, 641–651.

Robins, R. W., Norem, J. K., & Cheek, J. M. (1999). Naturalizing the self. In L. A. Pervin & O. P. Oliver (Eds.), *Handbook of personality: Theory and research* (2nd ed., pp. 443–477). New York: Guilford Press.

Robins, R. W., Tracy, J. L., & Sherman, J. W. (2007). What kinds of methods do personality psychologists use? A survey of journal editors and editorial board members. In R. W. Robins, R. C. Fraley, & R. F. Krueger (Eds.), *Handbook of research methods in personality psychology* (pp. 673–678). New York: Guilford Press.

Robins, R. W., Tracy, J. L., & Trzesniewski, K. H. (2008). Naturalizing the self. In O. P. Oliver, R. W. Robins, & L. A. Pervin (Eds.), *Handbook of personality: Theory and research* (3rd ed., pp. 421–447). New York: Guilford Press.

Ross, A. O. (1992). *The search of self: Research and theory*. New York: Springer.

Roysircar-Sodowsky, G., & Maestas, M. V. (2000). Acculturation, ethnic identity, and acculturative stress: Evidence and measurement. In R. H. Danna (Ed.), *Handbook of cross-cultural and multicultural personality assessment* (pp. 131–172). Mahwah, NJ: Erlbaum.

Sampson, E. E. (1978). Personality and the location of identity. *Journal of Personality, 46*, 552–568.

Scheier, M. F. (1976). Self-awareness, self-consciousness, and angry aggression. *Journal of Personality, 44*, 627–644.

Scheier, M. F., Buss, A. H., & Buss, D. M. (1978). Self-consciousness, self-report of aggressiveness, and aggression. *Journal of Research in Personality, 12*, 133–140.

Scheier, M. F., & Carver, C. S. (1977). Self-focused attention and the experience of emotion: Attraction, repulsion, elation, and depression. *Journal of Personality and Social Psychology, 35*, 624–636.

Scheier, M. F., & Carver, C. S. (1980). Public and private self-attention, resistance to change, and dissonance reduction. *Journal of Personality and Social Psychology, 39*, 390–405.

Scheier, M. F., & Carver, C. S. (1985). The self-consciousness scale: A revised version for use with general populations. *Journal of Applied Social Psychology, 15*, 687–699.

Scheier, M. F., Carver, C. S., & Gibbons, F. X. (1979). Self-directed attention, awareness of bodily states, and suggestibility. *Journal of Personality and Social Psychology, 37*, 1576–1588.

Schlenker, B. R., & Weigold, M. F. (1990). Self-consciousness and self-presentation: Being autonomous versus appearing autonomous. *Journal of Personality and Social Psychology, 59*, 820–828.

Sedikides, C., & Skowronski, J. J. (1997). The symbolic self in evolutionary context. *Personality and Social Review, 1*, 80–102.

Sennett, R. (1974). *The fall of public man*. New York: Random House.

Shaffer, D. R., & Kipp, K. (2007). *Developmental psychology: Childhood and adolescence* (7th ed.). Belmont, CA: Thomson/Wadsworth.

Shikanai, K. (1978). Effects of self-esteem on attribution of success–failure. *Japanese Journal of Experimental Social Psychology, 18*, 47–55.

Silvia, P. J., & Gendolla, G. G. E. (2001). On introspection and self-perception: Does self-focused attention enable accurate self-knowledge? *Review of General Psychology, 5*, 241–269.

Simon, B., Loewy, M., Stürmer, S., Weber, U., Freytag, P., Habig, C., et al. (1998). Collective identification and social movement participation. *Journal of Personality and Social Psychology, 74*, 646–658.

Smith, J. D., & Shaffer, D. R. (1986). Self-consciousness, self-reported altruism, and helping. *Social Behavior and Personality, 14*, 215–220.

Snyder, M. (1974). The self-monitoring of expressive behavior. *Journal of Personality and Social Psychology, 30*, 526–537.

Snyder, M. (1987). *Public appearances/private realities: The psychology of self-monitoring*. New York: Freeman.

Snyder, M., Berscheid, E., & Matwychuk, A. (1985). Unpublished research. University of Minnesota.

Snyder, M., & DeBono, K. G. (1984). Unpublished research. University of Minnesota.

Snyder, M., & DeBono, K. G. (1985a). Unpublished research. University of Minnesota.

Snyder, M., & DeBono, K. G. (1985b). Appeals to image and claims about quality: Understanding the psychology of advertising. *Journal of Personality and Social Psychology, 49*, 586–597.

Snyder, M., & Gangestad, S. (1982). Choosing social situations: Two investigations of self-monitoring processes. *Journal of Personality and Social Psychology, 43*, 123–135.

Snyder, M., Nettle, R., & DeBono, K. G. (1985). Unpublished research, University of Minnesota.

Suddendorf, T., & Whiten, A. (2001). Mental evolution and development: Evidence for secondary representation in children, great apes, and other animals. *Psychological Bulletin, 127*, 629–650.

Takata, T. (1987). Self-deprecative tendencies in self-evaluation through social comparison. *Japanese Journal of Experimental Social Psychology, 27*, 27–36.

Tesser, A., Felson, R. B., & Suls, J. M. (Eds.). (2000). *Psychological perspectives on self and identity*. Washington, DC: American Psychological Association.

Tice, D. M., Buder, J., & Baumeister, R. F. (1985). Development of self-consciousness: At what age does audience pressure disrupt performance? *Adolescence, 20*, 301–305.

Tobey, E. L., & Tunnell, G. (1981). Predicting our impressions on others: Effects of public self-consciousness and acting, a self-monitoring subscale. *Personality and Social Psychology Bulletin, 7*, 661–669.

Trafimow, D., Triandis, H. C., & Goto, S. G. (1991). Some tests of the distinction between the private self and the collective self. *Journal of Personality and Social Psychology, 60*, 649–655.

Trapnell, P. D., & Campbell, J. D. (1999). Private self-consciousness and the Five Factor Model of personality: Distinguishing rumination from reflection. *Journal of Personality and Social Psychology, 76,* 284–304.

Triandis, H. C. (1989). The self and social behavior in differing cultural contexts. *Psychological Review, 96,* 506–520.

Triandis, H. C. (1995). *Individualism and collectivism.* Boulder, CO: Westview Press.

Triandis, H. C. (1996). The psychological measurement of cultural syndromes. *American Psychologist, 51,* 407–415.

Triandis, H. C. (1997). Cross-cultural perspectives on personality. In R. Hogan, J. Johnson, & S. Briggs (Eds.), *Handbook of personality psychology* (pp. 439–464). San Diego, CA: Academic Press

Triandis, H. C. (2001). Individualism–collectivism and personality. *Journal of Personality, 69,* 907–924.

Triandis, H. C., & Trafimow, D. (2001). Cross-national prevalence of collectivism. In C. Sedikides & M. B. Brewer (Eds.), *Individual self, relational self, collective self* (pp. 259–276). Philadelphia, PA: Psychology Press.

Tropp, L. R. (1992). *The construct of collective identity and its implications for Wellesley College context.* Unpublished BA Honor thesis, Wellesley College.

Tulving, E. (1993). Self-knowledge of an amnesic patient is represented abstractly. In T. K. Srull & R. S. Wyer (Eds.), *The mental representation of trait and autobiographical knowledge about the self: Advances in social cognition: Vol. 5* (pp. 147–156). Hillsdale, NJ: Erlbaum.

Turner, R. G., Gilliland, L., & Klein, H. M. (1981). Self-consciousness, evaluation of physical characteristics, and physical attractiveness. *Journal of Research in Personality, 15,* 182–190.

Velichkovsky, B. M., Klemm, T., Dettmar, P., & Volke, H. J. (1996). Evozierte koharenz des EEG II: Kommunikation der Hirnareale und Verarbeitungtiefe [Evoked coherence of EEG II: Communication of brain areas and depth of processing]. *Zeitschrift für EEG-EMG, 27,* 111–119.

Whyte, L. L. (1960). *The unconscious before Freud.* New York: Basic Books.

Wink, P. (1997). Beyond ethnic differences: Contextualizing the influence of ethnicity on individualism and collectivism. *Journal of Social Issues, 53,* 329–349.

Ybarra, O., & Trafimow, D. (1998). How priming the private self or collective self affects the relative weights of attitudes and subjective norms. *Personality and Social Psychology Bulletin, 24,* 362–370.

Yik, M. S. M., Bond, M. H., & Paulhus, D. L. (1998). Do Chinese self-enhance or self-efface? It's a matter of domain. *Personality and Social Psychology Bulletin, 24,* 399–406.

Zanna, M. P., & Olson, J. M. (1982). Individual differences in attitudinal relations. In M. P. Zanna, E. T. Higgins, & C. P. Herman (Eds.), *Consistency in social behavior: The Ontario symposium: Vol. 2* (pp. 75–104). Hillsdale, NJ: Erlbaum.

Zillmer, E. A., & Spiers, M. V. (2001). *Principles of neuropsychology.* Belmont, CA: Wadsworth/Thompon Learning.

Chapter 12

Abele, A. E. (2000). A dual-impact model of gender and career-related processes. In T. Eckes & H. M. Trautner (Eds.), *The developmental social psychology of gender* (pp. 361–388). Mahwah, NJ: Erlbaum.

Abramson, P. R., Goldberg, P. A., Greenberg, J. H., & Abramson, L. M. (1977). The talking platypus phenomenon: Competency ratings as a function of sex and professional status. *Psychology of Women Quarterly, 2,* 114–124.

Adelman, C. (1991). *Woman at thirtysomething: Paradoxes of attainment.* Washington, DC: Department of Education.

Adler, P., Kless, S., & Adler, P. (1992). Socialization to gender roles: Popularity among elementary school boys and girls. *Sociology of Education, 65,* 169–187.

Allgood-Merten, B., & Stockard, J. (1991). Sex role identity and self-esteem: A comparison of children and adolescents. *Sex Roles, 25,* 129–139.

Anderman, E. M., Eccles, J. S., Yoon, K. S., Roeser, R, Wigfield, A., & Blumenfeld, P. (2001). Learning to value mathematics and reading: Relations to mastery and performance-oriented instructional practices. *Contemporary Educational Psychology, 26,* 76–95.

Antill, J. T. (1983). Sex role complementarity versus similarity in married couples. *Journal of Personality and Social Psychology, 45,* 145–155.

Archer, J. (1988). *The behavioral biology of aggression.* Cambridge, UK: Cambridge University Press.

Bailey, J. M., Kirk, K. M., Zhu, G., Dunne, M. P., & Martin, N. G. (2000). Do individual differences in sociosexuality represent genetic or environmentally contingent strategies? *Journal of Personality and Social Psychology, 78,* 537–545.

Bandura, A. (1986). *Social foundations of thought and action: A social cognitive theory.* Englewood Cliffs, NJ: Prentice Hall.

Bandura, A. (1989). Social cognitive theory. In R. Vasta (Ed.), *Annals of child development: Theories of child development: Revised formulations and current issues: Vol. 6* (pp. 1–60). Greenwich, CT: JAI.

Bandura, A. (1999). Social cognitive theory of personality. In L. A. Pervin & O. P. John (Eds.), *Handbook of personality: Theory and research* (2nd ed., pp. 154–196). New York: Guilford Press.

Bandura, A. (2001). Social cognitive theory: An agentic perspective. *Annual Review of Psychology, 52,* 1–26.

Bandura, A. (2002). Social cognitive theory in cultural context. *Journal of Applied Psychology: An International Review, 51,* 269–290.

Bandura, A., & Bussey, K. (2004). On broadening the cognitive, motivational, and sociostructural scope of theorizing about gender development and functioning: Comment on Martin, Ruble, and Szkrybalo (2002). *Psychological Bulletin, 130,* 691–701.

Barash, D. P. (1982). *Sociobiology and behavior* (2nd ed.). New York: Elsevier.

Baron, R. A., Byrne, D., & Branscombe, N. R. (2006). *Social psychology* (11th ed.). Boston: Allyn & Bacon.

Baron, R. A., & Richardson, D. R. (1994). *Human aggression* (2nd ed.). New York: Plenum.

Barrett, L. F., Lane, R., Sechrest, L., & Schwartz, G. (2000). Sex differences in emotional awareness. *Personality and Social Psychology Bulletin, 26,* 1027–1035.

Baumeister, R. F., & Tice, D. M. (2001). *The social dimension of sex.* Boston: Allyn & Bacon.

Bell, L. C. (2004). Psychoanalytic theories of gender. In A. H. Eagly, A. E. Beall, & R. J. Sternberg (Eds.), *The psychology of gender* (2nd ed., pp. 145–168). New York: London.

Bem, S. L. (1974). The measurement of psychological androgyny. *Journal of Consulting and Clinical Psychology, 42,* 155–162.

Bem, S. L. (1975). Sex-role adaptability: One consequence of psychological androgyny. *Journal of Personality and Social Psychology, 31,* 634–643.

Bem, S. L. (1977). On the utility of alternative procedures for assessing psychological androgyny. *Journal of Personality and Social Psychology, 45,* 196–205.

Bem, S. L. (1978). Beyond androgyny: Some presumptuous prescriptions for a liberated sexual identity. In J. Sherman & F. Denmark (Eds.), *Psychology of women: Future directions of research* (pp. 1–23). New York: Psychological Dimensions.

Bem, S. L. (1981). Gender schema theory: A cognitive account of sex typing. *Psychological Review, 88,* 354–364.

Bem, S. L. (1983). Gender schema theory and its implications for child development: Raising gender-aschematic children in a gender-schematic society. *Signs: Journal of Women in Culture and Society, 8,* 598–616.

Bem, S. L. (1985). Androgyny and gender schema theory: A conceptual and empirical integration. In R. A. Dienstbier (Series Ed.) & T. B. Sonderegger (Vol. Ed.), *Nebraska symposium on motivation: Vol. 32. Psychology and gender* (pp. 179–226). Lincoln: University of Nebraska Press.

Bem, S. L. (1987). Gender schema theory and the romantic tradition. In P. Shaver & C. Hendrick (Eds.), *Sex and gender: Review of personality and social psychology: Vol. 7* (pp. 251–271). Beverly Hills, CA: Sage.

Bem, S. L. (1993). *The lenses of gender: Transforming the debate on sexual inequality.* New Haven, CT: Yale University Press.

Bem, S. L., & Lenney, E. (1976). Sex-typing and the avoidance of cross-sex behavior. *Journal of Personality and Social Psychology, 33,* 48–54.

Bem, S. L., Martyna, W., & Watson, C. (1976). Sex-typing and androgyny: Further explorations of the expressive domain. *Journal of Personality and Social Psychology, 34,* 1016–1023.

Benbow, C. P. (1988). Sex differences in mathematical reasoning ability in intellectually talented preadolescents: Their nature, effects, and possible causes. *Behavioral and Brain Sciences, 11,* 169–232.

Benbow, C. P., & Stanley, J. C. (1980). Sex differences in mathematical ability: Fact or artifact? *Science, 210,* 1262–1264.

Benjamin, J. (1998). *Shadow of the other: Intersubjectivity and gender in psychoanalysis.* New York: Routledge.

Berkowitz, L. (1993). *Aggression: Its causes, consequences, and control.* New York: McGraw-Hill.

Bettencourt, B. A., & Miller, N. (1996). Gender differences in aggression as a function of provocation: A meta-analysis. *Psychological Bulletin, 119,* 422–447.

Biernat, M., & Vescio, T. K. (2002). She swings, she hits, she's great, she's benched: Implications of gender-based shifting standards for judgment and behavior. *Personality and Social Psychology Bulletin, 28,* 66–77.

Billimoria, D., & Piderit, S. K. (1994). Board committee membership: Effects of sex-based bias. *Academy of Management Journal, 37,* 1453–1477.

Block, J. H. (1976). Issues, problems and pitfalls in assessing sex differences. *Merrill-Palmer Quarterly, 22,* 283–308.

Bogard, M. (1990). Why we need gender to understand human violence. *Journal of Interpersonal Violence, 5,* 132–135.

Boldizar, J. P. (1991). Assessing sex-typing and androgyny in children: The children's sex-role inventory. *Developmental Psychology, 27,* 505–515.

Brehm, S. S., Kassin, S., & Fein, S. (2005). *Social psychology* (6th ed.). Boston: Houghton Mifflin.

Brehm, S. S., Miller, R. S., Perlman, D., & Campbell, S. M. (2002). *Intimate relationships* (3rd ed.). Boston: McGraw-Hill.

Bretl, D. J., & Cantor, J. (1988). The portrayal of men and women in U.S. television commercials: A recent content analysis and trends over 15 years. *Sex Roles, 18,* 595–609.

Brody, L. (1999). *Gender, emotion, and the family.* Cambridge, MA: Harvard University Press.

Brody, L. R., & Hall, J. (2000). Gender, emotion, and expression. In M. Lewis & J. Haviland-Jones (Eds.), *Handbook of emotions* (pp. 338–349). New York: Guilford Press.

Brodzinsky, D. N., Messer, S. B., & Tew, J. D. (1979). Sex differences in children's expression and control of fantasy and overt aggression. *Child Development, 50,* 372–379.

Bromberger, J. T., & Matthews, K. A. (1996). A "feminine" model of vulnerability to depressive symptoms: A longitudinal investigation of middle-aged women. *Journal of Personality and Social Psychology, 70,* 591–598.

Broverman, I. K., Vogel, S. R., Broverman, D. M., Clarkson, F. E., & Rosenkrantz, P. S. (1972). Sex-role stereotypes: A current appraisal. *Journal of Social Issues, 28,* 59–78.

Buntaine, R. L., & Costenbader, V. K. (1997). Self-reported differences in the experience and expression of anger between girls and boys. *Sex Roles, 36,* 625–638.

Buss, A. H. (1995). *Personality: Temperament, social behavior, and the self.* Boston: Allyn & Bacon.

Buss, A. H. (2001). *Psychological dimensions of the self.* Thousands Oaks, CA: Sage.

Buss, D. M. (1994). The strategies of human mating. *American Scientist, 82,* 238–249.

Buss, D. M. (1995). Psychological sex differences: Origins through sexual selection. *American Psychologist, 50,* 164–168.

Buss, D. M. (1998). The psychology of human mate selection: Exploring the complexity of the strategic repertoire. In

C. Crawford & D. L. Krebs (Eds.), *Handbook of evolutionary psychology: Ideas, issues, and applications* (pp. 405–429). Mahwah, NJ: Erlbaum.

Buss, D. M. (2000). *The dangerous passion: Why jealousy is as necessary as love and sex.* New York: Free Press.

Buss, D. M. (2003). *The evolution of desire: Strategies of human mating* (rev. ed.). New York: Basic Books.

Buss, D. M. (2004). *Evolutionary psychology: The new science of the mind* (2nd ed.). New York: John Wiley.

Buss, D. M. (Ed.). (2005). *The handbook of evolutionary psychology.* Hoboken, NJ: John Wiley.

Buss, D. M., Larsen, R. J., Semmelroth, J., & Westen, D. (1992). Sex differences in jealousy: Evolution, physiology, and psychology. *Psychological Science, 3,* 251–255.

Buss, D. M., & Schmitt, D. P. (1993). Sexual strategies theory: An evolutionary perspective on human mating. *Psychological Review, 100,* 204–232.

Buss, D. M., Shackelford, T. K., Kirkpatrick, L. A., Choe, J., Hasegawa, M., Hasegawa, T., et al. (1999). Jealousy and the nature of beliefs about infidelity: Tests of competing hypotheses about sex differences in the United States, Korea, and Japan. *Personal Relations, 6,* 125–150.

Bussey, K., & Bandura, A. (1984). Influence on gender constancy and social power on sex-linked modeling. *Journal of Personality and Social Psychology, 47,* 1292–1302.

Bussey, K., & Bandura, A. (1992). Self-regulatory mechanisms governing gender development. *Child Development, 63,* 1236–1250.

Bussey, K., & Bandura, A. (1999). Social cognitive theory of gender development and differentiation. *Psychological Review, 106,* 676–713.

Bussey, K., & Bandura, A. (2004). Social cognitive theory of gender development and functioning. In A. H. Eagly, A. E. Beall, & R. J. Sternberg (Eds.), *The psychology of gender* (2nd ed., pp. 92–119). New York: Guilford Press.

Bussey, K., & Perry, D. G. (1982). Same-sex imitation: The avoidance of cross-sex models or the acceptance of same-sex models? *Sex Roles, 8,* 773–794.

Buunk, B., Angleitner, A., Oubaid, V., & Buss, D. M. (1996). Sexual and cultural differences in jealousy: Tests from the Netherlands, Germany, and the United States. *Psychological Science, 7,* 359–363.

Buunk, B. P., Dukstra, P., Fetchenhauer, D., & Kendrick, D. T. (2002). Age and gender differences in mate selection criteria for various involvement levels. *Personal Relationships, 9,* 271–278.

Bylsma, W. H., Major, B., & Cozzarelli, C. (1995). The influence of legitimacy appraisals on determinants of entitlement beliefs. *Basic Applied Social Psychology, 17,* 223–237.

Cameron, J. A., Alvarez, J. M., Ruble, D. N., & Fuligni, A. J. (2001). Children's lay theories about ingroups and outgroups: Reconceptualizing research on "prejudice." *Personality and Social Psychology Review, 5,* 118–128.

Campbell, A. (2005). Aggression. In D. M. Buss (ed.), *The handbook of evolutionary psychology* (pp. 628–652). Hoboken, NJ: John Wiley.

Campbell, L., & Ellis, B. J. (2005). Commitment, love, and mate retention. In D. M. Buss (ed.), *The handbook of evolutionary psychology* (pp. 419–442). Hoboken, NJ: John Wiley.

Carli, L. L. (1981, August). *Sex differences in small group interaction.* Paper presented at the 89th Annual Meeting of the American Psychological Association, Los Angeles.

Carli, L. L. (1989). Gender differences in interaction style and influence. *Journal of Personality and Social Psychology, 56,* 565–576.

Carli, L. L. (1990). Gender, language, and influence. *Journal of Personality and Social Psychology, 59,* 941–951.

Carli, L. L., & Bukatko, D. (2000). Gender, communication, and social influence: A developmental perspective. In T. Eckes & H. M. Trautner (Eds.), *The developmental social psychology of gender* (pp. 295–331). Mahwah, NJ: Erlbaum.

Carmickle, M., & Carducci, B. J. (1993, March). *Examining the internal structure of and gender differences in the Multidimensional Jealousy Scale.* Paper presented at the meeting of the Southeastern Psychological Association, Atlanta.

Chatzky, J. (2003). *You don't have to be rich: Comfort, happiness, and financial security on your own terms.* New York: Portfolio-Penguin.

Chen, C. (2005). Processes underlying gender-role flexibility: Do androgynous individuals know more or know how to cope? *Journal of Personality, 73,* 645–673.

Chodorow, N. J. (1978). *The reproduction of mothering.* Berkeley: University of California Press.

Chodorow, N. J. (1999a). From subjectivity in general to subjective gender in particular. In D. Bassin (Ed.), *Female sexuality: Contemporary engagements* (pp. 241–250). Northvale, NJ: Jason Aronson.

Chodorow, N. J. (1999b). *The power of feelings: Personal meaning in psychoanalysis, gender, and culture.* New Haven, CT: Yale University Press.

Colapinto, J. (2000). *As nature made him: The boy who was raised as a girl.* New York: HarperCollins.

Comer, R. J. (2007). *Abnormal psychology* (5th ed.). New York: Worth.

Correll, S. J. (2001). Gender and the career choice process: The role of biased self-assessment. *American Journal of Sociology, 106,* 1691–1730.

Costa, P. T., Terracciano, A., & McCrae, R. R. (2001). Gender differences in personality traits across cultures. *Journal of Personality and Social Psychology, 81,* 322–331.

Crocker, J., Major, B., & Steele, C. (1998). Social stigma. In D. T. Gilbert, S. T. Fiske, & G. Lindzey (Eds.), *Handbook of social psychology: Vol. 2* (4th ed., pp. 504–553). Boston: McGraw-Hill.

Crutchfield, R. A. (1955). Conformity and character. *American Psychologist, 10,* 191–198.

Cuddy, A. J. C., Norton, M. I., & Fiske, S. T. (2005). This old stereotype: The pervasiveness and persistence of the elderly stereotype. *Journal of Social Issues, 61,* 267–285.

Dabbs, J., M., Jr., & Dabbs, M. G. (2000). *Heroes, rogues and lovers: Testosterone and behavior.* New York: McGraw-Hill.

Dacey, J., Kenny, M., & Margolis, D. (2000). *Adolescent development* (3rd ed.). Carrolton, TX: Alliance Press.

Davies, P. G., Spencer, S. J., Quinn, D. M., & Gerhardstein, R. (2002). Consuming images: How television commercials that elicit stereotype threat can restrain women academically and professionally. *Personality and Social Psychology Bulletin, 28,* 1615–1628.

Davies, P. G., Spencer, S. J., & Steele, C. M. (2005). Clearing the air: Identity safety moderates the effects of stereotype threat on women's leadership aspirations. *Journal of Personality and Social Psychology, 88,* 276–287.

Davies, T. L. (1995). Gender differences in masking negative emotions: Ability or motivation? *Developmental Psychology, 31,* 660–667.

Davison, G. C., Neale, J. M., & Kring, A. M. (2004). *Abnormal psychology* (9th ed.). Hoboken, NJ: John Wiley.

Deaux, K. (1982, August). *Sex as a social category: Evidence for gender stereotypes.* Paper presented at the meeting of the American Psychological Association, Washington, DC.

Deaux, K., & Emswiller, T. (1974). Explanations of successful performance on sex-linked tasks: What is skill for the male is luck for the female. *Journal of Personality and Social Psychology, 29,* 80–85.

Deaux, K., & Kite, M. E. (1993). Gender stereotypes. In M. A. Paludi & F. Denmark (Eds.), *Psychology of women: A handbook of issues and theories* (pp. 107–139). Westport, CT: Greenwood Press.

Deaux, K., & LaFrance, M. (1998). Gender. In D. T. Gilbert, S. T. Fiske, & G. Lindzey (Eds.), *The handbook of social psychology: Vol. 1* (4th ed., pp. 788–827). Boston: McGraw-Hill.

Delgado, A. R., & Prieto, G. (2004). Cognitive mediators and sex-related differences in mathematics. *Intelligence, 32,* 25–32.

DeSteno, D. A., & Salovey, P. (1996). Evolutionary origins of sex differences in jealousy: Questioning the fitness of the model. *Psychological Science, 7,* 367–372.

DeSteno, D. A., Bartlett, M. Y., Salovey, P., & Braverman, J. (2002). Sex differences in jealousy: Evolutionary mechanism or artifact of measurement? *Journal of Personality and Social Psychology, 83,* 1103–1116.

Diamond, M. (1982). Sexual identity, monozygotic twins reared in discordant sex-roles and a BBC follow up. *Archives of Sexual Behavior, 11,* 181–186.

Diamond, M. (1996). Prenatal predisposition and the clinical management of some pediatric conditions. *Journal of Sex and Marital Therapy, 22,* 139–147.

Diamond, M. (1999). Pediatric management of ambiguous and traumatized genitalia. *Journal of Urology, 162,* 1021–1028.

Diamond, M., & Sigmundson, H. K. (1997). Sex reassignment at birth: Long-term review and clinical implications. *Archives of Pediatric and Adolescent Medicine, 151,* 298–304.

Diener, E. (2000). Subjective well-being: The science of happiness and a proposal for a national index. *American Psychologist, 55,* 34–43.

Diener, E., Sandvik, E., & Larsen, R. J. (1985). Age and sex effects for emotional intensity. *Development Psychology, 21,* 542–546.

Dimitrovsky, L., Singer, J., & Yinon, Y. (1989). Masculine and feminine traits: Their relation to suitedness for and success

in training for traditionally masculine and feminine army functions. *Journal of Personality and Social Psychology, 57,* 839–847.

Dion, K. L., & Dion, K. K. (1973). Correlates of romantic love. *Journal of Consulting and Clinical Psychology, 41,* 51–56.

Dion, K. L., & Dion, K. K. (1975). Self-esteem and romantic love. *Journal of Personality, 43,* 39–57.

Dipboye, R. L., Fromkin, H. L., & Wiback, K. (1975). Relative importance of applicant sex, attractiveness, and scholastic standing in evaluations of job applicant resumes. *Journal of Applied Psychology, 60,* 39–43.

Dorans, N. J., & Livingston, S. A. (1987). Male–female differences in SAT-verbal ability among students of high SAT-mathematical ability. *Journal of Educational Measurement, 24,* 65–71.

Eagly, A. H. (1987). *Sex differences in social behavior: A social-role interpretation.* Hillsdale, NJ: Erlbaum.

Eagly, A. H. (1995). The science and politics of comparing men and women. *American Psychologist, 50,* 145–158.

Eagly, A. H. (1997). Sex differences in social behavior: Comparing social role theory and evolutionary psychology. *American Psychologist, 52,* 1380–1383.

Eagly, A. H., Beall, A. E., & Sternberg, R. J. (Eds.). (2004). *The psychology of gender* (2nd ed.). New York: Guilford Press.

Eagly, A. H., & Carli, L. L. (1981). Sex of researchers and sex-typed communications as determinants of sex differences in influenceability: A meta-analysis of social influence studies. *Psychological Bulletin, 90,* 971–981.

Eagly, A. H., & Karau, S. J. (1991). Gender and leadership style: A meta-analysis. *Journal of Personality and Social Psychology, 60,* 685–710.

Eagly, A. H., & Karau, S. J. (2000). *Few women at the top: Is prejudice a cause?* Unpublished manuscript, Northwestern University.

Eagly, A. H., & Karau, S. J. (2002). Role congruity theory of prejudice toward female leaders. *Psychological Review, 109,* 573–598.

Eagly, A. H., & Mladinic, A. (1994). Are people prejudiced against women? Some answers from research on attitudes, gender stereotypes, and judgments of competence. In W. Sroebe & M. Hewstone (Eds.), *European review of social psychology: Vol. 5* (pp. 1–35). New York: John Wiley.

Eagly, A. H., & Steffen, V. J. (1986). Gender and aggressive behavior: A meta-analytic review of the social psychological literature. *Psychological Bulletin, 100,* 309–330.

Eagly, A. H., Wood, W., & Diekman, A. B. (2000). Social role theory of sex differences and similarities: A current appraisal. In T. Eckes & H. M. Trautner (Eds.), *The developmental social psychology of gender* (pp. 123–174). Mahwah, NJ: Erlbaum.

Eagly, A. H., Wood, W., & Johannesen-Schmidt, M. C. (2004). Social role theory of sex differences and similarities: Implications for the partner preferences of men and women. In A. H. Eagly, A. E. Beall, & R. J. Sternberg (Eds.), *The psychology of gender* (2nd ed., pp. 269–295). New York: Guilford Press.

Eccles, J. S. (1989). Bringing young women to math and science. In M. Crawford & M. Gentry (Eds.), *Gender and thought: Psychological perspectives* (pp. 36–58). New York: Springer.

Eccles, J. S., Freedman-Doan, C., Frome, P., Jacobs, J., & Yoon, K. S. (2000). Gender-role socialization in the family: A longitudinal approach. In T. Eckes & H. M. Trautner (Eds.), *The developmental social psychology of gender* (pp. 333–360). Mahwah, NJ: Erlbaum.

Eckes, T., & Trautner, H. M. (Eds.). (2000). *The developmental social psychology of gender.* Mahwah, NJ: Erlbaum.

Ecuyer-Dab, I., & Robert, M. (2004). Spatial ability and home-range size: Examining the relationship in Western men and women (*Homo sapiens*). *Journal of Comparative Psychology, 118,* 217–231.

Ehrhardt, A. A. (1985). The psychobiology of gender. In A. S. Rossi (Ed.), *Gender and the life course.* New York: Aldine.

Etcoff, N. (1999). *Survival of the prettiest: The science of beauty.* New York: Doubleday.

Evans, M. A., Metindogan, A., & Carter, D. B. (2003, April). *Gender constancy and sex-typed preferences: A meta-analytic integration.* Paper presented at the meeting of the Society for Research in Child Development, Tampa, FL.

Fagot, B. I. (1977). *Sex-determined parental reinforcing contingencies in toddler children.* Paper presented at the biennial meeting of the Society for Research in Child Development, New Orleans.

Fagot, B. I., & Hagan, R. (1991). Observations of parental reactions to sex-stereotyped behaviors: Age and sex effects. *Child Development, 62,* 617–628.

Fagot, B. I., & Leinbach, M. D. (1989). The young child's gender schema: Environmental input, internal organization. *Child Development, 60,* 663–672.

Fagot, B. I., Rodgers, C. S., & Leinbach, M. D. (2000). Theories of gender socialization. In T. Eckes & H. M. Trautner (Eds.), *The developmental social psychology of gender* (pp. 65–89). Mahwah, NJ: Erlbaum.

Federal Bureau of Investigation (1997). *Uniform crime reports of the United States 1996.* Washington, DC: U.S. Department of Justice.

Felson, R. B. (2002). *Violence and gender reexamined.* Washington, DC: American Psychological Association.

Fischer, A. H., & Manstead, A. (2000). The relation between gender and emotions in different cultures. In A. Fischer (ed.), *Gender and emotion* (pp. 71–94). Cambridge, UK: Cambridge University Press.

Fiske, S. T., Bersoff, D. N., Borgida, E., Deaux, K., & Heilman, M. E. (1991). Social science research on trial: Use of sex stereotyping research in Price Waterhouse v. Hopkins. *American Psychologist, 46,* 1049–1060.

Fiske, S. T., Cuddy, A. J. C., Glick, P., & Xu, J. (2002). A model of (often mixed) stereotype content: Competence and warmth respectively follow from perceived status and competition. *Journal of Personality and Social Psychology, 82,* 878–902.

Fiske, S. T., & Taylor, S. E. (1991). *Social cognition* (2nd ed.). New York: McGraw-Hill.

Flaherty, J. F., & Dusek, J. B. (1980). An investigation of the relationship between psychological androgyny and components of

self-concept. *Journal of Personality and Social Psychology, 38,* 984–999.

Fletcher, G. J. O., Tither, J. M., O'Loughlin, C., Friesen, M., & Overall, N. (2004). Warm and homely or cold and beautiful? Sex differences in trading off traits in mate selection. *Personality and Social Psychology Bulletin, 30,* 659–672.

Frable, D. E. S., & Bem, S. L. (1985). If you're gender schematic, all members of the opposite sex look alike. *Journal of Personality and Social Psychology, 49,* 459–468.

Fredricks, J. A., & Eccles, J. S. (2002). Children's competence and value beliefs from childhood through adolescence: Growth trajectories in two male-sex-typed domains. *Developmental Psychology, 38,* 519–533.

Fuchs, D., & Thelen, M. H. (1988). Children's expected interpersonal consequences of communicating their affective state and reported likelihood of expression. *Child Development, 59,* 1314–1322.

Galliher, R. V., Rostosky, S. S., & Hughes, H. K. (2004). School belonging, self-esteem, and depressive sysmptoms in adolescents: An examination of sex, sexual attraction status, and urbanicity. *Journal of Youth and Adolescent, 33,* 235–245.

Garcia, L. T. (1982). Sex role orientation and stereotypes about male–female sexuality. *Sex Roles, 8,* 863–876.

Garland, H., & Price, K. H. (1977). Attitudes toward women in management and attributions for their success and failure in a managerial position. *Journal of Applied Psychology, 62,* 29–33.

Garnets, L., & Peck, J. (1979). Sex role identity, androgyny, and sex role transcendence: A sex role strain analysis. *Psychology of Women Quarterly, 3,* 270–283.

Glaude, B. A. (1991). Aggressive behavioral characteristics, hormones, and sexual orientation in men and women. *Aggressive Behavior, 17,* 313–326.

Glick, P., & Fiske, S. T. (1996). The Ambivalent Sexism Inventory: Differentiating hostile and benevolent sexism. *Journal of Personality and Social Psychology, 70,* 491–512.

Glick, P., & Fiske, S. T. (2001). Ambivalent sexism. In M. P. Zanna (Ed.), *Advances in experimental social psychology: Vol. 33* (pp. 115–188). San Diego, CA: Academic Press.

Glick, P., Fiske, S. T., Mladinic, A., Saiz, J., Abrams, D., Masser, B., et al. (2000). Beyond prejudice as simple antipathy: Hostile and benevolent sexism across cultures. *Journal of Personality and Social Psychology, 79,* 763–775.

Glick, P., Zion, C., & Nelson, C. (1988). What mediates sex discrimination in hiring decisions. *Journal of Personality and Social Psychology, 2,* 178–186.

Goldberg, P. A. (1968). Are women prejudiced against women? *Transaction, 5,* 28–30.

Goldschmidt, O. T., & Weller, L. (2000). "Talking emotions": Gender differences in a variety of conversational contexts. *Symbolic Interaction, 23,* 117–134.

Goldstein, E. B. (2005). *Cognitive psychology: Connecting mind, research, and everyday experience.* Belmont, CA: Thomson/Wadsworth.

Goodwin, S. A., & Fiske, S. T. (2001). Power and gender: The double-edged sword of ambivalence. In R. K. Unger (Ed.), *Handbook of the psychology of women and gender* (pp. 358–366). New York: John Wiley.

Graves, L. M. (1999). Gender bias in interviews' evaluations of applicants. In G. N. Powell (Ed.), *Handbook of gender and work* (pp. 145–164). Thousand Oaks, CA: Sage.

Green, L. R., Richardson, D. R., & Lago, T. (1996). How do friendship, indirect, and direct aggression relate? *Aggressive Behavior, 22,* 81–86.

Halpern, D. F. (2000). *Sex differences in cognitive abilities* (3rd ed.). Mahwah, NJ: Erlbaum.

Halpern, D. F. (2003). Sex differences in cognitive abilities. *Applied Cognitive Psychology, 17,* 375–376.

Halpern, D. F. (2004). A cognitive-process taxonomy for sex differences in cognitive abilities. *Current Directions in Psychological Science, 13,* 135–139.

Halpern, D. F., & LeMay, M. L. (2000). The smarter sex: A critical review of sex differences in intelligence. *Educational Psychology Review, 12,* 229–246.

Hanko, K., Master, S., & Sabini, J. (2004). Some evidence about character and mate selection. *Personality and Social Psychology Bulletin, 30,* 732–742.

Haring, M. J., Stock, W. A., & Okun, M. A. (1984). A research synthesis of gender and social class as correlates of subjective well-being. *Human Relations, 37,* 645–657.

Harlow, H. F., & Suomi, S. J. (1971). Social recovery by isolated-reared monkeys. *Proceedings of the National Academy of Sciences, U.S.A., 68,* 1534–1538.

Harris, M. B. (1992). Sex, race, and experiences of aggression. *Aggressive Behavior, 18,* 201–217.

Harris, M. B. (1994). Gender of subject and target as mediators of aggression. *Journal of Applied Social Psychology, 24,* 453–471.

Harvey, J. H., Flanary, R., & Morgan, M. (1986). Vivid memories of vivid loves gone by. *Journal of Social and Personal Relationships, 3,* 359–373.

Hatfield, E., & Specher, S. (1986). Measuring passionate love in intimate relationships. *Journal of Adolescence, 9,* 383–410.

Hatfield, E., Sprecher, S., Pillemer, J. T., Greenberger, D., & Wexler, P. (1989). Gender differences in what is desired in sexual relationships. *Journal of Psychology and Human Sexuality, 1,* 39–52.

Heilman, M. E., Block, C. J., Martell, R. F., & Simon, M. C. (1989). Has anything changed? Current categorizations of men, women, and managers. *Journal of Applied Psychology, 74,* 935–942.

Helgeson, V. S. (2003). Gender-related traits and health. In J. Suls & K. A. Wallston (Eds.), *Social psychological foundations of health and illness* (pp. 367–394). Oxford: Blackwell.

Hendrick, C., Hendrick, S. S., & Dicke, A. (1998). The Love Attitude Scale: Short Form. *Journal of Social and Personal Relationships, 15,* 147–159.

Hines, M. (2002). Sexual differentiation of human brain and behavior. In D. W. Pfaff, A. P. Arnold, A. M. Etgen, S. E. Fahrbach, & R. T. Rubin (Eds.), *Hormones, brain, and behavior* (4th ed., pp. 425–461). San Diego, CA: Academic Press.

Hines, M. (2004). Androgen, estrogen, and gender: Contributions of the early hormone environment to gender-related behavior. In A. H. Eagly, A. E. Beal, & R. J. Sternberg (Eds.), *The psychology of gender* (2nd ed., pp. 10–37). New York: Guilford Press.

Hinsz, V. B., Matz, D. C., & Patience, R. A. (2001). Does a woman's hair design signal reproductive potential? *Journal of Experimental Social Psychology, 37,* 166–172.

Hoffmann, J. P. (2002). The dynamics of self-esteem: A growth-curve analysis. *Journal of Youth and Adolescence, 31,* 101–114.

Hrdy, S. B. (1999). *Mother nature: Maternal instincts and how they shaped the human species.* New York: Ballantine.

Hughes, S. M., Harrison, M. A., & Gallup, G. G., Jr. (2002). The sound of symmetry: Voice as a marker of developmental instability. *Evolution and Human Behavior, 23,* 173–180.

Hyde, J. S. (1986). Gender differences in aggression. In J. S. Hyde & M. C. Linn (Eds.), *The psychology of gender: Advances through meta-analysis* (pp. 51–66). Baltimore: Johns Hopkins University Press.

Hyde, J. S. (2004). *Half the human experience: The psychology of women* (6th ed.). Boston: Houghton Mifflin.

Hyde, J. S. (2005). The gender similarities hypothesis. *American Psychologist, 60,* 581–592.

Hyde, J. S., & DeLamater, J. D. (2003). *Understanding human sexuality* (8th ed.). Boston: McGraw-Hill.

Hyde, J. S., Fennema, E., & Lamon, S. J. (1990). Gender differences in mathematics performance. *Psychological Bulletin, 107,* 139–155.

Hyde, J. S., & Linn, M. C. (1988). Gender differences in verbal ability: A meta-analysis. *Psychological Bulletin, 104,* 53–69.

Ickes, W., & Barnes, R. D. (1978). Boys and girls together – and alienated: On enacting stereotyped sex roles in mixed-sex dyads. *Journal of Personality and Social Psychology, 36,* 669–683.

Idle, T., Wood, E., & Desmarais, S. (1993). Gender role socialization in toy play situations: Mothers and fathers with their sons and daughters. *Sex Roles, 28,* 679–691.

Imperato-McGinley, J., Peterson, R. E., Gautier, T., & Sturla, E. (1979). Androgyns and the evolution of male gender identity among male pseudohermaphrodites with 5 alpha-reductase deficiency. *New England Journal of Medicine, 300,* 1233–1237.

International Mathematical Olympiad (2008). *49th International Mathematical Olympiad Individual Results.* Retrieved from www.imo-official.org/year_individual_r.aspx?year+2008&co.

Izraeli, D. N., Izraeli, D., & Eden, D. (1985). Giving credit where credit is due: A case of no sex bias in attribution. *Journal of Applied Social Psychology, 15,* 516–530.

Jackson, L. A., Gardner, P., & Sullivan, L. (1992). Explaining gender differences in self-pay expectations: Social comparison standards and perceptions of fair play. *Journal of Applied Psychology, 77,* 651–663.

Jackson, L. A., & Grabski, S. V. (1988). Perceptions of fair play and the gender wage gap. *Journal of Applied Psychology, 18,* 606–625.

Jackson, L. M., Esses, V. M., & Burris, C. T. (2001). Contemporary sexism and discrimination: The importance of respect for men and woman. *Personality and Social Psychology Bulletin, 27,* 48–61.

Jose, P. E., & McCarthy, W. J. (1988). Perceived agent and communal behavior in mixed-sexed interactions. *Personality and Social Psychology Bulletin, 14,* 57–67.

Joseph, H. B., Reznik, I., & Mester, R. (2003). Suicidal behavior of adolescent girls: Profile and meaning. *Israel Journal of Psychiatry and Related Sciences, 40,* 209–219.

Jost, J. T., & Kay, A. C. (2005). Exposure to benevolent sexism and complementary gender stereotypes: Consequences for specific and diffuse forms of system justification. *Journal of Personality and Social Psychology, 88,* 498–509.

Kaplan, P. S. (2004). *Adolescence.* Boston: Houghton Mifflin.

Kashima, Y., Yamaguchi, S., Kim, U., Choi, S., Gelfand, M. J., & Yuki, M. (1995). Culture, gender, and self: A perspective from individualism–collectivism research. *Journal of Personality and Social Psychology, 69,* 925–937.

Kenrick, D. T., Trost, M. R., & Sundie, J. M. (2004). Sex roles as adaptations: An evolutionary perspective on gender differences and similarities. In A. H. Eagly, A. E. Beall, & R. J. Sternberg (Eds.), *The psychology of gender* (2nd ed., pp. 65–91). New York: Guilford Press.

Kimball, M. (2001). Gender similarities and differences as feminist contradictions. In R. K. Unger (Ed.), *Handbook of the psychology of gender* (pp. 66–83). New York: John Wiley.

Kinsey, A. C., Pomeroy, W. B., & Martin, C. E. (1948). *Sexual behavior in the human male.* Philadelphia, PA: Saunders.

Kinsey, A. C., Pomeroy, W. B., Martin, C. E., & Gebhard, P. H. (1953). *Sexual behavior and the human female.* Philadelphia, PA: Saunders.

Kling, K. C., Hyde, J., Showers, C., & Buswell, B. (1999). Gender differences in self-esteem: A meta-analysis. *Psychological Bulletin, 125,* 470–500.

Knight, G. P., Fabes, R. A., & Higgins, D. A. (1996). Concerns about drawing causal inferences from meta-analyses: An example in the study of gender differences in aggression. *Psychological Bulletin, 119,* 410–421.

Kohlberg, L. (1966). A cognitive-developmental analysis of children's sex-role concepts and attitudes. In E. E. Maccoby (Ed.), *The development of sex differences* (pp. 82–173). Stanford, CA: Stanford University Press.

Krahé, B. (2001). *The psychology of aggression.* Philadelphia, PA: Taylor & Francis.

Kring, A. M., & Gordon, A. H. (1998). Sex differences in emotion: Expression, experience, and physiology. *Journal of Personality and Social Psychology, 74,* 686–703.

Kurdek, L. A., & Schmitt, J. P. (1986). Interaction of sex-role self-concept with relationship quality and relationship beliefs in married, heterosexual cohabitating, gay, and lesbian couples. *Journal of Personality and Social Psychology, 51,* 365–370.

LaFrance, M., Paluck, E. L., & Brescoll, V. (2004). Sex changes: A current perspective on the psychology of gender. In A. H. Eagly, A. E. Beall, & R. J. Sternberg (Eds.), *The psychology of gender* (2nd ed., pp. 328–344). New York: Guilford Press.

Lao, R. C., Upchurch, W. J., Corwin, B. J., & Grossnickle, W. F. (1975). Biased attitudes toward females as indicated by ratings of intelligence and likeability. *Psychological Reports, 37,* 1315–1320.

Larwood, L., Szwajkowski, E., & Rose, S. (1988a). Sex and race discrimination from management–client relationships: Applying the rational bias theory of managerial discrimination. *Sex Roles, 18,* 9–29.

Larwood, L., Szwajkowski, E., & Rose, S. (1988b). When discrimination makes "sense": The rational bias theory. In L. Larwood, A. H. Stromberg, & B. A. Gutek (Eds.), *Women and work: An annual review: Vol. 3* (pp. 265–288). Thousand Oaks, CA: Sage.

Laumann, E. O., Gagnon, J. H., Michael, R. T., & Michaels, S. (1994). *The social organization of sexuality: Sexual practices in the United States.* Chicago: Univesity of Chicago Press.

Lavine, H., Sweeney, D., & Wagner, S. H. (1999). Depicting women as sex objects in television advertising: Effects on body dissatisfaction. *Personality and Social Psychology Bulletin, 25,* 1049–1058.

Leahey, E., & Guo, G. (2001). Gender differences in mathematical trajectories. *Social Forces, 80,* 713–732.

LeUnes, A. D., & Nation, J. R. (1989). *Sport psychology: An introduction.* Chicago: Nelson-Hall.

Leve, L. D., & Fagot, B. I. (1997). Gender-role socialization and discipline processes in one- and two-parent families. *Sex Roles, 36,* 1–21.

Levenson, R. W., Carstensen, L. L., & Gottman, J. M. (1994). The influence of age and gender on affect, physiology, and their interactions: A study of long-term marriages. *Journal of Personality and Social Psychology, 67,* 56–68.

Leyens, J. P., Désert, M., Croizet, J. C., & Darcis, C. (2000). Stereotype threat: Are lower status and history of stigmatization preconditions of stereotype threat? *Personality and Social Psychology Bulletin, 26,* 1189–1199.

Liebert, R. M., & Sprafkin, J. (1988). *The early window: Effects of television on children and youth* (3rd ed.). New York: Pergamon.

Lippa, R. (1995). Do sex differences define gender-related individual differences within the sexes? Evidence from three studies. *Personality and Social Psychology Bulletin, 21,* 349–355.

Lippa, R. A. (2005). *Gender, nature, and nurture* (2nd ed.). Mahwah, NJ: Erlbaum.

Lubell, K. M., Swahn, M. H., Crosby, A. E., & Kegler, S. R. (2004). Methods of suicide among persons aged 10–19 years: United States, 1999–2001. *MMWR, 53,* 471–473. *Retrieved from* www.cdc.gov./mmwr/PDF/wk/mm5322.pdf.

Lubinski, D., Tellegen, A., & Butcher, J. N. (1981). The relationship between androgyny and subjective indicators of emotional well-being. *Journal of Personality and Social Psychology, 40,* 722–730.

Lyness, K. S., & Thompson, D. E. (2000). Climbing the corporate ladder: Do female and male executives follow the same route? *Journal of Applied Psychology, 85,* 86–101.

Lytton, H., & Romney, D. M. (1991). Parents' differential socialization of boys and girls: A meta-analysis. *Psychological Bulletin, 109,* 267–296.

Maccoby, E. E. (1990). The role of gender identity and gender constancy in sex-differentiated development. In D. Schroder (Ed.), *The legacy of Lawrence Kohlberg: New directions for child development* (pp. 5–20). San Francisco: Jossey-Bass.

Maccoby, E. E. (1998). *The two sexes: Growing up apart, coming together*. Cambridge, MA: Belknap Press.

Maccoby, E. E., & Jacklin, C. N. (1974). *The psychology of sex differences*. Stanford, CA: Stanford University Press.

MacKinnon, C. E., Stoneman, Z., & Brody, G. H. (1984). The impact of maternal employment and family form on children's sex-role stereotypes and mothers' traditional attitudes. *Journal of Divorce, 8*, 51–60.

Mahay, J., Laumann, E. O., & Michaels, S. (2000). Race, gender, and class in sexual scripts. In E. O. Laumann & R. T. Michael (Eds.), *Sex, love, and health in America: Private choices and public policies* (pp. 197–238). Chicago: University of Chicago Press.

Major, B. (1989). Gender differences in comparisons and entitlement: Implications for comparable worth. *Journal of Social Issues, 45*, 99–115.

Major, B., Barr, L., Zubek, J., & Babey, S. H. (1999). Gender and self-esteem: A meta-analysis. In W. Swan, J. Langolois, & L. Gilbert (Eds.), *Sexism and stereotypes in modern society: The gender science of Janet Taylor Spence* (pp. 223–254). Washington, DC: American Psychological Association.

Major, B., Carnevale, P. J. D., & Deaux, K. (1981). A different perspective on androgyny: Evaluations of masculine and feminine personality characteristics. *Journal of Personality and Social Psychology, 41*, 988–1001.

Major, B., & Konar, E. (1984). An investigation of sex differences in pay expectations and their possible causes. *Academy of Management Journal, 27*, 777–792.

Major, B., Vanderslice, V., & McFarlin, D. B. (1985). Effects of pay expected on pay received: The confirmatory nature of initial expectations. *Journal of Applied Social Psychology, 14*, 399–412.

Manning, J. T., Koukourakis, K., & Brodie, D. A. (1997). Fluctuating asymmetry, metabolic rate and sexual selection in human males. *Evolution and Human Behavior, 18*, 15–21.

Markstrom-Adams, C. (1989). Androgyny and its relation to adolescent psychological well-being: A review of the literature. *Sex Roles, 21*, 325–340.

Markus, H. R., Steele, C. M., & Steele, D. M. (2002). Colorblindness as a barrier to inclusion: Assimilation and nonimmigrant minorities. In R. Shweder, M. Minow, & H. R. Markus (Eds.), *Engaging cultural differences: The multicultural challenge in liberal democracies* (pp. 453–472). New York: Russell Sage Foundation.

Martin, C. L. (1987). A ratio measure of sex stereotyping. *Journal of Personality and Social Psychology, 52*, 489–499.

Martin, C. L. (1991). The role of cognition in understanding gender effects. In H. Reese (Ed.), *Advances in child development and behavior: Vol. 23* (pp. 113–149). San Diego, CA: Academic Press.

Martin, C. L. (2000). Cognitive theories of gender development. In T. Eckes & H. M. Trautner (Eds.), *The developmental social psychology of gender* (pp. 91–121). Mahwah, NJ: Erlbaum.

Martin, C. L., Eisenbud, L., & Rose, H. (1995). Children's gender-based reasoning about toys. *Child Development, 66*, 1453–1471.

Martin, C. L., & Halverson, C. F., Jr. (1981). A schematic processing model of sex typing and stereotyping in children. *Child Development, 52*, 1119–1134.

Martin, C. L., & Halverson, C. F., Jr. (1983). The effects of sex-typing schemas on young children's memory. *Child Development, 54*, 563–574.

Martin, C. L., & Halverson, C. F., Jr. (1987). The roles of cognition in sex-role and sex-typing. In D. B. Carter (Ed.), *Current conceptions of sex roles and sex-typing: Theory and research* (pp. 123–137). New York: Praeger.

Martin, C. L., Ruble, D. N., & Szkrybalo, J. (2002). Cognitive theories of early gender development. *Psychological Bulletin, 128*, 903–933.

Martin, C. L., Ruble, D. N., & Szkrybalo, J. (2004). Recognizing the centrality of gender identity and stereotype knowledge in gender development and moving toward theoretical integration: Reply to Bandura and Bussey (2004). *Psychological Bulletin, 130*, 702–710.

McCrae, R. R., Terracciano, A., & 78 Members of the Personality Profiles of Cultures Project (2005). Universal features of personality traits from observer's perspective: Data from 50 cultures. *Journal of Personality and Social Psychology, 88*, 547–561.

McGhee, P. E., & Frueh, T. (1980). Television viewing and the learning of sex-role stereotypes. *Sex Roles, 6*, 179–188.

McKenzie-Mohr, D., & Zanna, M. P. (1990). Treating women as sexual objects: Look to the (gender schematic) male who has viewed pornography. *Personality and Social Psychology Bulletin, 16*, 266–308.

Mealey, L. (2000). *Sex differences: Development and evolutionary strategies*. San Diego, CA: Academic Press.

Michalos, A. C. (1991). *Global report on student well-being: Vol. 1. Life satisfaction and happiness*. New York: Springer.

Miles, C. C. (1935). Sex in social psychology. In C. Murchison (Ed.), *A handbook of social psychology: Vol. 2* (pp. 683–797). New York: Russell & Russell.

Miller, G. F. (1998). How mate choice shaped human nature: A review of sexual selection and human evolution. In C. Crawford & D. L. Krebs (Eds.), *Handbook of evolutionary psychology: Ideas, issues, and applications* (pp. 87–129). Mahwah, NJ: Erlbaum.

Miller, L. C., & Fishkin, S. A. (1997). On the dynamics of human bonding and reproductive success: Seeking windows on the adapted-for-human environmental interface. In J. A. Simpson & D. T. Kenrick (Eds.), *Evolutionary social psychology* (pp. 197–235). Mahwah, NJ: Erlbaum.

Miller, L. C., Putcha-Bhagavatula, A., & Pedersen, W. C. (2002). Men's and women's mating preferences: Distinct evolutionary mechanisms? *Current Directions in Psychological Science, 11*, 88–93.

Miller, R. S., Perlman, D., & Brehm, S. S. (2007). *Intimate relationships* (4th ed.). Boston: McGraw-Hill.

Money, J. (1987). Sin, sickness, or status: Homosexual gender identity and psychoneuroendocrinology. *American Psychologist, 42*, 384–399.

Money, J., & Ehrhardt, A. A. (1972). *Man and woman, boy and girl*. Baltimore: Johns Hopkins University Press.

Morrison, A. M., & Von Glinow, M. A. (1990). Women and minorities in management. *American Psychologist, 45,* 200–208.

Moskowitz, D. S., Suh, E. J., & Desaulniers, J. (1994). Situational influences on gender differences in agency and communion. *Journal of Personality and Social Psychology, 66,* 753–761.

Myers, D. G. (2000). The funds, friends, and faith of happy people. *American Psychologist, 55,* 56–67.

Myers, D. G., & Diener, E. (1995). Who is happy? *Psychological Science, 6,* 10–19.

National Center for Injury Prevention and Control. (2004). *Web-Based Injury Statistics Query and Reporting System (WISQARS).* Atlanta, GA: Centers for Disease Control and Prevention. *Retrieved from* www.cdc.gov/ncipc/wisquars.

O'Brien, L. T., & Crandall, C. S. (2003). Stereotype threat and arousal: Effects on women's math performance. *Personality and Social Psychology Bulletin, 29,* 782–789.

O'Connor, K., Mann, D. W., & Bardwick, J. M. (1978). Androgyny and self-esteem in the upper-middle class: A replication of Spence. *Journal of Personality and Social Psychology, 46,* 1168–1169.

O'Heron, C. A., & Orlofsky, J. L. (1990). Stereotypic and non-stereotypic sex role trait and behavior orientations, gender, identity and psychological adjustment. *Journal of Personality and Social Psychology, 58,* 134–143.

Oliver, M. B., & Hyde, J. S. (1993). Gender differences in sexuality: A meta-analysis. *Psychological Bulletin, 114,* 29–51.

Orlofsky, J. L., & O'Heron, C. A. (1987). Stereotypic and non-stereotypic sex role trait and behavior orientations: Implications for personal adjustment. *Journal of Personality and Social Psychology, 52,* 1034–1042.

Osborne, J. W. (2001). Testing stereotype threat: Does anxiety explain race and sex differences in achievement? *Contemporary Educational Psychology, 26,* 291–310.

Österman, K., Björkqvist, K., Lagerspetz, K. M. J., Kaukiainen, A., Landua, S. F., Fraczek, A., et al. (1998). Cross-cultural evidence of female indirect aggression. *Aggressive Behavior, 24,* 1–8.

Owens, L., Shute, R., & Slee, P. (2000). "Guess what I just heard!" Indirect aggression among teenage girls in Australia. *Aggressive Behavior, 26,* 57–66.

Paludi, C. A., & Paludi, M. (2003a). Developing and enforcing effective policies, procedures, and training programs for educational institutions and businesses. In M. Paludi & C. A. Paludi (Eds.), *Academic and workplace sexual harassment: A handbook of cultural, social science, management, and legal perspectives* (pp. 175–198). Westport, CT: Praeger.

Paludi, M., & Paludi, C. A. (2000, August). *Workplace sexual harassment: Legal, management, and psychological approaches to prevention.* Workshop presented at the International Coalition Against Sexual Harassment, Washington, DC.

Paludi, M., & Paludi, C. A. (Eds.). (2003b). *Academic and workplace sexual harassment: A handbook of cultural, social science, management, and legal perspectives.* Westport, CT: Praeger.

Pazy, A. (1992). Sex-linked bias in promotion decisions: The role of candidate's career relevance and respondent's prior experience. *Psychology of Women Quarterly, 16,* 209–228.

Peplau, L. A., & Garnets, L. D. (2000). A new paradigm for understanding women's sexuality and sexual orientation. *Journal of Social Issues, 56,* 329–350.

Perry, D. G., & Bussey, K. (1979). The social learning theory of sex differences: Imitation is alive and well. *Journal of Personality and Social Psychology, 37,* 1699–1712.

Pietrzak, R., Laird, J. D., Stevens, D. A., & Thomson, N. S. (2002). Sex differences in human jealousy: A coordinated study of forced-choice, continuous rating-scale, and physiological responses on the same subjects. *Evolution and Human Behavior, 23,* 83–94.

Pipher, M. (1994). *Reviving Ophelia: Saving the selves of adolescent girls.* New York: Putnam.

Pomerantz, E. M., Fei-Yin Ng, F., & Wang, Q. (2004). Gender socialization: A parent × child model. In A. H. Eagly, A. E. Beall, & R. J. Sternberg (Eds.), *The psychology of gender* (2nd ed., pp. 120–144). New York: Guilford Press.

Pomerleau, A., Bolduc, D., Malcuit, G., & Cossette, L. (1990). Pink or blue: Environmental gender stereotypes in the first two years of life. *Sex Roles, 22,* 359–367.

Powlishta, K. K., Sen, M. G., Serbin, L. A., Poulin-Dubois, D., & Eichstedt, J. A. (2001). From infancy through middle childhood: The role of cognitive and social factors in becoming gendered. In R. K. Unger (Ed.), *Handbook of the psychology of women and gender* (pp. 116–132). New York: John Wiley.

Prager, K. J., & Bailey, J. M. (1985). Androgyny, ego development, and psychological crisis. *Sex Roles, 13,* 525–536.

Prentice, D. A., & Carranza, E. (2002). What women should be, shouldn't be, are allowed to be, and don't have to be: The contents of prescriptive gender stereotypes. *Psychology of Women Quarterly, 26,* 269–281.

Propp, K. M. (1995). An experimental examination of biological sex as a status cue in decision-making groups and its influence on information use. *Small Group Research, 26,* 451–474.

Quatman, T., & Watson, C. M. (2001). Gender differences in adolescent self-esteem: An exploration of domains. *Journal of Genetic Psychology, 162,* 93–117.

Rathus, S. A. (2006). *Child and adolescence: Voyages in development* (2nd ed.). Belmont, CA: Thomson/Wadsworth.

Regan, P. C., & Dreyer, C. S. (1999). Lust? Love? Status? Young adults' motives for engaging in casual sex. *Journal of Psychology and Human Sexuality, 11,* 1–23.

Ridgeway, C. L., & Bourg, C. (2004). Gender as status: An expectation theory approach. In A. H. Eagly, A. E. Beall, & R. J. Sternberg (Eds.), *The psychology of gender* (2nd. ed., pp. 217–241). New York: Guilford Press.

Rimer, S., & Healy, P. (2005, February 18). Furor lingers as Harvard chief gives details of talk on women. *The New Times,* pp. A-1, A-20.

Rosen, B., & Jerdee, T. H. (1974). Influence of sex role stereotypes on personnel decisions. *Journal of Applied Psychology, 59,* 9–14.

Rosen, B., & Jerdee, T. H. (1975). Effects of employee's sex and threatening versus pleading appeals on managerial evaluations of grievances. *Journal of Applied Psychology, 60,* 442–445.

Rosenfield, S., Vertefuille, J., & McAlpine, D. D. (2000). Gender stratification and mental health. *Social Psychology Quarterly, 63*, 208–223.

Rosenkrantz, P. S., Vogel, S. R., Bee, H., Broverman, I. K., & Broverman, D. M. (1968). Sex-role stereotypes and self-concepts in college students. *Journal of Consulting and Clinical Psychology, 32*, 287–295.

Rosenwasser, S. M., Lingenfelter, M., & Harrington, A. F. (1989). Nontraditional gender role portrayals on television and children's gender role perceptions. *Journal of Applied Developmental Psychology, 10*, 97–105.

Rosenzweig, J. M., & Daley, D. M. (1989). Dyadic adjustment/sexual satisfaction in women and men as a function of psychological sex role self-perception. *Journal of Sex and Marital Therapy, 15*, 42–56.

Rudman, L. A., & Glick, P. (1999). Feminized management and backlash toward agentic women. *Journal of Personality and Social Psychology, 77*, 1004–1010.

Rudman, L. A., & Glick, P. (2001). Prescriptive gender stereotypes and backlash toward agentic women. *Journal of Social Issues, 57*, 743–762.

Scelfo, J. (2005). Bad girls go wild. *Newsweek, 145*, 66–67.

Schmitt, D. P. (2005). Fundamentals of human mating strategies. In D. M. Buss, (Ed.), *The handbook of evolutionary psychology* (pp. 258–291). Hoboken, NJ: John Wiley.

Schmitt, D. P., and 118 members of the International Sexuality Description Project. (2003). Universal sex differences in the desire for sexuality variety: Tests from 52 nations, 6 contents, and 13 islands. *Journal of Personality and Social Psychology, 85*, 85–104.

Scutt, D., Manning, J. T., Whitehouse, G. H., Leinster, S. J., & Massey, C. P. (1997). Relationship between breast symmetry, breast size, and occurrence of breast cancer. *British Journal of Radiology, 70*, 1017–1021.

Seidlitz, L., & Diener, E. (1998). Sex differences in the recall of affective experiences. *Journal of Personality and Social Psychology, 74*, 262–271.

Shackelford, S., Wood, W., & Worchel, S. (1996). Behavioral styles and the influence of women in mixed-sex groups. *Social Psychology Quarterly, 59*, 284–293.

Shackelford, T. K., Pound, N., Goetz, A., & LaMunyon, C. W. (2005). Female infidelity and sperm competition. In D. M. Buss (Ed.), *The handbook of evolutionary psychology* (pp. 372–393). Hoboken, NJ: John Wiley.

Shaffer, D. R. (2002). *Developmental psychology: Childhood and adolescence*. Belmont, CA: Wadsworth/Thomson Learning.

Shaffer, D. R., Pegalis, L. J., & Cornell, D. P. (1991). Interactive effects of social context and sex-role identity on self-disclosure during the acquaintance process. *Sex Roles, 24*, 1–19.

Shaughnessy, J. J. (2005, May 22). Happiness and money related – to a point. *The Courier-Journal*, p. E1.

Sheridan, J. E., Slocum, J. W., Jr., Buda, R., & Thompson, R. C. (1990). Effects of corporate sponsorship and departmental power on career tournaments. *Academy of Management Journal, 33*, 578–602.

Shields, S. A. (2005). The politics of emotion in everyday life: "Appropriate" emotion and claims on identity. *Review of General Psychology, 9*, 3–15.

Shotland, R. L., & Hunter, B. A. (1995). Women's "token resistant" and compliant sexual behaviors are related to uncertain sexual intentions and rape. *Personality and Social Psychology Bulletin, 21*, 226–236.

Silverman, I., & Choi, J. (2005). Locating places. In D. M. Buss (Ed.), *The handbook of evolutionary psychology* (pp. 177–199). Hoboken, NJ: John Wiley.

Sistrunk, F., & McDavid, J. W. (1971). Sex variable in conforming behavior. *Journal of Personality and Social Psychology, 17*, 200–207.

Skogman, K., Alsén, M., & Öjehagen, A. (2004). Sex differences in risk factors for suicide after attempted suicide: A follow-up study of 1,052 suicide attempters. *Social Psychiatry and Psychiatric Epidemiology, 39*, 113–120.

Slaby, R. G., & Frey, K. S. (1975). Development of gender constancy and selective attention to same-sex models. *Child Development, 52*, 849–859.

Slade, J. W. (2000). *Pornography in America: A reference handbook*. Santa Barbara, CA: ABC-CLIO.

Smith, B. (2007). *The psychology of sex and gender*. Boston: Pearson Education.

Spence, J. T., & Buckner, C. E. (2000). Instrumental and expressive traits, trait stereotypes, and sexist attitudes: What do they signify? *Psychology of Women Quarterly, 24*, 44–62.

Spence, J. T., & Helmreich, R. L. (1978). *Masculinity and femininity: Their psychological dimensions, correlates, and antecedents*. Austin: University of Texas Press.

Spence, J. T., Helmreich, R. L., & Stapp, J. (1975). Ratings of self and peers on sex-role attributes and their relation to self-esteem and conceptions of masculinity and femininity. *Journal of Personality and Social Psychology, 32*, 29–39.

Spencer, H. (1897). *The principles of psychology: Vol. 1*. New York: Appleton.

Spencer, H. (1902). *The study of sociology*. New York: Appleton.

Sprecher, S., & Metts, S. (1989). Development of the "Romantic Beliefs Scale" and examination of the effects of gender and gender-role orientation. *Journal of Social and Personal Relationships, 6*, 387–411.

Stanley, J. (1990, January). We need to know why women falter in math. *The Chronicle of Higher Education*, p. B4.

Stanley, J. C., & Benbow, C. P. (1982). Huge sex ratios at upper end. *American Psychologist, 37*, 972.

Steele, C. M. (1992, April). Race and the schooling of Black Americans. *The Atlantic Monthly, 269*, 68–78.

Steele, C. M. (1997). A threat in the air: How stereotypes shape intellectual identity and performance. *American Psychologist, 52*, 613–629.

Steele, C. M. (2002, October 18). *The specter of group image: Its unseen effects on human performance and the quality of life in a diverse society*. Tanner Lecture, University of Michigan.

Steele, C. M., & Aronson, J. (1995). Stereotype threat and the intellectual test performance of African Americans. *Journal of Personality and Social Psychology, 69*, 797–811.

Steele, C. M., Spencer, S. J., & Aronson, J. (2002). Contending with group image: The psychology of stereotype and social identity threat. In M. P. Zanna (Ed.), *Advances in experimental social psychology: Vol. 34* (pp. 379–440). San Diego, CA: Academic Press.

Steil, J., McGann, V. L., & Kahn, A. S. (2001). Entitlement. In J. Worell (Ed.), *Encyclopedia of women and gender* (pp. 403–410). San Diego, CA: Academic Press.

Stein, J. A., Newcomb, M. D., & Bentler, P. M. (1992). The effects of agency and communality on self-esteem: Gender differences. *Sex Roles, 26,* 465–483.

Steinpreis, R. E., Andres, K. A., & Ritzke, D. (1999). The impact of gender on the review of the curricula vitae of job applicants and tenure candidates: A national empirical study. *Sex Roles, 41,* 509–528.

Sternglanz, S. H., & Serbin, L. (1974). Sex-role stereotyping in children's television programming. *Developmental Psychology, 10,* 710–715.

Strauss, S. (2003). Sexual harassment in K-12. In M. Paludi & C. A. Paludi (Eds.), *Academic and workplace sexual harassment: A handbook of cultural, social science, management, and legal perspectives* (pp. 105–145). Westport, CT: Praeger.

Sugiyama, L. (2005). Physical attractiveness in adaptationist perspective. In D. M. Buss (Ed.), *The handbook of evolutionary psychology* (pp. 292–343). Hoboken, NJ: John Wiley.

Swim, J. K., & Sanna, L. (1996). He's skilled, she's lucky: A meta-analysis of observers' attributions for women's and men's success and failures. *Personality and Social Psychology Bulletin, 22,* 507–519.

Tavris, C. (1992). *The mismeasure of woman.* New York: Simon & Schuster.

Taylor, M. C., & Hall, J. A. (1982). Psychological androgyny: A review and reformulation of theories, methods, and conclusions. *Psychological Bulletin, 92,* 347–366.

Taylor, S. E., Peplau, L. A., & Sears, D. O. (2003). *Social psychology* (11th ed.). Upper Saddle River, NJ: Prentice Hall.

Terman, L. M., & Merrill, M. A. (1937). *Measuring intelligence.* Boston: Houghton Mifflin.

Terman, L. M., & Miles, C. C. (1936). *Sex and personality.* New York: McGraw-Hill.

Top, T. J. (1991). Sex bias in the evaluation of performance in scientific, artistic, and literary professions: A review. *Sex Roles, 24,* 73–106.

Trentham, S., & Larwood, L. (1998). Gender discrimination and the workplace: An examination of rational bias theory. *Sex Roles, 38,* 1–28.

Twenge, J. M. (1999). Mapping gender: The multifactorial approach and the organization of gender-related attributes. *Psychology of Women Quarterly, 23,* 485–502.

Unger, R. K. (Ed.). (2001). *Handbook of the psychology of women and gender.* New York: John Wiley.

Unger, R., & Crawford, M. (1992). *Women and gender: A feminist psychology.* New York: McGraw-Hill.

U.S. Department of Labor, Bureau of Labor Statistics. (2004). *Women in the labor force: A databook* (Report No. 973). Washington, DC: U.S. Department of Labor, Bureau of Labor Statistics.

Walker, S., Richardson, D. S., & Green, L. R. (2000). Aggression among older adults: The relationship of interaction networks and gender role to direct and indirect responses. *Aggressive Behavior, 26,* 145–154.

Waterman, A. S., & Whitbourne, S. K. (1982). Androgyny and psychosocial development among college students and adults. *Journal of Personality, 50,* 121–133.

Watt, H. M. G., & Bornholt, L. J. (2000). Social categories and student perceptions in high school mathematics. *Journal of Applied Social Psychology, 30,* 1492–1503.

Weiss, D. H. (2004). *Fair, square and legal: Safe hiring, managing and firing practices to keep you and your company out of court* (4th ed.). New York: AMACOM/American Management Association.

Weitzman, L. J., Eifler, D., Hokada, E., & Ross, C. (1972). Sex-role socialization in picture books for preschool children. *American Journal of Sociology, 77,* 1125–1149.

White, G. L. (1981a). A model of romantic jealousy. *Motivation and Emotion, 5,* 295–310.

White, G. L. (1981b). Some correlates of romantic jealousy. *Journal of Personality, 20,* 55–64.

White, G. L., & Mullen, P. E. (1989). *Jealousy: Theory, research, and clinical strategies.* New York: Guilford Press.

Whiting, B., & Pope, C. (1974). Across-cultural analysis of sex differences in the behavior of children aged three to eleven. *Journal of Social Psychology, 91,* 171–188.

Whitley, B. E., Jr. (1983). Sex role orientation and self-esteem: A critical meta-analytic review. *Journal of Personality and Social Psychology, 44,* 765–778.

Whitley, B. E., Jr. (1988). Masculinity, femininity, and self-esteem: A multitrait-multimethod analysis. *Sex Roles, 18,* 419–431.

Wisniewski, A. B., Migeon, C. J., Meyer-Bahlburg, H. F. L., Gearhart, J. P., Berkovitz, G. D., et al. (2000). Complete androgen insensitivity syndrome: Long-term medical, surgical, and psychosexual outcome. *Journal of Clinical Endocrinology and Metabolism, 85,* 2664–2669.

Wood, W., & Eagly, A. H. (2002). A cross-cultural analysis of the behavior of women and men: Implications for the origins of sex differences. *Psychological Bulletin, 128,* 699–727.

Yamada, E. M., Tjosvold, D., & Draguns, J. G. (1983). Effects of sex-linked situations and sex composition on cooperation and style of interaction. *Sex Roles, 9,* 541–553.

Zeman, J., & Garber, J. (1996). Display rules for anger, sadness, and pain: It depends on who is watching. *Child Development, 67,* 957–973.

Zuckerman, M. (2005). *Psychobiology of personality* (2nd ed.). New York: Cambridge University Press.

Chapter 13

Aaker, D. A., & Myers, J. G. (1982). *Advertising management* (2nd ed.). Englewood Cliffs, NJ: Prentice Hall.

Aiken, L. R. (2003). *Psychological testing and assessment* (10th ed.). Boston: Allyn & Bacon.

Anderson, P. L., Rothbaum, B. O., & Hodges, L. (2001). Virtual reality: Using the virtual world to improve quality of life in the real world. *Bulletin of the Menninger Clinic, 65,* 78–91.

Arkin, R., Lake, E., & Baumgardner, A. (1986). Shyness and self-presentation. In W. H. Jones, J. M. Cheek, & S. R. Briggs (Eds.), *Shyness: Perspectives on research and treatment* (pp. 189–203). New York: Plenum.

Aronson, E., Wilson, T. D., & Akert, R. M. (2002). *Social psychology* (4th ed.). Upper Saddle River, NJ: Prentice Hall.

Barlow, D. H. (Ed.). (2002). *Anxiety and its disorders: The nature and treatment of anxiety and panic*. New York: Guilford Press.

Baumeister, R. F., & Bushman, B. J. (2008). *Social psychology and human nature*. Belmont, CA: Thomson Higher Education.

Beck, A. T., & Weishaar, M. E. (2000). Cognitive therapy. In R. J. Corsini & D. Wedding (Eds.), *Current psychotherapies* (6th ed., pp. 241–272). Itasca, IL: F. E. Peacock.

Berkowitz, E. N., Kerin, R. A., Hartley, S. W., & Rudelius, W. (2000). *Marketing* (6th ed.). Boston: Irwin/McGraw-Hill.

Brown, L. L., Tomarken, A. J., Loosen, P. T., Kalin, N. H., & Davidson, R. J. (1996). Individual differences in repressive-defensiveness predict basal salivary cortisol levels. *Journal of Personality and Social Psychology, 70*, 362–371.

Buss, A. H. (1995). *Personality: Temperament, social behavior, and the self*. Boston: Allyn & Bacon.

Buss, D. M. (2004). *Evolutionary psychology: The new science of the mind* (2nd ed.) Boston: Allyn & Bacon.

Cannon, W. B. (1929). *Bodily changes in pain, hunger, fear, and rage*. New York: Appleton-Century-Crofts.

Carducci, B. J. (1999). *The pocket guide to making successful small talk: How to talk to anyone anytime anywhere about anything*. New Albany: Pocket Guide.

Carducci, B. J. (2000a). *Shyness: A bold new approach*. New York: HarperPerennial.

Carducci, B. J. (2000b). What shy individuals do to cope with their shyness: A content analysis. In W. R. Crozier (Ed.), *Shyness: Development, consolidation and change* (pp. 171–185). London: Routledge.

Carducci, B. J. (2005). *The shyness workbook: 30 days to dealing effectively with shyness*. Champaign, IL: Research Press.

Carducci, B. J., & Clark, D. L. (1994, August). *The personal and situational pervasiveness of chronically shy, socially anxious individuals*. Paper presented at the meeting of the American Psychological Association, Los Angeles.

Carducci, B. J., & Clark, D. L. (1996). *A twenty-year comparison of the pervasiveness of shyness*. Manuscript submitted for publication.

Carducci, B. J., & McLeish, A. C. (2000). *The shy alcoholic: Cognitive correlates of a shy subtype* (SRI Tech Report). New Albany: Indiana University Southeast Shyness Research Institute.

Carducci, B. J., Ragains, K. D., Kee, K. L., Johnson, M. R., & Duncan, H. R. (1998, August). *Identifying the pains and problems of shyness: A content analysis*. Poster presentation at the annual meeting of the American Psychological Association, San Francisco.

Carducci, B. J., & Stein, N. D. (1988, March). *The personal and situational pervasiveness of shyness in college students: A nine-year comparison*. Paper presented at the meeting of the Southeastern Psychological Association, New Orleans.

Carducci, B. J., & Zimbardo, P. G. (1995, December). Are you shy? *Psychology Today, 28*, 34–41.

Carlson, N. R. (2001). *Physiology of behavior* (7th ed.). Boston: Allyn & Bacon.

Caughlin, J. P., Huston, T. L., & Houts, R. M. (2000). How does personality matter in marriage? An examination of trait anxiety, interpersonal negativity, and marital satisfaction. *Journal of Personality and Social Psychology, 78*, 326–336.

Cheek, J. M. (1989). *Conquering shyness: The battle anyone can win*. New York: Dell.

Cohen, D. (1981). *Consumer behavior*. New York: Random House.

Cohen, R. J., & Swedlik, M. E. (2001). *Psychological testing and assessment: An introduction to tests and measurements* (5th ed.). Boston: McGraw-Hill.

Comer, R. J. (2007). *Abnormal psychology* (6th ed.). New York: Worth.

Crozier, W. R. (Ed.). (2000). *Shyness: Development, consolidation and change*. London: Routledge.

Diagnostic and Statistical Manual of Mental Disorders-IV-TR (2000). Washington, DC: American Psychiatric Association.

Dozois, D. J. A., & Westra, H. A. (2004). The nature of anxiety and depression: Implications for prevention. In K. S. Dobson & D. J. A. Dozois (Eds.), *The prevention of anxiety and depression: Theory, research, and practice* (pp. 9–41). Washington, DC: American Psychological Association.

Emmelkamp P. M. G., & Scholing, A. (1994). Behavioral interpretations. In B. B. Wolman (Ed.) & G. Stricker (Co-ed.), *Anxiety and related disorders: A handbook* (pp. 30–56). New York: John Wiley.

Fann, W. E., & Goshen, C. E. (1973). *The language of mental health*. St. Louis: C. V. Mosby.

Fiske, S. T., Morling, B., & Stevens, L. E. (1996). Controlling self and others: A theory of anxiety, mental control, and social control. *Personality and Social Psychology Bulletin, 22*, 115–123.

Freud, S. (1959). Inhibitions, symptoms, and anxiety. In *Standard edition: Vol. 18* (pp. 77–174). London: Hogarth Press. (Original work published 1926)

Ganzer, V. J. (1968). Effects of audience presence and test anxiety on learning and retention in a serial learning situation. *Journal of Personality and Social Psychology, 8*, 194–199.

Geen, R. G. (1976). Test anxiety, observation, and range of cue utilization. *British Journal of Social and Clinical Psychology, 15*, 253–259.

Geen, R. G. (1980). Test anxiety and cue utilization. In I. G. Sarason (Ed.), *Test anxiety: Theory, research and applications* (pp. 43–61). Hillsdale, NJ: Erlbaum.

Geen, R. G. (1995). *Human motivation: A social psychological approach*. Pacific Grove, CA: Brooks/Cole.

Goleman, D. (1995, June 21). "Virtual reality" conquers fear of heights. *The New York Times*, p. C11.

Greenberg, P. E., Sisitsky, T., Kessler, R. C., Finkelstein, S. N., Berndt, E. R., Davidson, J. R., et al. (1999). The economic burden of anxiety disorders in the 1990s. *Journal of Clinical Psychiatry, 60*, 427–435.

Greenberg, L. S., Watson, J. C., & Lietaer, G. (Eds.). (1998). *Handbook of experiential psychotherapy*. New York: Guilford Press.

Griez, E. J. L., Faravelli, C., Nutt, D., & Zohar, J. (Eds.). (2001). *Anxiety disorders: An introduction to clinical management and research*. New York: John Wiley.

Gudykunst, W. B., & Ting-Toomey, S. (1988). *Culture and interpersonal communication*. New York: Plenum.

Hodges, W. F., & Spielberger, C. G. (1969). Digit span: An indicant of trait or state anxiety? *Journal of Clinical and Consulting Psychology, 33*, 430–434.

Holroyd, K. A., & Appel, M. A. (1980). Test anxiety and physiological responding. In I. G. Sarason (Ed.), *Test anxiety: Theory, research, and applications* (pp. 129–151). Hillsdale, NJ: Erlbaum.

Holroyd, K., Westbrook, T., Wolf, M., & Badhorn, E. (1978). Performance, cognition, and physiological responding in test anxiety. *Journal of Abnormal Psychology, 87*, 442–451.

Hull, C. L. (1943). *Principles of behavior*. New Haven, CT: Yale University Press.

Ishiyama, F. I. (1985). Universality of social anxiety: Is social anxiety a special characteristic of the Japanese people? *Seikatsu-no Hakken Journal, 29*, 40–43.

Ishiyama, F. I. (1986). Brief Morita therapy on social anxiety: A single case study of therapeutic changes. *Canadian Journal of Counseling, 20*, 56–65.

Ishiyama, F. I. (1987). Use of Morita therapy in shyness counseling in the West: Promoting client's self-acceptance and action taking. *Journal of Counseling and Development, 65*, 547–551.

Jackson, J. M. (1994). Psychoanalysis and related methods. In B. B. Wolman (Ed.) & G. Stricker (Co-ed.), *Anxiety and related disorders: A handbook* (pp. 340–357). New York: John Wiley.

Jackson, T., Flaherty, S., & Kosuth, R. (2000). Culture and self-presentation as predictors of shyness among Japanese and American female college students. *Perceptual and Motor Skills, 90*, 475–482.

Jackson, T., Towson, S., & Narduzzi, K. (1997). Predictors of shyness: A test of variables associated with self-presentation models. *Social Behavior and Personality, 25*, 149–154.

Jones, W. H., Cheek, J. M., & Briggs, S. R. (Eds.). (1986). *Shyness: Perspectives on research and treatment*. New York: Plenum.

Josephs, L. (1994). Psychoanalytic and related interpretations. In B. B. Wolman (Ed.) & G. Stricker (Co-ed.), *Anxiety and related disorders: A handbook* (pp. 11–29). New York: John Wiley.

Kanar, C. C. (2001). *The confident student* (4th ed.). Boston: Houghton Mifflin.

Kendall, P. C., Finch, A. J., Jr., Auerbach, S. M., Hooke, J. F., & Mikulka, P. J. (1976). The State-Trait Anxiety Inventory: A systematic evaluation. *Journal of Consulting and Clinical Psychology, 44*, 406–412.

Kessler, R. C., & Zhao, S. (1999). The prevalence of mental illness. In A. V. Horwitz & T. L. Scheid (Eds.), *A handbook for the study of mental health: Social contexts, theories, and systems* (pp. 58–78). Cambridge, UK: Cambridge University Press.

Kitayama, S., Markus, H. R., Matsumoto, H., & Norasakkunkit, V. (1997). Individual and collective processes in the con-

struction of the self: Self-enhancement in the United States and self-criticism in Japan. *Journal of Personality and Social Psychology, 72*, 1245–1267.

Klavora, P. (1975). Application of the Spielberger trait-state anxiety theory and STAI in pre-competitive anxiety research. In D. M. Landers, D. V. Harris, & R. W. Christina (Eds.), *Psychology of sport and motor behavior II* (Penn State HPER Series, No. 10; pp. 141–143). University Park, PA: Penn State University.

Kotler, P., & Armstrong, G. (1994). *Principles of marketing* (6th ed.). Englewood Cliffs, NJ: Prentice Hall.

Kring, A. M., Davison, G. C., Neale, J. M., & Johnson, S. L. (2007). *Abnormal psychology, with cases* (10th ed.) New York: John Wiley.

Leary, M. R., & Kowalski, R. M. (1995). *Social anxiety*. New York: Guilford Press.

Mandler, G. (1972). Comments on Dr. Sarason's paper. In C. D. Spielberger (Ed.), *Anxiety: Current trends in theory and research: Vol. 2* (pp. 405–408). New York: Academic Press.

Mandler, G., & Sarason, S. B. (1952). A study of anxiety and learning. *Journal of Abnormal and Social Psychology, 47*, 166–173.

Martens, R., Vealey, R. S., & Burton, D. (1990). *Competitive anxiety in sports*. Champaign, IL: Human Kinetics.

McIlroy, D., Bunting, B., & Adamson, G. (2000). An evaluation of the factor structure and predictive utility of a test anxiety scale with reference to students' past performance and personality indices. *The British Journal of Educational Psychology, 70*, 17–32.

McNally, R. J. (1998). Anxiety sensitivity and information-processing biases for threat. In S. Taylor (Ed.), *Anxiety sensitivity: Theory, research, and treatment of the fear of anxiety* (pp. 183–197). Mahwah, NJ: Erlbaum.

Melchior, L. A., & Cheek, J. M. (1990). Shyness and anxious self-preoccupation during dating interaction. *Journal of Social Behavior and Personality, 5*, 127–140.

Mowrer, O. H. (1950). *Learning theory and personality dynamics*. New York: Ronald Press.

Mowrer, O. H. (1960). *Learning theory and behavior*. New York: John Wiley.

Mueller, M. (2002). How virtual reality can help you. *Current Health, 2*, 16–17.

Myers, D. G. (2008). *Social psychology* (9th ed.). Boston: McGraw-Hill.

Neese, R. M. (2005). Evolutionary psychology and mental health. In D. M. Buss (Ed.), *The handbook of evolutionary psychology* (pp. 903–927). Hoboken, NJ: John Wiley.

Neese, R. M., & Williams, G. C. (1994). *Why we get sick*. New York: Times Books/Random House.

Nevid, J. S., Rathus, S. A., & Greene, B. (2003). *Abnormal psychology in a changing world* (5th ed.). Upper Saddle River, NJ: Pearson Education.

Pederson, A. M. (1970). Effects of test anxiety and co-acting groups on learning and performance. *Perceptual and Motor Skills, 30*, 55–62.

Peter, J. P., & Olson, J. C. (2002). *Consumer behavior and marketing strategies* (6th ed.). Boston: Irwin/McGraw-Hill.

Pilkonis, P. A. (1977). Shyness, public and private, and its relationship to other measures of social behavior. *Journal of Personality*, 45, 585–595.

Purdy, J. E., Markham, M. R., Schwartz, B. L., & Gordon, W. C. (2001). *Learning and memory* (2nd ed.) Belmont, CA: Wadsworth/Thomson Learning.

Rachman, S. (1998). *Anxiety.* Hove, UK: Psychology Press.

Raffety, B. D., Smith, R. E., & Ptacek, J. T. (1997). Facilitating and debilitating trait anxiety, situational anxiety, and coping with an anticipated stressor: A process analysis. *Journal of Personality and Social Psychology*, 72, 892–906.

Räikkönen, K., Matthews, K. A., Floy, J. D., Owens, J. F., & Gump, B. B. (1999). Effects of optimism, pessimism, and trait anxiety on ambulatory blood pressure and mood during everyday life. *Journal of Personality and Social Psychology*, 76, 104–113.

Rains, G, D. (2002). *Principles of human neuropsychology*. Boston: McGraw-Hill.

Rathus, S. A., & Nevid, J. S. (2002). *Adjustment and growth: The challenges of life* (8th ed.). New York: John Wiley.

Ray, W. J., Katahn, M., & Snyder, C. R. (1971). Effects of test anxiety on acquisition, retention, and generalization of a complex task in a classroom situation. *Journal of Personality and Social Psychology*, 20, 147–154.

Rosen, J. B., & Schulkin, J. (1998). From normal fear to pathological anxiety. *Psychological Review*, 105, 325–350.

Rothbaum, B. O., Hodges, L., Smith, S., Lee, J. H., & Price, L. (2000). A controlled study of virtual reality exposure therapy for the fear of flying. *Journal of Consulting and Clinical Psychology*, 68, 1020–1026.

Sapp, M. (1999). *Test anxiety: Applied research, assessment, and treatment interventions*. Lanham. MD: University Press of America.

Sarason, I. G. (1957). The effect of anxiety and two kinds of failure on serial learning. *Journal of Personality*, 25, 282–292.

Sarason, I. G. (1972). Experimental approaches to test anxiety: Attention and the uses of information. In C. D. Spielberger (Ed.), *Anxiety: Current trends in theory and research: Vol. 2* (pp. 383–403). New York: Academic Press.

Sarason, I. G. (1973). Test anxiety and cognitive modeling. *Journal of Personality and Social Psychology*, 28, 58–61.

Sarason, I. G. (Ed.). (1980a). Introduction to the study of test anxiety. In I. G. Sarason (Ed.), *Test anxiety: Theory, research, and applications* (pp. 3–14). Hillsdale, NJ: Erlbaum.

Sarason, I. G. (1980b). *Test anxiety: Theory, research, and applications*. Hillsdale, NJ: Erlbaum.

Sarason, I. G., & Palola, E. G. (1960). The relationship of test and general anxiety, difficulty of task, and experimental instructions to performance. *Journal of Experimental Psychology*, 59, 185–191.

Sarason, I. G., & Sarason, B. R. (1990). Test anxiety. In H. Leitenberg (Ed.), *Handbook of social and evaluation anxiety* (pp. 475–495). New York: Plenum.

Sarason, I. G., & Stoops, R. (1978). Test anxiety and the passage of time. *Journal of Consulting and Clinical Psychology*, 46, 102–109.

Smith, R. E., & Smoll, F. L. (1990). Sport performance anxiety. In H. Leitenberg (Ed.), *Handbook of social and evaluation anxiety* (pp. 417–454). New York: Plenum.

Spence, K. W. (1956). *Behavior theory and conditioning*. New Haven, CT: Yale University Press.

Spiegler, M. D., Morris, L. W., & Liebert, R. M. (1968). Cognitive and emotional components of test anxiety: Temporal factors. *Psychological Reports*, 22, 451–456.

Spielberger, C. D. (1966). Theory and research on anxiety. In C. D. Spielberger (Ed.), *Anxiety and behavior* (pp. 3–22). New York: Academic Press.

Spielberger, C. D. (1972). Anxiety as an emotional state. In C. D. Spielberger (Ed.), *Anxiety: Current trends in theory and research: Vol. 1* (pp. 23–49). New York: Academic Press.

Spielberger, C. D., Gorsuch, R. C., & Lushene, R. E. (1970). *Manual for the State-Trait Anxiety Inventory*. Palo Alto, CA: Consulting Psychologists Press.

Spielberger, C. D., & Rickman, R. L. (1990). Assessment of state and trait anxiety. In N. Sartorius, V. Andreoli, G. Cassano, L. Eisenberg, P. Kielholz, P. Pancheri, et al. (Eds.), *Anxiety: Psychobiological and clinical perspectives* (pp. 69–84). New York: Hemisphere.

Stein, D. J., & Hollander, E. (Eds.). (2002). *Textbook of anxiety disorders*. Washington, DC: American Psychiatric Publishing.

Stewart, S. H., Samoluk, S. B., & MacDonald, A. B. (1998). Anxiety sensitivity and substance use and abuse. In S. Taylor (Ed.), *Anxiety sensitivity: Theory, research, and treatment of the fear of anxiety* (pp. 287–319). Mahwah, NJ: Erlbaum.

Suinn, R. M. (2001). The terrible twos – anger and anxiety. *American Psychologist*, 56, 27–36.

Taylor, J. A. (1953). A personality scale of manifest anxiety. *Journal of Abnormal and Social Psychology*, 48, 285–290.

Taylor, S. E., Peplau, L. A., & Sears, D. O. (2000). *Social psychology* (10th ed.). Upper Saddle River, NJ: Prentice Hall.

Terry, W. S., & Burns, J. S. (2001). Anxiety and repression in attention and retention. *The Journal of General Psychology*, 128, 422–432.

Wheatley, J. J., & Oshikawa, S. (1970). The relationship between anxiety and positive and negative advertising appeals. *Journal of Marketing*, 7, 85–90.

Winerman, L. (2005). A virtual cure. *Monitor on Psychology*, 36, 87–89.

Wolman, B. B. (Ed.), & Stricker, G. (Co-ed.). (1994). *Anxiety and related disorders: A handbook*. New York: John Wiley.

Yamaguchi, S., Kuhlman, D. M., & Sugimori, S. (1995). Personality correlates of allocentric tendencies in individualist and collectivist cultures. *Journal of Cross-Cultural Psychology*, 26, 658–673.

Zeidner, M. (1998). *Test anxiety: The state of the art*. New York: Plenum.

Zimbardo, P. G. (1977). *Shyness: What it is, what to do about it*. Reading, MA: Addison Wesley.

Zimbardo, P. G. (1986). The Stanford shyness project. In W. J. Jones, J. M. Cheek, & S. R. Briggs (Eds.), *Shyness: Perspectives on research and treatment* (pp. 17–25). New York: Plenum.

Credits

Figures:

2.1   From *Personality and Psychological Assessment*, by B. Kleinmuntz, 1982, New York: St. Martin's Press, p. 228, and *Handbook of Psychological Assessment* (2nd ed.), by G. Groth-Marnat, 1990, New York: John Wiley & Sons, p. 226. Reprinted with permission of John Wiley & Sons

2.2   Reprinted by permission of the publishers from Henry A. Murray, THEMATIC APPERCEPTION TEST Card 12F, Cambridge, Mass: Harvard University Press, Copyright © 1943 by the President and Fellows of Harvard College, Copyright © 1971 by Henry A. Murray

2.4   Adapted from "Reward, Motivation, and Emotional Systems Associated with Early-Stage Intense Romantic Love," A. A. Aron, H. Fisher, D. J. Mashek, G. Strong, H. Li, & L. L. Brown (2005). *Journal of Neurophysiology*, 94, 327–337. American Psychological Association

3.4   Reproduction with kind permission of Bil Keane, Inc. and King Features Syndicate

3.6   Ziggy © 2001 & 2005 Ziggy & Friends, Inc. Reprinted by permission of Universal Press Syndicate. All rights reserved

3.7   Getty Images

3.10   Ziggy © 2001 & 2005 Ziggy & Friends, Inc. Reprinted by permission of Universal Press Syndicate. All rights reserved

6.4   © Ted Levine/zefa/Corbis

7.3   From *The Causes and Cures of Neurosis: An Introduction to Modern Behaviour Therapy Based on Learning Theory and the Principle of Conditioning*, by H. J. Eysenck and S. Rachman, 1965, London, Hodder and Stoughton Reprinted with permission of Hodder & Stoughton Limited

7.4   From *The Biological Basis of Personality*, by H. J. Eysenck, 1967, Springfield, IL, Charles C. Thomas. Reprinted with permission

8.2   Adapted from "Powers and Organs of the Mind," according to J. G. Spurzheim. *Phrenology, or the Doctrine of Mental Phenomena*, 1834, Boston: Marsh, Capen, and Lyons

10.1   Figure "Changes in the scores on the locus of control scale for groups of married and divorced women over a 9-year period: The higher the score, the more external the orientation" from "Impact of Divorce on Locus of Control Orientation in Adult Woman: A Longitudinal Study" by W. J. V. Doherty, 1983a. *Journal of Personality and Social Psychology*, Vol. 44, pp. 834–840. American Psychological Association

10.3   Albert Bandura /Stanford University

10.4   Figure "The average number of approach responses for clients receiving different treatments for a snake phobia" from "Relative Efficacy of Desensitization and Modeling Approaches for Inducing Behavioral, Affective, and Attitudinal Changes" by A. Bandura, E. B. Blanchard and B. Ritter, 1969. *Journal of Personality and Social Psychology*, Vol. 13, pp. 173–199. American Psychological Association

13.2   From "Application of the Spielberger Trait-State Anxiety Theory and STAI in Pre-Cognitive Anxiety Research" by P. Klavora, 1975. In D. M. Landers, D. V. Harris, and R. W. Christina (Eds.), *Psychology of Sport and Motor Behavior II*, pp. 141–143. University Park, PA: Penn State HPER Series, No. 10. Reprinted with permission of the author

13.3   Figure "Mean STAI scores for high and low trait-anxiety students as a function of the stress condition" from "The State-Trait Anxiety Inventory: A Systematic Evaluation" by P. C. Kendall, A. J. Finch, Jr., S. M. Auerbach, J. F. Hooke, and P. J. Mikulka, 1976. *Journal of Consulting and Clinical Psychology*, Vol. 44, pp. 406–412. Washington, D.C.: American Psychological Association

13.4   Figure "Mean time scores for high and low test-anxiety subjects as a function of feedback on test performance" from "A Study of Anxiety and Learning" by G. Mandler and S. B. Sarason, 1952. *Journal of Abnormal and Social Psychology*, Vol. 47, pp. 166–173. American Psychological Association

13.5   Topfoto/ImageWorks

13.7a Vince Bucci/Getty Images

13.7b Lionel Cherruault / Alamy

13.7c PA Photos

Tables:

2.1   *MMPI®-2(Minnesota Multiphasic Personality Inventory®-2) Manual for Administration, Scoring, and Interpretation*, Revised Edition. Copyright © 2001 by the Regents of the University of Minnesota. Used by permission of the University of Minnesota Press. All rights reserved. "MMPI-2" and "Minnesota Multiphasic Personality Inventory-2" are trademarks owned by the Regents of the University of Minnesota

4.4   Table "Mean Scores for Different Groups on the Social Interest Scale" from "Adler's concept of social interest: Theory, Measurement, and Implications for Adjustment."

262-3 Excerpts from Chapter Three. 1929–1937 in *Letters from Jenny*, edited and interpreted by Gordon W. Allport. Copyright © 1965 by Houghton Mifflin Harcourt Publishing Company and renewed 1993 by Robert P. Allport. Reprinted by permission of the publisher

399 From "The Need for Cognition." *Journal of Personality and Social Psychology*, Vol. 42, by J. T. Cacioppo and R. E. Petty, 1982, pp. 116–131. Copyright 1982 by the American Psychological Association

417 American Psychological Association, 1966

478 A subset of modified AIQ items, adapted from Cheek, J. M., Tropp, L. R., Chen, L. C., Underwood, M. K. (1994, August), "Identity Orientations: Personal, Social, and Collective Aspects of Identity," paper presented at the meeting of The American Psychological Association, Los Angeles, CA

557 Extract from "Introduction to Test Anxiety," by Sarason, I. G. (1980a). In I. G. Sarason (Ed.), *Test Anxiety: Theory, Research, and Applications* (pp. 3–14). Hillsdale, NJ: Lawrence Erlbaum Associates, Inc. Copyright © I. G. Sarason. Reprinted with permission of the author

Name Index

Subject Index